Windows® XP

Terry William Ogletree
Contributing Authors:
Walter Glenn and Rima Regas

SAMS

Unleashed

Windows® XP Unleashed

Copyright © 2002 by Sams Publishing

International Standard Book Number: 0-672-32280-3

Library of Congress Catalog Card Number: 2001093496

Printed in the United States of America

First Printing: December 2001

04   03   02   01   4   3   2   1

Trademarks

Warning and Disclaimer

ASSOCIATE PUBLISHER
Jeff Koch

ACQUISITIONS EDITOR
Terry Neal

DEVELOPMENT EDITOR
Steve Rowe

MANAGING EDITOR
Matt Purcell

BOOK PACKAGER
Justak Literary Services

COPY EDITOR
Mamata N. Reddy

INDEXER
Johnna VanHoose Dinse

PROOFREADER
Lara SerVaas

TECHNICAL EDITOR
Dallas Reliford

TEAM COORDINATOR
Denni Bannister

INTERIOR DESIGNER
Gary Adair

COVER DESIGNER
Alan Clements

PAGE LAYOUT
William Hartman

Contents at a Glance

Introduction   **1**

PART I   **Architecture and Installation**   **5**

1   Looking Inside Windows XP Professional   **7**

2   Before You Install or Upgrade   **23**

3   Installing and Upgrading Windows XP   **53**

4   Unattended Installation and Sysprep   **81**

PART II   **Desktop, File Management, General Configuration**   **101**

5   Configuring Accessibility Options   **103**

6   Understanding the Startup Process   **127**

7   Up Front: The New Desktop   **141**

8   Other Applications and Accessories   **169**

9   Working with Files and Folders   **195**

10   Using Microsoft Outlook Express for E-mail, News, and More   **227**

PART III   **Administration, User Management, Technical Issues**   **269**

11   Running Legacy Applications under Windows XP   **271**

12   Installing and Removing Applications   **281**

13   Command Prompt Tools   **297**

14   Using the Control Panel   **329**

15   Managing Local Users   **359**

16   Auditing Windows XP Using the Event Viewer   **397**

17   Printing with Windows XP   **421**

18   Managing Disks and Partitions   **443**

19   Using the Task Manager   **483**

20   The Windows XP Registry   **497**

21   Using Backup on Windows XP   **521**

22   Performance Monitoring, Logs, and Alerts   **545**

23   Be Paranoid: Disaster Recovery Planning   **587**

24 Configuring Your Computer for Local Area Networking **617**

25 Configuring Your Computer for an Internet Connection **643**

26 Joining a Domain and the Active Directory **679**

PART IV Multimedia 693

27 Overview of Windows XP Multimedia Features **695**

28 Capturing Images and Video and Using Windows Movie Maker **707**

29 Windows Media Player 8 **729**

PART V Appendices 759

A Introduction to Transmission Control Protocol/Internet Protocol **761**

B Overview of the Lightweight Directory Access Protocol and Microsoft's Active Directory **797**

C Using Windows XP on a Notebook Computer **813**

D Basics of Internet Information Server **833**

Index **851**

Contents

Introduction **1**

PART I **Architecture and Installation** **5**

1 **Looking Inside Windows XP Professional** **7**

  The Windows XP Architecture: Kernel Mode and User Mode 9
    Kernel Mode and the Hardware Abstraction Layer 10
  Protected Memory and the Kernel 12
  Executive Services 12
    How Virtual Memory Works 13
  Multitasking and Symmetric Multiprocessing 19
  What Is DirectX? 20
  Summary 21

2 **Before You Install or Upgrade** **23**

  Hardware Prerequisites 24
    Check the Hardware Compatibility List 25
    Finding Support for Hardware Not Found in the Hardware
    Compatibility List 26
  Conduct a Pilot Program 28
    Application Compatibility 28
    Working with the Windows on Windows Subsystem 29
  Understanding Network Installations 29
    Recording Network Information for Windows 95/98 31
    Using the ipconfig Command with Windows NT 4.0 and
    Windows 2000 33
  Should You Upgrade or Install? 34
    Upgrading from Windows 95/98 and Windows Me 35
    Upgrading from Windows NT or Windows 2000 36
    Installing Multiple Operating Systems 39
  Preparing Your Computer for XP 41
    It's Cleanup Time: Uninstall Unnecessary Applications and
    Components 42
    Save Copies of Application Configurations 43
    Save Hardware Configuration Data 44
    Back Up Everything! 45
    Defragment the Disk Partition 48
  Make a List and Check It Twice 51
  Summary 52

3 Installing and Upgrading Windows XP 53

Overview of the Windows XP Setup Process 54

What Is Dynamic Update? 56

What Is the Files and Settings Transfer Wizard? 56

Installation/Upgrade Checklist 60

Starting the Windows XP Setup Wizard 61

Booting from the Windows XP CD 61

Running the Setup Wizard under Another Version of Windows 62

Running the Setup Wizard from a Network Connection 62

Lights Out: Performing an Unattended Installation 63

First, the Setup Wizard Needs Some Information 63

Select Special Setup Options 64

Performing Dynamic Update 65

After the First Reboot: Text Mode Setup 66

Welcome to XP! 66

Choose Your Partition 67

Time for Copy: Copying Files to the Hard Disk 72

After the Second Reboot: Read Me Now! 72

From Collecting Information to Finalizing Installation 73

Regional and Language Options 73

Personalize Your Software 76

Computer Name and Administrator Password 76

Date and Time Settings 76

Network Settings 77

After the Third Reboot 77

The Five-Step Program: Finishing the Installation 78

Summary 80

4 Unattended Installation and Sysprep 81

Syntax for the Setup Command 82

Using the unattend.txt Setup File for Automated Installations 85

Creating an Unattended Setup Answer Text File with the
Setup Manager Wizard 87

Using Sysprep to Install Windows XP 97

System Identifiers in Cloning Windows XP 97

Using Sysprep to Set Up a Single Computer 98

Using Sysprep to Clone an Installation 99

Using the Sysprep.inf File 100

Summary 100

Part II   Desktop, File Management, General Configuration   101

5   Configuring Accessibility Options   103

Configuring Accessibility Options Using the Control Panel 105

StickyKeys, FilterKeys, and ToggleKeys 107

Using StickyKeys 107

Enabling StickyKeys 107

Setting StickyKeys Options 108

Enabling and Configuring FilterKeys 109

Enabling ToggleKeys 110

SoundSentry and ShowSounds 111

Using High Contrast for Easier Viewing 112

"Mouseing" Around with the Keyboard 113

Using the General Tab for Accessibility Options 115

SerialKeys 115

Administrative Options 116

Using the Accessibility Wizard 116

Windows XP Accessibility Accessories 118

Using the Narrator 118

Using the Microsoft Magnifier 119

Using the On-Screen Keyboard Feature 121

What Is the Utility Manager? 122

Using Speech Recognition 123

Using Handwritten Recognition Devices 124

Summary 125

6   Understanding the Startup Process   127

How Your Computer Boots 128

How Windows Boots 129

A Brief Recap 131

The BOOT.INI File 132

Startup Options 135

Safe Mode 135

Enable Boot Logging 136

Enable VGA Mode 136

Last Known Good Configuration 137

Directory Services Restore Mode (Domain Controllers Only) 137

Debugging Mode 137

Troubleshooting Startup Problems 137

Check the Event Logs for Startup Problems 138

Boot Using Advanced Options 139

Summary 140

7   Up Front: The New Desktop   141

Taking a First Look at the Windows XP Desktop 142

Customizing the Desktop 144

Create Your Own Desktop Background 144

Customizing Desktop Icons 145

Clean Up Icon Clutter: Use It or Lose It 146

Placing a Web Page on Your Desktop 147

Choosing a Screensaver 150

Changing the Screensaver 150

Create a Slide Show Screensaver 151

Choosing an Appearance for Windows XP 152

Adding Font and Menu Effects and Other Advanced

Appearance Features 153

Choosing Display Settings Appropriate for Your Monitor 154

Choosing and Creating a Theme 156

Choosing the Windows 2000 Classic Desktop and Other

Themes 157

Creating Themes 157

Customizing Shortcuts 157

Adding Shortcuts 158

Rename a Shortcut 158

Configuring Shortcut Properties 158

The Overhauled Start Menu 160

High-Five: The Last Five Programs You Have Used 160

Pin Your Favorite Programs to the Start Menu 161

Using the Search Companion 161

Customizing the Taskbar 165

File Grouping 165

The Notification Area 167

Summary 167

8   Other Applications and Accessories   169

Using HyperTerminal 171

Starting HyperTerminal and Creating a Connection 171

Using Entertainment Accessories 174

Using Sound Recorder 174

Using Volume Control 175

Using System Tools 177

Using Character Map 177

Using System Information 178

Using General Accessories 180

Using the Calculator 180

Using Notepad 182

Using Wordpad 183
Using Paint 188
Playing Games 191
Summary 193

9   Working with Files and Folders   195
The New Windows Explorer 196
File Types and Associations 198
Performing Simple Tasks in Windows Explorer 199
Saving Space, Part One: Compressing and Uncompressing
Folders 202
Saving Space, Part Two: Using Zipped Folders 203
Encrypting Files and Folders 204
Creating New Folders and Other Tasks 205
Folder Options You Can Configure 206
Changing a Folder Icon or Picture 207
Changing the Folder Type 208
Using the Indexing Service for a Fast Find 209
Configuring the Indexing Service 209
Starting the Indexing Service 210
Finding Files in a Hurry 211
Mapping Network Drives to Access Network Resources 211
Burn That CD: Copying Files and Folders to a CD-R 212
The Data Files to Be Burned Are First Sent to a Staging Area 213
The Recycle Bin 214
Retrieving Files from the Recycle Bin 214
Emptying the Recycle Bin 215
Sharing Files and Folders 216
Sharing Files with Other Users on the Same Windows XP
Computer 216
Sharing Files on a Small Workgroup LAN 217
Sharing Files in a Domain or Active Directory Network 219
Using the Security Tab for Auditing Usage of This Resource 222
Summary 225

10   Using Microsoft Outlook Express for E-mail, News, and More   227
Getting Started with Outlook Express 228
Working with the Outlook Express Window 229
Establishing an E-mail Account in Outlook Express 232
Sending and Receiving E-mail 236
Composing an E-mail Message 236
Attaching Files to an E-mail Message 238
Sending the Message 238

You've Got E-mail: Reading E-mail Messages 238
Printing E-mail Messages 239
Replying To and Forwarding E-mail Messages 239
Configuring Outlook Express Options 240
General Properties 240
Read Properties 242
Receipts Properties 243
Send Properties 244
Compose Properties 245
Signature Properties 246
Spelling Properties 247
Setting E-mail Security Properties 247
Configuring Connection Properties 250
Choosing Maintenance Options 251
Creating Filters and Blocking Unwanted Messages or People 252
Using the Address Book 253
Creating Folders in the Address Book 254
Adding Information to the Address Book 254
Using Groups in the Address Book 257
How to Sort and Print Information in the Address Book 259
Using Outlook Express Folders 259
Creating New Folders to Categorize Your Messages 260
Importing and Exporting Messages and Other Information 260
Searching Folders to Find Important Messages 261
Managing Accounts in Outlook Express 263
Creating a Newsgroup Account 264
Subscribing and Unsubscribing from Newsgroups 266
Reading News Messages 267
Posting Replies to Newsgroup Messages 267
Summary 268

PART III   Administration, User Management, Technical Issues   269

11   Running Legacy Applications under Windows XP   271
Why Applications Break 272
What Happens during an Upgrade 273
After the Upgrade 274
Using Compatibility Modes 276
The Find Compatible Hardware and Software Help Feature 277
Using the Application Compatibility Toolkit 278
Use Windows Update Regularly 279
Summary 280

12 Installing and Removing Applications 281

What Happens When You Install an Application on Windows XP 282

System Restore Points 283

Solving Problems with Shared Components and Dynamic
Link Libraries (DLL) 283

Use Your Autorun CD 286

Using Add/Remove Programs 286

Removing an Application from Windows XP 290

Installing or Removing Windows XP Components 291

After the Application or Component Installation 294

Summary 295

13 Command Prompt Tools 297

Overview of the Command Prompt 298

Configuring the Command Prompt 299

Configuring Command Buffers, Display Options, and Edit
Options 300

The Font Tab—Changing the Character Font and Size 301

Choosing Window Size, Buffer Size, and Location Layout 302

The Colors Tab—Why Be Ordinary? 303

Using Standard Commands 304

Cleaning Out Commands That Are No Longer Supported 305

Commands You Can Use at the Command Prompt 307

Using the HELP Command 310

The NET Command 312

Using Redirector Commands for Input and Output 314

Pipes and Filters 316

Get More from Your Commands with Wildcards 317

Working with Batch Files 319

Using the Command Line Task Scheduler (schtasks) 321

Creating a Scheduled Task 322

Using SCHTASKS /CREATE 324

Check the Results of Scheduled Tasks 325

Network Commands 325

How to Create an MS-DOS Startup Disk 326

Summary 327

14 Using the Control Panel 329

Using the Classic or the Category View 330

Using the Appearances and Themes Category 331

Folder Options 333

The See Also Menu and Troubleshooters 338

Troubleshooters! 344

Network and Internet Connections 344
Add or Remove Programs 345
Sounds, Speech and Audio Devices 345
    The Sounds and Audio Devices Applet 346
    Speech 347
    Sound and Audio Devices Troubleshooters 347
Performance and Maintenance 348
    Device Manager 351
    Viewing Device Properties 351
Printers and Other Hardware 354
User Accounts 355
Date, Time, Language and Regional Options 355
Accessibility Options 355
The New Help and Support Application 355
Summary 357

15   Managing Local Users   359
Adding User Accounts During Setup 360
Adding User Accounts After Setup 360
Changing User Account Information 364
    Change the Username 364
    Add or Change the Account Password 365
    Recovering a Forgotten Password 367
    Removing a Password from an Account 369
    Change the Picture for a User Account 369
    Change the Account Type 371
    Deleting a User Account 371
Selecting the Logon and Logoff Method for a User Account 372
Creating a Group Policy on the Local Computer 373
    Configuring Security Settings on the Local Computer 375
    Setting Password Policies 376
    Setting Account Policies 377
Configuring User Settings 378
Using Administrative Templates 379
Monitoring User Activities 380
Assigning User Rights 383
Using Groups to Simplify Management Tasks and Grant
    Resource Access 385
    Adding Members to a Group 387
    Creating a New Local Group 388
Using Fast User Switching? 389

Using Remote Assistance and Remote Desktop 390
   Using Remote Desktop 390
   Using Remote Assistance 392
Summary 396

16 Auditing Windows XP Using the Event Viewer 397

Overview of the Event Viewer 398
   Types of Events 400
   The Event Logging Service 401
   Event Records 402
   The Application Log File 403
   The Security Log File 404
   The System Log File 407
Setting Options for Log Files 410
   Configuring the Location of Log Files 411
   Sizing a Log File and Setting Overwrite Parameters 412
   Using the Filter Tab on the Log File Properties Sheet 414
Archiving a Log File and Clearing Events 416
How to Halt the Computer When the Security Log Becomes
  Full 418
   Editing the Registry 419
   What to Do When the Computer Crashes Because of a Full
    Security Log File 419
Summary 420

17 Printing with Windows XP 421

Windows XP Printing Basics: Defining Some Terms 422
Using the Add Printer Wizard 424
   Connecting to a Local Printer 425
   Connecting to a Printer on a Networked Print Server 432
Managing Printer Properties 433
   The General Tab 433
   The Sharing Tab 434
   The Ports Tab 434
   The Advanced Tab 434
   The Device Settings Tab 438
Managing Printers 438
   General Printer Management Techniques 439
Finding Printers on the Network 441
Summary 442

18 Managing Disks and Partitions 443

Basic Disks and Dynamic Disks 444

Choosing Partitions and Volume Types 446

Comparing File Systems: FAT, FAT32, and NTFS 447

   Improvements in FAT32 448

   Using the NTFS File System 448

Using the Disk Management Utility 450

   Adding and Deleting Partitions 451

   Creating Logical Drives in the Extended Partition 455

   Converting Between Basic and Dynamic Disks 455

   Extending a Dynamic Volume 457

   Changing a Drive Letter or Drive Path 458

Managing Disks Through the Command Prompt 459

   Converting a Partition From FAT to NTFS 459

   Using the DISKPART Command 461

   Using DISKPART LIST 464

   Deleting a Partition or Volume 465

   Formatting a Disk 467

Configuring Partition Properties 469

   Using Disk Cleanup 470

   The Tools Tab 471

   The Hardware Tab 474

   Sharing the Disk Drive 476

   Enabling Disk Quotas 478

Sharing Files with the Computer Management Utility 479

   Sessions and Open Files 480

Sharing Disks When You Are Part of a Domain 480

Summary 481

19 Using the Task Manager 483

Managing Applications Using the Task Manager 484

   Ending a Task—Killing an Application 485

   Switching to an Application 485

   Starting New Tasks 486

   Menu Options 487

Managing Individual Processes 488

   Changing Process Priorities 489

   Ending Processes and a Process Tree 491

   Menu Options for the Process Tab 491

Using the Performance Tab to Track System Performance 493

Tracking Networking Adapter Usage with the Networking Tab 495

Summary 496

20   The Windows XP Registry   497

A Brief History of the Windows Registry 499

Registry Basics 500

Subtrees 502

Keys, Subkeys, Entries, and Values 505

Hives and Files 506

Backing Up and Restoring the Registry 508

Back up the Registry 509

Restoring the Registry 511

Using the Windows Registry Editor 512

Searching the Registry 513

Changing a Registry Entry 514

Adding a Registry Entry or Key 515

Deleting a Registry Key or Entry 516

Exporting and Importing Registry Information 517

Summary 518

21   Using Backup on Windows XP   521

Hardware Can Make a Difference 522

Developing a Backup Plan 524

Deciding What to Back Up 524

Deciding How and When to Back Up 526

Running the Backup Wizard 529

Performing a Manual Backup 532

Selecting Components to Back Up 533

Setting Backup Information 533

Setting Advanced Backup Program Options 534

General 534

Setting the Default Backup Type 536

Customizing the Backup Log 536

Excluding Files From the Backup Job 536

Restoring Data from a Backup 537

Using the Restore Wizard 538

Restoring Files Manually 540

Using Automated System Recovery 541

Running Backup from the Command Line 543

Summary 544

22   Performance Monitoring, Logs, and Alerts   545

Understanding Performance Issues for Windows XP 546

Hardware Factors Affecting Performance 547

Some Ideas to Improve Performance 552

Using Task Manager 564

Using System Monitor 566

How System Monitor Collects Information 566

Starting System Monitor 567

Selecting Performance Counters 568

Viewing Your Graph 572

Printing System Monitor Data 574

Setting System Monitor Properties 574

Baseline Your System and Examine Performance
Periodically 578

Configuring Logs and Setting Alerts 578

Creating a Counter Log 579

Configuring an Alert 582

Command Line Performance Monitoring Tools 585

Summary 586

23   Be Paranoid: Disaster Recovery Planning   587

Back Up Important Data! 588

Using the Automated System Recovery Wizard 590

Creating the Automated System Recovery Diskette and
Backup of Your System Partition 590

Restoring a System Using the Automated System Recovery
Method 593

Using the Last Known Good Configuration Feature 595

Booting into Safe Mode 596

Using the Recovery Console 599

Starting Recovery Console from the Windows XP
Installation CD 599

Select the Operating System 600

What Can You Do with the Recovery Console? 600

How to Install the Recovery Console on Your Computer 602

Using Device Driver Rollback 604

What Is a Signed Device Driver? 604

Using Device Driver Rollback 605

How to Use System Restore to Recover Previous Settings 607

What Gets Saved and Restored with System Restore? 609

Using the System Restore Wizard 611

Create Your Own Restore Points 613

Using System Restore to Revert to an Earlier Time 614

Summary 616

24 Configuring Your Computer for Local Area Networking 617

Using Dynamic Host Configuration Protocol or Static Internet
Protocol Configuration Information 618
Using Static Addressing 619
Automatic Private Internet Protocol Addressing 619
Installing and Configuring Transfer Call Protocol/Internet
Protocol and Related Components 620
Using Add/Remove Programs to Install Network
Components 620
Configuring the Transfer Call Protocol/Internet Protocol
Connection 622
Configuring the Network Adapter Card 625
This Connection Uses the Following Items 630
Transfer Call Protocol/Internet Protocol Configuration 630
Configuring Static Internet Protocol Address Information 632
Configuring Advanced Transfer Call Protocol/Internet
Protocol Settings 633
Using Other Local Area Network Protocols 638
Installing Additional Network Clients 638
Installing Additional Network Services 640
Installing Additional Protocols 640
Using File and Printer Sharing for Microsoft Networks 641
Workgroups and Domains 641
Summary 641

25 Configuring Your Computer for an Internet Connection 643

Dial-Up Networking Versus Broadband Connections 644
The Standard Modem 644
Cable and Digital Subscriber Line Modems 644
Integrated Services Digital Network Connection 649
Installing a Standard Modem 650
The Add Hardware Wizard 650
Detecting Your Modem 652
Configuring Modem Properties 654
The General Tab of the Modem Properties Sheet 654
The Modem Tab of the Modem Properties Sheet 655
The Diagnostics Tab 655
The Advanced Tab 656
The Driver Tab 658
The Resources Tab 659
The Power Management Tab 660
Working with Dialing Rules 660
The General Tab 661

The Area Code Rules Tab 662
The Calling Card Tab 663
Setting Advanced Modem Options 663
Creating a New Internet Account 664
Configuring an Existing Internet Account 664
Changing a Dial-Up Connection's Properties 667
Checking the Status of Your New Connection 668
Windows XP Internet Connection Firewall and Internet
Connection Sharing 669
Windows XP Internet Connection Firewall 669
Windows XP Internet Connection Sharing 672
Creating a Connection to the Network at Your Workplace 673
Setting Up a Home or Small Office Network 676
Obtaining an Internet Service Provider 676
Summary 677

26 Joining a Domain and the Active Directory 679
Understanding Windows Domains 680
How Domains Function 681
The Master Domain Model 682
Working with Trust Relationships 683
What Is the Active Directory? 684
How the Active Directory Works 685
Computer and User Accounts in the Active Directory 686
Joining a Domain Using Windows XP 687
Joining a Domain During the Windows XP Setup Process 687
Joining a Domain After the Setup Process 688
After You Have Joined a Domain 691
Using the Domain Account 691
Searching the Active Directory 692
Summary 692

PART IV Multimedia 693

27 Overview of Windows XP Multimedia Features 695
The New Windows Media Player 697
New Folders—It's Not Just My Documents Anymore! 697
The My Music Folder 698
The My Videos Folder 698
The My Pictures Folder 699
Publishing Photographs or Movies on the Web 700
View as a Slide Show 700
Order Prints Online 700

Burning CDs with Windows XP 701
　Burn that CD 702
Microsoft Plus! for Windows XP 703
Using Third-Party Programs 704
Summary 705

28　Capturing Images and Video and Using Windows Movie Maker　707

Installing a Scanner, Camera, or Video Source 708
　Using the Scanner and Camera Installation Wizard 708
Using Third-Party Software 711
Using Windows Movie Maker 712
　Starting Windows Movie Maker 712
　The Collections Area 714
　The Monitor Area 714
　The Workspace 714
How Do You Make a Movie? 715
　Recording Video Using Movie Maker 716
　Editing the Movie 719
　Adding Narration to Your Movie 723
　Saving a Movie 724
　Publishing on the Web or E-mailing a Movie 726
　Burning to a CD 726
Summary 728

29　Windows Media Player 8　729

Overview of Windows Media Player 8 730
　What's New for Windows Media Player 8? 731
　Supported File Types 732
A Quick Overview of the Interface 732
Now Playing 734
　Opening Files 735
　Opening Uniform Resource Locators 735
　Drag and Drop with Media 736
　Visualization 736
　Advanced Features 737
　DVD Playback 738
The Media Guide: A Guide to Media! 739
Copying from CDs 739
　What Is Digital Audio? 740
The Media Library 741
　Adding Media To The Guide 742
　Editing Media Information 743
　Creating Playlists 744

Tuning into the Internet 744

Music on the Go 746

Working with Skins 748

Options, Tab by Tab 749

    Player 749

    Copy Music 750

    Devices 752

    Performance 753

    Media Library 754

    Visualizations 754

    File Types 755

    Network 755

    Summary 756

PART V Appendices 759

A Introduction to Transmission Control Protocol/Internet Protocol 761

Transmission Control Protocol/Internet Protocol 762

    Internet Protocol 762

Understanding Internet Protocol Addressing 764

    Internet Protocol Addressing Makes Finding Computers

    Easier 766

    Dotted-Decimal Notation in Internet Protocol Addresses 768

    Internet Protocol Address Classes 770

    Subnet Masks and Subnetting a Network 774

How Ports Complete the Connection 777

    Transmission Control Protocol and User Datagram

    Protocol Ports 777

The Transmission Control Protocol 778

    The Three-Way Handshake Sets Up a Transmission

    Control Protocol Session 779

    Sliding Windows 781

    Ending a Transmission Control Protocol Session 782

    The User Datagram Protocol 782

    The Internet Control Message Protocol 783

    The Address Resolution Protocol 784

Serial Line Interface Protocol and Point-to-Point Protocol 784

    The Serial Line Interface Protocol 784

    The Point-to-Point Protocol 784

The Domain Name System 785

The Dynamic Host Configuration Protocol 786

Windows Internet Naming Service 787

Virtual Private Networks 788

Troubleshooting Tools for Transmission Control Protocol/
Internet Protocol 788

Using ping and tracert 789

Use IPCONFIG Command to View Your Internet Protocol
Configuration 792

Using the NETSTAT Command 793

Using the ROUTE Command 794

Using the NSLOOKUP Command 794

Summary 795

**B   Overview of the Lightweight Directory Access Protocol and
Microsoft's Active Directory   797**

The Development of Lightweight Directory Access Protocol 798

A Quick Look at the X.500 Standards 799

Schemas 802

Defining Schema with Lightweight Directory Access
Protocol 803

Working with Lightweight Directory Access Protocol 804

Conducting a Search in the Directory 805

Changing Information in the Directory 805

Microsoft's Active Directory 806

A Quick Look at the Microsoft Management Console and
Managing the Directory 808

Finding Objects in the Active Directory 808

C   Using Windows XP on a Notebook Computer   813

Using ClearType 814

Setting Power Management Options in Windows XP 816

Power Schemes 817

Using Alarms 820

Using the Power Meter Settings 821

Advanced Power Settings 821

Hibernation 822

Enabling Advanced Power Management 822

Using Hardware Profiles 822

Creating a Hardware Profile 823

Managing Profiles 825

Setting up Hardware for a Profile 826

Selecting a Profile on Startup 827

Synchronization and Offline Files 828

    Setting up Offline Files 828

    Setting up Offline Web Access 828

    Using Synchronization Manager 830

Summary 831

D   Basics of Internet Information Server   833

What's New in IIS 5.1? 835

Installing IIS 835

Creating a Web Site 836

Managing a Web Site 837

    Web Site Properties 839

    Home Directory 839

    Documents 841

    Directory Security 842

    HTTP Headers 843

    Custom Errors 843

Managing an FTP Server 843

    FTP Site Properties 844

    Security Accounts 845

    Messages 846

    Home Directory 846

Managing the SMTP Service 847

    General Properties 848

    Access 848

    Messages 849

    Delivery 849

    Security 849

Summary 849

Index   851

Dedication

This book is dedicated, as always, to my parents, Gordon and Billie Jean Ogletree.

About the Author

Terry Ogletree is a consultant who has worked with Windows operating systems for many years now, as well as Unix, Linux, and OpenVMS. He is currently working through The Computer Merchant of Norwell, MA (`http://www.tcml.com`). He is the author of several recent books, including *Scott Mueller's Upgrading and Repairing Networks, 3rd Edition*, *Practical Firewalls*, and *Windows NT 4.0 Networking*. In addition, he has contributed chapters to many other computer books published by other authors, and is the co-author of *The Complete Idiot's Guide to Creating Your Own CDs, 2nd Edition*. You can email him at two@twoinc.com, or visit his Web site at `http://www.twoinc.com`. Your comments and suggestions for improving this book are welcome!

Acknowledgments

This book is the result of a lot of effort put forth by many people. Given the timetable for the release of Windows XP and the difficulty of writing about an operating system that was refined and honed carefully during the beta and release candidate phases, this book would not have been possible without the help of my co-authors and the supporting cast of characters at Sams. With their great contributions, the book you hold in your hands contains the most up-to-date information about Windows XP that I think you will find for sale in your local bookstore. All of the co-authors of this book have computer book pedigrees that prove their writing skills as well as their technical knowledge. I could not have done this without them!

However, it is not just the authors who are responsible for making a book like this one as complete and accurate as possible. There are many people who work behind the scenes performing such chores as copy editing, technical editing and other tasks that are part of computer book publishing. I would like to thank Steve Rowe, the development editor of this book, for his suggestions during the early writing phase of this book. Steve knows the target audience very well and his approach as to how this book should be written will make it much easier for you to read and understand. He also played a large part in the organization of the material found herein, making it easier for you to find what you need to know in a hurry. In addition, Lorna Gentry assisted with the development work on this book and thus helped to make it a better book. If you look at the masthead of this book, you'll see the names of many other important behind-the-scenes people who helped with creating this book, including the copy editors, technical editor, and others. These people are rarely recognized for the valuable work they do. Without them, this book would not exist!

I would especially like to thank Vicki Harding, an agent who works for the Studio B literary agency, and Terry Neal, the Executive Editor at Sams, for giving me the opportunity to write this book. Both have prodded me along to try to get this book out as soon as possible, while keeping it accurate and loaded with useful information for the reader.

Thanks also go to Michael D. Parrott and Associates of Raleigh, NC who help keep me from having to deal with a lot of things so I can find time to write. Thanks also to Angelo Simeo and John Rogue of The Computer Merchant, who have kept me employed for many years and encouraged me to continue in the writing field.

Finally, I would like to thank my parents and family for supporting me in this and other writing efforts that I have worked on for many years.

Tell Us What You Think!

As the reader of this book, *you* are our most important critic and commentator. We value your opinion and want to know what we're doing right, what we could do better, what areas you'd like to see us publish in, and any other words of wisdom you're willing to pass our way.

As an Associate Publisher for Sams, I welcome your comments. You can fax, email, or write me directly to let me know what you did or didn't like about this book—as well as what we can do to make our books stronger.

Please note that I cannot help you with technical problems related to the topic of this book, and that due to the high volume of mail I receive, I might not be able to reply to every message.

When you write, please be sure to include this book's title and author as well as your name and phone or fax number. I will carefully review your comments and share them with the author and editors who worked on the book.

Fax: 317-581-4770
Email: feedback@samspublishing.com
Mail: Jeff Koch
        Sams
        201 West 103rd Street
        Indianapolis, IN 46290 USA

Introduction

For many years Microsoft has maintained two sets of operating systems that both used the Windows name. From Windows 95 and 98 to Windows Me, an inexpensive operating system that could be used for both home and business applications was produced. For the server and workstation market, Microsoft produced Windows NT and Windows 2000. But maintaining two different operating system kernels for these two markets caused problems for users, due to the fact that some applications worked under one operating system, but not the other since the Windows 95/98/ME line of operating systems used a different *kernel* than the Windows NT and Windows 2000 operating systems. The kernel is the heart of the operating system and is the most important component.

Windows XP is the result of a merging of the features that you enjoyed with the Windows 9.x operating system and with the Windows NT/2000 kernel. In addition, Windows XP has many more features that you'll learn about in this book that make it the most logical choice for anyone who buys a computer today. With the stability of the Windows NT/2000 kernel, you'll find that your system is less likely to crash and that many applications will run much faster. Since developers will now only have to write applications to run under a single operating system, you can expect to have a larger number of applications to choose from. Because Windows XP contains a lot of new features, especially in the multimedia area, you should find a lot of fun applications come out that exploit these capabilities.

This book is divided into five sections. In Part I, you'll learn about some of the technical details of the operating system, such as how virtual memory is handled by the kernel and how multitasking operates. There's a lot going on behind the scenes that lets you run multiple programs at the same time and allows multiple users to access your computer. You'll also learn in Part I about some important factors that you should consider before you attempt to install or upgrade to Windows XP. Indeed, if you haven't upgraded yet, this book can be a valuable reference for deciding whether or not to make that decision. Part I walks you through the installation process one step at a time, explaining the choices you can make when you do finally decide to upgrade or install Windows XP on your computer. The last chapter in this section discusses some of the options available for installing Windows XP on a large number of computers. This chapter should prove useful for administrators in a business environment where they need to install or upgrade their client computers in an orderly fashion.

In Part II you'll learn about what is happening when Windows XP starts up, and a lot about configuring and using the new Desktop that Windows XP presents. Microsoft seems to have done a major overhaul on the Desktop, so this section will definitely be required reading if you want to be come an expert on this operating system. This section contains information about accessibility options for people who have a physical impairment that makes using a computer difficult. Part II also introduces you to the latest version of Internet Explorer, as well as the newest developments in how to work with files and folders. Finally, you'll find an entire chapter devoted to using Outlook Express to manage your email, news group subscriptions, address book, and much more.

Part III covers administration and technical issues that the administrator of the computer will need to use. Here you'll find chapters on everything from running older applications to the new Control Panel and tools for managing users on the computer. The Registry, often ignored by casual users, is covered in a chapter by itself, as is the all-important topic of disaster recovery and what you can do to prevent as well as fix problems. If performance is a problem, you'll find a chapter on that. If backups are something you need to understand, there's a chapter on that, too. This section closes with three chapters devoted to networking issues for both the local area network and the Internet. Windows XP now contains a personal firewall that can help protect your computer. You can learn how to join a domain or create a workgroup for a smaller network.

Part IV contains chapters that will be of interest to most users since computers are being used more and more today for their multimedia capabilities. If you want to know how to hook up a camera to your computer or use the new Windows Media Player to download music from the Internet and record it to a CD, then this section is for you. Or if you want to learn how to take your old VHS tapes and record them to digital files and make your own movie, then you'll learn to use Windows XP's Movie Maker. Windows XP has so many new multimedia features that it's hard to describe them in a few sentences. There are three chapters in this section that will enable you to make the most of any multimedia capabilities of your computer.

Part V contains several appendices that serve as reference material for this book. If you need to brush up on your TCP/IP skills, then Appendix A can be used for a quick refresher course. Appendix B describes the Lightweight Directory Access Protocol (LDAP) and the Active Directory. If you are using Windows XP in a business environment, then this appendix is a valuable resource for understanding how LDAP and the Active Directory are used to store a vast amount of information about your network. For the traveler, Appendix C has some advice about using Windows XP on laptop computers, and include features new with Windows XP, such as ClearType technology, that might make reading your laptop's screen easier. Finally, Appendix D contains a ton of information about using Internet Information Server. IIS is a complex application that gives you the ability to create a Web presence that can be used on your local network or the Internet.

Windows XP is truly a revolutionary operating system, and I think that you'll enjoy using it on your computer. This book will show you how to do things that weren't available in previous versions of Windows. The organization makes it easy to quickly locate the topic you need to learn about and pictures of important windows are shown so that you don't to need to try to visualize them in your head as you read. I think you'll find this book to be the best reference book available on using and managing Windows XP Computers.

Architecture and Installation

PART

I

IN THIS PART

1 Looking Inside Windows XP Professional   *7*

2 Before You Install or Upgrade   *23*

3 Installing and Upgrading Windows XP   *53*

4 Unattended Installation and Sysprep   *81*

CHAPTER 1

Looking Inside Windows XP Professional

IN THIS CHAPTER

- The Windows XP Architecture: Kernel Mode and User Mode *9*
- Protected Memory and the Kernel *12*
- Executive Services *12*
- Multitasking and Symmetric Multiprocessing *19*
- What Is DirectX? *20*

The newest version of the Windows family of operating systems is truly a new Windows "eXPerience." Windows XP Professional is built on technology that has been crafted and finely tuned since Windows NT first appeared many years ago. Today, we have a multitasking, symmetric multiprocessing operating system for the desktop that will enhance your productivity. With this release of Windows XP, you will find not only a new, snappy-looking desktop, but also support for many new devices and a convergence of the Windows 9x and Windows NT/2000 basic code. The result is an operating system that will allow you to run the same programs at home that you do at work. In addition, new features like System Restore and Device Driver Rollback will help to eliminate many of the headaches you had to endure in the past when installing new devices or software.

In this chapter, we will start out by looking at the very basics of Windows XP—that is, the means by which it provides a large memory space and allows you to run multiple applications at the same time. These features are key ingredients for most modern operating systems that run on mainframe computers. You now can have these capabilities on your office desktop or at home.

The key components of Windows XP that we will examine in this chapter include:

- Protected memory—Windows XP takes advantage of the central processing unit's (CPU's) ability to run code in either *kernel mode* or *user mode*. The majority of the operating system functionality is implemented in kernel mode, and it is this part of the operating system that is responsible for controlling access to the physical memory installed in the machine. User applications must make requests to the operating system in order to access virtual memory. Since the kernel protects the physical memory from applications, it is much less likely that an application can hang up or crash your computer!

- Virtual memory—Windows XP supports up to just 4 gigabytes (GB) of virtual memory, but it uses a paging file where it stores portions of memory that aren't needed at the moment by an application or the operating system. This large memory address space isn't shared among competing applications. Each application is given its own 4GB range of virtual address memory, allowing for the development of some very complex applications such as those that use sound and graphics to make your computing experience much more pleasant. Game lovers will find that Windows XP can work as well or better than previous version of Windows 9x operating systems.

- Multitasking—This is the ability to run more than one program at the same time. For office productivity, you can't beat having the capability to run more than one application at the same time, switching back and forth, and cutting and pasting data at will. Windows XP does this with ease.

- Symmetric multiprocessing—Windows XP can run applications using multiple CPUs in the same computer. With this ability, response time can be greatly improved. Although high-end graphics workstations in the past were usually based on Unix or a proprietary operating system, you will find that Windows XP is now up to that task, at a much more reasonable cost.

- Hardware Abstraction Layer (HAL)—The HAL is a layer of code that stands between the operating system and the physical devices attached to a computer, such as a network card or disk drive, allowing the operating system to control devices. This helps to prevent crashes caused by badly behaving devices.

- DirectX technology—The latest version of DirectX overcomes the limitations imposed by the HAL so that games and other multimedia applications can communicate much faster with the underlying hardware.

In this chapter we will look at the operating system architecture used by Windows XP to provide for these features.

The Windows XP Architecture: Kernel Mode and User Mode

Windows XP is based on the same architecture as Windows NT and Windows 2000. It is a virtual memory operating system that uses two basic modes of operation. The *kernel mode* is the layer of the operating system's code that is responsible for handling such fundamental operating system items as virtual memory and scheduling which applications will run at any given time. Operating system code that executes in kernel mode has direct access to hardware and memory on the computer. You will sometimes see this referred to as *privileged mode*. Since the Windows XP Executive Services run in kernel mode, it protects the system's memory against applications that try to write to portions of memory that may otherwise cause a problem.

Note

Executive Services operate in kernel mode and can do things on the computer that user applications cannot. For example, if an application wants to retrieve data from a disk file, it does not contact the disk device drive directly. Instead, it uses the input/output (I/O) manager component of the Executive Services, which then makes the request for the application.

User mode is where your actual program runs and is controlled by components of the kernel. For example, the kernel is responsible for allocating the memory that an application uses. User applications make requests such as a need for memory allocation to the kernel code by calling system functions that are designed to help meet the needs of user applications. The Windows XP kernel mode code is thus able to stay in charge and, if necessary, terminate a misbehaving application.

Kernel Mode and the Hardware Abstraction Layer

The kernel is also in charge of communicating with most of the hardware devices for your application. A component of the kernel, called the *hardware abstraction layer (HAL)*, is responsible for the actual control of hardware devices attached to the computer. The exceptions to this are the device drivers, which communicate with file systems and the network, and the Win32K and GDI graphics subsystems, which are used to communicate with the display monitor and input devices. Figure 1.1 shows a general overview of the separation of duties as they are performed by various components of the operating system. We will discuss these components in greater detail in this chapter.

FIGURE 1.1
Windows XP is built on a layered architecture that protects important system components from direct access by user applications.

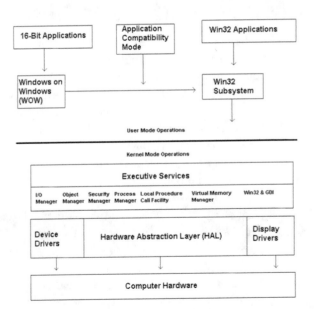

In earlier versions of Microsoft operating systems, applications could talk directly to the physical hardware devices attached to the computer. For several reasons, HAL was created when Windows NT was first developed. First, Windows NT was developed to run on multiple hardware platforms. These included the now standard Intel processor, along with others such as the PowerPC, Alpha, and MIPS processors. By providing an *abstraction* layer of code between the actual hardware devices and the applications, it was possible to port Windows NT to multiple platforms. Using HAL also prevented a single application from wreaking havoc on the machine by locking up a particular device, therefore making it necessary for you to reboot the computer.

Note

Abstraction layer is a layer of programming that allows an operating system to interact with an object at a general or abstract level rather than at a detailed level.

Support for PowerPC and MIPS was dropped during the development of Windows NT 4.0, and support for Alpha processors was dropped during the beta testing for Windows 2000. However, development efforts for Windows XP included not only the 32-bit Intel processors, but also the 64-bit Intel Itanium processor. HAL is still necessary in order to make it easier to separate system communications from the underlying hardware platform.

A second advantage that HAL provides is to prevent rogue application code from crashing the system. HAL is responsible for accessing the underlying hardware components of the operating system, and the code that runs in user mode cannot do such things as write over sections of physical memory buffers used by such things as network devices. Even components of the operating system that talk to device drivers and the graphics display are part of the kernel, so applications must still call system routines in order to access these devices. The separation between user mode and kernel mode is designed to make sure that under all but the most extreme circumstances, it will be very difficult for a single program to crash a Windows XP computer.

In Figure 1.1, the Windows on Windows (WOW) subsystem is shown, along with the Application Compatibility Mode subsystem. Older applications that were written for 16-bit processors can be emulated by the WOW subsystem. Although most 32-bit applications written for versions of Windows from Windows 95 up to Windows 2000 should run on a Windows XP computer, there are some that won't. For these programs a component called *Application Compatibility Mode* will allow you to emulate these previous operating systems. Application compatibility mode is discussed further in Chapter 12, "Installing and Removing Applications."

> **Note**
>
> You may find that some applications will not run reliably under Windows XP. Those that fall into the categories of antivirus programs, backup applications, and some system utilities may not work. However, vendors of the top-selling programs will produce upgrades for these programs, so you will still be able to use your favorite utilities under Windows XP. Just check the Windows Catalog Web site (http://www.microsoft.com/windowsxp/partners/catalog.asp) for the applications compatible with Windows XP. (You can also access this Web page within Windows XP by selecting Start, All Programs, Windows Catalog.)

In addition to running applications written for earlier versions of Windows (and even some MS-DOS programs), a 64-bit version of Windows XP will provide support for 64-bit applications. The 64-bit version of Windows XP will include another subsystem, called *Windows on Windows 64 (WOW64)* that will enable 32-bit applications to run with applications specifically written for the 64-bit version. Although most of us don't need the number-crunching capabilities of a high-end 64-bit workstation, this version of Windows XP will be very useful in environments such as computer-aided design (CAD) and 3-D animation. Since support for the 64-bit Alpha processor has been dropped, the 64-bit version of Windows XP will run on the Intel Itanium processor.

Protected Memory and the Kernel

Since physical memory is only used when allowed by the kernel mode code of the operating system, it is also known as *protected memory*. In early operating systems, such as MS-DOS, it was simple for a badly coded program to overwrite a section of memory that it should not. The results could be unpredictable, but usually resulted in a system crash. By separating the operating system into user mode and kernel mode, and thus protecting memory with privileged code, user applications will not find it easy to access memory locations that they should not.

Executive Services

Executive Services is simply a label given to a diverse set of components that provide the basics of an operating system. These basic services offered by the kernel executive include the following:

- Virtual Memory Manager—This component of the Executive is responsible for managing the 4GB virtual address space for each process, as well as paging in and out of physical memory all the pages of memory the operating system or an application needs at any particular time.

- Local Procedure Call Facility—This component is responsible for interprocess communications. This component is necessary because each process uses the same virtual address space.

- Process Manager—When it comes time to start or shut down a process, this component of the Executive is responsible for creating the necessary memory structures and starting up the threads of the process. From that point, other components of the Executive, such as the Virtual Memory Manager, become involved in controlling how a process functions and uses system resources.

- Object Manager—Windows XP uses the concept of an object for many different things. Consider an object as a basic unit that can be managed by the Executive. For example, system resources such as ports are considered objects. An object provides an interface that the application program can use to interact with a system resource in a uniform manner.

- Security Reference Monitor—This is a very important part of the Executive. The Security Reference Monitor is that component which controls all security mechanisms that are implemented in the operating system. This includes such things as the initial logon, validating a user's password, and checking whether a user can be granted access to a resource such as a disk file.

How Virtual Memory Works

A component of the kernel called the *virtual memory manager (VMM)* is responsible for taking charge of the physical memory installed in the computer and allocating it to individual processes on an as-needed basis. This is one of the most important features of not only Windows XP, but of all modern operating systems such as Unix and OpenVMS. The 32-bit Windows XP can support addressing up to 4GB of memory, although you likely won't find this much memory on a desktop PC at this time!

Note

The 64-bit version of Windows XP that will run on Intel's Itanium processor will support up to 16 terabytes of virtual memory. That is a huge increase in the virtual memory available to the more common 32-bit version of Windows XP Professional. By doubling the size of the numeric value that the processor can handle, it is easy to see why XP most likely will succeed. By allowing applications that require larger data structures and faster number crunching capabilities than a 32-bit machine can provide, users needing more powerful computing capabilities can find it in Windows XP.

Of the 4GB memory address range, 2GB are reserved for the operating system itself, whereas the other 2GB are reserved for the application. This means that an application can be written so that from the point of view of the application, there is actually 2GB of memory installed in the system. However, one important concept to keep in mind about virtual memory is that it is virtual. Another is that the range of memory addresses Windows XP can address is far larger and a separate entity from the actual physical memory installed on the computer. The two terms to remember here are *virtual memory addresses* and *physical memory*. Virtual addresses are simply numbered locations in the address space that a process can use. Physical memory is the actual memory installed in your computer. The VMM takes care of mapping virtual addresses to physical memory addresses on an as-needed basis.

It is the job of the VMM to keep track of a process's memory address space and to coordinate those addresses with the actual physical memory installed in the computer. The memory addresses range from 0000000016 to 7FFFFFFF16 (hexadecimal notation— something programmers like to use a lot). In addition, remember that each process uses the same range of addresses. You may think that the address range would be divided among the competing processes, with each receiving only a portion of the address range; however, this is not true. Each process can use the entire address range. The VMM keeps track of which addresses in this range a particular process is using and does so for each process on the system.

There is no doubt many of you are familiar with the story that the original architect of Windows NT was David Cutler, who was also the principal architect of Digital Equipment Corporation's Virtual Memory System (VMS) operating system, now called OpenVMS. It should come as no surprise then that Windows XP uses advanced virtual memory techniques that are similar to those used in OpenVMS.

Paged-Based Virtual Memory Addressing

The virtual memory management features provided by Windows XP may seem complex at first glance, but in reality, it is a simple process to mimic 4GB of memory when the actual computer contains a much smaller amount of physical memory. Several important concepts to keep in mind when talking about paged-based virtual memory follow:

- 32-bit Virtual Addressing
- Page Directories
- Page Tables
- Page Frames
- Translation Lookaside Buffers
- Pagefiles

32-Bit Virtual Addressing

Windows XP uses a 32-bit address to locate data in memory. However, all memory is accessed in segments that are 4096 bytes in size, called *pages*. The 32-bit address itself is broken down into three components, each of which is used to index into a table that eventually points to the actual memory location for the data required by an application. Keep in mind that we are talking about virtual memory addresses, not physical memory here. Once a particular byte is located using a virtual address, the byte may already be located in physical memory, or the page containing the byte may be located in a paging file. In such a case, that page will need to be brought back into memory before the data is accessible to the application. First, we will look at how the 32-bit virtual address is used to locate a byte of data, and then at how pages of memory are paged in and out of physical memory to a paging file.

In Figure 1.2, you can see how the actual address is divided into three separate portions, each of which serves a specific function.

FIGURE 1.2

The 32-bit memory address is actually composed of three components.

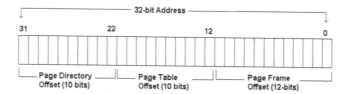

This figure shows the three components of the address that relate to offsets in the *page directory*, *page table,* and *page frame.* To locate the actual page frame, which is the actual page of application data, several steps are used by the VMM.

The Page Directory

The first 10 bits of the address are called the *page directory offset.* A page directory is nothing more than a page of memory, which, as you will recall, is 4096 bytes long. Each entry in a page directory is four bytes long, and is called a *page directory entry (PDE).* If you do the math, you will see that a single page directory can hold up to 1024 PDEs (1024 x 4 = 4096 bytes).

Each PDE is, by itself, an offset that points to another page structure called a *page table.*

Each process that runs on the Windows XP operating system has its own page directory. That may seem like a lot space to waste in memory, but as you will see shortly, the way the VMM handles memory takes care of a large number of page directories. The fact that each process has its own page directory is what makes it possible for each process to use the same address range. Because the addresses are virtual pointers and the VMM takes care of swapping in and out the actual data from the paging file to physical memory, a particular 32-bit address used by one process does not point to the same data byte as the same address used by another process! Each process has a unique set of data referenced by the range of addresses provided by Windows XP's VMM.

The Page Table

Once the first 10 bits of the 32-bit address have been used to locate an entry in the page directory for a process, the value found at that location is used to locate an entry in another page structure called the *page table*. Once again, this is a 4096-byte long page structure that is composed of entries called *page table entries (PTEs)*, each of which is also four bytes long.

The second 10 bits of the 32-bit address are used by the VMM to locate an entry in the page table that is pointed to by the PDE entry.

Once the VMM has used the PDE entry to locate the page table and then used the second 10-bit portion of the address to locate the entry in the page table, it uses the value found there to locate yet another page structure called the *page frame*.

The Page Frame

Finally, we get to where the actual data bytes are stored in memory. Remember that this is virtual memory, not physical memory. Once the VMM has found the actual page frame, it uses the last 12 bits of the 32-bit address to locate the actual data byte in the page frame where the address points. Because the last part of the address is 12 bits long, it can be used to point to individual bytes in the page frame. These last 12 bits do not point to another page structure. They are an offset into the actual page of memory that contains user or application data. Thus, it is possible to address each byte in the page frame individually. Remember that the PDE and PTE entries were only 10 bits long and were used to point to four-byte entries in their respective pages. Using 12 bits allows the VMM to address each individual byte in the page frame.

Figure 1.3 shows this process of using pointers to locate a page table, page frame, and then the actual data byte that resides in the page frame.

As you can see from this figure, the entries in the page directory do not point to entries in a page table. Instead, the PDEs point to a page table, and each process can have a large number of page tables, depending on the memory allocated to the process. The entry in the page table pointed to by the PDE doesn't point to the data byte in a page frame; it points to the actual page frame. The 12 remaining bits in the 32-bit address are used to locate the actual byte of data that is located in the page frame.

Now that was simple enough, wasn't it? But wait, there's more....

FIGURE 1.3

The page directory points to the page table that points to the page frame.

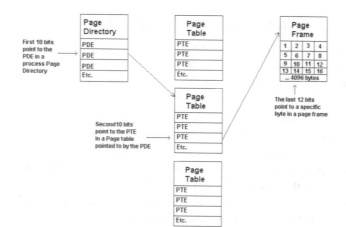

Page Files

Most desktop computers don't really have 4GB of physical memory installed. Because of this, the VMM must determine whether the page that contains the data is actually present in memory or whether it is being stored temporarily in a paging file on a disk drive. This situation happens when a PTE points to a page frame that is not valid or, to put it in other terms, is not present in physical memory. When this happens, a condition known as a *page-fault* occurs. This simply means that the page of memory pointed to by the PTE is brought into physical memory. If all of the physical memory is currently filled with data, then the VMM will select another page of data to swap out to the page file to make room in physical memory for the page required for the moment. The CPU assists in this process. Once the CPU has brought the requested page into physical memory, it causes the original instruction that pointed to the page to be executed again, and the application continues to function.

Note

Both the concept of breaking apart the 32-bit address to locate a byte of data and the process of swapping pages of memory in and out of physical memory using a paging file are not difficult ideas to understand. However, there is one more little thing you should know about this entire process. It is quite possible that the page directory for the process, the page table to which it points, and the actual page frame are all swapped out to the page file. Thus, when the processor executes an instruction that references a virtual memory address where this condition exists, it will take three page faults to locate the actual data: one to page in the page directory, one to page in the page table, and one to page in the page frame that holds the data location pointed to by the address!

What Is a Translation Lookaside Buffer?

In the memory lookup process just described, the VMM had to use three pages of memory to locate a particular byte. However, another method can help locate a byte a little faster. It is a hardware component of the actual CPU itself, called a *translation lookaside buffer (TLB)*. This buffer is basically a memory cache that resides on the CPU chip and stores the most commonly used physical addresses. Note that these are pointers to addresses of physical memory locations, not pointers to data stored in a paging file. Since it is much faster for a processor to look into this cache than it is to wait for a slow disk drive to page in a page of memory, the TLB can be consulted quickly to determine if the requested data is already present in physical memory. If not, then the regular process of paging can be used to bring the data into physical memory. The time spent looking in the TLB is miniscule compared with the process of swapping data between the paging file and physical memory.

The Page-Frame Database

Since each process that runs under Windows XP has its own page directory and all processes share the same virtual address range, it is important to understand that not all virtual addresses are alike. In other words, a virtual address for one process does not yield the same data as that same address for another process. In order to keep track of exactly what is present in physical memory, the VMM uses a database called the *page-frame database*, which holds an entry for every page of memory in the system and uses this database to keep track of the status of those pages.

In Table 1.1, you can see the six categories for classifying the status of a page of physical memory.

Table 1.1   Status of Physical Memory Pages

Page Status	Description
Valid	The page is in use by an active process.
Modified	The page has been written to, but the data has not been written to the paging file.
Standby	The page has been removed from a process's working set.
Free	The page is free for use after it has been zeroed (unless it is a read-only page).
Zeroed	A free page is ready for use by any process.
Bad	A page that has caused a hardware error; it is not available for use by any process.

In order to keep track of the status of physical pages of memory, the page-frame database is part of a section of memory controlled by the kernel called the *nonpaged pool*. Page directories, page tables, and pages of data can be sent to the paging file to make room for other pages, but the pages that make up the nonpaged pool are always resident in physical memory. Thus, it is a quick matter for the VMM to check the page-frame database to determine the status of a particular page of physical memory.

The actual organization of this page-frame database is a set of linked lists that group together pages based on their status. This means that when the VMM needs to find a few consecutive free pages so it can use them for a process, it can do so by following the linked list of pages in the free state. When the VMM needs to write a page of data out to the paging file to make room for another page to be swapped in, it can look for modified pages (those that have been modified since being swapped in from the page file), and then flush those pages out to the page file.

Another important concept associated with the page-frame database is that it contains a pointer back to the PTE that currently references the physical page location. This is how the VMM can determine which process is using that page of physical memory. To each individual process, then, a huge address space is available in which a program can execute. In actuality, the VMM takes care of translating among a process's virtual addresses and the addresses used by the computer's actual physical memory.

Multitasking and Symmetric Multiprocessing

MS-DOS and other simple operating systems allow you to run only a single program at a time. A *multitasking operating system* allows you to run multiple programs at the same time. Actually, in a single CPU system, only one process is active and running at any particular point in time. Processes can be further subdivided into units of instructions called *threads*, each performing tasks that can be run in parallel with other tasks that the application requires. Each thread is given what at first appears to be a very short amount of time in which to run, measured in milliseconds. However, keep in mind that today's fast CPUs can run millions of instructions per second, so even a small time slice granted to a particular program thread can be more than sufficient to accomplish a lot of work.

In a single CPU system, only one thread can execute at a time on the CPU. The method used to decide when it is time for a thread to stop executing and yield the processor to another thread is important. In Windows 3.1, for example, nonpreemptive multitasking was used. This method works by letting a particular task run until it is finished, and it voluntarily gives up the CPU to the next task. Of course, if the running program doesn't want to let go of the CPU, then your system can hang up. In preemptive multitasking, which is the method used by Windows XP, the operating system determines when it is time for a task to yield to another task.

The operating system grants each process thread a certain amount of time in which it can run, after which it must relinquish control of the CPU. When this happens, the operating system stores data necessary to keep track of the state the process thread was executing so that it can restore the process thread when it is time to let it execute again. The act of switching between one process thread and another is called *context switching*, and it occurs millions of times per second on today's fast CPUs.

Because the operating system is in control and not the application, preemptive multitasking helps to prevent conditions such as a single application hanging up the computer. For example, if you have an application running under Windows XP that for some reason or another hangs up, you can always bring up the Task Manager and kill the process. This is because Windows XP also uses a concept called *prioritization,* which grants some processes a higher priority when it comes to accessing the CPU. The Task Manager is granted a high priority so that it can be brought up no matter what other task is running.

As you can see, by using the concept of threads when writing applications, it is possible to allow an application to run at a faster rate. Instead of having to wait on some outside event, a process can schedule a thread to wait, and then continue with other threads to perform other chores that do not depend on the event on which that thread is waiting. This can be useful for I/O operations or network operations, where other processing can continue while, for example, a thread waits on a buffer to receive the data from the I/O subsystem.

In a multiprocessor system that uses more than a single CPU, it is a simple task to let different threads of a process execute on separate CPUs, and thus, an even greater speed advantage can be obtained. Although multiple-CPU systems are generally used as servers on a network, a high-end workstation can also be equipped with multiple CPUs in situations where intensive computations and other operations are necessary.

What Is DirectX?

When Windows NT was first released, all graphics devices, much like other hardware components such as memory, network cards, and so on, were controlled by the kernel, and the response time was much slower than on a MS-DOS machine, where, for example, applications could directly control the display driver. To make up for this, and thus allow high-speed graphics and input devices, DirectX was incorporated into the operating system. Windows XP supports DirectX Version 8, which includes the following components:

- DirectX Graphics—This combines earlier components known as *Microsoft DirectDraw* and *Microsoft Direct3D* into a single component. This simplifies the task of the application developer who creates those wonderful games or other graphics that make Windows XP a great platform for graphic-oriented applications.

- Direct Audio—This DirectX feature also combines earlier components, Microsoft DirectSound and Microsoft DirectMusic, into a single applications programming interface (API), again making it easier to develop audio applications on the Windows XP platform.

- Microsoft DirectInput—This feature provides support for a large number of input devices, including full support for force-feedback technology.

- Microsoft DirectPlay—If you like multiplayer games like those used on the Internet, then this component of DirectX Version 8 will allow you to create cooperative gaming applications that run at very fast rates.

- Microsoft DirectShow—Windows XP includes many multimedia features, including MovieMaker. This component of DirectX gives Windows XP the capability to capture high-quality audio and video, as well as the functions necessary to give you a high-quality playback experience.

- Microsoft DirectSetup—Finally, DirectX Version 8 allows for easy installation for all of the DirectX components. Installing multimedia applications has never been simpler.

The actual makeup of DirectX components is a subject for application developers and is not something easily explained in a book such as this that is geared toward the user of the system. As a matter of fact, you will find entire books written on the subject of programming using DirectX Version 8 technology. The important thing to remember is that applications written using DirectX Version 8 technology for Windows XP will greatly enhance your experience when using multimedia applications. We will get to some of those applications that are built into the operating system later in this book.

Summary

Windows XP Professional is an operating system that represents the next evolutionary step from the proven technologies of earlier Windows NT and Windows 2000 systems. Yet, because of advances in both hardware and software technologies, you will find that Windows XP is a whole new experience from the end-user point of view. In the past you probably used Windows NT or Windows 2000 for your desktop workstation in the business environment, and Windows 95, 98, or ME at home. Now you will find the same technology employed at both home and work. If you use an application at home using the low-end of the Windows XP operating systems, you will find that it will also run on the desktop or server you use at work.

In the next chapter we will look at a few things you need to consider before you upgrade or install Windows XP Professional on your computer. Following that, we will walk through all the steps necessary to install Windows XP Professional.

CHAPTER 2

Before You Install or Upgrade

IN THIS CHAPTER

- Hardware Prerequisites *24*
- Conduct a Pilot Program *28*
- Understanding Network Installations *29*
- Should You Upgrade or Install? *34*
- Preparing Your Computer for XP *41*
- Make a List and Check It Twice *51*

This chapter explains some things you should do before attempting to install Windows XP Professional or upgrade your current operating system to Windows XP Professional. Some of the topics discussed in this chapter may seem obvious, but it never hurts to make a list and check off each item when performing something as major as an operating system install or upgrade. By taking the appropriate steps upfront, you lessen the chance for something to go wrong, and you can also prepare a back-out procedure for recovering your system if anything out of the ordinary occurs.

Hardware Prerequisites

When preparing for an upgrade or installation you should first make sure that your computer meets the minimal hardware requirements for the operating system. Advances in hardware components have been made at a phenomenal rate during the past few years, along with a reduction in prices. A typical computer running Windows 95 or Windows 98 can get by with 16MB of RAM. However, Windows XP requires much more than that, but fortunately, prices for memory are probably not as high as when you first purchased your computer.

As this table shows, the most important items are the central processing unit (CPU) speed and the amount of random access memory (RAM) installed in your computer. The amount of free disk space depends on a number of factors. For example, if you choose to copy the setup files to your hard drive, either during an installation from the CD or by obtaining the setup files from a network connection, you will need additional space to store these files. A 2GB disk drive is the minimum size required for a Windows XP computer, but this doesn't leave much space for installing applications or data after operating system is installed.

Most keyboards and mice work with Windows XP, but you may find some features don't work as expected. For example, some keyboards have shortcut keys that do things like dial up to your Internet Service Provider (ISP). Depending on the keyboard and the features, you may be able to download a driver from the manufacturer to remedy these sorts of problems.

The same goes for other hardware components, especially disk drives. A disk drive with 5MB to 10MB of storage capacity was once considered enormous, but now a 60GB or larger hard drive is not only the norm but also available for a very low cost. Computers today also come equipped with better graphics adapter cards, DVD/CD-ROM drives, and in some cases, CD/RW drives. However, you don't have to have the latest and greatest system in order to load Windows XP on your computer. Table 2.1 lists the minimum hardware requirements your computer needs to perform an installation of Windows XP, along with the recommended and maximum values.

Table 2.1 Minimum, Maximum, and Recommended Hardware Requirements for
Windows XP Professional

Item	Minimum	Recommended
RAM	64MB	128MB (or more!)
CPU Speed	233MHz	Anything faster!
Disk Drive	2GB	Anything larger!
Free Disk Space	650MB	More for network installation
Display	VGA	SVGA for best results
Keyboard	Standard	n/a
Mouse	Standard	n/a
CD-ROM	CD-ROM	CD-ROM or DVD-ROM/CD-ROM
Network Card	Check the HCL	10/100Mbps card, for Category 5 twisted-pair wiring, RJ45 Jack

RAM, random access memory; MB, megabyte; CPU, central processing unit; MHz, megahertz; GB, gigabyte; VGA, video graphics array; SVGA, super video graphics array; CD-ROM, compact disc-read only memory; HCL, hardware compatibility list.

In general, your system should exceed the minimum requirements listed in Table 2.1, especially for memory and CPU speed. Although Windows XP will run on a machine equipped with the minimal requirements, you won't be able to achieve a very satisfactory experience. This is especially true if you decide to use some of the multimedia capabilities that are included with Windows XP or with applications written to take advantage of the DirectX 8 technology built into Windows XP. For example, if you are heavily into games, which depend on fast graphics and input devices, you will find that more memory and a high-end graphics adapter will make your gaming experience a lot more enjoyable. Similarly, if you are planning on using Windows XP as a graphics workstation for computer-aided design or another application of this sort, then you must upgrade your computer to a faster CPU and possibly a newer motherboard.

However, if you are only installing Windows XP to see if it's the operating system for you for the next few years, then the minimum requirements will allow you to do so. For simple office applications, the minimum requirements listed in Table 2.1 will suffice, as long as you have sufficient local disk space or space on network file shares to store your applications and data.

Check the Hardware Compatibility List

After you have made sure that your computer meets or exceeds the minimum requirements listed in the previous section, it is time to check out other hardware components in the system to make sure that they are supported by Windows XP. The simplest way to do this is to first check the hardware compatibility list (HCL). An up-to-date copy of this file can be found at Microsoft's Web site at `http://www.microsoft.com/hcl/`. You should compare your installed devices with that list.

The hardware compatibility list contains a list of devices that is updated frequently, so check back at a later date if you find that some of your hardware is not yet supported. In addition, when service packs or patches to the operating system are released, they usually include support for newer devices. You should again check out the HCL again. Don't bother printing out the entire listing, since it does change and because it is quite lengthy. It is much easier to search it online than to flip through the pages looking for a specific device.

Finding Support for Hardware Not Found in the Hardware Compatibility List

Just as devices are added to the HCL list, you may find that some hardware devices once supported under previous versions of Windows are no longer present on the list. This may be because they are so outdated that it wasn't worth the effort to provide support for them, or because the manufacturer is no longer in business or doesn't want to keep supporting these devices. If it is not on the HCL, however, all is not yet lost.

If your device is not listed on the HCL, it doesn't mean Windows XP will not support it. For example, when Windows XP detects that "new hardware" (Plug and Play feature) has been found, it will first try to determine if it has a driver written specifically for use for that device. If not, it will usually try to match up another driver that can be used in its place. The most common example of this occurs in the Display Adapters and Graphics Monitors categories. Although Windows XP may not fully support all the fancy features your expensive graphics adapter card provides, it can usually install a standard VGA driver that still works with the card. This is not the most optimal solution, and you are encouraged to keep checking with your device's manufacturer to see if they will release an XP-specific driver.

Of course, the best of all possible worlds is that you will find an XP-compatible driver for your hardware that has been digitally "signed" by Microsoft and is officially part of the Microsoft Logo program. This not only ensures full compatibility with XP, but in some cases the hardware will perform better on Windows XP than other platforms.

Some devices simply do not work under Windows XP. If you want to be able to use them to their fullest feature capacity, then check the Web site of the vendor to see if new drivers are available. Usually, it's a simple matter to download the driver and perform a quick install to get a hardware device up and running.

> **Note**
>
> In addition to the problems with hardware no longer being supported by Microsoft, is the problem that often occurs when you buy a computer from a major manufacturer who saves money by combining multiple functions into a single card, or worse yet, onto the motherboard. For example, it is quite common to incorporate the sound card functionality on a motherboard in a PC targeted to the consumer market. These original equipment manufacturers' (OEMs') computers also come with their own operating system and applications installation software, so you can use them to install the operating system on another computer. If you are stuck with one of these, again, try visiting the manufacturer's site (or better yet, ask more questions the next time you buy a cheap PC). More than likely, you will find that for many of these combination cards, Windows XP will install a basic driver (as with the VGA graphics driver) that will work with your system. If not, you may need to buy a separate card and install it in the computer.

It also pays to stay informed about hardware issues if you are anything but a casual user of a computer. Although there are many good sites on the Web that offer advice and can give you some "gotchas" about hardware problems and conflicts (and usually how to resolve them), here are a few sites to check out:

- Tom's Hardware Guide—`http://www.tomshardware.com`. This excellent Web site is highly regarded in the hardware community and reviews almost all important hardware components that make up your computer—from motherboards to memory to CPUs. Tom is also very adept at uncovering undocumented hardware features that you will not find in the vendor's inadequate documentation. As an example of Tom's prowess, Intel withdrew its Pentium III 1.13GHz from the market after Tom exposed some of the major flaws in this chip. If you can't try before you buy, at least check out Tom's site before you purchase anything.

- AnandTech—`http://www.anandtech.com/`. This Web site is another good place to visit to get in-depth reviews about computer hardware and up-to-date news about hardware issues.

- StorageReview.com—`http://www.storagereview.com/`. Another good Web site for hardware reviews, this site concentrates on storage technologies, from hard drives to optical drive technologies. You will find simple reviews and benchmark testing results. A LeaderBoard can be found here that makes it a simple matter to locate the best storage solution for your computer.

- Price Watch—Street Price Search Engine—http://www.pricewatch.com. Once you have selected what you want to add to your computer, find out where you can get the best price. This Web site can serve as a valuable source of street price information. Forget those "list" prices!

> **Tip**
>
> If you are a little savvy when it comes to assembling hardware but still need some help here and there, I recommend *Upgrading and Repairing PCs, 13th Edition*, by Scott Mueller (Que Publishing, 2001). You will find this book in just about every major bookstore chain, or you can purchase it online. This book has been in print for more than 10 years, has sold millions of copies, and is updated frequently. The author not only describes each component in your computer, he also provides tips and tricks for installing components that make the job look a lot easier than changing the oil in your car!

Conduct a Pilot Program

If you are deploying Windows XP on desktops in a business environment, then you should first conduct a pilot project to test the hardware and software currently in use in your organization. When it comes to applications, this is especially important, since purchasing, supporting, and maintaining applications is more expensive over the lifetime of a hardware platform than the price of the computer itself.

Although checking the HCL to determine if your PCs will run Windows XP Professional is a simple affair, applications are another matter entirely. For example, if an application can run on the new operating system, will it give the end user the response time they need?

Application Compatibility

Just as some hardware components may not be up to the task of running with Windows XP, you may find that some of your favorite old programs also won't install. Again, don't lose hope, since there are several things you should know about Windows XP and applications. Most 32-bit applications written with the Windows 2000 logo certification should run under Windows XP.

The same goes for many 16-bit programs that go back to the MS-DOS days. The good ol' Command Prompt (which I always call the MS-DOS box) is still present in Windows XP, and you will find it under the Accessories folder. From here, you can launch many standalone programs that weren't written for a Windows operating system.

Working with the Windows on Windows Subsystem

In addition to the Win32 subsystem used to run 32-bit applications, Windows XP uses another subsystem, called *Windows on Windows* (WOW), which can be used to run 16-bit applications. The problem with running these applications on earlier versions of Windows operating systems is that, unless you specify otherwise, all 16-bit programs will share the same address space. This is unlike 32-bit applications that each has the full range of 32-bit addresses available to them.

What this means is that if you simply run a 16-bit application by using the Start/Run command or by entering the program executable name in the Command Prompt box, then one misbehaving 16-bit application can cause any others also running in the same address space to hang or crash.

Fortunately, there is another way around this. For each 16-bit application running under Windows XP, try this test: Bring up the Command Prompt (Start, More Programs, Accessories, Command Prompt) and use the following command to start the program:

```
START /SEPARATE <executable program name>
```

Windows XP will run the application in its own separate virtual address space, usually referred to as a Virtual DOS Machine (VDM). Running 16-bit applications using this method means that if one program encounters a problem, then it won't interfere with other 16-bit programs that were started using the same method.

Additionally, Windows XP provides a special feature called *Application Compatibility Mode,* which allows you to search for and set up programs that ran on previous versions of Windows operating systems but that don't work properly under Windows XP. You can find out more about this and the Start command in Chapter 11, Running Legacy Applications Under Windows XP.

Understanding Network Installations

If you are planning on a fresh installation or upgrading your current computer's operating system and are connected to a network, then you need to understand how your computer participates in the network before you begin the installation or upgrade to Windows XP. If you operate a standalone system that isn't connected to a network (including the Internet), then you can skip this section.

Here are three ways in which you can participate in a Windows network:

- Workgroup—You can be part of a simple peer-to-peer workgroup, in which each computer has its own unique computer name. In this kind of network, each computer can offer resources such as file shares or printers to other computers in the same workgroup. This is the least secure method of networking but perhaps the easiest to set up. You won't find this in many business environments anymore, but it can be useful in the home environment. Here, you will usually create a username and password for logging onto your own computer. However, to access resources on other computers, you will need a username and password for each computer participating in the workgroup.

- Windows Domains—You can be part of a domain, which means that you have a user account that resides on a domain controller in the network. For Windows NT 4.0 and earlier versions of Windows NT, the main location of the account is on a primary domain controller (PDC), which is where changes to your account are made. Backup domain controllers (BDCs) replicate copies of the PDC database so that you can use your username and password to be granted rights to access resources within the domain (and in trusted domains) throughout the network.

- Active Directory Domains—With Windows 2000, the Active Directory can be used to store all sorts of information, including a username and password for each user, and this information allows you to log onto different computers in the network using a single logon.

However you access network resources, you need to be sure to keep a copy of the information used so that when you upgrade or install Windows XP, you will still be able to access the network in the same manner. Generally, if you are performing an upgrade, and you don't change the computer name or your username during the upgrade, you should be fine. However, if something goes awry with the upgrade, you should have the networking configuration information available in case you need to start over and do an install.

Note

If you plan to use Windows XP as the desktop operating system in your corporate network, be sure to read Part Four, "Networking Windows XP." Here you will find an in-depth discussion of the transfer call protocol/Internet protocol (TCP/IP) suite, as well as information about how to configure Windows XP in a network environment.

However, if you are installing a fresh copy of the Windows XP operating system, then you should record all the relevant information ahead of time so that you can once again join the network after the new operating system has been installed. During an installation of Windows XP, you will be required to select the networking components to install and hence, you will need the configuration information such as an IP address, subnet address, and other similar information.

Recording Network Information for Windows 95/98

If your computer is already configured for a local area network (LAN), and you are using TCP/IP (such as in a business environment) or for dial-up networking (such as in a home office), then you can use the utility `winipcfg` to get a listing of the pertinent network configuration information for your computer. You can start this utility by typing the command **winipcfg** in the Command Prompt window (Start, Programs, Command Prompt), or you can use the Start, Run method and enter the `winipcfg` command in the Run dialog box that appears.

Figure 2.1 is an example of the type of information that appears when this command is executed under Windows 98 Second Edition.

FIGURE 2.1

The winipcfg *command can be used to obtain the current network configuration information for your computer.*

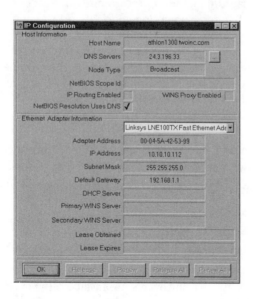

Note that in this figure, the Advanced button was clicked to show you a display with more information than the basic display provides. You can record this information by simply writing it all down, but that can be a tedious process prone to errors. A simpler method is to click once on the dialog box that displays the network configuration information so that it becomes the active window. Then press the Print Screen key while holding down the Alt button. This copies the active window to the clipboard.

To save the image data, you can then use Microsoft Paint:

1. Click Start, Programs, Accessories and then Paint.

2. When the Microsoft Paint accessory pops up, click on Edit on the menu bar and then click on Paste. The image will be copied from the clipboard to the Paint window.

3. Click on File and then Save As.

4. When prompted, choose a location and enter a filename to save this file. I suggest storing this on a floppy disk or a network drive share so that if anything goes wrong in the upgrade or installation, you will have an offline copy.

5. If you have a printer available, then click File, Print and print a copy of the image. Save it for use during the install or upgrade.

Tip

A well-managed network must include well-written and up-to-date documentation. Using the screen capture method to record network settings is a simple method you can use to begin documenting your network. If you use a special network file share folder to store these screen shots, and name them appropriately—using the computer's host name, for example—then you can find it easy to recover a crashed system. Additionally, you can take the information from these screen shots and record the information in a spreadsheet, database, or use some other method for storing network information.

If you are using another protocol, then copy the configuration information that can be displayed by using the Network applet in the Control Panel. For example, if you are on a Novell network, you will need to use the Network applet (see the following) to get the necessary information:

1. Click on Start, Settings, Control Panel.

2. When the Control Panel appears, double-click on the Network icon.

3. The Network properties sheet will pop up. Installed components appear in the pane titled The Following Network Components Are Installed. To view the details of a protocol, service, or adapter installed on the system, click once to highlight the item and click the Properties button. Another properties sheet appears, displaying several tabs that relate to the highlighted item.

4. Click OK to dismiss the Network properties sheet when you have finished record-ing any information you need to keep.

You can use the Alt+Print Screen method to take snapshots of the configuration informa-tion just like you did with `winipcfg` utility and use Microsoft Paint to save or print the screen captures.

Using the `ipconfig` Command with Windows NT 4.0 and Windows 2000

Windows NT 4.0 and Windows 2000 allow you to use a command line utility called *ipconfig* to display TCP/IP configuration information. However, unlike the `winipcfg` utility, `ipconfig` does not produce a graphical display. Instead, it displays the informa-tion in the Command Prompt window.

To save the information, you can use the redirector symbol (`">"`) to send the information to a file and then save or print the file for later use. In addition, using the `/all` parameter to the `ipconfig` command will cause it to display more information and should be used. To use `ipconfig` in this manner, use the following steps:

1. Click on Start, Programs, Accessories, Command Prompt.

2. When the Command Prompt window appears, enter the command `ipconfig /all > filename`. Substitute a filename you can easily remember for *filename*.

3. For example, if you want to send the output to a file on a floppy disk, the following command can be used: `ipconfig /all > a:ipinfo.txt`. This will create a file called *ipinfo.txt* on a floppy disk inserted in your floppy drive.

4. Again, save the floppy disk for future reference. It is also a good idea to print the file if you have a printer available.

To get additional network information if your network does not use TCP/IP, again you can use the Control Panel. For Windows NT 4.0 workstation, you can use the procedure detailed in the preceding section. Using Windows 2000 Professional, however, follow these steps:

1. Click on Start, Settings, Control Panel and then Network and Dial-Up Connections.

2. For each icon that shows up in the Network and Connections window, right-click and select Properties. A properties sheet will appear listing the installed networking components, including services and protocols (see Figure 2.2).

3. For each component that has the check box selected, highlight the component by clicking on it once and then click the Properties button.

FIGURE 2.2

The properties sheet for a network connection will display the components installed on the computer.

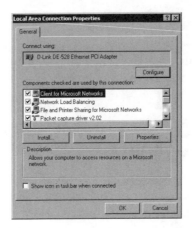

4. A separate properties sheet will appear showing configuration information for the component you've selected. Again, use the Alt+PrintScreen method to save the information to the clipboard and then use Microsoft Paint to save or print a copy of this information. Note that some properties sheets have more than one tab, as well as buttons that reveal additional information. Be sure to record all of the pertinent information you may need to reconfigure the computer.

For most situations, you will probably have just one local area connection icon in the Network and Dial-Up Connections window and possibly another icon for a dial-up connection if you connect to the Internet via a modem instead of your local network. Be sure to record the properties for each of these connections.

Should You Upgrade or Install?

This decision can be simple or complicated. When you upgrade to Windows XP, your currently installed applications should still be available for use after the upgrade is complete, assuming that the applications will run under Windows XP. During an upgrade, Windows XP will replace Windows files from previous operating system installations but should preserve your current settings for operating system components and your applications. For many users on a typical network, an upgrade is the most logical way to go. You won't have to first install the operating system and then undergo the tedious process of reinstalling every application from scratch once the installation is done.

However, if you have been using your computer for a long time, have had problems with some applications or the operating system, or have had to patch things here and there, it might be easier to just do a clean install and then reinstall the applications you need. For example, suppose that you have several important applications you use on a frequent basis, some that you never use, and a lot of others that you just installed so you could try them out. In this case a fresh, clean install can get rid of these applications you no longer use and you can simply install the few that you do currently need.

> **Caution**
>
> When you perform an install of Windows XP, keep in mind that the *files* for the now-defunct applications have not actually gone anywhere—it's just that all references to running the applications will be removed from the new Windows XP Registry.
>
> It is recommended that you remove the files and folders for the older applications right after installing Windows XP to properly clean your system.

When you perform an upgrade, keep in mind that other settings are also preserved. For example, your choice of desktop icons, security settings and other such things can be preserved. If you perform an installation from scratch, you will have to spend time reconfiguring the operating system to your liking.

Upgrading from Windows 95/98 and Windows Me

Upgrading from Windows 95/98 or Windows Me should not present many problems at all. These operating systems are based on a different kernel than the Windows NT/2000/XP code base, but the upgrade process takes this into account and preserves application and operating system settings that are applicable to the new Windows XP operating system. The following are some "Golden Rules" for upgrading:

- Be sure you have the original installation disks for all applications, just in case. No operating system is foolproof when it comes to an upgrade procedure.

- Often, application providers place different versions of their software on the same CD-ROM, so that a single disc can be used to install the product on more than one operating system. Make sure that you have the original source CDs (or other media) available so that if the upgrade to Windows XP does not migrate to your favorite application, you can always reinstall it after the upgrade has finished.

- Finally, be sure to create a Windows 98 or Windows Me startup diskette in case you find that the upgrade or install doesn't succeed. You can use the startup diskette to boot the system with CD-ROM support so that you can either fix the damage done to the computer or reinstall your previous operating system.

To create a startup diskette in Windows 98, use the following commands:

1. Click on Start, Settings, Control Panel.

2. Double-click on the Add/Remove Programs icon.

3. A dialog box titled Add/Remove Programs Properties will pop up. Click on the tab labeled Startup Disk.

4. Insert a newly formatted 1.44MB floppy disk into your floppy drive.

5. Click the Create Disk button.

The above procedure will take just a little over a minute to complete. Also, Windows may prompt you to insert the original source CD for your Windows installation if it can't find all the files on your hard disk that it needs to make the floppy bootable.

If for some reason the installation or upgrade fails, you can use this startup disk to boot the system with CD-ROM support so that you can reinstall a new copy of Windows. You can then use the Backup utility to restore your previous system from a recent backup.

Upgrading from Windows NT or Windows 2000

With Windows NT and Windows 2000 computers, the hidden file BOOT.INI is an important file. You will notice that when you boot the system, a menu appears that you can select from. If you have just installed one copy of Windows NT or Windows 2000, there will only be two entries in this file. The first is the VGA version that allows you to boot Windows NT/2000 in a basic VGA mode if you make a mistake and install a bad video driver and need to get back into Windows to correct your mistake. This entry will boot you into a Windows NT/2000 using a basic VGA driver so you can remedy the problem by resetting your video card parameters.

If you have used the computer to install multiple operating systems, from Windows 95 up to Windows 2000 (or even a beta of Windows XP), then you will see an entry in this file for every possible boot combination. When the system is initially powered on, after the power-on self-test (POST), you will be able to use the up and down arrow keys on your keyboard to select the operating system to boot.

Since it is always best to err on the side of caution, make a copy of the BOOT.INI file and save it so that if something does go wrong during the Windows XP installation, you can at least go back and get the information you need to reboot other operating systems installed on the computer.

> **Caution**
>
> Save a copy of the BOOT.INI file on a floppy disk or other offline storage media such as a Zip disk or a CD-R disc—not on the disk that you will be upgrading. Don't even copy the file to another partition on your computer's hard disk.

The BOOT.INI file is a hidden file, but you can "unhide" it by using the ATTRIB -H BOOT.INI command. Then copy the file to a floppy disk. If the system files on the boot partition (usually drive letter C:) become corrupted due to a bad upgrade problem, you will be able to copy this file back from the floppy disk after you recreate the boot partition and reformat it. Then you can use the BOOT.INI file to try to boot another operating system installed on another partition or disk so that you can start your trouble-shooting efforts.

For Windows NT and Windows 2000, you should also create an emergency repair disk (ERD). In this case you will need a 1.44MB blank floppy disk. The process for creating an emergency repair disk is different for these two versions of Windows. However, for both versions, the ERD will back up information stored in the directory %systemroot%/repair, to the ERD.

You should update the information in this repair directory every time you make major changes to your system, such as adding new hardware or applications. The repair directory contains compressed versions of some of the Registry files, as well as other files needed to repair your system. Table 2.2 contains a list of the files that are copies to the ERD.

Table 2.2 Files Copied to the Emergency Repair Disk

Filename	*Description*
AUTOEXEC.NT	Similar to the AUTOEXEC.BAT file, used by Windows NT to support legacy applications
CONFIG.NT	Similar to the CONFIG.SYS file, used by NT for configuring the MS-DOS environment when legacy applications are executed
Default._	Copy of the HKEY_USERS\.Default registry key
NTUSER.DA_	Copy of ntuser.dat
SAM._	Copy of the HKEY_LOCAL_MACHINE\SAM registry key
SECURITY._	Copy of the HKEY_LOCAL_MACHINE\Security registry key
SETUP.LOG	This file contains the locations of important system and application files and cyclic redundancy check (CRC) information used during the repair process
SOFTWARE._	Copy of the HKEY_LOCAL_MACHINE\Software registry key
SYSTEM._	Copy of the KHEY_LOCAL_MACHINE\SYSTEM registry key

2

BEFORE YOU
INSTALL OR
UPGRADE

As stated earlier, the registry files stored on the ERD are in a compressed format (those with the underscore character as the last character of the file extension), which makes it easier to fit all this information onto a single floppy disk. You will still need a recent backup of your data and application files to use in a recovery process if those files have become corrupted.

To create an ERD for a Windows NT 4.0 system, use the RDISK utility:

1. Click on Start, Run.
2. Enter RDISK into the Run dialog box and click OK.
3. The Repair Disk Utility dialog box will appear. Click on the second button, Create Repair Disk.
4. Place a 1.44MB floppy disk in the floppy drive and click OK when prompted.

In the Repair Disk Utility dialog box the first button is called *Update Repair Info*. Use this button whenever you make major changes to the system so that the changed info is copied to the %systemroot%\repair folder. If you forget to do this, then the information stored in the repair folder will simply be the default files created during an initial installation of Windows NT 4.0, and none of your user data or application information will be stored in the copies of the Registry hives that are in this folder.

Caution

Always use the RDISK update function right after any changes are made to the workstation that you want to be able to recover in case of an emergency.

Tip

Better safe than sorry. Always maintain at least two identical copies of the ERD. Floppy disks are magnetic media and are easily corrupted by such ordinary things as magnets in speakers, motors, and other common devices. This "double-copy" advice applies to the startup diskettes you create for Windows 98/Me also. In fact, you should keep two copies of every major backup you make on a system. You never know when one copy will become corrupted.

To create an ERD in Windows 2000, use the following steps:

1. Click on Start, Programs, Accessories, System Tools, Backup.
2. From the Welcome tab that appears, click the button labeled Emergency Repair Disk.

3. The dialog box in Figure 2.3 appears. If you select Also Back Up the Registry to the Repair Directory check box, a copy of your current Registry files is copied first to the /repair folder (this action is similar to using the Update Repair Info button when creating the Windows NT 4.0 ERD).

FIGURE 2.3

Select the check box to save the Registry along with other information on the emergency repair diskette.

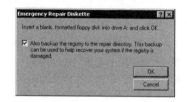

4. Insert a blank floppy diskette into the diskette drive and click the OK button. Creating the ERD should take a minute or less.

5. Label this diskette and store it away in a safe place!

The emergency repair disk can be used during a new installation of Windows NT or Windows 2000. During the installation, you are prompted to install the operating system or repair an existing one. Select the repair option, and you will be prompted for the ERD when it is needed to restore Registry settings and other files.

Installing Multiple Operating Systems

When trying out a new operating system, it is typical for the informed enthusiast to perform a multiple boot installation so that it is possible to switch back and forth between the "known" operating system and the new one. This can be a good idea for several reasons. First, it lets you try out the new operating system to decide if the features it provides are up to your needs and expectations. Second, it gives you time to learn the new operating system. In a pinch, you can always boot back into the older version to perform a task that needs to be done quickly until you figure out how to do it under the new operating system.

It is easy to install multiple versions of Windows operating systems on the same computer, but there are a few things to consider when doing so. First, you should install them in the order in which they were released. For example, if you want to keep Windows 98 and Windows NT on the same computer, as well as install a version of Windows XP, then you should install Windows 98 first, then Windows NT, and then Windows XP.

Second, although the BOOT.INI file will always reside on the boot disk (which, in most cases, is your C: drive), Microsoft recommends using separate partitions to install different operating systems. You can, if you want, just install them all on the same disk, using a different system root. For example, use /Windows for Windows 98 and then during the

Windows XP installation, specify a root directory of /Winxp. However, you should use a separate disk partition because when you install applications, you will most likely install them into default folders like /Program Files. When you reinstall applications under the different operating systems you choose to multi-boot; it is possible that one installation will install files that can interfere with the application (and even the operating system) under a different boot.

For this reason, it is also recommended that in addition to installing each operating system on a separate disk partition, you should *not* install an application on a partition that contains an operating system other than the one you will use for that application. For example, if you use Microsoft office, it is tempting to install Windows 98 on the C: drive and then install Windows XP on the D: drive. When it comes time to install Microsoft Office, you can save space by specifying the C: drive as the target for installing the application suite under each of the operating systems. However, doing so will produce unpredictable results when you run the applications. Instead, install Microsoft Office (or any other application) on the C: drive when you boot Windows 98 and on the D: drive when you boot Windows XP.

Therefore, when multi-booting a computer, first separate your disk drive into partitions so that you can use one for each operating system root. If you have multiple physical drives installed in the computer, that's even better. You can still use multiple partitions on either of the drives, but place the swap files on the drives that do not hold the particular system root. By placing swap files on a separate physical disk, you can speed up the paging process discussed in the "Paged-Based Virtual Memory Addressing" section in Chapter 1, "Looking Inside Windows XP." Placing a paging file on a separate disk partition doesn't do much to improve performance, since the same drive is accessed for paging, the operating system, and the applications if they all reside on different partitions on the same physical drive.

> **Tip**
>
> One of the best tools to partition a hard drive is PowerQuest's PartitionMagic 7.0 (http://www.powerquest.com/partitionmagic/). It can prep your hard drive for a multitude of operating system schemes. Best of all, it's compatible with Windows XP.

Speaking of partitions, if you choose to install Windows XP on a compressed partition, it must be an NT File System (NTFS) partition. Don't attempt to install Windows XP on a partition that was compressed using DriveSpace. Additionally, if you plan to multi-boot and include Windows 95/98 or Windows Me along with Windows XP, you will need to be sure that the earlier versions of Windows are installed on a FAT or FAT32 partition, since these partitions don't support the NTFS file system. The simplest method is to create the boot partition (usually your C: drive) using FAT or FAT32. The original version of Windows 95 supports only FAT partitions. The later OSR2 version supports FAT32, as does Windows 98 and Windows Me.

Windows NT 4.0 can also have problems with the type of partition on which it is installed. If you plan to multi-boot Windows NT 4.0 and Windows XP, then install Windows NT 4.0 on a FAT or FAT32 partition. Although NTFS is preferred for a standard Windows NT 4.0 installation, due to the security features NFTS offers, Windows NT 4.0 requires Service Pack 4 (or a later service pack) to enable it to access the newer versions of NTFS used by Windows 2000 and Windows XP. However, even with the Service Packs installed, Windows NT 4.0 cannot access all of the features of the newer versions of NTFS.

To summarize, if you want to multi-boot the whole range of Windows operating systems, from Windows 95 through Windows XP, your best bet is to format the boot partition using FAT and then format other partitions using FAT, FAT32 or NTFS, according to the operating system that will be installed on that partition.

Lastly, don't use the same hostname for the computer for every operating system you install, if you participate in a network. This is especially true for computers that use Windows NT domains or the Active Directory. In a domain, a computer account is created, along with a hostname, and a unique security identifier (SID) associated with the hostname. If you use the same hostname for each operating system you install, your computer account will not work for each operating system. This is because the SID will not be the same.

Preparing Your Computer for XP

As with any upgrade or install, there are several important steps to take before you stick in the new operating system CD and begin your upgrade or installation. These may seem obvious at first, but it is worth mentioning the obvious because today many people have become used to simple upgrades in which no problems occur. However, Windows XP is a significant upgrade. It is the convergence of the Windows 95/98 code base with the Windows NT/2000 (and now XP) code base, so things may not be as easy as they were in the past. The following precautions should be taken before you just pop in the CD and start an upgrade or install.

It's Cleanup Time: Uninstall Unnecessary Applications and Components

If you have applications or components of the operating system installed that you no longer use and don't intend to use, now is a good time to get rid of them. Cleaning unnecessary apps and components from your system can save time during the upgrade or installation of Windows XP.

In the Control Panel, use the Add/Remove Programs icon to bring up the Add/Remove Programs window. Figure 2.4 shows this window as it appears on Windows 2000 Workstation.

> **Tip**
>
> One thing to be aware of is the unfortunate tendency for Windows platforms to not completely erase every file associated with an uninstalled application. This should prompt you to manually check the folders in which the application was stored after the uninstall process is completed. You can also invest in a third-party application, such as Norton CleanSweep 2002 (`http://www.syman-tec.com/sabu/qdeck/`), which is compatible with Windows XP.

FIGURE 2.4

Use the Add/Remove Programs applet found in the Control Panel to remove programs or Windows Components you no longer use.

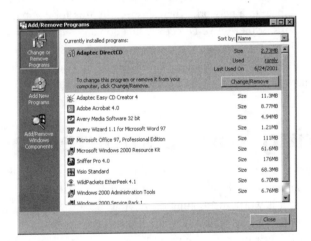

To remove an application, simply click once on the application and then click the Change/Remove button that appears. Depending on how the application was installed, you will be prompted to remove the program files, icons, and so on.

Caution

When you remove an application using the Add/Remove Programs utility, you may receive a message indicating that a file might be used by more than one application. You can choose to go ahead and remove the file, to remove all files that might be used by other applications (Yes to All button), or to leave the file on the system. To prevent the possibility of corrupting another application, the best thing to do in this situation is to leave the file. Removing the majority of the application's files and its Registry entries will still go a long way toward cleaning up your system.

Again, a third-party application such as CleanSweep will be able to track these duplicate entries and better safeguard your system.

To remove a Windows component, click the Add/Remove Windows Components button on the left side of this utility. The Windows Components Wizard dialog box will pop up and allow you to remove components by deselecting the check box associated with the component to be removed. After you deselect the component, click the Next button, and the wizard will prompt you through the process of removing the particular component.

When the wizard has finished removing the component, a dialog box will present you with an information message. Click Finish to dismiss this dialog box and then close the Add/Remove Programs window by clicking on Close at the bottom right of the window.

Save Copies of Application Configurations

When you install an application on a computer, you typically will have some aspects of the application that you can configure to make it function in a manner you prefer. Depending on the application, make a note of the configuration changes you make so they will be available if you need to reinstall the application.

For example, have you safely stored away the phone number, username and password, and any other information you may need to set up your Internet dial-up account again? Do you use a logon script? Do you use Serial Line Internet Protocol (SLIP) or Point-to-Point Protocol (PPP) Internet connections? You can use the Alt+PrintScreen method mentioned earlier in this chapter to take snapshots of configuration screens and store the data offline so that you don't have to write it all down.

> **Note**
>
> The next chapter discusses the Files and Settings Transfer Wizard for assisting in the process of saving your application configurations. However, this utility can't transfer settings for every possible application that you can buy for a Windows operating system, so if a particular configuration is important to you, keep a record of it!

Save Hardware Configuration Data

Just as you should save application-specific configuration information, you should also keep track of the hardware components that make up your system. First, you need to know the hardware components on your system so that you can compare them with the HCL, as mentioned earlier in this chapter.

However, it is also important to keep track of how each hardware device is configured. You can use the System Information accessory to do this. For example, on a Windows 98 computer, use the following steps to view information about your current system configuration:

1. Click on Start, Programs, Accessories, System Tools, System Information.
2. In Figure 2.5 you can see the System Information tool with the Network component selected.
3. Instead of taking screen shots for each device installed, it is easier to produce a report using this tool. To do so, click on File and then Save.

FIGURE 2.5

Use the System Information Tool to record specific information about your computer's configuration.

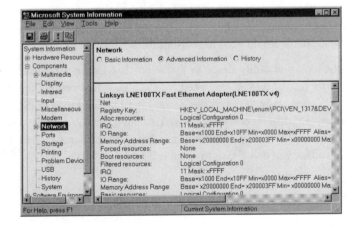

4. A dialog box will prompt you for a filename and what format you want to use to create the output file. Select Text File (.txt) and click OK. The output text file will be quite lengthy (probably between 75 to 100 pages), so be patient while it is created.

5. When finished, click on File and then Exit.

This report can be invaluable for troubleshooting purposes, especially when upgrading the operating system. It includes not only information about hardware components installed on your system, but also the drivers used, Registry keys, and other valuable information. If you upgrade to Windows XP and find that a device on the HCL no longer works, you can use the information about the device contained in this report to help solve the problem. It may be that an interrupt request line (IRQ) or other system resource has been incorrectly assigned.

As with other configuration information, you should save this report to a floppy disk, network file share, or some other place not located on your computer. If you want, use the printer icon on the toolbar to print the report.

Back Up Everything!

If you have, for example, all the application installation discs you need so that you can recreate your application environment, then a full backup of all disk partitions may not be necessary. A full backup can save time, but by using the original application discs (or new ones from the vendor) you can restore your entire operating environment if something doesn't upgrade as you expect it to.

However, I can't say the same thing about application data. Data created by applications is transitory and does not reside on the installation disc. The simplest example is that of a word processing program. The most popular office suite in use today is Microsoft's Office (in its many variations, from Office 97 to the newest Office XP and soon to be Office .NET). Although the application CDs can be used to restore the actual application, they cannot be used to restore the data files you created using them. Therefore, you need to make sure that you create backups of all your Office data—Word documents, Excel spreadsheets, and so on. If you use other applications, find out where the data files are located by reading the documentation and be sure to create backups.

Using a Tape Drive for Backups

The ideal situation would be to create a backup of everything before you begin to upgrade or install, using a tape backup (or other large capacity backup media) to back up every disk on your system. You can always use the backup to restore your system to its original state.

For corporate users, your administrator may already have in place the necessary measures to automatically back up your system on frequent basis. By placing applications and data on network drives, it is a simple matter to create complete backups using high-capacity tape drives on the servers that host the applications and data. For small office/home office users, a large capacity tape drive may not be cost-efficient. Disk drive sizes have increased dramatically in the past few years (it is not unusual to buy a new workstation with a 60GB or larger disk drive today), but the backup capacity of inexpensive tape drives has not kept pace.

Keep in mind the following things when considering using a tape backup on an individual workstation:

- Compatibility—Be sure that your tape drive will operate under the new operating system. Otherwise, all your work will be for naught!
- Capacity—How many tapes will it take to back up your entire system?
- Adapter—Does the drive use the standard IDE interface that is typical for most desktops or does it use one of the many different SCSI interfaces, which usually operate at much faster speeds?
- Backup Speed—How fast does the tape drive back up from disk to tape? What is the rate at which it can restore data?
- Price—This is an important factor if you are a home user or a small office user. Don't forget the cost of the backup tape media either, which can be quite expensive in some cases.

For example, you can purchase a small quarter-inch tape (QIT) drive for $100 to $1,000. QIC tape drives can be purchased at low cost, and the backup media isn't that expensive. You can find QIC tape drives that use a standard Integrated Drive Electronics (IDE) connection or a Small Computer System Interface (SCSI) connection to your computer. A typical system of this type can store, in compressed format, about 10GB to 20GB of data on a single tape. The transfer speed usually goes up to about 120MB per *minute* when using a SCSI interface. Although an inexpensive tape drive does offer the capacity to back up everything on a workstation that contains a large amount of disk space, backing up and restoring data can take a lot of time, and you will have to use more than one tape for the backup if your hard disk capacity is larger than about 20GB.

Another kind of tape drive that you might consider is a digital audio tape (DAT) drive. These drives generally cost more than QIC drives, but offer faster transfer rates, usually require a SCSI interface card, and also large storage capacity media. For just a little more than $1,000, you can purchase a DAT drive that can store up to 40GB of data on a single tape with a transfer rate of 330MB per minute—a considerable improvement over the transfer rates you can achieve with QIC tape drives.

Tape drives that use digital linear tape (DLT) cartridges are usually a lot more expensive (thousands of dollars), but also can store a lot more data and usually at a faster transfer rate. For example, a DLT drive (using a SCSI interface) can store between 20/40GB of data on a single tape, with a transfer rate of up to 3MB per *second*. (Yes, that's per second, not per minute!) The prices for a high-speed, large capacity DLT drive can put them out of the affordable range for use on a single workstation. However, for use on a large server, these kinds of drives are practically a standard. The newer Super DLT drives are even faster and accordingly, much more expensive.

> **Note**
>
> Keep in mind that while it may be a wise investment to spend a few thousand dollars to protect data that is worth a lot more, you will also have to buy the backup tape media. Like the tape drive itself, backup media can range from very inexpensive (under $10 for many QIC or DAT tapes) to very expensive (more than $50 for many DLT tapes).

Again, keep in mind the costs of having to recreate your data files when deciding whether a tape drive and the associated media are too expensive. When you do encounter a disaster during an operating system install or upgrade, having a complete backup of your system on tape can pay for itself in just that one restore!

Other Backup Choices

If a complete system backup to tape is not possible, then there are several other media you can consider using to back up important data files. These include the following:

- Floppy disks—If you only have a small amount of data, such as a few word processing documents and other data of a similar nature, you can use one or more floppy disks to back up your data. To make things simpler, you can use a program like WinZip to create a compressed backup that can span multiple floppy discs. For more information about WinZip, visit http://www.winzip.com/.

- Zip and Jaz drives—These removable media drives are very popular with home users and can be connected to a computer using a variety of methods, ranging from a parallel port, universal serial bus (USB) port and SCSI cards. If you decide to use one of these devices as a backup solution, go for the SCSI interface or USB connection. Neither is that expensive and the transfer rate is so much faster than a parallel port connection that the cost becomes insignificant. Note that Zip and Jaz drive media can be rewritten, like floppy disks, but hold a much large amount of data (from 100MB to 250MB for the Zip drive and up to 1GB for a Jaz drive). Zip disks can be purchased for around $10 to $15, whereas a Jaz disk will set you back about $75, depending on where you buy them.

- Recordable CDs—CD burners are very inexpensive compared to just a year ago. For less than $150 you can purchase a CD recorder drive if you don't already have one. Also, since you are upgrading to Windows XP, it supports built-in CD recording technology, so you might as well consider getting one now if you don't have one. CD-R and CD-RW (rewritable) media can store a lot more data than a floppy disk (between 650MB and 800MB, depending on the size of the media you buy), and it is ideal for backing up data. However, for creating a backup of a 60GB disk drive, this is obviously not a good solution! Consider CD-R technology as a solution that falls between using simple floppy disks and large capacity tape drives.

If you have multiple partitions or multiple disks installed in the computer, you may want to consider copying data files to other disk partitions or drives. However, keep in mind that if the system does become unbootable, you may have to wipe out a partition table (and thus lose all data on all partitions on the particular drive). Copying files to a separate physical disk is not a bad idea, but again, if something goes wrong with the system, you may not be able to recover the data from the drive in an easy manner.

Of all the choices you have, tape backups are probably the safest and offer the largest capacities and transfer rates. In terms of expense, recordable CD media is very inexpensive today, and the CD burners that you can buy support speeds of 16X and faster. Make your decision based on what data you need to back up, how much data you need to back up, and what it is worth to you.

Be sure to back up your data files before you attempt any computer install or upgrade. Remember Murphy's law—things that can go wrong will go wrong when you least expect them to. Having a good backup to recover from a botched upgrade or installation can be worth its weight in gold.

Defragment the Disk Partition

Although not a necessity, it is a good idea to defragment the disk partition on which you intend to install Windows XP. Defragmenting reorganizes the sectors of your disk so that files are written to consecutive sectors, rather than on sectors scattered all over the disk. Copying files to consecutive sectors makes the system read faster, with fewer movements of the read head.

Defragmentation also tries to group together sectors of free space. This means that when you write files to a disk that has just been defragmented, it's more likely that the disk controller will be able to write the file using consecutive sectors. Or, if it's a large file, at least there won't be as many fragments if most of the free space has been collected together into consecutive segments.

What does this mean for an upgrade or install of Windows XP Professional? Well, obviously, it means that if you have defragmented the disk, then the installation process will be able to write files to the disk a little faster since there will be larger sections of consecutive free sectors. If you choose an option to copy the source files to the hard disk before the install or upgrade begins, then they are also more likely to be written with fewer fragments. Hence, when they are read by the setup program, the process will proceed a little faster.

Defragmenting a hard disk before the install or upgrade is not a necessity, but if you have the time it can speed up the process a little. After you have finished installing Windows XP, you should perform another defragmentation of the hard disk since the installation or upgrade process itself involves writing and deleting a large number of files, which can put the disk back into a state where some of the files are badly fragmented.

You can defragment disks on Windows 95 to Windows 2000 systems. When the defragmentation has completed, a prompt will allow you to view a report, which will give you statistical information such as the number of files, number of files that are still fragmented (and the number of fragments), and so on. Note that the defragmentation utility cannot completely defragment every file on the disk. However, it will significantly reduce the number of fragmented files so that your disk will operate much more efficiently.

Defragmenting Windows 95/98 or Windows Me Disks

Use the following steps to defragment the C drive, and the partition on which you want to install Windows XP:

1. Click on Start, Programs, Accessories and then System Tools.
2. Click on the Disk Defragmenter.
3. A display will show you the disks and partitions on the system. Click on the disk partition you want to defragment and then click the OK button.
4. The Defragmentation utility prompts you before starting the procedure. Click Yes to continue.

Sit back and relax for a while. Defragmenting a disk can take quite some time, depending on both the size of the disk partition and the degree to which the partition is fragmented.

Defragmenting Windows NT 4.0 Workstation Disks

In Windows NT 4.0 the Disk Administrator utility is used to manage disks, and this includes, of course, the capability to defragment a disk partition. Note that you must be logged onto the workstation using an Administrator account, or a user account that is a member of the Disk Administrators group, to use this utility.

The following steps can be used to defragment any disk partition on the workstation:

1. Click on Start, Programs, Administrative Tools and then Disk Administrator.

2. The main window for the Disk Administrator will pop up showing a logical representation for each disk, as well as the partitions on each disk. If there is any unformatted space on the disk, that will also be displayed.

3. Right-click on the disk partition you want to defragment and select Properties from the menu that appears.

4. When the Properties sheet for the disk partition appears, click on the Tools tab.

5. On the Tools property sheet, click on Defragment Now.

Again, sit back and wait a while as the process of defragmenting a disk partition can take a considerable amount of time.

Defragmenting Windows 2000 Professional Disks

With Windows 2000 the Microsoft Management Console (MMC) is used for most system administration tools. Gone are the User Manager and Disk Administrator tools you were used to using with Windows NT 4.0. Instead, the common MMC interface makes it easy to switch from one task to another without having to learn the complexities of how the interface was written for each utility.

To defragment a Windows 2000 Professional disk partition, use the following steps:

1. Click on Start, Programs, Administrative Tools and then Computer Management.

2. When the Computer Management window appears, you will notice it is divided into two main sections (see Figure 2.6). The left pane contains a tree structure that allows you to select the computer management tool to use. The right pane will display information about that tool. Under Storage in the left pane, click on Disk Defragmenter.

3. After clicking Disk Defragmenter, the right pane will display the status of the disks installed on the system (see Figure 2.7). At the top of the right side pane, click once on the disk you want to defragment and then click Defragment.

4. The Analysis Display field in the right pane will slowly begin to display information about the degree to which the partition is fragmented. This will take a few minutes as the utility examines the disk partition. Following the analysis, the Defragmentation Display field will show you the progress it has made as the defragmentation process accomplishes its task.

5. When the defragmentation is complete, a dialog box will pop up, allowing you to view a report on the results of the defragmentation of the disk volume. Click OK to dismiss the dialog box and then click Close in the top right corner to dismiss the Computer Management utility.

FIGURE 2.6

Use the Disk Defragmenter tool found in the Computer Management MMC console to defragment disk partitions.

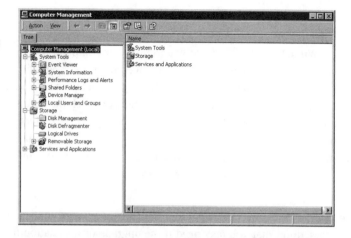

FIGURE 2.7

The right side pane of the MMC console will display the disk partitions you can select to defragment.

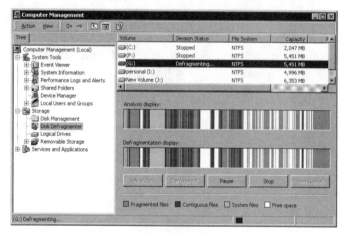

2

Make a List and Check It Twice

Now that you have cleaned up your system and recorded all the information required for networking and application configuration, you are just about ready to begin installing or upgrading to Windows XP Professional. However, just to be sure you have covered all your bases, consider making a checklist to use for each computer on which you are installing Windows XP and check off each item so that you can be absolutely sure you are prepared.

Create a checklist based on the topics covered in this chapter and add to it any additional items that may be helpful in your environment. For example, if you are upgrading a lot of computers in a corporate situation, you may want to include on the checklist such information as the user(s) who use the system, their manager, and the location of the computer.

Summary

Upgrading to Windows XP will enable you to use your computer more efficiently and give you access to new technologies that can make you more productive. However, careful planning can help you avoid the pitfalls that can occur during an upgrade or installation. Before you begin the installation, carefully check the hardware prerequisites and compatibility issues you will encounter with your system. Conduct a pilot installation program to test drive an installation before you put the real rollout in motion. If you are installing to a network, be certain to record all essential network information beforehand. Also, in any installation situation, weigh your options for upgrading or making a clean install.

Before you start an upgrade, back up important files and record configuration information and other settings that you may need if the upgrade or installation fails and you need to recover the system. Also, keep careful records of all backups, records, and configuration items you have checked during this preinstallation process.

In the next chapter, we will get right into the upgrade/installation process. Installing Windows XP is an easy task, and you will soon be using the new features it provides.

Installing and Upgrading Windows XP

IN THIS CHAPTER

- **Overview of the Windows XP Setup Process** *54*

- **Starting the Windows XP Setup Wizard** *61*

- **First, the Setup Wizard Needs Some Information** *63*

- **After the First Reboot: Text Mode Setup** *66*

- **After the Second Reboot: Read Me Now!** *72*

- **After the Third Reboot** *77*

CHAPTER 3

In the last chapter, you discovered some of the things you need to do before starting an upgrade or fresh installation of Windows XP. Of course, one of the main things that you need to decide is whether you want to upgrade your current Windows operating system to Windows XP or do a clean installation. In this chapter you will learn how to start the Setup process that will perform either of these functions. You will learn how to start the Windows XP Setup Wizard and what information you may need to supply the Setup program.

If you have performed an upgrade or installation of a previous version of Windows NT or Windows 2000, then most of the steps that the Setup program performs will be familiar, although the screen displays will look a little different. Windows XP has a new graphical user interface (GUI), and you will get your first look at this during part of the Setup process.

Note

For the purposes of this chapter, Windows XP Professional was used to demonstrate the installation process. The steps you see here will be very much the same if you happen to be installing the Home Edition for Windows XP.

Overview of the Windows XP Setup Process

The very first thing you should determine before you try an upgrade to Windows XP is whether there is an upgrade path from your current version of Windows. Table 3.1 lists the various choices for upgrading to Windows XP.

If your operating system is listed as having no upgrade path, then you really have two options: (1) you can perform a clean install of the XP operating system or (2) you can upgrade to a computer with Windows XP preinstalled.

If the upgrade path you need is available, then you will need to begin to set up Windows XP.

Setting up Windows XP is done in several phases. Once you start, the Setup Wizard will prompt you for a little information and then will copy some files to your hard disk. The system will then reboot into what is usually called *Text Mode Setup*. During the Setup process, you will be allowed to select whether to upgrade or install Windows XP and to choose the disk partition on which you want to place the system files. You can create partitions in unused portions of your hard disk, as well as delete and recreate partitions during setup. You can format the partition using either file allocation table 32 (FAT32) or NT File System (NTFS), both of which are supported by Windows XP.

Table 3.1   Upgrade paths to Windows XP Professional

Previous Version	*Upgrade?*
Windows 3.1	No
Windows 95	No
Windows 98/Windows 98 SE	Yes
Windows Me	Yes
Windows NT Workstation 3.51	No
Windows NT Workstation 4.0	Yes
Windows NT Server 4.0	No
Windows 2000 Professional	Yes
Windows 2000 Server	No*
Windows XP Home Edition	Yes

*A new release of Windows XP, Windows XP Server, will be available sometime in the first half of 2002 and will serve as the upgrade for Windows 2000 Server edition.

> **Tip**
>
> As you will learn in later chapters, one of the advantages of using the NTFS file system over FAT or FAT32 is that it provides for greater security. Although FAT and FAT32 are okay for Windows 95/98/Me versions of Windows, which are not capable of reading NTFS partitions), only NFTS allows you to set access permissions on a file-by-file or directory basis, and audit the access to those files or directories. If you are doing an install of Windows XP and don't need to let other operating systems have access to the installation partition, then I would recommend you use NTFS so that you can exercise this increased security over your operating system files.

3

INSTALLING AND
UPGRADING
WINDOWS XP

Starting the Setup process can be done by booting from the source CD, by inserting the CD in your CD-ROM drive while another version of Windows is booted, or by using a network connection to the Setup files. You can choose components you want to install, such as networking components or installing a modem, or you can choose to delay these until after the installation. Unlike previous versions of Windows, you can also create local user accounts during the Setup process, or you can create them later by using an applet in the Control Panel.

The time required to set up depends on the hardware installed on your computer. Obviously, the speed of your central processing unit (CPU), whether you are using the CD to run the Setup program or whether you are accessing the Setup files from a network, will make a difference for installation time. You can expect, however, that on a typical computer that meets the minimum hardware requirements discussed in Chapter 2, you will spend a little more than an hour setting up your computer to run Windows XP.

In the next few sections, we will look at some things you should do before you begin to upgrade or install Windows XP, such as creating a checklist. In addition, you will learn about the Files and Settings Transfer Wizard and Dynamic Update, both of which are designed to make the transition to a new operating system, or computer, an easier task.

What Is Dynamic Update?

One of the problems with distributing an operating system on a CD is that once the new operating system starts to become widely adopted, vendors of hardware components such as network cards, display drivers, and so on either create new drivers for the operating system or create updated drivers to fix problems that weren't anticipated when the driver was first created. You also may find that new hardware comes on the market after the Windows XP installation CD is created, so there is no driver for the device available during installation.

Dynamic update makes use of the Windows Update service and can be run during the Setup process to download new drivers if a better one is available from the Windows Update site than the one supplied on the distribution source CD.

If you are connected to the Internet during the Setup process (for either an upgrade or an installation), then you will be able to use the Dynamic Update service to check for additional device drivers so that you won't have to worry about installing them later. You can also use Windows Update at a later time to update drivers, if you want. However, by using Dynamic Update, you can be sure you have the most recent drivers and any other patches or updates that Microsoft has created since the installation CD was created.

What Is the Files and Settings Transfer Wizard?

If you are installing Windows XP on a new computer, you can save some time by using the Files and Settings Transfer Wizard. This wizard allows you to migrate some of the files, documents, and settings for some applications to the new computer. You do this by using a floppy disk or other removable media, or even a local area network (LAN) connection to transfer the data to the new computer. Although the wizard won't actually migrate the applications (you will have to reinstall those), it will migrate the settings for some of them.

The wizard will take you through a step-by-step process to collect the data on the old computer and transfer it to the new computer. Although the wizard doesn't support transferring settings for all applications, it does for many of the more popular packages like

Microsoft Office and will also allow you to select any additional files and folders that you want to transfer.

By default, the configuration settings for the following applications are supported by the wizard:

- Internet Explorer
- Outlook Express
- Dial-up connections
- Phone and modem settings
- Accessibility settings
- The classic Windows 2000 desktop settings (this is optional)
- Screen savers
- Fonts
- Folder options
- Taskbar settings
- Mouse and keyboard settings
- Sound settings
- Regional options (such as date/time settings)
- Microsoft Office settings and file types
- Network drive connections
- The Printers desktop folder
- My Documents, My Pictures, and My Favorites folders
- Cookies

As you can see, this migration wizard will save you a lot of time if you perform a clean install on a new computer. You won't have to spend time writing down a list of your current settings and then reapplying them once you have installed Windows XP on the new computer.

3

INSTALLING AND
UPGRADING
WINDOWS XP

Note

The Windows 2000 Resource Kit included a command-line utility called the *User State Migration Tool (USMT)*. This tool creates INF files to store settings and other information. The system administrator can edit this file to customize the settings and data that will be transferred to a new computer. A newer version

continues

of this utility will be available after Windows XP is released, and it can be used in conjunction with or instead of the Files and Settings Transfer Wizard to assist migration to new computer hardware for a large environment such as a business network.

Collecting Information from Your Old Computer

Since the Files and Settings Transfer Wizard is a new application included with Windows XP, you won't find it on an older operating system like Windows 98. However, there are two ways you can use the wizard to collect settings from your old computer. You can use the Windows XP installation CD on your old computer to run the wizard, or you can use the installation CD to create a floppy disk that will run the wizard. In a large network, creating a floppy disk and duplicating it for your users is a simple method for running the wizard. This is especially true if you have a site license for Windows XP and don't have a lot of copies of the actual CD.

To create a floppy disk that can run the wizard, use the following steps:

1. Insert the Windows XP CD into the CD-ROM drive of your computer. When the initial menu pops up, select Perform additional tasks.

2. From the next menu, select Transfer Files and Settings. The Files and Settings Transfer Wizard will start with an informational dialog box telling you about its function. Click Next.

3. The wizard will then present a dialog box asking if this is the old or new computer. Select the radio button labeled New Computer.

4. The next dialog box will as if you have the installation CD. Select the No radio button and click Next.

5. Another dialog box will then ask if you have a wizard disk. Select the radio button labeled I Want to Create a Wizard Disk in the following drive. Use the drop-down menu to select the floppy disk drive, or any other removable media drive on your computer. The floppy disk is all you need, since the wizard does not require more than one diskette. Click Next.

6. Insert a blank, formatted floppy diskette into the drive and click OK to the prompt the wizard presents. The wizard will copy the necessary files to the floppy disk. When it finishes creating the diskette, you can click Cancel to close the wizard. You now have a wizard floppy diskette that you can use on your old computer.

To use the wizard diskette, insert it into the floppy drive of your old computer and run the program FASTWiz.exe from the floppy drive. This will start the wizard on your old computer.

The wizard will be able to detect that it is not running on a Windows XP computer, so it won't prompt you as it did earlier to find out which computer you are running this from. Instead, after the welcoming dialog box, you will be prompted to enter the method that will be used to transfer the files. This can be either of the following:

- Floppy drive—This can be used if you are only transferring settings. If transferring both files and settings, the transfer process may require a number of floppy diskettes, depending on the amount of files you want to transfer.

- Other—This can be another removable drive or a network drive share. For a business environment, using a folder on a shared network drive is a good solution to transfer large amounts of information.

The wizard will then ask what you want to transfer. As you can see in Figure 3.1, you can choose to transfer settings only, files only, or both files and settings.

FIGURE 3.1

The Files and Settings Transfer Wizard will prompt you for the information to be transferred to the new computer.

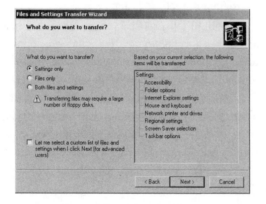

After you make your selection you can see in the right size of this figure a listing of what will be transferred. Click Next to start the process. The wizard will first scan your system and then copy the necessary information to a networked drive, or it will prompt you to insert a floppy disk if you chose that method. When finished, the wizard will tell you that it is done, and you can click Finish.

You have now saved information that you can transfer to your new Windows XP system. First, follow the steps outlined in the rest of this chapter to install Windows XP. When that is done, you can start the wizard by clicking on Start, More Programs, Accessories, System Tools and then Files and Settings Transfer Wizard. The wizard will prompt for the location of the data and restore your files or settings or both.

Installation/Upgrade Checklist

Before you start the Setup Wizard, be sure to read the previous chapter. Upgrading and installing operating systems is not a task to be taken lightly. When and if something does go wrong, you will need a back-out procedure (such as a good full backup and a set of startup disks or emergency repair disks) or a very good resume if you are performing this installation at work! Following are a few items you should be sure you have taken care of before starting the Setup Wizard:

- Create a full backup of your system. If this is not possible, create backups of application data that cannot otherwise be recovered if something goes wrong.

- Check that your computer meets the minimum hardware requirements such as CPU speed and memory.

- Get rid of applications and Windows components that you no longer use. This will help make the Setup program run a little faster.

- Check the hardware compatibility list (HCL) at `http://www.microsoft.com/hcl` to be sure that all the devices attached to your computer are supported under Windows XP. Replace components that are not compatible or obtain new drivers from the vendor if you have items not included on the HCL.

- Defragment the boot partition (usually your `c:` drive) and the partition on which you intend to install Windows XP. Keep in mind that you can create and delete partitions during setup, so if you are going to place the Windows XP system root on a different partition than the boot partition, you won't need to defragment anything other than the boot partition. This isn't a requirement, but just a good suggestion to make things run faster.

- Create a list of all hardware devices and configuration settings for devices installed in your computer. For example, what kind of network card do you use? Knowing the IRQs and other configuration settings for devices can be handy when troubleshooting the device if you have problems with it during the Windows XP Setup process.

- Exit from all other applications if you are starting the wizard from a booted system or via the network.

- Close any antivirus software that is running on your PC. Some may cause the Setup process to hang. This is especially true if you are upgrading from Windows 95/98/Me.

- Keep your fingers crossed except when entering information required by the Setup process.

Okay, now you are ready to start the Setup Wizard and install Windows XP. Good luck!

Starting the Windows XP Setup Wizard

As mentioned earlier in this chapter you can start the Windows XP Setup Wizard using several different methods. In past versions of Windows NT and Windows 2000, you could start the Setup process using floppy disks that would boot the system, gather hardware information, and then start copying files from the CD (or the network source). That option isn't available with Windows XP. If you boot from the CD, then you will get a full-screen menu that allows you to install Windows XP, browse the CD, or perform additional tasks.

Tip

Before you start to install or upgrade to Windows XP, I highly suggest that you use the Browse This CD option. This will allow you to locate and read any readme.1st or other similar files that may contain updated information that was not available on the first version of the Windows XP CD.

In the next few sections, you will explore the ways you can start the Setup Wizard.

Booting from the Windows XP CD

The distribution source CD for Windows XP is a bootable CD. Unless your computer is a very old one, you should have a CD-ROM drive that is capable of booting from the distribution CD. Simply place the CD in the drive and power up the system. The computer will boot from the CD and the wizard will pop up on your screen to start the Setup process.

Note

The El Torito Specification. You are probably aware that the BIOS of a standard PC will first look to the A: drive and then the hard disk when looking for sector. In 1995, the "El Torito" Bootable CD-ROM Format Specification Version 1.0 was published, which provides the information that computer manufacturers can use to provide support in a PC for booting from a CD-ROM disk. You can learn more about how this works by reading the specification, which is available at the following URL: http://www.phoenix.com/PlatSS/PDFs/specs-cdrom.pdf. Note that you will need to have the Adobe Acrobat Reader installed to read this, since it is presented in .PDF format.

Running the Setup Wizard under Another Version of Windows

The following operating systems can be upgraded to Windows XP:

- Windows 98 (all versions)
- Windows Millennium Edition (Windows Me)
- Windows NT 4.0 Workstation
- Windows 2000 Professional
- Windows XP (if you want to install a second copy!)

If you are running any of these operating systems, then you should be able to pop the Windows XP installation CD into your CD-ROM drive to start the Setup Wizard. If you have AutoRun enabled on the computer, then the wizard will start automatically. If not, simply use Windows Explorer to locate the Setup icon. The Setup program is found in the \i386 folder on the CD. You can double-click on the Setup icon in Windows Explorer, or you can execute the program from the Command Prompt by simply entering the program name as you would to start any other application.

> **Note**
>
> Starting with Windows 95 and Windows NT 4.0, the AutoRun feature is found in Microsoft operating systems. Basically, if the CD-ROM drive uses a 32-bit device driver (so it can detect when a CD is inserted into the drive) and if a file named autorun.inf is found in the root directory of the CD, then commands in that file will be used to run a program from the CD. You can disable AutoRun by changing values in the Registry, which we will cover in Chapter 20, "The Windows XP Registry."

Running the Setup Wizard from a Network Connection

If your network administrator has set up a file share that contains the source files for Windows XP, you can connect to the file share and execute the Setup Wizard program. In this situation, you may find that your network administrator has used a different folder than the standard \i386 folder, so be sure get the full path name you need to use to locate the Setup file.

Note

Although you cannot update an MS-DOS or Windows 3.1 computer to run Windows XP, you can run the installation program you are using under these operating systems. For example, in Appendix A you will find the steps you can use to create a bootable MS-DOS floppy disk to boot the computer, attach to the network file share that holds the Windows XP Setup files, and begin the installation. If you are starting the Setup Wizard using either MS-DOS or Windows 3.1, then the Setup program you will need to execute is called winnt.exe. If you are using Windows 98, Windows Me, or any version of Windows NT or later, then use the Setup program winnt32.exe to start the Setup Wizard.

Lights Out: Performing an Unattended Installation

If you are charged with the task of installing or upgrading a large number of computers, then it can be very tedious to have to go to each PC, run the Setup program, and wait around to respond to the prompts from the Setup Wizard. If this is the case, you can perform the installation in Unattended Setup mode. To do this, you will need to create an answer file that contains the information needed by the Setup application. The Windows XP CD contains a sample of this file, called unattend.txt, which you can customize not only to answer questions about the usual Setup process, but also to configure other applications or drivers to use during setup.

For more information on using Unattended Setup mode, see Appendix A.

First, the Setup Wizard Needs Some Information

After you have chosen to install Windows XP, you will get a Welcome to Windows Setup dialog box that will ask if you want to upgrade or install the new operating system. You can make your selection using a drop-down menu and then click Next to start the upgrade or installation.

The next dialog box is an important one, at least to Microsoft. It is the License Agreement. Be sure to read the agreement, using the scroll bars to view the entire text. When you have read it and are ready to continue, select the radio button labeled I Accept This Agreement and then click Next.

Another standard dialog box will pop up next. It is called *Your Product Key,* and this is where you enter the product key that comes with your Windows XP distribution CD. For a standard distribution CD, this is a 25-character product code that you enter into five fields, which makes it easier to correct mistakes. When you have entered the product key, click Next to continue.

Select Special Setup Options

The next dialog box, shown in Figure 3.2, is another important one. It allows you to perform the following several functions:

- Configure Language Options
- Configure Advanced Setup Options
- Configure Accessibility Options

FIGURE 3.2

Use this dialog box to configure language options and other Setup options.

Language Options

Select Language Options to bring up a dialog box that will allow you to select the language (and region) that you want to use. The choice you make here includes both language and region because many languages use different formats for such things as currency, date and time, and keyboard layout. For example, although the default is English (United States), you can also select to use English for other regions where the formats for the options just mentioned are expressed differently.

When finished making your selections, click OK.

Advanced Options

Choosing Advanced Options brings up a dialog box containing several important options. This is an important dialog box if you are going to multiboot (also known as *dual-boot*) different operating systems on your computer.

If you are going to multiboot different operating systems, then you should select the check box I Want to Choose the Install Drive Letter and Partition During Setup. This is important because, as you learned in Chapter 2, Microsoft recommends that you install each operating system on a different partition when you multiboot.

This dialog box also allows you to select the location of the distribution source files. This is typically your CD-ROM drive or a network file share. You can also change the name of the folder in which the operating system files will be stored. The default is /WINDOWS. However, you might want to change this to something like /WINXP if you multiboot so that you can easily determine what operating system is installed on a particular partition when browsing your disks.

In general, it is faster to perform the installation if you copy the Setup files to your hard disk instead of using a slow network share or a slow CD-ROM drive. You can use the check box Copy All Setup Files From the Setup CD to the Hard Drive, if this is the case with your system. Be sure you have sufficient disk space to store the files before choosing this option.

When you are finished choosing options from this dialog box, click OK.

Accessibility Options

Accessibility Options brings up a dialog box that allows you to select two of the accessibility tools for use during setup. These are as follows:

- Magnifier—This tool can be used much like a magnifying glass to enlarge portions of the screen to make them easier to read.

- Narrator—This tool will read the contents of the current screen and can be useful for those who have vision problems.

To enable either of these options, simply select the check box. When finished, click OK. Once back at the Select Special Options dialog box, click Next to continue the Setup process.

Performing Dynamic Update

This dialog box will allow you to select whether you want to use the Dynamic Update service, described earlier in this chapter, during setup. If you are installing Windows XP as soon as it is released, you can probably skip this step, especially if all the components of your computer are listed on the HCL. If you are performing this update or installation at a later time, then you can select the radio button labeled Yes and download the latest Setup files from the Internet. Otherwise, you can select the No radio button and click Next.

> **Note**
>
> Note that if you use Dynamic Update, you must have an Internet connection up and running during this Setup process!

After this dialog box has been dismissed the system will automatically reboot, and you will enter into Text Mode Setup. Now you can choose partitions, format partitions, and perform other Setup tasks.

After the First Reboot: Text Mode Setup

After you have started the Setup Wizard, it copies a small number of files to your hard disk and reboots the system. After this first reboot, the display will be in text mode instead of the usual Windows GUI. The Setup Wizard needs to gather some information about how you want to proceed, detect devices installed in your computer, and perform other tasks during this Text Mode Setup part of the process before it can reboot back into a GUI mode.

One of the first things that you will need to accomplish during this Setup phase is to detect the disk drives installed in your system. If you have a standard desktop PC that uses integrated drive electronics (IDE) disk drives, then these will be detected during setup. If, however, you use SCSI disks or have Redundant Array of Independent Disk (RAID) storage systems, you will see, shortly after the reboot, the following line of text displayed at the bottom of the screen:

`Press F6 if you need to install a third party SCSI or RAID driver...`

Pressing F6 will start a dialog that allows you to configure and install the drivers for your SCSI or other disk subsystem controllers. This option is usually used on server platforms that use large-capacity, high-speed, fault-tolerant disk subsystems. For most PCs, however, you won't need to use this option.

During the text mode part of the Setup process you will be presented with several text-based menus, which are described in the following sections.

Welcome to XP!

The first text menu that you will see will prompt you to continue setting up Windows XP to recover a previous installation or to exit setup:

Welcome to Setup.
```
This portion of the Setup program prepares Microsoft(R)
Windows XP to run on your computer.

*   To set up Windows XP Professional now, press Enter.
*   To repair a Windows XP Professional installation using Recovery Console,
    press R.
To quit Setup without installing Windows XP Professional, press F3.
```

To continue the Setup process, press Enter. At the bottom of the screen you will see text indicating that the Setup Wizard is searching for previous versions of Microsoft Windows.

Choose Your Partition

If you selected the option to choose the installation partition during the first phase of the Setup process, the next menu will display a list of the disk partitions it finds on your computer. It will list the type of file system (such as FAT, FAT32, or NTFS) for each partition or indicate that the partition has not yet been formatted. You will also see entries for any unpartitioned space present on your disk drives.

Use the up and down arrow keys to select the partition that you want to use for Windows XP.

Caution

Although you don't have to use the C: partition to install Windows XP, there will be some changes made to that partition during setup. If you are installing Windows XP on a system that contains Windows 95/98/Me, a BOOT.INI file will be created to record information. This information will be used to allow you to boot between one of those operating systems or Windows XP, if you are choosing to perform a dual-boot. If you are upgrading from one of these operating systems, then the BOOT.INI file will still be created, but you won't have the option to boot the earlier operating systems. If you have already installed any version of Windows NT or later, then this file will already be present on the system and the Setup Wizard will add an entry for the current installation or upgrade you are performing.

Once you have selected the partition you want to use to store the Windows XP system files, you are offered several options. The menu items presented to you are as follows:

```
The following list shows the existing partitions and
Unpartitioned space on this computer.
```

```
Use the UP and DOWN ARROW keys to select an item in the list.

*   Windows XP Professional on the selected item, press ENTER.
*   To create a partition in the unpartitioned space, press C.
To delete the selected partition, press D.
```

Following this text, you will see a list of partitions, one on each line, with a box drawn around the partition listing.

If you choose to delete a partition, you can then recreate the partition. This is useful if you want to change the size of a partition during the Setup process. Note that if you choose to install a copy of Windows XP on a partition that already has another version of a Windows operating system, you will get the following message:

```
You chose to install Windows XP Professional on a partition that
contains another operating system. Installing Windows XP Professional
on this partition might cause the other operating system
to function improperly.

Note: Installing multiple operating systems on a single partition
is not recommended. To learn more about installing multiple
operating systems on a single computer see
http://www.microsoft.com/windows/multiboot.asp
using Internet Explorer.

*   To continue Setup using this partition, press C
*   To select a different partition, press ESC
```

Before we continue, let's discuss disks and partitions.

What Is a Partition?

A single physical disk can be divided into more than one partition. Basically, a partition is just a section of a disk that is assigned its own drive letter. This was originally done because earlier versions of Microsoft operating systems couldn't address the larger disks that were being developed. You can learn more about physical disks and partitions in Chapter 18, "Managing Disks and Partitions." In the old MS-DOS days, you used the FDISK utility to perform this function, and you can still use an updated version of that utility to create and delete partitions. Each partition that you create on a single physical disk will be given its own drive letter so that it will appear that there are more drives installed in the computer than actually exist. Keep in mind that drive letters you see when running any Windows operating system can be a single partition that uses all the space available on a physical disk, or each drive letter can simply represent different partitions on a single disk.

Creating disk partitions is a good method for organizing the applications and files on your computer. For example, you might use a small partition for the drive letter C to store the operating system, and then one or more partitions to store data for different applications. Since each partition will appear to be a separate drive to the operating system, this can make tasks such as performing backups much simpler. For example, you might choose to create a single backup of the C: drive that contains the operating system, and then it would only be necessary to perform backups on the D:, E:, or other drives you create to store application data. Using a large disk (now available in sizes over 60GB) to store everything means you would either have to back up the entire disk or spend time creating a backup job by selecting just the folders and files you want to backup.

The Boot Partition Versus the System Partition

As mentioned earlier, the C drive letter is usually assigned to the first partition you create on a hard drive in your computer. The master boot record (MBR) is created in a special sector on the physical disk and is used by the BIOS when it boots from the hard disk. Thus, this partition is often called the *boot partition.*

For Windows XP (and earlier versions of Windows NT/2000), several other files are present on the boot partition, such as the BOOT.INI file, which is used to present a menu at boot time, along with other files that serve different purposes. From this menu that BOOT.INI enables, you can select which operating system to boot when you set your computer up for a dual boot scenario.

However, you don't have to store the Windows XP folder that contains all the operating system files on the boot partition. Instead, as described in "Choose Your Partition" earlier, you can select another partition to store the operating system files on. Additionally, as Microsoft suggests, it is a good idea to use a separate partition for each operating system you install.

Creating and Deleting Partitions During Setup

Under "Choose Your Partition," you learned about two useful options you can use during setup to repartition your hard disk drive. You can enter C to the menu choices to create a new partition if there is any unpartitioned space displayed, or you can use the D option to delete a partition and then use the C option to recreate one or more partitions in the newly unpartitioned space.

If you choose to delete the partition you have selected, the following text is displayed:

```
You asked Setup to delete the partition

G: Partition5 [NTFS] 11727MB (11727 MB free)

On 58644 MB Disk 0 at Id 0 on bus 0 on atapi [MBR]

*    To delete this partition, press L.
     CAUTION: All data on this partition will be lost.
```

```
*    To return to the previous screen without
     Deleting the partition, press ESC.
```

If you select unpartitioned space on the disk, and use the C option to create a new partition, the following text will be displayed:

```
You asked Setup to create a new partition on
58644 MB Disk 0 at Id 0 on bus 0 on atapi [MBR]

*    To create the new partition, enter a size below
     and press ENTER.
*    To go back to the previous screen without creating
     the partition, press ESC.

The minimum size for the new partition is 8 megabytes (MB).
The maximum size for the new partition is 11719 megabytes (MB).
Create partition of size (in MB): 11719
```

At this point, you can enter a new size or take the default size and create a partition using all of the unpartitioned space. Enter a value if you want to change the size and when ready, press Enter. The partition will be created, and you will be returned to the text menu that allows you to select the partition on which Windows XP will be installed.

Formatting a Partition During Setup

After you have played around with partitions and have selected the partition on which you want to store Windows XP system files, use your cursor keys (up and down keys) to select the partition and press Enter.

Text Mode Setup will continue and display another page, showing the partition you have chosen. If the partition already has been formatted and contains a file system, then you will see that information displayed also.

For example, you might see a display similar to the following:

```
D: Partition2 [NTFS] 11727 MB (11727 MB free)
On 58644 MB Disk 0 at ID 0 on bus 0 on atapi [MBR].

CAUTION: Formatting will delete any files on the partition.

Use the UP and DOWN ARROW keys to select the file system you want,
and then press ENTER to continue. If you want to select
a different partition for Windows XP Professional, press ESC to go back.

Format the partition using the NTFS file system (Quick)
Format the partition using the FAT file system (Quick)
Format the partition using the NTFS file system
Format the partition using the4 FAT file system
Leave the current file system intact (no changes)

Press ENTER to continue
```

Note

What is the difference in a regular format and a quick format? A regular format actually writes certain data out to the disk partition, such as the information needed by the file system (FAT or NTFS) to store directory information. A quick format doesn't go through that lengthy process but merely deletes all the files on the disk. If you are confident that your disk partition is in good shape, with no bad sectors or other things, then a quick format should be the logical choice. If you have time to wait for a full format to run, however, you will be playing it safe.

If you have changed your mind about which partition to use, press the Esc key to go back to the previous screen and select another partition. Otherwise, as instructed by Setup, you can choose to format the selected partition using FAT or NTFS. Use the arrow keys to select the file system and press the Enter key. Depending on the size of the partition, it will take a few minutes to complete the formatting process. You don't have to format a partition if it has already been formatted unless you want to either (1) use this as an easy way to delete any existing files on the partition or (2) change the partition's file system. For example, if you chose a partition that is currently formatted using FAT32, and you want to use NTFS, you can use the format option in this text menu to do that now during setup.

Tip

In Chapter 18, "Managing Disks and Partitions," you will find a lengthy discussion of the differences between FAT and NTFS formatted partitions. It is important to understand that if you want to be able to apply access permissions to files and folders on an individual basis, which can be used to grant or deny access by other users, then you need to use NTFS. The FAT file system does not support the ability to set resource protections on individual files or folders.

A second point to understand is that if you are going to multiboot the computer between any version Windows NT/2000/XP and an earlier operating system such as Windows 95/98/Me, you must leave the partition that contains those operating systems formatted as either FAT or FAT32. Windows 95/98/Me operating systems do not support NTFS. Again, this is another good reason to put each operating system on a separate partition so that you can use NTFS for your Windows NT/2000/XP installations, and FAT for earlier operating systems.

3

INSTALLING AND
UPGRADING
WINDOWS XP

Time for Copy: Copying Files to the Hard Disk

After the partition has been formatted, you will see text displayed at the bottom of the text mode screen indicating that the Setup Wizard is checking your disk. Next, a message will inform you that Setup is preparing a list of files to be copied to your hard disk. Since the Windows XP source CD contains many files for all the different hardware devices it supports, it doesn't need to copy the full CD to your hard disk. Instead, based on the examination it made of your hardware configuration, it builds a list of the files that will be needed.

After this file list is created, another blue screen will be displayed, with a bar graph showing the progress as files are copied to your system's hard drive. Be patient!

When the necessary files have all been copied, the system will again automatically reboot.

After the Second Reboot: Read Me Now!

After the second reboot, you will see a few messages indicating that Setup is collecting additional information, and finally, a graphical interface will be displayed. This screen will be divided into a left and right side. On the left side you will see:

- Collecting information
- Dynamic Update
- Preparing installation
- Installing Windows
- Finalizing Installation

As each of these functions completes, the text will change color so that you can keep track of what the Setup Wizard is doing. When a task has been completed, a check mark will appear to the left of the task.

At the bottom of the left part of the screen, you will see a bar graph that show the progress of each of these functions as they are performed. You will also see an Estimated Time to Completion field at the bottom left of the screen.

On the right side of the screen, you will be entertained by a collection of informational messages that are intended to introduce you to the new operating system. Each message is displayed for a short period, giving you some new tidbit of information about Windows XP. Reading these messages can keep you from falling asleep during the installation!

From Collecting Information to Finalizing Installation

Several dialog boxes will pop up during this phase of the Setup process, allowing you to further configure your Windows XP installation. These different options are discussed next.

Regional and Language Options

This dialog box allows you to select the locale for the system. The default user local is English (United States). To change this, click Customize. This will bring up the Regional and Languages Options properties sheets that allow you to select a number of things. The three tabs are Region Options, Languages, and Advanced.

> **Note**
>
> Selecting regional and language options during setup is not pertinent. These features can also be set using a utility found in the Control Panel after you have finished the installation. As a matter of fact, unless you are familiar with these options, I would recommend simply selecting the local and performing further customizations after the operating system has been installed.

Region Options

In Figure 3.3, you can see an example of this dialog box. Note that when you change Region Options, the fields under the word Samples will change to show you the kinds of formats that will be used for the region you select. Formats are provided for such things as numbers, currency, and time and date. At the bottom of this tab, you can click the Location drop-down menu to select a country. This information is used by Windows to provide you with local information.

From the drop-down menu, you can select from many languages and locales.

Click Customize if you want to change how any of the Samples fields are used. In Figure 3.4, you can see that the properties sheets that are used for customization are more complex.

To change any of the items in these properties sheets, just use the down arrow at the right side of the field to see the options available for customization.

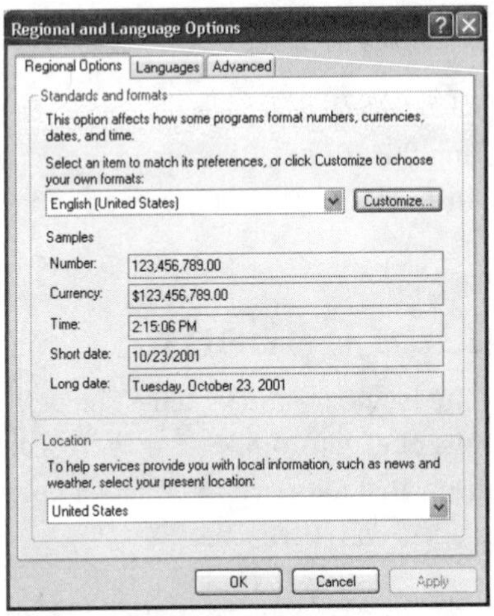

FIGURE 3.3

The Regional and Language Options dialog box allows you to set certain data formats depending on the Region you select.

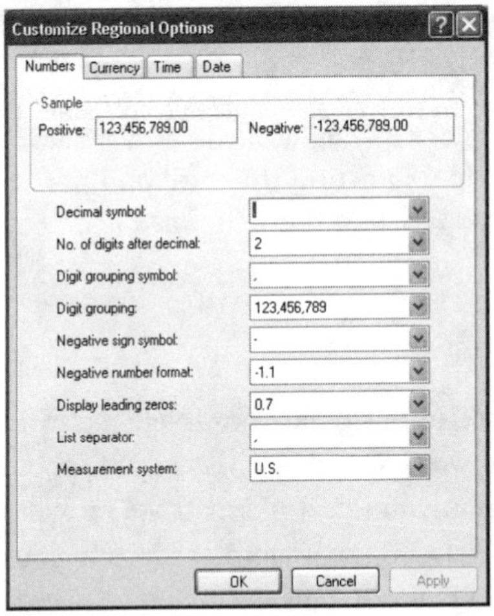

FIGURE 3.4

You can use Customize to bring up this set of property sheets to further customize how certain types of data are presented in Windows XP Professional.

The Languages Tab

As Figure 3.5 indicates, you can use this tab to install additional languages and to view details about the language you have selected.

Click Details to choose a default input language from the Text Services property sheet (see Figure 3.6).

In the Installed services section of this tab, you will see the language and keyboard type. To change the keyboard type, click Add. You can then select from the Add Input Language dialog box the type of keyboard you want to use. For example, if you have chosen English (United States) as your input language, the following keyboard layouts, among others, are available from the drop-down menu:

- United States-Dvorak

- United States-Dvorak for left hand

- United States-Dvorak for right hand

- United States-International

FIGURE 3.5

Use this dialog box to customize details about the language you have selected.

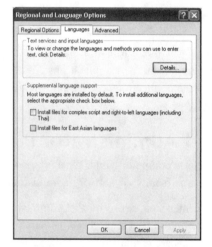

FIGURE 3.6

You can add additional languages and keyboard types using this dialog box.

The Advanced Tab

This tab allows you to set up the system for non-Unicode programs. Again, there is a drop-down menu from which you can select the language you want to use, and a section from which you can select code page conversion tables.

When you are finished using the Regional and Language Options properties sheets, click OK to continue Setup.

Personalize Your Software

This standard Windows dialog box will prompt you to enter your full name and the name of the organization to which you belong. This information is stored in the Registry and will appear later as the default when you install new applications. You don't have to enter anything here, but it can save time when applications use the information later. Click Next after entering the information.

Computer Name and Administrator Password

This dialog box will allow you to enter a computer name. If you participate in a network, then you should obtain a computer name from your network administrator.

This dialog box also prompts you to enter a password for the Administrator account. You need to enter it twice, in two separate fields. This is because the actual text you enter is not displayed. Instead, dark black circles are displayed for each character you type. By entering the password twice, the Setup Wizard can ensure that you didn't make a mistake. Click Next to continue.

Date and Time Settings

In this dialog box, you can set the current date and time. Default values will appear in these fields, but you can change them by using the up and down arrow keys. For example, to change the weekday, click on that portion of the field in the date field and use the up and down arrows to change to a different weekday. You can do the same for the month, month day, and field values in the time field.

The Time Zone section of this dialog box provides a drop-down menu that you can use to select the proper time zone for your location. Simply click on the down-arrow to display a list and then use the scroll bar that appears to find your time zone. Click once on the time zone to set it as the default.

Finally, if your location uses daylight savings time, you can enable an automatic change for this by selecting the check box Automatically Adjust Clock for Daylight Savings Changes. When finished, click Next.

Network Settings

This dialog box allows you to set up your computer's network configuration. The two choices are Typical Settings and Custom Settings. Typical Settings will install the Client for Microsoft Networks, along with TCP/IP with automatic addressing. If you choose Custom Settings, you will be able to enter network information manually.

> **Note**
>
> Information about how to manually configure network information is fully described in detail in Part 4 of this book. If you choose to manually set up the network during setup, then you should read the chapters in Part 4 first.

Click Next after making your selection. If you chose Typical Settings, the next dialog box will ask you if your computer is to be a member of a workgroup or a domain. In order to join a domain, your network administrator must set up an account for your computer and your username. If you want to join a workgroup, which is a peer-to-peer network in which authentication is done locally on each computer in the workgroup, you can enter the name of the workgroup. Click Next to continue with the Setup Process.

If you chose the Custom Settings options, you will see a dialog box that allows you to select which network components you want to install. Depending on the components you choose, additional dialog boxes will appear to prompt you for the information required. For example, you will be able to enter TCP/IP addressing information.

Setup will continue, performing functions like setting up the Start menu and registering components in the Registry. The Finalizing installation option on the left side of the page will now turn orange as Setup performs these last few functions. The last thing you will see is that Setup will remove temporary files, and then the system will reboot.

After the Third Reboot

After the system reboots, you have a few unfinished tasks to perform. Just press the F1 key to get help, or you can click on the circle with the question mark character. After this screen, you will have five tasks to complete in order to finalize the install.

3

INSTALLING AND
UPGRADING
WINDOWS XP

The Five-Step Program: Finishing the Installation

The five steps to complete configuring your Windows XP system follow.

Step 1: AU Pls. complete.

The first step asks you to slide your mouse over the mouse pad until it points to a particular location on the screen, at which point you click on the mouse button. This is just to test the mouse. Once you have tested your mouse, click Next.

Step 2: Setting Up an Internet Connection

This step allows you to set up an Internet connection for your computer. The options presented are as follows:

- DSL or cable modem
- Local area network (LAN)
- Telephone modem

If you select the radio button for any of these, then click Next to be prompted for the necessary information to set up the connection. If you want to perform these steps later, you can click Skip at the bottom of the screen.

For more information about making an Internet connection using a digital subscriber line (DSL), cable, or telephone modem, see Chapter 25, "Configuring Your Computer for an Internet Connection." For instructions on how to connect to the Internet through a LAN connection, see Chapter 24, "Configuring Your Computer for Local Area Networking."

You should simply select the radio button labeled Typical Settings if you are unsure. You will be made a member of a workgroup (with a default name of workgroup unless you choose to change it in the next dialog box that appears). If you do have information from your network administrator about network settings, then choose the Custom button and enter the information provided to you. Otherwise, for most home networking or small offices, you should choose Typical for all your Windows XP installations and upgrades and make changes (if necessary) after you have read the networking chapters later in this book.

Step 3: Activating Windows XP

One of the first things you did to install Windows XP was enter the product key code that came with your software. With this version of Windows you will find that you now have to "activate" the operating system. Next, you will be asked if you want to activate Windows XP now or at a later time. The purpose of an activation code is to prevent software piracy.

The choices presented in Step 3 are as follows:

- Yes, activate Windows over the Internet now.
- No, remind me every few days.

You have 30 days from the date of installation to activate Windows XP. To do so after the Setup process, simply click on Start/Activate Windows, and don't forget that if you take the second option above you will indeed be reminded every few days to activate the product. If you do not activate before the 30-day grace period expires, your computer will not boot into Windows XP!

According to the readme.1st document that comes with Windows XP, activation is only required for individual PC users. Corporations or other entities that use site licenses or PCs that include Windows XP preinstalled (an OEM version) will not require activation.

Click Next.

Step 4: Creating Local User Accounts During Setup

The last step in the configuration process allows you to create user accounts for other people who use your computer. You can do this now, or you can always perform this function later using the Control Panel. Select the Yes radio button to create user accounts now or select the No radio button to continue without creating additional accounts. When you have made your choice, click Next.

If you chose the *Yes* selection, then a dialog box entitled Who Will Use This Computer? pops up and provides a field in which you can enter your name, as well as fields for entering the names of five other users. You don't have to enter password information or anything else at this time, just the name that others will use to log onto your computer. When finished entering names, click Next. Note that you must enter at least one name or clicking Next won't work!

Step 5: Finishing the Configuration

The last screen simply says Thank You! and prompts you to click Finish. After you click on this, you will see some text such as Applying Your Personal Settings, and then you're done! The new Windows XP desktop, shown in Figure 3.7 will appear and you are ready to begin using the computer.

You will notice that the Start menu items are shown by default, and the Recycle Bin is present, but aside from the Windows XP Professional logo graphic, your new desktop is pristine. Your mileage may vary, however, if you purchased a PC that has Windows XP preinstalled. In that case you may see some icons other than the Recycle Bin on your desktop.

Figure 3.7

Finally, your first look at the new Windows XP Desktop! Setup has completed!

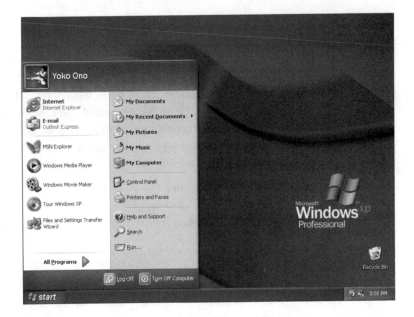

Summary

The Setup process for Windows XP doesn't differ that much from previous versions of Windows XP. You can select the partition on which you want to store the system files and customize your computer by entering locale information and creating accounts for other people who will use your computer. In the next chapter we will look at how Windows XP boots and some important files used in this process.

Unattended Installation and Sysprep

CHAPTER 4

IN THIS CHAPTER

- Syntax for the Setup Command   *82*
- Using the unattend.txt Setup File for Automated Installations   *85*
- Using Sysprep to Install Windows XP   *97*

In an environment in which a large number of similar computers will need to be upgraded or have Windows XP Professional installed, it is clearly not very feasible for the network administrator to visit each workstation and perform each installation or upgrade. As you saw in the previous chapter, the installation process can take some time to perform and a lot of prompts are used by the Setup program to help you customize the way you want Windows XP installed on your computer. You can do several things to ease this process. In this chapter, you learn how to use the command line syntax for the Windows XP Setup command, and how to use a file called unattend.txt to provide automated answers to the prompts that the setup process expects. To make your job easier, you'll also learn about using the Sysprep utility to assist you in creating an unattended answer file.

Syntax for the Setup Command

Although you can easily start up the installation of Windows XP by simply inserting the CD and choosing either an upgrade or install from the menu, you can also choose to use a command line to perform these functions. For 16-bit systems (such as Windows 95), the command is winnt.exe. For 32-bit operating systems (such as Windows NT), the command is winnt32.exe.

For a single installation, the menu is the easiest installation method to use. In environments requiring a large number of installations or upgrades, using the command can simplify matters and allow for automated installations. The system administrator can place the source files on a network share and avoid having to visit each PC with a CD in hand for running the Setup program.

The syntax for the winnt.exe command is as follows:

```
WINNT.EXE [/s[:sourcepath]] [/t[:temporarydrive]]
    [/u[:answer file]] [/udf:id[,UDF_file]]
    [/r:folder] [/r[x]:folder] [/e:command] [/a]
```

You can use the following command line switches and variables with the command:

- /s:*sourcepath*—This command line switch is used to specify the location of the source files. Use the format of *<driveletter>:path* or *\\servername\sharename[path]*.

- /t:*temporarydrive*—This switch tells the Setup program where to put temporary files used during the installation, and it tells Setup what disk drive you want to use to store the actual Windows XP system files. If you leave out the temporary drive letter and just use /t, then Setup will select a drive for you.

- /u:*answer_file*—Use this switch for an unattended setup. If you use this switch, then you will also have to use the /s switch. The value of the variable *answer_file* is the name and location of the unattended *answer file* (discussed later in this chapter). This file provides answers to the prompts that the Setup program uses so that you do not have to be present during setup.

- /udf:*id*[,*UDF_file*]—This switch allows you to specify an identifier (id). This id value is used with a Uniqueness Database File (*UDF_file*) from which some of the answers to Setup prompts are selected, overriding those values you may place in the unattended answer text file. If you use this switch but don't include the UDF_file, then the Setup program will prompt you to enter a disk that contains the file.

- /r:*folder*—Use this switch to specify that an additional folder (and its contents) be installed on the computer after the Setup program has finished.

- /rx[:*folder*]—This switch can be used to specify another folder that is copied to the system, but this folder and its contents will be deleted when Setup finishes.

- /e—Use this switch to specify a command that will be run after the end of the Graphical User Interface mode of Setup.

- /a—This switch will enable accessibility options.

The syntax for the WINNT32.EXE command is a little more complicated:

```
winnt32.exe [/checkupgradeonly] [/cmd:command_line] [/cmdcons]
[ic:ccc][/copydir:i386\folder_name] [
/copysource:folder_name] [/debug[level]:[filename]] [/dudisable]
[ic:ccc][/duprepare:pathname] [/dushare:
pathname] [/m:folder_name] [/makelocalsource] [/noreboot] [/s:sourcepath]
[ic:ccc] [/syspart:drive_letter] [
/tempdrive:drive_letter] [/udf:id [,UDB_file]] [/unattend[num]:[answer_file]]
```

The command line switches and parameters for this command are as follows:

- /checkupgradeonly—This tells the Setup program to check your computer to see if it is compatible for upgrading to Windows XP. The results will be displayed on the screen after the Setup program examines the computer. However, you can use the /unattend switch to cause the program to write the results of this check to the file %*systemroot*%\upgrade.txt. Use this if you are not sure if all the components on the target computer(s) will function with Windows XP.

- /cmd:<*command_line*>—This tells the Setup program to execute the command specified by the variable <*command line*> just before the final phase of Setup.

- /cmdcons—This command line switch will install the Recovery Console, which allows you to use a command-line interface for such things as accessing the local disk drives and starting and stopping services (including NTFS partitions) after Setup has finished. The Recovery Console can be useful for testing purposes in a computer laboratory where you are experimenting with different methods for installing or upgrading your company's computers to Windows XP.

- /copydir:i386*folder_name*—Use this switch to create another folder inside of the folder in which the Windows XP setup files are installed. This is useful when you need to modify the Windows XP setup for your particular site. If you need to install additional drivers, for example, you can create a directory and place them in this directory.

- /copysource:*folder_name*—This is similar to the /copydir:i386 switch, but Setup deletes the directory after it completes the install.

- /debug[*level*]:[*filename*]—This switch is used to create a debug file log. The variable level can be 0 for severe errors, 1 for errors, 2 for warnings, 3 for informational warnings and 4 for detailed debugging information. Recommended for advanced users only!

- /dudisable—Keeps the Dynamic Update feature from running. Only files supplied with the distribution source will be used during Setup. This switch will override a Dynamic Update selection in an unattended answer text file.

- /duprepare:*pathname*—This switch will use the Dynamic Update feature. The variable *pathname* should contain the updated files you have previously downloaded from the Windows Update Web site.

- /dushare:*pathname*—Similar to the previous entry in this list; use this switch after using the Dynamic Update feature on a computer. This switch tells the Setup program to only use the newly updated files and can shorten the time Setup requires.

- /m:*folder_name*—Use this to tell Setup to copy the setup files from a different location. If no files are present in *folder_name*, then the default location will be used instead.

- /makelocalsource—With this command line switch, Setup copies all the necessary files to the local system hard disk before proceeding with setup. This can be useful when you are using a single CD to perform Setup on multiple computers and don't want to leave the CD in one computer until Setup completes. Once the files are copied to the local hard drive you can remove the CD and proceed with the next computer.

- /noreboot—This switch tells Setup not to restart after the first file copying phase so that you can execute another command first and then restart the computer.

- /s:*sourcepath*—This tells Setup where the Windows XP setup files are located.

- /syspart:*drive_letter*—This switch tells Setup to copy the setup files to the local hard drive and mark that disk as the active partition. You can then take the disk and place it in another computer. When the second computer starts, it continues with the Setup process. The /tempdrive command line switch must be used with this one. Note that this only works on Windows NT/2000/XP computers. You cannot use this for Windows 95/98/Me computers.

- /tempdrive:*drive_letter*—This tells Setup where to place temporary files for the installation. This option differs from that used with the WINNT.EXE command, and it only tells the program where to place temporary files. It also specifies where the actual system files will be installed for an upgrade. For a fresh install, it works the same.

- /udf:*id* [,*UDB_file*]—This switch allows you to specify an identifier (*id*). This id value is used with a Uniqueness Database File (*UDF_file*) from which some of the answers to Setup prompts are selected, overriding those values you may place in the unattended answer text file. If you use this switch but don't include a value for the variable *UDF_file*, then the Setup program will prompt you to enter a disk that contains the file.

- /unattend—This switch, when used for upgrading Windows 95/98/Me or Windows NT/2000, in unattended setup mode will take settings from the previous installation. No unattended answer text file is required.

- /unattend[*num*]:[*answer_file*]—Use this switch for an unattended setup that does use an unattended answer text file. The value for *num* is the number of seconds that Setup waits after copying files before it restarts the computer. Of course, *answer_file* is the unattended answer text file you create to answer the prompts that Setup issues during the installation.

As you can see, there are many options available for using a command line installation, whether you are upgrading an older computer or a newer one. If you are going to use these commands in a large installation, it is recommended that you first experiment with the various command switches and take time to learn about the contents of the unattend.txt file.

Using the unattend.txt Setup File for Automated Installations

In the /i386 directory on your Windows XP installation CD, you will find a file called unattend.txt. You can use this file to provide answers to the prompts setup issues as it runs. Using this answer file solves part of the problem of automating the setup process. The unattend.txt file can contain a lot of information, or you can use the bare bones template included in the /i386 directory. A portion of the simple template provided by Microsoft is as follows:

```
[Unattended]Unattendmode = FullUnattended
OemPreinstall = NO
TargetPath = *
Filesystem = LeaveAlone

[UserData]
FullName = "Your User Name"
OrgName = "Your Organization Name"
ComputerName = *
ProductKey= "JJWKH-7M9R8-26VM4-FX8CC-GDPD8"

[GuiUnattended]
; Sets the Timezone to the Pacific Northwest
; Sets the Admin Password to NULL
; Turn AutoLogon ON and login once
TimeZone = "004"
AdminPassword = *
AutoLogon = Yes
AutoLogonCount = 1

[LicenseFilePrintData]
; For Server installs
AutoMode = "PerServer"
AutoUsers = "5"

[GuiRunOnce]
; List the programs that you want to lauch when the machine is logged into for
the first time

[Display]
BitsPerPel = 8
XResolution = 800
YResolution = 600
VRefresh = 70

[Networking]

[Identification]
JoinWorkgroup = Workgroup
```

As you can see, even in this simple template there are many sections (each are names
enclosed in square brackets) with variables separated from their values by equal signs. If
you require an intimate knowledge of the many variables that can be used, consult the
documentation on the Windows XP Setup CD or the resource kit. However, for most
users, a much simpler method for creating unattended answer files is available. You can
use the Windows Setup Manager Wizard. This wizard can be used to create an answer
file for both an unattended setup and for use with the Sysprep program discussed later in
this chapter.

Creating an Unattended Setup Answer Text File with the Setup Manager Wizard

The contents of an unattended setup file can become quite complex, and a misspelling here or there can lead to quite unexpected consequences. To assist you in creating the answer file that can be used for an unattended setup, for a remote setup, or with Sysprep, Microsoft provides the Setup Manager Wizard on the Windows XP setup CD. By using the wizard, you can simply answer a few questions, and the proper text file that contains your answers to Setup prompts will be created for you automatically.

Following is an example of how to use the Setup Manager Wizard. This example shows a simple setup and doesn't go into all the choices you can make using the wizard.

> **Note**
>
> If you are deploying Windows XP on a large number of computers, you might use some of the features that aren't used in this example. However, the Wizard is quite intuitive, so you should have little trouble choosing the appropriate options. You can also use the wizard to create an answer file, and then use a text processor to make changes to the file you create.

To use the Setup Manager Wizard, insert the Windows XP Setup CD into your CD-ROM drive and use the following steps:

1. When the CD menu appears, click on Perform Additional Tasks.

2. In the next submenu, click on Browse This CD.

3. Double-click on the Support folder and then the Tools folder; then the Deploy folder. Double-click on setupmgr program. Since the setupmgr program is stored in a compressed format, a dialog box will prompt you for a location you want to use to extract the expanded application to. You can browse for a folder, or just click on any drive letter. After you've done this, run the setupmgr.exe program by double-clicking on it using Windows Explorer, or you can simply enter the program name at the Command Prompt once you've navigated to the location of the expanded file.

4. The first screen the wizard presents will simply welcome you to the setup wizard and tell you what it is used for. Click Next and you will see the *New or Existing Answer File* wizard screen shown in Figure 4.1. You can choose to create a new answer file or modify an existing file; for the purposes of this example, choose the Create a New Answer File radio button.

4

UNATTENDED
INSTALLATION
AND SYSPREP

FIGURE 4.1

*You can use the
Windows Setup
Manager Wizard
to create a new
answer file or
modify an
existing one.*

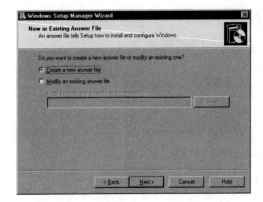

5. The next screen enables you to choose the kind of answer file you want to create. For the purposes of this example, choose Windows Unattended Installation (other options are Sysprep Install, or Remote Installation) and click Next.

6. Select Windows XP Professional in the next screen, where you are prompted for the product that the answer file is to be created for.

7. The User Interaction Level wizard screen (see Figure 4.2) lets you determine to what degree end-users will be involved in the installation. The choices are as follows:

   • Provide Defaults—You supply default answers, and the end-user can accept or override them during setup.

   • Fully Automated—You supply answers to all Setup prompts, and the end-user is not prompted or allowed to make any changes.

   • Hide Pages—You can supply answers for some pages and not for others, and the end-user will be shown only the dialog boxes for which you do not provide answers.

   • Read Only—Similar to Hide Pages except that all pages are displayed, and the end-user can only make changes on pages for which you do not supply answers.

   • GUI (Graphical User Interface) Attended—This automates only the text-mode portion of setup.

8. Click to select a choice; then click Next.

9. The next screen asks if you want to create a distribution folder or run the installation from the CD. In a large environment where it is not practical to distribute a CD to each user, it is easier to either install the setup files locally on the computer before giving it to the user or to use a network folder. For this example, choose Yes, Create or Modify a Distribution Folder. Select the first radio button, to create a distribution folder, and then click Next.

FIGURE 4.2

You can customize the end-user's involvement in the Setup process by using this page.

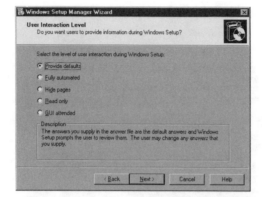

Tip

If you choose to give your users the CD for the setup process, they might just bypass your answer file and install Windows XP however they want. By using an answer file and copying the files to a distribution folder, you can use Sysprep (described later in this chapter) to further automate the Setup procedure so that the user cannot make unexpected, unwanted changes.

10. Since you chose to create a distribution folder in Step 9, the next Wizard screen (see Figure 4.3) asks where the existing setup files are located. Select the appropriate answer (either you have the CD or you have already copied the files to another directory on your network) and click Next.

11. In the next screen, choose Create a New Distribution Folder; then type a name for the new folder in the Distribution folder text box (see Figure 4.4). If you want to assign a share name, type it in the Share As text box. When you finish, click Next.

FIGURE 4.3

You need to tell the setup manager utility where the installation files are located so it can copy them to a distribution folder.

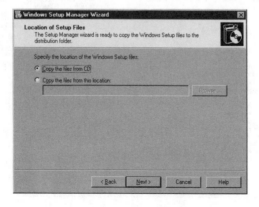

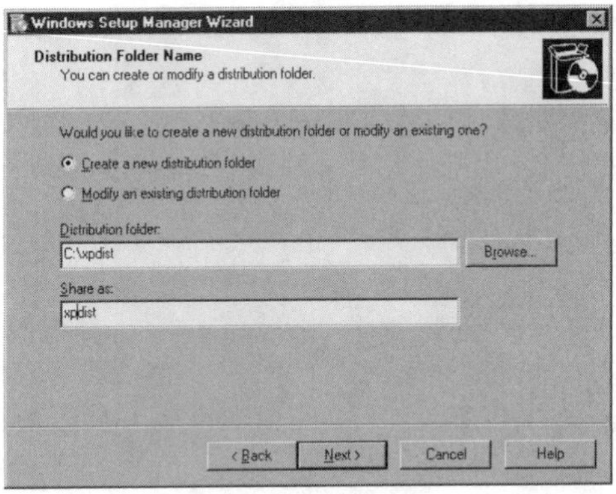

FIGURE **4.4**

You can choose the target distribution folder that will be used for the installation by the end-user. The Windows Setup Manager Wizard will create a new directory (or add one to an existing folder) if you so choose.

> **Tip**
>
> Another reason you might want to create a distribution folder, instead of letting the user have a copy of the Setup CD, is because you can add additional files, such as newer device drivers or other products, to a distribution folder. Another possibility is to burn your own distribution CD and add the extra files to that CD, but this extra step can make installation more cumbersome.

12. The wizard will now start prompting you for specific information about the Setup you want to automate. In Figure 4.5, the screens that were used earlier have been replaced by a larger one with a tree structure on the left side. It also contains prompts for information on the right side. In this Customize the Software screen, you will first need to enter a name and organization name, if applicable. These names are used as defaults during the Setup procedure. When you finish, click Next.

FIGURE **4.5**

Starting with this dialog box, you will be prompted for specific information about the software to be installed. As you enter information into the prompts on the right side, the tree structure on the left side shows your progress.

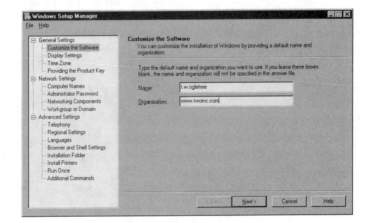

13. You are prompted for the display settings in the next screen. You can choose the colors, screen area, and refresh frequency from the options in this screens, or use the Custom button if you need to set specific settings for the monitor or graphics card you use. The Custom Display Settings dialog box will pop up and allow you to specify colors (bits per pixel), the screen resolution (such as 800 x 600 dpi, or dots per inch), and the refresh frequency (in Hertz) for the monitor.

14. Next, you are prompted for Time Zone information. Select the appropriate time zone and make sure that the date and time shown are correct for your location.

15. The next step is an important one, at least for Microsoft. Here, the wizard will prompt you for the product key that comes on the jewel case. Enter the product key and click Next to continue.

16. The next prompt (see Figure 4.6), allows you to add a computer name for the computer or specify that one be automatically generated. You can enter more than one name and click the Add button to additional ones if the answer file will be used for multiple computers. You can also create an ASCII text file with one computer name per line and use the Import button to import the file. Either way, one or more computer names will then show up in the Computers to be installed section of this dialog box.

FIGURE 4.6

Use this dialog box to enter one or more computer names with which the answer file will be used.

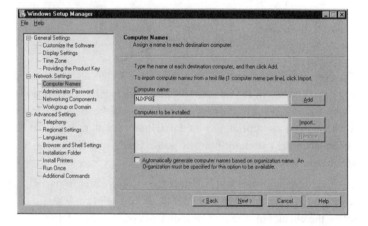

17. Use the next screen (see Figure 4.7) to specify an Administrator password for the local computer. Don't confuse this with the Administrator password used in a domain. You can also click the first radio button to cause Setup to prompt the user for an Administrator password during setup if you want them to have full control over their computer. Alternatively, select the second radio button and enter the Administrator password twice to confirm it. Use the check box Encrypt Administrator Password in Answer File to keep it from becoming available if

someone manages to get a copy of the file. A second check box labeled When the Computer Starts, Automatically Log On as Administrator will do just what it says.

> **Tip**
>
> If you specify a password, store it in a secure place so that you will have it ready if you later need to perform maintenance on the computer (such as install or remove programs).

FIGURE 4.7

You can enter a password for the local Administrator account or let the end-user create one during Setup.

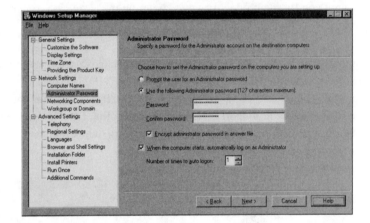

18. The Network Components screen next allows you to select a typical or custom network configuration. If you select Typical Settings, then TCP/IP, DHCP, and the Client for Microsoft Networks components will be installed. For many networks this should be appropriate, as the DHCP server can provide the necessary configuration when the computer boots. Choose Customize Settings if you want to provide specific services, clients or protocols, and values for each.

19. The next screen allows you to select for the computer to participate in either a workgroup or domain (see Figure 4.8). If you select a domain, then you should select the check box Create Computer Account in the Domain and then specify a domain administrator account and password that can be used to add the computer to the domain. If you do not do this, then you will have to manually create computer accounts for each computer yourself.

20. The Telephony screen prompts you to enter information such as your country or region, an area code, and other information of this sort. When you have entered the information, click Next to continue.

FIGURE 4.8

Choose whether the computer will be part of a Windows Workgroup or a domain.

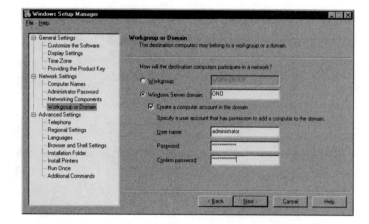

21. The Regional Settings dialog box next gives you three choices: Use the Default Regional Settings for the Windows Version You Are Installing, User Can Select Regional Settings During Setup, and Specify Regional Settings in the Answer File. The first or last of these choices should suffice for most installations. However, if you are setting up computers that will be used in a multinational corporation, the second choice may be a good idea, allowing the local user to specify the regional settings during setup.

22. The Languages dialog box allows you to add additional languages to the installation. This option doesn't give the user the option to specify a language; instead, it provides languages that can be used, for example, when a user views a Web page that uses a particular language.

23. Use the Browser and Shell Settings screen (see Figure 4.9) to decide how to set up a browser on the user's computer. Choose the first radio button, Use Default Internet Explorer Settings, if you want the typical standard installation, which will default to Microsoft's home page when the browser is first used. Choose to get settings from a customized script file created by the Internet Explorer Administration Kit that will be used during Setup to configure browser settings. Select Individually Specify Proxy and Default Home Page Settings.

24. In the same screen, choose Proxy Settings to specify a proxy server (or several proxy servers if you use multiple proxy servers for different Internet services). Choose Browser Settings to set the home page (a good idea in a corporate environment), as well as add a Help page, Search page, or list of Favorites to the browser's configuration. When you finish, click Next.

Architecture and Installation

FIGURE 4.9

*You can customize
the Internet
Explorer browser
that is configured
during Setup.*

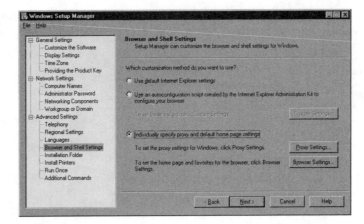

25. The next screen simply asks what folder on the user's computer you want to use
    for the Windows XP system files. You can choose from three radio buttons (a
    folder named Windows, a uniquely named folder generated by Setup, or This
    Folder:) and specify the folder name you want to use.

> **Tip**
>
> Using the installation folder option will create a unique name. This unique
> name may not make it obvious as to what it is for and may thus prevent your
> users from messing around in the system files folder.

26. If you want to install one or more printers for the user, the next screen allows you
    to do that. You can enter a printer name and use the Add button to add one or more
    printers that will be available to the users, provided that the appropriate permis-
    sions are also in place in the domain or Active Directory to enable the user to con-
    nect to the printers you specify. Remember, entering printers here does not grant
    access to the printers.

27. In the Run Once screen (see Figure 4.10), type the name of a command you want
    to run automatically after the user's initial login; click Add to add the command to
    the Run these Commands list. Repeat for each command you want to add to the
    list. When you finish, click Next.

28. In the Additional Commands screen, you can use the same process you used in the
    previous screen to specify commands that should run after the Setup process has
    finished, such as at the end of an unattended setup. Note that any command you
    enter in this dialog box must be a command that does not require that you be
    logged on in order for the command to execute. When you finish, click Next.

FIGURE 4.10

Here you can specify one or more commands that will run only once— the first time the user logs in after Setup has completed.

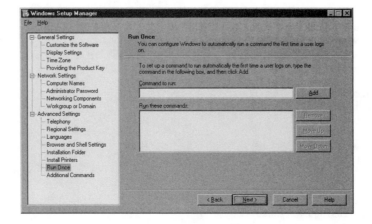

After all of these steps, which really doesn't take that much time to run through, the Windows Setup Manager Wizard pops up a dialog box (see Figure 4.11) telling you where the resulting file is located. Click the OK to dismiss this dialog box.

FIGURE 4.11

Windows Setup Manager will tell you where the file you've just created can be found so that you can use it.

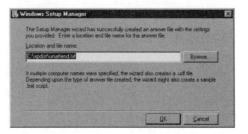

After you dismiss this dialog box, the wizard will begin to copy the installation files to the directory you specified, unless you chose to perform the Setup using a CD. After this, simply click on File, Exit to close the Setup Manager wizard.

The following is an example file created using this wizard:

```
;SetupMgrTag [Data]  AutoPartition=1

MsDosInitiated="0"

UnattendedInstall="Yes" [Unattended]
UnattendMode=ProvideDefault  OemPreinstall=Yes  TargetPath=winxp [GuiUnattended]
AdminPassword="ADMINISTRATOR"
  EncryptedAdminPassword=NO
  AutoLogon=Yes
  AutoLogonCount=1
  OEMSkipRegional=1
```

4

UNATTENDED INSTALLATION AND SYSPREP

```
[UserData]
  ProductID=DCBCB-KV2PF-897XX-M328F-CVCT8
  FullName="t.w.ogletree"
  OrgName="www.twoinc.com"
  ComputerName=NJXP66

[TapiLocation]
  CountryCode=121
  AreaCode=609

[SetupMgr]
  DistFolder=C:\xpdist
  DistShare=xpdist

[Branding]
  BrandIEUsingUnattended=Yes

[URL]
  Home_Page=www.twoinc.com
  Search_Page=www.dogpile.com

[Proxy]
  Proxy_Enable=1
  Use_Same_Proxy=1
  HTTP_Proxy_Server=proxy-server.bms.com:8080
  Proxy_Override=<local>

[Identification]
  JoinDomain=ONO
  DomainAdmin=administrator
  DomainAdminPassword=administrator

[Networking]
  InstallDefaultComponents=No

[NetAdapters]
  Adapter1=params.Adapter1

[params.Adapter1]
  INFID=*

[NetClients]
  MS_MSClient=params.MS_MSClient

[NetServices]
  MS_SERVER=params.MS_SERVER

[NetProtocols]
  MS_TCPIP=params.MS_TCPIP
```

```
[params.MS_TCPIP]
  DNS=No
  UseDomainNameDevolution=No
  EnableLMHosts=Yes
  AdapterSections=params.MS_TCPIP.Adapter1

[params.MS_TCPIP.Adapter1]
  SpecificTo=Adapter1
  DHCP=No
  IPAddress=10.10.10.93
  SubnetMask=255.255.255.0
  DefaultGateway=10.10.10.254
  DNSServerSearchOrder=10.10.10.5,10.10.10.7
  WINS=No
  NetBIOSOptions=0
```

For the setup of a large number of workstations, an unattended answer file can save the administrator a lot of work. Next, you'll learn about the Syspart utility, which can also help you when it comes to installing Windows XP on large number of computers.

Using Sysprep to Install Windows XP

Installing Windows XP Professional from scratch on each workstation in a large networked environment would be a daunting task. In this chapter, you learned how to create and use an unattended answer file to help automate the installation setup process. Here, you learn about another tool, called *Sysprep*. Sysprep allows you to run a Windows XP Setup once and then clone that installation so that you can deploy to multiple workstations quickly, without having to go through Setup each time.

You can use Sysprep in a variety of ways. Use it for simple cloning, for a full, unattended setup, as well as to add additional software or configure the Setup process. This appendix offers a basic overview of Sysprep; if you want to learn more, consult the resource kit or the documentation that comes on the Windows XP installation CD, as this is a very complex tool capable of performing many tasks.

System Identifiers in Cloning Windows XP

It is important to understand that although two computers in a Windows XP network may both be running the same operating system, there is a very important difference between the two computers. Each Windows XP computer you install will be given its own, unique system identification (SID). If you simply made a backup of a new system and copied it to the system disk of another computer, they would both have the same SID, which would cause a conflict on the network.

The SID is important for any computer that participates in a domain or the Active Directory. It is this ID that the domain security accounts manager (SAM) database or the Active Directory uses to identify the computer. The hostname you give your computer is just a user-friendly name that is easy for humans to remember. The networking components of modern Windows networks use the SID to identify your computer.

Using Sysprep to Set Up a Single Computer

One way you can use Sysprep is to create an initial installation that may include other applications that you may use in your business. You can pre-stage a common desktop environment for your user; when the user boots the system for the first time, he will have to complete just the last few steps of the Windows XP Setup process.

To do this, you begin by installing the Windows XP operating system (see Chapter 3). You can then customize the operating system and add applications that you want to include in the install. When you have finished tweaking the operating system and applications to your satisfaction, then it is time to configure Sysprep.

Keep in mind that in most companies not every desktop computer is configured exactly the same. For example, the applications used by an employee in the accounting department might not be the same ones needed by an employee who works in the manufacturing facility of your company. You can use Syspart to create customized installations for each of your different sets of users that need to share a common desktop setup. Then, when you need to install a computer for a new employee, just use the correct system image that was created using Syspart to prepare the new employee's PC.

For the following steps, you will need to have on hand a copy of the original Windows XP installation CD so that you can copy the Sysprep files to the computer you are using to create a system image for cloning. To use Sysprep, follow these steps:

1. Log onto the system using the Administrator account. If you are logged on under another account, simply log off and use Ctrl+Alt+Del to bring up a logon dialog box; then log onto the system using the Administrator account.

2. Insert the Windows XP Professional installation CD into the CD-ROM drive on the computer you used to create the install image.

3. Click Start/Run, and enter CMD into Open field of the Run dialog box.

4. Set your default directory to the root of the disk that holds the operating system. For example, use CD C:\, if you are using the drive letter C: for the system disk. If you are using multiple partitions, use the SET command at the command prompt and look for the value of the variable %SYSTEMDRIVE% to determine where your system files are stored.

5. Create a directory for the temporary Sysprep files: `MKDIR SYSPREP`.

6. Next, copy two files from the `Deploy.cab` file on the Windows XP Professional CD to this folder. First, set default to the new directory you created: `CD SYSPREP`.

7. Use Start, All Programs, Accessories, Windows Explorer to bring up the Windows Explorer program. Double-click on My Computer to expand the list of resources available. You should see the CD-ROM drive that holds the Windows XP Professional CD. Navigate to the folder `Support` and then `Tools`; then look for the `Deploy folder` and double-click on it.

8. Right-click on `sysprep` and from the menu; choose Extract. Extract the file to the Sysprep directory you created in Step 5. Do the same for the file `setupcl`.

9. Take the Windows XP installation CD out of the CD-ROM drive.

10. At the command prompt, execute the following command: `Sysprep -nosidgen`.

After you have issued the `sysprep` command, the system should automatically shut down. When the users boot the system, they will be prompted for the last few items required by the Setup process, such as accepting the license agreement, among other things.

In this example the `-nosidgen` parameter was used. This is because the installation is not being cloned, but you have simply set up a computer having completed most of the installation steps. The Setup process you went through when you installed Windows XP generated a unique SID for the computer.

Using Sysprep to Clone an Installation

Sysprep is usually used to clone an installation when a large number of computers need to be set up using Windows XP, and you have some means for duplicating a disk drive. This is the case with most computer vendors that sell computers with Windows XP already preinstalled on the hard drive. A large corporation may also use this method.

Use the same steps you did in the previous section to install and customize the operating system, as well as install additional drivers or applications. However, when you execute the `sysprep` command, omit the `-nosidgen` parameter.

When you have finished and the system has shut down, you can remove the drive from the computer and use whatever method you normally use to duplicate a disk. Place the copied disks in new computers. When the system is booted, the user will again have to answer a few prompts, but a new SID will be generated for the computer. After the user has finished answering the prompts, the Sysprep folder and its contents will be deleted automatically.

Using the `Sysprep.inf` File

You can make matters even easier for the end-user by supplying an answer file for Sysprep. Earlier in this chapter you learned how to create an unattended answer file to be used with the `winnt.exe` or `winnt32.exe` Setup programs by using the Windows Setup Manager Wizard. This wizard was used to generate an unattended setup answer file for use in installing Windows XP. You can use this same program to create a file called `sysprep.inf`, which will allow you to supply answers for some of the prompts that the mini-setup process issues when the user boots the computer. For example, you can supply a company name, regional settings, and so on.

To create the `sysprep.inf` file using the Windows Setup Manager Wizard, just select the radio button labeled *Sysprep Install* instead of *Windows Unattended Installation*, when prompted in the third screen presented by the wizard.

If you do create a `sysprep.inf` file, place it in the same Sysprep folder you created to hold the Sysprep program itself.

Summary

In this chapter you learned how to automate most of the process of installing Windows XP. By using an answer file you can supply answers to most of the prompts that the Setup program uses. You can also create multiple answer files if you have groups of users where each group needs to have their computer setup a little different from the other groups. The Windows Setup Manager Wizard can help you create the answer files that can be used by the Setup program (or by the Sysprep utility) so that you don't have to become intimately familiar with the hundreds of variables that can be used in an answer file. While the Syspart utility is usually needed only in a very large scale environment, it can be useful to ensure that you can clone a system that contains not just the Windows XP operating system, but also other applications that you need to install for a group of users.

Desktop, File Management, General Configuration

PART

II

IN THIS PART

5 Configuring Accessibility Options   *103*

6 Understanding the Startup Process   *127*

7 Up Front: The New Desktop   *141*

8 Other Applications and Accessories   *169*

9 Working with Files and Folders   *195*

10 Using Microsoft Outlook Express for E-mail,
   News, and More   *227*

Configuring Accessibility Options

IN THIS CHAPTER

- Configuring Accessibility Options Using the Control Panel *105*

- StickyKeys, FilterKeys, and ToggleKeys *107*

- SoundSentry and ShowSounds *111*

- Using High Contrast for Easier Viewing *112*

- "Mouseing" Around with the Keyboard *113*

- Using the General Tab for Accessibility Options *115*

- Using the Accessibility Wizard *116*

- Windows XP Accessibility Accessories *118*

- What Is the Utility Manager? *122*

- Using Speech Recognition *123*

- Using Handwritten Recognition Devices *124*

Windows XP Professional provides a number of features that help enable users with disabilities to unlock the full potential of their machines. Although we have not yet reached the Star Trek level of computer sophistication, the options discussed in this chapter can be used to make computers more accessible to a wider range of users, even those who are not functionally disabled. For example, the Magnifier is a useful option for those with or without visual impairment, since it can provide an enlarged view of any part of the desktop. You may find this useful when viewing images in an application.

In this chapter, you will learn how to configure and use the following accessibility features that Windows XP provides:

- StickyKeys, FilterKeys, and ToggleKeys
- SoundSentry
- ShowSounds
- High Contrast
- Mouse Keys
- Serial Keys
- Narrator
- Magnifier
- On-Screen Keyboard

In addition to learning how to configure and use these accessibility features, you will learn about speech and handwriting recognition. However, although Windows XP supports these two important features, you will have to supply an "engine" for speech or handwriting recognition by purchasing another application such as Microsoft Office XP. It may also be the case that the maker of your PC has installed Microsoft's speech engine as part of their OEM package of software. To check and see if a speech engine is installed, click on Start, Control Panel, (and using the Category View of the Control Panel), then Sound, Speech and Audio Devices. From the next menu select the Control Panel icon labeled Speech. If you see a Speech Recognition tab on the properties sheet that pops ups, then you have a speech engine installed.

If you find that you do not have a speech recognition engine installed on your computer, you might want to consider evaluating the cost of Office XP by comparing not only the enhancements to the overall product and its tight integration, but also to the speech recognition capabilities that come with Office XP.

Most of the features described here can be configured by using the Control Panel or the Accessibility Wizard. We will begin with the Control Panel, since this method provides the finest degree of control in setting up individual features. Alternatively, the

Accessibility Wizard is a simple-to-use wizard that prompts you with a few dialog boxes and then automatically sets up the same features that could be configured using the Control Panel. The Narrator and the Magnifier are also discussed, which separate accessories that you can use any time or that can be configured to start automatically using the Utility Manager.

Configuring Accessibility Options Using the Control Panel

Many of the options described in the following sections are configured using the Control Panel. The new desktop allows you to choose between the "new look" for the Control Panel or the Classic View. To bring up the Control Panel, click on Start, Control Panel. Figure 5.1 is the new version of the control panel. Instead of showing all of the Control Panel icons, which is what appears in Classic View, it presents specific categories from which to choose.

FIGURE 5.1

The new look for the Control Panel presents a list of categories instead of applet icons.

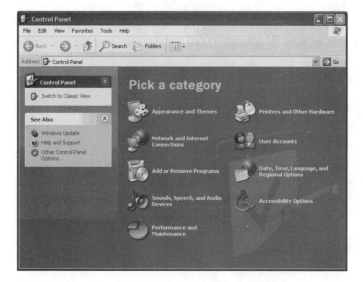

You can also click on Switch to Classic View in the top left corner of the Control Panel and then double-click on the Accessibility Options icon. To continue with the new Control Panel, click on the Accessibility Options category at the bottom right side of the Control Panel. This will bring up another Control Panel screen (see Figure 5.2), which offers a choice of several different Accessibility Options.

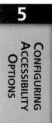

FIGURE 5.2

Use the Accessibility Options icon in the newly designed Control Panel to bring up the properties sheet to configure many of the Accessibility Options.

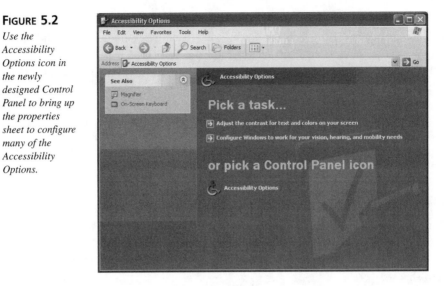

For the Accessibility Options first discussed in this chapter, click on the Accessibility Options under the section of this screen, which you'll find under Or Pick a Control Panel Icon. Through either the Control Panel Category View or the Classic View method, the Accessibility Options properties sheet (Figure 5.3) comes up, complete with a set of tabs for the different functions described in the next few sections.

FIGURE 5.3

The Accessibility Options properties sheet contains tabs for configuring different accessibility options.

To begin the configuration of the Accessibility Options using these property sheets, simply click on the property sheet tab associated with the option you want to configure.

A lot of options can be configured through the use of a few properties sheets, requiring little input from the user. Next, we will look at each of the options, describe what each does, and then explain how to configure them on your computer.

StickyKeys, FilterKeys, and ToggleKeys

Today's modern computer keyboard has many options over the alphabetic, numeric, and punctuation keys of yesterday's typewriters. The Esc key, a row of function keys, and additional specialized keys on computer keyboards are all useful for accessing the Internet or conducting other features offered by a particular computer manufacturer. This greater number of keys provides a lot more capabilities than the original typewriter; for example, it is often necessary to press more than one key at the same time to send a signal to a computer, a task not useful on typewriters.

The most obvious example of this is Ctrl+Alt+Del, which calls up a request to log off or restart the computer. For some people, this can be a difficult task. If you have arthritis or are just a hunt-and-peck typist, holding down three different keys can be difficult.

Using StickyKeys

StickyKeys allows you to set up your computer so that these key combinations can be entered by pressing each key singularly, instead of pressing and holding down all keys at the same time. In other words, instead of holding down the Ctrl, Alt, and Del keys at the same time, with StickyKeys, you can press the Ctrl key, then the Alt key, and then the Del key, and Windows XP will respond as if you had pressed all three at the same time.

StickyKeys works for the Ctrl, Alt, and Shift keys, as well as the Windows Logo key, and will keep these keys in a "pressed" state until you complete a particular key combination such as the Ctrl+Alt+Del combination.

Enabling StickyKeys

You can enable the StickyKeys feature in two ways. The feature can remain on full time, which is useful if there is only one user, or the check box labeled Use StickyKeys (see Figure 5.3) can be checked each time there is a need to employ them. However, if there is more than one user, it may be better to create a shortcut for enabling StickyKeys only when needed so that each user can employ the feature as necessary. To do this, click Settings next to the Use StickyKeys check box, and the Settings for StickyKeys dialog box (see Figure 5.4) pops up.

FIGURE 5.4

*Use this dialog
box to enable the
StickyKeys short-
cut or to further
customize how
StickyKeys work.*

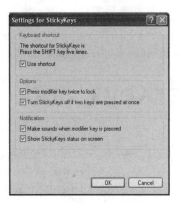

Select the Use Shortcut check box to enable the shortcut. As indicated in Figure 5.4, pressing the Shift key five times in a row is the shortcut for enabling StickyKeys. Since the purpose of the shortcut is to enable StickyKeys for only certain users of the computer, another dialog box pops up when you use the shortcut, stating that StickyKeys is enabled. Click OK or select the check box Turn Off Keyboard Shortcut for this accessibility feature. Note that this check box will disable the shortcut, so reenabling it requires recreating the shortcut.

This dialog box enables you to get back to the properties sheet to modify settings for StickyKeys, or you can use the check box provided on the dialog box to disable the shortcut.

Refer to Figure 5.4 for a few other options for controlling how StickyKeys work.

Setting StickyKeys Options

By using the shortcut method, multiple users of one machine can enable or disable StickyKeys as needed. To leave StickyKeys enabled, just select the check box shown in Figure 5.3. However, in the Settings for StickyKeys dialog box, several other options are available for specifying how to turn on or off the StickyKeys functionality. Two notification check boxes are also indicated so that you know when StickyKeys are in use. The options and notification check boxes on this property sheet are as follows:

- Press modifier key twice to lock—The particular StickyKey (Ctrl, Alt, Del or the Windows Logo Key) stay locked in a "pressed" state until you press that key again.

- Turn StickyKeys off if two keys are pressed at once—You can turn off StickyKeys by pressing any two of them at the same time.

- Make sounds when modifier key is pressed—Your computer's speaker will sound a beep tone that rises in pitch when StickyKeys are turned on and one that lowers in pitch when StickyKeys are turned off.

- Show StickyKeys status on screen—An icon on the taskbar is displayed to show you that StickyKeys is enabled.

Enabling and Configuring FilterKeys

FilterKeys can also be turned on by selecting the appropriate check box shown in Figure 5.3. The FilterKeys feature is useful for people who have problems with involuntary hand movements or who are just poor typists. You can use FilterKeys settings to make Windows XP ignore a key if it is pressed twice within a short period of time, and you can also change the rate at which a character is repeated on the screen when you hold down a key. To enable FilterKeys, simply select the check box in Figure 5.3. To configure how you want the FilterKeys feature to work, click Settings next to the check box. Figure 5.5 is the Settings for FilterKeys dialog box.

FIGURE 5.5

Use the Setting for FilterKeys dialog box to make Windows XP ignore repeated keystrokes or to change the rate at which a character is repeated when a key is held down.

A shortcut can also be used to maintain this feature full-time, especially if there is more than one user. The shortcut for FilterKeys is to hold down the right Shift key for eight seconds.

Under the Filter options section of the dialog box in Figure 5.5, you can choose from two of the following radio buttons:

- Ignore repeated keystrokes—This feature is useful for people with involuntary hand movements who may inadvertently press the same key twice. When this feature is enabled, the second key press of the same key will be ignored.

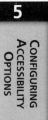

5

CONFIGURING
ACCESSIBILITY
OPTIONS

Click Settings, which is next to this radio button, to bring up a dialog box for setting time (from one half second up to two seconds), during which the second key press of the same key will be ignored. This settings dialog box also has a test area to type in so that you may practice making adjustments to the time.

- Ignore quick keystrokes and slow down the repeat rate—Select this to either disable the repeating feature entirely or slow down the rate at which characters are repeated when a key is held down. Use this feature to tell Windows XP to ignore quick keystrokes. Click Settings, which is next to this radio button, to get the Advanced Settings for FilterKeys dialog box.

As you can see from this dialog box, you can disable keyboard repeating entirely by selecting the No Keyboard Repeat radio button. You can also slow down the rate by selecting the second radio button and then using the two drop-down menus to specify the Repeat delay (how long a key must be held down before it starts to repeat) and the Repeat rate (the rate at which characters start to be repeated on the screen once repeating has started).

At the bottom of this dialog box is the SlowKeys drop-down menu, which specifies how long a key must be pressed before it counts as a keystroke. This can be useful in cases where you may occasionally strike keys by mistake. By selecting a longer rate of time here, you can make sure that a stray brush against the keyboard doesn't result in a keystroke.

At the bottom of this dialog box is a test area for fine-tuning the FilterKeys features. Refer to Figure 5.5 to see how the Notification section specifies a beeping sound to be made when a key is pressed or accepted or to indicate the status of FilterKeys on the screen.

Enabling ToggleKeys

The last section of the Keyboard tab in Figure 5.3 enables ToggleKeys. Basically, ToggleKeys will play a sound when the Caps Lock, Num Lock, or Scroll Lock keys are depressed. How many times have you hit one of these keys by mistake? If you have impaired vision, a sound indicates that you have pressed one of these keys. If you choose to enable ToggleKeys, then clicking Settings brings up a dialog box in which you can set a shortcut for turning them on. The shortcut for ToggleKeys is to hold down the Num Lock key for five seconds.

Like the StickyKeys shortcut, a small dialog box pops up stating that you have just turned on ToggleKeys. Click OK to leave them turned on or click Cancel if you did this by mistake. You can also click Settings on this small dialog box to bring back the Accessibility Options property sheet shown in Figure 5.3—that is, if you want to change some of the settings for the options defined by this Control Panel applet.

SoundSentry and ShowSounds

For the hearing impaired, you can use the SoundSentry and ShowSounds accessibility features to configure Windows XP. These will provide visual cues to the user when the computer's speaker sounds.

To configure these features, use the Sound tab in the Accessibility Options property sheet shown in Figure 5.3. With this tab (see Figure 5.6), you can enable either of these options.

FIGURE 5.6

Use SoundSentry and ShowSounds to give visual cues when the computer's speaker sounds.

Select the Use SoundSentry check box to enable this feature. Then use the Choose the Visual Warning drop-down menu to select how you want to have Windows XP indicate to the user that the computer's speakers have sounded. You can choose among the following options:

- None—This effectively turns off SoundSentry.
- Flash active caption bar—The caption bar at the top of a dialog box or window flashes momentarily.
- Flash active window—The current window flashes.
- Flash desktop—As the most striking effect of the three, the entire contents of the desktop flashes.

Test each of these options to see which one is the easiest for you to recognize. This feature is intended to assist those who have problems with hearing; however, if you are slightly visually impaired, it is also recommended that you test each option.

Use the ShowSounds check box to enable this feature. Programs use this feature to display an icon or some text on the screen when a sound from the computer's speaker would normally be used. Simply select the check box to enable this feature.

5

CONFIGURING
ACCESSIBILITY
OPTIONS

When you have finished making changes on the Sound tab of the Accessibility Options property sheet, click Apply and then OK to dismiss the property sheet.

Using High Contrast for Easier Viewing

High Contrast is an accessibility feature that makes it easier to see the contents of the Windows XP desktop for those who are visually impaired. You can choose from among a wide variety of color schemes, from simple, high-contrast, black-and-white screens to many different color schemes. To enable the High Contrast feature, click on the Display tab in the Accessibility Options property sheet shown in Figure 5.3. Two different methods enable High Contrast, as shown in Figure 5.7. You can also permanently enable this feature by selecting the High Contrast check box and then clicking Settings to further define the preferred color scheme.

FIGURE 5.7

Use the Display tab to configure High Contrast features.

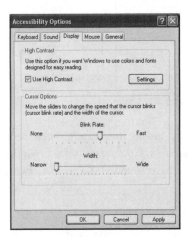

Once you click Settings, the Settings for the High Contrast dialog box will pop up (see Figure 5.8). You can use the shortcut method for this accessibility feature by selecting the Use Shortcut check box, if you don't want to leave High Contrast as the default setting. If you enable the shortcut, then to use the feature, simply press the following three keys at the same time: left Alt key, left Shift key, and the Print Screen key.

With the drop-down menu under this shortcut section of the dialog box, you can select your preferred color scheme. You will find a wide variety of choices here.

FIGURE 5.8

You can choose a shortcut to select the color scheme for the High Contrast accessibility feature.

Note

You can create custom color schemes by using the Display Settings feature on the Desktop, described in Chapter 7, "Up Front: The New Desktop." Any custom color schemes you create using the method described in that chapter also appear as selections in this menu.

The bottom half of the Display tab in Figure 5.7 indicates the rate at which the cursor blinks and its width. This feature can be useful to make it easier to see the cursor onscreen. Use the slider bars to make these adjustments and test them until you find a cursor rate and size that you will notice.

When you have made your selection, click OK to dismiss the dialog box.

"Mouseing" Around with the Keyboard

For those who would prefer to use the keyboard over a mouse or other pointing device, you can select the Mouse tab in the Accessibility Options property sheet to enable a feature called *MouseKeys*. MouseKeys allows you to use your keyboard's numeric keypad (typically to the right of the regular keyboard) to perform mouse movements. The numeric 8 key moves the mouse upward, whereas the numeric 2 key moves the mouse downward. In a similar manner, the numeric 4 key moves the mouse to the left, and the numeric 6 key moves the mouse to the right. Note that this does not apply to the numeric keys at the top of the keyboard.

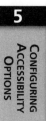

As with other accessibility features, you can simply select the check box labeled "Use MouseKeys" and then click Settings to configure the MouseKeys to your preferences.

Clicking Settings brings up the Settings or MouseKeys dialog box (Figure 5.9), in which you can use a shortcut to enable MouseKeys only when needed. The shortcut for turning on MouseKeys is to simultaneously press left Alt, left Shift, and Num Lock.

FIGURE 5.9

Use this dialog box to set a shortcut or to configure MouseKeys properties.

This dialog box controls the top speed at which the cursor will move when a numeric MouseKey is held down by using a slider bar. The Acceleration slider bar controls how the mouse will accelerate, or move faster the longer you hold it down.

If you select the check box, Hold Down Ctrl to Speed Up and Shift to Slow Down, then these keys can also be used to control the speed at which the pointer on the screen moves when you are using MouseKeys. For example, if you are using the numeric 4 key to move the mouse in a left direction onscreen and you then press the Ctrl key and hold it for a short time, the rate at which the pointer on the screen moves accelerates rapidly. The Shift key works in an opposite manner, causing the pointer to move more slowly as the Shift key is held down.

The radio buttons (On and Off) can be used to indicate when MouseKeys will be active. If you click On, then MouseKeys will operate when the Num Lock key is locked. This way, you can simply unlock the Num Lock key when you want to disable MouseKeys. For example, when the Num Lock key is not pressed, the 2, 4, 6, and 8 keys can be used like cursor keys to move the cursor in a Word document, instead of moving the mouse pointer onscreen. When the Off button is selected and you then use the Num Lock key, the 2, 4, 6, and 8 keys can be used for numeric input, which is their proper function when Num Lock is engaged.

Finally, you can use the check box Show MouseKey Status on Screen if you want a small icon to be displayed on the Task Bar to indicate when MouseKeys is enabled.

After making your selections, click OK to return to the Accessibility Options property sheet.

Using the General Tab for Accessibility Options

The last tab on the Accessibility Options property sheet allows you to set some specific configuration options for StickyKeys, SoundSentry, MouseKeys, FilterKeys, ToggleKeys, and High Contrast after the computer has been idle for a period of time. You can configure these by using a drop-down menu, as shown in Figure 5.10.

FIGURE 5.10

Use this dialog box to set configuration options that apply to most of the Accessibility Options that can be configured using the Control Panel.

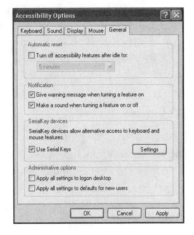

Using this method can be convenient, again in situations when you use shortcuts to enable features and when there is more than one user. Once the computer has been idle for the amount of time you set, then the features are turned off. When users that require the features start to use the computer again, they can use the shortcut method to turn on the feature(s) they need.

The Notification section also applies to these same features, and you can use the check boxes here to enable these audio or visual notifications.

SerialKeys

The SerialKey devices section allows you to use an alternative input device that is attached to one of the computer's serial ports (e.g., COM1 to COM4). Click Settings to select the serial port and set the baud rate for the port. A number of devices can be used to control mouse or keyboard functions, but these are beyond the scope of this book. Check out Microsoft's web site at http://www.microsoft.com and search for Accessibility Tools to find out more about the kinds of devices supported by the SerialKeys functionality.

5

CONFIGURING
ACCESSIBILITY
OPTIONS

> **Note**
>
> The term baud comes from an earlier method used to measure the speed of telegraph communications. Jean-Maurice-Emile Baudot was the French engineer to develop this technique. Basically, the baud rate measured the number of electronic states per second during a transmission. The term bps (or bits per second) is sometimes used as a replacement for the term baud.
>
> While a telegraph or early modem (those blazingly fast 300 baud modems, for their day), used the term baud to measure the speed of transmission, the term bps (bits per second) is more useful today, since the methods of transmission have improved greatly since the telegraph. To put it in terms that many network users will understand, when you see the word "baud," you can almost certainly interpret that word today to mean bits per second instead.

Administrative Options

Finally, with the General tab of the Accessibility Options property sheet, two check boxes allow you to indicate whether your selections apply to a specific user when he or she logs on. In other words, each user who logs onto the computer with a different username can have his or her own Accessibility settings. The second check box sets up Accessibility Options that you have configured as the default for new users added to the computer.

Using the Accessibility Wizard

You know that the accessibility features included with the Windows XP operating system are configured using the Accessibility Options applet in the Control Panel. Now you will learn about a few other accessibility features that can be configured by using the Accessibility Wizard. To get started, click on Start, All Programs, Accessories, Accessibility, Accessibility Wizard.

The first screen presented by the Accessibility Wizard is simply a welcoming screen. To continue, simply click Next. In this screen the Accessibility Wizard prompts you to select the smallest readable text size.

Simply use your cursor key to select between the following three options:

- Use usual text size for Windows
- Use large window titles and menus
- Use Microsoft Magnifier and large titles and menus

Figure 5.11 shows how the next dialog box allows you to choose additional options, based on the selection you made in the previous dialog box.

FIGURE 5.11

*With the next dia-
log box, you can
further configure
the size of text
used with
Windows XP, by
employing default
selections based
on your previous
selection.*

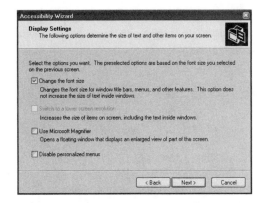

If you had chosen to use the Microsoft Magnifier, then in Figure 5.11, you would see that check box selected. Additionally, the Magnifier would automatically start up so that you could use it as you continue to use the Accessibility Wizard.

After you click Next (see Figure 5.11), you will get a dialog box that asks you to select from a set of statements describing various degrees of disability.

You can choose from the following statements:

- I am blind or have difficulty seeing things or You need a screenshot here for the reader to follow.
- I am deaf or have difficulty hearing sounds from the computer.
- I have difficult using the keyboard or mouse.
- I want to set administrative options.

The check boxes here help determine how the Wizard will continue from this point. The prompts will be used to decide which of the accessibility features discussed in the first part of this chapter will be enabled. Since each of these features has already been discussed in detail, we won't go through all the possible dialog boxes that the Accessibility Wizard can present. However, since you have already learned about the basic accessibility features configured by using the Control Panel's Accessibility Options applet, you can continue using the Wizard and should have no trouble understanding the prompts and features that will be enabled.

Keep in mind that any features you enable using the Accessibility Wizard can also be fine-tuned or reconfigured using the Control Panel applet. The Wizard can simply be a quick-and-easy method to configure a PC for a particular user once you are familiar with the accessibility options that can be configured using the Control Panel.

Windows XP Accessibility Accessories

In addition to the control panel accessibility options, several other accessibility features are available through the Accessories folder. The path to bring up these features is Start, All Programs, Accessories, Accessibility.

Here, you will find Narrator and Magnifier, which can be used to enlarge portions of the screen over which your cursor is placed. Additionally, the On-Screen Keyboard can be used with a pointing device instead of a regular keyboard.

Using the Narrator

The Narrator program is designed to work with some applications and can read text from the screen, as well as menu items and text that you enter yourself. Applications that Narrator works with include the following:

- Windows Setup
- Notepad and Wordpad
- Control Panel Applets
- Internet Explorer
- The Windows XP Desktop

Narrator isn't the best text-to-speech application you can buy, but it is the cheapest, since it comes with the operating system. For people who are severely visually impaired, Microsoft's Web site describes other applications that do a better job. Narrator only provides a very basic reading functionality.

For example, if you use Narrator while typing in Wordpad, then the Narrator voice will read each character as you type. After you have finished entering text, you can put the cursor at the beginning of some text and Narrator will begin reading the words aloud from that point. Unfortunately, using it as you type in Wordpad can be distracting. However, for reading text after it is entered, it does perform very well.

Having Narrator available for use with Windows Setup can make it easy to upgrade or install Windows XP. During the Setup process, you are first presented with the choice to use Narrator or Magnifier. Therefore, when installing Windows XP, you can use Narrator if you have not installed a better text-to-speech application.

To start Narrator, use the key combination Ctrl+Esc, press the R key, type in **narrator**, and press Enter. You can also use Start, All Programs, Accessories, Accessibility,

Narrator. Using the latter approach would present some difficulty for someone with vision impairment. That method can be used by another person to set up the system for a visually impaired user.

When you launch the Narrator program, a dialog box pops up stating that better programs are available and that you should visit Microsoft's Web site for better options. Click OK and the Narrator configuration dialog box asks you to select what you want Narrator to read.

As you can see in the figure, Narrator will read menu commands and dialog box options, so it can be useful for navigating through the Start menu to launch other programs. You can also have Narrator perform any of the following:

- Announce events on screen
- Read typed characters
- Move mouse pointer to the active item
- Start Narrator minimized

When this dialog box first appears on your screen, Narrator starts reading its own configuration dialog. In addition to reading the actual text that appears in the dialog box, Narrator reads the check box options and states whether an item has been selected ("check box checked"). It also says what types of controls are on the dialog box ("Help, pushbutton").

Help launches the Help Text window, which Narrator will then read. Clicking Voice brings up a dialog box in which you can select a voice and manipulate it using the following three controls:

- Speed—To set the speed at which text is read
- Volume—To set the volume of the Narrator voice
- Pitch—To change the pitch of the voice from low to high

The Narrator comes with a default voice supplied by Microsoft, but if other voices have been installed, simply select which voice to use. Each of the controls can be adjusted using values from 1 to 9, but a value of 3 is the default for each.

Using the Microsoft Magnifier

The Magnifier is a tool for enlarging part of the Desktop or any application window. For those who have only slight vision impairment, this feature can be very handy. The Magnifier feature can also invert colors that appear on the screen to make reading text easier.

To start up the Magnifier, use Start, All Programs, Accessories, Accessibility, Magnifier. A new window (see Figure 5.12) appears onscreen for configuring your settings for the Magnifier feature.

FIGURE 5.12

Use the Magnifier Settings dialog box to configure the Magnifier feature.

In addition to this configuration dialog box, a separate window called *Magnifier* is opened. At this point, there is nothing in the Magnifier window. You must first configure how you want Magnifier to work. The options for configuring the Magnifier Settings dialog box are as follows:

- Follow Mouse cursor—The portion of the Desktop is displayed wherever the cursor is placed. When you move the cursor, the Magnifier window displays, in a magnified view, the contents close to the cursor.

- Follow keyboard focus—The contents of the Magnifier window display a portion of the Desktop, depending on keyboard commands such as the Tab or arrow keys.

- Follow text editing—The portion of the desktop showing where you are currently entering text is displayed, such as during use of a word processor.

- Invert Colors—The Magnifier inverts colors to make them easier to read. For example, if a window shows white characters against a black background, this option can change it to black characters on a white background.

- Start Minimized—When the Magnifier is started, the Magnifier Settings dialog box is minimized but available on the Taskbar. This is useful if a particular set of configuration options has been selected and there is no need to change them. Otherwise, it becomes necessary to minimize the Magnifier Settings dialog box each time the Magnifier is started.

- Show Magnifier—A default selection, this option displays the Magnifier window when this Magnifier Settings dialog box is being used. Here, the Magnifier can be used to change the settings.

Using the On-Screen Keyboard Feature

Another accessibility feature for users who have problems using a keyboard is the On-Screen Keyboard option. You can start the keyboard using Start, All Programs, Accessories, Accessibility, On-Screen Keyboard. Figure 5.13 shows how the keyboard mimics a normal PC keyboard. Click on any key using a pointing device, and it will operate just as if the equivalent key on the computer's keyboard had been pressed.

FIGURE 5.13

The On-Screen Keyboard enables using a pointing device to click on each key for data entry.

Although this isn't exactly the fastest method for typing a long document, it can serve well for some simple tasks like answering an e-mail message or entering text into a search engine on the Internet.

The keyboard also has a menu at the top. The File menu allows you to exit the keyboard. With the Keyboard menu, you can select the type of keyboard you prefer, such as a standard or enhanced keyboard (which includes the numeric keypad) and the number of keys on the keyboard (101, 102, or 106). You can also select Regular Layout or Block Layout, which merely displays the keyboard using two different visual methods. In Regular Layout, it looks like a modern keyboard (see Figure 5.13). The Block Layout keyboard appears in Figure 5.14, a keyboard that may be easier for some users to navigate.

FIGURE 5.14

The Block Mode layout may be easier for some users to use with a pointing device.

The Settings menu allows you to select the option Always on Top, which simply means that the keyboard will always be the window in the forefront when other windows are opened. However, since you can change the size of another window, such as the one used by Internet Explorer or Notepad, you should be able to leave the keyboard at the forefront while working with other applications, since it doesn't take up the entire screen. You can also set up a clicking sound when you select a key; a different font (used to display each key); and more importantly, a typing style. The typing styles you can select are as follows:

- Click to Select—Use your pointing device to point to a key and then click to select the key.

- Hover to Select—Hover the cursor over the key for a specified amount of time, and the key will be selected without needing to click.

- Joystick or Key to Select—This allows you to use a joystick as the pointing device. It works similarly to the Hover to Select mode, and you can set the interval using the Scan Interval drop-down menu. This mode also has an Advanced option. Selecting Advanced brings up the Scanning Mode Options dialog box where you can select how the device is attached to the computer (serial port, parallel port, or game port) and a keyboard key for actually selecting the key. The default key is the space bar, but other keys are available.

The On-Screen keyboard is not a perfect solution for heavy-duty text input, but it can be useful for moderate input such as entering small amounts of text into e-mail messages or Notepad or for entering text into fields on an Internet web page.

What Is the Utility Manager?

The Utility Manager can be used to automatically start up some of the accessibility features discussed in this chapter. For example, the user can employ the key combination of the Windows logo key + U at the Welcome screen before logging on. By using this key combination, users who are impaired can automatically start the accessibility features they need when logging onto the system. The features for which the Utility Manager provides support are as follows:

- Magnifier
- Narrator
- On-Screen Keyboard

When the Utility Manager starts up, the Narrator also kicks on and begins reading the screen.

You can also start the Utility Manager by using Start, All Programs, Accessories, Accessibility, Utility Manager. When you start the manager in this fashion, however, you can only use it to start and stop the accessibility features that it supports. Simply click on the feature in the window at the top of the Utility Manager's dialog box and then click Start or Stop.

When started using the Windows logo key + U, three startup options for the accessibility features are available, as shown in Figure 5.15.

You can tell the Utility Manager to start the accessibility feature automatically every time you log on, when you lock your desktop, or every time the Utility Manager itself is started.

FIGURE 5.15

You can use the Utility Manager to control the startup of three accessibility features of Windows XP.

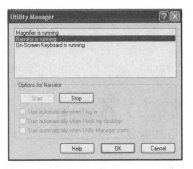

Using Speech Recognition

Windows XP supports input using a microphone for some programs. At this time, you can use speech recognition to dictate using any Microsoft Office XP application, as well as Internet Explorer 6 and Microsoft Outlook Express 6. In addition to enabling dictation of text into an application, speech recognition also permits the issuing of commands for some programs, and this will depend on the particular program. Programs like Wordpad and Notepad are not supported at this time. However, Microsoft may release code in a future service pack that will enable this feature in additional programs.

Before using the speech recognition feature, it is necessary to first install a speech recognition engine. At this time, a speech recognition engine is not included with the basic Windows XP operating system. However, Microsoft Office XP contains the necessary files for installing a speech recognition engine. Once this is done, the Speech icon in the Control Panel can perform speech recognition.

In addition to Microsoft Office XP, a number of speech recognition products are available on the market. However, make sure that the version you purchase supports Windows XP. Most current products such as IBM's ViaVoice were written for Windows 98 and other operating systems but may require an update to work with Windows XP.

To support speech recognition, your computer needs at least 128MB of memory and a 400MHz or faster processor. You will also need a microphone with gain adjustment support, a feature that changes the amplification of sound detected by the microphone to a

5

CONFIGURING
ACCESSIBILITY
OPTIONS

level that can be understood by the speech recognition engine. Microsoft recommends a microphone that connects to the computer via a universal serial bus (USB) port, but one can connect successfully to an ordinary sound card's microphone port.

Before you begin using Microsoft's speech recognition engine or one from any other vendor, you need to go through the training utility. A specialized training utility first gauges the level of background noise (such as an air conditioner or noise from other devices in your environment). Next, the training utility will ask that you read a pre-scored text file presented in the screen. It may require you to read the file several times, and during each pass, the program will be looking for patterns in your speech that will help it better understand you when you actually start using the program.

Using Handwritten Recognition Devices

This feature, like speech recognition, does not come bundled with the operating system, although some OEM (Original Equipment Manufacturer) computer vendors may choose to install a handwriting recognition engine in the version of Windows XP installed on their machines. Otherwise, you will again have to purchase another Microsoft product such as the Office XP suite in order to take advantage of this feature. Use the following steps to see if a handwriting recognition engine is installed on your machine:

1. Click on Start, Control Panel. From Category View, click on Date, Time, Language, and Regional Options.

2. From the next screen, click on Regional and Language Options.

3. Choose the Languages tab from the properties sheet that appears.

> **Tip**
>
> If you use the Classic View of the Control Panel, just Click on Start, Control Panel and then the icon Regional and Language to get to this same properties sheet.

4. At the top of this dialog box, click Details in the Input Languages and Methods section. The Text Services dialog box pops up. Under the section titled Installed Services, click Add.

These steps will bring up the Add Input Language dialog box. A Handwriting Recognition option indicates that a handwriting engine is installed on your computer. If the engine is installed, select the language from the Input Language drop-down menu, and a check box comes up for enabling handwriting recognition.

If you do have a handwriting recognition engine installed on your computer, then a variety of devices can be used to input text into the programs that support it. You can use a digital pen or tablet, but be sure that the device is on the hardware compatibility list. You can also use a mouse by holding down the button normally used for clicking and then using the mouse to draw your text. The text you enter, if it is recognized by the handwriting recognition engine, will be converted to characters on the screen. Note that in Office XP, you can also choose Ink mode, in which case your handwriting is not converted to text but rather remains in the document as-is.

Summary

Although not a complete solution for all people with impairments, the accessibility features built into the Windows XP operating system do offer quite a lot. For a user who doesn't need to input much, these features probably suffice for simple tasks. However, if you or one of your employees has a severe impairment, Microsoft's Web site may help determine what other programs and resources are available for use with Windows XP. These days, no one should be denied access to a computer because of a physical impairment. Many programs and special devices on the market today can provide assistance beyond the basic operating system.

Understanding the Startup Process

CHAPTER 6

IN THIS CHAPTER

- **How Your Computer Boots** *128*
- **How Windows Boots** *129*
- **Startup Options** *135*
- **Troubleshooting Startup Problems** *137*

Understanding how Windows XP Professional starts up is an important part of understanding Windows XP. Once you understand the startup procedure, you will have a better idea of what you can modify about the way Windows starts and how to troubleshoot startup problems.

Your computer really starts in two distinct phases. First, the computer itself boots, and then the operating system boots. In this chapter, you will learn a little about how your computer boots and a good bit more about how Windows XP boots. You will look at the important files involved in the startup process and what those files do. You will also learn what options you can control during Windows startup. Finally, you will learn ways to solve some of the more common Windows startup failures.

How Your Computer Boots

When you press the power button on your computer, power is provided to all the components and the boot process begins. This process happens basically as follows:

1. As soon as power is supplied to your main system board, a process called the *Power On Self Test (POST)* begins. This process is controlled by read-only memory (ROM) chips on the main board that test the more important pieces of hardware on the computer.

2. Control of the testing process is first passed to your graphics adapter so that it can test itself. This is why the first screen you see on starting a computer is usually a blank screen with information on your graphics adapter at the top.

3. Next, control is passed back to the regular POST routine and the main POST screen appears, similar to the screen shown in Figure 6.1.

4. The POST routine tests your processor and displays the processor version on your screen.

5. Once the processor test is complete, POST hands control of your system over to the Basic Input Output System (BIOS). BIOS is firmware coded on a chip on your main board that controls the behavior of your computer before any software loads and the basic configuration settings for most of the hardware attached to the computer (e.g., hard drives, CD-ROM drives, parallel and serial ports, memory, and so on). If, during setup, you hit the Delete key (or whatever key enters setup on your computer), it is the BIOS settings that will appear for you to configure.

6. Assuming you do not enter the BIOS setup, BIOS next tests your memory. This step (the memory countdown) is probably the one you are most familiar with. The memory is displayed on the next line after the processor.

Understanding the Startup Process

CHAPTER 6

129

6

UNDERSTANDING
THE STARTUP
PROCESS

FIGURE 6.1

The main POST screen when starting a computer.

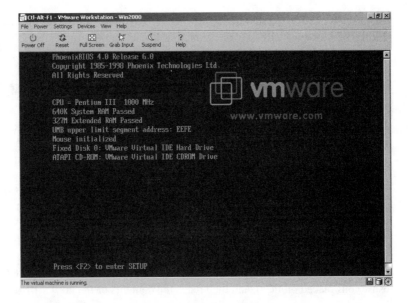

7. BIOS then proceeds to check the connection to your various hard drives, CD drives, and floppy drives. If the connections are not present or are different from what is listed in the BIOS settings, you will get an error message and the boot process won't continue. You will have to enter BIOS setup to fix things.

8. Assuming all goes well, BIOS next displays a screen that summarizes the state of your system.

9. BIOS then calls a special code, named the BIOS operating system bootstrap interrupt (Int 19h). This code first finds a bootable disk using the guidelines for which drive should be booted first as set in the BIOS settings.

10. Once BIOS finds a bootable disk, it loads the program found at the Master Boot Record (MBR) of the disk into your computer's memory, and then passes control of the computer to that program. The startup phase now passes from the booting of your computer to the booting of Windows.

How Windows Boots

This is where things start to get interesting (or should I say, complicated). The MBR is a small program typically found on the first sector of a hard drive, though it can also be located on removable media such as a floppy disk. If this is the case, you can configure your BIOS to point directly at the removable media drive where the MBR can be found.

Because the MBR is so small, not much can really be done with it. In fact, the MBR used in Windows XP has only one function. It loads a program called NT Loader (NTLDR) into memory.

> **Note**
>
> NTLDR is probably a name you recognize. When a computer tries to boot from a disk that is not bootable, but has been formatted with a Windows XP-compatible file system, you will often see the message, "NTLDR is missing. Press Ctrl+Alt+Del to restart." If you see this message, Windows is basically telling you that either the disk you are trying to boot from is not a valid boot disk (maybe that floppy disk is still in the drive), or that the NTLDR file is invalid. You will find ways to fix this later in the chapter.

NTLDR switches your computer to a flat memory model (thus bypassing the 640KB memory restrictions placed on PCs), and then reads the contents of the BOOT.INI file. The BOOT.INI file contains information on the different boot sectors that exist on your computer.

Each partition on a hard drive contains its own boot sector, which is the first sector on a disk. When an operating system such as Windows XP is installed, it creates its own boot sector on the partition on which it is installed. That boot sector is used to start Windows.

> **Tip**
>
> Windows XP includes a wonderful utility called *Recovery Console*, which can be used to repair an installation of Windows XP that has failed. Two recovery commands in particular, FIXMBR and FIXBOOT, can be useful in repairing a faulty boot process. Use of the Recovery Console and these commands is covered in Chapter 23, "Disaster Recovery."

If your computer has multiple partitions that it can boot (for instance when dual-booting is configured), NTLDR uses the information in the BOOT.INI file to display a menu. That menu contains options on the various operating systems (or versions of Windows XP, depending on how things are configured) from which you can choose. When you choose a version of Windows XP, NTLDR opens yet another program into memory called *NTDETECT.COM*.

Understanding the Startup Process

Chapter 6

131

6

UNDERSTANDING
THE STARTUP
PROCESS

> **Note**
>
> If only Windows XP is installed on your computer, NTLDR will not display a menu at all, but will just go ahead and load NTDETECT.COM anyway.

NTDETECT.COM performs a complete hardware test on your system. After determining the hardware that is present, NTDETECT.COM passes that information back to NTLDR. NTLDR then attempts to load the version of Windows XP that you selected. It does this by finding the NTOSKRNL file in the System32 folder of your Windows XP directory. NTOSKRNL is the root program of the Windows operating system, or the *kernel*. Once it is loaded into memory, control of the boot process is passed to it and another file named HAL.DLL is also loaded. HAL.DLL controls Windows' famous Hardware Abstraction Layer, which is the protective layer between Windows and a computer's hardware that enables such stability in the Windows XP environment.

> **Note**
>
> If you chose to boot another operating system besides Windows XP on the boot menu (such as Windows 98 or DOS), NTLDR loads the contents of a file named Bootsect.dos into memory and then forces a warm reboot of the computer. The Bootsect.dos code is then executed, which causes the computer to boot as if a DOS-based MBR had been loaded.

NTOSKRNL handles the rest of the boot process. First, several low-level system drivers are loaded. Next, all the additional files that make up the core Windows XP operating system are loaded into memory. Next, Windows determines whether there is more than one hardware profile configured for the computer (see Appendix C, "XP on Notebook Computers"). If there is more than one profile, you are shown a menu from which to choose one. If there is only one, no menu is shown and Windows loads the default profile.

Once it knows the profile to use, Windows next loads all of the device drivers for the hardware on your system. By this time, you are looking at the Welcome to Windows XP boot screen. Finally, any services that are scheduled to start automatically are started. While services are starting, the logon screen becomes available.

A Brief Recap

The Windows boot process is a pretty complicated one, by any measure. Now that you understand what happens, the briefer version that follows may serve as a simple recap:

1. You turn on the power switch.

2. The POST routine checks some of the hardware in your system and then passes control to BIOS.

3. BIOS checks the remaining hardware in your system, applies any configuration settings, and then loads the MBR into memory.

4. The MBR loads NTLDR into memory and passes control to it.

5. NTLDR reads the BOOT.INI file and displays a startup menu, if needed. If it does, you choose an OS to boot.

6. NTLDR loads NTDETECT.COM into memory.

7. NTDETECT.COM performs another hardware test and passes the hardware information back to NTLDR.

8. NTLDR loads the NTOSKRNL into memory.

9. NTOSKRNL loads the rest of the Windows files, the device drivers, and then starts any services scheduled to start automatically.

The BOOT.INI File

The BOOT.INI file is used by Windows XP (specifically the NTLDR file) to display a menu of operating system options during startup. If only one version of Windows XP is installed on your computer (the situation for most people), you will never see this startup menu; Windows bypasses it and simply starts up.

For the most part, you won't ever need to directly access the BOOT.INI file. You can change the most important aspects of the file using the System Control Panel (described later in this chapter). Nonetheless, there are a number of advanced options you can control by modifying the BOOT.INI file yourself.

First, you should be aware that BOOT.INI is marked with the read-only, hidden, and system attributes by default. You can remove these attributes by opening the file's properties and disabling them (or by entering the command ATTRIB -S -H -R C:\BOOT.INI) at the command prompt, but you should return the file to its original state after editing it. Once you remove these attributes, you can open the file in Notepad by double-clicking it. The following is an example of a typical BOOT.INI file:

```
[boot loader]
timeout=30
default=multi(0)disk(0)rdisk(0)partition(1)\WINDOWSXP

[operating systems]
multi(0)disk(0)rdisk(0)partition(1)\WindowsXP="Windows XP Professional"
/fastdetect
multi(0)disk(0)rdisk(0)partition(2)\Windows98="Windows 98"
```

Understanding the Startup Process

CHAPTER 6

133

6

UNDERSTANDING
THE STARTUP
PROCESS

As with most .INI files, the BOOT.INI file is divided into sections that are named using brackets. A BOOT.INI file contains two sections: [boot loader] and [operating systems].

The [boot loader] section contains the amount of time that must expire before the menu times out and the default operating system is booted. The default timeout value is 30 seconds. This section also contains a line specifying the default operating system.

The [operating systems] section contains the paths to any operating systems installed on the computer. Each path has its own line in the file. Although the path to the operating system looks a little strange, it is not difficult to decipher. Take the following example:

```
multi(0)disk(0)rdisk(0)partition(1)\Windows="Microsoft Windows XP Professional"
/fastdetect
```

Let's break that line into the following parts:

- Each line starts with the word *multi* or *scsi*. These refer to whether the bus the hard drive uses is an AT-bus (multi) or a SCSI-bus (scsi). The number in parentheses after the bus type refers to the adapter being used. The first adapter is 0, which is usually the boot adapter.

- The *disk* value is only used on scsi-bus adapters and refers to the SCSI ID for the drive.

- The *rdisk* value is used on both scsi and AT busses and refers to the ordinal number of the disk on its adapter (0 for the first disk, 1 for the second, and so on).

- The *partition* value is the ordinal number of the partition on the disk (1 means the first partition as opposed to the 0 used in the other values).

- The *directory information* (\Windows in this case) refers to the actual path of the Windows installation on the partition.

- The text surrounded by quotes is the name for the operating system displayed on the boot menu.

- Finally, any switches used for selecting the operating system are added to the end. (More on switches later in this chapter.)

Thus, the example given above tells you that the menu entry, Windows XP Professional, will start the operating system that is in the \Windows folder that is on the first partition on the first disk on the first adapter on the AT bus on the computer.

Fortunately, you can perform the most commonly needed alterations to the BOOT.INI file without ever opening it. Open your Control Panel window and double-click the System icon. In the System Properties dialog box, switch to the Advanced tab and click the Settings button in the Startup and Recovery section. This opens the Startup and Recovery dialog box shown in Figure 6.2.

FIGURE 6.2

Adjust BOOT.INI
*parameters using
the Control Panel.*

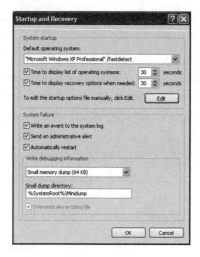

In the System Startup section of the dialog box, you can adjust the following properties:

- The default operating system booted when the timeout value is reached
- The timeout value, which is the number of seconds the boot menu is displayed before the default operating system is booted automatically
- The time to display recovery options, which are covered a bit later in this chapter

Knowing that common adjustments can be made using the Control Panel, there are some not-so-common adjustments that you can make directly to the BOOT.INI file. These come primarily in the form of switches that you can add to the operating system lines in the BOOT.INI file. Table 6.1 shows the available switches.

Table 6.1   Switches for the BOOT.INI File

Switch	*Description*
/basevideo	Forces the OS operating system to boot into 640x480, 16- color Video Graphics Array (VGA) mode.
/baudrate=nnnn	Sets the baud rate of the debug port. (The default is 19,200.) Using this switch automatically turns on the /debug switch.
/bootlog	Writes a log of the boot process to %systemroot%\ntbtlog.txt.
/crashdebug	Enables the COM port to be used for debugging.
/debug	Enables the kernel debugger to perform debugging through the COM port.
/debugport=comx	Specifies the COM port used for debugging.
/fastdetect	Tells NTDETECT.COM not to check parallel and serial ports during boot. These ports will be detected by system drivers instead.

Understanding the Startup Process

CHAPTER 6

135

6

UNDERSTANDING
THE STARTUP
PROCESS

Switch	*Description*
/intaffinity	Forces the multiprocessor HAL to set interrupt affinities so that only the highest numbered processor receives interrupts.
/nodebug	Disables the kernel debugger.
/noguiboot	Stops initialization of the VGA driver responsible for presenting graphical screens during the boot process. Using this switch prevents the boot progress indicator and the blue screen display used for Stop errors.
/noserialmice:comx	Disables the mouse port check for the specified COM port.
/pae	Enables the x86 kernel to use the Intel Physical Address Extensions (PAE) even when a system does not have more than 4GB of memory.
/nopae	Forces the x86 kernel not to use the PAE.
/nolowmem	Only valid if the /PAE switch is also used, this switch tells the kernel not to use the first 4GB of physical memory.
/sos	Forces the loader to display the names of modules that are loaded into Windows.

Startup Options

In addition to displaying the regular boot menu, another menu is lurking behind the scenes of the Windows startup process. If you have a problem booting Windows XP, the Advanced Options menu can be a lifesaver. You can display it by pressing the F8 key while the normal boot menu is showing. If your boot menu isn't shown during startup, press the F8 key once just after the POST routine finishes to display the boot menu and then press F8 again to get to the Advanced Options menu. The Advanced Options menu is shown in Figure 6.3.

Use the arrow keys to select the option you want to use and press Enter to return to the regular boot menu. Next, select the operating system you want to start using the advanced option you selected and press Enter. Windows should start using that option. The available advanced options are covered in the next several sections.

Safe Mode

Safe mode loads only the basic files and drivers needed to get Windows running and to allow access to your disks. It is designed for when you configure something in Windows (like installing a new driver) that causes Windows not to start properly. You can boot into Safe Mode, restore the original settings or make other changes, and then hopefully restart Windows in normal mode again.

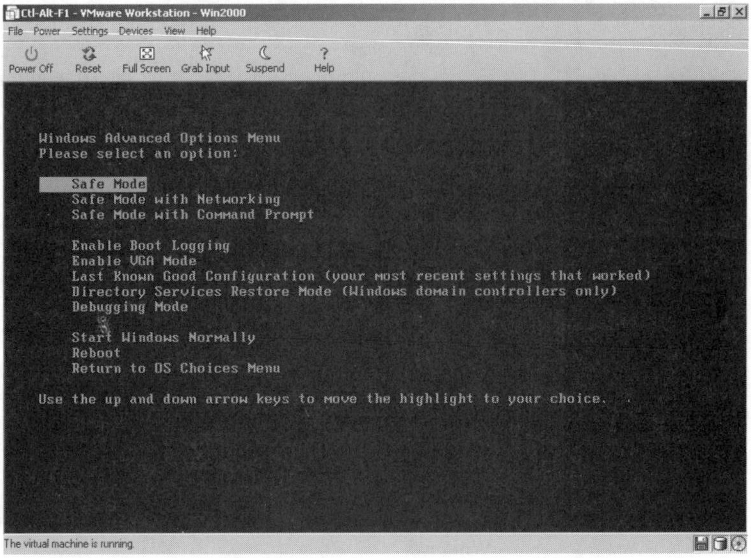

FIGURE 6.3

*Using the
Advanced
Options menu.*

The following Safe Mode options are also available:

- Safe Mode with Networking—This option boots into Safe Mode but also starts the device drivers for your networking hardware. Note that this will not work with PCMCIA network adapters.

- Safe Mode with Command Prompt—This option boots into Safe Mode except it does not load the Windows Graphic User Interface (GUI). Instead, you are left in a command-line only mode.

Enable Boot Logging

This option starts Windows XP normally, but create a log file that displays all the drivers loaded when Windows starts. This log file is found at %SystemRoot%\ntbtlog.txt. Figure 6.4 shows a portion of an example boot log.

Enable VGA Mode

This option starts Windows XP normally, but uses a standard VGA driver and is particularly useful if you have installed a video adapter driver that doesn't display correctly. This driver is also used when starting Windows XP in Safe Mode.

FIGURE 6.4

A sample
ntbtlog.txt file
showing device
drivers loaded
during startup.

Last Known Good Configuration

This option starts Windows XP using the hardware configuration that was saved the last time Windows XP successfully shut down. If you have installed a new device and driver only to find out that Windows can no longer start, you can shut down your computer, remove the device, and then restart using the last known good configuration.

Directory Services Restore Mode (Domain Controllers Only)

This option is used to restore Active Directory settings and is only used on domain controllers running Windows Server.

Debugging Mode

This option starts Windows normally but sends debugging information to another computer through a serial cable. This option is primarily useful when developing software for Windows XP.

Troubleshooting Startup Problems

Problems in the startup process can take many forms, from corrupt files to bad driver software to improper configuration. Sometimes, startup problems are caused by hardware failure. Whatever the problem you are having, the tips in the following sections should help.

Note

This section presents tips for dealing with normal startup problems that can be fixed without resorting to extreme solutions. For more serious problems, such as a complete system failure, bad MBR record, or corrupted system files that prevent Windows from starting at all, you should read Chapter 23, "Disaster Recovery."

Check the Event Logs for Startup Problems

The very first place you should check for information on suspected startup problems (or for any type of problems for that matter) is the Windows event logs to which Windows XP logs much of what happens during startup (and at other times). You can view the logs of both local and remote servers by using the Event Viewer utility, which you can find by opening the Control Panel and double-clicking the Administrative Tools icon.

Windows XP maintains the following three distinct logs:

- Application—The Application log is a record of events generated by applications. If any applications are scheduled to start up when Windows starts and these applications are having problems, this is where to check.

- Security—The Security log is a record of security events and is really only used if your computer is part of a Windows domain.

- System—The System log is a record of events that concern components of the system itself, including such events as device driver and network failures. This is the most important log to check when troubleshooting startup errors.

Figure 6.5 shows events listed in a typical System log. Double-click any event to find out more information about that particular event. Sometimes the event description will have suggestions on fixing any problem that might have occurred. You will encounter three types of events in the three logs, and a unique icon identifies each event type so that you can easily distinguish between the information entries and the error entries. These events include the following:

- Error—This event is noted with a stop icon. It indicates that a significant problem has occurred, such as a service not starting properly.

- Warning—This event is noted with an exclamation point icon. It indicates an event has occurred that is not currently detrimental to the system but may indicate a possible future problem.

6

UNDERSTANDING
THE STARTUP
PROCESS

- Information—This event is noted with an information mark icon. It indicates a significant event that describes a successful operation has occurred, such as a service starting successfully.

FIGURE 6.5

Viewing events in the System log.

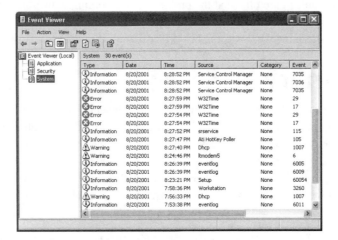

Boot Using Advanced Options

If you are unable to boot into Windows XP at all (and assuming that at some point after installation you could), you may find that the following steps (most of which were covered earlier in the chapter) will at some point resolve your problem:

1. If the MBR or boot sector is found to be invalid, see Chapter 23. Use the procedures there for starting the System Recovery mode. You may find that you can repair the MBR or boot sector.

2. If you boot and get a message that NTLDR is missing, first check to see if you have left a floppy disk in your drive. If you haven't, you will need to repair NTLDR. The best way to do this is to use the System Recovery console, although you may also be able to copy the file from another location.

3. If you get a message that any of the other startup files (NTDETECT.COM, NTOSKRNL, or BOOT.INI) are missing, you can replace them using the System Recovery console.

4. If you get past the initial boot phase and then Windows fails to start, try booting using the Last Known Good Configuration. This feature starts Windows using the hardware settings that were saved the last time Windows shut down. This often solves problems related to new hardware installations.

5. Boot using VGA mode if you have recently installed a new video adapter or drivers. Use this solution if the Last Known Good Configuration option does not work to start Windows and remove the new video drivers.

6. If video drivers aren't the problem (or you are not sure what is), try booting into one of the Safe Modes. You can often remove newly installed drivers or fix other problems this way.

7. If you can't figure out what the problem is, try booting with Boot Logging enabled. Then boot into Safe Mode and check out your boot log (ntbtlog.txt). You can often determine what was the last driver that tried to load this way.

Summary

The startup process for Windows XP is fairly complicated and happens in two distinct stages. First, the computer boots up. This process is primarily controlled by the system's BIOS, which detects and applies settings to your computer's hardware. Once BIOS is finished, it passes control to the MBR, which in turn passes control to the boot sector of a particular hard drive partition. When you boot into Windows XP, several files (including NTLDR, BOOT.INI, NTDETECT.COM, and NTOSKRNL) are loaded into memory one after another.

You can control the way Windows XP starts up in two ways. The first is by configuring the BOOT.INI file, which controls the operating systems that NTLDR can load when starting the computer. You can modify the BOOT.INI file using either the System Control Panel or by directly modifying the file using a program like Notepad. The other way to control startup is to specify any of a number of advanced options when Windows XP first starts to load. You can start Windows into a number of Safe Modes, create a boot log file during startup, and even start up using a debugging mode.

Up Front: The New Desktop

IN THIS CHAPTER

- **Taking a First Look at the Windows XP Desktop** *142*

- **Customizing the Desktop** *144*

- **Choosing a Screensaver** *150*

- **Choosing an Appearance for Windows XP** *152*

- **Choosing and Creating a Theme** *156*

- **Customizing Shortcuts** *157*

- **The Overhauled Start Menu** *160*

- **Customizing the Taskbar** *165*

CHAPTER 7

You may have heard a lot about the new features Windows XP brings to your computer, but one of the most startling things is the new Desktop. The XP Desktop has come a long way from the Windows for Workgroups model, with its separate windows for different functions or programs. On Windows 95 Desktop that followed, the Start button and a Taskbar proved so popular with users that Microsoft incorporated that Desktop design into Windows NT 4.0.

In Windows XP, Microsoft has merged the Windows 95/98/Me and the Windows NT/2000 product lines, and the Windows Desktop has undergone even more change. The new Windows XP Desktop design makes finding files, folders, and programs easier—and · it can make you more productive.

This chapter takes a close look at the Desktop itself, drilling down to the details of customizing such things as the toolbar, color schemes, screensavers, shortcuts, and so on. You learn about the Desktop's new "self-organizing" features, such as moving unused icons out of the way and grouping multiple invocations of the same application on the taskbar. This time around, you have a more intelligent Desktop!

Taking a First Look at the Windows XP Desktop

The first thing that probably comes to mind when you think about your current Desktop is *all* those icons! Each new program you install is placed on the Desktop (although some applications are polite enough to ask if you want that done). You can also create your own icons. Eventually, the Desktop can become so crowded with icons that it is harder to find a program by looking on the Desktop than by simply using the Start menu.

When you install Windows XP, you start with a clean slate and can build from there. When you finish Windows XP Setup and log in the first time, you may wonder if Setup actually completed because there are no icons on the Desktop—no My Computer or Network Neighborhood and no more icons trying to get you to sign up for MSN or to use Internet Explorer. Instead, all you see is a blank Taskbar with the Start button on the left and a clock on the right. The only icon in site is the Recycle Bin, which you easily can hide. Figure 7.1 shows the new Desktop without the Recycle Bin.

In addition to that clean, new Desktop, the Start button and taskbar have a fresh look in Windows XP. These features have softer, more rounded edges than their predecessors. The same goes for properties sheets and dialog boxes. It is a new, more comfortable look in Windows XP.

FIGURE 7.1

You get a clean slate for the Desktop when you first install Windows XP Professional.

Note

If you purchase a new computer that already has Windows XP Professional installed, then you may indeed see something more cluttered than the Desktop shown in Figure 7.1. Computer vendors that preload the operating system are free to place icons on the Desktop.

You can choose from among a number of Desktop themes in Windows XP. The Desktop shown in Figure 7.1 uses the Windows XP Desktop theme. You can select any of the built-in Desktops, or you can create your own. You can design your computer interface to look exactly like you want it.

Tip

Don't worry! If you don't like the new look and feel of Windows XP, you can always switch back to the good old standard Windows Desktop by using what is now called the *Classic Windows* theme. The same goes with other components of the operating system. For example, in Chapter 14, "Using the Control Panel," you learn how the Windows XP Control Panel has a whole new look and feel that is based on categories. You can also change the Control Panel back to the classic view from Windows 2000 or Windows NT.

Customizing the Desktop

If you don't like the Desktop in Figure 7.1, then you can begin customizing it by simply right-clicking anywhere on the Desktop and choosing Desktop from the Display Properties sheet pop up (see Figure 7.2).

FIGURE 7.2

Right-click any-where on the Desktop and select Desktop from the proper-ties page to change the Desktop appearance.

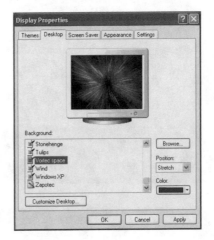

At the top of the properties page you see a preview display of the currently selected Desktop background. Click on any of the Background Options to see them in the preview pane before you apply one to your desktop. Use the scroll bars to move through the Background selections (there are a lot of them). Figure 7.2 shows the Vortec Space back-ground as it appears in the preview pane.

Create Your Own Desktop Background

If you don't like any of the built-in Desktop backgrounds, choose the first one in the Background menulist, (None). This background choice puts a blank screen on your mon-itor with the Start button and toolbar at the bottom. You can, of course, change the color of this backdrop, using the Color drop-down menu on the Desktop tab.

In addition to using the built-in Desktop backgrounds, you can use the Browse button to browse for a picture to use as a background. Since Windows XP supports many multime-dia features, you can even import your own pictures from a digital camera or a scanner to use as your Desktop background. Corporate customers can customize the backdrop by using a company logo. The possibilities are endless.

If the picture that you choose for a backdrop isn't large enough to fill the entire screen, use the Position drop-down menu to choose from the following options:

- Stretch—This option enlarges your picture to fill the entire screen. The success of the stretch depends on the quality of the picture you have chosen. If you take a picture using a low-resolution digital camera, you may not get good results using this option.

- Center—This selection centers the picture you select in the middle of the screen.

- Tile—This option covers the screen with multiple copies of the image you have chosen,, "tiling" the screen with the image. This selection works well with both patterns and pictures.

Customizing Desktop Icons

The last button on the Desktop tab of the Display Properties page is called *Customize Desktop.* This button leads you to a number of options for customizing the presentation of your Windows XP Desktop. Click this button to produce the Desktop Items properties sheet shown in Figure 7.3.

FIGURE 7.3

Clicking the Customize button produces the Desktop Items properties sheet with a number of customization options on the General and Web tabs.

If you would prefer to use the Desktop shortcuts that were present in previous Windows versions, you can use this properties sheet to restore those icons to the Desktop. Just select the check box next to a familiar icon, and it will reappear on the Desktop. The default options that will appear under the Desktop icons section are as follows:

- My Computer—This icon lets you explore all of the resources of your computer, from disk drives to printers and many others. My Computer now includes a lot of other items that were not present in earlier Windows versions, including a section called *Other Places,* which includes My Network Places and the Control Panel.

- My Documents—This icon will allow you quick access to any documents you choose to store in the My Documents folder. Note that the My Documents folder now includes My Pictures and My Music folders, which will be discussed in later chapters in this book.

- My Network Places—You can also access this from the My Computer icon and place it on the Desktop as its own icon if you want to be able to quickly find the information you are looking for.

- Internet Explorer—Of course, you should expect to see that you can restore this icon.

Under the generic category of Desktop icons, you will see a list of other icons to add to the Desktop. In addition to the Recycle Bin, most of these icons are the same as those included in the list above. Options in this section of the properties sheet are as follows:

- Change Icon—You can choose a new icon you want to use for the particular item. Since Windows XP has so many multimedia features incorporated into it, you may want to include your own images for standard Desktop icons; this option lets you do that.

- Restore Default—If you don't like the changes you have made, use this option to restore the default icon for the selected item.

Clean Up Icon Clutter: Use It or Lose It

At the bottom of the Desktop Items General properties sheet there's another section called *Desktop Cleanup*. This feature is intended to help you keep your Desktop clean and pristine. By default, Windows XP automatically sweeps away icons that you have not used for the last 60 days. You can deselect the check box titled Run Desktop Cleanup Wizard every 60 days if you want to disable this feature. Do give this option careful thought before you dismiss it. If you keep adding programs and each adds a Desktop icon, how many of those icons do you really use on a frequent basis? A half-screen filled with icons makes it difficult to locate the icon you need in a hurry.

With the Desktop Cleanup feature in place, after 60 days of inactivity for any icon, Windows XP prompts you to see if it is okay to sweep the unused icons off your Desktop. You can tell Windows XP not to perform this task. In addition, you don't have to go back and reinstall programs or otherwise to restore any icons you *do* use infrequently. Instead, icons removed from the Desktop are stored in a special folder so that you can restore any of them that you find you later want to use again. Note also that this feature *only removes the icons*, it *does not* remove the programs or data files associated with the icons it cleans up.

Tip

If you want to remove not only the icon but also the programs and files associated with it, use the Add/Remove Programs feature found in the Control Panel. You can learn more about this in Chapter 14.

Suppose your Desktop becomes so cluttered with recent application installations that you don't want to wait 60 days to remove unused icons. Open the Desktop Items properties sheet and click the Clean Desktop Now button to launch the cleanup process. The Desktop Clean up Wizard pops up to prompt you for which icons to remove.

Placing a Web Page on Your Desktop

With Windows XP, you are relegated to any single background picture, color, or texture. You can make your Desktop a Web page so that when you log into your computer, you are automatically connected to your favorite site. To install a Web page on your Desktop, click the Customize Desktop button on the Display Properties page and then choose the Web tab. Figure 7.4 shows this tab selected, along with the available options.

FIGURE 7.4

The Web tab of the Desktop Items properties page allows you to further customize your Desktop by specifying a Web page for use as a Desktop background.

If you have already selected a home page, then the check box My Current Home Page is already selected in this dialog box. Click New to specify a home page you want to use as your default Desktop. When the New Desktop Item dialog box appears, enter a Web address in the Location field or use Visit Gallery to select from a number of default Web site pages Microsoft suggests.

> ### Tip
>
> The Visit Gallery button can be useful for corporate users who don't have a specific Web page in mind for the Desktop. In this gallery, Microsoft suggests several types of pages that may be useful for businesses. For example, selecting Microsoft Investor gives you a Desktop background that delivers the latest stock quotes, or you can choose to use your company's home page as your Desktop background. This item makes any Web page available to your Desktop.

Microsoft pages in the Visit Gallery options are likely to change over time, but at the time of this writing, they include the following:

- Microsoft Investment Ticker—For those of you watching your stocks on a frequent basis!
- CBS Sportscenter Baseball Live—For the sports enthusiasts.
- J-Track Satellite Tracking—For the space enthusiast who wants to know just where a particular satellite is at the moment.
- Weather Map from MSNBC—Useful for mobile employees who travel and need to know the current weather conditions.

To choose a Web page not listed in the Microsoft gallery, enter the URL in the Location Field and click OK.

A dialog box titled Add Item to Active Desktop pops up to ask if the URL requires a password. You can use the Customize button to launch the Offline Favorite wizard shown in Figure 7.5. This wizard lets you further refine how the URL is used for the Desktop. The first thing you do in the wizard is set a schedule for synchronizing the Web page.

The Offline Favorite Wizard lets you set a specific schedule for updating the Web page background with new data from the site, as shown in Figure 7.5. Later screens let you determine how many levels of pages will be stored offline when the URL is accessed, an important option, since so many sites offer simple home pages with links to more useful pages.

Once a day is the minimum frequency you can set for your synchronization schedule in the When Would You Like to Synchronize This Page? area of the Offline Favorite Wizard screen. You can also set the time that you want the computer to contact the Web site for updates in this section. Give a name to this schedule that will make it easy for you to recognize. Lastly, If you want your computer to make a connection to the Internet when the scheduled update time comes up, select the check box under the Name field and the computer will do so. Click Next to move on.

FIGURE 7.5

*The Offline
Favorite Wizard
can be used to set
up a schedule for
updating your
Desktop with Web
page content.*

If you are online when you click OK, a Synchronizing dialog box pops up and the system attempts to contact the URL you entered and place the content on your Desktop. When it has finished, you are returned to the Web tab of the Desktop Items dialog box. Click OK if you are finished. If you want to further customize the Web page background and its offline contents, click Properties and use any of the options shown in Figure 7.6.

FIGURE 7.6

*Use Properties to
access additional
options for your
Web page back-
ground schedule,
such as other
schedules for
downloading the
Web site.*

The Web Document tab merely displays information about the URL, the number of times the Web page has been visited, and statistics such as the amount of data downloaded. The Schedule tab adds or removes additional schedules so that the page can be downloaded more often than once a day. The Download tab provides you with many more features for customizing how this Web page is used for your Desktop, including the following:

- Content to Download—Here you can select the number of page levels that will be downloaded when the page is downloaded. This merely tells Windows XP how many levels of links to follow (and then download) starting with the first page of the Web site. You can also use the check boxes in this section to allow or disallow downloading pages from links to pages from a different Web site, and you can limit the amount of disk space that will be allowed for the pages that are downloaded.

• When This Page Changes, Send E-mail To—Use this if you want to receive notice when content on any of the Web pages you have chosen has changed. This can alert you to, for example, the fact that a second level page has changed so you can check the link from your Desktop. You can also specify the simple mail transport protocol (SMTP) server that should be used to send the e-mail.

Under the Content to Download section, you will see an Advanced button with which you can further customize what content will be downloaded. You can choose from images, sound, and video, as well as ActiveX controls and Java applets. You can also use this button to specify that only links to HTML pages should be followed. Use Login to change your username and password for a password protected Web site.

When you have finished selecting the URL and have customized everything you want, click your way back out (using the OK buttons) and exit the Display Properties pages. You will see your Web site appear on the Desktop. You can resize the window by dragging the sides of the display so that it fills your entire Desktop or just a small portion of it. This is a handy way to keep your favorite Web page on the Desktop all the time, automatically, without having to bring up Internet Explorer (or that other browser). When you initially set up a Web site to be on your desktop, you must indicate how many levels of links that you want to store offline. If you click on a link that goes beyond that level, then a browser will pop up and attempt to find the Web page the link represents.

Choosing a Screensaver

Although many manufacturers and computer experts claim that screensavers aren't necessary for preventing "image burn" on modern monitors, screensavers continue to be popular and practical. A good screensaver provides an interesting display, but it also allows you to lock the machine so that when the screensaver kicks in (after a predetermined "idle" time), you need a password to turn it off and return to your work screen. That is a good feature in the office, when you may not want to log off your computer each time you need to step away for a short break. A password-protected screensaver keeps others out of your onscreen business while you are away; you save time *and* privacy.

Changing the Screensaver

To change the screensaver you can buy a third-party product, or you can use one that comes with Windows XP. To select a Windows XP screensaver, use the following steps:

1. Right-click anywhere on the Desktop.

2. Select Display Properties and then open the Screensaver tab.

3. Use the Screensaver drop-down menu to select from the built-in screensavers; an example is displayed in the terminal picture that fills the top of the property sheet.

4. Use Settings to change settings for the screensaver you select. The available items vary according to the screensaver you have chosen. Click OK when you are done.

5. Click Preview for a full-screen demo of your new screensaver; move the mouse to return to the Screensaver tab.

6. Use the Wait drop-down menu to specify the amount of idle time that should elapse before the screensaver kicks in.

7. Click the On resume, password protect check box to enable the password protection feature.

Note

At the bottom of the Screensaver tab, you will see the Monitor Power section. Click Power to bring up the Power Options Properties pages. This set of properties pages allows you to create different power schemes for turning off the monitor and hard disks, as well as to put the system into standby or hibernate mode. See Chapter 14 for more on this feature. It describes the Power Options Properties in greater detail. This is especially useful in an environment where the computer is left on all the time, or if you use a laptop computer where battery power needs to be conserved during idle times.

Create a Slide Show Screensaver

You can create a really personal screensaver by using the photographs in your My Pictures folder.

When you have collected the pictures you want to use for your slide show, create a slide show screensaver by selecting My Pictures Slideshow from the Screen Saver menu. If you want to customize this particular personal screensaver, click Settings. A My Pictures Screensaver Options dialog box pops up, and you can specify the directory from which you want to choose the images for your slide show by using the Browse button. You also can choose how often pictures are changed (from six seconds to three minutes), and the size of the pictures as they appear onscreen.

You can also select two additional options from this dialog box using the following check boxes:

- Use transition effects between pictures—Windows XP will use a variety of effects to go from one picture to the next. Experiment to see if you like the transition effects that are employed. Otherwise, each picture will simply be displayed, then the next, and so on.

- Allow scrolling through pictures with keyboard—You can use the arrow keys on your keyboard during the screensaver presentation to navigate through your pictures.

Tip

You can scan in photographs if you have an ordinary film camera, or you can directly import pictures from a digital camera or flash card reader to create your slide show. E-mail friends and relatives and ask them to send you pictures from any special occasions. You may consider this the best screensaver you can put on your Desktop! When your computer is idle, a continuous, random, sequence of your favorite photographs will be on display.

Choosing an Appearance for Windows XP

The Display Properties sheet's Appearance tab, shown in Figure 7.7, allows you to change several other aspects about how your Windows XP Desktop and programs look. Each time you select an item from the three drop-down menus on this page the upper portion of the tab's display will show you an example of the item you have chosen.

FIGURE 7.7

The Appearance tab shows you an example of the selections you make before you commit your changes using the Apply *and* OK *buttons.*

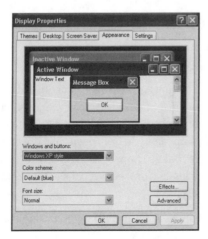

The three main drop-down menus on this tab are as follows:

- Windows and buttons—Use this to select from Windows XP style or Windows Classic Style. The default entry you choose on this menu will depend on the Theme you select or create (covered later in this chapter).

- Color scheme—Use this to change the colors that Windows XP uses for window backgrounds, title bars, menus, and so on.

- Font size—Here you can choose a font size from Normal (the default) to Extra Large. Experiment to see which size works best for you.

Adding Font and Menu Effects and Other Advanced Appearance Features

By default, Windows XP uses a fade effect to dissolve and fade into menus as they transition on and off the screen. If you would rather go back to the "scroll-in" menu styles from previous Windows versions, click the Effects button on the Appearance tab and choose the Fade or Scroll effect (see Figure 7.8). Both of these effects are difficult to describe, so experiment to see which you prefer.

FIGURE 7.8

The Effects dialog box can control many characteristics of how Windows menus, fonts, and dialog boxes are presented on the screen.

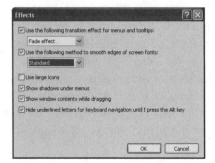

Other options in the Effects dialog box enable laptop users to choose a method for smoothing the edges of screen fonts. These options allow you to select from the standard True Type screen font and the new Clear Type font. Clear Type is a new font technology recently developed by Microsoft to make reading text on flat-screen monitors easier.

Note

Clear Type technology was developed mainly to make it easier to read text on a laptop computer screen. For more information about Clear Type, see Appendix C, "Using Windows XP on a Laptop Computer."

Other options in the Effects dialog box let you choose large icons, use shadow effects, determine dragging effects, and so on.

> **Note**
>
> The Hide Underlined Letters for Keyboard Navigation Until I Press the Alt Key eliminates the underline of hotkeys for keyboard shortcuts. When you press Alt, the underline appears for each hot key in the menu, so you can choose the correct combination key for the shortcut you want to use.

Clicking Advanced in the Appearance tab brings up the Advanced Appearance dialog box. You may never need to use the options in this dialog box. If you change other settings for windows and buttons, options in the Advanced Appearance dialog box may override other settings you choose. This Advanced Appearance dialog box allows you to further specify selected attributes, such as your preferred size, color, and font instead of the defaults for anything other than the Windows Classic theme.

The Item section of the Advanced Appearance dialog box allows you to select a particular component of the Windows XP display to modify, such as the Desktop, title bars, menus, fonts, and so on. You can use the Size drop-down menu to set the size of some objects (if the item is grayed out, you can't choose a setting for it). Next to the Size menu, however, are the Color 1 and Color 2 menus. From Color 1 you can select the background color to be used for the Windows component you've selected. For the Color 2 option you can select the gradient colors, which is how smooth shading from one color to another occurs in such things as title bars. For some Windows XP components, one or both of these color menus may be grayed out, which means you cannot make changes for that particular Windows component.

Choosing Display Settings Appropriate for Your Monitor

The Settings tab of the Display Properties page contains options for changing the screen resolution for your monitor and determining the color quality it displays (see Figure 7.9).

The settings available on this tab depend on the graphics adapter installed in your system, as well as the actual monitor attached to the card. In the example shown in Figure 7.9, screen resolution is set to 800 by 600 pixels. This is a standard size that is used for capturing screen shots to be published in books such as the one you're reading. But you can set this value much higher; higher screen resolution means more clarity and detail, but a smaller onscreen image. Use the Screen Resolution slider bar to change the screen resolution. Click the Apply button; Windows XP will ask you to preview the settings first so you can be sure that you will be able to use these settings on your monitor. Click Yes to apply the change. Don't worry. If nothing shows up after about 20 or 30 seconds, your screen will automatically return to its previous settings.

FIGURE 7.9

The Settings tab allows you to change the monitor resolution and color quality that is displayed on your screen.

Likewise, you can use the drop-down menu labeled Color Quality to choose the number of colors; then use the Apply button again. If you have trouble with any of these settings, Troubleshoot and Windows XP will prompt you with a series of questions designed to narrow down the problem and help you resolve it.

Using the Advanced button, you can select from a large number of configurable items. Figure 7.10 shows the set of properties sheets for the Advanced settings you can configure for your monitor and graphics card.

FIGURE 7.10

The Advanced Button presents a series of tabs, the exact nature of which depends on your graphics adapter and monitor.

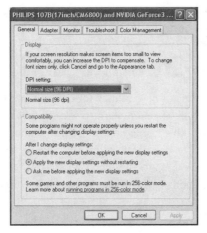

As you can see in Figure 7.10, the monitor and graphics adapter make a big difference regarding which specific tabs appear in these properties sheets. Since the graphics adapter involved in this example has a very high-resolution capability, you may not see several items when using a simpler card or monitor.

Regardless of what monitor and graphics adapter you use, you need to know about a few of these properties sheet tabs. The General tab, for example, includes a section labeled Compatibility. You can use the options here to set the color mode to 256 colors, which is an older standard. You may need to use that old-time standard, even though you may still be playing some of those fun old computer games that have been out-of-date for a number of years. Most newer games are written exclusively to run on higher priced graphics adapters and monitors; however, if you are a gaming fanatic, you will not have to bother with this option.

> ## Caution
>
> The Adapter tab allows you to identify the graphics adapter installed in your computer and to change some properties of the adapter. Unless you are a graphics-adapter guru, *don't make changes here unless you have documentation instructing you to do so*. You can render your display unreadable and have to use a recovery mechanism (such as what is described in Chapter 23, "Disaster Recovery").

The Monitor tab is another important tab. Here you can see a description of the monitor connected to the graphics card. You can also see which screen refreshes values your monitor supports. Again, don't fool around with different refresh rates (Hertz) in the Adapter tab unless you have checked the Monitor tab first to be sure it supports that refresh rate. You may end up with a garbled or blank screen.

Choosing and Creating a Theme

The Windows XP Theme tab offers lots of possibilities for customizing the Desktop display theme, such as icons, cursors, sounds, and other display properties, that make your Desktop come alive. Up to now, you have learned about all of the other ways you can customize the appearance and functions of your desktop. Most people use those options before they choose or create a new Desktop theme. The Windows XP theme is the default setting, but you can choose another built-in theme or create your own.

Choosing the Windows 2000 Classic Desktop and Other Themes

If you just don't like the new look of the Windows XP Desktop, you can switch back to the Windows 2000 look (as with the rest of life, it seems that anything more than a few years old is called *Classic*). To set your Desktop back to the Windows 95/98/ME or NT appearance to which you have probably grown accustomed, use the following steps:

1. Right-click anywhere on the Desktop to bring up the Display Properties Page.

2. From the Themes tab, use the Theme drop-down menu to select Windows Classic.

3. Click OK to dismiss the Display Properties sheet, and your Desktop will return to the classic look of previous Windows releases.

> **Note**
>
> Note that changing to the Classic theme will not change the actual way the Start menu, Taskbar, or other components of Windows XP work. You will still see the last five programs accessed when you click the Start button, and dialog boxes will have their familiar old sharp edges.

Use the Theme drop-down menu to select other themes. Use the Browse selection to explore for additional themes on your computer or to search for a theme using Internet Explorer. Choose More Themes Online, which will bring up a browser and take you to a Microsoft Web site.

Creating Themes

With Windows XP, you too can be a Desktop artist! You can use the other tabs in the Display Properties sheets to create your own theme. Use the other tabs to choose colors fonts and other things from among the items discussed earlier in this chapter. From the Themes tab, click Save As to save your selections as a new theme for yourself. Choose a storage location and name for your new theme and then click OK. Your new theme will then be available in the Theme menu on the Themes tab of the Display Properties page.

Customizing Shortcuts

Although Windows XP has changed many things, it still offers multiple customization options for shortcuts. You can add shortcuts, rename them, or configure their properties. Shortcuts are an important time-saving feature in Windows; the following sections outline techniques for making them look the way you want.

Adding Shortcuts

Adding shortcuts in Windows XP is much like the process you have used in earlier versions of the operating system. Simply use the Start menu to locate the program and then right-click on the program name. In the context menu, choose Send To. A submenu appears, and from this you can select the option Desktop (create shortcut). The icon for the program appears on the Desktop so you can access it quickly. (Remember, however, that if you don't use the icon within 60 days or if you choose to manually clean up the Desktop icons, it can be hidden away!)

You can add shortcuts for a lot of other things too, such as drives or folders. Simply click on the item once to highlight it, then click on the File menu and select Create Shortcut. You may have to resize the program you are in (such as Microsoft Explorer) to reveal the Desktop. From there, you simply drag (click and hold down the mouse button) the shortcut to the Desktop.

Rename a Shortcut

This is an easy one—just right-click and select Rename from the menu that appears (or very slowly double-click on the icon) on the Desktop icon you want to rename, and a box appears allowing you to enter the new text for the name you want to use for the shortcut.

Note that in an icon name, you can use most of the letters, numbers, and punctuation marks available via your keyboard. However, you cannot use the following keys: \:/*?"><|.

Configuring Shortcut Properties

Shortcuts, like most anything else in Microsoft Windows XP, have a set of properties sheets associated with them. Figure 7.11 shows how you can see the shortcut Properties sheet associated with a simple program: the Command Prompt.

In the Shortcut tab of the Command Prompt properties page, you can change the target location of the shortcut, in case you want to move a program to a different location. The Start in field is generally the same as the target directory, but for some programs you may find other files in other directories that the program's shortcut needs to access. Use this field for specifying the other directory, if different from the original program's directory.

In the Shortcut key field, you can specify a sequence of keystrokes that will bring up this shortcut automatically. A shortcut key *must* include the Ctrl+Alt keys to start the shortcut key sequence. In this field, press Ctrl+Alt, and the key you want to automatically activate a shortcut to this program.

FIGURE 7.11

The Shortcut tab will allow you to configure properties for a shortcut you create.

Note that you cannot use the following keys for shortcuts:

- Esc
- Enter
- Tab
- Spacebar
- Print Screen
- Delete
- Backspace

You must also be sure that your shortcut doesn't conflict with another shortcut or with any of the Alt+<keystroke> combinations that are already associated with shortcuts in Windows XP.

Under the drop-down menu labeled Run you can choose to have the program run in a normal, minimized, or maximized window. Choose from this menu the way you like to use the program being accessed by the shortcut. Another field allows you to enter a comment about the shortcut.

The three buttons at the bottom of this property sheet allow you to manage the shortcut even further:

- Find Target—This will open the folder in which the executable program for the shortcut was originally located. Use this if you find the shortcut no longer works because someone has changed a file name. You can also browse other folders to find the program.

- Change Icon—Use this button to change the icon used for the shortcut. This will not change the icon associated with the original program itself, just for this particular shortcut.

- Advanced—The Advanced Properties dialog box will pop up and offer two choices. First, you can choose the check box labeled Run with Different Credentials, which can be used to run the program associated with the shortcut using a different logon identity without granting you all the rights and permissions for that identity except to run the shortcut. The second check box allows you to run the program in a separate memory space, and is useful for 16-bit applications.

The Overhauled Start Menu

Now that you have learned how to change the style and color of your Desktop, it's time to get on to some additional features that make using Windows XP easier to use. You already learned that Windows XP can help keep your Desktop clean by hiding unused program icons that you rarely use. Now let's learn about the Start button.

High-Five: The Last Five Programs You Have Used

In the previous versions of Windows, the Start button would bring up a lot of items, and you had to navigate through all of them to find the particular program you wanted to use. The new Start button brings up a much different looking menu, as shown in Figure 7.12.

FIGURE 7.12

The Start button will show you a much different view than in earlier versions of Windows.

In the new Start menu, Programs has been replaced by All Programs. Click this if you want to see all of the programs installed on your computer. This is where you will find such things as the Accessories and System Tools folders. The left side of the display lists the last five programs accessed. This means that if you frequently use a small selected number of programs, they will be visible here so you don't have to navigate through several levels of clicking to find the program you want. The alternative, of course, is to fill your Desktop with icons—something Windows XP works hard to help you avoid.

> **Tip**
>
> In Figure 7.12 you see that the last six programs I've used are shown, instead of the last five that I told you that you would see. This is because you can change the properties of the Start Menu and set a value from 0-30 to indicate how many programs to list here. I choose six, since these are programs I use frequently.
>
> Another neat thing you can do with the properties page for the Start Menu is to select the "Classic" Start menu, if you prefer the one that you used with Windows 9.x, NT and Windows 2000.

Pin Your Favorite Programs to the Start Menu

One very important fact to note here is that you can change this "last five" behavior. If you do use more than five programs on a frequent basis, but have several you use most often, you can "pin" them to the Start menu list. Using this method, important programs are always easily available. The "first five" menu remains the same, but above it, you will see items you have pinned, since they are now much more easily attainable.

To pin your favorite programs, do the following:

1. Right-click on the program that you want to pin to the Start menu. You can right-click on the program as it already appears in the Start menu or as it shows up in Windows Explorer, or on a Desktop icon for the program.

2. From the menu that appears, select Pin to Start Menu.

3. The program will now appear in the area above the first five programs.

Using the Search Companion

Another feature on the new Start menu is the Search Companion. This replaces the old Run, Search capability of previous Windows operating systems. It also allows you to search not only your local computer or network, but also the Internet. In addition, the built-in indexing service can index all of the files stored on your computer. You can also specify what you want to search for, including places, people, files, folders, or Windows

XP support. Figure 7.13 shows the default window that appears through Search Companion (Start, Search).

FIGURE 7.13

The Search function from earlier Windows incarnations is now the Search Companion.

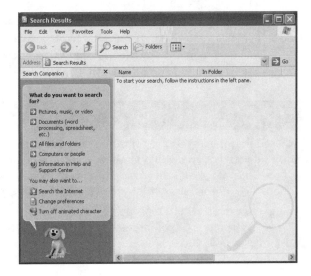

Unless you just like seeing animated animals on your Desktop, turn off the dog that appears at the bottom of the dialog box by clicking on Turn Off Animated Character.

You can also select from the Search dialog box that has the following options:

- Pictures, music, or video
- Documents (word processing, spreadsheet, and so on)
- All files and folders
- Computers and people
- Information in Help and Support Center

In addition there are a few other items you can select to search:

- Search the Internet
- Change preferences
- Turn off animated character

> **Note**
>
> It is always possible that you won't see all the items listed in the list of places to search, including the Internet. The Change Preferences option may have been used by you (or someone else who uses your computer) at another time to change the categories of how a search will be performed.

Click Change Preferences to change the way a search is performed and how the Search Companion operates. Use the Change preferences option to do the following:

- Get rid of the Search Companion animated figure or use a different character (of which there are several you can choose from).

- Enable or disable indexing the files on your computer, which is done during idle time, to make possible searches for text within files. You can also choose how the indexing service operates so that you can create indexes of all text or just abstracts of text within files, among other things.

- Change how files and folders are searched.

- Select a standard search for Internet searches that allows you to specify from a list of search engines available on the Internet what you want to use instead.

- Show or hide tips that pop up in balloons to help you through the search process.

- Turn the Autocomplete feature on or off, which anticipates the text you enter based on text you have previously entered.

Don't underestimate the capabilities of this new search feature. Not only can you search using standard techniques, like entering text that might appear in a document or e-mail title, but you can also search for text within a file. You can search for the last file you worked on and for printers and other resources based on such things as the capabilities of the printer or the location.

To search for a file or folder, click on All Files and Folders shown in the left pane of the Search Results page; the criteria dialog box shown in Figure 7.14 appears.

FIGURE 7.14

What used to be a simple search now allows you to specify many different criteria for searching for a file or folder.

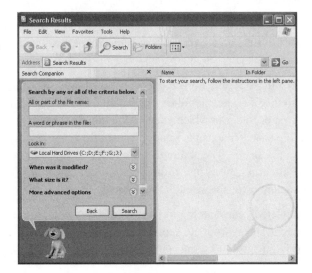

Do you remember part of a filename but not all of it? You can enter text in the first field to specify part or all of a file or folder name, or if you can't remember the document name but you know something about the subject matter that's in the file, use the second field and enter text to search for inside a file. The Look in drop-down menu allows you to expand or limit your search to your computer's hard drives. You can also choose to include network drives, the Desktop, or just any place on your computer, including the Recycle bin. After you enter the information you want to use for the search, click Search. Files or folders matching your query will appear in the right pane of the Search Results dialog box.

You also can use the following three search criteria modifiers:

- When Was It Modified?—Using this selection, you can specify one of the following radio buttons: Don't Remember (the default); Within the Last Week; Within the Past Month; Within the Past Year; or Specify Dates. Thus, you can find all documents you have modified within a wide range of times, or you can specify an exact range of date to search.

- What Size Is It?—This selection also brings up a set of radio buttons: Don't Remember (yes, it is the default for all of these menus); Small (less than 100 KB); Medium (less than 1 MB); Large (more than 1MB); or Specify Size (in KB). For example, if you have been working on a rather large document, it should be easy to locate it based on this option.

If you choose the More Advanced option, another dialog box appears offering even more options for refining your search. You can specify what type of file to search, the size of the file, and whether to search system folders, hidden files, and more. One option even allows you to search backup tapes for the item you are searching.

Figure 7.15 shows the results of a search for the name Yoko; this search didn't use any of the modifiers discussed in the preceding paragraphs.

Notice in Figure 7.15 that not only do you get the name of the file or folder but also an icon associated with the file type, the folder in which the file is found, the size of the file or folder, and the type of folder in which your information was found. Note also that if you have network file shares mapped to your computer, then you can extend your search capabilities to those file shares. The ability to search for just about anything, anywhere, using Windows XP is simply awesome! If this search had included the Internet, you can imagine how many more results it would have returned.

After you have completed your search, just double-click on one of the results, and it will pop up on your screen. The appropriate application for displaying the file (document, picture, and so on) will be used to show you the file.

FIGURE 7.15

Depending on the search criteria you enter, you may get back a lot of files that contain your information!

When the Search Companion asks if you found what you were looking for, you can change the search criteria to further refine your search to make it even easier to find what you want. There are also options to sort the results in a different format—sorting by name, date modified, size or file type—or view the results in a different format—showing all details, thumbnails, or tiles.

Customizing the Taskbar

The Taskbar has also undergone some changes that will make it easier for you to use Windows from now on. In this section you'll learn about file grouping, which helps to cut down on the number of items that appear on the Taskbar, as well as making it easier to close multiple instances of the same application. You'll also learn that the System Tray is now called the Notification Area.

File Grouping

In earlier editions of Windows, every new program opened would earn a space on the Taskbar. If you only opened a few applications, this feature was not so troublesome, but as you opened more applications, the size of each application icon on the Taskbar grew smaller and smaller. Additionally, if you opened more than one copy of the same program, a new application icon appeared for each version. File Grouping has changed all of that in Windows XP.

To help eliminate "Taskbar crowding," the new Taskbar uses a concept called *File Grouping*. Now, when you open more than one instance of the same application, instead of having multiple instances of the application appear on the Taskbar, you will instead see a file group entry. You can tell that it is a group of multiple instances of the same application because the entry on the Taskbar has a small down-arrow associated with it. If you click on this group, you will find that it expands to show you all the instances of the particular program (see Figure 7.16). From this menu, you can select your program in a much easier manner.

FIGURE 7.16

By grouping multiple instances of the same application on the Taskbar, you can more easily find the program you want to restore.

The group entry on the Taskbar also shows you the number of entries in this group. Thus, you can see if you have multiple instances of the same program running, along with the menu to pick the one you want to work with.

Now, suppose that you choose to open several different applications that are in the same group, maybe to switch between multiple instances of Microsoft Word. When you finish working in Windows, you have to close each application separately. With File Grouping, you can simply right-click on the Taskbar group entry and select Close Group to close all of the applications that are in the group at the same time. Another time-saving Windows XP feature to make you more productive.

The Notification Area

In earlier versions of Windows, the area to the right side of the Taskbar was called the System Tray. Lots of applications could put icons there, and it could become quite an overcrowded space. This area is now called the *Notification Area*. Instead of maintaining a huge list of icons that you probably would never use anyway, the new functionality will only show recently used icons. If you want to change how this works, use the following steps:

1. Right-click on Start.
2. Select Properties from the menu.
3. Click on the tab labeled Taskbar.
4. Make any changes you want and then click OK.

Summary

The new Desktop that comes with Windows XP is designed to make your job easier by eliminating items you don't use often and making it easier to find things you want. You begin with a clean, uncluttered Desktop and can add to it as you please. Yet, unless you turn off this feature, the Desktop Cleanup Wizard will come along periodically and put away all of those icons you aren't using; you can then retrieve them later when you want them. Windows XP offers many new features for customizing the colors, icons, cursors, font sizes, sounds, and backgrounds for your new Desktop and programs as well. Windows XP search functions have been updated from previous Windows versions to include more features for customizing and refining your search criteria. The new Taskbar eliminates overcrowding, so you will find it easier to use.

Other Applications and Accessories

IN THIS CHAPTER

- Using HyperTerminal   *171*
- Using Entertainment Accessories   *174*
- Using System Tools   *177*
- Using General Accessories   *180*
- Playing Games   *191*

CHAPTER 8

Throughout much of this book, you have learned to use the various components provided by Windows XP Professional to configure system settings, set up a network, customize your desktop, make and view various types of media, and how to get the most out of the Internet. Windows XP also includes a number of built-in accessories, which are small programs designed to provide extra functionality to Windows. These accessories include items like the Calculator, Notepad, and Sound Recorder.

In this chapter, you will learn about a number of these accessories and applications, including the following:

- Hyperterminal lets you connect to other computers, bulletin board services, or host computers using a modem or null modem cable.
- Sound Recorder can be used to record, mix, play, and edit sounds.
- Volume Control is used to adjust the volume, balance, bass, and treble settings for sounds played by your computer's components.
- Character Map is used to copy and paste special characters not normally available from the keyboard.
- System Information is used to collect and display configuration information about your computer's hardware and software.
- Calculator can be used to perform calculations.
- Notepad can be used to create and edit relatively small text files.
- Wordpad is a very basic Word processor that can be used to create and edit text files that contain formatting or graphics.
- Paint is a drawing tool that cab be used to create bitmap images.
- Games, there are quite a few included with Windows XP.

If you are familiar with previous versions of Windows, you will also be familiar with most of these accessories. But don't let that lull you into thinking you know everything there is to know about these old favorites, because Microsoft has made quite a few improvements to them. If you are not familiar with Windows, you may be surprised at the number of useful built-in features included.

Note

Looking at the Accessories folder on your Start Menu, you may notice a number of items not covered in this chapter. Some of these items such as the Network Setup Wizard and Remote Desktop Connection are found in other discussions in this book. Other items, such as Windows Media Player and the Command Prompt, have been given chapters of their own (Chapter 29, "Windows Media

Player 8," and Chapter 13, "Command Prompt Tools"). If you are looking for a specific item in the Accessories folder (or anywhere else on the Start menu, for that matter), look up its name in the book's index.

Using HyperTerminal

HyperTerminal is a terminal emulation program that has been bundled with Windows since Windows 95 (when it was called the Dial-Up tool). HyperTerminal is used to connect to remote computers using either your modem or a null modem cable. The remote computer also must be running some sort of software to accept the connection. HyperTerminal can be used both to receive and initiate connections.

HyperTerminal is often used for the following:

- Connect to a remote computer to exchange information
- Connect to a host computer on a network to provide remote terminal access
- Connect to network devices using VT100 emulation, such as Unix systems, routers, hubs, and so on
- Connect to Internet telnet sites
- Connect to bulletin board services (BBSs)
- Connect to online service not available over the Internet
- Communicating with some types of modems or remote connection hardware

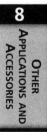

Although the usefulness of HyperTerminal has diminished with the phenomenal growth of the World Wide Web, HyperTerminal is still a useful program for many. This simple program is often used on a laptop to connect to disk controllers on large enterprise server systems. It provides a standard that has been around for a long time—since the Digital VT-100 became the standard interface between most computers and the end user—at least until the PC graphical user interface (GUI) revolution! You can also use HyperTerminal to connect to other devices that allow you to manage the device through a serial port connection. Routers and switches usually have a dedicated serial port used for just this purpose.

Starting HyperTerminal and Creating a Connection

Start HyperTerminal by going to Start, Accessories, Communications, and clicking HyperTerminal. You can also start HyperTerminal from the command prompt or a batch file using the command `hypertrm.exe`.

The first time HyperTerminal starts, you are asked to create a new connection and enter the phone number for the connection, both shown in Figure 8.1. HyperTerminal uses the telephony and location information configured using the Phone and Modem Options Control Panel utility (see Chapter 25, "Configuring Your Computer for an Internet Connection") to create connections. Once you have created a connection, you can modify the connection settings within HyperTerminal using the Properties command on the File menu.

FIGURE 8.1

Creating a new connection in HyperTerminal.

> **Tip**
>
> HyperTerminal saves connections in files with an `.ht` extension, which are saved by default in the HyperTerminal program group folder (`\Documents and Settings\`*username*`\Start Menu\Programs\Accessories\Communications\ HyperTerminal`). This means that any connections you save become available to you on the Start menu.

Once you are connected, the main HyperTerminal window is displayed, as shown in Figure 8.2. The main portion of the window is a large box that becomes the terminal emulation screen. What you see on this screen is entirely dictated by the remote service to which you have connected. Usually, you will be asked for a username and password and then presented with a menu of choices for navigating the remote system.

Although most of the functionality of HyperTerminal is dictated by the remote system to which you are connected, you should be aware of the following few extra tools and settings:

- The Properties command on the File menu opens a dialog box that provides a number of settings in addition to the basic dialing properties. You can configure how certain keys work, what type of terminal emulation you want to use, how many lines the backscroll buffer should save, and even custom ASCII text setup and input translation settings.

- You can copy information from the terminal window and paste plain text into the terminal window using the commands on the Edit menu. This provides a good way to save information from a session or to enter complicated commands.

- The Call menu provides commands for dialing and disconnecting the remote connection. It also provides commands for directing HyperTerminal to enter a receiving state where it can accept incoming calls from other terminal emulators. This means you can use just HyperTerminal to provide a connection between two computers.

- The Transfer menu holds commands for sending and receiving files between connected systems (a great way to transfer information between two computers if no other connection is available) and for capturing HyperTerminal text to a text file or your printer.

FIGURE 8.2

Navigating a remote connection in HyperTerminal.

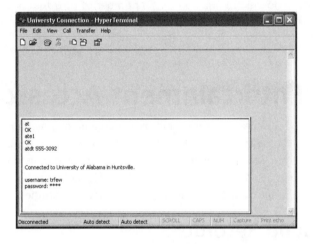

8
APPLICATIONS AND ACCESSORIES
OTHER

In addition to serving as a reliable terminal emulator, HyperTerminal is also useful as a tool for troubleshooting modem connectivity. Because HyperTerminal records all information passed over the connection, you can use it to view your modem's settings by sending Hayes-compatible modem commands through HyperTerminal and checking the results.

For example, you might enter the following command in the HyperTerminal window to check basic modem functionality:

`ate1`

If your modem is functioning, it should return a value of OK or 0.

Note

If you really want to delve into the world of Hayes-compatible modem commands, a good place to start is on the Hayes support Web site: `http://www.hayesmicro.com/Tech_CS/docs.htm`. You will find a number of AT command-reference documents.

Tip

HilGraeve, the company that makes the version of HyperTerminal included with Windows, has an enhanced version available on its Web site: `http://www.hilgraeve.com/htpe/`. This version, named HyperTerminal Private Edition, is a free download and contains a number of new features, such as enhanced terminal support, better printing control, macros, Transfer Call Protocol/Internet Protocol (TCP/IP) support, and much more.

Using Entertainment Accessories

Windows XP includes a few accessories that are featured in the Entertainment subfolder on the Start Menu. These include Windows Media Player, Sound Recorder, and Volume Control. Media Player, which lets you control the playback of various sound and movie formats, is covered in detail in Chapter 29, "Windows Media Player Version 8." This section covers the use of the Sound Recorder and Volume Control utilities.

Using Sound Recorder

Sound Recorder lets you control the recording and playback of .wav files, a sound format common among all versions of Windows and many other systems. It is a relatively simple utility, as you can tell by the interface shown in Figure 8.3. The buttons across the bottom offer tape recorder–style controls for playing, fast-forwarding, rewinding, stopping, and recording a .wav file. The slider above the buttons lets you position the playback anywhere within the sound file. The position reading to the left of the playback window shows the location in the sound file of what is currently being played, and the length reading to the right shows the total length of the file. A waveform display gives a visual readout of the sound as it plays.

FIGURE 8.3

Playing a .wav file with Sound Recorder.

By default, Windows XP actually uses Windows Media Player to play back .wav files, as well as most other sound files. Since Windows Media Player offers better control over sound files, you will almost never need to use Sound Recorder for simple playback. If you have a sound card on your computer, however, Sound Recorder can be used to record .wav files from any recognized source (such as a microphone, audio CD, DVD, and so on).

Once you have a sound loaded into Sound Recorder, regardless of whether you recorded it or opened an existing .wav file, you can perform some limited editing of the file:

- The Edit menu contains commands for mixing and inserting other .wav files with the sound currently loaded and for cutting portions of the sound before or after a selected point.

- The Effects menu contains commands for increasing and decreasing the volume in 25% increments. These commands work by increasing or decreasing the amplitude of the sound. When you increase or decrease the volume level of recorded speech, you may lose a little sound quality. When working with music files, however, increasing and decreasing the volume are likely to create considerable distortion.

- The Effects menu also contains commands for increasing and decreasing the speed of the sound in 100% increments. Other than working with speed of playback instead of volume, these commands work much as do the volume commands.

- The Reverse command on the Effects menu causes the sound to play in the opposite direction.

- The Echo command on the Effects menu creates a synthesized echo effect on the sound. However, be careful using this one. There is no way to undo the effect without reverting to a previously saved version of the file.

Using Volume Control

You can control the overall volume of your computer by clicking the speaker icon in your System Tray (next to your clock) and sliding the main volume control. The Volume Control utility is an extension of that control. You can open Volume Control by double-clicking the speaker icon, running sndvol32 from the Command Prompt, or using the Volume Control shortcut on the Start menu.

The main Volume Control window is shown in Figure 8.4. The screen displays a series of sliders that control the volume and balance of various sound devices on your system, including the main system volume (labeled Volume Control in Figure 8.4), the .wav file driver, line in, and CD audio. You can also mute any individual device.

Figure 8.4

Adjusting volume levels for sound devices.

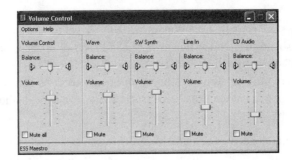

By default, only the most commonly used devices available on your computer are displayed. You can enable the display of additional devices using the Properties command on the Options menu. This opens the Properties dialog box shown in Figure 8.5. If you have more than one mixer device (usually meaning more than one sound card), you can select a specific device using the Mixer device drop-down list. Available volume controls for the selected device are shown in the list at the bottom of the Properties dialog box. Check any control to display it in the main Volume Control window. Use the Playback and Recording options in the middle of the Properties dialog box to filter the list to display only playback or recording controls.

Figure 8.5

Enabling the display of additional sound devices in Volume Control.

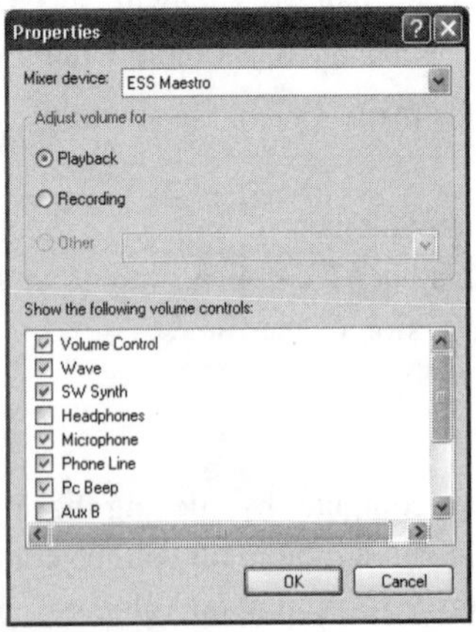

Using System Tools

Windows XP comes with many built-in tools for maintaining and troubleshooting your System. Most of these tools are covered elsewhere in this book. Scandisk and Disk Defragmenter, for example, are discussed in Chapter 19, "Using the Task Manager," and the Disk Cleanup utility is discussed in Chapter 22, "Performance Monitoring and Performance Logs and Alerts."

Two additional tools you may find quite useful are Character Map and System Information.

Using Character Map

Character Map is a utility that displays every available character in each font installed on your system. This includes those characters normally available using the keyboard and many special characters that are not. Character Map can display Windows, DOS, and Unicode character sets in a number of different languages.

You will find Character Map in the System Tools subfolder of the Accessories folder on the Start Menu. The main Character Map window is shown in Figure 8.6.

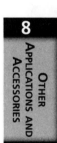

8

OTHER APPLICATIONS AND ACCESSORIES

FIGURE 8.6

Using Character Map to display additional available characters.

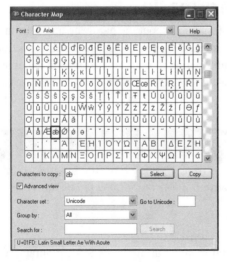

Here is the basic procedure for using Character Map to copy characters to the Clipboard so that you can then paste them into a document:

1. Select the font that contains the character from the Font drop-down list.

2. Scroll through the list of available characters to find the one you want. Hover your pointer over a character momentarily to see a pop-up description of the character. You can click any character once to see a magnified view of that character. Be mindful though that once you do that, there is no easy way to get out of the magnification state. Clicking anywhere just opens the magnification window for another character.

3. Double-click any character to add it to the string of characters you want to copy to the Clipboard. You can also add a selected character to this field using the Select button. You will see a list of characters being built into a string in the Characters to Copy field.

4. Once you have the character or characters you want to copy, click the Copy button. This copies the characters to the Clipboard.

5. Return to your document and use the Paste command to paste the characters in place.

If you click the Advanced view option, the Character Map window extends (see Figure 8.6) to provide controls for choosing a character set (Windows, DOS, or Unicode) to use, and for searching for particular characters in the specified character set.

Using System Information

System Information collects information about the hardware and software configuration of your computer and displays it in a tree view that makes the information fairly easy to browse. You can use System Information to find out information about hardware configurations (such as interrupt request line (IRQ) and input/output (I/O) use), computer components, signed and unsigned device drivers, and even some software settings.

Note

One thing to keep in mind is that depending on the amount of information that has to be gathered, System Information may take quite a while to report its findings.

The main page of the System Information utility is the System Summary page, which is shown in Figure 8.7. This page displays basic information about your system, such as the operating system name and version, processor type, BIOS information, and hard disk configuration.

FIGURE 8.7

Using the System Information utility.

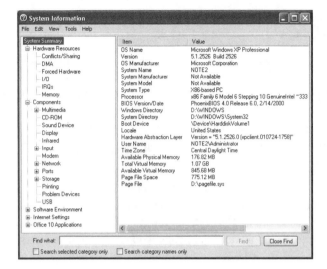

Under the System Summary, you will see five additional nodes (only four if Microsoft Office is not installed on your system):

- Hardware Resources—This category displays information about the configuration of resources among various hardware devices. You can view IRQ, direct memory access (DMA), and I/O allocation, as well as available memory resources. This category is one of the most useful in troubleshooting hardware problems.

- Components—This category displays information about specific components of your system, such as CD-ROM drives, hard drives, ports, and network adapters. You can use this category to find information not only on the actual hardware, but also on Windows settings relating to that hardware. For example, the Network subnode displays information on network adapters, installed protocols, and WinSock settings.

- Software Environment—This category contains information about Windows configuration and software currently loaded into memory, such as installed drivers and environmental variables. This is the best place to find out what is running currently on your system.

- Internet Settings—This category contains information about Internet Explorer configuration, such as security settings, cache information, and file versions.

- Office x Applications—*x* refers to the version number of Office installed on your computer. This node, which is only visible if Office is installed, has a subnode for each installed Office application that lists program configuration information, such as the install directory, loaded add-ins, and even active document information.

In addition to browsing the nodes on the System Information tree, you can also search the tree by entering a keyword in the Find What field at the bottom of the window.

You can also do a few other things with the system information data. Using the File menu, you can export the whole set of information to a text file for archival purposes or for sending to someone. You can also print the system information, but you can only print the entire thing. This tends to be a pretty big print job. Finally, you can save the information as a .NFO file that can then be loaded into the System Information utility on another computer. This is good for sending your system information to a technical support department.

You can also open the system information for a remote computer on your local network. Open the View menu and select Remote Computer. In the dialog box that opens, select the Remote Computer on the Network option and type in a computer name or IP address. Unfortunately, this dialog box does not allow you to browse computers, so you must know the exact name or address of the computer. You can always use Network Neighborhood to browse the network if you are unsure of the computer name. To connect to a remote computer, the Windows Management Instrumentation component must be installed on the remote computer and you must have sufficient permission to access it.

> **Tip**
>
> The Tools menu in System Information contains shortcuts to other valuable system tools that are otherwise hard to access in Windows, including Net Diagnostics, DirectX Diagnostics, and Dr. Watson, a network management tool.

Using General Accessories

You are assuredly familiar with most of the applications in the main Accessories folder, especially those discussed here, such as Calculator, Wordpad, Notepad, and Paint. Nonetheless, these programs offer important functionality of which many people are not aware.

Using the Calculator

Calculator is likely one of the most frequently used built-in programs in Windows (well, maybe after Solitaire). It is shown in its standard view in Figure 8.8. Aside from basic arithmetic functions, the standard calculator doesn't offer much.

FIGURE 8.8

Using the standard Calculator.

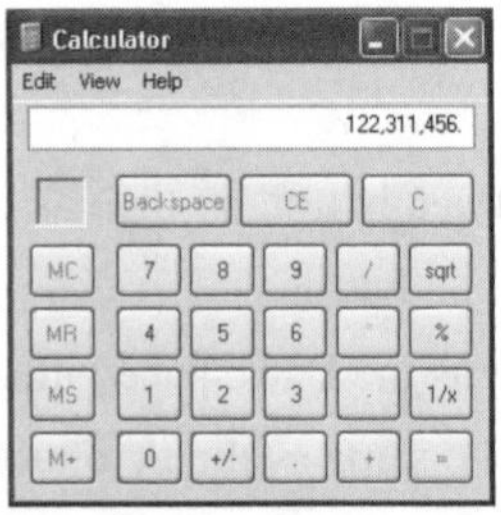

Tip

One thing you can do with both the Standard and Scientific calculators that many people aren't aware of is digit grouping. When you select the Digit Grouping command from the View menu, Calculator breaks up large numbers with commas, making them much easier to read.

If you need to perform more complex calculations, Calculator also offers a Scientific mode. To enter it, just choose Scientific from the View menu. Note that any calculations already entered are lost when you switch modes. Calculator remembers the last mode it was in, so if you exit while in Scientific mode, you will start in Scientific mode next time. The Scientific mode is shown in Figure 8.9.

FIGURE 8.9

Using the Scientific Calculator.

As you can see, the Scientific mode offers many more features than its standard sibling does. We won't go into the actual functions here because we are assuming that if you need a scientific calculator, you already know the purpose of the functions. Nonetheless, there are a few things about the actual program that it may be helpful to know.

To begin with, you can use the numeric keypad on your keyboard to enter calculations. Just make sure that the Numlock key is turned on. All the numerals and operators work just as you would expect. In Additionally, there are other keyboard commands that you can use while calculating:

- Esc—Clears all calculations; the same as the C button on the calculator
- Del—Clears the last entry; the same as the CE button
- Backspace—Clears the last digit; the same as the Backspace button
- Ctrl+L—Clears the calculator's memory; the same as the MC button
- Ctrl+R—Recalls the calculator's memory; the same as the MR button
- Ctrl+M—Stores a number in memory; the same as the MS button
- Ctrl+P— Adds the displayed number to the number in memory; the same as the M+ button

---

Tip

The Scientific calculator can display numbers and perform calculations in hexadecimal, binary, octal, and decimal number systems. Just click the option for the system you want to use. To convert a number from one format to another, select the system you want to convert from, enter the number; then select the system to which you want to convert. The converted equivalent of the number is displayed. As mentioned in the Appendix A, "Introduction to TCP/IP," using the Scientific mode of the Calculator can save you oodles of time when it comes to converting from binary to dotted decimal notation. You can convert from binary to decimal, from decimal to binary, and easily solve those problems associated with calculating subnets and subnet masks.

Using Notepad

Notepad is used primarily for editing small ASCII text files without layout. Notepad will open a text file of up to about 57K. Anything beyond that requires Wordpad or some other program. Notepad is configured as the default program for opening files with the .txt extension in Windows. Figure 8.10 shows the Notepad window.

For the most part, using Notepad couldn't be simpler. Enter and edit your text in the main window. There is no formatting (bold, italic, and so on) or layout available—just text. This offers the advantage of creating small files. Many system files (such as .ini and .bat) can be edited using Notepad, as can most Web pages.

FIGURE 8.10

Using Notepad.

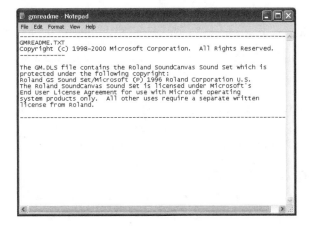

Following are a few extra features that Notepad includes:

- By default, text you enter scrolls off the right side of the screen indefinitely. Choose the Word Wrap command from the Format menu to make text wrap to the next line when it reaches the right edge of the window.

- Even though there is no formatting available, you can use different fonts in notepad. Choose the Font command from the Format menu to choose a font and size. Only one font can be used for an entire text file.

- You can enter the current time and date by pressing F5 or by choosing the Time/Date command from the Edit menu. The date and time are derived from the system clock.

Tip

If you type .LOG (must be in uppercase) as the first line in a text file, Notepad will automatically insert the time and date at the bottom of the file (with the cursor right after it) each time you open the file.

Using Wordpad

Although Wordpad is normally billed as an advanced text editor with layout capabilities, it is actually a stripped down version of Microsoft Word 95. Wordpad performs many of the basic functions you find in more advanced word processing programs.

One of the reasons for incorporating Wordpad into previous versions of Windows, as well as XP, is due to the large number of documentation (including white papers to entire articles or books) in Word format. Wordpad may not allow you to create spectacular documents, but it will permit you to read most of those you find on the Internet.

For the most part, using Wordpad is similar to using any other Windows-based program. Type text into the main window to create your document; use the File menu to open, save, print, and close documents; and use the Help menu to get Help. Aside from the obvious, however, Wordpad does include a few features worth getting to know. The next few sections cover formatting and laying out text, setting up a page, configuring program options, and using Wordpad in conjunction with other programs.

Formatting and Layout

The Wordpad window, shown in Figure 8.11, looks like a typical word processor. The main part of the window is for typing and editing text. In addition to the normal toolbar that provides shortcuts for file operations (such as open, save, and so on), a formatting toolbar provides quick access to common formatting features. You can also access these features using the commands found on Wordpad's Format menu. These features include the following:

- Selecting a font, font size, and font style—All fonts installed on Windows are available within Wordpad.

- Choosing basic formatting—Boldface, italics, underlined text, and different text colors are all present.

- Choosing basic layout—This includes text alignment (left, center, and right) and bulleted list formatting.

FIGURE 8.11

Using Wordpad.

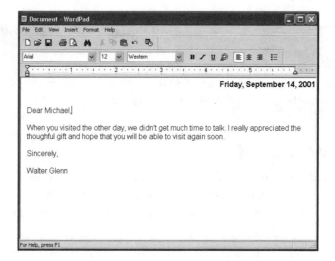

The ruler just above the text window lets you adjust the left and right margins. These ruler controls are shown more closely in Figure 8.12 and include the following:

- First line indent—This indicates the indent used by the first line of a paragraph.

- Hanging indent—This specifies the indent used by subsequent lines of lines of a paragraph after the first indent. When you move the hanging indent marker, the first line indent marker does not move. This can change the relationship of the first line indent as the rest of the paragraph changes.

- Left indent—This specifies the indent from the left margin used by all lines of a paragraph. If the paragraph also includes a first line indent, the first line indent marker moves along with the left indent marker when you use it.

- Right indent—This specifies the indent from the right margin used by all lines of the paragraph.

Note that most of these options can also be set using the Paragraph command on the Format menu.

FIGURE 8.12
Using Wordpad's Ruler.

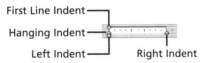

First Line Indent
Hanging Indent
Left Indent
Right Indent

Setting Up a Page

Wordpad's Page Setup feature is used to control the appearance of printed documents. Selecting the Page Setup command from the File menu opens the Page Setup dialog box shown in Figure 8.13. Use this dialog box to do the following:

- Specify the size of paper on which you are printing. The default setting is Letter. Other options include Legal, European measurements such as A4 and A5, and several envelope sizes.

- Specify the Source of the paper, which should include an option for each paper tray installed on your printer. The default is to have Windows automatically decide the paper source.

- Select whether the page should be printed vertically (portrait) or horizontally (landscape).

- Specify the exact measurements used for the top, bottom, left, and right margins of the page.

FIGURE 8.13

Setting page options in Wordpad.

Setting Options

Use the Options command on the View menu to configure general options for the Wordpad program. Note that settings made on the Options dialog box affect all documents opened in Wordpad.

The Options tab of the Options dialog box, shown in Figure 8.14, lets you configure two settings. The first is the measurement unit that should be displayed in Wordpad documents. The second option, Automatic Word Selection, instructs WordPad to select one word at a time (instead of one letter at a time when the option is not selected) as you drag the mouse pointer over text.

FIGURE 8.14

Setting Wordpad Options.

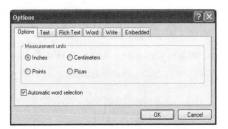

The other five tabs on the Options dialog box are all identical, but they each affect a different type of document. Available tabs include Text; Rich Text; Word (used for Wordpad documents); Write (used for older Windows Write documents); and Embedded (used for other documents inserted into a Wordpad document). Each of the tabs offers the same choices. For each type of document, you can specify the following two options:

- Whether the word wrap feature, which causes continuous lines to wrap to the next line on your display, is turned on—If word wrap is used, you can have it wrap according to the border of the Wordpad window or wrap to the document margin.

- What toolbars are displayed by default for each type of document—Toolbars include the main Wordpad Toolbar, Format Bar, Ruler, and Status Bar. Once a document is opened, you can toggle the display of toolbars using the View menu.

Inserting Objects

If you have used Windows before, you are probably familiar with the concept of embedding documents into other documents. In brief, embedding a document actually inserts an entire document into another document. Once inserted, you can modify the embedded document using the program registered for that document type.

The embedded document can be any document type created by a program on your computer that supports Object Linking and Embedding (OLE). You can insert a number of different document types into a Wordpad document, including other Wordpad documents, Excel spreadsheets and graphs, graphics files, and even sounds.

You can either insert a blank document that you can then fill out, or a document you have previously created. Once a document is inserted, there is no link between the embedded document and the original document.

Use the following procedure to embed a document into a Wordpad document:

1. Click on Start, All Programs, Accessories, and then Wordpad.
2. Create a new Wordpad document or open an existing document.
3. Place the insertion point (or cursor) at the point in the document where you would like to embed another document.
4. From the Insert menu, choose the Object command.
5. Select the Create New option to create a blank document of the selected type or select the Create from File option to browse your computer for a previously created document.
6. If you are creating a new document, choose the type of document you want to create, and then insert from the Object Type list.
7. If you are creating a document from a file, type the location of the file or click the Browse button to locate the file.
8. If you want to insert the file as an icon that you can then click on to open the embedded document rather than displaying the entire contents of the embedded document, select the Display as Icon option.
9. Click OK.

Using Paint

Paint is a drawing tool used to create bitmap images. Paint can be used to create both black-and-white and color images, view scanned images, create desktop backgrounds and icons, and print pictures.

Since you are probably familiar with Paint or one of the many other similar drawing programs available, only a brief description of the more interesting features is presented here.

Using the Drawing Tools

The main Paint window, shown in Figure 8.15, is made up of three key areas. The first is the canvas, the large area in the upper right where your drawing appears. The background color of the canvas in this figure is white. The second key area, to the left of the canvas, holds all of the drawing tools—16 in total, presented in two columns. Beneath the actual tools, a separate box shows any available options for the selected tool. The third key area, at the bottom of the window, is the color palette, the colors available for drawing.

FIGURE 8.15
Using Paint.

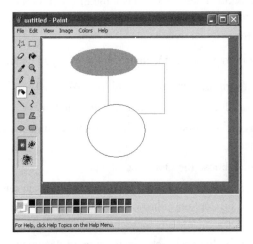

Pick any color to use as your main foreground color by clicking it. Pick a color to use as a background color by right-clicking it. At the left end of the palette, two color squares represent the selected colors—that is, the foreground color shown on top of the background color. As you work with most of the drawing tools, you will find that drawing with your left mouse button uses the foreground color and drawing with the right-mouse button uses the background color. You can also use the Colors menu to open a dialog box that lets you create custom colors using the entire palette of colors available to Windows.

Once you have selected colors to use, select a drawing tool by clicking it once. Drawing tools include the following:

- Free-form Select and Select—These tools let you select part of a picture. You may then move the selection or apply any image effects to it. The Free-Form Select tool lets you create the selection by drawing a free-form outline around it. The Select tool lets you create the selection by dragging a rectangle.

- Eraser/Color Eraser—The Eraser works by painting a wide swath in the selected background color wherever you drag your pointer. Right-click any color in the palette to select the background color.

- Fill With Color—This tool fills any closed shape in your drawing with the foreground color if you left click and the background color if you right-click. If the shape has even a one-pixel gap in its border, the fill color will spread to the rest of the picture. Click outside any shape to fill the entire background of the picture.

- Pick Color—This tool lets you select any color in your drawing as your foreground color (by clicking) or background color (by right-clicking).

- Magnifier—This tool lets you zoom in (click) or zoom out (right-click) on your drawing. You can zoom from regular size (1x) to eight times the regular size (8x).

- Pencil—This is the most basic drawing tool. Move your pointer around with the left mouse button pressed to draw a free form line in the foreground color. Use the right button to draw with the background color.

- Brush—This tool is similar to the Pencil tool but lets you choose a variety of different sizes and shapes for the head of your brush.

- Airbrush—This tool "sprays" a random pattern of dots onto the page meant to simulate an airbrush effect.

- Text—Use this tool to enter text into your drawing. First, you will drag a rectangle shape onto the drawing to serve as a bounding box for the text. Once that is done, you can start typing inside the box. A Fonts toolbar appears so that you can format the text.

- Line—Use this tool to draw a straight line of a specified thickness. Click where you want the line to start and, holding down the mouse button, drag to where you want the line to end.

- Curve—Use this tool to create and manipulate curved lines. First, draw a straight line the same way you would with the Line tool; then click where you want the arc of the curve to be and drag the pointer to adjust the curve.

- Rectangle, Rounded Rectangle, and Ellipse—Use these tools to draw the various shapes. Click where the shape should start and then drag the pointer to adjust the size of the shape. For each shape, you can choose whether to draw just the outline of the shape or fill in the shape with the foreground or background color.

- Polygon—Use this tool to draw a multisided shape. First, drag the pointer to draw a straight line. Next, click once at each position where you want a new line segment to appear. Double-click when you are finished.

Working with an Image

Paint also includes a number of tools for working with your image as a whole. These tools are available on the Image menu and include the following:

- Flip/Rotate—Use this tool to flip the entire image or a selection of the image vertically or horizontally. This tool is also used for rotating the image or selection by 90, 180, or 270 degrees.

- Stretch/Skew—This tool is used to resize the image or selection. You can stretch or shrink the image by a specified percentage of its original size. You can also skew the image along its horizontal or vertical axis.

- Invert Colors—This tool inverts an image. Each color becomes the opposite color, creating a negative effect.

- Attributes—This command displays the current attributes of the image. It also lets you adjust the size of the image by specifying precise measurements, control the units of measurement used, and specify whether the image should be in color or black and white.

- Clear Image—This command erases the entire image, leaving a blank page filled with the background color.

- Draw Opaque—This command turns opaque drawing on or off. Drawing in opaque mode allows the background color of the image to show through, potentially masking other images on top of which you are drawing. Drawing in Transparent mode allows any images you are drawing on top of to remain visible.

Using Advanced Viewing Features

While creating and working with your images, you may find some of the Advanced Viewing features of Paint useful. You can view your image in full screen using the View Bitmap command on the View menu. This is especially useful if you are creating or editing an image that will be used as a desktop background.

The other viewing commands are available on the Zoom submenu of the View menu. They include the following:

- Normal Size, Large Size, and Custom—Normal Size is regular 1x viewing mode. Large Size zooms your image to 800% of (8x) its original size, allowing you to work on individual pixels of your drawing. The Custom command opens a dialog box that lets you choose a zoom level of 100, 200, 400, 600, or 800%. You can also use the Zoom drawing tool to achieve the same effect, except that the 400% option is not available.

- Show Grid—When viewing the image at a zoom level of 400% or greater, the Show Grid command displays a grid overlaid on the entire image (see Figure 8.16). This grid helps distinguish between individual pixels of the drawing. For cleaning up images you have pasted into a Paint file, this is a very useful view. You can literally change things one pixel at a time. For those who create line drawings (such as a network design), this tool allows you to do a sloppy job in 1X view, and then clean up your mess one pixel at a time!

FIGURE 8.16

Using the Grid feature of Paint.

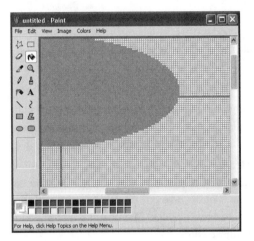

- Show Thumbnail—The Show Thumbnail command opens a separate window that contains a reduced overview of your entire image (see Figure 8.17). This window remains on top even when you are working on your drawing in the main Paint window. The Thumbnail view is very helpful when working on small details at a high zoom level in that it lets you see changes to the overall image as you are working.

Playing Games

Windows includes a number of games, from the classic Solitaire that has been included with almost every version of Windows ever shipped to Internet versions of Checkers, Spades, and Backgammon that automatically find a player of your skill level and set up a game for you. Since there are numerous games included with Windows XP, each

FIGURE 8.17

Using the Thumbnail feature of Paint.

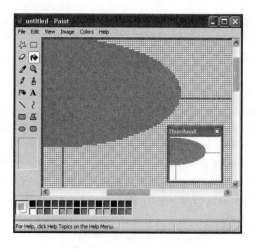

with its own rules and strategies, and because games are really outside the scope of this book, this section presents only a brief description of the games available. These include the following:

- FreeCell—A Solitaire game, in which you must move all cards to their home cells (stacks), using free cells as placeholders. To win, you must create a stack for each suit in its home cell, stacked in order of rank.

- Hearts and Internet Hearts—A four-player (you and three computer-controlled opponents) card game whose object is to have the lowest score at the end the game. At the end of each hand, you receive one point for each heart in your hand plus 13 points for holding the Queen of spades. The object while playing each hand, of course, is to get rid of these cards.

- Internet Games—These are versions of the classic games Backgammon, Checkers, Reversi (more commonly known as *Othello*), and Spades that are played against other Windows users over the Internet.

- Minesweeper—A game in which you must locate all of the mines on a grid within a time limit without actually uncovering any of them.

- Pinball—A 3D pinball game (meaning that the game actually looks like a pinball machine).

- Solitaire—The classic solo card game in which you must build a stack for each suit of cards from lowest to highest value.

- Spider Solitaire—Another solo card game in which you must uncover all of the cards from ten stacks using the fewest possible moves.

> **Tip**
>
> The Internet-based games included with Windows XP are quick and easy to set up, but offer pretty limited communications with other players. If you really enjoy playing games with others on the Internet, you will probably have a lot more fun at Microsoft's Internet Gaming Zone (`http://zone.msn.com`). On the Zone (as players call it), you will find a lot more games and better chat features.

Summary

Windows XP comes with a number of games, programs, and other accessories that can make your work and play a little more interesting. Using these accessories, you can perform calculations, create documents, connect to a remote computer or BBS, draw and edit images, and play a variety of games.

Working with Files and Folders

IN THIS CHAPTER

- The New Windows Explorer   *196*

- Folder Options You Can
  Configure   *206*

- Using the Indexing Service for a Fast
  Find   *209*

- Burn That CD: Copying Files and
  Folders to a CD-R   *212*

- The Recycle Bin   *214*

- Sharing Files and Folders   *216*

CHAPTER 9

Like the title says, in this chapter, you will learn to work with files and folders. Since most of you have been using the Windows graphical user interface (GUI) for many years now, this chapter will concentrate on new or advanced features dealing with files and folders. The basic features, such as cut/paste, copy, and delete are still present, and you can access them in the same manner as before. You can use the check box labeled Do Not Move Files the Recycle Bin, Remove Files Immediately When Deleted. For all intents and purposes, this option eliminates the use of the Recycle Bin and deletes items immediately. In other words, items will not be saved to the Recycle Bin before they are deleted.

The Windows Explorer application has been updated for Windows XP Professional and gives you a fantastic new interface into the files and folders that exist on your computer and on file shares you may use in a network environment. Using Windows Explorer is a lot like dealing with an Internet browser. Indeed, many of the concepts of browser technology have been incorporated into this application.

There are many places in the operating system where files or folders are represented as objects. If you learn the basics about how to use files and folders, configure their properties, and manipulate files and folders using Windows Explorer, you will be able to perform those same functions in other Windows XP components. For example, you will find that some folders such as My Documents and My Pictures are accessible from both Windows Explorer and the Start Menu.

The New Windows Explorer

In Figure 9.1, you can see that Windows Explorer has taken on a new look.

FIGURE 9.1

The New Windows Explorer is a little more refined than previous versions, and it looks a lot like an Internet Browser.

Note

The folders listed under My Documents, such as My Pictures and My Music, are *your* folders—that is, if more than one person uses the computer and each person logs on using a different username, then each username account has its own set of these folders. You can share your files and folders with other users, both on the local computer and on the network. One thing to keep in mind, though, is that although you may have your own separate set of folders, you must use the NT file system (NTFS) on the partition in order to enforce access permissions. You will learn more about this later in this chapter.

Several other Folders are listed on the Folders pane. They are as follows:

- Desktop—This folder contains items that appear on your desktop. Each of the items you place on the Desktop actually has a link somewhere in the underlying disk file system.

- My Documents—As explained above, this is a folder that contains other folders used to categorize certain types of files on your Windows XP computer.

- My Computer—This folder contains many items, including the floppy, hard disk, and CD-ROM drives on your computer, as well as file shares you may have mapped to your computer from other servers.

- My Network Places—This folder contains shortcuts to both dial-up networking connections, as well as any local area network (LAN) connections you may have created on your computer. For more information about connecting to the Internet or a LAN, see Chapter 25, "Configuring Your Computer for an Internet Connection," and Chapter 24, "Configuring Your Computer for Local Area Networking."

- Recycle Bin—This is another folder, appearing as a Desktop icon and containing items you delete when using Windows Explorer and other utilities. *NOTE: If you delete files or folders using the Command Prompt, they will not be sent to the Recycle Bin and will be gone forever!* Using Windows Explorer to send items to the Recycle Bin allows you to retrieve items you deleted by mistake. You should check the Recycle Bin frequently and empty it when you no longer need the items you have sent to this holding place.

The toolbar at the top of the window contains the familiar buttons going Back and Forward, muck like an Internet browser). There are also buttons labeled Search and Folders. The Search button will bring up the Search Companion (a powerful search utility described in Chapter 7, "Up Front: The New Desktop." The Folders button changes the Windows Explorer window so that the left Folder pane now becomes a pane containing menus for performing specific tasks or taking you to Other Places, such as your computer and network resources (see Figure 9.2).

FIGURE 9.2

If you click on the Folders button on the toolbar you will get a different view of Windows Explorer.

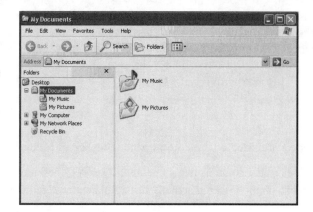

Later in this chapter you will learn about using these menus to create new folders, publish folders on the Internet, and share your data with other users. However, there are some fundamental things that you need to know about how Windows XP manages files and folders. For example, when you click on a Word document, how does Windows XP know what program to use to open the file? Alternatively, if you don't like the way files and folders are displayed on the Windows Explorer menu, how do you change the view to one that is more meaningful to you?

File Types and Associations

File associations allow you to specify a data file name and the program associated with the file extension (the part of the file name that follows the final period character), to automatically launch and open the file for you. To view the current file extension associations (such as .doc for a Word document), use the Folders applet in the Control Panel.

If you use the Category view of the Control Panel, simply click on Appearances and Themes and then from the bottom of the screen where it says to pick a Control Panel icon, select Folder Options. If you use the classic view, just click on the Folder Options icon. Figure 9.3 shows this Control Panel applet with the File Types tab selected.

The list in Figure 9.3, under the section titled Registered File Types, tells you what kind of file type each file extension represents.

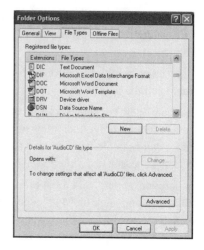

FIGURE 9.3

You can view the file types associated with specific programs, change them, or add new associations using this tab.

To find out what program will open a particular file type, just highlight it in this pane. At the bottom of the properties page under the Details For extension, you will see the program associated with this file type. You can use the Change button to change this to a different program if you want. You can also use the button labeled New to create a new association for a file type and a program, if the application itself doesn't do this automatically. The Delete button does just what it says. This particular Control Panel applet is covered in greater detail in Chapter 14, "Using the Control Panel."

Performing Simple Tasks in Windows Explorer

Now that you know how to launch the Windows Explorer application, let us look at some of the things you can do to configure the way information is presented, as well as how you can perform such simple operations as copying, moving, or deleting files or folders. Alternatively, you might want to do some customizing by changing the way Windows Explorer displays files and folders through use of the View menu.

Change the View

In the first few figures in this chapter, you saw folders displayed as icons. The View menu allows you to choose from several different views. Depending on the information you wish to see and your personal preferences as to how the display should look, you might want to use the View menu to select a different view. The views you can select from this menu include the following:

- Thumbnails—This view is useful when you want to identify the contents of a folder by an image. If you select the Thumbnails option from the View menu, then

9

WORKING WITH
FILES AND
FOLDERS

you will see a folder icon if the folder contains only ordinary files like word processing documents. However, if the folder contains pictures, then up to four miniaturized pictures will be displayed instead.

- Icons—This is the default view and shows a folder icon for each folder with the file or folder name displayed underneath the icon.

- Tiles—This view is similar to the Icons view but shows a larger icon. Additionally, if you choose to sort your files in a particular order, then the sort order is displayed along with the file or folder name. As an example, you can sort files by type (based on the file extension) so that the Tiles appear in order based on the type of files.

- List—This view will display smaller icons, along with a list of the contents of a folder. For example, if you use this view and click on My Documents, you will see in the left pane of the Windows Explorer window that both My Music and My Videos appear as subfolders —that is, the contents of the My Documents folder.

- Details—This view will show the contents of an open folder, and you will also see details about the contents of the folder. This view is shown in Figure 9.4.

FIGURE 9.4

The Details view gives you the most information about the contents of a folder.

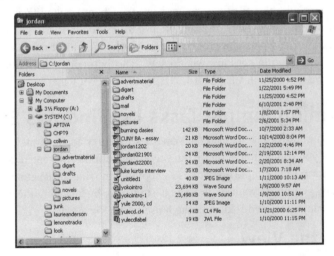

In this figure you can see that the details are very sparse by default. All you see here is the Size, Type, and Date Modified columns. However, you can customize the details that are displayed using this view. Again, use the View menu and select the option labeled Choose Details to select what kind of information you want to see. Figure 9.5 shows the dialog box that allows you to choose what columns will appear in the Details view.

FIGURE 9.5

You can choose what information to display using the Details view in Windows Explorer.

You can also select the width of each column by using the field at the bottom of this dialog box. You can use the buttons labeled Move Up and Move Down to change the order in which the columns will appear on the screen. Once you have selected the items you want to appear, you can use the vertical bars that appear between the columns in the Details view to resize the column width.

In addition to the views listed above, there are two other things you can do to control how files and folder are displayed. If you select the My Pictures folder a new item will appear in the View menu called *Filmstrip*. This view will show your pictures as thumbnails, which you can scroll through by using the left and right arrow buttons. Using this view, you can also click on a picture in this view to see it displayed in a larger size. You can also double-click on the picture to get to a menu that allows you to print, edit, or save the picture in another folder. For more information about using the Filmstrip view, see Chapter 27, "Overview of Windows XP Multimedia Features." The Filmstrip view is shown in Figure 9.6.

You can use the selection labeled Arrange Icons By in the View menu to bring up a submenu from which you can select the following options:

- Name
- Size
- Type
- Modified
- Show in Groups
- Auto Arrange
- Align to Grid

9

WORKING WITH FILES AND FOLDERS

FIGURE 9.6

The Filmstrip view is available only in the My Pictures folder.

Most of these selections should be obvious. However, the Show in Groups selection could use a little explanation. It is similar to the Type selection, which will arrange icons based on their type, or file extension. The Show in Groups selection allows you to do the same thing, but instead of just using the file type, you can select to show files in groups based on other attributes like filename or the date the file or folder was modified. To use this feature, first select the attribute you want to use for grouping by selecting View, Arrange Icons By and then the attribute (the available selections will depend on the details you have chosen to display on the screen). After that, use the same sequence: View, Arrange Icons By and then select Show in Groups.

Saving Space, Part One: Compressing and Uncompressing Folders

To compress a file or folder, right-click on the file or folder and then select the Properties option. When the property sheet for the file or folder appears, click on Advanced, which appears on the General tab.

Note

You can only compress files or folders that are on an NTFS formatted partition. For more information about File Allocation Table (FAT) and NTFS partitions, see Chapter 18, "Managing Disks and Partitions."

To compress the file or folder, simply select the check box labeled Compress Contents to Save Disk Space. Then click OK and the file will be compressed.

To mark an entire drive partition for compression (NTFS only), you can simply right-click on the drive partition in Windows Explorer, and you will see a check box right there on the General properties tab, allowing you to set the disk partition to compressed mode. After you click this button, the root directory and files in the root directory of the drive will become compressed. A dialog box pops up, asking if you also want to compress subfolders and files on the drive. If so, simply click OK, since this is the default. Another window will open and show you the progress as the disk is compressed. It can take quite some time to compress the disk, depending on whether you choose to compress just the root directory and files or the entire disk. Additionally, if you choose the latter, then obviously, it will take longer to compress the disk, depending on the amount of data to be compressed.

> **Note**
>
> You may not see a large amount of disk space freed up by using the compression option. This is because some files like Zip files are already compressed. Some image formats are also compressed in their normal state. In addition, the amount of space that can be freed up depends on each file, since some files can be compressed more than others can. For example, files that contain a lot of repetitive characters can be compressed more than those containing a random assortment of data.

The following are a few things to note about compressed files and folders:

- You can access compressed files and folders the same way as regular files and folders.
- Compressed files and folders cannot be encrypted.
- If a file is moved from one NTFS folder that is not compressed into a folder on the same NTFS partition, then the file maintains its uncompressed state.
- You might notice a slight decrease in performance when accessing compressed files.

Saving Space, Part Two: Using Zipped Folders

In addition to allowing you to compress files and folders by setting an attribute in the NTFS file system, you can use another form of compression on NTFS or FAT partitions. In this case, you can't compress (or zip up) the entire disk—just folders. First, create the zipped folder, which will be identified with a WinZip icon, and then drag files to the folder. To create a zipped folder, simply right-click at the location where you want to create the folder and select New from the File menu. From the menu that appears, select WinZip File. A new file will appear in Windows Explorer containing the WinZip icon, and a box will be drawn around the folder name. By default, the text says "New WinZip File." Place your cursor in the box and change the text to whatever you want to name the folder.

To add files to a zipped folder, just drag them to the folder. A dialog box pops up, allowing you to specify some aspects of how the file will be added, such as the level of compression (maximum, normal, fast, or super fast). Click OK to add the file to the zipped folder.

To view the contents of a zipped folder, just double-click on it like you would a regular folder. It is possible to run some programs by double-clicking on them in a zipped folder, but this will depend on the program. However, if a program that is in a zipped folder has a dependency on some other file or files, it may or may not run directly from the zipped folder. In that case, you need to move the file from the zipped folder to a new location.

To move a file from a zipped folder, double-click on the zipped folder to open it and just drag the file to a new location like you would a regular file. This places a copy of the file in the new location. To delete a file from a zipped folder, right-click on the file and select Delete from the menu that appears.

You can also drag a zipped folder itself to another drive, and it will stay in its zipped format. Using zipped folders is a good way to save space on non-NTFS partitions that do not support compression. You can also use zipped folders to transfer files to and from work using a floppy disk.

Encrypting Files and Folders

When you first attempt to open an encrypted file, It may come up unencrypted format. This is because the author of the file has the right to open any file they have encrypted. If you log in as another user and attempt to use the file that way, you will receive an Access Denied dialog box.

The following are a few things about encrypted files and folders:

- If you move a file from an encrypted folder to a folder not on a non-NTFS partition, the file becomes unencrypted.
- If you move a file that is not encrypted into a folder that is encrypted, the file will become encrypted.

- If you move a file from an encrypted folder to a folder that is not encrypted, then the file remains encrypted until you manually change it to an unencrypted file.

- You cannot encrypt the system folder that holds the Windows XP operating system files. You also cannot encrypt any file that has the system attribute set.

- Encrypted files and folders remain encrypted when they are backed up to other media such as tape or a removable storage device.

Keep in mind that encryption merely keeps others from seeing the data in your files or folders. If a user has access permissions to the file or folder, however, he can delete it. Encryption is not a substitute for using permissions! Therefore, for important data, use both the encrypting file system (EFS) and apply the appropriate access permissions.

To decrypt a file you can simply deselect the check box used to encrypt the file. If you are not the owner of the file, then you must ask the designated recovery agent assigned to the network to decrypt the file. On a Windows XP computer that is not part of a domain or the Active Directory, the Administrator of the computer can do this. If you are part of a network that uses the Active Directory, then certificates are used in the encryption process. Consult your system administrator to determine which user is the designated recovery agent. Note that in the Active Directory environment, certificates can be copied to a floppy disk or other location so that you can use them to decrypt a user's files. This can be useful in cases such as when a user leaves a company, making it necessary to decrypt their data.

Creating New Folders and Other Tasks

Earlier in this chapter, you discovered a set of tasks you can perform after clicking the Folder button on the Windows Explorer tool bar. This set of tasks includes the following:

- Make a new folder
- Publish this folder to the Web
- Share this folder

Making New Folders

Creating a folder is much the same as it always has been in Windows Explorer. Simply navigate to the drive or folder where you want to create the new folder and from the File menu, select New and then Folder. You can also right-click in the right-side pane of Windows Explorer to see this same menu. On the right side of the Windows Explorer application, a new folder will appear with a highlighted field next to it labeled New Folder. Place your cursor in this field and give a name to the new folder you want to create.

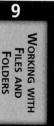

Publish This Folder to the Web

Windows XP also allows you to publish a folder to the Web. Perhaps you have a folder containing files that several people are using but which are in geographically diverse places. You may also have a project on which several people are working inside the company, so placing a collective folder on the Web or corporate Intranet will allow for ease of sharing. Placing the folder and its contents on the Web allows for greater accessibility to important files.

To begin the process of putting a folder on the Web, you need to start the Web Publishing Wizard. The first dialog box is simply informational, telling you that you can use this wizard to publish files so that others on your local network or the Internet will be able to see them. Click Next to continue with the wizard. The next dialog box allows you to change the selection of folders you initially selected to publish to the Web. Click Next to continue.

The next dialog box downloads information about providers from the Internet and provides a list of host providers from which you can choose to publish your pictures. These include MSN Communities and Xdrive. You will see more of these appearing as Windows XP rolls out and more providers sign on to the service. Pick a provider and click Next. Some sites may require you to register as a user and establish an account. Just follow the prompts until the Wizard completes.

E-mail This Folder's Files

Another helpful feature with Windows XP's advanced file management is the ability to e-mail files from a folder. Use this option if you want to e-mail some files such as photograph image files to another user. Select the file(s) first and then click on this option under the File and Folders Tasks menu. Windows XP will automatically create the e-mail message for you (see Figure 9.7). Just fill in the e-mail address where you want to send the files and then simply click Send.

Folder Options You Can Configure

You have already learned about some of the ways you can configure Windows Explorer's display via the View menu. Now you will learn how to configure some other interesting options like changing the icon or picture associated with a folder, as well as the type of folder. The type of folder determines what options Windows XP will allow you to perform on the folder or its contents, as well as some of the options available under the View menu. For example, if a folder is created using the Document template, you won't find the Filmstrip view available. That doesn't mean you can't store picture files in a document folder. It only means that the Filmstrip view won't be available for you to use.

FIGURE 9.7

Windows XP will create the e-mail message and attach the file you want to send.

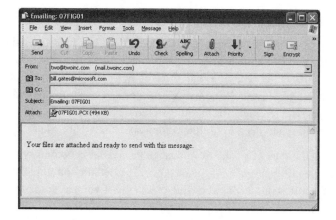

Changing a Folder Icon or Picture

If you don't like the icon or picture that shows up for a folder on your display, you can easily change that. Simply right-click on the folder you are looking at to change and select Properties. The directory's properties pages will be displayed; next, click on the Customize tab (see Figure 9.8).

FIGURE 9.8

The Customize tab of the folder's properties sheets will enable you to select a new icon or picture to associate with the folder.

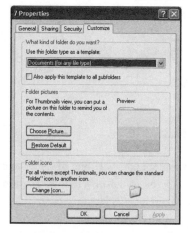

9

Click on the Choose Picture or the Change Icon buttons to browse for a new picture or icon. If you choose to change the picture, a dialog box appears in which you can look for a picture file in the My Pictures folder. If you click the second button to change the icon, you will get a colorful display of icons to choose from. The icon change capability also allows you to browse for other icon graphic files that aren't included as part of the Windows standard distribution. Thus, you can create your own icon graphic files using a graphics card or possibly find some fun ones on the Internet.

Changing the Folder Type

Figure 9.8 indicates that at the top of the Customize tab is a field labeled Use This Folder Type as a Template. Click the arrow on this option to see a list of the possible choices. In general, don't change the type of a folder that comes with the operating system or with an application file you install. Windows XP creates its system folder and subfolders using the appropriate template for the files stored there. Instead, use this option when you create new files and need to use them for a specific type of file.

Since changing the type of a folder can change the available options, you should become familiar with the different types of folder types. The default option is Documents, which can be used for just about any kind of file, especially if you are going to mix file types in a directory.

Figure 9.9 shows the expanded list of file template types from which you can choose.

FIGURE 9.9

Windows XP provides several different folder templates.

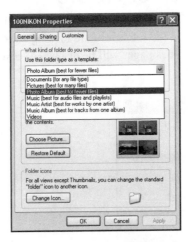

For example, if you choose to create a folder and select one of the Music templates shown in Figure 9.9, then, when you open the folder in Windows Explorer and click on the Folders button, the left pane will contain tasks related to music files such as playing the music files or shopping for music online. If you use the Pictures template, then you will see a different set of tasks such as viewing the pictures in the folder as a slide show or ordering prints online among other things.

Although the Documents template can be used to create a folder that can store any kind of file, using templates to create folders that hold a specific kind of file can make it easier for you to work with the files in the folder since the tasks and view options will be different, depending on the template.

Choosing the type of directory will cause a folder template to be associated with the directory. Unless you are going to create a special kind of file such as one to store pictures or audio/video files, just leave the default file type set to Document.

Using the Indexing Service for a Fast Find

Windows XP includes an indexing service for indexing almost everything on a disk. Placing indexes on your files is done as a search-and-replace measure that will hopefully seek out files faster. You can selectively disable or enable a file as a candidate for the indexing service. You do this through the file or folder's properties sheets. Select the General tab and then click Advanced. This will generate a dialog box similar to the dialogs used to compress and encrypt files. To index your files, simply use the section titled Archive and Index Attributes. The first check box allows you to select the archive attribute for this file. A backup program may examine this attribute to determine whether to back up a file or folder. Therefore, if you want to make sure a file is being backed up, select this check box.

The second check box allows you to decide whether the file or folder is to be indexed for use by the indexing service. The contents and filename are indexed on files you select. Documents, applications, and other items that you may frequently need to find should be candidates for the indexing service. For example, if you have a group of developers working on a large project, you might want to index the files shared by your programmers. By indexing those files, you have simplified the search for a file using the Search Companion instead of the old-fashioned method of sifting through files and folders and trying to determine where the file you want is located.

> **Note**
>
> The indexing service can also index files on network drives, if the attribute is set. This can make it easy to find files anywhere on your network.

Configuring the Indexing Service

To configure the Indexing service, you need to use a Microsoft Management Console application. To do this, use the Control Panel applet labeled Computer Management. It is found in the Administrative tools folder. For more information about this applet, see Chapter 14. However, let's go over how to manage the indexing service using this applet here.

9

WORKING WITH FILES AND FOLDERS

Open the Computer Management Console (MMC) and look in the console tree. The Indexing Service can be found under the Services and Applications branch (see Figure 9.10). Right-click on the indexing service and select the Properties menu selection. This service's property sheet has two tabs, Generation and Tracking. By default, the indexing service will index files of all types. You can deselect the first check box on this property page to change this behavior. If deselected, then only file types using registered file associations will be indexed. The second check box allows you to select that an abstract or short summary of the file be stored so that it will be displayed when the file comes up as the result of a search. You can use a field on this tab to select the maximum number of characters to include in the abstract. If disk space is limited, then deselect this check box, which is selected by default.

FIGURE 9.10

You can configure how the indexing service works using these properties sheets.

The Tracking tab simply has a single check box for enabling or disabling the indexing of files and folders on network file shares mapped to your computer. Again, your choice depends on two things. If the Search tool is useful for you, then you might want to leave this selected. However, if disk space is short and you have a lot of file shares, then you may want to deselect this check box.

Starting the Indexing Service

To start the indexing service, click on the Indexing Service in the console tree and from the Action menu, select Start. That's all there is to it!

You can also configure the degree to which the indexing service uses system resources. To do this, again click once on the Indexing Service and from the Action menu, select All Tasks and then Tune Performance. A dialog box pops up, specifying how often the indexing service is used on the computer. You can select from Used Often, in which case, the service will increase the frequency at which it scans for new files and updates the index.

You can also select Used Occasionally so that the service performs this function less often. If the radio button Never Used is selected, the service will not update the index.

If you click the Customize button, you can select slider bars that range from Lazy to Instant. One slider bar allows you to select the resource utilization the indexing service itself uses to index files. The second slider bar determines the system resources that will be used to query the indexed database when you do a search.

To stop the indexing service, click once on the service in the MMC pane and from the Action menu select Stop. If you only want to stop the service temporarily, you can use the Pause option from the Action menu.

Finding Files in a Hurry

You can use Windows XP's new Search Companion to find files, folders, and even search the Internet. You can also use this enhanced Search feature to find people in a directory database if you are connected to an Active Directory based network. This function is covered in greater detail in Chapter 7. This new searching feature allows you to do more than just supply a word or phrase to search. You can use advanced search functions that allow you to specify things like all words, any words, and the like.

Mapping Network Drives to Access Network Resources

Windows Explorer makes it easy to associate a drive letter with a shared network file resource. Mapping a drive to frequently used network resources is an efficient way to keep quick access to your files. Instead of having to search your entire network, particularly if it is a large network, every time you want a file, you can map a drive directly to the folder in which the files are kept. This will appear as an independent drive, much like your C: or D: drives in the Windows Explorer interface. A file share can be offered by another Windows XP computer or perhaps by a Windows server computer in your domain or workgroup. To map a file share, follow these steps:

1. In Windows Explorer, click on the Tools menu and select *Map* Network Drive. A dialog box will appear, as shown in Figure 9.11.

2. In the field labeled Drive, accept the default drive letter that will be assigned to this mapped file share or enter another drive letter that isn't used on your system.

3. In the Folder field, enter the file server and the file share you want to map to this network drive (using the Universal Naming Convention (UNC) syntax of *servername**sharename*. If you are not sure about what file shares are available, use the Browse button.

9

WORKING WITH
FILES AND
FOLDERS

FIGURE 9.11

This dialog box allows you to specify the drive letter for a file share and to browse the network to find the file share you need to use.

4. If you select the check box named Reconnect at Login, then the drive will be mapped automatically every time you log in so that you won't have to repeat these steps again!

5. You can also use the links at the bottom of the dialog box, including Connect Using a Different User Name (although you will need the password), Sign Up for Online Storage, or Connect to a Network Provider.

6. When finished mapping the drive, and click Finish.

Step 5 indicates how to connect using a user account that has access to files and folders your logon user account does not. This is most useful when an administrator wants to let a user connect for a file share for just a short period of time, after which this file share can be deleted. By connecting in this manner, the administrator doesn't have to give advanced privileges or grant additional access rights for the user's own account.

The second link mentioned in Step 5 leads you to a wizard for signing up for an online storage service. There are many of these on the Internet, and you can even have one on your LAN. File shares offered by other servers on your network may be available using this link.

Burn That CD: Copying Files and Folders to a CD-R

One of the new features incorporated into Windows XP is the capability of burning CDs without having to buy additional software. When you buy a CD burner and install it into your Windows XP machine you usually get a stripped-down copy of some other commercial CD burning product. This usually provides only the basic burning capabilities.

Windows XP now supports a lot of different features for burning CDs, including using them to store data files, as well as using your CD burner to create audio CDs. For more information about using the CD burning features of Windows XP to create audio CDs, see Chapter 29, "Windows Media Player 8." Here, we will learn about the process of creating a data CD.

The Data Files to Be Burned Are First Sent to a Staging Area

Windows XP lets you send files and folders to a staging area on your hard drive so that when you are ready to burn the CD, you will have all those files just waiting for you. This is a more efficient method because it conserves space on the CDs you burn.

To send a file to this staging area, simply right-click on the file or folder and select Send To. Then, from the next menu, select the CD-burner drive. A small balloon message pops up indicating that you have files waiting to be written to a CD. If you click on the balloon, you can see a list of files in this staging area.

The following steps make up a more direct method for burning several files to a CD:

1. In Windows Explorer, click on My Computer.
2. Select the files and folders to be sent to the CD burner. Use the Shift+Click or Ctrl+Click methods to select multiple files or folders.
3. From the File and Folder Tasks menu, which is present if you click on the Folders button (IMPORTANT!), depending on your choices, you can select Copy This File, Copy This Folder, or Copy the Selected Items. The selections that will be present in this menu will depend on whether you selected a single file, folder, or multiple items, as described in the previous step.
4. A Copy dialog box (or Copy Items if you have multiple selections) will appear. Select the CD burner drive and click Copy.
5. To view the files/folders waiting to be burned, click on the CD burner's drive letter in Windows Explorer under the My Computer section (see Figure 9.12).

FIGURE 9.12

You can see the files being staged for the burning process by clicking on the CD burner's drive letter.

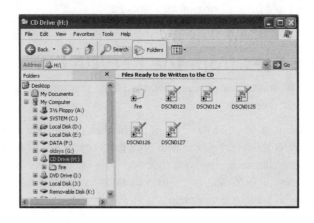

9

WORKING WITH FILES AND FOLDERS

6. Select Write These Files to CD from the File menu to start the burning process. The CD Writing Wizard will pop up and guide you through the process. You can give a name to the CD in the first dialog box of the wizard (or accept the default) and then click Next to continue.

7. Another dialog box appears, indicating several steps for preparing to write the file, such as creating the CDs table of contents, and then the actual writing process. (Be patient or buy a faster burner!)

8. A dialog box appears when the process is finished. You can use the check box labeled Yes, Write These Files to Another CD, if you want to create additional backup copies; otherwise, click Finish.

As you can see, it is not at all difficult to stage or write data files to a CD using Windows XP.

As you can see from this figure, the first menu selection is to write the files to the CD burner. You can also delete these temporary copies of files if you have changed your mind

The Recycle Bin

The Recycle Bin is where items go when you delete them. Deleted items using GUI interfaces send files to the Recycle Bin instead of actually deleting them. However, you are still taking up disk space, since the files are not really erased until you empty the Recycle Bin. You can either retrieve things from the Recycle Bin or permanently delete them.

Caution

Keep in mind that if you delete a file or folder from the Command Prompt, a floppy disk, or a network file share, these do not get placed into the Recycle Bin. These files have been permanently removed.

Retrieving Files from the Recycle Bin

If you delete a file by mistake or change your mind later, you can open the Recycle Bin window in many different ways.

To restore a file, shortcut, or other item, simply right-click on the item in the Recycle Bin's listing and select Restore. You can also open the Recycle Bin window on the desktop and click and drag the items you want to restore onto the desktop. Additionally, you can open the Recycle Bin in Windows Explorer and drag restored items directly to the folders you where you want to return them.

Emptying the Recycle Bin

If you are certain all items in the Recycle Bin are no longer useful to you, then you can simply "empty" the Recycle Bin by selecting this menu item under the Recycle Bin's File menu. This will permanently remove the items from your computer, just as if you had deleted them at the Command Prompt.

You can also simply right-click on the Recycle Bin icon on the desktop and select from the menu that appears, Empty Recycle Bin, which will delete all items in the Recycle Bin from your computer. Keep in mind that once you do this, *they are gone forever*, unless you have a backup copy.

Setting Properties for the Recycle Bin

The Recycle Bin can be either a lifesaver or something you hate, depending on how you configure the properties for this Windows XP component. Figure 9.13 shows the properties pages for the Recycle Bin. To get here, simply right-click on the Recycle Bin on the Desktop and select Properties.

FIGURE 9.13

The Global properties tab of the Recycle Bin allows you several options.

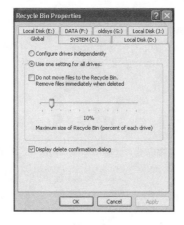

The first two radio buttons are as follows:

- Configure Drives Independently—You will notice that the other tabs on the Properties pages for the Recycle Bin are labeled according to the disk partitions on your disk hard drive partitions. Select this button if you want to configure the way the Recycle Bin works for each drive; then select the appropriate choices for each of the drive partitions that show up as tabs on your computer.

- Use One Setting for All Drives—The Global tab allows you to set the same settings for all disk partitions. If you select this, you have several choices, which are described below.

9

WORKING WITH
FILES AND
FOLDERS

You can use the check box labeled Do Not Move Files to the Recycle Bin, Remove Files Immediately When Deleted. This effectively eliminates the Recycle Bin and deletes items immediately. This can be a disk space saver in a system short on disk space. However, using the Recycle Bin and emptying it on a regular basis simply for safety's sake is recommended. The next item you will notice is a slider bar that allows you to determine how much disk space (per drive) will be devoted to storing "deleted" items. This choice is up to you. Keep in mind that if the Recycle Bin exceeds this percentage of the total disk drive's space, then when you send further items to the Recycle Bin, older items will be automatically deleted, and you will no longer see them in the Recycle Bin. The slider bar can be used to indicate the amount of storage per disk to allocate for deleted files stored in the Recycle Bin. If you allocate only a small amount of space, don't be surprised to see a file you previously deleted has been "aged out" of the first-in/last-out queue the Recycle Bin provides.

Finally, keep in mind that if you try to delete a file larger than the amount of space available in the Recycle Bin, then the file will be deleted. There will be no copy in the Recycle Bin to recover, if necessary. It is always best to err on the side of caution. Don't delete files about which you are uncertain.

The last check box, Display Delete Confirmation Dialog, allows you to display a confirmation dialog box when you use a GUI interface to delete files. If you use the check box labeled Do Not Move Files to the Recycle Bin check box, then this setting will have no effect.

Sharing Files and Folders

Because Windows XP can be used in so many different environments, from a standalone workstation to a computer on an Active Directory controlled network, there are several options for sharing files.

Sharing Files with Other Users on the Same Windows XP Computer

One way you can share files is to let other people who log onto your computer share some of your files. To do this, you can simply drag them to the Shared Documents folder, which you can see on the left in Figure 9.14.

Files and folders placed into the Shared Documents folder by any user on the computer are then available to all other users that log onto the computer locally.

FIGURE 9.14

The Shared Documents folder can be used to share information with other users on the same computer.

Sharing Files on a Small Workgroup LAN

Simple file sharing can be enabled to allow others on a small, workgroup-based LAN access to some of your files. Earlier in this chapter you learned about mapping a file share to your computer. Here you will see that you can offer a file share yourself to other users.

To do so, just right-click on the folder and select Properties from the menu that appears. Then click on the Sharing tab, which is shown in Figure 9.15.

The figure shows how you can choose the check box labeled Make This Folder Private, in which case it will not be shared. You are also instructed to simply drag the folder to the Shared Documents folder, as described in the previous section, if you only want to share the data with other users who log on locally to the computer.

FIGURE 9.15

You can use the Sharing tab of a folder's properties pages to allow others on the network to access your files.

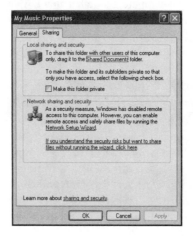

9

WORKING WITH
FILES AND
FOLDERS

However, at the bottom of this dialog box is a section titled Network Sharing and Security. Here, you can choose from two hyperlinks. The first will invoke the Network Setup Wizard, whereas the second will allow you to go ahead and create the file share. The Network Setup Wizard option is described in detail in Chapters 24 and 25. If you take the second selection, then another dialog box will pop up and warn you that simple file sharing will make your files available and possibly make your computer vulnerable to attacks from other computers. In a small office LAN that is not connected to the Internet, or which uses a firewall to connect to the Internet, you should use the radio button seen in this warning box labeled Just Enable File Sharing.

After you make this selection, click OK, and the bottom section of the Sharing tab will now allow you to select the check box labeled Share This Folder on the Network. Note that there is a field for naming the file share. You can also select the check box that allows others not only to read or execute the files that will be part of the file share, but also to make changes to them.

> **Note**
>
> You cannot share every folder on your Windows XP computer using this method. For example, you won't find the Sharing option available for several important folders such as Documents and Settings, Program Files, and the Windows system folder (or the name you gave to the system installation directory during the Setup process). Additionally, you cannot share the information found in the profiles of other users who have local accounts on your computer.

Again, only use this simple method of file sharing if you are isolated from the Internet by a firewall or if you just connect a few computers together in a LAN and do not use the Internet. In Chapters 24 and 25, you can learn more about networking under Windows XP. Chapter 18 also contains a lot of useful information for using file sharing in a more secure environment.

> **Tip**
>
> A quick method for finding out what file shares are offered on your system is to use the Command Prompt and issue the following command, NET VIEW. This will show you the computers in your local workgroup and any file shares offered by that computer. Additionally, although you can use the technique described earlier to map a network drive by using Windows Explorer, you can also do so from the Command Prompt (or in a script file). To learn more about the NET command and what it can be used for, see Chapter 13, "Command Prompt Tools."

Sharing Files in a Domain or Active Directory Network

One of the most common ways people share resources is over a domain-driven network. Windows XP has considerable capabilities for participating in these types of networks, and it is especially useful for connecting to a Windows Active Directory Network. You can make files and resources on your computer available to others participating in your domain or Active Directory network. To make items available for others to use, right-click on a folder and bring up the properties pages for a Windows XP computer participating in a domain or the Active Directory. From here, you will see the Sharing tab. This is where you can make items available for other network users.

Figure 9.16 shows the properties page for a folder with the Sharing tab selected. Note the Permissions and Caching buttons along with that Security tab.

FIGURE 9.16

The Sharing tab of a folder's properties sheets includes new items when your computer joins a domain.

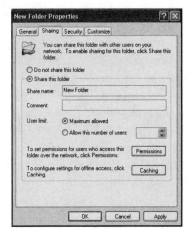

To create a new file share, click on the New Share button. A dialog box will pop up, allowing you to give a name to the file share and to set a limit to the number of users who can connect simultaneously to the share.

After you specify the new share name, you can choose between two radio buttons, one to limit the number of concurrent users of the share or another labeled Maximum Allowed. (This is a licensing issue, so you will need to check with your network administrator.) On this properties sheet is also that Permissions button, which you can use to grant or deny access to this file share by specifying users or user groups and the permissions you want to allow for each.

9

WORKING WITH FILES AND FOLDERS

FIGURE 9.17

You can use the Add and Remove buttons to control access to this file share.

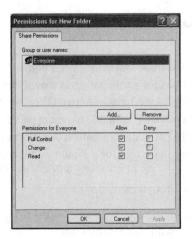

When you click Add, you will get the Select Users, Computers, or Groups dialog box. Here, you can add names of users or groups of users for whom you want to specifically set permissions. The first button you see on this dialog box is called Object Types. As a part of an Active Directory domain, you can grant or deny access to different objects in the Active Directory tree. An object can be an individual user account or a user group, as well as any other container object in the directory tree. The default objects you will see here are Users, Groups, or Built-in Security Principals. Click the Objects Types button, and you will also be allowed to select Computers. You can also use the dialog box that the Object Types button brings up to deselect Users, Groups or Built-in Security Principals. For more information about the Active Directory, see Appendix B, Overview of the Lightweight Directory Access Protocol (LDAP) and the Active Directory.

Since this computer participates in a domain, you may not be able to remember all of the user groups and names in the domain. If you click Advanced, on the lower left of the dialog box, your view will be expanded to give you a section where you can list users and groups who can access the resources you are sharing.

To select a user or group, use the Common Queries section of this dialog box and search through the Active Directory to locate a computer, user account, or an organizational unit. If you want to use this method, place text in the dialog box that relates to your search query and from the Name drop-down menu, select either Starts With or Is Exactly, depending on whether the text you entered is an exact match. Then click on Find Now to begin your search.

After you select Find Now, any matching results will show up in the bottom portion of this dialog box, as you can see in Figure 9.18.

Note

If you know your way around your domain or the domains in your Active Directory setup, you don't have to use the searching capability just described. You can simply click Find Now without inputting search text, and you will obtain a big list in the results section at the bottom of this dialog box, allowing you to scroll through the user groups and other objects in your network database. Also notice that the Locations button at the top of this dialog box allows you to select the "root" location from which the search should start. It can be one domain or all the domains in the Active Directory.

FIGURE 9.18

The results of your search will show up in the bottom portion of this dialog box.

To add a user or group, just use the scroll bar at the bottom of the dialog box and locate the user or group; then click OK. You will be returned to the Permissions dialog box, and you will see the new users or groups for which you have added permissions. Note that by default, the group Everyone has full access to a file share you create. If the file share contains sensitive data, you may want to change this. In addition, the permissions you can set on individual files and folders will still apply when the information is accessed across a network share. In other words, although the group Everyone may have full access to the file share (to save you the trouble of having to grant individual access for a share), they don't necessarily have access to all the files and folders on the file share unless you have set up the NTFS permissions to grant this access.

9

WORKING WITH FILES AND FOLDERS

Here, you can choose three types of permissions to allow or deny to any user or group appearing in the upper pane of the dialog box. These are as follows:

- Full Control—This permission lets the user read, write, delete, and execute files on the share. This user can create new directories and delete them. However, Full Control does *not* give the user the ability to add permissions for other users. That is granted by a *right*, which is discussed in Chapter 15, "Managing Local Users."

- Change—The user can do everything that is granted by the Read permission (the next in this list), but in addition, the user can add new subfolders, delete subfolders and files, and change data in files.

- Read—The user can read files on this file share but cannot delete them or create new files. The user can also traverse (pass through) a folder with this permission to view other folders and files that fall under this folder. The Read permission also grants the user the ability to execute application files.

After you click OK to dismiss the properties dialog box for the new share you have created, you can use the Caching button, which falls directly under the Permissions button on the Sharing tab. This dialog box allows you to configure how files are cached (or not) by clients.

Since there is always the possibility that your computer may be down when a user wants to update a document stored on a file share on your computer, Windows XP offers a feature called Working Offline. When using this feature, copies of a file are stored on both the file share and on the user's computer who connects to the file share. When your computer becomes available again, the files can be reconciled so that the most recent copy is available on the file share. The options you can choose from the Setting drop-down menu include the following:

- Manual caching of documents
- Automatic caching of programs and documents
- Automatic caching of documents

Decide on which files for which you want to allow caching or deselect the check box labeled Allow Caching of Files in This Shared Folder.

Using the Security Tab for Auditing Usage of This Resource

Although the Sharing tab is used to set up permissions for allowing users to connect to a file share and access files and folders on your computer, the Security tab allows you to set similar permissions for users who log on locally to the computer. These can be local

users or users who have a domain account, so the dialog boxes you use to add and
remove users and set their permissions are similar, as you can see in Figure 9.19.

FIGURE 9.19

*You can control
how users access
files when they log
on locally to your
computer.*

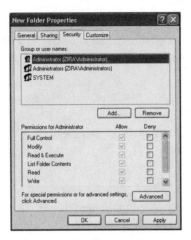

In this figure, however, note that there is a finer granularity of permissions to allow or
deny. This is a very important concept to understand when working with *rights* on a
Windows 2000 or XP computer. However, you should first understand that the permissions shown in the previous section, are really *groups* of permissions that are simply
given a special name to make your job easier. The list of the permissions shown in
Figure 9.20 is really groups of permissions that make it more convenient for you to
assign permissions. The following list details the actual granular permissions and how
they apply to the permissions you can select using the check boxes:

- Traverse Folder/Execute File—Here, you can move through a series of folders to
  get to a folder containing permissions that allow you access. For example, you
  might not have access to the folder `C:\applications`, but you might have been
  granted access to execute files in the folder `C:\applications\wordprocessing`.
  This permission allows you to skip over the `C:\applications` folder to get to the
  folder you to which have been granted access. In other words, as it says, you can
  traverse a series of folders. The Execute File portion of this permission allows or
  denies you, depending on the check box you select, to execute files in the folders
  to which you have been granted access.

- List Folder/Read Data—This allows or denies, depending on the check box you
  select, the ability to see the contents (list) of a folder, including both files and subfolders in the folder. This applies to folders only. The Read Data permission allows
  you to view data in files contained in the folders to which you have access.

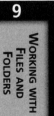

9

WORKING WITH
FILES AND
FOLDERS

- Read Attributes—Each file or folder has attributes associated with it. This permission grants or denies you access to these attributes, such as read-only, hidden, system, and so on.

- Read Extended Attributes—This is similar to the Read Attributes permission, but some applications may define additional extended attributes to a file or folder, and this is the granular permission that gives you the capability to view those attributes (or denies you the permission).

- Create Files/Write Data—For folders, this allows you to create files in the folder and to overwrite existing files.

- Create Folders/Append Data—This permission also allows or denies creating folders. It also allows or denies you the capability of making changes to files or overwriting existing files.

- Write Attributes—This permission grants or denies you the capability of changing the attributes of a file (such as read-only, hidden, and so on). This applies only to the attributes of a file or folder, not the capability to create folders or write to data files.

- Write Extended Attributes—This is similar to the previous permission but applies to extended attributes that NTFS allows to be created by applications.

- Delete Subfolders and Files—You can use this permission to allow or deny the capability to delete subfolders and files.

- Delete—This permission allows or denies you the permission to delete a file or a folder. If you already have the Delete Subfolders and Files on the parent folder to the subfolder, then this right is inherent.

- Read Permissions—This permission allows or denies you to read the actual permissions set on the file or folder. It does not grant read permission to the file or folder.

- Change Permissions—This is similar to the previous entry but also allows you to change the permissions on a file or folder.

- Take Ownership—This is a very powerful permission. Although the users who create files are usually the owners of the file (and they can set permissions on the files they create), this right allows you to take ownership away from the creator. This right makes you king of the hill! Once you take control, you can do anything with the file or folder. This is useful when a user leaves a business and the administrator needs to access the former employee's files.

- Synchronize—This allows or denies different threads, or part of a process that executes independently, to wait for a file or folder and synchronize with another thread that may signal it. This right is used more often in the 64-bit version of Windows XP, which will definitely support superior multiprocessing capabilities.

FIGURE 9.20

Click the Advanced button to get to the actual granular permissions that can be granted or denied.

Windows XP allows both the ease of administration by using groups or permissions, and it enables you to deny or grant very specific access permissions.

Summary

This chapter discussed how to use Window Explorer to manage files and folders. Keep in mind that on the Start menu you will also find menu entries like My Documents, which simply brings up the Windows Explorer application with the Folders button selected so that you can choose from the tasks available to you. Security is an issue that becomes very important if you share files on a computer or a network, and in this chapter, you learned the basic mechanisms used for managing security. Once you grasp the fundamentals of managing files and folders, you will find the concept is employed in other parts of the operating system, such as in some administrative tools, along with other applications. However, as an old timer, I still recommend you become familiar with ways to perform the same or similar functions at the Command Prompt, which you can read about in Chapter 13.

9

WORKING WITH
FILES AND
FOLDERS

CHAPTER 10

Using Microsoft
Outlook Express
for E-mail, News,
and More

IN THIS CHAPTER

- Getting Started with Outlook Express *228*

- Sending and Receiving E-mail *236*

- Configuring Outlook Express Options *240*

- Using the Address Book *253*

- Using Outlook Express Folders *259*

- Managing Accounts in Outlook Express *263*

After word processing and Web surfing, e-mail may be the most important productivity tool on your computer. It's fast, free, lets you exchange text, photos, video, and other files at lightening speeds, and it opens doors to a vast number of newsgroups populating the Internet. Windows XP Professional includes one of the world's most popular e-mail clients, Microsoft Outlook Express. In this chapter, you learn how to configure Outlook Express for use as a Mail and News client.

Outlook Express is a smaller version of Microsoft Outlook, a program that handles much more than e-mail and newsgroups. However, for most users, Outlook Express is all you are going to need to keep your e-mail and news messages organized and easy to manage. In this chapter, you learn how to use Outlook Express to manage your e-mail and news-group communications, not to mention one of your system's most important security features: blocking the transmission of malicious files via e-mail.

Getting Started with Outlook Express

Many people ask why Microsoft has churned out two very similar versions of what is essentially the same product: Outlook and its diminutive sibling Outlook Express.

The confusion is understandable, if you are only looking at how each application is used: both are primarily e-mail messaging clients. But to call Outlook just an e-mail client is something that drives the marketers at Microsoft nuts, because that is not how they wanted Outlook to be perceived.

The e-mail functionality of Outlook was originally supposed to play a smaller role in the overall Outlook package. It was a means to an end, not the end itself. Outlook, with its Task and Calendar tools, was designed to work in tandem with Microsoft Exchange primarily as a business collaboration tool. It was positioned as a direct competitor to the popular Lotus Domino/Notes server-client combination that provided collaborative tools to many businesses worldwide.

To Microsoft's chagrin and dismay, the Outlook/Exchange combination has never proved as popular as Notes/Domino toolset. People tended to treat Outlook as nothing more than a glorified e-mail client and Exchange as a glorified e-mail server and rarely did businesses tap into the full potential of Outlook and Exchange.

To try to further distinguish Outlook as being more than just an e-mail client, Microsoft decided to create and release Outlook Express. Outlook Express, the Redmond marketers proclaimed, *was* just a snazzy e-mail and newsreader client. Use this, we will give it away for free, they declared, and it will handle all your e-mail and newsgroup needs. And use Outlook for much, much more, like time management and task assignments.

Whether this strategy proved to be a success is a matter left for other forums. But it has left us with Outlook Express being present in every release of Windows. And, if you don't want to fork over the dough to buy Outlook, Outlook Express is a more than acceptable application to use for your e-mailing and news posting.

Working with the Outlook Express Window

The main Outlook Express window is made up of components familiar to any Windows user (see Figure 10.1). The menu bar at the top of the windows gives you access to main menus, icons below the menu bar provide one-click commands for major functions, a directory tree in the left pane offers quick access to folders, and the main pane serves as the Outlook Express "task" area. The top of the main pane displays the contents of any folder you have selected, such as Inbox, whereas the pane beneath it displays the text or graphics of any of the items you select from the pane above.

FIGURE 10.1

This is the main window you will see with Outlook Express unless you choose a different view.

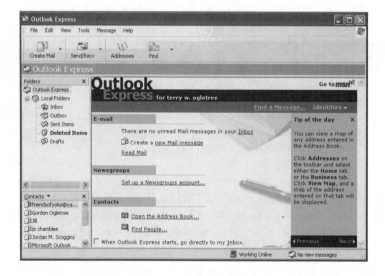

The Outlook Express controls also are familiar to any Windows user. Use the Menu bar to access File, Edit, View, Tools, Message, and Help menu options. Icons in the Command bar give one-click access to frequently used commands for the active folder. When the Inbox folder is open, for example, these icons include Create Mail, Send/Recv, and Address. To customize the contents of the icon bar, right-click any blank space in the bar, choose Customize from the pop-up menu, and then use the options in the Customize dialog box to add or remove icons.

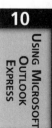

10

USING MICROSOFT OUTLOOK EXPRESS

> **Note**
>
> Notice that at the end of the Inbox icon bar you see two chevrons (>>). These indicate that more command icons are available off screen. You can maximize the window (or drag corners to make it larger) to reveal these icons.

Click any of the following items in the Folders pane to display their contents in the main Outlook Express screen:

- Local Folders—These include the Inbox, where incoming messages are stored; Outbox, where composed messages are stored before sending; Sent Items, where copies of mail you have sent are stored; Deleted Items, where deleted messages go; and Drafts, a "holding place" for messages you aren't yet ready to send.

- Contacts—This is Outlook's "fact file," where you can store names, addresses, business information, and more about personal and business associates. The Contacts list gives you fast access to people with whom you have corresponded or who are in your address book (more on this later in this chapter).

> **Tip**
>
> Although the initial view of Outlook Express can be useful, it is not very convenient. You might prefer to start the application with the Inbox selected, so you can immediately see new e-mail messages. You use the Options dialog box to select a new opening Outlook Express screen. Learn how to do that in "General Properties," later in this chapter.

For a quick lesson in navigating the Outlook Express window, begin by opening the Inbox, as has been done in Figure 10.2. In this example, quite a few e-mail messages are listed in the top pane, which is the message pane. An e-mail message is selected in the message pane, and its contents appear in the bottom, content pane.

You can use all of the typical Windows methods for resizing the Outlook Express window. You can drag the edges to resize the window and then drag the window dividing lines to resize individual panes within the window. You might want to make the content pane of the Inbox window larger, for example, so you have more space for reading message contents. Like any Windows program, you can use the Minimize, Maximize, and Full Screen buttons in the right corner of the title bar to trigger those size changes in the overall window display.

Message bar   Message pane   Content pane

FIGURE 10.2

This view of Outlook Express shows you the contents of your e-mail Inbox. Use the message bar to sort the contents by subject, sender, receipt date/time, flag status, level of importance, and more.

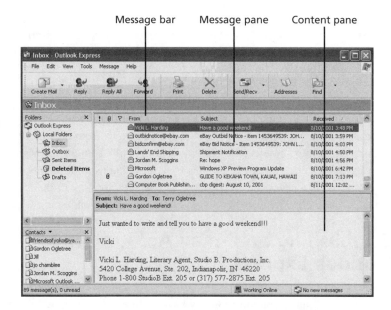

As stated before, when you choose any messages in the message pane of the Inbox, a preview of the unopened e-mail message appears in the content pane. To open the e-mail message and view it in a larger space, double-click on it, and the message comes up in its own window.

The Message bar is used to identify the columns of information included in the main Inbox message pane—that is, information describing the messages. This information includes message importance, whether the message has attachments or a flag status, who the message is from, its subject, and receipt date and time. You can click any item in the Message bar to sort the Inbox contents by that field. Sorting by subject groups all messages that share the same subject; you can also sort by Sender in order to create an alphabetized list of messages grouped by the senders' last names. Reverse the order of the sort by clicking the Message bar icon or subject header again.

Tip

By default, Outlook Express sorts the e-mail messages in the order in which they received, based on date and time. You can also use the sort capabilities to help find specific messages. For example, you might want to find all of the messages from a particular person or all the messages you have flagged. Clicking the Message bar item performs an ascending sort (A to Z, earliest to last, and so

continues

10

on). Click again to do a descending sort. After you have located the message, you should return the sort to the Received field so that new messages appear in order of receipt at the top of your main message pane in the Inbox.

If you don't want to see all of these columns of information, you can get rid of them. Right-click on any column header and choose Columns from the pop-up menu. In the Column dialog box, deselect the check box next to any column you want to eliminate from the display. Use the Move buttons to move columns to different positions in the display and type in a new pixel size in the text box at the bottom of the dialog box to change the width of a selected column. When you finish making changes, click OK.

Establishing an E-mail Account in Outlook Express

You need to set up an e-mail account before you can send or receive e-mail, but in order to set up the account, you must already have an Internet account with an Internet service provider (ISP) (see Chapter 25, "Configuring Your Computer for an Internet Connection"). In addition to giving you a dial-up number, your ISP should also give you one or more e-mail usernames. Most ISPs will let you specify the username you want to use, along with a password. You should also get the name of the mail server(s) that will be used to provide the service. You learn more about mail servers such as POP3 and SMTP later in this chapter, but you should be aware now that this information is needed to set up your Outlook Express e-mail account.

Note

Most ISPs will allow you to have more than one mailbox for a single connection. If multiple users in a household share an Internet connection, setting up separate e-mail accounts will maintain everyone's e-mail "privacy." You also might want to set up separate logon accounts for Windows XP; learn how in Chapter 15, "Managing Local Users."

With your ISP account in place, you are ready to set up your Outlook Express mail account. Begin by clicking Start, Outlook Express. This action launches the Internet Connection Wizard. The first screen asks you to type in your name. You can use your real name here, a nickname, or anything you want. Type in the name you prefer e-mail correspondents to see; then click Next.

The next Wizard screen (see Figure 10.3) asks you to type in your e-mail address—the one given to you by your ISP. The address is a string of text in the format of yourname@internetprovider.com. The @ character separates your username from the domain name of your ISP.

FIGURE 10.3

Enter the e-mail address provided to you by your ISP.

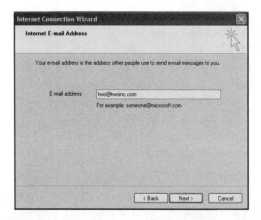

Note

The username you use to dial in to your ISP doesn't necessarily have to be the same username on your e-mail account. As you learned a few paragraphs ago, you can associate more than one e-mail account with a single Internet connection, so the name and password you use to connect to the Internet can be different from your e-mail username and password

Remember, too, that the e-mail address you enter here is used for the Reply To field that the recipient of the e-mail message sees. If someone receives an e-mail from you and clicks the Reply button, this is the address his or her reply is sent to. If you maintain several mail accounts but only want replies to come back to a single account, then you should use that e-mail address here.

The next screen asks you for your e-mail server names (see Figure 10.4). Get out that information from your ISP and begin here by correctly filling in the text box called *My Incoming Mail Server Is a Server*. Use the drop-down menu to select the type of mail server you are going to be receiving e-mail from.

10

USING MICROSOFT
OUTLOOK
EXPRESS

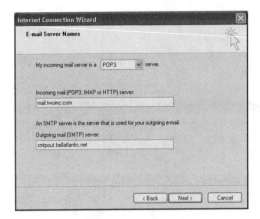

Your ISP will specify the server type you need to use, but here is a brief description of the server types:

- Post Office Protocol, Version 3 (POP3)—This is perhaps the most popular method that most ISPs use for letting you download e-mail from their mail servers.

- Internet Message Access Protocol (IMAP)—Currently at version 4, IMAP offers more flexibility in that you can download just the headers (such as From, To, and Subject fields) from the server and selectively download only the messages you want to read. You can also create folders on the ISP's mail server using IMAP, among other features. Since most ISPs have limited space on their servers, IMAP is used more frequently in a business environment than in the home Internet market.

- Hypertext Markup Language (HTML)—This is the language of the Web. In addition to the traditional mail services offered by a particular ISP, many places on the Internet, such as Microsoft's Hotmail service, offer free mail accounts that are read as Web pages. Outlook Express allows you to retrieve and send mail using a mail account you have set up with one of these HTML mail services if you desire.

Enter the address of the server in the field labeled Incoming Mail (POP3, IMAP, or HTTP) server. In the next field, enter the name of the simple mail transfer protocol (SMTP) server provided by your ISP and click Next to continue.

In the next screen (see Figure 10.5), enter the actual username and password for the e-mail account. In the Internet E-mail Address screen you saw earlier, you could enter any e-mail address to be used as the Reply To address. However, in this Internet Mail Logon screen, you have to enter the e-mail account username—that is, just the username without the @ symbol and the ISP's domain name. In the field labeled Password, enter the password for this account.

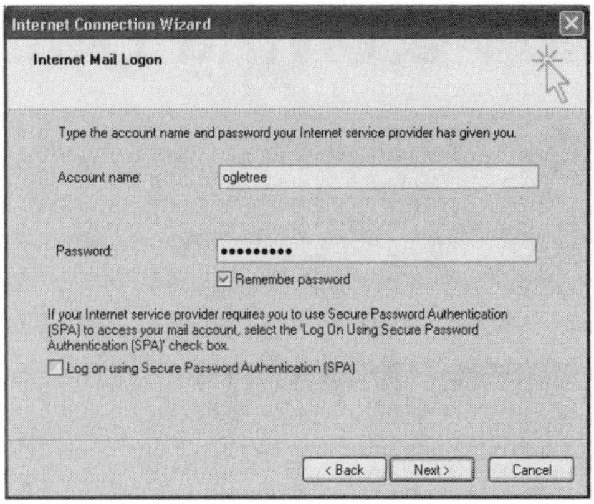

FIGURE 10.5

Enter the user-name portion of your e-mail address along with the password for the account.

Remember that some ISPs use case-sensitive names and passwords, so be aware of this, especially when entering the password.

Select the Remember Password check box if you want Outlook Express to remember the password so you won't have to enter it again each time you check your e-mail. Click to select the Log On Using Secure Password Authentication (SPA) only if your ISP has indicated that it uses SPA. Click Next to move to the final wizard screen and click the Finish button.

When the wizard closes, the main Outlook Express window (the one you saw at the beginning of this chapter) appears. Now you are ready to test the success of your e-mail account setup by sending yourself a message.

Tip

Sometimes, it is useful to have more than one "identity" on the Internet so that you can be known by a unique identity in newsgroups or mailing lists you participate in. To create a new identity, simply click on the File menu and select Identities; then click on Add New Identity. A dialog box will prompt you for a new name for this identity and ask if you want to use a password for this identity. If so, another dialog box will prompt you for the password. If you want to change identities during a session with Outlook Express, simply click on File and then Switch Identities.

10

USING MICROSOFT
OUTLOOK
EXPRESS

Sending and Receiving E-mail

You have learned about the Outlook Express window and how to navigate within it; you have also set up your e-mail account. Now you should test your new account by sending yourself an e-mail message. In this section you learn to compose and send an e-mail message and to configure the way your outgoing mail looks to recipients. You also learn to receive, read, and otherwise process messages in your Inbox.

Composing an E-mail Message

To compose an e-mail, begin by clicking the Create Mail button at the top left side of Outlook Express command bar. The New Message dialog box appears (see Figure 10.6).

FIGURE 10.6

Compose e-mail messages in the New Message dialog box.

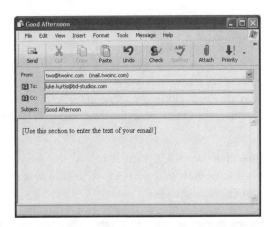

Enter the e-mail address of the person to whom you want to send the message in the To: field (for this example, enter your e-mail address); if you want to copy the message to someone else, enter the address(es) in the CC: field. You can click in a field to move to it, or use the Tab key move between the fields.

Type in the message subject in the Subject field; then click in the message pane to begin typing your message.

Tip

By putting some meaningful text in the Subject field, you help your message stand out when the recipient downloads e-mail. Choose a descriptive subject line to help the recipient find your message later.

> **Note**
>
> Outlook Express lets you blind carbon copy (BCC:) recipients of your message. To blind carbon copy someone is to send a copy of your message to the specified recipient, without showing the recipient's name in the CC: field. That way, other recipients will not know this individual was copied on the message. You can turn on the BCC: feature for Outlook Express by selecting All Headers from the View menu in the Create New Message dialog box. You only have to do this once, not each time you create a new message. Likewise, you can remove this field by clicking on View in the Create New Message dialog box and deselecting this feature

To write your e-mail message, place your cursor in the message pane and start typing. You learn about configuration later in this chapter; following are a few simple tools you can use while composing your message:

- Use the Format menu to switch from sending a plain text e-mail to one that uses rich text format (although Outlook Express actually uses HTML for this); choose Format and then Rich Text (HTML).

- Use the Cut, Copy, and Paste buttons to do exactly what they say. First, select text and then click Cut or Copy. Click where you want to insert cut or copied text your message; then click Paste.

- Click the Priority button to assign a high, medium, or low priority to your message. Your message is marked with the appropriate priority icon when it arrives in the recipient's inbox.

- Click the Check button to check your spelling (you learn how to configure this feature in Spelling Properties, later in this chapter).

- Use the Priority button if you want to let the recipient know that the message is of a high or low priority.

> **Tip**
>
> You can make your e-mails appear as though they have been composed on fancy stationary. To learn this simple trick, see Compose Properties in the Configuring Outlook Express Options section later in this chapter.

Attaching Files to an E-mail Message

You can attach any type of file (photograph, Word document, Excel spreadsheet, and so on) to an Outlook Express message. When you have finished composing your new message, attach a file by clicking on the Attach button (with the paper clip icon) in the New Message dialog box. A dialog box allows you to browse for the file. When you have found it, highlight it in the directory list and then click OK. The file is attached to your outgoing e-mail message. When the recipient receives the message in his or her Inbox, a paper clip icon appears next to the message listing to signify that an attachment is included. The recipient can transfer the attachment to his or desktop and then open and view it, as long as the recipient has the appropriate program for viewing the file type.

Sending the Message

When you have finished composing your message, click the Send button at the top of the dialog box to send the message to your Outbox. The Outbox folder item in the left pane will now have the number 1 in parentheses next to it, indicating it is holding an outgoing message.

To send the message, click the Send/Recv button on the main Outlook Express window.

You've Got E-mail: Reading E-mail Messages

When you click the Send/Recv button, new e-mail messages appear in your Inbox. Unopened mail shows a closed envelope icon and bold type. To read an e-mail message, just click on the header once, and the text will show up in the bottom pane. You can scroll through this message text or double-click the header to bring up the message in its own dialog box.

When you finish reading the message, you can close it to move to the next message. Messages you have read are marked with an open envelope icon and remain in the Inbox unless you file or delete them. If you no longer want to keep the message you have read, highlight it in the Inbox and click the Delete button. The message moves to your Deleted Items folder. You can save messages to other folders or directories in your Windows XP system, or use Outlook Express folders (see Using Folders later in this chapter).

Tip

If you receive a lot of e-mails that you know you don't want to read, you can create rules to automatically delete the messages. You learn more about this in Creating Filers and Blocking Unwanted Messages later in this chapter.

Printing E-mail Messages

Although it is convenient to keep e-mail online, safely stored away in an organized database that is easily searched, you can also print any of the e-mail or newsgroup messages. Simply click once on the message header and then click Print. If you have double-clicked a message to bring it up in its own window, you will find another Print button in that window. The standard Windows XP print dialog box will pop up, allowing you to choose the printer and change the printers' features if you need to, and you can then print the e-mail by clicking the Print button in the Print dialog box.

Replying To and Forwarding E-mail Messages

If you receive an e-mail and want to send a message back to the sender, you don't have to go through all the trouble of filling in the header fields of the Create New Message dialog box. Instead, click once on the message header and then click the Reply button. A message box pops up with the From: and To: fields already filled in, as well as the subject line (you can change the subject line if you choose).

If multiple recipients were included in the original message, choosing Reply to All sends your reply to the entire list. Reply sends the reply only to the original sender of the message. To copy additional recipients, use the CC: or BCC: fields just as you can with a new message. To forward an e-mail to a new recipient, open the message and click the Forward button and enter the appropriate e-mail address (or addresses) in the To: and CC: fields.

Whether replying or forwarding a message, by default, the text of the original message appears in the message pane with your cursor sitting on a blank line just above it. Start typing your reply message and when you are ready to send it, click the Send button to send the message to the Outbox folder. The open envelope icon on messages to which you reply are marked with a left-facing arrow; when you forward a message, the icons are marked with a right-facing arrow.

Caution

Whenever you reply to multiple recipients or forward a message to a new recipient, be very careful that the information in the message is appropriate for *all* of the recipients. This is especially important when you are working with a message with many replies. After a series of messages have passed back and forth several times, it is very easy to forget about the contents of the original messages. Many people have embarrassed themselves by forwarding inappropriate information to "late" recipients of a long chain of e-mails.

10

USING MICROSOFT OUTLOOK EXPRESS

Configuring Outlook Express Options

A whole book could be written on the options available to you for configuring Outlook Express, but the next few sections discuss some of the more important ones. Outlook Express is a supreme news and mail client. If you like what you read in this chapter, I suggest you research additional options further.

Most Outlook Express configuration options are contained in the Options dialog box; to access that dialog box, select Tools, Options.

General Properties

The General tab of the Options dialog box (see Figure 10.7) offers a number of startup and send/receive configuration options. The General options are as follows:

- When Starting, Go Directly to My Inbox Folder—When you start up Outlook Express, you go immediately to the Inbox. Since this is the folder most users work with most often in Outlook Express, most users select this option.

- Notify Me If There Are Any New Newsgroups—This informs you of any new newsgroups that have been added since you last logged into the Internet so that you can choose whether to subscribe.

- Automatically Display Folders with Unread Messages—Any mail or newsgroup folders are automatically displayed if they contain new messages.

FIGURE 10.7

Use the Options properties pages to set Outlook Express to automatically send and receive e-mail at a predefined interval.

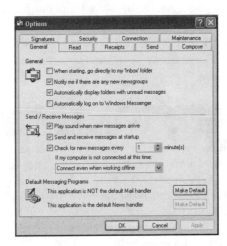

Use these options to configure Send/Receive message options:

- Play Sound When New Messages Arrive—Check this to hear a beep when new messages arrive (Outlook Express must be running).

- Send and Receive Messages at Startup—Select this to have Outlook Express automatically download and send messages as soon as you start up the application.

- Check for New Messages Every __ Minute(s)—Use the scroll arrows in this feature to determine at what interval Outlook Express should check for new messages and send messages waiting in the Outbox. Next, use the If My Computer Is Not Connected at This Time drop-down menu to tell Outlook Express how to proceed. Choose Do Not Connect, Connect Only When Not Working Offline, or Connect Even When Working Offline.

  If you choose the first option, then nothing will happen until you log back into the Internet. If you choose the second option, nothing will happen until you decide to work online. The third option causes the program to dial in for a connection at the specified interval.

Tip

If you receive lots of e-mail, you can select Check for New Messages Every __ Minute(s); then select an appropriate time interval (such as every 60 minutes) and tell the system to Connect Even When Working Offline. That setup has Outlook Express working through the night to download any new messages you receive so they are all waiting for you in the morning. However, it also ties up your phone line. To avoid that problem, Open the Connections tab and select Hang Up After Sending and Receiving. That way, your system dials in, downloads new messages, and then hangs up.

In addition, at the bottom of the General tab are the following two Make Default buttons:

- This Application Is NOT the Default Mail Handler—Click the Make Default button if you want Outlook Express to be your default mail client.

- This Application Is NOT the Default News Handler—Again, click the Make Default button if you wish to make Outlook Express the default client for reading news.

10

USING MICROSOFT OUTLOOK EXPRESS

Read Properties

The Read tab configuration options let you determine the appearance of received messages. These configuration options apply to mail or news messages and in some cases, both. The check boxes you can enable here include the following:

- Mark Message Read After Displaying for __ Second(s)—Use this option to mark a message read after a timer counts down the number of seconds you enter here, beginning as soon as you click on the message header. The default is five seconds; use the arrows to raise or lower the time. If you quickly scan messages, lower this to zero or perhaps one second. Otherwise, your messages remain marked as unread, and you may find yourself going back to the same messages when you next use Outlook Express.

- Automatically Expand Grouped Messages—Selecting this check box shows the entire thread of news messages in the top pane of the main Outlook Express window. This is useful when you are reading news and following a thread of messages. If you leave this check box unselected, you will just see the first message and have to expand it by clicking on it to see responses.

- Automatically Download Messages When Viewing in the Preview Pane—The text or body of the message is automatically displayed in the bottom message pane when you select a message header in the top message list pane. If you don't select this check box and choose only to download headers, you can retrieve the actual message text by clicking on the message header and pressing the spacebar.

- Show ToolTips in the Message List for Clipped Items—Selecting this check box displays ToolTips even if the message columns cut off this view.

- Highlight Watched Messages—Watched messages are those you want to track; use this option to select a highlight color for those messages.

Tip

To select a mail or news message and the replies to watch, select the conversation (a message) and then, from the Message menu, select Watch Conversation.

The next section of this dialog box contains two check boxes that apply to just newsgroup messages. The first check box, when enabled, allows you to select the number of news headers to download when you select a group. Use the up and down arrows in the field next to this check box to specify number between 50 and 1,000.

The second check box in the News section of this dialog box is labeled Mark All Messages as Read When Exiting a Newsgroup. This can be a good idea if you regularly read your newsgroup messages and don't want to actually have to click on each one to mark it as read.

> **Tip**
>
> Another way you can mark all messages in a newsgroup as having been read is to select Edit menu in Outlook Express and from the menu select Mark All Read.

Use the button at the bottom of the Read tab to change the fonts and international settings used for newsgroup messages.

Receipts Properties

The Receipts properties let you choose to send and receive receipt notifications for messages that leave and enter Outlook Express. This tab can be very useful when you want to know if someone has read an e-mail you have sent, which is an important function in many business environments. This tab can be used to enable the function for messages you send, as well as to enable or disable replies when you receive messages that request a return receipt.

Use the check box labeled Request a Read Receipt for All Sent Messages if you want to receive return receipt messages from the people to whom you send mail messages. They actually do not have to send back a receipt; the feature does it for them. However, keep in mind that some mail programs do not actually support this feature.

> **Note**
>
> If you don't want to turn on the Request Read Receipt feature globally for every message you send, you can do it on a message-by-message basis. When composing a new message, in the Create New Message dialog box select Request Read Receipt from the Tools menu.

Choose these options to control whether you send receipts back when you receive a request:

- Never Send a Read Receipt—You can use this if you don't want others to know if you have read their e-mail.

- Notify Me for Each Read Receipt Request—A dialog box pops up telling you that a read receipt has been requested, and you can choose at that time if you want to send a receipt back or not do so.

- Always Send a Read Receipt—This button causes Outlook Express to automatically send a reply to a read receipt without prompting you when it receives an e-mail that contains such a request. If you select this feature, then you have a check box you can use: Unless It Is Sent to a Mailing List and My Name Is Not on the To: or CC: Lines of the Message.

Send Properties

The properties in this sheet determine how sent messages are handled by Outlook Express. Select from the following Sending options:

- Save Copy of Sent Messages in the Sent Items Folder—Select this option to go back and read any message you have sent in Outlook Express. (You can regularly empty this folder, much like the Deleted Items folder, so you don't have to worry about it taking up a lot of space.)

- Send Messages Immediately—Select this to automatically send e-mail or newsgroup messages without having to wait on a timer to expire or use the Send/Recv button. As soon as you complete a message, click the Send button. Outlook Express sends the message if you are connected.

- Automatically Put People I Reply to in My Address Book—You learn more about this in Using the Address Book, later in this chapter. However, selecting this option stores the addresses of anyone you reply to in your Address Book. If you reply to many people that you know you won't later correspond with, don't select this option.

- Automatically Complete E-mail Addresses When Composing—This Autocomplete feature finishes an e-mail address that you are typing, if it matches an address in your Address Book. If it "guesses" the wrong address, just keep typing. It will continue guessing until it gets it right (or you type the whole address yourself).

- Include Message in Reply—Choose this to include original messages in your reply. If the recipient needs to see the original information, this option is helpful. However, it can also end up creating really long messages, especially after a number of replies.

- Reply to Messages Using the format in which They were Sent—You can choose to send e-mail in text format or HTML format, by default. This check box allows you to send a reply in the same format that of the message you are replying to.

In the Mail Sending Format section, choose from the radio buttons labeled HTML or Plain Text. You can then use the buttons HTML Settings and Plain Text Settings to further customize your choice. Similar options appear in the News Sending Format section, but they apply to news messages instead of e-mail messages.

Compose Properties

This tab allows you to choose the font for your mail and news messages. The default is 9 pt. Arial, but you can use the Font Settings button for either mail or news to change this. If you want your e-mails to look snappier than just a plain text message, you can spiff them up by using the Stationary options on this sheet. This feature presents the text you enter with a background (the stationary) of your choice in order to make the messages appear as if written on stationary.

> **Tip**
>
> Windows XP provides a number of stationary templates you can use, but many more are available for download. For example, for a particular holiday you may want to us a stationary background appropriate for the holiday. To find other templates, click the Download More button.

To set up stationary, use the Compose tab. Before you choose the stationary options, however, you must activate HTML sending options. Click Tools, Options, Send and choose HTML from the Mail Sending format options. Then click on the Compose tab again and follow these steps:

1. In the Stationary section, check Mail and/or News check boxes to use stationary for either or both kinds of messages (see Figure 10.8).

FIGURE 10.8

Use the Compose tab of the Options properties sheets to select your stationary.

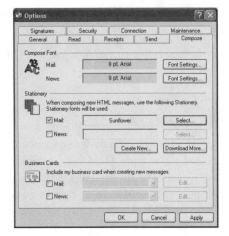

2. Press the Select button for each of the check boxes you have enabled to select the stationary you want to use. A Select Stationary dialog box enables you to preview available stationary patterns. Highlight a pattern in the Directory listing to view it in the Preview pane. When you have selected a stationary you want to use, click OK. (If you are skilled in the graphic arts you can also choose the Edit or Create New buttons first, to edit the pattern).

> **Tip**
>
> Using stationary makes your mail and news messages into larger files than simple text files. If you only want to use it on an occasional basis for a particular message, you can do that, too. Simply Click on the Message menu and select New Message Using. You will find options there to select a stationary to use for just that particular message.

3. Click Apply and OK to dismiss the Options properties sheets.

The Business Card options on this properties sheet works just like the stationary options. You select a business card file, which is essentially an entry from the Address Book that can be picked up and read by an Outlook-based client on the receiving end. You can even attach different cards to Mail and News messages.

Signature Properties

At the bottom of some e-mail or news messages you may sometimes see a person's name, some snappy graphic created using the alphabet, or even a quotation of some kind. This text is called a *signature,* and you can program Outlook Express to apply it automatically to every message you send. You create signatures in the Signature tab of the Options properties (see Figure 10.9).

The first two options in this tab are grayed out until you have created your signature. You return to the following options later:

- Add Signatures to All Outgoing Messages
- Don't Add Signatures to Replies and Forwards

Choose New to create a signature; this adds to the Signatures pane the text, Signature #1 Default Signature. You can then use the lower pane, titled Edit Signature, to enter the text to be associated with this signature. If you have already created your signature elsewhere in Windows, you can click File and then enter a filename (or use Browse to find the file).

FIGURE **10.9**

The Signatures tab allows you to create text that will appear at the bottom of your e-mail or news messages.

You can add additional signatures, for example, to create business and personal signatures simply by clicking New. The signatures will be created with names like the first one, using sequential numbering. Use the Set as Default button to determine which signature will be used by default when you create a message. Simply click on the signature in the Signatures pane and then click the button.

Spelling Properties

This tab can be used to turn on a spell checker, similar to the one used with Microsoft's Word application. There are several check boxes you can use to control how the spell checker functions. Select options familiar to all Windows programs, including Always Check Spelling Before Sending, Suggest Replacements for Misspelled Words, and so on. Experiment with checks using these options to find the set that work best for you.

> **Tip**
>
> You can also use the spell-checking feature just on a single message, without having to turn on this feature for all messages. When composing a new message in the Create New Message dialog box, simply select Spelling from the Tools menu.

Setting E-mail Security Properties

Security issues have never been more important due to the widespread use of viruses and "hack attacks." Many of the worst security offenses occur through e-mail. The options in

10

USING MICROSOFT OUTLOOK EXPRESS

the Security tab enable you to protect your computer from viruses and prevent it from being used as a tool to spread viruses to others. Options in the Security tab allow you to select a security zone for Outlook Express and to use Digital Identification (ID) with your e-mail.

Configuring Virus Protection

As with Internet Explorer, Microsoft uses a "zone" metaphor for how it handles security in Outlook Express. In fact, Outlook Express uses two of the exact same zone rules as Internet Explorer: Internet Zone and Restricted Zone. Which one you pick depends on how secure you want your e-mail to be.

Choose from these options in the Virus Protection section of the Security tab to select a security zone:

- Internet Zone—Although less secure but more functional, selecting this button makes the ActiveX Controls and scripts, which can be embedded in e-mails, run when you receive e-mails in HTML format. Selecting this option can present a security hazard since it opens the doors to viruses spread through e-mail.

- Restricted Sites Zone—This is a more secure selection but is not often used by many users. Essentially, it blocks access to any Web page that is not pre-approved by the user. In a business environment where you have a firewall and good virus protection software, you can probably just use the first selection instead of this one.

Two other check boxes appear directly under these radio buttons:

- Warn Me When Other Applications Try to Send Mail as Me—Enable this check box, and Outlook Express will warn you whenever someone is trying to send messages from your address book. Some viruses have the ability to read your address book and then use the addresses to spread themselves via e-mail to other systems. This is a good check box to enable because it lets you know if an e-mail attachment is trying to run itself as an executable on your system. You can quickly shut down the application and then run a virus-checking program to see if you have already been infected.

- Do Not Allow Attachments To Be Saved or Opened That Would Potentially Be a Virus—If you use this check box, you will practically eliminate your ability to receive e-mail attachments of any kind. Leave this unchecked, but don't open attachments unless you know who the sender is *and* have good virus protection software installed on your computer.

Caution

As a good practice, you should regularly delete e-mail from people you don't know, especially if that e-mail has an attachment. Don't open the e-mail, don't read it, and don't download the attachment!

Understanding Digital IDs and Digital Signatures

Digital IDs and Digital Signatures are used to encrypt e-mail messages and digitally sign them. A Digital ID ensures that the message and its contents have not been tampered with since they left the sender. Digital Signatures verify that the e-mail came from the person listed in the From field in the e-mail.

Digital IDs are issued by certificate authorities. You can sign up for one at http://www.verisign.com, or your company can use Microsoft's Certificate Server to issue its own digital certificates. Digital IDs are based on public key encryption, which uses two key codes—one public and one private. You give your public key to correspondents, and they use it to encrypt e-mail and other documents they send to you. You can decrypt those documents using your private key.

Digital IDs attach a digital signature to the files, verifying that those files were sent by the person whose name appears as the sender. A person sends you the e-mail or document signed with his or her private key, which only that person knows; then, you can use his or her public key to see if it matches up with the private key used to sign the document. In other words, encrypting the document is done using your public key; digital signing is done by using the sender's private key. You learn more about public key digital encryption later in this chapter.

Note

Encryption and digital signing are two separate procedures. A document doesn't have to be sent encrypted in order for it to be digitally signed.

If you already have a Digital ID, then you can use the check boxes at the bottom of the Security tab. The first check box encrypts all of your outgoing messages (and attachments) using your private key. Only those who have a copy of your public key will be able to read these messages. The second check box allows you to digitally sign all outgoing messages.

10

USING MICROSOFT OUTLOOK EXPRESS

Configuring Connection Properties

Use the options in the Connection tab (see Figure 10.10) to determine how Outlook Express uses and chooses the Internet connection to use. In the Dial-up section, choose from the following options:

- Ask Before Switching Dial-up Connections—If you have more than one connection to the Internet, select this check box, and Outlook Express prompts you before it switches to use a different connection. This prompt tells you the current connection isn't functioning so that it can provide a valuable "heads-up."

- Hang Up After Sending and Receiving—This check box tells Outlook Express to go offline as soon as all new outgoing messages have been sent and new incoming messages have been received. This option is helpful if you have your computer checking for new messages at scheduled intervals (as you learned about earlier in this chapter. However, if you want to remain online regardless of e-mail status, don't check this box.

FIGURE 10.10

Using the Connection tab you can tell your computer to drop the connection after it has downloaded your e-mail.

Under the Internet Connection Settings section of this dialog box you will initially see the text "Outlook Express shares your Internet Connection settings with Internet Explorer." Use the Change button to access the Internet Properties dialog box and change the way your system connects to the Internet when checking for mail.

Tip

If you want to keep your online time to a minimum, you can configure Outlook Express to let you work offline. Working offline, Outlook Express dials in, downloads messages, and then hangs up; you read messages, compose replies, reconnect, and send those messages. To switch to working offline, open the General tab on the Tools/Options properties page. Select Connect Only When not Working Offline; then close the page. Return to the main Outlook Express window and choose File, Work Offline. When you are ready to download new messages or send those you have composed that are waiting in your Outbox folder, just click Send/Recv; then choose Yes when the dialog box asks if you want to go online. Your computer dials into the Internet, downloads all new messages, and delivers the ones you composed offline.

Choosing Maintenance Options

It's housekeeping time! The Maintenance tab allows you to set up some automatic options for deleting messages or compacting the databases used by Outlook Express. By performing either of these actions, you can reduce the size of the message database within Outlook Express by either simple elimination or compression of message entries.

The first section of this tab is appropriately titled Cleaning Up Messages. You can choose from these options:

- Empty Messages from the Deleted Items' Folder on Exit—Unless you are absolutely certain that you will never want to retrieve an accidentally deleted e-mail, don't select this option. You can manually clear deleted items whenever you want by simply right-clicking on the Deleted Items folder and choosing the menu selection to empty the folder. If this option is selected, you will not get a "second chance" to retrieve a message from the trash; it will be permanently deleted when you exit Outlook Express.

- Purge Deleted Messages When Leaving IMAP Folders—This is similar to the previous check box. However, remember that when using IMAP instead of POP3, the folder exists on the IMAP server. Again, it is safer to leave this unchecked; you can manually clean your IMAP folders on a regular basis.

- Compact Messages in the Background—Outlook Express compacts its databases as a background process transparent to you so that you can continue to work. Enable this feature so you don't have to wait until Outlook Express warns you that you need to perform this function manually.

- Delete Read Message Bodies in Newsgroups—If you read a lot of newsgroups, choosing this option can save space on your hard drive. Newsgroups can use a significant amount of disk space, and typically, the text is not as important to you as are your e-mail messages. You can save newsgroup messages to file, if you need to keep them.

- Delete News Messages __ Days After Being Downloaded—Here, you simply fill in a preferred number (the default is five days). If you haven't read newsgroup messages in five days, you may never find the time! If you subscribe to a lot of newsgroups, you may want to even consider lowering this value to one or two days.

- Compact Messages When There Is __ Percent Wasted Space—Choosing this option makes searches and other operations work faster. Again, you fill in a percentage here, the default for which is 20%. This option, used in conjunction with Compact Messages in the Background, can keep your databases well organized.

Choosing Clean Up Now compacts your databases, removes messages in your Deleted Items folder, and purges your downloaded newsgroup messages.

The second button, labeled Store Folder, allows you to change the location where Outlook Express stores its databases. Unless you have a good reason to make a change, such as disk space problems, leave things as they are.

Use the options in the Troubleshooting section to have Outlook Express create a log file containing all commands sent to and received from a server. Don't turn these on and leave them on, or you will quickly find yourself running out of disk space. Instead, use them when you suspect problems and then examine the log files.

Creating Filters and Blocking Unwanted Messages or People

If you receive a lot of e-mails you know you don't want to read, you can use Message Rules to automatically delete the messages, copy them to a particular folder, or forward them to someone else. If you know you don't want to receive messages from specific addresses, you can block those messages entirely so that they never reach you.

Click on the Tools menu and select Message Rules. From the submenu that appears, you can select one to create a rule for mail or news messages. You can also create a list of users you want to block messages from.

Create rules by selecting the appropriate check boxes in the New Mail Rule dialog box and then specifying the criteria to match the item you have selected. Begin by selecting the conditions for the rule (a condition that will "trigger" the rule). In the second section, select the action to be taken, such as automatically deleting the message or moving them to a particular folder. The third section contains text based on the selection you make in the first section where you select the condition on which the rule is based.

For example, if you select the second check box labeled Where the Subject Line Contains Specific Words, then the text Rule Description appears at the bottom pane (see in Figure 10.11). Click on the underlined text, which, in this case, contains specific words and another dialog box.

FIGURE 10.11

When you click on a check box, you will be able to create a rule by clicking in the underlined text at the bottom pane.

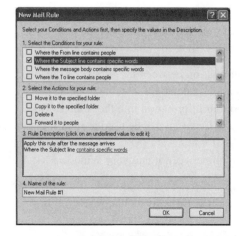

Just as text appears in the Rule Description section at the bottom of the dialog box when you select a rule condition, the same thing happens when you select the action in the second section of this dialog box. If you specify the action Move It to the Specified Folder, for example, then the text in the Rule Description portion of this dialog box contains the text Move to the <u>Specified</u> Folder. When you click on the underlined word <u>Specified</u>, a dialog box prompts you for the folder name.

You can also create multiple rules. The name of the rule appears in the fourth section of the New Mail Rule dialog box. By default, each rule is simply called *New Mail Rule #* followed by a number. However, you can place your cursor in this field and edit the name of the rule to make it easier for you to manage if you decide to create a large number of rules.

If you select Tools, Message Rules, Blocked Senders List, then you will get the New Mail Rule dialog box with the Blocked Senders tab selected. You can then use the Add button to block messages (both news and/or mail) from the e-mail address you specify. You can use the second tab News Rules in the same manner you do the New Mail Rule dialog box, specifying the condition and action to be taken.

Using the Address Book

Keeping track of information about people you know or do business with can be a daunting task. Binder-style planners have been popular for many years, but with personal digital assistants (PDAs) and computers becoming important business tools, address book programs are gaining popularity. Windows XP includes an Address Book that you can access from within Outlook Express. It can also store all kinds of information about personal and business contacts. You can store names and addresses, telephone numbers,

10

USING MICROSOFT OUTLOOK EXPRESS

e-mail addresses, and other personal information such as birthdays and anniversaries. You also can store Vcards (electronic business cards) in the Outlook Express Address Book, and you can use the Address Book to create your own Vcard.

You can import and export information between the Address Book and other applications, so if you have a current address database in another application, such as Eudora or Netscape Mail, you can import that information into the Address Book. You can create an output text file from the Address Book that can be used to import the information into other applications. For example, if you have a PDA, you can connect it to your computer and exchange address information between it and your Windows XP Address Book.

To bring up the Address book, simply click on Addresses at top of the Outlook Express. Figure 10.12 shows what the Address Book looks like when you first view it.

FIGURE 10.12

The Address book can help you store contact and other information about people you know.

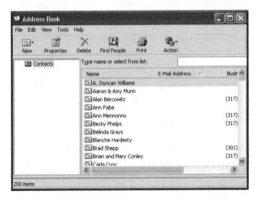

Creating Folders in the Address Book

Before you begin to store contact information about people in your address book, you might want first to create folders to store them in. By using folders, you can make managing a large address book a much easier task. For example, you might have one folder for personal contacts, such as friends, while you can have another for business purposes. You can create a folder for any category of information you enter into the Address book.

To create a folder, simply click on the File menu and select New Folder, or click New and select New Folder. Either way, a small dialog box pops up asking you for a name for the folder. Enter a name and click OK; the folder then appears in the folder list.

Adding Information to the Address Book

You can manually enter information into the Address Book, import it from another program, or have information automatically added by configuring this option in Outlook Express.

Automatically Add People to Your Address Book

When you receive an e-mail and reply to it, you can add the sender's e-mail and other available information automatically to the address book. To enable this function, use the following steps:

1. Click on Tools and select Options from the menu that appears.
2. Click on the Send tab and select the check box labeled Automatically Put People I Reply to in My Address Book.
3. Click Apply and then OK to close the Options properties pages.

Now, whenever you reply to a message from someone who is not already in your Address Book, he or she will be added in automatically.

Manually Enter a New Contact

If you want to enter contact information manually, you can either click on File/New Contact or click the New button at the top of the Address Book and select New Contact. Figure 10.13 shows the Properties dialog box open to the Name tab.

FIGURE 10.13

The Properties pages for a new contact allow you to store a lot of information.

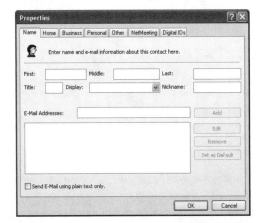

Tip

If you use folders to categorize your contacts, click the folder in which you want to store the new contact *before* you open the Properties dialog box. Follow the steps outlined in this section for entering the information for the new contact, and the contact will be created within the folder you have selected.

Note that you don't have to fill in every field. Indeed, when you use the automatic addition feature for adding a new contact to the address book when you reply to an e-mail message, only a small fraction of the total amount of information you can enter is actually stored in the Address Book. You can, however, double-click on an entry in the Address book to bring up these Properties pages so that you can add additional information or edit existing data.

The Name tab is used to store the contact's name and one or more nicknames, as well as one or more e-mail addresses for the person. You can use the Send E-mail Using Plain Text Only check box to override the global option, if you have selected to use HTML or stationary in your e-mails. To add more than one e-mail address, enter each address in the E-Mail Addresses field and then click the Add button. The Edit and Remove buttons can be used to change or remove any e-mail addresses you enter. The Set as Default button can be clicked when you have highlighted the default e-mail address for sending e-mail to this person. For example, the Autocomplete feature would use this address when assisting you in entering an e-mail address.

Click the Home tab to enter the person's home address, phone numbers and Web site. Click the View Map button if you are connected to the Internet; a browser pops up, showing you a map of the contact's home address. Click the Go button next to the person's Web site, and a browser will take you there.

Use the Business tab to store information related to the contact's work place. In a business environment, this can be very useful. You can enter the name of the company the person works for, along with addressing information; job title; department name; telephone, fax, and pager numbers; and so on.

This tab, as well as the View Map button and Web page field, also has the ability to set this address as the default for this individual.

The Personal tab is used to store exactly what it says. There are fields to record the individual's spouse's name; children's names; and person's gender, birthday, and anniversary. This sort of information can be useful for both personal contacts (your friends) and for business contacts.

The Other tab follows the Personal tab and is used to allow you to simply record notes about the person. There is a field into which you can enter text you may find helpful in the future. Use this as a general-purpose field to record information that cannot be stored in other fields available in the Address Book. In addition, if you use groups in the Address Book, then the user's group memberships are also displayed on this page.

The NetMeeting tab is use to store information used with the NetMeeting application and includes a field labeled Conferencing Server, as well as the ability to add one or more addresses for conferencing addresses. Just enter each address in the Conferencing Address field and then click the Add button. The standard Edit and Remove buttons can be used to manage these addresses. In addition, you can highlight an address and use the button labeled Set as Default or the button Set as Backup for the selected conferencing address. At the bottom of the property sheet is the Call Now button for setting up an Internet conference call after first selecting an address (or by using the default).

The Digital IDs tab is an important one, and it is becoming more important as the Internet continues to grow and becomes necessary to prove one's identity. However, the point is that on the Digital IDs tab you can store, by e-mail address, the public keys for people with whom you communicate. Storing public keys in one place is typically referred to as *creating a key ring*, which is the function provided by this tab in the Address Book.

To use this tab, simply select an e-mail address from the drop-down menu labeled Select an E-Mail Address and then click the Import button. You will be prompted for the file containing the public key the user has sent to you. (Remember that only the private key needs to be kept secret.) In fact, there are many "key ring servers" on the Internet that allow you to post your public key so that anyone who wants to contact you via an encrypted e-mail can retrieve your public key, encrypt their message, and send it to you.

Note

You can also exchange public keys via a floppy disk. However, as digital signatures become more important on the Internet, it won't be long before we all have one, and our public keys are posted on known servers. This technology is expanding rapidly, and you can expect that in a year or two, it will be just as normal to have a public key posted on the Internet as it is to have an e-mail address.

Using Groups in the Address Book

Groups are simply collections of different contacts in your Address Book that you want to address as a single entity. For example, if you are the manager of a department at your work, you might want to create a group that contains the e-mail addresses of all of the employees you manage. Then, when you need to send an e-mail message to all the employees in your department, you can use the group instead. In some mailing programs, a group is called a *mailing list*.

> **Tip**
>
> Don't confuse "groups" with "folders." Although folders can be useful for cate-
> gorizing your contacts, a folder is not a mailing list. Folders are simply a conve-
> nient method to store contacts that are related in some way so that you don't
> have to look through a long list to find someone. Groups are used to address a
> number of different contacts at the same time.

First, you need to create the group and then you can add and remove contacts from a group.

To create a new group, Click File and from the menu, select New Group. (You can also click the New button and select New Group.) When the Properties dialog box appears (see Figure 10.14), enter a name for the group in the Group Name field.

FIGURE 10.14

*Using the Group
Properties dialog
box for a group
allows you to give
a name to the
group and add
members to the
group.*

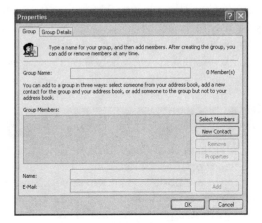

Once you have entered a name for the group, click the Select Members button. The Select Group Members dialog box (see Figure 10.15), showing you a list of contacts from which you can select who to include in the group. Just select the appropriate con-tact and click the Select button to add them to the Group list. After you are finished, click OK to close the Select New Members dialog box.

If the list of group members is satisfactory, you can click on OK to close the Properties dialog box.

FIGURE 10.15

You can easily select the members of the mailing group you are creating.

How to Sort and Print Information in the Address Book

You can sort the information in the Address book by clicking View menu and then Sort By. A list of address book fields appears so that you can choose the one by which you want to sort Address Book entries (the default is Name). However, as we all know, some people use an e-mail address that has nothing to do with their names. If you have used the Outlook Express configuration feature to add to your address book anyone to whom you have replied, it may be easier to find that person by his or her e-mail address.

Using Outlook Express Folders

Outlook Express folders are listed in the left pane of the Outlook Express window. As you learned earlier, the Inbox folder is used to store incoming e-mails, and the Outbox stores messages until it is time for Outlook Express to send them. The Sent Items folder can hold copies of messages you have sent, and the Deleted Items folder stores deleted messages until you empty the folder. "In progress" messages are stored in the Drafts folder.

To move a message to a different folder, simply drag the message from one folder to the next. For example, if you accidentally delete a message, click on the Deleted Items folder and then drag the message header back to your Inbox folder or any other folder in which you want to store it. Alternatively, you can right-click on a message header and select either Move to Folder or Copy to Folder, depending on whether you want to copy or simply move the message.

Creating New Folders to Categorize Your Messages

You can also create your own folders, which can be very useful if you receive a lot of incoming e-mails. You can then move messages to different folders to categorize your messages, making them easier to find later. You can create folders within folders to further organize messages. To create a new folder, simply click on File, New, Folder. A small dialog box prompts you for the name you want to give the folder. To create a subfolder under an existing folder, simply right-click on the folder and select New Folder and then fill in a name for the folder when prompted.

Importing and Exporting Messages and Other Information

If you have more than one computer and have used Outlook Express, or one of many other popular programs for your e-mail, you can import all of these messages, address information, and so on into Outlook Express. You need to have a method of transferring the data, such as a network connection or perhaps burning the data to a CD and then using it as your source to import the information.

To import information from another source, use the following steps:

1. Click on the File menu and choose Import.

2. Select from one of the following: Address Book, Other Address Book, Messages, Mail Account Settings, or News Account Settings.

3. If you choose to import messages from another source, Outlook Express prompts you for the application from which you are importing the data. This is important since different mail and news applications use different formats for storing data.

4. Select the appropriate application and click Next. A dialog box will prompt you for the location of the data. This can be on your local computer, a network drive, or perhaps a CD-ROM drive. If you installed Windows XP on your computer as a dual boot with another version of Windows, you can even find the location of your previous Outlook Express messages and import those. To change the default location, click the Browse button.

5. Depending on the program and the amount of data to be imported, you may be prompted with additional dialog boxes. The time it takes to import the data may be more than just a few minutes. When the wizard is finished, click Finish.

To export data so that it can be incorporated into another news or mail reader (or perhaps a spreadsheet or other database-like program), use the export function of Outlook

Express. Simply choose Export from the File menu and then select either Messages or Address Book.

You can then select to produce an output file compatible with either Microsoft Outlook or Microsoft Exchange.

Searching Folders to Find Important Messages

If you have a large database of messages stored in your Inbox or other folders, you may find that you need to locate a particular message quickly. Using such things as the flagging feature will only work for a small number of messages. For example, if you have flagged hundreds of e-mails as important messages, it can be very time consuming to search through them all manually to find the one you want. Instead, use the Search feature provided by Outlook Express.

Simply click on the Edit menu and select Find. From the submenu presented, you can select Message; Message in this Folder; Find Next; People; and if you read a message, Text in This Message.

In Figure 10.16 you can see the dialog box that pops up when you take the first selection, Message.

FIGURE 10.16

The Find Message dialog box offers an assortment of fields for searching for a message.

As you can see, you can choose to find a message using a variety of criteria, and you can specify the folder to look through. In Figure 10.16, Local Folders is selected. This means the search will look through not only the Inbox, but also your Outbox, Sent Items, and so on. You can use the Message in This Folder option from the Edit/Find submenu to look for a message in a specific folder.

After you enter the search criteria into any of the fields you are using for the search, click Find Now. Be patient if you have a large database of messages, since a search can take a few minutes if you have several hundred messages. The dialog box expands to show the message headers when the search is complete. You can double-click on the headers to bring up the messages so that you can find the particular one you were look-ing for if more than one result is returned.

Click Advanced to specify conditions for the search. Since this computer is also a mem-ber of a domain that uses the Active Directory, select that from the Look In field. Under the Default Criteria section, the first field, which has a drop-down menu, allows you to select from the following:

- Name
- E-mail
- First Name
- Last Name
- Organization

After you select one of these fields, the second field, also a drop-down menu, allows you to specify the following conditions of the search:

- Contains
- Is
- Starts With
- Ends With
- Sounds Like

The third field is where you can put the text that will be used for the search in the Active Directory, based on the field you have selected and the search condition.

However, if you are not part of a domain, you can instead use the Look In menu to select from your address book or an Internet directory. The default directories listed in this menu include the following:

- Bigfoot Internet Directory Service
- VeriSign Internet Directory Service
- WhoWhere Internet Directory Service

Remember that you can sign up for additional directory service accounts, and if you do, they will also appear here. Therefore, you can search through your company's Active Directory or even the Internet to find someone.

As you can tell, the search capabilities of Outlook Express are extensive. You can search for messages in folders on your computer, as well as for people all over the world.

> **Tip**
>
> If you use Outlook Express a lot, then you might want to memorize some of the keyboard shortcuts for performing the more common functions. Table 10.1 lists some keyboard shortcuts you can use from the Main window of Outlook Express or the View Message window.

Table 10.1   Outlook Express Keyboard Shortcuts

Key Command	Function
Ctrl+P	Prints the current message.
Ctrl+M	Sends/receives mail.
Ctrl+D	Deletes the selected message.
Ctrl+N	Creates a new mail or news message.
Ctrl+Shift+B	Opens the Address Book.
Ctrl+R	Replies to a message.
Ctrl+Shift+R	Replies to all mail message recipients.
Ctrl+F	Forwards a message to someone else.
Ctrl+I	Opens your Inbox.
Ctrl+>	Goes to the next message.
Ctrl+U	Goes to next unread mail message.
Ctrl+Shift+U	Goes to next unread news conversation.
Ctrl+<	Goes to the previous message.
Alt+Enter	Shows properties page for the message.

Managing Accounts in Outlook Express

Microsoft Outlook allows you to read both e-mail and newsgroup messages. You can create additional e-mail accounts, if you use more than one e-mail address. For example, you may have a work e-mail address, another with your ISP, and yet another with a Web-based service such as Yahoo or Hotmail. You can add accounts for directory services servers existing within your company or on the Internet. A directory service is a database that contains information about, for example, different people and their e-mail addresses. You can add your own e-mail address to a directory server.

10

USING MICROSOFT
OUTLOOK
EXPRESS

At the beginning of this chapter, you learned how to create an e-mail account. To create another, simply select Accounts from the Tools menu. Figure 10.17 displays the All tab, indicating all of the accounts created in Outlook Express. To create a new mail account, select the Add button and then Mail. You can use the same steps from when you added your first e-mail account.

FIGURE 10.17

The Internet Accounts dialog box will allow you to create additional e-mail, news, and directory services accounts.

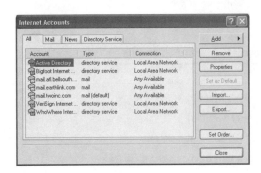

In the next section you will learn how to set up an account with a news server so that you can subscribe to newsgroups and start exploring the huge amount of information available through these ongoing conversations.

Creating a Newsgroup Account

If you think that surfing the Web to find information is useful and a lot of fun, you will probably become just as fascinated with newsgroups. In a newsgroup, you don't just look at Web pages and static information. Instead, you read and post messages that anyone else who subscribes to the newsgroup can see.

To create a news account, you need the name of a news server. Most ISPs operate a news server and will give you this address when you sign up for your Internet service. However, you can add other news servers to your accounts list. Microsoft, for example, operates news servers containing newsgroups about their products.

Once you have the news server address, simply click Add in the Internet Accounts dialog box. From the menu that appears, select News to start up the Internet Connection Wizard. The first dialog box is similar to the one you used to create an e-mail account. Just fill in the field with the name you want others to see when they read messages you post to a newsgroup. This is not your e-mail address, but it can be your real name, a nickname, or whatever. Click the Next button, and another dialog box prompts you to enter an e-mail address that newsgroup posters can use if they want to send a message directly to you instead of posting it to the newsgroup.

In the Internet News Server Name screen (see Figure 10.18), you are asked to type in the name of the network news transport protocol (NNTP) server your ISP has provided. (NNTP is the standard newsgroup protocol used on the Internet today.) Enter the name; then check the My News Server Requires Me to Log On check box, if appropriate.

FIGURE 10.18

Enter the address of your news server in this dialog box.

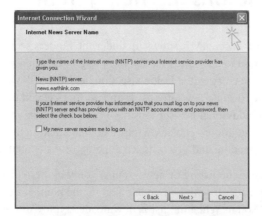

Note

Some news servers are reserved for private use. For example, Microsoft hosts news servers for beta testers, and in order to access these servers, you will need a name and password. You should click My News Server Requires Me to Log On if your news server has formal logon procedures for its users. If you are adding such a news server, a dialog box prompts you for the username and password that this news server requires for access. If you don't want to be prompted for your password each time you access the news server, select the check box labeled Remember Password.

After you click Next, a dialog box will tell you that you have completed the news account setup process. You can then click Finish to dismiss the wizard. Next, click Close on the Internet Accounts dialog box. When you do this, you will see another dialog box asking if you want to download the list of newsgroups from the news server at this time. You can click Yes or No. If you click Yes, it may take a few minutes, especially over a slow connection, to download the thousands of names of newsgroups hosted by the server. However, you can't read a newsgroup's messages until you subscribe to the newsgroup, so the first part of this process is to download the list of available newsgroups.

10

USING MICROSOFT OUTLOOK EXPRESS

Click Yes if you want to look through the newsgroup list at this time and possibly subscribe to a few newsgroups. If you click the No button, you can always choose to download the list at a later date when you have more time to search through the listing.

Subscribing and Unsubscribing from Newsgroups

After you have added a news account, it shows up under the Folders section of Outlook Express. If you didn't choose to download the list of newsgroups when you first created the account, just click on the entry in the Folders section, and you will be prompted again. If you did subscribe to some newsgroups when you first created the account, you can always check to see if additional newsgroups have been added, or you can look at the listing again and make additional choices. Simply double-click on the newsgroup server name in the Folder section, and you will see a listing of the available newsgroups.

When you initially download the listing of newsgroups, you will see a dialog box indicating the progress being made. It will then update you on the number of newsgroup names it has downloaded so far. When the list is downloaded, you will see the Newsgroup Subscriptions dialog box (see Figure 10.19). To subscribe to a newsgroup, simply double-click the newsgroup name (or click once and then click the Subscribe button).

FIGURE 10.19

When the list of newsgroups has been downloaded, you can select the ones you want to subscribe to.

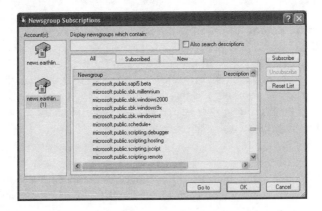

Click on the Subscribed tab to see what groups you have subscribed to. (This makes it easier to unsubscribe!) The New tab contains any new newsgroups that have been created.

You may find the list of newsgroups quite intimidating. Actually, lots of them are rarely used and are leftovers from previous years. There are even some quite outrageous ones. However, you can use the search field at the top of the listing to search for newsgroups that contain specific topics that may interest you.

Reading News Messages

To read newsgroup messages, click the newsgroup icon in the folders pane (see Figure 10.20). You can download the headers for the messages in the newsgroups, or you can download the entire messages for later viewing offline. Click the Settings button for the following options:

- Download all messages.
- Download only new messages since the last time you check the newsgroup.
- Download only the headers to the messages.

Unless you have lots (and that means *lots*) of disk space to spare, select to download only the headers. Then click on a message header to download the message. You can download selected headers and/or messages to your computer by double-clicking on any newsgroup in the listing.

FIGURE 10.20

When you view newsgroups, you can see the headers to messages that exist in the newsgroup.

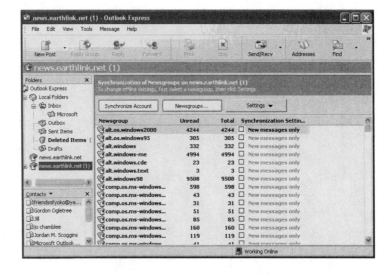

To view the text of a downloaded message, just click on the message header, and the text will be displayed in the pane beneath the headers.

Posting Replies to Newsgroup Messages

Newsgroups are an ongoing conversation. If you find a message to which you would like to reply, click the Reply button at the top of the Outlook Express window. You can also use the New Post button to start a new conversation by posting a message. Newsgroup conversations are organized based on the subject of the posting. Each time you post a

10

USING MICROSOFT OUTLOOK EXPRESS

message with a new subject, then a new conversation begins. If you have a question about a particular topic, then post a new message and check back later to see if someone has posted replies to your post. If you know an answer or have something else to contribute to a current conversation, then use the Reply button.

Summary

Whether you like to use Outlook Express for e-mail or newsgroups or both, clearly Microsoft has taken the best messaging functions from the Outlook application and fit them into one neat package.

In this chapter, you learned how to maximize the use of Outlook Express as an e-mail and newsgroup client as well as expand its security and delivery capabilities to that your messaging is always safe and efficient.

Administration, User Management, Technical Issues

IN THIS PART

11 Running Legacy Applications under Windows XP   *271*

12 Installing and Removing Applications   *281*

13 Command Prompt Tools   *297*

14 Using the Control Panel   *329*

15 Managing Local Users   *359*

16 Auditing Windows XP Using the Event Viewer   *397*

17 Printing with Windows XP   *421*

18 Managing Disks and Partitions   *443*

19 Using the Task Manager   *483*

20 The Windows XP Registry   *497*

21 Using Backup on Windows XP   *521*

22 Performance Monitoring, Logs, and Alerts   *545*

23 Be Paranoid: Disaster Recovery Planning   *587*

24 Configuring Your Computer for Local Area Networking   *617*

25 Configuring Your Computer for an Internet Connection   *643*

26 Joining a Domain and the Active Directory   *679*

Running Legacy Applications under Windows XP

IN THIS CHAPTER

- Why Applications Break *272*
- What Happens during an Upgrade *273*
- After the Upgrade *274*
- Using Compatibility Modes *276*
- The Find Compatible Hardware and Software Help Feature *277*
- Using the Application Compatibility Toolkit *278*
- Use Windows Update Regularly *279*

Because the Windows XP operating system merges what were essentially two separate product lines—the Windows 95/98/Me platforms and those based on the Windows NT kernel (such as Windows 2000)—problems may arise with running legacy applications. Microsoft has done a considerable amount of work to make the transition to this new, single kernel platform much easier for both developers and end users. Many Windows XP features are intended to intercept problems with legacy applications to make them work in spite of themselves.

This chapter contains information targeted to both the application developer and the end user. It describes the primary causes of application incompatibility and introduces utilities you can use to test and perhaps fix applications that don't work quite as they should under Windows XP, including compatibility modes and the Application Compatibility Toolkit.

Why Applications Break

In the past, application developers were bound by the stringent requirements of the operating system under which the application they created was to run. Some coded their applications so that specific files, links, and other elements were installed to operate correctly based on the computer's operating system. Others created applications specifically for Windows 95/98/Me or Windows NT/2000. Applications designed for a single platform are more difficult to migrate to Windows XP.

Some of the factors that limit an application to a single interface are as follows:

- Application Programming Interfaces (APIs)—These are simply libraries of code used to access specific functions (such as operating system functions) or for simple things such as soliciting input from the user. Although a data structure for a particular API may have used one set of data variable structures for Windows 95/98/Me, this may be entirely different for Windows NT/2000/XP. When a new operating system is introduced it usually includes new features. The data structures for an API entry point may change, depending on the operating system, and conversely, so can the resulting data structure that is returned to the program.

- Information locations—Some programs depend on finding user information in a specific location. Under Windows XP, the location may not be the same as it was under Windows 9x or even Windows NT/2000.

- Temporary Folder Locations—Some programs expect temporary folders to be in a specific location, and it may be different than that used by Windows XP.

- Version code—Developers sometimes code in the specific version of the operating system for which their program is written. You might find that when the application makes a check and finds out that it's running under a higher version number of the OS, the application might fail to install or run.

Although things such as device drivers and other low-level code will have to be rewritten to work with Windows XP, the operating system includes features that enable programs to run in an XP environment that simulates the operating system for which they were originally designed.

Microsoft classifies the strategies used to help with these sorts of problems into two categories: migration compatibility technologies and compatibility fixes, modes, and help. Migration compatibility technologies are used during the upgrade process to identify applications that may not function correctly after the upgrade. In some cases, Windows XP warns the user and in others, a minor fix is made to the application without the user even knowing.

For other programs, Microsoft has compiled a list of common applications that can easily be fixed by interfacing between the application and the application that translates the data exchanges. In the next few sections, you will learn about how these are implemented in Windows XP.

Finally, Microsoft offers several tools for testing and applying specific fixes to programs if nothing else seems to work. These tools are especially helpful when the source code for your application is no longer available. The Microsoft tools help identify the problem so that you can determine whether a fix is available.

What Happens during an Upgrade

When you upgrade to Windows XP from a previous Windows operating system, the Setup procedure uses two files when it finds a potential problem with an application on your system:

- `MigDB.INF`—This file is used when you upgrade to Windows XP from Windows 95/Me.
- `NTCompat.inf`—This file is used when you upgrade to Windows XP from Windows NT/2000.

Some older 16-bit applications, for example, attempt to directly access hardware, such as the hard drive or a network card. Under Windows XP, the OS accesses hardware via the Hardware Abstraction Layer (HAL). Programs make calls to APIs, and the HAL layer of the operating system is responsible for communicating with the hardware and returning any data or response codes to the application.

During the upgrade from Windows 95/98/Me, the `MigDB.INF` file is used to generate warnings to users about any programs that may not function correctly after the upgrade. If the program is absolutely essential, this warning gives the user or system administrator the opportunity to abort the upgrade procedure. Otherwise, the warning lets you make a note of the application so that you can proceed with the upgrade and install an updated version of the application after the upgrade.

The file NTCompat.INF performs a similar function, but it is used when upgrading from Windows NT/2000. You are less likely to encounter a problem with this kind of upgrade, as long as the program was specifically written to run under Windows NT/2000. A few programs out there do have compatibility problems; however, this file can help identify them and warn the user during the upgrade process. In addition, it is possible for some of the compatibility problems to be fixed during the upgrade procedure, based on the data in this file; The NTCompat.INF file actually contains fixes for many common applications. For other applications that are noted during the upgrade as incompatible, you may need to download patches from the application manufacturer following the download or run the application using one of the compatibility modes described later in the chapter.

After the Upgrade

After an upgrade has been performed, you can use Windows XP compatibility files to handle some of the basic compatibility issues known to exist with a set of tested programs. The information for these "fixes" is contained in the following two files:

- SysMain.sdb—This file tries to match up information when a program written for another operating system makes a call and coordinates the interaction between the program and the operating system.

- AppHelp.sdb—This file is used to provide a Help message with information for solving the compatibility problem. A dialog box pops up stating that the program may run (in which case you can continue), or it simply won't run under Windows XP (in which case it is "blocked").

The first file, SysMain.sdb is known as a *shim file.* It intercepts calls from a list of known programs for which fixes exist and returns to the calling program a value that keeps the program running. A program may issue a call for the operating system version number. The SysMain.sdb file intercepts the call and returns to the calling program a value of 5—the value that program expects to see. With this value returned, the program continues to run.

The initial Windows XP release contained about 200 compatibility fixes of this sort. You can expect that over the course of time this file will be updated as more programs are found to have compatibility problems. You can find this file in the %systemroot%\AppPatch directory. Note that it cannot be modified to add your own fixes; this is for security reasons.

Running Legacy Applications under Windows XP

CHAPTER 11

275

11

RUNNING LEGACY
APPLICATIONS
UNDER XP

The file `AppHelp.sdb` informs users of such things as the availability of a patch for updating its program when Windows XP encounters an incompatibility problem. The file may give the user a specific URL from where to retrieve a patch or other helpful information about the problem. This file is found in the directory `%systemroot%\AppPatch` also.

`AppHelp.sdb` usually gets involved only when the problem is severe. When the help message is generated, a dialog box appears and describes the problem to the user. Depending on the severity of the problem, one of the following two things can happen:

- The dialog box contains a yellow triangle with an exclamation mark inside of it (see Figure 11.1) warning the user that a potential compatibility problem exists and that Windows XP can't guarantee the program will function correctly. The user can continue using the program to determine if it will work or not.

FIGURE 11.1

A yellow exclamation mark doesn't mean the software won't work, but proceed at your own risk!

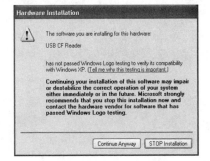

- The dialog box contains a red stop sign and blocks the application from continuing. If this type of dialog box pops up, then click Details to get additional information about the problem. If you are connected to the Internet at this time, details of the help text may come directly from a Microsoft Web site. When you do get a red stop sign and you are not connected to the Internet, then do so and see if there is updated information instead of just the canned info stored in `AppHelp.sdb`!

You will most likely encounter the red stop sign help messages for applications such as antivirus programs or older games that need to access hardware directly. Just click Details to get help on any problem you may encounter. If you receive the less severe warning message, read the details provided, then you can decide whether to continue the installation. If the program is functional, it should be available the next time you boot the system.

Tip

The first type of warning dialog box (with the yellow exclamation point) means only that the application has not been tested to pass the Windows Logo testing procedure for Windows XP, and that it is not an application listed in the SysMain.sdb database. *That doesn't mean it won't work!* This experience is another reason why a large corporate entity considering a switch to Windows XP should follow the advice given in the Resource Kits (described in the *Resource Kits* sidebar in this chapter). Create an experimental lab with a small network and test all your applications thoroughly before you think about deploying them. Don't wait until the last minute and assume they will work.

Caution

Don't take unnecessary chances! If you are worried that a program may cause instability in your system, then be sure to read Chapter 23, "Disaster Recovery," so you can back out of the installation if something truly does go wrong.

Resource Kits

Microsoft Resource Kits are books that come with a collection of software utilities created by Microsoft for use with particular products. For the most part, Resource Kits are aimed at high-level users—administrators, consultants, and others that may support the product in a large-scale production environment. The *Microsoft Windows XP Professional Resource Kit* contains valuable information on deploying, supporting, and troubleshooting Windows XP Professional in a network environment. You can find a copy of the *Resource Kit* in most bookstores or order it directly from Microsoft's Web site.

Using Compatibility Modes

Windows XP includes a set of compatibility modes, or collections of fixes that relate to specific operating systems. You can use a compatibility mode, for example, to run a Windows 95 program under Windows XP. This mode contains about 50 of the fixes from the SysMain.sdb file that are targeted specifically at Windows 95 programs. Because Windows XP has changed the location of certain folders, the compatibility mode "fix" translates between the different paths when data files need to be accessed.

To assign a compatibility mode, right-click on the program's icon (or its entry in the Start menu) and select the Properties menu item. Figure 11.2 shows the properties for a product called *NTI CD-Maker 2000 Professional.* To assign a compatibility mode for the application, click the Compatibility tab.

FIGURE 11.2

Use the options in the Compatibility tab to specify that Windows XP is to emulate another operating system with this application.

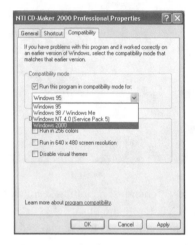

Use the drop-down menu to select a compatibility mode that matches the operating system you have always used to run the application (or for which the application was written). Then change display settings to match those used for the program under its original operating system.

This feature enables the system to accommodate older programs that weren't written for today's higher resolution monitors but offer true color and other features. You also can use the check boxes shown in this figure to disable the Themes feature that Windows XP offers (see Chapter 7, "Up Front: The New Desktop") which may interfere with the way some programs present dialog boxes and other visual elements.

This direct method of setting compatibility options works with most programs and is easy to get to without having to use a wizard. If your application doesn't work "as is" under Windows XP, then try using this tab on the application's Properties sheets to experiment with the different options available.

The Find Compatible Hardware and Software Help Feature

The Program Compatibility Wizard can be found in the Windows XP Help and Support Center. Simply click on Start, Help and Support Center. When the support window appears select Find compatible hardware and software for Windows XP, as shown in Figure 11.3.

FIGURE **11.3**

Select the Find compatible hardware and software for Windows XP selection from the Help and Support Center.

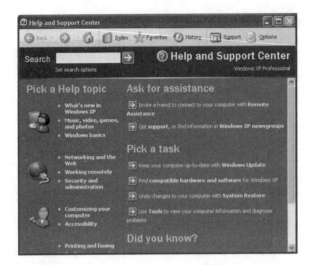

This wizard allows you to perform several functions, including searching for programs that are known to work under Windows XP. If you are unsure if your application will work, then use this option in the Help and Support Center. You should connect to the Internet to use this option, so the latest database of applications that have been certified by Microsoft can be checked.

Using the Application Compatibility Toolkit

If you have a large number of applications that need to be tested to determine if they will work correctly under Windows XP, you will need to download the Windows XP Application Compatibility Toolkit. The uniform resource locator (URL) may go through periodic updates, but you can find it by going to http://www.microsoft.com and searching for the Application Compatibility Toolkit.

This toolkit contains a number of products and documentation that may be of help if you are encountering problems with your existing applications on Windows XP. These include the following:

- Compatibility Administration Tool—Use this to browse for fixed applications on a drive or to turn on or off some of the fixes described earlier in this chapter. You can also use this utility to create your own package, based on the fixes that are present in the aSysMain.sdb file for particular applications.

- Application Verifier Tool—This utility helps you locate problems that are otherwise difficult to diagnose in existing applications so you can determine how to fix them.

- WfixApp—This tool can be used to test an application and apply some of the fixes found in the SysMain.sdb file. You can experiment until you get the right fixes and then distribute the application, with fixes, to other computers in the network. Remember that the SysMain.sdb file was created for a select set of popular applications, and it will be used for them automatically. Here you can pick and choose from the fixes and customize your application so that it will function correctly.

- PageHeap—This utility can help diagnose bugs related to memory leaks and memory allocation routines in older programs.

Tip

Although most end users won't care much about such things as software development kits (SDKs), an experienced network administrator may well understand the importance of obtaining not only the operating system, but also tools that can be used with it. Most network administrators purchase Microsoft Resource Kits so they can further tweak, probe, and troubleshoot the new operating system. If you are a system administrator, make sure to get a copy of the Resource Kit and read the documentation cover to cover so you can become familiar with the tools in the Resource Kit.

Use Windows Update Regularly

An operating system is an evolving creature; that is why there are bug fixes, patches, and service packs. By using the Windows Update service regularly, you can be sure that your system is operating with the latest files. Although your hardware devices may be working just fine right now, it is quite possible that the vendor has certified a newer driver with Microsoft, which would be available through Windows Update.

Caution

Regular use of Windows Update is an important part of your security regimen. As new viruses and other malicious programs make their way around the Internet, using the latest Windows security patches and protection helps you guard your system against attacks from these invaders.

Windows Update offers you several options. You can choose to have components automatically downloaded and installed, or you can have it prompt you first, letting you select what you want to install. For system administrators, you can download the update files and make them available on your network for your Windows XP client computers.

Summary

Windows XP is the result of the merging of two very different operating system kernels. Because of this, programs written for previous Windows versions may not run on Windows XP. In this chapter you have learned about some of the features built into Windows XP that can help older programs run without user intervention. You also have learned how to step in, when necessary, to use compatibility modes and fixes to help older programs make the transition to Windows XP.

In the next chapter, we will take a quick look at some of the traditional applications and accessories you have grown accustom to using in a Windows operating system, and point out how they were integrated into Windows XP.

Installing and Removing Applications

IN THIS CHAPTER

- What Happens When You Install an Application on Windows XP   *282*

- Use Your Autorun CD   *286*

- Using Add/Remove Programs   *286*

- Installing or Removing Windows XP Components   *291*

- After the Application or Component Installation   *294*

Windows XP Professional builds on technologies that were first introduced in Windows 98 Second Edition and Windows 2000 to help make installing applications much easier for you. You will learn about some of these techniques in this chapter, but before you begin to install a new application on your computer, there are three important things you should do first.

First, create an emergency repair disk (see Chapter 23, "Disaster Recovery Planning"). Second, back up your system, especially the system partition (see Chapter 21, "Using Backup on Windows XP").

The third thing you should do is read all the documentation that comes with the application. Although that may seem obvious, it is just so tempting to buy a new application and rush home and install it, only to find out that it doesn't install correctly or some other application no longer works after you installed the new application. So be sure to do your reading first. Application providers have tested their applications, and you should heed any advice given to you about performing the installation. Always check the package to ensure that the application will work with Windows XP. Although most applications that worked under Windows 98 and Windows NT/2000 also will probably work with Windows XP, you cannot be certain. Remember that the kernel used by Windows 98 is vastly different from the one Windows XP inherited from the tried-and-true Windows NT kernel base.

Tip

In addition to the printed documentation with the application, be sure to browse the CD for any `readme.1st` or other similar files. It is often easier for a vendor to create a new CD for distributing software than it is to update printed documentation. As a matter of fact, many vendors include not only readme files on their installation CDs, but also copies of the printed documentation (usually in Word or `.pdf` format) that has been updated since the original documents were printed. You can use Microsoft Word (or Wordpad) to read Word documents. You can also download Adobe's Acrobat Reader to read `.pdf` files by visiting their Web site at `http://www.adobe.com`.

What Happens When You Install an Application on Windows XP

When you install an application on Windows XP, it is usually accomplished by using the Windows Installer utility, which not only installs the program but also keeps track of the files copied to your system and the entries made to the Registry. This makes uninstalling an application a much easier task.

Other installation programs also exist, especially in older programs, but most installation programs will perform the following tasks:

- Create an installation directory (usually under the Program Files directory unless you choose a different location).
- Copy files to the installation directory.
- Copy files to other directories, such as \Documents and Settings or \Windows.
- Create entries in the Windows XP Registry.
- Create a file of information needed to remove the application.

This, of course, is a general idea of what most installation programs do. They also verify that you have a legal copy of the software (by performing a calculation based on a key code you enter), and some store files in temporary directories before moving them to the installation directory. Additionally, they also perform some other tasks that may go on behind the scenes, which may include linking files with other files.

However, from the user's standpoint, installing and removing programs under Windows XP should be a very painless process.

System Restore Points

Windows XP makes recovery easier because every time you install a new application, the operating system records the status of things like registry entries and Create a System Restore Point. You can read more about how these restore points are created manually or automatically in Chapter 23. Note that later in this chapter you can also find out how to "rollback" the system to a previous restore point if you find it performing in unpredictable ways after installing an application.

Solving Problems with Shared Components and Dynamic Link Libraries (DLL)

Files called *dynamic link libraries* (DLL) have caused problems in past versions of Windows operating systems. Most applications serve a specific purpose, but they often share common functions such as dialog boxes to solicit input from the user. Writing code for each application to perform the same function would only make your computer's hard drive more crowded with programs and operating system code than it is now. Windows operating systems were designed from the beginning to have shared components of code, the most common of which are DLL files but can include COM and Win32 components, which applications can share. Some DLLs come with the operating system, and applications provide some as well.

The two major problems with shared files are as follows:

- Although there are strict coding recommendations on how developers should use shared components of the operating system, some discover undocumented features (sometimes called *bugs*) that may work to their advantage and then use them in the code. Thus, when a patch, service pack, or a new version of Windows is released and this bug has been fixed, the application no longer works!

- Application providers sometimes have more than one product, and depend on using the same DLL. If they provide a DLL for product number 1 and make changes to that DLL file when they release a later product, it may cause the earlier product to no longer work. How many times have you tried to uninstall a program and have the Uninstall feature tell you that the file is being used by more than one application, and then query you to leave it or remove it?

Tip

While you can often safely remove DLLs that uninstall routines tell you are no longer needed, it is usually safest to just leave them on your hard drive. Of course, this can clutter up your hard drive so you may want to make a note of their location, and then remove them after you have tested your system following the application's removal.

Side-by-Side Components

Beginning with Windows 98 and Windows 2000, Microsoft started implementing a technique called *side-by-side sharing* to help overcome these kinds of problems. Since most computers made today are not as restricted to disk space or memory capacity as in the past, it is possible to use multiple copies of what used to be a shared component such as a COM or Win32 component. Another name for this technology, which is present in Windows XP too, is called *selective isolation*. Although it is not practical to have multiple copies of all of the files that all applications could share, it is now possible to install an application so that certain DLLs and other components have multiple "side-by-side" copies installed.

However, most shared code is stored in the system root directory, so when side-by-side technology is used, the copy of an updated file is no longer stored in the system directory root. Instead, provided your vendor correctly wrote the application, the COM or WIN32 component is stored in a directory or subdirectory under the application's own installation directory. This way, other applications that may use another version of that component, which the vendor previously distributed, will each have their own copies in their own installation directories. Each component can be loaded into memory separately and used by the correct application.

Additionally, application vendors are encouraged by Microsoft to put references to their application's shared files in the Registry and include a version number as part of the Registry key. This way, each individual version of the component can be tracked separately. When it comes time to uninstall, the Uninstall program knows which registry entry to remove. Using a single Registry key for a component that may actually exist on your system in several locations can be confusing to an uninstall program, and it may delete the wrong component.

Solving DLL Problems—DLL/COM Redirection

This approach to multiple versions of shared files can be implemented by the developer or, perhaps, by a smart system administrator who recognizes the problem. Again, the newer copies of the shared components are stored in a directory along with the new application. However, rather than making changes to the Registry, a file is created in the application's directory to notify the operating system that the shared components may be located there.

The file created in the application directory should be named the same as the application's executable name, but you need to add the file extension .local to the name. For example, if you have an application executable called *makemoremoney.exe*, create a file called makemoremoney.exe.local and place it in the same directory as the application. You will then end up with two files in the directory, the .exe file and the .exe.local file. The .local file isn't a copy of the application file. As a matter of fact, it can be an empty file. It is the existence of this filename in the application's directory that tells Windows XP that DLL/COM redirection should be used.

What happens next is simple. If the .local file exists in the application's directory, then Windows XP will look there first to find the shared component. If it doesn't find the shared component there, it then will look for the component in the path that is defined for the system. If you are unaware of what the path variable is, use the Set command at the command prompt. A list of directories will appear that the operating system can sift through, in the order listed in the path, to find programs and other files when you don't specify an exact location.

These two new techniques—side-by-side sharing (which requires the vendor to change installation code to create new Registry entries), and the DLL/COM redirection method (which requires no code and can be done by the vendor or by a smart administrator who recognizes the problem)—won't solve all the shared component problems on Windows XP, but it should take care of most of them.

Windows File Protection

Another feature that helps eliminate DLL problems is the fact that now only operating system installs/upgrades (or patches or service packs) can update certain DLLs existing in the system directory. In the past, application providers could pretty much replace any file they wanted—typically, the uneducated programmers who were writing shareware code in a hurry, who didn't fully understand the implications of their coding. However, now there are several thousand (yes, that many!) DLL files in the system directory that can't be modified or updated by a simple application installation. If an application does replace a DLL file that is in this protected category, Windows XP will notice it and simply will retrieve a copy of the original DLL from its own stored cache of protected files.

Use Your Autorun CD

You can easily install most programs because they come with their own CDs with the Autorun feature enabled. You simply insert the CD into the CD-ROM drive, wait a few seconds, and the installation wizard program pops up to guide you through the installation process.

For older programs, use the Command Prompt or Windows Explorer to search for a file called *setup.exe* or *install.exe* on floppy disks or CDs if the application was created before the Autorun feature became popular.

Again, once the Setup program starts running, just follow the directions to install the application. A point made earlier in this chapter bears mentioning again for older applications: *Read the documentation first.* It may be that your older application won't run with the devices or the operating system you are using, and if you install it, there is no guarantee that an uninstall program (if one exists for an older application) will work. In that case, go back to Chapter 23 and use the System Restore Point function to get back to where you started. And, keep that Emergency Repair Disk (ERD) and backup of your system handy, especially when installing older applications!

Using Add/Remove Programs

The Control Panel has a utility called *Add/Remove Programs* that can be used to install programs, even if they do use the Autorun feature. It also can be used to install older programs and to add or remove specific components of the operating system.

To start the Add/Remove Programs utility, click on Start, More Programs, Control Panel. As you can see in Figure 12.1, the Control Panel's category view gives you several menu-like options from which to choose.

FIGURE 12.1

Use the Control Panel to access the Add or Remove Programs option.

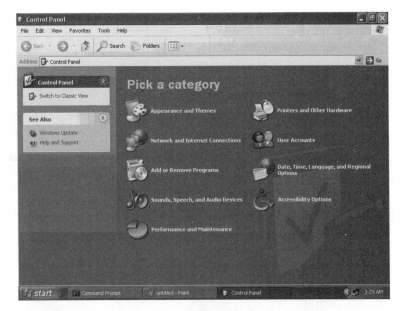

Simply click Add or Remove Programs found in the first column under the Pick a Category listing. Alternatively, you can select Switch to Classic View from the left side of this figure to see the old familiar Control Panel, and then click the Add/Remove Programs icon. In either case, Figure 12.2 shows you the Add or Remove Programs utility.

FIGURE 12.2

The Add or Remove Programs utility enables you to add or remove programs or Windows XP components.

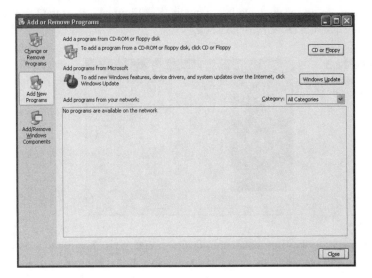

As you can see from this figure, there are three buttons on the left side of the window:

- Change or Remove Programs
- Add New Programs
- Add/Remove Windows Components

Use the first option, Change or Remove Programs, if you want to change the configuration of a particular application or select the second button, Add New Programs.

Notice also that there are other options available here. You can use the buttons on the far right side of the window:

- CD or Floppy—Use this if you have a CD that doesn't automatically start an installation program using the Autorun feature or if you are installing a program from a floppy disk.
- Windows Update—With this feature you can periodically check for and download new drivers, bug or security fixes, or other features directly from Microsoft using an Internet connection.

Yet another choice appears in this window. If your network administrator has set up programs so that you can access the installation files from a shared network drive, then they will appear in this window. You can simply double-click on one of these entries to start the installation process.

For our example, let's choose the CD or Floppy button so you can see how Windows XP will prompt you for the installation media. See Figure 12.3 for the Install Program From Floppy Disk or CD-ROM dialog box.

FIGURE 12.3

Insert the floppy disk or CD-ROM before clicking Next.

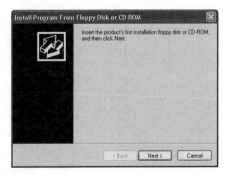

In Figure 12.4, the Run Installation Program dialog box has found a program called *INSTALL.EXE* on the E: drive (a CD-ROM drive in this computer). If this is not the correct program, use Browse to look for the correct program. For example, you may have a CD-ROM with many directories of different applications, and you may want to navigate through these directories to find the installation program for the application you want to install. When you have found the correct install or Setup program name in the Open: dialog box, Click Finish to start the installation.

FIGURE 12.4

The Run Installation Program dialog box displays the installation program, or you can also browse for another.

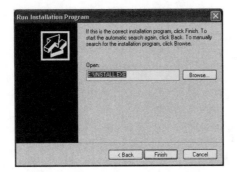

From this point, the particular installation or Setup program will run, and you should answer the prompts according to how you want to set up the program on your computer. For example, many installation programs give you the option of choosing the location for the applications files. For example, if you have more than one disk or disk partition, it can be a good idea to install programs on a separate disk (or partition) than the operating system. You then can make a single backup of the system disk for your backup needs, and also use more frequent backup schedules for the disk containing your applications and data.

Other options often available in installation programs are reading the release notes when the Setup finishes or placing an icon on the desktop.

When the installation program finishes, the Add or Remove Programs window shown in Figure 12.2 above displays. If you click the Close button at the bottom right of this window, you will see a different view of the Add or Remove Programs window (see Figure 12.5), which shows you the programs currently installed on your computer. Note that this view is also the one you will see if you had selected the Change or Remove Programs option in Figure 12.2.

As you can see, one of the programs I just installed is called *NTI CD-Maker 2000 Professional*. This is a CD-burner program that I recommend, in addition to others such as Nero Burning Rom and Roxio's Easy CD Creator 5 Platinum. Each of these programs function in much the same way and enable you to copy most music or data CDs. Although it is against the law to copy a program CD and give it to someone else to install on their computer, I *highly* recommend taking advantage of this feature if your computer has a CD burner by immediately making a backup copy of every application CD that you buy. You never know when the original may become defective or lost.

FIGURE 12.5

You can use this view to see the programs currently installed on the computer.

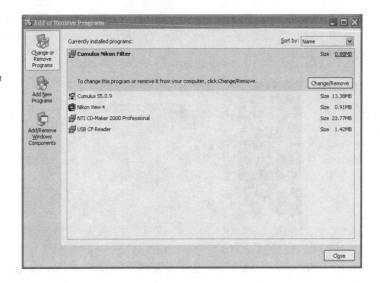

You should make it a habit to make a copy before installing any application, and then safely store the original CD. You then can use the backup copy for the installation to ensure it works. There is no such thing as a good backup until you have tested it. Hence, if you have a CD burner, make backup copies of all the CDs that come with your applications and use the backup copies, which is quite legal, to install your applications. If you have ever had to wait on replacement disks or pay for additional disks from the vendor, then you know exactly what I mean. In some cases you may not even be able to purchase a new copy of the program if the company has gone out of business or the software is no longer produced. Now you can see how valuable a backup CD can really be.

Removing an Application from Windows XP

Removing an application is actually much simpler that installing one. Again, use the sequence of Start, More Programs, Control Panel, and from the Category View select Add or Remove Programs from the items presented. When the Add or Remove Programs window appears, click on the button at the top left labeled Change or Remove Programs. You will see a listing similar to Figure 12.5. Now all you have to do is click on the program to highlight it. A Change/Remove button will then appear next to the program. Click this button, and it will invoke the particular program (most likely, Windows Installer, for most modern applications) for removing the application.

Note that some of these application programs will prompt you to repair an existing application or perform a reinstallation. You can use the repair option if you think the files may be corrupt or deleted. You can use the reinstallation feature if you didn't select all the program's components during the initial installation. For example, when installing

Microsoft Office (any version), you may have installed only Microsoft Word. If, at a later time, you want to install additional applications that come with Microsoft Office, you can use this Change/Remove feature to restart the installation program without reinstalling Microsoft Word.

However, if you simply want to remove a program, a dialog box will show the progress of the uninstall, which means it is removing files, removing Registry entries, and other features related to the program. If you want to save data files stored with the application directory's files—that is, if you are moving the application to a different computer, then be sure to back up those files before removing the application.

Installing or Removing Windows XP Components

When you first install Windows XP, you should perform a typical installation, as directed in Chapter 3, "Installing and Upgrading Windows XP." However, you will also notice on the menus presented by the installation CD that there are additional components to install. To add or remove additional components of Windows XP, you can use two methods.

One option is to insert the installation CD into the CD-ROM drive and select Install Additional Components from the menu.

However, in a corporate environment and during many installations performed by users who are savvy at working with Windows NT/2000, there is an alternative—copying the Windows installation files to a local or shared hard disk. This method is often used on networked drives so that the CD is not needed to reinstall Windows XP or install additional components. You can learn more about this in Chapter 3, "Installing and Upgrading Windows XP."

When adding or removing components of a Windows XP installation, you can use the same command sequence mentioned earlier: Start, More Programs, Control Panel, and then Add or Remove Programs. When the Add or Remove Programs window appears, click on the third button on the left side of the window labeled Add/Remove Windows Components. This will display the Windows Components Wizard (see Figure 12.6)

As you can see, you can select or deselect check boxes for the various components of Windows XP, depending on whether you want to install or remove the component. For example, I will select the check box labeled Fax Services. I wasn't sure I wanted this feature when I first performed my installation, but now I have changed my mind. Notice that at the bottom of this Wizard's dialog box there is a description for any of the components. Just click the component to see the text next to Description: change. You can also see the total amount of available disk space left on your hard drive and the amount of space that will be used when you select components. This can help you make better choices about which components to install. As you can see in Figure 12.7, after I select the check box for Fax Services, the Total disk space required field (at the bottom of the dialog box), shows 2.5MB. If you select more than one component, this number will change to reflect the total for all components selected, not just the last one you've click on.

You only need to click once on the check box (to select it), and then click the Next button.

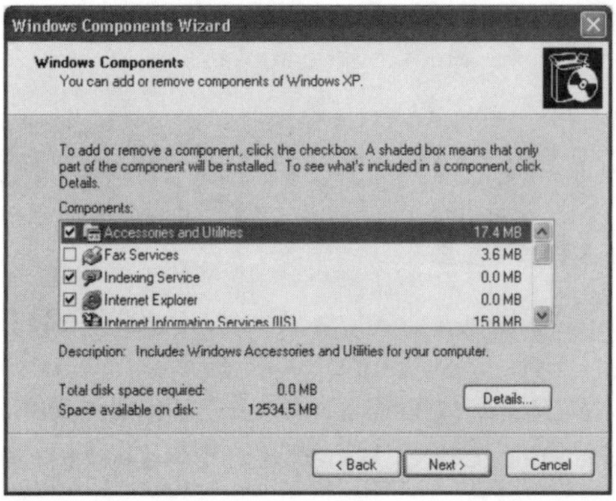

FIGURE 12.6

Use the Windows Components Wizard to add or remove components of the Windows XP operating system.

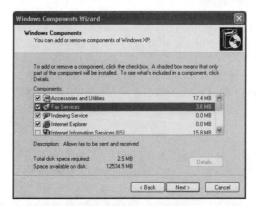

FIGURE 12.7

As you select components for installation, the Total disk space required field keeps track of how much disk space the installation will use.

Tip

Note that some of the check boxes you see in the Windows Components Wizard may have a check mark in them, but the check box will be gray in color instead of white. This means that particular component has other options you can select from and all of them are not currently selected or installed. To find out about other subcomponents, click the item once, and then click the Details at the bottom of the wizard. Another dialog box will appear, looking much like the same one in Figure 12.6 above; however, it will list the individual subcomponents of this Windows XP feature. Click once on each subcomponent to get a description of it and use the check boxes in this dialog box to select or deselect the subcomponents you want to install or uninstall.

Figure 12.8 shows a dialog box called *Insert Disk,* which prompts you to insert the Windows XP CD so it can copy the necessary Setup files for the installation of the selected components. However, if you want to use another source, such as an /i386 directory on your local system or a network drive, just click OK. When the wizard doesn't find the CD, it will prompt you to enter the specific location of the source files or browse for the location.

Finally, the wizard will start copying the files (see Figure 12.9).

FIGURE 12.8

The wizard will now prompt you for the location of the source files it needs for the installation.

FIGURE 12.9

The wizard uses a bar graph to show you the progress of the component installation.

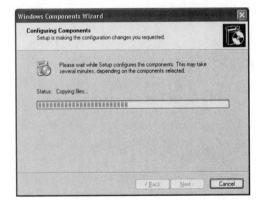

The amount of time required will depend on the following considerations:

- The number of components you chose to install.
- The size of the files needed for the components you chose to install.

- The source of the installation files; you may have a fast or slow CD-ROM drive, or your network drive may be slower than your CD-ROM drive.

The wizard shows a bar graph for keeping track of its progress (see Figure 12.9) so that you can tell how fast the process is going. If it appears to be going slowly, it may be a good time for a coffee break!

When the component or components you have selected are installed, one last dialog box from the wizard will display telling you its work is finished. Click Finish. Although most Windows XP component installations don't require a reboot, some do. If so, you will be prompted to restart your computer now or at a later time. If a reboot is required, the components you selected won't be available until you perform the reboot.

When the Wizard disappears, click Close at the bottom right of the Add or Remove Programs window to close the utility.

> **Note**
>
> After you have installed one or more Windows XP components, you still may not be finished with your task. Some components, such as networking components or the Internet Information Server (IIS) components will require configuration after they have been installed. So after installing the components and possibly rebooting the system, be sure to check each component to see that it is properly configured. For information on configuration options, see the appropriate chapter or appendix in this book that relates to the component.

After the Application or Component Installation

Just as you had to create an ERD and perform a backup before you added a new component or application to your system, it is also a good idea to do the same thing as a post-installation procedure. Your ERD should *always* be kept up to date whenever you make any changes on your system. A backup can come in handy if you have installed an application or component correctly and later encounter errors in configuring the application or component. Rather than restoring from the backup you created before the installation, use the post-installation backup, and then start your configuration steps again.

Summary

Adding and removing applications and components of the Windows XP Professional operating system is an easy task. It just takes a little time, and it helps to understand the purpose of the application or component you are installing. If you take the appropriate precautions (create an ERD, along with a good backup of your system, and also read the documentation before modifying your system), you will have less to worry about if something goes awry.

Command Prompt Tools

IN THIS CHAPTER

- Overview of the Command Prompt *298*

- Configuring the Command Prompt *299*

- Using Standard Commands *304*

- Working with Batch Files *319*

- Using the Command Line Task Scheduler (schtasks) *321*

- Network Commands *325*

- How to Create an MS-DOS Startup Disk *326*

CHAPTER 13

From the earliest IBM PC and the many compatibles that followed, there has been a command-line interface for the operating system. In years past, MS-DOS was the operating system, and what is now called the Command Prompt in Windows XP Professional *was* the interface into the operating system. Long before graphical user interfaces (GUIs) were in widespread use (such as in the Apple Macintosh, and later Microsoft Windows), the character-cell–based Command Prompt was where you executed commands, ran programs, and got to see the output.

Over the years, as Microsoft operating systems have become more and more sophisticated, the Command Prompt has been moved from the Programs folder, which is now the All Programs folder in Windows XP, to the Accessories folder. It is almost as if Microsoft was trying to rid itself of its heritage! MS-DOS was the operating system that standardized computing in the very early 1980s and, to this day, you can still find things to do with the Command Prompt by using good ol' MS-DOS style commands that are more difficult or less intuitive when using a GUI.

In this chapter, you learn several things about the Command Prompt. First, the chapter explains how you can customize the window in which the command prompt appears; then it goes on to discuss several of the commands you can use. If you have always been a point-and-click type, you can pick up some tips in this chapter that allow you to use your computer more efficiently.

This chapter also describes how to create a bootable floppy diskette—a function that Windows 2000/NT was missing. A bootable floppy disk can help you diagnose problems on a computer that won't boot and can be very useful for other things too, as you will see.

Overview of the Command Prompt

To bring up the Command Prompt, click Start, All Programs, Accessories, Command Prompt. The command prompt appears, as shown in Figure 13.1.

Not much to look at, is it? The screen contains just the drive letter of the default drive for your home directory, along with your home directory's pathname.

One thing you should understand about the Command Prompt is that it isn't the same in Windows XP that it was in the old MS-DOS days. There are actually two different applications that come into play when you execute MS-DOS–like commands on a Windows XP machine.

FIGURE **13.1**

The Command Prompt window opens with just a black screen and a prompt, showing you the default drive and user-name.

The program CMD.EXE is the Windows XP command shell that starts up when you use the Command Prompt found in the Accessories folder. The application COMMAND.COM is the old MS-DOS style command interpreter that runs only 16-bit applications. COMMAND.COM runs in what is called a *virtual DOS machine* (VDM), and it is included with Windows XP so that you can run old MS-DOS programs. However, to add an interesting twist to the situation, when you execute a command in the older COMMAND.COM environment, it actually isn't processed by COMMAND.COM. Instead, COMMAND.COM sends the commands you execute to the newer CMD.EXE 32-bit application and returns the results to you.

13

COMMAND
PROMPT TOOLS

> **Note**
>
> You can use the Task Manager to see how the command "hand off" works (you learn more about the Task Manager in Chapter 19, "Using the Task Manager"). Bring up the Command prompt and look in the Task Manager at the Processes tab; you will see that Windows XP has created a virtual DOS machine (process name NTVDM.EXE) to execute the Command Prompt. Next, execute a command that takes some time to complete, such as a directory listing on a large disk. If you look at the Processes tab in the Task Manager again, you see another process, with a name of CMD.EXE has been started up to process the command you executed in the Command Prompt.

Configuring the Command Prompt

You can configure the Command Prompt to make it more suitable to your tastes. You can choose a larger character size or a different font, for example, or you can change the color of the background or characters.

As with other features in Windows XP, you use Properties pages to configure the command prompt. If you want to set options that apply to all Command Prompt windows, then go to the Control Panel and use the Console icon to access the settings for the default values for the new Command Prompt windows you create.

If you already have a Command Prompt window open, simply right-click on the blue title bar that is at the top of the Command Prompt window and from the menu that appears, select Properties to produce the Properties pages (see Figure 13.2).

FIGURE 13.2

The Command Prompt can be configured using Properties pages, just like other Windows XP components.

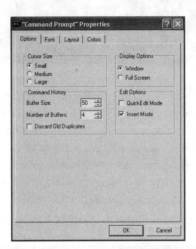

You can also simply click once on the MS-DOS icon on the left side of the blue title bar and select Properties to configure the appearance and operation of the Command Prompt window. When you use either of these last two methods to make changes, a dialog box appears, offering you the options to make changes for just the current window, or for the shortcut that started the window. Note that this only applies to shortcuts you create to start up the Command prompt.

To demonstrate this technique, right-click on the Command Prompt in the Accessories menu and use the Send To-> and then Desktop (Create Shortcut) selections to create a shortcut on the Desktop for the Command prompt. If you make changes and decide to apply them to the shortcut, it applies just to Command Prompt windows started by the shortcut. It doesn't affect Command Prompt windows you start from the Accessories menu. Changes made in the Console applet in the Control panel, however, apply to the Command Prompt menu selection in the Accessories menu.

Configuring Command Buffers, Display Options, and Edit Options

The Options tab enables you to change the cursor size, Command History, and cursor display options. The Command Prompt cursor is that blinking white box that shows you where text will appear when you start typing commands in the Command Prompt. Use the options in this tab to choose a larger size, if you prefer.

You may have used the `doskey` command in Windows 95/98/Me to activate Command History. In Windows XP, it is enabled by default (though the `doskey` command is still with us, and can be used to modify command-line buffer recall). When you enter commands in the Command Prompt, the system stores them in a buffer. Use the options in the Command History to specify the size of the Buffer field used to store these commands. You can recall stored commands by using the up and down arrow keys. You can also change the number of buffers, which is the number of different processes that can have their own buffers. Increasing either of these values increases memory usage.

The check box labeled Discard Old Duplicates condenses the command recall buffer to eliminate duplicate commands in storage.

The Display Options section of the Options tab allows you to specify whether the Command Prompt should be presented as a window, as shown back in Figure 13.1, or if it should fill the entire screen. Generally, you should select the Window option so that you can see the remainder of the Desktop and switch easily between applications.

> **Tip**
>
> If you do decide to change the Display Options to Full Screen, you can use Alt+Tab to switch between other applications that are currently running. Hold down the Alt key and press the Tab key until the application you want to switch to is highlighted; release the keys to open that application's window on your screen.

Use the Edit Options to select two modes for editing within the Command Prompt:

- QuickEdit Mode—Allows you to use your mouse to cut and paste rather than using the Edit menu.
- Insert Mode—Toggles between insert mode and overstrike mode. Insert moves text to the right as you type new text within a line of existing characters; overstrike replaces existing characters as you type.

The Font Tab—Changing the Character Font and Size

Use the options in the Font tab to select the font type and size for characters displayed in the Command Prompt (see Figure 13.3).

FIGURE 13.3

Use the Font tab to change the size and style of characters used for the Command Prompt.

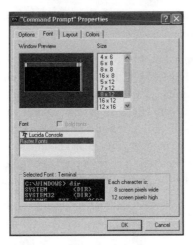

Choose a font size in the Size scroll box. Larger font sizes occupy more room in the Command Prompt window, as you can see demonstrated in the Window Preview area of the Font tab. The Font list box offers a variety of fonts types from which you can choose (your options are determined by the fonts installed on your system). The Windows XP default is Raster Fonts (Terminal), which is the font most people are accustomed to seeing in the Command Prompt window. Choose a font type by clicking it in the list. The Selected Font area at the bottom of the Font tab lets you preview what the font you have selected looks like in the size you have selected. This area also indicates the character height and width.

Choosing Window Size, Buffer Size, and Location Layout

By default, the Command Prompt window is 80 columns wide and 33 rows deep. You can use options in the Layout tab in Figure 13.4 to change both the actual size of the window as well as the buffer that stores lines that scroll off the screen. You can use the scrollbar on the side of the Command Prompt window to look at text that scrolls off the screen.

Under the section titled Window Position, you can specify whether or not to let the system automatically position the Command Prompt wherever it pleases, or you can specify a position (in pixels) for the top-left corner of the window.

FIGURE 13.4

You can change the size of the window, the buffer that stores text that scrolls off the screen, and the position of the window.

> **Note**
>
> Provided you have enough space on your desktop, you can drag the edges of the Command Prompt window to enlarge the area it takes up, as long as you don't exceed the buffer size you have enabled. This action can be very useful if you are using commands that produce output longer than the typical 33 lines, and you don't want to scroll or use the MORE command to view off-screen text. Drag the bottom of the Command Prompt window to increase the number of rows you can see.

The Colors Tab—Why Be Ordinary?

This Colors tab is a fun one. As you can see in Figure 13.5, you can change the colors of the characters, the screen, and Popup Colors.

Select a radio button to choose the color you want to set. You can use the Selected Color Values (Red, Green, Blue) to create a color, or you can click on the bar of predefined colors. You can select colors for the following items:

- Screen Text—The characters that appear in the Command Prompt window.
- Screen Background—Change the background color from black to any color you want. Just make sure that the Screen Text and Screen Background colors aren't the same, or you won't be able to read anything on the screen.

- Popup Text—Some programs open separate windows that display specific information. For example, the F7 key shows the commands in the recall history buffers. You can change the color of the text that appears in these popup windows.

- Popup Background—You can also change the background color of the popup windows by using this selection.

FIGURE 13.5

You can use this tab to change the colors used for the Command Prompt.

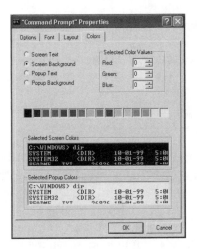

To change a color, select the appropriate radio button for the item you want to change and then use the up and down arrows for the Red, Green, and Blue color values to produce your own color. You can also click on one of the predefined colors in the row of colors found in the middle of the properties sheet.

Note that at the bottom of the properties sheet you will be able to preview the colors you have selected for both the main Command Prompt window and the popup windows.

Using Standard Commands

Windows offers a good set of commands, operators, and pipes (special symbols used to redirect output from commands) that can help you accomplish a lot of work from the Command Prompt. You can also use batch files or script files to run a number of commands in sequence automatically.

If you have worked with MS-DOS or the command prompt before, you may have created batch files in previous versions of Windows. Before you learn about using MS-DOS commands at the Windows XP Command Prompt, it is a good idea to get rid of outdated MS-DOS commands in existing files; some of those older commands aren't supported in Windows XP. The next section explains how to clean out these old commands from your files.

Cleaning Out Commands That Are No Longer Supported

Some MS-DOS commands are no longer supported, so they are of no value in Windows XP. This section contains a list of commands that worked in some of the previous incarnations of the Command Prompt or MS-DOS, but which are no longer included in the Windows XP version. Use this table to check any batch files you may have created for previous versions of Windows to be sure that you do not include them.

Table 13.1 Obsolete Command Prompt Commands for Windows XP

Command	*Former Usage/Replacement*
Assign	Used to redirect command output from one drive to another. Now, you can use the Subst command instead to redirect output from a folder to another drive.
backup	Use the System Tools/Backup utility instead.
choice	Used to prompt user in batch file.
ctty	No longer supported.
dblspace	Use compression for files and folders instead.
deltree	Use rmdir /s to remove a directory, and everything beneath it.
dosshell	This is now the Command Prompt.
drvspace	Use compression for files and folders instead.
emm386	With virtual memory, who needs this anymore?
fasthelp	Use help, help [*command*] or *command* /? instead.
fdisk	Use the diskpart command instead.
include	Multiple configurations for the MS-DOS subsystem are no longer supported.
interlnk	No longer supported. Clients can connect to Windows XP using Remote Access Services (RAS) instead.
intersrv	Same as interlnk.
join	Used to join drives. Larger disks and partitions have made this unnecessary.
memmaker	Used to optimize memory. This is now done automatically by Windows XP for MS-DOS programs.
menucolor	Multiple configurations for the MS-DOS subsystem are no longer supported.
menudefault	Multiple configurations for the MS-DOS subsystem are no longer supported.
menuitem	Multiple configurations for the MS-DOS subsystem are no longer supported.
mirror	Instead, use the System Restore tool.
msav	Use a third-party virus checker instead.

continues

13

COMMAND
PROMPT TOOLS

Table 13.1   continued

Command	Former Usage/Replacement
msbackup	Use the System Tools/Backup utility instead.
mscdex	Used to provided access to CD-ROM drives. Windows XP does this for MS-DOS based programs automatically.
msd	Use Start/Run/msinfo32 instead for system information, or look in the Control Panel.
numlock	Windows XP preserves the state of this key from one logon to the next—hence the command is no longer needed.
power	See the Power applet in the Control Panel instead.
restore	Use the System Tools/Backup utility instead.
scandisk	Use chkdsk command instead.
smartdrv	Caching is automatic for the MS-DOS subsystem in Windows XP.
submenu	Multiple configurations for the MS-DOS subsystem are no longer supported.
sys	Used in the creation of a system floppy disk. Windows XP does not fit on a floppy disk.
undelete	Retrieve deleted files from the Recycle Bin using Windows Explorer. Files deleted from the Command Prompt cannot be retrieved.
unformat	Yeah, right. This hasn't been offered in any Windows NT/2000/XP environment! Check that disk before you format it!
vsafe	Use a third-party virus checker instead.

In addition, if you are running the 64-bit version of Windows XP, the following Command Prompt commands will not be available.

Table 13.2   Obsolete Command Prompt Commands for 64-bit Windows XP

Command	Former Usage/Replacement
append	Allowed a program to open a file as if it were in the current folder.
debug	Executes the debug.exe program, to test MS-DOS applications.
edit	An MS-DOS ASCII text editor. Use Wordpad or Notepad instead.
edlin	A command-line ASCII text editor.
exe2bin	Used to convert executable (.exe) files to binary format.
expand	Used to expand compressed files.
fastopen	This command is accepted for compatibility with MS-DOS files, but is not used by Windows XP.

Command	Former Usage/Replacement
forcedos	Used to start programs in the Command Prompt that are not recognized by Windows XP as being MS-DOS programs.
graphics	Used to load a program to print the contents of the screen when using a color or graphics adapter.
loadfix	Used to load a program above the first 64KB of memory and then run the program. Memory is now managed by the operating system.
loadhigh	Used to load a program into the upper memory area. Memory is now managed by the operating system.
mem	Used to display information about memory usage.
nlsfunc	Used to load country/region specific information.
setver	Used to set the MS-DOS version that the MS-DOS subsystem returns to a program.
share	Accepted for compatibility with MS-DOS files, but not used by Windows XP.

Commands You Can Use at the Command Prompt

There are still plenty of commands left for working with the Windows XP Command Prompt. Although the list in this section is by no means complete, it does give you a good set of commands for use in the Command Prompt dialog box. Table 13.3 contains a list of the basic set of commands available using the Command Prompt under Windows XP. This list is just the straight text, as it appears when you issue the Help command in the Command Prompt. This book includes this table as a useful desktop companion. When you are sitting at your computer and you can't remember a command, this list makes an easy reference. (Later in the chapter, you learn about the MORE operator, another option for finding a command when all the help text scrolls off your screen.)

> **Note**
>
> The commands in Table 13.3 are just the basic Command Prompt commands. Later in this chapter, you learn about other commands that depend on Windows XP components, such as networking.

There isn't enough room in this book to discuss all the commands listed in Table 13.3. However, you should be aware of a few, which are discussed in next few sections of this chapter.

Table 13.3   Basic Command Prompt Commands for Wndows XP.

Command	Usage
ASSOC	Displays or modifies file extension associations.
AT	Schedules commands and programs to run on a computer.
ATTRIB	Displays or changes file attributes.
BREAK	Sets or clears extended Ctrl+C checking.
CACLS	Displays or modifies access control lists (ACLs) of files.
CALL	Calls one batch program from another.
CD	Displays the name of or changes the current directory.
CHCP	Displays or sets the active code page number.
CHDIR	Displays the name of or changes the current directory.
CHKDSK	Checks a disk and displays a status report.
CHKNTFS	Displays or modifies the disk check at boot time.
CLS	Clears the screen.
CMD	Starts a new instance of the Windows command interpreter.
COLOR	Sets the default console foreground and background colors.
COMP	Compares the contents of two files or sets of files.
COMPACT	Displays or alters the compression of files on NT File System (NTFS) partitions.
CONVERT	Converts File Allocation Table (FAT) volumes to NTFS. You cannot convert the current drive.
COPY	Copies one or more files to another location.
DATE	Displays or sets the date.
DEL	Deletes one or more files.
DIR	Displays a list of files and subdirectories in a directory.
DISKCOMP	Compares the contents of two floppy disks.
DISKCOPY	Copies the contents of one floppy disk to another.
DOSKEY	Edits command lines, recalls Windows commands, and creates macros.
ECHO	Displays messages, or turns command echoing on or off.
ENDLOCAL	Ends localization of environment changes in a batch file.
ERASE	Deletes one or more files.
EXIT	Quits the CMD.EXE program (command interpreter).
FC	Compares two files or sets of files, and displays the differences between them.
FIND	Searches for a text string in a file or files.
FINDSTR	Searches for strings in files.

Command	*Usage*
FOR	Runs a specified command for each file in a set of files.
FORMAT	Formats a disk for use with Windows.
FTYPE	Displays or modifies file types used in file extension associations.
GOTO	Directs the Windows-command interpreter to a labeled line in a batch program.
GRAFTABL	Enables Windows to display an extended character set in graphics mode.
HELP	Provides help information for Windows commands.
IF	Performs conditional processing in batch programs.
LABEL	Creates, changes, or deletes the volume label of a disk.
MD	Creates a directory.
MKDIR	Creates a directory.
MODE	Configures a system device.
MORE	Displays output one screen at a time.
MOVE	Moves one or more files from one directory to another directory.
PATH	Displays or sets a search path for executable files.
PAUSE	Suspends processing of a batch file and displays a message.
POPD	Restores the previous value of the current directory saved by PUSHD.
PRINT	Prints a text file.
PROMPT	Changes the Windows command prompt.
PUSHD	Saves the current directory then changes it.
RD	Removes an empty directory.
RECOVER	Recovers readable information from a bad or defective disk.
REM	Records comments (remarks) in batch files or CONFIG.SYS.
REN	Renames a file or files.
RENAME	Renames a file or files.
REPLACE	Replaces files.
RMDIR	Removes a directory.
SET	Displays, sets, or removes Windows environment variables.
SETLOCAL	Begins localization of environment changes in a batch file.
SHIFT	Shifts the position of replaceable parameters in batch files.
SORT	Sorts input.
START	Starts a separate window to run a specified program or command.
SUBST	Associates a path with a drive letter.

13

COMMAND
PROMPT TOOLS

continues

Table 13.3   continued

Command	Usage
TIME	Displays or sets the system time.
TITLE	Sets the window title for a CMD.EXE session.
TREE	Graphically displays the directory structure of a drive or path.
TYPE	Displays the contents of a text file.
VER	Displays the Windows version.
VERIFY	Tells Windows whether to verify that your files are written correctly to a disk.
VOL	Displays a disk volume label and serial number.
XCOPY	Copies files and directory trees.

Using the HELP Command

HELP is the first command you should learn how to use at the Command Prompt. As mentioned earlier, Table 13.3 is taken directly from a listing produced by the HELP command. But Table 13.3 *doesn't* give you the actual syntax or an example of how to use the command. To get the syntax of any command, you can type HELP <COMMAND> at the command prompt, where <COMMAND> is the command with which you want more help. You also can use the format <COMMAND>/? to get help for a command. Either way, you will find that by using this additional method to get more information about each command, using commands in the Command Prompt window can be made a simple process.

You can work with the XCOPY command to see an example of the HELP command in action. The text says that XCOPY allows you to copy files and directory trees, XCOPY is a much more powerful command than that information indicates. To learn about the command, type HELP XCOPY, then press return. You will see the following:

```
Copies files and directory trees.

XCOPY source [destination] [/A | /M] [/D[:date]] [/P] [/S [/E]] [/V] [/W]
       [/C] [/I] [/Q] [/F] [/L] [/H] [/R] [/T] [/U]
       [/K] [/N] [/Z]

source        Specifies the file(s) to copy.
destination   Specifies the location and/or name of new files.
/A            Copies files with the archive attribute set,
                  doesn't change the attribute.
/M            Copies files with the archive attribute set,
                  turns off the archive attribute.
/D:m-d-y      Copies files changed on or after the specified date.
                  If no date is given, copies only those files whose
                  source time is newer than the destination time.
```

```
/P          Prompts you before creating each destination file.
/S          Copies directories and subdirectories except empty ones.
/E          Copies directories and subdirectories, including empty ones.
                Same as /S /E. May be used to modify /T.
/V          Verifies each new file.
/W          Prompts you to press a key before copying.
/C          Continues copying even if errors occur.
/I          If destination does not exist and copying more than one file,
                assumes that destination must be a directory.
/Q          Does not display file names while copying.
/F          Displays full source and destination file names while copying.
/L          Displays files that would be copied.
/H          Copies hidden and system files also.
/R          Overwrites read-only files.
/T          Creates directory structure, but does not copy files. Does not
                include empty directories or subdirectories. /T /E includes
                empty directories and subdirectories.
/U          Copies only files that already exist in destination.
/K          Copies attributes. Normal Xcopy will reset read-only attributes.
/N          Copies using the generated short names.
/Z          Copies networked files in restartable mode.
```

13

COMMAND
PROMPT TOOLS

Caution

There is a difference between using HELP <COMMAND> and <COMMAND> /?. Both versions work for all the commands in Table 13.1, but for commands that are not part of the basic command set, you need to use the /? syntax to get help. This condition is true because most of these commands are based on specific utilities and contain their own help text.

As you can see in the listing above, XCOPY has a number of command line switches you can use, and you can use it to copy files and all the files and subdirectories to another location. Without using the HELP command, you might never have known that XCOPY can copy hidden files, or prompt you before copying files so you can select some and not others.

Practice regularly using the HELP command or the /? variation. Either version works not just with these built-in Command Prompt commands, but also with commands you can execute at the Command Prompt for other Windows XP components. For example, while you can map network file shares using Windows Explorer, it is much simpler to create a script file for a user so that when they log on file shares are automatically mapped by using NET commands contained in the script file. You might want to use one file for each user or create a single file that all users share. However, by creating a script, or batch file, you can automate a lot of processes. Note the IF command in Table 13.3. You can make the mapping of drives conditional based on environment variables, for example.

The NET Command

The NET command, as you just learned in the previous section, can be used to map a network file share (or a printer) so that your computer can access it as if it were directly attached to your computer. Yet, this is one of those commands that is not included in the basic set of Command Prompt commands. This is because NET was added to provide support for networking components of the operating system. If your computer isn't networked, then you have no use for this command.

To get help for this command, use NET /? at the Command Prompt. Entering this command will produce the following help text:

```
The syntax of this command is:

NET [ ACCOUNTS | COMPUTER | CONFIG | CONTINUE | FILE | GROUP | HELP |
  HELPMSG | LOCALGROUP | NAME | PAUSE | PRINT | SEND | SESSION |
  SHARE | START | STATISTICS | STOP | TIME | USE | USER | VIEW ]
```

As you can see from this, you still don't get a good idea of how to use the NET command. However, one other feature of the built-in help that most of these external commands have that the regular HELP command doesn't is the ability to ask for still more help. For example, what does the command NET USE do? Enter NET USE /?, and you will get the following response:

```
The syntax of this command is:

NET USE [devicename | *] [\\computername\sharename[\volume] [password | *]]
  [/USER:[domainname\]username]
  [[/DELETE] | [/PERSISTENT:{YES | NO}]]

NET USE [devicename | *] [password | *]] [/HOME]

NET USE [/PERSISTENT:{YES | NO}]
```

As you can see, this command can be used to connect to a shared resource on another computer. The help text even gives you the example. Note here that when a vertical bar is used between choices contained in brackets, which are optional components you can use with the command, it means you can use one or the other, but not both at the same time.

For example, if you want to use a file share called ACCTFILES offered by a server called NJADVSRV on a network using a domain account (domain=TWOINC.COM, username=OGLE-TREE), you could use the following syntax:

```
NET USE G: \\NJADVSRV\ACCTFILES /USER:TWOINC.COM\OGLETREE
```

This command tells the operating system to connect to the file share called ACCTFILES that resides on the server NJADVSRV, and to authenticate the user using a domain account (domain=TWOINC.COM, username=OGLETREE). Since the command text specified a drive letter (G:), you can now access files on the ACCTFILES file share as if they were simply on a drive G: on your computer. You can open files from applications, use Windows Explorer, and so on, and G: will show up so you can access files just like they were on your local computer.

If you look back at the help text for NET USE /? you can see that in addition to using a drive letter (G: in this example), you can also use the asterisk. This is an example of using one or the other. If you use the asterisk, for example, in the same NET USE command you used to connect to the ACCTFILES file share, then the operating system would choose the drive letter to use. Hence, these are mutually exclusive options. You can specify the drive letter or use the wildcard * to let the operating system choose what drive letter to use. You will see this sort of thing in a lot of commands that you can execute at the Command Prompt.

Another useful thing you can use the NET command for is to find out just what the network scene looks like. For example, you might not know what file shares you are connected to and want to see the specific details. You can use the NET USE command with no other parameters to see this information. When used in this format it will show a display similar to the following:

```
New connections will be remembered.Status Local Remote Network
-------------------------------------------------------------------------------
OK    X:   \\twoinc-njadvsrv\ishare Microsoft Windows Network
OK    Y:   \\twoinc-njadvsrv\cshare Microsoft Windows Network
OK    Z:   \\twoinc-njadvsrv\jshare Microsoft Windows Network
The command completed successfully.
```

However, suppose you want to connect to a network file share on another computer, and you don't know the name of the servers that you have access to, much less what file shares they offer. You can use the NET VIEW command by itself to find out the other computers on your network and the NET VIEW \\<SERVERNAME> to see the shares offered by a particular server. In the following example, we begin with NET VIEW:

```
Server Name Remark--------------------------------------------------------------
-----------------\\TWOINC-NJADVSRV
\\ZIRA    XP Professional Multi Media
The command completed successfully.
```

Now that you can see there is a server called TWOINC-NJADVSRV, you can find out what shares it offers to the network that you might be able to connect. Use the syntax NET VIEW \\TWOINC-NJADVSRV: and you get the following response:

```
Shared resources at \\twoinc-njadvsrvShare name Type Used as Comment
-------------------------------------------------------------------------------
CSHARE        Disk       Y:
fshare        Disk
HPLaserJ      Print   HP LaserJet 6L
```

```
ishare          Disk      X:
jshare          Disk      Z:
NETLOGON        Disk   Logon server share
ono             Disk
Room999p        Print   NYC, Bldg. 8, B/W Laser printer
SYSVOL          Disk   Logon server share
The command completed successfully.
```

There is simply not enough room in this chapter to go into all the specifics of the NET command, so a few helpful uses of two of the other command line options are as follows:

- NET USE <*driveletter*>: /DELETE—This will disconnect you from a file share.

- NET USE <driveletter>: \\<*server*>\<*sharename*> /PERSISTENT:YES—Use the YES or NO qualifier. If you use YES, then the file share connection will be reestablished when you reboot the computer and log in. If you use the NO option, then it won't be reconnected. Using NO for temporary connections can help keep your computer from becoming cluttered with a lot of file shares that keep reconnecting everything you log onto the computer.

Using Redirector Commands for Input and Output

Many Command Prompt commands produce output text on the screen. For example, if you type the DIR command, the program produces a list of your current directory's files. If the directory holds a lot of files, however, the listing might scroll off the screen.

You can use the Command Prompt window's scrollbars to reach off-screen text, but two other methods can be more useful if you want to do more than just view the output of a command. You can use a filter to "page" the input, a process explained in the next section of this chapter. You can also use a redirection symbol to send the output somewhere else like a file.

You can use the following redirection symbols:

- >—The "greater than" sign on your keyboard sends the output of the command to some place other than the screen, such as to a file. The command DIR > C:\MYDIRECTORY.TXT produces a file called C:\MYDIRECTORY.TXT that contains the output of the directory listing.

- <—The "less than" sign on your keyboard causes the command to accept input from a source other than the keyboard, such as from another command. For example, using the command SORT < C:\MYDIRECTORY.TXT applies the SORT command to the output from the mydirectory.txt file.

- >>—Two greater than signs with no spaces in between are used to add to a file that already exists, instead of overwriting it. The > redirector can create a file if it doesn't exist; if a previous file does exist, it is overwritten by the > redirector. If it does exist, it will be overwritten. Therefore, if you want to add to a file that already exists, instead of overwriting it (and losing the previous contents), use >> instead. For example, using the `DIR >> C:\MYDIRECTORY.TXT` adds a listing from the new directory to the directory file you previously created. Adding `C:\` to the filename locates the output file in the same place so you can add to it. For example, you can specify any path such as `C:\STUFF\`, if you want to store the information in a particular place on your disk.

- >&—The greater than symbol and ampersand together with no space between create a redirection symbol used to redirect input/output (I/O) streams. The Command Prompt uses three input/output (I/O) streams, each of which is numbered. Table 13.4 shows the three streams and the names associated with them.

Table 13.4   Standard I/O Streams

Numeric Value	Stream Name
0	stdin (standard input)
1	stdout (standard output)
2	stderr (standard error)

The first two redirectors in the preceding list are used in many Command Prompt commands. As a matter of fact, you can even combine them on the same command line. For example, look at the following commands closely and try to figure out what they do:

```
C:> DIR > MYDIRECTORY.TXT
C:> SORT < MYDIRECTORY.TXT > SORTED.TXT
```

You have already seen the first line in this chapter; it creates a file that contains the output from the `DIR COMMAND`. In the second line, the `SORT` command, which is also a filter (again, discussed in the following section), takes as its input the text you stored in the file `MYDIRECTORY.TXT` and then sends the output from the sort command to the new file called `SORTED.TXT`. If you use the `TYPE` command to display the contents of a file on your screen, you see that `SORTED.TXT` is nothing more than the same lines of text found in `MYDIRECTORY.TXT`, only sorted alphabetically.

Using the >& redirector is more complicated and typically is reserved for batch files. For example, the Command Prompt uses the `stderr` stream to send error messages to the screen, as shown here:

```
C:\>DIR YOKO.TXT
Volume in drive C has no label.
Volume Serial Number is BC32-E130
Directory of C:\
File Not Found
```

This error message occurred because the file YOKO.TXT does not exist, at least in the current directory, but consider this example:

```
C:\>DIR YOKO.TXT > FILELIST.TXT 2>&1

C:\>TYPE FILELIST.TXT
Volume in drive C has no label.
Volume Serial Number is BC32-E130
Directory of C:\
File Not Found
```

The DIR command in the first line above produces a directory listing and requests the output be sent to the file named FILELIST.TXT. That same command line, however, goes on to redirect the standard error output (value of 2) to the standard output stream (value of 1). Because the > redirector has already sent the standard output to the file FILELIST.TXT, the error message appears in the output file instead. The second command line uses the TYPE command to type the contents of FILELIST.TXT, producing the error message.

Although this seems unnecessarily complex, the >& symbol can be a useful tool when you are writing complicated batch files. In those cases, sometimes it is easier to receive input from one file, output it to another (and possibly use a command in between), and then parse the output file without seeing anything on the screen. Temporary files, like FILELIST.TXT, can be deleted by the batch file during its execution, so you never have to know it even exists.

You can get quite creative in using these operators in batch files to allow your script to search for results in temporary files you create, and then use IF and other commands to determine the flow of control in the batch file. However, you should do lots of testing when you write batch files and look at the intermediary results to be sure that your batch file is operating as you intended.

Pipes and Filters

Filters are much like commands, with one important difference: filters process input and produce output. You can use the following filters to manipulate the input or output from a command you execute at the Command Prompt:

- MORE—This filter will displays the output from a command or file one page at a time. By pressing the spacebar, the MORE command displays data one line at a time. By pressing the Enter key, the command displays one screen of data at a time.

- FIND—Use this filter to search through files (or the output from a command) and to display only those files that contain the text you are trying to find. The FIND command displays the name of the file(s) containing your search text, as well as just the lines from those file(s) that contain the search text.

- SORT—This filter, as you learned in the preceding example, sorts the output from a command or file.

A pipe is the vertical bar (|) symbol, and it is a useful tool for working with filters. In general, you should use the > redirection symbol to send the contents of a file to a command, but the | symbol when sending the output from a command to another command.

For example, with the MORE command, you can use the following syntax to see a page listing of all the files on your C: drive, although it would take some time to page through that many files:

```
DIR C: | MORE
```

In this example, the DIR command is used to get a listing of all the files on the C: drive. The | takes the output from the DIR command and sends it to the MORE filter, which pages the output. Alternatively, you could use the > redirector to send the output of the DIR command to a file named MYLIST.TXT and then use the following syntax:

```
TYPE MYLIST.TXT | MORE
```

Note here the difference between redirection and the pipe symbol. By using | with the DIR command, you can eliminate the necessity of creating a temporary file. The output of the command, when used with |, is sent via stdin to the command that follows it.

> **Tip**
>
> Another interesting trick you can use to manipulate Command Prompt commands is to separate multiple values for some commands with a comma or semicolon. For example, DIR A*.*, B*.*, C.* returns all files that start with the letters A, B, or C, and the commas in this command line help produce three executions of the directory command instead of a single list containing all the files that match these patterns.

Get More from Your Commands with Wildcards

Wildcards are symbols that take the place of unknown or random characters in commands. Wildcards are used to indicate in a filename that all or part of the filename (or the filename extension) doesn't matter. Wildcards tell the command to just match up certain specified characters and return all files that match, ignoring other characters.

The two wildcards that you can use are as follows:

- *—The asterisk character wildcard, when used in a filename, means that the command should ignore all characters other than those you specify when matching and returning filenames. For example, in the filename adam*, the match would return file names adam, adams, adamson, adamsley, and so on.

- ?—The question mark wildcard tells the command to ignore a specific number of characters when matching up filenames. Using the preceding example, the filename adam?, would return matches for adams, adama, adamt, and so on.

To examine these wildcard characters a little further, take a look at the following command:

DIR *.DOC

This command tells the DIR command to display all files that end with .DOC, regardless of what characters come before the extension period. You can use the * wildcard anywhere in a filename:

- DIR ABC*.DOC—This command lists all files that have as the first three letters of their filename ABC, regardless of what else follows in the filename up to the period character. For example, ABCD.DOC and ABCDEFGHG.DOC would both be listed to the screen using this version of the DIR command. The * wildcard makes a command use the characters you specify, as well as finds all files that have those letters, regardless of how many characters follow.

- DIR A*.DOC—This command lists all files that begin with the letter *A* and end with the file extension .DOC.

- DIR ABC*DEF.DOC—Note here I have placed the asterisk character in the *middle* of a filename. This will return a directory listing of all files that start with ABC and end with DEF, regardless of what other characters are in between.

- DIR MYFILE.*—This causes the DIR command to return all files that have MYFILE as the filename, regardless of their extension. MYFILE.DOC, MYFILE.RTF, and MYFILE.TXT all will show up in the directory display.

The ? wildcard can be used in the following ways:

- DIR FEB0?.DOC—This command produces a list of files such as FEB01.DOC, FEB02.DOC, and so on but does *not* list files like FEB10.DOC, since the original command line specified that the first character following FEB in the filename must be 0 and not 1.

- DIR FEB??.DOC—This example uses two question marks, so it returns a listing of such files named FEB01.DOC and FEB02.DOC, but it also includes in the listing FEB10.DOC, since in this example, you have two question marks indicating the two specific wildcard positions.

- `DIR MYFILE.W??`—This example uses the question mark again, and will return only files that start with `MYFILE`, followed by the W character in the first position and any characters in the next two positions. The `DIR` command then lists files such as `MYFILE.WPF` or `MYFILE.WP3`. However, since the question mark only "wildcards" a single character, you would not see a file such as `MYFILE.WXYZ` because it contains four characters in the file extension where the question mark wildcard characters are used.

Wildcards are useful feature especially with the `DIR` command. However, they can be useful with other Command Prompt commands such as `FIND` and others. Learn to use wildcards, and they will make it a lot easier to narrow your search for files.

Working with Batch Files

A batch file is a file that contains Command Prompt commands and commands from other utilities, such as the `NET` command. Batch files have many uses, but perhaps one of the most common is to create user logon scripts. You can configure a batch file that uses specific commands to configure a user's environment when the user logs into the system. Unix developers use batch files to simplify system administration tasks. Scripting and batch files are a topic for an entire book, but here just remember that many of Windows XP's GUI applications (such as Dynamic Host Configuration Protocol, or DHCP, and Dynamic Name System, or DNS) have an equivalent set of commands that can be used at the Command Prompt, and thus with batch files.

To create a batch file you use an ordinary ASCII text editor. Enter the commands you want to execute one line after another. You can use pipes and filters in batch files so that the input or output from one command can be used by another command. You can create temporary files. You can also use a few other items in your batch files to make them act almost like programs. For example, in Table 13.3, you may have noticed the `if` command, as well as the `goto` and `for` commands. These can be used to make your batch file execute some commands, depending on the results of previous commands. This conditional branching gives you the capability to make creating batch files that can adapt to different conditions or selections made by users.

The basic set of batch commands used to control program flow and execution are as follows:

- `call`
- `echo`
- `endlocal`
- `for`

- goto
- if
- pause
- rem
- setlocal
- shift
- %

The syntax for these commands can become very complex. For more information about using these commands use the /? help command line switch.

You can also use the Windows Scripting Host to run script files that are written using VBScript or Jscript. In the next section of this chapter, you will learn about using the Task Scheduler command line tool schtasks to schedule batch files, programs, and commands. Here is the syntax for using the cscript command to execute script files:

```
Cscript [scriptname] [host options] [script arguments]
```

The scriptname is the name of the script file to run. You will need to include the path and the file extension so that cscript will know where to find the file and how to execute it. The script arguments are command-line switches that get passed to the script. Note that you should always precede script command-line switches with the slash character (/). The host options are command-line switches that control certain features of the Windows Scripting Host features, as follows:

- //B—This runs the script in batch mode, so you will not see any alerts or script errors or be able to solicit input using prompts.
- //D—This turns on the debugger, so you can troubleshoot script problems.
- //E:engine—Use this to specify the scripting language of the script file.
- //H:cscript or //H:wscript—This will register which scripting host you wish to use for the default when running script files. The default is wscript.
- //I—The opposite of batch mode, this indicates the script should be run interactively.
- //JOB:xxxx—This specifies the job identified in a .wsf script file. Substitute the job for xxxx.
- //LOGO—The Windows Script Host banner is displayed in the console window when a script runs. This is a default you can override by using //NOLOGO instead.
- //S—This will save the current command-prompt options for the current user.

- //T:nnnn—This indicates the maximum amount of time (in seconds) that a script can run. The maximum you can specify is 32,767 seconds. If you do not use this, then the amount of time a script file can run is infinite.

- //X—This starts the script in the debugger.

> **Note**
>
> For more information about using the Windows Script Host, read the articles at Microsoft's Web site or the documentation that comes with the scripting language you choose to use. Since Microsoft has announced that it will not be including Java support in the new Internet Explorer, it may be that Jscript will no longer be supported. As things stand at this time, however, many PC manufacturers have announced that they will provide Java support on PCs on which they preinstall Windows XP, and some Web sites will allow you to download the necessary code to run Java on Windows XP.

Using the Command Line Task Scheduler (schtasks)

The schtasks command is the command line interface that can be used instead of the GUI application Scheduled Tasks in the Control Panel. If you are a die-hard command line worker, you will like schtasks.

> **Note**
>
> The schtasks command is the replacement for the old AT command. Windows still supports that command, but schtasks is much more flexible. If you have written script or batch files that use the AT command, you might want to consider rewriting them to use this newer command, which more closely matches what you can do with GUI to the Schedule service.

The syntax for schtasks is as follows:

```
schtasks /parameter [arguments]
Parameter List:
 /Create  Creates a new scheduled task.

 /Delete  Deletes the scheduled task(s).
```

13

COMMAND
PROMPT TOOLS

```
/Query   Displays all scheduled tasks.

/Change  Changes the properties of scheduled task.

/Run    Runs the scheduled task immediately.

/End    Stops the currently running scheduled task.

/?      Displays this help/usage.
```

Although this syntax looks relatively simple, it truly is a powerful interface into the scheduling of batch files. As the help text shows, you can schedule a new task (`/create`), or you can delete a scheduled task (`/delete`). You can also use the other command-line switches to perform a variety of tasks, from changing the run-time particulars of a specific task, or even running a task immediately to test if it does what you want.

Creating a Scheduled Task

After you have created a batch file containing the commands you want to execute on a scheduled basis, use the `schtasks/create` command to create the task. After the task is created, it will run, as you further specify. For example, you can specify a task run every five minutes, every week, or even when a user logs onto the system, but the first thing to do is to create the task. The options to the `/create` option are numerous. Let us examine the following command-line switches you can use with the `schtasks/create` command:

- `/S system`—This switch (SYSTEM) can be used to specify a remote system on which the task will run. If you do not include this switch, then the task will run on the system on which you created it.

- `/U username`—This switch indicates the user context that the command should be executed under.

- `/P password`—This switch specifies a password for the account if you use the `/U` switch. This prevents just anyone from running a task under your name.

- `/RU username`—This switch can be used to specify the username of the account that the scheduled task will be run under. Keep in mind that the user account must possess the necessary rights and access privileges to access any resources your scheduled batch file requires. You can use NT AUTHORITY\SYSTEM or SYSTEM if you want this task to run under the built-in system account that the Windows XP system uses itself. However, you cannot run tasks that will require user interaction, such as Notepad, because the internal system account, by default, does not have the right to log on interactively.

- `/RP password`—This is the password for the user account under which the task will be run. If you use the asterisk character (*), the system will prompt the user before executing the task to enter the password. For the system account, this is not necessary.

- `SC schedule`—This switch defines when the task will be run. You can specify the following: `MINUTE, HOURLY, DAILY, WEEKLY, MONTHLY, ONCE, ONSTART, ONLOGON,` or `ONIDLE`.

- `/MO modifier`—This switch allows you to further control the frequency under which the task is scheduled to run. Consider it a fine-tuning control for the `SC` switch. You learn more about this in other command-line switches in this list.

- `/D days`—This switch allows you to choose the days of the week on which the task will run. You can use the following values with this switch: MON, TUE, WED, THU, FRI, SAT, SUN. If you are using a monthly schedule, then you can use the numeric values of 1 to 31 to specify the days of the month on which the task should be run.

- `/M months`—This is the MONTHLY switch. If you only need a batch file to run certain months (like those darn quarterly audits), you can use this switch to specify the month. The valid options for this switch are JAN, FEB, MAR, APR, MAY, JUN, JUL, AUG, SEP, OCT, NOV, and DEC. The task will run on the first day of the month you specify.

- `/I idletime`—This is the IDLE TIME switch. The task runs after a specified amount of time, during which the system is idle. You can specify from 1 to 999 minutes of idle time using this switch.

- `/TN taskname`—This switch gives you the capability to name a task so that it is more recognizable when you view the scheduled task list.

- `/TR task`—This switch can be used to specify the path and filename of the program that the task will run. Remember that you can execute both programs and batch files using the Task Scheduler.

- `/ST starttime`—This switch is used to indicate the time of day to start running the task. Keep in mind that a 24-hour clock is used, so you cannot specify a.m. or p.m. Instead, use the 24-hour format. For example, to run a task at 1:00 in the afternoon, use 13:00 instead of 1:00, which would run the task at 1:00 a.m.!

- `/SD startdate`—Use the format MM/DD/YYYY to specify the date on which the task will first start. Valid for all schedule types, but required for the ONCE type.

- `/ED enddate`—Use the same MM/DD/YYYY format to specify the last day a task should run. This switch cannot be used with the ONCE, ONSTART, ONLOGON or ONIDLE schedule types. If you don't specify an ending date, a task will continue to be scheduled (unless is scheduled to run ONCE).

13

COMMAND
PROMPT TOOLS

A few things to note is that when you submit a task using this command, it does not verify that the password you entered is correct, and if you change the password for a user account before or between runs of this command, the task will fail to run. No checking is done either to see if the command, batch file, or other entity exists that you wish to run, so it is a good idea to perform a run of the task once to make sure it is going to work.

> ### Tip
>
> The syntax for the `schtasks` command is quite complicated! If you forget the exact syntax you need to use (and you don't have this book handy), just remember that you can always use the built-in help for this kind of command. For example, you can enter either SCHTASKS /? or SCHTASKS CREATE MONTHLY /? to get specific information on how to use the command.

Although `schtasks` can be used to run GUI programs that pop up and with which users can interact, it will not do so for those that run under the Internal System Account, since this account is usually reserved for running system components and does not possess the interactive logon right.

If you are going to run a command or program, you can either create a separate task for each of them or just one batch file that contains multiple commands. You cannot stack up commands or program executable names on a single command line.

Using SCHTASKS /CREATE

Just giving you the syntax for a command is usually enough to get you started. However, since this command is so powerful, take some time to review the following examples of how to create new tasks.

To schedule a task to run every 15 minutes, you could use a command line like the following:

```
schtasks /create /sc minute /mo 15 /tn "disk cleanup" /tr c:\utils\diskclean.bat
```

This example will create a task that runs every 15 minutes (`/sc minute` and `/mo 15`), and it will run a batch file called `diskclean.bat` located in the `C:\UTILS` directory. After you enter the command, you are prompted for your username, since another user was not specified on the command line.

You can also create tasks to run under someone else's user account, as with the following:

```
schtasks /create /sc hourly /u johndoe /p password /tn "disk cleanup" /tr
c:\utils\diskclean.bat
```

This task will run every hour under the account name of johndoe, and since the command line supplies the password, the schtasks program won't prompt for one.

You will find lots of help about how to use the schtasks command in the help file. For example, you can use the /change switch to modify a task that is already in the schedule. This could be used, for example, to modify a user account name or password. Using /change, you don't have to recreate the entire task again. To test a task command line that you have created, use the /run switch to see if the task will run immediately and do what you expect it to do. This can be very useful for debugging problems with your command syntax.

The /end switch can be used to stop a task that is currently running. Note that this doesn't remove the task from the schedule. It will run again if you have set up a task to run on regular basis. Use the /delete switch to remove a task from the schedule.

To get a listing of tasks that are currently scheduled on your system, use the switch /query. Actually, you can simply enter the schtasks command by itself to get a listing. However, /query allows you to do such things as control the format of the listing.

Check the Results of Scheduled Tasks

The scheduled tasks you create are run by the scheduler service and a logfile is produced that you can examine periodically to ensure that things are running smoothly. The log file can be found in %systemroot%\SchedlgU.txt. This is the Task Scheduler service transaction log, so you will find records here for both the tasks you create using the schtasks command, as well as those you use the GUI interface to create.

> **Note**
>
> The GUI equivalent of schtask is covered in Chapter 14, "Using the Control Panel."

Network Commands

In Chapters 24 and 25, you learn about networking your computer with other computers and making connections to the Internet. Although most people are familiar with using a network browser to search for interesting content on the Internet, you should be aware of a few commands that have been around for a long time. Diagnostic commands, such as ping and tracert are discussed in Chapter 23, "Disaster Recovery." However, several applications are available at the command line that you may find useful. Use the /? switch to obtain further help for these commands:

- Telnet—This is standard remote terminal application developed early in the development of the transfer call protocol/Internet protocol suite (TCP/IP). As with the rest of the commands listed here, Telnet requires a server and a client program. You can use the syntax `telnet servername` or `telnet ipaddress` to establish a remote character-cell (that is, Command Prompt–like interface) into a remote system that runs a Telnet server service. For example, a Windows XP client could use telnet to make a connection to a Windows 2000 or Windows 2002 server to execute commands, if allowed by the server. Telnet is an important tool for administrators who remotely manage systems. However, when used on a wide area network like the Internet, your username and password are sent as clear text! Use a dial-up connection to your server or a virtual private network (VPN) connection instead.

- FTP— File Transfer Protocol (FTP) is a very useful utility. Again, Windows XP includes client software, and servers include the server side of this equation. You can post files to another computer using this command to list the directories (provided you have permission to do so), as well as to upload or download files.

There are other standard TCP/IP commands to issue at the command prompt, such as `nslookup` (to find the name or address of a remote system); `ping` (to determine if a remote system is reachable); and `tracert` (to see the route your packets are taking to get to their destination or where they are stopping when problems occur). Another useful command is `hostname`; it returns the computer's TCP/IP name.

How to Create an MS-DOS Startup Disk

In Windows 95/98/Me you can create an MS-DOS startup disk to assist you when you are troubleshooting serious problems on your computer. Windows NT and Windows 2000 didn't offer this capability, but it is back in Windows XP. Just use the following steps:

1. Insert a floppy disk into the disk drive.
2. Click on Start and then My Computer.
3. Right-click on the floppy drive. From the menu presented, select Format.
4. In the Format Options dialog box, select the check box Create an MS-DOS Startup Disk, as shown in Figure 13.6.
5. Click Start to begin the formatting procedure. When the warning dialog box appears, click OK.

FIGURE 13.6

*You can create an
MS-DOS startup
floppy disk using
Windows XP.*

> **Tip**
>
> You should have a bootable floppy disk (or two) around and stored in a safe place. A bootable disk of any kind can be a lifesaver when you are having problems booting the computer.

Summary

Although this chapter only touches on its capabilities, the Command Prompt is a powerful tool. You can use the built-in commands or commands that other Windows components provide. The NET command can quickly give you an overview of your network connections and help you map or unmap network drives.

In this chapter, you learned to configure the Command Prompt window fonts, buffers, and screen colors to make the Command prompt seem more attractive and user friendly. You also learned how to use several Command Prompt commands, filters, and redirectors to issue and manipulate command results. You saw that the capabilities provided by these schtasks can either intimidate you or if you are used to command-line utilities, make the GUI version seem insignificant.

This chapter also explained how to use the help command to get the syntax for each of the available commands listed in the chapter and to see just how far you can go with these commands. You may be surprised to find that many tasks are more easily accomplished using the Command Prompt than trying to find one or more GUI applications that do the same thing.

Using the
Control Panel

CHAPTER 14

IN THIS CHAPTER

- Using the Classic or the Category View   *330*

- Using the Appearances and Themes Category   *331*

- Network and Internet Connections   *344*

- Add or Remove Programs   *345*

- Sounds, Speech and Audio Devices   *345*

- Performance and Maintenance   *348*

- Printers and Other Hardware   *354*

- User Accounts   *355*

- Date, Time, Language and Regional Options   *355*

- Accessibility Options   *355*

- The New Help and Support Application   *355*

Most Windows XP configuration is handled using a number of utilities found in the Windows Control Panel, often called *applets* because they are like small programs. You can configure settings ranging from keyboard and display preferences to network connections to user accounts using various Control Panel applets. In this chapter, you will learn how to use the Control Panel to configure many different Windows settings.

> **Note**
>
> A number of the utilities in the Control Panel are covered in other chapters. If you don't find what you are looking for here, look for the name of the Control Panel utility in the index of this book.

Using the Classic or the Category View

You can open the Control Panel window directly from the Start menu. If you have used previous versions of Windows, you will notice a change the first time you open the Control Panel. By default, a category view (see Figure 14.1) is used that is supposed to make it easier for new Windows users to get around. This view presents a number of broad categories that, when clicked, open other windows with tasks pertinent to that category. For example, clicking the category named Appearance and Themes leads to tasks such as changing the desktop background and screensaver. At the bottom of each category window, you will also find links to the actual Control Panel applets that fit within the category.

If you have used Windows before, the classic view of the Control Panel, which simply lists all of the Control Panel applets in a single window, is still offered. Just click the Switch to Classic View link at the left of the Control Panel window.

> **Note**
>
> Most of the traditional Control Panel utilities fit neatly within the categories listed in the Control Panel's Category View window. However, many applications that you install also create their own entries in the Control Panel. You can get to these by clicking the Other Control Panel Options link at the left of the Control Panel window.

FIGURE **14.1**

The new Control Panel presents a menu to the user.

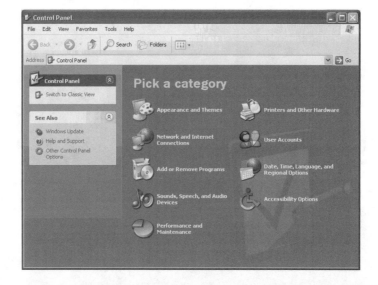

Tip

If you use the Control Panel often, you may find it useful to display the Control Panel item on the Start menu as a folder rather than a simple shortcut. Right-click anywhere on the Windows Task Bar and choose Properties. On the dialog box that opens, switch to the Start Menu tab and click Customize next to the Start Menu option (if you are using the classic Start menu view, click that Customize button). On the Customize Start Menu dialog box that opens, switch to the Advanced tab. In the Start Menu Items section of the Advanced tab, choose Display as Menu option in the Control Panel group.

14

USING THE
CONTROL PANEL

Throughout this chapter, you will learn to use the Control Panel using the Category View. Each of the major sections in the chapter presents a category, and is broken down into the tasks you can perform within that category. Once you are familiar with the Control Panel, you may find it easier and faster to use the Classic View first.

Using the Appearances and Themes Category

The Appearance and Themes category (see Figure 14.2) is used to control the way your desktop looks. You can choose a task to perform or select one of the Control Panel applets from the bottom of the window.

FIGURE **14.2**

Use the Appearance and Themes category to configure the look of the desktop.

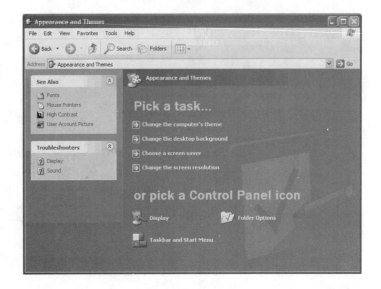

Using the task list and Control Panel applets are really just two different ways of doing the same thing. Clicking an applet opens a tabbed dialog box for configuring that aspect of Windows, the same as opening the applet from the Control Panel's Classic View. For example, clicking the Display icon opens a dialog with tabs for controlling desktop background, themes, screensavers, and more.

Each of the tasks available in a category are really just shortcuts to one of the tabs of the dialog boxes you can open using the icons at the bottom of the window. For example, clicking the Choose a Screen Saver taskbar opens the Display applet and then switches automatically to the Screen Saver tab.

The tasks available in the Appearance and Themes category include the following:

- Change the computer's theme
- Change the desktop background
- Choose a screen saver
- Change the screen resolution

Configuring all of these tasks and other display properties, as well as using the Taskbar and Start Menu applet, are covered in detail in Chapter 7, "Up Front: The New Desktop."

This section focuses on the remaining applet available in this category, Folder Options.

Folder Options

The Folder Options dialog box consists of four tabs, which contain settings that govern how folders work in Windows XP. These four tabs include the following:

- General—Configure basic folder options, such as whether opening a folder opens a new window.

- View—Configure advanced folder settings and change the default folder options used in Windows.

- File Types—Configure file extensions recognized by Windows and the programs associated with them.

- Offline Files—Configure how Windows handles offline files, which are shared files on a network that are made available when your computer is not attached to the network

General Properties

The General tab lets you configure a few minor settings. These options include the following:

- Tasks—Use the Show Common Tasks in Folders option to have Windows display links for tasks relating to a folder's contents within the folder window. These are common tasks, such as deleting items, creating new folders, and renaming files. The Use Windows classic folders option leaves folders looking much the way they have in previous versions of Windows.

- Browse Folders—Choose whether opening a folder opens the folder inside the same window you are currently using or opens a new window in which to display the folder you are opening. Whichever setting you use, you can override it (and use the opposite action) while opening a folder by holding down the Control key.

- Click Items as Follows—Choose whether it takes a single-click or double-click to open a folder or launch an item. Using the single-click feature makes Windows look and feel a little more like a Web page, but it does require some getting used to. If you choose the single-click feature, you can also elect whether to have Windows underline the icon titles (making them similar to links on a Web page).

If you have made settings on the General tab that you are unhappy with, just click the Restore Defaults button to revert to the default Windows settings.

View Properties

The View tab lets you configure a number of items governing how folders are presented in Windows XP (see Figure 14.3).

14

USING THE
CONTROL PANEL

FIGURE 14.3

Use the View tab to configure how Windows presents folders.

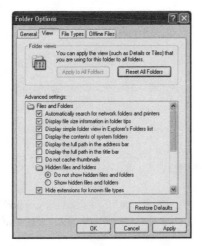

At the top of the tab, you will find the following two buttons:

- Apply to All Folders—Any changes you make with the Advanced Settings list at the bottom of the tab become the default for all folders on the computer. Note that this button makes all view settings configured for the current folder the default, including some that are not made using the View tab. You can learn more about customizing folder views in Chapter 9, "Working With Files and Folders."
- Reset All Folders—This button reverts the default folder settings back to the standard default settings used when Windows is installed.

The Advanced settings section features a long list of folder view settings, including the following:

- Automatically search for network folders and printers.
- Display file size information in folder tips.
- Display simple folder view in Explorer's Folders list.
- Display the contents of system folders.
- Display the full path in the address bar.
- Do not cache thumbnails.
- Hidden files and folders.
- Hide extensions for known files types.
- Hide protected operating system files (recommended).
- Launch folder window in a separate process.
- Restore previous folder windows at logon.

- Show Control Panel in My Computer.
- Show encrypted or compressed NTFS files in color.
- Show pop-up description for folder and desktop items.
- Use simple file sharing (recommended).

Tip

You can get a description of what each of the Advanced settings on the View tab does by right-clicking the option and choosing the What's This? command from the shortcut menu.

File Types Properties

Every file in Windows can have a three-letter extension appended to its file name (the letters following the "dot" or "period"). These extensions are registered with Windows and associated with particular programs so that Windows will know what program to use to open a given file. The File Types tab, shown in Figure 14.4, lists the file extensions associated with programs on your computer.

FIGURE **14.4**

The File Types tab shows file extensions associated with programs.

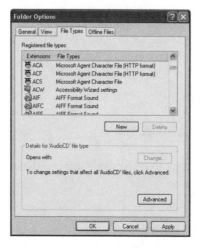

14

USING THE
CONTROL PANEL

Under the Registered Files Types section, you will see one column that displays the file extension and a second that gives a description of the type of file for which the extension is used.

Use the New button to open a simple dialog box that lets you add a new three-letter extension to the list. Use the Delete button to remove an extension from the list.

Select any extension on the list and click the Change button to choose a program with which to associate the extension. The dialog box that opens presents a simple list of programs installed on your computer, grouped into programs recommended for the file extension and other registered programs. The dialog box also offers a Browse button for locating programs not on the list.

> **Note**
>
> When you install some applications, you are prompted to mark the application as the default for supported file types. Some install programs do not offer this feature. That is why you can change the file association manually. However, remember that an association only specifies which application will be launched automatically when you select a file with the particular file extension. This doesn't control whether that program will be able to use the specified file type.

The final button available on the File Types tab is labeled Advanced, and clicking it opens the Edit File Type dialog box shown in Figure 14.5.

FIGURE 14.5

Editing advanced file types properties.

You can use the Edit File Type dialog box to perform a number of functions, including the following:

- Change the icon used in Windows for files with this extension.
- Change the default action used when a file with this extension is double-clicked. Select a file from the list and click Set Default. Other actions show up on the shortcut menu that appears when a file with the extension is right-clicked.
- Create a new action that can occur using the file. The new actions you can create really depend on the type of file and what program you use.
- Edit an existing action, which allows you to control what program is used to perform the action and set other options that depend on the program being used.

- Remove an action from the list.

- Specify whether files of this type should be automatically opened as soon as they are downloaded.

- Specify whether extensions for files of this type are shown in Windows.

Offline Files Properties

The Folder Options tab lets you enable the use of offline files on your computer and configure a few settings that control how they are used. The Offline Files feature allows you to use files that are shared on a network when you are working offline. Windows does this by copying temporary versions of the files to a local database on your computer.

> **Note**
>
> Appendix C, "Using Windows XP on a Notebook Computer," explains the use of Offline Files in detail. This section focuses only on the settings you can configure on the Offline Files tab of the Folder Options Control Panel applet.

By default, Offline Files are disabled. You can enable the feature by selecting the Enable Offline Files option on the Offline Files tab, as shown in Figure 14.6. Note that if this option is disabled, all of the other options on the tab are unavailable. Also, if you have the Fast User Switching feature of Windows XP enabled, offline files are not available at all; this tab will contain a note to that effect. You will have to disable Fast User switching before you can use Offline Files, a procedure covered later in this chapter.

FIGURE 14.6

Use the Offline Files tab to enable and control the Offline Files feature.

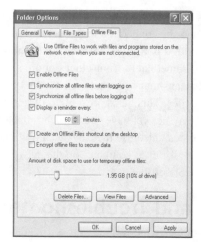

14

USING THE
CONTROL PANEL

Settings available for controlling Offline Files include the following:

- Synchronize All Offline Files When Logging On—A full synchronization is performed when you log on. Any files you have changed on your local computer are updated on the network, and any files that have changed on the network are transferred to your computer. If you leave this option unchecked, a quick synchronization is performed instead, in which only the files you've selected for offline access are downloaded to your computer.

- Synchronize All Offline Files Before Logging Off—This works the same way as the log on option, but the synchronization occurs when you logoff the computer.

- Display a Reminder Every nn Minutes—A balloon warning pops up from the notification area on the Taskbar when your computer is offline.

- Create and Offline Files Shortcut on the Desktop—This option puts an Offline Folders icon on your desktop so you can quickly get to offline items.

- Encrypt Offline Files to Secure Data—Selecting this checkbox will cause the temporary files stored on your computer to be encrypted.

- Amount of Disk Space to Use for Temporary Offline Files—Use the slider to configure the percentage of disk space that the offline files cache may use.

- Delete Files—Use this button to delete offline files stored locally. This button *does not delete the original network file*. It only deletes the offline temporary copies of these files stored on the local hard drive.

- View Files—This button is a shortcut to the Offline Files folder, which contains all the offline files stored on the local computer. The actual folder is stored on your desktop.

- Advanced—This button opens a dialog box that lets you configure what happens when you are working online and the connection to the network is suddenly lost. Your first option is to have Windows notify you that the connection is down and to start working with Offline files immediately. Your other option is to never allow the computer to go offline, which means that if the network connection fails, you will *not* have access to any network files. This helps prevent you from working on locally stored offline files that may not yet have been synchronized with the permanent files on the network. You can also use the Advanced Settings dialog box to configure these same two options for each computer on the network that has files you have configured to be available offline.

The See Also Menu and Troubleshooters

On the left of the Appearance and Themes window (see Figure 14.2), you will find a See Also menu that contains other options relating to the category. In the Appearance and

Themes category, there are three See Also options: Fonts, Mouse Pointers, and High Contrast.

The High Contrast option lets you change the colors of your screen for high contrast viewing and is covered in Chapter 5, "Accessibility Options." The Fonts and Mouse Pointer options are covered in the next two sections.

Fonts

Windows XP comes loaded with enough fonts that you may never have to add another. However, you can get additional fonts if you need them, since Windows offers an easy way to add, delete, and manage them. Clicking the Fonts link opens a Fonts window similar to the one shown in Figure 14.7.

FIGURE 14.7

Selecting Fonts from the See Also menu helps you manage the fonts on your Windows XP computer.

Right-click on any font and select Properties from the shortcut menu to open a dialog box for managing that font. The General tab of this dialog box shows the name and type of the font (such as TrueType), as well as other basic file information. The Summary tab shows additional file properties that may or may not be filled in, such as the title, subject, and author of the file. There is not a lot of useful information on these two tabs for most users. It can be useful, however, for determining when font files were created and stored on the computer and, in some cases, where the fonts originated.

14

USING THE
CONTROL PANEL

> **Note**
>
> The Change button on the General tab of a font's properties dialog box allows you to change the file association for this type of font. The Windows Font Viewer is the default application used to open font files. If you have installed a third-party font application, you can configure it to be the default manager for specific types of fonts.

To add a font to Windows XP, select the Install New Font command from the File menu of the Fonts window. The Add Fonts dialog box opens, which you can use to browse for the font file to install. At the bottom of the Add Fonts dialog box is the option Copy fonts to Fonts folder, which is probably a good idea if this is a font you intend to use a lot. Doing this will make it easier to manage your fonts, since they will all reside in the same location.

For the most part, the other elements of the Fonts window work the same way as a regular folder window. You can rename, delete, copy, and paste fonts the same way you would any other file. The View menu lets you choose from all the normal window views (list, icons, and so on) and also offers two additional views:

- List Fonts by Similarity—This provides a way to view fonts based on how similar they are to any given font you choose, as shown in Figure 14.8. Choose a font from the drop-down list just below the Address bar; all fonts are ordered based on how similar they are to the chosen font.

- Hide Variations (Bold, Italic, and so on)—Many fonts have a number of variations. Examples include Arial and Arial Bold. This view hides the variations so that only the main font family name (Arial in this case) is displayed.

FIGURE 14.8

Viewing fonts based on how similarity to a chosen font.

Mouse Pointers

The Mouse Pointers link on the Appearance and Themes' See Also menu is a shortcut to the Pointer Options tab of the Mouse Properties Control Panel applet, as shown in Figure 14.9.

FIGURE 14.9

Use the Pointer Options tab to configure how the mouse pointer operates in Windows.

You can configure the following settings on the Pointer Options tab:

- Select a Pointer Speed—Move the slider to adjust the speed at which the pointer moves relative to the distance you move your mouse.

- Enhance Pointer Precision–The pointer on the screen can be controlled a little more precisely when moving at slow speeds. If you do precision work, you will find this option invaluable. However, some people find that it slows down their pointer speed considerably.

- Snap To—The option in this section makes the cursor automatically position itself over the default button in any dialog box you open. You may find this convenient or distracting.

- Display Pointer Trails—The cursor on the screen leaves a trail of disappearing cursors behind it as it moves about the screen, much like a trail of smoke. It is helpful on displays (such as those on older notebooks) on which the pointer is often hard to see. You can also adjust the length of the trail.

- Hide Pointer While Typing—If you find that your pointer often obscures the text beneath it, this option will help. The pointer disappears when you start typing and reappears when you move your mouse.

- Show Location of Pointer When I Press the Ctrl Key—This is another option that is great for people who use displays on which it is sometimes hard to see the pointer. Pressing the Ctrl (Control) key highlights the location of the pointer by flashing a series of concentric circles.

14

USING THE
CONTROL PANEL

The other tabs available on the Mouse Properties dialog box let you control such things as the primary button used for clicking, graphics used for various pointers, and how the wheel on your mouse works (if you have one). The following sections examine the other tabs you can configure using the Mouse Control Panel applet.

The Buttons Tab

The Buttons tab, shown in Figure 14.10, lets you configure how Windows interprets the buttons on your mouse.

FIGURE 14.10

The Buttons tab lets you configure the buttons on your mouse.

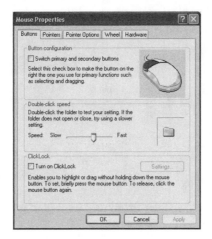

You can control the following settings:

- Switch the Primary and Secondary Buttons—Use this option to toggle the actions of the mouse buttons. When the option is selected, the right mouse button is used to click and double-click, and the left mouse button is used to open shortcut menus. This option is great for left-handed mouse users.

- Adjust the Double-Click Speed—Drag the slider to adjust how fast two clicks must be made to make a double-click. Double-click the folder icon to the right of the slider to test the setting before applying it.

- Turn on ClickLock—Normally, you drag items in Windows by holding down the mouse button while moving the mouse. This option lets you click once (a slightly longer click than a regular single click) to "hold" an item, move your mouse to drag it, and then click again to release it. This option is great for anyone who may have difficulty holding down a mouse button. Click the Settings button to set how long the mouse button must be held down before the single-click is considered locked.

The Pointers Tab

The Pointers tab lets you control the graphics used for the various pointers in Windows. The most common pointer is the small arrow that points up and to the left that you use to manipulate most objects in Windows. You may have noticed, however, that this pointer often changes to indicate other actions that will be performed. For example, the pointer changes to an hourglass to indicate that Windows is busy, to a double arrow when resizing a window, and so on.

Use the Pointers tab to pick custom graphics to represent the different pointer states. Just select a pointer state, click the Browse button, and find the graphic on your system. Click the Use Default button to revert the selected pointer state back to its default.

Finally, Windows offers a large number of preset pointer schemes that offer coordinated graphics for all the pointer states. Just use the Schemes drop-down list to select a scheme. If you have customized pointer graphics, you can click the Save As button to save your settings as a scheme that will appear on the list.

Tip

If you have trouble seeing the pointer on your display, try using the Magnified pointer scheme. This scheme uses graphics that look like the default pointers, but are about 30% larger and have bold black outlines.

The Wheel Tab

The Wheel tab is used if your mouse has a dial or wheel that is used to scroll window displays. This tab has the following two options:

- Use the wheel to scroll a set number of text lines for each notch of the wheel.
- Use the wheel to scroll a whole page at a time, much like using the Page Up and Page Down keys.

The Hardware Tab

The Hardware tab is used to configure the hardware characteristics of your mouse. Only one mouse will most likely show up on this tab. However, many people use multiple input devices, and those too will all show up here. You can adjust the properties for any item by selecting it and clicking the Properties button. This opens the same dialog box you can use to get to the Device Manager and allows you to configure resource and driver settings for the hardware. Using the Device Manager and configuring hardware is covered later in this chapter.

14

USING THE
CONTROL PANEL

Troubleshooters!

Underneath the See Also list in the Appearance and Themes window, you will find two Troubleshooters, now standard features in many Windows components. The two troubleshooters available here are labeled Display and Sound.

Figure 14.11 shows the opening window of the Video Display Troubleshooter. The troubleshooter will ask a series of multiple choice questions that will attempt to narrow down the problem you are having. Once the problem is isolated, the Help and Support system can offer suggestions on fixing the problem.

FIGURE 14.11

The Video Display Troubleshooter offers assistance based on the problem you are having.

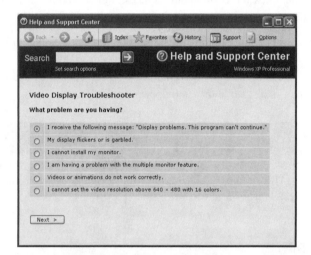

> **Note**
>
> For most common problems, these troubleshooters (and the others in other Windows XP components) work quite well. However, complicated issues like hardware and driver conflicts can be difficult for a troubleshooter to solve. In that case, the troubleshooter will often recommend that you visit Microsoft's or another developer's support site and will often provide you with links to do so.

Network and Internet Connections

The Network and Internet Connections category on the main Control Panel window is used to control Internet options, as well as to create and manage network connections. There are three tasks featured in this category:

- Set Up or Change your Internet Connection—This is a shortcut to the Connections tab of the Internet Options Control Panel applet (which itself is available at the bottom of the Network and Internet Connections window).

- Create a Connection to the Network at Your Workplace—This is a shortcut to the New Connection Wizard.

- Set Up or Change Your Home or Small Office Network—This is a shortcut to the Network Setup Wizard, which is also available on the Start menu. The Network Setup Wizard is covered in Chapter 24, "Configuring Your Computer for Local Area Networking."

You will find complete details on how to configure a local area network (LAN) connection in Chapter 24, "Configuring Your Computer for Local Area Networking." and more about making a connection to the Internet in Chapter 25, "Configuring Your Computer for an Internet Connection."

Add or Remove Programs

The Add or Remove Programs category on the main Control Panel window is really not a category at all. Instead, it is a link that directly opens the Add/Remove Programs Control Panel applet. You can use this applet to add and remove not only applications, such as Microsoft Office but also optional components of Windows XP, such as the Fax Client service. Chapter 12, "Installing and Removing Applications, covers this applet in detail."

Sounds, Speech and Audio Devices

The Sounds, Speech, and Audio Devices category is used to control a number of different configurations having to do with playing different kinds of media on your computer. There are three tasks available in this category:

- Adjust the system volume

- Change the sound scheme

- Change the speaker settings

All three of these tasks are shortcuts to tabs on the Sounds and Audio Devices applet, a link for which is also found at the bottom of the category page. This section covers the Sounds and Audio Devices and the Speech applets, as well as the troubleshooters available in this category.

The Sounds and Audio Devices Applet

The Sounds and Audio Devices applet is used to control volume settings for your computer, the sounds associated with different system events, and any audio hardware you have installed. The next several sections describe the tabs available for this applet.

The Volume Tab

The Volume tab controls your speaker volume and several other related functions. Use the slider at the top to control the volume level for sound output for the computer. The Mute option disables all audio output. The Place Volume Icon in the Taskbar option puts a small speaker icon in your System Tray so that you can quickly locate the volume controls on the taskbar without having to resort to going through all the Control Panel selections. The Advanced button in the upper portion of the Volume tab just brings up a dialog box with sliders that you can use to specify volume levels for different kinds of files or input devices, including CD Audio, MIDI input, WAV files, and many others.

At the bottom of the Volume tab, you will find two other buttons. The Speaker Volume button opens a dialog box with a slider control for setting the volume output to your speaker system. The Advanced button opens a dialog box that lets you choose a basic speaker setup (such as headphones, desktop speakers, or notebook computer speakers) for your system and also lets you control a couple of advanced features that can affect the performance of your system. These performance properties include the following:

- Hardware Acceleration—This slider specifies the level of hardware acceleration used for sound mixing. The default level is Full and, unless you experience problems, you should leave it there. If you are experiencing audio problems or hindered performance, you might try backing off this setting a little.

- Sample Rate Conversion Quality—This slider controls the level of quality for converting sample rates on your system. Again, unless you are experiencing problems, leave it at the Best setting.

The Sounds Tab

The Sounds tab lets you associate sounds with important Windows events. The Program Events window shows a list of all events to which sounds may be assigned. Select any event and the sound currently associated with it is displayed in the Sounds drop-down list. You associate another sound by selecting it from the drop-down list or by clicking the Browse button and locating a sound file on your system. Click the Play button to sample the selected sound.

Sound schemes are collections of sounds associated to events. Windows comes with two schemes: Windows Default and No Sounds. If you have custom desktop themes (or other applications) installed, you may have more schemes from which to choose. Just select a scheme from the list to reassign all the events to custom sounds in that scheme all at once.

If you customize your own sounds, you can save your collection as a scheme by clicking Save As and giving your scheme a name.

The Audio Tab

The Audio tab lets you select the device used to play sounds on your computer, the device used for recording, and the device used for MIDI music playback.

Under each section, you will see one or more devices in a drop-down menu, depending on the hardware installed on your computer. There are two buttons associated with each section. The Volume buttons set the playback or recording volumes for the selected device. The Advanced buttons open a dialog box much like the Advanced dialog box on the Volume tab discussed previously. Advanced settings are used to specify speaker type and performance settings for the devices.

The Voice Tab

The Voice tab lets you select voice playback and recording devices. The features on this tab work in the same way as those on the Audio tab.

The Hardware Tab

The Hardware tab displays a list of the many hardware devices on your system involved in audio recording and playback. You can select any device and click Properties to open a dialog box with configuration and driver settings for that device. The Properties dialog box is the same dialog box you can access using the Device Manager utility, which is discussed later in this chapter.

Speech

The Speech applet is used to control the voice properties used in text-to-speech translation, which is really just a fancy term meaning that Windows can read text to you in a canned computer voice. The Speech applet has only one tab with which you can choose the voice used to read text (only one, Microsoft SAM, actually comes with Windows) and adjust the speed at which text is read.

Sound and Audio Devices Troubleshooters

As you learned earlier, Windows troubleshooters work by asking you questions about a problem, isolating the problem based on your answers and then recommending specific help files for dealing with the problem. The Sounds, Speech, and Audio Devices category also contains two troubleshooters to help with problems configuring devices:

14

USING THE
CONTROL PANEL

- Sound—helps isolate problems with sound cards, volume controls, sound settings, and so on.

- DVD—helps isolate problems with DVD configuration and playback.

Performance and Maintenance

The Performance and Maintenance category, shown in Figure 14.12, is used to adjust certain settings that can affect your computer's performance; set power options; schedule automatic tasks; and access tools for backing up, cleaning up, and defragmenting your disk.

FIGURE 14.12

The Performance and Maintenance category lets you control a large number of options.

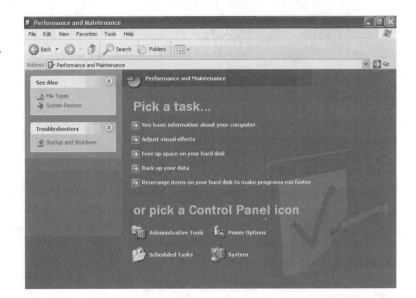

The following five tasks are offered in this category:

- See Basic Information About Your Computer—This is a shortcut to the General tab of the System applet, which is itself available at the bottom of the category window.

- Adjust Visual Effects—This is a shortcut to a special dialog box that you can also access by using the Advanced tab of the System applet. The dialog box contains a list of visual effects used by Windows XP that can adversely affect performance. You can find a detailed description of the effects in Chapter 22, "Performance Monitoring and Performance Logs and Alerts."

- Free Up Space on Your Hard Disk—This is a shortcut to the Disk Cleanup utility, which is also available on the Start menu. This tool is also described in Chapter 22.

- Back Up Your Data—This task is a shortcut to the Windows Backup program, which is covered in Chapter 21, "Using Backup on Windows XP."

- Rearrange Items on Your Hard Disk to make programs run faster—This is a short-cut to the Disk Defragmenter program, a program that is also available on the Start menu. You will find full coverage of this utility in Chapter 18, "Managing Disks and Partitions."

File Types and System Restore can be found on the See Also menu on the right side of the window. *File Types* refer to associating a filename extension (such as .doc or .txt) with a particular application. This was covered earlier in this chapter. The System Restore selection is covered in Chapter 23, "Disaster Recovery."

In addition to these tasks and See Also elements, the Performance and Maintenance category holds links to a number of Control Panel applets, including the following:

- Administrative Tools—These tools, such as Computer Management, the Event Viewer, and Performance, and others, are covered in chapters relating to those specific topics. You should check the index for the name of each of the administrative tools.

- Power Options—This applet controls how Windows controls power usage on your computer and is discussed in detail in Appendix C, "Using Windows XP on Notebook Computers."

- Scheduled Tasks—This icon opens the Scheduled Tasks window, which allows you to add, delete, and modify tasks that are scheduled to run at the time, or on a schedule, you specify. The command-line version of this utility, called `schedtasks` is covered in greater detail in Chapter 13, "Command Prompt Tools." Scheduled Tasks is simply the graphical version of this scheduling tool

- System—This icon opens the System Control Panel applet that is used to configure a host of Windows features and settings.

Since so many of the tasks and applets in the Performance and Maintenance category are covered elsewhere in the book, you will find that the remainder of this section is devoted to the System applet, shown in Figure 14.13.

The System applet consists of a number of different tabs, including the following:

1. General—This tab provides information about the current operating system and the computer, including the CPU, its speed, and the amount of memory on your system. This is an informational page, meaning that there are no options that you can modify.

14

USING THE CONTROL PANEL

FIGURE 14.13

*The System
Control Panel
applet.*

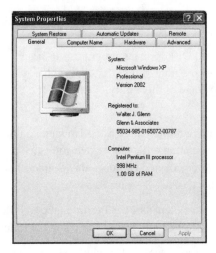

2. Computer Name—This tab is used to set the name of your computer and to control domain and workgroup membership for computers connected to a network. This tab is covered in detail in Chapter 28, "Joining a Domain and the Active Directory."

3. Hardware—This tab has the following four functions:

    • You can start the Add Hardware Wizard, which walks you through the steps of installing hardware devices not automatically detected by the system.

    • You can get details about signed drivers used on your computer. This is covered in depth in Chapter 23, "Disaster Recovery."

    • You can open the Device Manager, a tool for managing the hardware settings on your computer. This tool is covered later in this chapter.

    • You can configure hardware profiles.

4. Advanced—This tab is used to control performance settings (discussed in Chapter 22, "Performance Monitoring and Performance Logs and Alerts"), user profiles (discussed in Chapter 15, "Managing Local Users"), and the Startup and Recovery Processes (discussed in Chapter 6, "Disaster Recovery").

5. System Restore—This tab controls whether the System Restore feature is active and how related files are stored on your computer. System Restore is covered in Chapter 23, "Disaster Recovery."

6. Automatic Updates—This tab lets you choose whether Windows should automatically search for and download updates that become available on the Windows Update site.

7. Remote—This tab controls the Remote Assistance and Remote Desktop features.

Device Manager

The Device Manager utility lets you view and configure information about all of the hardware devices installed on your computer. You can also use Device Manager to enable and disable devices, view a comprehensive report of devices on your system, manage hardware drivers, and access a number of help and troubleshooting tools.

Viewing Device Properties

Device Manager, shown in Figure 14.4, organizes all the hardware on your computer into categories. You can expand any category to see the actual devices inside, much the same way you would expand a folder in Windows.

FIGURE 14.14

Device Manager lets you view and configure information about all of the known devices on your computer.

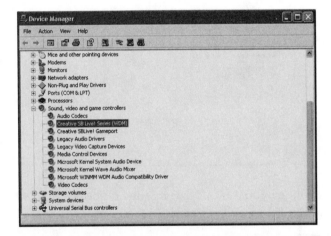

Tip

You can change the way information is displayed in the default Device Manager window. Click the View menu and select the view you want to see. You can choose from Devices by Type, which is the default view; Devices by Connection, which shows devices by the type of connection (for example, an SCSI device connection); Resources by Type, which shows you software resources such as input/output (I/O) ports, Interrupt Request (IRQs), and so on; and Resources by Connection, which works like the second option but from a resources point of view.

14

USING THE
CONTROL PANEL

In the example in Figure 14.14, you can see that a Creative Sound Blaster sound card is installed on this computer and listed in the Sound, Video, and Game Controllers category. This category also contains some software-based devices such as Audio Codecs and Video Codecs that interact with Windows as if they were hardware devices.

To view the properties for any of these devices or supporting software components, double-click the item or right-click it and select Properties from the shortcut menu. This will open a properties dialog box for the object, as shown in Figure 14.15.

FIGURE 14.15

You can bring up properties pages for each hardware or software device on your computer.

For each device, the tabs available on the properties dialog box may differ. However, there are a few tabs that you will encounter for most devices.

General Tab

The General tab provides basic information, such as the manufacturer of the device and where it is located in your computer (in the example in Figure 14.15, the device is installed in PCI slot number 1). The Device Status section tells you if the device is working or if there is a problem. If the device is not working properly, you may find information here suggesting a solution. You may also see in this section a Problem Code that can be used when you call for technical support. The Troubleshoot button opens one of Windows hardware troubleshooters, the specific troubleshooter based on the type of device you are viewing. At the bottom of the General tab is a drop-down list that lets you enable or disable the device. This can be very useful when troubleshooting to determine if one device is interfering with another or when using different hardware profiles on your computer (see Appendix C, "Using Windows XP on Notebook Computers").

Driver Tab

The Driver tab for any device is an important tab, as it contains controls for upgrading device drivers, rolling back drivers after a troublesome upgrade, and getting driver details. The use of this tab is covered in more detail in Chapter 23, "Disaster Recovery."

Resources Tab

The Resource tab, shown in Figure 14.16, lets you view (and sometimes modify) the resources used by the hardware device. Such resources include the I/O address, IRQ, and Direct Memory Access (DMA) settings. Most modern devices, especially Plug & Play devices, do not need to be directly modified in this fashion. In fact, many will simply not allow you to make changes at all. For some older devices, however, it is still useful to be able to specify the settings used by the hardware so that it does not conflict with other hardware.

FIGURE 14.16

Viewing the resources used by a hardware device.

Preparing a Hardware Report

Device Manager also lets you print or save a report of all the hardware on your system. Reports can be useful for sending to a tech support person or for archival purposes. To prepare a report, use the following steps:

1. In Device Manager, click the computer name to prepare a report on the whole system or click a specific category or device to prepare a more focused report.

2. From the Action menu select the Print command. This opens the Print dialog box.

3. Select the type of report to create. Types include the following:

    • System Summary report, which is basically a listing of important services on the system.

- Selected Class or Device report, which includes just the category or device that was selected in Device Manager when you issued the Print command.

- All Devices and System Summary report, which is a comprehensive (and usually very long) report that includes all devices on your system and their configuration settings.

4. If you want to print the report, select your printer, and click the Print button.

5. If you want to save the report as a file, select the Print to File option and click Print. This produces an output file based on the selected printer. This file includes the printer devices escape code and other character sequences that tell the printer how to print the document. This is a good option if you just want to produce a file now and then in case you need to look back to see what has changed when a problem creeps up on you.

Tip

You can actually create the report printed to file as an ASCII text file format. Just use the Add Printer wizard, which you can learn about in Chapter 17, "Printing and Faxing," to add a local printer and choose the port FILE: (Print to File). When asked for the name of the printer manufacturer, select Generic. For the Printers that fall under the Generic "manufacturer" you will have several choices. Select Generic/Text Only to produce a readable ASCII text file.) By printing to a file you can use a text editor or word processing program to narrow down the report to just the devices about which you need information.

Printers and Other Hardware

The Printers and Other Hardware category covers a lot of hardware. With the exception of game controllers, all the tasks and applets available in this category are covered in other chapters. For example, Chapter 17 covers printing and faxing in great detail.

For those of you who do have a game controller attached to your Windows XP computer, the Game Controllers applet offers a simple dialog box that lists any installed game controllers. Opening the properties for a particular device usually lets you calibrate the controller and configure what the various buttons will do. The properties for any particular game controller differ enough between devices, however, that it is not really possible to cover all the options here. Consult your documentation for the hardware device before making changes using this Control Panel applet.

User Accounts

The User Accounts category offers a selection of tasks, as well as a listing of the current local accounts on the computer. You can select an account to change or select a task to perform a specific function. You can find out more about managing user accounts in Chapter 15, "Managing Local Users."

Date, Time, Language and Regional Options

The Date, Time, Language, and Regional Options category lets you change your system time and date, as well as many different language functions. For more information about the changes you can make, see Chapter 3, "Installing and Upgrading Windows XP."

Accessibility Options

Many books often cover this subject in just a page or two, but this book devotes an entire chapter to Accessibility. Check out Chapter 5, "Accessibility Options," for a very detailed explanation of all the options that come with the Windows XP operating system.

The New Help and Support Application

While this application appears as a separate entry on the Start Menu, it also appears on the first page of the Control Panel if you use the Category View. Since Windows XP Help can be very useful in learning new tasks and troubleshooting problems, you may want to take some time to learn how it works.

You can launch Help and Support, shown in Figure 14.17, from the Start Menu, by pressing the F1 key (although if you are inside an application, F1 may open help for that particular application instead), from within the Control Panel, and from many other locations throughout Windows.

As you can see, there is a lot more to the traditional Help function than that offered in previous versions Windows. The opening screen provides a huge number of options from which to choose, ranging from the canned support text files that reside on your computer to getting information from Microsoft's online Knowledge Base to searching for an answer in a Windows XP Internet newsgroup.

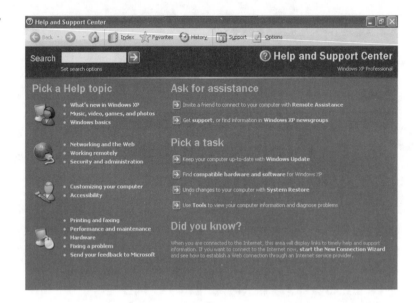

At the left side of this window, you can choose from a variety of topics if you want to browse for solutions on your own or just explore a new subject. These topics are almost an exact match for the topics you will find in the Control Panel's new Category View.

You can use the Ask for Assistance section to get someone else to help you with a problem.

The Pick a Task section contains links for performing a number of actions, including connecting to the Windows Update Web site and accessing the System Restore utility. You can use the Tools option in this section to invoke a variety of tools used to diagnose problems with your computer. These tools include Disk Cleanup, Backup, Disk Defragmenter, and more.

One of the most important new features of Help and Support is that it not only includes solutions with canned text written for the operating system but also allows you to retrieve information from the Internet when you use the Search option. Since all operating systems, including Windows XP, change over time, with patches, bug fixes, new drivers, and other software changes, it is a good idea when you suspect a problem to use the online database of information provided by Microsoft using the search feature. Combined with the Windows Update feature, you can be assured that your system is the most up-to-date of any. Additionally, if you do have a problem, at least you may be able to find a fix or a way around the problem by using the online Help search capabilities.

Summary

This chapter has covered a lot of territory because the Control Panel is a central component of Windows XP. Many of the functions you will find in this concentrated view of the operating system can be accessed from other applications, as was pointed out in this chapter. However, for some, you have to go to the Control Panel itself to find the right program to make your configuration changes.

For those who are used to the old standard Control Panel, you can always use the Classic View and invoke each individual applet icon by icon and avoid the use of the Category view, which is intended to make it easier for the novice to use the Control Panel.

14

USING THE
CONTROL PANEL

Managing Local Users

IN THIS CHAPTER

- Adding User Accounts During Setup *360*
- Adding User Accounts After Setup *360*
- Changing User Account Information *364*
- Selecting the Logon and Logoff Method for a User Account *372*
- Creating a Group Policy on the Local Computer *373*
- Configuring User Settings *378*
- Using Administrative Templates *379*
- Monitoring User Activities *380*
- Assigning User Rights *383*
- Using Groups to Simplify Management Tasks and Grant Resource Access *385*
- Using Fast User Switching? *389*
- Using Remote Assistance and Remote Desktop *390*

As you learned in Chapter 3, "Installing and Upgrading Windows XP," during the Setup process for Windows XP, you can create up to 10 user accounts. Just enter the actual username. You can't select the type of account or give it a password during this setup phase, though. You must configure accounts later using the Control Panel, a process described in this chapter.

You can add user account names during Setup and modify them after you have finished installing or upgrading to Windows XP. You can also add and manage user accounts after installing or upgrading the operating system. In this chapter, you learn how to use both processes. You learn about using the Control Panel to create or modify user accounts so that you can control who can log onto your computer and limit the things that they can do while working on the system. Additionally, this chapter discusses Fast User Switching, an option that keeps the programs and computer running while switching to a new user on a multiuser setup.

Learn about using Group Policy Objects, the Local Security utility, and the Component Services Utility. You can also find out how to create a password recovery disk, so you never have to worry about forgetting your password.

Adding User Accounts During Setup

One of the last steps in the Windows XP installation Setup process is the assignment of usernames. The Setup wizard presents you with a dialog box that allows you to enter up to 10 usernames. Windows XP uses these usernames to automatically create accounts; when you log onto the system, you can use the Control Panel to further customize these accounts.

Even if only one person uses the computer, it is a good idea to create at least one user account during the Setup procedure so you can use it (instead of the built-in Administrator account) to manage the system. If more than one person uses the computer, set up an account for each user. That way, you can assign privileges appropriate for each user, track user activity, and control access to change functions.

After you have created user accounts during Setup, return to the Control Panel to assign each user a password and account type, as well as to make other modifications.

Adding User Accounts After Setup

To add a new user to the computer after Setup, open the Control Panel by choosing Start, Control Panel. The Control Panel opens in Category View, as shown in Figure 15.1. To continue adding a new user to the computer, select User Accounts.

FIGURE 15.1

In the Control Panel, choose User Accounts to add a new user to the computer.

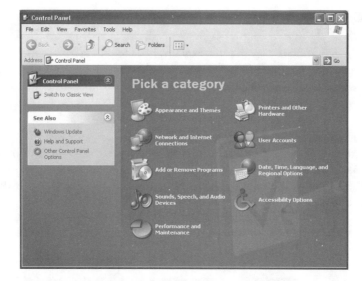

The User Accounts screen (see Figure 15.2) asks you to choose the account-management task you want to perform.

FIGURE 15.2

The User Accounts dialog box lets you manage user accounts that are local to the computer. You can use these options to create new accounts, delete accounts, and modify user accounts.

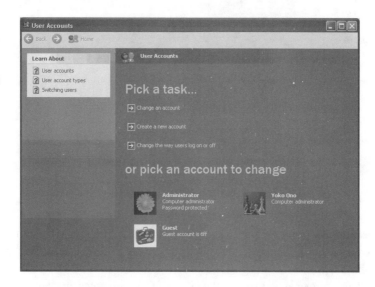

In the Pick a Task section, click Create a New Account. A series of pages then prompt you for information about the account you want to create. The first of these pages (see Figure 15.3) asks you to enter a username for the account.

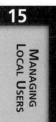

15

MANAGING
LOCAL USERS

> **Tip**
>
> The information in this chapter explains how to create an account that resides on your local computer. If you have a single standalone computer, you can create a separate logon for each person who uses the computer. If you participate in a workgroup, you also can create local accounts that others can use when they want to access shared resources on your local computer.
>
> If you are part of a domain, however, your network administrator probably has created a domain user account for you, which is either on a Windows NT 4.0 domain controller or on a Windows 2000 domain controller that is part of the Active Directory. Domain account usernames can give logon access throughout the domain (or in multiple domains in an Active Directory setup). Additionally, even if you are part of a domain, you can still set up local accounts on your computer. Local accounts only provide local access, though, not network access.

FIGURE 15.3

Enter the name you want to use for the user's logon name; be sure to choose a name the user will recognize.

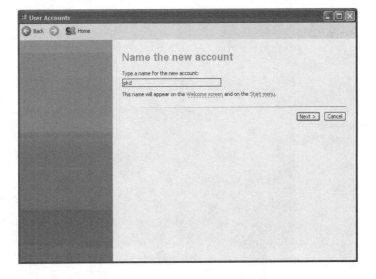

By default, the Windows XP system presents a Welcome screen when the system is booted or when no one is logged onto the computer. The Windows XP Welcome screen contains a list of users, along with a picture associated with each user account; users click their usernames to logon to the system. The usernames also appear on the Start Menu, as you will see later in this chapter.

Enter a logical, easy-to-identify username, then click Next to open the Pick an Account Type.

In Windows XP, you can create the following two account types:

- Computer Administrator—This type of account gives the username the same powers as those given by the local Administrator account. The user of a Computer Administrator account has access to most computer management functions, such as adding new users, installing new applications, editing the registry, and taking ownership of files created by other people. Again, you should create at least one account of this type so you can manage the computer without accessing the full Administrator account. In a business environment, you may want to create more than one Computer Administrator account in order to grant appropriate privileges to other users.

> **Caution**
>
> Always be sure to keep the Administrator account password a secret and force users who have administrative rights and privileges to use their own Computer Administrator accounts. Otherwise, you will have no audit trail to inform you who is making changes to the account.

- Limited—This is the type of account you should create for most users. As its name indicates, this type of account assigns limited access to the username. Users with Limited accounts can change (and even delete) their password, the picture associated with their account, the theme, and other desktop settings. All Limited account users can view files that are stored in the Shared Documents folder. Limited account users also can install some applications, depending on each application's installer program and the system changes it makes.

> **Note**
>
> You can learn more about choosing theme and desktop settings in Chapter 7, "Up Front: The New Desktop." Also, review Chapter 9, "Working with Files and Folders," to learn the details of working with shared files.

Table 15.1 outlines the differences between a Computer Administrator account and a Limited account.

15

MANAGING LOCAL USERS

Table 15.1   Differences between a Computer Administrator Account and a
Limited Account

Functionality	Computer Administrator	Limited
Install programs and hardware	Yes	No
Make system-wide changes	Yes	No
Access and read all nonprivate files	Yes	No
Create and delete user accounts	Yes	No
Change other people's accounts	Yes	No
Change your own account name or type	Yes	No
Change your own picture	Yes	Yes
Create, change, or remove your own password	Yes	Yes

Choose a radio button to select the account type, then click Create Account at the bottom of the Pick an Account Type screen. You just finished the process of adding a new user to the computer! However, you have some security settings to complete before you can give the user access to the new account.

Changing User Account Information

All changes to the user account information, including the assigning or changing of passwords, takes place in the Change an Account screen, located in the User Accounts screen (see Figure 15.2). Choose the Change an Account selection or simply double-click on the account name listed in the section titled or pick an account to change. To use the "pkd" account created in the previous example, double-click that name; a new screen appears, asking, What Do You Want to Change about pkd's Account? (see Figure 15.4).

Change the Username

In the preceding example, the username "pkd" represents the user's initials. In a business environment, usernames typically are made up of the user's first and middle initials and full last name to avoid confusion if several users share the same last name.

In this example, if you choose the Choose a New Username option, the Provide a New Name for pkd's Account screen appears. Enter the new name you want to associate with this account.

FIGURE **15.4**

The Change an Account screen lets you make many modifications to user accounts.

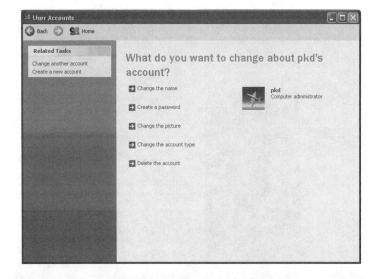

> ### Note
>
> Why does Windows XP allow you to change the user account name when you could just as easily create a new account with the new name? When you create a user account, Windows XP associates a security identifier with the account. The system uses this identifier to locate the files and folders created and owned by the user and to grant the user access to files, folders, printers, and other resources. If you create a new account for a current user, that user would no longer own the files and folders he or she had previously created. Using this name change feature avoids such complications.

Once you have entered the new name in the single field on this screen, click Change Name.

Add or Change the Account Password

Use the Create a Password selection in the What Do You Want to Change About pkd's Account? screen to add a password to the account. When you click this selection, a dialog box appears, enabling you to create a password (where the account currently has none) or modify the existing password. In this example, the pkd account was created during the Windows XP Setup, so it has no password; the window is labeled Create a Password for pkd's Account (see Figure 15.5). If an account has no password, the user can log onto the computer by entering the user account name or clicking on it in the Welcome screen.

15

MANAGING
LOCAL USERS

FIGURE 15.5

This screen allows you to add or change a password for a user account.

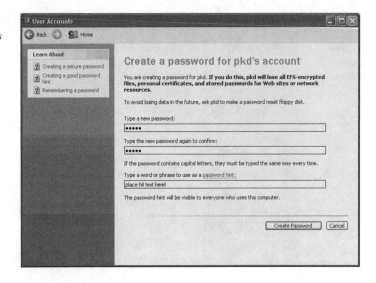

Just like nearly all other computer applications, Windows XP asks you to enter your chosen password twice, and the characters you type don't appear on the screen. After you have finished that drill, move to Type a Word or Phrase to Use as a Password Hint field. The hint feature is designed to help remind the user of a forgotten password, but, as useful as this hint may be, it can make your system less secure. Anyone who enters an incorrect password can read these hints; if the hint is too specific, anyone can use it to guess the password. Do take some time to choose your hints wisely.

For example, lots of people use their pet's or favorite baseball team's name as a password. If this is also your "trick," don't use a hint like "Fetch, boy!" or "Batter up!" as your password hint.

Tip

A quick word about passwords. Make them easy to remember, but difficult to guess. A common technique is to combine upper- and lowercase letters and to substitute numbers for parts of the password. For example, a password that might be easy for you to remember could be something *similar to* Yankees; just don't use the actual text, Yankees, as your password. Instead, choose something like Yank33s, where the two 3s take the place of the e letters. Then, as a password hint, you could simply put in "baseball team." Even this example is not truly a good example of a secure password. I'm sure someone would figure this one out after a few tries. You could also use YanK33s, or Yank3es, or other similar combinations that make it more difficult. You get the picture!

Remember the following as a rule:

- Choose passwords that are not direct names of sports teams, spouses, children, or pets.

- Don't use curse words, since this is also common and easy for hackers to guess (you would be surprised just how common).

- Try to use some obscure password, like the typical "mother's maiden name" you will find many Internet Web sites use.

- Use a combination of upper- and lowercase letters and add numbers to the password.

- The longer the password, the more difficult it will be to guess.

After you have filled in the password and entered the hint, click Create Password to add a password to this user's account.

Recovering a Forgotten Password

When users forget their passwords, an administrator can log onto the computer and use this control panel applet to reset the password to a known value. When users log back on after this procedure, they should change their individual passwords so that even the administrator doesn't know it. A password known by *anyone* other than the user to which it was assigned is useless.

Another option in the User Accounts applet lets you create a floppy disk (called a *password reset disk*) that enables you to log onto the computer, even when you have forgotten your password.

Using the disk is simple. If you enter an incorrect password at the Welcome screen, a message asks if you forgot your password. If you have, click on Use Your Password Reset Disk. A wizard pops up and allows you to create a new password (which will also be updated on the password reset disk, so you don't need to recreate it). If you enter the wrong password when logging onto a domain computer, a Logon Failed dialog box appears. Click on Reset and insert your password reset disk into the floppy drive; then follow the wizard to create a new password.

If your computer isn't part of a domain, follow these steps to create a password reset disk:

1. Open the User Accounts Control Panel utility.

2. In the User Accounts window, click your account name, then click Prevent a Forgotten Password in the Related Tasks section of the User Accounts screen (see Figure 15.6).

15

MANAGING LOCAL USERS

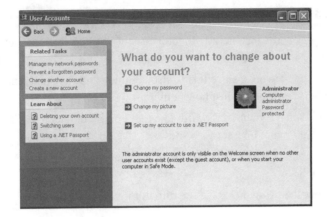

FIGURE 15.6

You can use the Prevent a forgotten password task to create a password reset floppy disk.

3. The Forgotten Password Wizard appears and warns you that anyone who has possession of this disk will be able to use it to log onto the computer using your username. Click Next.

4. The wizard prompts you for the location to be used to save the password information; the default is the floppy disk drive, usually A:. Insert a floppy disk in the drive and click Next.

5. The wizard prompts you to enter your current password (this step prevents someone else from creating a password reset disk for your account). Enter your password and then click Next.

6. The wizard copies a file to the floppy disk as a progress meter tracks the progress. When the process is complete click Next, and then Finish in the final screen.

Caution

Anyone who has possession of your reset disk can use it to access the system under your name. For obvious reasons, you should store the floppy disk in a safe place when you have finished creating it.

If you are part of a domain environment, the process is just a little different. To create the password reset disk use the Ctrl+Alt+Delete key combination to bring up a dialog box titled Windows Security. Click on Change Password and then click on Backup to start the Forgotten Password Wizard. Follow steps 3 through 6 in the preceding list to create a password reset disk.

Removing a Password from an Account

Once you have given a password to a user account, a new task shows up on the User Accounts page allowing you to remove the password. Removing the password is never a good idea unless the computer is strictly for home use and you fear that your children won't be able to remember a password. When this is the case, however, you can use the User Account applet to remove a password.

To remove a user password, log into the computer using an Administrator type of account and choose Control Panel, User Accounts. Select the user, then select Remove Password in the What Do You Want to Change About [username]'s Account? window. A warning (see Figure 15.7), alerts you of the consequences of removing the password.

If you are certain about removing the password, click Remove Password.

FIGURE 15.7
The User Accounts screen warns you of the consequences of removing the user password. Click Remove Password if you are sure you want to proceed.

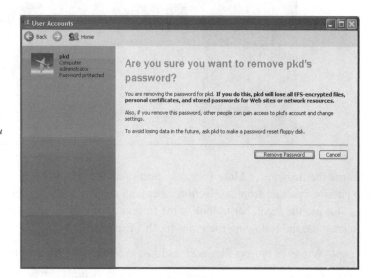

Change the Picture for a User Account

Windows XP comes with a set of pictures you can choose from to associate with a local user account. Although this may seem silly at first, these pictures allow users to personalize the Welcome screen. You also don't have to use just the built-in pictures that come with Windows XP. You can download pictures from Web sites or transfer images from your digital camera or scanner (see Chapter 30, "Capturing Images and Video).") You can even put a picture of the user next to the username on the Welcome screen.

15

MANAGING
LOCAL USERS

To change the picture associated with the user account, choose Change an Account on the User Accounts page. Select the account or just double-click on the user account at the bottom of that screen. When the What Do You Want to Change? screen appears, select Change the Picture.

Figure 15.8 shows the Pick a new picture for pkd's account screen.

FIGURE 15.8

You can select a picture from this page, browse the computer or the Web, or use one of your own digital images for the account.

You can use the Browse for More Pictures selection at the bottom of the screen if you want to choose a picture from a selection other than the Windows XP default location. You can also use the scroll bar to look at the full range of built-in pictures that are available. You can use the following file types for this feature:

- .bmp—Windows bitmap files such as those created using Microsoft Paint.
- .gif—CompuServe graphics interchange format pictures can be created by many different graphics programs.
- .jpg—This is a standard format that comes in many varieties, depending on the compression algorithms used. The initials come from the Joint Photographic Experts Group, which was responsible for creating this image standard.
- .png—Portable network graphics images are used by many different imaging programs and are widely used on the Internet.

If you select the browse option, an Open dialog box appears, as shown in Figure 15.9, so you can search other folders on your computer to find a suitable picture.

FIGURE 15.9
This dialog box allows you to look for pictures elsewhere on your computer.

Use the drop-down Look In menu at the top of the dialog box to select another drive or folder, or you can use the buttons on the left of the dialog box to navigate to the location of the picture. When you have found the picture you want to use, click Open. This will return you to the previous screen where you can then click Change Picture.

Change the Account Type

When you created an account at the start of this chapter, you had to specify whether to create a Computer Administrator or a Limited type of account. You can change the account type assigned to any username through the What Do You Want to Change? screen you used in the preceding set of instructions. Open this screen, select the Account type radio button, and then click Change Account Type.

Deleting a User Account

When you no longer need a user account, you can delete it. Indeed, this is a good idea, since the fewer the accounts that exist on the system, the less opportunity for someone to guess a password and log into your computer. To delete local accounts on a Windows XP computer, use the What Do You Want to Change screen, and select Delete the Account, which produces the screen shown in Figure 15.10.

FIGURE 15.10

When you delete an account, you don't have to delete the user's files unless you want.

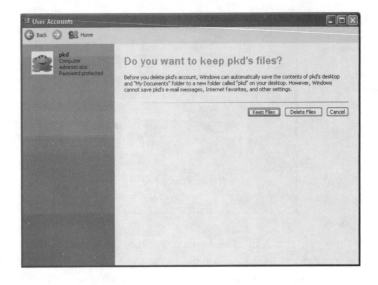

A warning at the top of this screen tells you that if you want to keep the user's files, a folder will be placed on your desktop to store the contents of the user's desktop and anything stored in the user's My Documents folder. The user's e-mail messages, favorites, and other settings will not be retained. Remember that you don't need to delete the user's account to change the user's account name. Instead, use the rename account feature described earlier in this chapter; all of the user's files and settings will remain in place, and only the account name will change.

However, if you want to permanently remove this user and his or her files from your computer, use Delete Files. If you want to retain the files, choose Keep Files.

Selecting the Logon and Logoff Method for a User Account

As mentioned earlier, the standard mechanism that Windows XP uses when your computer is not part of a domain is to present a Welcome screen that displays the user accounts (and pictures) that are stored on the local computer. If you prefer to use the standard Windows logon dialog box, you can change this default setting.

In the User Accounts screen, choose the Change the Way Users Log On or Off option. To use the standard Windows logon dialog box, deselect the Use Welcome Screen check box.

> **Note**
>
> When you open the Select Logon and Logoff Options window, you may see a dialog box warning that Fast User Switching can't be used because Offline Files is enabled. The Offline Files feature enables you to work with copies of files that normally exist on the network by using a copy stored locally on your computer when you aren't connected to the network. For information about how to turn off this feature, see Chapter 9, "Working with Files and Folders."

Creating a Group Policy on the Local Computer

On standalone and workgroup computers, you can control many aspects of how the computer can be used and enforce certain policies on the users who log onto the computer. To do this, you can use the Group Policy editor to create a Group Policy object for your local computer, which is used to assign policies and restrictions to certain groups of users. (If your computer is part of a domain, a domain policy object may override some of the settings you make in your local group policy object). You also can enforce security issues using the Local Security Policy applet found in the Administrative Tools section of the Control Panel.

> **Note**
>
> MMC stands for Microsoft Management Console. The MMC provides a common interface for performing many different management tasks on Windows computers. Snap-ins are the application-specific components that you can use within the MMC to manage certain computer functions.

You can use Group Policies to control a variety of computer views, menus, and functions. Group policies determine, for example, what items appear on the desktop or in the Start menu. Table 15.2 provides a more complete list of items you can administer by using a group policy object.

If you come from a Windows NT 4.0 background, then you will remember the System Policy Editor—a function that allows you to set configuration entries for all computers in a domain, to control desktop settings, and so on. A Group Policy is similar to the System Policy Editor, but it provides even more control. Keep in mind also that in this chapter,

15

MANAGING
LOCAL USERS

we are talking about a *local* Group Policy—that is, for a single computer. If you are part of a domain, you can create multiple levels of Group Policy objects, which may override some of the settings in the local Group Policy object.

Table 15.2   Group Policy Object Capabilities

Functionality	*Description*
Administrative Templates	Similar to the System Policies in Windows NT Server 4.0, templates let you set policies by creating Registry entries.
Folder Redirection	Redirects a user's folder to a folder located on the network.
Software Installation	Publishes applications (optional for the user) and assigns applications, which are installed automatically
Security Settings	Activates specific groups or set of security features on the computer

A Group Policy can exist in an Active Directory-based network at the Site level, the organizational unit (OU) level, and domains. To learn more about the Active Directory, see Appendix B, "Overview of the Lightweight Directory Access Protocol (LDAP) and the Active Directory."

To open the Group Policy MMC Console:

1. Click on Start and then Run.
2. Enter the command `gpedit.msc` and click OK. The Group Policy window opens (see Figure 15.11), which is used to modify user and computer configuration policies.

> **Tip**
>
> You can also enter the `gpedit.msc` command while using the Command Prompt interface.

> **Tip**
>
> If you are curious, the actual file that contains your local group policy can be found in the directory `%systemroot%\System32\GroupPolicy`.

FIGURE 15.11

*You can set poli-
cies for the local
computer using
the Group Policy
snap-in.*

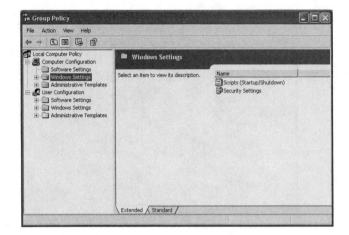

You can set policies based on two categories: the computer and the user(s). Computer
policies are applied when the computer boots up, and can be used to specify such things
as the desktop and application settings, as well as security settings and script files that
can run when the computer boots or is shut down. User policies are applied to specific
users (or user groups) and can also affect desktop and application settings, and logon and
logoff scripts for each user.

It would take an entire book to discuss all the configuration capabilities of the local
Group Policy object (there are more than a thousand settings you can manage), so the
next few sections discuss only some of the more important settings.

Configuring Security Settings on the Local Computer

One of the most important features you can control with Group Policy Objects is the
computer's security settings. For example, you can enforce a policy that makes users
change their passwords periodically or causes an account to be locked out after a specified number of failed logon attempts.

You access the Security Settings options in the left pane of the MMC console for the
Group Policy object, as shown in Figure 15.12. When you click the Security Settings listing, the groups of settings you can control for security policies appears on the right.

If you double-click on Account Policies in the right-side pane, you see two items:
Password Policy and Account Lockout Policy. These items make up the local security
policy options.

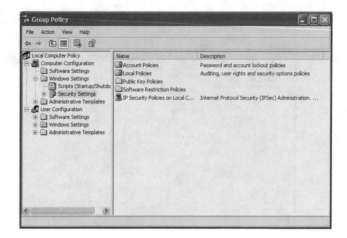

Setting Password Policies

The Local Security Settings window gives you access to a number of items for which you can create settings that control the password functions for all users on the local computer. These items include the following:

- Enforce password history—Use this setting to tell Windows XP how many passwords for each user to store in a history file so that the password cannot be reused until it is flushed from the history file. This feature can keep the user from reusing common passwords over and over again when it comes time to change a password. You can specify a value of between 1 and 24 for this setting.

- Maximum password age—This is the maximum length of time (the number of days) that a password can be use before Windows XP will force the user to change the password. You can specify between 1 and 999 days for this setting.

- Minimum password age—This is the opposite of the previous entry. Although you may have little need for this setting, it is designed to allow you to set the number of days a password is used before it can be changed. In other words, you can prevent users from changing a password until it has been used for a specific period of time. Avoid hassles by leaving this at the default of zero, so the users can change their password at any time.

- Minimum password length—This is an important setting. This is the minimum number of characters, including both alphabetic and numeric characters that a password must be. Users cannot create passwords that are shorter in length than this value. You can set this to between 1 and 14 characters (most businesses use eight or more characters) to make sure the user chooses a secure, hard-to-guess password.

- Password must meet complexity requirements—The operating system has a dynamic link library (DLL) that can examine a password and decide whether it is complex enough to be considered secure. A complex password is one that contains both letters and numbers, as well as upper- and lowercase letters. For strong security, select this setting.
- Store password using reversible encryption—This setting enables the administrator to decrypt a password stored in the security database. *Always disable this setting!*

To demonstrate these settings in action, the following example changes the number of passwords that the operating system stores in the history file so that a user cannot simply switch back to a previously-used password. To make this change, double-click on the Enforce Password History selection in the Local Security Settings window. The Enforce Password History dialog box appears, as shown in Figure 15.13. Use the raster arrows or type in a new amount to change the setting. Click Apply and then OK.

FIGURE 15.13

The Enforce Password History Properties dialog box lets you determine how many passwords are stored in a user's password history file.

You can change the other Password Policy items by using the same method; just double-click on the item in the MMC's right-side pane, and a dialog box pops up to allow you to specify a value, or to enable or disable a feature.

Setting Account Policies

The Account Lockout feature is designed to guard against password guessing, an important function in an environment where security is essential. You can set Account Lockout values that make the account unusable for a set period of time after a series of unsuccessful login attempts.

This feature can help prevent users from trying to log onto the machine both locally and via the network. If the computer is connected to the Internet, this setting can ward off attacks by vicious programs that try to break into computers by attempting one password after another to find the password of a known account—one form of a dictionary attack!

15

MANAGING
LOCAL USERS

Double-click the Account Lockout Policy item to produce the following policies in the right pane of the Local Security Settings window:

- Account lockout duration—This is how long an account remains locked-out (unusable) after the number of failed login attempts has been reached. This field can have a value of between 1 and 99999 minutes.

- Account lockout threshold—This field sets the number of failed logon attempts that will invoke the lock-out feature. The account will remain locked-out until the Account lockout duration timer has expired.

- Reset account lockout counter after—This controls the time between failed logon attempts that will trigger the lock-out. You can set hits to 1 to 999999, but this value must be less than (or equal to) the Account lockout duration. In other words, once the first failed logon attempt occurs, this counter starts decrementing. If it reaches zero before the second failed logon attempt, the counter restarts. If the number of failed logon attempts defined by the Account lockout threshold occurs before this timer expires, then the account is locked-out.

Setting the values for these items is quite simple. Just double-click on the item in the right side of the MMC pane and a dialog box pops up. Use the settings in the dialog box to set new values.

To experiment with this policy, set the Account Lockout Duration to 60 minutes. Next, set the Account Lockout Threshold value to 5. Finally, set the Reset Account Lockout Counter After to a value of 30 minutes. With these settings in place, if a user uses the wrong password five times within a 30-minute period, then the account will be locked for one hour (60 minutes). If the user only tries to login four times, and then waits for some time (more than 30 minutes) and then tries and fails again, the counter will have been reset and the user can continue trying to log in.

Configuring User Settings

In addition to setting policies for passwords and accounts, you can use the Group Policy Object to modify what the user sees on the desktop and the Start Menu, as well as to create logon and logoff scripts.

To access these settings, open the User Configuration folder in the left pane of the Group Policy window. Click the Windows Settings folder, as shown in Figure 15.14. The following items appear in the right pane:

- Scripts (Logon/Logoff)
- Security Settings
- Internet Explorer Maintenance

FIGURE 15.14

You can control the user's environment using the User Configuration settings in the Group Policy Object.

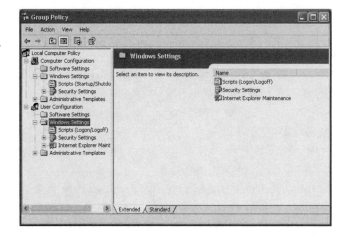

Logon and logoff script files can be used to map network drives and printers or run other programs. You can use any text editor to create a logon or logoff script file (for more information about creating script files, see Chapter 13, "Command Prompt Tools"). Select the items to use with the Group Policy Object to assign these script files to users or groups.

Using Administrative Templates

The Administrative Templates folder in the Group Policy Object tree gives you the most options for controlling how the computer environment is presented to the user. You can perform a number of functions in this folder, including the following:

- Windows Components—You can enable or disable certain Windows components with this selection.

- Start Menu and Task Bar—This selection allows you to remove items from the Start Menu and the Task Bar. You can remove links to Windows Update for example, or common program groups, the My Documents icon, the Search Assistant, the Help Menu, the Run menu, and so on.

- Desktop—With this selection, you can hide and disable all items on the desktop, remove the Recycle Bin icon from the desktop, and otherwise determine what functions users can access from the desktop.

- Control Panel—You can use this option to hide certain Control Panel applets or to completely prohibit the user from accessing the Control Panel. You also can use this selection to force the Control Panel to be presented in Classic View, rather than the new Category View.

- Shared Folders—You can use this setting to allow folders to be shared and Distributed File System (DFS) roots to be published in the Active Directory (if you are part of a domain).

- Network—You can use this option to enable or disable such things as offline files or to configure a large number of network capabilities.

- System—This entry in the MMC tree allows you to control a large number of items ranging from user profiles in order to prevent access to the command prompt and Registry editing tools.

Double-click the Administrative Templates folder to open it, then take some time to examine all of its subentries. Before deploying any of these settings in a large network, take time to experiment with them. Most small networks or home users have little use for these settings.

Monitoring User Activities

One good reason to have a separate account for each person who logs onto a computer is that you can use each person's username to track individual activities. If everyone uses the same username to logon (such as Administrator—a really dumb idea), then you have no audit trail to use for tracking down who, where, when, and what happened to your computer.

To track events on the computer you can do the two following things:

- You can set up the events to track in a process called *setting up auditing*.

- You can use the Event Viewer utility to review the events that get written to the audit files.

To set up auditing, use the Control Panel to bring up the Local Security Settings dialog box on your Windows XP computer, as shown in Figure 15.15. Select Performance and Maintenance.

The next screen asks you to pick a task or a Control Panel icon; choose Administrative Tools at the bottom of the screen.

In the Administrative Tools window, select Local Security Policy, to produce the Local Security Settings options shown in Figure 15.16.

> **Tip**
>
> When the Local Security Settings window pops up, the left pane of the MMC console also has entries in the tree for Password Policy and Account Lockout Policy. You can use either the Group Policy Object or the Local Security Settings applet in the Control Panel to access these entries.

FIGURE 15.15

Select Performance and Maintenance from the Pick a category listing.

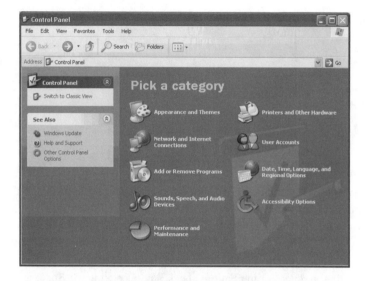

FIGURE 15.16

You can select the Audit Policies from this window.

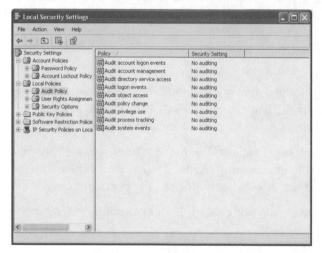

In the left pane of the Local Security Policy window is a list of events to audit (under the Policy column) and the current setting (under the Security Setting column). Using this applet, you can set up the events that will be stored in the security log file and that can be examined by using the Event Viewer.

Before you enable auditing on any of these items, you should understand that there are two sides to auditing. You can audit (or record to the log file) successful uses of these items or you can audit failed attempts to use these items. Double-click on Audit Account Logon Events in the left pane to produce the dialog box shown in Figure 15.17.

15

MANAGING
LOCAL USERS

FIGURE 15.17

You use this dialog box to decide if you want to audit an item, and which kind of event to audit: success or failure.

You can use the options in this dialog box to audit successful events, failed events, or both–that is, you can have a record created in the log file every time someone successfully logs onto the computer, or you can choose only to create a record each time someone fails to log in. If you are suspicious about when a particular user is logging into the computer, then choose to log success attempts. If you only want to know when someone is not getting in, then use the Failure check box. Checking the Success check box can help you track when users use the computer. Checking the Failed check box not only tracks valid users who are fumble-fingered and keep entering the wrong password, it also warns you of attempts to break into the computer by guessing passwords.

So as you can see, making decisions about auditing policy can be a daunting task. Keep in mind that you still will have to use the Event Viewer to review the records that are created, so you want to limit the amount of data collected to a reasonable amount. If you collect too much data, you are more likely to miss something as you scan the events log.

Another thing to keep in mind is that in this window, you are only choosing items to audit that appear in the Security log file. The Event viewer has three different log files, which you will learn about shortly. The security events you can audit are as follows:

- Audit account logon events—This creates audit records for logons for accounts on the local computer.
- Audit account management—This creates audit records for changes made to user accounts.
- Audit directory service access—If you are part of an Active Directory domain, this will allow you to create records in the audit file when a directory object that has a security access control list (SACL) attached to it is accessed.
- Audit logon events—This creates audit records for both local logons, and also network connections made to the computer as well.
- Audit object access—This creates audit records for any object that has a SACL attached to it.

- Audit policy change—This creates audit records for all policy changes—including changing the actual audit policies, assigning rights to users, and other similar events that grant access to the system.

- Audit privilege use—This feature tracks all attempts to use rights. You can grant certain rights such as audit privileges, which give even Limited account users permission to perform specific rights actions. Choosing to audit all use (both success and failure) of rights can quickly fill up the log file. However, if you suspect someone is trying to access files to which they have no rights, for example, then you might want to audit failure attempts.

- Audit process tracking—This will cause a record to be created for every process that runs on the system. If you activate this audit category, it will quickly generate massive amounts of auditing information. (If you don't think so, just use the Task Manager, described in Chapter 19, "Using the Task Manager," to see how many individual processes actually are running when just one person is logged into the computer.) Don't activate this audit category unless you need to use it for debugging purposes.

- Audit system events—This category causes audit records to be created when something happens that affects the system's security or the security log file. It is a good idea to enable both success and failure for this category.

Coming up with a good security auditing policy is something with which you will have to experiment. As you will learn later in this chapter, you can extract data from the logs and use other programs such as databases or spreadsheet applications to help evaluate the data collected. Once you get an idea of the uses your computer is being put to, whether in a standalone or network environment, you will be better able to determine which events you will need to audit.

Assigning User Rights

Given the complexities of the Windows XP operating system and the actions that it can perform, the two account types, Computer Administrator and Limited, are too general for most business environments. You have to choose all or nothing. An account created with all the rights of an administrator account can do anything on the system. A Limited user account basically allows users to do things with their own files and with resources to which the administrator of the computer grants them access.

You can grant rights to tailor a Limited account by assigning rights to a user or group or by placing a user into a group that possesses certain rights.

> **Note**
>
> Rights differ from permissions in important ways. *Rights* are very specific actions a user can perform; *resource permissions*, on the other hand, give users the ability to perform certain kinds of actions on specific resources. Resource permissions are discussed in other chapters. For example, you learned about controlling access permissions on files and folders in Chapter 9, "Working with Files and Folders." If you want to know more about granting access to printers, see Chapter 17, "Printing and Faxing."

You can grant a large number of very specific rights to a user or a user group to enable that group or user to perform certain actions on a Windows XP system. For example, an Administrator can make backups, look at all files on the system, install programs, and so on. That is because the Administrator account possesses a large number of rights that grant the capability to perform these actions.

To view a list of all of the individual rights you can make use of, open the User rights Assignment folder under the Local Policy entry in the Security Settings tree of the Local Security Settings Window. As shown in Figure 15.18, when you select User Rights Assignment, a list of User Rights appears on the right side of the window.

FIGURE 15.18

You use the User Rights Assignment security setting to grant rights to users or groups.

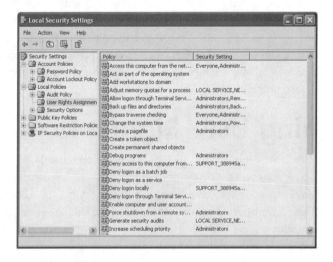

The right pane of this window lists the rights under a column labeled Policy. The users or groups who possess a particular right are listed under a column labeled Security Setting. Use the bars in the column headers to expand the space by dragging the bars so that you can expose the full text of the column you want to examine further.

Some rights are self-explanatory; for example, assigning the Change the System Time right enables the user to change the time on the system. If a user possesses the right called *Shut Down the System*, then that is exactly what they can do.

If you want to create user accounts that have the capabilities to do some of the things a Computer Administrator account can do but not everything that this super account can do, then you can grant rights to the user based on the actions (rights) you want them to be able to perform.

To grant a right to a user or group, simply right-click on the user or group and select Properties. In the dialog box that appears, use Add to select users or groups that have this right.

Using Groups to Simplify Management Tasks and Grant Resource Access

It is much simpler to create groups of users and then assign rights to the group than to assign rights to individual user accounts. Once you assign a user to a group, the user is granted all the rights that are associated with that group. Remember, too, that a user can be a member of more than one local group.

Windows XP comes with several built-in groups, which may be all that you need for your environment. Otherwise, you can create your own new local groups and customize the rights granted to the group. The built-in groups are as follows:

- Administrators—Members of this group can do anything on the system.

- Backup Operators—This group can override resource protections that you place on files or folders, but only for the purposes of performing a backup or a restore. This group does not grant members the ability to read another person's files.

- Guests—This is a limited group that is used for granting access to users who do not have an account on the system. Windows XP also offers a Guest user account, so you can safely disable the Guest's account.

- Network Configuration—Members of this group can perform some network configuration tasks.

- Power Users—This group is just a small step down from the Administrators group; members can perform many tasks on the computer but not as many as the Administrators group. For example, Power Users can create new accounts and can modify only those accounts they create. Members of this group also can remove users from the Power Users, Users, and Guests groups. This group cannot, however, modify the Administrators' or Backup operators' groups and (unlike Administrators) cannot take ownership of some other user's files.

- Remote Desktop Users—Members of this group have permission to access the local desktop remotely.

- Replicator—This is used for the file replication service in a network scenario. This is usually an account created for replication purposes, and not an ordinary user account. By placing the replicator account from a domain into the Replicator group on your system, replication processes can be performed by different network services.

- Users—Ordinary users of the computer. This group is limited in what it can do, and is the group from which most of the users should be a member.

- HelpServicesGroup—This group is provided for users who are part of the Help and Support Center. This group is populated by Windows itself when you issue a remote assistance invitation to someone. You should not modify the membership directly.

You can use the Computer Management tool found in the Administrative Tools folder of the Control Panel to view the built-in groups, create new groups, and add or remove users from groups. Figure 15.19 shows the Computer Management window, with the Users and the Groups folders displayed.

FIGURE 15.19

Use the Computer Management utility to manage user and user groups.

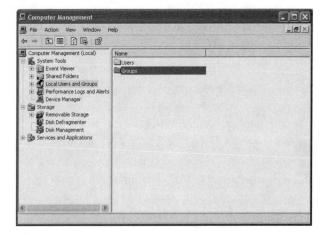

Adding Members to a Group

You can add members to a group using the group's property pages. For example, to add a member to the Backup Operators group, first open Groups folder and then double-click Backup Operators. The Backup Operators Properties page opens. Click Add to produce the Select Users dialog box, shown in Figure 15.20.

FIGURE 15.20

Use the Select Users dialog box to select the users to add to the group.

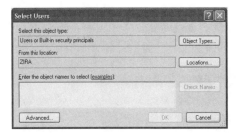

If you know a user or group name that you want to add to this group, type the name in the Enter the Object Names to Select text box and Windows attempts to fill in the username for you. If you have a number of users, though, this is not a very useful method for managing users, as it requires you to remember exact names. Instead, click Advanced to open a separate dialog box that lets you browse a list of users and groups to select from, as shown in Figure 15.21.

FIGURE 15.21

Click Advance in the previous dialog box to expand it to this display.

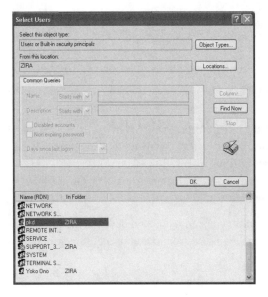

15

MANAGING
LOCAL USERS

In Figure 15.21, Find Now was clicked, so the bottom of the dialog box contains a listing
of all the user groups and users on the local system. In this example, the user name
"pkd" is highlighted. To add pkd to the Backup Operators group, click OK; pkd is added
as a member of this group, as shown in Figure 15.22.

FIGURE 15.22

*Members of the
group will show
up on the proper-
ties page after you
have added them.*

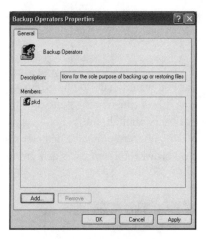

To remove pkd from this group, highlight the username in the Members section of the
dialog box and click Remove.

Creating a New Local Group

You also can create your own new group by using the Computer Management applet,
found in the Administrative Tools folder of the Control Panel. To do this simply click on
the Groups folder and from the Action menu, select New Group. The New Group dialog
box appears, as shown in Figure 15.23.

In the New Group dialog box, you can name and describe the group. You use the same
method described in the preceding section to add users to the group.

FIGURE 15.23

Use this dialog box to give a name and description to a new group, and also to add members to the group.

Using Fast User Switching?

Fast User Switching is a technique that you can use to quickly change from one user account on Windows XP computer to another, without first closing your applications and logging off the computer. True, you do use the log off feature, but you get to leave any applications that are executing in their current state; when you switch back, you can resume your work.

For example, suppose you are at home working on some business spreadsheet or a Word document, and your son wants to quickly use the computer to check his e-mail messages. You can use Fast User Switching to allow him to check e-mail, without disturbing the state of the programs you are running.

To use Fast User Switching, keep in mind that the computer cannot be a member of a Windows domain. For standalone or workgroup computers (on which the computer administrator has selected to allow Fast User Switching) follow these steps to use Fast User Switching:

1. Click on Start and then Log Off.
2. If Fast User Switching is enabled on the computer, you should see a selection labeled Switch User. Click on this selection.
3. The user accounts that are available on the local Windows XP computer will be displayed. Click on the account to which you want to switch.
4. When you have finished, you can use Start and Log Off again, and pick the previous user to return to your previous logon session.

Note that you can actually have more than just two logon sessions running at the same time. It is possible to have many sessions logged on, each being placed on hold when you switch from one account to another. When you return to your session, your open programs are still opened and running, so you don't lose any of your work.

15

MANAGING
LOCAL USERS

> **Tip**
>
> Fast User Switching can be useful in a small business environment where users on different shifts use the same computer. You can simply leave your applications open and running and use Fast User Switching to let the second shift user log on.

Using Remote Assistance and Remote Desktop

Remote Desktop and Remote Assistance features are built-in features of Windows XP. These features can make getting work done on your computer easier, and they can enable others to help you when you have problems. The following sections show you how to get the most from these useful features.

Using Remote Desktop

Remote Desktop is a feature that allows you to connect to another computer such as your work computer when you are at home and for all practical purposes, operate as if you were sitting at that remote computer. You will have access to the applications and resources on the remote computer, just as though they were on your local computer.

The concept of Remote Desktop comes from the technology developed for Windows Terminal Services. The display output, keyboard, and mouse input are transmitted between the two computers, using the Remote Desktop Protocol (RDP). RDP can be used by many different types of connections, including a dial-up line, a TCP/IP network connection, and even a wide area network connection such as the Internet (although if you use the latter, a virtual private network [VPN], connection would be a good idea).

> **Tip**
>
> Windows XP computers and computers that use Terminal Services can be used to connect to your computer using Remote Desktop. However, if you want to enable other computers such as Windows 95/95/Me or Windows NT 4.0/2000 computers that are not using terminal services you have to install software on them to enable this feature. Insert the Windows XP Professional installation CD in one of these computers and select Perform additional tasks from the first menu that appears. From there, select Set Up Remote Desktop Connection and follow the installation prompts to install the software component.

To enable Remote Desktop on your computer, follow these steps:

1. Click on Start and the Control Panel.

2. From the Category View, select Performance and Maintenance.

3. From the next window, click the System icon.

4. On the Remote tab (see Figure 15.24), enable Remote Desktop by selecting the check box labeled Allow Users to Connect Remotely to This Computer.

FIGURE 15.24

Use the Remote tab of the Control Panel System applet to enable Remote Desktop.

5. Click on Select Remote Users.

6. A list of the users that are already allowed to connect to the computer appears; click Add if you wish to select additional users.

7. If you use Add, a Select Users dialog box appears. Use it to select any users that have local accounts on the computer or users who are members of your domain, if you want to allow them to remotely connect to your computer.

8. Click OK to dismiss the Remote Desktop Users dialog box.

Note

If you want to turn off Remote Desktop for a while, you don't have to remove all the users that you have granted remote access to your computer. Temporarily suspend Remote Desktop access by deselecting the check box labeled Allow Users to Connect Remotely to This Computer. When you decide at a later time to re-enable the feature, the user names will still be there. Just select the check box and, if necessary, add or remove users from this list of those allowed to use this feature.

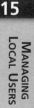

15

MANAGING
LOCAL USERS

> **Caution**
>
> Windows XP also provides the capability for using a Web server connection to use Remote Desktop, but it is not a feature that is well-suited to the Internet's lack of security. Unless you use a VPN connection, you probably should avoid the Web server connection capability in XP. Instead, use a modem for a dial-up connection. For more information on using a web connection, see the Help and Support Center in Windows XP.

Using Remote Assistance

The Remote Assistance feature allows another user such as a help desk operator or administrator to view your computer's screen remotely and (if you give permission) to take over control of your computer. Using this feature, the remote operator can show you how to perform the functions that you are having problems with on your computer.

In order to allow someone to assist you using Remote Assistance, you first have to issue an invitation to that person. You can do this through the following steps:

1. Click Start, then click Help and Support.

2. Click the Invite a friend to connect to your computer with Remote Assistance link from the column labeled Ask for Assistance. This opens the Remote Assistance page shown in Figure 15.25.

FIGURE 15.25

You need to send an invitation to get remote assistance.

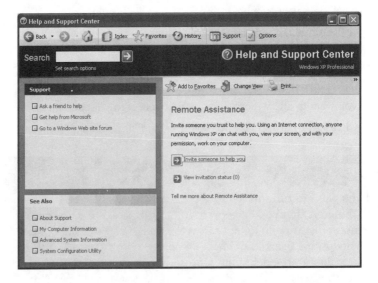

3. On the Remote Assistance page, click the Invite someone to help you link, which lets you to send an invitation for remote assistance.

> **Note**
>
> You can assign a password for Remote Assistance, and you can set a time limit on the remote password so that it is only usable for a short period of time. When the remote user receives the invitation, he or she will have to enter the password before they can take control of your desktop and further assist you. If you use a password, be sure to telephone or separately e-mail the recipient of the invitation to communicate the password to him or her.

4. You can choose from two methods for inviting remote assistance help: You can sign into Windows Messenger and select from your contact list; or you can send an e-mail to the person to whom you want to issue an invitation. For this example, click on the button underneath the e-mail address labeled Invite This Person.

5. The next screen prompts you to compose an e-mail message you can use to describe your problem and request help. Click the Continue after composing your message.

> **Tip**
>
> If you expect that you will want assistance in the future from the same person, you can save the invitation to a file. Simply select the Save Invitation as a File (Advanced) option.

6. When the remote assistance person receives the invitation, he or she can double-click on the attachment to be prompted to assist the sender of the e-mail. You can exchange messages (chat) with each other during the assistance session. If you have allowed it, the remote help person can click Take Control and actually work on your computer remotely. At the same time, the user who is being assisted remotely can also use his or her keyboard and mouse to access the computer.

7. Set the parameters for the length of time for which the invitation is valid, a remote password, and so on, as shown in Figure 15.26.

8. The recipient receives a message indicating that you are requesting help. The message also warns the recipient about opening attachments from unknown senders, as shown in Figure 15.27.

9. To assist the user who has sent the help message, the recipient opens the attachment, clicks on Yes, and enters any password you have put in place.

FIGURE 15.26

You can set the limit an invitation is available for use, as well as create a password for the connection.

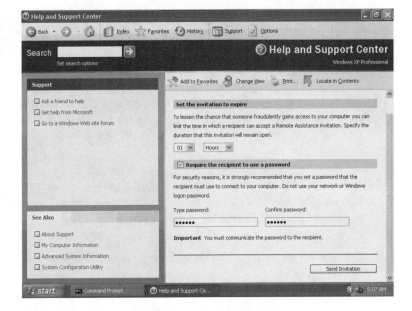

FIGURE 15.27

The recipient of your help request receives an e-mail message requesting help.

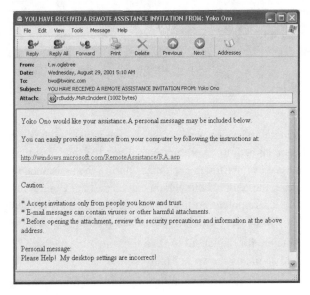

Following acceptance of the request, the recipient can connect to the user who is requesting help and see on his or her monitor the contents of the sender's display.

Although a text-based chat can be useful, if both ends of the connection have speakers and a microphone, the sender and receiver of the help request can actually converse while the remote assistance session is active. This capability can greatly enhance the ability to offer help, especially for users who have nominal typing skills.

You can also use Windows Messenger to send an invitation for Remote Assistance. To do this, follow steps 1 through 3 of the preceding list, next choose Windows Messenger in the Pick How You Want to Contact Your Assistant screen, and then sign in. If you don't already have a Microsoft .NET Passport, you must create that before you can use Windows Messenger. If you get this dialog box, click Next and sign up for a Passport. This chapter won't go through all the screens for this process, but when you have finished, you can then sign in to Windows Messenger.

When you have signed in to use Windows Messenger you can then send an invitation to a person who is on your contact list to request help. After you select the person you want help from, keep in mind that this person must be online or you won't be able to use Windows Messenger to use this feature. In that case, select another contact, or send an e-mail if the help request can wait.

To use Windows Messenger for remote assistance, simply right-click on the person from whom you want to request help. Then click on Invite and To Start Remote Assistance. The recipient of your message can accept or decline the help request. If they decide to help, you will get a dialog box asking you if they can take control of your computer. Select Yes.

> **Note**
>
> You should definitely be concerned about offering to let someone take control of your computer, but if you are using someone from your corporate IT department or other professional environment, you needn't worry too much. If the person messes things up, you can always call his or her boss in the morning and get your computer reconfigured! However, just because you allow someone to take control of your computer, it does not mean it's the end of the line. At any time you can click on Stop Control if you want to end the remote person's assistance. Pressing the Escape (Esc) key will also do the same thing.

15

MANAGING LOCAL USERS

To start working on your computer, the remote operator clicks Take Control; at that point, a dialog box enables you to grant the person permission to take control. The person you choose to help you with remote assistance will literally see your desktop on their screen and be able to enter commands as if he or she was sitting at your keyboard. To keep the person from being confused about which desktop with which he or she is working, the remote help person will see two different Start menus—one for his or her own computer and one for your computer. You can stop the remote control at any time by clicking Stop Control or by pressing the Esc key.

> **Tip**
>
> Send File is another useful feature provided with Remote Assistance. A help desk employee can use this feature, for example, to send a new driver file or other patch file to your computer and then use Remote Assistance to install it for you.

Summary

This chapter has covered a lot of territory! You learned to create a user account for yourself and others who will use the computer. You also learned how to control access to the computer by adding passwords and selecting the type of account for each user. You can even delineate capabilities further by assigning either specific rights to users or by making users members of groups who have a predefined set of right. You can also create your own groups if you find the built-in groups aren't exactly what you need.

You also learned in this chapter that in a workgroup environment, local user groups and user accounts are your main source of control over computer resources (although this isn't so in a domain environment). If you are using Windows XP Professional as your main operating system in a workgroup, then you should become familiar with the concepts covered in this chapter (and others), which tell you how to restrict access to resources and how to track the on-system activities of those using your computer.

Auditing Windows XP Using the Event Viewer

In This Chapter

- Overview of the Event Viewer   *398*
- Setting Options for Log Files   *410*
- Archiving a Log File and Clearing Events   *416*
- How to Halt the Computer When the Security Log Becomes Full   *418*

The Event Viewer is the tool you can use to monitor events recorded by Windows and other applications and to audit actions that users, applications, and the operating system itself perform within Windows XP. Windows XP Professional keeps log files based on three kinds of events:

- Security events
- System events
- Application events

> **Note**
>
> Although Windows XP uses only these three basic log files to record significant events that occur on the system, a Windows Server computer (such as a domain controller) can record events for a few more categories. For more information about the Active Directory and domain controllers, see Appendix B, which is an overview of the Lightweight Directory Access Protocol (LDAP) and the Active Directory. If you want to learn more about joining a domain or participating in a domain that is part of an Active Directory tree, see Chapter 26, "Joining a Domain and the Active Directory." To learn how to monitor the actual performance of software and hardware components, you use the Performance Monitor, which is described in Chapter 22, "Performance Monitoring and Performance Logs and Alerts."

It is important to note here that *not all events are recorded by the operating system by default*. As explained in Chapter 15, "Managing Local Users," you must enable security logging by using the Group Policy Microsoft Management Console (MMC) snap-in. With this snap-in installed, the Local Computer Security applet appears in the Control Panel. This applet enables you to set configuration options and capabilities with the Group Policy Editor, which can make auditing setup easier.

Because applications decide what kinds of events to write to the Application log file, choosing the events is left to the programmer. The Windows XP operating system is configured to write events to the System log file. The Security log file contains nothing, however, until you use the Group Policy Editor to set up a local security policy, and then set up the security events you want to audit.

Overview of the Event Viewer

The Event Viewer is a simple tool to use. You can use the graphical user interface (GUI) applet found in the Control Panel, or you can use the Command Prompt to issue commands that can be used to examine events in the log files. The GUI version is the most

Auditing Windows XP Using the Event Viewer

CHAPTER 16

399

16

AUDITING XP
USING THE
EVENT VIEWER

common method used to review audited events. The command-line version is more useful for system administrators who are creating script files that will perform automatic system maintenance tasks.

To start the Event Viewer, first click on Start, Control Panel to display the Control Panel. In the Pick a Category area, choose Performance and Maintenance; the Performance and Maintenance window appears (see Figure 16.1).

FIGURE 16.1

Use the Performance and Maintenance window to access the Administrative Tools.

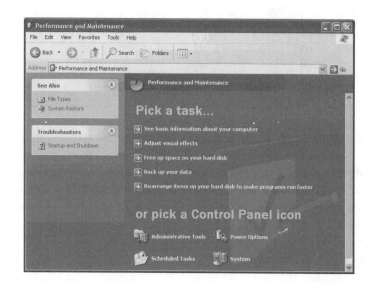

Click the Administrative Tools icon at the bottom of the window to open the Administrative Tools folder. This folder contains a number of important applets such as the Local Security Policy applet (used to set up selected security events for auditing on the local computer), and the Performance Monitor (used to measure the performance of hardware and software components). For now, double-click the Event Viewer icon. The MMC, a tool used for nearly every management application that runs on Windows XP, pops up with the Event Viewer snap-in (see Figure 16.2).

Note

If you have not yet used the Group Policy Editor snap-in, you may not see all of the icons displayed in Figure 16.2. Don't worry, just make sure you read the chapters referenced earlier to learn how to set up a security policy, and you then should see all of these icons.

FIGURE 16.2

The Event Viewer management tool is implemented as a snap-in for the MMC.

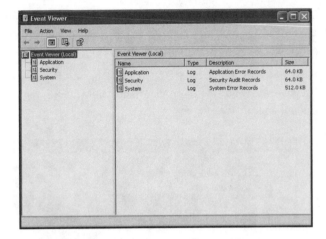

Using the MMC for management tasks helps simplify learning how to use a new management tool because the interface is similar across all the tools. The Event pane (on the left of the Event Viewer window) lists entries for the three basic log files that Windows XP supports. The Details pane, on the right of the window, lists details of the contents of a selected log file. The next few sections discuss these log files and some of the events they record.

Types of Events

To learn more about Event types, you can open one of the log files to view its contents in the Event Viewer Details pane. To make it easier for you to scan through the details of a log file, the Type field for each log file includes a small icon and name that identify the item type. The following types of events are recorded in the event log:

- Error—This type of event record is important, and it is marked with an *X* in a red sphere. An event of this type indicates that some significant event (such as the loss of data or failure of a hardware component) has occurred. Be sure to routinely review all events of this sort in each of the three log files.

- Warning—This event type is marked by an exclamation point inside a yellow triangle, and it records an event that, although problematic, wasn't bad enough to generate an error. For example, a Warning type of event occurs when the system detects that you are running low on disk space. The system issues a Warning message, but your work can continue (until the disk space is completely full, that is).

- Information—Marked by an *i* inside a balloon, an information event occurs when the system issues messages to keep the user or system auditor informed of the

Auditing Windows XP Using the Event Viewer

CHAPTER 16

401

16

AUDITING XP
USING THE
EVENT VIEWER

progress of a process on the system. For example, when an application or service starts up, the system might issue a series of information messages, each of which is recorded as an information event in the Application Event log. If something goes wrong on the system, reviewing the record of information events can help you determine what went wrong; if an information event is missing, you can start troubleshooting by looking for warning or error events relating to the service or application.

- Success Audit—This type of event is marked by a key icon, and it shows up in the Security log file only if you have enabled security logging. Success Audit events record the issuing of message boxes when users log in or access records. There are good reasons to track even successful login efforts. For example, if records indicate that someone is logging in during hours when they should not, you know that the person may be abusing computer privileges or that someone else is logging in with that person's username and password.

- Failure Audit—This event type is marked by a padlock and it indicates that someone tried unsuccessfully to log in or access a resource. This sort of event can tell you that someone is trying to break into your system, "probing" to see what can and cannot be accessed, or that person is simply incapable of using his or her password for a logon. In any case, multiple events like this should encourage you to spend some time reviewing security procedures with the user.

The Event Logging Service

Early in the boot process for Windows XP, the event logging service is started. This is so that it can record events relating to other components of the operating system (such as services) that are started during the boot process. The log files are not purged when the event logging service starts; the logs contain historical information until the log file becomes full.

The events that are logged by default can be viewed using the Event Viewer by anyone using the computer. However, only a user account that has administrator rights can view the Security log file.

Note

You can set the computer to halt when the Security log file becomes full. That way, you don't overwrite important Security log history. You will learn this technique later in this chapter.

> **Tip**
>
> If you are using Windows XP as a home-based computer system, don't discount the importance of the Security log file. If you connect to the Internet (and who doesn't today?), the Security log file can be just as useful to you as it can be in a corporate environment. You need to know who, when, and what account is being used when a potential hacking attempt occurs. The Security log file can tell you.

Event Records

By default, the Event Viewer displays a single line of information for each event record after you select the file you want to view. The records are displayed in a sorted order according to the date and time fields in the record, and the newest record appears first on the display.

In the Details pane, you see a limited amount of information. To view all of the information about a particular record, you can double-click on the record in the Details pane, which brings up Event Properties pages that contain additional data recorded in the event record.

Event records can contain all kinds of data, but the specifics of any particular record depend on the kind of event and the log file (Application, System, or Security). All event records contain a field called *Event ID*, which is a numeric value that can be very useful if you need to call Microsoft for support. Other fields, such as User or Computer may or may not have values—again, this depends on the kind of event being recorded. Each record should have a field labeled Source, which tells you the component or application that logged the event. Some event records also have a Category field. Each record has a Date, Time, and Type field.

The Events Properties page contains a Description field, used to give a brief explanation of the event record. For example, you may find informational text telling you that a service has started or stopped. Some records contain binary data, which is usually not very helpful, unless you are a programmer and are familiar with the component that generated the event record.

The Description field also contains a uniform resource listing (URL) that you can click on to go to a Microsoft Web site, set up to provide additional relevant information. If you click on this URL, specific information about the event record and perhaps some information from the Registry, the product name, version, and filenames associated with the event are sent to Microsoft. This information is used to construct a query that may return

Auditing Windows XP Using the Event Viewer

CHAPTER 16

403

16

AUDITING XP
USING THE
EVENT VIEWER

information from the Microsoft Knowledge Base. This information can help you determine what caused the event, as well as provide a possible remedy to the problem.

> **Caution**
>
> When using the Description field URL to get further information or assistance with an event record, remember that even information contained in Microsoft's Knowledge Base should be taken with a grain of salt. For example, if you receive information telling you that you can fix your problem by editing the Registry, consider taking precautions such as making a backup of the system (including the Registry) before you start hacking away. If you have a support contract with Microsoft, talk to a support technician directly before making any significant changes to the system.

> **Note**
>
> According to Microsoft's documentation, using a URL contained in an event record will not send any information to Microsoft about your email address, or the names of files that are not related to the event record. In other words, no personal information will be sent. Only the necessary information that is used to construct a query will be sent, if you decide to use this option. Of course, it goes without saying, if you want to use the URL option, you already must have established an Internet connection before this will work.

The Application Log File

The events that are logged in this log file do not require that you perform any configuration. Applications that are written for Windows operating systems contain code that, depending on the developer who writes the application, can send records to this log file.

Figure 16.3 shows how the right side of the Details pane changes when you click on the Application log file entry in the left pane.

The Details pane for this Application log contains Information, Warning, and Error event records. Some columns of data to the right of the window are cut off due to the size of the window (you can enlarge the window to full-screen size or use the scroll bars to view more columns).

To view the details about a specific record, double-click on the record (or right-click on the record and select Properties). Figure 16.4 is an example of an information event record's properties page.

FIGURE 16.3

When you click on a log file in the Event pane, the Details pane will display the records for that log file.

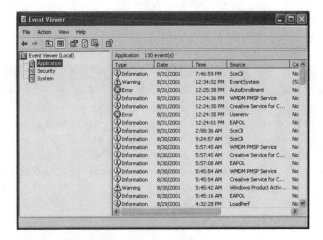

FIGURE 16.4

Double-click on an event in the Details pane to view the properties of the event record if you want to see all the information contained in the event records.

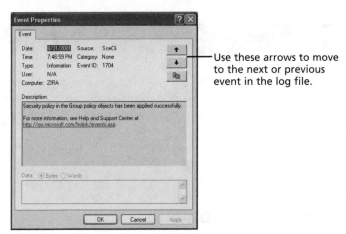

Use these arrows to move to the next or previous event in the log file.

Some problems can generate multiple records. To quickly scan through the details of events that precede and follow the current record, use the up and down arrow buttons on the right side of the properties page to see the next or previous event in the log file. In the Description section of this event record is the URL to the Microsoft Web site. Since this is an information type of message reporting that security policy created for the computer has been applied, you probably have little to learn by using the URL.

To dismiss the Event Properties dialog box, simply click OK, or Cancel.

The Security Log File

If you are concerned about protecting your data, consider this your most important log file. If you use the computer at home for merely recreational uses, then you probably

Auditing Windows XP Using the Event Viewer

CHAPTER 16

405

16

AUDITING XP
USING THE
EVENT VIEWER

don't care about recording when someone logs in or out of the computer, or when certain files or folders are accessed. For all other environments, however, you should set up a security policy and enable auditing on the resources you want to monitor using the Event Viewer.

Figure 16.5 shows the Event Viewer with the Security log file selected. Note that the event types in the Details pane consist of Success Audit or Failure Audit records.

FIGURE 16.5

The Security log file records significant events such as successful and failed logon attempts.

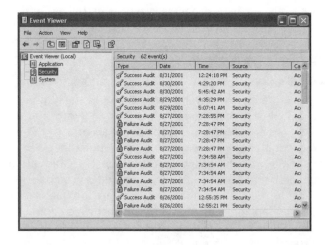

You use the same method to view the Event Properties page of any event in the Details pane. In Figure 16.6, the Success Audit record has been double-clicked to review its properties.

FIGURE 16.6

This record shows that a user was successful when logging onto the local computer.

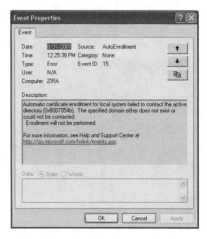

Here, the Event Properties dialog box looks similar to the one shown earlier for the Application log. However, some of the fields are different. For example, under the User field, you would think a successful logon would indicate the name of the user that logged onto the computer. However, that is not the case. Instead, it shows the user account (which, in this case, is the Windows XP system account that runs the components of the operating system that authenticate users) that logged the record. In the Description field, you can see the name of the user account, the name of the workstation and, as usual, a URL you can use to find out more about the event record. But again, since this was simply a successful logon, there is no need to use the URL at this point.

Tip

Don't forget that the System account is not the same thing as the Administrator account. The System account is one that you don't log into. The Windows XP operating system uses the System account to run services and to perform other functions. You won't find it in the Control Panel applet that is used to configure user accounts though. Keep in mind that most services, which are usually the basic components of the operating system and add-on components, use the System account. You can, however, as you will learn in Chapter 14, "Using the Control Panel," use an applet found there to select which user account a service should be run under. This is a feature to allow users to add their own services (a process that runs in the background).

Figure 16.7 shows an example of a Failure Audit event in the Security log file. In this case, you can see a different number is used for the Event ID field; and, in the Description section, you can see the name of the account that someone tried to log into, but was unsuccessful at doing so.

FIGURE 16.7

This is an example of a Failure Audit record, showing the name of the account from where the failed logon attempt was made.

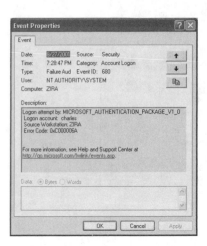

Auditing Windows XP Using the Event Viewer

CHAPTER 16

407

16

AUDITING XP
USING THE
EVENT VIEWER

The Security log file can also show attempts (both successful and failed) to access system resources such as files, folders, and printers. This chapter can't list every kind of event record that can be generated, but keep in mind that you would look for the Security log file to find records of these events, if you set them up for auditing.

> ### Tip
>
> If you want to audit access to files and folders, then you can only do so on NT File System (NTFS) partitions. If you install Windows XP on a File Allocation Table (FAT) partition, then you will not be able to set up security auditing. The FAT and FAT32 file systems do not contain the necessary data fields to store access control lists (ACLs), which track who is and isn't allowed to access a file or folder. Therefore, if you want to audit file-and-folder access, use NTFS.

The System Log File

The last log file is the System log file (see Figure 16.8). This log records a number of system events, including those that occur during service startup. The records in this log may tell you, for example, that a service failed to startup because it depended on another service that hadn't started properly.

FIGURE 16.8

This figure shows the details recorded by the System.

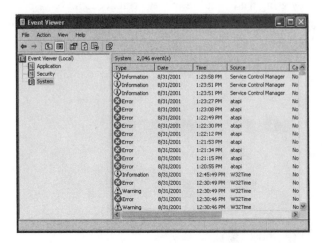

Hardware components that do not function as they should, cause the system to generate records in this log, too. Figure 16.9 shows the record generated when a standard disk drive (in this case a CD-ROM drive) failed to respond when an application was trying to write to it.

FIGURE 16.9

The system can log a large number of significant events in the System log file.

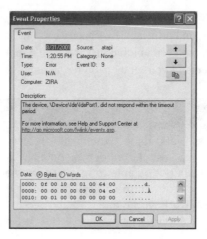

Here, the description indicates that a timer expired before the disk drive responded to a request made by the system. In this kind of situation, you may indeed want to use the URL listed in the Description field to get more information about this kind of event. Note that the system doesn't just log Error type events in the System log file. Figures 16.10, 16.11, and 16.12 show the properties pages for three Information event records of a successful use of the CD-Burner application.

As you can see, by using the Event Viewer, you can get some very specific information about what is going on behind the scenes when your Window XP computer is performing tasks for you. What may seem like a simple process to you might generate many event records. If you become familiar with the records maintained by the System log when things work as they should, you will be better equipped to troubleshoot problems that arise.

FIGURE 16.10

This Information record tells you that the CD-burning component of Windows XP sent a message to the CD burner to start burning a CD.

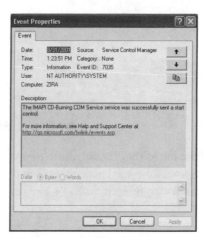

Auditing Windows XP Using the Event Viewer

CHAPTER 16

409

16

AUDITING XP
USING THE
EVENT VIEWER

FIGURE 16.11

In this example, the CD burning process is running.

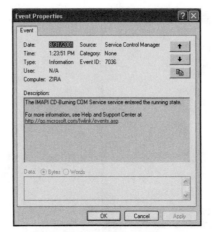

FIGURE 16.12

Finally, you can see that the burning of the CD was completed successfully.

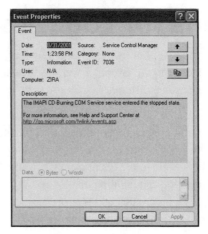

For example, if your computer is a member of a domain, you may know nothing of many domain management–related services that happen in the background. In Figure 16.13, for example, a record was generated in the System log file when this computer, which is a member of the domain twoinc.com, used the time synchronization service provided by a domain controller. Keeping computer clocks synchronized in a domain is an important function because many domain-related tasks use time stamps to coordinate information.

Because applications can sometimes make use of system services, you should always consider looking at event records in the System log file, as well as the Application log file when troubleshooting problem applications. An example of this is the CD burning event records mentioned earlier in this chapter. These were generated by an application, using a service offered by the operating system and not by the application itself.

FIGURE 16.13

The System log file records many significant events, even for things you probably don't know your computer is doing.

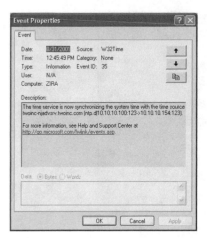

Setting Options for Log Files

Windows XP offers fantastic capabilities for configuring just about every feature of the operating system. This capability extends to the Event Viewer log files, and is an especially important feature for these files, since different log files may be more important to one user than another.

To begin the configuration process, bring up the properties pages for the log file you want to make configurable. For the purposes of this chapter, use the Application log file. To open the properties page, right-click on the log file in the Event pane, and from the menu that appears, select Properties; alternatively, you can highlight the log file in the Event pane, then select Properties from the Action menu or click on the Properties icon (which looks like a hand holding a piece of paper). The properties page appears (see Figure 16.14).

FIGURE 16.14

The properties pages for a log file enable you to control where the log file is stored, among other properties.

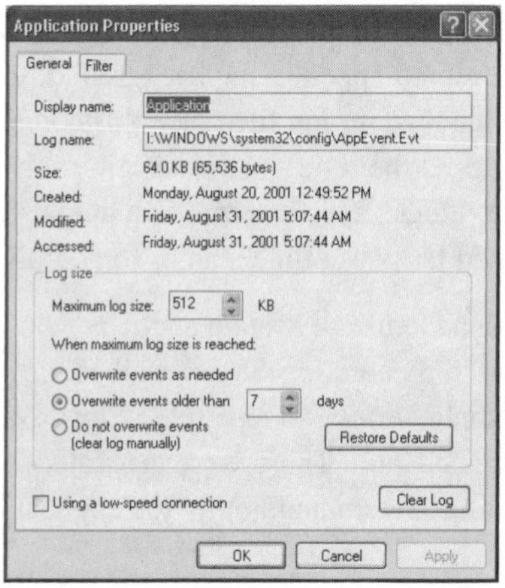

Configuring the Location of Log Files

In the General tab of the Application properties page is a field called *Display Name*. This is the name the log file uses when you see it in the MMC console. This field is configurable because it lets you change the name of log files you work with when using the files. That capability is useful when you archive log files. You can add archived log files to the left side of the MMC console as if they were current log files. Keeping historical information available from archived log files can be useful when you consider that many security infractions or virus infections and other such things may take more than a month or two to show up.

> **Tip**
>
> When renaming log files for archiving, it is a good idea to give some indication in its name of the date range of the archived data. For example a name like `APPLIC0802` makes it easy to recognize that this archived log file stores the Application log file for the month of August 2002.

Underneath the Display Name field is another field that you can use to specify the actual path and filename for the file that will store the logged events. Although it is a good idea on a Windows XP computer to accept this default setting, a system administrator may decide to use another path and/or location. You can use this field for that purpose.

The next few fields are informational only:

- Size—This is the current amount of information stored in the log file. You can use another field on this page to change the maximum log file size or indicate that you wish to use a round-robin approach and have older events overwritten by newer events.

- Created—This field shows you when the current log file was created. If you archive log files on a periodic basis, the information in this field may be useful to you.

- Modified—This field simply tells you the last date/time that a record was added to this log file.

- Accessed—This field will also tell you the last date/time that this log file was written to, but it will also tell you the last date/time that the file was read. In other words, you learn the last time someone looked at this file.

These fields can be helpful when you set out to plan a security policy about the frequency at which a log file should be examined or archived. In the next section, you will learn how to control the size of log files and set the method for how events are written to the log file.

Sizing a Log File and Setting Overwrite Parameters

Again, depending on the type of log file and how important the information is to you, the decisions you make about how much disk space a log file should take up and whether to allow older events to be overwritten by newer events all depends on your particular environment.

If you experience very little application, system, or security problems and you check these log files on a frequent basis, then you probably can use the defaults provided by the initial installation of Windows XP. Let us look at the following fields:

- Maximum log size—The default for all log files is simply 512MB. That may seem like quite a lot of disk space, but if you configure the Security log to log a large number of events, then you may want to consider changing the log file size to a larger amount. No matter which type of log file, simply use the up and down arrows on this field to increase (or even decrease) the amount of disk space you will allow this log file to use. To be safe, you should increase each log file's size to at least 1MB. Today's computers come with such large disk drives that allocating 3MB to three files doesn't really take up that much space, especially when you consider how valuable the information can be when troubleshooting.

Caution

If you set a small log file size for the events that are sent to the log file and if you don't use the next few choices to allow older events to be overwritten, then you will receive a message on your screen when a file becomes full. In such a case, change the settings to let the log file overwrite older events or change the size of the log file.

Also note that although you can increase the size of a log file while it is in use, you must clear events in the log file before you can reduce its size. Don't worry; when you clear the events in a log file, you are given a chance to archive the data first. Now you don't have to worry about losing any information.

Auditing Windows XP Using the Event Viewer

CHAPTER 16

413

16

AUDITING XP
USING THE
EVENT VIEWER

- Overwrite events as needed—Using this radio button causes the log file to act as a first-in, first-out (FIFO) buffer, where older events are deleted from the file when it becomes full so that newer events can be written. I don't recommend this for the Security log file, since security problems can take possibly weeks or even months to become known.

- Overwrite events older than—This field allows you to specify a number of days after which older log file entries will be overwritten. Again, this option isn't appropriate for the Security log file. If you are having a problem with an application you should notice it quickly. The default here is seven days, but you can use the field that follows this line to change the number of days by using the up and down arrows.

- Do not overwrite events (clear log manually)—This is the selection to use for the Security log. If you are having an application problem or a system problem and haven't noticed it in 7 days, which is the default, you aren't paying attention. However, if security is important (and where is it not?), then you should choose this option.

The Restore Defaults button simply resets the settings on this page to what they were when Windows XP was installed. The Clear Log button, however, empties all event records from the selected log file. When you use this button, a dialog box will pop up and ask if you want to save the data in an archived log file. If so, select Yes, and you will be given another dialog box, which is the typical Save As dialog box that most applications present. However, the options here for the file format of the archived file include the following:

- Event Log (`*.evt`)—This file format stores all of the information—including the binary information, if present in the event records—and it's the selection you should use when archiving log files that are important to you.

- Text (tab delimited) (`*.txt`)—This type of file separates individual data elements by a tab, but does not include binary information. Use this for importing data into an application, such as a database, word processor, or spreadsheet that supports this format.

- CSV (Comma delimited) (`*.csv`)—This is similar to the tab delimited format, but commas are used instead of tab characters to separate record fields. Check your application to see which type of import file it supports!

Select the Yes button if you want to save the log file data. If you select the No button, then the events in the log file are cleared, and are gone forever!

Using the Filter Tab on the Log File Properties Sheet

The Filter tab works much like the Find selection found in the View menu. However, when you use the View menu, it is a one-time thing. You can set options on the Filter tab that will show you only the events you want to see each time you bring up the particular log file that you are customizing. Click on the Filter tab, and you'll you will see a property sheet like that shown in Figure 16.15.

FIGURE 16.15

The Filter tab allows you to set criteria for those events to be displayed.

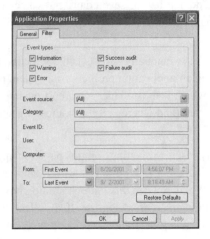

At the top of this dialog box are the five types of event records that were discussed earlier in this chapter. Just select the check boxes for the types of event records you want to see. This can be useful if you don't really care to see Information messages, since they just log events that tell you that things are actually working as they should. Information messages are more useful when something has gone wrong, and when you go looking for them they *don't* show up!

> **Tip**
>
> Don't worry about losing data when you set filter options. These options control only the records that are displayed, not the data, which is stored in the log file. When you use a filter, the system still keeps storing the entire event record for the log file you are customizing. Using a filter (or the Find function in the View menu) is simply a method to help you quickly review pertinent information in a log file.

Auditing Windows XP Using the Event Viewer

CHAPTER 16

415

16

AUDITING XP
USING THE
EVENT VIEWER

The Other fields that follow the Event Type check boxes include the following:

- Event source—This is a long list, and you can use the down arrow to select a source. Using this field in a filter can be helpful to eliminate a lot of records from your view if you already know the source of the record. The number of sources can be numerous, depending on the log file, and can range from system components to specific applications. So use this option carefully so that you don't inadvertently filter out records that might help you in troubleshooting a problem.

- Category—Similar to the Event Source field, this drop-down menu contains selections that are based on the log file you are customizing. For example, in the Security log file, the categories are those for which you set up security audit logging, such as Logon and Logoff, Policy Change, Privilege Use, and so on.

- Event ID—This is a numeric value. You can download a list of these values if you have the time to perform an exhausted search at Microsoft's Web site. However, keep in mind that Event IDs can change over time as service packs, patches, and additional Windows components are added to your system. This is most useful for troubleshooting problems that are occurring on a frequent basis because you already know the Event ID from looking at a current record, and you will want to quickly determine if there are any other instances of this type of event record in the log file.

- User—You can enter a user's logon account name here to filter out all records for a particular user or to track what the user is doing on your system.

- Computer—If other computers connect to your computer (for instance, to a printer or to files that are shared on the network), then you can enter a computer name here to find all of the records pertaining to a particular computer.

At the bottom of the dialog box, you can use the From and To fields to narrow your view so that you only see records for a particular date range. The Restore Defaults button will simply set all fields back to the way they look in Figure 16.15 above, which sets the filter to show all events.

Sorting Event Records

As you learned earlier, by default, the Event Viewer sorts records and displays them by date and time with the newest records at the top of the list, followed by the remaining records in descending order. You can change the sort order by using the View menu and selecting Newest First or Oldest First.

If you want to change the data on which the records are sorted, just click on the column you want to sort by. The records will be redisplayed (according to the sort order you have selected from the View menu), and then sorted by using data in the column on which you clicked. If you click twice on the column, the sort order will be reversed.

Adding and Removing Columns From the Details Pane

Since space is limited and a lot of data can be displayed in the Details pane, you can pick and choose the columns of data you want to see. Simply use the View and then Add/Remove columns, to produce the Add/Remove columns dialog box shown in Figure 16.16. Always remember to highlight the log file for which you want to change columns before you use the Add/Remove column option.

FIGURE 16.16

Select the column to add or remove and click the appropriate button.

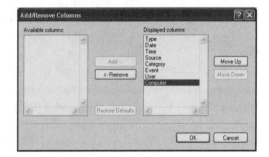

Here you can see that by default, all columns are selected and are listed under the Displayed columns list. To remove a column from the display, click on it once and click the Remove button. The column name then appears in the Available columns list so that you can select it again in the future should you change your mind. To change the order in which a column appears in the Display pane, simply click on the column in the Displayed Columns list and use the Move Up or Move Down buttons to change its order in the list.

Click OK to dismiss the dialog box.

Archiving a Log File and Clearing Events

Since today's disk drives take up so little space and there are many different types of removable media, from floppy discs to CD-R recordable disks, you may never need to clear the events in a log file without first archiving the log file. Once you have archived a log file, you can then copy the archived file to removable media or include it in your normal backup schedule so that it is saved for a long period of time. Keep in mind that viruses and Trojan horses may take many months to either start causing problems or to draw attention! If you keep your log files archived, you may be able to use them (talk to your lawyers) to provide an audit trail that can help you identify how the system became infiltrated in the first place. For example, you might find in an old log file that a user account was used during off-hours, indicating that the employee has some explaining to do. Keeping log files archived for at least a year is a good idea.

To archive a log file, follow these steps:

1. Highlight the log file you want to archive; from the Action menu, select Save Log File As; the Save Filename As window appears, as shown in Figure 16.17.

FIGURE 16.17

Use this dialog box to archive a log file for future reference.

2. Use the options in the dialog box to select the location to store archived log files and specify a name for the log file.
3. Click the Save button to save the archived data.

Note also that when you use this method to archive a log file, the event records remain in the log file and are not cleared. To archive a log file and clear all of the events, use the Clear all Events selection from the Action menu.

Caution

The type of archive file you choose to create does make a difference in the data, which is saved in the resulting file. If you use text in a comma-delimited file format (which is more suited for creating a data file that you can import into another program such as a spreadsheet or database program), then the binary data of the event record (which can be all important when diagnosing a tricky problem), will not be saved in the file! In order to make sure the entire record, including the binary data, is saved in your archived log files, use the `.evt` file format.

When you want to view the contents of an archived log file, simply use Open Log File from the Action menu and select the archived log file.

How to Halt the Computer When the Security Log Becomes Full

If you are serious about tracking security, then you won't want security logs overwritten. To avoid that situation, Windows XP gives you the option of halting the computer when the security log becomes full.

> **Tip**
>
> Because broadband, fast connections are becoming more available today, and because they basically leave your computer connected to the Internet day in and day out (unless you turn off the computer), you are an easy target for a hacker on the Internet. Be sure to read Chapter 25, "Configuring Your Computer for an Internet Connection." You will need to learn to use the built-in Internet Firewall that is provided with Windows XP. Although this simple firewall may not be a complete solution to the hacker problem, it does a very good job of keeping out a lot of potential problems.

You have already learned in this chapter about setting a large file size for your security log and archiving the security log files. Setting the computer to automatically shut down when the Security log file becomes full is the third part of the formula for configuring and managing your security log file for optimum safety.

> **Caution**
>
> **Danger! Danger, Will Robinson!** You are about to edit the Registry! Every text you read about Windows NT or Windows 2000 always gives you a warning that when you make edits to the Registry, you may make your computer unbootable or cause other damage. Before you proceed, create a backup of your system disk partition, and especially make sure to include the Registry. See Chapter 21, "Using Backup on Windows XP," for details.

Editing the Registry

Setting the computer to halt when the security log fills requires that you edit the registry. This section presents the changes you will need to make. If you are unfamiliar with editing the Windows Registry, you really need to read Chapter 20, "The Windows XP Registry," before you go any farther.

Before you edit the Registry, you first need to change the settings on the Properties sheet for the Security log file, as described earlier. Specifically, select the option Do Note Overwrite Events (Clear Log Manually).

Now that you have that out of the way, you are ready to edit the Registry. To begin editing the Registry, type REGEDIT at the Command Prompt. Using your mouse to navigate the Registry tree structure, select:

- Registry Hive: HKEY_LOCAL_MACHINE\SYSTEM
- Registry Key: \CurrentControlSet\Control\Lsa
- Name: CrashOnAuditFail
- Type: REG_DWORD
- Value: 1

Note that you may have to create this entry if it does not already exist on your computer. Also, you must reboot the computer before this change will take effect. If you didn't follow the previous advice and make a backup of your system partition before editing the Registry, please don't send angry emails to the author or the publisher!

What to Do When the Computer Crashes Because of a Full Security Log File

When the log file fills up and the system crashes, you will need to have an Administrator on hand to reboot the computer and make some more changes. As a matter of fact, no one but an Administrator account will be able to boot the computer and log on when it has been halted because of a full Security log file. If a normal user boots the computer and tries to log on, they will get a pop up message saying Audit Failed. This is your indication that it is time to find an Administrator.

After logging on as an Administrator, bring up the Event Viewer and use the procedure described earlier to archive the Security log file. Once this is accomplished, clear the events from the file so that it is no longer full.

Use the Registry editor again and delete the item labeled CrasOnAuditFail and then recreate it again. You must do this step and reboot the computer, or the computer will no longer halt when the Security log becomes full.

Summary

The Event Viewer is a police officer and detective for your Windows XP computer. Many users may skip this chapter thinking, "It will never happen to me." However, with the rapid growth of the Internet and corporate networks, keeping track of the actions performed on your computer can serve two important purposes. First, event logs can help you track down security breaches or application failures. Second, this record can also act in your favor by showing the actions you have taken. As you have learned in this chapter, both types of records can help you monitor the events on your computer. Using the Event Viewer can help protect the innocent and track down those who would take advantage of a system that has not been properly secured.

Windows maintains three primary event logs: Application, System, and Security. Windows records its own events to the System log and other Applications record events to the Applications log. The Security log is used only for auditing events that you or an administrator has enabled. Within each log file, different types of events (such as information, warning, and error events) let you examine the behind-the-scenes activities of Windows.

Printing with
Windows XP

IN THIS CHAPTER

- **Windows XP Printing Basics: Defining Some Terms** *422*

- **Using the Add Printer Wizard** *424*

- **Managing Printer Properties** *433*

- **Managing Printers** *438*

- **Finding Printers on the Network** *441*

CHAPTER 17

Windows XP Professional can send output to almost any kind of printer you can find on the market today. Of all the topics in this book, setting up a printer is perhaps one of the easiest tasks you will have to do. Since Windows XP supports plug-and-play, many printers connected to a local port such as LPT1: are detected automatically. You may have to use the Add Printer Wizard to select the manufacturer and model of the printer you are adding. With Windows XP, you can use printers connected directly to your workstation, the Internet, and print servers. A print server can be a Windows server-class computer or a printer appliance often used to connect several printers to a single network connection.

In this chapter, you will learn how to configure printing on your computer, as well as some basic terms that are used with Windows XP when describing the printing process.

Windows XP Printing Basics: Defining Some Terms

Before you connect a printer to your computer, you should understand some of the terms that the Windows XP documentation uses when it discusses printing. These are as follows:

- Printer—This is the actual physical printer that renders your output onto paper or some other material. In previous versions of Windows NT, this was referred to as the *printer device,* whereas the term printer was an abstract software concept that acted as an interface between the application and the physical printer.

- Logical printer—Windows XP uses the term logical printer to refer to the interface between your application and the printer device. In other words, a logical printer under Windows XP is a software abstraction of the actual physical printer. Because of this separation, it is possible to create more than one printer, each of which sends its output to the same physical printer device. This can be useful when you want to set up printers that have different characteristics but use the same device. This can make the end-user's job a lot simpler, since she can choose a printer that supports the characteristics it requires, instead of having to configuring these characteristics for a single printer each time something different needs to be done. You can also set up printer pools, where output sent to a single logical printer is divided among several physical printers.

- Print server—This is a computer dedicated to managing printers on a network. It can be any computer on the network and it can manage printers attached to local ports, as well as printers attached to the network. Clients can send their print jobs to the print server, which then sends the print job to the appropriate printer. One advantage of using a print server is that you do not have to load the drivers for all the printers the client uses on the client's workstation itself. Instead, when the client wants to print, it downloads the correct driver for the printer from the print server. Thus, when you install a physical printer, it is necessary to install the correct drivers on just the print server.

- Print spooler—This term originated as an acronym for *simultaneous print operations online*. For Windows XP, the print spooler is a collection of dynamically linked libraries that receives, processes, schedules, and distributes documents for printing purposes. Documents can be stored in memory or on disk while the print spooler is manipulating them. You can view the documents currently "spooled" to print by double-clicking on the printer icon that appears when you send documents to print.

- Print monitor—This term has two definitions: a language monitor and a port monitor. The language monitor is used if the printer can support bi-directional printing, which allows the spooler to obtain information about the printer from the printer. More important is the port monitor, which actually controls the input/output (I/O) process of sending the print job data to the physical printer.

- Print processor—This is the component of the printing process that receives a print job and makes alterations to the data if necessary to make sure that the print job prints correctly. The print processor works with the printer driver to instruct the spooler on how to send the print job to the printer.

- Print job—This is both the data to be printed and any code or commands needed to make the printed document print correctly.

- Data types—Windows XP supports several printing data types. The spooler sends the raw data type to the printer with no changes made. This is the default for non-Windows clients. The Raw [FF appended] data type is the same as the raw type, but a form feed character is appended to the last page. The raw [FF auto] data type adds "FF" to the end of the last page of a print job only if one is not already present. The NT EMF (enhanced metafile) data type is the default for documents created by Windows clients. The file output is smaller than would be produced by a raw print type. Finally, the text data type is simply ANSI text.

- Printer port—This is an interface between the printer and the computer. This can be a local physical port such as LPT1 or COM1, or it can be a network address for printers that reside on the network or on a print server.

When you create a printer using the Add Printer Wizard, you create a logical printer. The port you select for the printer will depend on where the printer is located. When you send a document to print, the logical printer will use the print processor and print spooler to control how the document is printed, while the print monitor will send the data to the printer.

Now that you have learned about a few of the basics, the next few sections will show you how to set up a printer on your Windows XP computer.

Using the Add Printer Wizard

You can make connections from Windows XP to printers that are physically attached to a local port on your computer to other computers that act as print servers, and to computers that have their own network cards and are directly attached to the network. In this section, you will walk through the steps for using each of these methods to connect to a printer. First, it is important to understand the difference between creating a local printer and connecting to a print share.

A local printer is one that is either directly cabled to your computer or directly attached to the network. That second option may not make sense when you first think about it and it requires some clarification. By local printer, Windows XP is differentiating between which computer controls the spooling and interaction with the printer. When you create a local printer, Windows XP can use the LPT ports or COM ports on your computer to perform I/O, or it can use a network port you create to send data to the printer.

In Figure 17.1 you can see an illustration of this concept.

FIGURE 17.1

Windows XP can connect to local printers, networked printers, or printers on a print server.

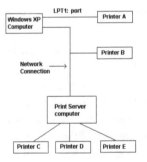

In Figure 17.1, Printer A is connected to the LPT1: port on the Windows XP computer. Thus, the print jobs that get sent to that computer are under the local control of the Windows XP computer. Printer B is connected directly to the network. Many printers come equipped with a network connection, or you can buy a device such as the HP JetDirect card to make the network connection. If you want to set up the Windows XP computer to send print jobs to Printer B, then this is also considered a local connection since the Windows XP computer will be responsible for managing the communications between itself and the printer. The only difference between Printer A and Printer B is the port used. To the Windows XP computer, both are local ports. One is a parallel port (LPT1:) while the other is a network port.

However, if the Windows XP computer wants to send a print job to Printer C, D, or E, then it does not control the communications with those printers. Instead, the print server to which those printers are attached is in charge. Hence, in this case you would, when using the Add Printer Wizard, choose to make a connection to a printer.

Now let us look at setting up a local port using the Add Printer Wizard.

Connecting to a Local Printer

You will need a little information about the local printer port before you can use the wizard. If the printer is directly attached to the computer, then you will need to know the port name (i.e., LPT1: or COM1:). If it is a networked computer, then you will have to know its address. For a networked computer, you may also need to know a print queue name (we will be getting to that shortly).

Using a Printer Connected Directly to Your Computer

To add a local printer to your computer, use the following steps:

1. Click Start, Control Panel. When the Control Panel appears, select Printers and Other Hardware (if you are using the classic view of the Control Panel, simply double-click the Printers and Faxes icon).

2. The Add Printer Wizard dialog box pops up. Click Next to continue.

3. The next dialog box the wizard presents (Figure 17.2) asks if you want to connect to a local printer or to a printer attached to another computer. If the printer is directly attached to your computer, then choose the first radio button, Local Printer. For directly connected printers you can also use the check box labeled Automatically Detect and Install My Plug and Play Printer.

FIGURE 17.2

Choose Local Printer to set up a printer connected to your computer or for one connected directly to the network.

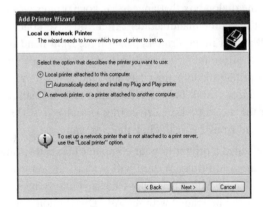

4. If you selected the Plug and Play option and the wizard is unable to locate a plug-and-play–enabled printer attached to your computer, you will get an error message. Otherwise, it prompts you to search for a suitable driver and to select one from a list. If you get this error message, click Next. If a driver is located, then it will be installed and you can skip to step 8 of this procedure. If a driver is not found or your printer is not plug-and-play compatible, then you will see the Select a Printer Port dialog box that lets you select an existing port or create a new port (Figure 17.3).

FIGURE 17.3

You can select a port to use for the printer connection or create a new port.

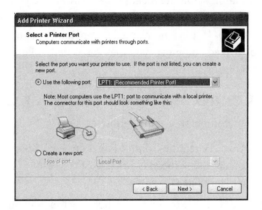

5. The radio button titled Use the Following Port can be selected if you are using one of the default ports (such as LPT1: or COM1:). It can also be used if you have previously created a port. For this example, we will assume that the printer is connected to one of these local ports (we will discuss networked printers later). After selecting the radio button, click Next to continue.

6. Figure 17.4 shows the dialog box that appears, if your printer was not detected by Plug and Play. First select the manufacturer. After you have done that, a list of supported printers will appear in the Printers pane on the right-hand side of the window. Select the printer from this list and click Next. You can also use the Have Disk button if your printer manufacturer has supplied you with a driver for a new printer that is compatible with Windows XP. In that case, a small dialog box will pop up and ask for the location of the driver files (usually your floppy disk drive). Once the driver is read from the disk, click the Next button.

7. If you have already added a printer to your computer that is the same model and manufacturer, then the Add Printer Wizard will next ask if you want to keep the existing driver or replace it with a new one. Unless you have received a new driver (or example, one that can be loaded with the Add Disk button), you should probably choose to keep the existing driver. If the manufacturer has rewritten the driver,

then you should use the Add Disk button in Step 6 and select the radio button
labeled Replace Existing Driver. Otherwise, select the radio button labeled Keep
Existing Driver (Recommended) and then click Next.

FIGURE 17.4

*If your printer
isn't plug-and-
play compatible,
then you must
select it from a list
of supported
printers.*

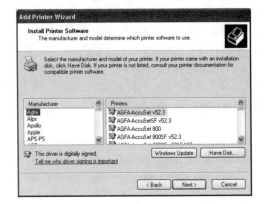

17

**PRINTING WITH
WINDOWS XP**

8. The wizard will next ask you to name your printer. You can use up to 31 characters
   for the name. Keep in mind that some applications won't permit a long printer
   name, so as the dialog box suggests, keep the name as short as possible. From this
   same dialog box, you can select from the Yes or No radio buttons under Do You
   Want to Use This Printer as the Default Printer. Click Yes if you want this to be the
   default printer that applications will use. Click Next when you have named your
   computer and made this selection.

9. Figure 17.5 shows the Printer Sharing dialog box that pops up next. Use the radio
   buttons to decide if you will allow other computers to connect to this printer
   through your computer. If you do choose to share the computer, you will also have
   to enter a share name for it. As usual, when you have made your selections, click
   Next to continue.

FIGURE 17.5

*You can choose to
share the printer
on the network.*

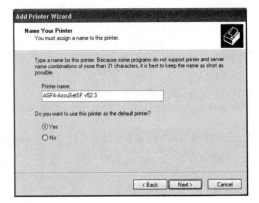

10. The Add Printer Wizard will then ask you to supply some optional information about your printer. This is useful if you are going to share it on the network, as other Windows computers will be able to see this information. The first field, Location, allows you to enter text describing where the printer is located. The second field, Comment, can be used to describe the printer's capabilities or for any other comments you want to use. Click Next to continue (you are almost finished).

11. Finally, the wizard will display a dialog box that asks if you want to print a test page. Use the Yes or No radio buttons, and then click Next. It is recommended that you do perform this test now to be sure that the printer is working. Note that the test page won't actually print when you click Next; there is still one more step to the finish line.

12. The Completing the Add Printer Wizard dialog box will pop up and display the choices you have made. If you're not satisfied with a selection you've made, use Back to go back and make changes. Otherwise, click Finish. If you have chosen to print a test page, then a dialog box (see Figure 17.6) will be displayed as the test page is sent to the printer. If the test page prints, then click OK on this dialog box. If it does not, click Troubleshoot.

FIGURE 17.6

Click OK if the test page prints, or you can troubleshoot the printer setup.

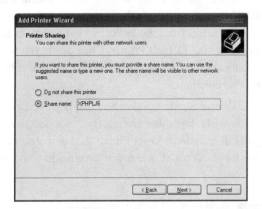

Once you click OK after the test page has printed, the printer will be available in the Printers folder and ready for use. If the test page did not print correctly and you clicked the Troubleshoot button, then the Printing Troubleshooter component of Windows XP Help and Support Services will pop up and prompt you through the troubleshooting process. To start the troubleshooting process, select one of the options and click Next

Using a Printer Connected Directly to the Network

As you will recall from Figure 17.1, a printer connected directly to the network can also be managed as a printer on your Windows XP computer. As a matter of fact, more than one computer can set up a logical printer to use the same networked printer. This printer connection is considered to be a local connection because your computer will be responsible for spooling, queuing, and rendering the print job into the correct format and then sending it to the networked printer, just as if it were a printer connected by one of your parallel or serial ports.

To install this kind of printer, use steps 1 through 4 in the previous section. However, as you can see in Figure 17.7, you should select the Create a New Port radio button, and then use the drop-down menu to select the kind of port to create.

FIGURE 17.7

Use the Create a New Port radio button for a networked printer.

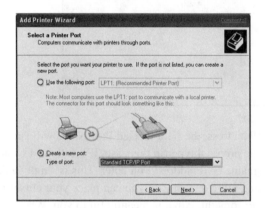

The options you will see on the Type of Port menu depend on the networking protocols you have installed. For most situations, you will use the selection Standard TCP/IP Port. If you have installed Microsoft's Services for Unix (an add-on package for Windows XP), then you will also see an LPR Port in this menu.

Unless you have an old printer or one with an old network card, the choice you make here will most likely be Standard TCP/IP port. We will use that for an example. After making this selection from the drop-down menu, click Next.

This starts up another wizard (yes, a wizard inside a wizard!) that creates the port. As instructed in the opening dialog box of the Add Standard TCP/IP Printer Port Wizard, be sure that the printer is turned on and your computer has been correctly configured to operate on the network. When ready to create the port, click Next.

Figure 17.8 shows that you need to fill in either a TCP/IP hostname or the IP address of the printer. Most printers won't allow you to assign them a hostname, but it is possible to create an association between a hostname and an IP address using the Domain Name System (DNS). Check with your network administrator to see if you should use a hostname instead of an address. The advantage to using a hostname is that if the printer's IP address changes, then a change needs to be made only in the DNS server in order for you to keep using the printer. However, in most cases, you will probably end up using the printer's IP address.

FIGURE 17.8

Enter the host-name or the IP address of the printer in this dialog box.

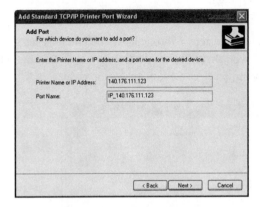

As you type the name or IP address, the field labeled Port Name will automatically create a port name based on the protocol type (in this case, IP), followed by an underscore character and then the hostname or IP address you enter. This is simply a default name. If you want to use something more descriptive, you can place your cursor in this field and change the port name to something that is meaningful to you. When finished, click Next.

The Add Printer Wizard will then attempt to contact the printer to see if it actually exists on the network. If it does not, you will get an error message, as shown in Figure 17.9.

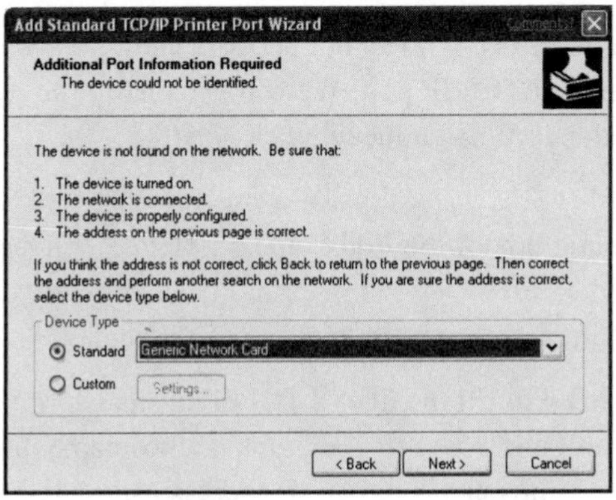

FIGURE 17.9

This dialog box will tell you that the printer is either not found on the network or it is possibly con-figured differently.

This dialog box doesn't necessarily mean that the printer isn't located on the network, only that it can't be contacted using the information that the wizard has received so far. Figure 17.11 shows the feature Standard selected at the bottom the Device Type field. If you think the printer's network card has been configured differently, click Custom. The Settings button will then become available. Click Settings, and another dialog box (Figure 17.10) will show the current settings for the typical TCP/IP port, allowing you to make changes.

FIGURE 17.10

You can make changes to the standard TCP/IP printer port configuration using this dialog box.

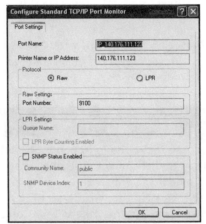

Under the Protocol section of this dialog box are two selections: Raw and LPR. Raw simply means that the computer will use a standard TCP/IP connection to exchange data with the printer. LPR stands for Line Printer Remote, which is an older protocol that was originally developed to allow for networked printer access on Unix machines. You will usually see this referred to as *LPR/LPD,* where LPD stands for Line Printer Daemon. A Daemon is a background process that runs on a computer, much like a service in Windows XP that listens for network requests. The LPR/LPD protocol was adopted in some of the first network printer cards. You should be able to consult the manual for your printer or print a test page to determine if it is using LPR/LPD. If this is the case, then change the protocol by selecting the LPR radio button here.

In most cases, a networked printer that uses LPR/LPD won't have a queue name; this is a holdover from the Unix implementations where one server could have several printers (for example, print queues) available for sharing through the same IP address. However, if your manual or test print sheet indicates that the printer network card does use a queue name, then enter that name in the LPR Settings portion of this dialog box.

If you determine that the printer is using the Raw TCP/IP connection, then look at the port number in the Raw Settings section of this dialog box. Port number 9100 is typically used for this purpose, but it is quite possible that someone has changed this on the printer. Most printers have a small LED screen and several menus that you can go through to set up the IP address, or if you prefer a different port to use. Check the printer to see if something other than 9100 is being used on that printer.

The last section of this dialog box has a check box labeled SNMP Status Enabled. SNMP is the Simple Network Management Protocol, and is used to allow a central management station to gather information about SNMP-enabled devices on the network. You should not have to do anything here in order to get your printer to work. Enabling SNMP on the printer's port monitor is a job best left to your network administrator.

When you finish making any changes, click OK, and the wizard will again attempt to contact the printer. If it fails, check with your network administrator to find out how to further troubleshoot this problem.

Tip

Troubleshooting TCP/IP connections is covered in Appendix A, "Introduction to TCP/IP." In that appendix you can find out how to use utilities at the command prompt, such as `ping`, to determine if the printer is reachable from your computer. If you can't get there from here, so to speak, then it is a network problem and you should inform your administrator. Otherwise, it could simply be that you have been given the wrong IP address for the printer!

After this port has been created, you will be returned to the Add Printer Wizard and can continue to create the printer by selecting the appropriate driver, naming the printer, and conducting the other steps listed in the previous section.

Connecting to a Printer on a Networked Print Server

If the printer you wish to connect to is offered on the network as a print share, then there are several ways you can go about finding the printer and connecting to it. Use the Add Printer Wizard as described earlier but when you get to step 3, select the radio button labeled Printer Connection. When you click Next, another dialog box then prompts you to enter the share name for the printer to which you are connecting by using the syntax of *servername**printername*. You can also use the Browse button to locate printers on your network, if you are not sure of the exact name of the server or printer to which you want to connect.

Managing Printer Properties

Once you have created a printer, it will show up in the Printers and Faxes folder. From this folder, you can manage the properties of the printer. To do so, simply right-click on the printer icon and select Properties. Figure 17.11 shows the Properties sheet for a typical printer.

FIGURE 17.11

You can use the tabs on this Properties sheet to change settings for your printer.

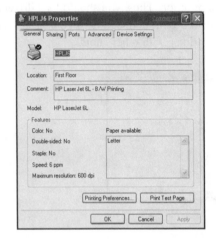

The General Tab

The first tab indicates the name of the printer, location, and comment that you have set up. You can change any of these fields by placing your cursor in the field you want to change and making any necessary edits. Under the Features section of the General tab, features specific for the printer are displayed. At the bottom are two buttons, Printing Preferences and Print Test Page. You already learned what Print Test Page does, but keep in mind that it is there in case you have problems with the printer in the future. If the test page won't print, then you can rule out a corrupted document as being the source of your problem.

The Printing Preferences button brings up a dialog box for setting certain characteristics of the printer, and the contents of this dialog box depend on the kind of printer you are using. Some typical preferences are for layout purposes, such as portrait or landscape printing. Other include such things as which paper bin to use, print quality (dots per inch), and duplex (two-sided) printing. Again, the items you configure depend on the type of physical printer and its capabilities.

The Sharing Tab

If you did not elect to share the printer on the network during the setup phase, you can do so anytime you wish. The Sharing tab of the printer's Properties sheet allows you to give a share name to the printer. Figure 17.12 indicates something else you can do at this tab. The Additional Drivers button allows you to load drivers for different operating systems. When a computer connects to your print share for this printer, it will download the appropriate driver before it sends a print job. Thus, you should load drivers for each operating system you expect clients to use for connecting to your print share. You can also use this tab to stop sharing the printer with other clients.

FIGURE 17.12

The Sharing tab allows you to share the printer on the network and to load drivers for clients that use another operating system.

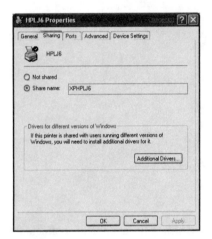

The Ports Tab

Earlier, when you learned how to create a printer, you had to select a local port, which could be either a physical communications port on the computer or a networked computer for which you could create a protocol port. The Ports tab on the printer's Properties sheet allows you to change this. This might happen if, for example, you reconfigure your computer and move a locally connected printer to a different physical port. Another scenario is a networked printer that is shared through your Windows XP computer as a printer share that has changed its network address. In either case, you can use this tab (see Figure 17.13) to add, delete, or configure a port.

The Advanced Tab

This tab (see Figure 17.14) can be a very useful tab in a busy office environment. You can configure many features using this tab.

FIGURE **17.13**

*You can change
the port to which
a printer is
connected using
this tab.*

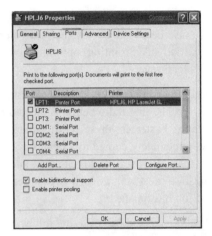

FIGURE **17.14**

*You can configure
several options for
this printer using
the Advanced tab.*

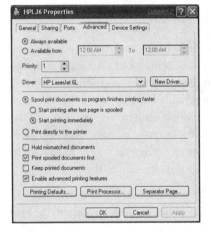

At the top of this Properties sheet, you can see how to specify a time for the printer to be available. This can be useful when you prohibit printing during certain time periods. For example, in a highly secure environment, you may want to be sure that the printer will not work after office hours. You can select Available From and then use the time fields to specify the exact period for which the printer can be used.

The Priority field allows you to specify a value from 1 to 99, with higher values granting access to the physical printer device above higher priorities.

The Driver field and the accompanying New Driver button show the current driver installed for this printer, so you can add a new driver if the manufacturer has created one. Since Windows XP is a new operating system, you may want to change the printer driver at a later date, especially if the printer is a newer one and a minimal driver was submitted to Microsoft just to get on the hardware compatibility list. Newer drivers that take advantage of additional printer features can also be added. For example, if you purchased a basic printer and later added a duplex (two-sided printing) option, you may be required to load a new driver that supports this feature.

In the Spool section, there are several things to consider. You should think about how you want documents to print for this section. The first radio button is labeled Spool Print Documents So Program Finishes Printing Faster. If you select this, then the document received from an application will be immediately copied to a temporary file by the spooler, and the application (for example, Microsoft Word) can continue. If you choose not to use this option, then the application must wait as each page is sent to the printer, and the user must wait until the print job has finished!

If you select to spool documents, then you can choose from the following two additional radio buttons:

- Start Printing After Last Page Is Spooled
- Start Printing Immediately

In most cases, you should select Start Printing After Last Page Is Spooled so that the spooler is both receiving data from the application and sending data to the printer at the same time. This can speed up the total time between when the user decides to print a document and when the printer finally outputs hard copy. The first option will delay the start of printing until the spooler from the application has received all data. This can result in the spooler using a larger amount of memory or disk space, since it must store the entire document before it can start sending data to the printer.

The second major radio button in this section, labeled Print Directly to the Printer, causes the data received from the application to be sent immediately to the printer, and no spooling will be involved. Therefore, your computer uses no extra disk space or memory to store print jobs awaiting printing.

The next section of this Properties page consists of a series of check boxes, which are as follows:

- Hold Mismatched Documents—This option enables the printer to check the document setup to make sure it can be printed on the print device as expected. If not, the document is held in the printer queue so that you can diagnose the problem.
- Print Spooled Documents First—This option sends documents that have finished spooling (those received from the application) to print before documents that have a higher priority, if those documents are still spooling. If no documents are

spooling, then the spooler mechanism prints larger documents before smaller ones. This option is recommended, as it can improve the speed at which documents are printed. If you disable this check box, then only the priority mechanism is used to determine which document prints next.

- Keep Printed Documents—This check box keeps spooled documents in their temporary queue-file state after they have printed. Thus, you can reprint them directly from the printer queue instead of using the application to recreate the printer job.

- Enable Advanced Printing Features—This option determines whether any advanced features supported by our printer are enabled by default. This can include such things as page order, booklet printing, and pages per sheet, in addition to other features, depending on the model of the printer. For most purposes, you can leave this turned on. If you have problems printing to the printer, try disabling advanced features. Note that when you disable advanced features in this Properties sheet, those features will not be available in the print dialog box when you print from an application.

At the bottom of this Properties sheet tab are the following three buttons:

- Printing Defaults—This button allows you to specify specific characteristics for the print job for all users who connect to your printer to send print jobs.

- Print Processor—Earlier in this chapter you learned about the different kinds of data types that are supported by Windows XP printer processors. For the most part you should not have to use this button. However, some older applications may require that you use this button to select a specific print processor and data type.

- Separator Page—this feature is useful when you share a printer. You can use this button to select a separator page, which is a page printed before a print job, specifying information about the printed document to follow, such as the username, document name, and other details about the print job.

Tip

Separator pages can be useful for identifying different users' print jobs when more than one user shares the printer. Another useful feature that separator pages can serve is to change a printer from PCL mode to PostScript mode. You can create your own separator pages, and the best way is to look at the examples you will find in the directory %systemroot%\system32. The sample separator pages all have a file extension of .SEP.

17

PRINTING WITH
WINDOWS XP

The Device Settings Tab

This section of the printer's Properties sheet shows information about the physical printer. It includes things such as assigning forms to specific trays, changing the font substitution table, and installable options, such as extra memory for the printer.

Forms are definitions you can create that define a paper size and margins. If your printer has multiple paper trays, you can create a form for each tray, depending on the kind of paper loaded in the tray. For example, one tray can hold ordinary letter-size paper, whereas another can be loaded with legal-size paper. You may also use one tray for envelopes. When the user selects the form in the print dialog box, the correct tray is chosen, based on an assignment you can make in this page.

You can use the font substitution table to change True Type to PostScript font mapping. Note that not all printers support PostScript, so you will probably not have to change this.

Managing Printers

In the last few sections, you learned how to use the Properties sheet for a printer to manage the capabilities of the printer and how clients that need to print can use it. In this section, you will learn about how to manage the printer itself—that is, managing tasks like removing documents from the queue, pausing and restarting the queue, and so on. Figure 17.15 shows the Control Panel view of the Printers and Faxes category. The HP LaserJet icon has been clicked once to select the printer. Because of this, the list of things you can do under Tasks (on the left side of the page) has expanded to include additional items. Initially this list includes only the Add a Printer task.

FIGURE 17.15

When you select a printer in the Control Panel, the Tasks list expands to include features for managing the printer.

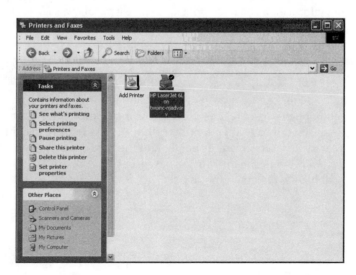

This Tasks list is a general way to manage any printer. You can use See What's Printing to bring up a dialog box that displays any documents in the queue. You can use Select Printing Preferences, which simply brings up the same dialog box you would get if you had clicked the Printing Preferences (see Figure 17.11 above). If you click Pause Printing, then the queue will stop sending documents to the printer. The Pause Printing task entry changes to Resume Printing so that you can stop and start the queue without having to remove pending documents.

The Share This Printer task simply brings up the same Sharing tab of the printer's Properties sheet from Figure 17.12. (You can probably guess what Delete This Printer does!) Finally, the last task, Set Printer Properties is just a quick way to bring up the printer's Properties sheet. Earlier, we did this by right-clicking on the printer and selecting Properties from the menu.

17

PRINTING WITH
WINDOWS XP

> **Tip**
>
> When you right-click on the printer icon, the menu includes several other items than just Properties. You can also select from this menu Printing Preferences, Pause Printing (and Resume Printing), Sharing, and Delete. Perhaps the most useful item, however, is the Create Shortcut menu selection. A dialog box pops up stating that it can't create the shortcut here, but it can place it on the Desktop instead. This way you won't have to go through the Control Panel to manage the printer.

General Printer Management Techniques

If you double-click on the printer icon or if you select the printer and then select See What's Printing from the Tasks list, a window will open (see Figure 17.16) for viewing documents waiting to print. It shows the status of each document, its owner, the number of pages, the size of the data file, and the time the document was submitted to print. You can also open this window by using the Desktop shortcut, if you chose to create one.

You can manage both the printer and the documents themselves using this window. For example, from the File menu, you can perform the following:

- Set As Default Printer—Make this your default printer. When you print from an application, this will be the printer that is selected by default.

- Printing Preferences—This brings up the Printing Preferences dialog box described earlier.

- Pause Printing—Again, this allows you to temporarily stop the print queue. Similar to the same item under the Control Panel task menu, this option changes to Resume Printing if you click it to pause the queue.

- Cancel All Documents—This is a convenient way to flush the queue of all documents waiting to print. You may want to do this when someone has erroneously sent a large number of documents to print or when you need to take a printer offline for an extended period of time for repair work.

- Sharing—This option brings up the printer's Properties sheet with the Sharing tab selected so that you can configure whether to share this printer on the network or make changes to the sharing configuration.

- Properties—This simply brings up the Properties sheet for the printer.

- Close—This closes the printer window.

FIGURE 17.16

Double-click on the printer icon to view the status of the printer and what documents are waiting to print.

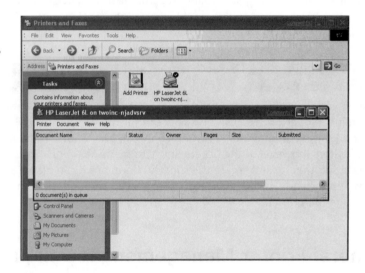

The Document menu allows you to control individual documents in a manner similar to the way in which you use the File menu to control the printer itself. To use the Document menu, first click on a document listed in the queue and then from the Document menu, select one of the following:

- Pause—This temporarily stops the queue from sending any more data for this document to the printer.

- Resume—This is a separate option in this menu. Use this to resume printing the document you paused.

- Restart—The spooler resends the print job from the beginning. This can be useful in situations where a paper jam or other malfunction at the printer has caused you to lose some of the output.

- Cancel—This removes the document from the queue. Use this to delete individual documents if you don't want to use the File menu to delete all documents in the queue.

- Properties—This brings up a Properties sheet showing details about the document, such as the size, number of pages, data type, owner, time the document was submitted, the print priority, which you can change here to make your document print before others in the queue, and other items.

Using the File menu and the Document menu, you can pretty much manage the printer and any documents sent to print.

Finding Printers on the Network

So far, you have learned about how to set up and manage a printer under Windows XP. However, in most cases such as in a business environment, you are part of a larger network, and if it is a Windows-based network, you will most likely be using Microsoft's Active Directory. If so, then locating resources such as a printer can be easy to do. In the typical print dialog box (see Figure 17.17), a button labeled Find Printer has been added.

FIGURE 17.17

The Print dialog box now includes Find Printer to help you locate a printer in the Active Directory.

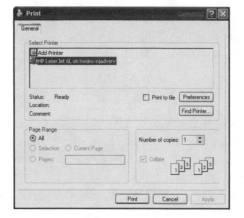

If you click on this button, a new Connect to Printer dialog box pops up (see Figure 17.18) for browsing through the available printers. Select a printer by clicking on it and then clicking OK, or simply double-click on the printer itself.

If you are not part of a Windows domain and do not use the Active Directory, then your computer is set up as a member of a workgroup. In this situation, another feature called *NetCrawler* is available in both Windows XP Professional and the Home Edition. Whenever you open or refresh your Printers and My Net Places folders, NetCrawler will check for new printers on the network. Not only will NetCrawler find printers on the network for you automatically, but it will also establish the link so that you don't have to go through the process of installing or connecting to a printer.

FIGURE 17.18

Use the Connect to Printer dialog box to browse for a printer on your network.

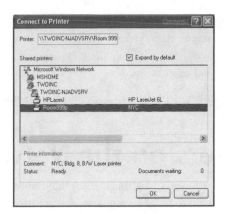

If NetCrawler does not see a particular printer share for a period of 48 hours, it will then be purged from the My Network Places folder, since NetCrawler will assume that the printer share no longer exists.

For home users or small offices that don't need the capabilities of the Active Directory (or the administrative overhead it requires), this solution makes networking computers and printers a much simpler task. Windows XP just does it all for you!

Summary

In this chapter, you learned about how Windows XP printing works, including how to install a printer and connect to a printer offered as a print share by another computer. In addition, you learned how to manage printers and documents. In Windows XP, printing and managing printers is not a complicated process, since the Add Printer Wizard walks you through the process of setting up a printer, and the printer Properties sheet makes it easy to further configure the printer.

In the next chapter, we will look at something more complicated but still easy to understand when using Windows XP—disks, partitions, and file systems, as well as techniques for managing them.

Managing Disks and Partitions

IN THIS CHAPTER

- Basic Disks and Dynamic Disks *444*
- Choosing Partitions and Volume Types *446*
- Comparing File Systems: FAT, FAT32, and NTFS *447*
- Using the Disk Management Utility *450*
- Managing Disks Through the Command Prompt *459*
- Configuring Partition Properties *469*
- Sharing Files with the Computer Management Utility *479*
- Sharing Disks When You Are Part of a Domain *480*

The most immediate storage options available to a central processing unit (CPU) are its own cache memory and the registers built onto the CPU board. Next is the computer's physical memory (SIMM, DIMM, and so on), followed by the hard disk and other fixed media, and finally the machine's removable media. Managing all of this memory for optimum computer performance can be a challenging task. Windows XP Professional's most important memory-management tools are partitions. In this chapter, you learn how to partition disks and manage the disk volumes in your computer. Not only do you learn how to create partitions on the fixed hard drives in your computer, you also learn about sharing disks and partitions with other users in a network, along with other offline storage techniques such as CD burning.

This chapter also discusses basic and dynamic disks, volumes, and file systems. Windows XP offers many different ways to store data, so you should be able to easily decide how you want to partition the disks in your computer, create partitions, and manage the disk volumes in your computer when you finish reading this chapter. In addition to the usual tasks provided by a file system, you will also learn how to encrypt and compress files and folders (if you choose to use the NT file system (NTFS)), as well as how to defragment a hard disk to dramatically improve performance when using disk-intensive applications.

Basic Disks and Dynamic Disks

Windows XP's disk management tools go beyond anything Windows 9x system had, although Windows NT users will certainly recognize them.

Every operating system uses partitions to help organize the data stored on hard drives. In all Windows and DOS machines, all physical hard drives are (usually) completely filled with one partition each, unless you indicate otherwise. These partitions are denoted by a drive letter (C:, D:, and so on). You can divide these physical partitions into what is known as a logical partition. Logical partitions look and behave like separate physical drives on your computer system. Each logical partition gets its own drive letter and directory system, separate from the other partitions.

In Windows XP, such partitions, physical or logical, are referred to as basic disks. They are what Windows 95/98/Me and Windows NT users have grown accustomed to using. In Windows 2000, a new type of disk volume, the dynamic disk, was introduced, bringing with it some interesting new features.

A dynamic disk is a physical hard drive that foregoes the use of physical and logical partitions. Instead, it contains only dynamic volumes that you create in the Disk Management console. Dynamic volumes do not use any drive letter notation and can even be extended on the computer without restarting the system.

To get all these features, though, you have to upgrade your drives from basic to dynamic. This procedure is relatively painless, but you should be aware of some limitations:

- You cannot use dynamic disks on a portable computer; nor can you use them on removable drives, detachable disks, or disks that share a SCSI bus. If you have any of these configurations, you're out of luck.

- You cannot access dynamic volumes with any operating system other than Windows 2000 and Windows XP Professional, no matter what file system you're using for the volume. This means that MS-DOS, Windows 95/98, Windows ME, Windows NT, and Windows XP Home Edition are right out. You can, however, get to any folder that is shared from the network, just as before. Because of this access limitation, though, you will have greater difficulty booting multiple operating systems on any system with dynamic drives. It is strongly recommended that you don't even try.

You should also note that although the change to dynamic disk is reversible, reverting from a dynamic disk back to a basic disk is not an easy matter because the disk must be completely empty before you convert it back to basic.

18

Note

Most computers use a disk-partitioning scheme that creates a master boot record (MBR), which is read by the computer's BIOS when the system is booting. Some high-end workstations with the Itanium 64-bit processor also use the Extensible Firmware Interface (EFI) scheme. EFI supports a partitioning mechanism known as the GUID partition table, also known as GPT. GPT enables you to create up to 128 partitions per disk and volumes in sizes up to 18 exabytes (an exabyte is 2 to the 60th power in bytes). GPT also supports the creation of a backup partition table in case the main one becomes corrupted. Most people using Windows XP Professional, however, need only a simple basic disk with a few partitions

You can install Windows XP on mirrored or simple disk volumes. You cannot install Windows XP on a basic partition you converted to a dynamic volume, unless the partition was a former boot or system partition. The Setup procedure only recognizes these partitions because they have entries in the partition table. Later in this chapter, you will see that by using the Disk Management tool, you can determine the disks, partitions, and volumes on your computer.

Choosing Partitions and Volume Types

A partition is a section of a basic disk that represents an isolated block of memory. As mentioned earlier, partitions are useful for running multiple operating systems on a single computer, and they can make the computer's memory more efficient. Most people will add a partition to their computer in order to help manage their files, which is definitely one of the best reasons for using partitions.

Partitions come in two varieties, primary and extended. For Windows XP, only a primary partition can be bootable, and will always get "lower" drive letters assigned than other partitions. An extended partition is used to store the logical partitions. In Windows XP, you can have up to four primary partitions on a disk. Additionally, you can use primary partitions to hold different versions of Windows XP or other operating systems such as Windows 2000 or 2002 by assigning a drive letter to each primary partition you create.

An extended partition allows you to further divide the disk into multiple drive letters. If you use extended partitions, you reduce the number of primary partitions on your drive to three. You can create only one extended partition on a single disk.

Volumes can consist of one or more partitions and span a single disk or multiple disks. You can assign a drive letter to each volume on a dynamic disk, and use each volume to support a single file system. Regardless of whether you choose to use a basic disk partition or create a dynamic volume, you will want to consider how to set up your computer. To make the choice, consider the amount of disk space you need for a particular drive letter, whether you want to break up a single disk into multiple partitions or multiple volumes, and whether you want to extend dynamic volumes.

You can create the following types of volumes on a dynamic disk using Windows XP:

- Simple and Spanned Volumes—This volume type consists of a single region of space occupied by a file system. A simple volume can be one of many on a single disk.

  You can join together partitions on the same or other disks to create one larger simple volume (with no fault tolerance), which is known as a *spanned volume*. Using a spanned volume makes it easy to work with multiple disks partitions under a single drive letter. This technology also offers an easy way to create significant space, which high-end workstations and some applications like multimedia may need for their huge files). However, although this technique uses multiple disks, it doesn't provide redundancy. If one disk goes bad, you have to replace it and reconstruct the volume in a spanned set.

- Striped Volumes—This is a RAID technology, which can be very useful when you need fast volume access. Striped volumes store data in small chunks across a set of two or more disks. This storage technique can increase the computer's read and write speed, since more than one disk controller can write information to the volume at the same time. However, as with spanned volumes, if one disk in a striped volume fails, you have to replace the disk and restore the data from a backup copy. Striped volumes are not fault tolerant; you cannot mirror or extended striped volume sets in Windows XP.

- Mirrored Volume—Another RAID technique, a mirrored volume consists of two disks that store exactly the same information; mirrored volumes provide redundancy and protect information if one of the disks is damaged. Using mirrored volumes can slow down write speeds on a system, since there is a little overhead in ensuring that both disks are updated correctly. However, if one disk is damaged, the system can continue to use the single remaining member of a mirrored volume until the bad drive has been replaced.

- RAID-5 Volume—This is a technique commonly found on large disk arrays used by large enterprise servers to provide a moderate level of redundancy. RAID-5 uses a striping method to write data in small chunks across three or more drives, but it also writes a parity stripe. The parity stripe calculates the data being stored, so if a disk fails, the disk driver can use the information on the parity stripe to determine what data is missing from memory on the remaining disks. A RAID-5 volume in Windows XP cannot be mirrored; therefore, if more than two disks fail in a RAID-5 volume, you have to recreate the volume and restore from a backup.

18

MANAGING DISKS
AND PARTITIONS

Caution

Remember, you cannot use dynamic disks on laptop computers, removable disks, or other removable media drives. It also is impossible to create dynamic disks connected to the system by the universal serial bus (USB) or a FireWire (IEEE 1394) interface. You also cannot create disks that exist on a shared Small Computer System Interface (SCSI) bus like what is found in a Windows cluster environment. Remember that if you dual boot with some earlier operating systems, you cannot use dynamic disks.

Comparing File Systems: FAT, FAT32, and NTFS

Data is scattered all over memory disks, in bits and clusters. An operating system uses a file system to find and organize data. One of the most common file systems used in early Windows versions is the file allocation table (FAT), a table that operating systems use to locate files on a disk. The table resides on the disk, and it contains an entry for each file or directory (folder) on the disk.

The FAT system divides a disk into clusters of bytes (usually from 2048 to 8192 bytes long), and each 16-bit entry in the FAT is used to point to a cluster on the disk. Because the FAT uses only 16 bits, it is not practical for hard drives larger than 128MB. The FAT system is not very good at managing disk clusters; it simply allocates the next available cluster when looking for free space on a disk. This means that a file can be made up of a large number of clusters that are stored all over the disk. The drive heads must jump all around the disk, reading both the file information and consulting the FAT table for each cluster to retrieve.

> **Note**
>
> When a disk is formatted using the FAT file system, two copies of the actual allocation table are maintained at fixed locations on the disk. In addition, the root directory, which stores the names of files and folders on the disk, must be located in a fixed location. The disk is formatted with pointers to clusters of bytes on the disk, and each cluster on the disk is represented sequentially by an entry in the File Allocation Table (FAT). A record for a file in a directory contains a pointer to the first entry in the FAT that stores the first cluster of bytes for a file. Each entry in the FAT contains a number that points to another FAT entry, which represents the succeeding clusters of bytes that make up the file.

Improvements in FAT32

Beginning with later versions of Windows 95, Microsoft used the FAT32 system, which supports larger disks and more efficient storage than its predecessor. FAT32 was developed and can address up to about two terabytes of disk space. FAT32 was first released with Windows 95 OSR2 and allows for 32-bit entries, which is why it can be used with larger disks.

Even so, the FAT32 system has limitations. The directory structure of FAT and FAT32 offers limited file attribute storage. No security information is stored, so on a FAT system, anyone with access to the disk also can access all information. However, if you choose to multiboot with other operating systems, you will need to use FAT and FAT32.

Using the NTFS File System

In addition to FAT and FAT32, Windows XP can use the NT file system, or NTFS, a system designed to organize data across multiple physical disks, which enables it to store incredible amounts of data. NTFS also provides greater reliability and security for your data by enabling tracking logs and controlling access to files, in addition to allowing for compression, encryption, and indexing. If you use only Windows XP on your computer, using NTFS for all of your file system partitions is the best way to go. Since NTFS uses a transaction log file, it can roll back incomplete transactions if a system failure causes problems for you. Thus, the chance of losing data on an NTFS-based disk is minimal because NTFS uses a master file table (MFT) as a directory for all files and folders on the disk. Like the FAT or FAT32 table, the MFT also stores the starting cluster for a disk, but the MFT is not a disorganized listing of files that were added to the computer. Instead, NTFS uses a B-tree (a term programmers will know), making it much more efficient when it comes to finding a file or folder.

Other advantages of NTFS include the following:

- Access control lists (ACLS)—These are the file and folder permission mechanisms (see Chapter 9, "Working with Files and Folders"). NTFS stores permissions that grant or deny access based on username or user group to protect files from those whom they are not intended for.

- Support for very large file sizes—This feature is for up to about 16 billion bytes and may be more useful on Windows Servers systems. However, Windows XP users with the necessary storage devices can rest assured they won't be running out of room anytime soon.

- Compression for files and folders that are stored on the disk volume or partition—Compression can reduce the amount of some files dramatically. You can use this NTFS feature in Windows XP for a disk or just selected folders.

- Unicode support—NTFS allows for the use of Unicode. Many computers use the standard ASCII character set that uses 8 bits of information (or 1 byte) to represent up to 256 characters. Unicode uses 16 bits (2 bytes) of information per character, which provides for 65,536 different characters. For written languages based on Latin or Cyrillic characters, this is a bit much. But for written languages with pictographs, such as Japanese or Chinese, Unicode is much more appropriate. Unicode support allows for native language support in all countries in which Windows XP is used.

- File encryption—You can encrypt a file stored on an NTFS disk volume or partition.

When it comes down to it, unless you plan to use your computer to multiboot other operating systems, then just use NTFS for all partitions on the computer. In the following sections, you will learn more about some graphical ways to look at disk drives and share them on the network.

18

MANAGING DISKS
AND PARTITIONS

Using the Disk Management Utility

You can use Windows XP's Disk Management utility to manage disks, volumes, and partitions. To start the program, choose Start, Control Panel (in Category view, select Performance and Maintenance) and then from the next window, select Administrative Tools. Double-click on the icon for Computer Management in the Microsoft Management Console (MMC).

The utility divides computer management into System Tools, Storage, and Services and Applications. In the Storage area, double-click on Disk Management. Figure 18.1 shows the Computer Management utility with the Disk Management tool selected. In this example, a single hard drive (disk 0) is installed on the computer, along with two CD-ROM drives.

FIGURE 18.1

The Computer Management MMC console is used by the Disk Management Utility to display important information about the computer's memory.

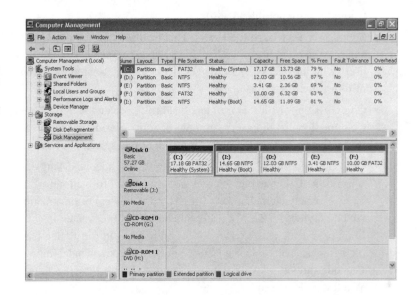

The top pane on the right side shows the disk drive letters assigned to each volume on this computer and lists important information about each drive except Drive A. Columns in this pane list each drive's layout; in this example, each drive is actually a partition. Other columns list drive type, file system, status, and available space.

The bottom part of the Details pane shows a graphical view of the details for each drive. Note the removable disk (J) on the example system; when you insert media into a removable drive and choose Action, Rescan Disks, information about the drive appears in this window.

> **Tip**
>
> The Disk Management details pane also contains a column called *Overhead*. When creating dynamic volumes, the operating system uses up a small amount of disk space on each disk participating in the volume. This overhead space stores information needed to manage the volume.

You can use the Disk Management utility to view the status of existing drives, create and delete partitions and volumes, and format drives with a selected file system. The next few sections explain how to do so.

Adding and Deleting Partitions

Since the example disk shown in Figure 18.1 is fully populated, you can begin learning to use the Disk Management utility by deleting a partition. Here, the first drive, C:, is on a primary partition created on the system, whereas the remaining drives are logical drives in an extended partition on the disk. To delete partitions, you must first delete the logical disk drives.

To delete a logical drive, right-click on the drive listing in the upper detail pane and select Delete Logical Drive. A dialog box reminds you that doing so will delete all information stored on the drive; click Yes to continue. In Figure 18.2, the D:, E:, and F: drives that were present in Figure 18.1 have been deleted using this method.

FIGURE 18.2

Before deleting a partition, you must delete the logical drives in the partition.

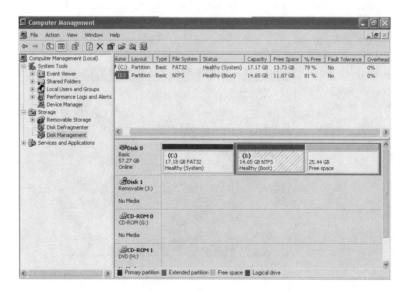

The example system has just the C: and I: partitions remaining with a combined free space of 25MB.

> ## Caution
>
> You cannot use the Disk Management utility to delete the partition that holds the operating system running the utility. If you need to delete a partition that holds the utility's operating system, you can boot into another operating system, including another installation of Windows XP, and then delete the original system partition.

Creating partitions with the Disk Management Utility is equally simple. We'll take a look at how to do this on another example PC.

To create a partition, right-click on the unallocated space disk region and select New Partition from the menu that appears. The New Partition wizard launches; click Next to move past the opening window. The Wizard asks you to choose whether to create a primary partition or an extended partition.

In this example, you create partitions for installing additional instances of the Windows XP operating system. Thus, you can choose to create another primary partition by leaving that radio button selected and clicking Next. The next window the wizard presents asks you to select the size of the partition. The default value displayed in the Partition Size in MB field is the total amount remaining free space on the disk. If you want to install Windows XP several times on this machine, you need to use smaller partitions, as shown in Figure 18.3.

FIGURE 18.3

You can choose the size of the partition to be created.

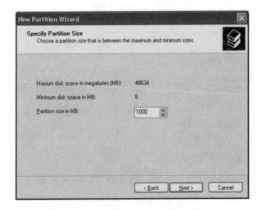

> **Tip**
>
> It is a very good idea to know exactly how much space each of your new partitions will need to accomplish their purpose. While creating a new partition is not very difficult, it is time-consuming enough that you won't want to do it that often.

Choose the partition size and click Next. In the next window, use the drop-down box to assign a drive letter. You can also choose not to assign a drive letter to the partition or to mount the partition in an empty NTFS folder on an existing disk partition (such as the C: partition) and assign it a drive path instead of a drive letter.

While most people will be content to assign a new drive letter for a new partition, drive paths are useful to help manage the data on a computer without disrupting the workflow of the applications using that data. For example, assume that you have several applications that constantly reference a particular folder on your C: drive. C:\My Documents is a good example of this. One day, you notice that your C: drive is getting rather full and that your My Documents folder is in danger of running out of room.

In the past, you could simply move the My Documents folder to another, larger drive. But then you would have to go into all of the applications that were used to accessing C:\My Documents and tell them that the folder is now D:\My Documents, or E:, or whatever. The solution is accomplished, but it takes a while to do.

With drive paths, you can move the folder wherever you want but then assign it a drive path of C:\My Documents. This will let any application (including the Windows Explorer) access that folder as if were located on the C: drive, even if it's off on another partition or another hard drive altogether.

For purposes of this example, choose the first option and leave the default drive letter of F: selected; then click Next.

The next window prompts you to go ahead and format the partition you create. If you aren't certain what file system you want to use on this partition, select Do Not Format This Partition, and you can format the partition later

You can choose to format the partition as FAT, FAT32, and NTFS; if you are using the partition for a Windows XP installation, choose NTFS in the File System field. Unless you have a very large disk size (such as one provided by a disk controller that uses RAID techniques to present many disks to the operating system as a single disk), you should leave the settings in the Allocation Unit Size at its default setting (see Figure 18.4).

18

MANAGING DISKS AND PARTITIONS

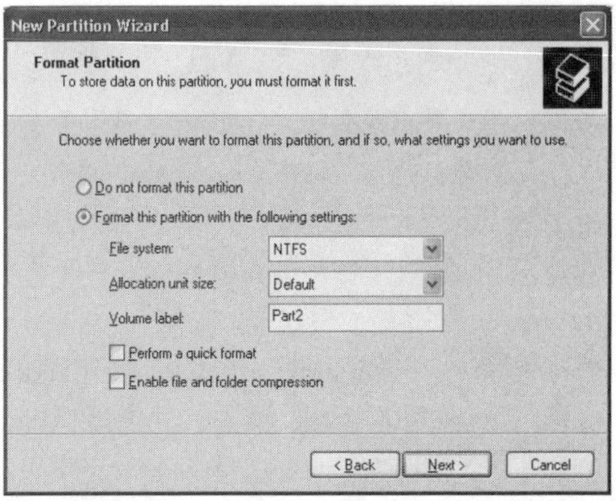

FIGURE 18.4

On this page of the wizard, you can specify file system, unit size, and volume label.

> ## Tip
>
> Disk space is allocated by the Allocation Units you choose when formatting a new partition. Choosing a larger cluster size can improve performance when you write large files, since more data is written as a unit. You can choose up to 65KB for this field, but if you don't use all of those bytes, they are wasted. That is why choosing a smaller sector size (or letting the operating system decide, based on the size of the disk) is a good idea.

Next, give the partition a name by deleting the text "New Volume" in the Volume Label field and entering your own descriptive label; this example uses the text "Part2" to indicate that this is the second partition (you later learn how to change the volume name).

Then choose to perform a quick or full format. A quick format only writes certain structures of the file system to the disk and leaves the disk's old data intact. If you want to fully format a partition, leave the Perform a Quick Format box unchecked to write the file system structure to the disk and erase the old contents.

Checking Enable File and Folder Compression. This can save space on your disk. Unless your PC is a very old system, the amount of time spent by the operating system compressing and decompressing files is virtually transparent. (Older systems have slower hard drives and thus compression activity can really make a big impact.) You should also consider the compression option carefully if you have an application that is disk intensive. The more an application has to access the disk for data, the more time the compression/decompression activity will take. You can always enable this feature later, if you choose not to check it now.

After making selections in the window, click Next. The wizard presents a summary page, detailing your selections; click the Finish button to close the wizard.

When the wizard disappears, the system begins creating the new partition. In the Disk Management window, the disk region for the partition tracks the progress of process (see Figure 18.5).

FIGURE 18.5

As the system creates the partition (in this example, drive F:), the formatting percentage that is shown tracks the partitioning progress.

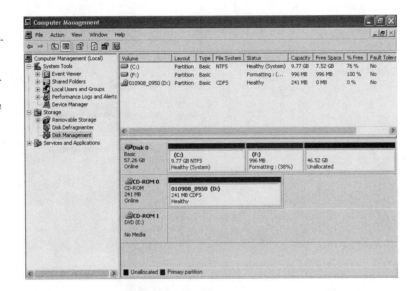

Creating Logical Drives in the Extended Partition

To create a logical drive, right-click on the extended partition in the lower pane of the Disk Management utility window, and from the menu that appears, select New Logical Drive. Again, the New Partition Wizard appears, and its windows prompt you through the process of creating the new logical drive.

As you saw when creating a partition, the wizard asks you to choose the size of the logical drive, the drive letter, the file system, and whether to enable compression by default on the drive. In Figure 18.6, you see the results of the partitioning of one example system. This system contains three primary partitions, one extended partition containing two logical disk drives, and a little over 8 GB of free space left to use for other purposes.

Converting Between Basic and Dynamic Disks

When using the Disk Management tool, you can easily convert a basic disk to a dynamic disk. First, click on the disk drive—that is, Disk 0, Disk 1, or whatever comes before the partition listing—in the lower-right pane of the Disk Manager screen. Do NOT mistake the C: or other drives for the basic disk.

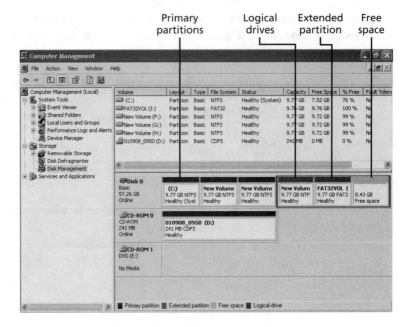

FIGURE 18.6

With all partitions and drives in place, the display changes to show the new organization of the system memory.

Choose Action, All Tasks, Convert to Dynamic Disk. (Alternatively, you can right-click on the disk; then choose Convert to Dynamic Disk from the context menu). The Convert to Dynamic Disk dialog box displays all physical disks on the system that you can convert, with a check mark in the check box next to the disk you have selected. Click OK to start the process.

Figure 18.7 shows the next dialog box indicating the contents of the disk that you have chosen to convert. Click Details to see a list of the drive letters that will be converted into volumes on the new dynamic disk.

FIGURE 18.7

The Disks to Convert dialog box shows you the partitions on the disk you are about to convert.

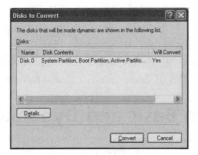

Once you are ready, click the Convert button; then click Yes in the warning box if you want to continue. Another dialog box warns you that any file systems on the disk to be converted will be dismounted first; click Yes again. If you are converting the system disk, another message tells you to reboot the computer to start the conversion process; click OK to finish the conversion.

When the computer reboots it will detect a new device, the newly converted system disk, and it will prompt for another reboot. Click Yes again; the disk is converted and appears as such in the Disk Manager utility window (see Figure 18.8).

FIGURE 18.8

After the conversion is complete, the Disk Management utility can be used to see that disk 0 is now a dynamic disk with dynamic volumes.

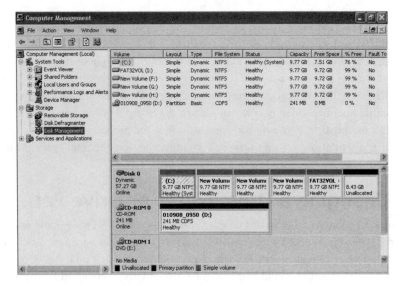

To reverse this process is not so simple. You have to back up all data on the volumes that are on the drive you want to change and then delete each volume (right-click on a volume and select Delete Volume). You then must recreate partitions and restore data after the conversion. When you have deleted all volumes, right-click on the disk and select Convert to Basic Disk.

Extending a Dynamic Volume

Provided you have extra disk space or other disks in your computer with free space, you can extend a simple dynamic volume to create a spanned volume. Spanned volumes can be spread across any space on a given disk but will give the appearance and performance of a single contiguous volume.

Right-click on the disk volume in either the upper or lower pane of the Disk Manager utility window and choose Extend Volume from the context menu. This action launches the Extend Volume Wizard, which walks you through the process. Click Next on the first welcoming screen.

The next screen shows you any other physical drives that appear on the computer and the amount of free space left on the drive that can be used to extend the partition. Use the Select the Amount of Space in MB field to set the amount of space to add to the partition. You can select the entire remaining disk space or use this field to select a lower amount, depending on your needs.

The last window of the wizard simply shows you the settings you have chosen; to close the wizard, click Finish. Refresh the display using the View menu, and you see that the disk volume has been extended to the amount of your choosing. However, the extended volume is still shown as two separate partitions in the bottom pane of Disk Manager. Right-click on the original partition and select Properties to view the properties for the entire volume, which is now made up of the original volume and the free space that was left on the disk. If you do the same to look at the properties for the last volume on this list, it will also show up as the new volume, showing the total space for both partitions that make up the single extended volume.

Changing a Drive Letter or Drive Path

As mentioned earlier in this chapter, you can view an NTFS volume with a drive letter, or it can be mounted with another drive path on another partition. To change the drive letter or drive path associated with a partition, right-click on the disk region and select Change Drive Letter and Paths. In the Change Drive Letter and Path dialog box, click Change to type in a new drive letter to be associated with the volume.

To mount the partition onto the drive path of another NTFS file system, click Add in the Change Drive Letter and Path dialog box. In the Add Drive Letter or Path dialog box (see Figure 18.9), choose Mount in the Following Empty NTFS Folder; then add the drive letter and path for the new the drive path. Choose OK and then OK again to close both dialog boxes.

> **Tip**
>
> You can create a drive path on another volume and give it a particular meaning as one method of linking partitions under Windows XP. All the files and folders of the partition you mount using a drive path become available (based on permissions of course) to users of the disk that have access to the drive path.

FIGURE **18.9**

You can enter the partition and path to a particular location from which this partition will be made available as if it were on the same partition.

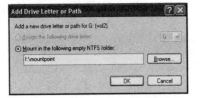

Managing Disks Through the Command Prompt

As you have seen in previous chapters, the Command Prompt offers you fast, flexible options for executing many processes in Windows XP. The following sections outline the Command Prompt techniques for performing basic disk management tasks.

Converting a Partition From FAT to NTFS

The easiest method to convert from a FAT or FAT32 partition is to use the CONVERT command. Suppose, for example, you chose to initially format the C: drive with FAT32, install Windows 98, and then install Windows XP on another partition. You can, if you decide not to use Windows 98 any longer, convert the C: partition to NTFS and then manually delete the Windows 98 system directory to free up some disk space. You can convert any partition using the CONVERT command, but you will be forced to reboot if it is a system partition or a boot partition. The conversion process will then happen during the boot process. Otherwise, the conversion will take place online, and you can watch the progress of the command. The syntax for the CONVERT command is as follows:

```
Converts FAT volumes to NTFS.
```

```
CONVERT volume /FS:NTFS [/V] [/CvtArea:filename] [/NoSecurity] [/X]
```

When using the command, substitute the drive letter of the drive you want to convert for volume (you can also use a mount point or volume name). If you use a drive letter, be sure to specify the colon character (for example, C:, not C). The switch /FS:NTFS is required, which simply tells the command that you are converting to the NTFS file system. At this time, no other formats are supported by the /FS: switch. The other command line switches are optional and include the following:

- /V—This means verbose mode and causes the conversion utility to display more information than when run without this switch.

- /CvtArea:*filename*—Use this to specify a contiguous file in the root directory that will be used as the placeholder for the system files.

- /NoSecurity—This will set the security settings for files and folders on the disk as available to the group Everyone.

- /X—This switch will force a volume to dismount if any files are currently opened on the disk to be converted. It is a better idea to exit the applications that have files opened on the disk to be converted if you can so that you won't suffer the possibility of some loss of data.

The following listing uses a command to convert the I: drive from FAT32 to NTFS:

```
I:\>CONVERT I: /FS:NTFS /V
The type of the file system is FAT32.
Enter current volume label for drive I: FAT32VOL
Convert cannot run because the volume is in use by another
process. Convert may run if this volume is dismounted first.
ALL OPENED HANDLES TO THIS VOLUME WOULD THEN BE INVALID.
Would you like to force a dismount on this volume? (Y/N) y
Volume dismounted. All opened handles to this volume are now invalid.
Volume FAT32VOL created 9/8/2001 3:17 PM
Volume Serial Number is C8D4-C35B
Windows is verifying files and folders...
0 percent completed.
100 percent completed.
File and folder verification is complete.
Windows has checked the file system and found no problems.
 10,231,392 KB total disk space.
 10,231,384 KB are available.

     8,192 bytes in each allocation unit.
 1,278,924 total allocation units on disk.
 1,278,923 allocation units available on disk.

Determining disk space required for file system conversion...
Total disk space:       10241406 KB
Free space on volume:   10231384 KB
Space required for conversion:  64010 KB
Converting file system
Conversion complete
```

As this listing shows, the utility warns you of potential data loss. In this example, it is due to another process using opened files on the disk being converted. After supplying the name of the volume and telling the CONVERT utility to close all open files on the disk, you see that the command goes on to display statistical information showing you important things (such as the 8192 cluster or allocation unit size).

> **Note**
>
> Keep in mind that when a single byte of a cluster is used (such as the last clusters in a file) the entire cluster is wasted, since another file must allocate its own unique clusters and cannot use part of a cluster. Instead, it must use the entire space of each cluster.

Using the DISKPART Command

The DISKPART command allows you to can add, delete, and view the status of the partitions on the disk. The syntax for this powerful command is as follows:

```
DiskPart [/s <script>] [/?]
```

You can also use user commands interactively with DISKPART to execute commands. By creating script files, you can set up a series of computers at a business all with the same disk partitions, provided the equipment is all similar. This arrangement enables you to perform other tasks while the script file performs lengthy operations such as disk formatting.

The easiest way to get acquainted with this command is to have on hand a computer on which you have data that you need to keep and to use DISKPART in interactive mode. Enter the command DISKPART at the Command Prompt; then enter the following DISKPART commands:

- LIST—This switch allows you to see the currently defined disks, partitions, and other information about the current partition setup. You can use LIST DISK, LIST VOLUME, and LIST PARTITION commands to see these disk structures, or objects, as they are now called in the DISKPART command. Use the LIST qualifiers to see what is on disk or disks before you begin to contemplate changes.

- SELECT—This qualifier forms the second step in trying to focus in on a specific object after you have used the LIST switch to find out the available objects. Similarly, you can use the following types of the SELECT switch: SELECT DISK, SELECT PARTITION, and SELECT VOLUME.

- ACTIVE—This will activate the basic partition you select so that on boot, it will be the active partition.

- ASSIGN—Use this to assign a drive letter to a mount point or a volume. The syntax is ASSIGN [{letter=*driveletter* | mount=*pathname*}] [noerr]. Substitute the drive letter you want to use for *driveletter* or the mountpoint you want to use for *mountpoint*.

18

MANAGING DISKS
AND PARTITIONS

Note

You cannot use ASSIGN to change the drive letter of a system volume or boot volume to any volume on which you may have placed a paging file. 64-bit Itanium users cannot use this command on GPT disks.

- CLEAN—This command qualifier will remove any previous partition and volume information from a disk. For standard MBR disks, only the MBR and the information about partitioning and hidden sector information are replaced. On a 64-bit system using GPT partition, information is overwritten. Use CLEAN ALL if you want to zero every sector in order to delete the current data on the disk as well as remove partitioning information.

- CONVERT BASIC—This command will convert a dynamic disk into a basic disk.

- COINVERT DYNAMIC—Use this to do the opposite of the previous command and convert a dynamic disk to a basic disk.

- CONVERT GPT—This can be used on 64-bit Itanium workstations to convert an empty basic disk from the MBR to the GPT partition table type. Use this command when you are upgrading your system to a newer one.

- CONVERT MBR—As you can guess, on an Itanium-based computer, this will convert an empty GPT type of partition to a MBR partition.

- CREATE PARTITION EFI—For Itanium users, this will create the extensible firmware interface (EFI) system partition on a GPT disk. You can then select this partition to perform further commands. See the Help online for further information about using this command.

- CREATE PARTITION EXTENDED—This is the equivalent of creating an extended partition on a disk after one or more primary partitions have been created. You are allowed to specify the size (in MB) of an offset into the disk free space. If you do not supply the offset value, it will default to the first free space available on the disk.

- CREATE PARTITION LOGICAL—This allows you to create an extended logical drive in an extended partition. You can also specify an offset and size for the disk. If you omit the offset, the disk will be created according to the size parameter. If you omit both, then the remainder of the extended partition will be used for the logical drive.

- CREATE PARTITION MSF—This command creates a partition reserved by Microsoft on GPT disks. This area follows the first partition on an EFI system, unless it is a on a disk used only for data storage, in which case, it is the first partition. Do not use this command unless you have a specific need, as it is a special partition that Microsoft uses and cannot be used for data or other storage needs.

- CREATE PARTITION PRIMARY—This will create a primary partition on a basic disk.

- CREATE VOLUME SIMPLE—This is used to create a simple volume on a dynamic disk.

- CREATE VOLUME RAID—Use this to create a raid volume on dynamic disks. As parameters to this command, you specify the size of the volume and the disk numbers that will be used for the RAID-5 volume.

- CREATE VOLUME STRIPE—You can use this command to create a striped volume on a set of dynamic disks.

- ADD DISK—This command can be used to mirror simple volumes. First use the SELECT command to choose a simple disk and then use this command to add another simple volume as a mirror image.

- BREAK DISK—This command can be used to separate mirrored volumes. You can choose the NOKEEP parameter to mark the simple volume that was a mirror as free space, or you can retain the copy.

- DELETE DISK—This syntax will delete a missing dynamic disk from the disk list. You can use this to delete any or all simple volumes on a disk.

- DELETE PARTITION—Use this to delete partitions on a basic disk. Remember, you cannot delete a partition that is the system or boot partition or one that contains a paging file in use.

- DELETE VOLUME—Use this syntax to delete any volume. The same restrictions apply from the DELETE PARTITION command, in that you cannot delete a system or boot volume or a volume that contains an active paging file.

- DETAIL DISK—This will display the properties of the disk you have selected.

- DETAIL VOLUME—This will display the disks on which a volume resides.

- EXTEND—This will extend a volume that you have selected into additional contiguous space. For a basic volume, of course, the space must be on the same disk. For a dynamic disk this can be used to extend a volume to new space on an additional disk. A boot partition or the current system partition from which you have booted cannot be extended. This command only works with volumes using the NTFS file system, which will be automatically extended to account for the new space.

- REMOVE—Use this command, specifying a drive letter or mount point, to remove the drive letter from the current volume. This cannot be used for the boot or system volumes or for one that holds an active paging file. If you don't specify a mount point or drive letter, the command will remove the first drive letter it can.

- RESCAN—Use this to cause the DISKPART utility to look for any new disks added to the computer.

- EXIT—Use this to exit the DISKPART interactive session.

18

MANAGING DISKS AND PARTITIONS

You can use the utility interactively or just enter single commands. You can also create a script file and use the syntax DISKPART /S *scriptfilename*. If you use a script file to automate setting up a large number of computers, it would be a good idea to keep a log of the actions taken by the utility. In that case, use the > redirection symbol to direct the output to a file: DKSKPART /S *scriptfilename* > *logfile.txt*.

Using DISKPART LIST

To get used to using this command, first try using the LIST commands to view the disk, partitions, and volumes on your computer. The following is an example of this command in action:

```
C:\>DISKPART

Microsoft DiskPart version 1.0
Copyright (C) 1999-2001 Microsoft Corporation.
On computer: ZIRA

DISKPART> LIST DISK

  Disk ### Status    Size  Free  Dyn Gpt
  -------- ---------- ----- ----- --- ---
  Disk 0   Online     57 GB 188 KB *

DISKPART> LIST PARTITION

There is no disk selected to list partitions.
Select a disk and try again.

DISKPART> LIST VOLUME

  Volume ### Ltr Label     Fs   Type    Size   Status   Info
  ---------- --- --------- ----- ----- -------- ------- --------- --------
  Volume 0   C             NTFS Simple  10 GB Healthy  System
  Volume 1   F vol1        NTFS Simple  10 GB Healthy
  Volume 2   G vol2        NTFS Simple  10 GB Healthy
   F:\mountpoint
  Volume 3   H vol3        NTFS Simple  18 GB Healthy
  Volume 4   I vol3        NTFS Simple  10 GB Healthy
  Volume 5   D 010908_0950 CDFS CD-ROM   241 MB
  Volume 6   E                  DVD-ROM    0 B

DISKPART>
```

As you can see, there is only one disk on this computer, but it is a dynamic disk. Since this was a basic disk that was converted to a dynamic disk, you can see that the LIST PARTITION command fails, because there are no disk partitions. Instead, the LIST VOLUME command shows the new dynamic volumes that were created from the partitions on the old basic disk. You can see from this listing that you can access drive letter G: through its drive letter or a mount point F:\mountpoint.

This listing also indicates the file system and disk type for each disk, as well as the size and drive letter associated with volumes.

Deleting a Partition or Volume

You can use DISKPART DELETE VOLUME command to remove a volume to free up space on a disk you might want to use for other purposes. For example, the following listing uses the command to delete the I: volume. Notice first that you must select the volume using the SELECT command to make it the current volume.

```
C:\>DISKPART

Microsoft DiskPart version 1.0
Copyright (C) 1999-2001 Microsoft Corporation.
On computer: ZIRA

DISKPART> LIST VOLUME

  Volume ### Ltr Label     Fs   Type     Size  Status  Info
  ---------- --- ---------- ---- -------- ----- ------- --------- --------
  Volume 0   C             NTFS Simple   10 GB Healthy System
  Volume 1   F   vol1      NTFS Simple   10 GB Healthy
  Volume 2   G   vol2      NTFS Simple   10 GB Healthy
   F:\mountpoint
  Volume 3   H   vol3      NTFS Simple   18 GB Healthy
  Volume 4   I   vol3      NTFS Simple   10 GB Healthy
  Volume 5   D   010908_0950 CDFS CD-ROM  241 MB
  Volume 6   E             DVD-ROM   0 B

DISKPART> SELECT VOLUME I

Volume 4 is the selected volume.

DISKPART> DELETE VOLUME

DiskPart successfully deleted the volume.

DISKPART>
```

Now, as in the following, go back and reuse that free space so to see how DISKPART can be used to extend a current disk volume:

```
DISKPART> LIST DISK

  Disk ### Status     Size  Free  Dyn Gpt
  -------- ---------- ----- ----- --- ---
  Disk 0   Online     57 GB 10 GB  *
```

```
DISKPART> LIST VOLUME

  Volume ### Ltr Label     Fs  Type      Size  Status   Info
  ---------- --- ----------- ----- ---------- -------- --------- --------
  Volume 0   C           NTFS Simple    10 GB Healthy  System
  Volume 1   F  vol1      NTFS Simple    10 GB Healthy
  Volume 2   G  vol2      NTFS Simple    10 GB Healthy
   F:\mountpoint
  Volume 3   H  vol3      NTFS Simple    18 GB Healthy
  Volume 4   D  010908_0950 CDFS CD-ROM   241 MB
  Volume 5   E              DVD-ROM   0 B

DISKPART> SELECT VOLUME H

Volume 3 is the selected volume.

DISKPART> EXTEND SIZE=500 DISK=0

DiskPart successfully extended the volume.

DISKPART>
```

If this had been a basic disk, you would have used the command DELETE DISK PARTI-TION instead of DELETE DISK VOLUME. Using the LIST DISK command quickly gets you info on whether a disk is a basic disk or a dynamic one. It also showed that this disk had 10GB of free space, so you could list the volumes to see what remained and then use the SELECT command to set the focus on the H: volume. The EXTEND command then extended the size of the partition by 500MB.

Now, since there is a little more than 9GB left on this disk, why not create a new volume? In the following listing, you can see how to use the CREATE VOLUME SIMPLE command to create a simple volume:

```
DISKPART> LIST DISK

  Disk ### Status   Size  Free  Dyn Gpt
  -------- ---------- ------- ------- --- ---
  Disk 0  Online    57 GB  9 GB  *

DISKPART> CREATE VOLUME SIMPLE SIZE=5000 DISK=0

DiskPart successfully created the volume.

DISKPART> LIST VOLUME

  Volume ### Ltr Label     Fs  Type      Size  Status   Info
  ---------- --- ----------- ----- ---------- -------- --------- --------
  Volume 0   C           NTFS Simple    10 GB Healthy  System
  Volume 1   F  vol1      NTFS Simple    10 GB Healthy
  Volume 2   G  vol2      NTFS Simple    10 GB Healthy
```

```
  F:\mountpoint
Volume 3  H vol3    NTFS Simple    19 GB Healthy
* Volume 4          Simple   5000 MB Healthy
Volume 5  D 010908_0950 CDFS CD-ROM   241 MB
Volume 6  E          DVD-ROM   0 B

DISKPART> ASSIGN LETTER=I

DiskPart successfully assigned the drive letter or mount point.

DISKPART> LIST VOLUME

Volume ### Ltr Label    Fs   Type    Size  Status  Info
---------- --- ----------- ----- ---------- ------- --------- --------
Volume 0  C          NTFS Simple    10 GB Healthy  System
Volume 1  F vol1     NTFS Simple    10 GB Healthy
Volume 2  G vol2     NTFS Simple    10 GB Healthy
  F:\mountpoint
Volume 3  H vol3     NTFS Simple    19 GB Healthy
* Volume 4  I        Simple   5000 MB Healthy
Volume 5  D 010908_0950 CDFS CD-ROM   241 MB
Volume 6  E          DVD-ROM   0 B

DISKPART>
```

As this listing shows, all that the command did was to create the new volume. The ASSIGN command was used to assign a driver letter to the newly created partition.

If you have more than one disk drive in your computer, you can then use the other CREATE commands to create dynamic disks like mirrored sets or RAID-5.

Formatting a Disk

To format a disk while still at the Command Prompt, use the FORMAT command as follows:

```
C:\>FORMAT /FS:NTFS I:
The type of the file system is RAW.
The new file system is NTFS.

WARNING, ALL DATA ON NON-REMOVABLE DIS
DRIVE I: WILL BE LOST!
Proceed with Format (Y/N)? Y
Verifying 5000M
Volume label (ENTER for none)?
Creating file system structures.
Format complete.
 5119996 KB total disk space.
 5091980 KB are available.
```

18

MANAGING DISKS
AND PARTITIONS

This example uses the /FS (file system) command line switch to specify that the disk volume be formatted using the NTFS file system. The syntax for the format command takes into consideration a lot of different things like disks from floppies to larger disk drives, as well as the type of file system to place on partition or volume. The syntax for the FORMAT command in Windows XP is as follows:

```
FORMAT volume [/FS:file-system] [/V:label] [/Q] [/A:size] [/C] [/X]
FORMAT volume [/V:label] [/Q] [/F:size]
FORMAT volume [/V:label] [/Q] [/T:tracks /N:sectors]
FORMAT volume [/V:label] [/Q]
FORMAT volume [/Q]
```

Wherever volume is the drive letter of the volume or partition you want to format, the following command line options can be used:

- /FS—This indicates the file system and can be FAT, FAT32, or NTFS).

- /V:label—This can be used to give the volume a label. You can also use the LABEL command to assign a label name at a later date.

- /Q—This performs a quick format by resetting certain file structures. Individual disk blocks are not erased or checked.

- /C—If you specified NTFS as the volume to format, then you can use this switch to indicate that any files created on the volume will be compressed (unless you later choose to modify a folder or disk's properties (discussed later in this chapter).

- /X—This switch can be used to force an online volume to dismount so that it can be reformatted. If any applications have open files on the disk, they will lose this data.

- /A:size—You should generally accept the default allocation size that the operating system determines is appropriate for the size of the volume. However, the FORMAT command allows you to use this switch to set the size to a different value if you want. You may want to set a smaller allocation size, for example, if you are going to use the disk for a lot of small files. This will cause less disk space to be wasted for files that use multiple clusters on the volume. However, if you are only going to have a few large files on the disk, you may want to specify a larger size. This is because reads and writes will most likely improve since fewer clusters have to be read or written to.

- /F:size—Use this to specify the size of a floppy disk. Generally, you should just ignore this switch. Most every floppy disk is 1.44 MB, high-density, double-sided disk, and a simple FORMAT A:/U command will unconditionally format the disk to its correct size. However, this may be useful if you have older disks; you can specify a wide number of sizes, ranging from 160KB up to 20.8MB.

- /T:*track*—Specifies the number of tracks for each side of the disk. This should not be needed unless you are using older disks.

- /N:*sectors*—This tells FORMAT the number of sectors to provide per track. Again, you probably will rarely, if ever, use this command, unless you have anything but the standard 1.44MB floppy disk.

> **Caution**
>
> If you decide to change allocation sizes, be aware that NTFS compression won't function on disks with an allocation unit size larger than 4096.

Configuring Partition Properties

Each folder file in Windows XP has a set of properties pages that you can view to find information about and configure the file/folder properties. To produce the properties pages for a partition, right-click on the drive listing in the lower-right pane of Disk Manager and choose Properties (see Figure 18.10). If you are viewing disk drives using Windows Explorer, just right-click the folder that represents the drive and make the same selection.

FIGURE 18.10

Each drive has a set of properties pages associated with it; here, the General tab is selected.

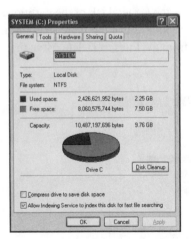

The General tab shows the label you assigned to the partition (or it is blank if you don't choose to give the partition a name), the disk type, the capacity of the disk, and the amount of free space it holds.

In the General tab, you can choose the Compress Drive to Save Disk Space check box to compress most of the files on your disk drive. You can still read and write to the files, and the process is transparent to the user, but the files will take up less space on the disk. You are asked to decide if you want to compress only the files and folders that reside at the top directory for the disk or all files and folders on the disk. Make your selection and click OK to continue.

Use the Allow Indexing Service to Index This Disk for Fast File Searching. Use this check box if you frequently use the Search Assistant tool to locate files. Note that this option will use up more disk space, since the index itself must contain some text and pointers to the files.

Note

When compressing files and folders, you might get a message box indicating that a file or folder cannot be compressed because it is in use by another program, especially on the system partition. If so, click Ignore to skip the particular file or Ignore All to skip all files that might cause this dialog box to pop up.

Using Disk Cleanup

You can use the Disk Cleanup option in the General tab of the partition's property pages to delete unnecessary files from your disk, thus making more space available on it. Click the Disk Cleanup button; then select from the Files to Delete list in the Disk Cleanup dialog box (see Figure 18.11).

FIGURE 18.11

Select the types of files to be removed during the disk cleanup procedure. Each listing indicates the amount of space occupied by the files; under the list, you see the total amount of disk space that deleting checked files will free up.

To view the files that will be eliminated during disk cleanup, select a check box and then click View Files. This can help you decide if you want to use that particular file type during disk cleanup.

For additional clean-up possibilities, click the More Options tab of the Disk Cleanup utility.

In this tab, you can choose any of the following:

- Windows Components—This tool will let you remove Windows applications to gain more space. You can also use the Add/Remove Programs applet in the Control Panel to perform this function.

- Installed Programs—This tool will let you remove third-party applications to gain more space. Again, you can also use the Add/Remove Programs applet in the Control Panel to perform this function.

- System Restore—You can remove restore points (described in Chapter 23, "Disaster Recovery." This option will remove all but the most frequent restore points. Each restore point stores some Registry settings and selected files that allow you to return your computer to a previous point in time. Don't choose this option.

On the Disk Cleanup tab, simply click OK once you have made your check box selections.

The Tools Tab

The Tools tab of a disk's properties page gives you quick access error-scanning, defragmenting, and backup disk management tools (see Figure 18.12).

FIGURE 18.12

The Tools tab allows you to use other utilities to manage the disk.

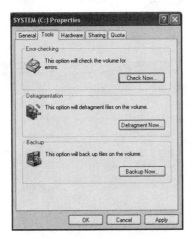

18

MANAGING DISKS AND PARTITIONS

The following is a closer look at these options:

- Check Now—This works like the old Scandisk, looking for problems on your disk drive. It can also be used to find bad blocks and fix common errors that may occur in the file system.

- Defragment—Over time, as files are created and deleted, the free space on the disk becomes fragmented into smaller chunks. Defragmenting a drive will optimize read and write functions by reorganizing the data on the disk so that most similar file data and free space is contiguous. That way, drive heads don't have to jump all around the disk to find different parts of the file.

- Backup Now—This option invokes the Backup program.

The Backup utility for Windows XP is described in Chapter 21, "Using Backup on Windows XP," but you will learn in the next two sections how to use the options described above to check a disk for errors and how to defragment the disk drives (or partitions) in your computer to help improve performance dramatically.

Checking a Disk Partition for Errors

If you chose the first selection in the Tools tab for the disk's properties pages, then a utility similar to what you used (such as Scandisk utility) will check your hard disk drive partition and give you two options:

- Automatically fix file system errors.

- Scan and attempt recovery of bad sectors.

Click appropriate radio buttons to make your selection; then click OK to start the process. Depending on the options you select and the size of the disk partition, this can take some time to complete, so be patient.

Caution

If you have chosen a system partition, a dialog box pops up telling you that it is not possible to do this check at the present time. You will then be asked if you want this check performed during the next reboot; in most cases you should select Yes. Even the system disk (or *especially* the system disk partition) needs to be examined for possible errors on a periodic basis because all your other disks, which may contain applications or data, depend on the operating system itself.

This function will report any disk or file system error it finds and repair them if you made that choice. You should consider first running this feature without selecting a repair option. If errors show up, then make a backup of the partition and rerun this utility to allow it to attempt to repair the damage.

Defragmenting a Disk Partition

From the Tools tab of the disk partition's properties page you can choose to defragment the disk partition. Disk defragmenting is an important "housekeeping" tool, due to the way disks record data. Files are written to disks in sectors (a set number of bytes). These sectors can be scattered across a disk. As you add and delete files, sectors from the same file can be scattered, and empty file space occurs in these scattered sectors. Noncontiguous file data and empty sectors create inefficient read and write processes, since the read/write heads must then scatter all over the drive themselves, trying to find and organize data. Defragmenting groups all similar files and empty sectors together, making read-write processes more efficient. Therefore, it only makes sense to regularly defragment your disks, including the system partition and all partitions in which data or applications change on a frequent basis.

To begin, click Defragment Now to open the window shown in Figure 18.12.

FIGURE 18.12

The Disk Defrag-menter utility allows you to reconfigure your storage of disk files to make them available at a faster rate.

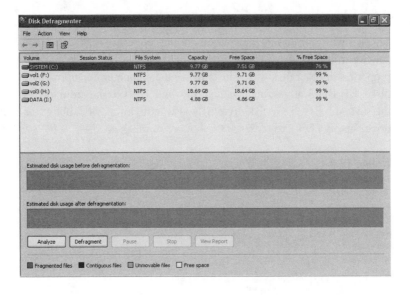

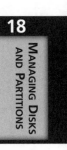

The top pane of this window displays the disk partitions for all of the disk drives installed on your computer. Click a disk partition and then click either Analyze to view the degree of fragmentation on that disk. Click Defragment to both analyze and defragment the disk. The Defragmenter window shows you the progress of the defrag-mentation process. One bar graph shows you the analysis of your disk partition before the defragmentation, while a chart changes as files are moved around. You can also see which files on the disk cannot be moved.

When the process is completed, a dialog box pops up asking if you want to view a report of the actions that were done to defragment the disk. Unless you are just really curious, click Close to dismiss the dialog box and then close the Disk Defragmenter utility by using Exit from the File menu or the X at the top of the window.

> ### Tip
>
> While defragmenting a disk, you may get an informational message saying that some files could not be defragmented. This is always the case on the system partition, since some system files are always in use and hence cannot be moved. If you have applications opened on a disk you are defragmenting, they will also not be moved. Therefore, it is a good idea to close all other applications before defragmenting a disk partition.

The Hardware Tab

This tab will give you information about the properties for the disk drive on which the active partition resides. As you can see in Figure 18.14, it also allow you to view the properties of other disk drives installed in the computer, including hard disks, floppy disks, CD-ROM drives, and even a removable USB flash card reader, which the operating system treats like a disk drive. If you want to know more about the particular disk drive, simply click Properties at the bottom of the page.

FIGURE 18.14

The Hardware tab shows the disk drive that holds the partition, as well as the other drives on the computer.

The Policies tab offers caching and safe removal options for the disk drive. The following three choices are available on this tab (note that the first two choices are mutually exclusive radio buttons that pertain to removable media and may be grayed out if you are looking at the properties for a fixed disk drive installed in the computer):

- Optimize for Quick Removal—This will disable write caching. Generally, to improve performance, you should enable caching whenever possible. Write caching means that when your application issues a command to the operating system to write data to the disk, it is instead stored in a buffer and written at a later time (usually just a few seconds or less) when it is convenient for the operating system to do so. For a removable device, however, you may want to disable caching so you can remove the device at anytime.

- Optimize for Performance—This will enable write caching for the drive. Before you remove the disk, be sure to use the Safely Remove Hardware icon that is located on the taskbar on the far right side in what is now called the *notification area*.

- Enable Write Caching on the Disk—As mentioned earlier, this will delay writes to the disk to make them more efficient, and an application that is disk intensive in its operation will probably run faster. Note, however, that when caching is enabled, if you suffer a power outage or some other fault, you can lose data. Generally, I recommend you use this check box to improve performance.

The first time you click on the Volumes tab, all fields are blank. Although the Volumes tab of the disk drive property sheet displays information about partitions created on the drive, you must first "populate" the tab to update the fields. Click Populate to populate the fields, as shown in Figure 18.15.

FIGURE 18.15

The Volumes tab contains no information until you populate it. After you click the Populate button, the fields contain data, and the button is grayed out.

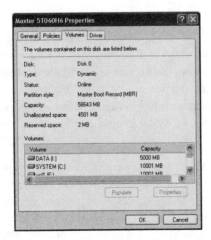

18

MANAGING DISKS
AND PARTITIONS

As you can see, the current disk drive contains the MBR for storing information that the BIOS of your computer uses to initially boot the operating system (or another utility, if you use one of the various multiboot programs available today). At the bottom of the display is a listing of the drive partitions and the letters associated with each. To view the information about any partition, click on the partition and then click Properties at the bottom of the property sheet. Another dialog box pops up, giving you information about the particular partition.

The Driver tab lists the provider of the following four driver options:

- Driver Details—You can get more information about the driver from this button. For the most part, you probably won't care to use this button at all unless you are a service technician.

- Update Driver—This button can be used to update a driver. If you install Windows XP from the distribution CD and the manufacturer later releases a newer driver, you will want to use this button. It will prompt you to insert the floppy disk, or browse for the location of the driver to install.

- Roll Back Driver—Here is another example of one of the improved features you get with Windows XP. If the new driver doesn't perform as expected or conflicts with another driver, you can boot into Safe Mode and use the Roll Back Driver button to remove the driver and replace it with the one that it replaced.

- Uninstall—Use this button to uninstall a driver. For example, if you have a removable disk drive and decide to no longer use it on this computer, then you can use this button to remove the driver. Simply disconnecting the removable drive doesn't remove the driver.

Sharing the Disk Drive

You can select a folder or an entire disk drive to share with others on the network. If you use an NTFS partition, you can even pick the users and choose what kind of access they are allowed to have. Figure 18.16 shows the Sharing tab as first seen when you decide to offer an entire disk as a file share. As the warning suggests, it is better to create folders for specific kinds of data and share those folders instead. Although the process is similar, you can learn more about how to share a folder by reading Chapter 9, "Working With Files and Folders."

After you click the warning link on this properties page, another dialog box enables you to configure how the disk drive volume will be shared. You can choose to share this disk volume with other users who log onto the computer, such as those who have local user accounts. If this computer were part of a domain, you would also be allowed to select users and user groups from the domain to which you want to grant permission. Drag the drive to the Computer Management's console tree and drop it onto the entry labeled Shared Folders.

FIGURE 18.16

The first time you use it, the Sharing tab will warn you about sharing an entire drive volume.

The technique for sharing the drive with others in a network depends on the kind of network you are using. If you are using the workgroup method, where you simply set the same workgroup name for each computer in the same workgroup, then you can run the Network Setup Wizard at this time.

Note

For more information about the Network Setup Wizard, see Chapter 24, "Configuring Your Computer for Local Area Networking," and Chapter 25, "Configuring Your Computer for an Internet Connection."

For purpose of this example, click If You Understand the Security Risks but Want to Share Files Without Running the Wizard, Click Here. Windows XP gives you one last chance to change your mind and use the wizard. Click the radio button labeled *Just Enable File Sharing;* then click OK.

When you click OK, the Sharing tab will change (see Figure 18.17). In this example, two important check boxes are selected: *Share This* Folder on the Network and Allow Network Users to Change My Files. Use the Share Name field to change the share name to be something more informative than the volume label and drive letter. In this example, the F: drive is being shared, so the share name is changed to fshare (this will remind you where the file is coming from when you connect from another computer in the office). Feel free to be more creative in your file names and name a share based on the content or use of the file share.

To finish the process, simply click Apply and then OK.

18

MANAGING DISKS AND PARTITIONS

FIGURE 18.17

The Sharing tab creates a file share name and shares the disk volume with the network.

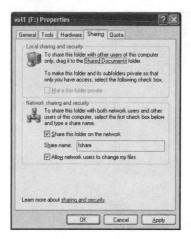

Enabling Disk Quotas

The last tab on this set of properties pages for a disk volume is the Quota tab. A quota is the maximum amount of a resource of which a user is allowed to make use. This helps control disk space usage. You can use the Quota tab (see Figure 18.18) to set file space quotas for selected users or groups, and to decide how quotes are enforced.

FIGURE 18.18

The Quota tab allows you to restrict disk space by user or group on a disk resource.

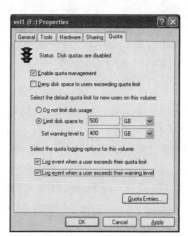

Enable disk quotas on the disk partition by using the check box labeled Enable Quota Management. Select Deny Disk Space to Users Exceeding the Quota Limit to strictly enforce disk quotas; users will not be allowed to exceed the maximum amount of disk storage space you decide is appropriate for them. Of course, as an alternative, the user can always save a file to another disk or file share, but this is a powerful management technique to keep users aware that disk space is limited and that they should respect it.

If you don't want to limit user access to disk space, select Do Not Limit Disk Usage. Otherwise, select Limit Disk Space To; then enter information in the accompanying fields to set disk space limit in KB or MB and to tell Windows XP at what amount of disk space usage to issue users a warning that they are nearing their limit.

The last two check boxes on this tab allow you to select to log an event record (to be viewed using the Event Viewer, described in Chapter 16, "Auditing Windows XP Using the Event Viewer") as users exceed the warning or quota limit you set. By reviewing records using the Event Viewer, you can get a better understanding of how the user is making use of your resource and perhaps negotiate a better quota size. Click Quota Entries to see a quick view of users who are approaching or have exceeded the limits you set.

Sharing Files with the Computer Management Utility

In Chapter 9, "Working With Files and Folders," you learned how to share files and folders using the Windows Explorer. As a system administrator, you have the option to use the Computer Management utility to share files, folders, and volumes quickly and easily.

Windows XP creates some file shares automatically to give those with administrative rights the ability to connect to the root of any disk volume. The share name of these files is composed of the drive letter follow by a dollar sign. Thus, the `F:` drive for which you just created a file share for called `fshare` also has a hidden file share called `F$` to which administrative personnel can connect. You can use the Computer Management utility and select Shared Folders and then Shares to view all the shares offered on the network by your computer (see Figure 18.19).

FIGURE 18.19

You can use the Shared Folders subfolder Shares to see all of the file shares offered by our computer, including the hidden ones.

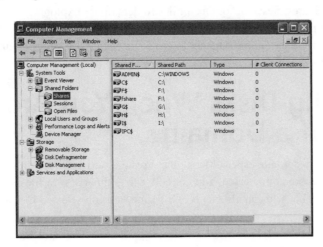

You can also use the Sessions and Open Files entries under Shared Folders in the Computer Management utility to view information about the usage of the shares you offer.

You cannot see hidden file shares unless you connect with an administrator type of account. If you want to share this drive or any folder on the drive, just bring up the properties sheet and select the sharing tab. Then create a file share with a recognizable name. The hidden file shares are meant for administrators and for some network programs that require them. For this reason, it is not generally a good idea to delete the hidden file shares.

Sessions and Open Files

In the Computer Management utility, you will find a few other things you can do to manage the sessions and opened files on your computer being used by remote users. Simply click on the Shares folder, Sessions folder, or the Open Files folder in the left explorer pane. You can then either right-click and select a menu option, or you can highlight folder and select the Action menu.

From this menu, you can do the following:

- Use the All Tasks menu selection to get the Send Console Message—A dialog box pops up in which you can type a short message and then select which users should receive the pop-up message. This can be useful if you want to warn users of a scheduled shutdown shortly before the downtime.

- Disconnect All Sessions—This will work for the Sessions folder and allow you to disconnect the sessions currently underway with the file share.

- Disconnect All Open Files—If you must close all files on a disk volume, use this menu selection.

Opening the Shares, Sessions, or Open Files folders in the Explorer pane displays information in the right-side pane, indicating pertinent information for what you have chosen. You can use this to determine whether to use some of the disconnect commands discussed above.

Sharing Disks When You Are Part of a Domain

When you join a domain, especially one that uses the Active Directory, then file sharing becomes a bit more complicated. You not only can grant access to files to general users on the network, but you can also set NTFS permissions on selected files and folders that allow certain kinds of access to files and folders. This is covered in detail in Chapter 9 for other users in the domain. The same techniques used for granting access to folders on disk volumes can also be used from Windows Explorer for file shares you create or from the built-in $ administrator shares.

Summary

This chapter covered a lot of territory, and although it may at first seem like a lot information to absorb, keep in mind that most of you will be using Windows XP on a desktop system and not a high-end workstation. In that case, using a single, basic disk and creating the partitions you want will be more than sufficient for your needs.

However, if you want to operate your computer more like a server computer or you use high-end workstations that do things like animation, then you may want to create larger disk volumes. Network administrators may want to provide some fault-tolerant disk systems, such as RAID-5 on the computer. As you have learned in this chapter, the Disk Management utility and the DISKPART commands enable you to configure and reconfigure, your system so that it fits your situation and hardware environment. If security is important, then you should use the NTFS file system, set permissions appropriately, and grant rights to users. Using FAT or FAT32 partitions will not offer you security from other users who log on locally to the computer.

Using the Task Manager

IN THIS CHAPTER

- Managing Applications Using the Task Manager   *484*

- Managing Individual Processes   *488*

- Using the Performance Tab to Track System Performance   *493*

- Tracking Networking Adapter Usage with the Networking Tab   *495*

CHAPTER 19

Ever have one of those days when a misbehaving application just wouldn't exit when you wanted to close it? How about when everything on the computer just runs slower than usual? If you have plenty of time and expertise, you can use the System Monitor to find the problem (see Chapter 22, "Performance Monitoring, Logs, and Alerts"). However, if you want to use a much simpler tool, turn to the Task Manager. The Windows XP Professional Task Manager allows you to do several things. Like the System Monitor, it can show you performance statistics in a real-time fashion to give you quick glance at how memory and the central processing unit (CPU) in your computer are being used. In addition, you can get statistical information about how well your network card is handling the load on your local area network.

In addition to these functions, you can use the Task Manager to check on applications and the many processes that make them up, as well as system processes. You can also use the Task Manager to kill an application that is not responding and has "gone to lunch." In this chapter, you learn how to use the Task Manager for these and other functions as a single utility that replaces more complicated tools in the Administrative Tools folder and the Control Panel.

Managing Applications Using the Task Manager

One of the main complaints of Windows users in the past few years is that Windows 95/98/Me applications sometimes tend to hang or freeze, requiring a system reboot. The Windows XP architecture should go far toward eliminating that problem. As you learned in Chapter 1, "Looking Inside Windows XP Professional," each process that runs under Windows XP has its own separate virtual address space. With the virtual memory management keeping track of all the page tables, pointers, and so on, there should never be a reason for you to reboot the computer to get rid of an application that isn't working as it should.

If an application hangs up in Windows XP, you can open the Task Manager in one of two ways:

- Right-click on the Desktop toolbar in any unused space and select Task Manager from the menu.
- Use the Ctrl+Alt+Del key combination to bring up the Task Manager.

Select the Applications tab (see Figure 19.1).

FIGURE 19.1

The Task Manager allows you to see what applications are running and to end an application that is not responding.

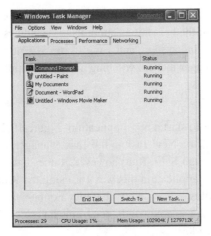

Ending a Task—Killing an Application

The Task Manager Applications tab lists every open application and its status, regardless of whether they are Running or Not Responding. When an application seems to hang up, check here to see if the application's status is Not Responding. If that is the case, you can choose to wait to see if the problem clears up (not recommended), or you can kill the application and restart it.

To kill an application, click its name in the Task column and then click End Task.

> **Caution**
>
> Although you can kill a running application that is responding normally, that is not a good idea. The normal shutdown process allows the program to clean up after itself; if you kill it, you might lose your changes. As a rule, only kill applications when they hang up.

Switching to an Application

You can also use this view of the Task manager to switch among running applications. This feature can be helpful if you are running a lot of applications at the same time and you cannot locate the correct icon on the Task Bar. Click on Task Manager and then click once on the application you want to continue using. Next, click the Switch To button or simply double-click on the application to accomplish the same result. The application will be restored on the Desktop, and you can continue working with it.

Therefore, the Task Manager can be a focal point for managing and switching among multiple applications. This is one of the best things about using Windows XP—it is a true, preemptive multitasking operating system, and you can run several programs all at the same time. Using the Task Manager makes switching among the applications a cinch!

Starting New Tasks

You can also use the Task Manager to start a new application. Figure 19.2 shows the dialog box that pops up when you click on New Task in the Task Manager. It is exactly the same as the dialog box you get through Start, Run; however, it does have a different title—Create New Task. Starting an application this way (or using the Run command) is a useful way of running program files or commands that may not be available on the Start menu. This includes command-line commands, programs on removable disks, and even programs located on the network.

FIGURE 19.2

You can start up new applications by using the Create New Task button on the Applications tab of the Task Manager.

Not only can you enter the name of a program, folder, or a document that you want to open, but you can also enter the uniform resource locator (URL) for an Internet resource. If you enter a folder name (such as C:\windows), then you will see a display of all the files and folders in that folder. This is a handy method to use when you are not sure of the name of an application but do know the name of the folder. You can then select from the listing that appears with the application you want to run, or you can double-click on folders within the folder you entered in order to keep browsing until you find what you want.

If you want to access an Internet resource like a Web page, just enter the correct syntax (e.g., http://www.twoinc.com) into the Open field, and Internet Explorer or your default browser will display the page for you.

If you are unsure of exactly where the application or file you want is located, then use the Browse button. At the top of the Browse window is the Look in: drop-down menu for browsing virtually anywhere you want, from your computer to the Internet (Figure 19.3).

FIGURE 19.3

Using the Look in: drop-down menu, you can browse your entire computer, as well as the entire network to find what you want to open.

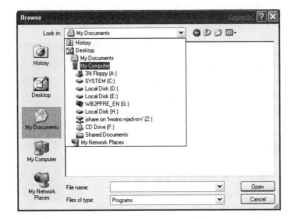

As you can see, this is much like combining the capabilities of the Windows Explorer accessory into the Task Manager. Again, keep in mind that that the Task Manager can be a handy central resource so that you don't have to use other accessories or programs to perform routine chores.

Menu Options

At the top of the Task Manager, you will find several menus. Some of these menus operate the same no matter which tab you have selected, while others offer different menu options. The Options menu allows you to specify the following:

- Always on Top—This selection means that regardless of which other programs are running, the Task Manager window will be in the forefront of the graphical user interface (GUI) display. You can move it around by clicking on the task bar of the Task Manager and moving it to a different portion of the screen if you want to look at a different application's window while remaining in the main window.

- Minimize on Use—Use this if you want the Task Manager to be running but not displayed as a window on the desktop until you choose to maximize it. The Task Manager will be available from the Task Bar.

- Hide When Minimized—When minimized, the Task Manager is not visible on the Task Bar.

19

USING THE TASK MANAGER

The View menu in the Applications tab offers you the following options:

- Refresh Now—The information display of applications running on the system can be immediately updated. You can learn more about the performance monitoring features of Task Manager in Chapter 22, "Performance Monitoring and Performance Logs and Alerts."

- Update Speed—From this, you can select High, Normal, Low or Paused. Each of these speed states will determine the rate at which the Applications tab data is updated. The default is Normal, but you should change this to High if you are monitoring a system and need to get immediate notification of application status. Use the Low setting if you are causally monitoring a system and don't want to check the information very often. Use the Paused setting to pause the update of the Applications tab information.

The other options of the View menu allow you to choose between a display that includes large or small icons, or a Details format that shows a small icon with the name of the application. The Large Icons option shows a larger icon for each application along with descriptive text under the icon. The Small Icon view simply shows the same thing but in a more compact format.

The Help menu does the same thing, no matter which tab is selected. It allows you to get online help.

Managing Individual Processes

The Processes tab contains information about all of the processes running on your computer. Each application that runs under Windows XP can run as a single process, or it may launch several processes. Additionally, the operating system itself runs a large number of processes in the background. For each network service, for example, one or more processes run on your computer. Processes for the printing spooler function wait in the background, ready to accept printing requests, and then send them out to the designated printer.

Figure 19.4 shows the Task Manager with the Processes tab selected. Here, you can see each and every process that runs on your computer. If more than one user is logged into the computer, use the check box at the bottom of this window labeled Show Processes from All Users to get a complete listing.

Note that in this display, you can see the image name, which is the actual executable program running as a separate process. Some entries have other entries indented beneath them, which are subprocesses (sometimes referred to as *child processes*) launched by the main process.

FIGURE 19.4

Using the Processes tab will give you more specific information about exactly what your computer is doing.

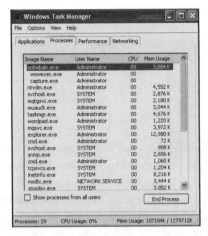

Caution

Choosing to kill a process can be dangerous! If you kill a process that the system runs as part of the operating system, you could potentially put the computer into an unstable, unknown state and cause more harm than good. If you are unsure whether the process is running on behalf of an application or the operating system itself, then don't kill it! In general, if you think the operating system is not working as it should, exit all applications normally, saving your data, and then reboot the computer instead. Only someone who is highly skilled in the internal operations of Windows XP should take on the task of killing a system process.

Changing Process Priorities

The Process tab also enables you to change the priority of a process. However, unless you are a programmer, you should *never* manipulate process priorities. The priority value assigned to a process or process thread determines how often it can run. Priorities range from 0–31. A priority of zero is reserved for the system to use, and processes can execute threads in a priority range of 1 to 31. When context switching occurs (a process time slot has expired or it has been preempted by another process with a higher priority), Windows XP selects the process with the highest priority (that is ready to execute) to run next.

Again, only programmers and those who are intimately familiar with the workings of the Windows XP operating system should change the priority of a process. If you fall into one of these categories, you can change the priority by clicking on the process in the listing and selecting Set Priority. A submenu will pop up, giving you the following choices:

19

USING THE TASK MANAGER

- Real-time
- High
- AboveNormal
- Normal
- BelowNormal
- Low

By leaving most processes in the Normal state, you enable other processes (such as the Windows XP kernel code itself) to perform important tasks, like managing other processes, the paging file, and the GUI. If you offer your Windows XP computer's resources to others (through either file shares or print shares), then don't do anything that might cause your system to respond more slowly to those who might connect to your machine.

> **Tip**
>
> You might want to consider lowering the priority of a process if you aren't concerned about its elapsed running time. For example, if you have a financial application that does intensive floating-point computations and you don't need the report until tomorrow, then you could lower that application's process priority. That allocates less CPU time to the process. You can then continue to use your Windows XP workstation, knowing that during idle CPU times, your reporting application is still chugging away and you will get your report later.

Raising the priority of a process, on the other hand, can actually lock out all other processes, if the process you decide to tinker with remains CPU bound. Your only option if this happens is to wait for the process to complete.

If you elect to run a process in "real time," then that process will be scheduled every time it wants to execute, regardless of what other processes are running on the system. For some unique circumstances, this might be a good idea. For example, in a factory automation environment where a process control program is monitoring a number of critical instruments, setting this process to real time would allow it to respond immediately to input/output (I/O) events for the devices that are attached to it.

In general, however, don't mess around with priorities unless you have tested them in advance.

Ending Processes and a Process Tree

As mentioned in an earlier caution, while you can kill processes, you rarely should do so or only with great caution. If you are not sure of exactly what functions the process performs, don't touch it. For example, you can kill the spoolsv.exe process and then find that you can no longer print. Indeed, if you try to print after killing this process, you'll be prompted to add a printer to the system.

If you feel that you can (and *must*) kill a process, right-click on the process and choose End Process or End Process Tree from the menu. If you have trouble ending an application using the Application tab of the Task Manager, then you might want to try to end a process here. You can also end processes that are not applications you launched. Remember that the processes you see under the Processes tab are all of the individual and child processes running on your computer. You can end background processes, such as services and other programs that the Windows XP operating system runs. These background processes will depend on the particular components of the operation system you chose to install.

You can also highlight any process and use the End Process button at the bottom right of the display to kill the process.

> **Tip**
>
> In a multiprocessor computer such as a high-end desktop workstation you can use the Processes tab to assign certain processes to a particular CPU. Right-click on the process you want to assign to a CPU and select Set Affinity from the menu. You can then select the processor to which the process should be assigned. This menu item will not show up on single-CPU systems, however.

Menu Options for the Process Tab

The Options menu for the Processes tab holds many of the same items it holds for the Applications tab but with one addition. You can select Show 161-bit Tasks to add 16-bit tasks to the process list, along with the usual assortment of 32-bit processes. If you are using a number of older applications then you might want to enable this option.

The View menu includes the same Refresh Now and Update Speed options, but does not have the selections for icons or details. Since icons are usually associated with an application and not an individual process, this only makes sense.

However, a new menu item is present in the View menu: Select Columns. This menu selection (see Figure 19.5) allows you to choose which information the Processes tab will display.

19

USING THE TASK MANAGER

FIGURE 19.5

The Select Columns dialog box allows you to select from a wide variety of statistical information that will be displayed for each process.

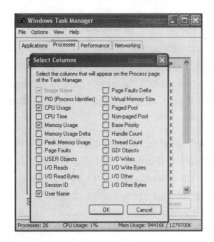

By default, this tab displays the CPU Usage, Memory Usage, and User Name options. However, the Windows XP operating system is capable of tracking a lot more information about each process. By experimenting with some of the other data items you can familiarize yourself with just exactly how a process is using system resources. For example, you can use the I/O data items to decide if you have a process that makes heavy usage of I/O devices and to improve performance by possibly moving that application's data files to other disks or devices. If CPU usage seems to be consumed by a process, you can consider running fewer applications on the machine or possibly buying a computer that supports multiple processors.

> **Tip**
>
> When you add additional data items for display on the Task Manager window, you don't have to delete others to make room for the new columns of data. Instead, use your cursor to drag the edge of the Task Manager window and you will see it widen to accommodate the new columns so that all can be seen on the screen at one time.

For a fuller description of all the statistical data items you see here, I recommend you purchase the *Microsoft Windows XP Professional Resource Kit*. Also, if you have an Internet connection, check out the free online documentation for the platform Software Development Kit at `http://msdn.microsoft.com`. You don't have to be a programmer to be able to read and understand the concepts you will find here for free.

Select the check boxes for the data items you want to see displayed under the Processes tab. If you leave the Username check box selected, keep in mind that those processes with usernames like System are operating system processes or possibly those services run by the operating system. You really don't want to go fooling around with those without a complete understanding of what these processes are doing. However, for individual usernames, you can pretty much look at the process name, switch back to the Applications tab, and then decide if you need to ask a user to scale back usage of the application or reschedule tasks for off-hours when the usage of the workstation is not being taxed as heavily as it is during normal hours.

Using the Performance Tab to Track System Performance

This is one of the more revealing views that the Task manager can give you. The Performance tab presents you with two graphic displays, one for CPU usage and another for memory usage, which display charts updated in a real-time mode so that you can see clearly what is happening on your system (see Figure 19.6).

FIGURE 19.6

The Performance tab gives you a graphical view of what is happening on your system.

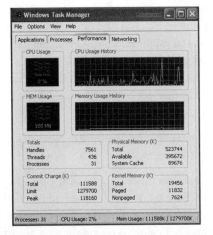

> **Note**
>
> You can learn about using the Task Manager and other Windows tools to monitor performance in Chapter 22, "Performance Monitoring and Performance Logs and Alerts."

The CPU Usage and MEM Usage charts show current use of both resources. The History charts show how those resources are being used over time.

> ### Tip
>
> Another interesting thing you can do while in the Performance tab of the Task Manager is to double-click almost anywhere on the Task Manager display to produce the CPU Usage and CPU Usage History charts in a format that fills the entire Task Manager window. To return to the normal view, just double-click again. If you do this in the blank space on the Applications tab, the Task Manager will be minimized and placed on the Tool Bar. You can also drag one edge of the Task Manager window to widen the view if you want to see information displayed for a longer historical period.

Beneath these two graphical indicators you will find several other more specific statistical counters. These are grouped by default into Totals (Handles, Threads, Processes); Physical Memory (Total, Available, System Cache); Commit Charge (Total, Limit Peak); and Kernel Memory (Total, Paged Nonpaged). Keep in mind that nonpaged kernel memory is always resident in physical memory and is not swapped out by the virtual memory manager. If your system is running slowly and you find that a large part or all of your physical memory is being used, then you might improve performance by moving the paging file to a separate physical disk rather than using a disk that does not contain your applications or operating system. (You can learn more about this in Chapter 22.) If this doesn't improve performance, then it is time for a memory upgrade, or time to stop running so many applications on this workstation!

The View menu for the Performance tab contains the Refresh Now and Update Speed menu items, as well as the following two items:

- CPU History—On multiprocessor machines, this menu option allows you to select between a single graph for all CPUs, or it shows an individual graph for each CPU. If you have a multiple-CPU workstation, then obviously, you might want to use the second option to ensure that the applications you are running are written correctly to take advantage of multiple CPUs.

- Show Kernel Times—If you select this option, then the CPU Usage bar graph and the CPU Usage History graph will be displayed in the usual green color for CPU usage; Windows XP kernel usage is shown in a red color. Thus, you can again get a good idea if your system has enough physical memory. If too much CPU time is spent in kernel usage, then it is time to upgrade the system to faster processors or to a multiprocessor system.

Tracking Networking Adapter Usage with the Networking Tab

If there is a networking adapter installed in your PC then there will be a Networking tab in the Task Manager. As you can see in Figure 19.7, this tab displays graphically the extent to which the adapter is being used. At the bottom of this display you see information about each adapter, if more than one is present in the system.

FIGURE 19.7

The Networking tab gives you a graphical view of your network adapter's status.

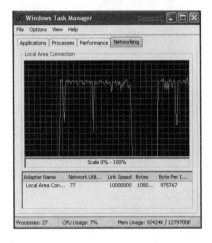

Note that directly under the graphical display is a small box that indicates the scale for the graph. This starts out a 0% to 5%, but in order to display adapter status meaningfully, the ratio may change (up to 0% to 100%) if a lot of activity is happening on the adapter.

Similar to the Performance tab, you can double-click on the graphical display and it will enlarge to fill up the entire Task Manager window. Double-click again to return to the normal view.

The Options menu for the Networking tab has the standard Always On Top, Minimize On use and Hide When Minimized entries. Other entries in this menu for this tab are as follows:

- Tab Always Active
- Show Accumulative Data
- Auto Scale
- Reset
- Show Scale

19

**USING THE
TASK MANAGER**

Under the View tab, you will find the Refresh Now and Update Speed entries, as well as the following:

- Network Adapter History—Bytes Sent (Red), Bytes Received (Yellow) and Bytes Total (Green).
- Select Columns—As you can see in Figure 19.8, you can select the data items related to network statistics that you want to have displayed.

FIGURE 19.8

You can choose the data items you want to appear on the Networking tab by using Select Columns from the View menu.

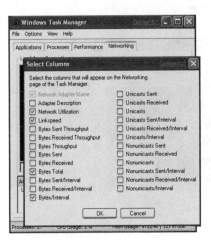

Don't forget that if you choose a large number of data items, you can again drag the edges of the Task Manager window to widen the view so that more columns appear on the screen at the same time.

Summary

The Task Manager can be a useful tool for finding and keeping track of information about what your computer is doing. You don't have to set up a number of statistical counters that you may want to view (although you can select some items if you know what they represent), but instead can get a quick look at the CPU and memory usage in a convenient graphical format. You can also see which applications and processes are running on the system, and kill an application or process that might be causing you problems. Consider the Task Manager to be a quick and convenient tool for judging system performance and for getting rid of misbehaving applications.

CHAPTER 20

The Windows XP Registry

IN THIS CHAPTER

- A Brief History of the Windows Registry *499*
- Registry Basics *500*
- Backing Up and Restoring the Registry *508*
- Using the Windows Registry Editor *512*

Let's face it. Just the mention of the Windows Registry makes most people a bit nervous. After all, Microsoft has gone to great pains ever since the introduction of the first Registry in Windows 3.1 to make people aware that editing the Registry can cause serious problems; improper changes can even prevent your computer from being able to start. However, if you take the proper precautions (such as backing up the Registry before editing it); learn to use the proper tools; and perhaps most importantly, learn when editing the Registry is the proper choice, you will find that the Windows Registry is one of the most powerful tools at your disposal.

The Windows XP Professional Registration Database, more commonly called the *Registry,* is essentially a database of the operating system, hardware driver, and application configuration settings. The Registry contains information ranging from user account settings to default application settings to the color of your desktop. The Registry is stored in a hierarchical database that often seems a little cryptic and can be modified directly only by using a special program named Windows Registry Editor that you won't find on the Start menu.

Indirectly, however, you edit the Windows Registry on a daily basis without even realizing it. Every time you install or remove a program or set up a new hardware device, you are editing the Registry. Every time you change your desktop background, create a new network connection, or change a program's preferences, you are editing the Registry. In fact, the vast majority of changes that you can make in the Registry are available in the multitude of dialog boxes and property pages you find scattered throughout Windows. Why, then, would you want to edit the Registry directly? The simple answer is that a number of configuration settings are available in the Registry that you just cannot access in other ways.

This chapter introduces you to the Registry with a brief history, and a look at how the Registry is organized. You then learn how to back up the Registry, and how to use the Windows Registry Editor.

> **Warning**
>
> As you have probably noticed, just about every discussion of the Windows Registry leads off with a stern warning that you can do irreversible harm to your system by editing the Registry directly. This is true. You should *never* edit the Registry files unless you have a very good reason. Even then, you might want to try out your edits on an experimental computer where it won't matter so much if you make a mistake. Before you start editing the Registry, create a backup of both the Registry and your hard disk. If something goes awry, then you can restore the data and try again.

A Brief History of the Windows Registry

Before there was the Registry, Microsoft operating systems used simple text files to control system settings. In the early days of MS-DOS, configuration of the operating system was controlled using the following two files:

- `Config.sys` contained configuration information required by MS-DOS to operate. This information was mostly general settings for hardware that multiple applications would use, such as how low and high memory was handled.

- `Autoexec.bat` was a batch file used to automatically execute startup procedures when MS-DOS was finished loading.

For the most part, MS-DOS–based applications were in charge of all their own configuration settings, including how they used hardware devices shared with other applications, for example, printer and sound settings. Applications stored these settings in text files called *initialization files* (`.INI` files).

When Windows was first introduced, it ran as an MS-DOS–based application that provided a simple graphical interface for DOS commands. When Windows 3.0 came along, however, things changed a bit. Windows 3.0 was the first version of Windows to really get behind the idea that there should be a system-wide set of configuration data for the operating system and that applications should use that data set instead of managing their own settings. Windows 3.0 did this by adding four `.INI` files that contained information about the computer's hardware, configuration, device drivers, and application settings. These four `.INI` files, which loaded after the two DOS configuration files, included the following:

- `Progman.ini`—This file contained settings for the Windows Program Manager, which provided the main graphical user interface (GUI) for working with Windows.

- `Control.ini`—This file contained many of the user-customized settings found in earlier versions of Windows, including desktop, sound, and printer settings.

- `Win.ini`—This file contained the visual appearance of Windows and settings for installed applications.

- `System.ini`—This file contained hardware configuration settings governing how Windows interacted with a computer's hardware.

In theory, all applications would use settings found in these four files to control resources that were shared by all applications. Applications should store their own settings in the `win.ini` file. In addition, applications could create their own `.INI` files to control settings particular to the application. There were a number of problems with this setup, however. Because they were text files, `.INI` files were easy for users to edit. This made them vulnerable. It was very easy for users through applications to change settings and cause all kinds of system problems. Another problem that arose from using text files was that each file suffered a 64K limit.

Windows 3.1 was the first version of Windows to include a Registry and offer a solution to many of the problems caused by using `.INI` files. The most important solution was that the Registry offered a single place for storing configuration data and that it had a clearly defined hierarchical structure that application programmers could easily follow. However, a few nagging problems remained. The Windows 3.1 Registry was stored in a single file that still suffered the same 64K size limit that plagued the `.INI` files. Another major problem with the Windows 3.1 Registry is that it did not do a very good job of synchronizing its contents with the state of applications, fonts, drivers, and other items loaded on the computer. Perhaps the biggest problem of all was that most programmers just didn't use it, continuing to rely instead on `.INI` files.

When Windows NT was first introduced, a whole new Registry was introduced with it. The 64K size limit was removed and the Registry could now grow to take up as much space as it needed. Instead of using a single file, multiple files were used to make up the Registry while still maintaining the appearance of a single hierarchical set of entries. Microsoft also began to strongly encourage application programmers to use the Registry instead of continuing to use `.INI` files.

Since the introduction of Windows NT, the Registry really has not changed much. Of course, you will find different entries in Windows 95/98/Me, as well as Windows NT/2000, and XP, but at its heart, the structure is the same.

Registry Basics

The Windows XP Registry is structured using a number of components. To begin with, the Registry is stored in several different files on your computer. These files are named *hives* and are located in the `\Windows\system32\config` and `\Documents and Settings\username` folders (we will come back to hives and files a bit later in this chapter). However, when you use the Windows Registry Editor (`regedit.exe`), the Registry is presented to you as one seamless hierarchy that looks much like a folder tree you would see in Windows Explorer, as shown in Figure 20.1.

FIGURE 20.1

The Windows Registry Editor.

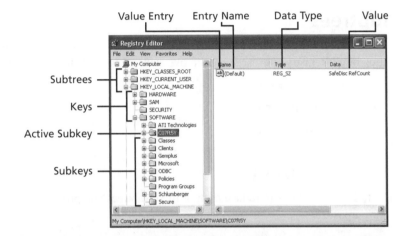

Value Entry   Entry Name   Data Type   Value

Subtrees

Keys

Active Subkey

Subkeys

Note

In previous versions of Windows, such as Windows 2000, two Registry editors were included: `regedit.exe` and `regedt32.exe`. `Regedit.exe` was the Registry editor first introduced in Windows NT. `Regedt32.exe` came along a bit later and supported a few extra features. In Windows XP, there is only one editor, the Windows Registry Editor. This program opens whether you run `regedit.exe` or `regedt32.exe` from the command prompt or Run dialog box.

As you can see from Figure 20.1, the Registry Editor presents the registry in a tree form that looks much like any other file list in Windows. The major components of this hierarchy include the following:

- Subtrees—The entire Registry for a computer is shown as one tree that is divided into five subtrees. Each of these subtrees has a specific purpose and is further divided into keys, subkeys, and entries. You will learn the purpose of the five subtrees later in this chapter.

- Keys—A key is something like a folder you would find in Windows Explorer. It can contain any number of subkeys and value entries.

- Subkeys—A subkey is simply a key that exists inside another key. Subkeys can hold additional subkeys and value entries.

- Value Entries—Value entries define the various properties of a key. Each entry has three parts: a name, a data type, and the value assigned to the entry. It is these entries you will edit when working in the Registry.

20

THE WINDOWS
XP REGISTRY

Subtrees

Subtrees are the top-level unit of the Windows Registry and represent the initial classification of all Registry entries. There are five subtrees in the Windows XP Registry:

- HKEY_CLASSES_ROOT
- HKEY_CURRENT_USER
- HKEY_LOCAL_MACHINE
- HKEY_USERS
- HKEY_CURRENT_CONFIG

The following sections introduce each of these subtrees and provide a brief description of their purpose.

HKEY_CLASSES_ROOT

The HKEY_CLASSES_ROOT (HKCR) subtree exists mostly for compatibility with 16-bit Windows applications. HKCR contains information about file associations on the computer—that is, what file types are opened with which applications. More importantly for most people, however, is that HKCR also holds definitions of every object that exists in the Windows XP environment. The keys that control these definitions control information about objects' shell interfaces, such as what commands are contained on the shortcut menu for an object.

Thirty-two-bit applications access all of this same data but do so through an identical copy of the data found in the HKEY_LOCAL_MACHINE subtree in the Software\Classes subkey. Actually, these aren't really copies so much as they are two different views of information held in the same Registry hive. If you change a value in one location, it also changes in the other location.

There are two major types of keys found within the HKCR subtree:

- File extension keys are named after the three-letter file extension they represent (.doc, .txt, and so on). Value entries for these keys define what program is used to open a file with that extension. File extension keys may also hold subkeys that control other features like the list of programs that appears on the Open With submenu of an object's shortcut menu.

- Class definition keys contain information on Component Object Model (COM) objects, a model that lets programmers develop objects that can be accessed by any COM-compliant application. Microsoft's Object Linking and Embedding (OLE) and ActiveX technologies are both based on COM.

HKEY_CURRENT_USER

The HKEY_CURRENT_USER (HKCU) subtree contains the profile for the user who is currently logged onto Windows. A profile contains customized system, hardware, and application settings for a particular user. All of this information is stored in a hive called USER.DAT, one copy of which exists for each user of a computer and is located in a user's Documents and Settings folder.

> **Note**
>
> Actually, as you will learn in the HKEY_USERS section later in the chapter, the HKCU subtree is really just a link to a specific key in the HKEY_USERS subtree, which holds profiles for all local users of the computer.

Many of the keys found in the HKCU subtree are created by applications installed on a computer, so the exact list will vary according to your situation. However, there are a number of keys that Windows itself creates, which you will find on any computer. These keys include the following:

- AppEvents—This key holds values for application events such as what sounds play when certain Windows events (errors, startup, and so on) occur, as well as any saved sound schemes.
- Console—This key holds values that control the appearance of the Windows command prompt.
- Control Panel—This key holds values representing settings made in the Windows Control Panel. This key is roughly analogous to the WIN.INI and CONTROL.INI files used in older versions of Windows.
- Environment—This key holds environmental variables set using the System Control Panel applet.
- Identities—This key holds values that describe the default user and the last user identification (ID) that successfully logged on to Windows.
- Keyboard Layout—This key holds values that define the language of the current keyboard layout.
- Printers—This key holds values that describe all printers available to a user.
- Software—This key holds values for all application settings defined for the current user and has roughly the same structure as the HKLM Software key.
- UNICODE Program Groups—This key will only exist if you upgraded to Windows XP from a previous version of Windows (or if you installed Windows XP to dual boot with a previous version).

HKEY_LOCAL_MACHINE

The HKEY_LOCAL_MACHINE (HKLM) subtree is probably the most important in the Registry. HKLM contains entries that describe the central processing unit (CPU), system bus, and all other hardware configuration information collected by Windows during startup. HKLM also contains installed drivers, settings, and configuration data. In addition, some security information (such as network logon preferences) can be stored in this subtree.

The HKLM subtree is divided into the following five keys:

- Hardware—All of the subkeys of the Hardware key are generated by Windows XP during the startup process and actually exist only in memory; they are not stored on disk. The reason for this is that Windows must register hardware that it finds during startup, even if it has not yet registered a disk on which to store that data. This key is really not very useful from an editing standpoint, as much of the data in the key cannot be edited.

- SAM—This key holds the Security Account Manager (SAM) database, which contains information about users and groups configured on the computer. This key is another one you probably won't bother with too much, as it is much easier and safer to change security information using the built-in administrative tools in Windows XP.

- Security—This key holds additional security information pertaining to policies and user rights.

- Software—This key holds settings for much of the system and application settings on the computer. It is one of the most important that you will deal with when using the Registry. It holds the vast majority of information that you will be interested in editing.

- System—The System key holds information about how Windows boots and where various system files are located. While it is one of the more important subkeys in the Registry in terms of how Windows operates, it is not very useful from an editing standpoint.

HKEY_USERS

The HKEY_USERS (HKU) subtree contains the profile information for all local users on the computer. There will always be at least two keys in the HKU subtree. The first, .Default, contains a default group of settings that are applied whenever a user that does not already have a profile logs onto Windows. When a new user logs on, Windows creates a new key for that user and then copies all of the information from the .Default key into the new key.

The second key you will always see in the HKU subtree will be for the built-in Administrator account. Additional keys are created for each user configured on the computer.

Keys in the HKU subtree (aside from the .Default key) are named according to the user security ID and hence appear as a long string of numbers.

Within the key for each user, you will find subkeys that are pretty much identical to those described for the HKEY_CURRENT_USER subtree. The reason for this, of course, is that the HKCU subtree is really just a link to the key in the HKU subtree that represents whatever user is currently logged on. The reason behind this is simple; providing this shortcut makes it much easier to find and edit values for the current user than guessing at security ID codes.

HKEY_CURRENT_CONFIG

The HKEY_CURRENT_CONFIG subtree (HKCC) holds information about the hardware profile currently being used, and device information that is gathered during Windows startup. This subtree is actually just a link to a key found in HKLM:

HKEY_LOCAL_MACHINE\System\CurrentControlSet\Hardware Profiles\Current.

Keys, Subkeys, Entries, and Values

Any key or subkey in the Registry can hold zero or more value entries. A value entry defines a specific property for its key. Take, for example, the following subkey:

HKEY_LOCAL_MACHINE\Software\Microsoft\Outlook Express\5.0\Default
Settings\Recent Stationary List

This key (at least on my system) has seven value entries aside from the blank *(Default)* entry that most keys have. Each of these value entries represents a file recently used as stationary (a colorful e-mail background) in Outlook Express.

All value entries have three parts: a name, a data type, and a value. The name is the easy part and is usually a string of standard text. There are several different data types that may be used for a value entry and the actual value assigned to the entry depends on the data type.

Data types you will find in the Registry are listed below. Note that each has two names. The first is what you will see when you use a dialog box to create a new key or value. The second, all in capital letters, is what will show up under the Type field when you are looking at Registry entries in the Registry Editor.

- Binary Value (REG_BINARY)—This is for raw binary data. Note that while the internal hardware information is stored in a binary format, REGEDIT.EXE displays it in hexadecimal format. As a quick tip, you can use the Scientific menu selection from View on the Windows Calculator, found in the Accessories folder to quickly translate from decimal to binary to hexadecimal, and so forth.

- `DWORD Value (REG_DWORD)`—This is a four-byte–long data field that is used to store a numeric value.
- `Expandable String Value (REG_EXPAND_SZ)`—This is a field that contains a variable-length amount of text, both alpha and numeric characters.
- `String Value (REG_MULTI_SZ)`—This is a fixed-length string.
- `Multi-String Value REG_FULL_RESOURCE_DESCRIPTOR`—This field contains a series of nested arrays. These arrays are used to store a resource list for hardware components or drivers.

By including the data type with the key or Registry entry, applications that make use of the data can quickly determine how to interpret the value. You will learn more about using value entries later in this chapter when you learn the ins and outs of using the Windows Registry Editor.

Hives and Files

While the Registry appears to be a single entity, it is actually made up of several different hives. Each hive is a separate file or block of memory that contains a Registry subtree. Windows XP maintains a list of hives in the following subkey:

`HKEY_LOCAL_MACHINE\System\CurrentControlSet\Control\hivelist`

Each value entry for this subkey contains the location of the hive in the Registry (as the value entry's name) and the physical location of the hive (as the value entry's value). You will see the following six basic value entries in this subkey:

- Hardware—This entry corresponds to the `HKLM\Hardware` subkey. This entry does not have a value because it is not stored on disk.
- SAM—This entry corresponds to the `HKLM\SAM` subkey.
- Security—This entry corresponds to the `HKLM\SECURITY` subkey.
- Software—This entry corresponds to the `HKLM\Software` subkey.
- System—This entry corresponds to the `HKLM\System` subkey.
- `.Default`—This entry corresponds to the `HKU\.Default` subkey.

You will also see an additional value entry for each local user configured on the computer that points to the `NTUSER.DAT` file in that user's Documents and Settings folder.

The files that represent these hives have ordinary sounding filenames, but there are also four file extensions that serve to indicate the purpose of the data file that Registry information is stored in. These are as follows:

- No extension—If the filename has no extension, it is a complete copy of the hive data.
- `.alt`—This extension is used to create a backup copy of the `HKEY_LOCAL_MACHINE\System` hive. This is the only hive that uses this extension.
- `.log`—This is a transaction log file for a particular hive, storing the changes you make.
- `.sav`—During setup, the Setup program uses this extension to store the hive files as they were at the end of the text-mode setup stage. If something goes wrong during the graphics mode portion of Windows XP setup, then these `.sav` files can be used to recover hive information.

Some of these keys are simply subsets of other keys. Indeed, the information for a particular key may come from more than one file. It isn't really important to keep in mind which file (or hive) in which the information resides, since the operating system will keep you from deleting these files. However, it is useful to know when you are trying to figure out where a particular configuration value is coming from during troubleshooting efforts.

Some of the files that are used to store information on your local machine are listed in Table 20.1.

Table 20.1 Registry Keys and File Storage

Registry Hive	*Files*
HKEY_LOCAL_MACHINE\SAM	Sam, Sam.log, Sam.sav
HKEY_LOCAL_MACHINE\Security	Security, Security.log, Security.sav
HKEY_LOCAL_MACHINE\Software	Software, Software.log, Software.sav
HKEY_LOCAL_MACHINE\System	System, System.alt, System.log, System.sav
HKEY_CURRENT_CONFIG	System, System.alt, System.log, System.sav
HKEY_CURRENT_USER	Ntuser.dat, Ntuser.dat.log
HKEY_USERS\.DEFAULT	Default, Default.log, Default.sav

All of these files, except for `HKEY_CURRENT_USER`, are stored in `%systemroot%\System32\Config`. The `HKEY_CURRENT_USER` files are stored in `%systemroot%\Profiles\Username`.

20

THE WINDOWS XP REGISTRY

> **Note**
>
> It is interesting to compare the local computer's Registry with the Active Directory, which is discussed in Appendix B. Both can be used to store security information, and the Active Directory can be extended easily to store just about any kind of information by extending its schema. In this chapter, you will learn about the local Registry on your Windows XP workstation. Keep in mind, however, that if you are part of a domain that is using the Active Directory, some settings in your local Registry get overwritten by those applied from the domain's Active Directory information. This is especially true for things like Group Policy Objects in the Active Directory, which can define security and other items for all users, computers, or other objects that exist in container objects in the Active Directory.

Backing Up and Restoring the Registry

When you make a change to the Registry using the Windows Registry Editor, the change is made to your system *immediately*. You don't get the luxury of being able to review your changes and save the file and there is no undo function. Changes just happen. For this reason, it is extremely important that you back up your Registry before making any edits.

There are a couple of different ways you can back up your Registry. The easiest way to back up the Registry is to use the Windows Backup program to back up your System State information, which includes the Registry and other important system settings. You can also include the System State information in your routine system backups for good measure (and if you are not doing routine backups of your system, put this book down, slap yourself on the back of the hand, and then turn to Chapter 21, "Using Backup on Windows XP," before you do anything else).

The other way to back up Registry data is to export important pieces of the Registry (those you'll be editing) to a separate file on your disk. You can then import those settings back into the Registry later if something goes wrong.

The advantage of using Windows Backup to back up all the System State data on your computer is that it is easy to do, easy to restore, and you can be sure that everything you need is backed up. The only real disadvantage is that it takes several minutes to do the backup—usually around 10 minutes on a typical Windows XP computer.

This section describes briefly how to back up your System State data using Windows Backup. You can find a more detailed description in Chapter 21, "Using Backup on Windows XP." You can find information on importing and exporting Registry data later in this chapter.

Back up the Registry

Windows Backup (go to Start, All Programs, Accessories, System Tools and click Backup) allows you to back up all of the drives on your computer, along with the Registry, or just the Registry and other system settings. Once the Backup program is started, it immediately launches the Backup and Restore Wizard, which walks you through the steps for backing up or restoring your computer. If the Backup program is set up to use Advanced Mode instead of Wizard Mode, you will see an initial screen with buttons for launching separate wizards for the backup and restore processes. Use the Tools menu of the Backup program to switch between Wizard and Advanced modes. This section assumes you are using Advanced mode to launch the Backup Wizard, a method that gives you finer control over the backup process than using the Wizard mode.

The Backup Wizard (shown in Figure 20.2) allows you to select the option Only back up the System State data.

FIGURE 20.2

The Backup Wizard prompts you to back up System State data.

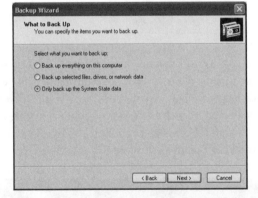

Note

The selection in the Backup Wizard that allows you to back up your registry also will back up some other important files. For example, the other files that are backed up include the COM Class Registration database and some files necessary to boot the system.

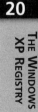

> **Tip**
>
> You can also use the following command at the command prompt or Run dialog box to backup the System State information: `ntbackup backup systemstate /j "backup name" /f"backup path"`.

Starting a backup opens the Backup Progress dialog box (see Figure 20.3). From this box, you can monitor which files are being stored in the backup file. This dialog box will also help you monitor how much time the backup takes.

FIGURE 20.3

The Backup Wizard opens a dialog box that shows you the progress of the System State backup.

Note that the file extension `.bkf` is the standard one used by the Backup Wizard. You can copy this simple backup file to removable media. The resulting file will be a lot larger than what will fit on a floppy disk (several hundred megabytes), so it is a good idea to store the backup file on another type of device, such as a CD-RW (rewritable CD) drive. You can use this disc repeatedly (although I recommend you keep a series of two or three previous backups at the very least) and use it with the Restore Wizard if it becomes necessary.

> **Tip**
>
> If you plan to do a good bit of mucking around in the Registry, here's a suggestion.... Chapter 23, "Disaster Recover," describes the Backup program's Automated System Recovery (ASR) Wizard. This is the best method you can use to ensure that you can recover your system. It creates a floppy disk, which stores important system settings and also backups up the disks you select. If you use ASR on a regular basis, you will be covered for most disasters until the point the

ASR backup is created. Hence, if you have time and want to play with the Registry, set aside another disk partition or use a tape or other removable media device and, along with a simple floppy disk, use ASR to create a total backup of your system disk.

Restoring the Registry

Windows Backup makes restoring a backed-up Registry almost as easy as backing it up in the first place. You can start the Restore Wizard from the main Backup program screen or using the Tools menu. If you are in Wizard Mode, you may need to switch to Advanced mode first as described previously. After the first welcome screen, the Restore Wizard displays the backups available to be restored. Recall that a System State backup stores more than just the Registry data. Figure 20.4 shows the backup items expanded so that you can see the actual contents. If you want to restore just the Registry, select it in the right pane of the window. If you are not sure whether your changes might have affected settings outside the Registry (and assuming you have not made other major system changes such as installing software or hardware), it is best to restore all the System State information.

FIGURE 20.4

The Restore Wizard allows you restore just the backed up Registry.

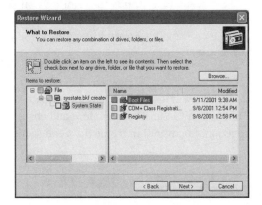

The Restore Wizard prompts you with other dialog boxes, such as whether it should replace existing files, or if you want to restore the files to an alternate location. When you've finished answering the prompts, select Finish, and the restoring process begins. You can learn about the restore process in detail in Chapter 21, "Using Backup on Windows XP."

20

**THE WINDOWS
XP REGISTRY**

Using the Windows Registry Editor

While Windows NT and Windows 2000 allowed you to pick from two different programs (REGEDIT.EXE or REGEDIT32.EXE), Windows XP includes only one editor, the Windows Registry Editor. If you type either command (regedit or regedt32) at the command prompt or the Run dialog box, the same Windows Registry Editor program runs. For convenience, the remainder of this chapter refers to the program as regedit.

> ### Note
>
> If you are using Windows XP 64-Bit Edition, which runs on the Itanium processor, your Registry will contain both 32-bit and 64-bit keys. Most of the 32-bit keys use the same names as their 64-bit corresponding keys. By default, however, when you run REGEDIT.EXE on a 64-bit version of Windows XP, only the 64-bit keys will be displayed. If you want to use an editor that also displays the 32-bit keys, first make sure you don't have the 64-bit of the Registry editor opened. Then run the 32-bit version, by clicking on Start, Run and entering the path %systemroot%\syswow64\regedit.
>
> Does syswow64 ring a bell? Syswow32 (wow stands for Windows on Windows) has been around for some time and is used in a 32-bit environment for running 16-bit Windows programs. Syswow64 provides an environment for 32-bit applications to run on a 64-bit processor.

Figure 20.5 shows the initial regedit window and the five major subtrees discussed earlier. Once you get here, you can search for, add, delete, view, and change value entries in the Registry. Each of these functions is covered in the next several sections.

FIGURE 20.5

The Opening window of the Registry Editor displays the key entry points you can use to navigate the data stored by the Registry.

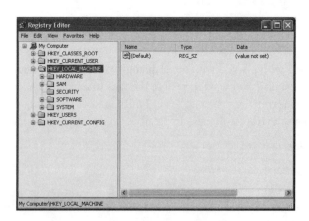

Searching the Registry

The best way to make changes to the Registry is to have the instructions for a well-documented change sitting in front of you. That way, you can browse right to the appropriate subkey, make the change, and be done with it. If you don't know the exact location of the subkey you want or if you just want to poke around for something interesting, regedit offers a pretty good search function.

You can search for the key name itself or even the data stored in keys. This can be a useful way to find out where important information is stored.

> **Warning**
>
> If you are reading a Microsoft Knowledge Base article or a tip you found on the Web and it recommends that you change a Registry key value, first make sure that the Knowledge Base article applies to Windows XP. Don't count on Registry keys in an article based on Windows XP to work as it did in previous versions of the Windows operating systems.

To use the search function, open the Edit menu and select Find. The Find dialog box, shown in Figure 20.6, allows you to specify the parameters of the search. Notice that you can enter the string (a sequence of characters), a numeric value, or the name of a key you want to find in the *Find What* field. Use the check boxes labeled *Keys*, *Values*, *Data*, and *Match whole string only*, if you wish to narrow down your search.

FIGURE 20.6

Use this dialog box to search for information in the Registry.

In Figure 20.6, you see that regedit will find only keys containing the string doc. This would be a good way to find the HKCR key for the file extension .doc, where you might alter the list of programs that appear on the Open With submenu on the shortcut menu for files of that type.

When you are ready, click Find Next. Regedit will jump to the first instance it finds that matches the search parameters. Figure 20.7 shows the results of the search for keys with .doc in them.

20

THE WINDOWS XP REGISTRY

FIGURE 20.7

The results of a search of the Registry are shown in this figure.

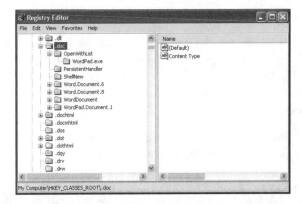

If the first instance that regedit finds is not what you are looking for, you can use the F3 key to jump to the next instance that matches the search without bothering with the Find dialog box again.

When you have found the key you want, you can save it as a favorite so that you can quickly get to it again. For Registry keys you manipulate (or need to examine) frequently, this is a good idea. Simply find the key first, as described above, and then click on the Favorites menu and select Add to Favorites. A small dialog box opens and you can keep the same name (which defaults to the Registry key name), or you can enter other text that will be more helpful in reminding you what the Registry key is used for. In the future, to get back to this key, just select it from the Favorites menu.

Tip

You can go ahead and add a few to your Favorites menu that I guarantee you'll use in the future. These include HKLM\Software, HKLM\Software\Microsoft\ Office (if you use it), and HKLM\Software\Microsoft\Internet Explorer.

Changing a Registry Entry

Once you have located an entry you want to change, click once on the entry in the right-side pane and then from the Edit menu, select Modify. You can also right-click on the item and select Modify, or you can just double-click the entry. Figure 20.8 shows two typical Edit dialog boxes used to change values for an entry. The dialog box on the top is used to change a string value, and the dialog box on the bottom is used to change a Dword value. Note that the data type for the value affects both the name of the dialog box and what kind of data you can enter.

FIGURE 20.8

Use Edit dialog boxes to change the values for an entry.

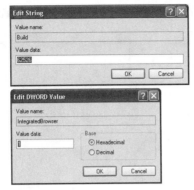

To change the value for this item, just edit the text or change the values. Different data items require different input, depending on the data type of the entry. Figure 20.9 shows another example of an Edit dialog box; only this time, it is for binary data.

FIGURE 20.9

The format of a dialog box changes for the data type you are editing.

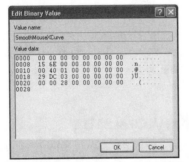

> **Tip**
>
> Right-clicking any value entry yields some additional possibilities. Most values (even those that are not binary) have an option for modifying binary data, which lets you change the data using binary code. You can also Rename and Delete keys from the shortcut menu.

Adding a Registry Entry or Key

To add an entry to the Registry, you need to decide under what key you want to create your entry. Once you have navigated to the key and selected it by clicking it once, create a new entry by clicking the Edit menu, selecting New, and then pointing to one of the listed data types that you can create. As you can see in Figure 20.10, the New submenu also allows you to create a new subkey under the selected key.

FIGURE 20.10

The Edit menu allows you to create new keys or new entries under a selected key.

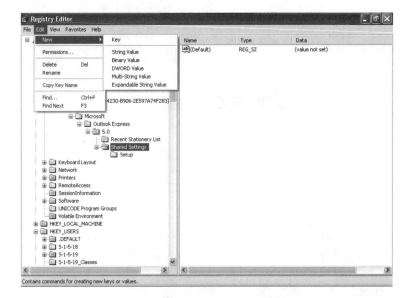

Once you create a new entry, it appears in the right pane with the name selected. Just start typing to name the entry (New Value #x is the default name). To add a value to the new entry, click the entry and use the Modify command. Entering a new value works the same way as modifying an existing value.

Deleting a Registry Key or Entry

Deleting an entry is just as simple as adding or editing one. Simply right-click on the entry and choose Delete from the shortcut menu or select the entry and use the Delete command on the Edit menu. A dialog box prompts you before allowing you to proceed. Click the Yes button to delete the entry.

Warning

It almost goes without saying that you should be extremely careful when deleting keys. If you try to delete a key with entries or one that has other keys and entries below it in the Explorer pane tree structure, the prompt you receive will let you know. There really aren't many good reasons to remove multiple keys and values unless you are trying to remove entries for a program that may not have been removed when you uninstalled a program.

Exporting and Importing Registry Information

Earlier in this chapter, you learned to use the Backup Utility to create a System State backup, which includes the Registry and an assortment of other configuration settings. Another way to back up Registry data and also to take Registry data to other computers is to export keys or subkeys to a file. You can then import this file back into the Registry to restore data or import it into another computer's Registry to transfer data.

To export a key, you first need to select the key by clicking it once. Next, select the Export command from the File menu. In Figure 20.11, you can see the Export Registry File dialog box that prompts you to export the file. In this example, the top-level key HKEY_LOCAL_MACHINE is being exported.

FIGURE 20.11

You can export Registry keys or the entire Registry to a file.

Note that in this dialog box there are several choices under the Save as Type field. The .reg file extension is used by default, but you can also save files as a text file (.txt file extension). This allows you to examine the files using Notepad or the EDIT command from the Command Prompt. You can also select to export a file to a .reg file that is compatible with Win9x/NT4 .reg files.

> **Warning**
>
> For some reason, viewing exported Registry information saved in a .txt file with Notepad can corrupt the information so that it cannot be imported back into a Registry. If you are using the export command to back up the Registry, it's
>
> *continues*

20

THE WINDOWS
XP REGISTRY

> best just to use the .reg format. If you want a .txt file to examine, export it in both formats. If, for some reason, you must use .txt files for export and want to preserve their integrity, do not use Notepad to view them. Use the EDIT command instead.

At the bottom of the dialog box in Figure 20.11, you can choose to back up the entire Registry. Under the Export Range section, select one of the following two radio buttons:

- All—Backup the entire Registry to the file.
- Selected Branch—Allows you to select a key further down the tree-like structure of the Registry hierarchy.

Click Save, and the file is created. Although the size of the file created depends on whether you create a file of the entire Registry data or just selected portions, it can be quite large. The file in Figure 20.11 was a little over 38MB in size. Again, it is a good idea to store this snapshot of the Registry in a safe place such as removable media or network storage.

To import a saved file, use Import command on the File menu. A dialog box opens that is similar to the one used to export Registry data. You only need to specify the filename and click Open to restore the data. A small window pops up, showing the progress of the restore using a bar graph. If you are restoring keys opened by the running system, you will get a warning stating that some of the data could not be restored.

Tip

If you exported Registry information as a .reg file, you don't even need to open Regedit to import the data. You can simply double-click the .reg file, and Windows will offer to add the data to the Registry.

Summary

The Registry is a powerful collection of data, without which Windows XP and the applications that run on it could not function. The elimination of many of the legacy .INI files that the Registry is now used for is reason enough to create such an information store. You should not make it a regular habit to make changes to anything in the Registry, especially when the change can be done using other utilities like the Local Security Policy utility. However, it is a good idea to become familiar with the data tree in order to better understand how a single Windows XP machine stores information specific not only to the operating system or applications but also to the users themselves.

The Registry is complicated and should be respected, but there is no reason to fear it if you take the time to understand it and to back it up before you make changes. Most of the time, you will probably edit the Registry to use an interesting tip found in a book or magazine article or to apply a fix found somewhere like the Microsoft Knowledge Base. Just browsing around through the Registry, however, can give you some powerful insight into how Windows works. You may even very well be the next person to come up with an interesting tip for others!

CHAPTER 21

Using Backup on Windows XP

IN THIS CHAPTER

- Hardware Can Make a Difference   *522*

- Developing a Backup Plan   *524*

- Running the Backup Wizard   *529*

- Performing a Manual Backup   *532*

- Setting Advanced Backup Program Options   *534*

- Restoring Data from a Backup   *537*

- Using Automated System Recovery   *541*

- Running Backup from the Command Line   *543*

Regardless of how up-to-date your computer is, how careful you are, or how secure your files are, a regular backup is essential. Computers die, people make mistakes, and no security scheme is perfect. Backing up provides protection against all of these situations.

A tool for backing up your computer has always been included with most versions of Windows. Usually, this tool has just been called *Backup* and despite its simple appearance and the fact that it is a built-in utility, it is a pretty powerful tool.

The backup utility in Windows XP Professional provides the following three functions:

- Back up files on your computer to another location—This involves selecting the files to back up, showing the backup utility where to save the backup file, setting any special options for the backup, and optionally scheduling the backup to occur regularly.
- Restore files from backup—This involves choosing the backup from which to restore, choosing the specific files in the backup that should be restored, and setting any advanced options.
- Using the Automated System Recovery Wizard—This is a specialized backup routine that creates an emergency floppy disk containing your system settings (so that you can boot and begin a backup after a system failure) and creates a backup of your entire computer. Using the Automated System Recovery Wizard is covered in Chapter 23, Disaster Recovery.

In this chapter, you will learn about the different types of hardware for backing up in Windows XP, as well as how to develop a backup plan, how to perform a backup, and how to restore your computer.

Hardware Can Make a Difference

Some previous versions of Backup in Windows only allowed you to back up to a supported tape drive. In Windows 2000 and now in Windows XP, backups are created as a single file that can be stored on any drive accessible by Windows. This includes tape; CD-R (recordable); CD-RW (rewriteable), Zip, hard, and floppy disks (if you happen to have a few hundred lying around). They can also be stored on a shared folder on a network and even in a folder on the Internet.

For the most part, backing up to all of these devices works the same way (although Backup does have some special features for working with tape drives); you just select the drive as the place to store your backup file when you run the backup. Nonetheless, each type of device has its advantages and disadvantages. Here are a few tips for using different types of backup media:

- Windows XP supports backing up directly to many CD-R and CD-RW drives. However, backing up directly to a CD-R or CD-RW may require direct-access software such as Adaptec's Direct-CD and a formatted CD. This software lets Windows write to a CD as if it were any other type of drive.

- Backing up directly to a CD-R or CD-RW drive can be a bit slow. It is best to do it when you will not need to use your computer for a while. Alternately, you could back up to a file on your hard disk and then copy that file to a CD later. The advantage of backing up to CDs is that they hold a good bit of information and have a long shelf life.

- Backing up to tape drives can also take a while, although modern tape drives are pretty fast. Unfortunately, you usually don't have the option of backing up to a hard disk and then transferring the file to tape later like you can with a CD. Try to schedule tape backups for when you won't need your computer for a while.

- Tape is a linear media, meaning that files are stored in a long string on the tape. To find a single file or group of files can take a considerably longer time than with other backup media. If you need to be able to quickly retrieve individual files out of your backups, tape is not the ideal choice.

- If you have two identical tape drives installed on your computer, Backup can only recognize the first drive. If, for some reason, you need two tape drives on your computer and need Backup to recognize both, you will have to make sure they are different models.

- Versions of Windows previous to Windows 2000 supported QIC and other floppy interface-based tape drives. Starting with Windows 2000, this support was dropped. IDE, SCSI, parallel, and PCMCIA tape drives are still supported.

- Backing up to floppy disk is pretty much a bad idea, unless you are backing up a few very small files and you just don't have any other choice. Even then, it would be better just to copy the files to a floppy disk.

- A fast, reliable, and relatively inexpensive method of backing up is to another hard disk, whether it is on your own computer or one on a network. On one office computer, you could install a removable hard drive kit—a $20 setup that includes a holder that fits into your computer (it connects to power and hard drive cables) and a tray that holds the actual hard drive. You can back up to that hard drive, pop the tray out of your computer, and then take it home so that your backup is offsite.

- If you have a small network, it is very inexpensive to build a computer that is just for storing backup files. You just need a computer that is capable of running Windows and has a hard drive big enough for the job.

Note

Okay, some people will argue that a removable hard drive isn't the cheapest solution. After all, once you spend the several hundred dollars for a tape or CD-R drive, the media is really pretty cheap. This may be true, but as of the writing of this book, an 80GB hard disk can be found for less than $200. Additionally, unlike a tape drive, you can copy files straight to a hard drive for the occasional extra backup copy of that really important file. If you use your computer for a small business, consider this a minimal cost to what it would cost you to recreate the data if you lost it because it was not backed up.

Your choice of backup media will likely be determined by price, reliability, speed, and capabilities of the device. For example, why buy a new, expensive tape drive when a CD-RW lets you do other things besides backing up files? Whatever your choice of hardware, the most important thing about backing up is creating a good backup plan and then sticking to it.

Note

Lots of the information in this chapter is directed toward people who will be backing up their individual computer or computers on a small network. That is because most large networks have a server-based backup solution that probably consists of banks of high-end tape drives and doesn't use the Windows Backup utility. Several third-party backup utilities provide more functionality for larger networks.

Developing a Backup Plan

Everyone has a preference in choosing what data to back up and when to do it. Think about how you organize your files and use your computer and then do some experimenting to come up with the best solution for you.

In developing a backup plan, your first step is to decide what you need to back up. Then you can decide how often to back it up.

Deciding What to Back Up

The easiest kind of backup to configure is a full system backup—that is, one in which you back up your entire hard drive at one shot. This kind of backup takes the longest, but ensures that you will be able to return your system to pretty much the state it was in before a catastrophe.

Another option is to only back up your personal files: e-mail folders, favorite Web pages, documents, and so on. If your computer fails, you have to reinstall Windows, reinstall your programs, and then restore your personal files from backup. Although it takes more work to restore than a full system backup, people use this type of backup for a couple of reasons. The first is that some people just like reinstalling Windows once in a while. It provides a good chance to reconfigure and clean things out. The other reason is that backing up only your personal files takes considerably less space and time when performing the backup. Many people can get away with backing everything up to a couple of 150MB Zip disks or to a single CD, something you can't do very well when you are backing up gigabytes of Windows and application files.

If you choose to do a full system backup, you won't need to give the matter much more thought. If you choose to back up only select files, it may be helpful to know where Windows XP keeps important files. Table 21.1 details the common default file locations in Windows XP that you will want to consider when backing up.

Table 21.1   Common Default File Locations in Windows XP

Path	Subfolder	Description
`C:\Documents and Settings\username`	Application Data	Holds saved program files and information for many programs; Outlook Express e-mail and news folders are saved in this folder in a subfolder named Identities.
	Cookies	Holds small files saved by Internet Explorer that contain personal settings (username, password, etc.) for some Web sites.
	Desktop	Holds all items placed on a user's desktop.
	Favorites	Holds all Web pages added to the Favorites menu in Internet Explorer.
	Local Settings	Holds settings and files for many programs by default, such as Microsoft Outlook, which stores its personal folders that hold locally stored e-mail, as well as settings in this folder.
	My Documents	The default location where many programs like Microsoft Office store documents the user has created.
	Start Menu	Holds customized shortcuts.

continues

Table 21.1   continued

Path	Subfolder	Description
`C:\Inetpub`		Holds the Web site and file transfer protocol (FTP) site created by Internet Information Server.
`C:\Program Files`		Holds folders for each installed program on your computer; although many programs now store their settings and saved files in the Documents and Settings folder, many others like games and some graphics editing programs still save files in their own folder within the Program Files folder.
`C:\Windows`		Although some programs may save settings in the Windows folder, most now use the Documents and Settings folder instead, making backups easier.
	Fonts	Holds all fonts installed on Windows; if you have installed any of your own fonts, you should back them up from this folder.
	Offline Web Pages	Holds offline Web pages synchronized using synchronization manager (see Appendix C).
	Resources\Themes	May hold any custom desktop themes you have downloaded and installed.
	Security\Logs	Holds any security logs created on your computer.
	Tasks	Holds any tasks you have created using Task Scheduler.

Deciding How and When to Back Up

Once you have decided what files to back up, you need to decide how and when to back them up. You can perform five basic types of backups using the Windows XP Backup utility (and most other backup utilities). The key difference between these backup types is how each one handles the archive bit in every Windows file. When a file is created or modified, the archive bit is set to On, as shown by the A in the Attributes column in Figure 21.1. When some types of backups run, the archive bit is set to Off, which indicates that the file has been backed up.

FIGURE 21.1

The Attributes column in the Details pane is indicated by an A where the archive bit is active on a newly created file.

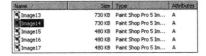

The five backup types are as follows:

- Normal—During a normal backup, all selected files are backed up, regardless of how their archive bit is set. After the backup, the archive bit is set to off for all files, indicating that those files have been backed up.

- Copy—During a copy backup, all selected files are backed up, regardless of how their archive bit is set. After the backup, the archive bit is not changed in any file. This provides a way to make an additional backup without disturbing any other backup procedures you may have pending.

- Incremental—During an incremental backup, all files on which the archive bit is located are backed up. After the backup, the archive bit is set to off for all files that were backed up.

- Differential—During a differential backup, all files on which the archive bit is located are backed up. After the backup, the archive bit is not changed in any file.

- Daily—During a daily backup, all files that changed on the day of the backup are backed up, and the archive bit is not changed in any file.

Given the five types of backups, most people have three favorite backup methods. These methods all start with performing a full backup of your computer on a regular basis. One continues with full backups daily, another performs an incremental backup every other day of the week, and the last does a differential backup every other day of the week. The difference is as follows:

- Daily Full Backup—Every day of the week, complete a full backup of your computer. Given the storage capacity and speed of modern backup devices and that the Windows XP Backup utility allows you to back up to any available drive, daily full backups are the choice of most people.

- Full Plus Incremental—A full backup is done on one day each week, such as a Sunday. Each day after that, an incremental backup is performed that backs up the new and changed data, since the last full or incremental backup (whichever is more recent). This method saves some backup time over the Daily Full Backup method because you only have to back up files that have changed in the last day. However, the restore time takes longer because you will have to restore the full backup and then each incremental backup in turn until you have restored the latest.

- Full Plus Differential—A full backup is done on one day each week. Each day after that, a differential backup is performed that backs up the new and changed data since the last full backup. This backup strategy takes the most time to back up files, since each day, the backup gets progressively longer. However, this method does take less time to restore, since only the last full backup and the last differential backup must be restored.

Tip

If you have enough space on your backup media and it is fairly quick, then only conduct full backups every day. It is much easier to configure and remember. The other methods are presented here on the off chance you find yourself required to use one.

Once you have decided what type of backup to use, you still need to consider how long old backups need to remain available. Assume, for example, that you use one removable hard disk for backing up. At the end of each day, you should back up the entire hard drive to your backup drive. This likely means that each day, the previous day's backup is erased. What if you discover that a file was accidentally deleted six days ago? What if you learn your computer has a virus, but it doesn't "explode" on your computer until several days or possibly months down the road? Unfortunately, in both cases, data is lost.

The solution to this, of course, is to use more than one backup drive or tape. If you are performing full backups each day, the simplest method is to decide how many days you need backups to be available and to use that many backups. For example, if you are using a tape drive and want to be able to access old backups for seven days, get seven tapes. Label each one by the day of the week on which it gets used. At the beginning of each week, the oldest tape gets written over.

Of course, if you are using a large hard drive for your backup and are not performing full backups every day, you may be able to fit a month's worth of backups on a single drive. You will have to come up with a plan of your own. In developing your plan, ask yourself the following questions:

- How long should my backups remain available? One day? One week? One month?
- How much space will it take to back up my drive? If backing up your whole drive, just find out how much disk space is used. If backing up only select files, use the

backup program to help estimate the amount of space the backup needs before you run a real backup.

- How much will my backup media hold?
- How often will I create a new backup?

> **Note**
>
> A truly secure backup is recorded on removable media and kept off-site. In the event of a catastrophe, such as a fire or flood, backup tapes stored on the shelf near your computer won't do you too much good. Consider using a backup mechanism such as tape, CD-R, or a removable hard drive that lets you pop the backup out of your computer and take it offsite. If security is a big concern for your offsite backups, consider renting a safety deposit box.

Running the Backup Wizard

When your backup hardware and plan are in place, you can perform an actual backup. You can run the Backup utility by going to Start, Accessories, System Tools, Backup. The opening Backup screen offers three options: running the Backup Wizard, the Restore Wizard, and the Automated System Recovery Wizard.

> **Tip**
>
> Before you begin any backup operation, it would be a good idea to defragment your hard drive and also scan for viruses. These actions will ensure an efficient and clean backup.

To run the Backup Wizard, follow these steps:

1. In the Backup Utility Window, click Advanced to launch the Backup Wizard.
2. Click Next to go past the welcome page of the wizard.
3. Select what you want to back up. You can back up everything on the computer, only selected files, or only the System State data (Windows settings). If you want to back up files on another computer on the network, you must choose to back up selected files. Click Next when you have made your choice.
4. If you chose to back up only selected files, the next page of the Wizard (see Figure 21.2) lets you choose what files to back up. Use the directory tree on the left to

find the folders and files you want to back up. Use the My Network Places icon to find files on other computers on the network. Place a check next to any items you want to include. If you chose to back up everything on the computer or just the System State data, you will not see this page. When you have chosen your files, click Next.

FIGURE 21.2

Select the folders and files to back up in the Items to Back Up window.

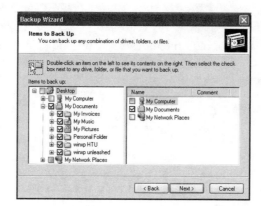

5. On the next Wizard page, you first need to select the backup type. If you have a tape drive in your computer, you have the option of backing up to tape or to a file. If you don't have a tape drive, you can only back up to a file; the Select the Backup Type option is grayed out, as shown in Figure 21.3.

FIGURE 21.3

If you have a removable media backup hardware option, you can select backup type in this Wizard screen. You also use this screen to set the backup type and destination.

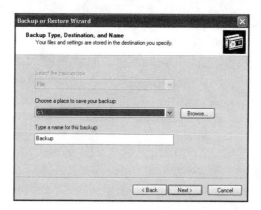

6. Next, choose the place to save the backup. If you are backing up to a tape, only your tape drive is shown in the list. If you are backing up to a file, you can browse your computer or your network to specify the location the backup should be saved.

7. Then type a name for the backup. When you are done, click Next to go on.

8. A summary page for the Backup Wizard is displayed, as shown in Figure 21.4. If you want to specify additional options for your backup, click Advanced. This takes you into several more wizard pages for configuring extra features. If you do not want to configure additional options, click Finish to begin the backup. Steps 9 through 13 of this procedure carry on as if you had clicked the Advanced button. If you do not set advanced options, just skip to Step 14.

FIGURE 21.4

Check the summary information listed in this screen, then click the Advance button to Set advanced backup options.

9. The first advanced setting you can configure is the type of backup to perform (Normal, Copy, Incremental, Differential, or Daily). The default setting is Normal (these backup types are discussed earlier in the chapter). After you select a backup type, click Next.

10. The next page (see Figure 21.5) lets you configure three settings. The first is whether Backup should verify the data after backup by comparing the backup to the original. This takes some extra time but may be worth it for the added security. The second option is for using hardware compression, which is usually available only on tape drives. Compression takes a bit longer but saves space. The final option is for disabling or enabling a shadow copy (enabled by default), which allows the backing up of files even if they are being written to. Once you have made your selections, click Next to go on.

11. The next page lets you choose whether to append the current backup to any other backups already on the backup media (the default option) or to replace any other backups. Make your selection and click Next to go on.

12. Next you get a chance to schedule your backup for later or run it now, as shown in Figure 21.6. If you run it now, the backup job is executed when the wizard finishes. If you set it to run later, you can click the schedule button and configure the days and times that the backup should run. Click Next to go on after setting your scheduling preferences.

FIGURE 21.5

The How to Back Up screen lets you configure other backup options.

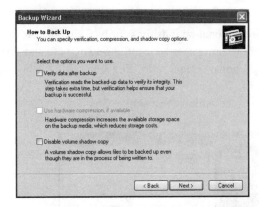

FIGURE 21.6

Decide when to back up by naming your job and setting a schedule.

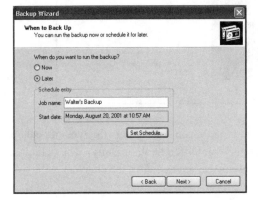

13. A summary page is displayed letting you confirm the choices you have made during the wizard. If you elected to run your backup now (the default choice), clicking Finish will begin the backup process. If you scheduled your backup for later, clicking Finish will exit the Wizard and return you to the Backup utility.

14. If you decided to run your backup now, Windows goes right ahead with the backup job. When it is finished, a summary of the backup is displayed (see Figure 21.7). Click Close to finish.

Performing a Manual Backup

If you choose, you can perform your backup manually instead of using the wizard. You provide the same information as in the wizard; you just have a little more control. To perform a backup manually, switch the Backup tab, which is shown in Figure 21.8.

FIGURE 21.7

This summary lets you view the details of your backup.

FIGURE 21.8

Creating a manual backup.

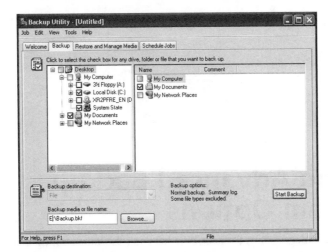

Selecting Components to Back Up

As you can see, the Backup tab shows a hierarchical directory of your entire system. You can back up anything on your computer that you like. You can even back up files from another computer on a network using the My Network Places icon.

After you have selected all of the components you want to back up, you must specify where to back them up. Use the Backup Destination drop-down list to specify whether you want to back up to tape or file. Then use the Backup Media or Filename box to specify the tape drive or the drive and filename you want to backup to. When you are satisfied with your choices, click Start Backup.

Setting Backup Information

After you select all the components and click the Start Backup button, the Backup Job Information dialog box opens (see Figure 21.9). You will need to supply the name of the backup set and whether the media should be overwritten or appended if there is already a backup present on the media.

If you want to perform a backup type other than Normal, click the Advanced button to open the Advanced Backup Options dialog box. From the Backup Type drop-down list, you can choose to perform a normal, incremental, differential, copy, or daily backup (covered earlier in the chapter). You can also use the Advanced Backup Options dialog to set additional options, such as verifying and compressing data or disabling shadow copy.

When you are ready to go, click Start Backup, and the backup will begin. You are shown the progress and a summary when the backup is finished.

FIGURE 21.9

The Backup Job information dialog box lets you determine whether to overwrite existing data on the backup media.

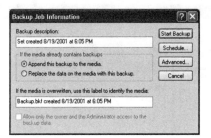

Setting Advanced Backup Program Options

In addition to setting options for a specific backup job while creating that job, you can set a few options for the backup program itself. To get to these options, open the Tools menu and select Options. This opens an Options dialog, the various tabs of which are covered in the next several sections.

General

The General tab (see Figure 21.10), contains a number of advanced options for how backups are handled. These options include the following:

- Compute Selection Information Before Backup and Restore Operations—This option makes Backup estimate and display the number of files and disk space that will be backed up during the current backup job. This computation may take a little extra time but can be valuable in determining whether your backup media has enough space. If this is not a concern, turn this option off to save time. This option is enabled by default.

- Use the Catalogs on the Media to Speed Up Building Restore Catalogs on Disk—This option indicates that you want to use the catalogs built into your backup media (usually available on tapes only) to build the catalog used for restore operations. If this option is not selected, Backup will scan your media to create a catalog. This takes more time but is usually more accurate. This option is enabled by default.

- Verify Data After the Backup Completes—Backup to checks the veracity of the backed up data against the original when a backup job is finished. It consumes a fair bit of time but helps make sure that backups are valid. This option is not enabled by default.

- Back Up the Contents of Mounted Drives—This option allows Backup to back up the information on mounted drives (such as Zip disks). If this option is disabled, only the path information for the drive (and not the data) can be backed up. This option is enabled by default.

- Show Alert Message When I Start the Backup Utility and Removable Storage Is Not Running—Removable Storage is the component of Windows XP that manages tape drives. If you don't use a tape drive, turn this option off. If you do use a tape drive, this option alerts you when the Removable Storage component is not running for some reason. This option is enabled by default.

- Show Alert Message When I Start the Backup Utility and No Recognizable Media Is Present and Show Alert Message When New Media Is Inserted—These options display alerts when new tape media is recognized by the Removable Storage component or when new media is inserted. Turn these off if you do not use a tape drive. These options are enabled by default.

- Always Allow Use of Recognizable Media Without Prompting—This option allows Backup to automatically use any new media detected by the Removable Storage component without prompting you. This option is disabled by default.

FIGURE 21.10

Setting General backup options in this dialog box determines how the backup program itself functions.

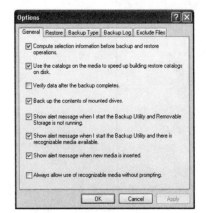

Setting the Default Backup Type

The Backup Type tab lets you configure the default backup type used in new backups, such as Normal, Copy, Differential, Incremental, or Daily. Of course, you can change this backup type to anything you want when you create a particular backup job. These backup types are covered earlier in this chapter.

Customizing the Backup Log

The Backup Log tab lets you configure how detailed a log the Backup Utility keeps. The three options available are as follows:

- Detailed—This option logs all information, including the names and files of all folders. This type of log is useful if you need written verification of your backups so that you can see whether certain files are being backed up. This level of logging is also useful in troubleshooting any backup problems.

- Summary—This is the default logging option. It logs only key operations such as starting and finishing the backup and any backup errors that occur.

- None—This option turns off logging.

Excluding Files From the Backup Job

The Exclude Files tab (see Figure 21.11), lets you pick certain types of files and certain folders that should be excluded from all backups. The tab is divided into two portions: a list of files excluded for all users of Backup and a list of files excluded for the current user only. You can add files to either list by clicking the appropriate Add New button and entering the file information.

FIGURE 21.11

Options in the Exclude Files tab let you exclude certain file and folder types from all backups.

Restoring Data from a Backup

Windows XP makes restoring files from a backup just as easy as backing them up in the first place. Before you get started with a restoration, however, there may be a few other actions you need to take first. This really depends on what you are restoring and why.

The first action is to get your hands on the right backup sets to do the job. The following will help you decide what you need:

- If you run only full backups and you are going to restore your whole system, the only thing you will need is the last full backup you created. If you need to dig through a backup to find an individual file, you will need the backup set that you think contains the file.
- If you perform differential backups, you will need your last full backup and the most recent differential backup.
- If you perform incremental backups, you will need your last full backup and every incremental backup that you have performed since the last full backup.

The next action is to determine what you intend to restore. If you are going to restore a few files or a folder, you have a couple of choices on how to do that. You could just restore them to their original location on your computer. You could also restore them to an alternate location (such as a new folder), so that you can compare the restored files to any originals and decide what to keep. Finally, you can restore them to a different computer entirely. This can be useful if you don't want to disturb your computer with a restore job or if you want to move files to another computer using the Backup Utility. How to do each of these is covered later in this chapter.

If you are going to restore your entire system (maybe after a crash), you will need to take a couple of additional steps before performing the restoration:

1. Fix whatever caused the computer to crash.
2. Reinstall the same version of Windows you were using before and use the same volume, hardware, and configuration options as on the previous system. This step is necessary because Windows XP will need to be there before you can run the Backup Utility.
3. Finally, restore the backup with System State information.

Just like with backing up, you can restore from backup in one of two ways: using a Restore Wizard or manually.

Using the Restore Wizard

The Restore Wizard steps you through the process of restoring a backup. To run the Restore Wizard, follow these steps:

1. Click Start, All Programs, Accessories, System Tools, Backup.

2. Click the button next to Restore Wizard (Advanced). This launches the Restore Wizard.

3. Click Next to go past the welcome page of the wizard.

4. The first (and arguably, most important) step of the wizard is to select the files you want to restore, shown in Figure 21.12. On the folder tree on the left, you will find a list of backup sets available. Expand the appropriate backup set and find the files and folder inside that you want to restore. Select files by checking the box next to them. If you are restoring an entire backup set, just select the set itself. Once you have made your selection, click Next.

Figure 21.12

Selecting files to restore.

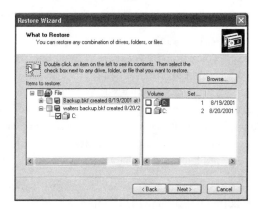

5. Next a summary page for the Restore Wizard is displayed; if you want to specify additional options for your restore, click Advanced. This takes you into several more wizard pages for configuring extra features. If you do not want to configure additional options, click Finish to begin the restore. Steps 6 through 9 of this procedure carry on as if you had clicked the Advanced button. If you do not set advanced options, just skip to Step 10.

6. The first page of advanced options lets you choose where you want to restore files. By default, files are restored to their original location. You can also elect to restore them to an alternate location that you specify or to a single folder. If you restore

them to a single folder, the original directory structure of the folders and files in the backup is recreated in full inside that folder. After you have made your choice, click Next.

7. The next page lets you choose what happens when existing files on the computer and files being restored have the same name. By default, the existing files on the computer are left alone and the files in the backup set are not restored. You can also have Backup replace the existing files if they are older than the ones in the backup set or replace the existing files no matter what. Click Next when you make your choice.

8. The next page, shown in Figure 21.13, has three options. The first is whether to restore security settings (permissions and so on) on files that are restored. The second is to restore junction points, which is a physical location on your hard drive that points to data stored at another location on the hard drive or on another storage device. If you don't select this option, junction points are restored as a simple directory that no longer points to the appropriate data. The Final option is whether to preserve existing volume mount points. This option prevents Backup from writing over any existing mount points that you have created on the partition or volume you are restoring to. If you are restoring to a replacement drive that you have just formatted but have not created mount points on, disable this option so that mount points are created for you during the restore process.

FIGURE 21.13

Choose the Advanced Restore options carefully.

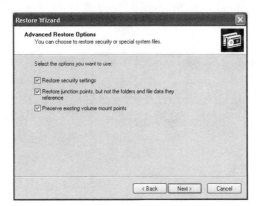

9. A summary page is displayed letting you confirm the choices you have made during the wizard. Clicking Finish will begin the restore process.

10. When the restore process is finished, a report is displayed (see Figure 21.14). Click Close to finish.

FIGURE 21.14

Displaying a report for the restore job.

Restoring Files Manually

In addition to restoring files using the Restore Wizard, you can also restore files manually. In the Backup Utility, click the Restore and Manage Media tab. All available backup jobs are displayed, and you simply have to drill down and select what backup job and components of that job you want to restore (see Figure 21.15).

You also need to specify whether to restore files to their original location, an alternate location, or an individual folder. Do this using the Restore Files to drop-down list. If you are restoring your entire computer, you will use the first option. If you are using a backup to move items to another server or to a newly installed server, you will usually use the second option. Restoring to an individual folder is useful if you want to try to find some particular piece of data within the backup job.

FIGURE 21.15

Choosing components to restore.

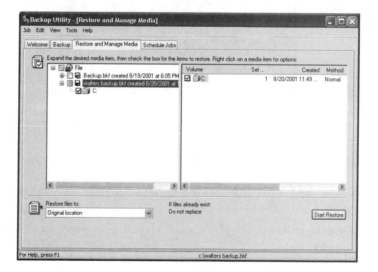

When you have made your choices, click the Start Restore button. This opens a Confirm Restore dialog box on which you can begin the restore process immediately or open another dialog box with some advanced options. The Advanced Restore Options dialog box is shown in Figure 21.16. You can use this dialog to control a number of options, such as restoring security, restoring junction points, and preserving mount point, all of which are covered in the previous section.

When you have set your options, click OK and then click OK on the Confirm Restore dialog to begin the restore process. When the process is complete, you are shown a summary of the job.

FIGURE 21.16

Setting Restore Options.

Tip

You can control the default action that happens when Backup attempts to restore a file that already exists on the computer. You can get to this option by opening the Tools menu of the Backup utility and selecting Options. On the dialog that opens, switch to the Restore tab. The normal default action is not to replace the file on the computer. You can also set the default action to either replace the file on the computer if it is older than the one in the backup or always replace the file on the computer. No matter what default action you set (Microsoft recommends leaving it at the normal default, and I agree), you can set a different option during the actual restore process, as you learned earlier in the chapter.

Using Automated System Recovery

Those of you coming from earlier versions of Windows (such as Windows 2000/NT) may remember the Emergency Repair Disk feature. In Windows XP, this feature has been replaced by Automated System Recovery (ASR), which works in much the same way.

During the ASR process, the following two actions occur:

- A complete backup of your computer's system files and settings.
- An ASR floppy disk that can be used to boot your computer in the event of a complete system failure and restore your system settings and files from backup

Backup provides a wizard that makes it very easy to set up the ASR backup and floppy disk. To create an ASR backup and floppy disk, use the following steps:

1. Click Start, All Programs, Accessories, System Tools, Backup.
2. Click the button next to Automated System Recovery Wizard. This launches the Wizard.
3. Click Next to go past the welcome page of the wizard.
4. Select the type of backup media to use. If you are backing up to a file, specify a file location. When you are done, click Next to go on.
5. Click Finish. The Backup utility will now perform the backup of your system files and settings.
6. When the backup is done, you are asked to insert a blank, formatted floppy disk. Insert the disk and click OK.
7. After the files are copied to floppy disk, the ASR wizard is finished. Remove your disk, label it, and click OK.
8. Click Close to exit the backup summary dialog box and return to the Backup program.

To recover your system from a failure using ASR, you will need to have the following items in hand:

- The ASR floppy disk
- The ASR backup media
- Your Windows XP Professional installation CD (or other access to the installation files)

To perform the recovery process, you will start your computer using your Windows XP Professional installation CD, as if you were going to install Windows. You will be prompted during setup as to whether you want to repair the current installation of Windows using ASR. When the Setup program asks, you will need to supply your ASR floppy disk and the ASR backup you performed. Setup will walk you through the recovery.

Running Backup from the Command Line

Like most components of Windows XP, you can run the Backup Utility from the command line. In previous versions of Windows, this was normally done to schedule backup jobs to occur automatically. Since Windows 2000, however, Backup has included a graphical interface for scheduling backups (which makes things much easier). Nonetheless, you can still use the command-line interface to run backup and there are still a couple of good reasons for doing so. The first is that it is an easy way to manually run a backup job on a remote computer. The second is that the command line can be included in batch files.

The basic command on the command-line interface for running backup is as follows:

```
Ntbackup [systemstate] [.bks name] path parameters
```

These parameters and available switches are detailed in Table 21.2.

Table 21.2   Parameters and Switches for `ntbackup`

Parameter or Switch	Description
/A	Sets backup to append mode, where backups are added to the end of the backup media
/N "name"	Specifies a media name
[.bks "name"]	Specifies a backup set filename, which can be used to show backup which specific files are to be backed up
Path	Specifies the path for the backup file
/M {}	Specifies the backup type (Normal, Incremental)
/F "name"	Specifies the filename when backing up to a file
/DS or /IS "server name"	Backs up directory information for Exchange Server (will not be used on a computer running Windows XP)
/V	Causes all operations to be verified.
/R	Restricts access to saved information to Administrators and file owners
/RS (yes|no)	Backs up the removable storage database
/D "description"	Enters a textual description of the backup
Systemstate	Backs up system files, including the Registry
/HC:{on/off}	Turns hardware compression on or off

continues

Table 21.2   continued

Parameter or Switch	Description
/T {option}	Specifies the tape name
/L f,s,n	Specifies the log file type (detailed, summary, or none)
/J "name"	Specifies the job name
/G "name"	Specifies the GUID name
/P "name"	Specifies the Pool name

Summary

The Backup utility provided with Windows XP is a powerful tool, easily up to the task of backing up a professional workstation. It includes the ability to back up and restore an entire computer, specific files on a computer, files in shared folders on a network, and the system state (Windows settings and Registry information) for a computer. Backup also provides the ASR feature, which creates a backup of Windows settings and a floppy disk that can be used to boot your computer and restore those settings in an emergency.

When planning a backup routine for your computer, you should first decide what files you want to back up and how often the backup needs to happen. You should then decide on backup hardware appropriate to your situation. When running backups, the most important thing is that you be regular and consistent. Like most plans, a backup plan is only as good as its execution.

Performance Monitoring, Logs, and Alerts

IN THIS CHAPTER

- Understanding Performance Issues for Windows XP   *546*

- Using Task Manager   *564*

- Using System Monitor   *566*

- Configuring Logs and Setting Alerts   *578*

- Command Line Performance Monitoring Tools   *585*

Along with the host of other features that Windows XP Professional brings to the table, it also brings improved performance over previous versions of Windows. All things being equal, a computer running Windows XP should show a small performance boost over the same computer running Windows 2000 Professional and a significant boost over the same computer running Windows Me.

In fact, increasing performance was one of the main design goals behind Windows XP. Designers tried to tweak the performance of just about every aspect of Windows' operation. XP starts faster and resumes from standby and hibernation more quickly. In addition, applications start faster and disk and video handling is better than ever before.

When Windows XP is first installed, it should be configured for optimum performance. Over time, however, after installing and uninstalling applications and drivers, creating and deleting files, and loading your computer up with more features, performance can begin to suffer. Monitoring and improving performance is the focus of this chapter.

This chapter describes some of the performance issues you might encounter and ways to address those issues. Next, you will learn about the three primary monitoring tools provided by Windows XP: Task Manager, System Monitor, and Performance Logs and Alerts. Task Manager offers an immediate overview of system activity and performance, useful for examining immediate problems you may be having on a system. System Monitor and Performance Logs and Alerts are both part of a Microsoft Management Console snap-in named *Performance System Monitor*. This feature lets you record information about hundreds of different aspects of your computer. Performance Logs and Alerts provide a way for Windows to notify you when certain performance thresholds are crossed.

Understanding Performance Issues for Windows XP

Before you start monitoring your system, and especially before you start trying to improve its performance by buying new hardware or uninstalling applications, it is important that you understand some of the underlying factors that influence your computer's performance. It is useful to divide these factors into three broad categories: hardware, Windows configuration, and installed software. This section takes a look at the general hardware issues relating to performance and then looks at some ways that you can configure Windows and additional software to improve performance.

Before going too far, however, you should set yourself some realistic expectations and take an honest look at your system. If your computer has always been fast enough for you, but you have noticed a significant slowdown over a fairly short period of time, the techniques in this chapter will probably help you a good bit. Likewise, if you are just the type of person that likes to keep their computer running in top form, this chapter can help.

However, if your system is a few years old and you have taken pretty good care of it but just don't find it fast enough anymore (maybe because you got that nice, fast, new computer at work or home), the techniques in this chapter can only do so much. A 1GHz Pentium III with plenty of random access memory (RAM) and a fast disk subsystem is going to outperform a 400MHz Pentium II with limited RAM and a slower disk subsystem just about every time, regardless of how perfectly configured is the slower system or how poorly configured is the faster system.

Hardware Factors Affecting Performance

Hardware is the single biggest determining factor in the performance of your computer. For the purposes of monitoring and improving performance, most people divide hardware up into the following three broad categories:

- Memory
- Processor
- Disk Subsystem

These three categories are certainly the easiest to monitor with software tools like Task Manager and System Monitor, and they are probably the most important in terms of overall system performance. However, the following three additional categories affect performance as well:

- Network
- Video Adapter
- System Bus

Windows XP is tuned to take better advantage of today's hardware. In many cases Windows XP is able to adapt itself to a changing hardware environment, letting you enjoy better performance with less work. However, understanding the major categories of hardware and how they affect your computer's performance is the first step to get the most out of your system.

The next several sections examine each of these hardware categories and the effect each has on system performance.

Memory

By far, memory and processor speed are the two most popular benchmarks by which people like to measure system performance. Adding memory to a computer also has the distinction of being one of the easiest and cheapest ways to improve performance, at least up to a point. Adding memory follows the law of diminishing returns. If, for example, you have 32MB of RAM and you upgrade to 64MB, you will see a pretty amazing difference. Upgrade again to 128MB, and you will see an impressive difference, although not quite as dramatic. The higher you go, the less the performance boost. The average desktop user, for example, may not notice any difference at all between 512MB and 1GB of RAM.

According to Microsoft, the minimum amount of RAM required to run Windows XP Professional is 64MB. However, it does admit that some features and performance may be limited by this amount, so it recommends a minimum of 128MB. In practice, I have found that even 128MB is not really enough to do anything but run Windows by itself at an adequate level of performance.

At the writing of this book, the price of 512MB RAM is less than $100. This makes it fairly easy and inexpensive to equip a computer with 512MB or even 1GB of RAM, which most modern computers will support.

You can determine the amount of physical memory installed on your computer using the following procedure:

1. Click Start, Control Panel.
2. If your Control Panel window is currently in Category View, click the Switch to Classic View link.
3. Double-click the System icon.
4. The amount of RAM installed on your computer is listed near the bottom of the General tab in a section labeled Computer:.

Note

Before you go out and buy more RAM for your computer, you need to double-check a few things. First, know the kind of RAM your computer needs. Different styles of RAM have been used over the years. In older systems, memory modules called *SIMMS* are often used. Currently, most computers use modules called *SDRAM*, although many of the new Pentium 4–based motherboards require a new type of memory called *DDR*. You should consult your computer's or motherboard's manufacturer to determine the type of memory it uses. Also, look out for different motherboards with different abilities. Some limit the maximum size of each memory module to 128MB, 256MB, or 512MB. Others limit the maximum amount of total memory a system can handle. Again, check with the manufacturer of your system.

Processor

The processor (or central processing unit [CPU]) is the other major component, in addition to memory, that affects system speed. Microsoft's minimum requirement for running Windows XP is a 233MHz processor, although it recommends 300MHz. A 300MHz processor from either the Intel or AMD line will run Windows XP; truthfully, however, you are probably going to want something more. An Intel Pentium III or AMD Thunderbird greater than 800MHz will do the job admirably and meet the needs of most users.

You can determine the processor installed on your computer using the following procedure:

1. Click Start, Control Panel.
2. If your Control Panel window is currently in Category View, click the Switch to Classic View link.
3. Double-click the System icon.
4. The Processor installed on your computer is listed near the bottom of the General tab in a section labeled Computer:.

Unlike adding more memory, upgrading your processor can be a bit tricky. The following are some things to watch out for:

- Different processors normally require different motherboards. For example, if you have a system with a Pentium III processor, you will probably be able to upgrade to a higher-speed Pentium III processor, although you may still want to check to make sure. You would not, however, be able to upgrade that same computer to a Pentium 4 or AMD processor.

- Even if you decide to get a different motherboard along with your new processor, you may not be able to use your current memory. You will need to check to make sure that your memory can be used on the new motherboard or buy new memory as well.

- For the most part, components like disk drives, video cards, and modems will work just fine with the various motherboards and processors that support Windows XP. Nonetheless, you should always check to make sure before upgrading.

Tip

Unless you are the type who must have the latest and greatest technology, the most cost-effective processor upgrade is usually only one or two steps below the current leader. For example, if a 2GHz Pentium 4 is the current speed leader, you will probably notice a sharp price difference between it and the next fastest processor. From the next fastest down, you will usually notice a more regular price difference.

22

PERFORMANCE MONITORING, LOGS, ALERTS

Disk

Obviously, having a nice, fast disk drive that operates on a nice, fast system bus will make the common operations of reading from and writing to the disk drive faster. A faster drive will make your computer start faster and your applications load faster because data can be read faster. However, the speed of your disk drive, as well as the amount of free space on the drive, also affects system performance in other ways.

Performance of your disk drive is interrelated with the performance of other components of your computer, particularly your memory. Windows supplements your computer's physical memory with a large paging file that is stored on disk, a setup referred to as *virtual memory*. When Windows anticipates that virtual memory will be needed, it begins a process of transferring the older contents of memory to disk, a process known as *paging* because of the way that information in memory is stored in pages. For this one reason alone, a fast hard drive with plenty of free space is essential to good system performance.

Additionally, Windows itself and many other large applications spread program files across your drive that must be accessed, so you can see why system performance is largely dependent on hard disk throughput.

Network

When working with material on a network or on the Internet, the network connection almost always presents the performance bottleneck. This is because your computer's components, along with the internal transfer rate between those components, are faster than your network or Internet connection. For this reason, it is important that your network connection perform its best.

Generally speaking, the real limiting factor in network speed is usually out of your hands. The network that your computer is on will have a maximum speed and so will any Internet connection. Nonetheless, you can make sure that your system is configured properly for network use. The most important thing is to make sure that your network adapter is up to the job. If possible, use a peripheral component interface (PCI)–based network adapter (see the discussion on System Busses later in this chapter for more on PCI), which is capable of using the full speed of your network. For example, if your network is a 100Mbps Ethernet network and you are using a 10Mbps network adapter, you are not realizing your full potential.

Video

Your video adapter (graphics card and the quality of its driver software) profoundly affects Windows XP performance. Windows XP makes greater demands on video memory compared with earlier versions of Windows. If your video adapter provides little or no memory, system memory is used for bitmaps and other graphics data. This reduces the memory available for use by Windows and applications.

Most modern video adapters come with a good bit of video memory built onto the card, fast graphics processors, and the ability to handle three- and two-dimensional (3D and 2D) graphics quite well. Unless you need outstanding 3D performance (maybe for games or intensive graphics or video work), you can probably get by with a moderately priced card from any of the major vendors.

If possible, you should also use a video adapter that uses the newer accelerated graphics port (AGP) bus, which is explained in the next section.

System Bus

A bus is a set of wires through which data is transferred from one part of your computer to another. People normally use the word bus (at least in relation to computers) to mean the internal bus or busses that connect each of the computer's components to the processor and memory. Every bus has a clock speed measured in MHz that determines the maximum speed at which data may be transferred.

The busses you might run into include the following:

- PCI—As the most popular bus in use in computers today, the peripheral component interface (PCI) bus is found on all modern PCs and even Macintosh computers. Most of the cards (network adapters, modems, and so on) available today are PCI-based.

- ISA—A bus popular in older models of PCs, the industry standard architecture (ISA) bus was the original bus used on the IBM PC/XT and the PC/AT. Although use of ISA has been supplanted almost entirely by the PCI in modern computers, many computer manufacturers still include an ISA slot or two to maintain compatibility with older hardware. The ISA bus is slower than the PCI bus.

- AGP—A relatively new bus, the accelerated graphics port (AGP) bus is based on PCI but is designed specifically for high-demand graphics use. Many modern video cards require an AGP slot and most modern computers come with one.

In general, your best bet is to configure a system so that the most critical components run on a higher-speed bus. If possible, use the AGP bus for your video adapter and the PCI bus for your network cards or SCSI adapter cards. The ISA bus is fine for plugging in older modems, sound cards, or other devices that don't require high-speed throughput.

Some Ideas to Improve Performance

Aside from upgrading its hardware, there are a number of ways to improve the performance of your computer. Windows XP includes several utilities and configuration settings for optimizing the performance of various components of your computer and to eliminate some of the delays you may experience within the Windows interface.

The next section covers a several methods for improving the performance of your computer, including the following:

- Optimizing Windows startup
- Using the Disk Cleanup tool to maximize free disk space
- Using Disk Defragmenter to optimize the storage of information on a disk
- Removing unnecessary applications and services that may consume disk space and other system resources
- Removing unneeded restore points created by System Restore to maximize free disk space
- Managing virtual memory paging files
- Managing display settings and effects to optimize the performance of the Windows interface

Note

Windows XP does a better job of managing resources than previous versions of Windows by taking advantage of idle times to perform system maintenance activities. Rather than relying on timers that may start up while you are working, Windows XP manages resources when the system is idle. Idle time activities include optimizing the layout of files and directories on the hard drive. Other system and service cleanup activities can also take place at this time.

Tip

A fresh installation of Windows XP on a clean hard drive will generally have a performance advantage over an upgrade, since it can exert greater control over the placement of files on the disk. Disk partitions converted from the FAT to the NTFS file system may have less than optimal cluster sizes too. For the best performance, install Windows XP onto a clean hard drive and use the Windows XP setup program to format the hard drive using NTFS.

Optimizing Windows Startup

When Windows XP is first installed and booted, the operating system observes your system's behavior. With the very first boot, Windows begins a process of optimization that quickly speeds up subsequent boots. Similarly, the first launch of an application is likely to be slower than subsequent optimized launches. It is important to recognize that this optimization is taking place and to allow a sufficient number of reboots and launches to train the system before deciding whether you need to optimize the Windows startup system (or indeed judge the performance of your system at all).

Windows startup is a fairly complicated process and there are a number of ways that you can optimize that process for a quicker startup time. These include the following:

22

PERFORMANCE
MONITORING,
LOGS, ALERTS

- Check the BIOS settings for your computer to see whether there are unnecessary actions you can eliminate from the startup process. For example, on many computers, you can skip the memory check that occurs when you turn on your computer—something that can take quite some time when you have a lot of memory.

- If you have your system configured for dual booting, you can reduce the amount of time Windows displays a menu of operating system choices at startup. Configure this setting by opening the Advanced tab of the System Properties dialog box, (Start, Control Panel, Performance and Maintenance, System), and clicking the Settings button in the Startup and Recovery section. This is covered in detail in Chapter 4, Unattended Installation and Sysprep.

- If you have more than one hardware profile configured for your system, you can reduce the amount of time Windows displays a menu of profile choices at startup.

- Remove any unnecessary applications that start automatically with Windows. This is covered a bit later in this chapter.

- When you remove a hardware device from your computer, make sure that any drivers and software installed with the device are also removed.

The Windows startup process and the methods for making the adjustments mentioned on the previous list are covered in detail in Chapter 6, Understanding the Startup Process.

Using Disk Cleanup

Disk Cleanup is a utility included with Windows that scans your hard drive looking for unnecessary files such as temporary files, Internet cache files, and old program files and then deletes them. Disk Cleanup is a simple and effective way to help make sure that the free space on a hard drive is maximized.

The basic procedure for using Disk Cleanup is as follows:

1. Click Start, All Programs, Accessories, System Tools, Disk Cleanup.

2. A dialog box with a single drop-down list appears. Choose the drive you want Disk Cleanup to examine and click OK.

3. The main Disk Cleanup window appears, as shown in Figure 22.1. Disk Cleanup informs you of how much disk space it can free up by eliminating the most common forms of unneeded files. These include the following:

   • Downloaded Program Files, which are all files contained in the \Windows\Downloaded Program Files folder.

   • Temporary Internet Files, which are contained in the \Documents and Settings*username*\Local Settings\Temporary Internet Files folder

   • Temporary Offline Files, which are contained in a hidden folder on your desktop

4. If you want, you can also customize the kinds of files that will be removed by selecting or deselecting items from the Files to Delete list.

5. Highlight any category of files and click the View Files button to see a list of the actual files that will be removed in a separate dialog box. From this dialog box, you can specify individual files to remove or keep.

6. Click OK.

7. Disk Cleanup asks whether you are sure you want to perform the actions you have selected. Click Yes and Disk Cleanup will begin deleting the selected files.

FIGURE 22.1

Using Disk Cleanup.

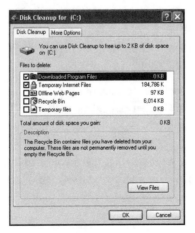

> **Tip**
>
> It is always a good idea whenever you undertake a significant housekeeping task on your computer to back up your system beforehand. This will ensure you can recover anything you might errantly delete.

Aside from selecting the specific files you want to have deleted, there is really not much else to configure about Disk Cleanup; it is really just a fancy file deleter. The More Options tab on the Disk Cleanup window (refer to Figure 22.1) hold shortcuts for opening the Add/Remove Programs Control Panel window and the System Restore window, both of which you can use to free up more disk space. These methods are discussed later in this chapter.

Using Disk Defragmenter

When you delete a file on your computer, Windows doesn't really remove it. It just marks that space as available for new information to be written. When a new file is written to disk, part of the file might be written to one available section of disk space, part might be written to another, and part to another. This piecemeal writing of a file is called *fragmentation*. It is a normal process and Windows keeps track of files just fine. The problem is that when a drive has a lot of fragmentation, it can take Windows longer to find information it is looking for. You can speed up drive access significantly by periodically defragmenting your drive.

Performance is strongly influenced by the layout of files on disk. Files and directories that are heavily fragmented or dispersed across the disk hurt performance. Although Windows XP automatically repositions some files to improve performance, this is done infrequently and usually includes only a small fraction of the files on the disk. Therefore, it is a good idea to defragment the disk after an installation and then periodically after that.

Windows includes a utility named Disk Defragmenter that examines your disk and then rewrites the information on the disk so that files are stored in a contiguous manner. Using Disk Defragmenter is covered in detail in Chapter 18, "Managing Disks and Partitions."

Removing Unnecessary Applications and Services

Over time, a computer accumulates a surprising amount of clutter. When you install an application, files are copied to your hard disk, Registry entries are created, and shortcuts are created on your Start menu, as well as your desktop. Often, large programs install smaller programs or services that start with Windows and are intended to provide you with added functionality or preload certain program components into memory so that the larger programs seem to start faster.

One example of this would be Microsoft Office, which installs a shortcut in your Startup folder to a component named Office Startup. This component preloads common pieces of the Office application code into memory so that the various office applications start faster. If you use Office applications all the time, then this is probably okay. If you don't, it is wasting system resources.

Additionally, many people never bother removing applications no longer in use and are often unaware of what components are starting with Windows. Therefore, the typical installation of Windows could almost always use a good bit of pruning.

To start with, it is always best to remove applications from Windows that are no longer in use. The uninstall routines included with today's programs remove program files, clean out Registry entries, remove shortcuts from your Start menu, and even remove links to programs scheduled to start with Windows. To remove applications, go to the Control Panel and use the Add/Remove Programs wizard. Its use is detailed in Chapter 12, "Installing and Removing Applications."

If you don't want to remove a particular program, Windows does provide ways to control the programs that start with it.

The first place to check is the System Tray. Many programs that load with Windows are represented by icons in the System Tray. Although their actual use varies by program, you can usually click or right-click an icon to find options for controlling the program. Some programs have an option for turning off the loading at Windows startup.

The next place to look is the Windows Startup folder. This is a special folder inside the Windows folder on your computer. Anything in this folder is executed during startup. The easiest way to see it is to open the Start menu and point to the All Programs folder. The Startup folder is listed inside. You can delete items from the folder by right-clicking them and choosing Delete from the shortcut menu that appears.

Tip

Instead of simply deleting items from your Startup folder, try moving them to your desktop first. That way, should removing them have an adverse effect, you can easily move them back.

The other type of program that loads during Windows startup is called a *Service*. A service is usually a small piece of code that provides support to Windows or another application. They usually work closer to the hardware level than the other types of programs that start with Windows. For this reason, you need to be a little more careful working with them than with other programs. Many provide functions vital to Windows. Therefore, it is fairly easy to control the services that load during Windows startup.

To view and control the installed services on your system, use the following procedure:

1. Click Start, Control Panel.

2. If your Control Panel window is currently in Category View, click the Switch to Classic View link.

3. Double-click Administrative Tools.

4. Double-click Services.

5. The Services Dialog box appears (see Figure 22.2). This dialog shows all the local services on your computer, along with their status (whether they are started or not) and their startup type (automatic or manual). Click Service.

FIGURE 22.2

The Services dialog box.

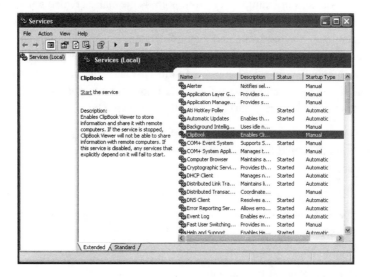

6. A description of the service appears to the left of the list of services. This description not only tells you what the service is for but also what will happen if the service is disabled.

7. Use the control buttons on the toolbar or the commands on the action menu to control the service. Commands include starting, stopping, pausing, and restarting (which stops and then starts) the service.

8. Right-click a service to open its Properties. From the Properties dialog, you can configure whether the service starts automatically with Windows, as well as a host of other options.

Tip

Windows also includes a great but little-known utility called the *System Configuration Utility.* You can run it from the command line, using the Run command `msconfig`. The utility is a tabbed dialog box that gives you detailed control over many of the Windows startup processes. You can choose a specific type of startup; edit the three major startup files (`SYSTEM.INI`, `WIN.INI`, and `BOOT.INI`); control what services start with Windows; and examine many programs scheduled to start with Windows that you cannot find elsewhere.

Controlling System Restore

System Restore is a component of Windows XP that periodically saves snapshots of your system files and settings so that you can roll your settings back to a previous state should a problem occur. For example, a restore point is normally created before installing any new hardware drivers. If the new hardware or drivers cause a problem with your system, you can remove the hardware and then use System Restore to return all settings to their previous state. Although this utility is one of the best new features of Windows XP, this kind of safeguard comes with a price. In this case, it is that restore points can take up a fair bit of disk space and System Restore's automatic monitoring (the ability to know when to create a restore point) can slow things down a bit.

However, you can control these aspects of System Restore. To control what System Restore monitors and how much disk space it is allowed to consume, use the following procedure:

1. Click Start, Control Panel.

2. If your Control Panel window is currently in Category View, click the Switch to Classic View link.

3. Double-click System.

4. Click the System Restore tab (see Figure 22.3).

5. Use the Turn Off System Restore on All Drives option if you want to disable System Restore's automatic monitoring of your system. If you do this, you are strongly urged to make manual restore points periodically and before any major software or hardware installation.

6. If you want to leave automatic monitoring on but control its use on individual drives, select a drive on the Available Drives list and click on Settings. This opens a separate dialog box with settings for that drive (see Figure 22.4).

7. Use the Turn Off System Restore on This Drive option to disable automatic monitoring of the selected drive.

FIGURE 22.3

*Setting System
Restore options.*

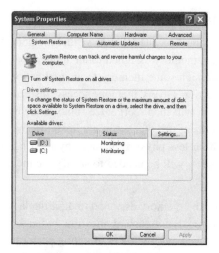

FIGURE 22.4

*Setting System
Restore options
for individual
drives.*

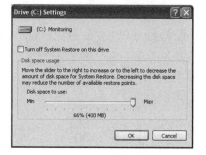

8. Use the slider control to specify the amount of disk space on the drive that System Restore is able to use for creating restore points.

In addition to reigning in the behavior of System Restore, you can also delete restore points that you will no longer need to help free disk space. To delete all restore points except for the most recent, use the following procedure:

1. Click Start, All Programs, Accessories, System Tools, Disk Cleanup.

2. A dialog box with a single drop-down list appears. Choose any drive and click OK.

3. The main Disk Cleanup window appears. Click the More Options tab.

4. In the System Restore section, click Clean Up.

5. On the Disk Cleanup dialog box that appears, click Yes. Once you do this, all but the most recent restore point will be deleted, so make sure that your system is in working order.

You will find a full discussion of using System Restore in Chapter 6, "Understanding the Startup Process."

Managing Paging Files

Windows XP, like most modern operating systems, uses virtual memory. Virtual memory is created by extending the physical memory assigned to an application on the computer's hard drive. Windows may assign some memory to an application, but not necessarily enough to satisfy that application's every memory access. Instead, some accesses will be detected by Windows, which will then reorganize some of the memory structure. By correctly anticipating the patterns of use of a set of applications, the operating system allows a computer to operate with far less physical memory by figuring out what combination of physical and virtual memory will be needed to satisfy the memory requirements of that set of applications.

Windows XP regularly checks that the memory assigned to a particular application is actually in use and maintains an estimate for each application, indicating the amount of memory that could reasonably be taken away without affecting performance. A reserve of memory is kept on hand to be used as needed. When this reserve sinks too low, it is replenished by paging some of the contents of memory to disk.

When Windows stores memory to hard disk, it uses a special file known as a *paging file*, or *swap file*. You can configure some aspects relating to how Windows uses the paging file by referring to the Virtual Memory dialog in Figure 22.5. To get to this dialog box, use the following procedure:

1. Click Start, Control Panel.
2. If your Control Panel window is currently in Category View, click the Switch to Classic View link.
3. Double-click the System icon.
4. Click the Advanced tab.
5. Click the Settings button in the Performance section. This opens a new dialog box named Performance Options.
6. Click the Advanced tab.
7. Click the Change button in the Virtual Memory section.

The Virtual Memory dialog box shows the size of the paging file for each disk on your computer and the total paging file size for all drives combined. The files on all disks are aggregated and treated as a single area for paging memory to disk. Breaking the file up across multiple disks (especially disks on different disk controllers) can decrease the time it takes to write memory information to the paging file.

FIGURE 22.5

*Setting Virtual
Memory options.*

For the most part, Windows manages the size of the file itself pretty well. If you want to change the size of the file, first select the drive and then choose the Custom Size option. Enter an initial size, which is the minimum size that the page file cannot shrink below, and a maximum size. When you are done, click Set.

> **Tip**
>
> If possible, try to avoid having your paging file on the same disk as your system files. Also, try not to put your paging file on fault-tolerant drives, such as mirrored or RAID-5 drives. Paging files do not need fault-tolerance, and fault-tolerant drives are often slower when writing information to disk.

Managing Display Settings and Effects

One often overlooked aspect of controlling performance is adjusting the display settings and effects used by Windows. Settings may include higher color depths and higher screen resolutions than are necessary. Effects that can slow a system down include showing a window's contents while it is being dragged across the desktop and using fancy transitions (such as a fade effect) when displaying menus.

Windows XP attempts to match the visual effects in the user interface to the capabilities of individual computers. There are a number of effects such as animations, drop shadowing, and menu fading that have the potential to interfere with response time if they cannot be rendered fast enough on a particular computer. To avoid this problem, Windows XP tries to gauge the capabilities of the system during installation and adjust the user interface settings accordingly.

Of course, Windows isn't perfect, and even if it determines that you have the system resources for a particular setting or effect, you may find it unnecessary, distracting, or even that it slows your system down. Fortunately, all of these settings and effects are pretty easy to control.

Many of these settings and effects can be found in locations throughout Windows, particularly on the various tabs and dialog boxes associated with the Display control panel. Windows also offers way to control all the aspects that may affect performance in one place: the Performance Options dialog box (Figure 22.6). To get there, open the System Control Panel, switch to the Advanced tab, and click the Settings button in the Performance Section.

FIGURE 22.6

Controlling display settings and effects that relate to performance.

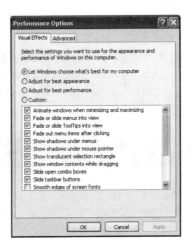

On the Visual Effects tab of the Performance Options dialog box, you can choose from the following four options:

- Let Windows manage the visual effects based on your system resources
- Adjust the effects for best appearance, which actually just selects all the effects
- Adjust the effects for best performance, which disables all the effects
- Manage your own effects by using the Custom option

Table 22.1 lists the available effects along with a description and notes whether or not the effect is included in the best performance or best appearance setting.

Table 22.1   Visual Effects in Windows XP

Visual Effect	*Notes*
Animate windows when minimizing and maximizing	A zoom effect occurs when you minimize or maximize a window.
Fade or slide menus into view	This setting not only uses up some resources, but it also makes you wait a bit longer to access menu items.
Fade or slide ToolTips into view	ToolTips are the pop-up descriptions that appear beside certain items when you hold your pointer over them.
	Fade out menu items after clicking
	Show shadows under menus
	Show shadows under mouse pointer
Show translucent selection rectangle	This feature draws a filled-in rectangle when selecting multiple items on the desktop instead of just a rectangle outline.
Show window contents while dragging	This setting really hogs the resources, since Windows must redraw the window multiple times while it is being moved.
Slide open combo boxes	A combo box is a drop-down list of items that you open from within a dialog box.
Slide taskbar buttons	This causes taskbar buttons to slide to the left when other programs are closed or to the right when new programs are opened.
Smooth edges of screen fonts	This setting does consume some resources, but is probably one of the more useful visual effects, making screen fonts easier to read, especially at higher resolutions.
Smooth-scroll list boxes	This causes the contents of a list box to scroll smoothly when you click the scroll bar rather than just jump down a few items in the list.
Use a background image for each folder type	Different types of folder in Windows XP can use different background images. Many of the special Windows folders such as Control Panel make use of this effect.
Use common tasks in folders	This setting causes folders in Windows to show the list of available tasks related to the files in the folder to the left of the actual file list.
	Use drop shadows for icon labels on the desktop
Use visual styles on windows and buttons	This setting is an important one in that it controls the new look of Windows XP. If you disable it, your desktop will look like the old Windows 2000 desktop.

22

PERFORMANCE MONITORING, LOGS, ALERTS

Using Task Manager

Task Manager provides information about applications and processes currently running on your system, and real time (although somewhat limited) system and networking performance levels. Task Manager is an important utility in managing Windows XP and, as such, has its own chapter in this book, Chapter 19, "Using the Task Manager." This section takes a look at the performance aspects of Task Manager.

You can start Task Manager in a number of different ways:

- Press `Ctrl+Shift+Esc`.
- Right-click the taskbar and then Task Manager.
- Press `Ctrl+Alt+Del`.
- Enter `taskman.exe` at the command prompt or using the run command.

The Task Manager window is divided into five tabs: Applications, Processes, Performance, Networking, and Users. The Performance and Networking tabs are the only ones relevant to this discussion of monitoring performance. While Task Manager is running, the status bar always displays the total number of processes, CPU usage as a percentage, and virtual memory use for the system.

The Performance tab, shown in Figure 22.7, features the following four gauges that help you gauge the current performance of your system:

- CPU Usage—This graph indicates the percentage of processor cycles that are not idle at the moment and is the prime indicator of processor activity. If this graph displays a high percentage continuously, your processor may be overloaded and you should perform some more sophisticated monitoring with System Monitor, covered later in this chapter. While Task Manager is running, an accurate miniature of this graph appears in the System Tray. Placing your mouse over it opens a pop-up tip with the percentage value.

- PF Usage—This is the percentage of the paging file that is currently being used. If this value runs near 100% continuously, you may need to increase the size of the paging file or decide whether you need more memory.

- CPU Usage History—This graph shows how busy the processor has been recently, although it only shows values since Task Manager was opened. You can use the Update Speed command on the View menu to specify how often the values are refreshed. The High value updates about twice per second, Normal once every two seconds, and Low once every four seconds. You can also pause the updates and update the view manually by pressing F5, a useful method if you want to monitor some specific activity. The length of time shown by the graph varies, depending on the update speed selected, but is never more than a few minutes unless the update is paused.

- Page File Usage History—This graph shows how full the page file has been over time, although it also only shows values since Task Manager was opened. Values set using the Update Speed command affect this history as well.

Note

If you have more than one processor on your computer, Task Manager is capable of graphing them. Use the CPU History command on the View menu to control how the information from each processor is displayed.

FIGURE 22.7

Monitoring performance with Task Manager.

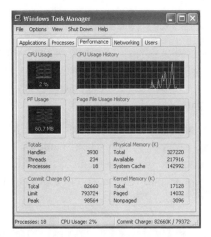

The Networking tab (see Figure 22.8) indicates the current network traffic over various network connections on your computer. Note that if you do not have any networking connections configured, this tab will not be visible. If you have more than one connection, a separate line is shown on the graph for each connection.

Tip

If you run Task Manager frequently and do not want to see its button on the taskbar, click Hide When Minimized on the Options menu. To open an instance of Task Manager when it is hidden, click the Task Manager CPU gauge on the taskbar.

FIGURE 22.8

Monitoring basic network performance with Task Manager.

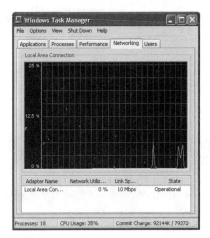

Using System Monitor

Although Task Manager is good for getting a quick overview of the current performance of your system, it pales in comparison to the functionality provided by System Monitor. System Monitor is one of two parts of a Microsoft Management Console (MMC) snap-in called *Performance,* with the other part being the Performance Logs and Alerts tool.

System Monitor works in much the same way as the old Performance Monitor application that came with various versions of Windows NT. When Windows 2000 came out, the utility was retooled as an MMC snap-in and given the name System Monitor. Not too much has been added since the Windows 2000 version, so those of you familiar with that version may just want to skim this material.

How System Monitor Collects Information

System Monitor is used to measure the statistical data generated by various components of your computer. System Monitor breaks down that data into the following three distinct pieces:

- An object represents a major system resource that is either physical or logical in nature. Examples of physical objects are physical disks, processors, and memory. An example of a logical object is transfer call protocol (TCP), which represents one of the major networking protocols of the TCP/IP (internet protocol) suite.

- A separate instance of an object exists for every type of component the object represents on your computer. For example, if you have three hard disks attached to your computer, there would be three instances of the physical disk object.

- Each instance of an object is further broken down into counters, which are the actual aspects of the object that can be measured. For example, the physical disk object includes a number of counters such as %Disk Time, %Idle Time, and Average Disk Bytes per Read.

Starting System Monitor

As mentioned previously, System Monitor is part of an MMC snap-in called *Performance*. You can use the following procedure to start the Performance snap-in:

1. Click Start, Control Panel.
2. If your Control Panel Window is in Category View, click the Switch to Classic View link.
3. Double-click Administrative Tools.
4. Double-click Performance. This opens the Performance window.

Windows can also show the Administrative Tools folder right from the Start menu. If you use these tools often enough, it can save time. To do this, use the following procedure:

1. Right-click the Taskbar and then click Properties.
2. Click the Start Menu tab.
3. Click the Customize button next to the Start menu option.
4. Click the Advanced tab on the Customize Start Menu dialog box that opens.
5. On the Start Menu items list, find the System Administrative Tools Section.
6. The default action is for the Administrative Tools folder not to be displayed. Other options include displaying it as a folder that opens when you click it and displaying it as a submenu that contains shortcuts for the items in the folder.

Once you start the Performance snap-in, it automatically switches you to System Monitor and begins monitoring your system using three very common counters: Pages/sec, a memory counter; Avg Disk Queue, a physical disk counter, and %Processor, a processor counter. These three counters actually offer a good look at the overall performance of the three main sources of hardware performance bottlenecks on a system. The Performance snap-in with the System Monitor active is shown in Figure 22.9.

The System Monitor display consists of the following elements:

- A toolbar with capabilities such as copying and pasting counters, clearing counters, adding counters, and so on. The toolbar buttons provide the quickest way to configure monitoring, but you can also use a shortcut menu (just right-click on the display) to add counters and configure properties.

Figure 22.9

*The basic System
Monitor window.*

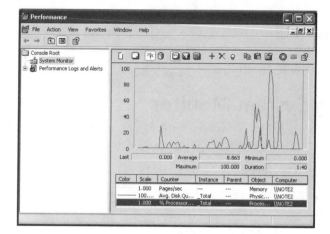

- The System Monitor node, which is the utility being described here.

- The Performance Logs and Alerts node, a utility for logging performance over time and having Windows alert you when performance thresholds are crossed. This utility is covered later in the chapter.

- The Graph View where counter values are displayed as graph lines. You can vary the line style, width, and color of these lines. You can also change the color of the window and of the chart within the window.

- A Timer Bar that moves across the graph indicates the passing of each update interval. Regardless of the update interval, the view shows up to 100 samples. System Monitor compresses log data as necessary to fit it in the display. For example, if there are 1,000 samples, the display might show every tenth sample.

- A Value Bar, where you see the last, minimum, maximum, and average values for the counter that is currently selected. The value bar also shows a Duration value that indicates the total elapsed time displayed in the graph (based on the update interval).

- A legend showing the selected counters and associated data such as the computer name, parent object, and instances.

Selecting Performance Counters

The default System Monitor display automatically graphs three of the more commonly used counters for major system objects, but you can still add hundreds of different counters on dozens of objects to the display. You can add counters to the current display, or you can clear the current counters and create a new counter set. To do this, just click the New Counter Set button on the toolbar.

To add a counter to the display, use the following procedure:

1. On the System Monitor toolbar, click the Add button (a plus sign) to open the Add Counters dialog box (see Figure 22.10). You can also open this dialog box by right-clicking anywhere in the graph view and choosing the Add Counters command or by simply pressing Ctrl+I.

FIGURE 22.10

Adding counters to a System Monitor display.

2. If you want to monitor a remote computer, make sure the Select Counters from Computer option is selected and type the full network path to the computer (for example, \\computername). Monitoring a remote computer is a great way to make sure that the overhead created by the graphical display of the System Monitor itself is not included in the performance results being graphed.

Tip

You can launch multiple instances of the Performance snap-in. Each open version of System Monitor can be configured to monitor a different computer on the network. Many people dedicate a computer to running multiple instances of System Monitor to track the performance of various servers or workstations on their network.

3. From the Performance Object list, choose the object that you want to monitor. Major objects include Memory, Processor, Networking, and Physical Disk.

4. Once you select an object, you must make sure you choose the correct instance of that object to display. For many objects, the instance won't matter so much (for some, you cannot choose an instance at all). For other objects such as Physical Disk the instance indicates which disk drive on your system will be monitored.

5. Once you have chosen an object and an instance of that object, you must choose the counters you want to display. When you first select an object, System Monitor automatically chooses the counter that is most commonly used for that object and it is usually a pretty good choice. Often, the default counter represents the overall performance of a particular object. Choose a counter from the list by clicking it once.

6. If you need a description of the counter, click the Explain button. This opens a separate dialog box that includes a description of the currently selected counter, as shown in Figure 22.11. Select another counter without closing the Explain Text dialog box and the explanation changes to match the new counter.

FIGURE 22.11

Getting a description of a counter.

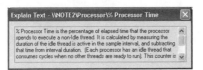

7. After you have decided on a counter, click Add to add the counter to your graph.

8. The Add Counters button remains open so that you can add additional counters. When you are finished, click Close to return to your graph, which will already be displaying performance data from the selected counters.

> **Tip**
>
> Although you can include any number of counters to your display, it is best to keep the number to a minimum just to make the display easier to read. If you want to record the performance of a number of different objects and counters, it is usually better to create a log (described later in this chapter).

Table 22.2 lists many of the most important objects in System Monitor along with some of the more useful counters for each. The default counter for each object is also noted. Note that this is not a complete list of available objects and counters; this is a minimum list of items you should monitor to get a good picture of the performance of your hardware.

Table 22.2   Major Objects and Counters in System Monitor

Object	Counter	What to watch for
Logical Disk	%Free Space	This counter shows the free space on a drive. Typically, you should watch for it to fall below about 10% to 15%.
	% Disk Time	This counter shows the amount of time the disk is busy servicing read and write requests. Watch for it to stay above 90%, indicating that the disk may not be fast enough or that there may not be enough memory on your system. Low memory results in large amounts of disk activity as more paging must take place.
Physical Disk	Disk Reads/sec Disk Writes/sec	These counter values can be tricky to read. For the most part, you should watch for any drastic changes in these values over time, which often indicates a low memory situation, as described above.
	Current Disk Queue Length	This counter represents the number of requests outstanding on the disk drive at the time the data is collected. Higher requests often mean that the disk cannot keep up with demand. Compare this value to the baseline you have established. As with other disk situations, this can indicate a disk or memory problem.
Memory	Available Bytes	This counter represents the number of bytes available at the time the data is collected. If this value falls below around 4MB, it may indicate a memory bottleneck.
	Pages/sec	This counter represents the number of memory pages written to disk in a second. It is usually recommended that this value remain below 20 pages/sec. Higher values could indicate not enough memory.
Paging File	%Usage	This counter represents the amount of the paging file currently being used. Watch for it to rise frequently above 70%. Consistently high values could indicate not enough memory.
Processor	%Processor Time	This counter represents the percentage of time that the processor spends on nonidle threads. Watch for it to rise often above 85%, which could indicate that a processor bottleneck.
	Interrupts/sec	This counter measures the average rate at which the processor receives hardware interrupts. A dramatic increase in this value that is not accompanied by an increase in system activity often indicates that another hardware device (such as a network card or disk controller) is sending spurious interrupts.

22

PERFORMANCE
MONITORING,
LOGS, ALERTS

Viewing Your Graph

Once you have selected the counters for System Monitor to measure, System Monitor begins graphing the results of those measurements immediately. An example of a graph is shown in Figure 22.12. As you watch, the timer bar will move from left to right across the screen, trailing behind it a separate line for each of the selected counters. Each line is color-coded and the colors are indicated in the legend at the bottom of the graph, along with other information on the counter, such as the scale of measurement, instance being measured, the counter's object, and the computer being measured.

FIGURE 22.12

Viewing a graph in System Monitor.

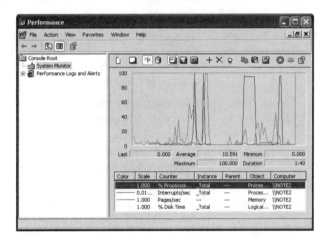

Just above the legend, the Value Bar shows the last measurement of the selected counter, along with the minimum, maximum, and average measurements recorded. Also shown is the duration of measure.

There are a number of ways to affect the display, all of which are represented by buttons on the toolbar. The available commands for working with the System Monitor display are as follows:

- New Counter Set—This command removes all active counters from the list and clears the display. Use this command to "start over" and select a new batch of counters to monitor.

- Clear Display—This command clears the display but does not remove any of the counters. The timer bar starts over at the left side of the display and continues to graph the counters.

- View Current Activity—This command works as a toggle with the View Log Data command (described next). Only one of these two views can be active at a time.

22

PERFORMANCE
MONITORING,
LOGS, ALERTS

View Current Activity displays a chart of the current counters' measurements and is the default view for the display.

- View Log Data—Use this command to have System Monitor display activity from a saved log file instead of activity currently being monitored. You will learn how to create a log file later in this chapter. Once you open and view log activity using this command, it works very much the same as viewing current activity.

- View Graph/Histogram/Report—There are three basic ways that System Monitor can display current or logged activity: as a graph (the default view that you've seen already in this chapter); as a histogram (or bar chart); and as a report (which shows aggregate values much like those seen in the value bar of the graph display). These three commands work as a three-way toggle; only one view can be selected at a time. All three views are shown side-by-side in Figure 22.13.

FIGURE 22.13

Different views in System Monitor include graph (top), histogram (middle), and report (bottom).

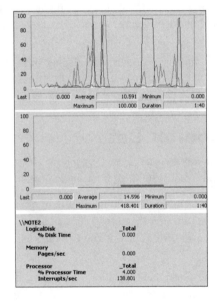

- Add—With this command, discussed previously in the chapter, you can add counters to the display.

- Delete—This command deletes the counter currently selected in the legend from the display.

- Highlight—This command draws attention to a particular counter's data by replacing the colored chart line with a thick line. For white or light-colored backgrounds, this line is black; for other backgrounds, this line is white.

- Copy Properties—This command copies properties of the currently selected counter to the clipboard in HTML format. You can paste this information into a Web page (or other document capable of displaying HTML), and the page will then include a working graph that displays those counters. You can also create a Web page from a System Monitor display by right-clicking the display and choosing Save As from the shortcut menu or pasting the information into another version of System Monitor.

- Paste Counter List—Use this command to paste the counter properties you have copied to the clipboard from another instance of Performance Monitor.

- Properties—This command opens a Properties dialog box for System Monitor, which allows you to configure many program options. These options are covered later in the chapter.

- Freeze Display—This command freezes the display of all counters, giving you time to look at the graphs without them being written over. Data is still collected while the display is frozen.

- Update Data—This command manually updates the display and is typically used to update a frozen display.

- Help—This command starts the Help feature for System Monitor.

Printing System Monitor Data

System Monitor does not include a way to print a graph or report. However, there are a few ways you can print information from System Monitor, including the following:

- Copy the current screen to your clipboard as an image file by pressing Alt+Prt Scr. Next, start a graphics program (the Paint program that comes with Windows will do) and paste the image from the clipboard. You can then use the graphics program to print the image.

- Save the System Monitor control as an HTML file by right-clicking the System Monitor display and choosing the Save command. You can then open the HTML file and print it from your Web browser.

- Import a performance log file you have created in comma-separated (.csv) or tab-separated (.tsv) format into Microsoft Excel, Word, or Access (or any program that handles such files) and print from that program.

Setting System Monitor Properties

A number of general program options are available for you to configure in System Monitor. All of these options are configured using the System Monitor Properties dialog box. To get to this dialog box, click the Properties button on the System Monitor toolbar or right-click anywhere in the display and choose Properties from the shortcut menu. The available options are spread across five tabs, each of which is discussed in the following sections.

General Properties

The General tab, shown in Figure 22.14, lets you configure a number of basic options for how System Monitor displays data. These options include the following:

- View—Whether the default view in System Monitor is a graph, histogram, or report.
- Display Elements—Whether the legend, value bar, and toolbar are shown in the System Monitor display.
- Report and Histogram Data—How much data reports and histograms display. Usually, it is best to leave this setting at the default value. Increasing the data displayed can slow the performance of your system and thus skew System Monitor results.
- Appearance—Whether 3D elements such as the recessed display of the graph are shown.
- Border—Places a border around the graph display.
- Sample Automatically Every—Specifies whether System Monitor should sample data periodically based on the value that you enter.
- Allow Duplicate Counter Instanced—Specifies whether to display an index for each instance name to make each instance on the system unique.

FIGURE 22.14

Configuring general properties in System Monitor.

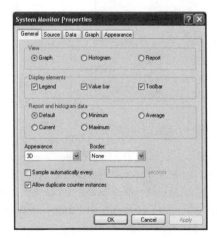

Source Properties

The Source tab (see Figure 22.15) lets you specify the source of data for the current display in System Monitor. By default, the activity being currently measured on the computer is displayed. You can specify that log file data be used instead. Select the Log Files option and choose a log file from the list to display. Click the Add button to browse your computer for log files to add to the list. Finally, you can use the Database option to display performance data stored in a database. To do this, you must select a valid Open Database Connectivity (OBDC) Database Source Name (DSN) and the particular log set for the data you want to display.

Tip

If you are working with a log file that is currently collecting data, you need to click the Select Time Range button and keep moving the Time Range bar to the right to update the display with new samples.

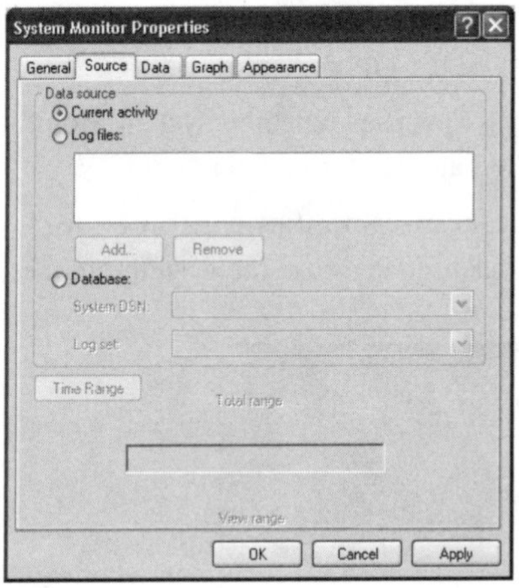

FIGURE 22.15

Configuring source properties in System Monitor.

Data Properties

The Data tab (see Figure 22.16) lets you control the index lines used for each counter currently being displayed. For each counter, you can specify the color, width, style, and scale of the displayed line. Varying styles and colors helps you group common counters and differentiate between counters when a large number of them are displayed.

FIGURE 22.16

Configuring data properties in System Monitor.

Graph Properties

The Graph tab (see Figure 22.17) is used to control the display of the graph in System Monitor. You can give the graph itself and the vertical axis a name, toggle the display of vertical and horizontal grids, and choose whether to display the vertical scale numbers on the graph. If you display the vertical scale numbers, you can also specify the minimum and maximum values of that scale.

FIGURE 22.17

Configuring graph properties in System Monitor.

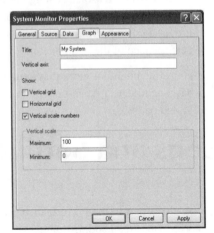

Appearance Properties

The Appearance tab (see Figure 22.18) is used to set the color for various elements in System Monitor, including the graph background, control background, text, grid, and time bar. You can also change the font used in the System Monitor display.

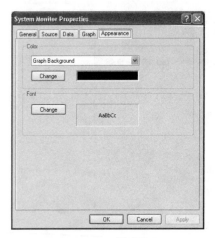

FIGURE 22.18

Configuring appearance properties in System Monitor.

Baseline Your System and Examine Performance Periodically

After becoming familiar with System Monitor and the process of configuring graphs and logs, you are ready to start monitoring. The first thing you will want to do is establish a baseline of performance.

A baseline is a measurement of performance over a reasonably long period of time that encompasses various times during which a computer is used. The baseline is a good indicator of how a computer's resources are used during periods of normal activity. It also gives you a good idea of the normal performance of the computer.

Once you have created a baseline, you can then monitor current system activity occasionally and compare the results to your baseline to detect when bottlenecks are developing or to watch for long-term changes in usage patterns.

Configuring Logs and Setting Alerts

The Performance Logs and Alerts tool, also a part of the Performance snap-in, provides a more sophisticated way to monitor performance than adding counters to System Monitor and watching a graph. Performance Logs and Alerts provides the following three basic services:

- You can create a counter log that logs the performance of specified counters over time. A counter log measures data in much the same way as System Monitor but logs the data to a comma or tab-separated value file instead of displaying it. The log file can be opened later in System Monitor to view a graph of performance or to be imported into a program like Excel or Access.

- You can create a trace log that records detailed system and application events to a log file when certain performance events occur. This differs from counter logs in that performance is not measured at regular intervals but only in response to events. The data is measured from start to finish, rather than sampled in the manner of System Monitor. The built-in Windows kernel trace data provider supports tracing system data; if other data providers are available, developers can configure logs with those providers as appropriate. A parsing tool is required to interpret the trace log output.

- You can create alerts that send messages or trigger other events when they detect that a specified performance threshold has been crossed.

Logging is typically used for detailed analysis and record-keeping purposes and for establishing a baseline of performance. Retaining and analyzing log data collected over a period of several months can be helpful for capacity and upgrade planning if you are administering computers on a network.

22

PERFORMANCE MONITORING, LOGS, ALERTS

> **Note**
>
> Trace logging is a fairly complicated subject and is typically used in conjunction with third-party trace providers and not on a simple desktop system. For that reason, this chapter does not include a detailed description of trace logging and instead focuses on the tasks of creating a counter log and configuring alerts.

Creating a Counter Log

The Performance Logs and Alerts tool appears as a node in the Performance snap-in (see Figure 22.19). Inside this node, separate folders contain all counter logs, trace logs, and alerts configured on the system. Selecting any of these folders displays a list of available logs or alerts in the details pane.

To create a new counter log, use the following procedure:

1. Right-click the Counter Logs folder.

2. From the shortcut menu, choose New Log Settings to create a new log with blank settings. You can also choose New Log Settings From to create a new log based on settings from an existing log.

3. The New Log Settings dialog box appears. Type in a name for the new log file and click OK.

FIGURE 22.19

Performance Logs and Alerts.

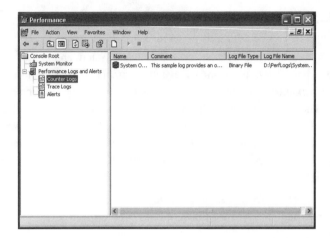

Once you create and name for the new log, a dialog box appears that contains three tabs: General, Log Files, and Schedule. When you modify the properties of an existing log (by right-clicking the log and choosing Properties), the same dialog box opens, and the same tabs are used to configure the log's properties. These tabs are discussed in the following sections.

Once a log has been created, it is started automatically. You can stop the logging process by selecting the log in the Performance Logs and Alerts window and clicking the Stop button on the toolbar. You can use the techniques described for using System Monitor previously to view a graphical display of the log data while it is running or after you have finished collecting data.

Setting General Log Properties

The General tab (see Figure 22.20) is where you will do most of the configuring of your log. Use the Current Log File Name field to change the location and name of your log file. The Counters list shows all of the counters currently set to be monitored by the log. Use the Add Objects button to pick an object for which you want to include all counters to the log. Use the Add Counters button to open a dialog much like the one used in System Monitor that lets you choose specific counters to add to your log. The General tab also holds commands for specifying the interval at which counters are sampled (the default is fifteen seconds) and for entering a username by which the log can log onto a system.

Setting Log Files Properties

The Log Files tab (see Figure 22.21) lets you specify settings governing the format of the log file. You can set the following options on the Log Files tab:

FIGURE 22.20

Setting General Log Properties.

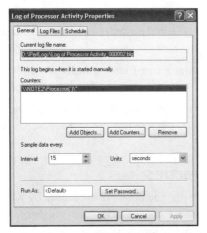

FIGURE 22.21

Setting Log Files Properties.

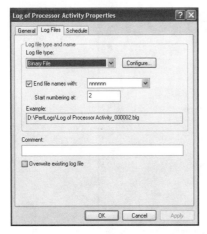

22

PERFORMANCE
MONITORING,
LOGS, ALERTS

1. The Log File Type option lets you choose the format for the log file. A log can be recorded in several different formats, including the following:

   - Comma or tab-separated text files, which provide the ability to import the log file into a spreadsheet or database program

   - Binary file, which can only be read by System Monitor (this is the default choice)

   - Circular binary file, which records data until the file reaches a user-defined size limit and then starts over

   - SQL Database

2. The End File Names With and Start Numbering At options make Windows automatically generate file names based on a convention you specify. Files are named

by appending the title of the log you supply on the General tab with the ending you specify and then an incremental number. An example of the naming convention is shown.

3. The Comment field lets you enter a free-form comment to help you better identify the log file.

4. The Overwrite Existing Log File option lets Windows create a new file even if one by the same name already exists. Disable this option to preserve your existing log files.

Setting Schedule Properties

The Schedule tab (see Figure 22.22) lets you create the schedule by which the log will run. You can specify when the log starts, when it stops, and whether to start a new log or run a custom program when the log file is finished.

FIGURE 22.22

Setting Schedule Properties.

Configuring an Alert

With the alerting function, you can define a counter value that will trigger actions such as sending a network message, running a program, or starting a log. Alerts are useful if you are not actively monitoring a particular counter threshold value but want to be notified when it exceeds or falls below a specified value so that you can investigate and determine the cause of the change. You might want to set alerts based on established performance baseline values for your computer.

You create an alert in much the same way you create a new counter log, as shown in the following procedure:

1. Right-click the Alerts folder.

2. From the shortcut menu, choose Alert Settings to create a new alert with blank settings. You can also choose New Alert Settings From to create a new alert based on settings from an existing alert.

3. The New Alert Settings dialog box appears. Type in a name for the new alert and click OK.

Once you create and name the new alert, a dialog box appears that contains three tabs: General, Action, and Schedule. When you modify the properties of an existing alert (by right-clicking the alert and choosing Properties), the same dialog box opens and the same tabs are used to configure the alert's properties. These tabs are discussed in the following sections.

Setting General Alert Properties

The General tab (see Figure 22.23) is where you will do most of the configuring of your alert. Use the Comment field to enter a free-form comment that helps you identify the alert. The Counters list shows all of the counters currently set to be monitored by the alert. Use the Add button to open a dialog much like the one used in System Monitor that lets you choose specific counters to have the alert monitor. For each counter on the list, you can specify the value threshold that triggers an alert.

You can also set the interval at which counters are sampled (the default is five seconds) and enter a username by which the alert can logon to a system.

FIGURE 22.23

Setting General Alert Properties.

22

PERFORMANCE
MONITORING,
LOGS, ALERTS

Setting Action Properties

The Action tab (see Figure 22.24) lets you control what happens when an alert is triggered. Available actions include the following:

- Record an entry in the Windows application log. This action is the only one selected by default.

- Send a network message to another computer on the network. Enter the full path of the computer to which you want to send the message (for example, \\computer-name). The message that appears is a simple system dialog box (see Figure 22.25).

- Start a performance data log. This action automatically starts a preconfigured log whenever an alert is triggered and is a great way of setting up automatic system monitoring. The drop-down list shows all logs configured using the Performance Logs and Alerts tool.

- Run a custom program. You can browse your system for a program to run and use the Command Line Arguments button to specify how the program should run. You could use this, for example, to run a backup or virus check when certain thresholds are triggered.

FIGURE 22.24

Setting Action Properties.

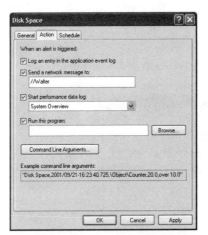

FIGURE 22.25

A network alert message.

Setting Schedule Properties

The Schedule tab (see Figure 22.26) lets you create the schedule by which the alert will run. You can specify when the alert starts, when it stops, and whether to start a new alert scan when the current alert scan is finished.

FIGURE 22.26

Setting Schedule Properties.

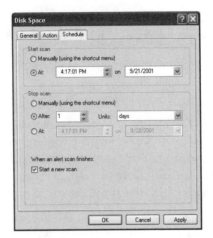

Command Line Performance Monitoring Tools

In addition to the monitoring tools already discussed in this chapter, there are also some command-line options for monitoring a computer's performance. Most of these work in conjunction with the tools already discussed. The following commands are available to you:

- Logman—Manages and schedules performance counter and event trace log collections on local and remote systems. This command is particularly useful for creating, starting, stopping, and managing logs from batch files and on remote computers.

- Relog—Extracts performance counter data into a comma or tab-separated file from other log file formats. This is useful if you need to pull performance data into a spreadsheet or other document from a file that is in binary format.

- Tracerpt—Processes trace logs or real-time data from trace providers and allows you to generate trace analysis reports and CSV (comma-delimited) files for the events generated

- `Typeperf`—Displays real-time data from System Monitor counters in a command window. You specify the counters and the update interval in a command-line string; `TypePerf` returns the values of the requested counters at the specified intervals and displays them in the command prompt window until you stop it by pressing any key.

To get details on running any of these commands, just enter the command followed by `/?`. At the command prompt, Windows provides a complete command reference to assist you in using these commands.

Summary

As you can see, there are a number of factors involved in a computer's performance, including hardware, configuration, and software. Windows provides a number of utilities for improving your computer's performance. These range from the more mundane tools like Disk Cleanup, which helps free hard disk space by deleting unnecessary files, to the more interesting System Configuration utility, which you can use to exert fine control over your Windows startup routine.

In addition to the utilities used to improve overall performance, Windows also includes three utilities for monitoring performance and determining where performance bottlenecks may occur on your computer. Task Manager provides a real-time snapshot of current activity. System Monitor lets you choose from literally hundreds of different counters that represent the various hardware and software components on your computer and then graph measurements of those measurements in various ways. Performance Logs and Alerts provides a way to log performance data over time for later study and to have your computer alert you when performance thresholds are crossed.

Be Paranoid: Disaster Recovery Planning

CHAPTER 23

IN THIS CHAPTER

- Back Up Important Data!   *588*
- Using the Automated System Recovery Wizard   *590*
- Using the Last Known Good Configuration Feature   *595*
- Booting into Safe Mode   *596*
- Using the Recovery Console   *599*
- Using Device Driver Rollback   *604*
- How to Use System Restore to Recover Previous Settings   *607*

It does pay to be paranoid when you work with computers. Although we now have PCs that can talk and be updated via the Internet, they are not yet perfect. Because of this, taking precautions to protect the data that you have entrusted to your Windows XP Professional workstation is important. In this chapter, we will discuss methods for accomplishing this. I will remind you regularly to back up your system, and I have included an entire chapter devoted to using Windows XP's own Backup Utility. In addition to regular backups, we will focus mainly on the many other features of Windows XP available for when you are in a fix (or, should I say, in need of a fix!). These features are as follows:

- Automated System Recovery
- Using Last Known Good Configuration
- Booting into Safe Mode
- Using the Recovery Console
- Using Device Driver Rollback
- Using the System Restore Utility

I suggest that you read this entire chapter even if you are acquainted with previous versions of the Windows operating systems. For example, in Windows NT, you could create an Emergency Repair Disk (ERD), and in Windows 98 you could create an Emergency Startup Disk. In Windows XP, the available recover options that you can make use of are a little different. If you keep important data on your local workstation (as opposed to a networked drive regularly backed up by a corporate server), then reading this chapter just may save your behind, so to speak!

It is also important that you understand the differences between how the features in the preceding list work. Although you may think that all you need to do is use the Device Driver Rollback feature to fix a renegade device driver—that isn't true. This feature is useful if you have *replaced* a driver, and a copy of the previous driver is available on the system to replace the newer one. Other features some people get confused about are the Automated System Restore and the System Recovery utilities. These sound similar, but they are entirely separate utilities performing very specific and different functions. Read this chapter thoroughly if keeping your computer up and running with a good safety net means anything to you!

Back Up Important Data!

Chapter 2, "Before You Install or Upgrade," emphasized that before you attempt to perform an upgrade to Windows XP, you should first perform a backup of the system or at least the data files. Back up those files as well as any other files you may need to restore the system in the case of a problematic failure. Although modern PCs can be very reliable, anything can happen that may cause a loss of data. This is especially true for users of Windows XP. Many redundant capabilities like the feature called *redundant array of inexpensive disks* (RAID) are not often found on a personal computer. These expensive techniques are usually reserved for high-end servers.

> ### Tip
>
> **Redundant Array of Inexpensive Disks (RAID).** This term was conceived back when large computer servers used much more expensive disks than the ones installed on today's PCs. Now, the term stands for Redundant Array of Independent Disks, since they aren't necessarily inexpensive anymore, and RAID is not just a single technology. It comes in all sizes and types. For example, disk striping—which uses a set of disks as if they were a single disk and divides up disk writes and reads so that data gets stored in "chunks" across multiple disks—can improve read or write performance, since more than one disk is at work storing a smaller portion of the input and output (I/O).
>
> Other techniques were developed over the years, such as adding a parity stripe to allow for the continued operation and recovery if a single member of a striped disk set was lost. Additionally, disk striping is referred to as *RAID level 0*. Disk mirroring is known as *Raid level 1* and is simply a technique where the disk controller writes the same information to two or more disks. This way, if one disk becomes defective, the other has a complete copy. There are other RAID levels, and readers are encouraged to research the topic further. Several Web sites explain the basic RAID techniques in use today.

23

DISASTER RECOVERY PLANNING

After you have upgraded to Windows XP, regular backups should still be part of your regular maintenance activities. In Chapter 21, "Using Backup on Windows XP," you will find all the details you need to know about how the backup utility functions on Windows XP, and how to create backup jobs. That chapter also contains the steps for restoring data from a backup should it become necessary.

Keep in mind that having a good backup can also mean storing the backup offsite. For example, if you operate a home business and the data you keep on your Windows XP computer is important to you (for example, accounts receivable records), then you should conduct regular backups and store them somewhere else such as a bank safety deposit box. You don't have to do this every day, just as you don't have to enter accounting information every day. In most small businesses this is done in batches. After you have entered a significant amount of data, back up the system and store the backup file in a safe place!

Using the Automated System Recovery Wizard

In previous editions of Windows NT, an Emergency Repair Disk (ERD) was used to store portions of the Registry and other important information that could be used in the event of a disaster to help recover your system. Of course, you also needed to create a backup of your system disk partition on a regular basis to use with the ERD if you wanted to be able to completely recover from a disaster.

In Windows XP, this feature is incorporated into the Backup utility, where you can create not only a floppy disk (what we used to call the ERD), but also a backup of the local system partition. Now, the floppy disk is called the Automated System Recovery (ASR) disk.

> **Caution**
>
> We are discussing the Automated System Recovery feature of Windows XP at the start of this chapter because you should be fully aware of this feature and make absolutely sure that you update your ASR disk and back up your system on a regular basis. This does *not* mean that using the ASR disk and a backup of your system partition is the best method to use for a system recovery! However, as a regular maintenance chore, it should be on your list. Usually you can recover simple problems by using techniques such as booting into Safe Mode and the Last Known Good Settings feature, which is described later in this chapter. However, those techniques may or may not work. An ASR disk and a good backup of the system partition are good insurance.

Creating the Automated System Recovery Diskette and Backup of Your System Partition

There is a two-part process to using the ASR feature, which you can use to make a special floppy diskette and then make a backup of your system partition so that you can restore your system. In this section, you will learn how to create these two important items. In the section following, you will also work through restoring your system partition in case a dire emergency should make this a necessity.

To begin the process, use the following steps:

1. Click Start, All Programs, Accessories, System Tools, and then select Backup.
2. If the wizard is enabled, click the check box to disable the wizard and repeat Step 1. When the Backup utility reappears, you will see a display similar to that shown in Figure 23.1.

FIGURE 23.1

With the Backup Utility, you can create a floppy disk and a backup of the system partition for an emergency recovery.

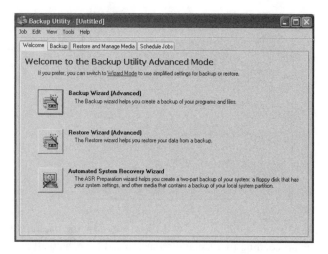

3. Click on the last button, Automated System Recovery Wizard. The first dialog box of the wizard will appear (see Figure 23.2), telling you to use the Backup Wizard after you create the ASR disk in order to have a complete snapshot of your system. Click Next to continue.

FIGURE 23.2

The wizard warns you that the ASR disk is not enough, so you also will need to create a backup of any partitions that contain data or application files.

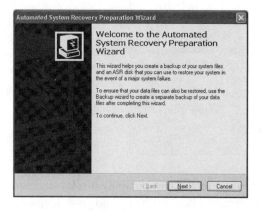

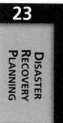

4. In the next dialog box, you are prompted for the location to use for creating the backup of the system disk. You may use a tape drive or another disk partition. You can take the default or use the Browse button shown in Figure 23.3 to select another source. For this example, we will use a disk partition, which is faster and can be copied later to tape. Click Next to continue.

5. In the next dialog box, the Automated System Recovery Preparation Wizard tells you that it is ready to create the disk. Click Finish.

FIGURE 23.3

The wizard will prompt you for a location to create the backup of your system disk.

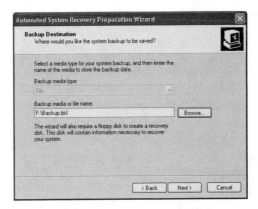

6. The Backup Progress dialog box will show you how the backup of the system disk partition is proceeding by displaying the elapsed time, as well as estimated time to completion. Under the field labeled Processing, the files being backed up at this time pass by quickly. See Figure 23.4 for an example of this.

FIGURE 23.4

You can watch the progress of the backup of your system partition in the Backup Progress dialog box.

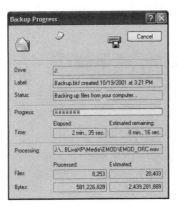

7. When the backup is complete, the Backup utility displays a dialog box asking you to insert a 1.44 MB formatted floppy diskette into your floppy disk drive. Information necessary to start the recovery process, using the backup that was just created, will be stored on this floppy diskette.

8. A dialog box comes up, stating that ASR files needed for the recovery are being copied to the floppy diskette. Finally, a dialog box tells you to store this floppy away in a safe place, just like you did your Windows NT Emergency Repair Disk!

9. Click Close on the Backup Progress dialog box to close the Backup Utility.

You have now created the necessary backup and ASR diskette needed to restore your system in an emergency. However, as suggested earlier, this is only for a severe emergency. Try the methods that follow in the next few sections first.

Restoring a System Using the Automated System Recovery Method

Assuming you have kept your backups up-to-date, as well as your ASR diskette, it is possible to restore the system partition when all other methods fail. Again, if your problem is simply a device driver or other minor problem, use the techniques described later in this chapter to recover your system. ASR is a last resort! This chapter discusses it early on to ensure that you read about it and not to depend on other simpler methods during a crisis situation.

Restart the Windows XP Professional Startup Procedure

To start the recovery process, place the ASR floppy diskette in the floppy disk drive and boot the system. Be sure to boot from the original Windows XP Professional CD. Watch closely as you boot the computer. It should simply ask you to press any key to boot from the CD-ROM. When Windows Setup starts running, it states at the beginning of the process to press the F2 key to start the Automated System Recovery Process.

This message comes directly after the Setup program asks you to press F6 if you want to load a third-party SCSI (small computer systems interface) or RAID disk driver. Press F2, and you will be notified (see the bottom of the display) that the ASR process has begun. Windows Setup will then continue. Setup will format the system partition then start to install a *minimal* set of Windows XP files. During this Setup procedure, you won't have to answer any of the questions from the normal Setup procedure. This is because the backup you are that was creating from your system will be used to restore important files and settings after this mini-setup is completed. System Restore reads the information it needs from the files it has stored when you created the ASR backup and floppy diskette. Be patient! You are going to start from scratch and then restore the backup. The Setup process will proceed at a faster pace than a normal Setup or Upgrade because only a subset of the operating system files are being restored, so you will not be prompted for configuration information.

> **Tip**
>
> If you are curious about partitions and how they are formatted, or you would like to learn about the normal Setup procedure, see Chapter 3, "Installing and Upgrading Windows XP." Reading this chapter again can help keep you informed about the procedures that are occurring when you use ASR.

After Setup has restored important system files to the newly formatted partition, it will then reboot. Then it will continue with the Setup process, as a normal Setup would proceed. You will see the regular screen showing that the Setup procedure is Installing Windows.

Finally, the Setup process will hand off the task of restoring your system to ASR. Be patient, this takes time! The Automatic System Recovery Wizard will present a dialog box stating it has taken over and will continue with the full restoration of your system. A dialog box titled Restore Progress will pop up, showing the progress of the restoration of the system files that you backed up when you initially used ASR to create a backup. This dialog box looks just like the one shown in Figure 23.4 above, except that this dialog box indicates that a restore process is being performed. After the restore is complete, the system will then reboot.

When the restore is finished, the system will reboot, and you should be able to use it just as if nothing had happened. Keep in mind that if you store data on the system partition (such as in My Documents), only the files saved when you created the ASR backup and floppy diskette will be available now. Any applications installed after the ASR utility was run will also have to be restored. For this reason, I strongly suggest the following steps be taken:

1. As mentioned already, use ASR as *a last resort*! First, try the other methods described later in this chapter, especially if you use the default installation and store data files on your system partition!

2. Use ASR in place of your regular system partition backup so that it will be performed on a more frequent basis—that is, if you decide to keep your data files on the same partition that you use for the system.

3. Use the Backup utility, described in Chapter 21, "Using Backup on Windows XP," to create a backup job that selectively performs a backup on just your data files, and schedule it to run every night! Don't forget that ASR does not backup those other partitions, just your system partition, so be sure to perform regular backups of important data partitions!

Using the Last Known Good Configuration Feature

If your system doesn't boot, there can be a number of reasons. Perhaps you didn't heed the warning that most books give you when they caution you to be careful when you make changes to important system files such as the Registry. Perhaps you installed an unsigned device driver that makes the system unstable. The first step in trying to boot the system should be to use the Last Known Good Configuration feature available during boot time.

This feature can also be helpful if your computer does boot but exhibits strange behavior, which is another indication that a configuration setting was incorrectly modified or a driver isn't working like it should.

> **Note**
>
> Using the Last Known Good Configuration feature will restore Registry settings, as well as driver files, if you have recently installed new drivers. It will not help you if a driver file has become corrupted and there is no previous version. If this is the case, you should consider booting into Safe Mode and replacing the file; or if the situation is not recoverable using that method, consider using ASR.

The Last Known Good Configuration feature will restore your registry settings to a successful state so your machine can boot to a usable configuration. This is accomplished by using the last known stored registry settings that the system knows will perform a successful boot. It will also, if possible, restore device drivers you may have replaced since the last time the system was booted successfully. Hence, if the system doesn't boot normally, try using the Last Known Good Configuration feature as your first step to correct the problem.

> **Note**
>
> Configuration issues aren't alone in preventing a system from booting. An important system file may become corrupt, perhaps due to a disk drive error or some other similar event. In that case, using the Last Known Good Configuration feature may not work to boot the system. Consider this method as the first step in trying to recover your system. If it does not work, then proceed onto using other methods such as booting into Safe Mode or using System Restore.

When resorting to the Last Known Good Configuration feature, use the following steps:

1. Shut down the computer by clicking on Start and then Shut Down. Select the Restart option when the Shut Down Windows dialog box pops up. This option can be found in the What Do You Want the Computer to Do? drop-down menu. Click OK to shut down and restart the computer.

2. If the computer is already powered off, power it on to start the boot process.

3. When the Please Select the Operating System to Start menu is displayed, after the power-on self-test (POST), press the F8 key.

4. You will see a display with many choices, defaulting to Start Windows Normally. Use your arrow keys to move to the entry that says Last Known Good Configuration (Your Most Recent Settings that Worked), and then press the Enter key.

5. You will be returned to the Please Select the Operating System to Start menu, but at the bottom of the screen, you should see the text Last Known Good Configuration (Your Most Recent Settings that Worked). Select Microsoft Windows XP Professional from the menu (which should be selected by default, unless you are using your computer in a multi-boot scenario and another is selected by default), and then press the Enter key.

When the computer has rebooted, log on and begin your troubleshooting efforts. For example, what was the last driver you installed? What was the last configuration change you made? You may want to experiment to determine what caused the previous system instability.

Booting into Safe Mode

If your computer encounters a problem during the boot process and hangs up or it just won't boot normally, then you may need to use the capability provided by Windows XP to boot into Safe Mode. When you boot into Safe Mode only, standard drivers such as a VGA monitor driver are installed, as well as only those other drivers needed to boot the system. The purpose of Safe Mode is to allow you to boot the computer to fix a problem. You may not have access to all of your devices or their advanced features, but Safe Mode can be very useful for fixing minor problems.

For example, you may make some application or hardware driver setting changes and then attempt to reboot your system, only to find that it no longer boots. In this kind of situation, boot into Safe Mode and undo the changes made.

You have several options when you boot into Safe Mode. First, you can undo the changes you made manually, which can come in handy if you have selected different options on a device's properties pages. Additionally, if you receive an error message when the system was previously booted stating that an important system file was corrupted, write down the name and location of this file. Then, after booting into Safe Mode, copy the file from the Windows XP setup installation CD to the correct system directory and then attempt to reboot the computer.

Making manual changes (for example, replacing files or changing configuration settings) should be performed by someone who is knowledgeable about the changes being made. You can do further damage to your system if you just start copying files of which you may not be certain.

Another alternative when you boot into Safe Mode is to use the System Restore utility, discussed later in this chapter, to revert your system to a point in time when you knew it operated correctly. You can then reevaluate the changes you made and try to determine the problem.

Keep in mind that when you boot into Safe Mode, you won't have all the capabilities that you do when booting the system normally. There will be limitations.

To boot into Safe Mode perform the steps described below, which are similar to those described in the previous section about booting Last Known Good Configuration. The are as follows:

1. Shut down the computer by clicking Start and then Shut Down. Select the Restart option when the Shut Down Windows dialog box pops up. This option can be found in the What Do You Want the Computer to Do? drop-down menu. Click OK to shut down and restart the computer.

2. If the computer is already powered off, power it on to start the boot process.

3. When the Please Select the Operating System to Start menu is displayed, after the power-on self-test (POST), press the F8 key.

4. You then will see a display that has many choices, defaulting to Start Windows Normally. You can then choose from the three Safe Mode options at the top of the menu. These are Safe Mode, Safe Mode with Networking, and Safe Mode with Command Prompt. Use your arrow keys to move to one of the menu items and press the Enter key.

5. You will be returned to the Please Select the Operating System to Start menu. At the bottom of the screen, you should see the text for the Safe Mode menu item you selected. Select Microsoft Windows XP Professional from the menu (which should be selected by default, unless you are using your computer in a multi-boot scenario and another is selected by default), and press the Enter key.

6. As the computer boots, you will see a list of the drivers it is loading, which may be helpful in your diagnostics efforts.

23

DISASTER RECOVERY PLANNING

7. When the computer has rebooted, log on and begin your troubleshooting efforts. For example, what was the last driver you installed? What was the last configuration change you made? Again, you may want to experiment to determine what caused the previous system instability.

In Figure 23.5 you can see the dialog box that will appear after you log onto the system in Safe Mode.

FIGURE 23.5

After you boot into Safe Mode and log into the system, a dialog box will inform you that you are in Safe Mode.

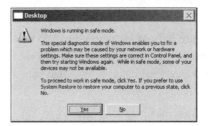

Notice that this dialog box will also let you know that if you can't fix the problem yourself while in Safe Mode, then you may want to use the System Restore utility, which is discussed later in this chapter. To continue working in Safe Mode (so that you can try to fix the problem yourself, which I recommend), if you made a specific configuration change and you may know how to change it back to a previous value, click Yes. If you want to use the System Restore utility, then click No.

At the boot menu choices for Safe Mode, you can also choose, as noted above, to boot into Safe Mode with networking components loaded. This will allow you to use the network if you need to in order to retrieve files you may need to replace or to perform other network tasks.

The other Safe Mode option allows you to boot into Safe Mode using only the Command Prompt. This option is a last resort when the other Safe Mode options won't work. It will boot the computer (if it can) into a state that allows you access only to the Command Prompt, with no networking or other programs available. You will still have to log into the system, however. When at the Command Prompt you can access other drives, such as your CD-ROM drive, which can be useful if you need to copy a system file from the Windows XP installation CD back to the appropriate system directory. This is not something that should be done unless you are knowledgeable about the specific problem and know what file or files are corrupted or missing.

To shut down or reboot the system while in Safe Mode with Command Prompt, use the Ctrl+Alt+Del key combination. This will bring up a window for shutting down the computer, since there will be no Start button.

Using the Recovery Console

The Recovery Console feature is not for the uninitiated! You need to have a very good understanding of how Windows XP works before using this feature. Additionally, in order to use Recovery Console, you need to either boot from the Windows XP installation CD or you can install the Recovery Console onto your workstation so that it shows up in the list of operating system choices presented by the BOOT.INI menu.

Starting Recovery Console from the Windows XP Installation CD

Some computers are set up to check the A: drive, then the CD-ROM drive, and finally the C: drive to look for a boot sector. Some will prompt you to ask if you want to boot from the CD-ROM. To boot from the Windows XP CD, you will need to know which method your computer uses. Place the CD in the CD-ROM drive and reboot the computer. If you see a prompt, respond to it.

> **Note**
>
> Can you boot from your CD? While most modern computers—those less than a few years old—have the capability of booting from a CD drive, you might have to configure your computer's BIOS settings to do so. When you initially power on your computer you'll probably see some message that tells you to press F1 or any key (or some other key) to enter SETUP. This SETUP is the setup mode you can use to change certain computer configuration settings. This includes the hard drives installed, and many other configurable items. While it's usually best to leave these items alone, you may find it necessary to change your BIOS settings when you install a new hard drive, for example.
>
> However, there is also a setting, usually called something like "BOOT" or "BOOT SEQUENCE." Look for this and see if it includes your CD-ROM drive in the list of bootable devices. If it doesn't, you can change this by following the directions and help that are supplied by your BIOS . Note that the CD-ROM drive that you boot from may not be the one you think it is. For example, if you install a CD-burner in your computer, it may be the bootable drive, depending on whether it is installed on a separate controller or whether it is the master or slave device on an IDE controller, for example.

The Windows XP Setup program will start. On the blue screen menu titled "Welcome to Setup" you will see three options:

- To set up Windows XP now, press Enter.
- To repair a Windows XP installation by using Recovery Console, press R.
- To quit Setup without installing Windows XP, press F3.

Select the second option to start the Recovery Console.

Select the Operating System

When the Recovery Console starts, you will see a black screen and a list of the operating systems (Windows XP) located on the partitions on your computer. It will show you a numbered list, each of which lists the drive letter and system root such as `D:\Windows`. Each of these listings, if more than one exists, is an entry from an installation you have performed on your computer. For example, you may choose to dual-boot between Windows 2000 and Windows XP. In this case, you would see the drive letter and the main folder that contains the system files for each installation. You would be prompted to enter a number corresponding to the installation with which you want to work with using Recovery Console. To exit the Recovery Console, simply press the Enter key without entering a number. Otherwise, enter the number, which will be 1 if you have installed only one copy of Windows XP and don't multi-boot several copies, and press the Enter key.

You will then be prompted to enter the Administrator password for this installation, which is for the local Administrator account stored on this computer—not the password for an Administrator account in a Windows domain.

Once you enter the correct password, you will get a prompt just like you would if you were using the Command Prompt. The default directory will be the drive and system root of the Windows installation you chose earlier.

What Can You Do with the Recovery Console?

While the Recovery Console interface looks much like an old-fashioned, MS-DOS computer, it does have some powerful capabilities. If you type HELP, a list of the commands becomes available, indicating all the standard commands available at the Command Prompt (see Chapter 13, "Command Prompt Tools"), as well as a few others. At the Recovery Console Command Prompt level, you can do such things as disable services, copy files from other drives such as your CD-ROM, and even format disk drives. You can even use the DISKPART command to create or delete partitions.

In effect, the Recovery Console provides an interface into your computer without loading all the code, such as background services and many device drivers. You can use simple commands to manipulate files, disks, and partitions on the system. If you want to begin using this tool, first understand the nature of the problem you want to correct. For example, you may have received an error message telling you that a particular file could not be found during the boot sequence. You can copy the file from the Installation CD using Recovery Console. Perhaps you made an error while trying to install another operating system over Windows XP, and now the master boot sector has become unusable for Windows XP.

Some of the basic helpful commands, other than the standard copy, delete, and type commands, include the following:

- DISKPART—As explained earlier, this is Windows XP's version of the old FDISK utility. You can create or delete partitions, or display partition table information using this command.

- FIXBOOT—Use the syntax FIXBOOT *<driveletter:>* to write a new boot sector if you suspect the boot sector was overwritten or corrupted by some other means.

- FIXMBR—This command, using the syntax FIXMBR *<driveletter:>* will repair the master boot record. If you omit the drive letter, then the default boot device will be used.

- BOOTCFG—This command has many options and variations for its syntax, based on how you use it. Use the HELP command for more information on the exact syntax. This command can be used to scan all of your disk partitions for Windows installations. You can then use the command to add a particular installation to the boot list that is presented when you boot Windows XP. You can list entries already in the BOOT.INI file, cycle through them, and select which one you wish to be the default.

- LISTSVC—This command will list all of the available services and drivers installed on this computer. This command is handy if you need to use one or both of the next two commands. The list is displayed in a page format to make it easier to view. In addition, you will see a column indicating whether the service is currently set to be disabled or enabled, and there will be a description for some services.

- DISABLE—This is an important command for disabling a service so that on the next boot, the service you selected will not start. If you have reconfigured your computer recently and enabled a service that is causing problems for the computer, you can use the syntax DISABLE *<servicename>* [*START_TYPE*] to keep the service from starting. The *START_TYPE* is optional and can be one of the following, depending on when and how the service starts: SERVICE_DISABLED, SERVICE_BOOT_START, SERVICE_SYSTEM_START, SERVICE_AUTO_START, or SERVICE_DEMAND_START. When you use the DISABLE command, it will print on the screen the current value for START_TYPE so that you can write down the

23

DISASTER RECOVERY PLANNING

information. This is so you can restore the service to the correct mode once you have tracked down the problem.

- ENABLE—Use this command to enable a service using the same syntax as the DIS-ABLE command.

- EXPAND—Use this command to expand a compressed file. You will note that the majority of files on the Windows XP Installation CD are stored in a compressed format. These files have a trailing underscore as part of the file extension. If you are copying a file from the Windows XP Installation CD to a system directory, use this command to expand the file to its normal state so that it will run correctly.

> **Caution**
>
> If you know what you are doing, you can use Recovery Console as a powerful means to get right to the problem and fix it. If you are unsure about what you want to accomplish, then using Recovery Console can be as dangerous as editing the Registry. You can literally destroy your operating system while using Recovery Console if you don't understand the actions you are taking!

To exit the Recovery Console, use the EXIT command or the Ctrl+Alt+Del key combination. To answer the question that is the title of this section, you can do just about anything by using Recovery Console, so be careful!

How to Install the Recovery Console on Your Computer

You can install a copy of the Recovery Console on your computer's hard disk so that you won't have to keep a copy of the Windows XP Installation CD around all the time. Once installed, Recovery Console shows up as an item in the boot menu selection when you start your computer. To install Recovery Console, use the following steps:

1. Place the Windows XP Installation CD in your computer's CD-ROM drive.

2. Click Start and then Run. In the Open field of the Run dialog box enter D:\i386\winnt32.exe/cmdcons. In this example, D: is the CD-ROM drive letter for your computer. Substitute the appropriate letter if you have multiple drives or partitions on your computer. A dialog box will display (see Figure 23.6) informing you that you are about to use 7MB of disk space to install the Recovery Console as a startup option on your computer.

FIGURE 23.6

The first dialog box will tell you that you are about to install the Recovery Console as a startup option on your computer.

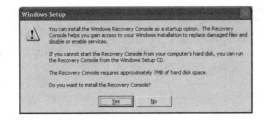

3. The Setup program will attempt to connect to the Windows Update Web site so that it can download any files that may be newer than those on the installation CD. If it cannot contact the Web site, then you will see a dialog box telling you that it was unable to reach the Windows update site. If you are not currently connected to the Internet, select the radio button labeled Skip This Step and Continue Installing Windows. You can also connect to your Internet provider and restart the installation of Recovery Console.

4. Figure 23.7 shows an example of the dialog box that Setup presents when it is able to connect to the Windows Update Web site and download new files.

FIGURE 23.7

By using the Windows Update Web site, you know your installation of Recovery Console contains the latest files.

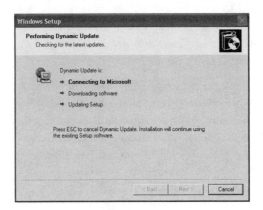

5. The next dialog box will show you the progress of files being copied from the Windows XP Installation CD to your hard disk. Finally, a dialog box explains that Recovery Console has been installed as a boot menu option on your computer.

> **Tip**
>
> If you are going to install the Recovery Console on your local computer, then another good idea is to also install the Windows XP installation files, found in the /i386 directory on the Installation CD. Since you may be using Recovery Console to correct a boot partition that is experiencing problems, I recommend creating an /i386 directory on another partition. This way, if you need to use Recovery Console to restore files that have become corrupted, they will be locally available and you won't need the Windows XP Installation CD.

Using Device Driver Rollback

Device drivers are software components that act as "middle men" between the operating system and a hardware device. The operating system makes standard system function calls, which the device driver intercepts. The driver then uses its own code to communicate with the hardware device and return any data resulting from the call to the operating system. A device driver is basically just an interface between the operating system and hardware. This makes it easy to write the operating system because Microsoft doesn't have to write code for every possible device you can hook up to your computer. Instead, vendors (and in some cases Microsoft) can write device drivers and when the hardware component is installed, the appropriate device driver is as well.

Microsoft tries to make installing drivers a simpler, safer process by using a technique called *Device Driver Signing.* However, even though a device driver may be digitally signed and work perfectly with the device for which it is intended, other problems can occur from loading a new device driver. For example, the new driver may interfere with system resources used by another driver already installed, and hence can cause system problems and instability.

What Is a Signed Device Driver?

A signed device driver is one that has passed rigorous testing procedures to ensure that it is compatible with Windows XP, and has been digitally signed. A digital signature, when used for device driver signing, is a public key encryption method used to ensure that the contents of a file have not been altered. For Windows XP, this means that the vendor must use tools provided by Microsoft to ensure that the driver will work properly with Windows XP, and then submit the driver files to Microsoft who will digitally sign the driver.

In order to qualify for inclusion on Windows XP's Hardware Compatibility List (HCL), the driver is submitted to the Windows Hardware Quality Labs (WHQL) at Microsoft. Before submitting the driver, the vendor can download various tools to perform testing themselves so that they can be reasonably sure that the driver will meet the specifications set forth by Microsoft. The device driver setup file (also known as the .inf file) will reference a catalog (CAT) file produced by Microsoft that contains a digital signature issued by Microsoft. If you look in a driver's .inf file, you can see an example of a CAT file under the file's [Version] section. The file you will see may look something like the following example:

```
CatalogFile=filename.cat
```

Using this syntax, the vendor can specify the filename for the catalog file in order to differentiate it from other vendor's catalog files.

The digital signature is created using a hashing algorithm on the device driver files, which is stored in the CAT file, and then cryptographic methods are used to create the digital signature for the CAT file. If you are curious about the specifics, you can find the CAT files in the %systemroot%\CatRoot directory. The actual .inf files can be found in the %systemroot%\Inf directory.

When it comes time to load a driver, the operating system will compare the hash codes found in the CAT file with the hashes it computes on the files for the device driver. In this way, the operating system can detect if a device driver has been altered and can warn the user. When you get that pop-up dialog box asking if you want to install an unsigned driver, be sure you know the vendor and from where you received the installation files!

23

DISASTER
RECOVERY
PLANNING

Using Device Driver Rollback

When Windows XP detects Plug-and-Play hardware it attempts to locate a driver and load it for the device. In most cases, this may be exactly what you want; it may also be the case that the driver XP selects doesn't work as well as a newer one you may have received from the manufacturer. For example, Windows can support most any kind of monitor or sound card on the market that adheres to certain standards. Yet, you may have a driver that enables other features that the standard driver installed by Plug and Play does not support. In this case, you can install the new driver.

It may also be the case that Windows XP does not have a driver for a device you are trying to install, and you must install a driver supplied by the manufacturer. Yet, as time goes on, the manufacturer of the device may update the driver used by the device you have installed or plan to install. In this case, you may later update the driver you initially installed to a newer version that you download from the vendor's Web site.

Sometimes, however, installing a new device driver can cause havoc on your system, especially if the new device driver tries to overwrite system files or other important files it should leave alone. If this happens to you, the Device Driver Rollback feature found in Windows XP removes a driver if it is causing problems after you install it. Device Driver Rollback will reinstall the previous driver that did work.

Tip

Use Device Driver Rollback as your first attempt to recover from a bad driver installation. You might be tempted to use System Restore, discussed later in this chapter. System Restore does keep track of driver files and can also be used to restore the system to a previous state. However, if you install the driver and make other changes to your system before you notice the instability of the device driver, using System Restore will not only undo the driver, but also the other changes you made. Therefore, always try to use Device Driver Rollback first, and if that fails, proceed to using the System Restore utility.

Figure 23.8 is an example of how to use the rollback feature for device drivers. The properties pages for the modem installed on the computer are shown. Under the Driver tab is a button labeled Roll Back Driver. Click this button and Windows XP will remove the current driver and reinstall the driver that was in place before the current one was used to update it.

A dialog box will inform you if there is no previous driver available on the system. Otherwise, the previously stored driver will be reinstalled.

FIGURE 23.8

Use the Roll Back Driver *button on a device's properties pages to return to a previous version of the driver.*

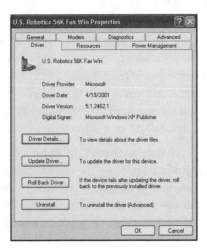

If you have an older device you are trying to install, then you might have to just throw it out and buy a newer one. Device Driver Rollback only allows you to remove a driver and replace it with its predecessor. It doesn't do anything to help you create a driver or tweak settings that will make the driver work with Windows XP. So, if you have a device driver that doesn't work with XP (and you'll find this out during the installation of Windows XP or when you later install the device), then contact the manufacturer. The vendor may or may not produce a new driver that is compatible with Windows XP. However, for a product (such as a network adapter card), many vendors only create new drivers for products that are recent or still for sale. You can't expect a vendor to write a new device driver for a five-year-old product every time Microsoft releases a new operating system! You can usually find out quickly if a compatible driver is available by visiting the manufacturer's Web site. Be sure you know the make and model of the device before you start downloading files.

How to Use System Restore to Recover Previous Settings

Another powerful feature that Windows XP offers you is called *System Restore*. When you make major changes to your system by installing an application, by making application changes, by changing device drivers, and so on, the System Restore feature can help you back out of these changes in a nice clean way. System Restore is one of the better features on Windows XP when it comes to correcting your mistakes (or those of a software vendor on which you counted!).

> **Note**
>
> To use System Restore to revert your computer to a previous state, you will have to boot the system first. With System Restore, you can recover the system by restoring files to a previously saved state, and it can be used by booting the computer normally or when you boot the computer using Safe Mode. Therefore, before you try to use Automated System Restore, discussed at the beginning of this chapter, first try to boot the system normally. If that fails, try using Last Known Good Configuration. If that fails, then boot into Safe Mode and try using System Restore.

Please note that you must be logged on as an administrator in order to use the System Restore utility, both to create a manual restore point or to use the utility to revert your system to a previous state. However, you do not have to be logged on for restore points to be created that the system does for you on a periodic basis, as described below.

23

DISASTER
RECOVERY
PLANNING

> **Tip**
>
> Although System Restore can be used to help out when you have installed a device driver that messes up, you should first attempt to use the Device Driver Rollback feature mentioned earlier in this chapter. Use System Restore to fix a device driver problem only when the Device Driver Rollback feature does not fix the problem.

System Restore takes regular snapshots of your system, and when you install a new application, a snapshot of the system this is usually triggered as well. The System Restore capability will, at the time of a major change or a timed-event, store configuration settings and files that can be used to roll back to that time.

Maybe this doesn't seem like such a great a feature. What if you have created that all-important Word document for your boss and you find your system unstable and hence need to use System Restore to recover from this event? System Restore only saves (and restores) important information such as Registry settings and certain configuration files. Except under unusual circumstances, like when you name a data file with an extension used by protected system files, such as `.sys`, System Restore doesn't touch the data files you created (but you still need to keep those backups running on schedule!).

To summarize, System Restore creates System Restore Points using the following methods:

- By default, when the system is up and running, a System Restore point will be created every 24 hours, saving a snapshot of your system.

- If you choose to install an unsigned device driver, a restore point is created. Earlier in this chapter, you learned that a signed device driver is one that has passed testing by Microsoft and is distributed with a digitally signed catalog file that contains hash codes used to verify the integrity of the device drivers files. When an unsigned driver is installed, the operating system takes notice and automatically creates a restore point.

- When you use the Windows Backup utility to restore data to your computer, a restore point will be created.

- When you install a new application, you may see a dialog box telling you that a System Restore Point has been created. This is not true for all application installations. The installation must be done using an installation program that makes a call to the application programming interface (API) called *RestorePT.API*. The normal Windows Installer program used by most application vendors does this. If you are not sure, create a manual restore point before you install an application.

- When the Windows Update feature is used to download a new component from Microsoft's Web site, a restore point will be created before the component is installed.

- You can manually create a System Restore point anytime you wish, using the System Restore tool found in the System Tools folder.

- When System Restore is used to restore the system, you run the System Restore program to return to a previous restore point. The System Restore feature even creates a new restore point so that you can effectively undo a system restore!

In the sections that follow you will learn how to create a manual restore point, what restore points exist on your system, and how to use System Restore to revert your system to a previous state.

What Gets Saved and Restored with System Restore?

Unlike the ASR utility, System Restore does not save the entire contents of your system partition and the Registry. Instead, it saves just the information it needs to restore the system to a point in time before the restore point was created. The utility will need at least 200MB of space on the system disk to store this information in an archived file. Keep in mind that restore points exist in a queue—that is, when there isn't enough room in the archived file to add a new restore point, the information for the oldest restore point will be deleted so the new information can be added. Therefore, although you can depend on System Restore to revert your system to a previous point in time, the length of time depends on how often you create restore points, such as by installing applications or creating manual restore points.

The information stored consists of a snapshot of the Registry and some specific dynamic files.

23

DISASTER
RECOVERY
PLANNING

Tip

The System Restore archive data is kept in the system volume directory, and it is one of those hidden directories. You can check out the contents, if you have the permission to do so, by using Windows Explorer or the DIR command at the Command Prompt. Since it is a system directory, you'll have to choose to see all files if you use Windows Explorer. For the DIR command, you can use the syntax DIR /A:S, which tells the DIR command you want to see files that have the system attribute set.

The types of files stored in the archive include the following:

- The Registry files, with the exception of the Security Accounts Manager (SAM), and files that store local user account and password information)
- Local profiles (note that roaming profiles are *not* saved)
- COM+ DB files
- WFP.dll cache
- WMI DB files
- IIS Metabase

Unless you are a programmer, not much of the above list will make a lot of sense. They are listed simply for those who do understand these kinds of files and the data they manage. The one object that is discussed at length later in this book is the Registry, which you can learn about in Chapter 20, "The Windows XP Registry." Note also in the preceding list that passwords do not change when you use System Restore. This is an important feature! For example, a good system management practice is to change passwords on a very frequent basis, depending on the security needs for your site. If you have recently changed your password but then need to use System Restore, you would be out of luck if System Restore also restored the old password and you had forgotten it. As you can see, the utility does operate with some intelligence when it comes to deciding what needs to be saved and later restored.

In addition to the list above, the utility will save copies of a significant list of files. The files are saved based on the text used for the file extension portion of the filename—that is, the text following the period in the filename. This includes such common file extensions such as .exe, .sys, and .dll. Therefore, you should not use these file extensions when you create a data file. If you do, then the saved version will be restored when you use System Restore to revert to a previous restore point. If you have changed any data in a file that uses a monitored file extension, then you will lose the data in that file if you have changed it since the restore point was created.

There are several-hundred file extensions System Restore monitors, which are too many to list here. In addition, this list will probably change over time. If you are interested in a copy of the complete list, visit Microsoft's Web site and search for Monitored File Extensions. You will find the list in the documentation section for the Platform SDK (software development kit).

System Restore does not restore certain kinds of files. For example, files ending with .doc should not be restored, since these typically are Microsoft Word documents. Although System Restore may restore some of the application files and dynamic link library files used by Microsoft Word if something goes awry, it won't replace your documents with older versions! Hence, for most applications that have been around for some time and use well-known file extensions for storing data, you don't have to worry about losing your data files if you use System Restore.

To be more specific, the files that will not be restored include the following:

- Files that use an extension not listed as <included> in the Monitored File Extensions List in the System Restore portion of the Platform SDK
- Data files created by the user and stored in the user profile
- The contents of any redirected folders
- Anything listed in the Registry under HKEY_LOCAL_MACHINE\system\controlset001\control\backuprestore\filesnottobackup
- Anything listed in the Registry under HKEY_LOCAL_MACHINE\system\controlset001\control\backuprestore\keysnottorestore

Therefore, you can consider System Restore a good way to recover from a bad application installation, a corruption of system files, and other situations of this sort. Its basic function is to restore operating system and application files and settings, along with most of the Registry. The utility tries not to step on your data and leaves your passwords intact. Now you can probably see that this is a better method to attempt to recover from many system problems that you would normally use ASR to do. In this way, at least you won't lose any data, provided your applications use standard file extensions for data files.

Using the System Restore Wizard

To start the System Restore Wizard, click on Start, All Programs, Accessories, System Tools, and System Restore. Figure 23.9 shows the first dialog box displayed by the wizard.

As shown in this dialog box, you can use one of two radio buttons on the right side of the dialog box. With these buttons you can either create a manual restore point to save your computers settings as they are at this particular moment, or you can take the default selection Restore My Computer to an Earlier Time. If you choose either of these, then simply click Next.

On the left side of the dialog box is a link entitled System Restore Settings. This link goes to the System Properties applet, which is located in the Control Panel with the System Restore tab selected, as shown in Figure 23.10. You can use the link provided here or access this properties page through the Control Panel. For more information about using the applets found in the Control Panel, see Chapter 14, "Using the Control Panel."

23

DISASTER RECOVERY PLANNING

FIGURE **23.9**

With the first dialog box of the System Restore Wizard, you can create a manual restore point or restore your system to an earlier time.

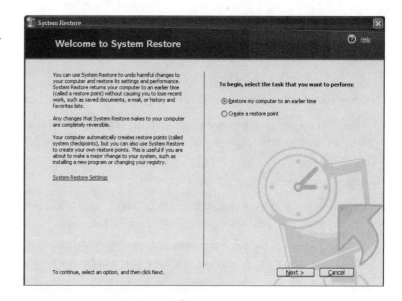

FIGURE **23.10**

The System Properties applet in the Control Panel can be used to configure how System Restore works.

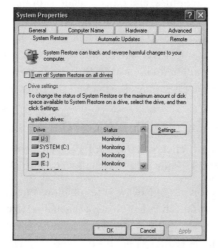

In this figure, you can turn off System Restore for all drives by selecting the check box at the top of the properties page. Otherwise, you can see which drives the utility is monitoring, under the Available drives section. To view the settings for a particular drive, just click on it once and then click Settings. In Figure 23.11 you can see the Settings dialog box for the system partition. Here, you are told that you can't turn off monitoring on this drive (since it holds the system partition), unless you elect to use that check box to turn off the System Restore utility entirely for all drives.

FIGURE 23.11

The settings for the system partition are shown in this dialog box.

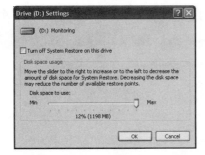

Notice that the only thing you can set here is the amount of disk space to allow for storing restore point information in the archive. Don't worry about setting this to the maximum, since the actual archived files will be limited to a total of about 200 MB anyway. In Figure 23.12, you can see the settings for the C: drive. Here, you can use a check box to specifically turn off monitoring by System Restore for this drive, since it is not the system partition. Notice also that the slider bar is also set to the maximum amount, but the amount of disk space used, despite being 12%, is not the same as that shown in Figure 23.11 for the system partition. That is because each disk has its own archive, and the partitions are of different sizes.

FIGURE 23.12

You can turn off monitoring by System Restore for drives that are not the system partition.

23

DISASTER
RECOVERY
PLANNING

If you install applications on different disks instead of just the typical Program Files folder on your system partition, then it is probably a good idea to let System Restore create an archive and monitor each disk. Better safe than sorry, right?

Create Your Own Restore Points

Although System Restore does create restore points on a 24-hour basis, and for the other events listed previously, you can always choose the second radio button shown in Figure 23.9 above to create your own restore point. Just click the radio button, and then Next at the bottom of the screen. Figure 23.13 shows the Create a Restore Point dialog box, where you can enter descriptive text to recall later why you created the restore point.

FIGURE 23.13

Enter some descriptive text to make it easier for you to recall at a later time why you created this manual restore point.

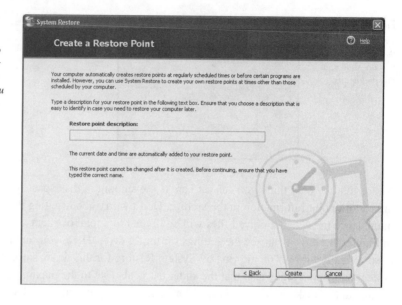

When you have finished entering the text, click Create; or if you have changed your mind, use Cancel or Back. The final dialog box will tell you that the restore point has been created, showing the date and time and your descriptive text. Click Close to finish.

Using System Restore to Revert to an Earlier Time

When something does go wrong and you decide you want to go back in time (hey, Windows XP is a time machine!), you can take the default radio button selection shown above in Figure 23.9 (Restore My Computer to an Earlier Time). Click Next for a calendar to be displayed that shows all the restore points that have been created on the computer (see Figure 23.14).

Note

In Figure 23.14 only one restore point is shown for the date selected. As things go, you may see multiple restore points. For example, if you do several application installations on the same day, each one will cause a restore point to be created, in addition to the 24-hour periodic basis that the system uses to create a restore point. Additionally, if you had created any manual restore points on that date, those would also show up. Before you click Next, be sure to select the restore point you want to use.

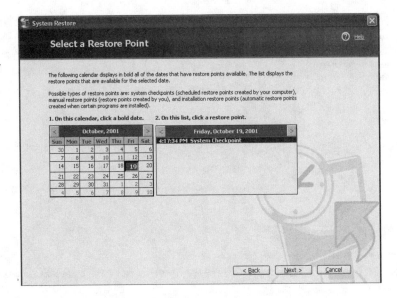

The previous date is selected so that you can see that the system had created an automatic restore point. If you want to go back to that restore point, just click Next.

Before such a serious operation as restoring to a previous time is actually executed, Windows XP will alert you (see Figure 23.15) as to what you are about to do. It tells you that you won't lose things like e-mail or documents and that the process is reversible (remember that a restore point will be created *now* before the system is restored to an earlier time).

You are also warned that a system shutdown will be necessary, so close any applications that are opened before proceeding. You can close applications by right-clicking them on the taskbar at the bottom of the screen and selecting Close from the menu, or you can use the Alt+Tab key combination to move from one application to another and close each application still open.

When you are ready to proceed, click Next.

The Start button, taskbar, and any icons on your desktop will disappear, and a dialog box appears stating that System Restore is doing its job of restoring files and settings. This should only take from a few seconds to a minute, depending on the amount of data to be restored and your computer's speed. The system will then shut down and reboot. Log back on when the computer has finished rebooting.

The system will display a screen on reboot that tells you that the system has been restored to the point in time you selected.

23

DISASTER
RECOVERY
PLANNING

FIGURE 23.15

You must confirm that you really want to perform the system restore.

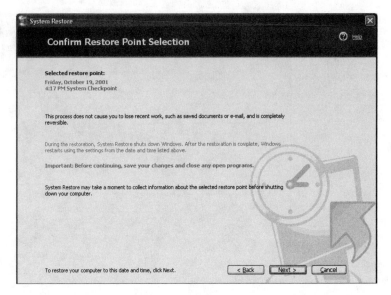

If you click on the link called *Renamed Files/Folders*, another dialog box shows the files and folders changed by the system restoration. To close the dialog box and get back to working with your Windows XP computer, click OK.

Summary

Windows XP gives you several avenues of recovery, depending on the situation. By using simple techniques such as starting in Safe Mode or using Device Driver Rollback, you can lick most common problems. Using the System Restore feature can also be a great benefit, since the system applications and settings are restored to a specific point in time where you were certain everything was working as it should, and you don't have to lose any data you have created between restore points.

Using the ASR tool is perhaps the most important action for you to consider. If you believe a regular backup will take care of all of your needs, then you may be misguiding yourself. ASR is the last resort, but it works. That is why it was presented first in this chapter. ASR can recover the system when all other methods fail.

In the next chapter, I will show you how to get over your paranoia (but keep those backups running), and start exploring the new interface that Windows XP provides. No more desktops cluttered with unwanted icons. An easier to use Start Menu and taskbar are waiting for you in the next chapter.

CHAPTER 24

Configuring Your Computer for Local Area Networking

IN THIS CHAPTER

- Using Dynamic Host Configuration Protocol or Static Internet Protocol Configuration Information   *618*

- Installing and Configuring Transfer Call Protocol/Internet Protocol and Related Components   *620*

- Configuring the Transfer Call Protocol/Internet Protocol Connection   *622*

- Configuring Static Internet Protocol Address Information   *632*

- Using Other Local Area Network Protocols   *638*

- Using File and Printer Sharing for Microsoft Networks   *641*

- Workgroups and Domains   *641*

Whether you are using Windows XP Professional at home or at work, you will probably need to know a little about how to configure the networking components. For a business environment, this is practically a must. Except in a very small business, it is rare to find a standalone computer today that is not linked to other computers in an office or perhaps to a networked printer.

You may find that purchasing an Ethernet card, which can be found for under $20, for each PC, as well as a small, inexpensive hub or switch can make exchanging data between multiple PCs not only affordable but also much easier than using floppy disks or other removable media. Computers on a network can also share a single Internet connection, which may save you the cost of using multiple connections.

Today's mobile workforce, armed with their laptop computers, can also benefit from using a network connection at home and at work. You can connect to the company's network at work, or just plug into the local area network (LAN) at home and use a broadband connection to send and receive data from your work LAN.

Note

Laptop users, see Appendix C, "Using Windows XP on Notebook Computers." It contains several valuable tips on how to better utilize your laptop computer using new features provided by Windows XP.

In Appendix A, "Introduction to TCP/IP," you can learn the incredibly boring details about how Transmission Control Protocol/Internet Protocol (TCP/IP) works. In this chapter, we will have more fun! You can learn in less than half an hour how to set up the networking components that are part of Windows XP so that your computer can start talking with other computers.

Using Dynamic Host Configuration Protocol or Static Internet Protocol Configuration Information

Appendix A, "Introduction to TCP/IP," discusses how being a part of a TCP/IP network requires, at a minimum, an IP address and subnet mask. If you are connecting your LAN to another network, such as the Internet, then you also will need the IP address of the default gateway, as well as the address of one or more domain name system (DNS) servers. Fortunately, dynamic host configuration protocol (DHCP) can automate the entire process so you don't have to enter all this information yourself.

For the most part, using DHCP is efficient. If you simply want to network a few computers and have either a Windows NT/2000 or .NET server machine to provide the DHCP service, you can configure your Windows XP computer to dynamically obtain its IP address from that service. The DHCP server takes over and automatically configures computers with addressing information each time they boot into the network.

> **Tip**
>
> A cable or DSL modem offers the alternative option of getting DHCP up and running on your Network. Companies such as Linksys (http://www.linksys.com) and NetGear (http://www.netgear.com) both sell inexpensive switches for use in a central wiring box to which all of your computers can connect. The switch itself can be connected to the cable or DSL modem and can use the IP address that your broadband provider assigns to your connection. It is important to use the address the provider gives you, since it is unique on the Internet and most providers charge for additional addresses. However, the switch, using a technique called *network address translation (NAT),* uses one of the reserved address spaces that cannot be used on the Internet to provide addresses to your individual computers. The switch keeps track of Internet requests from your computers and the responses as they come back and makes sure information is transferred to the correct location. For more information about how NAT works, see Appendix A, "Introduction to TCP/IP."

Using Static Addressing

If you have several computers at work or home and you don't want to connect to the Internet, then you can always manually configure static IP addressing information and use any of the valid IP addresses discussed in Appendix A. You may also connect your single computer to the Internet, but your ISP may assign you static IP addressing information instead of using DHCP. If that is the case, then refer to a later discussion in this chapter on how to enter that information so that Windows XP uses the correct address.

Automatic Private Internet Protocol Addressing

Your Windows XP computer can be configured for automatic addressing. If you configure Windows XP to use DHCP, then when the computer boots, it will send out a request to try and locate a DHCP server to download the address configuration information it needs to communicate on the Internet. However, Windows XP also supports a feature called *automatic private IP addressing (APIPA).* If the Windows XP computer boots and doesn't get a response back from a DHCP server within one minute or so, then it will use APIPA to establish a private IP address. APIPA uses the IP address range of 169.254.0.1

through 169.254.255.254 (and a subnet mask of 255.255.0.0). If the DHCP server cannot be contacted, then the Windows XP computer will simply pick a random address from this range and probe the network to make sure the address is not already in use. If it is not in use, then the Windows XP computer assumes it can use this address and will automatically perform the configuration.

This simple method can be used to create a small network if you don't want to set up a DHCP server or manually configure IP addressing information for each of your Windows XP computers. Just set the computer to automatically acquire IP configuration information and then boot up your computers!

Installing and Configuring Transfer Call Protocol/Internet Protocol and Related Components

As with most configuration tasks, configuring Windows XP networking components depends on whether you choose to install the necessary components during setup. You will then need to use the Control Panel to configure the networking components you want to install. The next section explains the steps required for installing TCP/IP components after the initial Windows XP setup has been performed. This is necessary if you skipped the installation of networking components during the Windows XP setup procedure. After installing the required components, you then will learn how to configure them.

Using Add/Remove Programs to Install Network Components

If a network adapter card is installed in your computer when you install Windows XP, Windows XP will recognize it; so by default, the Setup procedure will install the card and some of the software used for local area networking. If you choose the Typical setup, only a minimal number of components will be installed. These are as follows:

- Client for Microsoft Networks
- File and Print Sharing for Microsoft Networks
- Quality of Service (QoS) Packet Scheduler
- TCP/IP (with automatic addressing enabled)

If you choose the Custom selection during Setup, you can assign configuration information at that point. Regardless, you may find that after the Setup procedure is completed that not all of the networking components you needed may have been installed. If so, then you can install the components you need. To install any other necessary software on your computer, use the Add/Remove Programs applet in the Control Panel. Figure 24.1 shows the Control Panel with its new category look. From this page, select Add or Remove Programs.

FIGURE 24.1

You use the Control Panel to access the Add or Remove Programs function.

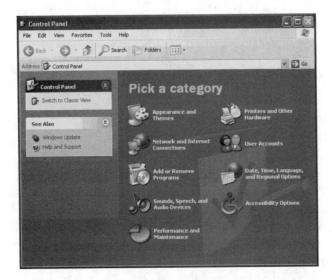

When the Add or Remove Programs dialog box pops up, click on Add/Remove Windows Components. A dialog box pops up stating that Windows XP Setup is being started. The Windows Components Wizard pops up next (see Figure 24.2).

FIGURE 24.2

You can choose which network components to install using the Windows Components Wizard.

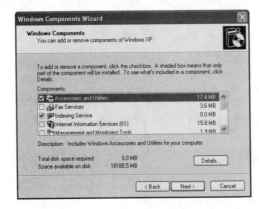

This wizard will allow you to install many optional components for Windows XP. However, for the purposes of this chapter, just install the components related to networking.

The following is a list with brief descriptions of the other networking components available from this wizard. Depending on what you want to do with your network, you will end up choosing some or all of the following:

- Internet Information Services (IIS)—You can use your computer to create a Web site using Microsoft's IIS. This is a comprehensive set of Web services and an entire appendix in this book (Appendix D, "Basics of Internet Information Services") is devoted to this topic. However, installing IIS is not recommended until you have read that appendix first!

- MSN Explorer—Install this component if you want to use Microsoft's own MSN service for connecting to the Internet. For a LAN connection or if you use another Internet service provider, you don't need this networking component.

- Networking Services—This component is made up of three other services. Click on the service and then click the Details button to find out about these services. The first is RIP Listener, which is used to listen for routing updates from routers that use RIPv1. You can read more about routing and RIP and routing in Appendix A. This is a service that most users will not need. The second is called *Simple TCP/IP Services,* another service you probably don't need, but it won't hurt to install it. These services include Character Generator, Daytime, Discard, Echo, and Quote of the Day services. Again, Appendix A explains these services in more detail. The last service is called *Universal Plug and Play.* This can be useful if you plan to interoperate with other computers on the Internet, especially when using a firewall. Game players will want to select this component. To install any of these components, simply select the check box next to the service and when finished, click OK.

- Other Network File and Print Services—This component is also made up of several services. Clicking Details shows Print Services for Unix. This component lets Unix computers communicate with your Windows XP computer and uses any printer to which your computer has access.

Configuring the Transfer Call Protocol/Internet Protocol Connection

As you know, you can either configure a TCP/IP connection to use DHCP, which will automatically configure your computer's IP addressing when it boots (or to use APIPA), or you can enter static IP addressing information for the computer. Let's look at both of these options. To begin the process, bring up the Control Panel (see Figure 24.1). Select the category labeled Network and Internet Connections. This brings up the window shown in Figure 24.3. From this window, select Network Connections near the bottom right of the window.

FIGURE 24.3

Select Network Connections from the Control Panel's Category View to configure a LAN connection.

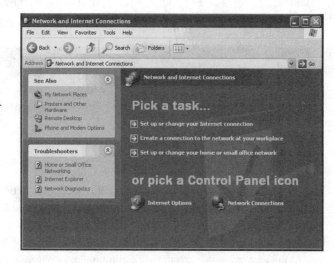

If a network card was installed in your computer during the initial setup of Windows XP and it is one that Windows XP recognizes, then this network card will be ready for a LAN connection. Figure 24.4 indicates how after you select Network Connections in the Control Panel, an entry for the Local Area Connection appears.

FIGURE 24.4

The Network Connections dialog box shows you the Local Area Connection entry created for your network card.

24

CONFIGURING FOR LOCAL AREA NETWORKING

If you only have one network adapter in your system and you choose the Typical option during Setup, then by default, Windows XP will create a connection and configure it to automatically obtain an IP address using a DHCP server or APIPA. Right-click on the connection that was created and choose Properties from the menu that appears.

> **Tip**
>
> As with most right-click menus, you can also simply highlight the network connection and then use Properties from the File menu that appears in the dialog box.

However, if you chose the Customize option during Setup (and didn't select to install any of the networking components), the Properties page for this local connection will then list a series of check boxes for determining what components can be used for the connection. I chose this method during setup so that you can see how each component is configured instead of relying on automatic configuration during the Setup procedure. It is important for you to understand how each network component is configured so that you can troubleshoot or make changes should the need arise.

After selecting the Properties page for the LAN connection (right-click and select Properties), you can further configure the IP addressing data for the connection, as well as many other aspects of the network connection. Figure 24.5 shows the Properties page for a typical LAN connection that was created during the Setup process. Note that all the check boxes are deselected.

FIGURE 24.5

The properties sheets of a LAN connection helps configure how the connection operates.

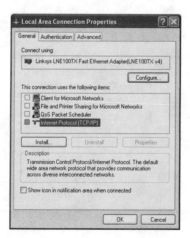

Figure 24.5 shows the three tabs for the Local Area Connection Properties page. In this chapter, you will learn about the use of each of these tabs.

However, before you start to configure network protocols, clients, or services, you will want to look into how the network adapter card was set up. The next section covers this topic.

Configuring the Network Adapter Card

The General tab is displayed by default, and the first thing at the top of this page is the network adapter used for this connection. Click Configure to make changes to configuration items that determine how this network adapter will work. For example, the adapter shown in Figure 24.5 states that it is a 100TX Fast Ethernet Adapter, which means that it operates at 100Mbps. If you are installing a new Windows XP computer in a home network with a hub and other computers that operate at 10Mbps, then this adapter may not be capable of communicating with those slower devices. You then need to look first at the configuration options for the adapter.

Clicking Configure makes Windows XP display a set of properties sheets that apply to your specific adapter. Figure 24.6 is an example of this, but keep in mind that your mileage may vary.

FIGURE 24.6

The Properties sheets for a network adapter can vary, depending on the configurable items for the adapter.

24

CONFIGURING FOR
LOCAL AREA
NETWORKING

This figure shows the name of the adapter, along with the manufacturer and the PCI slot in which the adapter is installed. This can be very handy information when troubleshooting PCI cards! Under the Device status section, you can see that to Windows XP, the device appears to be working as it should. If you do not see text here saying The Device Is Working Properly, then click on Troubleshoot to determine the cause of the problem.

It may be that your network adapter card conflicts with an interrupt request line (IRQ) of another card installed in the system, or it could be one of a host of other problems. However, the troubleshooter will prompt you through a series of questions and can help you resolve the matter.

At the bottom of the General tab shown in Figure 24.6, you can see a field labeled Device usage. You can use the drop-down menu under this section to enable or disable the device. For most users who only have one network adapter, you want to be sure that the selection here reads, Use this device (enable). However, if you have multiple network adapters installed and are performing troubleshooting tasks, you may want to choose the second option—Do not use this device (disable)—to eliminate this adapter as the cause of the problem you are troubleshooting.

Figure 24.7 shows the Advanced tab selected for this adapter. Note that the items you see in the Property section of this dialog box will vary, depending on your network card's capabilities.

FIGURE 24.7

The Advanced tab shows a list of the capabilities that can be configured for your adapter.

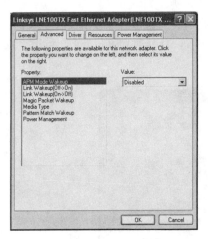

If you are simply an end-user of the Windows XP system, then you should not change any of these values. You can highlight a value under the Property section and then select a value for the property under the Value section. Since the card used as an example here is an advanced card that supports many modern technologies, such as Wake on LAN and power management, you will see entries for these capabilities. However, one important Property of many network adapter cards you will find on the market today is the Media Type. This property determines the network media to which the network card is attached.

The majority of LANs today consist of Ethernet technologies, with a few still using the Token Ring technology. In this case, the Ethernet adapter is an all-encompassing term that supports many different underlying physical media specifications, and those can support many different speeds for network communications. The most common of these in use today are as follows:

- *10BaseT*—This is the standard twisted-pair wiring that operates at 10Mbps (megabits per second, hence the name starts with 10), using baseband signaling and twisted-pair cables (hence the T in the name). If you purchase an inexpensive home networking kit from your local computer store, this is probably what you will get—a few network cards and a hub that support 10BaseT.

- *10BaseT Full_Duplex*—This is similar to the item above but supports full duplex communications—that is, your network adapter is probably connected to a switch, and by using additional wires available in the twisted-pair cable, you can both send and receive data at the same time, hence the name Full Duplex. Standard 10BaseT, which uses a hub, can only send or receive, but it cannot do both at the same time.

- *100BaseTX*—This is the twisted-pair standard for Fast Ethernet, which is similar to 10BaseT, but operates at 100Mbps instead of 10Mbps. That is a ten-fold increase in speed! However, in this case, it can only send or receive data but not both at the same time. This means you are probably using a hub. The letters TX are appended to the name to imply twisted-pair cabling, since the 100Mbps Ethernet standard also allows for other physical media connections such as fiber optic cables.

- *100BaseTX Full_Duplex*—This means you are probably using a switch in Full Duplex mode, and the network card can send or receive at a speed of 100Mbps.

Another value you may see for most Ethernet cards is AutoSense. This means that the network adapter card is capable of sensing the speed on the network and making the necessary adjustments to operate at the speed that the other computers are using. However, do NOT depend on this feature. If you find that AutoSense is selected as the value for the Media Type property and that you cannot communicate on the LAN, then use the Value menu to select the appropriate network speed and whether the network uses Full Duplex. In general, a hub does not use Full Duplex, while many switches do. You can find out more about hubs and switches in Appendix A.

24

CONFIGURING FOR
LOCAL AREA
NETWORKING

Tip

Figure 24.7 shows strange entries under the Property section. Just what is a magic packet and magic packet wakeup? These, along with the power management and link wakeup properties, are all part of a general strategy to make managing computers from a central location an easier task. The Magic Packet Wakeup property, if supported by your network adapter, allows an administrator at a central console to essentially wake up your computer when it is turned

continues

off. Using this capability, the administrator can perform such tasks as installing new software or running auditing software to ensure no programs are installed that shouldn't be—easy tasks to complete after hours. If you want to find out more about properties of modern network adapters, check out *Upgrading and Repairing Networks, Third Edition* (Que Publishing, 2001) by yours truly, or visit `http://developer.intel.com/ial/WfM/index.htm`. This is Intel's Web site for researching the Wired for Management technologies that may become a part of your networking future.

The remaining tabs in the network adapter's properties sheets deal with drivers, resources (IRQs and memory locations), and power management capabilities. For the most part, you won't need to worry about the configurable settings displayed on these pages.

However, since new hardware is being developed and sent to the market at a rapid pace, you may benefit from an upgraded driver if the manufacturer offers one after the initial release of Windows XP. In that case, select the Driver tab to display what is shown in Figure 24.8.

FIGURE 24.8

The Driver tab gives details about a particular driver; you can load or roll back a new driver for the network adapter.

If you received a floppy diskette (or more likely today, a CD-ROM) from your network card manufacturer, then see if the `readme.1st` (or similar) documentation instructs you to install a new driver or keep the one that Windows XP selects by default. Keep in mind that when a new operating system is distributed, the manufacturer (in this case, Microsoft) must supply a large number of device drivers for a huge number of possible devices and network adapter cards. The driver originally included with the operating system may work fine. However, it may not take advantages of all of the features of which the card is capable.

In this case, you can use the Driver tab to install a newer driver. Select Update Driver, and Windows XP will prompt you to insert the floppy diskette or CD-ROM containing the newer driver. You can also select a driver from another location. This can be useful when your network administrator has obtained the driver and placed it on a network share, for example. In either case, you can install the newer driver by using this button.

What happens if the newer driver doesn't work as well as the one it replaces? Just go back to the Driver tab and select the button labeled Roll Back Driver. This removes the new driver and reinstalls the previous driver, which Windows XP never really eliminated; it just removed it from current duty. If you have not updated the driver and only one driver was installed at the time you selected this option, you will be notified of this. In that case, don't roll back the driver! It is the only one you have! Instead, talk with your network administrator to determine what to do.

If you have installed a new network card, you can use the Uninstall button to remove a previous driver. Note that if you do this for a network adapter card currently installed in your computer, you will render it useless. Use this as a "clean-up" measure and not as a casual matter.

The Resources tab contains resources (like memory and IRQs) that the adapter is using. This can be useful for documentation purposes in a LAN and for troubleshooting problems. If another card uses the same IRQ or memory range, then you will have problems. This tab can help resolve problems like this.

At the bottom of the Resources tab is a section entitled Conflicting device list. If something shows up here, then you probably do have a problem and need to investigate further. Have you recently installed another hardware expansion card in your system, such as a video graphics adapter or modem or other device? In that case, this section will show you the device that is trying to use the same resources as your network adapter card. Using a software program changes the properties of some devices, whereas other, typically older, devices require that a jumper on the card itself is changed. This is territory for the experienced network administrator to explore and not the casual computer user.

The last tab is the Power Management tab. You have the following two options with this tab:

- Allow the computer to turn off this device to save power—This is useful with laptop computers when you are traveling and not connected to a network. By turning off power to the network adapter, you can conserve limited battery reserves.

- Allow this device to bring the computer out of standby—This is related to the Wake on LAN feature mentioned earlier. If you participate in a networked environment, and are plugged into an AC adapter, then this is a good selection to use. Note

24

CONFIGURING FOR
LOCAL AREA
NETWORKING

that under this selection is another check box labeled Only Allow Management Stations to bring the computer out of standby. This means that only a central management station can wake up your computer. If operating on battery power only, do NOT choose this selection. Your computer can be awakened and the battery power drained when you are not present.

This Connection Uses the Following Items

Figure 24.5 showed the section that describes your network card, which is in another section entitled This connection uses the following items. Since all the check boxes are cleared, none of these are enabled for the connection but are suggestions of defaults you can use for most purposes.

The first item in this list is Client for Microsoft Networks. Unless you participate in a Novell NetWare network, you should enable this client by selecting the check box next to it. The second item, File and Printer Sharing for Microsoft Networks, is discussed later in this chapter, and you should consider carefully whether you want other computers to be able to access your computer before enabling this feature.

The third item is called *QoS Packet Scheduler*. This service provides quality-of-service features, and you generally should enable this feature on Windows XP Professional desktop computers.

The last item in this list is the TCP/IP configuration, which requires a more lengthy discussion.

Transfer Call Protocol/Internet Protocol Configuration

After confirming that your network adapter card is working as it should, you will next configure a network protocol to be used to exchange data on the network. For most networks today, except for a few AppleTalk LANs and older NetWare LANs, this protocol is TCP/IP. TCP/IP is the network protocol that glues the Internet together, and it is the most popular LAN protocol on the market today. See Appendix A for an overview of this feature.

Figure 24.5 shows the Internet Protocol (TCP/IP) as listed under the section labeled This connection uses the following items. To configure how the protocol operates, click on it once and then click the Properties button. Figure 24.9 shows that if you do not choose otherwise during setup, TCP/IP will be configured to automatically obtain IP addressing configuration information.

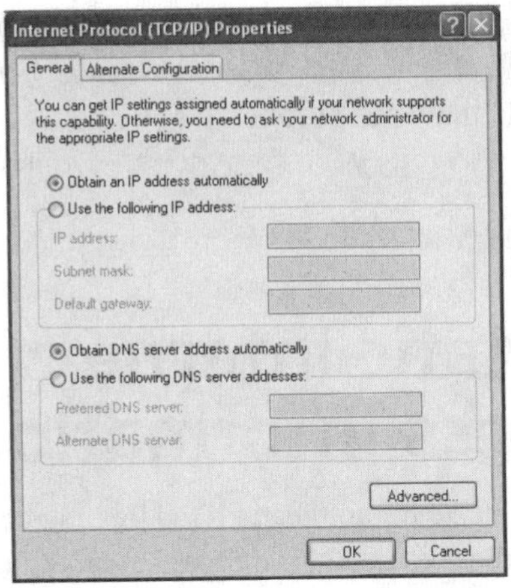

FIGURE 24.9

The default settings allow for autoconfiguration of TCP/IP using DHCP or APIPA.

Remember that when the computer first boots, it will attempt to contact a DHCP server to get an IP configuration. If that doesn't work within one or two minutes, then APIPA kicks in and the computer attempts to self-configure using private address ranges set aside for this use.

In most environments, automatic IP configuration through DHCP is the best choice; it is easier to design, implement, and maintain automatic IP addressing. If a computer provides certain services (for example, it serves as a DHCP or other type of server), it may be best to configure the computer with a static IP address. Naming services, such as Windows Internet Naming Service (WINS) and Domain Name Service (DNS), can resolve computer names to IP addresses in most situations, but there are certain services that can only be contacted by IP address.

> **Note**
>
> In most modern networks, WINS is a declining feature that was a stop-gap measure so that Microsoft could provide a dynamic name-to-address translation service while the traditional Domain Name System (DNS) services lagged behind. However, with dynamic DNS, the entire landscape has changed. Dynamic DNS allows domain name system servers to register name-to-IP address records dynamically, much like the WINS service did for earlier versions of Windows. If you have down-level clients such as Windows 95/98 or Windows NT 4.0 clients who still use WINS, then you will have to continue to provide a WINS server on your network if you want to locate services on those computers.

Configuring Static Internet Protocol Address Information

Figure 24.9 showed the selection to make for automatic IP addressing configuration. If you select Use the following IP address, you will have access to other fields on this page, as shown in Figure 24.10.

FIGURE 24.10

You can choose to enter specific IP addressing information by choosing Use the following IP address.

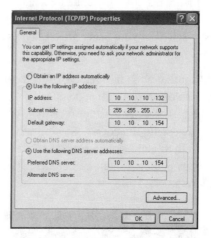

Typically, a server computer will use a static IP address, whereas workstations or a desktop computer with Windows XP will use DHCP to get their configuration information from a DHCP server. However, if you need to assign a static IP address, you can enter the following information:

- IP address—This is the static IP address you want to use for this computer. As explained in Appendix A, it is expressed in what is known as *dotted-decimal notation;* hence there are four sections in this field separated by dots. Any decimal number greater than 255 is not permitted in any part of this address.
- Subnet mask—This is a mask written in dotted-decimal notation, like the IP address, and is used to mask out portions of an IP address. This is done so that

another computer can determine what part of your IP address is the address of your network (or your subnet) and what part of the IP address is the address of your individual computer on that network or subnet. Again, the maximum value you can enter for any part of this field is 255.

- Default gateway—This is the address of a router (or possibly a server acting as a router) that is a gateway linking your local network to a larger network, such as your business network or the Internet.

- Preferred DNS Server—This is the address of a DNS server that your computer will first contact when it wants to resolve a human-friendly computer or resource name (such as http://www.twoinc.com to the actual IP address. Communications on the TCP/IP network and the Internet use IP addresses, not names.

- Alternate DNS Server—This field allows you to specify a secondary DNS server. You never know when a primary DNS server will be down because of problems with the server or for routine maintenance. By entering two DNS servers, you increase the chances that you will not have any problems resolving computer names to IP addresses.

Configuring Advanced Transfer Call Protocol/Internet Protocol Settings

At the bottom of the General tab, you will see Advanced. This button will bring up another set of properties pages called *Advanced TCP/IP Settings,* as shown in Figure 24.11

Four tabs are available for use: IP Settings, DNS, WINS, and Options.

FIGURE 24.11

The Advanced button brings up a set of properties pages that allow you to enter more specific TCP/IP configuration information.

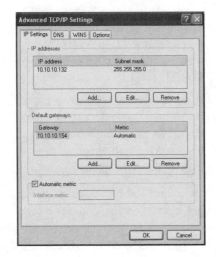

24

CONFIGURING FOR
LOCAL AREA
NETWORKING

The Internet Protocol Settings Tab

The first is the IP Settings tab, where you can enter several items. First, you can use the IP addresses section to specify more than one IP address for the network connection. This means that your network adapter can have more than one IP address bound to it. For most users, this is something you will never need to use. To add additional IP addresses for use on the local LAN, click Add and enter the IP address and an appropriate subnet mask. You can also use the Edit and Remove features to change or remove an IP address bound to an adapter.

Under the section titled Default gateways, you can also use the Add, Edit, and Remove additional gateways that connect your network to other networks. Under the column titled Metric, you can select Automatic, in which case the computer will calculate the best gateway to use based on the speed of the interface. Otherwise, you can specify a metric when you add a new gateway. The interface with the highest speed will have the lowest metric when automatic is selected. You can use the Command Prompt command `route print` to view the computer's routing table if more than one default gateway is entered. Here, you can look under the column labeled Metric to see which route (or gateway) will be used. If you use the Add or Edit buttons, you can change the metric to force a particular gateway to be used instead.

To disable the Automatic metric feature for this particular interface (network card), simply deselect the check box of the same name at the bottom of this property sheet. Next, enter a value you want to use for the metric for this interface on the computer. Note that this check box and the Interface metric field are used to determine the metric for all routes in your routing table that come from this particular interface. If the computer has more than one network card, then you can configure each separately. Using the Automatic metric check box or the associated Interface metric field does not apply to any default route (gateways) you manually enter with a metric value.

The Domain Name System Tab

This tab on the Advanced TCP/IP Settings properties sheets helps specify information about DNS servers that your computer will use. In the General tab, you could enter a primary and a secondary DNS server. Using this advanced option, you can specify additional DNS servers to use. Similar to the previous tab, there are three buttons to use (Add, Edit, and Remove), and they work in the same manner.

Sometimes it is easier to enter just a hostname and not the fully qualified hostname. For example you can enter the hostname of a computer in a command such as `ping mycomputer`, where `mycomputer` is the hostname you assigned to a computer when you first set it up on the Network. However, a fully qualified hostname would include the DNS domain name, such as `mydomain.com`. Two radio buttons help you choose the DNS domain name (the suffix) for creating a fully qualified DNS name when you enter only a hostname for a command. These radio buttons are as follows:

- Append primary and connection-specific DNS suffixes—When you enter a host-name that doesn't specify the fully qualified DNS name, the domain suffixes of the primary suffix (or any connection specific suffix) will be added to the name. For example, enter the command telnet zira. If the local DNS suffix or the connec-tion suffix is twoinc.com, then the fully qualified name use for the telnet com-mand would be zira.twoinc.com. You can check the value of the primary DNS suffix in the Control Panel by using the System applet. Chapter 14, "Using the Control Panel," describes this in more detail.

- Append these DNS suffixes (in order)—Here you can specify a list of DNS suf-fixes to be used instead of your primary DNS or connection-specific DNS suffixes. Again, you can Add, Edit, and Remove items from this list. If you use this radio button, then these suffixes will be used when attempting to create a fully qualified hostname instead of those used for the connection or as defined in the Control Panel.

At the bottom of this property sheet, you will see a field that can be used to enter a DNS suffix for this connection, as well as two other check boxes. If you use DHCP, then the DHCP server will generally assign you a DNS suffix for this LAN connection. However, you can use the field here to override that DHCP supplied value. The two check boxes are as follows:

- Register this connection's addresses in DNS—Your computer's hostname (again, as defined in the System applet in the Control Panel) and its associated IP addresses will be dynamically registered in a DNS server. This is dependent, of course, on whether you are using a DNS server that supports dynamic registration. The DNS server supplied with Windows 2000 and Windows 2002 does support dynamic reg-istration. By using dynamic registration with DNS, the older WINS database may no longer be needed for name resolution, provided you do not have any older com-puters on your network that still use WINS.

- Use this connection's DNS suffix in DNS registration—This check box can be selected only if the previous check box has been enabled. If selected, the connec-tion's DNS suffix will be included with the computer's hostname for dynamic reg-istration with a DNS server.

The Windows Internet Naming Service Tab

The WINS tab was developed to address the problem of dynamic name registration dur-ing a time that DNS servers did not support this feature. Although with the DHCP ser-vice you can automatically configure your network clients with IP addressing information, there was no guarantee that a client would keep the same IP address for an infinite amount of time. Yes, you could enter reserved addresses into a DHCP server, but by having to manually enter this information for each client in the DHCP server, you defeat the purpose of having DHCP automatically administer your IP address space.

The other half of the equation is name resolution. If the IP address of a client changes and your network uses DNS to resolve hostnames to IP addresses, you may spend a lot of time finding out what IP address was assigned to a particular client, then manually entering that information into the DNS server.

WINS was developed to resolve this problem. WINS acts much like a DNS server, but it allows clients that are properly configured to dynamically register their hostnames and IP addresses with a WINS server. Now that Dynamic DNS servers are becoming the norm, WINS can be considered a declining technology. However, for computers that use operating systems such as Windows 95/98/NT, you may still need to use WINS, as well as DNS, to ensure that all clients can resolve hostnames to IP addresses.

The WINS tab on the Advanced TCP/IP Settings property page is used for this purpose. Here you can use the Add, Edit, and Remove buttons to add or change WINS servers on your network. When your computer needs to find the IP address of another computer that has registered with WINS, it will use this list of WINS servers and contact each by trying to find out if it has a registration for the computer name in question. For fault tolerant purposes, it is best to use more than one WINS server on the network, just as you use more than one DNS server. WINS servers can be configured to replicate information, so if one server is down, another may still be able to resolve the name in question.

On this tab you will see a check box labeled Enable LMHOSTS lookup. This is another feature that is quickly becoming a declining technology. In Appendix A, you will learn about the TCP/IP hosts file, which is a flat ASCII text file that contains a list of computer hostnames and their IP addresses. The LMHOSTS file was created for a similar purpose—to resolve NetBIOS names to IP addresses. Using this check box will cause your computer to check for the existence of a LMHOSTS file to resolve a name when it cannot get an answer from a WINS server. Next to this check box is a button labeled Import LMHOSTS, which can be used to specify a location of a LMHOSTS file that you want to copy to your computer. Using this button makes it easier to create a single LMHOSTS file and then copy it to multiple computers so you don't have to enter the information manually on each client.

Under the section labeled NetBIOS, you will see three radio buttons. NetBIOS has a long history with Windows and Microsoft's LAN Manager software. Before Microsoft networking began to shift toward the TCP/IP method of network communications, NetBIOS was the technology used. Once again, if you have older operating systems (pre-Windows

2000) that still use NetBIOS for network communications, then you may need to configure how NetBIOS is used. The three radio buttons you can use are as follows:

- Default—This button tells your computer to use whatever settings it receives from a DHCP server for NetBIOS settings.

- Enable NetBIOS over TCP/IP—This button should be used if your DHCP server doesn't provide any NetBIOS configuration information. It tells your computer to use the TCP/IP protocol for NetBIOS communications (also known as *NetBT* and in some documentation, *NBT*). If you use WINS on your network for name resolution, then you should be sure that this option is selected or that the DHCP server provides this information.

- Disable NetBIOS over TCP/IP—Use this to disable NetBT. If your network consists of only computers that use operating systems from Windows 2000 onward, such as Windows XP, and you have no applications that require NetBIOS naming capabilities, then you don't need to use NetBIOS at all. Use this option to turn off this feature.

The Options Tab

This tab provides optional settings for your connection. Under Optional settings, you will see optional components that can be configured for TCP/IP. Currently, only TCP/IP filtering is listed in this section. Use the Properties button to view how this setting (or others that may be added at a later date) will operate.

With TCP/IP filtering you can filter the types of TCP/IP network traffic that is intercepted by your Windows XP computer. In Figure 24.12, you can see the TCP/IP Filtering dialog box that pops up when you click the Properties button.

This dialog box starts with a check box labeled Enable TCP/IP Filtering (All Adapters). You need to select this before you can further configure anything on this dialog box. Any ports or protocols that you choose to allow or deny will apply to all network adapters on the computer. You cannot filter these items on a per-adapter basis.

FIGURE 24.12

Use this dialog box to filter out unwanted TCP/IP network traffic.

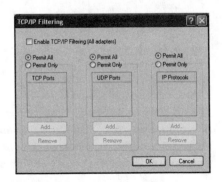

24

CONFIGURING FOR
LOCAL AREA
NETWORKING

As you can see in this figure, you can choose to permit or deny TCP ports, User Datagram Protocol (UDP) ports, or specific IP protocols. Do not use this dialog box unless you are thoroughly familiar with the TCP/IP protocol suite. Appendix A provides a good overview of the purpose of these ports, as well as some of the basic protocols that make up the TCP/IP protocol suite, such as TCP, UDP, and Internet Control Messaging Protocol (ICMP). However, note that this dialog box drops certain packets automatically if you find a need. Most users on a typical LAN never need to use this dialog box.

Using Other Local Area Network Protocols

TCP/IP is not the only protocol supported by Windows XP. Refer to Figure 24.3 under the section titled This Connection Uses the Following Items—there are three buttons: Install, Uninstall, and Properties. You have already learned how to use the Properties button for the TCP/IP protocol.

Install can be used to install additional network protocols, clients, and services on your computer. Using Install will bring up a dialog box for choosing what you want to install—a client, service, or protocol.

Installing Additional Network Clients

By default the Client for Microsoft Networks is installed when you perform a standard TCP/IP installation. However, if you select to install another client, you will also see in the list of possibilities Client Service for NetWare (see Figure 24.13). You can also choose Have Disk to install additional clients supplied by a third-party provider.

FIGURE 24.13
You can install additional network clients using this dialog box.

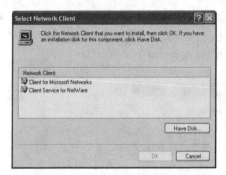

The NetWare client provided by Microsoft allows your Windows XP computer to access resources on a NetWare network. These can be resources that are accessed using Novell Directory Services (NDS) or resources accessed using the older NetWare bindery method. NDS operates in a fashion similar to Microsoft's Active Directory, in that you authenticate yourself to the NDS server and from there are granted rights and permissions to resources throughout the NetWare network. If you authenticate to a bindery server, then you can only access resources on that particular server.

If you choose to use this client, you will have to get authentication information (such as a username and password) from the administrator of the NetWare network. Additionally, NetWare versions 5.x now support the IP protocol, but Microsoft's Client Service for NetWare does not. If you choose to use Microsoft's client, then you will also have to install Microsoft's NWLink protocol, which is Microsoft's implementation of Novell's IPX/SPX proprietary networking protocol. You can also visit Novell's Web site and download their client service.

> **Note**
>
> Microsoft's Client Services for NetWare is not supported by the 64-bit version of Windows XP. Keep this in mind when planning your network and where you want to locate resources such as files or printers.

To install the NetWare client, simply highlight it once and click OK. You will be prompted to restart your computer. When the computer restarts, a logon box appears for specifying the logon credentials for the NetWare logon, such as the bindery server or the NDS tree context. You can also specify this information in the Control Panel applet labeled CSNW (Client Services for NetWare). This applet's dialog box is shown in Figure 24.14.

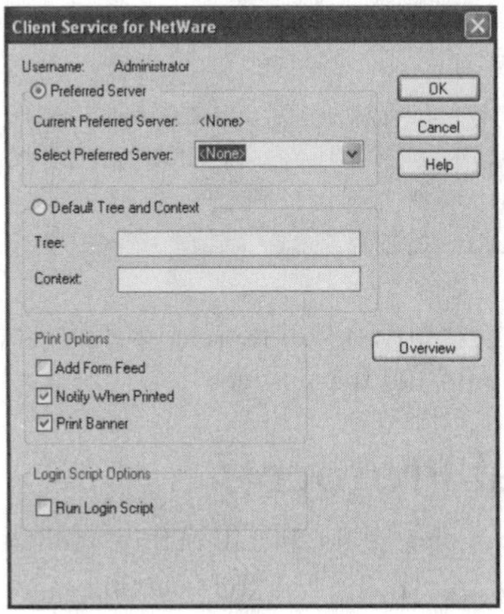

FIGURE 24.14

Use the CSNM applet in the Control Panel to configure a NetWare logon.

You will need to get information from your NetWare administrator in order to determine if you are using a Preferred Server (the bindery method) or Novell Directory Services.

Additionally, if you choose to install CSNW, then Windows XP will automatically install the following two network protocols for you automatically:

- NWLink NetBIOS
- NWLink IPX/SPX/NetBIOS Compatible Transport Protocol

These are installed because, as mentioned earlier, the Microsoft NetWare client does not support IP connections in a NetWare environment. You will have to get Novell's client for that functionality.

Installing Additional Network Services

Use the Install button on the Local Area Connections properties sheet to install additional network services. Similar to the method used in the previous section, a small dialog box pops up for selecting Client, Service, or Protocol. Select Service and then click Add.

Figure 24.15 shows a list of network services available for installation. This list depends on the networking components you have installed during Windows XP setup, as well as the services that are already currently installed. To install a service that is not on the list, use the Have Disk button. Otherwise, click on a particular service such as File and Print Sharing for Microsoft Networks and then click OK.

FIGURE 24.15

Choose the network service you want to install from this dialog box.

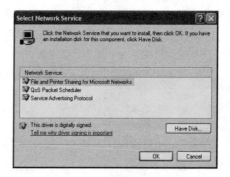

After you add a service from this dialog box, it will no longer appear here as a selection unless you choose at a later time to uninstall the service.

Installing Additional Protocols

Just like the last two sections, you can choose the Install button on the Local Area Connection properties sheet to bring up a dialog box for selecting to install a network protocol. For example, you can choose to install NWLink before from this dialog box, or you can choose to use the Have Disk button to install a protocol supplied by a third-party provider. Simply click on the protocol you want to install and click OK. When installing new protocols, you will usually be prompted to restart the system before the change will take effect.

Using File and Printer Sharing for Microsoft Networks

If you choose to install the File and Print Sharing service, then you are allowing other users on the network to access your computer. However, you will need to enable sharing for each resource. See Chapter 9, "Working with Files and Folders," for information on shared files, folders, or even entire disks on your computer with other users on the network.

If you want to share a printer, then you can use the Security tab for a printer's properties sheet to determine which users will be allowed to use the printer. For more information on how to do this, see Chapter 17, "Printing and Faxing."

Workgroups and Domains

This chapter covers the topics you need to know in order to make a physical (network card) and logical (IP address) connection to a network. In a managed network, you will find two basic methods used in Windows networking for allowing computers to share information with each other. The first is called a *workgroup*, which is nothing more than a group of computers with a common name for using as a workgroup name. In this case, each computer in the workgroup can decide which other computers or users are allowed to access resources on the local computer. In Chapter 28, "Joining a Domain and the Active Directory," you will learn about a more secure network. Joining a domain and using the Active Directory allow for much more control over resources on all computers throughout the network. If you use your Windows XP computer in a business environment, then you will most likely exist in a domain environment. Now that you have made a connection to the network, you can further explore whether you want to use a workgroup or domain for securing your computer's resources, as well as for accessing resources that reside on other computers.

Summary

This chapter introduced you to the basics for connecting a Windows XP computer to a network. More detail was probably provided than what is needed for a simple LAN. However, as you become more familiar with networking, you will find that more of this

24

CONFIGURING FOR
LOCAL AREA
NETWORKING

will start to make sense. Some of the topics covered in this chapter will be revisited in other chapters. For example, the next chapter will show you how to connect your computer to the Internet, using a dial-up connection. In that chapter, you will also learn about other important networking features such as how to use Windows XP's virtual private networking (VPN) features and the personal firewall accompanying the system.

CHAPTER 25

Configuring Your Computer for an Internet Connection

IN THIS CHAPTER

- Dial-Up Networking Versus Broadband Connections   *644*

- Installing a Standard Modem   *650*

- Configuring Modem Properties   *654*

- Setting Advanced Modem Options   *663*

- Creating a New Internet Account   *664*

- Windows XP Internet Connection Firewall and Internet Connection Sharing   *669*

- Creating a Connection to the Network at Your Workplace   *673*

- Setting Up a Home or Small Office Network   *676*

- Obtaining an Internet Service Provider   *676*

Whether you use your computer for business or personal reasons, an Internet connection is practically a must. The Web offers important sources of information, communication, data exchange, and financial tracking, and entertainment. An Internet connection not only gives your computer access to the world; it gives the world access to your computer.

In this chapter, you will learn the differences between various types of Internet connections, whether broadband or dial-up. You will also learn how to set up a dial-up connection to the Internet and create effective security with Windows XP's firewall and connection management tools.

Dial-Up Networking Versus Broadband Connections

Modems translate communications between computers and outside sources such as an Internet service provider (ISP). Standard modems convert the analog signals used on an ordinary voice-grade telephone line, as well as the digital signals used by computers. Newer devices such as cable modems and digital subscriber line (DSL) modems provide an end-to-end digital connection between your computer and your ISP and thus require no digital-to-analog conversion.

The Standard Modem

The standard modem, which originally worked at speeds of 150 to 300bps, now ranges up to 56Kbps. That speed is adequate for users who use the Internet for nothing more than sending e-mail and viewing Web pages. For downloading large files or playing games on the Internet, however, this connection speed can be much too slow. Additionally, even a modem rated at 56Kbps rarely connects at that speed. Poor connections, old wiring, and heavy traffic are just some of the factors that reduce modem speed.

If you have a 56K modem installed in your computer, and you plug it into a phone jack in your home or office, then you have a modem connection. By placing a modem on each end of the connection, a computer's digital signal can be converted to an analog signal for transfer over an ordinary telephone line and then converted back to a digital signal at the other end. Thus, computers can take advantage of the huge telephone network to exchange data.

Cable and Digital Subscriber Line Modems

Cable modems and DSL modems are devices used for broadband Internet connections. Broadband is the term given to high-speed, high-traffic Internet connections. Broadband devices are *not* modems at all in the traditional sense of the word *modem* because they don't provide any signal translation between analog and digital signals. Nevertheless, cable and DSL modems are quickly becoming the modems of choice for high-speed Internet connectivity.

Digital Subscriber Lines

The term *DSL* encompasses a number of different technologies. Most home users with DSL connections actually use ADSL, or asynchronous DSL. The term *asynchronous* means that the data does not flow at the same speed in both directions. Instead, ASDL provides a faster download speed than it does for uploading data to the Internet. ASDL was designed to accommodate the average home user who typically enters a few characters or points a mouse and makes a few clicks while the Web server (or other Internet service) at the other end sends much larger volumes of data back down the data pipe to the user. For typical Web surfing or downloading files, ASDL is an excellent solution.

For business purposes, you may want to consider a different kind of DSL, depending on what services are available in your area. Most ISPs offer SDSL (single-line digital subscriber line) or HDSL (High-bit data-rate DSL); both of these connection types offer the same upload and download speed.

> **Tip**
>
> If you are working from home and connect to your company's network, then you might want to use an SDSL or HDSL connection. These connection types will accommodate large uploads such as spreadsheets and large documents from your home to your businesses network.

DSL accomplishes high bandwidth using the same pair of copper wires that your voice-grade telephone service uses (and at the same time). It may sound complex, but this process is really simple to understand. Only the first four megahertz (MHz) of the total frequency range that a copper wire is capable of carrying is used for the voice channel. Copper wires are capable of much larger frequencies. DSL simply lets your telephone service keep using that first 4MHz frequency range and, after leaving a small separation to avoid interfering with that range, uses the higher frequencies on the line for its transmissions.

The higher frequencies are split off and sent to a device called a *DSLAM (DSL access multiplexer)*. This device links together signals from many DSL lines into a single stream of data sent to and from the actual ISP. The connection to the ISP is usually a much higher bandwidth connection, such as a fiber-optic connection, and it can use different high-speed networking protocols such as asynchronous transfer mode (ATM) to allow for very fast response times for the connection between the central office and the DSLAM equipment. The DSL challenge for phone companies is upgrading the lines so that they can handle the higher frequencies and getting enough customers to make it financially feasible to install the DSLAM equipment at the central office.

Caution

One thing you should keep in mind when signing up for either DSL or cable modem access is that while the local cable or telephone company may be providing you the actual physical connection, a separate ISP may be contracting to use the lines to provide the Internet access. This means that if you have problems with your service you may get the runaround as both companies point fingers at each other. Once you have the service up and running, you will probably be glad you got it. If you have problems later on, don't expect them to get resolved quickly and efficiently all the time!

Note

One of the limiting factors determining whether you can get DSL service is the distance you live from your central office. In general, if you are more than 10,000 to 18,000 feet, depending on the type of DSL service you require, then you probably won't be able to get DSL service. The primary reason for this limitation is that the further down a copper wire an electrical signal travels, the weaker it becomes—a process called *attenuation*. However, in recent years many telephone companies have begun to install digital boxes in neighborhoods that are connected to the central office by high-capacity fiber-optic cables. They then run the copper wires to your house from this box. If this is the case, then you may indeed be able to get DSL service.

Two basic types of DSL are in use today: carrier amplitude phase (CAP) and discrete multitone (DMT). CAP was widely employed during early DSL rollouts. CAP uses two channels in the higher frequencies, a smaller frequency range for uploading information from your computer and a much larger frequency range for downloading information to your computer. CAP is not the best choice for DSL. If you have a poor quality line, then the distortions created by the line can affect the single up- or downloading frequency range.

Unlike CAP, DMT divides the upper frequency range into many smaller units, called *bins,* and monitors each of these bins for any errors that may occur due to poor line quality. DMT adapts by sending data over the bins, which cover frequencies that provide the best transmission while avoiding frequencies that are compromised by distortions on the line. Because DMT can also monitor each bin on a periodic basis, it can change between bins if the distortion is a transient one, such as those caused by high traffic on a nearby line.

Thus, if you are going to get DSL service of any kind, it would be nice to know if you are using DMT instead of CAP. However, since broadband technologies are just now starting to become widespread, you may be at the mercy of your local provider and have to take what you can get.

Cable Modems

Just as a telephone company needs to install a device at the central office to handle the Internet-bound digital signals, your cable company must do the same to enable Internet connection over the coaxial cable that carries television signals. In most digital cable TV services, each television channel occupies 6MHz of bandwidth on the coaxial cable. To provide for Internet services, the company sets aside one or more of these channels for that use.

To allow different customers to access the Internet over a cable connection, time slots are set aside on the channels dedicated to cable service. Some of these time slots, called *contention slots,* can be used by any subscriber, whereas others are dedicated to individual subscribers. Because cable modems are targeted to home users, they are configured much like ASDL, providing a smaller upload bandwidth and a much larger download bandwidth.

There is a very important topological difference in the way DSL and cable modem technologies work. Although both combine incoming signals being sent to the Internet, DSL provides you with a single line back to the DSLAM; you are the only one who uses that line. With cable modems, multiple users share a single coaxial cable segment. The more households in your neighborhood that use cable Internet access, the slower your speeds will be in both directions.

Many users were overwhelmed by the high speeds they were able to get from a cable modem—that is, when it was first installed. A year or two later, that speed has dropped dramatically. Like your telephone company, in order to make a profit, the cable provider must sign up as many customers for its Internet service as it can so that it can pay for both the cable routers at its central office and managing the network.

To get an idea of the speeds of cable modem and DSL service, Table 25.1 compares the typical transmission rates for each kind of service.

25

CONFIGURING FOR
AN INTERNET
CONNECTION

Table 25.1   Cable versus DSL: Speed

Connection	Download Speed	Upload Speed
Cable	1–2mbps	128–384kbps
ADSL	384kbps–9mbps	128kbps
SDSL	1.5mbps	1.5mbps
ISDL	144kbps max	144kbps max

Tip

You may have little choice between broadband connection types in your area. DSL may not be available in your neighborhood, but cable access may be, or vice versa. If you decide to use either of these high-speed techniques, be sure to ask a lot of questions before you sign up for the service.

When you speak with a DSL provider, ask them what kind of DSL service they will provide to your location. See if the modem they provide will belong to you or if there is a monthly rental fee. If there is a fee, find out if you can provide your own DSL modem.

Ask cable providers the same question about the cable modem; it could save you some money down the road. Also, check to see how many users are currently subscribed to your network node. If the node is nearly full, find out when the cable company plans to expand the network to reduce the traffic load.

Pros and Cons of "Always-on" Internet Connections

DSL or cable modems technologies offer "always-on" connections, as opposed to a dial-up connection that you can disconnect when you finish using it. In general, your provider will use DHCP to assign an address to your cable modem or DSL modem. Typically, you use a standard Ethernet plug on the modem to connect to your PC.

Always-on connections are convenient and offer the advantage of constant information updates and (usually) fast connectivity with no dialing and connecting time. The disadvantage of these connections is that they can open your computer to attack by hackers. Crackers and hackers can use programs to probe the Internet, cycling through all the available IP addresses. If they find your machine and it is connected to the Internet, it is easier for them to plant a virus, Trojan horse, or other malicious program on it if it is always on.

If you use an always-on connection, you need to take advantage of Windows XP's built-in firewall protection (or some other firewall device or software) to protect your always-on computer from invasion by mischievous people. (You learn about the Windows XP firewall later in this chapter.)

> **Note**
>
> Cable and DSL modem connections require that you have a network adapter card on your PC. You learn how to install a network card and how to use a switch or router to connect more than one PC to this cable or DSL modem connection in Chapter 24, "Configuring Your Computer for Local Area Networking."

Point-to-Point Protocol Over Ethernet

Windows XP also supports point-to-point over Ethernet (PPPoE). PPPoE is a new broadband Internet connection standard that may eliminate the worry of always-on connections. PPPoE is similar to a typical broadband connection in that it offers high-speed connections. It differs from the standard broadband connection, however, in that it requires you to actually authenticate yourself each time you want to establish a connection with your DSL provider. Keep in mind that many ISPs don't have a lot of IP addresses that they can allocate to customers. In order to conserve valid IP addresses, many DSL providers are switching to using PPPoE. If your broadband provider uses this protocol, then you do *not* have an always-on connection.

PPPoE does require you to go through an authentication process each time you want to connect and that takes a small amount of time. However, it offers the advantage that you are not always connected, so if you don't use a firewall or other software to protect your computer(s) from hackers or others who would do you mischief, you need not worry about turning your computer off when you are not using it.

Integrated Services Digital Network Connection

Integrated services digital network (ISDN) is a digital communications standard, like DSL, but it is not an always-on connection. Instead, most ISDN services provide two 64Kbps bearer channels to carry digital data, as well as a third channel for call setup and a telephone line. Thus, if you have ISDN service, you can connect your computer to the Internet and use your telephone at the same time.

With ISDN, you must place a call, just like you do with an ordinary modem, each time you want to connect to the Internet. Thus, ISDN, although a digital technology, is also considered a dial-up connection.

25

CONFIGURING FOR
AN INTERNET
CONNECTION

Although ISDN technology provides a good connection to an ISP, it has its drawbacks. First, it is not all that fast. When you consider that you only have two 64Kbps channels (which can usually be combined to provide you with a 128Kbps connection if your ISP or corporate network supports it), this speed is nowhere near what you can achieve with a DSL or cable modem connection. Second, it is not all that inexpensive. For the price of an ISDN connection, you may be able to get a second phone line for dedicated modem connection that delivers speeds close to those you will get over ISDN. Third, it is not all that easy to obtain. You may have to wait weeks or even months to get an ISDN connection installed.

In other words, if you can get DSL or cable modem service at your home or office, you will end up with a less expensive service that provides the same or better connection to the Internet.

Installing a Standard Modem

If you have a new PC that came with a modem and Windows XP installed, you don't need to read through the information in this section. If that is not the case and you want to use a different modem or upgrade an existing computer to Windows XP, you need to install the modem.

The Add Hardware Wizard

To install a modem in your computer, click on Start, Control Panel, then select Network and Internet Connections. In the Network and Internet Connections window, choose the Phone and Modem Options task from the See Also list located on the left side of the screen (see Figure 25.1).

If a modem is installed in your computer and has already been configured to work with Windows XP, then it will show up in the next dialog box titled Phone and Modem Options (click the Modem tab to see installed modems). If no modem appears in the Modem tab, click the Add button to launch the Add Hardware Wizard.

Tip

If you are working in the Classic view of the Control Panel, you can click the icon labeled Phone and Modem to produce the Phone and Modems Options properties sheet.

FIGURE 25.1

To install a modem or check to see if one is installed, select Phone and Modem Options.

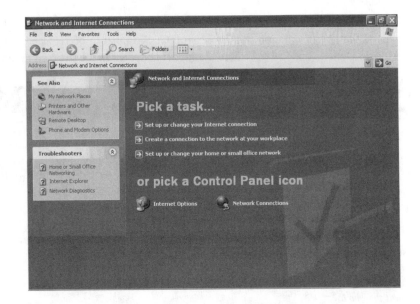

The first page of the wizard will tell you to be sure that the modem is turned on (if it is an external modem) before continuing. If you know that your modem is not supported by Windows XP but you have a driver diskette or CD from the manufacturer, then you can select the check box titled Don't Detect My Modem; I will select it from a list. Otherwise, leave this check box unselected and simply click the Next button. The next wizard screen tells you what it's searching for.

In Figure 25.2 you can see that if you didn't select the Don't detect checkbox then the wizard will inform you that it is looking for plug-and-play devices.

FIGURE 25.2

The Wizard searches for plug-and-play devices to detect your modem.

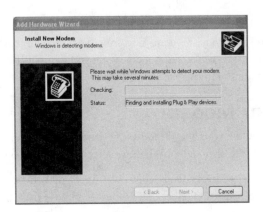

25

CONFIGURING FOR AN INTERNET CONNECTION

The Wizard screen tells you when it has located and installed your device; the final screen reports that the installation was successful. Click Finish to be returned to the Phone and Modem Options dialog box, where the modem appears in the list (see Figure 25.3).

> **Note**
>
> Note that you can install more than one modem in your computer, provided you have adequate Peripheral Component Interconnect (PCI) slots available for the hardware and enough interrupt request lines (IRQs) available for each device on the computer. If you have installed more than a single modem, then all of them should appear in the Phone and Modem Options dialog box.

FIGURE 25.3

When the modem has been successfully installed, it will show up in the Phone and Modem Options dialog box.

You can use the Add and Remove buttons at the bottom of the Phone and Modems Options dialog box to add additional modems or to remove a modem that you no longer want to use. For example, if you replace a modem, you can highlight it in this dialog box and click the Remove button to remove the driver for this modem from the system.

Detecting Your Modem

Although the number of modems on the Windows XP hardware compatibility list (HCL) is growing, there is always the chance that Windows XP won't detect your modem.

If that happens, don't worry; you very likely can select it by yourself from a list. You can also bypass the detection process altogether and request to choose from the list from the get-go.

In Figure 25.4 you can see that you have a choice at this juncture of allowing Windows XP to search for the modem, or you can use the check box labeled Don't Detect My Modem; I Will Select It from a List. Use this option if Windows XP does not detect your modem or if you have a driver file (on disk or diskette) that you would like to use for the modem.

FIGURE 25.4

You can choose to manually select the modem.

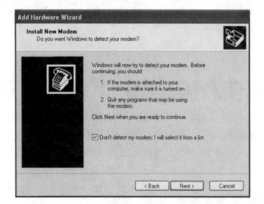

The next dialog box presented allows you to choose the manufacturer and model of your modem (see Figure 25.5). Click to highlight the correct items in the two lists; then click Next. If your modem does not appear in this list and you have a manufacturer's driver that is certified to work with Windows XP, click the Have Disk button.

FIGURE 25.5

Choose your modem's manufacturer and model number; then click Next. If you don't find your modem here, you may need to use a manufacturer's driver to install it.

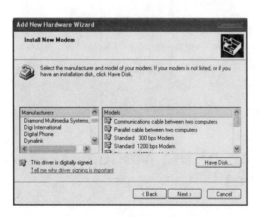

The setup wizard prompts for the location of the manufacturer's installation files. Make sure that the correct driver is listed in the text box and then click OK (use Browse to search for the driver, if necessary).

> **Note**
>
> If you have just purchased Windows XP, and the manufacturer of your modem has released a newer version of the driver software for the modem, then use the "have disk" feature to load the newer version. Manufacturers have to work from beta code, so after the final release of an operating system, they might create a new driver that is more efficient at using your modem than the original code they provided to Microsoft.

Configuring Modem Properties

The Properties button on the Modems tab of the Phone and Modem Options dialog box allows you to configure specific properties for the modem—something you rarely have to do. If your ISP or your corporate network instructs you to do so, then this is the button you should use. Figure 25.6 is an example of a modem's property sheet.

FIGURE 25.6

The Property sheet for a modem allows you to configure specific options for the modem.

The General Tab of the Modem Properties Sheet

The General tab of the modem's property sheet lists information about the manufacturer and connection type for your modem. In this example, it is installed in PCI slot number 5. The Device Status tells you whether the modem is working properly. As the text here indicates, if you are having problems with your modem, you can click the Troubleshoot button to produce a series of windows that ask you questions in an attempt to track down the source (see Figure 25.7).

FIGURE 25.7

The trouble-shooter will prompt you through the process of trying to find out why your modem is not working.

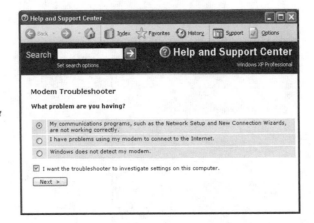

You can use the Device Usage drop-down menu to enable or disable the device. This can be useful if you have more than one modem installed and only want to use a particular one at this time.

The Modem Tab of the Modem Properties Sheet

This tab allows you to adjust the speaker volume and port speed, and to instruct the modem to wait until it hears a dial tone before it starts to dial a number. You can turn the speaker volume to Off or use the slider bar to adjust the volume. (Some folks listen to modem connection sounds to verify that the connection is in place.) You should leave the Maximum Port Speed set to the highest value unless your modem manufacturer suggests otherwise. This is not the speed of the modem itself but the speed at which applications can send data to the modem. Leave the check box labeled Wait for Dial Tone Before Dialing checked unless you have to dial the phone manually or unless you are in a different location such as another country, where your modem cannot detect the dial tone.

The Diagnostics Tab

This tab displays information about your modem and also helps troubleshoot communications problems (see Figure 25.8). The Modem Information field just displays general information about the modem, such as the Hardware ID that it is known by in the Windows XP Registry.

The Query Modem button, which was pressed before this screenshot was taken, sends several commands to your modem and displays the responses to help you determine if your modem is properly configured and functioning as it should.

25

CONFIGURING FOR
AN INTERNET
CONNECTION

FIGURE 25.8

This tab displays information about your modem and allows you to view a log file of commands and responses sent to/from the modem by the operating system.

The View Log button pops up the contents of the log of communications Windows XP uses when it initializes and talks to your modem. Notepad is the default text utility used to display the log file. You might want to send this file to Microsoft support services if you log a support call and let them examine the file to help further troubleshoot a modem problem.

> **Tip**
>
> You can also use another text viewer or word processor to view the modem operations log file at any time. It is stored in the same directory you used to install Windows XP (the `/WINDOWS` directory). The file will have, as its name, the text `ModemLog`, followed by the name of your modem and a file extension of `.txt`.

If you select the Append to Log check box each time you use the modem (which is a session), the logging text is appended to the existing log file. If you clear this check box, each session recreates a new log file that replaces the old one. Because this file can grow quite large in size, leave the check box unselected (the default) unless you are regularly experiencing problems with the modem.

The Advanced Tab

This tab enables you to enter an extra initialization string that needs to be sent to the modem during initialization. Under most circumstances, you shouldn't have to change this. However, consult your documentation to see if it specifies something other than the normal initialization string.

The Advanced Port Settings button brings up a dialog box that allows you to change settings in the receive and transmit buffers used by the modem. Use the slider bars to lower the settings if you are having problems connecting or maintaining a connection with a remote site. Keep the buffers at their highest values if you are not having problems, since this will result in faster transmission/receive times.

You also can use the Advanced Port Settings to change the COM port your modem uses. This is useful when you have more than one modem installed, but don't use them at the same time. Using this option, you can have multiple modems on the same COM port.

The Change Default Preferences button on the Advanced tab of the modem properties sheet brings up another set of properties sheets that you can use to configure your preferences about how the modem operates (see Figure 25.9).

FIGURE 25.9

You can select the General or Advanced tab on the properties sheets brought up by the Change Default Preferences button.

The General tab of the Default Preferences sheet holds the following configuration options:

- You can select the amount of time to disconnect a call when the modem remains idle (default is 30 minutes) and to cancel dialing a call if it is not connected within a certain amount of time (default is 60 seconds). You can also select the port speed, (which you can also do from the Modem tab described earlier).

- You can use the Data Protocol drop-down menu to determine how the modem handles error correction. Standard EC (the default) allows the modems at each end to negotiate the error correction method that will be used. Forced CD forces the V.42 standard to be used or terminates the connection if it is not available. Disabled disables error correction, but this can slow down communications if packets have to be retransmitted.

- The Compression drop-down menu allows you to enable or disable hardware compression on the modem. Most users should leave hardware compression enabled. If you use a communications program that performs software compression, however, or if you regularly transfer a lot of compressed files (such as WinZip files), you might want to experiment with disabling hardware compression.

- The Flow control drop-down menu determines how flow control (raising or lowering your computer/modem communication speed or throttling up or back the speed at which your computer communicates with the modem) is performed. Hardware flow control uses the ready to send/clear to send (RTS/CTS) hardware controls, whereas transmit on/transmit off (Xon/Xofs) uses software controls. Check your modem's documentation to see if it does not support hardware flow control, which is the default. If you select none, the results may be unpredictable.

The Advanced tab lets you configure hardware settings for the modem, depending on what modem you have installed. For example, you can set the data bits used to represent characters (most modems use 8 bits, some use 7 bits). You can enable parity checking (although most modems now use more sophisticated methods for error checking, so this should usually be left at none). You can also choose the modulation technique used which determines the type of codes and symbols modems use to talk to each other. Leave this setting at standard for most modems but change it if you are connecting to a modem that uses a non-standard modulation technique.

The Driver Tab

This tab shows you details about the device diver being used for the modem (see Figure 25.10). A device driver is the software component that the operating system uses to interface with the modem. Information on this tab gives a date and version number and, if the driver is a digitally signed driver, the name of the authority that signed the driver.

FIGURE 25.10

Use this tab to install, uninstall, update or roll back a driver installation.

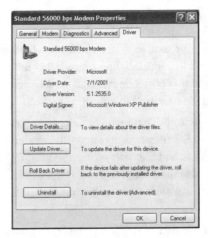

> **Tip**
>
> A digital signed driver has a digital signature that ensures that the signer has tested the driver to meet certain specifications and that the file has not been altered or changed (by a virus, for example, or overwritten by another installation procedure since the driver was signed). This signature helps ensure that your driver is functional and will perform up to the specifications you expect from your device.

The Driver Details button in the Driver tab gives you more information about the device driver, such as the files used, their locations on your system, as well as the original provider of the driver.

The Update Driver button start up the Hardware Update Wizard, allowing you to install a newer driver, if one becomes available. Usually this involves simply copying files from a new CD or floppy disk that your vendor or Microsoft has provided.

Use the Roll Back Driver button if you have updated a driver and find that the device no longer works. This feature returns your previously installed (and working) driver.

Lastly, the Uninstall button removes the driver from the system. You get a warning dialog box before this happens. Once you remove the driver, the modem will no longer function, so you will have to go through the reinstallation again. You might want to use this if you are removing a modem from the system and do not plan to use it again.

The Resources Tab

This tab displays the system resources used by the device, such as the memory usage and IRQ. If the device has been configured with values that conflict with another device, you will see a list that contains one or more devices with which the modem is in conflict.

> **Caution**
>
> Only advanced users should try to use the Resources tab options to change device settings to resolve system resource and IRQ problems. Check your modem's documentation to see to what IRQs it can be set. You may have to change a jumper on the modem card itself or run a software program supplied by the manufacturer to make changes.

25

CONFIGURING FOR
AN INTERNET
CONNECTION

The Power Management Tab

This tab contains two check boxes, which are available for selection only if supported by your modem. The Allow the Computer to Turn Off This Device to Save Power option can be useful in a laptop computer so that power to the device can be turned off when you are not using the modem, thus saving battery power. The Allow This Device to Bring the Computer Out of Standby option is useful if you use the Control Panel power options settings to allow your computer to be put into a low power state (such as hibernation). Enabling this option causes the computer to "come alive" if it detects an incoming call. This lets you leave the computer in a low power state when you are away from home because it will wake up when you dial in. Again, your modem must be capable of signaling to the operating system that it supports this functionality, or it will not work. Check the documentation to confirm.

Working with Dialing Rules

The Dialing Rules tab of the Phone and Modem Options dialog box (see Figure 25.11) lets you configure the way your modem dials in from a number of locations. If you use your mobile computer to dial from home, the office, and on the road, setting up specific information about each location lets you switch between locations without having to reconfigure your modem each time.

FIGURE 25.11

This tab allows you to add or edit Locations so that you don't have to reconfigure the dialing rules for your modem each time you use it from a different location.

For example, if you have to dial a 9 to get out of your workplace Private Branch Exchange (PBX) phone system before dialing a number you want to connect to, you can set up that dialing rule for that location. At home, you won't need this feature, so you set up a different location-dialing rule. If your Internet account uses a different phone number in each city, you will need additional location dialing rules to handle your dial-ups on the road. Click the Edit button to change information for an existing location. To add a new location, click New to produce the New Location dialog box shown in Figure 25.12.

FIGURE 25.12
The General tab allows you to give a name for the new location you are creating, along with other information.

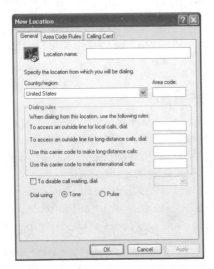

The General Tab

The General tab of the New Location dialog box (refer to Figure 25.12), enables you to give a name for each location so that you can easily switch between them. Use some text phrase that is easy for you to remember. For example, if you are changing between cities, then use the name of the city. If you have more than one ISP, you might want to use the name of one here. Whatever name you choose, just try to choose one that will help you remember for what this particular set of dialing rules is useful.

Use other options on the General tab to select a location country and region and area code. The section titled Dialing Rules offers these options:

- To Access an Outside Line for Local Calls, Dial—As described earlier, you may need to dial 9 to get outside your office PBX and connect to an actual telephone trunk line. If so, use this selection and enter the number in the box provided.

- To Access an Outside Line for Long Distance Calls, Dial—Similar to the previous item, your PBX may require you to enter a different number (such as 8) to access a long-distance line when you are at work. Use the space provided here to enter that number.

- Use This Carrier Code to Make Long Distance Calls—Enter the number of a long distance operator you need to dial before dialing a long distance number in this field.

- Use This Carrier Code to Make International Calls—Enter the international prefix used to make international calls in the box provided with this selection.

25

CONFIGURING FOR AN INTERNET CONNECTION

The check box To Disable Call Waiting, Dial is used to specify the telephone numeric sequence your local carrier has given you to disable call waiting. Call waiting (on some modems) can interrupt the current modem connection, so you may want to use this feature in such situations.

The Pulse and Tone radio buttons are pretty much becoming dated in the United States, but you may find them useful in some locations.

The Area Code Rules Tab

This tab allows you to configure how to dial numbers within and outside your area code. Since the proliferation of cellular phones and other phone services (such as fax machines and wireless personal digital assistants [PDAs]), it has been necessary for phone companies to create additional area codes to divide up the phone number address space. Indeed, many large cities have more than one area code. To make matters even worse, your neighbor across the street may have a different area code than you! In some places, area codes represent distinct areas, whereas some allow area codes to overlap geographic locations.

To add new rules to this tab, click New. Figure 25.13 shows the New Area Code Rule dialog box. As the dialog box says, these rules will apply only to calls made to the area code you specify and the prefix combinations you supply.

FIGURE 25.13

Use the New button on the Area Code Rules tab to create area code dialing rules.

In the Area Code field enter the area code to which this rule will be applied. In the United States, the prefix is the first three numbers of a local seven-digit telephone number. For example, the number 609-912-0470 consists of the area code 609, a prefix of 912, and a final number following that prefix. Use the radio buttons in the Prefixes area to select that all prefixes within this area code will be subject to this rule. You can also use the radio button labeled Include Only the Prefixes in the List Below to enter only the specific prefixes to which this rule will apply. To add a prefix, select the second radio button and then click Add. A pop-up dialog box allows you to enter a single prefix or a list of prefixes separated by commas. Click OK when finished entering a prefix or prefixes.

In the Rules section, you can specify the area code and prefixes you have defined in the dialog box:

- Dial—Use this check box to enter (in the field provided) a number that must be dialed first before dialing numbers that match this area code and prefixes. The number 1 is usually used, but your telephone company may use a different number.

- Include the area code—This check box determines whether to include the area code when dialing the number. In some cities, you must dial a 10-digit number when more than one area code is used in a single area. Again, check your local telephone company to determine how dialing works in your area!

The Calling Card Tab

If you travel and use a calling card to make long distance calls to your ISP or home computer, use the options in this tab. The default selections for calling cards are quite extensive, but you can always use the New button to bring up a dialog box to enter a different calling card. When you have entered your calling card, use the Account Number and Personal ID Number (PIN) fields to enter additional information that may be required by your telephone card service provider.

> **Tip**
>
> The calling card modem configuration options are especially helpful if you are a business traveler and use a company calling card. For salespeople who must make Internet connections from such places as airports or hotels, using a company calling card can be a lot more inexpensive than using the rates charged by local providers.

Setting Advanced Modem Options

The Advanced tab of the Phone and Modem Options dialog box contains options for selecting the telephone application programming interface (TAPI) provider you want to use on this computer. Figure 25.14 indicates available APIs supplied with the operating system. You can use the Add and Configure to add additional APIs or edit the configuration of any of those that appear in the list.

25

CONFIGURING FOR AN INTERNET CONNECTION

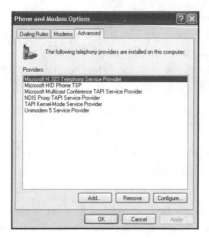

FIGURE 25.14

Choose a TAPI provider from this dialog box.

You can also use the Remove button when a particular provider is highlighted to remove that provider's API from your computer.

Creating a New Internet Account

When your modem is installed and configured, you are ready to create a new Internet account or enter the information about an existing account. Even if you are dialing into a corporate network, the account creation process is much the same. The following sections take you through the process of setting up your modem to dial into different kinds of networks using Windows XP.

Configuring an Existing Internet Account

To begin the process click on Start, Control Panel and when the Category view pops up, select Network and Internet Connections. From this window, choose one of the following three options in the Pick a Task category:

1. Set up or change your Internet connection.
2. Create a connection to the network at your workplace.
3. Set up or change your home or small office network.

For the purposes of this chapter, choose the first option to produce the Internet Properties dialog box (see Figure 25.15). In the Connections tab, click the Setup button to launch the New Connection Wizard.

FIGURE 25.15

Use the Setup button to configure a dial-up Internet account.

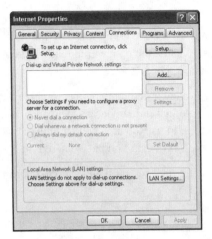

Click the Next button in the first Wizard screen to continue.

In the second screen, choose Connect to the Internet to create an Internet account on your computer; then click Next. The wizard asks you to select from a list ISPs, set up a connection manually, or use a CD that you have received from your ISP. For this example, select Set Up My Connection Manually and then click Next.

The next wizard screen (see Figure 25.16) asks you to choose the kind of connection you will use for your Internet service. If you are connecting to a DSL or cable modem broadband connection, choose Connect Using a Broadband Connection That Is Always On. If you are connecting to a PPPoE connection, choose Connect Using a Broadband Connection That Requires a User Name and Password. For the purpose of this example, choose Connect Using a Dial-up Modem.

FIGURE 25.16

Choose the type of connection you will use for an Internet connection.

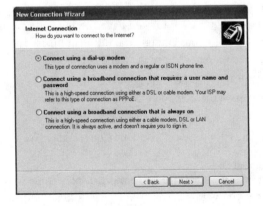

25

After you click Next, the wizard will ask you to provide a name for the connection. You can enter any text here that you want. If you are going to create multiple connections, then you should use some text here to name the connection that will help you distinguish it from others. After you enter the name, click Next.

The next item you will be prompted to enter is the telephone number of the ISP. Enter the number provided by your ISP. Note that in many areas, new area codes are overlapping geographical areas, so if you have to use the area code to dial the ISP, be sure to include it in the field provided. Click Next when you have entered the telephone number.

Figure 25.17 shows that you must enter the account name and password that your ISP has assigned.

FIGURE 25.17

Enter the account name and password using this dialog box.

Additionally, the three check boxes on this dialog box from which you can choose are as follows:

- Use This Account Name and Password When Anyone Connects to the Internet from This Computer—This is useful if you have one Internet account but have multiple users who log onto your computer at different times. This check box allows all users on the computer to use the same connection.

- Make This the Default Internet Connection—Use this if you have more than one Internet account set up on the computer, but want this one to be the default one to use.

- Turn on Internet Connection Firewall for This Connection—We will learn about this later in this chapter.

That's it! The last dialog box of the wizard will simply display some information about your selections and present you with a check box labeled Add a Shortcut to This Connection to My Desktop. You can use this check box or not. Whichever way, click Finish to complete the wizard and your account will be set up. Figure 25.18 shows the connection dialog box that pops up when you click on the Desktop icon for the connection.

FIGURE 25.18

Just click Dial to connect to the Internet.

Changing a Dial-Up Connection's Properties

After you have set up a connection, you may change your mind about some of the selections you made during the setup procedure, or you might just not remember everything you did. You can use the Properties button in Figure 25.18 to bring up the connection's Properties dialog box so that you can review information about each connection you create. The Properties dialog box will have the following several tabs:

- General—This shows you the modem type and allows you to use a Configure button to make changes to the modem configuration, as well as the phone number and dialing rules used for the connection.

- Options—This tab allows you to select from a number of items, such as displaying information about the dialing and connecting progress and whether to prompt you for a phone number or use the default one provided for this connection. You can also use a check box to include your Windows domain name if you are dialing into a business environment where this information is needed. Redialing options on this tab let you specify the number of redial attempts, time between each attempt, and to set an amount of time to hang up the connection when it is idle.

- Security—This tab allows you to select to send your password across the connection in an unsecured fashion (as clear text) or to use another method, such as an encrypted password or a smart card. You can also use an advanced Settings button to further configure a secure method for logging on. However, for most ordinary users, this will not be necessary. The advanced Settings button will bring up a list of protocols (PAP, SPAP, CHAP, and so on), about which only someone skilled in

25

CONFIGURING FOR
AN INTERNET
CONNECTION

network security can advise you. This tab also allows you to use a check box that will show a terminal window during the connection (so you can see how the connection is established) and to run a script file, if your ISP requires one. Today most ISPs do not require a script file, but this option is available if yours does.

- Networking—This tab has a list of the protocols and services you are using for the connection, such as TCP/IP. At the top is a drop-down list labeled Type of Dial-up Server I Am Calling that can be used to change between PPP and SLIP. As you learned in Appendix A, "Introduction to Transmission Control Protocol/Internet Protocol," SLIP is an older protocol, and you should probably stick with the default setting of PPP. A Settings button allows you to further configure the connection. You can use this button to enable link control protocol (LCP) extensions, enable software compression, and negotiate for multilink or single-link connections. Again, you probably won't have to change nay of these values unless instructed by your ISP.

- Advanced—This tab allows you to enable the Internet Connection Firewall (ICF), if you did not choose to do so during the connection setup. You can also use a check box on this tab to allow other computers on your local network to connect to the Internet through your computer using this connection. This is called *Internet Connection Sharing (ICS)*. Both of these will be discussed in greater detail in the next section.

Checking the Status of Your New Connection

After you have dialed into the Internet using your new connection, you can check the status of the connection easily. Double-click the "connected computer" icon at the right end of the Task bar in an area that used to be called the *System Tray*. A dialog box appears on your Desktop that shows you the status of the connection. The General tab of this dialog box indicates how long you have been connected and at what speed. You can also see the number of bytes sent and received, number of errors, and percentage of compression, if any, for the connection.

Tip

If you are attempting a long download it seems to have gotten hung up, use the connection status dialog box to see if any information is actually being exchanged. If the Bytes Sent and Received columns aren't incrementing, then you may have a problem. Perhaps the connecting server has frozen, or your computer can't access the Domain Name Server anymore. Usually, logging off and reconnecting with the ISP will fix the problem. If not, contact the ISP and see if they are having system problems. Be ready to provide your own system's information in case they need it. The Details tab of the dialog box shows you parameters about the connection, such as your computer's IP address, the server's IP address, the transport protocol (usually TCP/IP), whether compression is being used, and so on.

Windows XP Internet Connection Firewall and Internet Connection Sharing

A firewall is a fireproof barrier between connected rooms or buildings that is intended to help keep a fire from spreading from one to the other. In networking, a firewall serves a similar purpose. Since you are connecting your computer to literally millions of other computers when you connect to the Internet, you need to have some mechanism in place to protect your computer from malicious users, viruses, and other bad things that lurk on the net. The ICF that comes with Windows XP is a flexible means of protecting your computer when you connect to the Internet.

Internet connection sharing allows you to use one computer to make the Internet connection; it then allows other computers that are connected to yours via a local area network (LAN) to use that connection. This means you won't have to buy a modem for each computer in your home or small office.

Windows XP Internet Connection Firewall

Microsoft's ICF uses a process called *stateful inspection* to protect your computer. When you send out a request from your computer to the Internet like clicking on a link to download a Web page, the ICF makes note of this in a table. When the response comes back from the Web site, the ICF allows the data to pass through if it finds an entry in the table.

This keeps incoming traffic from the Internet limited to just things you request. As mentioned earlier, hackers can use programs that scan the Internet and probe all possible IP addresses looking to get a response back. In Appendix A you will learn about the ping program. It uses ICMP ECHO and REPLY messages. ICF wouldn't allow an ICMP ECHO message to come into your computer from the Internet; thus it would keep a hacker from discovering that your computer is online. However, if you choose to send out an ICMP ECHO request yourself to see if another computer is reachable, then ICF would allow the ICMP REPLY message back in, since it would have an entry in its table that you are the one who originated the data exchange.

25

CONFIGURING FOR AN INTERNET CONNECTION

To enable the firewall, click on the Properties button of the connection in question to bring up the Properties dialog box. Click the Advanced tab and click the check box found in the ICF section (see Figure 25.19).

FIGURE 25.19

Enable ICF by selecting the check box in the ICF section of the Advanced tab for a connection.

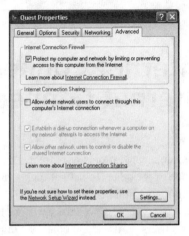

Once you select this check box, the Settings button at the bottom of the dialog box becomes available. Click on this button to see the items you can configure for the firewall within the Advanced Settings dialog box, as shown in Figure 25.20.

FIGURE 25.20

You can configure the firewall using this dialog box.

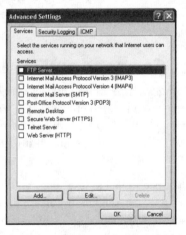

At times, you may want to allow incoming traffic from the Internet that is not in response to a request you have sent out. For example, you may want to allow another user to use FTP to retrieve a file from your computer, or you may operate a Web server and want to allow HTTP requests to come in. If you are using any of the services listed in Figure 25.20, you can allow incoming connections by clicking the appropriate check box. Each of these services uses a specific port number; these are the very basic Internet services you are likely to need.

You can add additional services, for example, to open up a port for a game shared by users on the Internet. To add additional ports (think of a port as a service), use the Add button at the bottom of the Advanced Settings dialog box. Figure 25.21 shows how you must provide information about the new service you want to add.

FIGURE 25.21

You can add additional network services to the firewall using this dialog box.

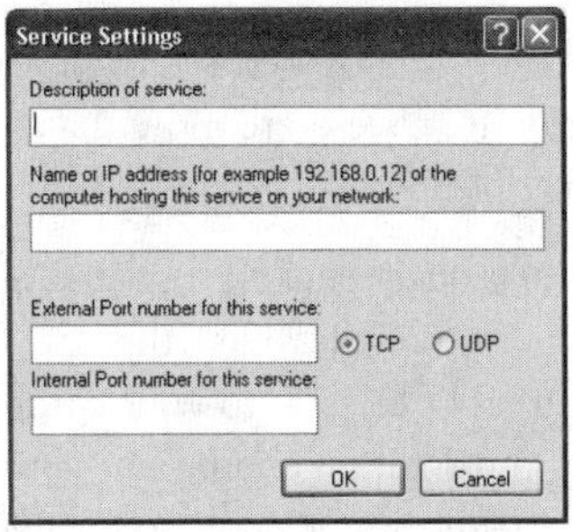

The items you will need to provide include the following:

- Description of Service—You can use any text here you want, and this is what will show up in the Advanced Settings dialog box shown in Figure 25.20 after you add the service.

- Name or IP Address of the Computer Hosting This Service on Your Network— This is exactly what it says it is. If you are operating a Web server, for example, then enter the IP address of that server here.

- External Port Number for This Service—This is the port number that an external request will use when accessing your service. You can visit the Web site of The Internet Corporation for Assigned Names and Numbers (ICANN) at http://www.icann.com to view a list of port numbers used for specific services. Depending on the service you offer, you will also have to use one of the radio buttons next to this field (TCP or UDP) to indicate which network protocol will be allowed to use this service. For more information about TCP and UDP, see Appendix A.

- Internal Port Number for This Service—Use this to specify the port number the server on your internal network uses for this service. This may be different than the port number used for the previous field.

You can also use the Edit button in the Advanced Settings dialog box to bring up a similar dialog box for the services the firewall supplies by default. Since these are

25

CONFIGURING FOR
AN INTERNET
CONNECTION

well-known services, you need only enter an IP address or hostname of the network computer to which you want this service limited.

Under the Security Logging tab you can elect to have ICF log both packets that are dropped (those that don't make it through the firewall), as well as successful connections. You can use this tab to change the location and name of the log file and limit its size. If you decide to allow any of the incoming services described in the previous paragraphs, you should enable logging and check the log often to ensure that your network is not being abused by someone attempting to hack into it.

You use the ICMP tab of the Advanced Settings dialog box to enable options for the ICMP. Unless you have a good reason for doing so and are more than a novice when it comes to TCP/IP matters, do not enable any of these.

For example, allowing incoming `ICMP ECHO` request packets can let a hacker with a port scanner find out that your computer is online. Once they have this information, they can then use a wide variety of tools on the Internet to break into your computer or network. Just as silence is golden, it is best to let all information about your network stop at the firewall's address. It can only work to an outsider's advantage to be able to obtain information about any computer on a LAN attached to your network.

Windows XP Internet Connection Sharing

If you have a small office or more than one computer at home, you can connect them in a LAN (see Chapter 24) and then allow a single computer to be used for Internet connections. Using Windows XP's ICS service, you can allow computers on your LAN to use this single connection.

Figure 25.22 shows the Advanced tab of the connection's property sheet with the Allow Other Network Users to Connect Through This Computer's Internet Connection option checked. That turns on ICS.

You have the following two options in the ICS section of the Advanced tab:

- Establish a Dial-up Connection Whenever a Computer on My Network Attempts to Access the Internet—Checking this option means that you don't have to stay connected to the Internet all the time in order for ICS to work. If the computer configured to connect to the Internet isn't connected when another computer on the network wants to communicate with the Internet, the second computer can dial into the Internet. If you leave this unchecked, you can control when the Internet connection is available from the computer that makes the connection.

- Allow Other Network Users to Control or Disable the Shared Internet Connection—Selecting this check box allows the client computers on your network to control the Internet connection. If the computer configured for an Internet connection is not currently connected, for example, the client can choose to connect (or disconnect) it.

FIGURE 25.22

You can use ICS to allow more than one computer in your network to use a single Internet connection.

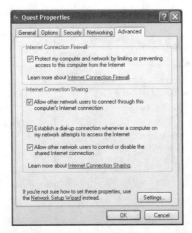

> ## Note
>
> One important note about ICS you should keep in mind is that the computer that connects to the Internet essentially has two network connections. The first is the Internet connection, and the IP address is usually supplied by the ISP. The second connection is through a network card that connects to other computers in your LAN. If you enable ICS, then the network adapter will be assigned a new static IP address, as determined by ICS. If you have already assigned network addresses to other computers in your LAN, then you will probably have to reconfigure them to be in the same network address range (and use the same subnet mask) to be compatible with the new address that ICS assigns to your network adapter. To determine how to view and change the IP address of a network adapter card, see Chapter 24.

Creating a Connection to the Network at Your Workplace

For most of this chapter you have learned how to set up a modem and configure a simple dial-up account to the Internet. However, if you will recall, two other options were found under Pick a Task when you clicked on Network and Internet Connections in the Control Panel. The second was to create a connection to the network at your workplace. You could use the simple dial-up method to connect to a workplace network. However, this second option allows you to more securely create a connection.

After you click on Create a Connection to the Network at Your Workplace, the New Connection Wizard will present you with two options (see Figure 25.23).

FIGURE 25.23

You can still use the New Connection Wizard to connect to your workplace network.

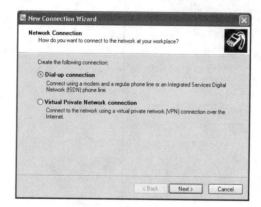

The first option is to create a simple dial-up connection, as was described earlier in this chapter. The second option, however, allows you to create a virtual private network (VPN) connection, which is a more secure method for communicating across the Internet to a workplace network.

Note

You can use the Dial-up Connection option, if you are dialing into a server that is on your workplace network, thus bypassing the Internet. Unless you think someone is tapping your phone line, this should create a simple, easy-to-use method for connecting to a computer at work. However, if you are using the Internet, a VPN connection provides a more secure solution. For example, if you are a mobile worker and dial into local Internet providers as you travel, using a VPN connection can help secure your communications with the home base network.

To set up a VPN, click the second radio button and then the Next button. Just like the dial-up version of the wizard, the next dialog box asks you to give a name to the connection. You can use the name of the server at your workplace for the name of the connection. Once you have provided a name for the connection, click Next to continue.

The next Wizard screen (see Figure 25.24) asks if you want to automatically dial an existing Internet connection when you decide to establish the VPN or whether you should be prompted first. The second radio button allows you to select among different connections if you use the VPN to dial in from different locations, each with its own phone number.

FIGURE 25.24

Select whether to automatically dial a connection when you use the VPN.

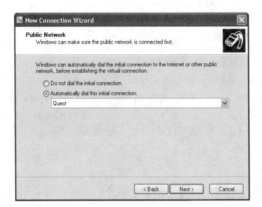

The next Wizard screen asks you to provide the IP address of the computer that you will connect to at your workplace. You will need to get this from your network administrator. Enter the address and then click the Next button to continue.

Finally, the wizard will again present you with a list of the choices you have made and give you a check box that allows you to add a shortcut to your Desktop for this VPN connection. Click the Finish button to terminate the wizard.

> **Note**
>
> You can learn more about VPNs and how they are implemented in Microsoft's Windows operating systems by reading Appendix A. Although creating the VPN is a simple task, as you have just seen, your network administrator will probably require that you make changes to the connection's properties, such as the method used for exchanging username and password information. Once the VPN has been set up and tested, you can send information through an encrypted tunnel that helps keep anyone on the Internet from intercepting your communications and deciphering the content.

25

CONFIGURING FOR AN INTERNET CONNECTION

Setting Up a Home or Small Office Network

The third option found under the Pick a Task listing in the Control Panel allows you to set up some of the basic things you can use in a small network, most of which you have already learned about in this chapter. Using this option, you can set up an Internet connection and firewall, as well as share files, folders, and printers.

Simply follow the directions the wizard presents, which will vary depending on the choices you make from one dialog box to the next. For example, you can use this wizard to set up the initial computer that will connect to the Internet, or you can use it to set up a computer for a client on your network who will use the Internet connection the other computer offers. This wizard can be considered a simple way to perform the other tasks we have discussed.

Obtaining an Internet Service Provider

Earlier in this chapter, when you learned how to set up a dial-up account for an ISP, it was assumed that you already had an ISP and the phone number you would need to connect to it. However, if you haven't already done that, Windows XP can help you with this too.

After you start the New Connection Wizard for a dial-up connection and select the Connect to the Internet option, the Wizard will proceed to the dialog box shown in Figure 25.25. Obviously, if you have a CD from an ISP like AOL, you can use the third radio button and click Next. The Wizard will then instruct you to insert the CD and follow the directions the ISP's setup program provides.

FIGURE 25.25

You can choose an ISP that has its own set up routine or pick from a list of ready-to-go service providers.

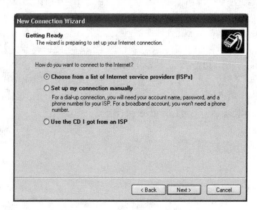

If you don't already have an Internet account or a setup CD from an ISP, then use the first radio button (Choose From a List of Internet Service Providers (ISPs)) and click the Next button.

The Wizard will then ask you to click Finish so it can provide you with some choices. After the Wizard closes down, the Online Services folder will appear in the Windows Explorer window.

Here, you can set up an account using Microsoft's own MSN service. Or you can select from a list of providers Microsoft has found in your location by clicking the shortcut called *Refer Me to More Internet Service Providers*. If you click on this shortcut, the Internet Connection Wizard will open and dial into a referral service number and download a list of providers for your location.

You can choose one of them, or you can obtain referrals from your friends and make your own decision about which ISP to use.

Summary

Setting up a modem with Windows XP is usually a painless process, since the operating system will automatically detect most plug-and-play modems. If it doesn't, you can always use the diskette or CD provided by the modem manufacturer to load a driver for Windows XP to use to communicate with the modem. Setting up a connection to the Internet can be a little more complicated, but it doesn't have to be. By using a wizard, the process is simplified, and you only need to enter a small amount of information for most of the major ISPs. Depending on the type of Internet connection you have, the Windows XP firewall may offer powerful protection for your computer. In this chapter, you learned how to enable and configure the firewall for your connection type.

25

CONFIGURING FOR
AN INTERNET
CONNECTION

Joining a Domain and the Active Directory

IN THIS CHAPTER

- **Understanding Windows Domains** *680*

- **What Is the Active Directory?** *684*

- **Joining a Domain Using Windows XP** *687*

- **After You Have Joined a Domain** *691*

There are three scenarios in which it makes the most sense to deploy Windows XP Professional:

- In a home environment
- In a small business
- In a large corporate network

In the home environment, many computer professionals install Windows XP so that they can continue to improve their skills and stay up-to-date with the latest technology. If you want to get your Microsoft Certified Systems Engineer (MCSE) or some other certification, then you will need to practice and learn on the actual operating system. Otherwise, home users should use Windows XP Home Edition and not Professional.

For small businesses, Windows XP Professional is a great choice. You can't beat it for creating a small business network using the workgroup model. Considering its heritage, this is an incredibly stable operating system.

If you are going to use Windows XP at a business (big or small) that already uses Windows Server computers grouped into domains or on a network that uses Windows 2000 or Windows 2002 servers and the Active Directory, then you need to read this chapter. This chapter only briefly touches on some of the concepts of the Active Directory, concentrating on showing you how to join a domain, and become part of and make use of the Active Directory.

> **Note**
>
> You can learn more about the Active Directory and how it dramatically improves the capabilities for storing and locating resource information for Windows networks in Appendix B, "LDAP."
>
> Before you can join a domain, you must first configure your computer to participate in the network. Appendix A, "Introduction to TCP/IP," covers the basics of the TCP/IP protocol suite that is used for most modern networks today, while Chapter 24, "Configuring Your Computer for Local Area Networking," will show you how to set up your Windows XP computer to participate in such a network.

Understanding Windows Domains

After you have successfully installed the networking protocols, clients and services, then it is time to look into becoming part of a domain or the Active Directory. Domains are a

Joining a Domain and the Active Directory

CHAPTER 26

681

26

JOINING A
DOMAIN AND
ACTIVE DIRECTORY

collection of computers that share a common security database. Thus domains present a security boundary.

The domain concept was developed by Microsoft early in the development of Windows NT to allow for a single logon for each user. In earlier networking models, such as Windows for Workgroups, accessing resources on other computers required that you remember a username and password stored on each of the other computers with which you needed to exchange data. This share level of access still exists in Windows XP, but with the NT file system (NTFS) access permissions are now more granular. That granularity allows the network administrator to exercise a large degree of control over what you can access and to audit your successful (or unsuccessful) attempts to do so.

> **Tip**
>
> When you first set up Windows XP and if you have a network card installed in your computer, you are prompted by the Setup program to use Typical or Custom settings for networking. If you chose Typical, then your computer is set up to use transfer call protocol/Internet protocol (TCP/IP), to automatically obtain an IP address (using Dynamic Host Configuration Protocol (DHCP)), and to be part of a workgroup. The default in this dialog box for the name of the workgroup is simply WORKGROUP, but you can change it to anything you prefer. For a small environment in which you do not need the security and control that domains or the Active Directory provide, this sort of setup can work perfectly for a small network. You should change the name from WORKGROUP to something more meaningful, because everyone who knows how Windows operates will know the default (and could potentially come in with a laptop computer and "join" your workgroup).

How Domains Function

When you become a member of a domain using Windows NT computers, the system stores information about your username and password in a database called the Security Accounts Manager (SAM) on a Primary Domain Controller (PDC). Backup Domain Controllers (BDCs) regularly receive security information updates to provide for redundancy, in case, for example, the PDC has been taken offline to perform maintenance. Administrators can also locate BDCs close to users in geographically dispersed networks in order to enable authentication to be done locally, rather than through an expensive network link to the PDC of the domain.

> **Note**
>
> The Security Accounts Manager (SAM) database in a Windows NT network resides only on Windows NT Server computers. You cannot use Windows NT or earlier versions of Windows operating systems such as Windows 98 for domain controllers. You can, however, use a Windows 2000 server computer to operate as a domain controller in a mixed-mode network that uses the Active Directory, yet still contains other Windows NT server computers acting as domain controllers.

The Master Domain Model

As mentioned earlier, Domains provide a means of defining a security boundary. For each domain, a boundary exists to protect resources belonging to the domain. For example, one popular method for implementing domains is called the *Master Domain Model.* In this model, a single domain stores all user accounts to make it easier to manage user accounts from a single location and to create resource domains containing the actual files, printers, and other resources that users need to access. The Master Domain model is shown in Figure 26.1.

FIGURE 26.1

In the Master Domain Model, all user accounts are stored in a single domain, and trust relationships make it possible for users to access resources in resource domains.

In this model, a trust relationship is set up between the master domain (called *ACME* in Figure 26.1) and each of the resource domains. Notice that the arrows that represent trust relationships point in a single direction. This is to show that a trust relationship in a Windows NT domain network is a unidirectional trust feature. In order for users in one domain to access resources in another domain, the following two things must be done:

- A trust relationship must be set up by the network administrators of the domains so that the resource domain "trusts" the users of the other domain.

Joining a Domain and the Active Directory

CHAPTER 26

683

26

JOINING A
DOMAIN AND
ACTIVE DIRECTORY

- The administrator of the resource domain must then grant appropriate permissions for resource access to users from the "trusted" domain.

As you can see, simply setting up a trust relationship between domains *does not compromise the security boundary that a domain creates*. It just opens a door. The administrator of the domain that trusts another domain still has control over the resources in the domain.

Opening this door allows the domain administrator of the trusting domain to grant access to resources in his or her domain to user or user groups in the trusted domain. By granting permissions to individual users or groups of users from trusted domains, the administrators of resource domains could grant or deny access to specific resources (down to the file level) in their respective domains. Yet, from a people management standpoint, it is easier to keep all user accounts in a single domain so that the human resources department, for example, can administer creating and deleting accounts as employees come and go.

> **Note**
>
> There is another way to let a user have access to resources in multiple domains without using trust relationships. You can set up a user account for the user in each domain, but this arrangement defeats the purpose of a single network logon that the domain/trust relationship model provides. If you create multiple accounts for a user in multiple domains, they are separate accounts. The user would have to provide a username and password each time he wanted to connect to a resource in any of the domains in which he has an account. Additionally, changing the password of an account in one domain would have no effect on the accounts the user has in other domains.

Working with Trust Relationships

As you can see, by providing a single logon for each user, security is greatly increased for the network as a whole. If each user has to remember a different password (much less username) for every file share or printer or other resource that they connect to, then the user is more likely to write down this information, making it easy to compromise security. By providing each user with a single username and a single password, domains allow for greater security.

Although trust relationships are unidirectional, you also can create two trust relationships between two domains—that is, one for each direction. Suppose, for example, two small companies have just merged and each company uses only a single domain for its network. By setting up two trust relationships, one for each direction, it is a simple matter to allow users to exchange information with users in the other domain.

Single-domain user accounts and resource-domain storage make up perhaps the most popular domain model in older Windows NT networks, but it isn't the only model. For example, in a company where users generally make access of resources only in their local domain and rarely have to access resources in another domain, using a multiple-domain model may be appropriate. Users can have their user account stored in a domain local to their environment, making it easy for the local administrator to grant and deny access to resources. Trust relationships between domains can allow users to cross domain boundaries to gain access to resources.

What Is the Active Directory?

The Active Directory changes the landscape dramatically. Active Directory uses domains, although simply as an organizational unit in the Active Directory database. The Active Directory also still allows for domain controllers, but it doesn't use PDCs and BDCs. All domain controllers in a domain are peers when the Active Directory is fully implemented. With this arrangement, changes to the security database can be made on any of the domain controllers. When using PDCs and BDCs, all changes to the security database must be made on the PDC (of which there can only be one in any particular domain). Additionally, those changes are propagated on a periodic basis out to the BDCs, which merely hold a copy of the security database.

You can probably notice a problem with this setup right away. What happens if the PDC is taken off line for some reason? In that case, no changes can be made to the security database. There is a provision that allows a BDC to be promoted to become the new PDC of a domain, and the process can be reversed when the PDC is brought back into service again. Network administrators can be thankful that using the Active Directory has eliminated this headache.

Another important difference between the domain-based Windows network of earlier times and the Active Directory network that is available today, is that the security database can now hold much more information. PDCs and BDCs held a limited amount of information about each user account and each computer that participated in the domain. The SAM also held information about trust relationships that a domain maintained with other domains.

How the Active Directory Works

The Active Directory is similar in many ways to NetWare's Novell Directory Services. It holds all the same user and computer information that the Windows NT domain controllers do but adds a lot more information so that the Active Directory can hold much more information about each user account than can NDS.

It is easy to see that a security database would need to maintain a copy of the user's logon username, password, and a few other things such as whether the user is allowed dial-up access and what rights the user is granted by the domain administrator. These are basic data items that most computer systems store in a security database.

The Active directory expands the amount of information you can store about each user account dramatically. For example, what is the user's telephone number? What is the user's cell phone number? Who is the user's supervisor? All these items, and many more, can be stored in the Active Directory. You can see an example of a typical user account in Appendix B. The Active Directory also stores an account for each computer that is part of a domain, as well as information about the shared resources, such as file shares and printers, for the domain.

Tip

The Active Directory comes with a number of built-in object classes, each of which can be used create an instance of a resource, such as a user account. In addition, the schema, which is a term that most database programmers will recognize, is extensible. In other words, you can create entirely new object classes (and thus track new kinds of resources), and you can add attributes (pieces of information) to existing object classes. So, if you want to be sure you don't forget to send the boss and his wife flowers on their anniversary, you can add an attribute to track such anniversaries to the Active Directory!

As if that isn't enough, the Active Directory also stores information for more than one domain. The directory database is a tree-like structure that can contain many domains, and all domains that are part of the same tree have implicit two-way trust relationships between them. This eliminates another headache for network administrators. They no longer need to establish, or keep track of, trust relationships. Instead, it is a simple matter for a domain administrator to grant users from any other domain in the domain tree access to resources in his domain. The domain then remains a security boundary in the Active Directory, but trust relationships aren't needed between domains in the same tree.

> **Note**
>
> When you create a domain, you can join it to a domain tree or create a new domain tree. As you can imagine, this leaves open the possibility of having more than one domain tree. When you have multiple domain trees in a network it is called a *forest*.
>
> Domains that reside in the same domain tree have implicit two-way trust relationships between all other domains in the same tree, but the same is not true for a forest. In that case, you must still create trust relationships if users in a domain in one tree need to access resources in a domain in a different tree in the forest.

In either case, using a Windows NT domain network or using the Active Directory to store domains, if your Windows XP computer is going to be in a network that uses domains, then an account will need to be created for both you and the computer itself.

Computer and User Accounts in the Active Directory

Each computer in the network has its own account in the domain, in order to prevent someone from simply placing a rogue computer onto the network and becoming part of your network. By requiring each Windows XP computer to have a computer account in the domain, the administrator has control over which computers can participate in the domain.

The domain administrator can also manage computers that are part of the domain. When a computer joins a domain, the Domain Admins group of the domain is automatically placed into the Administrators user group on the local computer. Although it is quite possible for the local computer administrator to remove the Domain Admins from the Administrators group, that would defeat the purpose of allowing domain administrators control over the computer in the domain. For example, the Administrator account on your computer can grant permission to users in the domain to have access to the printer on your computer. A user account that is a member of the Domain Admin's account can do this for all computers; in a large network you don't need to have a separate administrator for every computer.

Each user must also have a user account in the domain if the user wants to access resources on any computer other than his own local Windows XP workstation. Indeed, if you have a printer connected to your computer and all the applications and data you need are on your local computer, then you don't need a user account in the domain. You don't even need to be on the network if you have everything you need installed on a single computer. However in network environments, you will need access to files and other resources, so a domain user account is helpful.

> **Tip**
>
> Domain accounts, enable you to participate in a domain-based network and give you a single logon for the network. In a small network that doesn't use domains (or on a standalone computer), you can create a user account for each person who uses the computer. This arrangement can help you keep your own files and application and Desktop settings separate from those of others who use the same computer.

Joining a Domain Using Windows XP

You can join a domain when you first install Windows XP. When you get to the network selections dialog boxes, just enter the domain name. If your network administrator has already created a computer account for the computer, then it can join the domain automatically. You will be asked for a username and password of a domain account that has the right to join a computer to a domain. This feature again is to prevent just anyone from hooking up a computer to your network and joining it to the domain.

When the administrator creates a computer account in the domain, the administrator only has to give a name to the computer that will join the domain. The purpose of having an administrator username and password when the computer actually joins the domain is to prevent someone from finding out the names of computer accounts that have been created and simply using those names to install computers on your network. The administrator username and password is used to authenticate that the computer for which the account was created is indeed the computer joining the domain.

Ideally, the administrator will already have created a domain user account for you. If not, although your computer may be part of the domain, you will only have a local computer account that is good for accessing the files and other resources on your own Windows XP computer.

Joining a Domain During the Windows XP Setup Process

During the Setup process, you will be prompted to use Typical or Custom settings for network access. Choose Custom if you want to join a domain. You will also have to have an administrator present that knows a username and password for a domain account that has the right granted to it to join a computer to the domain.

> **Tip**
>
> Although it may be impractical to always have a domain administrator on hand when you are undergoing the Windows XP Setup process, it is always possible to use an unattended setup file (described in Chapter 4, "Unattended Installation and Sysprep"). If you use the Setupmgr.exe program to create the answer file, you can store an administrator password in the answer file in encrypted format, making it unnecessary for a domain administrator to be present when the actual Setup program is run.

Selecting Custom during the networking portion of the Setup process enables you to configure many other items, such as network protocols and services. If you have been assigned specific IP addressing information, you will also need that. For most computer networks today, however, DHCP is used to automatically assign IP and other protocol configuration information.

For purposes of joining a domain, you will only need the name of the domain and the domain user account and password. When the Setup process has finished and Windows XP has been installed on your computer, you will be able, if you have a domain user account, to begin using resources on the domain.

Joining a Domain After the Setup Process

If you chose the Typical setting during the networking portion of the Setup process, then your computer will be set up as part of a workgroup called WORKGROUP (unless you chose a different name for the workgroup). It will also be set to automatically configure its network addressing by using DHCP or Automatic Private IP Addressing (APIPA). You can choose a name for your computer or take the default name generated by the setup process when you install Windows XP.

If you want to join a domain, you may need to change the name to one your network administrator has reserved for your computer. You will also have to join the domain by using an administrator's username and password so that the computer can be authenticated when it joins the domain.

You use the System Applet in the Control Panel to change your computer name, domain, or workgroup membership, after the operating system has been installed. To join a domain, use the following steps:

Joining a Domain and the Active Directory

CHAPTER 26

689

26

JOINING A
DOMAIN AND
ACTIVE DIRECTORY

1. Click on Start, Control Panel.

2. From the Pick a Category view, select Performance and Maintenance.

3. From the menu presented, select System; the System Applet of the Control Panel appears (see Figure 26.2). In this example, the name of the computer, assigned during the initial Setup process, is `twoinc-tkfdyk5` (randomly generated names), and the computer was configured during the Setup process to be a member of the workgroup called WORKGROUP.

Tip

If you don't want to navigate through all these menus and submenus, select Start, Control Panel, Switch to Classic View, System.

FIGURE 26.2

The System applet (called System Properties in the Control Panel) allows you to make a number of changes to your computer.

4. To change the name, click Change; the Computer Name Changes dialog box appears (see Figure 26.3).

5. Select the radio button Domain and then enter the name of the domain you wish to join. In this example, the computer will join a domain called `twoinc.com`. You also can change the default computer name in this dialog box. (Note that it is unchanged in the example shown; check with your network administrator first.) When you have finished entering the computer name and the domain that you want to join, click OK.

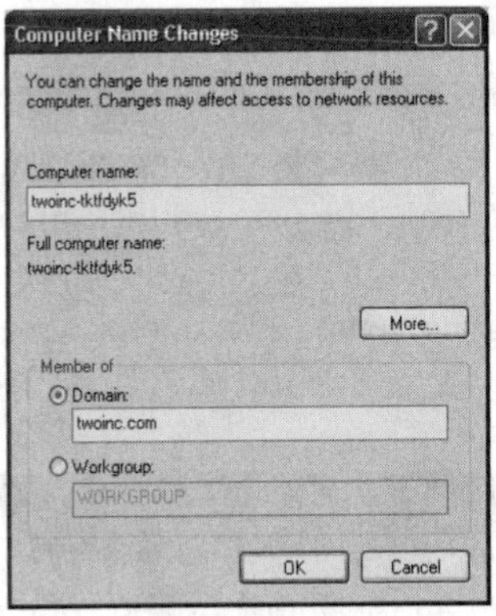

FIGURE 26.3

To join a domain, enter the computer name and domain name given to you by your network administrator.

6. Figure 26.4 shows another Computer Name Changes dialog box, which prompts you for a domain user account name and password that you will need to join the domain. Enter the appropriate information and click OK.

FIGURE 26.4

You will need to provide a domain user account name and password that has the right to join your computer to the domain.

7. A few seconds or maybe one or two minutes pass before you receive a response. The time lag depends on the size of your network, the load the domain controller is currently processing, and other factors. Be patient. If you are successfully granted a computer account in the domain, then you will see a welcome dialog box (see Figure 26.5). Click OK.

FIGURE 26.5

If everything works as it should, you will be welcomed to the domain!

8. The next dialog box will tell you that you need to reboot your computer before these changes will take effect. Click OK. When the System Properties pages reappear, click Apply. Another dialog box will again tell you that you need to restart

Joining a Domain and the Active Directory

CHAPTER 26

691

26

JOINING A
DOMAIN AND
ACTIVE DIRECTORY

your computer before you can fully join the domain. If you have other things you want to do on the computer, click No. If possible, however, click Yes to restart the computer and finish this process.

After You Have Joined a Domain

When your computer reboots, you will get the standard Welcome to Windows dialog box that prompts you to enter Ctrl+Alt+Del to bring up a logon dialog box. Click Options to access the following choices:

- Username—A field for entering a username.

- Password—A field for entering the password associated with the username.

- Log On To—The drop-down menu to select to log onto the local computer, which will be listed by name followed by the text This Computer, or to log into a domain name you can choose by using the down-arrow. If you want to log back on using a local account on the Windows XP computer, then choose the first option. If you want to log onto the domain, use the menu option and select the domain.

Also included in this dialog box is the check box Log on Using Dial-Up Connection. Use this if you are logging into the computer via dial-up line.

Using the Domain Account

When you log into a domain account, you can browse the domain to connect to other resources such as shared printers, applications, and file shares. Using a domain logon user account to access a computer registered in a domain opens up a whole new computing horizon before you.

Your network administrator can configure your Windows XP computer so that it automatically connects to other file shares. These are simply drives on other computers. Typically, these are large-capacity drives installed on very fast servers; you can have at your fingertips not only a local disk driver, which may be limited in capacity, but also a whole network on which to find or store data.

Tip

One advantage you can gain from storing important files on a network share in a domain is the fact that most network administrators will choose a reasonable backup schedule for the large servers that host these files shares. Thus, by placing your important files on a file share, you don't have to worry about creating

continues

a backup schedule locally (if you indeed need to back up your computer using a local resource like a tape drive). Instead, the network does it all, and when you accidentally delete a file, your network administrator should be able to restore it for you.

Searching the Active Directory

Once you have joined a domain, you will find that many parts of the operating system are integrated to allow you to search for resources in the domain. The Active Directory offers greatly enhanced search features. For example, if you want to find a printer, you can simply search for one using the standard Print dialog box (see Figure 26.6).

FIGURE 26.6

You can use the Find Printer button to search for a printer using the standard Print dialog box.

Select the Features tab to search for a printer with specific features such as duplex printing, stapling, or color. Use the Advanced tab to launch an even more specific search.

Summary

Joining a domain can let you access resources on many other computers. Domains add security to resource–sharing in ways workgroups cannot. By creating a domain account for your computer, you make it part of the computers that can be managed and maintained by domain administrators. You can create a domain user account for yourself in order to use a single logon username and password to access resources through the domain.

Multimedia

PART IV

IN THIS PART

27 Overview of Windows XP Multimedia
    Features   *695*

28 Capturing Images and Video and Using Windows
    Movie Maker   *707*

29 Windows Media Player 8   *729*

Overview of Windows XP Multimedia Features

IN THIS CHAPTER

- The New Windows Media Player *697*
- New Folders—It's Not Just My Documents Anymore! *697*
- Publishing Photographs or Movies on the Web *700*
- Burning CDs with Windows XP *701*
- Microsoft Plus! for Windows XP *703*
- Using Third-Party Programs *704*

CHAPTER 27

The emergence of Windows XP Professional is not only the first time that Microsoft has tried to create a convergence of home and business operating systems, but it is also an operating system that contains many features that were lacking in previous editions of Windows. Although such things as the Sound Recorder and Paint have been included in most editions of Windows, the capabilities for using imaging devices, especially CD recording technology, have been either lacking all together or found in one version of Windows but not the other.

For example, Windows Movie Maker's predecessor appeared first in Windows Me, but you can't find Movie Maker anywhere in Windows 2000! Although all of the operating systems have provided support for different imaging devices, you will find that Windows XP offers a wider variety of device drivers than you could find in previous editions of Windows operating systems.

This chapter will give you some insight into the multimedia features included in Windows XP, including a few tips on how to use them. As mentioned previously, Windows XP includes a combination of multimedia features not found in past Windows versions. Since this chapter is simply an overview of Windows XP's multimedia features, you will be referred to other chapters that include more detailed discussions of specific topics.

> **Note**
>
> Microsoft has also released a companion CD for Windows XP, called Microsoft Plus! for Windows XP. In addition to the multimedia technologies that have been incorporated into the new operating system, you can purchase this additional CD, which adds additional functionality to Windows XP's rich multimedia capabilities.

The main multimedia capabilities that come with the basic Windows XP operating system include the following:

- Windows Media Player 8
- My Music, My Videos, and My Pictures folders
- Publishing pictures and videos on Web sites
- Ordering prints of your digital pictures from Web vendors
- CD burning capabilities
- Windows Movie Maker
- Increased support for digital cameras, scanners, and other imaging devices

You will learn about Windows Movie Maker and other imaging products in the next chapter, Chapter 28, "Capturing Images and Video." You will also find an entire chapter, Chapter 29, "Windows Media Player 8," devoted to the new Windows Media Player. This chapter will only briefly touch on some of the features you may find useful and easy to use.

The New Windows Media Player

Windows XP is shipping with Windows Media Player 8. That much is certain. But like Internet Explorer, the Media Player tends to be upgraded more often than the operating systems. So while the initial distribution CDs for Windows XP include Windows Media Player 8, you may find a few months down the road after you purchase this book, that there is another version available as a free download from Microsoft.

27

OVERVIEW OF XP
MULTIMEDIA
FEATURES

> **Tip**
>
> Be sure to use the Windows Update feature to check on new upgrades for the Media Player application.

However, I think you will find that this new version 8, which you can download and use on earlier operating systems if you haven't made the switch to Windows XP yet, includes a lot of new features, including direct ripping of music from audio CDs and burning of music to CDs. On the more fun side, it also supports such things as "skins," which control how the application appears on the screen. Skins have been standard for many third-party media applications for years. Now you have the same capability with Windows Media Player.

New Folders—It's Not Just My Documents Anymore!

The My Documents folder has been around for quite some time now. However, as we continually advance into newer formats for storing data, the term *document* just doesn't cover the wide territory that is available on a modern computer. Instead, you have all sorts of files. You can classify some files under the My Documents folders. Examples of these types of files can be word processing files or perhaps spreadsheet or other data files. However, when it comes to multimedia, there are several ways you can categorize your files, and thus make them easier to find. These include the My Music, My Pictures, and My Videos folders.

Remember that if you are just one user of a computer running Windows XP, you will have your own set of the aforementioned folders. For each person who has a local account on the Windows XP computer, there is a separate user profile, as well as a separate collection of these folders. You can choose to share them or not. For more information about sharing folders and files, see Chapter 9, "Working With Files and Folders." You will also find additional information about what folders you can protect from access by other users, depending on whether you join a domain, by reading several other chapters, such as Chapter 18, "Managing Disks and Partitions," and Chapter 26, "Joining a Domain and the Active Directory."

The My Music Folder

If you use your computer at home or work, chances are you will be using it as a CD player or at least to play songs you have downloaded to your hard drive. The My Music Folder contains all the music (or other audio files) you download to your computer's local hard disk, unless you choose another location for storing the file. It is easiest, however, to store the files in one convenient location so you can quickly find the particular audio file you want.

The Windows Media Player, discussed in great length in Chapter 29, can tell you how to add music files to the media player library. However, if you like to record new files and store them in your own My Music folder or if you download files from the Internet and store them in this folder, you will find it easier to locate and add them to your music library using the media player. Alternatively, you may have some files you just want to examine and decide later whether to add to your folder. Use the My Music folder for this purpose, and you won't have to go browsing all over your hard disk drives or partitions to find a file you downloaded long ago.

The My Videos Folder

Since Windows Movie Maker, covered in Chapter 28, is an important, new addition to Windows XP, it is necessary for the movie file itself to have a folder you can use to quickly locate the movies or videos you create. This is the purpose of the My Videos folder.

Tip

You can also use subfolders in the My Videos folder to better organize your video collection.

The My Pictures Folder

As the name suggests, this folder is where you store your picture files. These can be photographs downloaded from your camera or scanner software or files you find on the Internet. Note that it is now quite a popular feature of film processors to post digital copies of your photographs on the Internet (or charge you extra and provide a floppy disk with the same images). This means that you can share your photos with others via e-mail or a Web site, after you have a digital copy of the photo.

The My Pictures folder is the default folder that most camera and imaging products designed for Windows XP will use. You will find subfolders created under this folder to store the various files you download. One interesting thing about the My Pictures folder, however, is that it adds an additional entry to the View menu. This is the Filmstrip view. Simply select this view from the View menu when you are looking at the My Pictures folder, and you will see a different way of looking at the files contained in a folder.

You can usually use icons or choose a detailed view, but the Filmstrip view allows you to see a strip of picture icons, and you can select any of them to get a larger view (see Figure 27.1).

As you can see in this figure, you can use the buttons on the screen or the left and right arrow keys to scroll through the pictures contained in this view.

FIGURE 27.1

The Filmstrip view is available from the My Pictures folder only.

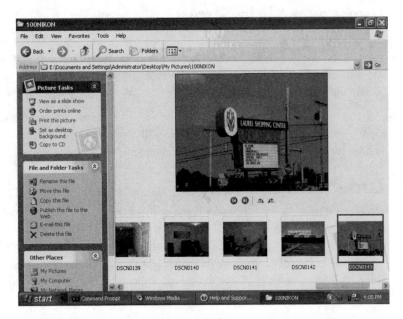

You can also use the other options from the View menu to look at files in the My Pictures folder. The Thumbnails view will show you a small version of each picture, similar to the Filmstrip view, but you won't have the option to see a larger view of a particular picture on the same display, as shown in Figure 27.1. Instead, you will have to double-click on the thumbnail to bring up an application that can display the picture. Then for the My Pictures folder, the Filmstrip view is probably the best thing for you to choose.

Publishing Photographs or Movies on the Web

In the next chapter, you will find out how to publish movies you make by using Windows Movie Maker on Web sites. Basically, this process simply involves uploading the movie file using file transfer protocol (FTP) to a Web site and then creating a hypertext markup language (HTML) link to the movie for the Web site.

Figure 27.1 illustrates how if you want to upload picture files, there are several menu items on the left portion of the screen that fall under the menu name Picture Tasks. This menu contains common things you can do with picture files.

View as a Slide Show

If you choose this selection from the Picture Tasks menu, then you will get a full screen view of each picture in the folder you have selected from the My Pictures folder. A slide show is just a continuing showing of all the pictures, one after another, until you decide to stop the process.

You can leave the slide show running to operate like a screensaver, or just for entertainment. The pictures in the folder you select will continue, cycling over when the last file is displayed. Press the Escape (Esc) button on your computer to stop the slide show.

Order Prints Online

This option from the Picture Tasks menu will start up a wizard appropriately called the *Online Print Ordering Wizard*. The first dialog box this wizard presents is just informational. It tells you that you can choose to order hard-copy prints of your digital photographs via an Internet company. You can select the size of the prints and enter billing and shipping information also. Click the Next for this wizard to start the online ordering process for those precious moments you have captured in digital format.

The second dialog box of the wizard will show you each picture in the folder with which you started, and it will allow you to use a check box next to each picture to select or deselect the files from which you want to have prints made. Select a check box to have a print made; you can see this dialog box in Figure 27.2.

FIGURE 27.2

The wizard allows you to use check boxes to select the digital photo files you want to get hardcopy prints made from.

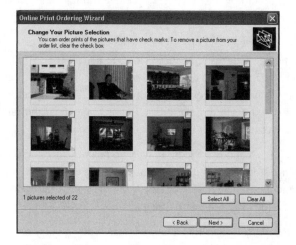

Note that you can use the buttons labeled Select All or Clear All to perform those functions and then select the individual check boxes of the prints you want to order. When finished making your selections, click Next to continue.

The wizard will then try to locate companies on the Internet that can provide a printing service for you. Of course, you must be connected to the Internet at this time for this to work. You can then follow the specific dialog boxes for the picture provider you select, providing all necessary information for uploading your digital files to the print vendor and obtaining copies of the prints you ordered.

Burning CDs with Windows XP

In other chapters, you learned that Windows XP can be used with a CD-recordable (CD-R) drive to burn your own CDs. You can create CDs that contain data files, or you can use this function with Movie Maker to create a CD that stores the movies you make.

It is important to distinguish between the capabilities offered by Windows XP and third-party applications. There are several things you should consider.

First, to record a CD to be played in a regular CD player, you will use Windows Media Player to create the list of audio files you want, and then you will save them to a temporary staging area for the CD-R drive to later burn onto a CD.

For example, using the software packages Easy CD Creator or NTI's CD-Maker, among others, you can select what kind of CD to create, from data to audio to many others. You then select the files to add to the CD layout, which determines the order of the items on the burned CD.

With third-party products, you can copy CD-DA (the Digital Audio native format on a CD music disc you buy at your favorite audio store) to a .WAV file. A .WAV file is really not much more than a CD-DA file with the individual bits of the recording stored in a different order. Hence, when you choose to record a new CD and select files from different .WAV files you have extracted to a hard disk, you get just about the same quality on your new CD as you would get from the original source recordings.

If you use Windows XP's Windows Media Player, you can extract audio tracks from a CD. However, they are stored in a different format specific to Windows operating systems. The format you choose can vary from low to high quality, but it does not equal the CD-DA format from which the file was extracted.

If you download MP3 files or other files that aren't up to the quality of an original CD, then you shouldn't worry about this. However, if you want to create your own compilation CD with your favorite tracks from other CDs, then using a third-party application is best.

If you are satisfied with the highest quality that Windows XP can record to a CD, then that's okay too. For many portable audio players, this quality is good enough. However, if you want to duplicate CDs or create copies that contain the same quality as the original, it is best to use a third-party application.

Burn that CD

As you will learn in other chapters, you can burn a CD from within Windows XP by simply dragging, or using other methods described in previous chapters, the files to the CD burner drive. Instead of recording a CD instantly, the files will be stored in a temporary staging area, ready to record to a CD. To actually burn the CD, you will need to bring up Windows Explorer. Select My Computer and then click on the CD burner drive. You will see a display that shows the files waiting to be burned to the CD (see Figure 27.3).

To burn the CD, whether it contains data or audio or video or photographic files, simply click Folders on the toolbar, and you will see another display (Figure 27.4) showing the tasks you can perform.

Under the CD Writing Tasks menu, you can choose to delete any files you have added to this temporary staging area. Choose Write These Files to CD to burn the CD.

FIGURE 27.3

By clicking on the CD drive in Windows Explorer, you see that the files are stored in temporary files for later burning to a CD-R.

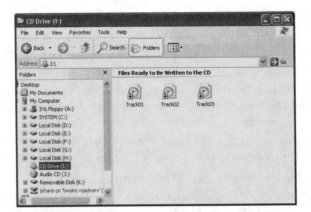

FIGURE 27.4

You can use the Write these files to CD selection to burn a CD.

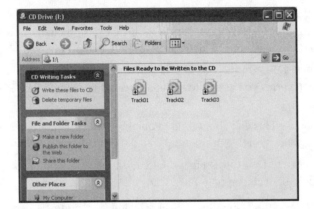

Microsoft Plus! for Windows XP

This CD, which is an add-on component for the standard Windows XP operating system was available on the same day that the operating system itself was released. So you have to spend a few extra bucks! The street price of this CD will be less expensive than taking a family to a movie!

The Plus! CD includes functionality that will only enhance your Windows XP "eXPerience," including the following:

- You Talk and Windows XP Responds—The companion CD will add voice recognition, which was previously available only in third-party products, or in other Microsoft products such as Microsoft Office. This voice recognition capability isn't complete—that is, you can't pretend you are in the Star Trek Enterprise and simply start talking! However, it is very well integrated into both Windows Media Player and a number of other programs.

- Enhanced Speaker Capabilities—Again, like third-party products, you may find that using the speak enhancements provided by this CD will take advantage of the capabilities of many different kinds of speakers. You will get digital quality on most of your desktop systems, and if you have a high-end audio card and speakers, you might find that this software can meet the quality of what you are getting from those third-party vendors. However, buyer beware! Usually, the manufacturer of a sound card or speaker system knows best how to produce output for their products. If your system doesn't have the latest, greatest sound system, then this feature on the Plus! CD may improve your sound "eXPerience" a great deal.

- Labels—Although Windows XP allows you to create CDs at a lower quality level than many other vendor's products, the one thing lacking was the capability to create labels for your CDs using Windows XP. This feature adds the capability to produce your own labels as well as the CD inserts.

- 3D Visualizations—As Microsoft puts it, this CD also includes new three-dimensional (3D) visualizations, which can be used with the Windows Media Player.

- The Personal DJ—This add-on allows you to create customized play lists based on selected categories you assign to the audio recordings stored in the Windows Media Player.

- MP3 Support—This CD allows you to quickly and easily convert MP3 audio files into Windows own native format.

- Screensavers and Desktop Themes—Of course, new desktop themes and screensavers would be included on a Plus! CD!

In addition to these features, the Plus! CD also includes several new games, which may or may not appeal to you, depending on whether you use Windows XP for home or business purposes.

Using Third-Party Programs

Again, although Windows XP offers several new features specific for multimedia applications, you may or may not find them suitable to your purposes. Keep in mind that many applications are available from other vendors that extend the capabilities of the multimedia hardware attached to your computer. In the next chapter, you will learn about using Windows Movie Maker to create your own digital movies to be posted to a Web site, e-mailed to a friend, or burned to a CD.

However, there are many other products to evaluate that go beyond the capabilities offered by Windows XP. For example, Ulead Systems has several multimedia programs ranging from inexpensive to several hundred dollars. You do get what you pay for, however. Check out the many multimedia products from Ulead Systems at http://www.ulead.com/. You can download trial versions of most of the site's software and make your own comparisons. Additionally, products such as those from Ulead allow you to save your work in a variety of formats. You will find that the nice thing about standards is that there are so many to choose from when it comes to multimedia products!

Another example is Roxio's Easy CD Creator 5 Platinum. This application will allow you to duplicate CDs exactly. Although Windows XP includes CD burning capabilities, it doesn't have a "copy" function that allows you to simply copy a CD. Instead, you have to first stage files in a temporary holding area and then tell Windows XP to burn a CD. You can extract CD-DA tracks from a CD, record them to a .WAV file, and then create a compilation CD from those .WAV files if you have Easy CD Creator. With Windows XP, you can also extract audio tracks from a CD, but you can't record them to a .WAV file. Instead, you record them to a Microsoft proprietary format. This format does allow you to store your favorite music in a more compact form, and it allows you to choose the quality. However, a .WAV file is basically nothing more than a CD-DA file with the bits in a different order. You don't lose anything when you record a CD from a .WAV file. When you record from a Windows media format, you don't get an exact replication of the original audio track. You can check out Roxio's products at http://www.roxio.com/.

Don't get me wrong—I think that that the multimedia capabilities included in Windows XP are a great step forward and will be more than sufficient for many people. However, if you are really into audio or video, you should consider third-party applications with additional features.

Summary

As you can see, Windows XP offers a lot of multimedia capabilities. For many users, these features that accompany the operating system will suffice. For advanced users, purchasing a third-party product from a different vendor may satisfy best. However, it all depends on what you want to accomplish. Read the remaining chapters in this section on multimedia and decide for yourself. Chapter 29 provides an in-depth look at Windows Media Player, along with other new or enhanced features, such as the new Internet Explorer.

CHAPTER 28

Capturing Images and Video and Using Windows Movie Maker

IN THIS CHAPTER

- Installing a Scanner, Camera, or Video Source *708*
- Using Third-Party Software *711*
- Using Windows Movie Maker *712*
- How Do You Make a Movie? *715*

Windows XP Professional allows you to capture video and audio from many different sources. You can also capture still pictures from a traditional scanner or digital camera, and you can even download pictures from the Internet. Many of you still using film cameras already know that some developers will give you a floppy disk with digital images of your roll of developed film. Some make them available online for download. In this chapter, we will briefly touch on adding an imaging device such as a camera and then walk you through producing your first movie file using Movie Maker.

Installing a Scanner, Camera, or Video Source

If you have a source device supported by Windows XP, then all you have to do is connect it to your system and let the plug-and-play functionality detect the device. If the source device is not one supported by Windows XP, you may need to obtain a driver from the manufacturer. This can be in the form of a floppy disk or CD-ROM, if it is a new device. For older devices, you may need to download a new driver from the manufacturer that was created for Windows XP. In any case, connecting a scanner should be a simple task. For devices that connect using a Small Computer System Interface (SCSI) card, you may need to install that hardware along with any software that comes with the product before you can connect your source device.

If your input device is one supported by Windows XP and you can check the Hardware Compatibility List at http://www.microsoft.com, then you should have no problems. Otherwise, you should insert the diskette or CD-ROM that comes with your device and follow the instructions provided by the manufacturer.

Using the Scanner and Camera Installation Wizard

If you are going to use a digital camera for the input device, then you will need to use the Control Panel icon labeled Scanners and Cameras to select the correct device driver for your camera. Note also that like many devices, an updated driver for Windows XP may be available for download at the vendor's Web site, or a diskette or CD-ROM may be available through the vendor for use when installing the camera. In addition, you might want to consider purchasing a card reader so that you can remove SmartCards, flash cards, memory sticks, and other similar storage devices used by cameras and other portable devices.

To begin, click Start, Control Panel. You can then switch to Classic View using the menu on the top left side of the Category View of the Control Panel. If you use this method, just select the Scanners and Cameras icon. Otherwise, from the Category View, select Printers and Other Hardware from the first Category View menu; then from the next screen select Scanners and Cameras. From the next screen, select the option Add an Imaging Device. The Scanner and Camera Installation Wizard will pop up and walk you through the process of adding a new device.

Click Next to continue past this welcoming screen. In Figure 28.1 you will see the dialog box the wizard uses to let you choose the type of scanner or, as in this case, camera, which you want to add.

FIGURE 28.1

You can use this dialog box to select the manufacturer and then the device you want to add.

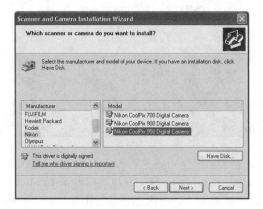

Choose from the Manufacturer listing the vendor of your camera and then under the pane labeled Model; click on the model of the camera or other imaging device. Click Next.

> **Note**
>
> If your scanner, camera, or other device isn't found in the listing in Figure 28.1 but you have a diskette or CD-ROM from the manufacturer containing a driver compatible with Windows XP, then select Have Disk, and you will be prompted to enter the file name and path of the driver. If your device is new, be sure to check out the manufacturer's Web site to see if a new driver is available for downloading that will work with Windows XP.

The next screen of the wizard allows you to select the port or use Automatic Port Detection to find out to which port your camera is connected, such as COM1. Once the port selection is made and you click the Next button, you will be presented with a screen that allows you to choose a name for the device. You can use the default, which is a combination of the manufacturer and model name, or enter your own text. Click Next.

28

USING WINDOWS MOVIE MAKER

The last screen of the wizard will simply tell you that the process is complete; you can now click Finish to close the wizard.

Figure 28.2 displays the new camera (or other device) that will now show up in the Scanners and Cameras display from the Control Panel.

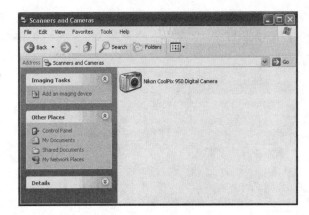

After you have installed a camera or a scanner, you can use a number of methods to download images to your computer. First, you can bring up the Control Panel and right-click on the device (see Figure 28.2). You will get a small menu that allows you to delete or rename the device, or examine its properties. Another option with a camera is Get Pictures. Click on this, and the pictures stored in your camera's memory will be downloaded to a folder in your my Pictures folder.

You will also notice that once you have installed the device, a new menu entry will be placed into the File menu of applications like Microsoft Paint, allowing you to also download pictures from the camera or scanner. Third-party applications can also acquire photographs in this manner.

The process is similar for adding other imaging devices like digital videocassette recorders (VCRs) and flash card readers.

Flash Card Readers

If you do use a digital camera, you should invest in a flash card (or other memory device) reader. These come in several types. Some will let you slip your memory card into an adapter that can be plugged into a floppy drive or even a Personal Computer Memory Card International Association (PCMCIA) slot on a portable computer. The memory card will look like a disk drive to the operating system.

You can also connect a card reader to a serial port, such as a universal serial bus (USB) or FireWire port and use it to download pictures from your cards. One good thing about having an alternative method to use instead of making a direct connection to your camera is that you can carry around several flash cards and not have to download each to your computer in order to erase and use the card again. Instead, carry several cards with you on your vacation and just pop them in and out of your computer as you fill one up and start on another. Then at the end of the day, use the attached flash card (or other device) reader to download the contents of any of the cards.

Figure 28.3 shows that a flash card reader was attached to a Windows XP computer using Windows Explorer. The user can see that it is a removable device (the flash card) and can even view the directory containing the pictures on the card. At this point, however, the pictures still remain on the card and have not been transferred to the computer. Since the device looks just like a disk drive (K:), you can use the standard methods for copying files or folders to move individual pictures, or the entire folder of pictures, to a hard disk for later use. This is a good idea if you want to set up a staging ground to store photos before you burn them to a CD.

FIGURE 28.3

You can use a flash card reader (or other portable memory device reader) to view the contents of a flash card or other storage device as you would any other drive.

Using Third-Party Software

In addition to making a direct connection to your camera using the drivers that come with Windows XP, you may find that some devices, especially cameras, come with their own software to load and use for transferring images from your camera. Even if your camera is supported by drivers supplied with the Windows XP installation CD, you will find a lot more software applications with scanners and cameras that go beyond some of the capabilities offered under Windows XP or that are simply easier to use. You should check out any additional software applications that come with your imaging devices and decide if the features they offer are ones you prefer.

> **Caution**
>
> Be wary of software that is shipped with hardware. While the quality of these applications can be excellent, sometimes they are trial versions that will require you to purchase a full version later on. So read the fine print.

Using Windows Movie Maker

In the past, it has been necessary to purchase expensive software to create video files called *movies* in Windows XP. Now you will find that an application called *Windows Movie Maker* is part of the Accessories included with the operating system, just like WordPad and the Calculator.

Because Windows Movie Maker allows you to work in a graphical user interface (GUI), it is very easy to use. You can make movies that vary in quality, depending on the purpose of the movie. As an example, if you are going to post a movie on a Web site, you will probably choose to create a low or medium quality movie, since bandwidth might keep some users with dial-up modems from being able to download a large file. The higher the quality of movie you produce, the larger the file that is created. You may also want to create a movie and burn it to a CD to send to relatives. In this kind of situation, creating a movie at the highest quality may prove the best choice.

Three kinds of files can be created using Windows Movie Maker. The first is the project file. This contains all the clips you have added to the project and any editing you have done. The second is a Collections file, which contains collections of clips from which you may choose to create a movie. The last type of file is a movie file, which is the final product you produce with Windows Movie Maker.

However, before we continue this discussion about the capabilities of Windows Movie Maker, let us first examine the application in general, obtain a good idea of what the layout of the application looks like, and find out what tools you have at your disposal as you step into the shoes of a Hollywood producer.

Starting Windows Movie Maker

To start the program, click on Start, All Programs, Accessories, Windows Movie Maker. If you have just installed Windows XP, you may see that the Movie Maker application is part of the first column of the Start menu, which typically stores a link to the five or six applications you used most recently. Either way, once you start the application, a window (see Figure 28.4) will be your first look at the application.

FIGURE 28.4

Windows Movie Maker starts out with just a lot of blank spaces to fill in.

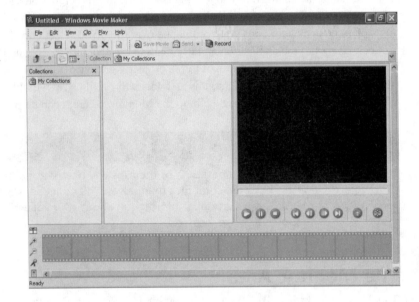

The first thing to learn is the different components of this window, and then we will move on to how to use them. This application window is divided up into toolbars, a Collections area, a Monitor, and a Workspace.

There are several toolbars at the top of the window, including the standard File, Edit, and so on toolbar present in most Windows applications. This is called the *Menu bar*. The toolbar underneath this one contains a collection of icons for performing specific tasks. This second toolbar is actually two different toolbars separated by a vertical bar. The first is called the *Standard toolbar* and contains basic icons used for such things as cutting, pasting, saving, and deleting. Next to it is the Project toolbar, which contains three important icons:

- Save Movie—Use this toolbar to save a movie after you have assembled the clips and done the necessary editing.
- Send—Use this toolbar to send your movie to a Web site or another user via e-mail.
- Record—This allows you to use a capture device such as a graphics capture card or an attached video camera device to record to a file.

Under these two toolbars are another set of two toolbars. The first part contains the Collections toolbar, which is used to manage collections of video clips, whereas the second toolbar on this line is called the *Location toolbar* and is used to locate your collections.

The Collections Area

This section of the application window looks like the tree structure you see in the Microsoft Management Console (MMC) and allows you to navigate among the collections of video and audio clips you accumulate over time. You select clips from the Collections part of the application and use them to create a movie. To add a clip to a movie in progress, you simply drag it to the project Workspace at the bottom of the application window. In Figure 28.4, this area looks like a filmstrip with blanks for all the pictures. You can also drag a clip to the Monitor, where it can be played.

> **Note**
>
> The Collections area is just a database of the clips you have chosen to use with a project. These are not the actual files themselves. The Collections listing in Windows Movie Maker just contains information about your collections of clips and where the source files are located

The Monitor Area

This Monitor looks just like a VCR. It is that big black screen off to the right side in Figure 28.4 with the typical VCR control buttons underneath. You can drag clips from the Collections area to the Monitor and play them, or you can play a movie you have created by using the Monitor. The Monitor is your basic viewing tool, allowing you to see the contents of a clip or movie project. The Monitor also allows you to perform other functions, which will be explained later in this chapter.

The Workspace

This is where you do most of the work, of course! Actually, the Workspace area is that area at the bottom of the application window that appears first like a filmstrip. This is called the *Storyboard View*. You can change this to a Timeline View by clicking on Timeline in the View menu. You can see the application with the Timeline View in Figure 28.5.

Two things to know about the Timeline and Storyboard Views are as follows:

- The Storyboard View doesn't show any audio clips you have added to the project. The Storyboard View is useful mainly in rearranging the order of clips in the project.

- The Timeline View does indicate in two separate bars both the video and the audio clips you added to the movie project. At this point, Figure 28.5 doesn't show anything but gray space in these views. Once you begin adding clips, that all changes.

28

USING WINDOWS
MOVIE MAKER

FIGURE 28.5

The Timeline View gives you a different perspective in the Workspace area of the application.

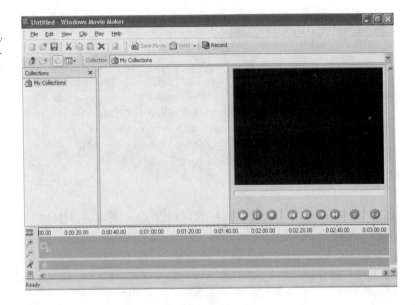

The Timeline View also enables you to conduct basic editing techniques, such as creating a cross-fade from one clip to another or adjusting audio levels when clips come from different sources that have different volume levels. You can also use the Timeline View to zoom in or out on a particular clip.

Note that you can use the View menu to switch back to the Storyboard View. You can also click the icon on the far left of the Timeline View, which resembles a filmstrip, to switch back. This same button will then change to an icon you can use to switch back to the Timeline View.

How Do You Make a Movie?

Now that you understand the basic layout of the application screen, it is time to get down to the nitty-gritty and make a movie. The steps involved are simple. First, record some video and audio files!

Tip

When you import video or audio clips into your Collections area in Movie Maker, you may get an error message telling you that Movie Maker doesn't use that format. Near the end of this chapter, you will find a table that can be of

continues

some help in deciding what settings to use when creating video clips using programs other than Movie Maker. For example, your video capture card may come with its own software to create video files. Yet, if you do not select the right settings for such things as frames per second or pixel size, Movie Maker may just reject your file. Check the table at the end of this chapter to make sure your existing collection of files is suitable for Movie Maker. If not, most video software applications that come with video capture cards will allow you to convert files from one format to another if you chose settings incompatible with Movie Maker when you first captured the file.

Recording Video Using Movie Maker

You can obtain video files to use in your movie in numerous ways. If you own a digital or analog video camera, then as long as the device is supported by Windows XP (check the hardware compatibility list), you can connect it to your computer and use the Record function of Movie Maker to transfer video and audio tracks to your hard disk. Second, you can use a video capture card that allows you to record from an external source, such as cable television or a VCR. Still another way to acquire files is to look on the Internet. Just be sure you don't use material under copyright protection if you are producing a movie for business or profit. You can use your video capture card with Windows Movie Maker much like you do a VCR, if you have large amounts of disk space. However, if you record from a source like television, make sure the recording is simply for your own entertainment and use.

Selecting a Recording Source

Unless you have been asleep the past few decades, you probably have amassed a lot of videotapes. If you don't think much about them, consider the fact that year after year, depending on the condition in which they are stored and the number of times they are played, videotapes are just like vinyl records—that is, they deteriorate over time. If you want to save a favorite movie, forget it! Just buy the digital video disc (DVD), if available, and you will get a better quality playback. However, for those home movies you made using your video camera (digital or analog), you can use Windows Movie Maker to convert these tapes into digital files to be used in a movie.

First, you need to be able to connect the device to your computer in order to provide a channel to send the analog or digital signal to the computer so Movie Maker can intercept it. Typically, a USB or FireWire port can be used. Once you have a connection established, simply use the following steps to record the incoming stream from your VCR:

1. Select Record from the File menu. The Record dialog box will pop up (see Figure 28.6). In this figure, use the first drop-down-down menu labeled Record to choose what you want to record. You can select to include video, audio, or both in the recording.

FIGURE 28.6

You can select many options from the Record dialog box.

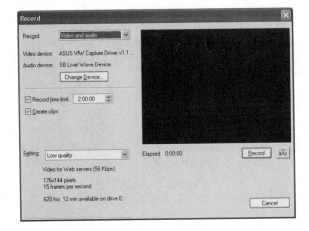

2. As you can see in Figure 28.6, you can use the Change Device button to select from a video capture card, a VCR, or another supported device. If you use the Change Device button to select another device, it will then appear in the fields under the Record field so that you will know from where your video/audio is coming.

3. Use the field labeled Record Time Limit if you want to set a maximum amount of recording. If you select this check box, use the Up and Down arrows in the time field next to it to set the maximum recording time. The default is 2 hours.

4. Select the Create Clips check box if you want Movie Maker to automatically chop up your video into separate clips when the scene changes significantly. Don't worry—you will just end up with more clips, which can be reassembled on the Storyboard. If you want to record one single clip, then deselect this check box.

5. Choose the quality you want to record from the source using the Setting field. You will also be able to use a similar selection when you create the final product. Choose the highest quality that you expect to produce in the final movies you create from the recorded clips.

6. When ready, click the Record button (off to the right side under the monitor screen) and then start the playback function of your source such as your VCR.

7. The recording will stop after the maximum time limit (if you set one in Step 3), or you can click on the Stop button, which the Record button changes to after you start recording, to stop the recording process.

28

USING WINDOWS
MOVIE MAKER

8. After you click the Stop button or the time limit expires, a dialog box will allow you to give a name to the file and select the path under which it will be stored. Enter the information and click Save. The video/audio file will be saved under this name, and you can then import it into your My Collections section so that you an use it in a movie.

Note that if you selected the check box labeled Create Clip, then you will see Movie Maker break the recording into several different clips before you are asked to save the data.

Using a Video Capture Card

For those who can afford these more expensive graphics cards, you might just find that they pay for themselves in little time. Simple graphics cards can be purchased for under $50, and graphics cards that can capture video start at $150. If you want to use your computer like a VCR, then spending a few hundred dollars on a video capture card may not seem expensive at all. If you buy a basic PC and only want to make the occasional movie, then this can be considered too much money to spend. At this time, the higher quality graphics cards that support good quality video capture usually go for $200 to $500. Be sure to check out the specifications for a video capture card before spending a lot of money. If you only want to make low-grade movies that can be easily downloaded from your Web page, then you don't need an expensive card. If you are going to transfer your family's old videotapes to digital format, then you might consider the cost of a high-end card.

Using a video capture card has many advantages. First, most cards come with additional software, although it may be a stripped down version of some video editing software application. If you like the application better than Movie Maker, then you can always go out and buy the full application. In addition, many third-party video applications can handle different types of video and audio files, and you may be able to use this capability to convert a file from one format to another. Video capture cards often allow you to convert your PC monitor into a television. You can be working on an important document or spreadsheet while watching the news in a small window up in the corner of the screen! As you can see, video capture cards serve a purpose other than just capturing and saving video.

Generally, you can plug into a video capture card just about any kind of video input, from an antenna to a cable box. You can also connect VCRs if you want to save that library you have of home movies that is slowly deteriorating as you read this book.

Importing Video Files

You can use your video capture card with Windows Movie Maker, or you can use other video capture software to create your multimedia files. If you use another application, then you can import these video clips into the My Collections tree structure easily. Just click on My Collections and from the File menu select Import. You will be able to use this dialog box to browse for your video files and select which ones to add to the My Collections section of Movie Maker.

Figure 28.7 indicates that a few files have been added, and those show up under the My Collections tree on the left pane in Movie Maker.

FIGURE 28.7

The My Collections tree stores information about multimedia files that you can add to your movie.

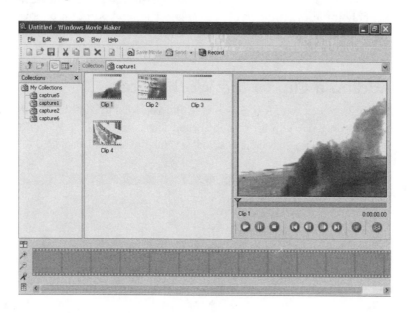

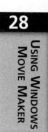

If you select a collection from the My Collections tree, then you will see the first frame of the video in the middle pane of the Movie Maker screen, the Collections pane. If you had chosen the option to let Movie Maker split a video file up into separate clips, then you would see each separate clip in the middle pane when you select the file to import, which is the display you also see in Figure 28.7.

Notice also that you can click on any clip in the Collections area, and it will show up in the monitor. You can click Play on the monitor to view a clip before you decide whether to add it to the Workspace area and make it part of your movie.

Editing the Movie

After you have created one or more collections of clips, you can then edit your movie. The editing techniques you will learn about here are really quite simple. The Workspace section of Movie Maker (at the bottom of the screen) can be set to Storyboard or Timeline View, as discussed earlier in this chapter. For general editing purposes, it is easy to simply drag a clip to one of the frames in the Storyboard View and later use the Timeline View to made adjustments or edits.

> **Tip**
>
> If you are working on a movie that will take some time to edit and assemble, then you can save your work at any time as a Project. Simply select Save Project As from the File menu. You can then use the Open Project selection from the same menu at a later time to continue editing. A project, however, is not the final output of Windows Movie Maker. The final output is a movie file that you can create when you are finished editing and making changes to your project.

Adding a Clip to the Workspace

This is a simple chore. Just click on the clip you want to add and drag it to the Workspace. You can drag one clip after another, and they will all be sequentially displayed in the Workspace. Figure 28.8 indicates how several clips have been added to the Workspace.

FIGURE 28.8

You can drag clips to the Workspace to make them part of the movie you are editing.

Alternatively, if you prefer, you can click once on a clip and then click the Clip menu. From this menu, select Add to Storyboard/Timeline.

Removing a Clip from the Workspace

If you change your mind after you have added a clip to the current movie, you can easily delete it from the Workspace. Although you cannot drag a clip off the Workspace, you can use the Edit menu to delete it. Right-click on the clip in the Workspace and select Delete from the menu that appears. You can also click once on the clip and select the Delete option from the Edit menu.

Cut and Paste: Moving Clips Around in the Workspace

You can also rearrange clips in the Workspace. Although you could technically delete a clip and then add it back from the original collection, it is easier to simply use the cut and paste method. First, you can simply select Cut from the menu that appears when you right-click on a clip in the Workspace. Next, position your cursor on the Storyboard (or Timeline) in the Workspace where you would like the clip to appear. Then right-click and select Paste.

Another easy method to rearrange clips in the Workspace is to drag the clip from one part of the Workspace to another. Just hold down the left button on your mouse and drag the clip to its new location. When you use this method, a vertical position bar will be displayed at the point at which the clip is inserted.

Tip

Another interesting thing you can do with a clip is to make a copy. Why would you want to do this? Well, you might decide later to trip part of a clip and perhaps use the trimmed portion elsewhere in the Storyboard. (You will learn about trimming a clip later in this section.) To copy a clip, just select it (either in the Collections pane or in the Workspace) and from the Edit menu, select Copy. Next, click once in the Workspace at the position where you want to copy the clip and from the Edit menu, select Paste. If you are in a hurry, just hold down the Ctrl key and drag a clip from one position in the Workspace to another. This will produce a copy instead of moving the clip.

Editing a Clip

You edit the movie by rearranging the clips in the Workspace so that they appear in the order you want. You can add some narration (more on this later) and other things like a title frame. However, you can also edit a clip that you have placed into the Workspace area. You need first to switch to the Timeline View of the Workspace. Figure 28.9 shows how the Timeline View has changed. From this view, you can see the number of seconds a clip will play. Some clips in this view are shorter than the actual picture associated with the clip is cut in order to fit into the shorter space.

FIGURE 28.9

If the collection consists of a set of clips produced by Movie Maker, then you will see the first frame of each clip in the middle pane.

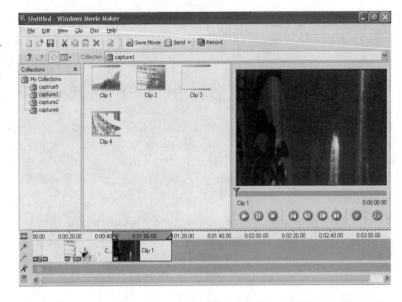

In Figure 28.9, you will also see that the last frame is longer than the space it takes to show the single frame in the Workspace, so it is followed by its name (Clip 1). The last clip is also selected (you can do this by clicking on it), and you can see in the section of the Timeline where the minutes and seconds appear. At each end of the clip are trim handles. These are the small triangles you see at each end of the clip. You can drag these handles to trim footage from either side of the clip. This doesn't destroy the original clip but instead selects the portion that will be included in the movie you make. This trimming capability makes it easy for you to use a wide variety of source files and know that they will always remain the same. You don't have to create a new file and edit it each time you want to include just part of a file in a movie. To trim, just click on a trim handle and move it to a new location.

As you move a trim handle, you will see the frames you are trimming in the Monitor. You will also see the number of minutes or seconds you are trimming from the clip. Keep in mind that at any time, you can preview your project or any clip by using the monitor.

You can also use the monitor and the Clip menu to trim a clip. Simply select the clip in the Workspace and then click Play on the monitor. When the playback reaches the point where you want to start, you set the left trim point by selecting from the Clip menu Set Start Trim Point. Then click the Play button again on the Monitor. When the playback reaches the portion of the clip where you want to stop, select Set End Trim Point from the Clip menu. Only the portion of the clip that is between the start and end trimming points will be included in the movie.

You can also use the option Clear Trim Points, which is also found on the Clip menu, to make the trim handles return to their original point.

Splitting or Combining Clips

You can split clips or combine them using the Clip menu. Splitting a clip is almost the same as setting a trim handle, but you use a different menu selection. Click once on the clip and start the playback in the Monitor section of Movie Maker. When the clip reaches the point where you want to split it into two separate clips, click on the Clip menu and select Split. The clip will be separated into two different clips and show up that way in the Workspace area. You can also join two clips together so that they appear as one clip in the Workspace. Just hold down the Shift key and click once on each contiguous clip to combine and select Combine from the Clip menu.

Fade Out/Fade In: Creating Transitions Between Clips

If you just add clips to your movie, then each clip will be played one after another. If you want, you can add a fade transition, where one clip starts to fade out as another fades in. To accomplish this effect, you must also work with Timeline View in the Workspace. Click on the second clip that will be part of this transition (the one that will fade in) and drag it back over the previous clip that will become the clip that fades out. The section on the Timeline that overlaps will become shaded, indicating where the fade out/fade in effect will happen.

You can undo a transition by simply dragging the second clip back to its original position.

Adding Title Slides or Still Pictures to a Movie

You can also add title slides and place them anywhere you want in the Workspace. You can use a graphics editor such as Microsoft Paint or PowerPoint to create the slide, or you can just use your favorite graphics editor. You can also add still pictures and even specify the amount of time they will be displayed. The graphics format supported for still pictures or title slides by Movie Maker are `.bmp`, `.jpg`, `.jpeg`, `.jpe`, `.jfif`, `.gif`, and `.dib`.

You can use the Import selection from the File menu, as discussed earlier, to import still photographs or title slides you create and add them to the Workspace like any other clip.

Adding Narration to Your Movie

Not only can you add both video clips and still pictures to your movie, you can also add narration. This is especially effective if you have several title slides or if you create a movie consisting mainly of photographs displayed for a short time. You can narrate what the end user will see.

28

USING WINDOWS
MOVIE MAKER

You can record your narrative text using the Sound Recorder and then simply import the resulting audio file into Windows Movie Maker like you do a video clip or still image. However, if you look closely at the previous figure which shows you the Timeline View of the Workspace area, under the section that displays your video clips, title slides and still pictures, there is a bar with a microphone next to it. This is where you drag audio clips that will be part of the final movie. You can also experiment with different levels of audio between clips, but that is beyond the scope of this chapter.

Saving a Movie

After you have assembled your clips, added fades or title slides and any narration, you can preview it using the Monitor. When you have it where you want it, you can then turn your Project into a Movie. To create a Movie file, select Save Movie from the File menu. Figure 28.10 shows the Save Movie dialog box, which allows you to make several choices about the resulting output file.

FIGURE 28.10

You use this dialog box to decide to save a Movie and select the quality of the resulting file.

Caution

The file system on your computer can limit the amount of space available for using Windows Movie Maker to capture video and audio for use in Movie Maker. For partitions formatted using the NT file system (NTFS), you can use the entire file system—that is, you can use the entire partition for an almost unlimited recording if you have a large enough partition. For a 32-Bit File Allocation Table (FAT32) partition, you are limited to a maximum of 4GB. This may seem like a lot of space. However, when recording video and audio, you will find that this really isn't a whole lot of space! For the older FAT16 file system you are limited to 2GB.

You can also use the Display information section at the bottom of the dialog box to insert information into the file about the movie, such as a title, author, and description. This is not the title that will be used for the actual Movie file; it is simply a place for you to store information about the properties of this movie file.

Selecting the Quality of the Finished Product and Saving the Movie

You need to decide the quality of the output movie file that will be created. This will depend on how you want to use the movie file. As was stated earlier in this chapter, if you have a Web site and want to put the movie up for downloading by others, you may want to choose a lower quality format. The same goes for sending a movie in an e-mail message. A broadband connection would have no problem sending out several megabytes of data in an e-mail message, but make sure that the recipient of your e-mail attachment has the same capacity. Otherwise, you may need to lower the quality of the movie.

> **Tip**
>
> When you have finished assembling the clips for a movie, experiment with different quality settings and then use Windows Media Player, version 8 (WPM 8) to play back the different versions you create. You can see what kind of difference the quality setting makes and then make your decision on what the final movie output should be. You might even produce several versions of your movie, one for the Web, and one for burning to a CD.

From the Setting drop-down menu, you can select from low, medium, or high quality. Once you have done this and filled in any other information you want about the properties of this movie, then click OK. A standard Windows Save As dialog box will pop up, allowing you to give the file a name. The file type (or file extension) will be .WMV, which is the Windows movie format. The default folder for storing your movie file is the My Videos folder. You can also use this dialog box to save the movie to a different location if you wish. After selecting a name and location for the output file, click Save.

A dialog box titled Creating Movie will appear and show you the progress as the output file is created. When this process is complete, another dialog box asks if you want to watch your movie. Click Yes or NO. You can always watch a movie file saved in the .WMV format by double-clicking on it in the My Videos folder (or wherever you saved it). WPM 8 now shows you your movie.

Publishing on the Web or E-mailing a Movie

After you have created your movie, you can use the File menu to send the resulting movie file to a Web site (using file transfer protocol [FTP]), or you can select to send the movie via e-mail to a friend.

> **Tip**
>
> Before you e-mail a movie (or any large file), be sure the recipient has the bandwidth to handle such a file and does not have mailbox memory limitations that would prevent them from receiving such a large file.

To start this process, click on the File menu and then Send Movie To. Next select either E-mail or Web Server. Anyone who receives your movie via e-mail can play it using WPM 8. If you want to upload to a Web site, you will have to edit the hypertext markup language (HTML) page for the Web site to include a link to your movie before it will appear on the Web page.

Burning to a CD

You can also use the new CD burning technology incorporated into Windows XP to create a CD of your movie file. (Of course, you must have a computer with a CD burner that is recognized by Windows XP!) To create a CD, use the same steps you used earlier to save a movie file (Save Movie from the File menu). This time, in the Save As dialog box, select the drive letter of your CD burner instead of the My Videos folder. Give the output file a name and click Save. The file will be stored in a temporary area for the moment. You will see the same dialog box telling you that the movie is being created.

To burn the actual CD, place a recordable CD in your CD burner drive and bring up Windows Explorer (Start, All Programs, Accessories, Windows Explorer). Select My Computer from the left Folders pane so that you can see all the drives on your computer (see Figure 28.11).

As you can see, the CD burner is selected. In Figure 28.11, Windows Explorer (in the right side pane) is saying that there are files waiting to be written to the recordable CD. To burn the CD now, click the Folders button on the toolbar, and the left side of the Windows Explorer screen will change to show you the tasks you can perform, including writing data to the CD. You can see this view in Figure 28.12.

FIGURE **28.11**

You can use Windows Explorer to burn the movie to a recordable CD.

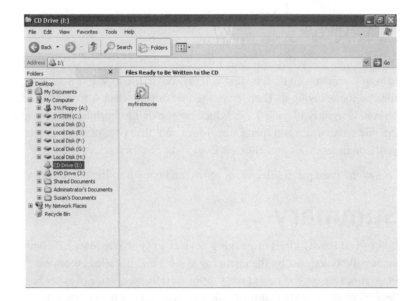

FIGURE **28.12**

After you click Folders on the toolbar, you can select the Write these files to CD option task.

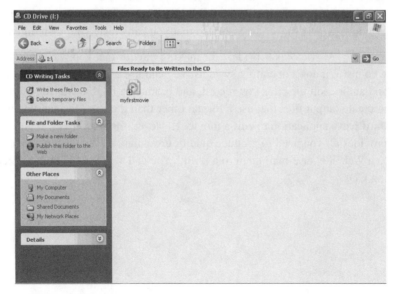

The CD Writing Wizard will pop up, allowing you to give a name to the CD. You can use the default name or enter any name you want. Click Next to this first screen of the wizard to start the process. The Wizard will show you a bar graph indicating the progress it makes as it writes the file to the CD. When the Wizard is done, click the Finished button, and your CD is ready to use!

To play a movie, just insert it into your CD-ROM drive and double-click on the Movie file. WPM 8 will then play your movie.

You can also use WPM 8 to save a move to a portable device if you have one connected to your computer. To do this, first add the movie file to WPM 8's Library by selecting the file and then playing it. Then, from the File menu, select Add to Media Library and click on Add Currently Playing Track. Once the movie has been added to your library, click on the File menu again and then Copy. Make sure that your portable device is connected to your computer. After you click on Copy, you can then select Copy to Portable Device.

Follow the prompts to select your movie and copy it to the portable device.

Summary

You can add many kinds of imaging devices to your Windows XP computer. Most of them will be detected by the operating system and installed automatically using Plug and Play. However, as you saw at the start of this chapter, you can also choose from the device drivers that Microsoft supplies, or you can use a disk from the manufacturer to install an imaging device. Most of this chapter, however, concentrated on using the Windows Movie Maker accessory so that you can create your own digital movies.

Windows Movie Maker is ideal for making movies that you want to share with others who use Windows operating systems. You can use Movie Maker to capture both video and audio, edit the clips you record, and produce a final movie file output. If you want to create output files that use a format other than the .WMV format, you will need to use a third-party application to edit a movie. However, for most users, Windows Movie Maker provides all you need to produce quality presentations. You can post movies you make to a Web site, or e-mail them to a friend. You can also use the built-in technology burning CDs.

Windows Media Player 8

CHAPTER 29

IN THIS CHAPTER

- Overview of Windows Media Player 8   *730*
- A Quick Overview of the Interface   *732*
- Now Playing   *734*
- The Media Guide: A Guide to Media!   *739*
- Copying from CDs   *739*
- The Media Library   *741*
- Tuning into the Internet   *744*
- Music on the Go   *746*
- Working with Skins   *748*
- Options, Tab by Tab   *749*

Microsoft has been quite busy since the release of Windows Media Player 7.1, because Windows Media Player, version 8, has gone through a bevy of changes, improvements, bug fixes, and a few new additions here and there. For the most part, Media Player 8 is an evolutionary step from 7.1.

Media Player had a rather meager and modest upbringing. Formerly named CD Player and capable of precious little, it was a poor competitor to the already powerful QuickTime from Apple and RealPlayer from RealNetworks. It was at around this time that rumblings about a new audio format were starting up.

Having used the MP3 format (the audio stream, or layer 3, portion of the MPEG-II codec) for some time, Internet users were not surprised as it began to take off. At the same time, radio stations were beginning to stream their broadcast over the Internet to avid listeners. RealNetworks had been introducing Internet users to video over the Internet for quite some time, and Apple was about to introduce its stream media server for the new Mac OS X Server. The year was 1997.

In the meantime, Microsoft was rapidly trying to catch up with these third-party vendors by heavily modifying its CD Player application to match the capabilities of something like RealPlayer. CD Player was used only to provide playback for audio CDs. Microsoft also had other applets to play some sounds and eventually those tiny little AVI video clips you could download off the Internet.

Eventually, CD Player and the rest of these applications were combined into the single Media Player application.

In this chapter you will learn more about Media Player 8, including how to copy music from CDs, playback audio and visual content, and yes, even play a CD or two.

Overview of Windows Media Player 8

Media Player is a collection of tools to play and manage audio and video files of various formats, integrated into a single application. Although WinAmp (www.winamp.com) will likely be the popular favorite for some time, Microsoft has brought to bear a formidable opponent. Microsoft is aiming at a number of perceived competitors, not just the digital audio market.

One thing that Media Player does *not* do is replace players like QuickTime 5, RealPlayer, and RealJukebox applications. In order for your system to support these file types, you will have to download and install each application from its respective vendor. Interestingly enough, RealNetwork licensed the Windows media formats from Microsoft and has integrated playback support of these file formats into their products. This agreement, however, does not include support for Microsoft's new Media Player 8 file formats.

What's New for Windows Media Player 8?

Media Player has the following new features and capabilities:

- Integrated DVD Playback Support—Media Player 7.1 for Windows 2000 and Windows Me required a separate player program for digital video disc (DVD) playback. You are still required to provide a hardware or software DVD playback solution, so Microsoft hasn't given you everything.

- Improved Audio CD Recording—Microsoft has already integrated CD burning capabilities into Windows+ XP, but now, the audio CD burning capabilities have been enhanced. Most of the speed benefits, however, come from increased support for faster CD-recordable/rewritable (CD-R/RW) drives and some improved caching techniques.

- Improved Support for MP3 Files and File Management—This is an excellent improvement, considering that file management support was practically nonexistent in Media Player 7.1. One neat trick is that when you move media files that have been added to the Media Library, the system will track their new location and update the database so that you won't break links. This is very Macintosh-like.

- Full Screen Controls—In Media Player 7.1, no controls were available while viewing files in full-screen mode. Now, when you move the mouse, controls appear from the top and bottom edges and disappear if you leave them alone for 5 seconds. Also, mode switching is now more intuitive.

- Enhanced Audio CD Ripping—When you rip a CD, or extract the audio files from the CD and convert them to digital media files that can be played back on a computer (hence the more compact term *rip*), Media Player 8 gathers all the information it can about the artist and album, including a picture of the cover.

29

WINDOWS MEDIA
PLAYER 8

Note

It should be noted that while Media Player 8 can play MP3 files, it cannot record in MP3 format. This means that any audio passage ripped from a CD will be recorded to the less standard Media Player file format. If you purchase a copy of Microsoft Plus!, MP3 recording capabilities will be made available.

- Video File Transfers to Mobile Devices—You were once limited to audio files on your Pocket PC, but you can now watch complete movies in your hand. FilmSpeed (www.filmspeed.com) has a number of movies that have been especially encoded for handheld devices.

Supported File Types

It may sound like a limitation to say that Media Player is used for the playback and management of just audio and video, but that would be disingenuous. Media Player is capable of playing back all Windows media formats (`.asf`, `.asx`, `.wax`, `.wm`, `.wma`, `.wmp`, `.wav`); CD audio (`.cda`); Audio Interchange File Format (`.aiff`); Motion Picture Experts Group (`.mpeg`) audio; Musical Instrument Digital Interface (`.midi`) files; and Unix audio (`.au`, `.and`, `.snd`). On the video side, Media Player 8 is able to play back Intel Indeo video (`.ivf`), all Windows Media files (`.wmv`, `.wvx`, `.avi`), `.mpeg` (`.mpeg`, `.mpg`), and DVD video (`.vob`, with a decoder).

Music Swapping, The RIAA, and The Law

When you buy a recorded product or even a book, what you are purchasing is the right to use the copy you purchased. Loaning a book or CD to a friend is within the license, but copying it onto a CD-R or uploading its contents as digital media for others to download from the Web is not.

This is because you have created a copy or copies of the product and still retain your original instead of purchasing new copies or loaning out your copy. This is what was at the heart of the matter of the Napster case. Napster lost because they could not substantiate their claim that what their users did was swapping.

When you swap something, you exchange it for something else. With Napster, you get something for nothing without either party really having to give anything up. Does this mean that you cannot legally copy a CD you just purchased? The answer here isn't as clear-cut. First, there are technical issues. Most record companies, for example, are implementing technologies that they hope will prevent piracy. For now, with the new technologies, you can listen to it in an audio CD player but not on a computer's CD-ROM drive. Fortunately, it probably won't be too long before this hurdle is eliminated as well.

A Quick Overview of the Interface

If you are already familiar with Media Player 7.1, then you pretty much have Media Player 8 in the bag. With the exception of some minor details and a sculpted look added to the Full Mode, there are no significant changes. If, however, you have not experienced Microsoft's new multimedia center, then there are a few things you should get familiar with, which will help in the following sections. First, get the big picture (see Figure 29.1).

FIGURE 29.1

The complete Media Player 8 interface in Full Mode.

The main interface can be viewed as having three distinct areas: component buttons, playback controls, and display area. Since Media Player 8 covers a wide range of functions, the interface is divided into components that are accessible by clicking the buttons to the left of the Full Mode display. Those components are as follows:

- Now Playing—Displays active media, controls for playback, equalization, SRS WOW effects, active playlists, and visualizations.

- Media Guide—Displays the Windows Media Web site (`www.windowsmedia.com`) and gives you integrated access to its resources.

- Copy From CD—Displays controls specific to making copies of your existing CD-based media.

- Media Library—Displays and manages cataloged audio and video media arranged in categories defined by artist, album, or song name, as well as other data.

- Radio Tuner—Displays and allows management of selected Internet-based radio stations. Stations can be added to sets and managed in groups.

- Copy To CD or Device—Displays controls and information regarding the copying of digital media to CD or device. Devices can be portable digital media players and Pocket PC devices.

- Skin Chooser—Displays available skins or visual themes between which you can switch

29

WINDOWS MEDIA PLAYER 8

While playing media of any kind, video or audio, you can move among these components, as you like. The media will not be interrupted, although if you have an older machine or one that falls under the minimum requirements for installation, it might skip.

What Is Streaming Media?

The Internet was once a place where you could find something interesting to read and that was about it. At least until some bright guy (Rob Glaser, CEO of RealNetworks Inc.) started a company in 1994 that would bring streaming audio and video to the Internet. Today, a number of streaming media types are available over the Internet. The three most popular are QuickTime from Apple Computer Inc., RealMedia from RealNetworks Inc., and Windows Media from Microsoft. But what, you ask, is streaming media?

The average consumer desktop computer can move large files around the hard drive very quickly. Even transferring files from CD-ROM is quite speedy with drives capable of 52x speeds (around 2MB of data per second). These speeds are more than enough for CD and DVD quality video. DVD drives and their associated hardware- or software-based decoders are capable of delivering high-resolution video and surround sound audio directly through your desktop's monitor and speakers.

All of the speed you can get locally means that you can listen or view a file almost as soon as you open it. However, since the data transfer rate is typically far slower through an Internet connection, even with DSL and Cable, a portion of the media file must load before playback can begin. That portion of the file, which loads before being displayed, is called *stored in a memory buffer.* In other words, the buffer is there to provide continuous play.

Like most things regarding the Internet, buffering is highly dependent on a good connection and servers that aren't overloaded. In other words, the stream must have a constant flow for this to work properly. If the site streaming the movie clip you want to watch has too many visitors, then you may have to wait a relatively long time for the clip to start playing, or you may not be successful in downloading your clip at all.

Now Playing

The Now Playing component is where most of the action takes place. Although playback can be started and stopped from any component, this one is where you can see Visualizations (more on that a little later) and video. Unless you use Media Player solely for multimedia file management and don't play back any files at all, this is where you will spend most of your time.

The Playlist (to the far right) and the Equalizer and Settings (across the bottom) bars are shown by default. You can toggle these on and off by clicking the rightmost buttons that appear to the left of the Playlist selector, as indicated in Figure 29.2. The third button is the control that changes from normal playback mode to shuffle playback mode and back again.

> **Tip**
>
> Shuffle mode will allow Media Player to act as a DJ for your audio files by playing them in a random order.

FIGURE 29.2

The Shuffle, Equalizer and Settings, and Playlist buttons.

Opening Files

Opening files in Media Player is like opening files in any other program. The most common way is as follows:

1. Click on File, Open.
2. Navigate to the directory where your media files are stored. Since this is Windows XP, this will likely be your My Music folder, although you can store media files anywhere you like.
3. Select one or more files by dragging over several or using the standard Shift+Click and Ctrl+Click functions. When you have selected enough, click OK.

Now, the files will appear in the Playlist pane (that is, if it is open), and the first file will start to play.

Opening Uniform Resource Locators

Opening uniform resource locators (URLs) for Web sites in Media Player is much like opening files as described above, with one exception. The most common way is as follows:

1. Click on File, Open URL.
2. Enter the address manually or copy and paste it from Internet Explorer. If the URL is stored as an Internet shortcut, navigate to the directory where the shortcut is

stored. If you created the shortcut by using the File, Send, Shortcut To Desktop command, it will be on the desktop.

3. Click OK.

Again, the files defined in the remote Playlist will appear in the Playlist pane (if it is open), and the first file will start to load. Since media files from a Web site need to be transferred using streaming technology before playing them, you will likely see the piece "buffering" before actual playback.

Drag and Drop with Media

Even more convenient than using the Open function is the ability to drag media files onto Media Player, specifically into the Playlist pane of the Now Playing component. Once you have dropped several files into the Playlist, you can reorder them by dragging them into the order of your choice. The only case where you cannot reorder tracks is from an audio CD in your CD drive. You can, however, reorder these if you copy them to a playlist file, a procedure covered in the Media Library section.

Visualization

Visualization is a graphical gizmoid that moves, changes colors, and otherwise gyrates to the music playing in Media Player 8. A commonly known example of a visualization is the sound meter (the green, yellow, and red light bars that bounce up and down) on a stereo system's amplifier. Visualizations in Media Player 8 (see Figure 29.3) can be much more complex and not necessarily as helpful as the old type, but that is not their reason for being.

Think of visualizations as being the lava lamp, black light, strobe light, and mandala of the modern age, all wrapped up into one neat, computerized package. Other than that, there is no clear, concise explanation. You really have to see them to understand them. Then again, you are also likely to sit and stare as they wheel and gyrate around your screen!

A number of visualizations are provided with Media Player. You can change which one you are viewing or select a "random" command from View, Visualizations and then select one of the items inside several oddly named categories like Particle, Battery, or Plenoptic. If you have no wish to view any visualizations, select the Cover Art option at the top of the list. If there is no cover art, a graphic bearing a CD and musical note will appear.

FIGURE 29.3

Media Player 8 showing a visualization for music.

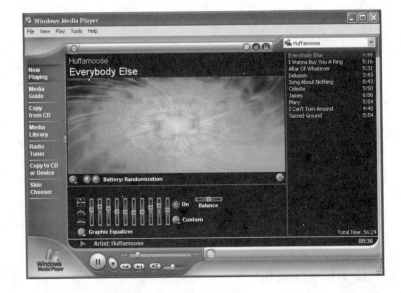

To manage your visualizations, follow these steps:

1. Click Tools, Options.

2. Select the Visualizations tab. A list of installed visualizations will appear with some option buttons across the bottom.

3. To add a visualization, click the Add button and locate the file. Click OK.

4. To remove a visualization, select it in the list and click the Remove button. If the button is not highlighted, you cannot remove it. Of all of the default visualizations, only Musical Colors can be removed.

5. To modify the properties of a visualization, select it in the list and click the Properties button. Most visualizations do not have any options to change. The ones that do are limited to setting screen resolution and buffer size. Click OK.

You can download additional visualizations by clicking on Tools, Download Visualizations on the Media Player Menu bar. This really just takes you to the http://www.windowsmedia.com/mg/visualizations.asp address.

Advanced Features

Several additional features are not only available via the regular menus, but also through the context menus that come up when you right-click on certain parts of the Media Player interface.

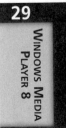

29

WINDOWS MEDIA PLAYER 8

- Right-clicking a visualization will give you a list of other visualizations from which to choose.

- Right-clicking the Equalizer will give you a list of controls and information panels to which you can switch.

- Right-clicking an item in the Playlist will give you a list of functions you can perform with it, including renaming the file.

A few final notes on this subject are as follows:

- If you click on the Windows Media Player logo on the lower left corner of the Full Mode window, you will be taken to a step-by-step guide to the software.

- Spend time fiddling with any new skins you try and always know that you should be able to right-click on nearly anything to get a menu with an available Return To Full Mode command.

DVD Playback

Despite all the hype from Microsoft about DVDs playing in Windows XP, Media Player does not have the capability to play DVDs right out of the box. Some system vendors may make this available to their customers or sell computers that already have the capability, but there is no way to predict which systems will have DVD playback capabilities.

If you have a DVD drive in your system, insert a DVD to see if it plays (it is cheaper and easier to rent a DVD if you don't happen to have one handy). You may have to open Media Player if you have turned off AutoRun (also called *Auto Insert Notification*), or you can click on Start, Run, type in dvdplay, and click OK, which will also try to load a DVD. If there is no hardware and/or decoder, you will see the error dialog indicated in Figure 29.4.

FIGURE 29.4

Nope, no DVD here!

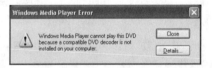

The only existing solutions for DVD playback are from third parties. That means another purchase. This shouldn't be, but it is so, and we have to deal with it. The best software-based DVD player is PowerDVD from Cyberlink (www.gocyberlink.com), which has great controls and excellent color reproduction.

The Media Guide: A Guide to Media!

Although it isn't much more than a Web site accessed through Media Player, the Media Guide (see Figure 29.5) is updated daily and often has something interesting. Most of the items listed will open up in Internet Explorer, and the media you selected to audition will likely appear in that same Web page in Internet Explorer and not in Media Player 8 itself. Regardless, you can set a single option as follows:

1. Click on Tools, Options.

2. Select the Player tab.

3. In the Player Settings section, you can deselect the Start Player In Media Guide option.

FIGURE 29.5

Media Player showing the movies section of the Media Guide.

Copying from CDs

By default, Media Player converts CD audio into .wma files, a Microsoft media format. Informal testing indicates that a 64 kilobits/seconds (Kb/s) .wma file is equal in quality to that of a 128Kb/s MP3 file. For example, an average MP3-rendered CD will take approximately 60MB of disk space; its .wma counterpart will take about 30MB, although Microsoft claims it is actually 28MB. The quality of .wma files is more than acceptable.

What Is Digital Audio?

Digital audio is the sum of three components: KHz, Bit depth, and Bit rate. They are defined as follows:

- KHz—KHz [pronounced **kee**-low-hurtz] describes the "sampling rate" at which audio is recorded. The higher the sampling rate, the better is the quality—that is, up to a point. For perspective, CD audio is sampled at 44.1 KHz, whereas FM radio is sampled at 22.050 KHz, AM radio at 11.025 KHz, and standard voice telephone at 8 KHz.

Note

Sampling is the act of capturing bits of an original sound at specific, regular intervals. The more often the sound is sampled, the more complete is the "picture" of the original sound. Resampling is the same thing, except that when you resample, you pick up bits of an already recorded sound to make yet another recording at a lower quality. The more frequently a sound is sampled, the more data exists for our ears to interpret. Of course, the more data we have, the fuller is the sound.

- Bit depth—The bit depth is the range of frequencies that comprise a sound as it is recorded. More specifically, the greater the range, or bit depth, the fuller is the "picture" of the sound. Common bit depths for digital recording are 8 and 16, although 24-bit audio is coming into use. Because music is more intricate than the spoken word, a wider range of frequencies must be used to accurately reproduce it. Thus, music is typically recoded at higher bit depths.

- Bit rate—The bit rate is the speed at which decompression of encoded audio takes place. This is measured in kilobits (Kb) per second. The more Kb passed and decoded per second the higher the audio "resolution."

Tip

Codec (pronounced **co**-dek) is a made-up word that is shorthand for compression/decompression. In reality, the only results of a codec that consumers tend to see is the decompression part.

Putting it all together, consider a common MP3 audio file. Because MP3 is used for music, it captures a wide range of sound frequencies. However, the sounds that fall on the outside ranges of human hearing are not included in the sound capture. By cutting out the frequencies that we can't hear, the file size is reduced. As a result, an MP3 audio file created directly from a 3.5-minute song from an original CD has the following properties:

- Sample Rate—44.1 KHz
- Bit Depth—16
- Bit Rate—176.4 Kb/s
- Size (MB)—~4.6

Most people sample their MP3s at anywhere from 128Kb/s to 256Kb/s. Digital audio tape (DAT) has a bit rate of 192Kb/s, higher than Redbook audio (the CD audio standard) of 176.4Kb/s. The higher bit rate compensates for some deficiencies in the DAT format, although the resulting difference in audio quality is such that few would be able to tell the difference.

Windows Media approaches its sampling in a completely different manner. What formula they use is a Microsoft trade secret. The result they achieve, however, is a high-quality file at a lower bit rate. As such, a 64Kb/s .wma file is the rough equivalent of a 128Kb/s MP3 file, as long as the other aspects of the media remain the same.

The Media Library

Unlike any simple player application, Media Player can store and organize your media. The Media Library (see Figure 29.6) will store detailed information about your CDs, including cover art and in some cases even lyrics, and sort them into folders. When you place a CD in a drive on your computer or tell Media Player to search your directories for media files, the information on what they are and where they are stored is immediately entered into a large database.

Unfortunately, the Media Library is clearly lacking in some areas. The primary complaint is that you cannot remove entire albums in the library. You must remove entire albums by right-clicking and individually removing each track. If you need to start over, be sure to check out the tip earlier in this chapter.

Of course, if you go along with Media Player's way of organizing things, you will be fine. Each artist is assigned a folder that contains subfolders for each separate album. When you rip CDs using one of the MP3 encoding utilities that comes with Plus!, you will also get lyrics, credits, and cover art, just like Microsoft's own Windows Media.

29

WINDOWS MEDIA
PLAYER 8

FIGURE 29.6

*The Media
Library main
interface with files
listed by artist.*

Tip

The database file for Media Player 8 is typically stored in C:\Documents and
Settings\All Users\Application Data\Microsoft\Media Index and will be
called something like wmplibrary_v_0_12.db. Why is this important? If you collect all of your MP3 files in one folder, you will have a problem. Every time you
search that folder to add new files, you will also add duplicate entries for everything already there. Trashing this database file can help you start all over again.
Just make sure to save all of your playlists to files first!

Adding Media To The Guide

If you elected to have Media Player search your accessible drives for media when you
first began using the program, the following steps will not be necessary. If, however, you
bypassed this offer, you may want to follow these instructions. This process adds media
files that are supported by Media Player, both audio and video, to the media library.

To automatically search your systems for media, do the following:

1. Click on Tools, Search for Media Files

2. In the Search for Media Files dialog, select the drives that you want Media Player
   to search. If you store all of your media in a single directory, you may elect to limit

the search to that directory by clicking Browse and navigating to the target folder. Click Search.

3. When the search has reached 100%, click the Close button. If you would like, make any additional searches to add more media. If not, click Close.

Windows XP installs a number of supported media files for use with the operating system. Although it is unlikely that you would want to add them to your library, you may if you so choose. To modify the search parameters, click the Advanced button in the Search for Media Files dialog. To specifically add the .wav files that the system uses, check the Include System Folder option. Otherwise, modify the size options for audio and video files as necessary.

Another option for adding files is to have them added as you play them. Of course, this assumes that you have a more direct hand in managing how and where you media files are stored. If you prefer to store files by hand, this option may be for you. You can set the option using the following steps:

1. Click on Tools/Options.

2. Activate the Player tab.

3. Place a check in the Add Items To Media Library When Played option.

4. Click OK.

Of course, if you can put them in, you can take them out. If you would like to delete a file or files from the Media Library your first option is to right-click on the offending file and select Delete From Library.

Warning

Deleting items from the Media Library does not remove the files from your hard disk. In order to remove media files from your hard disk, you will need to locate them physically in Windows Explorer and place them in the Recycle Bin manually.

Editing Media Information

To edit media file information, you right-click on the file for which you would like to edit the data and select Edit. Of course, Media Player also facilitates the editing of groups of files. For example, if you copy your Barenaked Ladies CD and the band name is incorrectly displayed as Bare Naked Ladies, then this means that someone entered the information incorrectly. You may fix this by doing the following:

1. Make the Media Library active.

2. Locate and select the copy of your CD under the Artist or Album listing in the left-hand pane of the Media Library interface. The track names will appear to the right.

3. Select all of the tracks in the album.

4. Right-click on any track in the Artist column and select the Edit Selected Items command.

5. Edit the Artist's name to read correctly and press Enter to save the changes.

Once you have done this, the files disappear and then reappear with the corrections made.

Creating Playlists

Not everybody likes to listen to entire records straight through. This is why there are playlists into which you can drop any song from any album and arrange them in the order you like. You can either create a new playlist, or you can add tracks to an existing playlist by doing the following:

1. To create a new playlist, make the Media Library active and click on the New Playlist button.

2. Enter a name for the playlist in the New Playlist dialog.

3. Click OK.

Your new playlist appears in the right pane and in the left pane listed in the My Playlists item. Now you are ready to add items to the playlist. To add tracks to your playlist, do the following:

1. Locate the track or tracks you want to add. If there are several, select them all.

2. Right-click on any selected track and select the Add To Playlist command.

3. In the Playlists dialog, select an existing playlist from the ones shown or click New and create a new playlist to which to add the tracks.

4. Click OK.

Repeat this process until you have added all the tracks you would like to add to the playlist. You can reorder tracks in a playlist by dragging them up and down the list or by clicking the Up and Down arrows just above the list area.

Tuning into the Internet

Internet radio started to attract interest in the mid-1990s. Today, literally thousands of terrestrial and Internet-only radio stations are broadcasting further then they ever could before. Media Player provides access to these servers through a special, regularly updated Web page (similar to the Media Guide) that allows you to store and search through currently operating stations. This is called *Radio Tuner* (see Figure 29.7).

FIGURE 29.7

The Media Player 8 Radio Tuner shown in its default appearance.

The Radio Tuner page is divided into five distinct areas: Featured Stations, My Stations, Recently Played Stations, Find More Stations, and Today's Hits. By default, the Featured Stations section appears listing the stations that Microsoft has chosen, whereas the My Stations and Recently Played Stations are rolled up. Clicking on a station name (such as BBC World, National Public Radio) calls up more detailed information about the station. Click the name again, and it rolls back up. Each featured station has the following links:

- Add To My Stations—Click this link to add the station to your My Stations list.
- *Visit Website*—Click this link to open an Internet Explorer browser window that displays the station's Web site.
- Play—Click this link to play the station in Media Player 8. This typically also takes you to the same Web site that you would get if you clicked the Visit Website link.

29

WINDOWS MEDIA
PLAYER 8

- Visit Website To Play—As an alternative to a simple Play link, this link indicates that you visit their Web site to listen to the station's stream.

The roll down/roll up function works the same way for each of the three sections that make up the left side of the page. For example, to see the contents of your My Stations section, click the My Stations name.

Music on the Go

New to Media Player is the ability to record CDs. Windows XP itself has the ability to burn CDs, as does Media Player. The application can still transcode and copy files to portable digital media devices and personal digital assistants (PDAs) (see Figure 29.8), but the addition of CD burning capability really increases portability.

FIGURE 29.8

Media Player copying music to a mobile device.

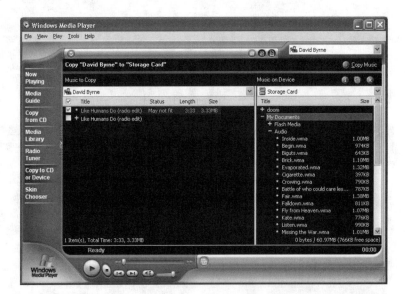

> **Tip**
>
> Transcoding is what Microsoft's term for converting one media format to another (MP3 to WMA) and resampling the media to make it smaller (128Kb/s to 32Kb/s).

There are three ways to get audio files to CD and device: audio CD, digital media file, and a playlist. (The procedure for all three is the same and is covered in the list below.) To prepare a list of digital media files to be copied to CD, follow these steps (these instructions assume that you have already added all existing digital media to your media library):

1. Insert an audio CD or create a playlist.

2. Click on the Copy To CD Or Device component button. The window has two panes. The left is what you are copying from and the right is what you are copying to.

3. In the Music To Copy drop-down menu, select the CD, album stored in the Media Library, or playlist that you want to copy.

4. In the Music On Device menu, select the device that you want to copy to. If you have just connected a universal serial buss (USB) device, you may have to refresh the list by pressing F5 before it is available.

5. Deselect items on the left that you either don't want to copy to CD or device or for which you have no room.

6. Click Copy Music in the top right corner of the window.

> ### Tip
>
> For more detailed information on making devices available to Media Player, see the section later in this chapter, "Options, Tab By Tab."

If you have elected to have Media Player transcode your files before transferring them to your device, there is one catch. You will note that Media Player shows you which files fit on the device. It bases this on the size of the source files. It does not calculate how large the files will be *after* the transcoding to see if they will fit. The following is a guide on how to assess the size of the files:

- 32Kb/s—About 14MB of space per CD and 800 to 1,100 KB per track
- 48Kb/s—About 22MB of space per CD and 1.2 to 1.5 MB per track
- 64Kb/s—About 28MB of space per CD and 1.6 to 2 MB per track
- 128Kb/s—About 56MB of space per CD and 4 to 6 MB per track

Using the lower settings will allow for more efficient use of space, but will result in lower quality sound. You would be surprised, though, to find how good 48Kb/s can really sound. Microsoft claims that 48Kb/s is "near-CD" quality. That is subjective, to say the least, but it does sound quite good.

> **Warning**
>
> Be prepared to wait. It generally takes me 35-45 minutes to transcode and copy 30-40MB of audio files to my Casio Cassiopeia EG-800-STD Pocket PC device, and that's over USB!

Working with Skins

The historical source for this particular application of the word skin is unknown, but what it means is far less gross than it sounds. In Media Player parlance, a skin is a graphical replacement for the Skin Mode part of the applications interface. Skins can make Media Player look like a face, a thin bar, a rubber ducky (see Figure 29.9), or a number of other things, depending on what the skin artist (no, not a tattooist) intends.

FIGURE 29.9

Selecting a Skin.

The Skin component is separated into two parts. The left pane lists all installed skins. The right shows a preview of the skin itself. With these skins, there are three operations you can perform. They are as follows:

1. Apply Skin—Click a skin in the list so you can preview it. If you like it, click this button.

2. More Skins—If you want more skins, click this button to go to the official Windows Media skin pages. For even more skins, check out WinCustomize

(www.wincustomize.com) and click the WinMedia link. The number that appears after the link is the number of skins that are in the archive.

3. X (Delete Selected Skin)—Remove the selected skin from the list.

The skins that you download from the Windows Media site will be automatically installed into Media Player when you fetch them. The skins from the WinCustomize site will be in Zip archives, and you will need to extract them before installing them manually. The skin files are located in C:\Program Files\Windows Media Player\Skins.

Options, Tab by Tab

The Options dialog is the heart and soul of Media Player. With this dialog you can modify the behavior of Media Player to suit your needs. We will go tab by tab here, starting with the Player tab.

Player

There are three sections to the Player tab (see Figure 29.10). Let's take a look at each of these options in more depth.

FIGURE 29.10

The Player tab of the Options dialog box.

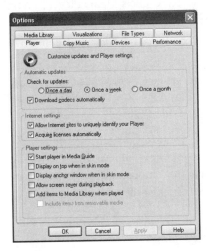

Automatic Updates

This option group sets how often you want Media Player to check for updates to itself. The options are daily, weekly, and monthly. The Download Codecs Automatically option toggles whether Media Player should fetch plug-ins that allow it to play back formats that it may not already be able to play.

Internet Settings

This section of the Player tab gives you options for the following:

- Allow Internet Sites To Uniquely Identify Your Player—This option gives Media Player the ability to deliver certain streaming media to Media Player that contains special features.

- Acquire License Automatically—This option grants Media Player the ability to download the required permissions some media require to play back correctly.

Player Settings

In this section you can do any of the following:

- Start Player In Media Guide—Sets Media Player to automatically load the Media Guide when you start it.

- Display On Top When In Skin Mode—Sets Media Player to float above all other windows when the Skin Mode is active.

- Display Anchor Window When In Skin Mode—Shows the Anchor window when in Skin Mode.

- Allow Screen Saver During Playback—Sets Media Player to run the screen saver if you have it set in the Display control panel.

- Add Items To Media Player When Played—Adds played media to the Media Library automatically.

- Include Items From Removable Media—Sets Media Player to add media from removable media formats like CD-ROM, Zip, and DVD. This is only active when the previous option is activated.

Copy Music

This tab offers options for controlling the various aspects of copying music over to Media Player (see Figure 29.11). Let's look at the options you can use from this tab more fully.

Copy Music to This Location

The default storage location is your My Music folder in your My Documents folder, but you can change that. Click on the Change button and navigate to the new location. It does not have to be on the same drive. Clicking the Advanced button opens the File Name Options dialog in which you can change how Media Player writes the filenames of copied tracks.

FIGURE 29.11

The Copy Music tab of the Options dialog box.

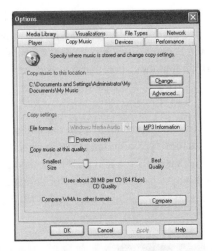

Note

If you plan on burning your own audio CDs, you won't have to worry too much about filename length; but if you have a portable or car CD player that can play CDs with MP3 files on the CD instead of standard audio files, you will. The ISO 9660 data CD standard supports up to 64-character filenames, even though Windows XP supports 256-character filenames.

Copy Settings

Media Player will copy audio to your hard drive based on the settings in this section. The default size used by Media Player is what Microsoft calls *CD quality*, or 64Kb/s encoding. Check or uncheck the Protect Content option based on your preferences, although it is best left unchecked if you have a number of devices or experience any compatibility problems with playback.

Media Player does not have the built-in ability to encode, or rip, MP3 files from CDs. Instead, Microsoft has opted to provide a plug-in architecture for third parties to make MP3 ripping and DVD playback available to users of Windows XP by obtaining their respective add-ons. The first three companies that have announced products are as follows:

- InterVideo—http://www.intervideo.com/jsp/Press.jsp?mode=xpmusic
- Ravisent—http://www.ravisentdirect.com/dv/dvdxp.html
- Cyberlink— http://www.gocyberlink.com/english/products/powerdvd/winxp_plugin.asp

29

WINDOWS MEDIA PLAYER 8

Cyberlink will be providing a standalone MP3 encoder, MP3 PowerEncoder, for $9.95, as well as a DVD player and a combined product ($14.95 and $19.95, respectively). Prices and availability for the InterVideo and Ravisent products were not available at the time of this writing, but Microsoft has clarified that they should all be ready by October 2001.

Devices

This tab (see Figure 29.12) lists all devices connected to your computer that can be accessed by Media Player. Devices that are typically detected can either act as a source for files to be copied from or a device that can store and play back media files. Generally, your CD-ROM or DVD drive or drives are added. Portable media players and Pocket PC devices are also recognized as they can play back either MP3s, .wma files, or a combination of the two.

FIGURE 29.12

The Devices tab of the Options dialog box.

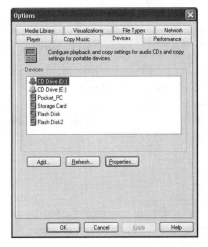

The three buttons are as follows:

- Add—Takes you to a list of compatible devices on the Windows Media Web site. There are no options here. In fact, it is just Internet Explorer.

- Refresh—Reloads the list of devices and checks to see if any new devices have been recently added. You may need to click this to have Media Player recognize a recently connected USB device.

- Properties—Opens the selected devices Properties dialog. For CD drives, you can select between digital and analog output, and error correction. For mobile digital media players, you can select the encoding level used when copying files to such devices. The smaller the files, the more you can fit, but at a cost of audio quality.

Performance

This tab (see Figure 29.13) controls how Media Player plays back and displays local and streaming media.

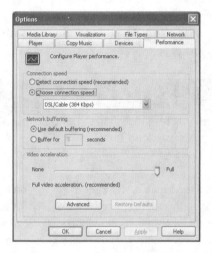

Connection Speed

The two selections here are used to define your connection speed. This allows Media Player to determine which media files to access, especially when streaming. You can either leave Media Player to determine how fast your connection is or you can elect to set the speed yourself. If you know your speed, you can select it; otherwise, just leave it alone.

Network Buffering

Although related to speed, this is a somewhat helpful option as it defines how much media is downloaded and stored before playback begins. The default is the automatic recommended setting, which works well with high-rate broadband connections (640Kb/s or better cable or DSL connection), but it can make for choppy playback for slower connections. The limit is 60 seconds, which is better than the 5 to 15 seconds that you get by default, but it can be extended.

Video Acceleration

Microsoft found out a long time ago that some playback problems can be alleviated by reducing the load on some video cards. Errors and bottlenecks can crop up when moving the video data from computer to the video card on certain models, so the control slider

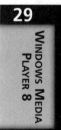

was added to the operating system. Although these problems are rare, Microsoft is still mindful of them and has even added the facility to Media Player.

If, for some reason, you have been able to eliminate all other possibilities for consistent video playback problems, move the slider to the middle position and restart the computer. If the playback problems persist, move the slider all the way to the left and restart again. Regardless of whether these changes fix the problem, find out who makes your video card and get the latest drivers for it.

> **Note**
>
> You are not required to restart your computer after changing the acceleration settings, but it is better to start from a clean slate.

Clicking the Advanced button opens the Video Acceleration Settings dialog. You will never need to touch most of what is in this dialog. The Digital Video slider is available if you need to adjust the size ratio of the video playback window for slower machines, but leaving it where it is will not limit fast computers. The remaining controls are for people who have specialty cards or other nonstandard hardware.

Media Library

This tab (see Figure 29.14) controls rights management and access for files cataloged in the Media Library. The sections are as follows:

- Access Rights of Other Applications—Controls how access to media stored in the Media Library is treated when local applications request access. The default is Read-Only.

- Access Rights of Internet Sites—Controls how access to media stored in the Media Library is treated when Internet sites request access. The default is No Access.

- Media Files—This single option, checked by default, tells Media Player to add digital media files purchased and then downloaded to be added directly to the Media Library.

Visualizations

This tab deals quite a bit with what we have already discussed about visualizations. (See the section on managing Visualizations earlier in this chapter). From this tab, you can choose from a large number of different visualizations and find one that you prefer.

FIGURE 29.14

The Media Library tab of the Options dialog.

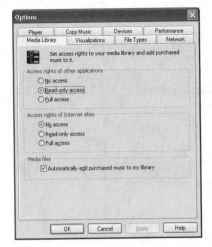

File Types

Simply put, Windows manages what files are "owned" by which applications and which applications are installed. By default, Media Player "owns" all media file types. If later you decide to install a copy of a third-party application such as WinAmp and don't change the default installation settings, it will take over "ownership" of MP3 files. This is what is referred to as file association in Windows. Thus, if you double-click on an MP3 file before installing WinAmp, Media Player will open it. After you install WinAmp, the MP3 files will open for their new owner.

If, for any reason, you want to manually manage which file types Media Player owns at any given time, come to this tab (see Figure 29.15). If the file type is checked, then it is associated with Media Player. If the file type is unchecked, something else owns it. Other than that, there is nothing to this tab!

Network

The Network tab (see Figure 29.16) contains setting sections for Protocols and Proxy Settings. The Protocols are for the four standard communications protocol that streaming media types use over the Internet. There is generally no reason to turn off any particular protocol, unless you are directed to do so by your Internet service provider (ISP) or a network administrator. If your internal network has a firewall, you may also be instructed to define specific ports for use with the User Datagram Protocol (UDP). A field to enter such ports is supplied with the UDP option.

29

WINDOWS MEDIA PLAYER 8

FIGURE 29.15

The File Types tab of the Options dialog.

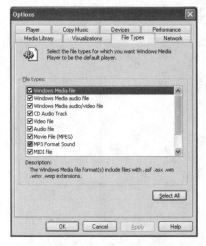

FIGURE 29.16

The Network tab of the Options dialog.

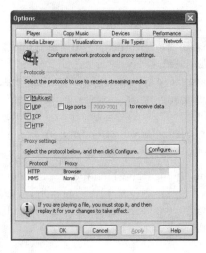

The Proxy Settings section is used to define servers that may be employed on your network to act as proxies over the Internet. Your systems administrator or ISP technical support department should supply the information you need to make this work.

Summary

In this chapter, we covered Windows Media Player 8 for Windows XP in significant detail. If anything, you learned that Media Player is quite a capable performer that can wear many hats. When it comes to cataloging and categorizing media, Media Player is one of the best.

Media Player has plenty of controls for customizing your sound and video quality. Playlist support is strong. The Media Guide provides a bevy of new material to look at and listen to every single day. Place a CD in the drive and, if you are connected to the Internet, Media Player will download everything it can find about a particular artist and album. Converting your CDs into digital media files and organizing everything into playlists is a breeze.

We also covered the various capabilities of Media Player including viewing video and listening to audio files, copying CD files, creating custom CDs, cataloging media file collections, tuning into radio online, and even making Media Player look like a duck!

That should keep you busy for a while!

Appendices

PART V

IN THIS PART

A Introduction to Transmission Control
Protocol/Internet Protocol   *761*

B Overview of the Lightweight Directory Access
Protocol and Microsoft's Active Directory   *797*

C Using Windows XP on a Notebook Computer   *813*

D Basics of Internet Information Server   *833*

APPENDIX A

Introduction to Transmission Control Protocol/Internet Protocol

IN THIS APPENDIX

- Transmission Control Protocol/Internet Protocol *762*
- Understanding Internet Protocol Addressing *764*
- How Ports Complete the Connection *777*
- The Transmission Control Protocol *778*
- Serial Line Interface Protocol and Point-to-Point Protocol *784*
- The Domain Name System *785*
- The Dynamic Host Configuration Protocol *786*
- Windows Internet Naming Service *787*
- Virtual Private Networks *788*
- Troubleshooting Tools for Transmission Control Protocol/ Internet Protocol *788*

Without the transmission control protocol/Internet protocol (TCP/IP) suite, there would be no Internet today or at least it would look and operate a lot differently than it does now! Although some might argue that better protocol suites have been developed over the years, none has lasted as long as or has adapted to new situations as well as TCP/IP. In the early 1980s, most computer manufacturers were still using their own proprietary networking protocols (such as DECnet). New upstarts like Novell's NetWare IPX/SPX and Microsoft's LAN Manager were trying to define the networking landscape. However, TCP/IP had already begun its eventual domination of the networking world. The Open System Interconnect (OSI) network protocols were developed to give a single set of protocols that could be run on multiple hardware and software platforms so that everyone could share the same protocols and therefore exchange data seamlessly. However, by the time these protocols were seriously considered, TCP/IP had already made itself the de facto standard by being the networking protocol suite used on the ARPANET, which was the forerunner of what is today's Internet.

Even as late in the game as Windows NT 3.51, the default network protocol installed in a typical installation was Microsoft's implementation of Novell's IPX/SPX. When Microsoft realized that the Internet was the future of computing, that default changed to TCP/IP, and it has remained the default ever since.

Therefore, if you are going to use your Windows XP Professional computer on a network, it is important that you get to know about TCP/IP and how it works.

Transmission Control Protocol/Internet Protocol

You will usually hear TCP/IP referred to as a *protocol suite* instead of just a protocol. There is a good reason for this. TCP is one protocol, and IP is another. To begin with, we have two protocols, not just one, and there are other protocols, services, and utilities that have been developed over the years to enhance the capabilities of what started out as a simple concept. Today, TCP/IP includes not only TCP and IP, but also things like dynamic host configuration protocol (DHCP), domain name system (DNS), as well as a host of applications and troubleshooting utilities that make operating a TCP/IP network really a quite simple task.

Internet Protocol

The basis of the entire protocol suite is IP. This protocol is used by both TCP and user datagram protocol (UDP). It may sound odd, but IP is considered an unreliable, connectionless protocol. (Doesn't sound like something you would bet your network on, does it?)

IP is the workhorse of the TCP/IP suite. It is a simple protocol that simply adds information to the data to be transported across a network and sends it on its way. Actually, there is more to it than that! In addition to encapsulating the data, IP is useful for the following two important reasons:

- Simplicity—IP is a simple protocol that doesn't require any session setup (like TCP does) or any acknowledgment mechanism to ensure that the packets it sends out actually make it to their destinations or even if the packets sent out arrive in the correct order. This function is left up to higher-level protocols (like TCP). By eliminating the acknowledgment function, IP can be used by many different higher-level protocols, each with its own requirements for checking on accurate delivery of the data.

- Addressing—IP provides for addressing both a host computer (or other network device) on a local area network (LAN) and the network on which the host resides. Since the Internet is a collection of many different networks, this network addressing function, which makes routing possible, is a very important feature of IP.

- Fragmentation—IP can accept data messages from higher-level protocols and can also break up data into more manageable sizes that the network links connecting the endpoints of the connection can handle. If it were not for this fragmentation capability, then the Internet would be limited to using the smallest maximum transmission unit (MTU) for any network link connected to it. IP allows higher-level protocols to send large data segments that can be fragmented into smaller ones and reassembled into their original state at the destination computer.

When I say that IP is a connectionless, unreliable, protocol that shouldn't give you cause for alarm, you should think of IP like you do the electrical socket into which you plug your computer. As long as a UPS is attached, it doesn't matter if the electricity suddenly gets cut off. The UPS can detect this and make up for the loss until the electricity is restored. IP works in a similar fashion. It simply accepts segments of data from other protocols, breaks them into manageable sizes, provides addressing and other information, and then sends the packets out onto the network. Routers and other devices examine the IP address information when making decisions on where to send a data packet or whether it needs to be dropped. If something goes wrong, such as an IP packet not reaching its destination, other protocols using IP can detect this condition and provide for a solution such as retransmitting the packet.

It is also quite possible that a router or other intermediary device standing between the origin and destination of an IP packet will drop a packet now and then. However, this isn't a capricious thing. It is done to make the connection between networks operate more efficiently by eliminating some of the problems that can crop up.

An IP packet can be dropped for several reasons. First, the router that a packet passes through may not know of an interim destination it can forward the IP packet to and still get the packet to its final destination. Second, it is always possible for routers to have been configured improperly. This means a loop can be created in the network-to-network routing tables. The IP header contains a field called *Time to Live (TTL),* which basically tells routers how long the packet can exist on the network before it should be dropped. Some routers decrement this value by one for each time a packet visits the router. Some routers decrement it by each second an IP packet waits in the router's queue. In any case, it is quite possible for an IP packet to be dropped or discarded because it has outlived its TTL value and may be circulating in an endless loop.

IP is also connectionless—that is, it doesn't need to contact the destination of the data and perform a setup before it starts to send data packets to the destination. Contrast this to your telephone system. When you dial a telephone number, especially a long distance one, it may take a few seconds before the call starts to ring the destination telephone. This is because the networking protocols used by the public switched telephone network (PSTN) first establish a path through its network to be used to carry packets of information (your voice, which has been converted to a digital format) before it starts to let you talk. The other side of the conversation must acknowledge this session setup (the user picks up the phone and says "hello").

IP doesn't work this way. It just puts addressing and other information into a packet that contains the data and sends it on its way, hoping for the best. If the packet makes it to the destination, then the computer there can determine (from other protocol headers discussed later in this appendix) what to do with the data. Because no session setup is required (and indeed, each IP packet can take a different route to the same destination, depending on conditions on the Internet), it is called *connectionless.*

Perhaps the most important function IP performs for Internet connections is addressing. Before we start to look at how higher-level protocols such as TCP or UDP can make up for the shortcomings of IP, let's see how IP addressing works. It is the IP address space that glues the entire Internet together. Without it, there would be no Internet or at least the one we know now. Yet, once you grasp the concepts of a network address and a host computer address, you will start to understand just how important IP is and why it is considered the workhorse of the TCP/IP suite.

Understanding Internet Protocol Addressing

Figure A.1 shows the layout of a typical IP packet. You should note that we have already discussed the TTL value. This field is used to keep an IP packet from circulating in an endless loop indefinitely when one or more routers have been misconfigured. The other important fields (perhaps the most important) are the source and destination address fields. The remainder of the IP packet is shown for completeness so that you can see how data is structured as it makes its way through the Internet.

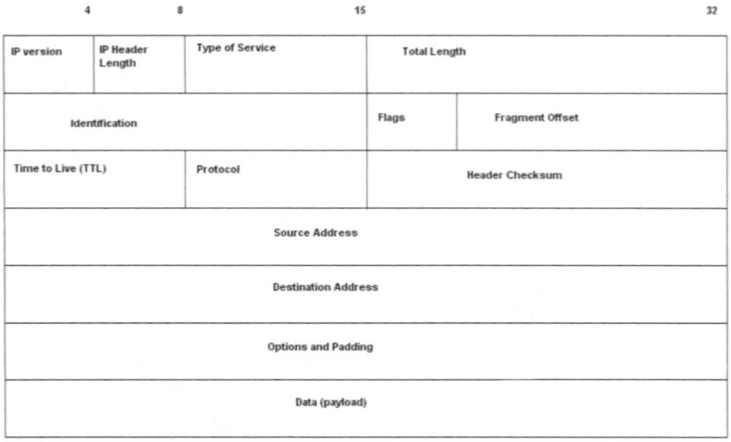

FIGURE A.1

The IP packet consists of many fields, but the addressing fields are of particular concern here.

Before we get into why IP addresses are so important, let's discuss the actual physical address programmed into your computer's network card. It is a 48-bit address that has no meaning other than to indicate the card's manufacturer and its own uniqueness in the cards the manufacturer produces. Each company that makes network adapter cards is assigned a specific prefix (the first part of the network card's physical address) that identifies the manufacturer of the card. The remainder of the address is simply a serialized unique number to identify the card uniquely. This addressing scheme creates what is known as a *flat address space*. You cannot use the address for such things as identifying networks (anyone can buy network cards from the same vendor and put them on different networks); however, the physical address of the network card does have local significance on your LAN. (We will discuss this later when you learn about the address resolution protocol [ARP].) Using this hardware address (usually called the MAC address, for Media Access Control) is the most important thing to remember. Although it can uniquely identify a network card on a local network, it cannot give you any other information such as where the network is located and to what computer the card is attached.

This is exactly the reason why IP addresses are so important to the Internet. An IP address provides a hierarchical address space divided into a network address and host computer addresses. The first part of this 32-bit address identifies the network on which the computer is located, whereas the remaining portion of the address tells the network to which host computer on that network the data is addressed. Simply put, an IP address allows you to identify both the destination computer's network and the computer itself.

A

Internet Protocol Addressing Makes Finding Computers Easier

At first, the concept of using a separate address to identify a network and yet another address to identify a computer on a network may not seem important. Indeed, some networking schemes such as ARCnet (perhaps the oldest networking technology still finding uses today) work only within single, small networks. Yet, if you want to connect two networks together, some sort of gateway between the networks and that gateway is needed (usually a router) in order to be able to determine to which network an IP packet should be sent.

Routers and Routing Tables

Routers are devices that have multiple network interfaces so that you can connect several networks together. Each interface has its own address, just like a computer's network interface card does. When an IP packet comes into the router from one network interface, the router examines the IP addressing information in the packet and then uses a routing table to decide how best to get the packet to its destination. It does this by extracting from the destination address the network portion of the address and looking up that network address in a routing table.

A routing table is simply a table that lists network device addresses and then pairs these addresses with the appropriate network interface for sending the packet on its way to its destination. Note that this doesn't mean that the router has to have a direct connection to the destination network. In most cases (the Internet, for example), an IP packet passes through many routers before it gets to its destination network.

The routing table, then, also keeps other information about distant networks in its memory tables, such as the number of hops (or the number of other routers) the packet will be sent through to get to its destination network. It is also quite possible that there is more than one way to get a packet to its destination. That is where the number of hops (called a *metric* by most routing protocols) comes into play.

Typically, if more than one route to the destination network is known, the one with the lowest metric is used. However, the network administrator can manipulate the routing table and make changes to the information stored there.

For example, it may be that one route uses fewer hops to deliver a packet than another route. However, the other route may be composed of high-speed links. Thus, the administrator could improve performance by changing the metric so that the route that uses the higher speed links would be chosen instead of the one with the least number of actual hops.

Having more than one route to a destination serves another purpose: redundancy. Should one router in a link go down (for maintenance, for example), then another route could be used to deliver a packet.

One last thing to keep in mind about routers is why IP addressing is so important. If a router had to maintain in memory a route for every single network card ever produced, it would be impossible to store that much information efficiently, nor would it be easy to look up the route. Thus, the flat address space provided by MAC addresses doesn't work well with routers. Instead, the router keeps in its table a number of network addresses it knows about and which network interface it should use to send the packet on its way. Just as it is impossible for a route to store every possible MAC address, it would also be impossible for a router to store every possible network address. To solve that problem, each router has, in addition to a list of addresses it knows about, a default route, which is the network address of 0.0.0.0. When an IP packet comes into the router and there is no match for the network for which the packet is destined, the router sends the packet to the default route.

You can see an example of a routing table by using the ROUTE PRINT command in the Command Prompt. The following listing shows the output produced by this command:

```
===========================================================================
Interface List
0x1 ......................... MS TCP Loopback interface
0x2 ...00 04 5a 42 53 99 ...... Linksys LNE100TX Fast Ethernet Adapter(LNE100TX
  v4) - Packet Scheduler Miniport
===========================================================================
===========================================================================
Active Routes:
Network Destination     Netmask     Gateway   Interface Metric
      0.0.0.0        0.0.0.0  10.10.10.254  10.10.10.100  30
  10.10.10.0    255.255.255.0  10.10.10.100  10.10.10.100  30
  10.10.10.100 255.255.255.255    127.0.0.1    127.0.0.1  30
10.255.255.255 255.255.255.255  10.10.10.100  10.10.10.100  30
    127.0.0.0      255.0.0.0    127.0.0.1    127.0.0.1  1
    224.0.0.0      240.0.0.0  10.10.10.100  10.10.10.100  30
255.255.255.255 255.255.255.255  10.10.10.100  10.10.10.100  1
Default Gateway:   10.10.10.254
===========================================================================
Persistent Routes:
  None
```

As you can see from this listing, routers aren't the only ones keeping routing tables. This computer has one network interface (the modem) hooked up to an Internet provider and another network card attached to a LAN. Thus, in order for my computer to keep track of where to send IP packets, it too needs to keep a routing table.

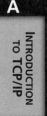

This listing indicates that there is a default route, along with several other network addresses. For each network address, there is an associated subnet mask (discussed later in this appendix); a gateway (where to send the packet); and a metric.

Dotted-Decimal Notation in Internet Protocol Addresses

Figure A.1 showed the IP address as a 32-bit address. Although computers just love using binary numbers to calculate and transmit data, humans aren't very good at that. For this reason, it is a common practice to take those 32 bits and divide them into four 8-bit bytes and then express each byte in decimal notation, a numbering system that you can understand. For example, in binary notation, the address 140.176.110.232 is a string of zeros and ones: 10001100101100000110111011101000. Which is easier for you to type into your computer? Table A.1 illustrates how the binary address is broken down into four groups of eight bits each (a byte), and then each of those bytes is then converted to its decimal equivalent.

Table A.1   Converting a Binary Address to Decimal Values

Binary Value	*Decimal Equivalent*
10001100	140
10110000	176
01101110	110
11101000	232

Hence, to express the actual 32-bit binary IP address in a format that is easier to remember, we simply join together the decimal equivalents and put a period in between each of the values. Now, 10001100101100000110111011101000 becomes 140.176.110.232 instead. Although you may not think this dotted-decimal notation is so easy to remember, it actually is. This is because part of this address is the network address portion, and if you are working on a particular LAN most of the time, you will eventually memorize the address portion of the address. Then, you will only have to worry about the part of the address used for the host computer address.

Now, you don't have to be a math whiz to be able to convert from binary to decimal. Later, when you learn about subnetting, you may have to do some conversions, however; so instead of having a lesson on the binary numbering system at this point, we are going to use a much simpler method to do these calculations—a calculator!

> **Tip**
>
> One thing to keep in mind when expressing an IP address in dotted-decimal format is that you can never have a decimal number greater than 255 for any part of the address. This is because the largest number you can express in eight binary bits is 11111111, which is 255 as a decimal value. Thus, if you try to enter an address such as 123.222.211.512, it will not work, since 512 cannot fit into a single byte. Another thing to keep in mind is that some addresses are reserved for special purposes. For example, it is common to use zeros to identify a network. It is also common to use the number 254 as a host computer address that acts as a router or gateway.

Use Start, All Programs, Accessories, Calculator. As you can see in Figure A.2, the basic calculator supplied with Windows operating systems pops up. The form you see in this figure is not much use, unfortunately.

FIGURE A.2

The standard Windows calculator view doesn't do you much good when it comes to converting from binary to decimal values.

Recall from earlier in the book that the calculator has computational capabilities beyond the basic interface. The scientific calculator that you find inside View menu at the top of the calculator is a stronger version of calculator that will help you do binary calculations. That's the secret that most people never bother to learn. Click on View and select Scientific, and you will get a much better calculator (see Figure A.3).

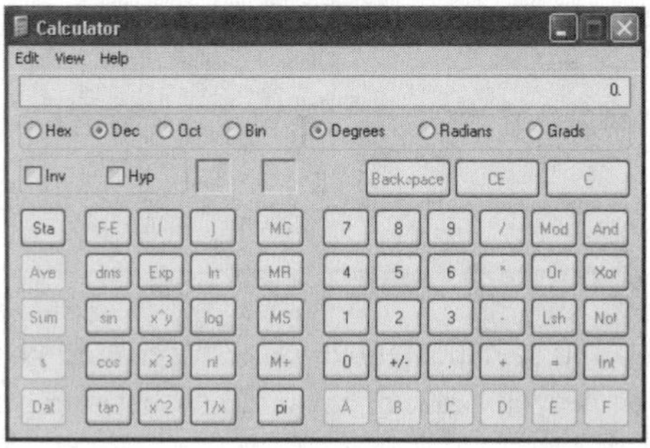

FIGURE A.3

The Scientific view of the Windows calculator allows you to convert a number from one base to another.

A

INTRODUCTION TO TCP/IP

If you want to convert 140 to binary, simply click on the radio button labeled Dec and then enter the number 140 using your keyboard or by clicking on the screen numbers. Then click the radio button labeled Bin. Voila! You can now see the binary equivalent of the decimal number 140. Note that this calculator supports several base numbering systems, and the ones supported weren't chosen at random. The other numbering systems are Hex(adecimal) and (Oct)al. These are two common numbering systems used in computers and programming, so this calculator can be very useful for many purposes other than just for converting from binary to decimal.

Internet Protocol Address Classes

You have already learned that an IP address is 32 bits long and that part of it is used for a network address while the remaining part is used for the host computer address. Now it is time to figure out which part of those 32 bits is being used for the network address. If life were so simple, then we would just have to set aside the first 16 bits as a network address and the second 16 bits as the host computer address. Unfortunately, life is not that simple, and networks are much more complicated than life!

IP addresses come in classes. The reason for this is that there are large and small networks (and yes, there are even medium-size networks). Therefore, if we simply use 16 bits for the network address and 16 bits for the host computer addresses, we end up with a total of 65,535 network addresses, each with 65,536 computer addresses. There are not a lot of LANs that have 65,536 computers! The original implementation of TCP/IP provided for IP address classes, each of which uses a different number of bits for the network portion of the address and the host computer portion of the IP address. By using IP address classes, it is possible to have a few large networks, some medium-sized ones, and a lot of smaller ones. Table A.2 shows a breakdown of how IP address classes can be determined by examining the first four bits of the address itself.

Table A.2   IP Address Classes

Address Class	*Binary Bit Values*
Class A	0xxx
Class B	10xx
Class C	110x
Class D	111x
Class E	1111

In this table the x character is used to indicate that it doesn't matter what the value is for this position in the address. As you can see, any address that starts with a zero as the first bit of the binary address has to be a Class A address. Any address that starts with a 10 as the first two bits must be a Class B address, and so on. The main classes you need to be concerned about are primarily A to C. Class D and E addresses are used for special purposes.

Obviously, the first four bits that define the address class can be converted to decimal values to determine from a dotted-decimal address to what class an address belongs.

Class A Addresses

A Class A address always starts with a zero. Class A addresses use the least number of bits of the available 32-bits to identify a network. Hence, not many Class A network addresses are available, as compared with the other classes, since fewer bits are used. However, the opposite is true for the number of host computers existing on each Class A network.

Class A addresses use only the first byte (eight bits) of the IP address to specify a network address. Taking this into account, it becomes obvious that the range of network addresses is from 00000000 through 01111111. In decimal notation, this is 0 through 127, so if a dotted-decimal address has a value that ranges from 0 through 127, then it is a Class A IP address.

Tip

There is one address that falls into the Class A address range that you normally don't use on a network. Instead, it is reserved by the IP and is used to identify the local host computer. It is 127.0.0.1, and it is also known as the *loopback address* because it actually does serve a purpose. Once you set up TCP/IP on a computer, you can use test commands such as `ping` to test to see if the protocol stack is working properly. You simply `ping` your own local computer!

Doing the math, then, you can see that Class A addresses fall between the ranges of 0.0.0.0 through 127.255.255.255. Again, keep in mind that 0.0.0.0 is also a reserved address used to indicate the default route in a routing table, so while it technically falls in the Class A address range, you can't use it on a computer.

Considering that you only have 127 possible network addresses, that means there are very few Class A networks in the world. If you take the remaining three bytes (24 bits) and use them for computer addresses, then each of these 127 Class A addresses can have up to 16,777,215 unique addresses (111111111111111111111111 in binary notation is 16,777,215). Remember that we are not counting zero as a host address, or this would be 16,777,216.

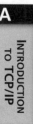

Now a word about network addresses. In a routing table, just the network portion of the IP address is used to indicate the network, whereas the remaining parts of the dotted-decimal address are set to zeros. A network address for a computer with an IP address of 125.110.222.111 would then be 125.0.0.0. (Note that the last three bytes are used for computer addresses, not network addresses, so they are set to zeros in our example.)

Class B Addresses

A Class B address always starts with the first two bits being 10—that is, binary one and zero, not decimal 10. Class B addresses use more bits of the IP address to identify networks than Class A addresses do. Thus, there are more Class B network addresses than Class A network addresses. This also implies that since more bits are used for the network portion of the address, fewer are left for the host computer addresses. Thus, a Class B network has fewer host computer addresses available—more networks, fewer computers!

Class B addresses use the first two bytes (or half the IP address, 16 bits) of the IP address to specify a network address. Taking this into account, it becomes obvious that the range of network addresses is from 10000000 through 10111111. In decimal notation, this is 128 through 191. So, if a dotted-decimal address has a value that ranges from 128 through 191, then it is a Class B IP address. You would think that since both the network and the computer host portions of the address are each two bytes in length, you would have the same number of possible network addresses as you do computer addresses. However, that is not the case.

A Class B address must have a zero in the second bit position so that you can use all of the possible values that can be expressed in binary for use as network addresses. Instead, Class B addresses range from 1000000000000000 through 1011111111111111, which is 128.0.0.0.0 through 191.255.255.255. This gives you a total possible number of network addresses of 16,384. Why are there so few addresses when the binary number 1011111111111111 is 49,151? Because part of the numbers that fall in that range are Class A addresses (49,151 – 32,767 = 16,384). The Class B address space doesn't start at zero in decimal notation. It starts at 128, whereas class A addresses ended at 127.

Since there are no such restrictions on the last two bytes used to create host computer addresses, you can have a range from 0000000000000000 through 1111111111111111, which is 0.0 through 255.255 in dotted-decimal notation. This means that if you find an address that ranges from 128.0.0.0.0 to 191.255.255.255, then the address is a Class B address. However, we still have the reserved network address (x.0.0.0.0), as well as a few other reserved addresses we will discuss later.

The Class B address range then has a total of 65,535 possible host computer addresses because we are subtracting the address of 191.255.255.255.0, since the zero is a reserved address.

Class C Addresses

Now we get to the more practical address class. Most networks don't have such large numbers of host computers attached to them that are eligible for Class A and Class B address classes. The Class C address class uses the first three bytes of the 32-bit IP address to identify a network and only the last byte (eight bits) to identify host computers.

You should get a total number of networks of 2,097,152, each having computer addresses ranging from 0 to 255 (but again, remember that zero is reserved).

Class C addresses always start with the values of 110 for the first three bits of the total 32-bit address. Thus, in dotted-decimal notation, you can figure out that an address is a Class C address if it falls in the range of 192.0.0.0 through 223.255.25.255. This is a very useful address class because it allows for a large number of networks, each with a reasonable amount of computers attached to them. If necessary, simply get additional Class C addresses and then use a router to link together separate LANs so that they all can participate in a network together.

Other Address Classes

The Class D and E addresses ranges aren't used for normal addressing of individual computers. Class D is used for a process called *multicasting*, in which a message is sent to more than one computer. This is technically outside the scope of this book, but in short, the range is from 224.0.0.0 to 239.255.255.255. Class D addresses do not break down the address bits into network or host computer addresses but do use the entire address as a single entity. Computers that receive these multicast addressed packets must be programmed to do so. These can be used for streaming data to many hundreds (or thousands) of computers on the Internet.

Class E is reserved for experimental usage at this time. The address range for Class E addresses is from 240.0.0.0 to 255.255.255.255.

Private Network Address Classes

As you learned earlier in this appendix, some addresses are reserved for specific purposes. The address 127.0.0.1 (and on some older computers, 127.0.0.0) is the loopback address used when troubleshooting the local TCP/IP stack. Using this address simply tells the TCP/IP layered software components to send a message down the stack and back up to make sure things are configured correctly. From there, you can proceed to other troubleshooting efforts to solve your network connectivity problems.

Another set of addresses that you should be aware of are the following:

```
10.0.0.0 to 10.255.255.255
172.16.0.0 to 172.31.255.255
192.168.0.0 to 192.168.25.255
```

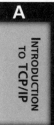

These address ranges are set aside by the Request For Comments document RFC 1918, Address Allocation for Private Internets. These addresses cannot be used on the Internet. Then why do we have these address ranges set aside for "private" networks? When the Internet began to grow in leaps and bounds, it became obvious that some day the limited number of IP addresses would become exhausted. Sooner or later, all of the address space would be assigned. Since the Internet is nothing more than a collection of many separate but interconnected networks, it is important for every computer on the Internet to have its own unique address. It is just like your postal mail address. The same address can receive letters all the time.

However, some networks aren't connected to the Internet but might want to make that connection at a later date. These private networks can use any of the three address ranges listed above.

As for networks that do have to connect to the Internet, a technique called *network address translation (NAT)* makes it possible to use one of these large private address ranges for your entire business (or home) network but still use a different address for Internet communications. NAT is a router or firewall (or a box that is a combination of both, which is becoming quite common now) that serves as a gateway to connect your private network to the Internet. The router's interfaces connecting to the Internet are assigned valid IP addresses that can be used on the Internet. When a computer inside your private network wants to send a request out to an Internet server, the router or firewall intercepts the packet. It then substitutes its own valid IP address for the private address and sends the packet out onto the Internet. When the response is received from the Internet server, the router or firewall performs a reverse operation and puts the original address of the computer inside your network into the IP packet as the destination. Thus, the router keeps track of the connections and which packets need to go to which computer on the Internet and on your host computer.

Several techniques are used for NAT. One easy method is to manipulate port numbers. The router or firewall simply uses a unique port number in its internal table to keep track of the request it sends out onto the Internet. Then, when a response is received, it can look up the port to determine which private address it should use to send the IP packet back to the originator of the request.

Subnet Masks and Subnetting a Network

One commonly misunderstood concept about IP addresses is the subnet mask. First, the Class A, B, and C address classes all have subnet masks associated with them. Subnet masks are also 32-bit binary values used to mask out portions of the IP address so that a router can tell which part of the address is actually the network portion and which part is the host computer part of the address.

You can tell from the first four bits of the original IP address class what part of the IP address is the network address, but subnet masks are still necessary. If all we used on the Internet were simple Class A, B, and C addresses, then subnet masks would not be necessary.

However, consider the numbers discussed earlier when you learned about address classes. Table A.3 shows the actual number of networks and host computer addresses for each of these classes that can be used after taking into consideration the special exceptions such as the loopback address and the use of zeros to indicate a network address.

Table A.3   IP Addresses Available for Use

Address Class	Number of Networks	Number of Hosts
A	126	16,777,214
B	16,384	65,534
C	2,097,152	254

It should be quickly apparent that if you have a Class B address, then it is going to be very difficult to connect more than 65,000 computers and let them all talk to each other. First, there are topological considerations. For example, if you use Ethernet (the most common LAN technology), there are limits to the lengths of cables and the number of computer that can be connected to any particular cable segment, hub, or switch. It is just not possible to practically network together 65,534 computers in one LAN.

The concept of subnetting is quite simple. It involves borrowing a few bits from the host computer address portion of the IP address and using it for a subnet address. Thus, you can effectively create more network addresses (consisting of different subnets), each having a smaller number of host computers attached.

In a subnet mask, a value of 1 in the subnet mask means that this particular bit is used for part of the network address, whereas a value of zero indicates that the bit is used for the host computer address.

By convention, subnet masks are still used for traditional Class A, B, and C addresses. Thus, a Class A address, which uses the first eight bits of the address for the network address component, would have a subnet mask in binary notation of 11111111000000000000000000000000. If you translate this to dotted-decimal notation it comes out to be 255.0.0.0. This subnet mask makes it easy to see that the first byte is set to all ones (255 is eight bits all set to 1). Class B addresses would have a subnet mask of 255.255.0.0, since the first 16 bits of the address are used for the network address component. Class C addresses, which use the first three bytes of the address (or the first 24 bits) for identifying a network, have a subnet mask of 255.255.255.0.

However, the purpose of the subnet mask (first described in RFC 950) is to further break down the IP address so that a few bits can be borrowed from the host computer address portion to create additional networks with fewer host computer addresses. For example, not many Class B address ranges originally assigned ever had the capability of using up the entire number of possible host computer addresses and thus a large amount of the IP address space is wasted. The same goes especially for Class A addresses.

By using subnet masks to divide up these large address ranges, we can create a larger number of networks with smaller host computers.

Let's look at a simple example using the subnet mask 255.255.255.128. This subnet mask can be used to divide a Class C address space into two separate subnets. If you take the last byte (128) and convert it to binary, you get 10000000. This means that a single bit is being borrowed from the host computer portion of the IP address. The 1 at the beginning of this binary representation of the mask simply means that the first bit of the computer address portion of the IP address will now be used for network addressing purposes. Of course, this leaves you with fewer bits to use to create host computer addresses. Since a single bit can be only a zero or a one, then you can use a subnet mask that borrows a single bit from the host computer address space to create two subnets (subnet 0 and subnet 1).

Using this mask with a network address of 192.113.255.0 then you would end up with one subnet with host addresses ranging from 192.113.255.1 to 192.113.255.128 and a second subnet with host addresses ranging from 192.113.255.129 to 192.113.255.254. This excludes, of course, the special reserved addresses of using all ones or zeros for the host portion of the address.

You can continue borrowing bits from the host computer portion of the IP address to further subdivide a single network address into more subnets. For example, a subnet mask of 255.255.25.192 when used with a Class C address would divide the address space into four subnets. That's because the value of 192 decimal, when expressed in binary notation, is 11000000. Thus, you are borrowing two bits from the host address space. Using those two bits you can express up to four unique values in binary notation, thus you can create four subnets.

If you want to know more about subnetting, consult a good book on TCP/IP. However, it is only important for you to understand the principles behind subnetting so that you will know why you use them when you enter IP addressing information into your computer's configuration, which learn how to do for Windows XP in Chapter 24, "Configuring Your Computer for Local Area Networking."

How Ports Complete the Connection

So far you have learned that IP addresses are used to make sure that data gets delivered to the correct destination. However, since the IP address only identifies the computer network card, then how does the computer know what application the data it receives is intended for? For example, let's use the postal service as an example again. You can send letters simply to an address but without putting a person's name on the envelope; then when the letter gets delivered, who gets to open it?

Ports are the solution to this problem in the TCP/IP suite. In addition to an IP address, a port number is used to identify the source and the recipient of data transmitted using TCP/IP. However, IP doesn't have fields in its header to support port numbers, it only handles the source and destination computer IP addresses. It is the higher-level protocols such as TCP and UDP that use port numbers.

Transmission Control Protocol and User Datagram Protocol Ports

Both the TCP and UDP ports use port numbers so that data exchanged between computers can be delivered to the intended application. An IP address combined with a port number is often referred to as a socket.

The Internet Corporation for Assigned Names and Numbers (ICANN) is an organization that assigns applications to what are called *well-known ports* (those ranging from 0-1023). These ports have been defined in numerous RFC documents. However, the 16-bit port field allows for port numbers of up to 65,535. If you visit the ICANN Web site (http://icann.com), you can obtain a listing that shows both the usage of the first range of well-known ports, as well as how some of the other ports are used. In general, everything above 1023 is up for grabs, and many applications can actually use the same port. However, there are so many antiquated port number associations in the listing that if an application simply chooses a large port number at random, the odds of it conflicting with another already in use between two computers is quite remote.

> **Tip**
>
> In Chapter 25, "Configuring Your Computer for an Internet Connection," the Internet Connection Firewall that Windows XP provides will allow you to configure a firewall to prevent certain data packets from coming into your
>
> *continues*

computer from the Internet. The Internet Connection Firewall uses port numbers and shows you a list of basic TCP/IP applications like Telnet and FTP, and the port numbers they use. You can also configure additional services to allow (or disallow) for the firewall, and for this, it is important to understand that the port numbers represent applications. When you read Chapter 25 and if you decide to allow incoming requests for certain services, be sure you understand what the port is being used for before you allow incoming requests from the Internet!

The Transmission Control Protocol

Now, let's start talking about a protocol that does a lot of other important work in the TCP/IP suite. Remember that IP just tries to get your packets delivered and provides the addressing capabilities as its basic functions. Also, remember that IP doesn't allow for a reliable connection between two different computers. It leaves that function up to higher-level protocols, and TCP is one of those.

TCP controls the transmission of packets between two computers. IP provides the information needed to transport a packet along its way through the myriad of routers that make up the Internet, whereas TCP uses IP to create sessions between the two computers. TCP keeps track of the data it sends to IP for transmission, and it is the protocol that determines that a packet was dropped or that packets are arriving out of the order in which they were sent.

TCP is called a *reliable, connection-oriented protocol*. Before two computers can begin exchanging information, a "three-way handshake" is performed to set up a session between the two computers. Just like IP adds its own header information to the data it receives from TCP (and other higher level protocols), TCP does a similar thing. TCP receives messages from an application, for example, and first breaks down the messages into manageable segments. It then attaches a header that identifies the application. It uses port numbers for this function, which are discussed shortly.

A basic summary of what the more important fields are used for is as follows:

- Source Port—This field is 16 bits long and is used to identify the port (the application) sending the data.
- Destination Port—This field is also 16 bits long and is used to identify the port (the application on the destination computer).

- Sequence Number—When a message that TCP receives from an application is broken into smaller segments for transmission, this 32-bit field is used to identify where a segment fits in the larger message so that it can be reassembled and delivered to the destination application intact.

- Acknowledgement Number—This field is 32 bits long and is used to indicate what the next sequence number in the session exchange should be. This value is the next byte in the data stream that the receiver expects to receive from the sender.

- Data Offset—This field is only four bits long and is used to specify the number of 32-bit words (a word is eight bytes) that make up the header. This value makes it possible for TCP to determine where the payload or actual data portion of the packet starts and where the header information ends.

- ACK Flag—This is the acknowledgement bit. If set to 1, the packet is an acknowledgment. If set to 0, the packet is not an acknowledgement.

- RST Flag—This bit, if set to 1, is a signal that the connection is to be reset; otherwise it is set to 0.

- SYN Flag—This bit, if set to 1, indicates that the sequence numbers are to be synchronized. If set to 0, the sequence numbers are not to be synchronized.

- FIN Flag—This bit, if set to 1, specifies that the sender is finished sending information. Otherwise it is set to 0.

- Window—This field is 16 bits long and is used to tell the sending computer how many blocks of data the receiving computer is able to accept at this time.

- Checksum—This 16-bit field is a calculated value used to verify the integrity of both the header and data portions of the packet.

Because the size of the header can vary, it may also include padding bits of zeros to allow it to end on a 32-bit boundary before the payload begins.

The Three-Way Handshake Sets Up a Transmission Control Protocol Session

TCP is connection-oriented. This means that a session is set up and packets of information are not independent units to be dealt with separately. Instead, a flow of data between both computers that participate in a TCP session is possible. For example, when you use the Telnet application to establish a terminal window on a remote computer, your keystrokes are sent via TCP to the remote computer and the responses to the commands you enter are returned, all in the correct order. Although IP does the actual transporting of the packets of information across the network, TCP ensures that the packets are interpreted properly in a session-oriented connection.

A

INTRODUCTION TO TCP/IP

To set up a session, a simple process is followed:

1. The computer that wants to start a TCP session sends a segment to the remote computer with the SYN field (synchronize) of the TCP header set to a value of 1. This SYN bit tells the remote computer that a session setup is being requested. The originating computer also sets an initial sequence number in the TCP header, indicating what sequence number it wants to start for the synchronization process. The final important field in the header that the originating computer sets is the port number. Keep in mind that port numbers generally indicate what service of application the TCP session wants to connect to.

2. When the remote computer receives this TCP segment, it sends a segment back to the computer that originated the connection. The remote computer also sets the SYN bit and also supplies a sequence number that it wants to use for synchronizing segments on its side of the connection. Keep in mind that TCP is a two-way communication (full-duplex) process. Each side has to keep track of the order of segments received from the other side. Each side has its own starting sequence numbers. Additionally, to let the originating computer know that its first segment was received, the ACK (acknowledgment) bit is also set in this segment. Lastly, this packet will contain a field that contains the originating computer's initial sequence number that has been incremented by 1, indicating that the first segment was received.

3. The client that started this whole process receives the acknowledgment segment from the remote computer and sends another segment to the remote computer acknowledging the receipt of the segment. This third segment that is part of the handshake contains the initial sequence number that the remote computer included in its segment, incremented by one.

After this process is complete, the session is established and communications can take place between the two computers. One important thing to keep in mind about sequence numbers is that they are not always incremented by a value of one. The sequence number is used to tell the remote side what byte of data it expects to receive in the next segment. Thus, when the actual data exchange takes place, this value can be incremented by much larger amounts. If the data received doesn't match the expected number of bytes, then TCP can determine that something has gone wrong. For example, IP may have dropped a datagram, or a datagram may have arrived out of sequence. TCP can track this information and either hold segments in memory and wait for the other missing segments, or it can ask the other side to retransmit the expected data.

> **Note**
>
> The initial sequence number for each side of the TCP connection is a seemingly random number generated by each computer. For each application that uses TCP for a connection, a different starting sequence number is used. This is because you might want to use the same application between two computers at the same time. Since the IP address and the port numbers identify the applications to which data is to be sent, it is the sequence numbers that also help distinguish between multiple instances of the same application sessions. This is why you are able to open several Telnet or FTP sessions between the same two computers. The port numbers keep track of what application receives the data, while the sequence numbers help TCP figure out which particular session the packet belongs to.

Sliding Windows

Since each exchange between two computers using TCP requires that each side acknowledge the other side's sequence numbers, a simple exchange of one segment at a time would be the easiest method to use. However, it would also be the slowest method. Depending on the speed of the network link, one side would send a segment and then wait until the other side acknowledged it before sending another one. A concept called *sliding windows* allows for a single segment to acknowledge more than one segment. Thus, TCP can send multiple segments and determine if they were correctly received by a single segment. This received segment will come back acknowledging all of the segments that were sent. By default, the window size, which is the maximum number of segments that can be sent before an acknowledgment is required, is 12 segments. Note that it only takes a single segment from the remote computer to acknowledge any number of segments up to this window size.

TCP also keeps track of statistical information about the number of segments sent, acknowledged, and so on. It can negotiate to change the window size if a connection deteriorates. Thus, during a TCP session you will sometimes see high rates of data exchange, and at other times, the rate may slow to a crawl. TCP adjusts to make the best it can of the transmission medium, based on the actual data that does get through to the other side and acknowledged. Because the window size can change and because more than one segment can be outstanding without an acknowledgment, the term *sliding windows* is applied to this technology.

A

INTRODUCTION
TO TCP/IP

To be sure that a segment is received properly, TCP uses timers when it sends segments to IP for delivery on the network. For example, a retransmission timer is set when a particular segment is sent. If the timer expires before the segment is acknowledged, then the segment gets retransmitted.

Ending a Transmission Control Protocol Session

Because TCP is a full-duplex protocol (data can travel in both directions for the session), then when it is time to close the connection, it must be done for each side of the session. In actuality, however, two methods can be used. The first is called a *half-close,* in which one side tells the other it is finished sending data and wants to terminate the connection. To indicate that it wants to close the connection, the computer sends a TCP segment with the FIN (finished) bit set. The other side will send back a packet acknowledging this (with the ACK bit set). The same process must be performed in reverse, with the remote computer sending a segment with the FIN bit set, and this segment must also be acknowledged with a segment that has the ACK bit set.

However, it doesn't always happen just like that. For example, one side may be finished sending information, but the other side may have more data to send. In this case a half-close is performed, where one side sends a FIN segment, and it is acknowledged. However, that computer keeps the necessary memory data structures in place to continue receiving data from the remote computer until it does finally receive a segment with the FIN bit set, which it then acknowledges. This often happens when you use TCP to send a command to a remote computer, which then turns around and sends lots of output for the command back to you. You don't need to send any more commands, so your side of the connection can be closed. Yet, you must leave the other half of the connection opened so that you can receive the output from the command.

Many different applications use TCP. You have already learned that Telnet and FTP use TCP, which, in turn, uses IP. There is another protocol that also uses IP to transport data across the network. It is similar to TCP because it uses IP, but it does have some significant differences. This is the UDP, which is explained next.

The User Datagram Protocol

UDP, like IP, does not perform any session setup. This is one way in which it differs from TCP. Instead, consider UDP to be a best effort method for getting data delivered. Why is UDP necessary since IP can pretty much do the same thing?

It's the ports! Remember that ports are used to identify services or applications on the remote computer. IP doesn't have a field in its header to store information about port numbers, but TCP and UDP do. Thus, consider UDP to be a stripped-down version of

TCP. There is no session setup, but since the UDP header contains source and destination port fields, it can be used to make sure that, if the data does get through, it gets delivered to the right service or application.

As an example, many implementations of the DNS use UDP for communications. By using this simpler protocol, a DNS server doesn't have to manage large amounts of memory to store data structures relating to session setups and ending sessions. Instead, if a query to a DNS server isn't received within a short period of time, the originating computer can just send another query, which will hopefully get through. Many other utilities such as `ping` also use UDP, and we will talk about those near the end of this appendix when you learn about some troubleshooting utilities that can be used for TCP/IP.

The Internet Control Message Protocol

The Internet control message protocol (ICMP) is a protocol used mainly for maintenance operations on the network, and it is also used in a few utilities for troubleshooting network problems. ICMP uses UDP to send and receive messages. Although there are many kinds of ICMP messages, you only need to know about the following ones:

- ECHO REQUEST—This is a message sent to another computer requesting that it send back a reply that it successfully received the message. You will learn more about this when we discuss the `ping` and `tracert` utilities.

- ECHO REPLY—This is the reply message sent back in response to an ECHO REQUEST message.

- SOURCE QUENCH—This is a message that tells a computer or router that it is sending IP traffic faster than the destination can handle, so it should throttle back somewhat. Although IP doesn't have any built-in mechanisms for session setup or other maintenance functions, ICMP can be used for this rudimentary form of flow control.

- REDIRECT—This is a message, usually sent between routers, when a router is telling another router that it knows of a better route to a particular destination. This is also a message that hackers can use to forge packets that can harm your routing table.

The basic messages you will learn about in this appendix are the first two in the list above because they are useful for troubleshooting. The last two are important from a network standpoint, but you shouldn't need to worry about understanding them completely. It is important, however, if you use the Internet Connection Firewall provided with Windows XP to understand that turning on any of the ICMP message types can allow someone from outside your computer or network to gain information about your network (see Chapter 25).

The Address Resolution Protocol

Once a packet of information has arrived at the intended LAN, it is time to use those hardware addresses you learned about at the start of this appendix. This means that another level of translation comes into play. The address resolution protocol (ARP) is used on this last leg of the journey. When the packet gets to the router that is connected to the same network (or subnet network) that the destination computer is attached to, it must then resolve the computer host portion of the IP address to the hardware address. From there, communications take place using the hardware addresses instead of the TCP/IP addresses.

Serial Line Interface Protocol and Point-to-Point Protocol

A network adapter card attaches your computer to a network, and that card gets assigned an IP address. If you want to connect to the Internet using a dial-up modem, then you don't need a network card on your computer, just the modem. In that case, communications can be handled between your modem (a serial connection) and your Internet service provider (ISP) by using serial line interface protocol (SLIP) or point-to-point protocol (PPP).

The Serial Line Interface Protocol

SLIP is an older protocol developed to allow a serial line data exchange between two computers. SLIP is not used very much now because it is a very simple protocol and provides for no authentication. SLIP has, for all practical purposes, been replaced by PPP.

Basically, SLIP requires that each end of the connection first set up an address. Second, SLIP uses only a small header, and does no error checking on the information that flows through this data pipe.

Windows XP does still support SLIP (see Chapter 25), but if your ISP is still using SLIP, then it is probably time for you to find a better ISP!

The Point-to-Point Protocol

PPP is the most popular method used to create a dial-up connection to the Internet today. PPP was created to take care of the deficiencies of SLIP, and it is a much more robust protocol. For example, although SLIP can carry only a single protocol at a time across a link, PPP can multiplex (combine multiple signals) multiple protocols across the same serial link.

PPP also provides for mechanisms that set up the connection, provide for how authentication will be done, and other important administrative functions of this sort. The link control protocol (LCP) component of PPP is used to set up links so that different protocols can make use of the same PPP connection at the same time. It isn't really important for you to understand the mechanics of how PPP works; just know that if you use a dial-up connection to the Internet, then PPP is the protocol you should be using, not SLIP.

The Domain Name System

Earlier in this appendix you learned that IP addresses are expressed in dotted-decimal notation because that is an easier numbering method to memorize than a string of binary digits. Likewise, another abstraction has been incorporated into the system called *domain name system (DNS)*. Simply put, a DNS server is used to translate between a dotted-decimal IP address and a user-friendly name. For example, it is much easier to remember zira.twoinc.com than it is to remember 10.10.123.121. So, instead of entering an IP address when you surf the Web or use one of the TCP/IP troubleshooting utilities, you can instead enter the easier to remember computer name instead. It is much easier to remember zira.twoinc.com than the IP address.

A DNS server can be used to translate an IP address to a registered host computer name or for the reverse. In addition to storing records about host computer names, DNS servers also store other kinds of name translations such as popular URLs and services on the Internet. Although the actual mechanics behind how a DNS server operates can be quite complex, it is important to use one if you don't want to resort to using IP addresses for all your network communications.

You can use a DNS server inside your network and only for the computers on your network. If you connect to the Internet, you will find a hierarchy of DNS servers that can be used to search through many different DNS databases to return an IP address when your computer makes a query. On the Internet, you must register your domain name, and it must be unique throughout the entire Internet name space. This is because the actual data for each domain on the Internet is stored in a DNS server for that domain, and your request will be forwarded through the hierarchy of DNS servers until a DNS server is found that can perform the address translation. If the same domain name was used for more than one network, then it would be impossible to predict what address you will receive from a request.

Actually, all this usually happens without your knowledge. You just enter a URL in a browser window and the TCP/IP stack on your computer sends out a DNS request to get the actual IP address and then uses that IP address to contact the server holding the information you want.

A

INTRODUCTION TO TCP/IP

The Dynamic Host Configuration Protocol

Each computer on a TCP/IP network must have its own unique IP address. When the ARPANET was first put into place, it was a simple matter to manually assign an IP address to each computer on the network. However, complications could arise when using this manual method. For example, in a large network, if you didn't keep good records, you might assign the same address to two different computers. In that situation, how would a packet get delivered to the correct computer?

The dynamic host configuration protocol (DHCP) was designed to solve this problem. DHCP allows the network administrator to assign a range of addresses to a DHCP server that, in turn, leases the IP addresses out to individual computers, keeping track of which computer is using which address. As long as you properly configure your DHCP server (and you can have more than one on a network), then it is a simple matter to simply configure your computer (see Chapters 24 and 25) to automatically acquire addressing information from a DHCP server. Over the years, DHCP has been enhanced so that it now supplies not only an IP address to a computer that makes a request, but also a lot of other information such as the subnet mask, default gateway, and the address of DNS servers.

Thus, by using DHCP on your network, you don't have to manually configure each computer with any addressing information. You just select the radio button in the Network Configuration Wizard that says to automatically obtain the information, and when the computer boots, it communicates with the DHCP server and leases the information. The term *lease* is important here because networks can change rapidly.

For example, think of how an ISP supplies a unique address to your computer when you dial up to the ISP's network. You don't always get the same address. The ISP cannot possibly afford to have a unique address for every subscriber, although it can use one of the private address ranges discussed earlier in this appendix and use NAT. Instead, your computer is granted a lease of the configuration information for a period.

DHCP is also useful in large corporate networks. In this kind of setup, a lease is usually set for a period measured in days or weeks. Thus, when a computer is moved to a new location on a different subnet (this requires a different IP address), the lease that it held for an address at its old location will eventually expire and be allocated to another computer. To keep the same address, a computer usually will, about halfway through the lease time, send a request to the DHCP server to renew the lease. If, for some reason, the DHCP server doesn't answer back, which can happen if it is off line, the client will then request an IP address lease from any other DHCP servers that may be on the network.

Using this method, you can see that it is possible for your address to change over time even in a large corporate network.

Some computers, however, cannot use DHCP. This is because some computers such as Web servers need to keep the same address. This address is stored in a DNS database so that clients on the Internet can look up the server by name and get its address. In the last few years, a newer form of DNS has been developed, called *dynamic DNS,* which is what you will find in Windows 2000 and Windows XP Server and .NET Server that allows a computer to dynamically update a DNS server so that the server has the correct name-to-address translation. However, for the majority of DNS servers on the Internet today, each IP address and user-friendly name (such as `http://www.amazon.com`) must be entered manually. If a Web site were constantly changing the IP addresses of its servers, it would be quite difficult to keep making manual changes to DNS servers. Thus, DHCP is generally used by client computers, whereas static, unchanging addresses are generally used by servers on a network.

Windows Internet Naming Service

As you just learned, DHCP makes assigning IP addresses to each computer an easy chore. It is all done automatically, and there is not much that the network administrator needs to do once the computer is set up. However, when DHCP was first developed, a small problem occurred. DHCP can give your computer an IP address, but how do other computers determine what that IP address is when they need to communicate with your computer?

Before dynamic DNS was developed, Microsoft developed its own name service called the *Windows Internet Naming Service (WINS),* which essentially acts as a dynamic DNS. When a client computer has been configured with the address of one or more WINS servers and the client then boots up, it sends a message to the WINS server to issue its name and address. Actually, it does get a little more complicated than that, since WINS also allows for the registration of multiple names for a computer. This is because up until Windows 2000, NetBIOS was the primary method that Windows operating systems used to find resources on a network. NetBIOS over TCP/IP (NETBT) allowed the nonroutable NetBIOS naming scheme to be adapted to the routable TCP/IP suite. By using WINS servers, NetBIOS names could be used not only in a single LAN, but also on many networks connected by routers, as long as WINS was available to allow a translation between the NetBIOS name and an IP address.

With Windows 2000 Server and the upcoming XP Server and with current Windows XP computers, you may no longer need to use WINS servers and could just get by using DNS. This will depend on what applications you use and whether you have any older legacy clients in your network that still use NetBIOS.

A

INTRODUCTION
TO TCP/IP

Virtual Private Networks

One important thing to understand about TCP/IP is that it wasn't developed with a great deal of security in mind. In the early days of the Internet, only large corporations, the government, and educational institutions typically were connected to the Internet. In this small community, you didn't have to worry much about hackers or computer viruses.

Today, however, the situation has changed dramatically. Since the actual data that IP carries in the payload section of its datagram is not encrypted, someone else can easily intercept it. A network adapter can be put into what is called *promiscuous mode*, in which case it will send all packets it detects on the network up the protocol stack for processing. Generally, only packets of data intended for your computer make their way up the protocol stack.

Note that this promiscuous mode wasn't developed to be malicious. It does serve a purpose. For example, if you use a computer or network-troubleshooting device to monitor the network for problems, you need to see all of the packets that are traversing the network. Thus, you need a network adapter to pick up all of the packets that come its way.

However, today you can't depend on everyone being so polite on the Internet, so if you are going to use the Internet to transfer valuable or confidential information, then you need to use additional technologies, such as a virtual private network (VPN). There are several different protocols involved in creating VPNs today. Some involve proprietary technology using routers and other devices. However, Microsoft allows you to use Windows Servers and Windows XP computers to create a VPN through the Internet.

For users that travel frequently, it is much less expensive to dial into a local number of a national ISP and use a VPN to connect to the company network than it is to pay long distance rates to make a direct dial-up connection to that same network.

Troubleshooting Tools for Transmission Control Protocol/Internet Protocol

The TCP/IP suite is considered a suite because it encompasses not just TCP and IP, but many other protocols, services, and applications as well. Part of this suite includes several useful tools that can be used for testing your TCP/IP configuration and troubleshooting remote connectivity. In the next few sections, you will learn about how to use some of these tools supplied with Windows XP.

Using ping and tracert

The two most commonly used tools you will find in the TCP/IP suite are the ping and tracert (trace route) commands. The ping command simply sends an ICMP ECHO request message to a remote computer and lets you know if it receives a reply from the remote computer, along with some statistical information such as the number of milliseconds it took for the round trip. The tracert command will also use ICMP ECHO REQUEST messages but will manipulate the value of the TTL field so that it can discover each router or other device that lies in the path between your computer and the remote computer.

Using the ping Command

This is the most basic command for when you find you are unable to communicate with another system on the network. The syntax for Microsoft's version of ping is as follows:

```
ping [-t] [-a] [-n count] [-l size] [-f] [-i TTL] [-v TOS]
     [-r count] [-s count] [[-j host-list] | [-k host-list]]
     [-w timeout] destination-list
```

Although it is usually sufficient to use the simple version of this command, such as ping www.twoinc.com or ping 122.111.221.20, the following options can also be used to control how the ping command operates:

- -t—The ping command will usually just try to send ICMP ECHO requests to the remote system four times. If you want to have ping continue sending the ICMP ECHO requests until you stop the program (using Ctrl+C), then use ping -t.

- -a—This will tell the ping command to print hostnames instead of just addresses. If you ping a hostname, then both the hostname and address are normally displayed. Using this when you ping an IP address causes ping to attempt to get the name of the host associated with the IP address you are pinging.

- -n count—By default, ping will send four ICMP ECHO requests. Use this to specify a different value.

- -l size—By default, ping will send a packet 32 bytes long. You can use this to change to a larger size.

- -f—This tells ping that it should not set the Don't Fragment bit in the packet.

- - i TTL—This option can be used to specify a TTL value other than the default (104) that is used by ping.

- -v TOS—This option can be used to change the value for the Type of Service in this field in the packet.

- -r count—This will cause ping to record the route for count hops.

- -s count—This will cause ping to record a timestamp for count hops.

- -j host-list—Use this to specify a loose source route to get to the host.

- -k host-list—Use this option to specify a specific route to get to the host.

- -w timeout—This option will change the number of milliseconds to wait for an ECHO REPLY before ping prints a timeout message.

For the most part, unless you are an experienced network technician, a simple usage of the ping command along with an IP address or a host name will enable you to determine if your computer can communicate with another computer on the network or on the Internet. You can see an example of the output from the ping command in Figure A.4.

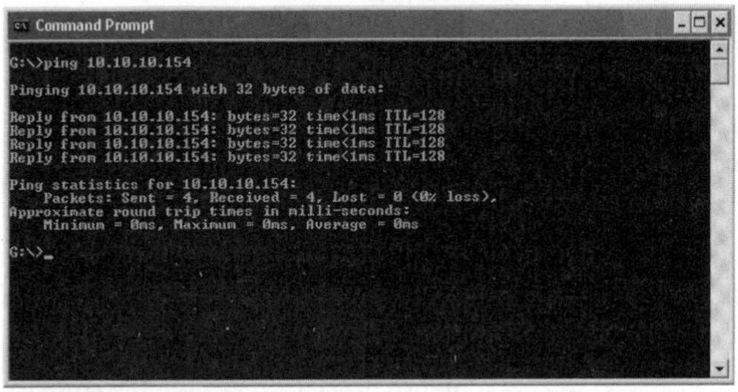

FIGURE A.4

The ping *command can tell you whether a computer is reachable on the network.*

Using the tracert Command

This command, like ping, uses the ICMP ECHO and REPLY messages to bounce packets off a remote host. ping sets the TTL value in the IP packet to a high number. However, in order for the packet to be able to pass through many routers or other systems to get to its destination (without being dropped), the tracert command takes advantage of the TTL value.

When the tracert command sends out its first ICMP ECHO packet, it sets the value of TTL in the IP packet to 1. Thus, the first router at which the packet arrives will decrement this to zero and return to the sender an ICMP DESTINATION UNREACHABLE message. The traceroute command has, through this method, learned the name of the first router the packet will take to get to its destination. It then increments the TTL value to 2, and sends out another ICMP ECHO packet. As you can guess, this allows the packet to pass through the first router but get dropped at the second router. This process continues until the packet eventually reaches its destination, and tracert prints a line for each hop along the way. Thus, in addition to letting you know if you can get there from here, tracert shows you how you got there!

The syntax for the `tracert` command is as follows:

```
tracert [-d] [-h maximum_hops] [-j host-list] [-w timeout] target_name
```

Again, you can use this command simply, such as `tracert www.twoinc.com`, or you can use some of the following command line options if needed:

- `-d`—This tells `tracert` to *not* try to resolve hostnames to addresses. This is sort of the opposite of what `ping` does.

- `-h maximum_hops`—This option can be used to limit the number of hops to be probed to get to the target destination. The default is to try for up to 30 hops.

- `-j host-list`—Use this option to specify a loose source to the destination.

- `-w timeout`—Use this option to specify the number of milliseconds to wait for the ICMP ECHO REPLY messages.

Again, unless you are an experienced network technician, using `tracert` with just a hostname or IP address should be all you need for most troubleshooting efforts. Using `tracert`, you can determine if the packet is being forwarded to the default gateway, for example, when the target resides outside your network. Otherwise, it can pinpoint places in the network where the replies stop coming back. If `ping` is unable to get to the destination, at least you can use `tracert` to find the last place along the route that the packet was able to get to and start your troubleshooting efforts at that point.

In the following listing, you can see the results of the usage of the `tracert` command:

```
Tracing route to www.nytimes.com [208.48.26.200]over a maximum of 30 hops:
  1  *      *      141 ms  envlnjewsap05.bellatlantic.net [192.168.125.169]
  2  *      *      145 ms  192.168.125.158
  3 143 ms  *      143 ms  QWEST.delawarevalley.iprs.verizon.net
[ic:ccc] [206.125.199.71]
  4 146 ms 149 ms 149 ms  jfk-edge-04.inet.qwest.net [63.144.129.221]
  5  *     147 ms 149 ms  jfk-core-03.inet.qwest.net [205.171.30.113]
  6 147 ms  *      *      ewr-core-03.inet.qwest.net [205.171.5.89]
  7  *     146 ms 144 ms  ewr-brdr-01.inet.qwest.net [205.171.17.98]
  8 147 ms 149 ms 149 ms  ibr02-p5-0.jrcy01.exodus.net [216.32.173.225]
  9 147 ms  *     150 ms  bbr02-g5-0.jrcy01.exodus.net [216.32.223.130]
 10 153 ms 154 ms 154 ms  bbr02-p0-0.nycm01.exodus.net [206.79.9.178]
 11 153 ms 154 ms 154 ms  64.15.224.19
 12  *     154 ms 154 ms  64.15.224.5
 13  *     163 ms  *      208.48.26.200
 14 169 ms  *      *      208.48.26.200
 15 169 ms  *     169 ms  208.48.26.200
Trace complete.
```

A

INTRODUCTION
TO TCP/IP

Use IPCONFIG Command to View Your Internet Protocol Configuration

Once you have configured Windows XP for use on the network, you can use the IPCON-FIG utility to display a lot of information about your IP networking configuration. This command can also be used to release or renew a DHCP configuration lease. You can use the simple format of just the command itself, which prints a short list of information, or you can use the following syntax:

```
ipconfig [/? | /all | /release [adapter] | /renew [adapter]]
```

The options available are as follows:

- /?—This displays help or this command, of course!
- /all—This produces a longer display, showing all IP configuration information for the Windows XP workstation instead of just the minimal amount (see examples below).
- /release[adapter]—Use this to relinquish the IP address for the specified adapter. You don't have to use adapter if there is only one network adapter card on the system. This can be helpful, along with the next option, for testing DHCP to ensure your computer can get an IP configuration. It can also be useful to release the IP addressing information when a computer is being taken out of service for an extended period of time and you don't want for the DHCP server to wait out the lease period before it reuses the address.
- /renew—This causes the Windows XP computer to begin the renewal process whereby it contacts a DHCP server to renew an existing lease or to try to obtain a new one.

If you use the command by itself with no other options, you will get just the IP address, subnet mask, and the default gateway that have been configured. The IPCONFIG /ALL | MORE command shows you all the information; by using the pipe to the MORE command, you get to see the data paged so it doesn't roll off your screen! An example of the output you will get from using the /ALL option is shown in the following listing:

```
Windows IP Configuration
        Host Name . . . . . . . . . . . . : twoinc-tktfdyk5
        Primary Dns Suffix . . . . . . . .: twoinc.com
        Node Type . . . . . . . . . . . . : Unknown
        IP Routing Enabled. . . . . . . . : No
        WINS Proxy Enabled. . . . . . . . : No
        DNS Suffix Search List. . . . . . : twoinc.com
Ethernet adapter Local Area Connection: Connection-specific
        DNS Suffix . . . . . . . . . . . .: twoinc.com
        Description . . . . . . . . . . . : Linksys LNE100TX Fast Ethernet
```

```
Adapter(LNE100TX v4)
        Physical Address. . . . . . . . . : 00-04-5A-42-53-99
        Dhcp Enabled. . . . . . . . . . . : Yes
        Autoconfiguration Enabled . . . . : Yes
        IP Address. . . . . . . . . . . . : 10.10.10.100
        Subnet Mask . . . . . . . . . . . : 255.255.255.0
        Default Gateway . . . . . . . . . : 10.10.10.254
        DHCP Server . . . . . . . . . . . : 10.10.10.154
        DNS Servers . . . . . . . . . . . : 10.10.10.154
        Lease Obtained. . . . . . . . . . : Tuesday, August 07, 2001 2:50:51 AM
        Lease Expires . . . . . . . . . . : Wednesday, August 15, 2001 2:50:51
AM
PPP adapter isp: Connection-specific
        DNS Suffix . . . . . . . . . . . .:
        Description . . . . . . . . . . . : WAN (PPP/SLIP) Interface
        Physical Address. . . . . . . . . : 00-53-45-00-00-00
        Dhcp Enabled. . . . . . . . . . . : No
        IP Address. . . . . . . . . . . . : 151.204.200.41
        Subnet Mask . . . . . . . . . . . : 255.255.255.255
        Default Gateway . . . . . . . . . : 151.204.200.41
        DNS Servers . . . . . . . . . . . : 151.204.0.84 151.197.0.39
        NetBIOS over Tcpip. . . . . . . . : Disabled
```

Using the NETSTAT Command

The command NETSTAT is another useful command for when troubleshooting TCP/IP connections because it can show you all of the sessions between your computer and other computers. It will show you the statistics about each protocol and the current TCP/IP connections. The syntax for NETSTAT is as follows:

NETSTAT [-a] [-e] [-n] [-s] [-p *proto*] [-r] [*interval*]

The options you can use are as follows:

- -a—This option shows all connections, including listening ports on a server side of the connection. By including this you can see if you have any open ports that may be a potential security risk! By default, these are not shown.

- -e—This option displays statistics about Ethernet, which is the underlying protocol your TCP/IP network is probably using to transmit data across the wire. You can combine this with the -s option.

- -n—This option causes address and port numbers to be displayed in numerical form. The default is to use hostnames.

- -p proto—You can limit the display to show only TCP or UDP connections by using those terms for proto. With the -s option, you will also see statistics for these protocols.

A

INTRODUCTION
TO TCP/IP

- -r—This will show you the contents of the routing table. This is similar to the route print command.

- -s—This will display statistics for the protocols selected.

- interval—You can use this to specify a number of seconds at which the command will update the display. Use Ctrl+C to end the display.

This command can be useful for troubleshooting because it can show you statistical information about each protocol, such as dropped packets and other like information.

Tip

In addition to the NETSTAT command, you should also check out the set of NET commands covered in Chapter 13, "Command Prompt Tools." These commands can be used connect to or view network resources and help you troubleshoot other network problems.

Using the ROUTE Command

This command is useful for manipulating the routing table, or displaying its contents. On a Windows XP computer, you simply use the route print command to display the routing table. If any changes need to be made to a routing table on your computer, then consult first with your network administrator before doing so.

Using the NSLOOKUP Command

This is a simple command that you can use to determine if a host name (or an IP address) is registered in a DNS server. You can use NSLOOKUP in two different modes. First, you can simply use the command followed by an IP address or a computer host name. The utility will contact one of the DNS servers you have configured in your Windows XP IP configuration and ask it for any information, which will then be displayed for you on the screen. The following listing shows you an example of this simple usage of the command:

```
C:\>nslookup www.twoinc.com

Server: dnshpw.net.xyz.com
Address: 134.83.112.99

Name:  www.twoinc.com
Address: 204.248.100.8
```

Note in this figure that the utility also shows you the DNS server from which it obtained its information.

Secondly, you can enter interactive mode by simply entering the command NSLOOKUP itself, without following it with a hostname or IP address. You will get a greater than symbol for a prompt (>) and can then keep entering commands until you type EXIT to terminate the interactive session. For most purposes, you will find that the simple command line version works for most troubleshooting needs: to determine if a hostname is recognizable by DNS and to make sure the correct hostname and IP address are associated with each other. For information on using NSLOOKUP in interactive mode, type help at the at the greater than prompt.

Summary

This appendix has covered a lot of territory if you are a beginner in the networking field. As you learn about setting up your Windows XP computer in a network or using it for a connection to the Internet, it is important that you understand some of the concepts involved. Knowing what an IP address is and the subnet mask associated with it can help you understand how the address space in a LAN can be divided up. Understanding the importance of DHCP and DNS servers will also help you better troubleshoot network problems.

APPENDIX B

Overview of the Lightweight Directory Access Protocol and Microsoft's Active Directory

IN THIS APPENDIX

- The Development of Lightweight Directory Access Protocol   *798*

- Working with Lightweight Directory Access Protocol   *804*

- Microsoft's Active Directory   *806*

Microsoft's Active Directory (AD) is useful for storing information that often needs to be looked up on a network. The AD extends the concept of a directory to include storing information about not just files on a computer, but all kinds of useful information in a networked environment. In this appendix, you learn about the pre-history of lightweight directory access protocol (LDAP), how to use LDAP, and Microsoft's implementation of directory services. You see what actual user and computer accounts look like in the directory.

If you are going to be using Windows XP Professional in a business environment, you are probably part of a workgroup, domain, or domain that is part of the AD. The information in this appendix is intended to supplement your knowledge of how Windows networking functions in a large environment. Understanding how the directory is structured, as well as the protocol (LDAP) used to access the directory is important. The more you know as an end-user of the network, the better able you will be in using the AD to your advantage for locating important system resources.

If you are using Windows XP as a standalone computer or in the home, then AD is probably of no interest to you; however, this appendix will still make for some interesting reading.

The Development of Lightweight Directory Access Protocol

In 1993 the X.500 protocol standards were approved by the International Telecommunications Union (ITU); later these standards were also adopted by the International Organization for Standardization (ISO). The purpose of the various protocols under this standard was to create a hierarchical database and the necessary protocols needed to access the database so that information from different applications such as those envisioned by the X.400 standards for e-mail could be located in a central database. Because the namespace provided by the X.500 standards was so flexible, developers realized that a directory could be created to store many different kinds of information, not just the e-mail data originally targeted by the development work on X.500.

The X.500 standards were developed to run on powerful machines (for their time) and were not intended to address the small, yet growing, PC market. Because of this, LDAP was developed as a "lightweight" set of protocol standards for accessing a directory, based (with some modifications) on the original directory envisioned by the X.500 developers. LDAP runs over transfer call protocol/internet protocol (TCP/IP) networks. Because IP is so flexible in providing a networking service to higher-level protocols, it was easy to develop LDAP to make use of IP.

A Quick Look at the X.500 Standards

The X.500 standard covers several different protocols. At about the same time these protocols were being developed, the Internet began to grow at a rapid rate. The growth of the Internet pretty much killed off interest in any of the Open System Interconnection (OSI) network protocols in all but a few large companies. Once the Internet began to allow commercial access, instead of allowing access only to large corporations, universities and government institutions, the de facto standard for communication on the Internet (TCP/IP) had started invading local area networks (LANs) as the protocol of choice. Although a lot of Novell NetWare networks were in existence, once the Internet took off, TCP/IP became the worldwide standard for LANs. Emerging 10-gigabit Ethernet standards show that using TCP/IP across very high-speed Ethernet links is now becoming a metropolitan area network (MAN) and wide area network (WAN) standard.

It is important to know a little about the OSI protocols so that you can understand *why* LDAP was developed.

> **Note**
>
> The domain name system (DNS) is also a hierarchical database. It is a distributed database that involves many thousands of DNS servers that operate to help resolve names on the Internet or possibly just your own LAN. You can learn more about DNS in Appendix A, Introduction to TCP/IP.

The original X.500 protocol standards consisted of several different protocols:

- Directory access protocol (DAP)
- Directory system protocol (DSP)
- Directory information shadowing protocol (DISP)
- Directory operational binding management protocol (DOP)

If those aren't enough abbreviations for you, don't worry, there's more to come!

The Directory Information Base and the Directory Information Tree

The actual data stored in the database is organized in a tree-like fashion based on the directory information base (DIB) standard. Records that exist in this directory hold data about an object. Each object is composed of one or more attributes. Basically, an object is just a collection of attributes, and for each object, there can be mandatory attributes, which means every instance of the object must have a value for these attributes.

Additionally, optional attributes may or may not be needed by a particular instance of the object. Think of an object as a template for creating records in a database. Think of the attribute as an individual data item that is stored in an object.

The directory information tree (DIT) is the standard that dictates how objects are organized in the directory. You will note that a real tree usually has one small branch sticking out at the very top, reaching for the sunlight. Under it fall many other branches, and on these branches are leaves. The DIT follows this format to create a logical way to organize (and thus locate) information in the DIB. Some branches have more branches attached to them, while some of the branches at the outer portions of the tree merely have leaves.

At the very top of the tree is an object called the *root object*. However, Microsoft changed the name so that in the AD it is called the *Top Abstract Class*. The naming is unimportant to understanding how the directory is organized. The root or top object in the directory is the starting point for organizing the directory. All other objects (and their attributes) fall under this first object.

Objects and Attributes

Because you can start at the top of the tree and search down through the branches, it is very easy to locate information in the directory database. However, to understand how this works, you need to know more about objects and their attributes. First, understand that one of the attributes of every object in the tree is the object's common name. Every object you create in the tree has a name, and that name can be expressed in the following ways:

- Relative Distinguished Name (RDN)—This is also known as the *common name* of the object. It is just an attribute of the object that is used to give it a name of local significance. For example, if you have two employees in your organization that have the same name, they can both have the same values for their relative distinguished name. In other words, it is relative to the location of the object in the tree structure. You can have several people in your organization named Yoko Ono, so long as they don't have user accounts in the same container object (another concept we will get to shortly).

- Distinguished Name (DN)—This name is more complicated, usually much longer than the RDN, and always much more useful. The DN of an object is its own common name (RDN), linked together with all of the RDNs of its parent objects in the directory. When you think about it, this means that the DN is virtually a map to point you to the object in the directory. It names each object that precedes the object in the tree.

By using an object's DN name, it is possible to navigate the tree and locate the object exactly in the database. There can be only one unique object in the database that has that DN name. The RDN name can vary, and you can have many objects with the same RDN name, since it has only local significance. The DN name of an object uniquely identifies it, as well as its location in the directory tree structure, since it contains not only the name of the object but also all of the parent objects that lie above it in the tree structure. It is like following a map. Once you have the DN name, you simply traverse the tree until you get to the object you want. Although you can have two objects in a directory with the same common name (or RDN), there cannot be two objects in the directory that have the same DN, since the DN points to a specific location in the directory.

Container Objects and Leaf Objects

It is important to note here that there are two kinds of objects: container objects and leaf objects. Container objects hold other objects and are generally used for organizing the data in the directory tree. Leaf objects are the actual objects that contain attributes that hold specific data. For example, a user account stored in the AD is an individual leaf object, because it holds information about a specific individual user account. Yet, that leaf object can be located under (or inside, depending on how you view it) a container object such as a domain. In the X.500 standards container, objects are usually called *organizational units* (OUs). These also exist in the AD. The domain, which was used to group together individual computers and users in pre–Windows 2000 computer networks, is now just another kind of Organizational Unit in the AD.

The OSI Protocols and Standards: Directory User Agent, Directory Service Agent, and Directory Access Protocol

As you just learned, the directory database is organized in a tree-like structure, composed of objects and attributes. However, the X.500 standards also contain protocols that were created to access the directory database, and for other purposes. There are also standards for the applications that run on a directory-enabled computer. The Directory User Agent (DUA) runs on the end-user computer, and the Directory Service Agent (DS) runs on the computer responsible for accepting requests from user agents to access the directory.

The following is important to remember about DUA:

- Read some or all the values for attributes of a particular object in the database.
- Compare a value with an attribute of an object in the database to see if they are the same.
- List objects that are subordinate in the tree structure to an object specified by the DUA.

- Search the database, either all or a portion of it, to find objects with attributes matching values supplied by the DUA. A search can return more than one object to the DUA, depending on the criteria the DUA supplies for the search filter.

- Abandon the search or any other request that the DUA has previously made to the directory database.

- Add an entry or a new object to the database, provided that the necessary access permissions allow this.

- Modify an object or one or more of its attributes in the database, provided that permissions allow for it and also that the new value the DUA wants to give to an attribute is allowable by the syntax associated with the attribute.

- Remove an entry from the database, provided that the client application has permission to do so.

- Modify a DN.

As if that is not complicated enough, let's throw in the Directory Access Protocol (DAP). This is the protocol the DUA uses to talk to the DSA. Again, keep in mind that these applications and protocols were developed to run on fast minicomputers and mainframes, and not the PCs of their day. Thus, the OSI protocols that were designed for use with the X.500 standard were never widely implemented except in high-end computing applications.

Schemas

When we talk about objects and the attributes that make them up, there has to be some definition of what kinds of objects and attributes can exist in the directory. The schema is a collection of rules and templates that dictate what kinds of objects and the syntaxes for their attributes can be created in the directory.

Simply put, for every object in the AD, there is a directory class that specifies the mandatory attributes and the optional attributes that can be used when a specific object is created. For example, a user object class allows the Windows 2002 administrator to enter some mandatory information about a user, such as the username and password, as well as optional information, such as the user's department, supervisor, telephone numbers, and other useful information. However, in order to include any type of information in a particular object, the object class must allow for it. The AD does allow you to modify the schema. You can create new object classes (and then create instances of those objects), or you can create new attributes for an object or a new object class. This is why the AD is so flexible. It comes with a set of built-in objects and attributes designed to serve the purposes of most networks. However, if your environment needs to store a different type of information, you can always modify the schema to create a new object, attribute, or both so that you can store virtually any type of information in the AD.

Defining Schema with Lightweight Directory Access Protocol

In today's environment, PCs are much more powerful than when the X.500 standards were developed. Servers on your network are more powerful than many mainframes of the early 1990s. LDAP was created to avoid unnecessary overhead on a PC and to cut down on network traffic. The original X.500 directory structure was retained (with some modifications), but the OSI protocols and other services were thrown out and replaced by a more concise, limited set of protocols. Microsoft's AD supports LDAP, and its set of protocols are used in Windows XP to update, interrogate, and otherwise use the information available in the AD.

As mentioned earlier, LDAP was designed to work with TCP/IP. Version 2 of LDAP (LDAPv2, described in RFC 1777) was the first practical implementation of LDAP. Version 3 (LDAPv3, described in RFC 2251) more fully explains the client/server nature of the functions required for accessing the directory database. Microsoft's AD supports both LDAPv2 and LDAPv3.

LDAPv3 provides for additional operations that were not supported in the older versions of LDAP, such as paging and sorting. Additionally, LDAPv3 is extensible. It defines a concept called *extended operations*, allowing future developers to implement operations not provided for in the current protocol. This extended operations capability allows a vendor to customize his version of LDAP applications but still allow his product to inter-act with other LDAPv3 compliant products (more or less).

LDAPv3 also lets you define the schema—that is, the definition of the objects and attributes that can be created in the directory itself. The DNS is a distributed database that allows you to associate user-friendly, or human-readable, names with IP addresses. However, most implementations of DNS require you to define name-to-address translations in a flat-file read when the DNS server starts up. LDAPv3 allows for the definitions of objects and attributes to be defined in the directory database itself, which means that you can use the graphical user interface (GUI) provided by Windows 2000 and Windows 2002 Server to modify the kinds of information you can store in the database.

This may seem inconsequential at first glance, but consider this: applications can query the directory database to find out what kinds of objects or attributes are stored in the directory, since these definitions are stored in the directory and not just a flat-file on some computer. Again, this makes the AD and other LDAP directories more flexible. Not only can an application look up information about specific objects and attributes of those objects, but it can also look into the directory to find out what kind of information is actually available.

> **Tip**
>
> If you want to learn more about the specifics of the LDAP protocol, check out the following Request For Comments (RFC) documents. The significant detail these documents offer cannot be included in this book due to space requirements:
>
> - RFC 2252, Attribute Syntax Definitions
> - RFC 2253, UTF-8 String Representation of Distinguished Names
> - RFC 2254, The String Representation of LDAP Search Filters
> - RFC 2255, The LDAP URL Format
> - RFC 2256, A Summary of the X.500 User Schema for Use with LDAPv3
> - RFC 2247, Using Domains in LDAP X.500 Distinguished Names
>
> These documents, available through a quick search on the Internet, can give you more insight into the details of how LDAP works. One location where you can find most all RFC documents is `http://www.rcf-editor.org`.

Working with Lightweight Directory Access Protocol

LDAP is sometimes called a *wire protocol*, which is merely a way of saying it defines the methods used for the exchange of information between the client and server. LDAP is a series of messages, called *protocol data units* (PDUs) that are exchanged between the client and server using either TCP or User Datagram Protocol (UDP). As you learned in Appendix A, both TCP and UDP in turn make use of the IP for sending data between computers.

LDAP PDUs are used to connect to an LDAP-compatible server and to authenticate the client to the server. Other PDUs are used to search the directory and manage error handling. In order to start a session with a directory server, the LDAP client first must bind to the server database. The PDU sent should contain the name of the directory object to which the client wants to bind, the version of the LDAP protocol the client is using, and specific information used to authenticate the client to the directory.

The server will respond with either an error message (as is the case if the server doesn't support the version of LDAP the client is using) or a number of other responses that will keep the client from accessing the server. For example, the server may not support the authentication method the client uses or may require the use of a stronger authentication method such as a digital certificate. The server might also refer the client to another directory server if it doesn't hold the data object to which the client wants to bind. This process is known as a *referral* and can be important when a large directory database is distributed across several servers. Another response that the server can send is a PDU informing the client that the server is shutting down at the moment so it will be unable to handle the request.

Conducting a Search in the Directory

If the client does succeed in binding to the directory (its authentication method is acceptable and the client presents the correct information), then the client can perform a number of different functions when interacting with the directory. The most common function is to search the directory database for some kind of information.

When performing a search, the client can help minimize the impact on the directory server by telling the server an appropriate place in the directory tree to begin the search. For example, when using Microsoft's AD, it wouldn't make sense to start at the very top of the directory tree structure to begin looking for a printer if you already know the print server managing the printer resides in a particular domain. You can then specify the domain, which is a container object in the directory and start the search at that point. If a domain is a large one, further divided into many OUs, then it may make sense to start the search further down the tree, beginning with the OU. For example, if you want to find a printer in the accounting department and there is an accounting OU, then you could specify for the search to begin at that point in the directory tree.

When making a search request, the client can also specify other information pertinent to the search effort. The LDAP client can specify a filter, which is a set of attribute values used to make comparisons to objects in the directory. With a printer, the client can specify that it wants to locate a color printer. The client can specify the maximum number of objects it can handle from the search. Depending on the kind of search, this can keep the client from being overwhelmed when a large amount of data is returned to it by the search. The LDAP client can also specify a maximum amount of time the server should spend on the search so that the client doesn't have to wait for long periods.

Changing Information in the Directory

If the client has the necessary permissions, based on how it is authenticated to the server, then the client can change, add, or delete objects or attributes in the directory. In order to do this, the client must specify the distinguished name of the object so that the directory can locate the object. Remember that the DN of an object is made up of the RDNs of the object plus all of the objects superior to that object in the directory. The server follows the name of each object down the tree until it locates the object to be modified or the location where the LDAP client wants to insert a new child object.

To add a new object, the client must specify values for all of the mandatory attributes of the object it wants to create and may, if it wants to, specify any additional optional attributes supported by the object class. In order to delete an object, the client also has to specify the distinguished name so that the directory can locate the specific object.

If the client wants to modify the object, then it is possible to add, delete, or modify any of the attributes of the object the client has permission on which to perform such operations. For example, if the object represents a user account in a domain, you might give a client the permission to modify the user object's attribute storing the user's password but not grant permission to the client to change other attributes of the object, such as the user's home directory. In addition to modifying an object, sometimes all a client wants to do is find out if the values of one or more of the attributes of an object match the values of the client.

The granularity of control that can be used in a directory database such as the AD is a very powerful tool. You can create groups of users who can perform specific functions and limit the portions of the directory tree (by domain, or organizational unit, for example) where they can perform these functions.

Microsoft's Active Directory

When Windows 2000 Advanced Server was released, it changed Windows networking dramatically. Before, computers and user accounts were organized into domains, and there were primary domain controllers (PDCs), which were used to hold the master copy of the security database, and there were backup domain controllers (BDCs), which held a copy of the security database and provided for redundancy. Changes could be made to the security database only on PDC and then propagated to the BDCs. In a large domain, this could take some time, and when the PDC was down, the administrator could either wait until it was online again to make changes like adding new users or promote a BDC to be the new PDC.

This is only a brief description of the PDC/BDC method of storing security information. In addition, if users wanted to access resources in other domains, special trust relationships had to be set up between domains and then administrators in the resource domains had to grant permissions to users or groups of users. All in all, it worked, but it was a complicated method for administering a large number of computers and users.

The AD, based on the X.500 directory model and the LDAP, has made the process much simpler. Now, there are only domain controllers, and all are equal peers within a domain. Each domain controller holds a copy of the directory database for its own domain, so changes can be made on any domain controller.

Domains are a special kind of organizational unit in the directory tree, and trust relationships do not have to be set up between domains that exist in the same directory tree. Instead, implicit transitive trusts are automatically created when a domain is added to the directory tree. Administrators in each domain still have control over the resources in their domain, but they no longer need to create and maintain trust relationships with other domains in the same tree.

> **Note**
>
> In addition to a directory tree made up of domains, the AD also provides for the concept of a forest. A forest, of course, is a collection of trees. When a new domain is created, you can attach it to an existing domain tree or create a new domain tree. If you have domains in separate trees, then you still have to create specific trust relationships between domains that exist in separate trees in the forest.

Because of the extensive schema provided by the AD, you can store all sorts of objects in the directory. You can have user accounts, computer accounts, printers, and many other kinds of objects that are useful in a networked environment. The schema itself is extensible so that if the object class you need doesn't exist, you can create a new one (this is necessary only in extreme cases).

Some of the standard container objects provided by the AD with which a systems administrator will interact on a frequent basis include the following:

- Namespaces
- Country
- Locality
- Organization
- Organizational Unit
- Domain
- Computer

Standard leaf objects representing real entities in the world are defined in the AD schema as follows:

- User
- Group
- Alias

- Service
- Print Queue
- Print Device
- Print Job
- File Service
- File Share
- Session
- Resource

Managing these built-in objects gives the administrator a large degree of control over managing the network users and resources. However, this is not a complete listing by any means.

A Quick Look at the Microsoft Management Console and Managing the Directory

Windows XP uses the Microsoft Management Console (MMC), along with snap-ins, to give a similar look and feel to most management applications. You no longer have to use the User Manager for Domains, the Server Manager, and other utilities that each had their own unique interface. Instead, the MMC organizes functions into a tree structure and makes it easy to use many different utilities if you have learned some of the basics of how MMC snap-ins work.

Snap-ins are just the separate utilities created to be used by the MMC. If you look in the Administrative Tools folder on a Windows 2000 Server computer you see a large number of utilities, nearly all of them using MMC.

In Figure B.1 you can see an example of the MMC administrative tool called *AD Users and Computers*.

As you can see, the left pane of the Active Directory Users and Computers window lists a number of container objects, including one for Computers and one for Users. If you double-click on one of these container objects it expands to show its contents. In the figure, the Users container object has been opened, and you can see user groups and individual user accounts in the twoinc.com domain.

Finding Objects in the Active Directory

Finding objects in the directory is a simple matter. In the MMC snap-in Active Directory Users and Computers, choose Action, Find to open the Find dialog box (see Figure B.2).

FIGURE B.1

The Active Directory Users and Computers MMC snap-in allows you to manage users and computers in the domain.

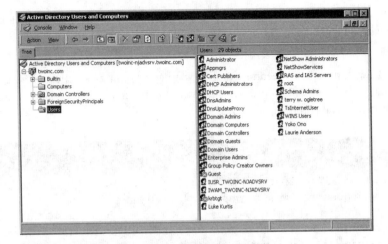

FIGURE B.2

You can find information in the directory easily by using the Find function.

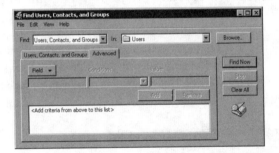

To search for an object (in this example, a user, contact, or group) in the directory, specify a field and then enter a condition and a value to be used in the search. The fields you can specify are dependent on the attributes of the object you are looking for. For example, if you are looking for a user account object, you can specify a first name, last name, e-mail address, and a host of other attributes. The Condition field allows you to specify a search condition to be used when comparing the value you enter into the Value field. You can enter one of the following:

- Starts with
- Ends with
- Is (exactly)
- Is not
- Present
- Not present

By specifying an attribute of the object (called a *field* in the search dialog box) with a condition and a value for the search, you can easily locate any object in the directory for management purposes.

Likewise, users who need to search for perhaps a printer can click on Find on the print dialog box, search for a printer, and enter search criteria, as long as they are part of a domain participating in the AD.

Note

The AD search capability may seem elementary at first, but consider its global consequences. A user in Princeton, N. J. can search for a printer to send output to for another use that may reside in Waterloo, Belgium. The AD truly makes global computing much easier to implement, provided it is structured correctly and managed by administrators who are knowledgeable in how the AD operates.

After you have located the object in the directory you are looking for, you can click on it in the search results to view the object and its attributes. Figure B.3 shows the eight tabs on the Properties page for a user object. Note that some applications such as Microsoft Exchange Server may add additional tabs or fields to an object such as this.

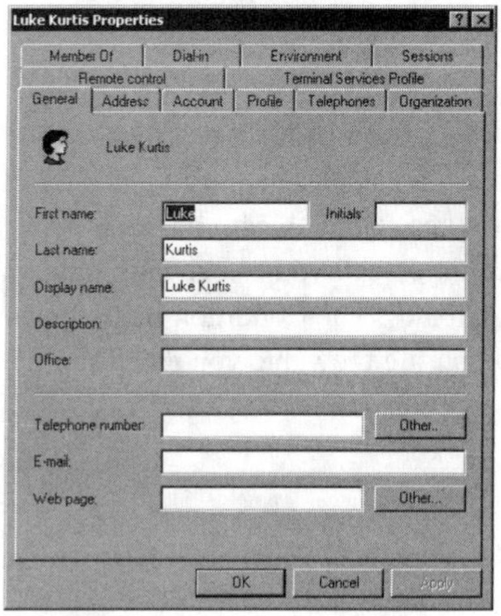

FIGURE B.3

The Properties page for the Active Directory User object.

The amount of information you can store in the AD overshadows the limited capabilities of the Security Accounts Manager (SAM) database of earlier versions of Window NT. It is beyond the scope of this appendix to tell you each and every field available for you to store information about a particular user. However, if your Windows XP Professional computer is participating in a corporate domain that resides in the AD, just keep in mind that you can store a lot of information about a person or any other object. This includes things like file shares, printers, and other things, all in a single object to be easily found with a quick search.

Using Windows XP on a Notebook Computer

APPENDIX C

IN THIS APPENDIX

- Using ClearType   *814*
- Setting Power Management Options in Windows XP   *816*
- Using Hardware Profiles   *822*
- Synchronization and Offline Files   *828*

Windows XP Professional is designed to take full advantage of the power of notebook computing. Windows XP provides real benefits when it comes to managing power—the single resource that remains limited on notebook computers. Windows XP can accurately determine the amount of battery life remaining and provide you with ample warning before you run out of power. Additionally, Windows XP gives you more control over which hardware devices use power (and sometimes even how much power) to extend the amount of work time you get from a battery charge.

In addition to providing better power management, Windows XP boasts three features that can make the life of almost any notebook computer user better:

- ClearType display technology boosts the horizontal resolution of your display and makes reading liquid crystal display (LCD) screens easier.

- Offline Files let you copy files from a network, work on those files offline, and synchronize the files when you reconnect.

- Hardware profiles let you configure the hardware on your computer for different situations and then switch between configurations easily. For example, you can create one profile governing the hardware that is enabled when you are connected to a network and one profile for when you are not connected.

In this appendix, you learn many ways to be more productive on your Windows XP notebook computer. You learn how to use the Remote Desktop feature (covered in detail in Chapter 15, "Managing Local Users") to access a home desktop computer from the road. You also learn how to enable ClearType, manage power settings, use Offline Files, and set up different hardware profiles.

Using ClearType

ClearType is a font technology originally designed for Microsoft Reader, a program for reading electronic books. ClearType characters have particularly smooth edges and higher horizontal resolution (three times that of predecessors), so they are crisper and easier to read on LCD screens. Figure C.1 shows a Web page in Internet Explorer displayed normally. Figure C.2 shows the same Web page displayed using ClearType.

> **Note**
>
> How does ClearType work? Regular fonts such as TrueType assume that each pixel in your display is turned on or turned off. This often results in a jagged onscreen appearance because characters are essentially formed of many tiny squares. ClearType technology is able to address the area surrounding a normal

pixel and provides an anti-aliasing effect based on information from the display itself. This means that ClearType is able to actively adjust the display of onscreen characters to smooth out the rough edges.

FIGURE C.1

Normal display methods can make characters look jagged on a laptop screen.

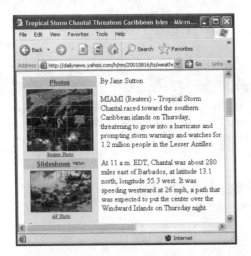

FIGURE C.2

ClearType has a better resolution, has less jagged edges, and appears a little bolder on a laptop display.

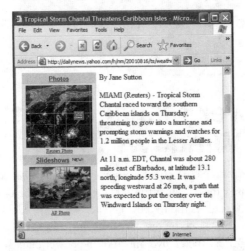

Enable ClearType in Windows XP using the following steps:

1. Click Start and then click Control Panel.

2. In the Control Panel window, click the Appearance and Themes link and then click the Display icon (in Classic view, just double-click the Display icon).

3. In the Display Properties dialog box, open the Appearance tab and then click the Effects button to open the Effects dialog box (see Figure C.3).

4. Select the Use the Following Method to Smooth Edges of Screen Fonts option. From the drop-down list under that option, choose ClearType.

5. Click OK to return to the Display Properties dialog box; click OK to return to Windows. At this point, everything on your display, including window text, title bars, menus, and so on, will be displayed using ClearType.

> **Note**
>
> The Standard font setting also softens the edges of screen fonts but not as dramatically as does ClearType. The standard setting is primarily intended for desktop monitors and not LCD screens.

FIGURE C.3

Use the Effects dialog to config-ure advanced display settings, such as ClearType.

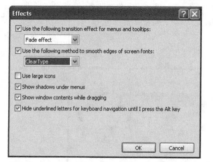

Setting Power Management Options in Windows XP

Since the real limiting factor for most notebook computer users is power (after all, battery life is finite), power management is an all-important feature. In the past, many of the details of power management were left up to the computer's BIOS—the built-in software that determines what a computer can do before accessing any programs on disk. With modern advances, Windows XP has taken over much of the power management from the BIOS.

Two basic power specifications can be found in computers today. These include the following:

- Advanced Power Management (APM)—Developed by Intel and Microsoft, APM is the technology that originally allowed a computer's BIOS to manage power.

Windows XP can take advantage of many of the features of APM to power down certain components automatically in order to save power.

- Advanced Configuration and Power Interface (ACPI)—Developed by Intel, Microsoft, and a few other companies, ACPI enables the operating system to control the amount of power provided to each piece of hardware on a system. If your computer supports ACPI, you will have the options of sending your computer into a standby mode, in which most of the hardware is powered down, and possibly of powering your computer up with a touch of your keyboard or mouse.

All of the power management features in Windows XP are controlled through the Power Options Properties dialog box. Open it from your Control Panel by double-clicking the Power Options icon or by right-clicking the Power icon in your system tray (a plug or a battery, depending on your power source) and selecting the Adjust Power Properties command.

The Power Options dialog box features a number of tabs, each of which is covered in the next several sections.

Power Schemes

A power scheme is a collection of settings for managing the power usage of your computer, and it works like many of the other schemes you see throughout Windows. You control power settings using the Power Schemes tab (see Figure C.4).

FIGURE C.4

Setting a Power Scheme for your laptop will prolong your battery life.

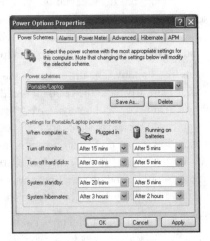

Using this tab, you get to specify what happens to your computer after it is idle (no mouse or keyboard activity) for a certain amount of time. If you have a notebook computer (or a desktop computer with a battery backup), you see two columns under the Settings section at the bottom of the dialog box. The first column represents what will happen when the computer is plugged in; the second column indicates what happens when the computer is running on batteries. If you don't have a battery (or if you don't have Advanced Power Management turned on), you see only one column of choices.

In each state (plugged in or on battery), you can have Windows XP perform any of the following actions after a specified amount of idle time:

- Turn Off the Monitor—The monitor is one of the most power hungry pieces of hardware around. When running on a battery, the default idle time before the monitor is turned off is five minutes. You might even consider shortening this to one or two minutes to help conserve battery power.

- Turn Off Hard Disks—Hard disks also consume a good bit of power. By default, hard disks are also turned off after five minutes when running on battery. When the hard drive or monitor is powered down, moving the mouse or pressing a key brings them back. The monitor should come back almost instantly; the hard drive may take a few seconds to spin up and be ready for access.

- Standby—In standby mode, power to the monitor and hard drives is cut, and the computer appears to turn off. Actually, just enough power is kept flowing to the computer's random access memory (RAM) to keep its contents intact. When you bring your computer out of standby, it should come back to the exact state in which you left it, with open windows, running programs, and so on. You can bring some computers out of standby by moving the mouse or pressing a key. Others require that you press the power button. Check your documentation. You can also send a computer into standby yourself by using the Turn Off Computer command on the Start menu. A computer that has only a few hours of battery life when turned on should easily last overnight (and maybe a couple of days) in standby mode.

- Hibernate—Hibernation is much like standby. The difference is that the contents of RAM are written to a file on your hard drive and the computer really is turned off. When you turn your computer on again (you will always have to use the power button for this), the computer returns to the exact state in which you left it. The advantage of hibernation over standby is that no battery power is used during hibernation. The disadvantages are that it does take a little longer to reactivate a hibernating computer, since it has to go through the boot process, and that writing the contents of RAM to a hard drive requires enough hard drive space to be free.

It is probably best that you spend some time figuring out the power settings that best suit you, but Windows XP offers several preset power schemes to get you started. The settings of each of these are detailed in Table C.1. Select the power scheme that most closely resembles your usage, modify it the way you want, and then use the Save As button to name and save your modified scheme.

Table C.1   Preset Power Schemes

Scheme	State	Settings
Home/office desk	Plugged in	Turn Off Monitor (20 minutes) Turn Off Hard Disks (Never) Standby (Never) Hibernation (Never)
	Running on batteries	Turn Off Monitor (5 minutes) Turn Off Hard Disks (10 minutes) Standby (Never) Hibernation (15 minutes)
Presentation	Plugged in	Turn Off Monitor (Never) Turn Off Hard Disks (Never) Standby (Never) Hibernation (Never)
	Running on batteries	Turn Off Monitor (Never) Turn Off Hard Disks (5 minutes) Standby (15 minutes) Hibernation (2 hours)
Always on	Plugged in	Turn Off Monitor (20 minutes) Turn Off Hard Disks (Never) Standby (Never) Hibernation (Never)
	Running on batteries	Turn Off Monitor (15 minutes Turn Off Hard Disks (30 minutes) Standby (Never) Hibernation (Never)
Minimal power management	Plugged in	Turn Off Monitor (15 minutes) Turn Off Hard Disks (Never) Standby (Never) Hibernation (Never)
	Running on batteries	Turn Off Monitor (5 minutes) Turn Off Hard Disks (15 minutes) Standby (5 minutes) Hibernation (4 hours)
Max battery	Plugged in	Turn Off Monitor (15 minutes) Turn Off Hard Disks (Never) Standby (20 minutes) Hibernation (45 minutes)

C

USING XP ON A
NOTEBOOK
COMPUTER

continues

Table C.1   continued

Scheme	State	Settings
	Running on batteries	Turn Off Monitor (1 minute) Turn Off Hard Disks (3 minutes) Standby (2 minutes) Hibernation (1 hour)
Portable/laptop	Plugged in	Turn Off Monitor (15 minutes) Turn Off Hard Disks (30 minutes) Standby (20 minutes) Hibernation (3 hours)
	Running on batteries	Turn Off Monitor (5 minutes) Turn Off Hard Disks (5 minutes) Standby (5 minutes) Hibernation (2 hours)

Using Alarms

Use the Alarms tab to configure the methods Windows uses to alert you when a low power state is reached. Alarms can display messages, make sounds, put the computer in standby or hibernation, and even run a custom program. The Alarms tab is only available on computers that support APM and for which the APM feature has been enabled.

The following two alarm levels are available:

- The low battery alarm is intended to alert you when the battery starts to get low so that you can take any necessary steps. By default, the low battery alarm is triggered when the battery reaches 10% of its full charge. A text message is displayed, letting you know that the battery is running low.

- The critical battery alarm is intended to let the computer handle the situation itself when the battery gets very low. By default, the critical battery alarm is triggered when the battery reaches 3 percent of its full capacity. A text message is displayed. The computer goes into hibernation mode if hibernation is enabled and into standby mode if hibernation not enabled.

You can control when and if each alarm state is triggered and exactly what happens when the trigger takes place. You can disable either option if you only want one alarm or disable them both if you want no warnings at all. The latter might be the case if your computer comes with its own software to handle low battery situations. For each alarm, drag the slider to set the power percentage that will trigger the alarm. To set what happens when the alarm is reached, click the Alarm Action button for either alarm. Both buttons works the same and bring up a Low Battery Alarm Actions dialog (see Figure C.5).

Tip

If you want to test your alarm settings, just drag the alarm threshold to 100% and unplug the AC power source for your notebook. The alarm should go off immediately.

FIGURE C.5

Setting Alarm Actions.

Windows can notify you when an alarm is triggered by displaying a text message, playing a sound, or both. Use the Alarm Action section to control whether Windows shuts down, enters standby, or hibernates when the alarm is triggered. If you choose one of these actions, you can also tell Windows to force the action even if a program stops responding. Finally, you can tell Windows to run a custom program when the alarm is triggered. When you finish making your alarm selections, click Apply.

Using the Power Meter Settings

The Power Meter tab, shown in Figure C.6, displays your current power source (AC or battery) and the current charge on each battery. You can also click a battery's icon to open a dialog showing the battery's status (online/offline, charging/discharging). The Power Meter tab is only available on computers that support APM and for which the APM feature has been enabled (this feature is described in depth later in this appendix).

Advanced Power Settings

The Advanced Power Settings tab is divided into two sections. The Options section at the top is always present and contains two simple settings, regardless of whether a power icon is shown in the system tray or you need to enter a password when coming out of standby. The Power buttons section is only displayed if your computer supports the ACPI power standard. This section controls what happens when you press the power button and sleep button (if you have one) on your computer. Choices include shutting down, going to standby, and hibernating.

FIGURE C.6

Checking on your remaining power.

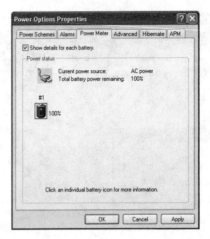

Hibernation

The Hibernate tab contains only one setting: enabled or disabled. This tab is only shown if your computer supports hibernation. The tab also shows how much free disk space you have and how much would be required for your computer to hibernate.

Enabling Advanced Power Management

The APM tab, shown in Figure C.7, is shown only if your computer supports the APM feature. You can use this tab to enable or disable APM. When APM is enabled, many of the following advanced power settings become available to you:

- Different power settings on the Power Schemes tab for when your computer is plugged in or running on battery
- Settings on the Alarms tab
- Settings on the Power Meter tab

Using Hardware Profiles

A hardware profile is a collection of configuration information about the hardware on your computer. Within a profile, each piece of hardware (such as networking adapters, ports, monitors, and so on) can be enabled, disabled, or given specific configuration information. You can have any number of hardware profiles on a computer and switch between different profiles when booting into Windows XP.

To better explain hardware profiles, here is an example of using hardware profiles with a notebook computer. Assume that you use a notebook computer as your main system at work and that you like to unplug it and take it home with you in the evenings.

FIGURE C.7

Enabling APM will further conserve precious power on your mobile system.

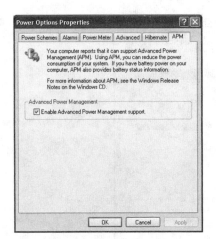

You have two networking cards in your computer. One lets you plug in the networking cable at the office so you can share information with other computers and take advantage of the office's Internet access. The other networking card is a wireless card that lets you communicate with a desktop computer at home (in which you also put a wireless card) and share that computer's Internet connection.

At the office, you connect your notebook computer to an external monitor, keyboard, and mouse. At home, you use the notebook's display, keyboard, and mouse.

Although you could leave all your hardware enabled all the time, you may have noticed that this can cause some conflicts. Your network also seems to run a bit slower when both networking cards are active.

A great solution for this situation is to create two hardware profiles. You could name one At Work and one At Home. For the profile at work, you can leave all the hardware enabled except for the wireless networking card. For the profile at home, you should enable the wireless networking card and disable the other networking card and the external monitor, mouse, and keyboard. Whenever you start your computer, a menu appears that lets you choose which hardware profile to activate. Sounds intriguing? The next several sections show you how to do it.

Creating a Hardware Profile

By default, one profile is created during the installation of Windows XP and is named Profile 1. To create an additional hardware profile, follow these steps:

1. Click Start, Control Panel.
2. Double-click the System icon.

3. Switch to the Hardware tab and click the Hardware Profiles button. This brings up the Hardware Profiles dialog box (see Figure C.8).

FIGURE C.8

Changing Hardware Profile settings will let your laptop adapt to new situations quickly.

4. Interestingly, you cannot just create a new profile. You must copy an existing profile and then modify it. Select Profile 1 by clicking it once and then clicking Copy.

5. The Copy Profile dialog box appears; type in a name for the new profile and then click OK. This returns you to the Hardware Profiles dialog box.

6. Select the new profile and click Properties. This opens a properties dialog for the profile (see Figure C.9).

FIGURE C.9

Setting properties for a hardware profile.

7. If you use a docking station with your notebook computer (and if that docking station is one that Windows XP supports), you should select the This Is a Portable Computer option and then specify whether the profile is to be used when the computer is docked or undocked. When a supported docking station is used, Windows

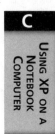

XP can determine whether a notebook computer is docked or undocked and apply the correct profile automatically. If you do not use a docking station (or just prefer to set up and control your own profiles), leave the This Is a Portable Computer option unselected and proceed with the rest of this procedure.

8. Select the Always Include This Profile as an Option When Windows Starts option and click OK. This returns you to the Hardware Profiles dialog box.

9. Select the Profile 1 hardware profile and click Rename.

10. Type in a name for the original profile and then click OK. You might use At Home and At Work (or something equally inspiring).

11. Click OK to return to the System Properties dialog and then click OK again to return to Windows.

Managing Profiles

After you have created a profile, you can manage a couple of things about how Windows XP treats those profiles. All management takes place on the Hardware Profiles dialog box (open Control Panel, double-click the System icon, switch to the Hardware tab, and then click Hardware Profiles), as shown in Figure C.10.

FIGURE C.10

Managing hardware profiles will maximize your laptop's performance.

The first thing you will want to do is tell Windows how to treat hardware profiles during startup. You have the following two options:

• Have Windows wait until you select a hardware profile before it continues booting.

• Have Windows automatically select the first hardware profile on the list and continue booting after a specified amount of time. If you select this option, you can tell Windows how long to wait before going on without you. The default is 30 seconds.

Next, you will want to specify the order of the profiles on the list. This is most important because it is the first profile on the list that Windows will boot if you have set it up to select one automatically. Select any profile on the list and use the up or down buttons on the right to move the profile around.

Setting up Hardware for a Profile

Once you have created your profiles and set Windows up to display and start them the correct way, your next step is to configure hardware settings for each profile. To configure hardware for a profile, you need to start the computer using that profile, return to the Control Panel, and open the System Properties again. On the Hardware tab, click Device Manager (see Figure C.11).

FIGURE C.11

Managing hardware with Device Manager.

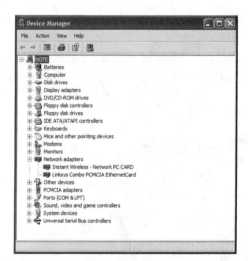

You learned to use Device Manager in Chapter 14, "Using the Control Panel," but here is a brief recap. Device Manager organizes hardware into a tree according to type: modems, monitors, network adapters, and so on. Within each category, you will find the actual hardware devices listed. Double-click on any device to open a properties dialog. Figure C.12 shows the properties for a network adapter card. The Device Usage drop-down list offers these options:

- Use this device (enable)
- Do not use this device in the current hardware profile (disable)
- Do not use this device in any hardware profiles (disable)

The only tricky part here is that you must remember what profile you are currently using, since the device properties dialog does not tell you. You can always switch back to the

System Properties dialog and open the Hardware Profiles window to find out your current profile, though.

FIGURE C.12

Setting properties for a device.

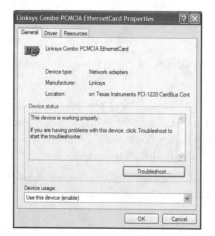

Selecting a Profile on Startup

After you have your hardware profiles created and configured, using them is the easiest part. Whenever you start your computer, you are presented with a menu early in the boot process that looks like the one in Figure C.13.

FIGURE C.13

Choosing a hardware profile on startup.

If you don't select anything within 30 seconds, the first profile on the list is selected for you. If you configured your startup menu not to start any profile automatically (described previously), you won't see the timer at the bottom of the screen. Use the arrow keys to select a profile and press Enter to start the computer.

Synchronization and Offline Files

Offline Files is a technology designed for those who take their computer away from the network or who dial into a network periodically with a modem, but don't want to stay connected all the time.

With Windows XP, you can make the following two types of files available while you are offline:

- Shared Folders— The contents of these folders are copied to a temporary location on the hard drive on your notebook computer. When you disconnect from the network, you can work on the temporary copy of these files. When you reconnect to the network, the files are synchronized with the originals.

- Web Pages—Web pages and any graphics they contain are copied to a temporary location on your computer when you disconnect, so they are available for browsing while you are offline.

Setting up Offline Files

You can set any shared folder on a network to be available offline. To set up an offline folder, follow these steps:

1. Browse to the shared folder using My Network Places or any other method you commonly use to access shared folders on your network.

2. Right-click the folder and select the Make Available Offline command. This opens the Confirm Offline Subfolders dialog box.

3. Choose whether you want to make only the selected folder and the files inside it available offline or whether you also want to make all the subfolders of the selected folder available offline too.

4. Click OK; the icon for the folder is overlaid with two blue arrows to let you know that it is now an offline folder, as shown in Figure C.14.

Setting up Offline Web Access

Offline access to Web pages is configured in Internet Explorer. To make a Web page available offline, follow these steps:

1. Use Internet Explorer to browse to the page you want to make available.

2. From the Favorites menu, choose Add to Favorites.

3. Select the Make Available Offline option.

4. Click Customize. This opens the Offline Favorite Wizard.

5. If you see a welcome page to the wizard, click Next to go past it.

FIGURE C.14

Offline folders' icons are marked with a small overlay.

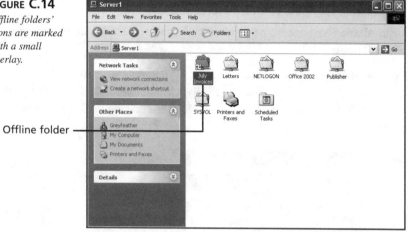

Offline folder

6. To make the pages available to which the page links, select the Yes option and then select the depth of links you want to make available. If you select a link depth of one, each page that the current page links to is made available. If you select a link depth of two, each page those pages link to is also made available. When you finish, click Next.

Caution

Be careful with adding depths of links for browsing offline. For each level to which you increase the link depth, you increase the number of pages to be made available exponentially.

7. Choose whether you want to synchronize the pages (download the most current versions) manually or set up a schedule for automatic synchronization. If you choose to synchronize manually (using the Only When I Choose Synchronize from the Tools Menu option), you will not see the wizard page in Step 8.

8. Configure a schedule for synchronizing these pages. Choose the frequency in days and the time of day for the synchronization. You can also specify for the computer to connect to the Internet to synchronize if it is not already connected.

9. If any of the pages that you are making available offline require a username and password for access, you can enter that information now. This enables Windows to synchronize the pages without prompting you for the information.

10. Click Finish. Windows synchronizes the pages immediately and then returns you to Internet Explorer.

Using Synchronization Manager

You use Synchronization Manager to perform manual synchronization and to configure automatic synchronization.

Start Synchronization Manager by choosing Start, All Programs, Accessories, Synchronize. You can also start it by selecting the Synchronize command from the Tools menu of any open folder in Windows. The Items to Synchronize dialog box shown in Figure C.15 opens.

FIGURE C.15

Use Synchronization Manager to synchronize files manually or automatically.

To start synchronization of any files and Web pages currently set up to be available offline, just check the specific items to synchronize (all are selected by default) and then click the Synchronize button. Windows closes Synchronization Manager, synchronizes the selected items, and informs you when the synchronization is complete.

You also use Synchronization Manager to configure automatic synchronization of files and Web pages. To do this, click the Setup button on the Items to Synchronize dialog box (refer to Figure C.15). This opens the Synchronization Settings dialog box shown in Figure C.16.

The following list indicates three ways to schedule automatic synchronization; each is represented by a tab on the Synchronization Settings dialog box:

- Use the Logon/Logoff tab to configure automatic synchronization when logging on or off Windows. For each connection, you can specify the offline files that should be synchronized. For example, you might want to synchronize Web pages when using the networking connection at work and at home but only synchronize the other offline files when at work. You can also specify whether files should be synchronized when logging on, logging off, or both. Finally, you can tell Windows whether or not to ask you before performing the synchronization.

FIGURE C.16

Configuring synchronization settings.

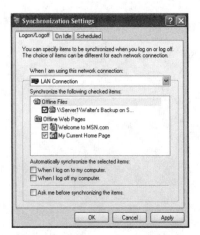

- Use the On Idle tab to configure whether offline files are synchronized during your computer's idle time. You can configure different settings for different network connections, select which offline files to synchronize, and even control how long a period of inactivity must occur before synchronization occurs.

- Use the Schedules tab to set up regularly scheduled synchronization. Click the Add button on the tab to have a wizard walk you through setting up synchronization on a daily or weekly schedule. You can even set up multiple scheduled synchronizations, which lets you schedule different files and Web pages to be updated at different times. For example, you might want offline files to be updated once per day, some Web pages to be updated once per week, and others to be updated once per month. In this situation, you could set up three scheduled synchronization events.

Summary

As you can see, the designers of Windows XP gave a good bit of consideration to users of notebook computers. Windows XP provides a number of features to the mobile user, including APM, ClearType display, hardware profiles, and offline files. These features and the general usefulness of Windows XP solidify its reputation as the best operating system to use on notebook computers.

Basics of Internet Information Server

IN THIS APPENDIX

- What's New in IIS 5.1? *835*
- Installing IIS *835*
- Creating a Web Site *836*
- Managing a Web Site *837*
- Managing an FTP Server *843*
- Managing the SMTP Service *847*

APPENDIX D

Internet access, particularly the Web, has become ubiquitous in the past several years—at work, at home, and even on the road.

Whenever you point your browser to a Web address, the browser retrieves the proper page from a Web server and displays it for you. Web servers run software that allows them to store, retrieve, and even modify all the pages and graphics that make up a Web site. Internet Information Server (IIS) is Web server software that comes with Windows XP Professional.

IIS provides a number of powerful features, including the following:

- Web Server—The main claim to fame of IIS is as a world-class Web server. It complies completely with the HTTP 1.1 standard and supports advanced features such as Active Server Pages, common gateway interface (CGI), Internet server application programming interface (ISAPI), and FrontPage server extensions.

> **Note**
>
> HyperText Transfer Protocol (HTTP) is the stateless `protocol` used by Web servers on the Internet. It defines how messages are formatted and transmitted, and what actions `Web servers` and `browsers` should take in response to various commands.
>
> Most Web clients and servers currently support HTTP 1.1, which in turn supports persistent connections. An example of a persistent connection would be when a browser client connected to a Web server, it could receive multiple files through the same connection.

- FTP Server—File transfer protocol (FTP) is used to transfer files over a TCP/IP network, such as the Internet. Files are transferred between an FTP client and an FTP server. IIS 5.1 provides a robust and completely configurable FTP Server.

- SMTP Server—Simple mail transfer protocol (SMTP) is a transfer call protocol/Internet protocol (TCP/IP) used to send e-mail messages between computers. IIS 5.1 provides a basic SMTP service that you can use to set up Intranet mail services.

In this appendix, you will learn the new features in IIS 5.1, how to install IIS, and how to manage a basic Web site, FTP site, and SMTP server.

What's New in IIS 5.1?

IIS 5.1 is the latest incarnation of Internet Information Server. IIS 5.1 ships with Windows XP. It is only a small upgrade over the IIS 5.0 version that came with Windows 2000, but it does offer a few new features.

New features in IIS 5.1 include the following:

- Advanced Digest Authentication—Digest authentication was introduced in IIS 5.0 and is a secure way to authenticate users across proxy servers and firewalls. IIS 5.1 provides a more secure and reliable version of digest authentication.

- Metabase Changes—The Metabase is a registry-like database of configuration settings for IIS. IIS 5.1 provides several enhancements to Metabase management. You can now restore the Metabase from backup to other computers on the network. IIS 5.1 also includes the Metabase Snapshot Writer, which uses the Component Object Model (COM) to ensure that Windows Backup creates a stable and reliable backup of the Metabase.

- Active Server Pages Template Caching—Active Server Pages (ASP) provide a way to deliver dynamic content to Web browsers. Now, changes to ASP Template Cache tuning provide enhanced control over the caching of ASP files on a server.

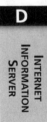

D

INTERNET INFORMATION SERVER

Installing IIS

Although IIS is included with Windows XP, it is not installed by default unless you upgrade a computer already using IIS. Fortunately, it is pretty easy to install.

To install IIS 5.1 on Windows XP, follow these steps:

1. Click Start, Control Panel.

2. In the Control Panel window, click the Add or Remove Programs icon. If your Control Panel window is in classic view (where all the Control Panel icons are shown in a single window), double-click the Add/Remove Programs icon instead.

3. On the Add or Remove Programs dialog box, click Add/Remove Windows Components. This opens the Windows Components Wizard (see Figure D.1).

4. Place a check next to the Internet Information Services (IIS) option.

5. If you want to include the FTP service in your installation (it is not included by default), select IIS option and click the Details button. Select the FTP Service option from the dialog box that opens and then click OK.

Figure D.1

Installing Internet Information Server.

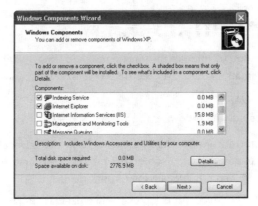

6. Click Next to go on. Windows XP copies the IIS files to your hard disk. Windows may ask for your installation CD now if it needs to copy files from there.

7. Windows informs you when the installation is finished. Click Finish to return to Windows. You are not required to restart your computer after the installation, but it would probably be a good idea to do so anyway.

You can also use this same procedure to add or remove specific components of IIS (or even remove the program altogether) if you have upgraded a computer that was already running IIS.

Note

When you remove IIS from Windows XP, the program files are removed and registry entries are cleaned out, but any Web pages you have created remain. This makes it easy to save a Web site and even use it with other Web server software.

Creating a Web Site

When you install IIS, a default Web site is created for you and is ready for you to start building Web pages right after installation. You can use any tool you feel comfortable with, including Microsoft FrontPage, Office 2000 or XP, or just good old Notepad.

By default, the folder for your Web site is C:/Inetpub/wwwroot, and you can start creating Web pages right in this folder. Just name your home page Default.htm or Default.asp, and when someone browses to your site, that page loads automatically.

Until you create your own home page, visitors to the site will get an Under Construction page.

You can open your site in a browser from your computer or from any computer connected to your local network by entering the address `http://[computername]` or `http://[IP_address]`.

If you want people on the Internet to be able to visit your site, then they will have to connect using an IP address or you will have to register a domain name that points to your IP address.

Managing a Web Site

Once you have installed IIS and regardless of whether you have created your Web site yet, all management takes place using a single tool—the Internet Services Manager (ISM).

ISM is a management console that allows you to administer IIS services. You can open ISM using the following procedure:

1. Click Start, Control Panel.
2. If your Control Panel window is not already in classic view, click the Switch to Classic View link at the left of the window.
3. Double-click Administrative Tools.
4. Double-click Internet Information Services.

D

INTERNET
INFORMATION
SERVER

> **Tip**
>
> If you find this method a bit of a pain to use on a regular basis, you could also add a shortcut to your Start menu that points to `%SystemRoot%\System32\inetsrv\inetmgr.exe`.

The main ISM window is shown in Figure D.2. Notice that it uses a typical hierarchical view arranged first by computer and then by the types of sites available on that computer (Web, FTP, and SMTP).

The default Web site created during IIS installation is simply named Default Web Site. You can rename this site by right-clicking it and choosing Rename from the shortcut menu. An expanded view of this site is shown in Figure D.3. Under the Default Web Site object, each of the folders configured for the site is displayed (these are all the folders in the `C:\Inetpub\wwwroot folder`).

FIGURE D.2

Exploring the IIS interface.

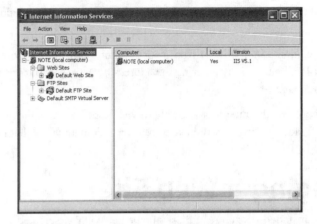

FIGURE D.3

The default Web site.

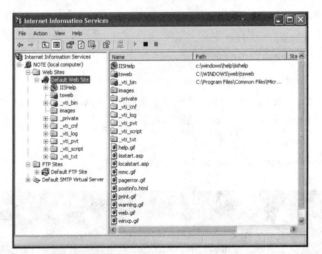

Note

In Windows XP, you are only allowed to have one Web site. If you need to host more than one Web site on a single computer, you must use Windows .NET Server instead.

As elsewhere in Windows XP, most of the management of IIS happens using property pages. To manage a Web site, right-click the site and choose the Properties command. The most important tabs available on the Web site properties are discussed over the next several sections.

> **Note**
>
> You can also manage the folders within a Web site by opening their property pages. The tabs available for an individual folder are a subset of those available for the Web site itself and do work the same way, except that settings made on a folder in a site override the same general settings made for the site. This appendix focuses on the management of the Web site, but the principles are the same for individual folders.

Web Site Properties

The Web Site tab, shown in Figure D.4, is used for the following three purposes:

- Web Site Identification—Use this section of the tab to name the Web site (use the Description field), configure an IP address for the site if it is different from the computer's main IP address, and set the TCP port used to connect to the site. Unless you have special requirements, you should leave the TCP port set to 80, which is the default used by all Web browsers.

- Connections—Use this section of the tab to specify the time in seconds that a connection may remain idle before the Web server terminates it. The HTTP Keep-Alives option lets Web browsers maintain open connections with your server rather than asking you to reopen a new connection with each request. You should leave this option enabled to help increase server performance.

- Enable Logging—Use this section to have IIS keep a log of connections to your Web server and choose the format of those logs. Formats include WC3 Extended Log File Format (the default); Microsoft IIS Log File Format; and NCSA Common Log File Format. The Properties button opens a separate dialog for configuring the period a log file should cover, the naming convention for the file, and a number of extended options you may include in the log.

Home Directory

A home directory is the root directory of a Web site. By default, the Default Web Site uses the home directory `c:\Inetpub\wwwroot`, which is a directory located on the local computer. You can change this directory to any other directory on the computer by entering the path in the Local Path field (see Figure D.5). You can also make the home directory for your site point to a shared folder on another computer on the network or even point to another URL (if you wanted to redirect client requests to your Web site from another one).

FIGURE D.4

Managing Web site properties.

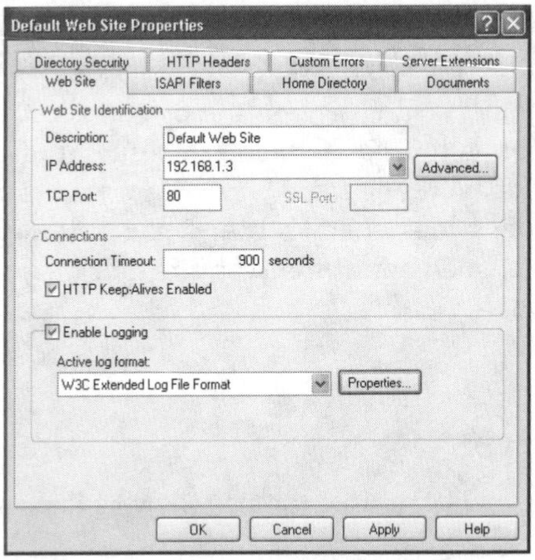

FIGURE D.5

Setting up a home directory.

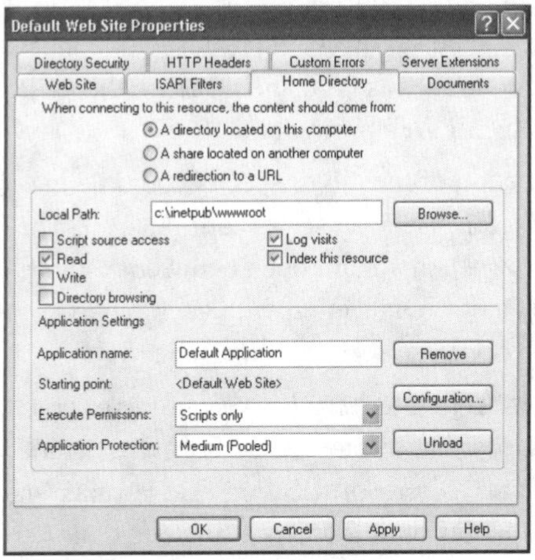

If you choose a local or shared directory, you can set detailed access permissions on the directory. These permissions include the following:

- Script Source Access—Allows a user to access source code for script in an ASP application.

- Read—Allows a user to access a Web page in the directory. Since this permission is required for basic Web access, the Read permission is enabled by default.

- Write—Allows a user to upload files to a directory and change content in existing files. This permission is required for anyone who will help author and publish the Web site.

- Directory Browsing—Allows a Web browser to display a DOS-like listing of files in the directory if a default Web page cannot be found.

- Log Visits—Records visits to the directory in the log file, if logging is enabled. See the section on the Web Site tab for information on enabling logging.

- Index This Resource—Allows Microsoft Indexing Service to include the directory when indexing a Web site.

In addition to setting permissions on a directory, you can also configure how Web-based applications are treated in the home directory, including what permissions and protection the application is given.

Documents

The Documents tab, shown in Figure D.6, is used for two purposes. The first is to configure the names of the default documents for the Web site. A default document is one that loads automatically when no other document is specified in a browser. For example, if you typed `http://www.microsoft.com/windows` and did not include the name of a specific file on the end of the URL, the default document in the windows directory would be loaded. Four default document names are already configured: `Default.htm`, `Default.asp`, `index.htm`, and `iisstart.asp`. These documents are used in the order shown on the list. For example, if both a `Default.htm` and a `Default.asp` document exist in a folder, the `Default.htm` document is used. Add a default document name by clicking Add and typing in the name of the document. Order the documents on the list using the up and down buttons to the left.

FIGURE D.6

Setting up the Documents tab.

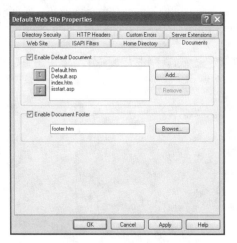

The other use for the Documents tab is to enable a footer document to be included on all pages delivered from the Web site. The footer document should be a standard Web page and is included at the bottom of each page of the site when the page is displayed in a browser.

Directory Security

The Directory Security tab, shown in Figure D.7, offers three different security configurations:

- Anonymous Access and Authentication Control—The Edit button in this section brings up a separate dialog box that lets you configure two things. The first is whether anonymous access is allowed to your site—something you will want enabled if Internet users will have access or if you don't want to limit access even in your own network. The second thing you can configure is what type of authentication is required for users who are not anonymous. Authentication methods include Basic, an unsecured method where a username and password is sent in clear text; Digest, which allows secure authentication using HTTP; and Integrated Windows authentication, which uses Kerberos V5 domain security.

- IP Address and Domain Name Restrictions—Unfortunately, this section is only available in Windows 2000 or 2002 Server. When active, the Edit button in this section opens a separate dialog that lets you grant or deny access to the Web site based on IP addresses or Internet domain names. For example, you could restrict a particular subnet in your company from accessing your site based on their IP address or you could prevent access by anyone with aol.com as part of their domain name.

- Secure Communications—This section lets you require certificates from users trying to access your Web site. Clicking Server Certificate starts a wizard that you can use to obtain a certificate from a certification authority on your network.

FIGURE D.7

Configuring directory security.

HTTP Headers

HTTP headers are special codes placed on all the Web pages in a site. These headers are not viewed by a typical browser but instead are used in the management of pages on a site. The HTTP Headers tab, shown in Figure D.8, is used for four types of configuration:

- Content Expiration—Removes pages or entire folders from a site automatically on a certain date or after a specified period

- Custom HTTP Headers—A special code you add to the pages in your site.

- Content Rating—Allows you to apply ratings to your site that are compatible with major content verification services.

- Mime Mapping—Allows you to associate certain types of files with certain applications so that the correct program is used when a file on your site is accessed.

FIGURE D.8

Configuring HTTP Headers.

Custom Errors

The Custom Errors tab, shown in Figure D.9, lets you configure customized error messages for communicating with visitors to your site. For example, instead of the typical error message, "404 HTTP Error," you could create a custom message that said something like "We're sorry, but we could not find that page on our server."

Managing an FTP Server

Web servers can be used to transfer files, but many people still prefer the ease and reliability of transferring files using File Transfer Protocol (FTP). The FTP service built into Windows XP is fully featured and, like the Web server, you will manage it using ISM.

FIGURE D.9

*Configuring cus-
tom errors.*

Compared to the management of a Web site, the management of the FTP site is pretty simple. Figure D.10 shows ISM with the Default FTP site selected.

To manage the FTP site, right-click it and choose Properties from the shortcut menu. The property pages involved in managing the FTP site are discussed in the next few sections.

FIGURE D.10

*The default FTP
site in ISM.*

FTP Site Properties

The FTP Site tab, shown in Figure D.11, lets you configure many basic settings for your FTP site. These settings include the following:

- Identification—Use this section to name the FTP site, configure an IP address for the site if it is different from the computer's main IP address, and set the TCP port used to connect to the site. Unless you have special requirements, you should leave the TCP port set to 21, which is the default used by all FTP clients.

- Connections—Use this section of the tab to limit the number of simultaneous connections your site will support (the maximum limit is 10 connections in Windows XP anyway) and to specify the time in seconds that a connection may remain idle before the Web server terminates it.

- Enable Logging—Use this section to have IIS keep a log of connections to your FTP site and choose the format of those logs. Formats include WC3 Extended Log File Format (the default) and Microsoft IIS Log File Format. The Properties button opens a separate dialog for configuring the period a log file should cover, the naming convention for the file, and a number of extended options you may include in the log.

- Current Sessions—This button opens a dialog that shows all users currently connected to your FTP site.

FIGURE D.11

Managing FTP Site properties.

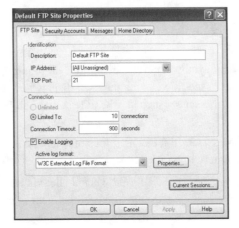

Security Accounts

Use the Security Accounts tab, shown in Figure D.12, to specify whether anonymous connections are allowed and to configure FTP site operators. If you do allow anonymous connections, you must select a specific Windows account that is used for anonymous connections. You can then configure permissions for this account on your FTP folders to provide security for your site. Use the FTP operator's section of the tab to assign Windows user accounts that are able to administer your FTP site.

FIGURE D.12

Configuring Security Accounts.

Messages

The messages tab, shown in Figure D.13, lets you configure four different messages that are displayed automatically to FTP clients at different times. These messages include the following:

- Banner—A special message displayed whenever an anonymous user logs into your site.

- Welcome—A message displayed whenever a client logs on to the FTP server. This message is commonly used to welcome the user, display any rules for using the server, and show alert messages (such as when the server will be down for maintenance).

- Exit—A message displayed every time a client logs off the FTP server. This is a short message intended simply to let users know they have successfully logged off.

- Maximum Connections—A message displayed when a client is refused a connection to an FTP server because the maximum allowable number of connections had already been made. This is also a short message.

Home Directory

A home directory is the root directory of an FTP site, as shown in Figure D.14. By default, the Default FTP Site uses the home directory `c:\Inetpub\ftproot`, which is a directory located on the local computer. You can change this directory to any other directory on the computer by entering the path in the Local Path field. You can also make the home directory for your site point to a shared folder on another computer on the network. The Home Directory tab also lets you choose how file lists are displayed to clients (UNIX-style or MS-DOS-style).

FIGURE D.13

*Setting up
Messages.*

FIGURE D.14

*Configuring
the FTP home
directory.*

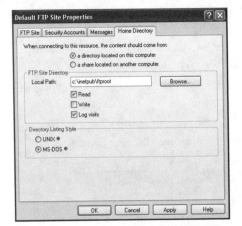

Managing the SMTP Service

SMTP is an Internet protocol used for sending messages to another computer, usually to a mail server. IIS provides a simple SMTP service that is primarily intended to be used in conjunction with your Web site. There are certain Web functions (such as submitting a form via email) that need SMTP in order to work. For example, a visitor to your site might fill out a form intended to be mailed to you. IIS would need to use SMTP to mail that form. In addition to being used by your Web site, you can also use the SMTP server to send mail from your e-mail clients (through Outlook Express, for example) to your Internet service provider's (ISP's) mail server. However, since your ISP almost certainly provides its own SMTP server, there is usually no reason for this.

As with the Web and FTP sites, the SMTP site is managed using property pages. Just right-click the Default SMTP Virtual Server in ISM and choose Properties to get started. The more important tabs are covered in the next few sections.

General Properties

The General tab is used to set the IP address for the site, the maximum number of connections allowed, a connection time-out value, and logging. This tab works just the same as the Web Site and FTP Site tabs discussed previously.

Access

The Access Control tab, shown in Figure D.15, is used to restrict access to the SMTP server. The sections on this tab include the following:

- Authentication—Use this section to specify whether anonymous access is allowed and to set authentication methods.

- Secure Communications—Use this section to require a security certificate from users that access the SMTP server

- Connection Control—Use this section to restrict the IP addresses or domain names allowed to use the SMTP server.

- Relay Restrictions—Use this section to set up a list of computers that are able to use the SMTP server to relay messages to other servers.

FIGURE D.15

Configuring SMTP access.

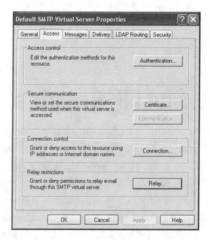

Messages

The Messages tab, shown in Figure D.16, is used to set up restrictions on messages delivered through the SMTP server. You can use this tab to limit the size of messages that may be delivered; the size of sessions (in which multiple messages may be delivered); the number of messages per connection; and the number of recipients allowed per message.

FIGURE D.16

Configuring SMTP message restrictions.

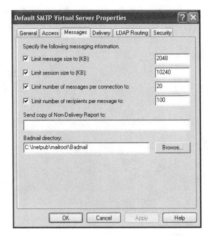

Delivery

The Delivery tab is used to control the advanced settings that govern connections to other SMTP servers and what the SMTP server should do with undeliverable mail.

Security

The Security tab is used to set up Windows user accounts that are allowed to manage the SMTP server.

Summary

Windows XP comes with one of the most powerful Web servers available, the Internet Information Server 5.1. With its standards-based design and support for advanced features, IIS provides users of Windows XP with a robust, easy-to-manage Web server right out of the box. IIS also includes an FTP server and SMTP server that feature the same ease of management as the Web server.

INDEX

>> on menu bar, 230
64-bit versions of XP, 12
   Intel Itanium processor, 13
32-bit virtual addressing,
   15–16
30-day grace period for activation, 79
10BaseT cabling, 627

A

abstraction layer, code, 11
Accessibility Options, 65, 355
   FilterKeys, 109–110
   High Contrast, 112–113
   MouseKeys, 113–114
   SerialKeys, 115–116
   ShowSounds, 111–112
   SoundSentry, 111–112
   StickyKeys, 107
   ToggleKeys, 110
Accessibility Wizard,
   104–105, 116–117
Accessories
   Calculator, 180–182
   Entertainment, 174–176
   handwriting recognition,
      124–125
   Magnifier, 119–120
   Narrator, 118–119
   Notepad, 182–183
   On-Screen keyboard, 121–122
   speech recognition, 123–124
   Utility Manager, 122–123
   Wordpad, 183–187
Accessories folder, 170
Account Lockout, 377–378
Account Policies, MMC,
   375–376
accounts. *See also* user
   accounts
   Active Directory, 686–687
   Outlook Express, 232–235,
      263–268

ACK flag, TCP, 779
acknowledgment number,
   TCP, 779
ACLS (access control lists),
   449
ACPI (Advanced
   Configuration and Power
   Interface), 814
action properties,
   Performance Logs and
   Alerts tool, 584
activation, 78–79
   grace period, 79
Active Directory Network,
   file sharing, 219–222
Active Server Pages, 834
   Template Caching, 835
AD (Active Directory), 680,
   798, 806–808
   accounts, 686–687
   domains, 30
   objects, 800–801
      classes, 685
      locating, 808–811
   overview, 684–687
   root object, 800
   schemas, 802
   searching, 692
   Top Abstract Class, 800
AD Users and Computers
   tool, 808
adapter cards
   Ethernet, 626–627
   graphics, 24
   tape drives, 46
Add Hardware Wizard,
   650–652
Add Printer Wizard, 422, 423,
   424–425
Add/Remove Programs, 42,
   286–290, 345
   network components, 620–622
   performance and, 555–558

address book, Outlook
   Express, 253–254
   contacts, adding, 255–257
   entering information manually,
      254
   folders, creating, 254
   groups, 257–258
   printing from, 259
addresses
   IP addresses, 619, 763–776
   virtual memory, 14
Administrative Templates,
   Group Policies, 374,
   379–380
Administrative Tools, 399
   Local Security Policy, 373,
      380
   Performance and Maintenance
      and, 349
   System Monitor and, 567
administrator password, 76
Administrators group, 385
ADSL (asynchronous DSL),
   645
Advanced Appearance Dialog
   box, 154
Advanced Digest
   Authentication, IIS, 835
Advanced Options, setup,
   64–65
Advanced TCP/IP settings,
   633–638
AGP (accelerated graphics
   port)
   AGP bus, 551
   video adapter, 551
Airbrush tool, Paint, 189
alarms, power management,
   820–821
alerts, Performance Logs and
   Alerts tool, 582–585
All Programs option, Start
   menu, 161
Allocation Unit Size, 453–454
Alt+Tab, switching between
   applications, 301

always-on connections, pros/cons, 648–649
AnandTech Web site, 27
API (applications programming interface), 21
  application limitations and, 272
APIPA (automatic private IP addressing), 619–620
APM (Advanced Power Management), 816–822
Appearance, 152–153
  color, 155
  fonts, 153–154
  hotkeys, 154
  large icons, 154
  monitor display settings, 154
  screen resolution, 154
  shadow effects, 154
Appearance and Themes, Control Panel, 331–332
  See Also menu, 338–344
  file types, properties, 335–337
  folders, 333
  fonts, 339–340
  graphics, pointers, 343
  hardware, 343
  mouse buttons, 342
  mouse pointers, 341–342
  Offline Files, 337–338
  pointers, 343
  properties, 333
    viewing, 333–335
  Troubleshooters, 344
  wheel mouse, 343
AppEvents key, HKEY_CURRENT_USER, 503
AppHelp.sdb file, 275
applets, 330
  Local Computer Security, 398
  Local Security Policy, 373
  Sounds and Audio Devices, 346
Application Compatibility Mode subsystem, 11, 29

Application Compatibility Toolkit, 278–279
Application log, 138, 403–404
application management, Task Manager, 484–488
Application Verifier Tool, 279
applications
  compatibility, pilot program and, 28
  configurations, saving prior to installation, 43–44
  events, Registry key, 503
  installation, 282–283
    Autorun CD, 286
    DLLs, 283–286
    side-by-side sharing, 284–285
    system restore points, 283
  killing, Task Manager, 485
  limitations, 272–273
  removing, 42, 555–558
  switching between, 301
  switching to, Task Manager, 485–486
architecture
  kernel mode, 9–10
  layered architecture, 10
  user mode, 10
archived files
  formats, 413
  log files, 416–418
  System Restore, 610
area codes, modems, 662–663
ARP (address resolution protocol), 784
Arrange Icons By, Windows Explorer, 201–202
ASR (Automated System Recovery), 541–542
  Automated System Recovery Wizard, 590–594
  disk, 590–593
  installations and, 282
  restoring system, 593–594

associations, files, 198–199
asynchronous DSL, 645
ATM (asynchronous transfer mode), 645–646
attachments to e-mail, 238
attenuation, DSL and, 646
Attributes tool, Paint, 190
audio. *See also* **sound**
  devices, 347
  digital audio, 740–741
  DVD, troubleshooters, 348
  hardware, 347
audio CDs
  burning, 212–214, 701–702
    filenames, 751
  CD-DA, 702
  legal issues, 732
  Media Player, 731, 739–741
  Napster, 732
  volume, 346
autoexec.bat file, 499
automated installation, unattend.txt file, 85–97
Automated System Recovery Wizard, 522, 529, 590–594
Automatic Updates, System applet, 350
Autorun CD, 286
AutoSense, Ethernet cards, 627
availability time, printers, 434

B

background, Desktop, 144–145
Background Options, 144
Backup Job Information dialog box, 533–534
Backup Log, custom, 536
Backup Operators group, 385
Backup Wizard, 509–511, 529–532

backups, 522
to another location, 522
ASR, 542
CD-ROMs, 48
CD-Rs, 523
CD-RWs, 523
command line, 543–544
copy, 527
daily, 527
default file locations, 525–526
differential, 527
Disk Cleanup and, 554–555
floppy disks, 47, 523
full plus differential, 528
full plus incremental, 527–528
hardware, 522–524
housekeeping tasks and, 554–555
incremental, 527
installation preparation and, 45
Jaz drives, 47–48
length of availability, 528
manual, 532–533
    advanced options, 534–535
    Backup Job Information dialog box, 533–534
    excluding files, 536
    selecting components, 533
    types, setting default, 536
normal, 527
partitions and, 69, 590–593
Performance and Maintenance, 349
plan development, 524–529
Registry, 508–509, 509–511
removable hard drives, 524
removable media, 529
restore points, 608
restoring files, 522, 537
    manually, 540–541
    Restore Wizard, 538–540
tape drives, 45–47, 523
upgrades and, 588–589
what to back up, 524–526
Zip drives, 47–48

bandwidth, DSL, 645
baseline, performance (System Monitor), 578
basic disks, 444
dynamic disks, converting between, 455–457
batch files, Command Prompt, 319–321
baud rate, 116
BDC (backup domain controller), 30
domains and, 681–682
bi-directional printing, 423
binary addresses, converting to decimal, 768–770
binary files, log files, 581
BIOS (Basic Input Output System), 128–129
bit depth, digital audio, 740–741
bit rate, digital audio, 740–741
blind carbon copies (bcc), e-mail, 237
blind users. *See* **Accessibility Options**
blocking messages in Outlook Express, 252–253
.bmp files, icons, 370
boot partition, system partition and, 69
booting
advanced options, 139–140
boot logging, enabling, 136
CD boot, 599
computer, overview, 128–129
kernel, 131
recovery and, 593–594
Safe Mode, 596–598
Windows, overview, 129–135
from Windows XP CD, 61
Boot.ini file, 36–37
partition selection, 67
Windows boot up, 132–135

breaking applications, reasons for, 272–273
broadband connections
ADSL (asynchronous DSL), 645
ATM (asynchronous transfer mode), 645–646
cable modems, 644–645, 647–648
CAP (carrier amplitude phase), 646
DSL (digital subscriber line), 645–647
DSL modems, 644–645
DSLAM (DSL access multiplexer), 645
PPPoE (point-to-point over Ethernet), 649
pros/cons of always-on connections, 648–649
Browser and Shell Settings screen, Setup Manager Wizard, 93
Brush tool, Paint, 189
buffer size, Command Prompt, 302–303
bugs, shared files and, 284
built-in groups, 385–386
burning CDs, 212–213, 701–703
filenames, 751
Media Player, 731
movies, 726–728
staging area, 213
business cards, Outlook Express, 246

C

cable modems, 619, 644–645, 647–648
always on pros/cons, 648–649
speed, DSL comparison, 648

cabling, networks, 627

Calculator, 170, 180–182

Call Waiting, modems, 662

calling cards, modems, 663

cameras, installation, 708–710

    flash card readers, 710–711

    third-party software, 711–712

canceling printing, 440–441

CAP (carrier amplitude phase), 646

capacity, tape drives, 46

Category View, 330–331

    Appearance and Themes, 331–344

CBS Sportcenter Baseball Live, 148

CD-DA (Digital Audio), 702

CD-ROMs

    as backups, 48

    booting from, 599

    booting from Windows XP CD, 61

    burning, 212–213, 701–703

    NTI CD-Maker 2000 Professional, 289

CD-Rs as backups, 522, 523

CD-RWs as backups, 522, 523

CD Writing Wizard, 214

centering background, 145

CGI (common gateway interface), 834

Change permission, file sharing, 222

Character Map, 170, 177–178

checklist prior to installation, 51

checksum, TCP, 779

child processes, 488

circular binary files, log files, 581

Class A addresses, IP, 771–772

Class B addresses, IP, 772

Class C addresses, IP, 773

class definition keys, Registry, 502

Classic theme, 157

Classic View, 330–331

    Control Panel, 105

Classic Windows theme, 143

clean install, 54

CleanSweep, 42

cleanup, 42–43

Clear Image tool, Paint, 190

ClearType, 153, 814–816

click speed, mouse, 342

ClickLock, mouse, 342

Client Service for NetWare, 638

clips, Movie Maker

    adding, 720

    combining, 723

    cutting/pasting, 721

    editing, 721–723

    removing, 720–721

    splitting, 723

cloning installations, Sysprep and, 99

CMD.EXE file, 299

code abstraction layer, 10

codec (compression), 740

Collections area, Movie Maker, 713, 714

color, 155

    Command Prompt, 303–304

    Magnifier and, 120

    Paint, 188–190

COM (Component Object Model)

    objects, Registry, 502

command buffers, configuration, 300–301

Command History, Command Prompt and, 300–301

Command Prompt, 298

    Backup, 543–544

    batch files, 319–321

    colors, 303–304

    commands, 304, 307–310

configuration, 299–300

    buffer size, 302–303

    command buffers, 300–301

    display options, 300–301

    edit options, 300–301

    location layout, 302–303

    window size, 302–303

CONVERT command, 459

converting partitions from FAT to NTFS, 459–461

disk formatting, 467–469

disk management, 459

DISKPART command, 461–464

filters, 316–317

fonts, 301–302

Help command, 310–311

I/O (input/output) streams, 315

input, 314–316

NET command, 312–314

output, 314–316

overview, 298–299

performance monitoring tools, 585–586

pipes, 316–317

popup background, 304

popup text, 304

redirector commands, 314–316

running applications, 286

Safe Mode with Command Prompt, 136

screen background, 303–304

screen text, 303–304

wildcards, 317–319

Windows Scripting Host, 320–321

COMMAND.COM file, 299

commands

    Command Prompt, 304–319

    network commands, 325–326

    obsolete, 305–307

    Recovery Console, 601–602

compacting messages,
Outlook Express, 251
compatibility
AppHelp.sdb file, 275
applications, pilot program
and, 28
printers, 435–436
SysMain.sdb file, 276
tape drives, 46
Compatibility Administration
Tool, 278–279
compatibility modes,
276–277
components, removing, 43,
290–291
Components, System
Information, 179
compression
files/folders, 202–203
New Partition Wizard, 454
NTFS, 449
zipping, 203–204
modems, 657–658
computer, boot process,
128–129
computer accounts, Active
Directory, 686–687
Computer Administrator
account, 363
compared to Limited, 364
Computer Management
utility, 479–480
computer name, 76
Computer Name, System
applet, 350
config.sys file, 499
configuration
applications, saving prior to
installation, 43–44
Command Prompt, 299–304
drivers, 66
finishing, 79
folder options, 206–209
hardware, saving prior to
installation, 44–45

Internet connection account,
664–667
last known good configuration, 137
NetBIOS, 637
network adapter cards,
625–630
networks, manual, 77
static Internet protocol address
information, 632–638
TCP/IP, 622–632
user settings, 378–379
Conflicting devices, 629–630
Connection Wizard, 232
connectionless sessions, 764
connections
HyperTerminal, 173
Outlook Express properties,
250–251
Console key, HKEY_
CURRENT_USER, 503
contact groups, address book
(Outlook Express), 258
Contacts, Outlook Express,
230
container objects, LDAP, 801
contention slots, cable
modems, 647
context switching, 20
Control Panel, 104–105
Accessibility Options, 355
Accessibility options,
105–107
Add/Remove Programs,
286–290, 345
Administrative Templates, 379
Appearance and Themes,
331–344
Classic View, 105
Date, Time, Language and
Regional Options, 355
Help and Support Center,
355–356

Network and Internet
Connections, 344–345,
622–623
Performance and
Maintenance, 348–345
Printers and Other Hardware,
354
Sounds, Speech, and Audio
Devices, 345–348
User Accounts, 355
Control Panel key,
HKEY_CURRENT_USER, 503
control.ini file, 499
CONVERT command, 459
copy backups, 527
copy/paste in HyperTerminal
window, 173
copying
CDs, 290
files to hard disk, partitioning
and, 72
music, Media Player, 750–752
corporate users, activation
and, 79
counter logs, Performance
Logs and Alerts tool,
579–580
CPU (central processing
unit), 24
multiple, 9, 565
Task Manager
CPU History, 494
CPU Usage charts, 494,
564
CPU Usage History,
564–565
multiple CPUs, 565
crashes, full Security log and,
419
Create a Restore Point dialog
box, 613–614
Curve tool, Paint, 189
Custom Settings
Internet connection, 78
network, 77

D

3D visualizations, 704
daily backups, 527
daily full Backups, 527
DAP (directory access protocol), X.500, 799
DAT (digital audio tape), 741
Data Offset, TCP, 779
data types
    printing and, 423
    Registry, 505–506
databases, page-frame database, 18–19
Date, Time, Language and Regional Options, Control Panel, 355
date settings, 76
Daylight Savings Time, 76
DDR memory, 548
deaf users. *See* Accessibility Options
debugging mode, 137
decimal values, converting from binary addresses, 768–770
decrypting files/folders, 205
defragmenting, 48–49
    partitions, 473–474
    Windows 95/98, 49
    Windows 2000 Professional, 50–51
    Windows Me, 49
    Windows NT Workstation, 49–50
Desktop, 142–143, 197
    Administrative Templates, 379
    background, 144–145
    customizing, 144–150
    icons, custom, 145–146
    Remote Desktop, 350, 390–392
    themes, 143, 704
    Web pages on, 147–150

Desktop Cleanup, 146–147
destination port, TCP, 778
Detailed Backup log, 536
Details view
    files, 199
    Windows Explorer, 200–201
Device Driver Rollback, 588, 604–607
    signed device drivers, 604–605
device drivers
    HAL and, 10
    restore points, 608
Device Manager, 351
    Driver tab, 353
    General tab, 352
    hardware profiles, 826
    hardware reports, 353–354
    Resources tab, 353
Device Status, modems, 654–655
devices
    conflicting, 629–630
    Media Player, 752
    printer devices, 422, 438
    properties, 351–352
    resources, 353
DFS (Distributed File System), 380
DHCP (dynamic host configuration protocol), 618–619, 762, 786–787
    APIPA, 619–620
    cable modems, 619
    DSL modems, 619
diagnostics, modems, 655–656
dial-up connections
    broadband connections and, 644–650
    Outlook Express, 250–251
    properties, changing, 667–668
dialing rules, modems, 660–661

DIB (directory information base), LDAP, 799–800
differential backups, 527
    full plus differential, 528
    restoring and, 537
digital audio, 740–741
    codec, 740
Digital Identification (ID), Outlook Express, 248
    keys, 257
Digital IDs, e-mail, 249
digital media devices, Media Player and, 746–748
Digital Signatures, e-mail, 249
Direct Audio, 21
Direct3D, 21
DirectDraw, 21
DirectInput, 21
directory security, Web sites, 842
directory services restore mode, 137
DirectPlay, 21
DirectSetup, 21
DirectShow, 21
DirectX, 9, 20–21
    Direct Audio, 21
    DirectX Graphics, 21
disconnect time, idle modems, 657
Disk Cleanup, 470–471
    performance improvement and, 553–555
Disk Defragmenter, 349
    performance improvement, 555
disk drives, 24
disk management. *See also* partitioning
    adding/deleting partitions, 451–455
    basic disks/dynamic disks, converting between, 455–457

Command Prompt, 459
CONVERT command, 459
converting partitions from
FAT to NTFS, 459–461
deleting partitions,
465–467
deleting volumes, 465–467
disk formatting, 467–469
DISKPART command,
461–465
compression, files/folders, 454
drive letters, partitions, 453,
458–459
extended partitions, 455
extending volumes, 457–458
logical drives, deleting, 451
MMC (Microsoft
Management Console), 450
New Partition Wizard,
452–453
partitions, converting from
FAT to NTFS, 459–461
Disk Management utility,
450–451
drive letters, 453
drive letters, changing,
458–459
drive path, changing, 458–459
partitions, adding/deleting,
451–455
disk quotas, 478–479
disk sharing, domains and,
480–481
DISKPART command, 461–464
List commands, 464–465
Recovery Console, 600
disks. *See* basic disks;
dynamic disks
DISP (directory information
shadowing protocol),
X.500, 799
display
Command Prompt and,
300–301
monitor, 154–156

performance and, 561–563
System Monitor, 575
Display Properties sheet, 144
distribution folder, 88–89
DIT (directory information
tree), 799–800
DLL/COM redirection, 285
DLLs (dynamic link libraries),
283–286
DLT (digital linear tape), 47
DMA (Direct Memory Access)
settings, Device Manager,
353
DMT (discrete multitone),
646
DN (Distinguished Name),
LDAP, 800
DNS (domain name system),
618, 785
as hierarchical database, 799
preferred server, 633
settings, 634–635
Domain Admins group,
686–687
domain-based networks, 687
domain controllers, directory
services restore mode, 137
domains
account use, 691–692
Active Directory and, 380
disk sharing, 480–481
file sharing, 219–222
forest, 686
joining, 687–691
Master Domain Model,
682–683
networks, 30, 641
overview, 680–684
trees, 686
trust relationships, 683–684
DOP (directory operational
binding management pro-
tocol), X.500, 799
DOS startup disk, creating,
326–327

dotted-decimal notation, IP
addresses, 768–770
Downloaded Program Files,
Disk Cleanup and, 554
downloading Web page on
Desktop and, 149
dragging, effects, 154
Draw Opaque tool, Paint,
190
drawing tools, Paint,
188–190
drive letters, partitions, 453
changing, 458–459
drive mapping, network
drives, 211–212
drivers
configuration, 66
Device Driver Rollback,
604–607
Device Manager, 353
installation, 66
keyboards, 24
modems, 658–659
networks, 628–629
Roll Back Driver, 629
signed device drivers,
604–605
DS (Directory Service Agent),
801–802
DSL (digital subscriber line),
78, 645–647
ADSL, 645
always on pros/cons, 648–649
asynchronous, 645
CAP, 646
DMT, 646
HDSL, 645
modems, 644–645
SDSL, 645
service, obtaining, 646
speed, cable modem comparison, 648
DSL modems, 619
DSLAM (DSL access multi-
plexer), 645

DSN (Database Source Name), 576
DSP (directory system protocol), X.500, 799
DUA (Directory User Agent), OSI, 801–802
dual-boot, 64–65. *See also* **partitioning**
DVD (digital video disc), 716
  Media Player, 731
DVD playback, Media Player, 738
DWORD value, Registry, 506
dynamic disks, 444
  basic disks, converting between, 455–457
dynamic DNS, 787
Dynamic Update, 56, 65–66
dynamic volumes, 444, 445
  extending, 457–458

E

e-mail. *See also* **Outlook Express**
  attachments, 238
  composing messages, 236–237
  files, 206
  forwarding, 239
  movies, 726
  multiple recipients, 239
  printing messages, 239
  reading messages, 238
  replying, 239
  sending messages, 236–237, 238
Edit File Type dialog box, 336
editing
  movies, Movie Maker, 719–720
  Registry, 498
    full Security Log, 419

effects
  performance and, 451–563
  Sound Recorder, 175
Effects dialog box, 153–154
EFI (Extensible Firmware Interface) scheme, 445
El Torito Specification, 61
Ellipse tool, Paint, 189
Emergency Repair Disk. *See* **ASR (Automated System Recovery)**
EMF data type (enhanced metafile), 423
emptying Recycle Bin, 215
encrypting files/folders, 204–205
  NTFS, 449
Entertainment accessories
  Sound Recorder, 174–175
  Volume Control, 175–176
Environment key, HKEY_CURRENT_USER, 503
Eraser/Color Eraser tool, Paint, 189
ERD (emergency repair disk), 37–38, 588
  post-installation, 294
  Windows 2000, 38–39
error checking, partitions, 472–473
Error event, 138, 400
Ethernet technologies
  adapters, 626–627
  LANs and, 626
  PPPoE (point-to-point over Ethernet), 649
event logs, 401–402
  Error event, 400
  Failure Audit event, 401
  Information event, 400–401
  startup problems, 138–139
  Success Audit event, 401
  Warning event, 400

Event Viewer utility, 138, 380, 398
  Application log file, 403–404
  clearing events, 416–418
  Details pane, 416
  Error event, 400
  Event ID, 402–403
  event records, 402–403
  Failure Audit event, 400
  Information event, 400
  log files, 410
    archiving, 416–418
    filtering, 414–415
    location, 411–412
    overwrite parameters, 412–413
    size, setting, 412–413
  overview, 398–400
  records, sorting, 415
  Security log, 401–402, 404–407
    full, 418–419
  Success Audit event, 400
  System account, 406
  System log, 407–410
  Warning event, 400
events
  recording, 398
  security events, 382–383
  sounds, 346–347
  types, 400–401
Events Properties page, 402
excluding files from backups, 536
Executive Services, 9, 12
  Local Procedure Call facility, 13
  Object Manager, 13
  Process Manager, 13
  Security Reference Monitor, 13
  VMM (Virtual Memory Manager), 12
expandable string value (REG_EXPAND_SZ), 506

exporting
    messages, Outlook Express,
        260–261
    Registry information, 517–518
Extend Volume Wizard, 458
**extended operations, LDAP,
    803**
**extended partitions, logical
    drives, 455**
extending volumes, 457–458

F

**fade out/fade in, Movie
    Maker, 723**
Failure event, 400–401
Fast User Switching, 389–390
FAT32, 447–448
    improvements, 448
**FAT (file allocation table),
    447–448**
    partitions, 71
        *converting to NTFS,
        459–461*
**FDISK utility, partitioning
    and, 68**
**File and Print Sharing service,
    641**
file extensions, 198–199
    Registry keys, 502
file formats
    archived files, 413
    .csv (comma delimited), 413
    .evt (event logs), 413
    .txt (text files), 413
**File Grouping, Taskbar,
    165–166**
file protection, 286
file services, 622
file sharing, 197
    Active Directory Network,
        219–222
    Administrative Templates, 380
    domains, 219–222
    new shares, 219

    permissions, 221–225
    same computer, 216–217
    security, 222–225
    workgroup LAN, 217–218
file systems, 447–448
    FAT32, improvements in, 448
    NTFS, 448–449
file types, 198–199
    Appearance and Themes,
        335–337
    Media Player, 732, 755
**File Types and System
    Restore, performance, 349**
filenames, CDs, 751
files
    associations, 198–199
    compression, 202–203
    copying
        to CD-R, 212–214
        *to hard disk, partitioning
        and, 72*
        *Windows Components
        Wizard, 293–294*
    decrypting, 205
    default locations, 525–526
    deleting, 196
    e-mailing, 206
    encryption, 204–205
    indexing, 209
    installation, copying to disk,
        290
    My Documents, 697
    Recycle Bin, retrieving, 214
    Registry, 505–508
    Registry keys, 507
    saving during System Restore,
        609–611
    Search Companion, 163–164
    shared backups, 522
    sharing
        *Computer Management
        utility, 479–480*
        *File and Print Sharing
        service, 641*
    video, importing, 718–719
    zipping, 203–204

**Files and Settings Transfer
    Wizard, 56–59**
**Fill With Color tool, Paint,
    189**
Filmstrip
    My Pictures, 699
    Windows Explorer, 201
FilterKeys, 109–110
filters
    Command Prompt, 316–317
    log filters, 414–415
    Outlook Express, 252–253
    TCP/IP, 637–638
FIN flag, TCP, 779
**FIND filter, Command
    Prompt, 316–317**
firewall, 777–778
FireWire, 710–711
flash card readers, 710–711
flat address space, 765
Flip/Rotate tool, Paint, 190
floppy disks, 47
    ASR, 542
    backups, 522, 523
    Files and Settings Transfer
        Wizard, 58–59
    password reset disk, 367
**Folder pane, Windows
    Explorer, 198**
**Folder Redirection, Group
    Policies, 374**
folders
    address book, Outlook
        Express, 254
    Appearance and Themes, 333
    compression, 202–203
    configuring options, 206–209
    copying to CD-R, 212–214
    creating, 205
    decrypting, 205
    distribution folder, 88–89
    e-mailing files from, 206
    encryption, 204–205
    icons, 207
    Outlook Express, 259–263
    pictures, 207

publishing to Web, 206
searches, 163–164
sharing, 197
   Administrative Templates,
    380
   backups, 522
type, changing, 208–209
zipped folders, 203–204
Folders button, Windows
Explorer, 197
fonts, 153–154, 339–340
adding, 340
ClearType, 814–816
Command Prompt and,
   301–302
listing, 340
Outlook Express messages,
   245
Raster fonts, Command
   Prompt, 302
variations, 340
Wordpad, 184
Forgotten Password Wizard,
367–368
forgotten passwords, recov-
ering, 367–368
formatting
partitions, at setup, 70–71
Wordpad, 184–185
fragmentation, 555
IP, 763
Free-form Select tool, Paint,
189
FreeCell game, 192
freeing hard disk space, 348
FTP (File Transfer Protocol),
326
server management, 843–847
site properties, 844–845
FTP Server, IIS, 834
full backups
daily full backups, 527
restoring and, 537

Full Control permission, file
sharing, 222
full plus differential backups,
528
full plus incremental
Backups, 527

G

Game Controllers applet, 354
Games, 170, 191–193
GB (gigabyte), 25
.gif files, icons, 370
grace period, 79
Graph View, System Monitor,
568, 572–574
graphics
adapter cards, 24
DirectX Graphics, 21
pointers, 343
grid, Paint, 191
Group Policies, 373–378
Account Lockout, 377–378
Administrative Templates,
   379–380
MMC, 373–375
password policies, 376–377
security, local computer,
   375–376
User Configuration folder,
   378–379
groups
address book (Outlook
   Express), 257–258
built-in, 385–386
local, creating, 388–389
management tasks, 385–389
members, adding, 387–388
permissions, 223
resource access, 385–389
Guests group, 385

H

HAL (hardware abstraction
layer), 9
kernel mode, 10–12
upgrade and, 273
handicapped users. *See*
Accessibility Options
handwriting recognition,
124–125
hard disk. *See also* basic
disks; dynamic disks
freeing space, 348
hardware
acceleration, sound, 346
Appearance and Themes, 343
backups, 522–524
compression, modems,
   657–658
configuration data, saving
   prior to installation, 44–45
Find Compatible Hardware
   feature, 277–278
HAL, 10
performance issues
   disk, 550
   memory, 547–548
   networks, 550
   processor, 549
   system bus, 551
   video, 550–551
resources, 353
System applet, 350
Web sites, 27
Hardware key,
HKEY_LOCAL_MACHINE,
504
hardware profiles, 822–823
creating, 823–825
management of, 825–826
setup, 826–827
Startup, 827
Hardware Profiles dialog
box, 824

hardware reports, Device Manager, 353–354

hardware requirements, 24–28

   unsupported, 26–28

Hardware Resources, System Information, 179

Hayes-compatible modems, 174

HCL (hardware compatibility list), 25–26

   Device Driver Rollback, 605

   support for items not found, 26–28

HDSL (high-bit data-rate DSL), 645

Hearts game, 192

Help and Support Center, 355–356

   compatibility issues, 277–278

Help command, Command Prompt, 310–311

HelpServicesGroup, 386

hibernate, power management, 818, 822

High Contrast, 112–113

HilGraeve, HyperTerminal and, 174

histograms, System Monitor, 575

hives, Registry, 500, 506–508

HKEY_CLASSES_ROOT (HKCR), 502

HKEY_CURRENT_CONFIG (HKCC), 505

HKEY_CURRENT_USER (HKCU), 503

HKEY_LOCAL_MACHINE (HKLM), 504

HKEY_USERS (HKU), 504–505

home directory

   FTP site, 846–847

   Web site, 839–841

home network setup, 676

hotkey underlining, removing, 154

.ht files, 172

HTML (Hypertext Markup Language), 234

HTTP headers, Web sites, 843

HTTP (HyperText Transfer Protocol), 834

HyperTerminal, 170, 171

   connections, 171–174

   properties, 172

   starting, 171–174

I

I/O (input/output)

   address, Device Manager, 353

   Command Prompt, 315

   printing and, 423

   System Information, 178

ICANN (Internet Corporation for Assigned Names and Numbers), 777

ICF (Internet Connection Firewall), 668, 669–672

ICMP (Internet control message protocol), 783–784

icons

   customizing, 145–146

   Desktop, 142

   Desktop Cleanup, 146–147

   folders, 207

   large, 154

   My Computer, 145

   user accounts, 369–371

   Windows Explorer view, 200

ICS (Internet Connection Sharing), 668, 672–673

ID (Digital Identification), Outlook Express, 248

IDE (integrated drive electronics) drives, 66

Identities key, HKEY_CUR-RENT_USER, 503

identities online, 235

IIS (Internet Information Services), 622, 834

   FTP Server, 834, 843–847

   installation, 835–836

   messages, 846

   new features, 835

   security accounts, 845–846

   SMTP server, 834

      management, 847–849

   Web Server, 834

   Web sites

      creation, 836–837

      directory security, 842

      documents, 841

      HTTP headers, 843

      management, 837–839

      properties, 839

images

   Paint tools, 190

   user accounts, 369–371

IMAP (Internet Message Access Protocol), 234

importing

   messages, Outlook Express, 260–261

   Registry information, 517–518

   video files, Movie Maker, 718–719

incremental backups, 527

   full plus incremental, 527–528

   restoring and, 537

indexing, Search Companion and, 163

Indexing service, 209

   configuration, 209–210

   networks, 209

   starting, 210–211

Information event, 139, 400–401

information locations, legacy applications and, 272

initialization files (INI files), 499

input, Command Prompt, 314–316

Insert mode, Command Prompt, 301

instability, legacy application and, 276

installation
applications, 282–283
  Autorun CD, 286
  DLLs, 283–286
  side-by-side sharing, 284–285
  system restore points, 283
cameras, 708–710
checklist, 60
clean install, 54
cloning, Sysprep and, 99
customized, Sysprep, 98–99
DirectX components, 21
drivers, 66
files, copying to disk, 290
IIS, 835–836
information from previous setup, 58–59
modems, 650–654
  detecting, 652–653
multiple operating systems, 39–41
network services, 640
networks, 29–34
  clients, additional, 638–640
  components, 620–622
  connections, 61
  protocols, additional, 640–641
  recording 95/98 information, 31–33
preparations, 41–51
Recovery Console, 130, 602–604
scanners, 708–710
Sysprep, 97–100
TCP/IP, 620–622
unattended, 63

unattend.txt file, 85–97
uninstalling items, 42–43
from Windows XP CD, 61

installation *versus* upgrade, 34–41

Installed Programs, Disk Cleanup, 471

international calls, modems, 661

Internet connection
configuring existing, 664–667
DHCP, 618–619
Dynamic Update and, 66
ISDN, 649–650
Media Player, 750
remote access, 345
setup, 78, 345
status checking, 668–669
workplace network, 673–675

Internet Explorer icon, 146

Internet Games, 192

Internet Hearts game, 192

Internet Naming Service, 635–636

Internet radio, 744–746

Internet Settings, System Information, 179

Internet Zone, Outlook Express security, 248

interprocess communications, 13

Invert Colors tool, Paint, 190

IP addresses, 764–765
APIPA, 619–620
binary addresses, 768–770
classes, 770–774
decimal values, 768–770
dotted-decimal notation, 768–770
flat address space, 765
local significance, 765
MAC, 767
network printers, 430
private network address classes, 773–774

routers, 766–768
static addressing, 619
subnet masks, 774–776

IP (Internet Protocol), 631, 762–764

IP Settings, 634

ipconfig command line utility, 33–34, 792–793

IRQ (interrupt request line)
Device Manager and, 353
System Information and, 178

ISA (industry standard architecture) bus, 551

ISAPI (Internet server application programming interface), 834

ISDN (integrated services digital network), 649–650

ISO (International Organization for Standardization), 798

ISP (Internet Service Provider), 24
modems, 644
Outlook Express setup and, 232
selecting and obtaining, 676–677

Itanium processor (Intel), 13

ITU (International Telecommunications Union), 798

J

J-Track Satellite Tracking, 148

Jaz drives, 47–48

joining domains
after setup, 688–691
at setup, 687–688

.jpg files icons, 370

K

56K modems, 644
kernel, 131
kernel mode, 8, 9–10
   Executive Services, 9
   HAL and, 10–12
   protected memory, 12
key rings, Outlook Express
   address book, 257
keyboard, 24
   Calculator and, 182
   FilterKeys, 109–110
   Magnifier and, 120
   On-Screen keyboard, 121–122
   StickyKeys, 107–109
   ToggleKeys, 110
   type, 74–75
   underlining hotkeys, remov-
     ing, 154
Keyboard Layout key,
   HKEY_CURRENT_USER, 503
keys, Registry, 501
   adding, 515–516
   deleting, 516
   exporting, 517
   file storage, 507
   value entries, 505–506
KHz (kilohertz), 740–741
killing processes, 489

L

labels, CDs, 704
LAN (local area network), 78
   connection properties,
     624–625
   Wake on LAN setting, 626
   workgroup file sharing,
     217–218
Language Options, setup, 64
Languages, Setup Manager
   Wizard, 93

Last Known Good
   Configuration, 590,
   595–596
last known good configuration, 137
last used programs, Start
   button, 160–161
layered architecture, 10
LDAP (lightweight directory
   access protocol), 798
   development, 798–804
   DIB, 799–800
   directory information, chang-
     ing, 805–806
   directory search, 805
   objects, 800–801
     container objects, 801
     leaf objects, 801
   schemas, 803–804
   wire protocol, 804–805
   X.500 standards, 798
leaf objects, 801
legacy applications
   APIs, 272
   AppHelp.sdb file, 275
   Application Compatibility
     Toolkit, 278–279
   breaking, reasons for, 272–273
   information location, 272
   instability in system, 276
   Program Compatibility
     Wizard, 277–278
   Resource Kits, 276
   SysMain.sdb file, 276
   temporary folders and, 272
   upgrades and, 273–276
   version code, 272
   warning dialog box, 275–276
   Windows Update, 279–280
legal issues with music
   recording, 732
License Agreement, 63–64
Limited accounts, 363
   compared to Computer
     Administrator, 364

Line tool, Paint, 189
List view, Windows Explorer,
   200
LMHOSTS lookup, 636
Local Area Connection,
   TCP/IP, 623
Local Computer Security
   applet, 398
Local Folders, Outlook
   Express, 230
local groups, creating,
   388–389
local printers
   connecting to, 425–432
     computer connection,
       425–428
     network connection,
       428–432
     networked printer servers,
       432
   creating, 424
Local Procedure Call facility,
   13
Local Security Policy applet,
   373, 380
   User Rights Assignment
     folder, 384
local significance, IP
   addresses, 765
local user accounts, 79
Location toolbar, Movie
   Maker, 713
log files, 410
   archiving, 416–418
   Backup Log, 536
   communications, 656
   counter logs, 579–580
   filters, 414–415
   location, 411–412
   overwrite parameters,
     412–413
   properties, Performance Logs
     and Alerts tool, 580–582
   size, 412–413
   trace logs, 579

logging on/off user accounts, 372–373

logical drives
deleting, 451
extended partition, 455

logical printers, 422
Add Printer Wizard, 423

logman command, 585

long distance calls, modems, 661

low battery alarm, 820

LPD (Line Printer Daemon), 431

LPR (Line Printer Remote), 431

LPR/LPD, printers, 431

LPT1 port, 422

M

Magnified pointer scheme, 343

Magnifier tool, 65, 119–120
Paint, 189
Setup and, 118

mail server, 232
HTML, 234
IMAP, 234
POP3, 234

mailing lists, Outlook Express, 257–258

manual backups, 532–533
advanced options, 534–535
Backup Job Information dialog box, 533–534
excluding files, 536
restoring manually, 540–541
selecting components, 533
types, setting default, 536

mapping drives, network, 211–212

Master Domain Model, 682–683

maximum hardware requirements, 25

Maximum Port Speed, modems, 655

MB (megabyte), 25

MBR (master boot record), 69
partitioning and, 445
Windows booting, 129–130

MCSE (Microsoft Certified Engineer), 680

Media Player, 697, 730
audio CDs, 731, 739–741
Automatic Updates, 749
connection speed, 753
copying music, 750–752
devices, 752
DVD, 731
DVD playback, 738
file types, 755
file types supported, 732
interface, 732–734
Internet radio, 744–746
Internet settings, 750
Media Guide, 739
Media Library, 733, 741–742
editing information, 743–744
playlists, 744
settings, 754
MP3 files, 731
network buffering, 753
network settings, 755–756
Now Playing, 734–735
drag and drop, 736
opening files, 735
URLs, 735–736
visualizations, 736–737
Options dialog box, 749–756
overview, 730–732
performance, 753–754
Player options, 749
Radio Tuner, 733, 744–746
screen controls, 731
settings, 750
shuffle mode, 735

skins, 697, 733, 748–749
Sound Recorder and, 175
streaming media, 734
transcoding, 746–748
video acceleration, 753–754
video file transfer, 731
visualizations, 754–755

MEM Usage charts, Task Manager, 494

memory
paging, 550
performance issues and, 547–548
physical, 14
physical, determining, 548
protected memory, 8, 12
virtual memory, 8, 550
addresses, 14
paged-based addressing, 14–17

menu bars
Movie Maker, 713
Outlook Express, 229

Message bar, Outlook Express, 231

Metabase Changes, IIS, 835

metrics, routers, 766–768

MFT (master file table), 449

mice, 24

microphone, speech recognition and, 124

Microsoft Direct3D, 21

Microsoft DirectDraw, 21

Microsoft DirectInput, 21

Microsoft DirectPlay, 21

Microsoft DirectSetup, 21

Microsoft DirectShow, 21

Microsoft Investment Ticker, 148

Microsoft Management Service. *See* MMC

Microsoft Plus!, 696, 703–704

MIDI input, volume, 346

MigDB.INF file, 273

migrating files, 56–59

Minesweeper game, 192
minimized windows,
    Magnifier and, 120
minimum hardware require-
    ments, 25
MIPS, 11
mirrored volumes, 447
MMC (Computer
    Management Console), 808
    Account Lockout, 377–378
    Account Policies, 375–376
    Disk Management utility, 450
    group policies and, 373–375
    Indexing service and, 209–210
    password policies, 376–377
    Performance snap-in, 566, 567
modems, 78, 644
    advanced options, 663–664
    area codes, 662–663
    cable, 644–645
    cable modems, 647–648
    Call Waiting, 662
    calling cards, 663
    detecting during installation,
        652–653
    Device Status, 654–655
    diagnostics, 655–656
    dialing rules, 660–661
    disconnecting idle, 657
    drivers, 658–659
    DSL, 644–645
    hardware compression,
        657–658
    Hayes-compatibility, 173–174
    installation, 650–654
    international calls, 661
    long distance calls, 661
    outside lines, 661
    power management, 660
    properties, 654–663
    resources, 659
    troubleshooting,
        HyperTerminal and, 173
modification date, searches
    and, 164

monitor
    display settings, 153–156
    power options, 151
Monitor area, Movie Maker,
    713, 714
monitoring user activities,
    380–383
MORE filter, Command
    Prompt, 316
mouse
    buttons, 342
    Magnifier and, 120
    pointers, 341–342
    setup, 78
    wheel mouse, 343
MouseKeys, 113–114
Movie Maker, 696, 712. *See
    also* video
    burning movies to CD,
        726–728
    clips
        adding, 720
        combining, 723
        cutting/pasting, 721
        editing, 721–723
        removing, 720–721
        splitting, 723
    Collections area, 713, 714
    e-mailing movies, 726
    editing movies, 719–720
    fade out/fade in, 723
    importing files, 718–719
    Monitor, 713
    Monitor area, 714
    narration, 723–724
    publishing to Web, 726
    recording source, 716–718
    recording video, 716
    saving movies, 724–725
    starting, 712–713
    still pictures, 723
    title slides, 723
    toolbars, 713
    transitions between clips, 723
    video capture card, 718
    Workspace, 713, 714–715

MP3 files
    burning to CD, 702
    Media Player, 731
    support, 704
MSN Explorer, installing, 622
MTU (maximum transmission
    unit), 763
multi-booting, 39–41
multi-string value
    (REG_FULL_RESOURCE_
    DESCRIPTOR), 506
multicasting, IP addresses,
    773
multimedia, 696
    audio CDs
        burning, 701–702
        CD-DA, 702
    burning CDs, 701–703
    CD-DA (Digital Audio), 702
    desktop themes, 704
    digital audio, 740–741
    Filmstrip, My Pictures, 699
    MP3 files, burning to CD, 702
    MP3 support, 704
    My Documents, 697
    My Music, 697, 698
    My Pictures, 697, 699–700
    My Videos, 697, 698
    Online Print Ordering Wizard,
        700–701
    Personal DJ, 704
    pictures
        commercially processed,
            posted to Internet, 699
        slide show, 700
    speakers, 704
    third-party programs, 704–705
    Thumbnails view, 700
    voice recognition, 703
    .wav files, 702
multitasking, 8, 19–20
My Computer, 197
    icon, 145
My Documents, 146, 197
    files, 697

My Music, 197, 697, 698
My Network Places, 145, 197
My Pictures, 197, 697,
  699–700
My Videos, 697, 698

N

name and organization infor-
  mation, 76
Napster, 732
narration, Movie Maker,
  723–724
Narrator tool, 65, 118–119
  Utility Manager and, 122
NAT (network address trans-
  lation), 619, 774
NDS (Novell Directory
  Services), 638–639
NET command, Command
  Prompt, 312–314
NetBIOS configuration, 637
  NetBIOS over TCP/IP
    (NETBT), 787
NETBT (NetBIOS over TCP/IP),
  787
NetCrawler, 441–442
netstat command, TCP/IP,
  793–794
NetWare clients, installation,
  639–640
network
  component installation,
    620–622
  workplace, connecting to,
    673–675
network adapter cards
  cable modems, 649
  configuration, 625–630
  DSL modems, 649
Network and Internet
  Connections, Control Panel,
  344–345
network commands, 325–326

Network Components, Setup
  Manager Wizard, 92
Network Configuration
  group, 385
networking adapter usage,
  Task Manager, 495–496
networking services,
  installing, 622
networks
  Administrative Templates, 380
  backups, 523, 524
  buffering, Media Player, 753
  cabling, 627
  clients, additional, 638–340
  configuration, manual, 77
  connections, items used, 630
  corporate, 30
  directory services restore
    mode, 137
  domain-based, 687
  domains, 30, 641
  drive mapping, 211–212
  drivers, 628–629
  Ethernet cards, 626–627
  file services, 622
  home network setup, 676
  IIS (Internet Information
    Service), 622
  Indexing service and, 209
  installation
    overview, 29–31
    recording 95/98 informa-
      tion, 31–33
    Sysprep and, 97–100
  Media Player, 755–756
  MSN Explorer, 622
  NDS, 638–639
  Networking Services, 622
  Novell, 32–33
  performance issues, 550
  print services, 622
  printer connection, 428–432
  printers, locating, 441–442
  protocols, installing
    additional, 640–641

QoS Packet Scheduler, 630
Safe Mode with Networking,
  136
services, installation, 640
settings, 77
Setup Wizard, 62–63
small office network, 676
subnetting, 774–776
Task Manager, 565
workgroups, 30, 641
New Partition Wizard,
  452–453
news messages, Outlook
  Express, 252
news servers, 265–266
newsgroups
  account creation, 264–266
  posting replies to messages,
    267–268
  reading messages, 267
  subscribing/unsubscribing,
    266
nonpaged pool, 19
normal backups, 527
Norton CleanSweep, 42
Notepad, 170, 182–183
Notification Area, Taskbar,
  167
Novell networks, 32–33
Now Playing, Media Player,
  734–735
  drag and drop, 736
  opening files, 735
  URLs, 735–736
  visualizations, 736–737
nslookup command, TCP/IP,
  794–795
ntbackup command, 543–544
NTCompat.inf file, 273
NTDETECT.COM, 130
NTFS (NT File System), 40,
  447–449
  ACLS, 449
  compression, 449
  encryption, 449

versus FAT32, 54
file compression, 202
MFT, 449
partitions, 71
    converting from FAT,
    459–461
performance, 552
Unicode support, 449
NTI CD-Maker 2000
Professional, 289
NTLDR (NT Loader), 130
NTOSKRNL file, 131
numeric keypad, calculator
and, 181–182

O

object classes, Active
Directory, 685
Object Manager, 13
objects, 800–801
    AD, 800–801
    container objects, 801
    inserting, Wordpad, 187
    leaf objects, 801
    System Monitor, 571
obsolete commands, 305–307
ODBC (Open Database
Connectivity), 576
OEMs (original equipment
manufacturers), 27
    handwriting recognition,
    124–125
office network setup, 676
Office *x* Applications, System
Information, 179
Offline Favorite Wizard, 148
Offline Files
    logon/logoff method, 373
    properties, 337–338
offline files
    setup, 828
    shared folders, 828
    Web pages, 828–829

OLE (Object Linking and
Embedding), 187
On-Screen keyboard,
121–122
online identities, 235
Online Print Ordering
Wizard, 700–701
Open Files folder, Computer
Management utility, 480
operating systems
    multiple, installing, 39–41
    Recovery Console, 600
OSI (Open System
Interconnection) network
protocols, 799
    protocols and standards,
    801–802
Other Places, My Computer,
145
OUs (organizational units),
801
Outlook Express, 228–229.
    See also e-mail
    account setup, 232–235
    accounts, 263–264
    address book, 253–254
        contacts, adding, 255–257
        entering information man-
        ually, 254
        folder creation, 254
        groups, 257–258
        printing from, 259
    attachments, 238
    bcc (blind carbon copies), 237
    blocking messages, 252–253
    checking for messages, prop-
    erties, 241
    compacting messages, 251
    composing messages,
    236–237
        properties, 245–246
    connection properties,
    250–251
    default mail handler, 241
    deleting messages, 251
    deleting news messages, 252

Digital Identification, 248
Digital IDs, 249
Digital Signatures, 249
exporting messages, 260–261
filters, 252–253
folders, 259
    message categories, 260
    searching, 261–263
forwarding messages, 239
importing messages, 260–261
keyboard shortcuts, 263
mailing lists, 257–258
maintenance options, 251–252
message previews, 231
multiple recipients, 239
newsgroups, 264–266
    posting replies to mes-
    sages, 267–268
    reading messages, 267
    subscribing/unsubscribing,
    266
printing messages, 239
properties, 240–253
reading messages, 238
    properties, 242–243
receiving messages, properties, 243–244
replying to messages, 239
rules, 252–253
security, 247–248
sending messages, 236–237,
238
    properties, 241, 244–245
signatures, 246–247
sorting messages, 231–232
spelling, 247
stationery, 237, 245–246
username, 233
virus protection, 248–249
window, 229–232
output, Command Prompt,
314–316
outside lines, modems, 661
overwrite parameters, log
files, 412–413

P

page directory, 32-bit memory addresses, 15–16
page directory entry (PDE), 15
page directory offset, 15
page-faults, 17
Page File Usage History, Task Manager, 565
page files, 32-bit memory addresses, 17
page frame, 32-bit memory addresses, 15, 16–17
page-frame database, 18–19
page table, 32-bit memory addresses, 15, 16
paged-based virtual memory, 14
32-bit virtual addressing, 15–16
PageHeap utility, 279
pages, 15
paging, memory, 550
paging files, performance and, 560–561
Paint, 170
Advanced Viewing features, 190–191
drawing tools, 188–190
Image menu tools, 190
paper, printing, 433
partitioning, 39–41, 64–65.
See also **dual-boot**
adding/deleting partitions, Disk Management utility, 451–455
backing up partition, 590–593
backups and, 69
compressing partitions, 203
CONVERT command, 459
converting partitions from FAT to NTFS, 459–461
creating partitions at setup, 69–70
defragmenting partitions, 48–49, 473–474

deleting partitions, 465–467
at setup, 69–70
DISKPART command, 459
drive letters, 453
changing, 458–459
drive sharing, 476–478
error checking, 472–473
extended partitions, logical drives, 455
FAT, 71
files, copying to hard disk, 72
formatting partitions at setup, 70–71
NTFS, 71
partition definition, 68–69
properties, 469–470
Disk Cleanup option, 470–471
disk quotas, enabling, 478–479
Hardware tab, 474–476
Tools tab, 471–474
selecting partitions, 67–68, 446–447
volume types, 446–447
PartitionMagic, 40
Password Hint field, 366
password reset disk, 367
passwords
Administrator account, 363
forgotten, recovering, 367–368
policies, MMC, 376–377
removing from accounts, 369
selection tips, 366–367
user accounts, 365–367
patches, 275
paths, upgrade path, 54
pausing printing, 439, 440
PCI (peripheral component interface)
network cards, 550
PCI bus, 551
PCMCIA (Personal Computer Memory Card International Association), 710

PDAs (personal digital assistants), Media Player and, 746–748
PDC (primary domain controller), 30
AD and, 806
domains and, 681–382
PDE (page directory entry), 15
PDUs (protocol data units), 804–805
Pencil tool, Paint, 189
performance, 546
baseline, System Monitor, 578
command-line tools, 585–586
display settings and effects, 561–563
hardware and
disk, 550
memory, 547–548
network, 550
processor, 549
system bus, 551
video, 550–551
improving, 552–553
Disk Cleanup, 553–555
Disk Defragmenter, 555
removing applications/ services, 555–558
Startup optimization, 553
System Restore and, 558–559
Media Player, 753–754
paging files and, 560–561
swap files and, 560–561
System Monitor, 566–578
Task Manager and, 493–494, 564–566
Performance and Maintenance, Control Panel, 348–350
Device Manager, 351
System applet, 349–350
Performance and Maintenance window, 399

performance counters,
  System Monitor, 568–572
Performance Logs and Alerts
  Node, System Monitor, 568
Performance Logs and Alerts
  tool, 578–579
    action properties, 584
    alerts, configuring, 582–585
    counter logs, 579–580
    schedule properties, 582
Performance Options dialog
  box, 562
Performance System
  Monitor, 546
permissions
    file sharing, 221–225
    Media Player, 750
    rights and, 384
Personal DJ, 704
PF Usage, Task Manager, 564
physical memory, 14
Pick Color tool, Paint, 189
pictures
    folders, 207
    processed commercially,
      posted to Internet, 699
    screen saver slideshow,
      151–152
    slide show, 700
    user accounts, 369–371
pilot program
    application compatibility, 28
    WOW and, 29
Pinball game, 192
ping command, TCP/IP,
  789–790
pinning programs to Start
  menu, 161
pipes, Command Prompt,
  316–317
Player options, Media Player,
  749
playlists, Media Library, 744
Plug and Play
    hardware and, 26
    Universal Plug and Play,
      installation, 622

Plus!, 696, 703–704
.png files, icons, 370
pointers
    Appearance and Themes, 343
    mouse pointers, 341–342
pointing devices
    mouse pointers, 341–342
    MouseKeys and, 113–114
Polygon tool, Paint, 190
POP3 server, 232, 234
popup background,
  Command Prompt, 304
popup text, Command
  Prompt, 304
ports
    printer ports, 423, 429
      setup, 434
    TCP/IP, 777–778
POST (Power On Self Test),
  128
    Last Known Good
      Configuration, 595–596
posting to newsgroups,
  267–268
power management,
  816–822
    advanced settings, 821–822
    alarms, 820–821
    hibernate, 822
Power Meter settings, 821
power options
    modems, 660
    monitor, 151
Power Options, Performance
  and Maintenance, 349
power schemes, 817–820
    preset, 819–820
Power Users group, 385–386
PowerPC, 11
PowerQuest PartitionMagic,
  40
PPP (point-to-point protocol),
  784–785
PPPoE (point-to-point over
  Ethernet), 649
preemptive multitasking, 20

preloaded software, 143
preparing for installation,
  41–51
    backups, 45
    checklist, 51
    defragmenting, 48–51
    saving application configura-
      tions, 43–44
    saving hardware configuration
      data, 44–45
    uninstalling prior to installa-
      tion, 42–43
preset power schemes,
  819–820
Price Watch Web site, hardware, 28
primary buttons, mouse, 342
print job, 423
print management, 438–447
print monitor, 423
print processor, 423, 437
Print Screen, 32
print server, 422–423
    connecting to, 432
print services, 622
print share, connecting to,
  424
print spooler, 423, 436
    simultaneous print operations
      online, 423
Print Test Page option, 433
printer devices, 422, 438
printer ports, 423
    setup, 434
    Type of Port menu, 429
printers, 422
    compatibility, 434–435
    default, 439
    defaults, 437
    local printers, 424
      computer connection,
        425–428
      network connection,
        428–432
      network print server, 432
    logical printers, 422

LPR/LPD, 431

NetCrawler, 441–442

network, locating, 441–442

properties, 433–438

sharing, 434, 440

Printers and Other Hardware, Control Panel, 354

Printers key, HKEY_CUR-RENT_USER, 503

printing

bi-directional, 423

canceling, 440–441

e-mail messages, 239

File and Print Sharing service, 641

Outlook Express address book, 259

pausing, 439, 440

restarting, 440

resuming, 440

separator page, 437

System Monitor data, 574

Printing Preferences, 433, 439, 441

prioritization, 20

processes, Task Manager, 489–490

private network address classes, IP, 773–774

privileged mode, 9

process management, Task Manager, 488–493

Process Manager, 13

process threads, context switching, 20

processor, performance and, 549

product key, 64

activating XP and, 78–79

profiles. See hardware profiles

progman.ini file, 499

Program Compatibility Wizard, 277–278

promiscuous mode, 788

properties

Appearance and Themes, 333

file types, 335–337

viewing, 333–335

devices, 351–352

dial-up connections, 667–668

HyperTerminal, 172

logs, Performance Logs and Alerts tool, 580–582

modems, 654–663

Offline Files, 337–338

Outlook Express, 240–253

partitions, 469–479

printers, 433–438

Recycle Bin, 215–216

schedule, Performance Logs and Alerts tool, 582

shortcuts, 158–160

System Monitor, 574–578

Volume Control, 176

protected memory, 8

kernel mode and, 12

protocol suite, 762

protocols

DAP (directory access protocol), X.500, 799

DISP (directory information shadowing protocol), X.500, 799

DOP, X.500, 799

DSP (directory system protocol), X.500, 799

FTP (File Transfer Protocol), 326

IMAP (Internet Message Access Protocol), 234

LDAP (lightweight directory access protocol), 798

network printer setup, 431

TCP/IP (transfer call protocol/Internet protocol), 30

wire protocols, 804–805

Proxy Settings, Setup Manager Wizard, 93

PSTN (public switched telephone network), 764

PTEs (page table entries), 16

publishing folders to Web, 206

publishing movies to Web, 726

Q

QIC backups, 523

QIT (quarter-inch tape) drives, 46

QoS Packet Scheduler, 630

quick format, partitions, 71

QuickEdit mode, Command Prompt, 301

QuickTime, 730

R

Radio Tuner, Media Player, 733

Internet radio, 744–746

RAID-5 volume, 447

RAID (Redundant Array of Inexpensive Disks), 589

RAM (random access memory), 24

increasing, 548

Raster Fonts, Command Prompt, 302

Raw data type (FF appended), printing, 423

RDISK utility (NT), 38

RDN (Relative Distinguished Name), LDAP, 800

RDP (Remote Desktop Protocol), 390

Read permission, file sharing, 222

RealJukebox, 730

RealNetwork, 730

RealPlayer, 730

rebooting
finishing installation, 78–80
informational messages,
70–72
Text Mode Setup, 70–72
**recommended hardware
requirements, 25**
recording
hardware, 347
Napster, 732
video, Movie Maker, 716
source, 716–718
voice playback and recording,
347
recovery. *See also* restoring
Device Driver Rollback,
604–607
Last Known Good
Configuration, 590, 595–596
partition backup, 590–593
Safe Mode, 590, 596–598
Setup and, 593–594
upgrades, 588–589
Recovery Console, 130
commands, 601–602
DISKPART command, 600
exiting, 602
installation CD startup,
599–600
installing, 602–604
Rectangle tool, Paint, 189
Recycle Bin, 197, 214
disk space allotted, 216
emptying, 215
properties, setting, 215–216
retrieving files, 214
**red stop sign messages,
upgrades and, 275**
**redirector commands,
314–316**
REG_BINARY, 505–506
regedit, 512
REG_EXPAND_SZ, 506
**REG_FULL_RESOURCE_DESCRI
PTOR, 506**

**Regional and Languages
Options properties, 73–76**
regional options, 73–76
**Regional Settings, Setup
Manager Wizard, 93**
**Registered Files Types,
Appearance and Themes,
335**
Registry, 498
backing up, 508–509,
509–511
data types, 505–506
DWORD value, 506
editing, 498
full Security Log, 419
files, 505–508
ERD, 38
history of, 499–500
hives, 500, 505–508
importing/exporting information, 517–518
keys, 501, 505–506
file storage, 507
Last Known Good
Configuration, 595–596
REG_BINARY, 505–506
REG_EXPAND_SZ, 506
REG_FULL_RESOURCE_D
ESCRIPTOR, 506
REG_MULTI_SZ, 506
restoring, 508–509, 511
searching, 513–514
subkeys, 501, 505–506
subtrees, 501, 503–505
value entries, 501, 505–506
Registry Editor, 512
entries
adding, 515–516
changing, 514–515
deleting, 516
keys
adding, 515–516
deleting, 516
REG_MULTI_SZ, 506
regular format, partitions, 71

relog command, 585
remote access
HDSL and, 645
SDSL and, 645
System applet, 350
Remote Assistance, 392–396
System applet, 350
Remote Desktop, 390–392
System applet, 350
**Remote Desktop Users
group, 386**
**removable hard drives, back-
ups, 524**
removable media
backups, 529
dynamic disks, 445
removing
applications, 42
components, 43, 290–291
renaming shortcuts, 158
**Repair Disk Utility dialog
box, 38**
reports, System Monitor, 575
resolution
ClearType, 814–816
monitor, 154–155
Resource Kits, 276
resource management, 552
restarting printing, 440
**restore points. *See* System
Restore**
**Restore Wizard, 509–511,
529, 538–540**
**restoring files from backup,
522, 537**
ASR, 541–542
manual restores, 540–541
Restore Wizard, 538–240
restoring system, 283
ASR, 542, 593–594
Last Known Good
Configuration, 595–596
rebooting, 593–594
Registry, 508–509, 511
Safe Mode, 596–598
System Restore, 607–616

Restricted Sites Zone, Outlook Express security, 248
resuming printing, 440
retrieving files from Recycle Bin, 214
rights, 223
  permissions and, 384
  users, assigning, 383–385
Roll Back Driver, 629
root directory, multiple installations, 40
root object, AD, 800
Rounded Rectangle tool, Paint, 189
route command, TCP/IP, 794
routers, 766–768
RST flag, TCP, 779
rules, Outlook Express, 252–253
Run command. *See* Search Companion
Run Installation Program dialog, 289

S

Safe mode, 135–136
  booting into, 596–598
SAM key, HKEY_LOCAL_MACHINE, 504
SAM (Security Accounts Manager), 98, 504, 811
  domains and, 681–382
sample rate conversion quality, sound, 346
sampling, digital audio, 740
saving movies, Movie Maker, 724–725
Scanner and Camera Installation Wizard, 708–710

scanners
  installation, 708–710
  third-party software, 711–712
schedule properties, Performance Logs and Alerts tool, 582
Scheduled Tasks. *See also* Task Scheduler
  Performance and Maintenance and, 349
scheduled tasks
  creating, 322–325
  results checking, 325
schemas, AD, 802
schemes
  pointers, 343
  sound schemes, 346–347
schtasks command, 321–325
Scientific calculators, 181
screen background, Command Prompt, 303–304
screen name, newsgroups, 265
screen resolution, 154–155
screen text, Command Prompt, 303–304
screensaver, 704
  changing, 150–151
  slide show, 151–152
scrolling screensaver slideshow, 152
SDKs (software development kits), 279
SDRAM, memory, 548
SDSL (single-line digital subscriber line), 645
Search button, Windows Explorer, 197
Search Companion, 161–165, 197–198, 211
  files, 163–164
  folders, 163–164
  indexing, 163
Search dialog box, 163

searches
  Active Directory, 692
  AD objects, 808–811
  directory, LDAP, 805
  folders, Outlook Express, 261–263
  Registry, 513–514
secondary buttons, mouse, 342
security
  events, auditing, 382–383
  Group Policies, local computer, 375–376
  Outlook Express, 247–248
    Digital IDs, 249
    Digital Signatures, 249
  sharing files/folders, 220, 222–225
  Web sites, IIS, 842
Security key, HKEY_LOCAL_MACHINE, 504
Security log, 138, 401–402, 404–407
  crashes and, 419
  full, halting computer, 418–419
  Registry, editing, 419
Security Reference Monitor, 13
Security Settings, Group Policies, 374
See Also menu
  Appearance and Themes, 338–344
  Performance and Maintenance, 349
Select tool, Paint, 189
selective isolation, 284–285
separator page, printing, 437
sequence number, TCP, 779
SerialKeys, 115–116
servers
  mail server, 232, 233–234
  news servers, 265–266
  print server, 422–423

services, removing, 555–558
Services dialog box, 557
Sessions folder, Computer
    Management utility, 480
setting up auditing, 380
Setup
    Accessibility Options, 65
    administrator password, 76
    Advanced Options, 64–65
    computer name, 76
    date settings, 76
    domains, joining, 687–691
    Internet connection, 78
    Language Options, 64
    Magnifier and, 118
    mouse, 78
    name and organization infor-
        mation, 76
    Narrator tool, 118
    network settings, 77
    partitions
        deleting/creating, 69–70
        formatting, 70–71
    rebooting
        informational messages,
            72
        Text Mode Setup, 70–72
    regional options, 73–74
    restoring system and, 593–594
    starting, 55
    Text Mode Setup, 54, 66
    time settings, 76
    unattend.txt file, 85–97
    user accounts, 79, 360
setup
    starting, 55
Setup command, 82–85
Setup Manager Wizard,
    87–97
Setup program, 286
Setup Wizard, 54
    License Agreement, 63–64
    from network connection,
        62–63
    starting, 61
    versions of Windows, 62

shadow effects, 154
Shared Documents folder,
    216–217
Shares folder, Computer
    Management utility, 480
sharing
    disks, domains and, 480–481
    drives, partitions, 476–478
    files/folders, 197
        Active Directory Network,
            219–222
        Administrative Templates,
            380
        backing up to, 522
        Computer Management
            utility, 479–480
        DLL/COM redirection,
            285
        DLLs, 284
        domains, 219–222
        File and Print Sharing
            service, 641
        new shares, 219
        offline availability, 828
        partitions, 476–478
        permissions, 221–225
        same computer, 216–217
        security, 222–225
        side-by-side sharing,
            284–285
        workgroup LAN, 217–218
    printers, 434, 439, 440
shim file, 274
shortcuts
    adding, 158
    custom, 157–160
    properties, 158–160
    renaming, 158
Show Kernel Times, Task
    Manager, 494
ShowSounds, 111–112
shuffle mode, Media Player,
    735
SID (system identification),
    Sysprep, 97–98

side-by-side sharing, 284–285
signatures, Outlook Express,
    246–247
signed device drivers,
    604–605
SIMMS, memory, 548
size of files, searches and,
    164
skins, 697
    Media Player, 733, 748–749
slide show
    My Pictures, 700
    screensaver, 151–152
sliding windows, TCP,
    781–782
SLIP (serial line interface
    protocol), 784
small office network setup,
    676
SMTP (simple mail transfer
    protocol) server, 232
    IIS, 834
    management, IIS, 847–849
SNMP (Simple Network
    Management Protocol)
    Status, 432
Software Environment,
    System Information, 179
Software Installation, Group
    Policies, 374
Software key, HKEY_
    CURRENT_USER, 503
Software key,
    HKEY_LOCAL_MACHINE,
    504
Solitaire game, 192
SORT filter, Command
    Prompt, 317
sound. *See also* audio
    events, 346–347
    hardware acceleration, 346
    sample rate conversion quality,
        346
    .wav files, 174–175

Sound Recorder, 170,
174–175
effects, 175
Media Player and, 175
sound schemes, 346–347
Sounds, Speech, and Audio
Devices category, Control
Panel, 345–346
Sounds and Audio Devices
applet, 346
Audio tab, 347
Hardware tab, 347
Sounds tab, 346–347
Speech applet, 347
troubleshooters, 347–348
Voice tab, 347
volume, 346
SoundSentry, 111–112
source port, TCP, 778
spanned volumes, 446
Speaker Volume, 346
speakers, multimedia, 704
Speech applet, 347
speech recognition, 123–124
spelling in Outlook Express,
247
Spider Solitaire game, 192
staging area, CD burning,
213
Standard toolbar, Movie
Maker, 713
standby, power manage-
ment, 818
Start button, 142
last used programs, 160–161
pinning programs to, 161
Start Menu, 160
Administrative Templates, 379
startup
boot logging, 136
debugging mode, 137
directory services restore
mode, 137
event logs and, 138–139
hardware profile selection,
827

last known good configuration, 137
optimizing, 553
Safe mode, 135–136
troubleshooting, 137–140
VGA mode, 136–137
startup diskettes
DOS, creating, 326–327
Windows 95/98, 35–36
Windows Me, 35–36
stateful inspection, firewall
and, 669
static Internet protocol
address information, con-
figuration, 632–638
static Internet protocol configuration, 618
static addresses, 619
static IP addressing, 619
stationery, Outlook Express,
237, 245–246
status checking, Internet
connections, 668–669
StickyKeys, 107–109
still pictures, Movie Maker,
723
storage capacity, 24
StorageReview.com, 27
Storyboard View, Movie
Maker Workspace, 714
streaming media, Media
Player, 734
Stretch/Skew tool, Paint, 190
stretching background, 145
string values
(REG_MULTI_SZ), 506
striped volumes, 446–447
subkeys, Registry, 501
value entries, 505–506
subnet masks, IP addresses,
774–776
subnetting networks, IP
addresses, 774–776
subscribing/unsubscribing to
newsgroups, 266

subtrees, Registry, 501
HKEY_CLASSES_ROOT
(HKCR), 502
HKEY_CURRENT_CONFIG
(HKCC), 505
HKEY_CURRENT_USER,
503
HKEY_LOCAL_MACHINE
(HKLM), 504
HKEY_USERS (HKU),
504–505
Success Audit event, 400–401
Summary Backup log, 536
swap files, performance and,
560–561
switching between applica-
tions, 301
Task Manager, 485–486
symmetric multiprocessing, 9
SYN flag, TCP, 779
synchronization
Offline Files, 338
Web pages on Desktop, 148
Synchronization Manager,
830–831
Synchronizing dialog box,
149
SysMain.sdb file, compati-
bility and, 276
Sysprep
cloning installations and, 99
single computer setup, 98–99
system identifiers, cloning
and, 97–98
Sysprep Install button, 100
Sysprep.inf file, 100
System account, Event
Viewer utility, 406
System applet, 349–350
Performance and
Maintenance, 348
system bus, 551
System Configuration utility,
558
System Control Panel, 349

System Information, 170, 178–180
System Information Tool, 44–45
System key, HKEY_LOCAL_MACHINE, 504
System log, 138, 407–410
system maintenance, 552
System Monitor, 566
  Administrative Tools, 567
  appearance properties, 577–578
  baseline, performance, 578
  data properties, 576–577
  graph properties, 577
  Graph View, 568, 572–574
  information collection, 566–567
  legend, 568
  objects, 571
  performance counters, 568–572
  Performance Logs and Alerts Node, 568
  printing from, 574
  properties, 574–578
  sources, 576
  starting, 567–568
  System Monitor Node, 568
  Timer Bar, 568
  Value Bar, 568
system partition, boot partition, 69
System Policy Editor, 373–374
System Restore, 607–609
  Disk Cleanup and, 471
  files saved, 609–611
  performance and, 558–559
  restore points, 283, 608–609
    creating, 613–614
  reverting to earlier setup, 614–616
  Safe Mode and, 597–598
  System applet, 350

System Restore Wizard, 611–613
System Tools
  Character Map, 177–178
  System Information, 178–180
System Tray, performance improvement and, 556
system.ini file, 499

T

tape drives, backups, 45–47, 523
Task Manager
  application management, 484–488
  Command Prompt and, 299
  counters, 494
  CPU History, 494
  CPU Usage, 494, 564
  Internet resources, 486–487
  killing applications, 485
  MEM Usage charts, 494
  menu, 487–488
  Networking tab, 495–496, 565
  New Task, 486–487
  performance and, 564–566
  Performance tab, 493–494
  PF Usage, 564
  prioritization and, 20
  process management, 488–493
    ending processes, 491
    killing processes, 489
    priorities, 489
    process trees, 491
  Show Kernel Times, 494
  switching to applications, 485–486
Task Scheduler, 321–322
  creating tasks, 322–325
taskbar, 142
  Administrative Templates, 379
  custom, 165–167

  File Grouping, 165–166
  Notification Area, 167
  volume control, 346
tasks, printers, 438–439
TCP/IP (transfer call protocol/Internet protocol)
  advanced settings, 633–638
  configuration, 622–625, 630–632
    network adapter cards, 625–630
TCP/IP (Transmission Control Protocol/Internet protocol), 30, 762
  ARP (address resolution protocol), 784
  configuration information, 33
  DNS (domain name system), 785
  firewall, 777–778
  ICMP, 783–784
  installation, 620–622
  ipconfig command, 792–793
  NetBIOS over TCP/IP (NETBT), 787
  netstat command, 793–794
  network printers and, 429
  nslookup command, 794–795
  ping command, 789–790
  ports, 777–778
  PPP (point-to-point protocol), 784–785
  route command, 794
  SLIP (serial line interface protocol), 784
  tracert command, 790–791
  troubleshooting tools, 788–795
  UDP (User Datagram Protocol), 782–783
  VPN (virtual private network), 788
  WINS, 787

TCP (transmission control protocol), 778–784
ACK flag, 779
acknowledgement number, 779
checksum, 779
Data Offset, 779
ending sessions, 782
FIN flag, 779
RST flag, 779
sequence number, 779
sliding windows, 781–782
SYN flag, 779
three-way handshake, 778, 779–781
Telephony screen, Setup Manager Wizard, 92
Telnet, 326
temporary folders, legacy applications and, 272
Temporary Internet Files, Disk Cleanup and, 554
Temporary Offline Files, Disk Cleanup and, 554
Text Mode Setup, 54, 66
partitions and, 70
Text tool, Paint, 189
themes, 143, 156
Classic, 157
creating, 157
desktop, 704
third party multimedia programs, 704–705
threads, 19
context switching, 20
three-way handshake, TCP, 778, 779–781
thumbnails
Filmstrip, 201
Paint, 191
Windows Explorer, 199–200
Thumbnails view, My Pictures, 700
Tiles view, Windows Explorer, 200

tiling background, 145
time settings, 76
Set Manager Wizard, 91
Timeline View, Movie Maker Workspace, 714–715
editing clips and, 721
Timer Bar, System Monitor, 568
title slides, Movie Maker, 723
TLB (translation lookaside buffer), 18
ToggleKeys, 110
Token Ring technology, Ethernet, 626–627
Tom's Hardware Guide Web site, 27
toolbars
Movie Maker, 713
Windows Explorer, 197–198
trace logs, performance, 579
tracerpt command, 585
tracert command, TCP/IP, 790–791
tracking user activity, 380–383
transcoding, Media Player, 746–748
transitions, screensaver slideshow, 152
translation lookaside buffer (TLB), 18
Troubleshooters, 344
Sound and Audio Devices, 347–348
troubleshooting startup, 137–140
TrueType fonts, ClearType and, 814–816
trust relationships, domains and, 683–684
TTL (Time To Live), 764
Turn Off Hard Disks, power management, 818
Turn Off the Monitor, power management, 818

typeperf command, 586
Typical Settings
Internet connection, 78
network, 77

U

UDP (User Datagram Protocol), 782–783, 804–805
unattended installation, 63
unattend.txt Setup file, 85–86
UNICODE Program Groups key, HKEY_CURRENT_USER, 503
Unicode support, NTFS, 449
uninstall program, 286
performance and, 556
uninstalling prior to installation, 42–43
Universal Plug and Play, 622
updates, Dynamic Update, 56, 65–66
upgrade
backups, 588–589
checklist, 60
device drivers, 353
effects afterward, 274–276
versus installing, 34–41
legacy applications and, 273–276
from Windows 95/98 and Me, 35–36
from Windows NT or 2000, 36–39
upgrade path, 54
***Upgrading and Repairing Networks, Third Edition,* 628**
***Upgrading and Repairing PCs, 13th Edition,* 28**
URLs (Uniform Resource Locators), Media Player, 735–736

USB (universal serial bus), 710–711

user accounts

Active Directory, 686–687

adding after Setup, 360–364

Computer Administrator, 363

deleting, 371–372

Limited, 363

logon/logoff method, 372–373

monitoring activity, 380–383

passwords, 365–367

removing, 369

pictures, 369–371

Setup, 360

setup, 79

types, 363–364

changing, 371

username, changing, 364–365

User Accounts, Control Panel, 355

User Accounts screen, 361

User Configuration folder, 378–379

user mode, 8, 10

User Rights Assignment folder, 384

usernames, 361

changing, 364–365

domains, 691

e-mail setup, 233

users

My Documents, 197

My Music, 197

My Pictures, 197

rights, assigning, 383–385

Users group, 386

USMT (User State Migration Tool), 57

utilities

ipconfig command line, 33–34

winipcfg, 31

Utility Manager, 122–123

V

Value Bar, System Monitor, 568

value entries, Registry, 501, 505–506

VDM (Virtual DOS Machine), 29

COMMAND.COM and, 299

version code, legacy applications and, 272

VGA mode, enabling, 136–137

ViaVoice, 123

video, 550–551. *See also* **Movie Maker**

acceleration, Media Player, 753–754

file transfer, Media Player, 731

importing files, Movie Maker, 718–719

mobile devices, 731

recording, 716

video adapter, 550–551

video capture card, 718

views

Category, 330–331

Classic, 330–331

System Monitor, 575

Windows Explorer, 199–202

virtual memory, 8, 550

64-bit XP, 13

addresses, 14

paged-based addresses, 14–17

Virtual Memory dialog box, 560–561

virus protection, Outlook Express, 248–249

Visit Gallery options, 147–148

visual effects

performance and, 562–563

Performance and Maintenance, 348

Visual Warning menu, 111

visualizations, Media Player, 736–737, 754–755

3D, 704

VMM (Virtual Memory Manager), 12, 13–14

virtual addresses, 14

VMS (Virtual Memory System), 14

voice playback and recording, 347

voice recognition, 703

volume, Sounds and Audio Devices applet, 346

Volume Control, 170, 175–176

volumes

deleting, 465–467

mirrored volumes, 447

partitions, 446

RAID, 447

spanned volumes, 446

striped volumes, 446–447

types, 446–447

VPN (virtual private network), 674–675, 788

W

Wake on LAN, 626

warning dialog box, 275–276

Warning event, 138, 400

.wav files, 174–175, 702

volume, 346

Weather Map from MSNBC, 148

Web

publishing folders to, 206

publishing movies to, 726

Web pages

on Desktop, 147–150

downloading to Desktop, 149

offline access, 828–829

synchronizing Desktop, 148

Web Publishing Wizard, 206
Web Server, IIS, 834
Web sites, IIS
    creation, 836–837
    directory security, 842
    documents, 841
    home directory, 839–841
    HTTP headers, 843
    management, 837–839
    properties, 839
WfixApp tool, 279
wheel mouse, 343
WHQL (Windows Hardware
    Quality Labs), 605
wildcards in Command
    Prompt, 317–319
WinAmp, 730
windows
    Magnifier, 120
    Outlook Express, 229–232
    size, Command Prompt,
        302–303
Windows 2000
    ERD, 38–39
    upgrading from, 36–39
Windows 95/98
    defragmenting, 49
    network information,
        recording, 31–33
    upgrading from, 35–36
Windows 2000 Professional,
    defragmenting, 50–51
Windows boot process,
    129–135
Windows Catalog Web site,
    12
Windows Components
    Administrative Templates, 379
    Disk Cleanup and, 471
Windows Components
    Wizard, 292–294, 621–622
Windows Components
    Wizard dialog box, 43
Windows Explorer, 196–197
    Arrange Icons By, 201–202
    Details view, 200–201

Filmstrip, 201
Folder pane, 198
icons view, 200
List view, 200
thumbnails, 199–200
Tiles view, 200
toolbar, 197–198
view, changing, 199–202
Windows Me
    defragmenting, 49
    upgrading from, 35–36
Windows Messenger,
    Remote Assistance invita-
    tion, 395
Windows NT, upgrading
    from, 36–39
Windows NT Workstation,
    defragmenting, 49–50
Windows Scripting Host,
    320–321
Windows Unattended
    Installation, 100
Windows Update
    Add/Remove programs and,
        288
    Dynamic Update and, 56
    Recovery Console installation,
        603
    regular use, legacy applica-
        tions and, 279–280
    restore points and, 609
win.ini file, 499
winipcfg utility, 31
winnt.exe command, syntax,
    82–83
winnt32.exe command syn-
    tax, 83–85
WINS (Windows Internet
    Naming Service), 631, 636,
    787
wire protocols, 804–805
wizards
    Accessibility Wizard,
        104–105, 116–117
    Add Hardware Wizard,
        650–652

Add Printer Wizard, 423,
    424–432
Automated System Recovery
    Wizard, 522, 529, 590–594
Backup and Restore Wizard,
    509–511
Backup Wizard, 529–532
CD Writing Wizard, 214
Connection Wizard, 232
Extend Volume Wizard, 458
Files and Settings Transfer
    Wizard, 56–59
Forgotten Password Wizard,
    367–368
New Partition wizard,
    452–453
Online Print Ordering Wizard,
    700–701
Restore Wizard, 529, 538–540
Scanner and Camera
    Installation Wizard, 708–710
Setup Wizard, 54
System Restore Wizard,
    611–613
Web Publishing Wizard, 206
Windows Components
    Wizard, 292–294, 621–622
Wordpad, 170, 183–184
    fonts, 184
    formatting, 184–185
    layout, 184–185
    Narrator and, 118
    objects, inserting, 187
    Options command, 186–187
    Page Setup, 185–186
workgroups, 30
    file sharing, 217–218
    networks, 641
workplace network connec-
    tion, 673–675
Workspace, Movie Maker,
    713, 714–715
    adding clips, 720
    removing clips, 720–721

WOW64 (Windows on Windows 64), 12
WOW (Windows on Windows) subsystem, 11
   pilot program and, 29

X–Y–Z

X.500 standards (LDAP), 798, 799
XCOPY command, 310
yellow triangle with exclamation mark in dialog box, 275
Your Product Key, 64
Zip drives, 47–48
   backups, 522
zipped folders, 203–204
zooming, Paint, 190–191

A Shore Thing

An Otter Bay novel

JULIE CAROBINI

PUBLISHING GROUP
Nashville, Tennessee

Published by B&H Publishing Group
Nashville, Tennessee

Dewey Decimal Classification: F
Subject Heading: LOVE STORIES \
BEACHES—FICTION \ ENVIRONMENTAL
PROTECTION—FICTION

For my children, Matthew, Angie, and Emma—
You are beautiful, each in your own way

Acknowledgments

Thank you, readers, for cheering me on to write seaside stories filled with faith, flip flops, and waves of grace. I have appreciated the letters, e-mails, and Facebook friendships immensely. I'd also like to give a shout out to those who willingly offered their time to help me in various ways while writing *A Shore Thing*.

Thanks to . . .

Tami Anderson, Sherrill Waters, and my husband, Dan, for reading, critiquing, and offering honest advice along the way. Appreciation also to Gary Anderson for the broken piano bench story!

Steve Laube for adeptly handling the business side of things. Karen Ball and Julie Gwinn at B&H Publishing Group—working with you both is a joy. Kudos also to Alton Gansky for your skillfulness and good humor in editing this manuscript.

My family—Dan, Matt, Angie, Emma, and Charlie the Dog, who must survive on mac 'n' cheese or something similar during writing season, along with my inattention—love you! My parents, Dan and Elaine Navarro, who deserve my forever gratitude for cheerleading me through life and storytelling.

A special, huge thank you goes to my architect brother, Daniel Navarro. You helped bring Gage to life and taught me so much about the journey of a hard-working, creative architect. Can't thank you enough, little brother!

My Lord and Savior Jesus Christ without whom I'd be living one empty life. Thank you for filling me daily.

Chapter One

 The rope in my hand resembled a noose. "Sorry, pal, but it was all I could find."

The stray doggy with the dewdrop eyes found me earlier today as I jogged along the shores of Otter Bay while trying to shake off a tough weekend. I slipped the makeshift leash around his skinny neck. It was almost evening now and our trot through the woods on the way to my sister's house for Sunday supper would serve as my halfhearted attempt to find this dog's owner.

Hopefully, they're long gone, because until this pup's arrival, I hadn't realized just how hollow my house with its reclaimed wood flooring and single occupant had begun to sound.

It wasn't supposed to be this way. By my age—and my mother's calculations—I should be living quite comfortably as a wife and mother and keeper of a house surrounded by a white picket fence. "Men aren't attracted to tomboys, Callie," my mother always said, clutching her heart and peering into the sky. She'd always been dramatic like that. Probably a leftover from her days in musical theater, an aspiration she eventually gave up to raise children.

If only *I* understood the rewards of marriage and motherhood. We had this conversation every year.

At thirty years old, though, I understood it fine. I just never seemed to have enough time nor decent prospects— at least not since *The One* got away three years ago—as my mother often put it. I tried never to think about that, but whenever one of my ex-boyfriend Justin's road-hog trailer trucks sped by on the highway, advertising the biggest and best interior plant design company the West Coast had to offer . . . well, a twinge of anger attempted to coil itself around my lungs and squeeze until I could no longer breathe.

I bought my cottage with the proceeds from selling that business to him.

My family contended that my living against the grain had kept my life from progressing to the place they deemed appropriate. And after a day like today, maybe it was time to slow down, to figure out what Callie Duflay's life really *should* look like, to finally admit that, yes, while I often saw the world through a different set of lenses than the rest of my siblings, it didn't have to stay that way.

I stepped it up, realizing that if I was late for supper again, my sister Sheila was going to be ticked.

In the few short hours since he wriggled his way into my unconventional life, Doggy here had already soothed a couple of newly opened wounds, starting with the one that happened soon after I arrived at the camp on the hill for my job as weekend assistant camp director.

I arrived early Friday morning to what might have been a grim discovery: a mouse had wedged itself inside a box of colorful two-by-three cards used for the night game. These things happen when cookies from the evening snack are packed away with games.

Fortunately, though, the little guy still had breath to breathe. So I headed back outside, trudged up a hillside until my calves burned, released him from his makeshift cell, and scooted him in a direction away from camp. He moved slowly at first as if still gasping for life and then his speed quickened as if he knew that sustenance was only one foraging session away. Although it was early spring, the air still held a chill, especially in the shady spot where my feet stood planted. Patches of frost clung to the ground.

I spied a large, wayward plastic disc half-buried in a nest of pine needles and the sand slide the counselors had made the previous week. Positioning the pink disc at the top of the gangly patch, I folded myself inside its tight borders and let go. Like an oversized junior camper, I scraped and slid along the sand, picking up enough speed to skip across cool earth and flatten new growth before landing at the bottom of the hill in a laughing heap.

It never occurred to me that someone might be watching.

"Looks like someone has too much time on their hands." Natalia Medina stood over me in a navy blue tailored suit, holding a clipboard and looking more like she was about to conduct a board meeting than visit camp.

I stood, wiped one hand down the side of my overalls, and reached out to the sole female board member of Pine Ridge Camp. "Hello, Natalia." She shook my hand.

"I'm looking for Thomas. Have you seen him?" She glanced up the hill I'd just rocketed down. An amused smile tugged at her lips. "Then again, perhaps not."

"Actually, Squid—I mean Tom—usually comes in by ten on Fridays. I had to, uh . . ." I turned toward the glistening hill not sure how a woman wearing red leather shoes would handle a mission of mercy for a mouse. "Retrieve a sand toy."

She nodded. "I see that. Well, given your age now, I suppose it's hardly easy to resist one last childhood fling." Her shoulders lifted in a shrug and she laughed, but the squeak that escaped her mouth sounded more like a scoff.

I leaned my head to one side. "Excuse me?"

Natalia patted my shoulder. "I only meant that someone with as much education and years behind you will surely be moving on from here soon." She wrinkled her nose and lowered her voice as if inviting me into her confidence. "Assistant camp director is merely a starter job, right?"

I leaned forward, my eyes fixed on hers. With one quick

draw of my verbal sword, Natalia would find herself backed against the hard trunk of a nearby pine. But did I want to jeopardize a job that allowed me so much freedom? "Actually, I don't plan to leave anytime soon, Natalia. I *love* that this job allows me to work with kids and to be outside so much. Besides, it gives me time to volunteer for some great causes during the week." I put on a smile. "Not many people can say that."

A pause dropped like a taut bubble between us. Natalia cleared her throat and her eyes flitted around. "Perhaps you have a point." She took a step back. "Well, I won't take up any more of your valuable time. Please let Thomas know that I was here to meet with him. Ask him to call my office, would you?"

She didn't wait for my answer.

By Sunday, after two packed days of camp, I had seen more bloody noses and blistered toes than even the most experienced mother would be called upon to care for in any given weekend. And this made Squid's invitation to join him in leading the kids down to the waters of Otter Bay all the more welcoming. Nothing erased a troubling memory quicker than that view, unspoiled by civilization, framed in the clearing.

"Forward, ho!" Squid led the charge through dense pine and fragrant eucalyptus trees. Far above us, clumps of Monarch butterflies still clung together as they hung from laden branches. It was going to be a late spring.

As I stepped up the pace, ten-year-old Xander marched alongside me and his fellow campers, his rigidity a protest against the apparent torture of a nature hike. "It's a bunch of trees!"

His proclamation stirred within me the desire to prove him wrong, so I laughed and patted his back. "Just *wait*, mister. Once you get to where we're going, you won't ever want to leave."

He crossed his arms. "Doubt that."

Squid spun around and marched backward while still moving us forward. I took another look at our illustrious leader at the front of the pack. Charismatic and brilliant with the children, yet down-to-earth and humble, he defied my usual aversion to ordinary men. I'd been thinking twice about him lately.

His eyes connected with mine. "You pullin' up the rear, Seabird?"

I sent him a smile from my place at the back of the group of mostly ten- and eleven-year-old campers. "I'm pullin' it up!"

He nodded and winked at me, continuing to walk backward. "Watchin' for escapees?"

I tossed Squid a playful salute. "That I am." At about that spot the campers, mostly boys, often became distracted by the meandering stream that wiggled its way through this land. Dreams of gathering sticks and creating dams danced through their minds.

A rugged smile broke out across Squid's closely-bearded face. The brightness of his smile dazzled. "Well then, carry on." He spun back around, and faced forward as he led us through the forest.

My senses filled with the crispness of pine-infused air, the effect so cleansing that it almost wiped away the sting of condescension that pricked me at the start of this particular weekend. Not quite, but almost.

Even as I inhaled the cool breeze that tickled my cheeks while we moved along on the hike, I continued to replay my conversation with Natalia. Who knew that I could be a victim of ageism at such a young age? Most of the college-aged counselors working weekends at camp liked to give me good-natured ribbing about my *wisdom* and *experience*, while I teased them about wearing diapers and sucking pacifiers. It's always been in jest because—really—is thirty all that much older than those fresh-faced souls who walk the hallowed halls of academe?

Excitement interrupted my wallowing. "The beach!" Xander, who only moments before had dug in his heels, lit up, enthusiasm glowing on his young face. "Woo! Yeah! The beach!"

Squid caught my eye and I went on alert, ready to corral campers who tried to dart for the sea which lay at the foot of the cliff. Most of the kids lived too far inland to be able to visit the beach very often, let alone a protected cove so saturated with marine life like this. My heart leapt at the thought of sharing this place with the kids, one of the few panoramic vistas untouched by development.

We stood at the edge and gazed at the beach below. Etched rock formations and drenched peaks rose from the bottom of the sea. Soon the pitted and crevice-carved home of bountiful marine life would lie exposed in the sun. A perfect day for tide-pooling. Squid raised the bullhorn along with the camper's sign of respect displayed on one hand: the thumb, forefinger, and pinky. He waited, his stance unruffled, until every eye was on him. His sober expression may shake up the kids, but I knew better. Lines at the corner of Squid's eyes stretched gently toward his temples, belying a smile.

The campers quieted. "Okay, my friends, listen up." Squid put on his tough voice. I've heard it so often that I could replay it in my dreams. "Pretty soon, we'll head down those stairs and do some tide-pooling at negative tide. That means the water level is lower than average. While it *is* possible to walk out further than the boundary markers we'll be giving you—don't do it."

"A-ah!" Xander protested.

I held my forefinger to my pursed lips, urging Xander and his buddies to listen.

Squid continued. "After lunch, my assistant Seabird over here and I will be explaining the rules of exploring to you—"

A hand went up.

Squid nodded at Megan, the youngest of our campers here this weekend. "Hang on, Meggy, and I'll get around to you in a second. For all the rest, get into your preassigned groups. The lunch wagon has arrived compliments of Tidal Wave—aka camp cook. And the counselors will be handing out *de-li-cious* ham and cheese sandwiches with all the fixins to the quietest groups first."

Rustling and shushing went on all around us, the hungriest campers urging their group mates to quiet down. Squid was about to signal the counselors that it was time to serve the lunches when Megan's petite hand rose above her curly brown hair again.

"Yes, Megan. Did you want to say something?"

Her grin barely fit across her face. "I was just wondering . . . is Seabird your girlfriend?"

The rest of Megan's group—older girls whose counselors had been coaxed into welcoming the young one to join their cabin—giggled behind hand-covered faces. A couple of boys in the back stood and crashed back onto the ground as if they'd been shot by wayward arrows.

Squid smiled and nodded. "All right, all right." He held up the sign of respect. "Seabird and *all* the counselors are my friends. Now eat your lunch or we'll miss out on that super-low tide." He shot me a wink that sent a quiver right down my leg.

Squid and I had been a team for more than a year. As my own duties had grown, though, I missed having more opportunities to participate in hikes like these—especially with him at the helm. Hiring Squid for camp director was the smartest decision the board ever made. At twenty-nine, he still wore youthful exuberance like a treasured baseball cap. And yet I'd have to be blind and stupid not to notice him as more than an energetic leader. How could I not notice the way his chiseled arms fit snugly against the flannel of his sleeves, or the way his white teeth flashed against dark facial hair when he smiled? Dare I admit how an unfamiliar warmth flowed through me when our eyes linked and I knew precisely what he was about to say?

"Sandwich?" Carp, one of the counselors, handed me a paper bag, and then another to Squid.

We stood, Squid and I, shoulder to shoulder while watching the children. He swallowed a bite. "Join me on that rock over there?"

I gave him a sideways glance. "Sure."

Settled on the rock, our lunches on our laps, we continued to eat in silence while watching the campers. There really was no place I'd rather be, and yet sitting that close to Squid my mind gave way again to uncharted thoughts. The late morning breeze wrapped us in its coolness, and goose bumps rose on my skin. I'd forgotten how to act around someone so intriguing. Did our sudden wordlessness seem awkward to him too?

Megan tossed her lunch sack into one of the trash bags held by a counselor, and then skipped toward us. She plopped herself next to me. "You know what? I think you *are* boyfriend and girlfriend!"

Squid laughed through a bite of sandwich. "Why's that?"

Megan giggled. "I know a lot of things. My sister is a teenager."

I wrapped my arm around her shoulder and gave her a squeeze, laughter in my own voice. "Well, then, that explains it."

Squid bumped my shoulder with his. "Shall we tell her then?"

My chin whipped to the side and I faced him then. I never realized the silver gleam in his eyes before this. "Tell her?"

Squid's bright grin filled his face. He sent me one of his familiar winks before bending closer to speak directly to Megan. "Seabird here is just too old for me."

GAGE

THE ALARM'S SHRILL ANNOUNCEMENT that daylight had come in all its complicated glory rousted Gage from the warmth of rumpled sheets. He hadn't slept well and couldn't sleep now if he wanted to—not with young Jeremiah's thunderous four-year-old footsteps to greet him.

Seven a.m. When had he begun to sleep in so late?

Gage smacked the alarm clock's snooze button. It felt wrong to get up on a Sunday morning knowing full well he ought to be attending church rather than working. He hoped his friend Marc wouldn't call under the guise of shooting the breeze when it was really a lame attempt to discover whether he had found a church yet in this little town.

He had, but no time today. Gage had work to do. He lolled in bed a minute more, listening to the commotion coming from the living room, trying to picture the scene. Jeremiah liked to roll his dump truck across the Spanish tile hearth before school. Suz, Gage's baby sister, would have the coffee brewing. Maybe there'd even be enough milk left for him to pour himself a bowl of granola to eat along with that coffee.

He startled at the soft rap on the door. "Gage? Coffee's on."

Gage pressed a weary hand to his face and rubbed his eyes. A slight smile raised the corners of his mouth at the sound of Suz's voice wafting in from the hall. "Thanks. I'm on it." He sat up in bed, determined to plant both feet on the floor in spite of the growing disquiet that had formed in his gut. He would not allow his anxiety to flourish, no matter what. If not for his own sake, then for the welfare of those he'd promised always to protect.

Chapter Two

Too *old*? First Natalia, and now . . . Squid. My eyes shut at the thought of him smiling at me so winsomely before delivering the deathblow to my daydream. Whoever said that fifty had become the new thirty had gotten it backwards. My face felt crimson, even though it had been hours since Squid made his proclamation about my advanced age to little Megan. How could I have been so stupid as to believe that Squid could have any feelings for me other than the kind of friendship that happened when two people worked together? We were cohorts, and nothing else.

I had returned to the scene of the crime with only a stray dog as my companion. The negative tide had long gone. Only the dramatic peaks of darkened rock appeared above the tide line, and soon that would be gone too. I always came here when troubled, and besides, walking the path was one of the best ways to prep myself for the Sunday suppers that my sister Sheila hosted each week.

By the number of lingerers found resting in contemplation on stumps of fallen trees or splayed atop blankets on the tall grass, others appreciated the solitude here too.

Three men stood together near the ridge all holding notebooks in front of them. My muddled mind nearly missed their curious presence until one of them pitched a lit cigarette over the cliff.

Startled, my chest reeled and anger sucked air out of my lungs. "What . . . What are you doing? Do you realize you just flicked your cigarette into a protected marine sanctuary?"

Even to me, my voice sounded acerbic, but *que sera sera*. As if I were invisible, the men looked past me. So I repeated myself.

One of them, the largest of the three, hunkering in stature, took a step toward me and I tightened my grip on Doggy's leash. The man squinted, his smile pinched and mocking. "Guess someone's not doing their job then."

My blood heated. I should have continued walking, but I was in no mood to back down from a fight. My mouth wouldn't hear of it. "Otters are finally making a comeback, but because of people like you, they're likely to choke and die off again."

Three looming men stood near the edge of one of the most pristine and undeveloped stretches of land here in Otter Bay and watched me, their expressions all too familiar. Patronizing. Insulting.

Except for the one who wore flip-flops, jeans, and a button-down shirt. Instead of the ridicule I'd come to expect from certain people, the laid-back one watched me with a sort of curiosity. *Don't expect brownie points for that.*

As if taking my side, the ocean surged. All three men sidestepped the cliff's precarious edge. Sea spray landed on the camera hanging around the neck of the bald man in the middle and he cursed.

I cocked my head. "Hope none of your pictures were sullied by litter."

He shook his head and sauntered away from the pack, pointing his lens at the land, his back to the ocean and to me. The lumbering one continued to glare at me as I proceeded along the path worn into the earth by thousands of pairs of feet that came before to this magical place. More than the view captivated people here. It was also the call of the otters, sea lions, and whales that roamed along the shore, and the song of the birds—pelicans, cormorants, and murres—that migrated overhead on the Pacific Flyway. Even those children we brought from camp, the ones bemoaning their fast from everything electronic and cellular, got lost in the adventure when they arrived.

I breathed in the clean air, and attempted to shake off the annoyance that crept up my back when I noticed that burning ash being tossed into the water. Tension still gripped my shoulders. With my mind focused on the horizon, I pulled Doggy along and failed to notice the tripod laying in my path—until tripping over it. I hung onto the leash and avoided falling by landing hard against the rough surface of a pine tree, both my right elbow and my dignity shredded. Laughter spiked the air a short distance away. Closer to me, a scraping sound chewed the earth as someone dragged the tripod off the path.

The man with the flip-flops and quizzical smile stepped toward me and his eyes homed in on mine. "Don't move."

My breathing caught for a moment, but then I ignored him and pushed myself away from the tree trunk using my other arm. Droplets of dark red blood oozed from the wound on my elbow and I winced, the breeze against my raw skin gave me a sickening chill.

"Here. Let me help." The man continued to stay by my side, his arm outstretched as if I needed steadying. His buddies were less than chivalrous, their snickers still alive.

"No. Thank you. You have done enough damage for one day." I glanced at the length of metal I tripped over, and then back at him. Doggy began to whimper. "That looks like survey equipment."

He shoved both hands into his pockets and nodded his head once. "It is."

"Well, why? This land isn't being developed."

He stood silent, the corner of his mouth turned upward. The furrow above his brow told me how wrong I was.

My hands found a place to steady themselves on my hips. I ignored the shooting pain in my elbow and shook my head. "Tell me you're kidding."

He shrugged. "It's not my call. Listen, you need to get that wound cleaned up. I've got a first aid kit in my truck." He pointed up the hill. "If you'll wait here I'll run up and—"

My head snapped side to side. "The Kitteridges own this property. They'd never sell it, and certainly not to someone who would put up houses on it—"

"Condos. Mixed-use, actually."

"Mixed-use? As in offices and residences? Here?"

He nodded but made no eye contact. "Largest development this county has ever seen."

His pronouncement hit me harder than my fall. June and Timothy Kitteridge opened up this property years ago as a thank-you to the community of Otter Bay. After their popular gallery, Kitt's on Display, burned to the ground, and the county's trail of red tape delayed the rebuilding of their store, the citizens of the town took it upon themselves to pitch in once the murky waters of bureaucracy had cleared.

I glanced toward the sea where a gull dipped against a cloudy sky. The Kitteridges closed their store last year, saying they were looking forward to retirement and spending more time with their only daughter, Chloe, who had moved to another state. I had ignored the rumors that told a sadder tale. The Kitteridges were broke and had no choice but to board up Kitt's for good.

A harsh voice barked from behind. "Dude. We're gonna finish up here and go get burgers. You can call the office for your survey. It's a doozy, so it might be awhile."

Heavy boots crunched against dirt as the other men left the area. I focused on the man in charge and cocked my chin. "It's not your call, huh?"

He held up two palms. "I'm just the architect. The survey will help in the design process, once the sale actually goes through, that is." His face looked as grim as I felt.

"It hasn't closed yet?"

He shook his head and then offered me his hand. "Gage, by the way. Gage Mitchell."

He had two first names. I read somewhere that people with two first names were suspect, but then again, what about Patrick Henry and John Adams? *Or Benjamin Franklin?* A sigh slipped away from me. "I'm just so surprised . . . and so sad." I glanced again at the swell of ocean water so teeming with unseen life, and then back to Gage. "I'm Callie, and you might as well know, you'll be hearing my name a lot in the coming days."

He smiled at me again. "Really? And why is that?"

I answered his smile with a frown. "Because I think I've just found a new cause."

GAGE

SO MUCH FOR THE 'friendly, small-town atmosphere' he'd read within the folds of Otter Bay's tourist brochure. *I've seen friendlier women at a boxing match.* He shook his head at the air, picturing the now-meaningless words splashed across a shiny page in a jaunty, coral-colored font.

Gage watched Callie take the hill as she'd probably done hundreds of times before, confidently and purposefully, like a doe might leap in and around forested land. She was no docile member of the deer family, though. He could tell by the way she snapped at the three strangers who had dared to finish their work in her presence, two of whom nearly doubled her in size.

Until last night when he'd lain awake fretting over the enormity of this endeavor, everything else about this project screamed "God is control." He'd acquired this job mere hours after watching his career implode, the developer wore deep pockets and stayed out of the limelight, and Gage had finally overcome the fear of launching a dream business, in a new location.

So why did his stomach churn after this chance meeting with the town grump?

He swiveled his gaze out toward the equally tumultuous sea, just beyond the rocky cliff. A fissure of doubt unsettled him. Not over his abilities as an architect—he knew he had the skills and the passion to create what his client desired. And he also believed that the community would be proud of the finished project, a sprawling and sustainable mixed-use development. Eventually.

Maybe it wasn't what she said, but the expression on her face as she questioned him. Her eyes had narrowed just so, even as her brows knit closer to one another and her lips parted, the corners weighted down. She looked wounded. His actions had somehow wounded the prettiest if not angriest woman in town.

That shouldn't have bothered him much, but unfortunately, it did.

Chapter Three

 I left Gage Mitchell behind to ponder my seriousness about fighting his new job, and stepped up what was supposed to have been a leisurely stroll to my sister's home. My legs moved faster, my elbow stiffer and more pain-filled with each stride. Surely even my high-strung older sister would understand when I told everyone—the whole family's having supper together—that the Kitteridge property was in peril.

Something brushed against my leg, and I skittered sideways before whipping a look down to find the dog with round, sorrowful eyes, and a long, skinny body staring up at me. Our eyes connected and, quite dutifully, he sat. Oh my. I knelt and gave him my hand to sniff which he did with little emotion. With a roll of my wrist, I petted him on the noggin. "Almost forgot about you, my friend."

Those eyes implored me with questions, but I was at a loss. I swept a look around while on my knees, massaging his body, unable to spy anyone searching for a lost dog. "Where's your family, kiddo?" I stroked his naked neck, exposing the area where a collar usually sat and the fur had worn off. He lowered himself until flat on the ground. The sun had long moved past its mid-day point, and my sister's chastising voice grew louder inside my head.

With reluctance, I gave the doggy one last pet and stood. "Sorry, pal. I'm late, and my sister will surely give me an earful about that. She's probably right . . . sometimes I do get distracted, but I have good reason. I really do." I peeked around again. "See, my sister is busy with her husband and her kids—Brenna and Blake; you'd love them. Anyway, she doesn't understand that when a passion burns inside me, I can't turn it off. Know what I mean?" He pitched his head to one side, making me laugh. "Okay, maybe not. We'd better go."

I broke into a jog with Doggy at my side along the winding path up a hill that led to Sheila's rambling ranch-style home in the pines. For as long as I could remember my family had never taken my causes—or me for that matter—seriously. I usually chalked it up to being the baby of the family, but I knew there was more to it than that. I had tasted success with Oasis Designs, yet, in their minds, my stubbornness made me walk away from everything I'd built.

Didn't they understand the real reason I took Justin's offer to buy me out?

I neared the top, my breathing jagged, my face overheated, when my stray friend raced me toward the peak. His tongue hung from his mouth, rubbery and pink like a warm strip of taffy. I stopped and bit my lip. *How would Sheila react if I brought him along?* As I stood there, debating how a four-legged date might disrupt our family gathering, my new friend hoisted himself on his hind legs, looking much like a miniature kangaroo. He sniffed my aching elbow and gave it a swift lick. How gross. *And precious.*

With my good arm, I placed a fist on my hip. "Okay, my new friend, you're invited. Just be on your best behavior." His tail wagged in agreement and we headed up the hill, Sheila's picture-perfect home framed in the clearing.

My sister welcomed me, if you could call it that, at the door. "You're late again." The rooster on her apron glared at me, and Sheila stared over my shoulder. "What is that?"

"Oh, Sheila, you're never going to believe—"

She turned her back on me. "With you, sure I would. Don't bring that thing in, and hurry up, we've already started eating." I watched her sidle away.

In one quick bend, I scooped up the doggy—really must find him a name—slipped along the side of the house and opened up the back gate to a long and wide expanse of manicured lawn. "Here you go, mister. Behave and maybe I'll bring you some quiche or something." He gazed at me with wondrous eyes. "Okay, some red meat. I'll find you some. Promise."

I slipped in through the slider door. "Auntie Callie, you're here!" My six-year-old niece Brenna rolled from her chair and into my arms. We laughed in unison, her hug sending us both onto Sheila's pomegranate-colored Oriental rug, the one she ordered from the Front Door catalog at half price.

She buried her chubby face into my hair, and I breathed her in. "How's my girl?"

"Ggrrreat!"

Sheila's agitated voice cut through our giggles. "Brenna, get off that floor. Go wash your hands again now."

Brenna scampered off and Sheila passed by with a platter of fish. She muttered into my ear. "You should know better."

I rose, smiled, shrugged, and glanced at the rest of the family. "Hey, everybody."

A spattering of hellos filled the air like an out of sync choir. My mother smooched my cheek and my father raised his glass in my direction. My brother Jim gave me a straight-mouthed smile, much like the one he might give my never-present nephew Kirk when he asked for the car keys one too many times, and his wife Nancy tossed me a parade wave, before glancing away.

Greta, my brother Bobby's wife, gestured to me with graceful fingers, while her other hand lay quite motherly across her burgeoning belly. As the second course made its way around the table, Bobby rose to greet me. Laughter lit his eyes as he found my ear. "Can't wait to hear what you're up to now."

I stuck out my tongue, surreptitiously of course, the way I learned to do when we were kids. With just seventeen months between us, we learned to say much without many words.

"Pass the potatoes, please." Blake, my five-year-old nephew was seated next to me. He giggled. I laughed back. "What?"

He raised his chin, showing me his shiny white teeth and impish smile. "That's a tongue twister—pass the potatoes please!"

Sheila corrected him with her eyes. "Close your mouth when you're eating, Blakey."

Greta bumped me with her shoulder. "Tell me something to keep my mind off all these contractions I'm having."

I sucked in a breath and turned to face her. My eyes roamed from her belly to her eyes. "You're having contractions already?"

Greta giggled. "Don't worry. Little Higglebottom or Mollysue still has time to play in there."

She had been teasing us with name ideas for months. I laughed and released a sigh of relief.

Sheila grunted from her spot at the one end of the table. "They're Braxton-Hicks—just some false labor pains—not the real thing."

I relaxed my shoulders, but swung my gaze back to Greta. "They sound serious to me."

Sheila passed a bowl of beans to her husband, Vince, before addressing me again. "Of course they do, Callie. Lots of serious things get your attention—always have. We all know how much you love your causes."

Vince guffawed. Jim nodded while taking in another bite of fish.

I set down my fork. "Did I miss something? I thought we were talking about Greta."

Greta touched my arm as Sheila shrugged. "I had asked you to tell me what you were up to these days."

I hesitated before picking up my fork and glancing around. "Same old thing. Working at the camp on weekends, and keeping busy on projects the rest of the time." I continued to hold my fork in midair, an empty sensation growing in my gut. "Did you all hear that the Kitteridge property is being developed?"

My mother clutched her heart. "Heavens, no! They would never!"

My father grunted something unintelligible.

I shook my head. "Well, somebody's trying to." I looked to Bobby. "Do you know anything about it?"

My brother, the younger of the two, shook his head. "Yes and no. I've heard talk through one of my investors. I didn't tell him this, but I've figured for a while this would never get past the planning commission. Are you sure that it has?"

"I'm not sure of anything. All I know is that a couple of goons were surveying the property, and that an architect has already been hired. Saw them all today." My heart thudded in my chest. "If we're going to try to stop this, we'd better get on it quick."

Sheila bolted upright against her chair. "Stop this? What makes you think *you* could do anything about it? What's done is, apparently, done." She turned to Blakey. "Eat your beans."

"Well, I have to at least *try*. Surely there's something the community can do to preserve that open space. There's hardly any of it left anymore, and property bordering the sanctuary should have special consideration. Don't you think?"

Sheila's grim expression and downcast eyes offered me her usual opinion. I'd seen that expression on her face many times.

Nancy twisted to look at Jim. "I would love to buy a home on that property once it's built. That would be fabulous!"

Jim, the oldest, sat back, his arm laid casually atop Nancy's chair. "We're not in the old USSR, Callie. Private property is just that; people can do what they want in our country, whether you care for their choices or not."

My bite of potatoes lodged in my throat like mush. I downed some water. "So if you decide to raze your house and put up a mini-mart, for example, your neighbors have no input at all? Is that what you're saying?"

Jim removed his arm from its perch on Nancy's chair, and his sober face matched Sheila's. "Take it from someone who's been around awhile longer, Callie. You may have been able to convince the church to bus homeless to services, but city hall is far too big for you to take on. Let it go."

Nancy nodded in agreement.

Greta, appearing serene amidst the thickening tension in the room, leaned toward me. "Maybe they're right, sweetie. Why bother?"

My chest tightened. I'd been in this place before, and not just physically, but emotionally too. Justin used the same tone of voice the first time he tried to talk me into selling a piece of our company to a high bidder.

"We'll never do this on our own, Callie," he had pleaded. "This guy has the bucks to help us make our dreams come true."

But the investor in question had wanted a controlling interest in the company. *Our* company. He wanted to jack up prices, use suppliers with less than reputable quality, and pay our employees dirt rates. We had only just begun, so why would I agree to give everything away before we'd even had a chance to try to make it on our own?

Jim advised me to take the money and run.

Sheila urged me to listen to Justin—then marry him quick.

Even Bobby said he doubted a better offer would ever come my way.

Not taking their advice had furthered the divide between my siblings and me, at least the older two who seemed to think it was up to them to provide parental guidance since our own were so often traveling. "Traveling away our golden years," as Mom always said.

And it definitely drove a wedge between Justin and me. If I had acquiesced early on, would our story have had a different ending?

At times I still wondered.

I took in the faces of each of my family members, aware of how quickly they moved on to other conversations and topics. Why hadn't the news about the Kitteridge property bothered them as much as it bothered me? They passed platters and flung jokes with ease. After Vince delivered a punch line, my brother Jim threw back his head and launched his booming voice to the rafters while our father smiled mildly at his model son with the comedic bent.

In the backyard my doggy companion smashed his nose against the clear French door, his breath and wet tongue leaving a mess that resembled my mood: foggy and in disarray. While my family had moved on—rather quickly even for them—I had not. I planned to call the Kitteridges first thing tomorrow. Maybe they would have a change of heart.

Chapter Four

Bobby's voice sounded groggy over the phone. "It's seven in the morning, Callie."

"You used to be an insomniac."

He sighed. "That was before we got pregnant."

I laughed. "We?"

"You know what I mean—Greta's pregnant, and she's been keeping me up late with baby projects." I heard him yawn. "And now my kid sister won't let me get my beauty rest."

Thank God for Bobby. Everyone called him Bob but me. I refused to be pulled into the stodginess that so much of my family had embraced. Despite his usual tailored, nine-to-five inspired appearance in a white starched shirt coupled with dark, pressed pants, one look at Bobby and in my heart we're five and six again, huddled at the cove during low tide, trying to pry an abalone from its rocky home—before learning that was a big no-no, of course.

He grunted into the phone. "You still there? Or did you wake me for nothing?"

"I've been thinking all night about the Kitteridge property."

Bobby groaned. "You're obsessed. You know that?"

I grimaced. "What? Am I really the only one who thinks that property is worth saving? Don't you remember all the hikes we took down there? We'd be gone for hours—"

"Of course I remember."

My left hand gestured while I talked, even though no one was around to see it. "If we don't at least try to intervene, your baby will never have the kind of childhood you and I did."

"So what do you want me to do?"

"Advise me. Help me figure out where to turn first."

"Before I've even had my coffee?" He sighed. "Don't you think you should call the Kitteridges first?"

"Of course, and I did that already. There was no answer, though. I haven't seen Timothy's old Ford pickup rambling through town in days, and I think they may have gone to visit their daughter." I tapped my pencil on the table. "You and I are both old enough to remember how they promised to leave that piece of land open for the community—that's what they've always wanted—so my guess is that they aren't aware of the buyer's plans."

Bobby sighed again. "Or maybe they are very aware of it and don't want to face the neighbors."

"You think they know?"

Bobby's low voice challenged me. "Maybe we shouldn't interfere, Callie. They might really need the cash."

My heart softened recalling the recent rumors about the Kitteridges' money troubles. "I've wondered that too, but maybe they can sell the property to someone else. Maybe the city should buy it for a park."

He scoffed. "Fat chance. Otter Bay is synonymous with 'cash-strapped' these days."

"Oh, shush. Financial hard times or not, this is one of the most beautiful spots on earth. All I'm asking is for help in collecting information."

The tone of Bobby's voice turned lighter. "That's it? Collecting info, huh? Sounds more like you're building a case."

My sigh was drenched in exasperation. "Against a project that just might ruin Otter Bay forever!"

This time Bobby's sigh blew through the receiver. "I don't know why you always fight so hard, but okay. You can start by calling the National Marine Sanctuary office. Try searching Google for the number."

I scribbled that down. "Check. What next?"

"How should I know?"

"What about your friend . . . the money guy? He seems well-connected."

"Henry? No, no. He's a private guy who prefers to stay out

of the limelight. Let's keep him out of this. Besides what he told me was said in confidence—and secondhand."

"But he may—"

"He's off-limits, Callie."

I huffed. "Okay. Fine. Thanks for the advice."

"Callie?"

My mouth twisted into a pucker. "Hmm?"

"I hope you get somewhere with all this."

I thanked my brother and hung up. Although I always put two feet forward into any situation that caught my heart, my family seemed to believe this would be my undoing. I finished college in three years including summers and took mostly night classes so I could keep the days open for whatever cause came my way: working at the garden co-op, teaching school children how to grow pumpkins from seeds, volunteering in the fight to keep the library open, things like that. After graduation, there was the interior plant design business I opened with Justin . . .

I turned to the computer, hoping to dig up the Sanctuary office phone number. Within seconds, the number appeared on the screen.

"National Marine Sanctuary. How may I help you?"

I cleared my throat. "I'm wondering about some property."

"We don't sell real estate, ma'am."

I squeezed my eyes shut, hoping to clear my head. Maybe Bobby was right. Certain things should not be tackled before the requisite caffeine boost. "Sorry. Listen, I've learned that property abutting a portion of the National Marine Sanctuary is being considered for a large development, and I'm wondering why this would be allowed."

The woman paused. Had I annoyed her? "I feel your frustration. I really do, but frankly, there is not much help we can offer you. We do not regulate development in the coastal zone, unless of course the structure is to be constructed over the water. Is that the case?"

"I'm not sure. All I know is that there are plans for some kind of mixed-use development—which would be great in town."

"But probably not-so-terrific along federally protected waters. I hear you."

My heart lifted. "So you might be able to help?"

"I wish we could, but you see, our jurisdiction does not extend inland beyond the mean high tide line. My guess is that you would have to work within your local jurisdictions for permitting clarifications on upland developments."

"I understand."

"Miss?"

"Yes?"

"Good luck."

My heart sank and I glanced at the Sunday paper still spread across my kitchen table. Not one mention of an impending shoreline project lay within its pages. And although a tattered welcome flag furled and snapped in the wind from its perch on the Kitteridge home, there was still no sign of the elderly couple in Otter Bay.

My mysterious doggy friend jostled my leg, and I gave him a pet while still sorting through my thoughts. It was going to take more than good luck to figure out what was really going on down by the shore.

Monday, my usual day to plow through the housework left behind by a busy life, and yet here I was, taking another trek along the bluffs at Otter Bay.

Lord, please don't let this area be fenced off from your people.

Sheila would come down hard on me for a prayer like that. She'd say, "Prayers are for important things, not the whims of your head."

What made her think my quest was a whim?

Doggy tugged at my homemade leash. His nose had been moving faster than a hungry squirrel since the moment we arrived here. "We need to find your owner, you know." I glanced around, deep translucent blue ocean water on my left and a slow rise of land to my right. There would be chances for searching out his owner later.

"Excuse me? Do you have the time?" The woman's voice sounded familiar.

I glanced back at her. "Sorry, no. Don't have a watch."

The woman shrugged. "Me neither." She stood tall and wiry and wore a floppy hat over moppish, blonde curls. Ruth. Her name was Ruth. We'd been thrown together on the library fund-raising project two years back. She had an obsession with lead ink in books and had lobbied to have testing added to the library's budget.

I smiled at her. "Ruth, right? It's been a long time, but we worked together awhile back."

She returned a feeble smile. "We did?"

My smile faded. "On the library project about two years ago?"

Her mouth puckered as she squinted and began a slow nod. "Yes, uh-huh."

I swallowed the sigh that wanted to barrel out of me. Why didn't I just say I didn't have a watch and keep on moving? Even in this small community, I had somehow managed to stay invisible to so many.

Ruth popped a gloved finger into the air. "Wait. You set up a composting system over at the library and helped build a rain garden. Right?"

Vindicated. "That's me."

She grasped my hand and gave it a few quick pumps, her glove rough and scratchy against my palm. "Sorry. Didn't recognize you at first. It's been a long time."

I put one foot in front of me to keep her at bay. She's a close talker and I'd forgotten about that. "Yes. Long time."

She lifted a bloated garbage sack with her other gloved hand. "I've been picking up trash all the way from south of the cove. I usually do this on Mondays. Never seen you here before."

I shrugged. "Probably the only day of the week that I don't make it here. I'm usually cleaning up the house after working the weekend up at Pine Ridge."

"The camp?" There. That's the expression I remembered from her. Ruth's right cheek muscle stuck in a grimace, causing one eye to remain half closed. "Bet there's a lot of mess up there."

"Not really." I considered the mouse trapped in the box with days-old crumbs. "Well, maybe a little. But teaching the kids to clean up after themselves is part of the program. By the time the weekend is over they're able to handle KP like pros."

"Glad to hear it." She dropped the bag and the doggy approached her. "Who's this?"

Again I shrugged. "Wish I knew. He followed me home yesterday."

She squatted and gave the doggy a good scrub. "He's skinny and without a collar, so that makes him yours. Adoptees are the best kind of pets in my book. And this one's already in love with you." She gave him one more pet before standing. He came back to me and sat at my heel. "Told you."

Her comment lifted my spirit and I let the leash drop to my side. My smile widened when I thought about telling Mom how I'd finally decided to start that family.

Far behind Ruth, a lone man paced the eastern path beneath some pine trees located at the top of the incline. His head hung forward; hands clasped behind his back. He walked to the left for several paces, and then to the right, and back again.

Ruth followed my gaze. "We get all kinds out here. Maybe he's one of those labyrinth walkers, although shouldn't he be going in a circle?"

I started to laugh, but air caught in my windpipe.

Ruth watched me. "What is it? He an old flame?"

"Not exactly." I pulled my stare away from Gage and his curious behavior. "He's an architect on a mission to turn this acreage into condos and office buildings."

"Impossible. The Kitteridges—"

"—are apparently selling this property."

She planted both hands on her hips. "Nu-uh."

"Uh-huh."

"Says who? What makes you think that could ever happen? Especially here?"

As I told her what I knew, she twisted in the breeze first looking to the dramatic sea and then back at the intense architect pacing the hill.

"But the property's not actually sold yet? Is that right?"

"I believe that's true."

"So we stop it. Plain and simple."

Relief gushed through me, a warmth cascading over my shoulders. Having an ally would be a great help, especially one with time and a can-do attitude. Hopefully she'd remember me the next time we met. "It's a daunting task, but I've got some ideas."

"I'll make some calls, you make some calls, and see who we can find to make some noise about this. Can you imagine Otter Bay without this open land?"

My listlessness returned. "No, I can't. I don't know what has happened to change the Kitteridges' mind, but it must be serious." I found Ruth's eyes. "I've been hoping to speak with them directly, to see if they might work with us to come up with a solution."

"Go ahead and do it, but I'm not holding my breath. Now, let's figure this out." She peered into the sky as if it had a mighty day planner stretched across it. "Let's meet at the RAG, say, Thursday morning at nine, after the breakfast crowd goes. You in?"

I hesitated, a tightness squeezing the muscles of my chest. I loved the beachside diner located near a spattering of quaint inns north of here. But had I gathered enough information yet for a meeting? "Okay." I paused. Still unable to fully fill my lungs with air. Agreeing to meet with others on this matter some how hadn't given me the lift I expected. "I'll come."

Ruth grabbed the bag of trash and slung it over one shoulder. She took another look at Gage in the distance and curled her lip, her cheek scrunching into that familiar grimace as she tossed me a wave and continued on with her volunteer work.

GAGE

FROM HIS POST ON the hill, Gage stopped mid-pace. He straightened and shaded his eyes with a notebook, the other hand poised in a greeting. Even from this distance, he could see the scowl forming on her face. Callie's dog tugged at the leash wound around her hand, and she spun toward the beach, giving Gage her back.

The congenial smile he hoped to convey, faded. He followed a path down the hill toward the sea, watching her use a boulder to steady herself for the climb down the cliff. He could've gone back to his work then. Maybe he should have. Instead, he found himself stopping an awkward distance away, watching her.

She spun back around then with a force that caused him to reel slightly before righting himself. He watched the sunlight glint of the waves of her hair as she stomped toward him, and wearing a look that told him she had something to say.

She cocked her chin. "Didn't take enough notes yesterday?"

He felt a smile glide back onto his face. "Hello, again, Callie. Beautiful day, isn't it?"

She paused. "You know, unless you're being paid by the hour, your wallet might be better off if you didn't spend so much time around here. Could be a big waste."

He shrugged, still smiling, and glanced around. He let his arms rest by his sides, one hand still grasping a yellow legal pad and a fat pencil. "I don't mind at all. I still have much to work through and besides." His eyes found hers again, and he concentrated so she wouldn't see laughter behind them. "Can't beat the view."

She gripped doggy's leash and he strained against it. "But that's exactly what you and your cronies are trying to do— beat the view."

"Actually, I'm trying to work within it." He held up his pad of notes. "That's why I'm here again now studying the site. I like to sit, and to listen . . . to get a feel for what the land is saying."

She crossed her arms, the leash still firmly in her grip. "I'll tell you what it's saying. It's saying, 'Mosey on now, there's nothing for you here.'"

He couldn't stop himself then and a guffaw blurted from him. Her eyes narrowed, the only reaction to his show of emotion. Gage cleared his throat and looked out to sea. "Have you ever watched closely where the sun falls at different times of day?"

"Sure. I guess."

"Whenever I build anything, I study the light carefully. Make sense?"

Her pursed lips twitched before answering him. "Energy efficiency is important."

"Sure it is. But there are other things to consider. For instance, northern light produces the most even rays. That's what your typical artist studio would need. On the other hand, southern light may provide the best illumination, but it's positioned so high that it won't provide optimum heat."

She pulled the leash taut. "So it wouldn't be the best in cool climates, then."

His smile grew across his face, slowly at first, then open and wide. She tried to keep up the bravado, but he could tell by the way her mouth and eyes relaxed, that she was softening. "You're following me."

She shrugged then, refusing to make eye contact with him. "I read."

He paused. "Still upset about the plans for this property?" He knew the answer before asking the question.

She turned her head toward the ocean and he did as well, taking in its variant blues and greens. Who wouldn't be upset to lose access to something so mighty yet peaceful all at the same time? But she knew . . . she *had* to know that the sea didn't belong to the people of this town, and neither did this land. Leaving it untouched as the Kitteridges had all these years was more than generous, and yet, if one could view a heart aching from disappointment, then Callie's appeared to need some medical attention.

The only kind he could offer was education. He detected a kindred spirit underneath all that animosity. If only he could explain to her his plans . . .

She swallowed, clearing her voice. "I played here when I was little."

He nodded. "So it's a sentimental attachment then?"

One side of her mouth clenched, and her eyes grew hard and small again, marring her pretty face. "Something's not right," she said, finally. "I can feel it, and I'm going to do everything in my power to halt this supposed project from going forward. Maybe the Kitteridges just need to rethink it." She dropped her gaze to the ground, as if trying to shake off some distant memory.

Gage felt his brows lift—both of them—and his mouth

tightened against his cheek. "What's to rethink? They're being offered a ton of money for bare land that runs to the sea. If they're like most people, they'll take the money and head out of here."

"This is where their friends are."

"They'll make friends elsewhere. Believe me, people do it all time, and with money in the bank, it'll be easy for them."

A beat of silence passed. He tried not to stare as she tamped down her frustration. He could almost read her mind: *Who is this man to suggest that the Kitteridges would turn away from their friends and their promises that easily?* But he knew the human condition could be greedy and unkind. Surely she wasn't as naive as she appeared.

Instead of acknowledging the truth in what he said, Callie toyed with the rope in her hand and challenged him with a stare. "Something you know about personally then?"

His jaw jerked upward and he shook his head slowly. "I'm not the enemy, you know.

"You just work for him."

He nodded once and stepped backward. If she wanted to feel his dismissal, then so be it. "Enjoy your walk, Callie. I don't doubt that we'll be running across each other in the near future." Even he knew that statement could not be accurate in a town so small that even stray animals run into each other.

A gull floated down on a gust of wind and landed on a rock. Callie's dog whined and tugged at his leash. Gage geared up to walk away from her then, even though he sensed that her every nerve stood at attention, as if preparing for battle.

She spoke to his back. "Once the Kitteridges return from wherever they've gone, we'll all see how wrong you are."

He sent her a wave knowing full well it looked more like a salute. A patronizing salute.

Chapter Five

"Still no one missing a dog, huh?" I lean into the receiver and swiveled my chair to take another peek at Doggy. Those soulful eyes melted me.

Aida, the harried director from the rescue shelter, assured me again that my new companion, the one with shedding hair, who begged for scraps and expanded my heart, was all mine.

After I hung up, I bent forward in my chair as the doggy scurried to my feet. "Well, boy, if you're going to live here, you're going to have to have a name." My hands dug into his fur and massaged behind his ears. "Do you prefer a regular guy name like Jack or Steve? Or how about a beachy name like the counselors at camp get?"

He leaned his head to one side, one floppy ear grazing his shoulder.

I cooed in his face. "So you're saying it's up to me, huh? All right then, I've decided. With those big round eyes of yours, you, my dear, are now *Moondoggy*." This time my head cocked to the side. "What do you think?"

In a flash his front paws landed in my lap and he leaned against me, his tongue bouncing. I laughed. "I take that as an approval." With a sneeze, he pushed away from me and his nails clacked down the hallway.

So like a man. With a sigh I dug into my purse. Unlike the rest of the world, I didn't carry my cell phone everywhere, so I was not surprised to find three voice mails. Did I have time for this? I still had to revise the cabin assignments for this coming weekend's camp and then fax them to our cabin coordinator, Luz. The mail symbol throbbing at the top of my screen won out and I dialed.

"Hello, Callie, it's Marie from the church. I'm wondering if you'll be here on Thursday for food distribution? Since it's still somewhat chilly outside, we'd also like to give away sweaters and sweatshirts that we've collected, which means we'll need you for a longer time. Oh, I hope you'll be here. Call me."

Food distribution! I'd forgotten all about that when making plans to meet Ruth. I made a note to call Marie with my regrets.

"Callie. Meredith Smythe from the American Cancer Society. Are you available to make phone calls for us this week? We'd sure love to have you. Please return my call. Thanks."

I jotted it down.

"Hello? Oh, my. Timothy! Timothy! Turn down that racket! I can't hear myself think. Callie? Oh, for heaven's sake. This is June Kitteridge returning your call from . . . yesterday was it? Oh, dear, I've already erased the message. Anyhow, we were out of town but we're home now and . . . Timothy! I can't hear! Oh, never mind. Feel free to call me back, dear, if you need something. So long."

Faster than rolling thunder, guilt spread through me like those hot flashes Mother always went on about, burning and unforgiving, making me sweat. Could I not have waited a few days before pursuing answers about the Kitteridge property? The more I played it over in my head, the more my body began to suffocate as if wrapped in a wool blanket during a summer heat wave.

I pictured my confrontation with those survey goons from yesterday. And today I blabbed about the development rumors to Ruth—a woman who had no qualms over making Steph Hickey, our perpetually pregnant town librarian, cry. Not to mention the tutorial Gage gave me today on sustainable housing that evolved into a standoff.

Maybe all of it was for naught. Could a heartfelt chat with June Kitteridge bring about a speedy antidote for our town's affliction?

My phone buzzed in my palm, causing me to yelp. Moondoggy came running and I hurried to pick it up from where it bounced across the hardwood then plopped onto the floor. "Hello?"

"Hello, Auntie Callie." Greta's voice sounded more like a giggle when she spoke.

My mind lurched toward another concern. "Hey G—you're not—"

"No baby yet." Greta giggled, this time for real. "Silly girl, it's still two months off. Just calling to see if you'll go paint shopping with me this afternoon."

I scooted my butt up against the wall and leaned back. Moondoggy licked my cheek and I pushed him away, trying not to get a mouthful of dog spit. "Pregnant women shouldn't be buying paint. It's not safe. How about we go check out this cool organic cotton store that just opened in downtown SLO instead." Greta loved San Luis Obispo, a college town just south of us.

"A lot of good that'll do me if I don't have a nicely painted room to put them in." Greta's voice picked up speed. "I want to buy low VOC paint for the baby's room."

Good for you. Low Volatile Organic Compound paint will be better for everyone. "Try no-VOC, if you can. Low still has some dangerous fumes."

"This is exactly why I called you, girlfriend. See? You know all about this *green* stuff. Anyway, since I've finally decided on a color, I want to see how it looks on the walls. Bobby promised me some time this weekend. Did I tell you? I'm going with teal."

My head rested against the wall and I smiled at the ceiling. "You sure? 'Cuz no VOC paint ain't cheap."

"I'm sure. So will you go? I need you to make sure I'm getting the right stuff and the correct shade of teal."

"There's more than one shade of teal?"

Greta's giggles filled the phone. "Stop that. Laughing
makes me have to tinkle. Yes, of course there's more than one
shade. Think of all those trees you're always going on about.
They're not all the same shade of pine green, now are they?"

"No, I guess not."

"No, they are not. So are you going to help me or is little
Tsunami or Bluebella going to have to live in a plain, ol' beige
room?"

I smacked my forehead and leaned my head into my hand.
"Enough with the weird baby names. Okay, I'll go. What
time?"

"Afternoon-ish?"

"I'll pick you up at one."

With plans for the rest of the day made, I considered
whether now would be the perfect time to call the Kitteridges
and ask the burning questions. Or not. The pacing began. Was
this really any of my business what the Kitteridges did with
their property?

Memories swept into my gut. My dad and older brothers
and other men carrying lumber into Kitt's on Display while
the kids from the village played hopscotch on the sidewalk
out front. Mom hiking up her skirt and joining in while other
mothers dropped off platters of food and pitchers of lemonade. After the last swath of golden paint had been swept

across the walls and the stunning new sign had been hoisted above the entry door, we all cheered. That afternoon we caravanned to the Kitteridge's property along Otter Bay, and it was then that June and Timothy gathered us around and announced the dedication of their land to the community.

On that land I tasted the lushness of my first locally grown olallieberry.

I learned to worship God with abandon and a few off-key notes when our teen group gathered there with guitars and youthful enthusiasm.

And Steven Diletto, high-school senior who hadn't glanced at me until that last semester of school, pledged undying love for me beneath the shade of a Monterey pine—after which he left for college.

With new resolve, I picked up the phone and dialed June Kitteridge.

GAGE

SUZ'S HOPEFUL FACE GREETED Gage as he stepped into his office. "Well? Is that progress I see on your notepad?"

Gage sank into his desk chair that squeaked with every shift of his body. He hid his annoyance and offered his sister a forced smile.

She leaned over his desk to peer at his notes. "Greek. I had no idea you could write in Greek. Do you speak it too, big brother?"

Suz gave way to light laughter and it nearly turned his stomach. It wasn't her laughter that bothered him—under other circumstances he would love hearing it. What worried him was the thought of telling her about the hiccup on the horizon of an otherwise straightforward and high-paying project.

Maybe straightforward wasn't the best term for this project. No matter. Gage had plans to create something that would take best advantage of the land and the light, something sustainable that people would appreciate for ages to come. Surely even his nemesis might find it in her heart to appreciate that.

Suz handed him a crumpled white bag. "Here."

Gage reached for it. "What's this?" He opened it, the aroma too inviting to ignore.

Suz plopped into the straight-backed wooden dining table chair opposite his desk. He had planned to outfit his new office with top quality furniture. It had yet to happen. He was lucky he had a few extra pieces to pilfer from his apartment. Regardless, Suz looked content and that's all that mattered. "A turkey burger. Just the way you like it, I hope. You haven't changed your taste over the past year and a half, have you?"

His nose drew in the mouth-watering smell. How long had it been since he allowed himself the pleasure of takeout? "Slathered in mustard?"

Suz nodded. "Yup."

"Roasted green chile on top?"

A playful grin brightened her face. "Sadly, two of them had to give their lives for your burger."

"Two?"

Suz rubbed the arm of her chair. "I told them it was for a starving architect so they gave me extra."

The bitter reality of that statement made him lose his appetite. He set the bag down onto his desk and looked away. His little sister didn't need to know how hard things might have to become before they turned around again.

Suz's face turned sober and she sat up. "I'm sorry." She reached across the desk. "I was just kidding, but that was over the line. Forgive me?"

How could he be angry with that face? Suz was the miracle child their mother had given birth to when Gage was already thirteen years old. He'd always felt somewhat fatherly towards her—except when she'd drag her dolls into the room his parents always referred to as his teenage cave. Never did like finding Barbie in his closet.

He mustered up the most award-winning smile he could and glanced back at her. "Nothing to forgive. My mind's just preoccupied. Lots to think about."

"Like how you're going to spend all that cash when you get the Otter Bay project going?" She smiled in a way that let him know she was teasing. And yet, a part of her had to understand that this project had the potential to skyrocket him out of obscurity and into the realm of the much sought-after. If only . . . if only he didn't need assurances about that right now.

His sister stood. "Eat your lunch. I'm almost done setting up your filing system and then I should leave. I have an errand to do before picking up Jeremiah from preschool—I had him stay for lunch today. Okay?" She waited in the doorway, her face expectant.

He waved her on. "Of course. Go when you need to. Give Jer a hug for me and tell him I've got something to show him when I get home." She smiled at him like she always did and turned to leave. "And Suz?"

Her hand still cradled the doorknob. "Yes?"

"Thanks for the burger."

When she'd left, Gage nestled his back into his chair. He stared out the window at the colorless, cinder block wall separating his office from the building next door. Why bother putting muscle to work on something so blah? In other times, he'd look at a dull wall like that and see a blank slate with endless opportunity. Today, it held little promise at all.

The phone rang and he lunged for it. "Gage here."

"Squawk-squawk."

Gage rolled his eyes. "Hey, Marc."

"How'd you know it was me?"

"I guessed." His shoulders bobbed when he tried to stifle a laugh. "Why are you bothering me?"

"So this is how it's going to be. You've got yourself a new best friend over there in beach town. Is that it?" Marc hollered off somewhere in the distance. "Hey, Lizzie, Gage just dumped me." He came back on the line. "She says, 'Good for you.' Sheesh. Even my woman's against me."

"Listen to that one," Gage said. "She's not called your better half for nothing." He relaxed against his chair. Nothing like an old friend's voice to ward off an overhanging cloud of doldrums. He and Marc had been friends for five years. Been through good times, like Marc's wedding, and not so good ones, like when a car accident snatched away the use of his friend's left arm.

"You got that right. Hey, you find a church yet?"

"I did. Stopped in my first weekend here. Met a few people and one of the guys invited me to a Bible study at his home."

"And since?"

He knew Gage well. "Haven't had the time."

"Not the study either?"

"Not yet. But I plan to go one of these days." He tried to thwart Marc's inquisition. "You remember that Suz and Jer are here now, right?"

"That working out good for you all?"

"Seems to be, although Suz's pretty quiet about it all. Don't want to pry, but she probably needs to talk to someone."

"Hopefully she'll meet a girlfriend, someone to do double duty and be your woman too."

"Oh, brother. No time for that, let me assure you."

"You hit your head or something? A guy always has time for women or as in my case, *woman*."

"Lizzie's in earshot, isn't she?"

"You got that right."

Gage roared, the sound tumbling through his gut. Leave it to Marc to provide him levity at just the right time. "Fine. If you must know, I met someone recently and she hates my guts."

"Oh, so you're handling her with your usual finesse, I take it."

"Nice."

Marc laughed. "Seriously, how long can she resist your charms, man?"

Gage groaned. "Please." For the next ten minutes they caught up on each other's lives and Gage felt lightness reemerge.

His friend laughed in his ear. "Okay, buddy, gotta go. Get yourself to that church, if you don't want me coming out there."

Gage nodded. "Promise."

Chapter Six

 "So that's it, then?" Greta hung onto her belly as I drove, my shocks bouncier than I remembered. I walked nearly everywhere, but could I ask that of a mother-to-be, especially when we're about to acquire two gallons of paint?

I nodded through my unease. "I guess it is."

"You don't sound too sure. Are you sure Mrs. Kitteridge said everything was okeydokey?"

I pulled into a spot in the paint store parking lot and switched off the engine. "She did say that, but . . ."

"You think she was lying?"

I released a sigh and focused on the store's glass doors. "Not lying, no, no. She's not the type." I turned to Greta. "You know that feeling you get when you say something but even you don't believe it?"

Greta nodded. "Like when you're sick and someone says they're praying for you and you agree and nod like you know you'll get better just like that." She snapped her meticulously groomed fingers.

My head bobbed up and down. "Yes, but even you don't really believe it's going to happen. Yes, like that. I had this feeling . . . this feeling that she had doubts even while trying to convince me that ownership of their property was still intact."

Concern veiled Greta's eyes. "Did you tell her what you were thinking?"

I gripped the steering wheel. "Not exactly, but I did get her to admit that they've toyed with finding a more permanent arrangement for the property. She said someone had approached them with promises of keeping the property open to the public."

For a moment silence sat between us. Greta, rarely the suspicious one in the family, heightened my unease another notch. "I don't really know about these things, but it sounds fishy. Maybe that's why you're feeling uncomfortable. You don't think she lied to you, exactly, but that maybe she's holding something back."

I leaned back and lifted my chin, noticing all the dust particles embedded in the ceiling liner. "Maybe." I glanced at my sis-in-law, trying to focus instead on why we'd come. "C'mon. Let's go find little Winklebottom some nice toxic-free paint for his or her bedroom."

Greta giggled all the way inside the store. And some store it was. Fisters prided themselves on not only stocking the latest in paints, lacquers, and finishes, but also a decorating studio in the back to rival any of the big box stores. A good thing too since the closest Home World was more than twenty minutes away.

I approached a wall-sized display in the back room. "So what's it going to be? Stippling, sponge painting, stenciling? Ragging? Trompe l'oeil?"

Knitted brows and a delicate frown marred Greta's normally serene expression. "Bobby would never go for all that. Don't they have regular ol', nontoxic paint that you can just put on with a roller?"

Her squinty eyes and contorted mouth made me want to laugh aloud, but wasn't it against protocol to show such emotion when you're sis-in-law was nearly ready to give birth? Wouldn't she think I was having fun at her expense? I grabbed her hand. "Over here. Plain old no-VOC paint. And look! They actually have more than three colors now."

The lines in her face disappeared. "Well, now, phew. But, oh no. Look at all those shades. How will I ever decide?"

If it's not one thing, it's another. I plunked a thick book of sample colors onto a table and she began to browse the pages one by one. My mind clipped along with each turn of a page.

At the next table, a woman with a brunette ponytail and heavy-looking black sweater pored over a catalog as a young salesman hovered nearby. The salesman, a cherry-cheeked twenty-something wearing loose-fitting khakis and the store's signature collared shirt, hovered behind her. We might as well have been invisible.

Greta squealed when viewing a particular page. "Oh!" Her shoulders sagged. "Never mind." We continued our search.

The salesman, apparently having acquired the nerve, approached the pony-tailed woman who continued the search for perfect paint. "May I help you, miss?"

She gasped, then placed both hands onto her chest as if trying to slow her heart. The salesman's pink cheeks reddened further. "Whoa. You scare easily."

The woman's eyes appeared guarded and she didn't meet his gaze. She turned slightly away from him. "You surprised me, that's all."

This did nothing to deter him and he pulled out the chair next to her and sat. "Can I help you find something?"

She shrunk back, as if questioning exactly how long he might have been watching her. After a long pause, she relaxed her shoulders. "I'd like to repaint the living room walls but I need to find paint that's green."

He squished his features into a quizzical state.

She straightened. "You know, as in nontoxic?" She flipped her fingers through the pages of the catalog in front of her. "I think I need low-TOX or something, but I don't see a thing in here about that."

The salesman fidgeted and nodded as if he had an idea. Greta's gaze caught with mine and she lifted her forehead as if to say, "Do something." I opened my mouth but wasn't quick enough.

The man in the collared shirt bent his head closer to hers. "It's really all malarkey, you know. Paint is paint, and we've got all kinds of it. Tell you what. You focus on the color you like and I'll have several quarts of it mixed up for you to try on your walls." He lowered his voice, but not enough that we couldn't hear him. "On the house."

Translation: while the fresh-faced salesman could spot a damsel in paint-store distress, he had no idea what VOCs were, nor why so many people were on the hunt for alternatives. By the way his customer abruptly stood and grabbed her purse from the back of her chair, it was obvious that he needed help with his pickup lines.

There were no other paint stores for miles, so I turned toward the woman as she attempted to pass by the wet-behind-the-ears sales guy. "Excuse me. I think we have what you need over here." I tapped the catalog that Greta fretted over. "And it's low- or no-VOC paint that you're looking for." I caught eyes with the salesman. "Trust me, they sell several kinds here."

"Really?" She rushed over and sat down. Several unruly strands of hair had slipped from her ponytail and swung beneath her diamond-shaped chin.

I gestured toward Greta's belly. "We're trying to find the same thing for my little niece or nephew's nursery."

The woman, who had moments ago appeared watchful

and restrained, gushed over Greta's impending motherhood. "Oh, I love babies. Is this your first?"

The glow emitting from Greta's countenance could have lit the room. "Yes, our first. Everybody else in the world thinks we should find out the baby's gender, but I want to be surprised. How about you? Any children?"

An almost imperceptible shadow dimmed the woman's smile. "I do." She cleared her throat and shifted toward me. "So you said you knew what kind of paint I was talking about?"

Her quick change of subject caught me daydreaming. "Y-yes. I think you meant you didn't want paint with VOCs."

Greta touched my arm. "What are those anyway?"

I scooted forward. "It means 'volatile organic compounds' and they are pollutants that evaporate into the air especially from paints and finishes. They've been around forever, but as people have become aware of how bad they can be for us, more and more companies have come up with alternatives."

The woman nodded, like this was all new. "Wow. I had no idea. I want to surprise my brother by sprucing up his living room, but I knew he'd want the most nontoxic paint I could find. He's really into all things green."

Greta laughed. "Your brother sounds just like Callie." She nodded in my direction. "She's always giving the rest of us advice on, you know, saving the world and stuff."

A sharp sigh escaped me. "Who dragged who in here today?"

Greta's serene smile, highlighted by a sliver of light shining through the side window, would make a charming painting. What's it like to be that composed all the time? In that up-and-coming motherly way of hers, she gave her complete attention to the harried young woman who shared our table. Greta pushed the catalog she'd been viewing over to her. "See if what you're looking for is in here. I'm Greta, by the way. This is my sister-in-law, Callie."

The woman gave us a closed-mouth smile and a single nod. "Thanks. I'm Suzanna. I'm sorry to cut in on you, but I have to get going soon. I appreciate this." She peered into the catalog.

Greta waved her off. "It's no problem. I'm in no big hurry these days. My husband will have to do the painting for me anyway."

Suzanna quirked an eyebrow. "How 'yucky' are the fumes? Can a child be nearby? I've got my brother's concerns and, um, a little one's too."

I brightened. "No reason to be scared off. Despite their lack of expertise"—I jerked my head toward the doorway that our flirtatious salesman slunk through—"this store has some great choices. It's not the end of the world if you can't, but if you *can* find the no-VOC product in the color you like, you'll be best off."

Suzanna's face relaxed and she continued to thumb through the book. "Thanks so much. Not sure what I would have done without you."

Greta giggled. "Probably would have bought the wrong paint *and* had a date for Saturday night."

Suzanna slid her gaze toward the door. She turned back to me and laughed. "How can I repay you?"

Even I was surprised by the snort that escaped from me. Greta gave a "woot" at my lack of propriety. Sometimes I have to remind myself that I'm in polite company. If this were camp, I'd get an award for a snort like that.

Greta fanned herself and rocked. "So, Suzanna, have you lived in Otter Bay a long time?"

Suzanna kept her eyes on the book in front of her, and her voice took on the air of forced nonchalance. "Um, not really. But my brother has a place here, so my son and I, we're staying with him for a while."

Greta stopped. "Your brother anyone we'd know? We've been here our whole lives, and it's growing so fast, but maybe we've met him before."

Suzanna rubbed her lips together as if mulling whether or not to continue this conversation. Why was she being so secretive? She shifted her shoulders as if still weighing her decision to divulge more about her life. "I doubt you'd know him. He's new in town too. Got here a few weeks before me." Her eyes flashed at the both of us. They appeared both sad and hopeful at the same time. She breathed in and pasted on a smile. "Anyway, Gage is a good guy—the best big brother a girl could have. Really."

She might as well have doused me with ice water. How many men named Gage could possibly live in a town as small as Otter Bay? My guess? Not many. Unless of course the Gage Mitchell I'd come to dread didn't live here at all.

Greta's touch on my arm broke my wanderings. "I don't know him, but it looks like you might. Do tell."

My brow furrowed at my sister-in-law's hopeful gaze. "Do tell, what? Do I have to know everyone in this bitty town? And isn't it possible there's more than one Gage around here?" That came out sharper than I had planned, and let's face it, that theory was thin at best. Greta's mouth fell open. She looked at Suzanna, who stared back at her. I hustled to make amends. "Sorry. I've got a lot on my mind, I guess. Didn't mean to jump on you, Greta. Besides, I know you were only kidding, right?"

Greta wouldn't look at me. "Suzanna, what's your brother's last name?"

Suzanna answered her, but focused on me. "Mitchell. So you two know each other?"

I shrugged her off, hoping my slack jaw wouldn't give away my distaste for the man. It wasn't her fault he hoped to tear apart Otter Bay (and rip out my heart while doing so). Besides, this was moot considering my conversation with June this morning. Gage Mitchell's plans were all but dashed.

I forced a smile. "Not really. We've met, but I don't know him well." *Thankfully.*

The room fell quiet as Suzanna jotted down a couple of numbers from the catalog. She stood and scooted her chair backward, taking her notes with her. "I just realized the time, ladies. I'm going to come back for my paint when I have time to wait for it. Thanks again for your help. It was really good meeting you both." She started to go, then stopped and spun around. "And I'll be sure and tell my brother 'hi' for you, Callie."

Greta stared me down.

I gave her a smirk. "What?"

She glanced toward the door, still looking like a painted vision with light streaming across her body. She stroked her swollen belly. "I'm not used to seeing you all fired up over a guy." She swung her face toward me, her eyes taunting me like a cat's. "That boy must've really said something feisty for you to clam up like that in front of his sister. You're usually pretty free with your opinions. Something tells me you didn't want to share this one."

I chuckled and nodded too many times in a row. "Practicing your parental psychology, I see. That's good. That's good. You'll be all practiced up once little Petunia or Oregano gets here."

"So happy you're finally coming around about my choice of names."

I stood and rolled my eyes. "Please. Can we go now?"

Greta didn't budge. "I haven't picked my color yet."

"Have Bobby bring you back. He'll help you pick the right one."

She shut the catalog and batted her eyes. "I want to know all about Gage Mitchell first."

"Not happening."

"Then I'm not going anywhere."

I fished around in my bag for the sports bottle I'd filled with water before we left this morning and plunked it on the table in front of her. "Drink this."

She snorted. "I will not. You just want my bladder to fill so I'll have to get up. You are a *naughty* young lady."

"Again with the parenting!"

"So then, who's Gage Mitchell?"

The paunchy paint salesclerk darkened the doorway. "Mr. Mitchell? He's that guy who builds all that weird eco stuff."

We slid our gazes toward the door.

He went on. "Yeah, he came in here talking about natural paints and asking if we had a green directory in the store. I think he draws up houses and such. Anyway, he wanted to talk to the manager about providing all that stuff for some big project and I said, 'Whoa! Hold it right there. We have *normal* wall coverings in this store.'"

Greta leaned her head to one side, surveying him. "So you never told your boss?"

He puffed out his chest. "Nah. Didn't need to bother him with that."

I wondered if I should bother because something told me this kid probably wouldn't be working here long anyway. Then again, why did every attempt to preserve health have to be mocked? I set my gaze on him, taking a quick look at his name tag. "Andy, is it?"

He nodded, his chest puffed out farther than a wind sail.

"Well, Andy, first off, this entire catalog . . ." I tapped the book on the table. ". . . has thousands of paints that are safer and healthier than the *normal* everyday paint you're so fond of. Not only is it better for our environment, but it's better for all of us. Did you know that VOCs can cause headaches and nausea? Why use something that can hurt you when we have better products now?"

He gave me the classic deer in headlights look, his eyes so wide that I feared his pupils would disappear into the whites. Tempted as I was to poke my forefinger into the air and shout, "Furthermore!" I bit back my voice and softened the approach. "Listen, caring for God's handiwork is a cool responsibility, and I'm sure your boss wouldn't be too thrilled to learn not only that you oppose doing so, but that you've also turned away customers with your negative attitude."

He straightened further, pulling his neck back so far that his round chin developed a second one beneath it. We watched as his cherry cheeks inflamed to the color of beets. He left the room without a word.

Greta patted the table, her laughter hushed. "That's the Callie I know and love. You go!"

I dusted my hands against one another, like making a tortilla. "Somebody has to teach the young 'uns."

Greta's cheek quirked. "I do have one question: Does Suzanna's brother happen to be the architect on the Kitteridge property?"

With a toss of my bag over one shoulder, I moved to the door and gave her an are-you-coming-or-not look. "Yeah, I think so."

"Huh." Greta continued to lounge and she stared after me. "After that little lecture you gave young Mr. Andy a minute ago, one might think you and the eco-conscious architect were actually on the same side."

Eco-friendly or not, my dear sister-in-law couldn't have been farther off base.

GAGE

GAGE TOOK A LONG sip of hot coffee, conscious of the attention his precocious nephew was attracting. Suz had appeared so worn and drawn last night that he had decided not to wake her and instead to whisk Jeremiah out of the house early and feed him some breakfast. He figured something shaped like a mouse with big ears would do the trick. His sister didn't have to know that he would be using a "buy one get one free" coupon to do so.

"Well, would you look at who we have here. Aren't you a

precious little thing?" Gage recognized her as Holly, the young manager of the rugged diner with a view of the sea. Word was that she helped her aunt run the Red Abalone Grill.

Jer put down the stubby crayon he'd been coloring his paper menu with and showed Holly three fingers. "I'm four."

She smiled wide at him. "You are? Wow. I was gonna say three, so you're a bigger boy than I thought." Holly pretended to assess Jeremiah, tilting her head to one side and tapping the end of her pencil on her chin. "I know you're a big guy and all, but somethin' tells me you still like your pancake to have a face on it. Am I right?"

A sheen of juice dribbled down his chin, but he lifted it toward her anyway with unashamed aplomb. "You're right!"

She tossed him a smile, then looked to Gage. "And what can I get you?"

Gage slid the coupon toward the edge of the table. "Two eggs and rye toast."

"That it? That's not enough for a man to be eatin', if you ask me." Holly grabbed up the coupon without a glance and stuck it in her apron pocket. "I'll make it three and add on a side of hash browns on the house—Jorge makes amazin' hash browns."

Gage opened his mouth to protest, but she had already spun away, all curls and bounce as she went. It didn't look like much could stop her except for perhaps an empty coffee mug to refill or meal to deliver.

He took another sip of that coffee wishing he'd asked for a refresher and watched as several women and one man gathered together near the entrance to the restaurant, each talking over the other. The man stood just outside the circle, hands in his pockets, jangling spare change.

The proprietor of the diner, an older woman with energy to match her niece's, grabbed a handful of menus and guided them all to a table in the rear. He might not have paid them much mind if it hadn't been for their loud, animated conversation, which was a sharp contrast to the previously quiet morning.

Jer hummed as he went back to his drawing. Without warning, the boy glanced at Gage catching his uncle mid-sip. "Where's my sand dollar?"

He asked as if curious, not demanding. Gage noticed little things like that about his nephew, and each time the revelations tugged at him. "It's in the garage at home, drying on my workbench. Remember?"

Jer smacked himself on the side of the mouth. "Oh, yeah. I remember. Where'd you get it 'gain?"

Gage put his empty mug down, and without hesitation Holly showed up, filled it, and scooted away. He clenched his thumb and forefinger around the handle. "Well, I was walking on the beach, and I found it buried in the sand. Do you remember what I told you?" Jer rested both elbows on the table and plopped his face into open hands. Though Gage feared the boy's interest might soon run out, he surprised him by staring at his uncle, rapt. "It was like a miracle to find that unbroken sand dollar there so late in the day. Especially among the rocks. Sand dollars usually live in very soft sand."

"Oh." Jer focused on the Formica table before flashing his eyes upward again. "Hey, maybe a pirate put it there!"

Gage swallowed down his sip of coffee before choking on it. "A pirate?"

"Yeah, maybe he stole the money and then put it there to hide it and, oh no, I have his pirate money now!" Jer slapped his dimpled cheek with one hand.

He warmed a smile right out of Gage. "I don't think you should worry, kiddo. I think pirates have special safes to keep their coins in. Besides, what pirate would leave his money right there in the open like that?"

His little face puckered as he considered this. "Then how come no one else took it 'fore you?"

Gage studied the little boy's face. "That's a good question. I would have to say that maybe God wanted you to have it."

Jer plopped both arms across the table in front of him, and then laid his head across them. "Yeah, God wanted Jeremiah to have it."

Holly appeared with two steaming plates of breakfast, just in time to delay the inevitable fidgeting that Gage expected. "Hope you boys are hungry 'cuz these plates weigh more than a fat tuna fish caught offshore."

Jer perked at the aroma of butter melting into a pool at the base of his happy face pancake. His eyes spied the maple syrup jug in Holly's hands. She held it over his plate. "Can I pour some on it for you?"

Jer nodded dramatically, as little boys often did, his blond hair catching wafts of air with each nod. And Gage noticed that just as he dug out his first bite from the pancake's middle, the little boy had begun to hum.

Chapter Seven

He didn't notice me. Late as it was, I scooted past Gage Mitchell and he didn't see me at all. Was he all alone with that little boy?

"There you are!" Ruth stood, her eyes nearly cloaked by the wide-brimmed mesh hat she wore. "Callie, I'd like you to meet Charity, Neta, Gracie." She turned toward the other end of the table. "And Bill."

Not one of them looked familiar. Did they even live in this town? They all nodded and murmured their greetings. As usual, I felt like the splash of cold water on a fire. Why was that?

Ruth stood CEO-like at the head of the table. She gestured my way as I took a seat. "It was at my chance meeting with Callie that I learned that the Otter Bay property is now subject to development. We cannot have this, and we must exercise every option there is to stop this audacious move."

I raised my hand as if needing permission to speak. "My apologies to all of you who took the time to come out here today, but I spoke to June Kitteridge by phone this week and she assured me that the property was not for sale after all." I hoped that sounded more convincing than it felt.

Ruth's familiar mouth quirk and the accompanying half-closed eye stared me down. "Au contraire."

Did Ruth know something I didn't? Or that I suspected? I tilted my head to one side. "Oh? Have you heard something different?"

She leaned forward. "My source tells me that someone recently called the city planning department to discuss procedures for applying for permits, and not just any permits, but ones specifically for the land along the coast."

Bill looked bored. "Doesn't prove anything, since there are still a few small empty lots ripe for building."

Ruth grimaced at him as if he was a piece of garbage she'd just plucked from the shore. "It was for the Kitteridge property, acres and acres of land. My source confirmed this."

I narrowed my eyes. "Your source?"

Ruth looked down her nose at me. "A neighbor who works as a secretary—that's all I have to say on that."

Peg, the diner's owner, arrived with a pot of hot coffee and an order pad. Neta, Charity, and Bill all signaled they would like a cup. When she finished, she plopped the carafe onto the table and positioned her pen over the pad. "What'll you have this morning?"

Ruth waved her off. "Nothing other than coffee. We're having a meeting."

Peg sighed and left without another word.

I plunked my elbows onto the table and rested on my fists. "Did they actually pull permits, Ruth?"

She hauled in a breath. "No, but now's the time to act, not after someone has already spent millions acquiring property behind this community's back."

She had a point, although could I go along with this considering June's earnest discussion with me the other day? Queasiness pulsated through my stomach. And what about Gage Mitchell? Something must be up or else this topic would not keep hanging over this town like a dark cloud.

Ruth stood stick straight, her gaze floating beyond the table to the view of beach outside the window. She exhaled slowly, allowing it to shutter through her as if the thought of losing Otter Bay had begun to weaken her. No doubt she took this as seriously as I did, but did she have to be so dramatic?

Finally she spoke. "We need a leader, someone who is passionate and driven. Someone who loves Otter Bay as we all do and who has the drive to see this hideous project laid to rest once and for all."

Gracie, Neta, and Charity nodded continuously.

Ruth was moving in for the role, I could see it in her face. And why not? She was leadership material and had the fortitude to follow her gut and fight for what she believed in. I saw that in her when we fought the closure of the town library several years back. So what if she came off as annoying and tactless at times? We all had our crosses to bear.

Something starrier had replaced her familiar grimace, as if Ruth could see into the future. She dropped her gaze to all of us. "And the person I nominate is . . ." Her straightforward eyes caught me in their beams. "Callie."

Me?

The women around the table nodded in agreement, and Bill tapped a forefinger on his temple and saluted me.

Ruth put a hand to her hip. "Well? Will you step up and run with this, Callie? We'll need investigations and financing, a motto and media coverage . . ."

My head swam with the possibilities, so much that I hadn't noticed Gage approaching our table. He strolled up without an ounce of timidity. By his congenial, open smile the others would never know why he was in Otter Bay.

Ruth, however, glared at him. I'd forgotten that Ruth had seen him before. "What's he doing here?"

He startled, but only for a moment; his grinning eyes only slightly dimmed. Holly had apparently taken a break because she was sitting at his booth with the little boy I guessed to be Suzanna's son—Gage's nephew.

Gage offered Ruth his hand. "Sorry? Have we met?"

Ruth narrowed her eyes, and now both fists had found her hips. "You're the reason we're having this gathering today."

His blue-green eyes connected with mine. I glanced away. Ruth ignored his hand, so Gage slowly pulled his arm back rather than have it dangle in midair. "I see. Since I'm new in town, perhaps I should take this as a compliment."

We caught eyes again, although I tried to avoid it. I really did.

He surveyed the table, his hands resting loosely at his sides. "I'm Gage Mitchell. Just stopped by to say hello to Callie." He paused, his smile seemingly earnest, although who knew how he managed it? "And introduce myself to all of you, of course."

Gracie glowed as if a mythical god had come to life before her. She batted her lashes and stood, holding her white fringed shawl closed with one hand while extending the other to Gage. "How do you do?"

He held her hand. A beat longer than necessary, if you asked me. "And you are?"

Gracie blushed. "Gracie Stormworty. Pleased to meet you, Mr. Mitchell."

The others weren't quite so accommodating and gave Gage an unenthusiastic nod. He planted his hands at his waist and released a satisfied sigh. "Well, I can see you're all busy on a project here, so I'll leave you alone. Nice to meet you all." He turned to me and winked. "Thanks for being so kind to my sister yesterday, Callie. I really appreciate that."

I opened my mouth but not a word managed to make it out.

Gracie still glowed like an ember. "He seems like such a nice man."

Ruth's grimace had returned. "Well, he's *not*. Someone has hired that man to do away with the pristine land down by the otter sanctuary, and I for one won't stand for it." She twisted her gaze in my direction. "I hope I haven't made a huge mistake in suggesting you lead our cause, Callie. He's one smooth character, that one. You do realize that, I hope."

She was right. A cringe worked its way through me as I considered how his presence had a way of knocking me off my game. He wanted to keep me from messing with his plans. Of course it was all an act. Right?

Ruth waited for my response. I had spent most of my life fighting for causes I believed in, but always as second fiddle. I've always been the worker bee, the volunteer justice-seeker, never the leader.

I looked from person to person, knowing this little group would need an infusion of passion if we were going to prevail. *If this fight truly existed, I would not want the Kitteridges to be harmed in any way.* I began formulating a new plan. I wondered if I possessed what it would take to see such a plan through.

I glanced across the diner to Gage's booth only to see him watching me. He had the audacity to send a wink my way. While I've never been at the helm of any of my causes, Gage Mitchell and his devastating idea—the paving over of the community's sanctuary—gave me all the courage I needed.

A smile came over me. "I accept the position. Thank you for the vote of confidence."

Ruth's half-closed eye widened until it matched the size

of the other one. "Excellent. I hope you will not sleep until you've put Mr. Gage Mitchell out of business."

I glanced over her shoulder to see Gage and an adorable towheaded boy leaving the diner. It occurred to me then that this fight might have further reaching consequences than I had originally imagined.

Chapter Eight

"One scoop in the morning, and another in the evening. He'll beg you for more, so you must stay strong, my friend." I handed the scooper to J.D. Moondoggy had chosen the boy as his favorite neighbor, so I offered him the job of taking care of my pup during the weekends while I was working at camp. Thankfully my cottage had a doggy door already installed when I bought it. "I'll be back on Sunday. Can you handle it?"

"Yup!" J.D. fetched Moondoggy's leash from the hook on my wall. "C'mon, boy."

Moondoggy pranced over, then shied away. He came forward again, slapped his two front paws on the floor, then skittered backward. It had become a regular game.

I leaned against the wall. "I was going to tell you that you didn't need to take him out yet, but I don't think he'd let you out of it now."

Like a pro, J.D. dropped to his knees and grabbed Moondoggy by the collar. With a quick twist of his wrist, he hooked up the leash and stood. "That's okay. I want to walk him before I go to school. And I'll make sure to walk him plenty all weekend too." J.D. gave me a grin that told me he would have taken this job for a penny.

I called out to him. "I have to run to camp now. Lock up for me too, okay?"

He nodded that he would, and I watched through my screen door as Moondoggy dragged the poor kid due west. I grinned, then began my weekly checklist, making sure I had everything necessary on hand for three days at camp: hiking boots, check; toiletries, check; Bible . . . rarely get the chance to use it, but check anyway; and overnight bag with all kinds of spares, check.

Oh, wait. My phone. Always seem to be forgetting that cellular wonder. I grabbed it making sure to unplug the charger, switched it on, and tossed it in my bag. Not more than a minute later, as I was about to pull from the driveway, a bell dinged. I had voice mail.

I cut the car engine and retrieved the messages.

"Callie! You coming soon? We've got a big mess here, and I need you. We're overbooked. Help!"

Luz, from camp, sounded frantic. But didn't I already lay out everything for her in my e-mail? Next message:

"Hello?" Pause. "Hello? This is June Kitteridge. Callie? Is that you?" A shrill alarm pierced the earpiece. "Oh, for goodness sake. That's my hearing aid again. Wait a moment will you?" Long, long pause. "Hello? This is June again. I'm back. Callie, I'd like to talk to you about something if you wouldn't mind, dear. Would you call me, please?"

I stared into the morning fog. Did this have anything to do with the building permits Ruth had mentioned? My finger hovered over the keypad, but I stalled. If the camp were really overbooked as Luz said, then I was going to be inundated with decisions about who to put where. I snapped shut the phone and spoke into the air. "First thing Sunday evening, June."

The drive to camp lasted less than ten minutes. This was only the second week of the spring season. Staffers new and old trickled on-site to prep for this season's new camp theme: "Standing on the Rock." I'd seen some of the sketches but had not had enough time to see an entire run-through.

The doors to the Adventure Room had been propped open, so instead of racing by as usual, I wandered in. Because other groups used the camp during the week, program staffers had to replace banners and other props before the start of each weekend.

Squid stood in the center of the organized chaos. His arms were crossed but his stance relaxed as he observed the staffers. My usual lift at seeing him had dulled considerably. Before I was able to turn away, he offered me a wave.

My smile felt weak, unimpressive. Continuing through the auditorium-sized space I halted at the massive banners hanging high on each side of the stage, their letters large and capped. One read SAND and the other ROCK.

Carp, who hugged a ladder beneath the first banner, called out to me. "Hey, Grandma Callie!" She smiled as if truly happy to see me, but she would change her mind if she knew how much I longed to knock over her ladder.

Squid jogged over to me. "Gotta minute?"

I hesitated. "Sure."

"I'm holding a midweek meeting for all senior staff. We have some kinks to work out." His eyebrows had a funny way of twitching up and down when he felt intense about something. "You in?"

"Well, it depends." I crossed a set of files in front of my chest, not unlike a high school student with her books. "I just agreed to head an important cause in town, and we'll be meeting a couple of times this week. When did you want to have your meeting?"

He tilted his head to one side. "What cause? Something to do with animals? Or the environment?"

"In a roundabout way, I'd guess you could say that." I lowered my voice. "I'd rather not say too much about it just yet. But between us there's been talk about a development going in on the Kitteridge property, and I'm working with a group of citizens to keep that from happening."

He scratched his beard, gaping at me. "First I heard of it."

His lack of reaction unnerved me. "Like I said, there still are plenty of unresolved issues. Suffice to say that SOS—that stands for Save our Shores—is very much in the planning stages."

He dropped his hand and gave a shrug. "Well if it's God's will, you'll know it."

We're in a Christian camp, so why did his response cause me to do a double take? I glanced toward the front as staffers ran a thick strip of masking tape down the center of the stage. My eyes found Squid again. "So you wanted to meet with me midweek?"

He blinked.

"I-I meant . . . you wanted to hold a staff meeting after this weekend. Right?"

He blinked hard, then nodded. "Oh right. Yeah. So can you be here Wednesday evening around six? Tidal Wave'll be bringing pizzas."

"Fine. Sure." From the doorway Luz waved me over with urgent, hard strokes of her hand. I inhaled for strength. "Have to go." I jogged away. Facing him wasn't nearly as tough as I thought it might be, considering my ego still smarted from his proclamation of last week that I was old and tired. So maybe that's an exaggeration? By the way it affected me, he might as well have said as much.

"It's hopeless." Luz's glasses slid down her shiny nose. She perspired when things didn't go as expected.

"Nothing's hopeless." I held out my hand for her clipboard. "May I see?"

She smirked and handed it over. "Good luck. Looks like we're going to have to make kids camp out in the Adventure Room or something."

I studied the list of cabin assignments. "What about the e-mail I sent?"

Luz puffed out a sigh laced with stale coffee. She pointed at line seven. "You forgot about them."

She was right. Somehow I'd missed the church from Bakersfield. My mind hummed, searching for an answer. I ran my finger down the list. "And you've checked with each of these church groups to make sure all their campers are coming?"

She nodded.

"Well, then. We've got our work cut out for us today."

GAGE

"I'M GLAD YOU CALLED." Gage leaned against the seat back of his creaky office chair. He figured the elusive developer who had hired him would be getting wind of the project's opposition soon. It wasn't, however, his job to deliver the bad news.

The gruff voice on the line was all business. "What's the status?"

Status? As in how powerful did he think that band of mostly elderly committee members could be, save Callie and that angry one? Come to think of it, there were two angry women in that bunch.

Gage decided to stick to discussing the project itself. "Still waiting on the survey, but I've been on the property several times and have developed further vision for it than represented in the schematic design we discussed. Once I receive that survey, I'll be ready to lay it out."

"What's the ETA of that?"

Gage tapped the fat tip of his pencil on a blank sheet of tracing paper. "They tell me they'll have it available by Friday."

"No mistakes on this." His client's voice was low and despite his urgent words, nearly monotone. "As soon as escrow closes, we'll want a complete set of plans into the planning commission ASAP. I'll keep you abreast of timing. In the meantime, make sure there are plenty of green elements in the design. We don't want no trouble with this community—lots of fringe in that area of the state."

He winced. Sustainable architecture was what he did. "Don't worry, Redmond. While waiting for the survey, I've been perfecting the placement of the buildings to maximize the best light and the naturally occurring breezes. Sitting your property well is my top priority."

"Just make sure to make it green. Stick some bamboo on the floors and solar panels outside, stuff like that, and that ought to make the rubberneckers happy."

Gage bristled at the assumptions. The idea of making

Julie Carobini

something sustainable should be foundational whenever possible, instead of designing something and then asking afterward, "How can I make this green?" The ideal was to understand what it meant to create something sustainable, and from there allow the design to naturally occur.

Explaining the truth of sustainable design to his client, however, would only fall on deaf ears. Gage's fingers tightened on the phone. "If this project gets off the ground, it will be compatible with the landscape and be an inspiration to the Otter Bay community."

"*If? If* this project gets off the ground?" Same gravelly voice; higher pitch. "You doubt your paycheck?"

Gage sat up and planted both of his feet back on the floor. "That's not what I meant." His fingers raked through rumpled hair. "I apologize if—"

"You've heard something, then." Redmond swore and spoke something unintelligible into the background. "If that guy thinks he's gonna pull this one from under me, he'll have more than a lawsuit to deal with. He'd better know that. Better yet, you tell 'im that if he tries to put any more doubts in your head. Got it?"

Gage's eyes shut. He tried to picture what his caller was saying, and who he was saying it about. "I'm not sure I—"

"Are we done? I've got a plane to catch."

Suz drifted in with a question in her eyes but stopped short at Gage's expression. She clutched a thick file closer to her chest and made a quick retreat back to her desk.

Gage's client's question hung between them until he shrugged it away, ready to be off that phone. "I'll be in touch."

"You do that." The line went dead.

Suz peeked through the doorway. "Tough customer?"

Gage stared at the bland wall outside his window, his voice sounding far away even to his ears. "And perplexing." He forced the conversation out of his head and swung around to look at his little sister.

"Did you want to ask me something?"

She approached him, a note in her hand. "You had a call from a realtor. A Rick Knutson."

Gage shook his head. "I've seen the guy's picture on signs around town but don't know him. Did he say what he wanted?"

"Just that he had some news on a property you were working on." One of her eyebrows lifted as if a question mark held it up.

"What's the look for?"

She relaxed her face in a hurry. "Nothing. He just reminded me of, you know, a used car salesman or something. He talked real fast and called me *honey*. Who does that?"

Gage laughed. "Hey, watch it. Our father sold used cars when he was in college." He sat forward and held the note in both hands. "A real estate agent, huh?" Gage didn't bother to ask which property the caller was referring to because, unfortunately, there was only one—hopefully, the one that would lead to more work than he could handle. He looked up. "Thanks, Suz. I'll give him a call."

Chapter Nine

 "How did you let this happen?" Squid paced as Luz and I continued to pore over the cabin assignments spread across her desk.

I turned up both hands. "Somehow I missed a church. It happens."

He paused and gave me a sideways glance. "It happens when your head's not in the game."

I frowned. "When have you known me to make a mistake like this?"

He took several more steps, then tossed up his hands. "Sorry, Callie. You're right. Mistakes happen."

Luz grimaced. "Just don't let it happen again, right?"

We both turned to stare at her.

She waved us off. "Ah. You both seem distracted lately, like you're here but your attention's somewhere else."

Squid and I exchanged glances. He tossed a strange little smile my direction and a sigh slid between his lips. "She's right. It's the second week of camp and something's just not jelling with the program." He stared at the fake wood paneling. "Can't figure it out and it's ticking me off."

I rubbed my lips together, my eyebrows raised. "Wish I could help, but um, we've got this little problem over here."

"What's your solution?"

Luz jumped in. "Hope that someone's bus breaks down?"

I cut her a look. "Nice. No. First off, I've never known a weekend where someone didn't fail to show up. It's a fact that people get sick. We don't like it or wish it on anybody, but it happens all the time. We'll just have to wait and see."

The lines in Squid's forehead deepened. I'd never seen him so stressed. "And if everyone shows up?"

My lips continued to run together as I considered my last resort. The boys would hate it. The newfound leader in me inhaled and let it out before announcing my decision. "The game room. We take bunks out of storage and move them in there. And, of course, move the foosball tables, etcetera, out."

One corner of Squid's mouth curled upward as he nodded, while a small smile lit Luz's face.

I continued. "Thankfully the bathroom's located just outside the cabin and it's warming up a little, enough that campers won't have to traipse outside in the early morning frost to use the facilities."

Squid slapped the sides of his jeans. "Well, okay. You have a plan."

"You doubted me?"

He bowed. "My apologies to the ever-resourceful Seabird."

"Oh, brother." Luz's previously hopeful expression had degenerated into a scowl. She glanced out the dusty window. "Don't look now but it looks like an early arrival."

Squid pulled the curtain aside, and I caught a glimpse of a renovated school bus pulling up the gravel driveway. He turned to Luz. "I'll help them unpack the bus while you get to your place at check-in." Before heading out, Squid caught my eye.

I waved him on. "It'll be fine. Go."

Luz stacked the papers on her desk and slipped them into her file. "I'm right behind you, Squid." She dropped her clipboard onto the file and scooped up the entire stack just as someone knocked on the door to the office.

"Callie?"

My breath caught. Her white hair had been swept into an elegant bun, but otherwise the elderly woman looked skinny and alarmingly frail. With her back bowed as it was, her taut shoulders pointed up like two upside down *V*s. "Mrs. Kitteridge? Hello." My questions for her collided with thoughts on camp. I needed to be where all the action was as the campers arrived. Why was June Kitteridge here? And why now?

June stepped through the door just as Luz slipped out, throwing a concerned, I-need-you expression as she did.

Mrs. Kitteridge kept her gaze fixed on me. "Please, call me June."

I drew in a breath and pasted on a smile. "Sure. Have a seat." Concern etched across her face, so to alleviate that I joined her by sitting in Luz's chair. "I received your voice mail this morning. I had planned to call you first thing Sunday evening after camp."

"I'm sorry to have bothered you. Shall I go?"

"No, no. Didn't mean it that way. How can I help you, June?" Even at my age it felt odd calling Mrs. Kitteridge by her first name.

She fingered her collar and her eyes had trouble settling on one place. "You've been asking about our property along the sanctuary."

I nodded. That familiar guilt wound through my gut. Was she about to confront me about my involvement in the opposition? Or would she finally tell me what was going on?

She clasped her hands and dropped them in her lap. "I may need your help. I know we don't really know each other very well, Callie, but I've seen you walking through town many times. Oh, and your mother is lovely."

She removed a floppy bag from one shoulder and placed it on her lap. Rifling through it, she pulled out page after page of documents and handed the array to me. As she continued to search her purse, I came across page one marked with the words, "Promissory Note."

Her face reddened and her breathing became pronounced.

My mind slipped back to my CPR training. I hoped I wouldn't have to use it.

June's bag deflated and I knew she had plucked the last of the papers from it. She dropped it on the floor and looked me in both eyes. "You mustn't tell anyone about this."

The urgency in her voice, her eyes, gripped me. "Of course. What is it?"

"It's Timothy. He's . . . he's . . ." June glanced away. Pain shadowed her eyes. "He's not well these days. He tells me things, and then forgets what he told me. Sometimes he denies he ever said what I heard." She returned her gaze to me. "And I'm beginning to wonder if maybe we signed something we shouldn't have."

Dread began slithering in and around me. "What do you mean?"

She eyed the papers in my hand. "We needed money to help our daughter start a business after her husband lost his job. It was some time ago. I wanted to go to the bank and take out a small loan, but Timothy wouldn't hear of it. He'd met a man who offered to loan us money against our home . . ."

"And?"

Regret saturated her voice. "We've been making the payments faithfully. I never thought . . . never knew . . ."

"What didn't you know?"

She covered her mouth for a moment. "There's a balloon payment due very soon, and we do not have the money to pay it."

Luz tapped on the window, her stressed-out expression burning through the flimsy curtain. I ignored her.

"Oh, June." I tried not to allow shock to permeate my voice. "Are you saying that you're about to lose your house?"

Her palm flipped upward along with one pointy shoulder. "I think so. I don't know."

My mind raced. "Have you talked with your daughter?"

She waved both palms in front of her. "Oh, no. Her husband spent most of the money we gave her, and then left her and our grandchildren. She couldn't handle this if she knew."

Silence fell like a dark night between us. What did I know about this type of thing? "Have you looked into refinancing?"

She deflated more. "Timothy gets angry when I bring it up. He says we borrowed too much for that. What are we going to do?"

I reached out to still her shaking hand, its skin loose and thin. "Why did you come to see me, June?"

She pulled her chin upward until our eyes met. "Forgive me for making assumptions, but I've always observed you to be the justice seeker of this community."

I shrunk back a little.

Those eyes were hopeful and searching now. "You may not think of yourself in that way—it's not as if your name's in the paper all the time—but I've seen you working behind the scenes on so many different causes. And that's what I want, someone who is behind the scenes helping me figure this out."

Would this be the wrong time to tell her I signed on to lead

SOS? I rubbed my lips together, trying to figure out my role in all of this. "Listen, June, my brother Jim is an attorney. He doesn't normally handle this sort of thing . . ." I didn't mention that never once had he been willing to help me with any of my causes. "But if you wouldn't mind me sharing this information with him, then maybe he could advise you on what you can do."

"Timothy hates lawyers."

"I'll make sure not to mention that to Jim."

Her head had dropped forward as if from shame, then she peered up at me. "And you're sure he won't tell anyone else?"

I nearly held my breath. "I'll make him promise."

The resolve on her face pricked my heart. "Then I would be very grateful. Very grateful, indeed."

GAGE

"GAGE MITCHELL FOR RICK Knutson. I'll hold." Suz set a second cup of coffee in front of him while he waited on the phone. The acid was bad for his stomach, but he could not do without the caffeine.

"Rick here."

He jolted forward and set his long arms on his desk. "Gage Mitchell, returning your call."

"Ah, Mr. Mitchell, the architect." Knutson's voice barreled on. "Good to finally meet you. How are you, sir?"

Gage rolled his eyes to the ceiling. What was this guy trying to sell? "Fine. What can I do for you?"

"Not into preliminaries. I appreciate that. Let's see now, oh right, I called you about the Kitteridge property, didn't I?"

Gage stayed quiet and pictured Rick Knutson's blindingly white teeth on all those realty signs.

Knutson cleared his throat, and after he did, his voice sounded deeper than when he had begun. "My client asked that I pass along the news to you that everything is on schedule to take over the property within thirty days."

Gage's forehead bunched. "Take over?"

"Acquire." He cleared his throat again. "What I meant was *acquire*. Now, I'll need you to get this information to your client ASAP. The planning commission has been breathing down my neck on this one."

"You're telling me the city government is actually asking for these plans?" Gage had never heard anything so ludicrous. Planning departments were notoriously slow about issuing permits. He'd known many architects who'd crossed the line with personal gratuities just to light a fire under the process.

Knutson's voice rose again, fired up. "I'm telling you that this project is hot. No one's been able to touch this property for years and the community is itching to see something state-of-the-art built there. You, my man, will be a hero."

He doubted that. His own aspirations for growing his own independent and eco-conscious firm aside, communities weren't usually gracious about prime property going to development. Case in point: Callie and her pals.

Gage leaned back against his squeaky chair and cringed. "I appreciate the information, Mr. Knutson." He couldn't imagine why the realtor had called him in the first place. "But I'm still waiting on the survey so we're only in the schematic design process at this point. Once the survey is complete, we can move into design development and begin taking bids from contractors. It will be awhile until the drawings will be ready to submit to the city planner's office."

"Huh."

Gage's eyebrows both shot up. "Is there a problem?"

"Well, it's nothing really." Knutson's voice oozed with arrogance. "Except that I'd heard you were the best and, frankly, I'm beginning to wonder now. Surely you understand the high cost of delays."

Who did this guy think he was kidding? Realtors, or at least *this* realtor, had no idea of all the hoops necessary to create plans that would pass muster with fickle planning departments. A dart of pain pierced his right temple. Gage wasn't sure if this guy was a mole or just stupid. Then again, this was the second time today he'd been told to get on something ASAP, and did he want to bite the single hand responsible for feeding him and his family? The answer to that tumbled through him like bricks.

Gage drew in an even breath, taking his time to respond. "Certainly I am aware that delays mean money, Mr. Knutson.

Be assured that my company will do everything in its power to provide the best design in a timely fashion."

Knutson's voice rose again. "Now we're talking."

Gage fixated on that blank wall outside his window. "If there's nothing else, I'll sign off."

"I'll be in touch."

Gage hung up the phone, sensing that Rick Knutson most certainly would keep in touch and more than he cared to imagine. The idea of future phone calls from that guy turned his stomach—almost as much as groveling.

Chapter Ten

"Sleep on *my* side!"

"No, sleep over here by us!"

Who knew that the church group I had to split up would decide to send only one female counselor? Half of their girls had to move into the game room for the weekend, and without an extra counselor, I had been elected—drafted—into duty.

It meant:

Tight quarters.

Schlepping outside to use the restroom.

Little to no sleep.

"Night, girls!" I smoothed my sleeping bag on the creaky bunk in the middle of the room amidst a choir of groans. "There." The mattress sagged and the coils squealed when I slid into it. As the girls settled into their spots for the night,

I lay awake awhile, contemplating this hectic day and how tempting a night in my own soft bed sounded. I whispered a prayer of thanks that J.D. had checked in on Moondoggy tonight, and began to shut my eyes.

In the dim glow of a night-light, a girl named Angel hung over the top of her bunk and stared at me upside down. Her long hair dangled like a privacy screen between me and one side of the room.

"Psst."

I peered at her with one eye, hoping to convince her I was already half-asleep. I'd been waiting for most of the day to contemplate the ramifications of June Kitteridge's surprise visit from this morning and didn't want another distraction.

She wiggled. "Are you sand or rock?"

I pulled my chin out from under the flap of my sleeping bag. "That sounds like a silly question to me."

"Really?" She flopped her arms over the rail, and I feared she would tumble out of the bed and onto the hard floor. "'Cuz that's what they asked us at camp meeting tonight."

Great, of course it was. I should have been aware her question was related to the camp's theme. Could they see my cheeks burning in the dark?

Another face appeared in the near darkness, this one small and round with a voice to match. Her name was Bailey. Apparently she and Angel had decided to double up above me. "Anthony got on the sandy side because he likes the beach."

I relaxed against my thin pillow, embarrassment averted. "He sounds like a man after my own heart."

A chorus of "ooohs" sprang up from inside the cabin.

Angel kept talking. "At the meeting tonight, they told us to choose sides. We went to the *rock* side, but it was kind of silly, I think."

Another voice, this one from Taylor, carried from the bed beyond the foot of mine. "Yeah, who cares if you want to sit on rocks or on sand? I didn't get it."

Some counselors relish times like this with their campers. Joy buoys their voices the next morning after they've had the opportunity to discuss deep, theological things with kids late into the night. Others find discussions like these terrifying. "Hmm, really?" I contemplated which camp I fell into. "Well, I missed all that tonight. Why don't you tell me about it?"

"I will, I will." Angel hopped down from her bunk, shuddering the cabin walls as she did. I slid my legs behind me as she plunked herself into my bunk. Two other sleepy girls dragged themselves over, probably unable to sleep with all this excitement. They sat on the floor in their pajamas.

"Okay." Angel showed no sign of the sleepiness that came with responsibility. "First we sang this song 'I Am the Light of the World' a bazillion times."

"I liked it." Bailey continued to peer at me from above.

Angel gave her a daggered look. "I did too. I was just sayin' that we sang it like a hundred times. So anyway, after that we talked about the devil."

Bailey shut her eyes and recoiled as if she'd been given peas for dinner. "I didn't like that part."

Another voice piped up. "I thought that was cool."

Angel sighed and started again. "Squid . . ."

Another chorus of "ooohs" went into the air. Angel gave me a knowing glance. "They all think he's cute, and I just think that's dumb." She shook her head. "So anyway, Squid talked about how sometimes we think things that aren't right because it's the serpent's job—he's the devil—to lie to us. If we follow those lies, we're listening to the wrong guy!"

Bailey nodded. "So we have to listen to God. Is that what Squid was saying?"

By now Taylor had slipped out of bed and joined the circle around mine. "I think so, but we're just kids. How would we know how to do that?"

Squid's words from this morning sprang into my consciousness. *If it's God's will, you'll know it, Callie.* I weighed his statement in my thoughts. What earth-shattering bits of wisdom could I impart to these fertile little souls sitting before me? At that moment, my respect for camp counselors everywhere grew tenfold.

I pulled in a silent, deep breath. "You know, it says in the Bible that the angels of little ones can always see God the Father's face. Somehow I think it might actually be easier for you guys to listen to God."

Angel's mouth sprung open. "What? So you don't hear God anymore?"

I sat up and bonked my head on the bunk above me.

"Oh-oh." Bailey's mane of upside down hair swished from side to side. "Maybe God was saying you should watch your head, but you weren't listening."

All signs of sleepiness had vanished. Amazing how a smack on the head could bring about a spate of unleashed giggling from a cabin full of ten- and eleven-year-old girls. I massaged my crown. "Actually, I didn't mean it like that. I do believe wholeheartedly in listening to God." *That a girl, skirt the issue.*

Angel wasn't buying it. "But do you *hear* him anymore?"

For the first moment since I arrived in the midst of this active cabin, all went quiet. They didn't want my interpretation of Squid's message, but my personal story. I had always advised counselors to be transparent with their campers, and yet I'd been too preoccupied to do that with mine.

Something in my brain fumbled. Should I be honest here, and tell Angel just how busy my life had become? Or will she recognize that for the cop-out it was?

"I'll be honest with you girls. Yes, I've heard God before, but lately, not as much as I'd like to."

"Really? You've heard him? Out loud?"

"Not really out loud—although I'm open to that, Angel—but I have heard him in here." I placed a hand over my heart. "He has a way of letting me know when I'm on the right track."

Angel snorted. "And when you're about to crash into another train." She rolled over on the floor with her own laughter.

Taylor's voice took on a worried pitch. "What if we can't figure it out? What if we go through this whole weekend and none of it makes any sense to us? What then?"

By now, I'd sat up, albeit in a crouched position. "Oh, Taylor, don't worry. And I mean *don't*. There's a question in the Bible that goes something like, 'Who by worrying can add a single hour to his life?' I want you to have fun this weekend. Laugh a bunch, and eat a ton, and soak up the lessons. You *will* learn something new—I've no doubt about that. But you can't force it, okay? Let God do what God's gonna do."

Angel screwed up her face. "'Gonna?' What kind of grammar is that?"

"Did you understand what I said?"

"Yeah."

"Well, then, my grammar did its job. Now, go to sleep. I love you all."

For the second time that night, the cabin wound down with "goodnights" all around. Bare feet padded about as the girls climbed onto beds that needed oiling, their voices twittering their myriad thoughts in hushed tones.

Bailey's voice floated above me. "Night, Callie." It took several twisting squeaks for her and Angel to settle down, but by the time they did, so had everyone else.

In the dark I contemplated what I could do for June, and for our community, and even more pressing at the moment, for the young girls in my care over the next couple of days.

Chapter Eleven

 "In my professional opinion, the Kitteridges are about to be financially devastated." My brother Jim stared down his nose at me, the hard line of his bifocals as unyielding as the opinion he had just delivered.

Still, I wasn't ready to give up. "Isn't there due process or something?"

He slapped the pages onto his desk. "Sure, maybe if they had borrowed from a bank or a reputable mortgage company. But they didn't do so, Callie. They took out a loan from a private lender—a sharp one." He drummed his fingers on the stack. "I will say this, whoever advised them to sign off on this kind of loan ought to have his license revoked."

I crossed my arms as I stood there in Jim's office. After the weekend I'd had, it took all the strength I could rally to call on my ultra-important sibling this rather hazy Monday morning. Especially when I'd missed the family's regular Sunday gathering. "What are their options?"

He grimaced. "If the balloon payment is not paid by the due date, the private party can file a lawsuit the next day. This contract allows for the lender to take possession in the event of nonpayment." He sat in his high-backed chair, looking lawyerly and quite definite. "Theoretically, a default judgment could be entered within 45–60 days and they could be evicted."

"It's that ironclad?"

"Appears so."

I uncrossed my arms and ran my fingers along the grain of Jim's desk, my voice losing steam. "Is there anything they can do?"

"Yeah, they could sell the land bordering their house—the same property you seem to think you have a vested interest in—and that will provide them with enough to pay off their loan. Brilliant stipulation—wish I'd thought of it."

"You can't be serious. That lender took advantage of the Kitteridges and you know it."

Jim shrugged. "Happens all the time. People shouldn't sign agreements they do not understand."

"And there's nothing else that you, my smart attorney brother, can suggest for them to do?"

"Yeah, they could come up with the money within the next six weeks in order to be safe." Jim threw both hands up and gave me his signature "See-it-my-way" expression. He did that whenever he had decided that a particular conversation was nearing its end. "Listen, Callie, you can't help them on this one. They were foolish in signing this."

I shook my head. "An old couple's home is at stake, Jim. We have to come up with a way to help them."

"Says who?" Jim let out an obvious sigh, the kind that told me that even if he could help, he wouldn't. It wasn't worth his time. "Callie, this is the same song and dance we've traded since you were a kid. Stop trying to save the world. It can't be done."

I crossed my arms again and cradled my elbows. "I'd like to think that it could."

Jim stood. He leaned both fists on his desk until his body stretched across its surface, causing me to take a backward step. "I wasn't going to be the bad guy and point this out, but weren't you the one who came tearing into Sunday supper last week ready to take the Kitteridges down?"

"I was just stunned by what those goons had said and how they treated me." I lowered my head until all I could see was the plush, ebony carpet at my feet. "I-I really hadn't had a chance to think of the Kitteridges' part in all of it at that point."

"Even though, technically, it was their property you were so bent out of shape over." He was bullying me. I could tell by the tone of his voice and I hated it. Why, after so many years, did I let him get away with that?

I lifted my head until our eyes met, which meant that I had to rise to my toes and crane my neck. "So what you're saying is that this is too tough for you to handle."

Now I'd done it. If skin could look warm, his had begun to sizzle. His silence roared through the office, taunting me to apologize. Instead I stood there. And waited.

His smile returned, the same patronizing smile I had seen as a child every time I asked to go along with him and his friends to a movie, or an ice cream. Even a trip to the grocery store would have been nice. Jim's normal skin tone had returned, and he lowered himself into his wide-armed chair. "My suggestion to you is to save all your money from your camp job and hope it's enough for a down payment."

"Down payment?"

He tossed the stack of Kitteridge documents to the edge of his desk. "Yeah, for a nice ocean-view loft at Otter Bay."

GAGE

GAGE PERCHED UPON A rock, his arms wrapped around his shins, one hand gripping his other wrist, as he stared into the far-reaching expanse of watery jade from the edge of Otter Bay. Moments like this, when the air and water kept reasonably still, reminded him of his childhood, a time when he'd run his dog Luke down a path through pine and scrub until they'd come to the edge of the lake. Lake Forever may have had a glorified name, but it was merely an oversized pond.

Still, he liked to go there and let Luke tear around wild while he rested on a rock and contemplated the ripples on the water. Much like he was doing now. Only this time the water reached farther than his eyes could see, and the ripples crested every once in awhile when the wind decided to blow.

The irony of his growing fondness for this spot, which was slated for development under his direction, was not lost on him. If only he had the resources to buy this plot himself, he would build something respectful and harmonious with the land—and then leave the rest wide open. For what, he didn't know. Squirrels to skitter about? Otters to coast by without worry over debris dropping off high-rises built by overzealous developers hungry for the profit margin that came with density?

Or maybe . . . a family?

Not now. He couldn't entertain such a proposition, because for one his sister and nephew depended on him for survival. Neither he nor they had planned on that fact, nor the more sobering reality of Suz's husband—Jer's father—landing in jail. He still couldn't believe the guy had done what he'd done.

Gage blew out a sigh with force. Truthfully, though, his sister's bad fortune had little, if any, effect on his immediate plans because Gage had not cared deeply for a woman in a long, long time. He glanced around. After being unceremoniously tossed from his last job, Gage could have settled anywhere. He had long since passed his exams and become registered in California. As a single guy with no one but himself to worry about, he had built up some savings and had determined to start his own company in a coastal community. So he landed here in Otter Bay. Who was he kidding? The lure of a mammoth-sized job awaiting him had everything to do with that. Still, he could not shake the sense that a larger force was at work.

A woman appeared before Gage, her shapely figure casting a shadow over him. "Praying?"

He blinked. After daring to wander back to this spot, Gage might have expected to hear Callie's voice, but somehow he hadn't, and now here she stood at the top of the rickety steps, glaring at him.

He shrugged a shoulder. "Maybe."

The gritty look on her face faltered. "So how does that work exactly?"

"Prayer, you mean?"

"What I mean is I'm praying one way . . ." She glanced around before making eye contact with him again. ". . . and my guess is you're praying the exact opposite."

Gage chuckled and unfolded his legs, allowing his feet to land on the ground. He rested against the rock he'd been sitting on and kept her gaze. "He's a big God, Callie. I'm sure he can handle it."

It happened again. Something faltered in her expression. Did she have a problem with God? Or the fact that Gage was not the godless enemy she had made him out to be? Or maybe she spotted a speck of chive stuck to his teeth.

"We're going to fight this all the way, you know."

"I understand. Quite a gang you gathered together for the fight, by the way." That wasn't called for and he knew it, but such a pain she was! He couldn't find it within himself to avoid frustrating her if only a little. He gripped the cold, rough surface of the rock beneath his fingers. What did she mean they were going to fight this all the way? How far did she think that pretty face would get her and the geriatric crew she'd recruited for her cause?

She stared at him as if stunned, and for the briefest instant, he felt another stab of remorse over his flippant comment. But then her eyes narrowed at him and if she had access to a kitchen drawer, he thought she might stab him on the spot. Such beauty, wasted on an angry woman.

Her intense stare bore into his. "First you carelessly make your presence known before all avenues for saving this property have been explored, and then you foolishly mock the people of this community." She shook her head slowly, deliberately, as if he were a child. "You are making this easier for me than I had given you credit for."

Ouch. He swallowed, trying not to show how bitter his pride tasted sliding down his throat. "Glad I could help." His voice sounded weak and insincere, even to his own ears.

"How altruistic of you."

"Okay, give." Gage adjusted his body against the boulder before flashing two open palms in an attempt to end the stalemate. "I don't care to fight with you, because as I've said before, I'm only here to do my job. Maybe if you'd give this thing a chance, you would see just how well the design for this project will complement your community."

Callie's laughter exploded in a wave of snorts, and Gage waited for her to blush and apologize for the unladylike outburst. She didn't flinch. Instead she took a step, halted, and looked him up and down from his sneakers to the tousled-hair tip of his head, as if daring him to cross her. Her chest rose and fell. Had her animosity tired her? "You go on thinking that, Mr. Mitchell. Just go on thinking it." She pushed past him, and as she did her face lingered uncomfortably close to his. "Enjoy the view."

He fought the urge to seize her arm. "Wait. What did you mean when you said you were exploring avenues to save this property? My understanding is that it has already been sold and is ready to change hands. Pretty straightforward—unless you have knowledge to the contrary." He paused, watchful. "Do you?"

She opened her mouth but it hung there, wordlessly. Her eyes flitted about as if unable to find a solid place to land. When she licked her lips, Gage looked away. He could hear the pattern of her breathing before she finally spoke. "Really, Mr. Mitchell, how silly do you think I am? Give away my strategy to the enemy?" He thought he heard her smirk. "Come on now and give a girl more credit than that."

Chapter Twelve

 That was close. After the disappointing
visit to my brother Jim's office—a cliché
if I ever heard one—it pained me to run into
Gage Mitchell at the Kitteridge property.
I had strolled the beach to regroup and planned on climbing
the hill on my way home. I was unprepared to see him there,
of all places. I tried, but he needled his way under my skin.
What's worse—I almost gave away June's secret. After she
begged me to keep the information to myself, I nearly threw
it into the architect's face as proof that all was not right with
this deal.

For the first time since Friday, I could see that keeping this
secret presented a challenge.

I disliked admitting this, even to myself, but there were
moments when I noticed glimpses of something pleasing about

Gage. When I reached the top of the stairs, he didn't notice me at first and I studied him briefly, noting a wistful, almost longing expression on his face. It felt familiar to me. Could he have been having second thoughts?

Our eyes met and good sense rematerialized within me. In his gaze I saw a flash of appreciation and it turned me cold. Worse, he talked of God, then followed that by mocking the townspeople.

I trudged up the hill toward home, shaking my head with each step. Instead of Gage being the person that, for one irrational instant, I considered someone to confide in, I realized he may be playing me.

"There she is—Madam President." Ruth stood to the right of the well-worn path, a sagging trash sack over one shoulder, her other hand formed in a salute.

My head jerked. "Didn't see you there."

"That's all right. You got your head in the details I'm sure. Wanna give me a heads-up on what you'll be reporting tomorrow night?"

I swallowed hard. The memory of June's desperation clenched at my heart. "Worked all weekend, but I do have an idea I'd like to run with."

Ruth's face went on alert and she leaned in.

I inhaled and thought out my words. "But let's wait until we're all together. I've got to get home to take my dog for a walk—been a busy day, you know?"

The hand that had been raised in a salute moved to Ruth's

hip. "Sure. All right." She raised her chin until her eyes were visible beneath the rim of her hat. "Been thinking about those Kitteridges lately. Have you talked to them yet? Must've been given some offer to go back on their word like that."

"Oh, I don't know. Things happen and people change their minds sometimes."

"So you haven't talked to them."

Why did I get the feeling that, in Ruth's mind, my leadership was in name only? "Actually I have. Like I said, I've got an idea, so I'll see you at the RAG, okay?"

Carp, from camp, pulled up next to us on a mountain bike, her back tire kicking up dust as she went into a skid. "Hey Seabird! Thought maybe I'd see you around."

Ruth cocked her head.

I smiled at the counselor, momentarily forgetting how much she likes to tease me about my age, then turned to Ruth. "Seabird is my camp name—it makes it more fun for the kids to call us by nicknames. And this is Carp. She's one of our weekend counselors." I gestured toward Ruth. "Carp, I'd like you to meet Ruth."

Ruth nodded. "Nice to meet you. Is that Carp for the town of Carpinteria down near Santa Barbara? Or for the fish?"

Carp giggled. "The fish, definitely. I've never been that far south."

Ruth puckered. "Haven't seen you riding around here before. You new in town?"

Carp straddled her bike, and let her hands drape down the front of her handlebars. "I go to college down in SLO but decided to stay around today to check out the town more." She flicked a look my way. "You're my inspiration, Seabird."

"Really?" My eyes widened. "Why?"

"Well, at first I was gonna drive down to my dorm last night, then drive back up here today. But then I started thinking about how you always talk about saving fuel and how you walk everywhere." She shrugged. "Seemed like a waste of gas to do all that driving around, so I stuck this bike into the trunk of my car on Friday and just spent another night at camp." She patted her bike. "You really can see a whole lot more when you're not stuck in a car."

I clapped my hands. "Cool. I love hearing that. You picked a perfect day weather-wise too."

"I'll say." Carp's gaze led to the horizon. "I'm usually so busy with the kidoodles at camp that I don't have the chance to just *be* out here on the bluffs. It's mesmerizing."

A sly smile creased Ruth's face and she slid a look my way. She was in recruiting mode, I could feel it. So I stepped to the plate—and changed the subject. "I've got a doggy that needs some love, so I'll leave you here to soak up the beauty. By the way, on Wednesday I am going to meet with Squid and a few others on the board. If you have any comments for me to take back, I'd—"

"I do! Some of the kids, well, they don't seem to be understanding the message as well as they should. The counselors have been doing a good job of filling in the gaps, but I don't know. I just think we need to make the presentation more clear." As soon as the words tumbled from her mouth, Carp waved both hands in front of herself, as if wanting to take them back. "I didn't mean that Squid or anybody was doing a bad job or anything."

I touched her shoulder. "I'm sure you didn't. If it helps, Squid's been reworking the presentation and looking for reviews and suggestions. Like you said, I had some great discussions with my kids over the weekend and that could go a long way."

Carp's face lit up. "Oh, that's right. You got a chance to play counselor. Fun, huh?"

"Oh, sure. No sleep, freezing toilet seat—yeah, that was cool." I laughed. "Seriously, though, the girls were so ready to grow. I'd forgotten how precious it was to see their transformation."

Ruth fidgeted. It appeared that she was looking for her escape so I addressed her. "I'll see you tomorrow night, Ruth."

She nodded, her hat flapping up and down. "That's right. And I'll be expecting a full report." She turned to Carp. "And good meeting you, missy. Just be careful you don't ride that bike of yours too close to the edge. There's some erosion going on that could be dangerous."

Carp hopped onto her bike. "Aw, thanks. That was sweet of you to warn me." We watched as she waved goodbye and coasted downhill.

"Warn her, my foot." Ruth muttered loud enough for me to hear as I hiked up the hill. "I'm just hoping not to see any more damage caused by careless humans."

I brushed aside Ruth's thoughtless comment and focused instead on my brief conversation with Carp. She was right. Something was missing in the weekend presentation. Still, as Gage said, our God is a big God and I had no doubt that he would fill in the gaps for our campers.

My feet froze in place. Did I just agree with something Gage said?

GAGE

GAGE TYPED IN HIS voice-mail code, hoping he didn't have to hear his client's gruff voice right now, issuing him commands. Hearing Marc's voice on the line, however, wasn't much easier.

"Dude, Lizzy wanted me to call you . . . you know, just to check on your status Are you settling in? Found a church? Things like that. Put me . . . I mean, help me put my wife out of her misery here, 'kay?" Marc lowered his voice to a conspiratorial tone. "You know how she worries about you."

Gage squeezed his eyes shut, drew in a breath through his nose, and stretched his shoulders toward his ears. He gave his head a tight shake. What did he ever do to deserve such a friend?

Gage dropped his face into his hands and muttered to himself. "Hypocrite." He felt his cheeks flush at the single word spoken into the air. Of course, he wasn't referring to Marc. Never! Instead, he spoke the word about himself.

Gage leaned back against his squeaky chair, his head a tangle of heavy emotion. He recalled the way he let Callie Duflay believe that he prayed on a regular basis. He knew better. Worse, God did too. He sighed, not the feathery exhalation of someone who's been inconvenienced, but the kind of wretched sigh that escapes from lungs held taut from discontent with oneself.

This move to Otter Bay had not solved all his problems. On the contrary, everywhere it seemed, he found land mines ready to explode. His phone rang again, but he immediately switched off the sound, not caring to see who was on the other end. Instead, he kept his head bowed, and began, "Dear God . . ."

Chapter Thirteen

 "Here, put this on." Greta handed a white face mask to me and snapped the elastic band.

I hopped backward. "Why do I have to wear one? I'm not pregnant."

My sister-in-law dug one elegant fist into her now ample hip and hung the mask from the fingers of her free hand. "Because if I'm going to look like an alien, then so are you."

I sighed. Pregnancy-brain affected us all. I secured the mask around my mouth and immediately felt remorse for having eaten so much garlic with dinner last night. "Where to?" My voice sounded muffled.

Greta motioned for me to follow her down the hall to a room with tall windows and partially painted walls. Bobby rolled color onto the previously dull surface while wearing ear buds and humming "I Heard It Through the Grapevine." He couldn't hear me cackling behind him.

Greta smacked his rump to get his attention, and I turned away from the marital display. *Please.*

Bobby pulled one bud from his ear. "Hey, Callie. What do you think?" He waved the saturated paint roller around his head.

"I think you should keep your day job."

He stuck out his tongue then leaned and gave me a swift smacker on the cheek. "You're in good spirits today I see. Nice mask."

I blew him a raspberry and quickly regretted it. With one hand, I pulled the thing off and handed it to Greta. She wagged a shaming mommy finger at me, but I only laughed. "So you really did go with teal." I paused and looked around. "You know, it really looks good."

Greta perked, her eyes smiling. "Really?"

I gave her an appraising nod. "Really, *really* pretty."

"You mean handsome." Bobby's paint roller froze midair.

I clasped my hands. "You're having a boy?"

Greta shook her head and led Bobby back to painting. "No. We don't know. He's just worried that if we do, this room will look too pretty."

I sent him a mock glare. "You're not into that whole pink for girls and blue for boys thing, are you little brother?"

He looked to Greta, then at me, as if this were a trick question. "No comment."

Greta laughed. "You two are so weird. Speaking of boys, I wanted to tell you that I gave out your number yesterday."

Bobby quipped. "Nice segue."

His wife slapped his shoulder, then grabbed me by the elbow. "Remember that girl we met? Suzanna? She was in the paint store yesterday at the same time we were, and we got to talking, and well . . . she asked for your phone number."

Bobby stopped but didn't look at us. "You'd better explain that, G."

She gave her head a tiny shake. "For her brother. The one who's the architect. Remember him?"

"Tell me you're kidding." I pulled away from her. "Why would you do that?"

"Well, she asked about you and thought you were so nice to help her. She said you saved her a trip to another paint store! Anyway, she thinks her brother is lonely and that he needs a friend and thought that since you two are so much alike that you'd be a good match."

Had pregnancy caused Greta to lose all sense? "You do remember who Gage Mitchell is, right? The architect who wants to desecrate the Kitteridge property?"

Greta smoothed back a curl. "Are you angry? It's just, I don't know. The more she told me about her brother—how cute he is, and 'green' he is—I just thought you might be able to get past your differences and at least show him around Otter Bay a little. He's new around here. Did you know that?"

Bobby stood in silence. He was like a cat. Maybe if he froze in place, I wouldn't see him. But oh, I saw him all right. "And where were you when I was being set up with the enemy? Huh?"

"*No me recuerdo.*"

"Right. Don't pull that high school Spanish on me. You *do* remember, mister. Thanks a lot for watching my back."

He dropped the paint roller into a pan, shrugged, and opened both palms. "You expect me to get in Greta's way when she's doing God's work?"

I threw my head back and scoffed. "Don't bring God into this!"

Greta gave her stomach several *there-there* pats. Her face had begun turning a darker shade. "I'm sorry I upset you, Callie. It just felt like a divine appointment to me. What were the chances of running into Suzanna at the same store two times in a row? I haven't gone to a paint store in years, then all of a sudden I'm in there twice and meet a woman whose brother speaks your language. He's single and you're single so . . ."

"So you figured you'd meddle." I unfolded my arms and glanced away once I became aware that tears were forming in Greta's eyes. "Listen, forget it. It was a nice thought, but be assured, Gage Mitchell would never call me, especially for anything personal. You can take that to the bank."

"Why?" Greta wasn't giving up. "Wait. Have you and he had more encounters?"

My pause swelled like Greta's belly. Silence hung for an uncomfortable beat. "Let's just say that I'm moving forward with a plan that will send him back to where he came from, and he's not too thrilled with me." I scoffed. "He even had the audacity to make fun of my group's efforts."

Bobby stepped up. Splatters of teal covered his shoes, pants, and fingers. "What's going on with that, by the way? Henry stopped by yesterday and when I casually mentioned your concern, he seemed to think the whole project was a done deal."

"How does he know?" The statement bothered me. "Does he have some inside information?"

Bobby shrugged. "Don't think so. But as you probably know, he's got a lot of friends on the new council, and from what he's heard, they're already poised to fast-track the project once the plans are completed."

Plans. Gage's plans. "Fast-track? Tell me more."

"Basically that means that once all the legalities are taken care of, development plans will be moved to the front of the stack for consideration, and if everything's in order, they'll get the stamp of approval more quickly than usual."

"But why? What's the hurry?"

Bobby picked up the roller again, dipped it in the paint, and rolled off the excess. "I really don't know, Callie. It was just a casual conversation. Henry was in to discuss my plans to expand the storage center, and Tim Kitteridge happened to be leaving after a visit to his unit. I didn't mention anything about it to him. Anyway, one thing led to another and suddenly Henry and I were talking about the Kitteridge property."

"So if I were to do a little snooping at the planning department—"

"Don't you dare. I need Henry's support to expand my business so don't let on that I've mentioned any of this to you. Wouldn't want him to think I can't be trusted with confidences."

My forehead scrunched. "So he said all this to you in confidence?"

"No, nothing like that." He stopped and sighed. "We were just shooting the breeze, but it would still look bad if he knew I was repeating our conversations."

Greta touched Bobby's arm. "Okay, you two. Either of you want a soda? All this shop talk is making me thirsty."

I turned to her. "Actually, you really should be off your feet and as far away from wet paint as possible."

"It's that healthy paint!"

"But still." I hugged her to me. "Come on, I'll go with you to the kitchen."

We left the room, but my mind lingered on the fresh news that SOS would have to work quickly to stave off the plans for the Kitteridge property.

GAGE

IT WAS EITHER A double espresso or this. A severe jolt of caffeine might have been the easier route, but coffee in the evening could have an adverse effect, one that might keep him up all night and put him back on the exhaustion treadmill. So he shed his jeans, pulled on a pair of shorts, and hit the ground running.

Maybe not *running*, but he was jogging all right. The stress of the past few months had put too much time between him and exercise, and to avoid injury he'd have to start slow.

He wound through the village, over the bridge, and past the inn-dotted road that abutted the beach. A couple and their two daughters sat at a window-side table at the Red Abalone Grill eating ice cream and something panged in his chest. Suz and Jer should be living that life. Instead, they had run away from their home and the stigma that came from living with a drug-addicted, incarcerated husband and father.

He pressed on, allowing the rhythm of his cadence to lull his mind away from the intricate knot that had formed in that impossible-to-reach space between the shoulder blades of his back. He hauled in a lung-filling breath. Seagulls sailed overhead, as did the occasional mallard, and even a formation of pelicans on their afternoon snack hunt. Although he felt a slight pull running down his calves, his breathing stayed even, and not surprisingly Gage felt stronger than when he had begun.

With his second wind providing the needed energy, he

charged up a brief rise in the road so enthralled with the land-scape that it had not occurred to him that once he crested that hill, he would be at the south end of the Kitteridge property. And there it was—the all-encompassing view, the rock he rested on, the man-made stairs down to the shore—all there. Not to mention, the memory of his verbal sparring with Callie yesterday.

Why did this woman he barely knew get to him so easily? His head dropped forward and he squeezed his eyes shut will-ing away anything that would hinder his workout.

Too late. He slowed to a pathetic jog and figured that at this point, he might as well consider it a brisk walk. He blew air from his lungs and glanced around. As the sun made its descent, so did the distraction of sound and memory. The sea had calmed, the scent from woody scrub surrounded him, and crickets had begun their night music early.

For once Gage wanted to walk this land without thinking about hindrances, to run across the expanse and consider the possibilities. True, in order to do that, he would also have to push away the snapshot in his head of preliminary drawings that showed just how thorough and far-reaching the coverage of this land would ultimately be. Still he dreamt. Progress was not evil in itself. If only he could find a way to be the bridge between the community and those who had hired him.

Heavy breathing galloped up from behind, and he spun around. A tan-colored dog with bright eyes greeted him, his pink tongue dangling out the side of his mouth. "Hey, boy. What are you doing out here all by yourself?" Gage squatted and petted the dog with one hand while grabbing his collar with the other. He fingered a makeshift tag. "Moondoggy, eh? Maybe your owner's not as hard-nosed as she acts." He rubbed Moondoggy's head and neck. "It's quite a mouthful but I like it."

Holding onto his collar, Gage craned his neck, searching for Callie. All he spotted was an elderly man in a plaid shirt and jeans hiked up to his waist. Concern furrowed his brow. He turned back and cupped Moondoggy's face, expecting to give him some reassurance before setting out to find the dog's home, only Moondoggy sprung from his grip like a kangaroo in the outback.

"Wait!" He forgot about the gentle strain in his calves and tore off after the dog. If it were his animal roaming the town by itself, he hoped someone would do the same for him. At least he told himself that's why he was doing this.

At the top of the hill, not far from where he'd met Callie and her new pet for the first time, Moondoggy halted like he had spotted a slab of raw beef hanging from a pine branch. Gage slowed not wanting to spook the dog again. The animal watched as Gage slowly ascended through a thick bed of dry pine needles. Then, just as he was about to take two final steps to reach the top, Moondoggy darted off again, this time back down the hill and in the direction of town.

Score: Moondoggy the mouse = one; Gage the cat = zero.

"Shoot." Gage rested his hands on his knees while gulping air and watching the dog romp along until he was a far-flung speck on the land. He moved his hands to his waist, took a few deep breaths, then hobbled back down the hill. He was not surprised to discover Moondoggy waiting for him at the edge of the property as if to say, "Just so you understand, I'm the one in charge around here."

Moondoggy stood on his hind legs and slapped his paws on Gage's midsection, scraping his long front nails down his shirt. He eyed the dog. "So you think I'm going to pet you now? After all that?" He reached out then and gave the dog a begrudging rub of his noggin. "Yes, well, let's get you home."

He didn't recognize the street name, so Gage had no choice but to follow the little guy home. Sure, he could've called Callie—his sister had given him her number for who knows what reason—but why give her fair warning of his arrival? He had her dog, and that meant he had leverage. She would have to put away her arrows and play nice.

A pang of something—guilt at the thought of watching her squirm—coiled through him.

He had barely reached the house when he heard, "Moondoggy!"

His remorse intensified when he saw her red-rimmed eyes. Callie dropped to her knees and threw her body over the pup with the wagging tail and happy jowls and hugged him. Gage stood there, trying not to look like a dork as he listened to her sniffling.

She looked up at him while still clinging to the dog. "Where was he?"

"Found him over at the Kitteridge property wanting to play. Tried catching him but he was too fast."

Her eyes showed relief. "Well, then, thanks for staying with him until he made it home."

Gage glanced at the cottage behind her. Simple structure with lime plaster exterior, frameless windows, and a meandering path of blue solar lanterns. "This your place?"

"It is."

A small plot of cannas, asters, and lilies flourished in tended soil set away from the home's foundation. A neatly formed berm surrounded the floral display. "You're into rain gardening, I see. Impressive."

A guarded look in her eyes returned. "It's not that hard."

"Some might disagree with you."

"They'd be wrong."

Of course, because everyone who has an opinion other than yours is wrong. He cleared his throat, opening his mouth to speak, but she beat him to it.

"Thanks again for bringing Moondoggy home. I don't know what I would have done—"

"Don't mention it, and I should be thanking you. He gave me the workout of my life." Gage laughed and something lifted in his heart when he saw a smile shaping Callie's lips. She had a natural beauty and might have been the first woman he'd ever met who didn't run to put on lipstick before heading outdoors. He wondered if her skin had ever seen a puff of powder or whatever it was that women used daily.

She stood and hoisted Moondoggy into her arms unbothered by the dog's weight and gangly limbs. "I've got a thing to get to. So, I'll see you, I guess." She batted thick eyelashes at him. Did she do that on purpose? He watched Callie climb the stairs of her porch, dash another look his way, then disappear inside.

Maybe, in another time, their friendship might have grown and flourished like that rain garden behind them. A beat passed as he stood on the path outside. When had he become so sappy?

Chapter Fourteen

"You're late!" Ruth met me at the door of the RAG, a clipboard in her arms.

I blinked back tears. "Couldn't be helped. Moondoggy got out and I couldn't leave until he was safe at home again." I didn't mention that my knight was the known enemy, nor that his presence at my home had caused me to reel almost as much as my dog's disappearance.

"Not to worry. I filled everybody in on the name of our group and got them all to give me their current contact info." She tapped her clipboard. "They are all ready to do what must be done."

My eyes hovered over her clipboard. Many of those I'd invited via e-mail had come. "Good. You can take notes."

Quickly it became apparent that we had doubled in size. Familiar faces of our community sat around not one table, but two, some chatting amiably, others sending waves of heat with their frowns. The scene accelerated my pulse. Was I ready for this?

Ruth pulled at the sleeve of one of the newcomers until he hauled himself from his chair. "Eliot, I'd like you to meet the leader of our group, Callie Duflay."

He was young and sprightly, with black hair spiked at the crown, and he wore wire-rimmed glasses in an apparent attempt to age him because he could not have been more than eighteen or nineteen years old. He slipped his pen and notepad into his left hand and reached out to shake my right. "Eliot Hawl, with the press, ma'am."

"The press?" And had he just called me ma'am?

"SLO Press, covering county news. Hope you don't mind if I sit in?" He puffed out his chest. "I will have questions."

Media coverage. I had toyed with getting the papers involved eventually, but so soon? My mouth went dry like cotton and I tried to pull my thoughts together, the thoughts that had scattered about the neighborhood during my search for Moondoggy this evening. It didn't help that when I called June this morning, she cried and begged me not to share their predicament with anyone else. She calmed way down when I presented her with my plan.

Now, it was time to convince everyone else.

You're a leader, Callie, not a follower. My mother's words propelled me forward. I shook Eliot's hand. "Pleasure to meet you. Glad you could join us today."

When he and Ruth had taken their seats, I motioned for Holly. "Would you leave us a couple of coffee pots with more cream and sugar?"

The waitress with the unruly ringlets and bright smile nodded. "Will do."

I glanced about the table, making eye contact and trying to remember everyone's names. "Thank you all for coming. I see more have joined our cause, and that's great."

Eliot's hand darted up. "Are you aware that the Kitteridge project is on fast-track status with the planning department?"

Stunned. The kid's done his homework. If I answered him in the affirmative, I'd probably have to tell him how I knew. I kept my expression calm. "I will take questions after the meeting. Now, getting back to—"

"Once I heard what those Kitteridges were up to, I had to come!" A woman with a sharp nose and angry eyes crossed her arms in a huff.

A man across from her dumped the last of the sugar into his coffee then stirred it so roughly some of it splashed onto his place mat. "Selling to developers after all this time. I'll tell you what—that Tim better watch his step at my feed store!"

Things were flying out of hand. Somehow I needed to grab hold of the string. "Friends, please, wait. Let's not get too upset with June and Tim." I paused and pressed my lips together. "Sometimes things happen for a reason."

There. Diplomacy. Didn't have a whole lot of experience with it, but I was trying.

"So you're defending them?" Oscar, one of our local fisher-men, spoke up. "We've got to be respectful of that area, Callie. The otters are coming back, but what's going to happen to them once the area begins to erode from overbuilding?" He shook his head, rattling the wire hooks hanging from his hat. "I can tell you that the quality of fish around here has already gone down from all the pollution that comes from dirty run-off. It's bad, Callie, really bad."

He was right. Yet somehow we had to strike a balance here. How in the world could I get them all to see?

Steph, our town librarian, raised her hand. "Callie, I sym-pathize with the Kitteridges. I thought they would never shut down their store, but when they did and the rumors about their money problems surfaced, well, I became very worried for them."

Ruth cocked an eyebrow. "What sort of money problems? That ol' dog Tim do some risky investments or something?"

I shoved my flexed palms toward the crowd. "Listen. Rather than speculate on all that . . ." Rumors had been flying for months about the Kitteridge's financial health, but it was not my place to give the specifics. I inhaled through my nose and put on a happy face. "I suggest we try something amazing and unchartered for this area. Please, hear me out."

Ruth stood and began shushing everyone, repeatedly flap-ping her right hand downward. Eliot crouched and snapped a picture of me from an unflattering angle. Holly breezed in to set coffee pots within arm's reach.

As the crowd grew quiet, my heart swelled with excitement. If we pulled this off, we might just have a win-win situation at our feet. I drew in a confident breath. "Okay, everyone, here's what I propose."

GAGE

"WHAT IS IT?" SUZ stood alongside Gage as he peered at an oversized document on his drawing board in the morning light.

"It's the survey I've been waiting for."

She bent over the document. "You, big brother, must be really smart because this thing looks like hieroglyphics to me. What are all the swirls and numbers about?"

Gage smoothed back the curled page. "They're all necessary parts of the survey, Suz. Actually, this one is actually more like a map showing natural and man-made features of the project site. It also provides exact height in feet above sea level. So what we have before us is a topographical map that encompasses all the open property at the Kitteridge property."

She eyed him. "So this will help you get going on your plan, then."

"Right." Gage studied the survey while making mental notes for later. "It will help me lay out drainage patterns and slopes and vegetation, things like that. Then I'll use it as an underlay beneath my own site plan."

"So exciting, isn't it?"

Gage looked away from his work and met his sister's gaze. Although in the midst of personal troubles, she didn't show it. She seemed downright happy to be carried along for the ride on this project. "You're right, it is. Some people like to drive around showing off the properties that they've built; and while I don't have a problem with that, per se, I'd say that this is the thrilling part for me."

"The journey."

He swallowed, noticing a tinge of sorrow pass across her face before her smile returned. "Yeah, the journey."

Suz straightened and smoothed away the crease in her skirt. "Then get to it."

After she left, he reached for his coffee mug only to realize it had been drained. No matter. A hot-off-the-press survey gave more of an adrenaline boost than caffeine did anyway.

"I forgot to bring these in earlier." Suz dropped a couple of local newspapers on Gage's desk. She also had a coffee pot with her and filled his empty mug.

"Bless you."

She laughed. A headline caught his attention and wiped the smile off his face.

SAVE OUR SHORES:
SOS GROUP AIMS TO OUST UNWELCOME
DEVELOPMENT

Gage ignored his coffee as he opted for the morning news instead.

> Callie Duflay, president of Save Our Shores, has
> a message for waterfront developers: You're not
> welcome in these parts. The riveting blonde and
> her mighty band of angry residents met last night
> at the Red Abalone Grill. Aside from drinking
> enough coffee to finance a third-world nation, their
> mission was simple—fight a project planned for
> the popular open land known as the Kitteridge
> property.

Gage set the paper down. The article's cheese factor aside, this was bad news on any day. He glanced at the survey on his desk. Especially today. His eyes followed the text to the bottom of the page, then he obeyed the directions and turned to page four.

> Speaking on the condition of anonymity, an aide to
> one of the town council members had this warning
> for SOS, "It would behoove Miss Duflay to stay out
> of the way of progress. The council is comprised
> of upstanding citizens within our own community,
> and I assure you, they all have the best interests
> of Otter Bay at heart."

Yes, sure, that would make her run away, cowering. He read on, noting the brief profile written about Callie and highlighting her many humanitarian efforts. Apparently she even sponsored children in other countries. He grunted and skipped to the last paragraph.

> Only time will tell if SOS will heed such advice. As of now, the group is moving forward with a plan to buy the property from under the developers. They are about to embark on an aggressive fund-raising campaign, one that will help them achieve their goal of making the Kitteridge property open to the community—forever.

Gage crumpled the newsprint with one hand. This must have been the "thing" she had to get to last night. She hadn't let on either. No, not a word about her plans to him—even after he saved her dog from certain danger. He reached for the warm coffee and took a bitter sip. Maybe if he had not chased that animal home, she would not have made it to her little gathering in the first place.

"What's got you?" Suz wore concern on her face. "Two minutes ago you were like a giddy eight-year-old, but now your upper lip is all twisted up."

"Bad news about the Kitteridge property."

"What? Already? You were just telling me . . ."

He pressed his thumbs to his temples and raked his fingers through his hair noting how much he needed a haircut. He motioned to the newspaper. "That woman you met at the paint store—Callie—remember her? She's heading up some group that's trying to thwart the project."

Suz's forehead crinkled. "Let me see that." She smoothed the paper and her eyes tracked the article. Gage tried to interject a comment, but each time she would stop him with a flick of her forefinger and a "shush." She made it to the end, inhaled, then handed the paper back. "I don't know much, but if there's one thing I do understand it's that people are broke and you can't squeeze money out of a dried up turnip. I think she's bluffing. There's no way this small town can come up with that kind of money that fast. Take it from one who knows, money's hard to get and even harder to raise from others."

He glanced at his sister. She wore her life lessons with fierceness, and for once in a long while he recognized her for the strong woman she had become. "So I should just forget about it, then? Is that your advice?"

She shrugged. "Of course not. When this thing crumbles, Callie's going to need some broad shoulders to lean on, and you'll be there."

"You can't be serious."

"I absolutely am. Dead-on serious, big brother."

He sputtered. He had no idea if he'd ever be able to say two words to the woman after this, let alone be a source of support. "That woman is a thorn in my side, or haven't you noticed?"

Suz laughed. "She keeps you alert. That's good."

"Or exposes my need for a tetanus shot!" He tossed the paper into the waste can.

His sister sighed. "Don't you get it? You need to get that girl on *your* side. Listen to her concerns, open the communication between you two, and when things fall apart, she won't see you as the enemy anymore."

"Oh, really. She'll just see me as the great guy that I am." He smirked, followed by a sigh. "And why would I even want to do this, Suz? Why should I care?"

Suz's gaze slid downward. "I missed out on the perfect guy, Gage. All because I was afraid of a little work. Good relationships take work, but I wanted things easy. Seth asked me to move across the country with him as he searched out a new life." She wrinkled her nose, pausing. "But I wanted to stick around with my friends and keep hanging out on Saturday nights. I wanted all the trinkets that money could buy, but I didn't want to wait around for Seth to find the perfect job and to build up his savings. So I let him go." Tears spiked her lashes. "When Len showed up and said all the right things— bought all the right things—I made a hasty, shallow decision and married him. And you know what's funny?"

He couldn't imagine.

"I ended up moving all the way across country anyway." The smile on her face didn't reach her eyes. "Isn't that a riot?"

Gage reached for her hand. "You've got Jer."

Suz sniffed and wiped away a tear with the back of her hand. "That's right. God's way of reminding me there is always a silver lining." Her eyes connected with Gage's. "I can't say if Callie's the one for you, Gage. But I do know that you've run into her more than once lately, and every time you do you come back looking like some lost puppy."

"You been spying on me?"

"It's a small town." She nudged him before slowly making her way to the office door. "So why don't you give her a call?"

Gage sat in the silence, thinking on the advice Suz had offered. It sounded crazy, ludicrous.

He picked up the phone and dialed.

Chapter Fifteen

"Greetings, Madam President!" Tidal Wave plopped a soggy triangle of pizza onto a flimsy plate and pushed it toward me.

Starved, I picked up the plate. Grease slid across my palm. "Really, TW, you can just call me President Callie."

"Hee, hee." Tidal Wave's chin bounced when he laughed, forcing evening stubble through the folds. "Saw your picture in the paper."

I nodded. Those were the same words Gage used when he surprised me with a phone call today. I had no idea just how many people in town kept up with the local news. By the number of times I'd been stopped on my walks, you'd think it was everyone. "That was me. Could've been a better angle, don't you agree?"

He blushed and kept his focus on slicing the monstrous pizza before him. "I cut it out and put it on my fridge."

I punched his solid shoulder. "Oh, you did not!"

He looked at me stunned, eyes wide, unsmiling mouth. My gut felt hollow. Did Tidal Wave have a little crush? A pause, and then he roared, a garble of laughter falling from him. "Just having some fun with you."

His was no longer the only red face in the room. I directed the most even look into his eyes; the most serious tone into my voice that I could muster. "I'll have a second piece."

His eyebrows shot up and he hesitated and bit his lip before quickly scooping up another drippy slice and plopping it onto my plate. "Yes, ma'am."

He didn't see the sly smile on my face as I walked away and headed to Squid and a gathering of board members at a nearby table.

"Hello, Callie." Natalia had shed her woman-in-the-board-room look for more casual low heels, capris, and a button-down blouse. "I've been reading about you. You have been a busy lady."

My mind hesitated. Did I need more opposition in my life? True she appeared welcoming, but then again, Gage sounded congenial on the phone today too. Suspicion rose in me then, and it reared itself again now. While I wished to find another table, I relented and took a seat across from Natalia. "It's been a whirlwind already. So far, there's been positive support in the community."

"But will that support translate into dollars?"

"I'm hopeful that it will. One of our SOS team members set up that Web page mentioned in the article, and already several thousand dollars in pledges have come in."

"Impressive!" She tasted a bite of the salad in front of her, obviously brought in from the outside, and then set down her fork before turning to Squid. "Maybe Callie should become part of our fund-raising team here at camp. We could use someone with fund-raising knowledge on future campaigns."

Squid downed a cola and shrugged. He glanced my way. "Yeah. Maybe."

I smiled. If she wanted to pump me up in front of Squid, I wouldn't stand in her way. "Thanks for the boost of confidence, Natalia. Right now is not the best time, but I would certainly love to share all I learn with the camp board. This place means a lot to me."

"Thank you, Callie. I can see that."

Probably the most civil, uncomplicated conversation that Natalia and I have ever had. One newspaper article and, like others in the community, Natalia seems to have developed an appreciation for my contributions. Squid, however, seemed more contemplative than usual.

Natalia wiped her fingers with a napkin. "Would you like to start the meeting, Thomas? Everyone appears to be here now."

Squid rose from the table. The faint lines at his eyes appeared deeper than usual. "Evening, everyone. Thanks for stopping by tonight. As you know I've been mulling over ways to make our weekend camps more viable for the kids. But before I get to that, we've got some quick business to discuss."

Squid seemed preoccupied tonight. His eyes flitted about rather than conveying the directness that those of us who worked with him were used to seeing. He cleared his throat. "Camp's busier than ever. We get calls every day with new registrations, but unfortunately we've had to turn away some great people."

Luz piped up. "Not always."

I slouched in my chair. *Really, Luz? Must my blunder of last weekend be brought up now? In front of both board and staff?*

"There have been few exceptions." Squid's mouth lay flat. "The board and I have been discussing the possibility of building more cabins. The problem is we use every square inch of our outdoor space already, plus we'd need to raise funds before we could even begin."

Natalia smiled, giving me a nod. You'd think this would make me feel honored and maybe even important. Instead, the idea of tackling anything larger than what I've already proposed to SOS boggled me.

Ted, one of the board members, held up a bent forefinger. "I have an idea, Tom. What about two-story cabins? More kids, yet we keep the same footprint."

Natalia leaned back in her chair, arms folded. "Too costly. That and we would probably have the fire chief after us all season. Also, I think there may even be a rule against younger children sleeping on the second floor."

Luz grimaced, elbow on table, and chin in hand. "So if we don't have just the right mix of kids, we could still find ourselves with too many campers and not enough beds. Great."

Squid fidgeted with his beard. I couldn't recall seeing him do that before. He rolled his shoulders back from their slumped position and raised his hand. "Maybe we're getting ahead of ourselves, eh? All of this is food for thought at the moment. We obviously can't do anything about this right away, but we will be looking thoroughly at all ideas. If anyone comes up with the miracle solution, you can call me or Natalia." He clasped his hands. "Moving on."

For the next five minutes or so Squid proceeded to work through a boring checklist of maintenance items that needed fixing. Normally Squid ran meetings the way he ran a night camp gathering for two hundred kids. He'd spiral footballs into the crowd and tell some groan-worthy jokes then follow up by using his megaphone for effect. Tonight, however, my former crush was off his game.

My mind wandered. Maybe I only imagined Squid's perplexing state. The past day and a half carried with it the low of nearly losing my dog (and having to humble myself, tear-stained cheeks and all, before Gage), and the incredible high from the huge community support for the Kitteridge property acquisition, complete with a media plug and name recognition. Not to mention that rather confusing phone call from Gage.

"I realize that we're on opposite sides of the court, Callie," he had told me. "But I'm not going to try to convince you to stop your fight. If you ever have any questions about my plans for this project, you just ask. Will you do that?"

I didn't know whether to pitch my phone across the room or present him with a lengthy list of questions, the answers of which would give me ammunition to up the fight. Could I do that to another person? Take what they freely gave and then turn it against them? Or maybe that was exactly what Gage Mitchell surmised: that my conscience would not allow me to use someone that way.

He was a crafty one, all right.

Squid stroked his beard again and the motion yanked me back into the meeting. He had made it to the bottom of his list and I couldn't recall a thing that had been on it. I set aside my plate and focused on him.

"Getting back to our campers, there's always the danger that their experience with us will be the high." He gestured to the airspace above him. "But we're not about mountaintop experiences that have nowhere to go but down. Are you tracking with me here?"

The room fell silent. Squid dropped his gaze to the floor, his eyes shut. When he lifted his head, his eyes were sharp, focused. "It's about giving them an experience that is so real, so vibrant, that they'll go home changed. Different. My hope is that people around them will want to know what they've been up to. Not what camp they attended, not the name of their counselor, but what happened *inside* them that has changed them for the better."

He spoke with deliberateness and passion. "At the same time, I don't want the message to get so convoluted that they can't even begin to live it. Does that make sense?"

I spoke out in the quiet room. "I think so. You want them to understand the essence of faith."

Squid cast his attention toward me. "And that is?"

As a person of faith, I knew this one by heart. "To serve God, of course. To live for him."

Squid watched me. "Exactly. Yet how can they do that if they don't understand how to hear his voice?" He stared at me for a beat longer than felt comfortable. Had he heard my middle-of-the-night confession to the girls in my cabin? I had admitted to them my struggles, yet had not spent one minute sorting them out for myself.

Ted cleared his throat and raised a finger again, offering his own take on what direction he thought the message could go, and I sat back, trying to rein in my buzzing thoughts. One thing I knew, I had better think of a way to work faith into my plans.

GAGE

GAGE CRACKED HIS NECK. First the left side, then the right. He winced and rolled his shoulders, but it did nothing for him other than accentuate his fatigue. With a few clicks, he shut down his computer and waited for it to power down.

Suz had asked him to work late tonight, fixated on painting his entire living room. She had planned to put Jeremiah to bed early, then finish up what she'd started earlier in the day. He shut his eyes, remembering the first week she and Jer had spent with him. She had found some leftover paint in his shed, paint he had used in his former house and didn't want to part with. While he was away at work one day, she painted his bathroom a rich shade of Chocolate Loam.

Initially, he reacted with a tinge of shock and a lot of apprehension. He had his own ideas of what he would like to do with his home once he had the time—and the resources. But Suz's eye for design and the meticulousness of her work won him over. Vaguely he remembered their mother saying Suz had artistic ability, but for all he knew at the time, it was nothing more than motherly bragging. He knew better now.

Although he had the utmost confidence in his sister's skill and designer eye, he was tired. Gage hoped she had all the time she needed to accomplish her goal for the day. He yawned, picked up his office phone, and dialed home.

Suz answered on the fourth ring. "Hey."

He sat back against his chair. "How's the painting coming along?"

"I'm in the homestretch." Her voice was breathless, as if rolling paint onto walls as she spoke. "Because of all that sun we get, the first coat dried enough for me to add another."

He shoved two soft pencils into his desk drawer and slid it shut. "Great. Can't wait to see your handiwork."

"Oh, but don't come home yet. I have a surprise and don't want you to see it until I'm finished. Okay?"

He stifled a sigh, and stretched his forehead in an attempt to hold his eyes open. "Well . . ."

"Stop at the RAG and have something to eat. I bet you haven't eaten all evening." She paused. "I'm right, aren't I?"

He chuckled. "You're such a mom."

"Of course I am. Why are you laughing?"

"Not laughing at you. It's just new to me, that's all." He glanced at the clock on his credenza and grimaced. "I guess I could use some dinner."

"Great! Chew slowly and I'll try to have this done and the place all cleaned up before you get home. See you."

She clicked off. He grabbed his coat and slipped out the door, the rumbling in his stomach holding at bay his other pressing need—to crawl into bed. When he arrived at the RAG, much of the patronage consisted of teenagers gazing at each other and the occasional, solitary diner. The hostess, Mimi, doubled as a waitress. She led him to a table against the window and took his drink order. Coffee. Black. Decaf.

She delivered it in seconds along with a kind smile. "You're in late tonight."

He smiled up at her. "Hunger knows no schedule."

She cackled. Mimi looked to be in her late forties. She leaned against the booth opposite him. "I've seen you here several times. New in Otter Bay?"

He sipped the coffee and nodded. "I am. Gage Mitchell. Glad to formally meet you, Mimi."

"Same here. Most everyone comes in here if they're in this town any length of time. I've been working for old Peg since my oldest was in diapers."

"Really? How many children?"

"Four. All of them girls. I love 'em to death, but all those hormones in one house gets more than I can handle sometimes. Work is a blessing."

He threw his head back, grateful for a hearty laugh. "I guess so."

Mimi glanced across the diner as a bell jingled announcing another diner had entered the place. She smacked him on the rotator cuff. "Now don't be getting the wrong idea about women from me. You fellas need us just as much as we need you!"

She laughed and Gage followed suit. He gave her an "I hear you" nod as she motioned with a flapping hand for someone to join them. Apparently his table was the designated gathering spot for the evening.

He held the mug in his hands and glanced over his shoulder. Callie approached. For someone who had sounded strained and suspicious during their five-minute phone call this morning, she sure had a nice smile on her face. Then he understood. She had no idea who sat in the booth next to where Mimi stood.

"There's the girl of the hour," Mimi called out and turning

her back to him. "I heard you were in the paper this morning, Callie."

"Yes, yes. Lot's going on."

"Well, now, I haven't had a moment to read it myself, but it sure seems like a big project to handle." Mimi rocked side to side when she talked, the bow of her apron rustling against his booth. "Are you sure this is what you want to do?"

Discomfort crept through him. He felt like he was eavesdropping even though the women stood not two feet from him on the other side of Mimi.

Callie spoke. "I'm doing this for all of us."

"Oh!" Mimi jumped to one side, exposing his presence. "Where are my manners? Callie, this is Gage Mitchell. He's new in town. And Gage—"

He didn't bother putting out a hand, but offered a friendly smile, albeit somewhat forced. "We've met. Hello, Callie."

Mimi bubbled. "How nice that you two know each other, what with him being new in town and you being a lifelong resident." She reached over the table behind Gage and snatched a menu from the two teens who seemed to have eyes only for each other. "Here's another menu. I supposed you'd like to sit together."

He had decided to help Callie out, one last time. "No, I don't—"

Callie plucked the menu from Mimi's hand. "Sure. That would be fine. Thanks, Mimi."

Mimi spun away still chattering. "I'll come right on back with a hot pot. It'll be just a second or two."

Callie slid into the seat across from Gage, a blend of tired and pretty all rolled into one exasperating woman. He continued to cradle his mug, searching for something to add to the phone conversation that went nowhere this morning.

He needn't have bothered because Callie had a lot on her mind.

"I don't know what that phone call was all about this morning, or what kind of tricks you have up your sleeve, Mr. Mitchell, but I'm not leaving here until we understand each other. Completely."

He took one last, slow sip, set down his mug, and realized his appetite had vanished.

Chapter Sixteen

 Gage needed to understand that I was no damsel in distress. Nor was I naive. On the contrary, I wondered just how much he knew about the Kitteridge's dire predicament and how that knowledge might be driving his own actions. Of course, I couldn't ask, because that would be betraying June's confidence. While his phone call from this morning may have caused me to wobble momentarily, I had been ruminating about it all day, and my suspicions had mushroomed.

Now as we sat with this table as a dividing line between us, I hoped to see on his face what I could not hear over the phone: his hidden agenda.

He set his coffee down and clasped his hands on the table. "As far as I'm concerned, my meaning was completely clear. But if you did not understand it, then I apologize for that."

I ignored his sarcasm. "People don't just call up their enemies and offer to help them. Did you really think I'd fall for that?" I stopped him with a raised palm. "Wait. Let me answer that. No. I would not."

Although his lips remained in a flat line, it looked like he was hiding a smile. Faint crow's-feet appeared.

I watched him through narrowed eyes. "Did you have something to add?"

He shook his head, but the smile in his eyes remained.

I gripped the table and slid from the booth. "This is a waste of time. You're just laughing about this."

"You've got me wrong. Completely." All trace of the smile vanished. Gage hung his head and moved it side to side, exposing waves of sun-streaked hair. With his tanned skin and untamed locks, Gage could pass for a surfer, if surfers wore Dockers and collars, that is. He raised his head. "I would never laugh at you."

I glanced away, suddenly fascinated with the classic yellow and red bottles at the far edge of our table. My heart pounded and I wanted to send it to bed without its supper. This made no sense. *He* made no sense.

His eyes captured mine and didn't waver. A golden shadow framed his lips and trailed down his chin. "Let's just lay it out on the line here, Callie. Can we do that?"

He sounded sincere. My mouth had gone dry. Annoyingly dry. But I managed to croak out, "Sure." I slid back into the booth.

Gage unhooked his hands and stroked the speckled design of the Formica tabletop with his fingertips. "I feel for you and for this community. Like you, I've begun to appreciate the land in question. I've spent time on it, watched the sea life, felt the bones of it, if you will." He sighed and lifted his head. Those eyes again. "It's a magnificent place."

My shoulders relaxed. "So you understand."

"To a point." Gage sat up straighter. "I've got a new business to run and this is, quite frankly, our first big project."

My forehead lifted. "You're a new architect?"

Gage shook his head. "No, not at all. I've worked under some of the best. I've learned what I like, and what I don't care for in this business, and this is one of the reasons I chose to open my own firm." He continued to stroke his fingers across the table surface. "I'm a big believer in divine appointments. Something tells me you feel that way too."

I hesitated. That seemed rather forward, even for him. "I do."

"That's exactly how I felt when this project fell into my lap. I have wanted to open my own eco-firm for months, but just needed a push or maybe more like a harsh shove." A closed mouth smile lit up his face, those eyes. He clasped his hands again. "I wasn't even sure where to settle. That's one reason why, when this opportunity arose, I embraced it."

"Why are you telling me all this?"

"Because I can see that you are a reasonable person. You know what it's like to pursue things that are meaningful to you. That newspaper article sure listed a lot of them. For instance, all those children you support . . . did the reporter get that number right?"

I stifled a sigh. Supporting children through Compassion International was a pet cause, but Eliot surprised me when he asked how many and I blurted out the truth: five kids. Even most of my family didn't know about them. "He did, but I shouldn't have admitted that to him. It isn't right to put myself on a pedestal. Anyone would—"

"Do the same thing? Hardly. No, I'd say that shelling out enough to feed and educate five children each month is not something ordinary people do."

"The Von Trapps did it—and then some."

Silence, followed by a burst of laughter, flowed from Gage. "You got me there." He continued to laugh. "Good one."

As his laughter dissipated, Mimi showed up with an expectant look on her face. I fidgeted with the menu, even though I knew everything listed on it. "Just a cup of your chicken soup tonight."

Her brows, painted a shade too light, rose and pulled together. "Well, I hope you're not feeling sick." She laid the oily back of her hand to my forehead. "Nope, you're cool as a cuke. And for you, Gage?"

He handed the menu to Mimi without looking at it. "Turkey burger, medium rare, mustard only, and a green chili on top."

"Some gal just ordered the same thing not more than a

couple of days ago. Must be a trend." She stuffed her notepad into a pocket and jetted to the next table.

Gage peered at me, a remnant of his laughter still warming his face. "Comfort food all around then, eh?"

"Yes, but not in a good way." I sighed. "Just came back in from a meeting at camp where I work. Collected enough grease from the pizza to fuel my car."

"Hmm. Not good."

Silence draped itself over us. And over me, fatigue, the kind that sneaks up on you after adrenaline courses through the body, much like a rushing river does along a mountainous pass, carving new grooves into the earth until it sputters dry. Without thinking, I shut my eyes and dropped my head forward to stretch my neck then rolled my chin all the way around. My eyes popped open to find Gage watching me. "Sorry."

He waved away my apology. "I'm with you. If Suz hadn't decorated my house with drop cloths and ordered me to stay away, I too would be asleep by now." He held up his coffee mug and winked at Mimi who zipped over with a hot pot. He took a fresh sip. "But then again, I can't complain. I intimated this before, but I received more confirmation that this move was the right one when just after I arrived, my sis and nephew showed up needing a home."

"May I ask? When we met, Suzanna seemed, I don't know, distracted maybe? Like she had a lot on her mind but didn't want to share it. Just a sense I got."

"You're right. Things have been rough for her and Jer. I probably should let her be the one to tell you about it; you were the first person in town to reach out to her. Despite our differences, that meant a lot, Callie. A whole lot."

"Thanks." His compliment threw me again. Second time today that Gage Mitchell had something surprising to say to me. My stomach churned. Was it hunger for real food, or an emotional stew of conflict brewing in my gut?

"All I'm trying to say here is that I believe God led me here to this job so I could provide the home that my sister and nephew need. I have no doubt in my mind about that. So I'm sorry if you thought I had some kind of trick up my sleeve." He smiled at me while folding his arms onto the table and leaning toward me. "But being hated just isn't on my to-do list. If truth be told, the only trick I could be accused of was trying to help you see that I'm not the ogre you think I am."

"And that maybe when I figured that out, I'd drop the SOS project?"

He shrugged. "Guess that was naiveté on my part, wasn't it?"

His face held a more rueful look now, although his eyes glimmered. Part of me wanted this whole thing to go away, but it wouldn't, so neither would I. There was too much at stake for the Kitteridges, the community, even for myself. I shrugged. "Sorry."

Mimi served me a steaming cup of soup and packet of crackers, and slid Gage's burger concoction in front of him. "Water?"

We both nodded yes.

"Right up." She scampered to the kitchen.

Gage picked up a fry. "My offer still stands. Even though you may reject me, I'd still like to give you an insider's glimpse into what I have in mind for the property."

I swallowed a spoonful of soup. It tasted bland. "I'm not rejecting you, just your work."

He raised an eyebrow.

I put down my spoon. "Don't get all artiste on me. I know all about the reject-my-art-and-you-wound-me theory."

He bit into his burger, then wiped his mouth with a napkin. "So you don't buy it?"

I shrugged, two palms up. "Whatever floats your boat."

"My sister might challenge you on that. She's the true artist in our family, and I'm only beginning to see how much art means to her."

"Yes. That's right, the painting."

"Not just any painting, but freehand art, applied directly to my walls. She made the bathroom a masterpiece in one day with a giant sunburst. Knocked my socks off."

I smiled. "Really."

"Well, no, not *really*, but it surprised me. She and I have a lot of years between us—"

"I've noticed."

Gage dropped his burger onto his plate and sat back, eyeing me. "Oh have you now? How subtle of you to say so."

Nimbly, I took another sip of soup, the second helping better than the first. "Anyone who knows me understands how little I care about age. That was my attempt at humor, but I apparently need work on delivery."

"Not necessarily. That Von Trapp line was good."

I glanced at the ceiling before looking back at Gage, unable to hide the glint that had formed in my eyes. "This is true."

Laughter erupted at our table as Mimi appeared with two glasses of ice water with slices of lemon floating on top. "Dang, I missed the joke." She winked at me. "Now see what breaking bread together can do for relationships?"

She sped off and I allowed the afterglow of laughter to keep my spirit buoyed. I tried not to think about how the fight ahead might affect the friendship with Gage that, despite my every attempt to avoid, continued to bud. Instead, I searched my mind for some common ground—other than the obvious.

A lightbulb switched on inside my head. "Do you think Suzanna might be interested in doing some painting for me . . . as a job?"

Gage's right eyebrow arched and he paused, as if considering the idea. "I think she would love that."

I pulled my gaze away from that highly-arched brow of his. "All this talk about painting has made me long for some fresh color in my cottage, but I just don't have the time to tackle that. I'd love it if she would consider working for me." I didn't tell him that depending on how she did there could result in more work for her at the camp. "Let me give you my number—"

"She has it."

"Oh. Right."

A moment passed and Gage raised his glass. "To finally finding something we can agree on."

I raised my own glass and clinked it with his. "Here, here. To common ground."

GAGE

ELVIS HAD NOTHING ON him, for as Gage drove the windy road to his quaint home near the shore, the lyrics of "All Shook Up" assailed his mind until he wished he could push a button and force the voice in his head to be silent. His daily thoughts about Callie and her righteous anger and cause-fighting spirit had turned tonight into something altogether new and fresh. Frightening, even.

Part of him welcomed the change. He wasn't immune to the hope that someday he might find a relationship worth sacrificing everything for, a woman whose body and heart would replace his round-the-clock consumption of work with a passion of another kind. Lack of enthusiasm from either side of the equation, however, would kill a bond in its infancy.

This is what shook him to his middle. Gage fought the stirrings within himself, almost wishing them away. He realized that it would do no good to allow himself to fan the flames of ardor only to have them doused by a gully-washer of a rainstorm. And yet desire had sprung up from some dormant place, and at the moment he was doing nothing to bat it away.

The front porch light welcomed Gage as he turned into the drive. Although the front bedroom was dark, a glow shone from the living room, a sign that Suz's artistic ambition had yet to wane for the night. Youth. Sometimes he felt much older than his thirty-five years. At the same time, some of Suz's zest for life had found its way beneath his skin and pumped the equivalent of fresh oxygen into his veins. Worries that may have buried a more cynical man had failed to throw him into despair.

Before he could slip his key into the lock, Suz flung the door wide open. "Hey, you're home!"

"I am."

Her hair ribbon had failed in its duties because uncombed strands sprung up every which way. And while an apron may have saved her clothing, finger-width smudges of paint swept across her cheeks, chin, and nose. Her almond eyes peeked from beneath unruly bangs reminding him of Jeremiah after a day at preschool.

She halted and tilted her head to one side. "What's up with you?"

Gage shut the door behind him. "Nothing much. Tired, but that's all."

"Right." She squinted at him. "You have a goofy look on your face. You got a secret?"

Astute question. If keeping feelings tucked away where they could not do damage meant he had a secret, then he supposed he would have to lie. "C'mon. Show me why you kicked me out of my own house."

She surveyed him warily but relented and lifted one lovely hand into the air à la Vanna White. "You like?"

His gaze riveted to the room. The giant sunburst that Suz had painted on his bathroom wall had surprised him. If she had told him about it ahead of time, he might have discouraged her and guided her toward a more masculine image. When he saw it, however, he was awed and glad he had not said a thing beforehand.

Now? Similar thoughts ran through his head. "Wow. This is beyond what I imagined."

"You like it, then?"

"Beyond words."

Suz had managed to transform his white living room into a warm, elegant sanctuary. The walls no longer appeared flat but uneven, textured, and layered with rich tones. "I've seen this technique before, but . . ." He turned to her. "How did you learn to do this? It looks like plaster but it's—"

"Paint! I know. It's a Tuscan technique, or at least a method that makes it *look* Italian." She took a breath; her smile dimmed slightly. "Probably the only other good thing to come out of my marriage."

"It's stunning. And the trompe l'oeil?"

"That I learned on six months worth of Saturdays at the rec center. I'm glad you like it because I hadn't time to sketch it out before putting it up there."

"Freehand?"

"Of course."

He shook his head, smiling. "Thanks for all the effort. It's classic and beautiful." He paused. "You know, you could make money doing this."

"What? This?"

He laughed. "Of course you could. It would probably be a lot more fun for you than hanging around my dull office all day." He didn't have to tell her that her income would skyrocket with a career change. *Any* career change. Until the Kitteridge project got completely off the ground and he began finding smaller in-between jobs, money would be tight.

"But don't you need me?"

Her face sent him back in time. She still could pout like the very little sister. "I'll always need you, kid, but I'll make do."

She thought a moment. "Then I'd like to try. If you really don't mind."

"Actually, I'm glad you said so. I mentioned your work to Callie, as a matter-of-fact, and she expressed interest in hiring you." He deliberately worked to make his voice sound even and nonchalant.

Suz's eyes popped open wide. "You ran into her tonight! You did. I can tell."

He slipped one hand into his pocket and glanced around the room, as if continuing to admire his sister's handiwork. "Yes, she happened to stop by the diner tonight and we talked." Gage turned his focus on Suz. "About you."

She blew a raspberry. "Right. You want me to believe that I was the main topic of conversation between the two best looking, single people in town. I'm not daft."

He threw his head back, laughter barreling from him. "You are too much."

She poked his shoulder with a paint-encrusted finger. "And you, my brother, are in denial."

He gave her a mock glare. "Are you interested in the job or not?"

"I'm more interested in that look on your face every time you run into her." She paused and when he did not react, she let out a sigh that threatened to awaken Jeremiah. "All right, yes. I'm interested. Guess I should give her a call, unless of course, you'd like to make it for me?"

He tried not to laugh at the sneaky grin lighting up her face. He rolled his eyes. She made him feel young with this high school style banter.

She slapped him on the upper arm. "Fine. I'll call."

Much like a teenage boy with his heart hung out for a wrenching, Gage's spirit lifted at the thought of his sister working closely with Callie. Strangely, it threatened to plunge at the very same thought.

Chapter Seventeen

"Why don't you ever answer your phone?" My sister Sheila's voice in my ear at half past eleven at night startled me. "I've been calling all evening!"

"I'm here now." I tossed my keys onto the table and slid into a chair as Moondoggy danced around me like a starved animal. "What did you want to talk to me about?"

"I saw the article, Callie. *Everyone* saw it. Well, I would have seen it if I had the luxury of time in the morning—like certain people."

Pow. Punch number one.

She continued. "I didn't need to read it anyway. That article was all *anyone* wanted to talk about. I could not shop or bank or pick up children without someone, somewhere stopping me to discuss the SOS campaign."

I bent to pet Moondoggy and he nudged my face with his wet snout. I returned the favor with a quick back-of-the-ears massage while balancing the phone between my own ear and right shoulder. "I'm so glad to hear that. We need all the support we can to make this happen."

"You're serious."

"Of course. Did you expect anything less?" I said this knowing she probably did. Sheila always seemed to have an opinion about how I spent my time. She never got past the fact that I had moved beyond baby-of-the-family status into full-fledged adulthood.

"Callie, this isn't a bake sale to raise money for kids in Africa; this is a war you are embarking on. People with money and a lust for developing prime land do not lay down their weapons at the first sign of retaliation. They turn up the heat."

"Who cares?" Moondoggy sat, so I flipped through the stack of mail on my kitchen table.

"And have you thought at all about how dragging the family name through the mud will affect our parents and your siblings?"

Pow. Punch number two.

It was always about her or them. My sister had been annoyed with me since I was two and refused to allow her to dress me in chiffon. Oil and water. That's how we'd always been. She broke in to my meanderings. "I don't think you're even listening to me."

"On the contrary, I heard everything you said and I'm disregarding it." I gave Moondoggy one more long stroke of my hand along his back, thankful for the friendly face that greeted me at the end of the day. "Sheila, you are the only soul in this town who seems to have a problem with me and/ or this project." I stuffed down the vague memory of Squid's skepticism. "Even the architect and I have talked and he's not standing in our way."

Sheila snickered. "Well, of course not, Callie. He's no dummy. He knows you don't stand a chance of winning against his client, so why would he want to burn a bridge? There's no doubt I'm right about that, and if you tell me he's single and handsome, then I'll *know* I'm right."

Pow. Punch number three. Only this one hurt. It may have even done some damage. I watched as Moondoggy scampered away. The adrenaline that gave me the boost to drive home withered and disappeared. She was right, of course. Gage and I may have called a truce, his sister Suz may freshen up these walls and paint me something fabulous, but in the end, my new architect friend hoped—probably even prayed—that I would fail.

"Can I ask you a question, Sheila?"

"You may."

"When all these people you talk about—the ones who approached you on the street about the newspaper article— when they mentioned my work with SOS, well . . ."

"Spit it out."

"Did they sound unhappy? Were they upset about the community raising funds to buy the property?"

Silence.

"Sheila? Did I lose you?"

"No. I'm still here." She sighed and in my mind's eye her mouth and eyes were closed and she was breathing deeply through her nose. "If truth be told, they were surprised and excited. Every one of them."

"Well good. I'm glad to hear that." My eyes shut. "Sheila, I know you and I haven't always agreed on environmental things, but I want you to know that I understand what I'm doing. It's just so hard for me to worship God with one eye and watch while every last bit of his creation is destroyed with the other. Know what I mean?"

"Fair enough, I suppose." Sheila's voice lost its edge. I knew she felt the same, even if she didn't have it at her mind's forefront. "Let me ask you something, Callie."

"Go for it."

"Why in the world, if you have been sponsoring all those children, did you not share that with the rest of the family?"

And then I knew—the real reason for my sister's late night call. Should I tell Sheila that I had hidden certain things in my life in order to protect myself from the opinions of my older siblings? And what if she learned that Bobby and Greta knew about my children in faraway lands? I had not set out to hurt her.

"Listen, Sheila, it just never came up. Come to think of it, Brenna and Blakey have seen their pictures when they've played in my bedroom. Hadn't they mentioned it?"

She let loose an exasperated, motherly sigh. "They are children. Of course they didn't mention it. I'm just disappointed that I had to read such important aspects of my little sister's life on the front page of the newspaper."

I frowned. "You mean the paper you didn't have a chance to read today?"

"Don't be so literal. You know what I mean."

She meant I'd snared her in a white lie and she hated that. In the long pause, I wondered what it might be like to have a big sister to share things with. Although if I tried harder . . . "Listen, Sheila—"

"It's late. Get some sleep, dear. I read that a cold snap might be blowing in this weekend, probably the last one before summer, and with all you are involved in, you will need your beauty sleep."

"Sure. Thanks. Kiss the kids for me."

We clicked off for the night and I couldn't have been more grateful.

Chapter Eighteen

 The flurry of interviews and phone calls and canvassing had made me more tired than a camp counselor after a night hike with a hundred ten- and eleven-year-old boys. Still, with several large sponsors pledging their support—including the possibility of a large contribution from the Otter Bay Banking Association—I could smell success on the horizon.

It was Friday morning and my other duty called, the one that helped me pay my mortgage. If Moondoggy hadn't poked his nose beneath my comforter, I would have slept clear through the sunlight and my alarm and everything.

At the first sign of my eyelids lifting, Moondoggy whined and chased his tail. In dog language, I interpreted this to mean he wanted breakfast.

"C'mon. Let's eat." I padded to the kitchen, slower than usual. Why my dog would not interpret my body language and hush up was beyond me. "Okay, I'm moving." I poured kibble into his dish and gave him fresh water, but he had disappeared.

I peered around the corner. "Moondoggy?"

He whined and stood nose to door at the front of the house.

I cinched my robe tighter. "What is it?"

He didn't budge so I cracked open the door. No one there. No cat or errant bird. No one, yet when I tried to shut the door, Moondoggy threw himself against it. "Oh brother. Wait." I gave him the command we'd practiced and he stopped short so I could slip onto the porch and investigate further.

There. A white envelope stood out among the green of my rain garden. The moist air licked my bare legs as I hurried to retrieve it. Unlike the foliage dressed in dew after a foggy night, the envelope felt dry to the touch. I glanced around, but saw no one.

Back inside Moondoggy continued to act agitated. "You are one perceptive pup." My words did nothing to calm him or my own growing unease. It took some effort, but I finally coerced him to settle down and eat by hand-feeding him. He developed a one-track mind for his breakfast after that so I sunk into my couch, tore open the envelope, and read the note inside:

Leave the land alone, lady.

I turned it over. Blank. That's it? Leave the land alone? My eyes narrowed. Or what? The sparsely worded note was in pencil, written as if done hastily in a moving car. I tossed it aside and watched it flutter to the wood floor.

Coward. I figured there might be some opposition to my idea to raise funds to buy the Kitteridge property, especially from the developer with plans to denigrate the land, but perhaps I had given him too much credit. I figured that at some point I might receive a phone call or an unannounced visit to the next SOS meeting.

But this? A threatening note left in my rain garden?

My cell rang, jarring the eventful morning. I touched my chest where my heart resided, neglecting to check the number on the screen. "Hello?"

"Callie? It's Steph Hickey, from the library. Great news!"

Blood raced through my body. "Hi, Steph." I steadied my breathing. "What's your news?"

"The Friends of the Library have decided to hold a book sale the weekend after next and here's the news: all proceeds will go into the fund to save the Kitteridge property! Isn't that wonderful?"

A shaky smile found its way to my face. "That is good news, Steph. It truly is."

"And already, a man from the valley stopped in and donated a very nice collection of books to sell."

I nodded, my thoughts in a jumble. "That's great. Really great."

"I couldn't wait to tell you. Remember, the rest of the prayer team and I'll be praying! Enjoy your day, Callie. Ta-ta." She clicked off.

What might a good book sale bring in? Seventy-five, maybe eighty dollars at best? I wagged my head. I had been fielding these types of calls for the past two days, thankful that so many had gotten behind the cause. Local businesses such as The Italian Bakery, Mott's Shoes & Pearls, and Simka's Shop on Alabaster Lane had all pledged significant amounts. Just last evening, only a day after my impromptu dinner with Gage, I learned that Holly over at the Red Abalone Grill had named an all-organic, dolphin-safe salad after me: the SOS Callie.

With a huff, I retrieved the unwelcome note from the floor and stuffed it into the pocket of my robe. Moondoggy laid at my feet and I brushed his fur. I felt my eyes flash. "I refuse to be scared off by a coward, Moondoggy."

My companion only quirked his head, but somehow, I knew he understood.

GAGE

"WHAT ARE YOU SCARED of?"

Suz paced in front of Gage's desk. "What if she doesn't like my painting?"

"Callie?" He leaned back in his chair, wincing slightly at the squeak. He stretched out his arms, threaded his fingers together, and cradled his neck into his open palms. "She'll love your work."

"How do you know that?"

"Because she appreciates art, and what you do qualifies. Trust me on this, okay?"

She slowed her pacing. "I'm meeting with her this week and Tori will be babysitting Jer."

"Tori Jamison?"

"You know any other Tori's?" She grimaced, flashing her eyes at him. "Sorry to be short. I'm just nervous. Yes, Tori Jamison. Her mom works at the preschool—I think I mentioned that, right?"

He chewed his lip as he thought. "And I read that her father's one of the new council members too. Busy family."

"She's a nice girl and Jer likes her, so she'll be helping me out here and there."

He released his hands, plopping them on the desk in front of him and leaning forward. "Good. If I can, I'll stop in and check on them."

Suz stopped pacing, her face filled with relief. She propped both hands on his desk. "Really? Thank you, Gage. I appreciate it."

"Go on now." He winked at her. "I've got work to do."

She hesitated, her brow knit by new concern. "You're moving forward on the Kitteridge property, aren't you?"

He nodded once. "Yes. We're in the design development stage and I'm ready to draw it up."

"Is that hard?"

"Well, I wouldn't call it hard, per se, but it is time consuming." He turned the computer screen so she could see. "This is when all those drawings you've seen me working on are fed into the computer, and we'll be able to see how far-fetched my plans might be. By the way, they won't be."

"You sound pretty confident."

He turned the computer back around and shrugged. "Never let them see you sweat."

"I see. So then what? You give it to the builder?"

"Almost, but not quite. After my client approves these plans— there's usually quite a bit of back and forth in that phase—I'll need to plot it all out to the highest degree of accuracy."

She stepped back, casually crossing her arms. "Sounds intense."

He nodded his agreement. "That it is. I probably won't be much fun in the coming days, but I will help you as much as I can."

"Do you run anymore? Swim?"

He pursed his lips. "That was random."

"With all this work you're going to need some kind of outlet to de-stress. I remember when we were kids, you would run for miles or swim at the park pool. Don't you do those things anymore?"

"Rarely. Well, I do run when I can." He thought back on the recent day when he found Callie's dog. It took deliberate strength to keep from smiling over the memory. He shoved it away. "I haven't been swimming in at least a year. Might drown if I tried now."

"Maybe you can get back into it by teaching Jer like you taught me."

"That's right, I did. Wow. How did you remember that?"

"I may have been little but I remember a lot, like what a great teacher you were—unless a bikini strolled by. You left me hanging on the side more times than I count!"

"Categorically untrue." He laughed.

She tapped her chin with a fingernail and peered at the ceiling. "Maybe I ought to rethink this idea of you teaching Jeremiah. Especially with that Callie around."

His smile faded and he rocked forward, dropping his eyes to the work on his computer screen. "No worries there."

"Why not?"

He exhaled a groan. "Don't you have work to do?"

She forced a laugh into the awkward moment. "C'mon. I'm just teasing you, though I really am serious about you finding a way to let off some of that stress. You will try, right?"

Her face held the fear that both of them knew. Their mother died from a heart attack at fifty and that fact lived somewhere behind their quest for healthy foods and protectiveness of each other. Still, Suz didn't need to keep meddling in his love life, now did she?

The phone rang and he reached for it but not before acknowledging his sister. "I will try. Promise. I have to get this." He put the phone to his ear. "Gage Mitchell."

"What do you know about this SOS group?" Redmond. His client cranked his gruffness up a notch.

He took a breath. "I know they're a serious group of locals who are opposed to development on the Kitteridge land."

"There's nothing they can do about it."

He thought about Callie and her plans, knowing Redmond was probably correct. "My understanding is that they are trying to raise enough money from the community to buy the property from the Kitteridges themselves. I agree that theirs is a tough hill to climb."

"You got that right." He swore. Twice. "This project's been moving as it should from day one. Ain't no little band of yokels going to stop it."

"Any chance of their fight slowing us down?"

"Not if I can help it."

"May I ask how far along escrow is? If they were to be able to raise enough money—"

"They won't. And don't worry about the other logistics—I've got that covered. You just get those drawings done and fast. Where are you on those plans? We have to be ready to pounce ASAP. We don't want that group to think they'll have any chance to win this fight."

Gage swallowed. "I should have something to you by the end of the week."

"Good. Do that. I'll be in touch."

They hung up and Gage fought off a swirl in his gut. Why did he sense that, despite his words to the contrary, Redmond was more worried than he let on?

Chapter Nineteen

 Twelve cell phone messages. Twenty-eight e-mail messages. And a driver sped up to greet me at a stop sign on my way home from camp. After the long, hot weekend I'd just endured with two hundred kids and a laundry list of duties that left me caked with dirt and longing for a cool bath, the last thing I felt compelled to do was attend Sunday supper at Sheila's house.

After missing last week, however, I saw no way out of it. I scanned all messages, answered two of them, grabbed a shower, and headed outside. The cool breeze brought on by a descending sun wrapped around me like a soft shawl, and I embraced every minute of my walk opting to leave the cell phone at home rather than endure its penchant for interruption.

Daffodils and tulips dotted the yard around Sheila's sprawling home, but that pretty packaging did little to help me forget my sister's late night phone call. Why did I let her bother me? My parents would be here after their latest trip, and I had not seen Brenna and Blakey since our last Sunday supper together. Reasons enough to chin up.

The door swung open at my touch and I stepped inside. As usual, the rest of the family had arrived before me and noshed on appetizers around Sheila's massive kitchen island. Thankfully that meant Bobby and Greta were here, my allies in the often strained world of my sister's home.

As the aroma of fresh baked food made my stomach tumble. My mother kissed my cheek. "Callie, my famous daughter! I've heard all about it. My you look . . ." She knit her brow. "Do you ever eat, my child? Come, come, and have some of Sheila's feast."

"Hi, Mom." I glanced at my father who sat in a chair drinking a beer. "Hey, Dad." I gave him a peck on the cheek, his smooth shaven skin cool to the touch. He smiled in his bland but congenial way, but said nothing.

My mother wore a scarf around her head, its colors reminiscent of an Impressionist painting. Her matching skirt swished as she moved. "Darling, we had the most fabulous time in Carmel. We visited every gallery and bakery in town and your father, the romantic devil, coerced me to walk for miles along the beach. You do know the sand is like powdered sugar, don't you?"

My father gave a guarded shake of his head, letting on that my mother, as usual, was exaggerating. In all likelihood, their walk was not much more than several yards.

"Well, you look very rested, Mom." I waved at the rest of the clan and threw my arms around Greta's neck, although it was getting tougher to do. "How's our baby today?"

Greta glanced down at her belly. "Weatherbee or Fruitashia has been keeping me up all night."

I laughed and searched out Bobby. "Keeping you up too, then?" I asked him.

He gave me a weak smile that disappeared quickly. His gaze flitted away.

Sheila swung through the kitchen, a stack of folded cloth napkins in her arms. She spied me. "Good, Callie, you're here. Take these and put them around the table."

If I weren't so startled that my usually punctual sister had yet to lay out her formal table, I might have been put off by her order. Since my hunger had been replaced by an awkward, sinking feeling in the hollow of my stomach, I was grateful for the opportunity to step away from the family, if only for a few moments.

Blakey stumbled into the room and scampered into a chair. Brenna followed close behind, tiny hands on equally miniscule hips. Her eyebrows furrowed. "We have a bone to pick with you, Auntie Callie."

I stopped. "Oh, really? What have I done?"

Blakey tipped his chin up. "Where you been, Auntie Callie? We never see you anymore."

I continued on with my table setting duties. "Well, I've been working and volunteering for all sorts of things."

Blakey pumped his legs beneath him, causing him to rock on his mother's good dining room chair. "Like what?"

"Yeah, what? Mother says you're making a lot of people really angry." Brenna's face, which made me chuckle when I first saw it, turned darker. I saw her future and my heart twisted.

"She said that? Well, honey, I don't think anyone is all that angry with me. Did your mother say she was?"

"She said *other* people." Her tone sounded too sharp for a six-year-old.

I bent to face her. "You might as well learn now that you can't control what other people think about you. My philosophy is to do what I think is right and *que sera sera!*"

"K what?" Brenna's face had gone from sinister to cute and confused. That was the girl I knew.

Blakey laughed. "I think she has a friend named Sara!"

Sheila marched in and set a stack of her best china onto the buffet adjacent to her table. "Blake and Brenna, you both go get washed. Hurry." She pulled a hinged, wooden box from beneath the buffet and set it on the table. "Here's the silverware."

She left without making eye contact. I stood wondering if I should bother setting a place for myself as the kitchen ought to be much warmer. I didn't have time to ponder this as the rest of the family trickled in and took their seats: Jim, Nancy, Vince, Mom and Dad, Greta and Bobby. Brenna and Blakey stomped to their places with Sheila pulling up the rear. The usual chatter came along with them all, but I neither jumped into the conversation nor sensed I was invited to do so.

Still I sat and joined hands with my family. After Vince said grace, Mom began to regale us with detailed descriptions of every morsel of gourmet food that she and Dad had tasted. ". . . and the lamb, braised with mint jelly, was superb . . ."

I spooned several in-season strawberries onto my plate and kept watch on Bobby, waiting to catch his eye. He and I used to pick wild strawberries behind an old lean-to shed by the camp. We never washed them and the telltale sign of red berry juice splotching our skin got us into trouble every time.

He hadn't looked at me since the meal began.

Vince spoke from the head of the table. "Maybe you ought to ask Callie." He motioned toward me with the tip of his knife.

Startled, I glanced around. "Sorry? What did I miss?"

My mother's hands froze in the air as she awaited my response. "I was just telling everyone that Carmel is filled with celebrities of all sorts, bit actors and politicians, we saw many of them." She turned and touched my father's wrist. "Didn't we, darling?"

My father nodded and touched the hand Mom had laid on his wrist.

"And I was wondering aloud what it must be like for those whose names are in the press to enjoy a breezy walk through downtown Carmel." She turned to Vince. "Are you saying that our Callie is becoming a celebrity in town?"

His shoulders rose and fell as he sliced a hunk of roast pork on his plate. "Some might think so. In a relatively short amount of time she has managed to whip up some of the town's folk into a frenzy. Listen to this, yesterday one of my clients wanted to talk more about Callie and her tenacity than his insurance policy. The guy wanted your number too, but Sheila wouldn't let me give it to him." He smiled and pushed a bite of pork into his mouth.

"Really!" Her mother clapped her hands and held them, her mouth agape.

I gasped and looked to Bobby for support. He just chewed his meal, giving me an occasional glance. "Is everything all right over there, Bobby?"

Greta patted his arm. "Poor man. Works all week, then paints all weekend."

I leaned my head to one side. "So you're tired?"

Bobby kept chewing, his eyes glaring, angry, like we were kids and I'd just eaten all the strawberries without offering him one. He swallowed his bite. "Something like that."

Jim coughed. "So, Bob, how's business?"

Bobby dropped his silverware onto Sheila's good china, its rattle sharp and reverberating.

Greta jerked. "What's wrong, honey?"

My brother glanced sideways at her, then back at me. "You couldn't just leave this one alone. Had to get involved and shake up the whole town."

I touched my fingers to my chest. "I don't understand. I thought you supported the fight for the Kitteridge property."

He rolled his eyes. "Yeah, sure, make a little noise. Get them to lower the density of their plans or dedicate a portion of it for parkland, but out-and-out purchase the property? Do you know how much money has already been invested?"

"No. Do *you?*"

The family peacemaker looked like a bull ready to charge. "I know you've been getting a lot of props lately, Callie. Some people do love what you are doing, but there are a whole lot of others out there affected by this campaign of yours. Have you thought this all out?"

"Who? You mean the developer? The architect? Future buyers of all those condos?" I glanced at Nancy who lowered her eyes.

He shook his head. "You are a brilliant woman, but you just don't understand business. Think about all the businesses in town that would benefit from a project like that." He pointed at Vince. "You could insure all those new residents."

I waved my hands. "Okay, so let me get this straight. My evil scheme to protect the Kitteridge property along the marine sanctuary from development is prohibiting local businesses from flourishing. Have I got that right?"

Greta's face paled. "I think he just means that this has happened so fast, Callie. We don't really understand all the consequences of your plan." She turned to Bobby. "Isn't that right, sweetie?"

I shook my head. "Something happened, Bobby. What is it?"

Greta's face registered surprise. She looked to me then her husband.

Sheila passed a tray of muffins. "I think I speak for all of us when I say that we've had enough of this subject for one evening. Oh, to have a Sunday supper without controversy." She fanned herself and I half expected Sheila to fall into a Gone-with-the-Wind type swoon.

Bobby crouched forward. "I'll tell you what it is, you know my chief investor, Henry? Remember him? He called this morning after reading yet another news story about the unstoppable Callie Duflay and told me quite bluntly that if SOS succeeds, he might not have a good reason to invest in phase two of my storage facility."

Greta gasped. "What? Why?"

He twisted his face toward her. "Because if our community refuses to grow, then he sees no need to continue adding storage space in town."

My shoulders drooped. "That's ridiculous and you know it, Bobby. You are already bursting at the seams without this development. Can't he see that?"

Bobby wouldn't meet my gaze. "Who am I to challenge his reasoning? The guy makes his living investing in other people's dreams. If he thinks losing this development will have a negative impact on business, then I take notice."

My mother's strained chuckle disrupted the thickness hanging in the room. "My Callie." She fingered the string of polished red beads hanging around her neck. "You've been a mighty busy girl. All this in just two weeks?"

Sheila licked her napkin and ran it over Blakey's face. "All this talk about how this will affect local businesses brings up something I've been meaning to ask, Callie." She turned toward me, while smoothing out her napkin and dropping it into her lap. "Have you considered how this will affect the Kitteridges?"

Jim and I exchanged a glance. Careful here. It would be too easy to betray June's confidence right now. One word of the Kitteridges' troubles, however, and this conversation would be over. The sliced potatoes on my plate were getting cold, but I nibbled on them anyway, taking my time to answer. I placed my fork back onto the plate. "June and I have spoken." I felt Jim's stare. "And they are more than willing to entertain a sale to the community should we be able to raise the money." In time.

Sheila shifted her eyebrows. "Well. Then they are generous people. You are lucky." She threw up her hands and reached into a drawer beneath the buffet table behind her. "I almost forgot. One of the parents from Blakey's kindergarten class asked me to give you this." She held out an envelope. "It's a donation to SOS, but don't expect it to be for too much. They drive an old van."

I accepted the envelope from her, still aware of Bobby's palpable anger. The last thing I wanted was for his business to suffer. "Thanks."

Our mother clapped her hands. "What say we all have a toast, hmm? Go on everybody, raise your glasses." She surveyed all of us. "Now, here's to adventure—for all of us."

"Here, here." Laughter burst forth. Water glasses clanked. Cheeriness, however, eluded me until Brenna and Blakey slid from their chairs and surrounded mine. While the rest of the family started up new conversations while continuing to dine, I swiveled to get a better look at my young niece and nephew.

Blakey sat on his heels and whispered up at me. "You should take us for ice cream sometime."

Brenna nodded, her voice also a whisper. "Yeah. You should. You have been very busy lately, Auntie Callie."

I smiled. "I have, haven't I?" I brushed her bangs away from her eyelashes.

She leaned in until I could smell her pure, childlike breath. "My mom wants me to cut them but I think I should make my own decision about that. Don't you?"

I sucked in my breath, trying not to laugh. "Well your mama has your best interest in mind. Still, I think you are smart to tell her how you feel."

Brenna's large eyes implored mine, her voice still a whisper. "I won't tell her you said so 'cuz that might make her mad."

I pressed my lips together. "Fine. How about I take you for ice cream after school tomorrow?"

Blakey bobbed his head and threw a fist into the air. "Yes!"

Aside from my parents whose job it was to love me, it was nice to know I still had a few fans left in this family.

Chapter Twenty

 Holly, rocketing by with a tray full of food, nearly ran me over as I ducked for cover after entering the RAG.

"Hey there, sorry!" she called over her shoulder.

I waved her off and righted myself. My mind had been a whirl from early this morning when I stepped outside to water my rain garden and I remembered the note I'd found over the weekend. It irked me that my brain continued to give the incident second thoughts.

In the back of the restaurant, the core leadership group of SOS had gathered to discuss the latest updates and news regarding the Kitteridge property. I hurried toward them when a voice snagged me from one of the side tables. "Callie!"

"Squid?"

He tapped a finger on his forehead, saluting me. I raised my hand in a wave and then noticed a wispy blonde sitting next to him. Her silken white hair split at her shoulders. "This is Peyton."

She waved four fingers at me.

"Hi." I cocked my head at Squid. "Thought you had already headed back to SLO for the week."

He shook his head, probably hoping I didn't notice the almost imperceptible look he sent Peyton. "I had some things to take care of up here. How about you? What brings you to this fine dining establishment?"

I glanced to the back. "A meeting with the SOS group."

His eyes lit with recognition. "Ah. Well, don't let us stop you, then." His eyes lingered a beat longer. "See you Friday?"

I smiled and shrugged. "Guess we will. Nice meeting you, Peyton."

She waved the same four fingers at me again, and I tried not to think about how young and skinny and, well, *young* she appeared.

The core group of SOS sat in the back sampling pastries and sipping coffee. I poured myself a cup and addressed them. "Thanks everyone for meeting here today. Great to see you all. I'm going to run down our list of officers and if you have something to share with the group, now would be a great time. Okay, let's start with PR. Ruth?"

Ruth stood, clipboard in her hands. Even inside, she wore

her signature floppy hat. "Heavens, it has been a busy week." She turned to me. "Plan to get even busier."

The group laughed.

She continued. "Now, Eliot, with the paper, will be running a regular feature on the progress of SOS. I've given him all of your contact information as he'll be wanting to get quotes from you all. And for heaven's sake, try to make yourselves sound intelligent. No 'uhs' or 'ums' or long-winded speeches that mean nothing—you're not politicians! Think: sound bite."

Gracie raised her hand. "I don't think I understand what that is."

"It's a snippet of a statement, Gracie." Ruth sighed and looked to me. "You're an expert now. You explain it."

I sat up straight, contemplating how to put this in simple terms. "A sound bite is usually just a few words or one sentence. The words have to be important so that newscasters and writers will replay or rewrite them over and over again."

Gracie nodded her hands folded in front of her. "Something pithy, then?"

I held back a smile. "Yes. Pithy. That's good."

"Moving on." Ruth looked at Bill. "You. How's the word of mouth going with the geezers down at the donut shop?"

"Good. Good." He bit into a peach Danish, chasing it down with a swig of coffee.

"All right then. Neta, did you get the latest report from the bank?"

"That I did! And you're going to be thrilled, just tickled." She groped around for her notebook while we waited. After retrieving it, Neta stood in silence.

"Well?" Ruth's eye had closed halfway. "Get on with it."

Neta jerked. "Oh. Sorry." She examined her notes, adjusting her reading glasses. "As of this morning, we have received $29,382.00 in pledges."

We all burst into applause. My mouth popped open. "Wow. Really? That's . . . it's fantastic. How much of that money has been received, roughly?"

Neta peered through her glasses again at the scrawling on her notepad. "Says here the bank has received a grand total of $1,200.50." She looked up. "Do you want me to read it again?"

I swallowed and shook my head. "No, but I think we'd all better impress upon people that there is a deadline. We must have cash in hand for the Kitteridges to be able to accept our offer."

"Phew, oh Callie, you're still here." Steph blew in, her cheeks flushed, her belly threatening to birth twins. "I gotta sit."

"Absolutely. Take my chair." I helped her into it. "What made you come all the way down here?"

She gaped at me. "Don't you remember? I said I'd be the head of the prayer team."

"Of course. Yes. I knew that."

"Just came by to tell y'all that we've got you covered."

Ruth bent forward. "Covered? What do you mean 'covered'?"

Steph blew out a few Lamaze-style breaths. "Covered in prayer. My team of women meets twice a week to pray about all our needs. We should meet every day—everybody seems to have so many needs. Anyway, we've been meeting and praying and listening to God and I don't know, just felt like I should be here."

Ruth batted at the gnat that crisscrossed in front of her face. "Can't imagine why."

I placed a hand on Steph's shoulder. "Thanks for coming. I'm grateful." I scanned the group. "Well, I don't know about you, but I've got much to do. I'll be working with our Webmaster this afternoon to set up ways to get the word out to the community. So if you won't mind, I'd better—"

"Wait!" Ruth held her clipboard out like a stop sign. "I forgot to mention that you're being interviewed today on the news."

"Today? What time?"

She glanced at her notes. "Down in SLO at 3:30. You'll be on around four. Meant to tell you but with you running late again and all the things I've been doing, I forgot. Here." She handed me a sheet of paper. "Here are the directions. Wear something dark and solid, so you look professional."

Television. Probably the best way to get out the message about our campaign, but I'd never been on camera; never even been in a crowd scene during a televised event. Would it be cowardly to admit how the thought of being interviewed on camera made my knees quiver?

It would and I knew it, so I glanced at Ruth. "Good job, PR Lady. I'm all over it."

Thing was, I had no idea what that entailed.

GAGE

HUNGER HAD DETERRED GAGE from inputting even one more piece of data into the Computer-Aided Design software on his computer. He pulled into his drive, grateful he lived close enough to dash home and eat a late lunch or really an early dinner, still able to return to the office for another long night.

A sleek, black car, far less practical than his truck, sat in his drive.

He called in through his front door. "Hello?"

"Hi, Mr. Mitchell."

The babysitter. He had been so focused on the intensity of his work that Gage had forgotten that Suz would still be at Callie's, and Jer's babysitter would be here with him. He scooped up Jer as he ran down the hall. "Hey, buddy. This your new sitter?"

Jer bobbed his head. "She's funny."

Gage leaned against the wall while Jer bounced in his arms. "Is that right? Nice to see you again, Tori. I just stopped in to grab a bite to take back to the office with me."

"That's fine. We're just playing. Wanna go get one of your toys, Jeremiah?" She plucked Jer from his arms and scampered with him down the hallway.

Since Suz and Jer moved in, the refrigerator held more surprises than it had with just a bachelor in residence. Leftovers made the world go 'round, he always thought, probably because their mother loved to cook. That and she sold Tupperware for a time, so something could always be found burped and sealed within the many-sized contain- ers they owned. From all the dated terra-cotta hued plastic inside their fridge, Suz had acquired much of their mother's collection.

He set an iron skillet atop the gas burner and began warming his lunch: turkey stroganoff over egg noodles. As the kitchen began to swirl with the aroma, Gage's stomach protested the long wait. He switched on the television in the living room to pass the time.

Commercials on every channel. He increased the volume and turned to check on lunch. Jeremiah's heavy steps clomped down the hall and followed him into the kitchen. His nephew clambered onto a chair. "Whatcha eatin'?"

"Your mother's stroganoff. You hungry?"

Jer pumped his head forward and back. Tori wandered in and laughed. "You eat a lot!" She looked at Gage, her eyes agog. "I already gave him a big lunch and an even bigger bowl of ice cream. And he's still hungry?"

Gage's smile grew deeper. "He's a growing boy!"

A voice wafted from the television. "Our visitor today is a young woman who is making quite a splash in her community and quite quickly, I might add."

Gage glanced at Tori. "Would you mind going and shutting off the TV? I've changed my mind about watching it."

"No prob."

The stroganoff sizzled and Gage dished up two bowls of different sizes. He called to Tori? "Would you like something to eat?"

She didn't answer so he peered through the doorway, into the living room. The young girl stared at the screen. With her hair pulled back into that ponytail, he could see the stern grit of her teeth, the furrow laced above her brow. "Tori?"

Both hands had found her hips. "This girl's got a lot of nerve."

Curious, Gage blew on Jer's food then set it in front of him. He carried his own steaming bowl with him to join Tori in front of the television. "Who is she . . . oh."

Callie sat opposite the reporter looking composed, confident, and . . . stunning.

Tori stayed focused on the screen. "My dad says she's a spoiled brat who gets whatever she wants. He says she's trying to steal some old peoples' land."

He couldn't take his eyes off Callie's face. "Why would your dad say that?"

She flicked him a backward glance and he tore his gaze from the screen. "My dad's on the town council. He knows all about this stuff. He says if she doesn't back off, there could be trouble."

"For who? For the old folks?"

She shrugged. "Don't know. But if I were votin' age, I'd make trouble for her. Listen to the way she sits there and acts like she's doin' what everybody wants."

Newscaster: "Tell us about your cause."

Callie: "Great. Thank you. Okay, well, SOS—Save Our Shores—is a grassroots effort to save the beloved open land on the bluffs in Otter Bay. We are citizens who believe in the benefits of land being available to the community. This particular area is right next to the national marine sanctuary."

Newscaster: "And your group is concerned for the animals in that sanctuary?"

Callie: "Yes, we are. That area is particularly popular with otters, and as you are probably aware, otters were nearly extinct not too many years ago."

"See? She's just some earth-lover with an agenda."

He nearly choked on a noodle. How many teenagers talked like that? He abhorred hearing Callie's reputation defamed, especially from someone so obviously guided by a parent's opinion. Yet he knew that news coverage like this couldn't be good for his project. He still held out hope that SOS would fail, of course, but didn't like the idea that the group's fight might also present an indefinite delay for the project.

"Just *wait* until my dad hears about this."

Gage swallowed another bite. "Is your father's interest in this cause related to his work with the town council?"

"Yeah, I think so. All I know is they were all getting ready for some big project when—whoosh—in comes this lady and her harebrained ideas."

Again, how many teen girls use words like *harebrained*? "I see. And your father would be aware of this because, around here, the town council and planning commission are made up of mostly the same folks."

She wrinkled her forehead and paused, as if thinking. "Yeah, that's right. I think so."

Newscaster: "How is your cause progressing?"

Callie: "We're doing well. I learned today that pledges are pouring in from businesses and individuals alike."

Newscaster: "Congratulations are in order then!" She laughed and flipped her hair, peering into the camera. "Quite a feat in a short space of time. Before you go, Callie, why don't you tell our viewers how they can help?"

Callie: "Sure! You can find more information about us by visiting this station's Web site. SOS is fighting for the community, for our visitors, and for the otter population swimming in those waters—but we can't do it without your help! I urge you to make your donation quickly to Save Our Shores."

Tori used the remote to turn off the television. "Grrr." She used a sassy, mocking tone. "SOS is fighting for the community, for our visitors, and for the otter population swimming in those waters. C'mon, Jeremiah, let's go find something fun to play with."

Jer slid from his seat and, leaving his bowl half full, ran into the living room. "Yeah!"

Gage finished his bowl of pasta and headed back into the kitchen to wash up. Callie had poise and presence on that screen, and if it weren't for this project between them, he might have picked up the phone to tell her so. He rinsed his and Jer's bowls and shook off the excess water. As it was, if he was going to be able to stay focused on the job at hand, he had to forget about Callie and SOS for the time being.

It didn't help, however, that Jeremiah's teenage babysitter could so readily recall Callie's carefully crafted sound bite.

Chapter Twenty-one

 June's gratitude-filled voice poured through the receiver. "Callie, I phoned to tell you how beautifully you handled that television interview, dear. Is it true? Are there really that many pledges coming in?"

Pledges, yes. Actual money? Not so much. I'd pulled my car to the side of the road to use my cell phone because I couldn't remember where I had stashed my ear buds. "Yes, June, pledges are definitely coming in. And hopefully, my interview today will spur people on to really get involved." *How's that for a positive attitude?*

"Wonderful!"

I pressed my lips together, thinking. "You know, June, I'm wondering if you have thought any more about going public about your predicament with the loan." I scratched my head and glanced in my rearview mirror as trucks and cars sped by me. "I just think that if people knew what you were up against—"

"Then they would feel sorry for us."

I swallowed before speaking. "It's nothing to be ashamed of, June. Your story is one people can relate to because, well . . . who couldn't have made a better money decision at one time or another?"

"You don't understand. Timothy has been getting worse. He walks that shoreline every day, like he's saying goodbye, but every time I bring up the subject, he won't hear of it. He doesn't want our private business splattered all over the news-paper." Her voice shook. "Says it'll kill him—and I don't want to be the one to put that man into his grave."

"I understand."

"He's confused. I'm confused. Sometimes I think I should not have bothered you. We can just turn over the house and take the money for the other property, then go and live a mod-est life with our daughter and grandchildren." Her voice still sounded shaky. "Wouldn't be so bad."

I clenched a fist. Traffic whizzed by rocking the car. "Not like this. I'm sure your daughter and the kids would love to be closer to you, but not like this. Let's not give up hope, okay? My voice mail is filled with messages I've yet to listen to, so something tells me the interview today had a great impact. Don't lose heart."

"Thank you, dear. I will try not to."

For the first time in hours I allowed myself a minute to think. My head found the seat rest and I nestled into it, closing my eyes to shut out the day's worth of noise and decisions. My phone buzzed.

"It's Ruth." She hollered into the phone like she too was parked on the side of a busy speedway somewhere. "You were somethin' on that telly, I don't mind pointing out to you."

"Thanks. Not too corny?"

"Nah, but who would care anyway? A little corn could do some good. Our Web guy says the site's been lighting up with pledges brighter than Times Square."

"Really?" My shoulders dropped. "Fantastic."

"Hold on. I haven't told you the half of it. It looks like we got ourselves a little clandestine meeting going on with the town council. My source tells me the developer of this property is in a snit about SOS. I hear they're trying to get some kind of go-ahead approval before the fact. Can you beat that?"

Unbelievable. I pressed a fist to my forehead. "That doesn't smell legal to me. Doesn't that violate the Brown Act?" Then again, Ruth had been known to befriend "sources" who might better be described as elderly women with nothing but time to watch the world through the split in their drapes.

"Any chance Kitteridge might have signed over the whole place right from under us?"

"Not a chance. I just . . . well . . . June promised me that as long as we come up with the money in advance of her deadline, the property will be sold to the community. And I believe her."

Ruth sniffed in my ear. "What deadline?"

My breath caught. "The uh, you know, date before the developer planned to buy the property. You know, before the community got involved. I've talked about it."

She huffed. "Maybe. Here's what I think: June Kitteridge could tell those people to go jump in the ocean if she wanted to, but she would never do it. That woman doesn't have the backbone of a flea. Now Tim, he could get rid of those people. Deadline . . . phshee. He oughta tell them to stick that deadline where—"

"Where and when is the meeting tonight?"

Ruth harrumphed. "Well, technically it's not a *meeting* because there are laws against that. It's just a *gathering* of friends, supposedly. Friends, who just so happen to be wanting to buy the Kitteridge property, at the home of a town council member, who just *happens* to be one of those in power to approve or disprove the project. So anyway, this non-meeting will be up at the Jamison house. Know where it is?"

I scoured my mind. Jamison. New council member. Teenage daughter. Pleasant-looking wife. This piece of information contained facts. "I can picture the family, but not where they live. He's new on the council, right? Are they up on Sutter's Way?"

"Yes, he's a new council member, which isn't saying much since most of 'em are new. And wrong about the house—they used to live there but now they moved to one of those sprawling places at the top of the hill on Cascade. Can see the whole ocean from up there."

"I see."

"So what do you think, Ms. President? You think we oughta crash their party, make 'em invite the public in to their little shindig?"

Ruth smelled blood. Her voice quivered in a low growl sort of way. No doubt she'd like nothing more than for me to lead our band of revolutionaries through the pines and across the Jamison's gleaming marble floors that led to a sanctuary of sorts for all kinds of underhanded business dealings. Maybe she was right. Nip secret activities in the bud before they can gather the steam necessary to blow away their competition.

Then again, wouldn't it be better to observe a malfeasance in the making firsthand? To allow questionable activities to play right into the hands of the enemy? Or had I been reading too many suspense novels?

I pulled in a breath and allowed it to flow out again. *Be the leader, Callie.* "Let them have their meeting, Ruth. Right now, I need you to follow up on the PR that you've so brilliantly choreographed already. Why don't you have the Web guy pull a clip of my interview today and upload it to YouTube." *Good, Callie, good.* "Let's beat them by creating an impenetrable campaign of goodwill, one that will endear our cause to the community we represent."

She chortled. "I've taught you well. Very good then. I'll trust your judgment on this one. I only hope we won't be sorry."

We clicked off the line and I glanced into the growing line of traffic. Nothing but brake lights as far as my eyes could see. I released a heavy sigh. Ruth needn't have worried. If it were at all possible, I would not allow this ill-timed meeting to go on without the benefit of evidence.

I only hoped that traffic would clear soon enough for me to make it home to Otter Bay—and up the winding hillside to the group that gathered on Cascade Court.

GAGE

BACK IN HIS OFFICE, Gage rubbed the heaviness from his eyes. They stung, which usually meant he had worn his contact lenses far longer than he should. He'd planned to remove them when he slipped home for his late lunch and replace them with glasses, but became distracted by Callie's undeniably alluring presence on his flat screen TV. That and the way she so confidently answered the reporter's questions while staying fully intent on burying his career.

His office phone jarred him with its ring. "Gage Mitchell."

"Gage, my man. Rick Knutson here."

Gage glanced at the clock on his desk. Its digits glowed red, much like his eyes. "Yes, Rick." He had no patience for the nettlesome realtor's games tonight.

"You're working late. I'm impressed. What say you shut it down for the night and come join the boss for a nightcap and some good old-fashioned conversation?"

He had to be kidding. Was he beckoning me? And at who's behest? Redmond's? "Thanks for the invitation. Maybe some other time."

"Whoa-whoa-whoa. C'mon, man. Take a break. No one can work all day and still be a prince." The man's voice oozed like butter through the phone. Nauseating.

Gage scraped his fingers over his scalp. "I really do not have the time—"

"Better make the time for this. Wasn't easy setting up this soiree tonight. Your boss'll be there along with various townspeople who have clout around here, if you get my drift." Rick snarled. "And if we're going to crush this merry band of revolutionaries trying to carve us out of jobs, we need to make sure we're all on the same page. Capiche?"

The cloak and dagger routine was getting old. If this meeting was that important, why hadn't Redmond phoned him himself? No sooner had this thought come to mind when a new e-mail popped onto the screen.

Rick sounded impatient. "So we'll see you at the Jamison house, then."

Gage clicked on the bold-faced message calling from his inbox. It was from Redmond, inviting him for drinks and conversation tonight on Cascade Court. He clicked "delete" and, reluctantly, gave Rick the answer he wanted to hear.

Twenty minutes later Gage made the drive up the hill toward the Jamison home, still kicking himself for not removing his contacts. The mixture of moist air and approaching headlights blurred his vision, causing him to squint. He had hoped to be home by now, tucking Jeremiah in for Suz and hearing about her day working on Callie's cottage. The kinds of things he'd be doing once his business took off—hopefully with a wife and child of his own.

No time for that. The custom homes perched on this undulating land were visions, the kind that pulled him out of the bed in the mornings. High-end, well-designed beauties, all of them. He checked the address highlighted on the curb with the one he'd memorized.

This was the one. The driveway was filled with expensive cars, sleek and dark, but polished so well that they glowed in the moon's light. He parked his truck on the street and weaved his way up the drive, recognizing Tori's car parked at the front.

Only a glimmer of artificial light seeped from the front windows and no noise whatsoever greeted him besides the cricket serenade drifting from an adjacent field. He took the first step up the wide, molded porch and stopped. His tired eyes picked up a movement to his right. Gage stood a minute, frozen, wondering if he was about to be accosted by a wild animal and if so, why he hadn't already hightailed it to the front door.

He took the second step and heard a sneeze. A human one. One dainty, human sneeze. His eyes had absorbed enough of the darkness now that he could more easily make out his surroundings. Someone ducked and ran behind a stand of trees.

Curious, he stepped away from the house and onto plush, wet grass. He followed a shallow rustling, winding his way around to the side of the property that lay unshielded by fence or wall. Instead, a newly planted stand of pines struggled to create a barrier between the home and curiosity seekers. And through that flimsy stand of baby pines, he saw a familiar figure crouched beneath a window.

"Callie?" He tried to force laughter and the tinge of shock from his voice.

She whipped him an annoyed look, her face illuminated enough by the partial moon for Gage to see the scowl forming in her eyes. She impatiently waved him over, one slender finger pressed against her lips.

Gage approached, bit back a smile, and squatted in the dirt, close enough to draw in her scent. The effect, a longing that tugged, startled him. "What are we doing here?" He didn't bother to keep the tease from his voice.

"Ssh!" Callie's fingers clung to a window ledge, keeping her from settling onto the cold ground. Seeing her there, holding onto that ledge, made him want to wrap his arms around her and allow her body to ease against his. He shook away the image.

A spike of laughter from inside the house jarred the silence between them. Gage moved his mouth closer to Callie's ear, a strand of her hair tickling his nose. "We toasted to common ground the last time we were together. Had no idea you were being so literal."

A soft groan slipped from her lips. Male voices churned together on the other side of the glass, volume turned up. Callie put a hand up to stop Gage from saying another word, only when she did her fingertips brushed his cheek, sending a heated ripple through him. Quickly she pulled her hand away.

As she did, a million thoughts surged inside Gage's head. He didn't care that his knees would soon begin to ache from his weight, nor that moist earth was oozing its way into the patterned crevices of his shoes, only that he and Callie were inexplicably alone, arms and hands brushing against each other, the mingle of fresh pine and her perfume buoying his senses.

As quickly as they had risen, the voices on the other side of the window died down, signaling that the party had moved deeper inside the house. Gage realized that he didn't care one iota that he wasn't inside that place, sucking down martinis and slapping backs over the next best project to hit Otter Bay. Sure as that crescent moon shined above them, he knew he would rather be in this precarious predicament than anywhere else.

Callie shifted and let out a sharp breath. She turned her face to meet his gaze and glared at him, her voice a hiss. "I knew it! So much for our truce! You're on the side of the enemy, I get it, but do you have to participate in something so . . . so . . ."

Her eyes glowed, burning him. "So . . . what?" He put the brakes on his voice, keeping it low, trying to keep the emotion out of it. He tried interjecting some levity. "You're upset that I didn't ask you to join me? Is that what this is? Would you have said yes if I had?"

Her face curled in disgust. "Join you for *what*? An old boy's club meeting? Come. On."

She turned her head toward the window, stretching herself just enough to peek through a sliver of an opening between two shutter slats. Her blonde hair spiraled down her back and it took all of his fading strength to keep from brushing it with his fingertips.

A sigh fumed out of Callie as she turned and slid down the home's outer brick wall, her shoes sinking into the dirt. "They're gone." Her eyes flashed at his. "Seriously, what are you doing here, Gage? Spying?"

He huffed out a sigh of his own, perplexed. "I could ask you the same thing, now, couldn't I?"

She crossed her arms and looked away. A glower tipped the ends of her mouth. "What do you think?"

He raised both eyebrows, willing himself to keep his fingers from smoothing out the downward curve of her lips. He steadied himself with one hand against the earth and took a moment to gather air back into his lungs. "Well, I think . . . I think . . ." He raised his chin and found her gaze locked on him, her breathing visible, her chest rising and falling in rhythm. Was she having as much difficulty resisting him as he was her?

He wouldn't wait to find out.

Gage's free hand found her chin and he held it gently between his thumb and forefinger. She gave no resistance to his touch. "I came here because I was invited." He controlled his breathing against a jagged heartbeat. "But strange as this may sound, especially after what we both represent, I would rather be hiding in the dirt with you."

A flicker softened her mouth and the girl who always had some retort on her tongue, said nothing. Instead she watched him with curious, imploring eyes, her vulnerability melting him. Before he could measure the impact of his actions, Gage's hand slipped along Callie's chin line until it cupped the base of her neck. He kissed her, reveling in the sweetness of her lips against his and the purr elicited when their mouths met, only vaguely aware that her initial acquiescence had been replaced by a subtle rebuke.

He pulled away from her—or had she pushed him?

Callie's eyes grew wide and fierce then, her brows pulled low toward her lashes. Her lips parted sharply, tempting him to cover them again with his own. "Go" she told him, her voice like a cry. "I just want you to go. Now. Please."

Chapter Twenty-two

 I didn't dare breathe. If I did, I knew the sound would come out rough and uneven like a wave colliding with coarse, chiseled rock. And then my presence would be discovered.

Again.

Reliving the kiss, my fingertips brushed my lips. They felt raw and cold in contrast to Gage's touch. This wasn't how it was supposed to happen. It was . . . it was unthinkable. Gage Mitchell and I were on opposing sides and even though we had taken the high road with each other and declared a truce, I had looked at it as more of a stay, a polite promise to keep out of each other's way.

Until he showed up here and turned my thinking—maybe even my heart—upside down.

He hadn't wanted to leave. His face registered a string of

emotions as I pushed him away, but what made me want to turn my head was the kindness I saw in his eyes. Deep green pools of tenderness that pleaded with me to give him more of myself.

But I held my stance—I always held my stance—and in the end I was relieved that he had, however reluctantly, gone. Instead of heading for the Jamison's front door, as I had guessed, Gage stuffed his hands into his pockets and took one step backward. He paused a moment, hovering over me as if he had something else to add, his expression flickering between passion and a touch of anger, and then he pivoted in the direction of his truck out on the street.

I swallowed back something that tasted awfully like remorse, but really, he shouldn't have been here in the first place. If this house contained more than one town council member, then this so-called gathering breaks the open meeting law. Did Gage approve of this kind of sneaking around? Did he realize how brazen an act this meeting might be?

Or could it possibly be that Gage was not fully aware of what he had been invited to?

A door closing, followed by slow footsteps pricked my ears. I pressed my back against the bricks, still sitting on the ground, my bum growing colder by the second. From an awkward angle, my eyes strained to watch the figure descend to the street below. Moisture from the ground had begun to absorb through the seat of my capris, sending a chill through me. I rubbed my arms.

After the lone figure got into a car and drove off, I gently lifted myself out of the damp dirt and peered into the window. A rumble of voices from inside the house caught my attention and I crouched beneath the sill. What was I doing here? The ludicrousness of my actions began to seep into my bones much like the slow absorption of moisture through my clothing. Gage must think I'm mad. Then again, how many crazy women was he likely to kiss the way he just did?

No use. I couldn't see or hear anything going on in the house. And now that someone had left, who knew if I'd ever be able to prove my suspicion that this meeting was an underhanded attempt to defy the law and the people of this community?

Reluctantly I stood and stretched my limbs, willing away the beginning of a cold ache. With a swift glance around the corner and toward the front door, I stepped through the damp blades of grass, intent on forgetting all about my sad attempt at espionage. Gravel crackled from somewhere behind the drive and I halted. Had I been too preoccupied with my own swirl of thoughts to notice that someone else had arrived?

My eyes darted for somewhere to hide, but how would that look? I stood still, thinking quickly, but coming up with nothing that would look less than suspicious. Another slide of gravel alerted my ears, but still, I saw nothing. Maybe the noise came from a raccoon in search of a stray morsel for a late night snack. My shoulders relaxed. I was hiding from a raccoon.

Shaking off my initial skittishness, I moved quickly across the lawn and toward the street where my car waited at the bottom of the hill. A bright flash blinded me both with its intensity and suddenness and I lurched sideways.

A familiar male voice sliced through the night. "Ms. Duflay?"

I shielded my eyes. "Yes."

He stepped out from behind a BMW parked in the driveway. "It's Eliot, Ms. Duflay. From the newspaper?"

I lowered my hand, hoping the action would slow the rapid beat of my heart, its second vigorous workout of the night. "What are you—"

"I was wondering what you were doing behind those bushes, Ms. Duflay?"

The boy with the notepad and camera had aged. Who was this man with the searing stare and pointed questions? I swallowed to wash away the dryness in my throat. "I think you must be mistaken." I forced myself to breathe. How much, exactly, had Eliot seen? "Is there a reason that you, Eliot, are standing outside here in the dark instead of joining the party?"

"So that's a party in there. Hmm." He glanced toward the closed front door. "Word was there was some big meeting going on tonight." His unwavering eyes taunted me. "Know anything about it?"

I shrugged and forced one foot in front of the other. "Can't say that I do. Nice meeting up with you, Eliot. Different, but nice." I moved past him, hoping he wasn't about to point that camera at me again, and dreading what might happen to the picture he had already snapped. "Night, now."

"Wait."

I glanced back at him, the cold night air beginning to give me shivers. "Uh-huh?"

"Do you need a ride home?" His voice sounded husky and almost man-like, until it cracked on the word "home."

Bless that young boy's heart. Who wouldn't appreciate someone of the male species who did not see anything wrong with a relationship between a man and a *slightly* older woman? "Thank you for the offer, but I will be fine. I've got my car nearby."

"Glad to hear that because if you were *my* mom, I wouldn't be happy to know you were out here on this ridge after dark."

I jerked to a stop, and this is where I made my mistake. I should have kept moving. *Just one foot in front of the other, Callie.* But no. For some reason, Eliot's *my mom* remark irked me such that I spun around, my face registering exactly the emotion his words had caused.

And that's when a second, blinding flash of light went off in my face.

Eliot glanced down at his camera screen and chuckled. "Perfect. This picture's way better than that other one."

Chapter Twenty-three

GAGE

Gage's head ached almost as much as his eyes burned. While sitting at the breakfast table, he hung his head forward and stretched the muscles in his neck. The action, however, reminded him too much of Callie and the way she made a similar move while seated across from him at the diner. He lifted his head and the throbbing continued.

Suz set a cup of coffee in front him. "Here. Drink this." She leaned through the doorway. "Jeremiah, stop that racket. Your Uncle Gage has a headache!"

Should he mention that shouting didn't help? He chugged the coffee, thankful he hadn't had to grind the beans and brew the pot himself.

"You seen the paper today?" Suz glanced at him over her shoulder, pursed her lips, and looked away. "Suppose not. You must've had a hard night, because your eyes are more red than the apples I picked up at the store. You want a slice, by the way?" She held out a crescent slice of apple to him.

He waved her away. "Not hungry. Thanks."

"I wasn't going to say anything, but here." She dropped the paper onto the table in front of him. "Thought you might be interested in this article mentioning my boss. Not a very good likeness, unfortunately. Sounds like she might be getting herself into some trouble."

Gage's forehead shifted forward. "What kind of trouble?"

Suz gestured toward the paper. "See for yourself."

He adjusted his glasses, blinked a couple of times to get his eyes to focus, and realized how old the prescription must be. His contacts had outworn their welcome last night, and he'd had no choice but to put on an old pair of specs. "Where?"

Suz sighed. "You are worse than Jeremiah today, you know that?" A slight smile flexed his mouth as Suz reached over him and turned to page A2. "There, see?"

He did see, and unfortunately Callie's scowl in the picture was all too familiar. She'd looked the same way at him when he'd found her last night, spying in that cleft of trees.

"Says there she might have been doing something suspicious." Suz ran a wet paper towel over Jer's mouth as he clamored into the chair next to Gage. "I really like working for Callie but didn't get to see her all that much yesterday, so I have no idea what that girl was up to. She's so funny. Did you know she has little verses tacked on her walls?"

Gage squinted at Suz.

"She really does. Psalms and proverbs—all kinds of inspirational sayings—hand printed on cards and tacked in weird spots. I spent most of yesterday patching the walls." His sister sighed. "Anyway, you think she was spying or something, like that reporter suggests?"

Gage's cheek twitched. She was doing something all right. With him. As for the spying, he'd have to take the Fifth. "Who knows."

Suz flopped down next to him. "Says there she was caught walking out of some bushes up at the Jamison's house late at night. Doesn't that strike you as strange?"

He forced his face into a bland expression. "If it's true. Did it say what she might be looking for . . . if she were actually spying?"

Suz eyed him. "Says here she told the reporter there was a party going on in the house, but see how he uses the words 'according to Ms. Duflay' and 'Ms. Duflay claimed he was mistaken'? You'd think we were reading the tabloids or something right here at the breakfast table."

"You say that like it's a sin."

"Maybe it's not as bad as all that, but it sure isn't healthy, reading about things that might not be true. It's called gossip and from someone who's been on the other side of all that ugliness, well, it's not good. I can attest."

For the most part Suz held in the pain that had brought her all the way across the country to live with him. Occasionally, though, a wound would surface the way a change in weather might arouse an old injury. Something in Gage's chest twisted at the thought of all his young sister and nephew had been through.

He closed the paper. "Then I think we should just let it be." Guilt flicked him. "Suz? I should mention that I, uh, was invited to a gathering up at the Jamison's last night."

She sat down. "Really? Did you go?"

He hesitated. If he told her yes and she asked follow-up questions, he might end up telling her about things that he had not fully vetted himself. Plus, Callie's presence on the property would certainly substantiate the reporter's claims— and how would that make her look to Suz?

He shook his head. "Should have, but didn't make it after all."

Suz nodded. "Well, it's a good thing. You've been working too late as it is. Just look at those eyes beaming like brake lights at me. Besides, if you weren't careful, you might've had your mug plastered all over the newspaper just like Callie."

Now there was a disastrous thought. He saw the title inked across his mind: "Architect Sleeping with the Enemy." He'd certainly have plenty of explaining to do—on all fronts.

Gage downed the last sip of coffee as Suz left the kitchen to get Jer ready for preschool. He winced as it trickled down his throat cold and thick. In the silence he had no control over his mind, which flickered over the memory of Callie and last night: her soft skin against his face as he kissed her so brazenly.

Awfully forward of you, Mitchell.

Yeah, but she didn't resist. At least, not at first.

No doubt about it. As the fight for the Kitteridge property dragged on, Gage felt certain that the tabloid-esque nature of the debate would become worse.

Chapter Twenty-four

 "Well. You didn't waste any time. Did you?" Sheila's voice provided my first human connection of the morning. I tried to think of what might have been worse, but nope, couldn't think of a thing.

I yawned as Moondoggy clicked down the hall toward my bedroom. "Not sure what you are referring to, sis."

"First you go on television, without telling your sister, and now I see your face in the morning newspaper. A less than becoming photograph too."

I sat up and shook away my early morning disorientation. "The newspaper?" Pulling on my robe, I slid into a pair of ratty slippers and padded to the front door, craning my neck to see where the paper delivery guy had tossed it.

"Page A2. Quite the story too. You weren't really sneaking around in someone's bushes, were you?"

Where is that paper? I spotted it near the front walk, *of course*, and padded out to get it. None of me had seen a mirror yet, like I cared, but in case Eliot lurked nearby with that camera of his, I'd rather not be discovered in my robe and slippers.

Pulling the rubber band and an attached envelope from the folded paper, I slipped back inside. "Where is it again? Oh. Wait. I've found it."

"Kind of hard to miss."

My heart sunk deep into my core and my skin prickled as if chilled. Not only was the picture hideous, but as I scanned the article it became obvious that Eliot had planted the piece with speculation and conjecture, having forgotten everything he'd learned in Journalism 101. Who cares if it was the truth? This ruined *everything*.

"Jim's concerned about you, Callie."

I slapped the paper onto the table. "Jim? I can hardly believe that."

"What a thing to say. He's your brother and he's concerned that you might find yourself with charges of trespassing leveled at you. I know your causes mean the most to you, but this is serious, little sister. Pay attention."

I sunk into the couch, wishing I could crawl back into bed and revisit the dream I'd been having about finding a treasure map and sailing away on calm seas to seek my fortune.

"Are you even listening?"

"Yes, Sheila, I heard you. I doubt seriously that any *charges* could ever be filed against me because it would be my word against that reporter's."

"But he has a picture!"

I glanced again at the unflattering shot and winced. My wretched, scowling face filled the whole frame. "That picture proves nothing. Well, other than my mood. He could've taken that at the RAG or in church, for all we know. You can tell big brother not to worry his legal mind over me. I'm not."

My sister sighed and paused, most probably to give me time to think about all I'd done. She sighed again. "For someone who's created such a stir and raised a lot of money in a short time, you've become downright surly. Look at that picture of yourself—you would think you had just fought off the enemy with that glare in your eye."

Sheila was right about that and her words gave me pause as I thought back on the night and all that had transpired. Although Eliot surprised me by showing up with his notebook and camera, Gage's sudden appearance startled me most. And not in a bad way, exactly. I barely had time to digest the emotions that had shown up with him, uninvited. Frustration, anger, and longing had all traced their way through me leading to that awkward, surprising, savory kiss.

I felt my body blush at the memory. "Probably had something else on my mind." I forced a laugh. "Like that time Brenna ran around with your camera on Thanksgiving, shoving it in everybody's faces. A lot of those pictures, as I recall, were less than attractive."

"Speaking of my darling daughter, you owe me seven dollars."

"Really? Why?"

"For ice cream. You didn't show up and the children were crestfallen. Don't worry. I covered for you *as usual*."

I covered my face with my hand. "Oh no, no, no." How could I forget the promise I had made to Brenna and Blakey? "I am so sorry, Sheila."

"It's no biggie, but you will have to tell them that."

"I will. How about later today? Could I pick them up in the afternoon and—"

"Not today. Brenna has gymnastics and, well, I would rather Blake not eat ice cream two days in a row. It will have to be sometime next week because our activity calendar is quite full already."

"Fine. See you Sunday?"

"I hope so."

"What's that supposed to mean?"

"Nothing. Never mind. Hopefully Jim's concerns will not come to fruition."

"You think I'll be in *jail*?"

"Let's not dwell on the negative, all right, Callie? I have got to get going on my errands." She paused again, her voice weary, almost fearful. "You be careful out there, little sister."

"Yeah. Thanks." I hung up the phone, fully awake now and equally aware of my new menacing ways. Much as I'd like to think otherwise, my sister, not to mention my niece and nephew, all had the right to be upset with me. If I could bend that way, I'd deliver a swift kick to my own behind.

And did I really hide out in bushes last night, hoping to catch townspeople violating the law? What if I had? It occurred to me that in a small town like ours, the story of my tactics just might trump the council's crime.

No matter how much I'd like to hide away the memory of last night's spy mission, that annoyingly clear black and white photo of me in the paper wouldn't allow it. One thing I could be thankful for was that there was no mention in the article of the friendly combat I entered into with Gage. *Really missed a scoop there, Mr. Eliot Hawl.*

I put a hand to my face, both eyes closed, my thoughts wandering back to Gage. He'd made me so angry, showing up like that. I had wanted to believe that despite his work with the land developer, Gage was above taking part in question-able government activities.

Niggles of doubt wormed their way through me. Gage *had* been quick to change course the minute he spotted me. He could have taunted me awhile before leaving, but instead he didn't hesitate to join me in my grimy hideaway on the side of the Jamison's house. I groaned. Maybe that was honesty talk-ing when he said he'd rather be playing in the dirt with me than be inside that house.

Didn't he understand, though, that I was not the type of woman to give up a cause over a guy? He could never change me, so why would he try?

The thought lingered along with a thousand others as I curled on my couch with Moondoggy in the crook of my lap. It would take strength of will to push me forward this morning. My eyes caught again on the picture in the paper, but no matter how I tried to snarl the image away, it stayed static, its ridicule aimed straight at me. If I hadn't forced myself to glance away, I might not have noticed the envelope that had fluttered to the floor when I had first opened the paper.

I snatched it up, the turn in my abdomen oddly familiar. When I unfolded the paper within, I became aware that my secret admirer had, unbeknownst to me, struck again:

You can hide, but you can't win, lady.

GAGE

"SO YOU DECIDED TO give us the ol' heave-ho last night, Mr. Mitchell?" Rick Knutson's voice on the other end of Gage's phone was almost too much to take so early in the morning. "That's all right, I know how it is. Probably got yourself a curvy little number to get home to. Don't sweat it."

He knew it was immature for an educated man in his late thirties to roll his eyes, but Gage couldn't help himself. "I had intended to be there, Rick, but had a last-minute change of plans. Couldn't be helped." That was stretching it, but whenever he thought back on the two choices he had last evening once he spotted Callie in those trees, well? He doubted he could have forced himself to make any other choice.

And what a choice it turned out to be.

"No matter. Word on the street is that the press scared away most of the council members anyway. Only Jamison was there, so Redmond had to put all his eggs in one basket with him. Know what I mean?"

"I'll give Redmond a call with my regrets." Gage jabbed the eraser end of his pencil into his desk. "Wait. Are you telling me this party was actually a front for a meeting with the town council? Behind closed doors?"

Rick's laughter soared through the phone. "As if you didn't know? Right. Good one!" His laughter reduced to a silly whine. "Keep up that holier than thou front—that's solid PR."

Steam rose within him, heat passing through his veins. "I don't think you understand the severity of the penalty for violating an open meeting law. Especially in light of the project's current opposition."

Rick spewed contempt. "Don't get me started on the so-called SOS group. Those people are laughable Ineffectual—"

"And receiving lots of press—" As soon as the words flew from his mouth, Gage wished he could retract them. Despite the whuppin' he hoped to inflict on the cocky realtor, he had no intention of exposing Callie in the process. He held his breath, hoping Rick hadn't seen the paper. Then again, if he had, wouldn't he have mentioned that news by now?

"That is exactly why we're able to fly under the radar so easily. Don't you see? SOS is so busy calling attention to their merry band of nitwits that nobody notices the swift plans we are making on this deal. Could not have planned this better myself."

Gage squeezed his eyes shut, forcing the burn from them. He tapped the tip of his pencil on his desk like it was sending out an SOS of its own. "Was there another reason for this call?"

"The plans. Where are you on the plans for the prop?"

Gage held his breath for fear of the barrage of sentiments that threatened to erupt. He'd been cordial to Rick to this point, but the guy was a realtor for crying out loud. He had no business sticking his nose into the design end of this business. "You'll have to take that up with Redmond. Now if you will excuse me, I've got a deadline to meet."

"Okay. All right. We can play that game, if you want. I don't have to tell you, though, Mr. Mitchell, that time is money. The longer you take to handle your end of this deal, the more money it's going to cost your client. That could affect you."

Did he really want to get into this with Rick Knutson, annoying real estate broker? Besides, he didn't see how this project would cost any more money if he got the plans to Redmond this week or next. Once his client approved them, he would have to meet with his engineering consultants to bring the drawings to the final level. Might set him back another week or so, but even though construction costs continued to climb, they would not do so *that* quickly. He wanted to call the realtor on his claims, but that would only prolong this conversation. "I'll bear that in mind."

"Good. Glad you see it my way. Talk soon."

Gage listened to the dial tone buzzing in his ear. *That guy's got to be kidding.* Disruptions like that made it much more difficult for him to go back to the drawing board, so to speak. He shook his head. Actually, much more than an unwelcome phone call distracted Gage this morning. This thing with Callie wasn't going away; rather, it was growing bigger and faster than the project he so diligently worked on for the Kitteridge property each day.

He glanced at his computer screen, which lay open, ready for more inputs. Soon he'd be meeting with Redmond for his sign-off, then plotting out the construction documents, then presenting the whole exhaustive design to the city. Although he respected Callie's drive to thwart something she felt so strongly about, like Rick and the others, he doubted that this community effort would win out over Redmond's longtime plans and seemingly endless supply of cash.

So what was he going to do about Callie Duflay?

His office line rang again, keeping him from coming up with the answer to his question. Did he dare answer the phone again? It could be that reporter snooping around, digging for more manure to spread across the paper.

"Gage here."

"Gage. It's Redmond." He didn't have to identify himself. His gravel-laced voice did that for him. "You didn't answer my e-mail."

Gage squinted. E-mail? He clicked over to his account but even before he did, he remembered. Rick had phoned him last night with an invitation to the "party" at Jamison's house, but Redmond had e-mailed him too. Thankfully he hadn't answered that. "Sorry, Redmond. Had a long night last night."

"As well you should have. Those designs ready?"

He breathed easier. "As a matter of fact, I was going to give you a call myself. If all goes well, I should have them ready for you to take a look at by Friday morning. If you like what you see, I will be able to move onto the next phase, which will ultimately mean bringing the finished designs to the planning department."

"Good. Let's meet at your office Friday, 9:00 a.m. sharp."

"Great. You're on my calendar."

A thick pause filled the air between them. "Want to talk to you about something that's come up."

Gage's chest stilled, like his lungs had quit functioning. Had Redmond gotten wind of Gage's romance with Callie outside the alleged party on the hill last night? "All right, Redmond. Shoot."

"Know anything about this Callie Duflay?" Redmond's garbled voice spat out Callie's name in a way that turned his stomach.

"I've seen her around town."

He huffed and it sounded like a seal's bark. "She's a piece of work. Seen the paper this morning?"

Gage swallowed. "Skimmed it over my morning coffee." He decided to take the proverbial bull by its pointy horns. "Wasn't impressed with the rag-like quality of the reporting, however. That picture of Ms. Duflay looked like something out of a tabloid. Quite a bit of speculation on the part of that reporter, in my opinion."

"Really. So you think the allegations are suspect, then?"

"If I remember correctly, Cal . . . Ms. Duflay did not confirm the reporter's accusation. And by the look on her face, I suspect she didn't pose for that picture either."

His laughter came through like a shout. "A hideous depiction, all right."

"Yes. Well." The only picture in Gage's mind was of the beauty who received his kiss in the dark of night. He shook it away. "I wouldn't let it bother you."

"Me? I'm not bothered. Jamison and I already had a discussion about the trollop and have decided to make her day and not investigate. Because if it were proven that the little minx was hiding in those bushes, trespassing charges could be made." He lowered his heavy voice until he resembled a stalker. "Let's just say that we would rather not draw attention to our soirée last evening. You with me?"

Yeah, he was with him all right, wishing he wasn't so privy to the obviously questionable aspects of this project. It wasn't lost on him that Redmond's admission to his and Jamison's discussion over why they weren't inclined to investigate the allegation against Callie made him both disturbed and relieved at the same time, the mixture unsettling.

Chapter Twenty-five

 Never had I been happier about the prospect of going to work. I slipped into the RAG early this morning, hungry for one of Holly's creations but hoping not to be noticed by those who read the paper. It was Friday, though, and shouldn't folks who read Tuesday's edition have moved on by now?

Here was hoping.

"Mornin' Callie." Holly greeted me with her usual big smile.

I took a seat along the side wall. "I'll have—"

"A peanut butter smoothie?" Holly finished my order. "And how about a rum muffin to go with that?"

"Sounds lethal."

"Oh, it is. It'll light a fire under you for the entire day, mark my words."

I shrugged. "Okay. Why not?"

A squeal of voices entered the diner and Holly's face lit up. "There's my girls." She glanced at me. "I'll be right back with your breakfast, hon."

I watched, awed, as Holly threw herself into the group of three women near the counter. The women were all fairly new in this town, but word was they were Holly's kin. What would it be like to squeal with abandon every time my family and I got together? The thought made my heart drop a little.

One of the women caught my eye and broke free from the group. I glanced away, believing I'd been mistaken, but sure enough, she approached my table. "Excuse me? Are you Callie Duflay?"

The woman's blonde waves framed her smiling face. She wouldn't smile like that if she had a complaint to file with me, now would she? "Yes. What can I do for you?"

She snapped open her bag and retrieved an envelope. "My sisters and I wanted to give you this, for your cause." She handed it to me. "We admire your tenacity."

Speechless, I reached for it. This week had started off well with donations pouring in as I made our case on the local television station. But after my mug appeared in the newspaper the next morning with Eliot's claims attached, the tide began to reverse its course.

While pledges and support continued their steady stream, an upswing of opposition had also begun to surface. Angry letters made the op-ed page, some from people outside of

Otter Bay who we'd surmised wanted to purchase a condo in the new development, but missiles from locals also appeared, many of them questioning our treatment of the Kitteridges. And I still wondered about the author of the "love notes" I had received. Rather than draw undue attention to ourselves, the SOS team had gathered by phone conference this week.

She continued. "I'm Tara Sweet, by the way." A bright diamond on her finger flashed when she pulled her left hand back after I'd taken the donation from her.

"Tara, thank you so much for this."

She tilted her head to one side, one shoulder slightly raised. "It's not a huge amount, but we hope it will help. That property's been open since I was a kid." She glanced out a far side window, her eyes wistful. "Have a lot of memories to hold onto over there."

I nodded. "Me too."

She gave her head a slight shake as Holly approached with my breakfast. "Well. I'll let you get back to your breakfast . . . hey! Peanut butter smoothie. That's my favorite."

Holly laughed. "And I talked her into a rum muffin too."

Tara smiled and winked at me. "You live dangerously, don't you?"

No kidding. I waved at her as she strolled toward her sisters who sat at a window-side table. Maybe I should take this as a sign that the blip in our campaign this week had only a momentary effect and that the generosity of these women with ties to Otter Bay would light a spark beneath the rest of the community.

Trying not to appear overly eager, I slipped a glance down at the envelope, noticing that its seal had been left open. I pulled the check up slightly and bit back a smile. We were another three thousand dollars closer to meeting our goal.

I enjoyed my breakfast more than anticipated and Holly was right—not sure if it was the rum muffin or not, but a fiery charge had lit into me and I couldn't wait to get to camp. I paid the bill then drove straight to work.

While hikers enjoyed a needle-softened path to get from the sea and back to camp, the drive was longer and windier. I didn't mind. Emerging from the bending road that tunneled through a canopy of Monterey pine gave an aerial-like view of the vast ocean the horizon muted by light fog. Up here, it seemed, cares were but a memory.

I pulled into a spot next to Squid's, surprised to see him here so early. *Must be working on some new activities.* To the left of the Adventure Room marked the beginning of a narrow pathway lined by plantings of eucalyptus that led to a circle of stones set around a wood cross. The outdoor chapel was one of Squid's ideas, a brilliant one, and another reason he was so good at what he did. Getting excited children to march single file could test the patience of Mother Teresa, however, so I created the path only one person wide with the "mysterious" stone circle at the other end.

The breeze carried the minty scent of eucalyptus, and I couldn't resist ducking down the path. On occasion, before or after particularly busy weekends, I liked to meditate or pray in that chapel beneath the forest where I was headed now. The air hung cooler along the shady path, and I took my time, inhaling the fresh scent and letting the stresses of this week filter out of my worry zones and into the brush at my feet.

A rapid flapping of wings caused me to flinch, then laugh, as a hummingbird whizzed overhead. All the money in the world couldn't replace this heady feeling of stepping through a natural wonderland. This is what my ex-boyfriend Justin never understood. Or it's what he had forgotten along the way. For him, the business had become the means to an end—his wealth. Well, *our* wealth until Tish and her father's money showed up.

If Justin's bus bench ads and truck fleet were any indication, he may have found a measure of success with Oasis Designs, but did he still have that spark that drew me to him like a moth to a candle? He used to drag me into the greenhouses at school and give me endless rundowns on the propagation of new plantings. The glee in his face over learning more about how plants grew and prospered reminded me of Blakey's the day he finally learned to tie his shoes. All out, abandoned joy.

Justin had lost that and though I had to fight the bitterness of his betrayal at times, I had begun to understand that had we stayed together, I too would have lost something meaningful to my life.

As I rounded a sweeping curve along the pathway, my breath caught. It always caught at this point because the children became so mesmerized. They anticipated what they would find at the other end when light flooded their eyes and curiosity had overtaken them. I slowed my pace, lingering in the quiet rustling surrounding me, knowing that something pleasing awaited on the other side, yet somehow wanting to slow its arrival. A crisp twig cracked beneath my heel. Water flowed through a nearby stream that had dug a meandering swath through the hill on its way to the ocean. I inhaled another deep breath and stepped into the morning's sunlight, refreshed and hopeful.

I opened my eyes expecting to see the grand cross rising alongside the pines. Instead, my gaze landed on two people wound so closely together that not a crack of light could pass between them. "Squid?"

A high-pitched gasp disrupted the breezy quiet and I recognized her as the woman Squid had introduced me to at the diner. Peyton.

Squid yanked his arms from where they'd been adhered to Peyton's body. I let my eyes flit away. "Callie, what are you doing here so early?"

I pulled my gaze back to him in time to observe Squid shoving both hands into the front pockets of his jeans. Peyton fumed at me, while smoothing her hands along the short length of her tankini dress. I shrugged, raising both palms. "Came to, uh, pray, but didn't realize anyone was here."

Squid's face reminded me of a hairy tomato as we stood there the three of us, no one quite sure how to ease the awkwardness that bound us.

Peyton rolled her eyes and huffed. "I need a latte."

Squid slid a compliant glance her way, his shoulders bowed. "It's all yours," he said with a nod of his head toward the stone circle at the base of the cross. He slowed as he passed and spoke with a low voice. "Saw the paper. I'll send Luz for you if you want to stay here and pray for awhile."

They left, Peyton marching ahead of Squid as he followed dutifully behind. I exhaled a full breath and looked upon the outdoor chapel. Lowering myself onto a cold rock, I realized that the wondrous moment of finding this place at the end of that twisting, shaded path had ebbed.

I blew another sigh, like a balloon that had been untied. Squid had this annoying way of using doublespeak. Hadn't really noticed that trait until now. It might work when trying to help children dissect real meaning behind a person's words, but when he used it on me, I vacillated between offering him my gratitude and suggesting he jump off the nearest cliff.

And what about him? What was it with men who found tiny, impatient—and *young*—women so attractive? Peyton had nearly stomped her petite and pedicured little toes when I'd appeared, messing up her early morning romance. *Like Tish.* Justin's girl-toy made a similar maneuver once when I showed up at Oasis Designs to clean out my desk. Instead of toe stomping, she tapped them continuously as if hoping I'd grow tired of her petulance and leave in a hurry. Didn't she realize behavior like that only slowed me down?

The cross stood unmoved before me, urging me to focus my mind on something other than the confusion that men and their quest for toys and prominence could cause. *Have I got it all wrong, Lord?*

After contemplating awhile, I picked myself up, no longer as enthused as when I'd wandered over here, but ready to take on whatever God had planned for the body of campers eagerly anticipating their weekend ahead. Somehow I hoped he had plans for me as well.

GAGE

REDMOND TOOK A SEAT in the plush, black armchair Suz had picked up at the dollar store one town north of Otter Bay. When he did, a dusting of stale smoke floated through the office. "Let's get this started."

Redmond Dane and Gage had spoken face-to-face only one time before. That rainy night the formidable developer stumbled into a coffee bar in Westwood after having a monstrous argument with his ex-business partner. Unknown to Redmond, Gage had just been laid off after having negotiated two high-end design projects, including one for a reality star in the Hollywood Hills. He discovered that his boss had planned to use non-licensed contractors and pocket the extra profit. What should have been a celebration was instead a caffeine-bender for Gage before heading home to his apartment overlooking The Getty Center. He planned to sit and stare at the museum's outer walls until he figured out what to do next.

Opportunity showed up before he left his counter stool.

As Gage walked around his desk, ready to lay out the Kitteridge project design for Redmond's approval, he hoped to live up to the expectations of the man who had hired him on the spot for this project. Although they had never worked together before this, they were both aware of each other's reputations. Destiny brought a tipsy Redmond and a discouraged Gage together that night in the coffee bar. They also both knew that Redmond's former business partner waited on the sidelines, hoping for failure, which meant that Gage's client had much to lose. As did he himself.

Suz stepped into the office with a stocked coffee tray. She bowed out of painting at Callie's house this morning, insisting instead on stepping in as Gage's assistant during his important meeting with his lone client. Gage waited as she set a large mug before Redmond on the side of the desk. "Coffee?"

The older man, his skin blotched and uneven, furrowed his brow. "Thought you'd never ask." Despite the steam rising from the top of his mug, Redmond guzzled down half the coffee, then cleared his garbled throat.

Suz refilled his mug. "I'll be in my office if you need me."

Gage thanked her, watched her leave, then turned to address his client. "I think you'll appreciate the project's cohesive transition from man-made to natural surroundings." He used a fat pencil to guide Redmond's eye through the design set spread across his desk. "I've woven in the natural elements you requested, offering organic styling while keeping with the quintessential beach town design."

Redmond stroked his chin. "Hmm."

Gage pointed out the shape of the buildings that flowed with the natural curve of the land, the cantilevered decks that provided views of the borrowed landscape, the plans for radiant heat in the floors and solar for everywhere else. Intact within the multi-use complex were places of refuge where dwellers could wander outside the confines of their condos and offices and sit among the pines and sustainable landscape—which included a wildlife pond to attract native and migratory birds and a rain garden added after Gage had stumbled across the miniature one near Callie's home.

Gage knew better than to talk too much, so he paused, giving Redmond a chance to collect his thoughts and formulate his comments and questions. Much like he did the night they met, when Redmond, slightly inebriated and wholly angry, offered Gage the chance of a lifetime—to design this property. He had been sitting at that counter that night, drinking a frothy latte in a tall glass, assessing his future, when in blew Redmond and his plans for Otter Bay.

Gage couldn't give his landlord two weeks' notice fast enough.

Gage stood by, waiting for Redmond to review the design he had been toiling over for weeks. He figured there would be many questions. More often, there would be inappropriate suggestions, the classless kind that made a designer's skin freeze and cause a chill deep in the bones.

Gage had already determined to answer all of Redmond's comments without cringing—at least visibly—at suggestions that would undoubtedly run counter to his design. This was the part of the project that could try an architect's confidence, when clients might look beyond the skill and vision of a particular design and be offended by what they see, mainly Gage believed, because they could not picture what the architect had drawn. Cockiness had ended his career once before, however, and that piece of history was never far from his mind.

Ultimately Gage knew he must walk that line between fighting to keep the design as he saw it and giving Redmond enough of what he wanted to secure the project's ultimate construction.

He held his breath, wondering if Redmond's silence indicated that they were about to head into battle.

But all Redmond did was peer up at him, a silver Cross pen poised between his thumb and fingers, a question in his high brows. "Sign at the top?"

No questions? Not even a rogue comment or scoff? Gage hesitated, knowing he should be leaping with relief. Redmond's reaction was highly unusual. So much so Gage was momentarily stunned like when handing a cashier a five-dollar bill for a cup of coffee and receiving eighteen dollars in change.

Gage mentally righted himself. "Yes. At the top." Gage understood that a verbal acceptance was more typical at this stage of the design process, but wariness had settled over him and he chose instead to allow Redmond to sign the set on his desk, thereby creating a paper trail.

After scrawling a large RD in the designated space, Redmond stood and handed Gage an orange business card with a woman's name and phone number printed in fancy script.

"Thanks," Gage said, still perplexed over the brevity of their meeting. "Who is this?"

"Call her." Redmond shuffled toward the door. "She'll be doing an artist's rendering of the design for a full page ad my staff will be placing in the local papers over the next several weeks. We'll also be posting an oversized sign on the property. She'll make your sketches so attractive the town'll be begging us to develop that land." He gave Gage a pointed stare. "You'll want to put those construction documents on the fast track. The council wants to see them within a week."

A week?

Gage stood, ready to balk, but Redmond put up a hand. "I'll see myself out."

Gage lowered himself into his desk chair, exhausted. Rocking back and forward, wincing at the squeak, he attempted to sift through an onslaught of varied emotions. *I knew it was too easy.* Redmond hadn't even mentioned SOS or the picture of Callie in the paper, almost as if neither existed. By signing off on the Design Development and hiring an artist renderer, Redmond seemed to imply that everything was moving forward as planned.

Except that he only gave Gage a week to draft a complete set of drawings for both permit and construction. Impossible.

Suz appeared in the doorway and leaned against the frame. "That was fast. Did he sign off on the project?"

Gage nodded.

"And? This is good news. Right?"

"Right." Regardless of the worries that hammered him, Gage gave his sister a thumbs-up and watched as she slipped away, beaming.

He tucked his elbows into his ribs and leaned on steepled fingers. If he had a drafting staff, plenty of time, and not a doubt in the world, then Gage would have no trouble admitting that this meeting had gone wildly beyond his expectations. Without all of that? It felt more like he stood on a precarious, rickety swinging bridge over a churning and unreliable current. And what worried him most was that a young mother and her little boy clung to that bridge with him.

Chapter Twenty-six

 The campers arrived in rambunctious spurts, dragging sleeping bags and over-stuffed suitcases off their buses and into tight-fitting cabin quarters. Giggles and shouts whizzed around camp, and the few times I ran into Squid, he was doing his big brotherly camp director thing—tossing footballs to the kids, proclaiming his favorite sports teams, asking campers if they were here to have F.U.N.—that sort of thing. Otherwise, he ignored me.

My work was fairly light that first night. No overbookings to worry about or ill children—although one first-time camper had to fight off a wave of homesickness. One hour and two ice cream sandwiches later (hers and mine), she blended back in with her group, which had begun to play the night's game: "Rock? or Sand?"

Maybe *ignore* wasn't quite the word for Squid's non-acknowledgment of me. He wasn't rude or surly. He didn't look me up and down, then purposely snub me (as far as I noticed). But the playfulness we often shared—the teasing winks and eye rolls, the private guffaws over a camper's dance moves—were all missing. If he needed me to do something, say, make sure the sound guy knew which songs were on the night's play list, he'd ask. Only his communication with me had turned sparse and robotic.

I wasn't sure if this had something to do with my surprise upending of his quiet moment this morning with Peyton, or if mentioning that he'd seen the newspaper on Monday was his way of letting me know that, as my boss, he was not amused.

The man was a mystery.

But today was a new day. The sun, and a nest of chattering wild finches near my open window, woke me early. Being up here, even though it was just a short drive from home, isolated me from the daily news and hometown gossip. I rolled my shoulders, luxuriating in the gentle pull of taut muscles as they stretched and relaxed.

Luz approached me. "Whee. Beautiful here today, isn't it?"

I let out a sigh. "Sure is."

The kids had assembled on the lawn at the base of the hill, the counselors corralling them with megaphones and toughness that was merely an act. The campers knew that.

Luz touched the cuff of my shoulder. "It's quiet in the office. You should go and watch the game today."

"You sure?"

"Yeah. Go on. It's fun."

As assistant camp director you'd think I would have more time with the kids as a whole, but I didn't. So watching more of the camp theme unfold during this sunny morning drew me like a butterfly to wild lupine. Besides, after a week like this one, I needed the distraction.

The rock wall had been erected two years ago near a hilly area so that kids could cheer on their friends from the sidelines. This year, though, the hill had been layered with a ton of sand. Instead of kids sitting on the hill to watch their friends, they lined up at the bottom, with their eyes on climbing their way to the top through nearly knee-deep sand. Squid said he got the idea for this activity after driving along Pacific Coast Highway near Malibu and spotting a similar sand hill that drew kids to its challenge.

I curled up on the lawn amid one of the groups waiting for their turn. Those at the front of the rock climbing wall strapped on helmets and pads and waited for instructions. At the base of the sand hill, counselors had to keep calling boys back down, telling them to wait for the whistle.

Squid's voice boomed through his megaphone. "Hello, my friends! Everyone will have the chance to climb both the rock hill." He pointed toward the towering setup. "And the sand hill."

The kids cheered.

"Settle down, settle down." The campers squealed and

hollered but Squid would not budge. Little girls pointed and whispered, their ponytails swishing in each other's faces as they assessed each activity. Several boys had to be reminded to sit. Squid held up the sign of respect and, slowly, the voices quieted.

He put the megaphone up to his mouth. "Now. I want you to think about a couple of things when you're doing your climbs. First, ask yourself, 'which one of these climbs is easier?'"

Shouts came from the peanut gallery.

"The sand, of course!"

"No way, the rock wall's much harder!"

Squid waited for the kids to quiet. He raised the sign of respect. "And which one of these hills do you think is stronger? Don't answer that now. Just think about it."

The girl next to me grabbed her friend's arm. "I think that was a trick question."

Her friend's eyes widened. "You do?"

The girl nodded vigorously. "Yeah. Adults are always asking stuff that's too easy."

Her friend nodded in agreement, her eyes and mouth stuck open.

I bit back a smile, although, really, the girl's proclamation carried some truth. Sometimes the answers to our questions seem so simple, yet it was not always the easy way that worked best. It would have been easier for me to say yes to Justin's desires for our business. Once while I watered a braided ficus tree inside a bank branch, a woman asked me a question. When I didn't respond right away—I hadn't actually realized that her question was directed to me—she jabbed an arched finger in my face and said, "What? No hablas Ingles?" Even after all this time, her condescending tone still flattened my smile.

It would have been easier to walk away from that kind of treatment, to give away ownership rights to the business, hire staff to handle the daily service to clients and marry Justin. Easier but not necessarily the right thing to do. After turning down that investor's offer, it didn't take much for Justin's eye to be drawn to the next tempting scenario. Only this one had long and shapely legs and the hip action to match. Not to mention a wealthy father.

If I had married Justin, who's to say he would not have strayed eventually anyway?

Squid raised the whistle to his mouth and blew, charging up the campers in the audience and those at the start of each hill. On my knees now, I clapped and shouted my support for the climbers along with the rest of the campers, my voice becoming one of the chorus. I'm not sure why I let my eyes wander from the frenetic activity at that moment, but when I did, Squid's gaze locked with mine and he sent me a wink. A deliberate, happy-eyed wink.

Not long ago a look like that from Squid would have turned my legs to boiled noodles. I would have interpreted it one way, when clearly, that wasn't how he meant it at all. My mind switched to Gage's kiss, that surprising, sultry, shocking kiss, and all at once I lost my balance and collapsed backward, landing on my backside in the dirt. Could I be wrong again?

I glanced back at Squid. This time all that moved within me was the sense that, although he may have read the paper, it did not appear that my boss was holding my indiscretion against me.

GAGE

GAGE NEEDED TO GET out more. Although this convenient office with its close proximity to town had caught his eye the moment he first drove into Otter Bay, he'd begun to tire of the arduous days spent splitting his time between the complicated design in front of him and staring at that dreary wall beyond his window.

Although he awoke to sunshine this fine Saturday, duty called and he had slid behind his desk with only a cup of coffee and one of Holly's muffins for company.

He wondered what Callie was up to today.

He reassigned that thought to somewhere in his mind's recesses, but strings of curiosity dangled in front of him, willing to be pulled, threatening to unravel him. She worked for a camp—that he knew. She also fearlessly spoke her mind and radiated beauty doing it. Callie had so much going for her that he wondered if something else kept her from realizing it. There was so much he didn't know about her, so much he wanted to learn. Gage battled the urge to call her, wanting, if nothing else, to hear the smooth purr of her voice in his ears.

As if in a trance, Gage picked up the receiver, only to slam it down when the dial tone jarred the air, breaking into his meanderings.

The wind he created fluttered papers across his desk. Why would he consider calling a woman who had let him know she wasn't interested? He'd probably stunned her with that kiss. Maybe if she'd known it was coming, she would have darted for the first break in those trees. *Smooth, Gage, real smooth.*

His eyes noted the hot orange card Redmond left with him. "Call her," his client had commanded. Gage twisted his lips and sighed. Somehow thinking of Callie and his design for the Kitteridge property all at once did little except remind him of the searing divide that—no matter how this played out—would always be between them.

He turned his thoughts to the number on the card, reading the name aloud, something he always did to make sure that he had the pronunciation correct. "Amelia Rosa Carr." Even her name had an artist's hum to it.

He dialed, his eyes flitting impatiently about the room as he waited for someone to pick up.

"Hello."

The bubbly pitch of her voice threw him. "Hello. I'm . . . calling for Amelia Rosa Carr."

"You've reached her."

Really? He figured the person attached to the youthful voice would excuse herself and fetch her mother. "This is Gage Mitchell calling. I'm looking for the artist who will be doing the rendering of the Kitteridge property for Redmond Dane."

"Like I said—you've reached her." Her singsong voice kept him off-guard. "I'm about to go to yoga, Mr. Mitchell, but I could stop by your office afterward to pick up a copy of the DD. Would that work for you?"

He straightened. Young or not, the woman knew her stuff. "That'll work. And call me Gage. Do you know where I'm located?"

"Sure do, Gage. My yoga class is a block from there. See you."

Over the next hour Gage cleaned up as many stray notes as possible and copied the design documents for Amelia. He also left messages for the structural engineer on the project as well as the contractor, Gus, who'd been chomping to get started for the past month—even though escrow had yet to close. Gage planned to spend the next forty-eight hours working on the next phase of the project and wanted to be sure all the players would be ready to consult with him Monday morning.

A woman with a brisk step and carrying a rolled up mat appeared in his office. He gave her a blank glance.

"Gage Mitchell?"

Perky . . . yoga mat . . . casual wear . . . "Amelia?" He stood and offered her his hand. "Come in. Have a seat." He pulled out her chair then moved to the side of his desk where he had laid the DD set for the artist to see. His ears had not betrayed him. Amelia was about Suz's age, with long, straight hair the color of wheat parted in the middle. She folded herself softly into the chair like a dancer and eased into it, her ballet slippers crossed at the ankles.

She peered at him, then at the pages on his desk. "I want you to know, Gage, that I will take good care of your baby."

He felt his mouth crook as he glanced at her. "Come again?"

"Your baby." She gestured at the DDs. "Trust me. As an artist, I understand how much of yourself you have put into this project. Art is always a personal investment whether we are talking about paintings on canvas or buildings along the coast." She blinked at him, as if waiting for him to comment, then must have decided he had not understood her meaning. "My interpretation of your design must not veer from your intent. I take that very seriously."

He considered her words. "Thanks." First Suz had impressed him with her creative spirit, and now Amelia was making a promise that sounded lyrical to this architect's ears. He wondered if he should take up art collecting.

Amelia leaned back. "I have a proposition for you."

Funny how she was doing all the talking.

She blinked her eyes again. Or maybe that was batting the eyelashes. Yes, she was definitely batting. "Let's discuss the rendering over dinner tomorrow night. Say Chez Rafe at six o'clock?"

Now it was his turn to blink. Marc would have a field day with this. Was the sunny artist about the age of his baby sister asking him out? His eyes flickered over her face and then back to his comprehensive drawings. Maybe she really did just want to discuss the rendering of multiple buildings and surroundings that she had exactly one week to complete. Possible. Then again, maybe Redmond had put her up to it. Was his client using her to keep an eye on him?

Mighty paranoid of you, Mitchell.

Then again, he had to eat. And what was it he'd been saying about needing to get out more? "Sure. Bring along your sketch pad."

She laughed, the sound reminding him of Cindy Lou Who talking to "Santy" Claus in *The Grinch*.

Chapter Twenty-seven

 The weekend had exceeded my expectations. Not only had I gotten the chance to interact more with campers, including s'more snacking at the fireside chat and this morning's worship-a-thon during chapel, but the reverberations from my brush with Eliot "investigative reporter" Hawl had no effect on anyone here at camp. Maybe no one other than Squid even noticed the picture.

Tidal Wave bounded through the cafeteria door where I restocked the game cabinet. I tensed, knowing how much he loved to sing out at the end of a successful weekend. He spotted me, halted, swept out a thick, hairy arm, and let loose in his best operatic baritone. "Cal-lie-e-e! Oh-o-oh, Cal-al-lie-e-e!"

"Pfsst."

He splayed wide fingers across his chest, his monstrous voice filling the dining hall. "What? You no like my singing?"

I jerked my face into a "lightbulb moment" expression. "Is *that* what you were doing?"

He grabbed a just-washed frying pan from the counter. "That's it." He raised it over his head and started for me.

A squeal escaped from me as I darted for the side door.

"You dare to ridicule my pipes!"

I pushed on the open bar, but the door was locked. Tidal Wave continued to bear down on me, pan held high, ridiculous scowl zigzagging across his face.

Another squeal flew from my lungs as I pushed two chairs out of the way and lunged behind a corner table.

"Raaaarrr!"

One of the main doors rattled as it opened, slamming shut seconds later. Tidal Wave spun around, both arms—and that fry pan—stuck in the air like he was under arrest. I stretched up on my tiptoes to see who had saved my life.

"There she is! Callie the hiker? Or huntress, perhaps?" Natalia stepped into the hall in her traditional suit and heels, a teasing smile belying the accusation behind her probing questions. "What would be the proper title for someone allegedly hiding in the bushes of a town council member's home?"

Tidal Wave lowered the pan and cast me a quizzical eye. "Stalker?"

I brushed back stray hairs that had slipped down around my face, working to keep the grin on my face from fading. "Hello, Natalia."

Her red lips stretched into a smile. "Callie."

I glanced at Tidal Wave who winked in a show of solidarity before he turned toward Natalia and lifted one of his big round hands in a wave. "Nice to see you again, Ms. Medina."

He exited the way Natalia entered. The door clicked behind him. "Not used to seeing you here on Sundays, Natalia." I resumed straightening the game cabinet. Plastic Candy Land people cavorted with Monopoly symbols and it must stop.

"Well, actually, I drove up here hoping to talk with *you*." Natalia strolled across the dining hall, dodging tables and chairs. "Quite a picture of you in the paper. Have you heard much backlash?"

I frowned. "Can't say that. No."

Natalia joined me in my quest to retrieve wayward fake money. She stacked the hundreds while I, ironically, chased after ones. "Because the board sure has been chatting about it."

I froze. "Are you saying they're concerned, Natalia? Because you should reassure them that SOS is doing well. I'm doing well. The campaign is moving forward." A shrug drew my shoulders upward. "Nothing to be worried over."

"I'm glad to hear it." Her face said otherwise. "I wonder. Have you thought about how your involvement in what is . . . hmm . . . in what is becoming a heated campaign might reflect on the camp?"

Her question hung between us. Even as my back stiffened

in defense, though, I could not deny that I had not thought about that until this morning as I recapped the weekend in my mind. Hadn't even considered how leading a fight for the Kitteridge property might affect anyone other than myself. At least not how anyone might be affected *adversely*.

I guess I'd always viewed my passion for this open space as altruistic in nature, something for the community at large. While I knew that those who wanted to wrest the property from the Kitteridges would be none too happy about this fight, I never thought this campaign could cast a negative glow on anybody. *Including my family*.

But that's not the point. I hadn't considered the affect of negative press, and as a board member she certainly had. And although I had successfully dodged answering direct questions about the night Eliot snapped that hideous picture of me, my heart knew the truth. No matter how often I justified my actions with suspicions over who attended that meeting, the truth remains that I had trespassed on private property.

A shudder chilled me. I'd been caught not just by a reporter, but also by Gage. Being away from home and the frenzy over the campaign, that reality of my brazenness weighed down my shoulders like an iron cape.

"I didn't know what to expect going into this, Natalia. The people of this town love the Kitteridge property and, I don't know, it seemed like a slam-dunk idea at the time."

Natalia wore a look of deep contemplation. "Have the donations come in to support that?"

"Well, there have been many. The problem is there's a deadline and—I don't even want to think about this—but if money doesn't flow in faster, we will have failed."

"I see. And then what?"

"I move far, far away." Natalia's mouth popped open and I laughed. "I'm kidding, of course. I haven't really let my mind go there, Natalia. I can't. Not yet."

"May I make an observation, Callie?"

Here it comes. Would it be acceptable to tell the camp's board chair no? "Sure."

"You are a gutsy woman. I've been impressed with how you defy convention and follow that beat of your heart. Thomas paid you an enormous compliment recently when he told me how tirelessly you work for this camp, and how much the children love you. He said it was a shame you did not get more time with them."

Thomas told Natalia that? About me?

"As someone who I've observed to be quite remarkable about thinking outside the box, I would encourage you to do the same thing about this quest you are leading up. As you reluctantly noted, the money necessary to purchase the property may be too little too late. It's a shame really, but a possible reality as well."

I swallowed back creeping disappointment even while fighting off the possibility that we could lose.

Natalia took hold of my free hand with both of hers. I'd never seen her be so . . . so . . . motherly. I struggled with a

sense that she had something to say but was not being forth-
right about it. "Be open to what God has in store, Callie. It
may or may not be as you hope, and yes, I absolutely believe
in the power of prayer, but what will be, will be. It's God's
will we should all be praying for. Wouldn't you agree?"

It may or may not be as you hope. Starting a business fresh
out of college with soaring dreams and idealistic expectations
made me understand the truth of Natalia's words. I had let go
of all the disappointment that came with losing those hopes to
Justin, though, hadn't I? Or maybe not. Maybe the memory of
dashed dreams had lingered.

Natalia watched, waiting for me to say something so
I nodded in agreement, still nursing the suspicion that she
had more to say—but wouldn't. The idea continued to niggle
at me. Were her admonitions really all for me? Or maybe
I was being too obstinate to recognize God staring me down.
If he wanted to do so by way of a woman with a not-a-hair-
out-of-place updo who wore nothing but wool blend suits,
he could. He was God. He could do whatever he wanted to
make his point.

GAGE

AMELIA STROLLED INTO CHEZ Rafe fifteen minutes late
wrapped in a gypsy skirt, her rubber slippers flapping across
the restaurant's burnished pavers. "Sorry to have kept you

waiting, Gage." She slipped into her seat and plopped a sketch pad, some files, and a case of pencils on the table.

"Do you eat here often?" As soon as he said the words, Gage had to stifle the gasp that caught in his throat. The bar scene had never been his thing, but there he was offering a variation of a standard pickup line, to a woman who reminded him of his little sister, no less.

To her credit, Amelia didn't blanch. "Actually, yes, I do." She looked at an approaching waiter. "Good evening, Terrance."

He kissed her on both cheeks like they were in France. "Amelia! How are you, darling?"

"I'm doing well, love." She gestured to Gage. "I'd like you to meet Gage Mitchell, architect extraordinaire."

With all the drama of a beginning acting student, Terrance pressed his fingertips into his chest. "An architect! How *fabulous*. Working on any projects around here?"

Gage ignored the waiter's appraising stare. "I am." He took a sip of water. "Transforming the Kitteridge property. Know it?"

The exaggerated smile on the man's face shrunk considerably. He glanced at Amelia and then back at Gage. "I'm afraid I do." He pursed his lips and paused, glancing around the restaurant as if to reformulate what he might say next. He took in a quick breath through his nose, his eyes continuing to focus anywhere but on them. "What can I get you both?"

Amelia smiled at him, unaffected by their waiter's

countenance change. "You mustn't react that way, Terrance." She tsked-tsked. "Gage here has put together a sustainable design that, eventually, the community will love."

Terrance stood stick straight, unable to make eye contact with Gage. "Perhaps. Now if there's nothing I can get you from the bar, I will return in a moment to take your orders." He spun away, his shoulders more tense than a new wooden fence.

Amelia turned to Gage. "I see you're quite the popular guy around here." She laughed lightly as if attempting to lessen the sting.

He shrugged. "Saw the welcome wagon riding down my street the other day, but all the driver did was spit on my lawn."

Amelia nearly choked on ice. She laughed so loud that several nearby diners glanced uneasily at their table. "You almost made me get my files wet!" She laughed with abandon, apparently unworried about the attention she garnered. She and Suz could be good friends.

"Speaking of files, I'm here to answer your questions." He paused. "Would you like to take a look at the menu first?"

She waved him off. "Nope. Already know what I'm having."

Gage smiled. "All right. I do too."

She held up her hand and Terrance came running. His stance had softened slightly, but he still appeared to have trouble making eye contact. They gave him their orders and he darted into the kitchen.

Amelia opened a file, pulled a pencil from her case, and looked at Gage. "Now, I've looked over the DD set carefully, Gage, and I definitely have some questions for you."

Gage nodded, knowing rendering consultants often flashed their claws at this point in the process. Less of this happens when renderers were working from construction documents—but he hadn't gotten to those yet and Redmond was hot to get this rendering completed for the upcoming ad campaign.

He nodded. "Shoot."

"Love the condo design, so free-flowing and all, but what especially intrigued me was the way you have structural support going through the middle of several floors of showers."

Gage kept his face neutral. "Like that, do you?"

"Oh, yes. Nice design, but where are you going to place those drains, I wonder?"

He leaned forward and clasped his hands on the table. "The ceiling?"

She laughed. "I take it you'll be fixing that."

He unclasped his hands. "I'm sure you are aware that you are working from the early schematics. The roofs haven't been worked out, windows still need detailing, haven't met with the engineer yet to coordinate all the mechanical, structural—"

"I get it. Okay. Still more to do."

Terrance arrived with their salads. "Pepper?" Just how did the waiter manage to so evenly grind pepper onto Gage's salad without looking?

Amelia tasted her salad. "I'd be remiss not to mention that

in Plan A's elevation, you're missing a chimney. Is your client going to just have to deal with the bellowing smoke or—"

"Tell you what. Why don't you just draw one in and we'll go with that."

She closed one eye and assessed him like he was one of her paintings. "You're kidding, aren't you?"

He shrugged. "Not really, like I said there are still many details to work out. Guess you're going to have to improvise."

She tipped her glass. "You're on, but we most definitely will have to stay in touch. If you don't watch out, Gage-man, I might have to put you in my speed dial."

She threw a smile at him, and he could see a glimpse of her tongue resting on the underside of her top lip. Queasiness turned his stomach. He wanted to kick himself under the table, hoping she hadn't mistaken his banter for something romantic. Reading a woman's signals never did come easy for him stretching all the way back to Franny Holmes in sixth grade. He'd taken her frequent phone calls asking for help with math to mean she wanted to go out with him, when all she really wanted was—help with math.

And Callie. She bristled when he came near, but when he'd kissed her underneath that ledge at Jamison's place, there was no mistake in the soft way she responded. Her faint groan still reverberated in his ears and the confusion in her eyes continued to melt him. One day soon he wanted to find out what was behind all that fight she had in her.

Amelia the artist sat across from him, a smoky smile lounging across her face. "That all right with you?"

He answered her with the professionalism she deserved. "Call me during office hours, and I'll be glad to answer your questions."

By the way her grin reduced, he figured he had not given her the answer she was after.

Chapter Twenty-eight

 Natalia's admonishment to seek God's will replayed in my head as I scooted across the Kitteridge property on my way to Sheila's house. The waters below had taken on a blue-green cast in the afternoon sun, making me think of the sea glass I'd collected over the years. Something touched me about the way an ordinary bottle came away beautiful after churning through chilly, salty waters. I'd felt tossed around lately too, or to be honest, more like the past few years.

The gentle music of the waves drew me, making me want to linger awhile on the great cliff overlooking the sea. Natalia had told me to be open to what God had in store and she was right. That's really what I should be seeking in everything I did, and yet, the thought scared me. Maybe God had no intention of blessing this campaign. Maybe he didn't care about such trivial things, not with so much human suffering to handle.

Or worse, maybe God would punish me for not seeking his will first before opening my big mouth to Ruth. If only I had been patient and prayed and sought his advice, this whole thing could have turned out much differently. I knew that the moment June Kitteridge came to see me with her sad tale. Guilt over having already set a campaign in motion gnawed at my heart.

For once, I remembered to bring my cell phone with me. Checking the time, I tore myself away from the cliff's edge and hustled toward Sheila's home determined to put more effort into these weekly gatherings.

Once there, Brenna answered the door, a stern furrow across her brow. "Hello, Aunt Callie."

I dropped to my knees and smiled right in her face. "Hello to you, dear niece Brenna."

A smirk turned the end of Brenna's petite mouth upward. "I'm trying to stay mad at you, Auntie."

I whisked her into my arms, one hand tickling her. "No way. You can't do it. I just know you can't!"

Brenna squealed and giggled. "Yes, I can. I'm really, really mad at you, Aunt Callie."

Blakey appeared, tugging at my pants. "I'm mad at you too!" Fat chance of that. All of his baby teeth showed when he smiled.

The three of us huddled on the floor, wrestling and laughing until my lungs were spent and both sides ached. I pulled Blakey onto my lap. "Listen, little man. You too, Brenna. I am so, so, so sorry that I forgot to take you to ice cream last week."

Brenna crossed her arms. "You broke your promise. You should never break promises."

I swallowed down but couldn't hide my regret. "That's right and I need you to forgive me. Can you do that?"

Brenna pouted. "I . . . don't . . . know . . ."

Blakey laid a pudgy hand on one of his sister's crossed arms. "C'mon. She said she was sor-ry!" He rose on his knees, placing his face inches from mine. "I forgive you, Auntie Callie. We gonna go to ice cream tomorrow?"

His earnest expression moved me and I wanted to cry. I'm going to buy this kid the biggest—

Two arms flew around my neck and squeezed. Any more strength in them and I might have had to be resuscitated. "All right, I forgive you too." Brenna's voice tickled my ear. "I can't stay mad at my auntie."

I grabbed their hands and tucked them into my sides. "You both have to promise me something, okay?"

They nodded, both waiting, eyes wide.

"You eat everything on your plates tonight with no squawking."

Blake wrinkled his nose. "Even the broc-lee?"

"Yes, even the broccoli. Promise me now because I'm going to talk to your mama about letting you both come out with me for . . . are you ready for this?"

Brenna's voice came out hushed like a whisper. "Yeah? Yeah?"

"Hot fudge sundaes with nuts and a big red cherry on top!"

Both kids squealed and tumbled over me. Somehow I landed on my stomach and the two kidlets climbed onto my back, bouncing like I was some kind of wild pony. An *oomph* escaped from my windpipe, but it was the approaching *click-click* of Sheila's heels across the laminate flooring that made me wince. I drew up on my elbows.

"Hey, Sheila."

"When I heard the children screaming, I should have known that Aunt Callie had arrived." She placed a hand on her waist. "You're early. This is a first."

"Glad to see me?"

Something flickered in her eyes. She paused. Sheila never paused. "Of course I am."

I didn't expect that.

"Come help me set the table."

Okay, now *that* I expected.

Vince offered me a hug in the kitchen as I grabbed the silverware drawer and headed for the dining room. He opened the fridge and hovered there. "Something to drink?"

"Mineral water, if you have it."

He followed me to the dining area where Sheila arranged giant hollyhocks and a spray of honeysuckle in a clear glass vase. I stopped, holding the large drawer on my hip. "Wow,

Sheila. I would never have thought of that combination. Pretty."

A smile lifted her cheekbones. "Just thought I would give it a try."

Vince entered the room and handed me a tall glass of mineral water. "How's the campaign coming?"

"Lots of donations and questions. I keep my phone turned off, otherwise the ringing drives me crazy."

"You never seemed to keep your phone on anyway," Sheila said.

I sipped my drink and shrugged. "This is true."

Vince's gaze pointed toward the west. "That sure is a beautiful piece of property. If I had the money—"

Sheila looked up, sharply. "Don't think about that, Vince. As it is, you already work too much."

A rueful expression fell on Vince. He lowered his eyes to his glass. "Guess so."

Sheila set down her shears and grabbed Vince around the shoulder. She planted a swift kiss on his cheek. "Don't go worrying about what we can't buy. I have all I need right here." She patted his rump. "Now please get my large blue platter down from the top shelf."

Vince snuck me a smile as he left. The doorbell rang.

I stopped wrapping silverware. "I'll grab it."

Greta pushed her way through the front door like a mother racing after her chick. "Oh, honey, get me a chair. I need to put these tree trunks up!"

Bobby ushered her in, his arm around her waist, a grim set to his mouth. He glanced at me and I wished I could wash away the worry I saw there.

My heart picked up speed at seeing my dear friend and sister-in-law in such a state. "Are you hurting? Can I get you a drink? A pillow?"

Bobby helped her lower into a chair and she seemed breathless. "I . . . just . . . want . . . a baby!"

Vince stepped into the room with a glass of water and Sheila on his heels. "Drink this." He thrust the glass into her hands as Sheila shoved a pillow beneath Greta's swelling calves.

Greta eyed him. "What is it?"

I scrunched my forehead. "Greta, it's just water. What's wrong with you?" I grabbed Bobby's arm. "What's wrong with her?"

He threw up both hands, using one of them to rake through his messy brown hair. "She wanted to walk, you know, to see if labor could start so I took her out to the Kitteridge property and we, uh, walked."

I felt my eyes widen. "*All* of it?"

He nodded vigorously, biting his lower lip. "Pretty much."

We turned to see Greta downing the water like a woman lost in the desert. I swung my gaze to Bobby. "That's miles of shoreline. Did you do the interior hikes too?"

The wince on his face gave it away.

"Oh, Bobby!"

He pressed his palm to his cheek. "Not all of them, of

course. She had all this energy this morning. Kept cleaning the house, even though it didn't need it. She washed all of the baby's new bedding—"

Sheila nodded. "Well, it's always a good idea—"

Bobby faced us, his expression bewildered. "But she'd already washed them and put them in the new cradle!"

Sheila's hand found Bobby's arm. "You're describing nesting. It's perfectly normal for a woman who's about to give birth to experience sudden bursts of energy. The trick is to know how to use that energy wisely."

Bobby blew out a long breath. "In other words, no long hikes." He glanced at his wife then back to us.

Sheila shrugged. "A nice brisk walk around the block would have been just fine."

I knelt next to Greta and stroked her belly, hiding the climbing panic within me. The thought of childbirth made my forehead perspire. "How's my little Clementine or Norwich today, huh?"

Greta's head lolled against the back of the recliner. "Giving me all sorts of trouble. He or she has been kicking me in some awful places."

The color had returned to Greta's cheeks as well as her sense of humor. Sheila was consoling Bobby over his regrets, and Vince was running around refilling everyone's drinks. Blakey rolled around on the floor with his toy diesel truck, while Brenna padded around behind her father, pretending to tend to everyone's needs.

Bliss like a fluffy cotton blanket wrapped comforting wings around me. It felt good to be part of this family. Flaws and all, when it came down to caring for one another, we were there. All of us. I leaned my head on Greta's shoulder and relaxed, noticing how her hands, clenched when she and Bobby arrived, now draped along the sides of the chair. She let go a ripple of a sigh.

I barely heard the door open and more family trail in. From somewhere beyond the living room wall, Jim's booming voice made it to my ears first.

"This may not be over yet. Callie has some serious explaining to do and without counsel she may find herself in a deeper pit."

Sheila shushes him. "Now, Jim, this is neither the time nor the place."

"Are you a lawyer, Sheila? Because last time I checked, I was the one who attended three hard years of law school. Trust me when I say that girl has made terrible choices and they may not only bury her, but this family as well!"

A frown replaced Bobby's panicked expression. He offered me a hand, pulling me up, and together we made our way out of the living room and into the dining room where Sheila stood toe-to-toe with Jim.

She spoke between gritted teeth, as Vince held her shaking shoulders. "I'm telling you that I'm tired of the way you treat this family."

Jim trivialized her with a sarcastic smirk. "You're tired of *me*? Spare me."

Sheila wouldn't let up. "We have been over this a thousand times and I already told you that Callie has it under control. Jim, I'm beginning to realize that you are nothing but a bully, always seeking your way, always bellowing about something."

Jim caught eyes with Vince. "What's wrong with her—that time of the month or something?"

One of Vince's brows stretched into his forehead. "Cool it, man."

This only served to make Sheila rise up more. "This is the way you've been for as long as I remember, Jim. But let me remind you how it really went when we were kids. While you were off hanging with your friends in high school, *I* was the one keeping things running around our house. Mom and Dad left *you* in charge when they traveled, but you were never around. *I* cooked, *I* cleaned up after everyone, and *I* tucked Bob and Callie into bed at night." Her face flamed red, her breathing loud. "Frankly, I'm surprised that all that pot you smoked didn't fry your brain. That was one thing *I* couldn't help you with!"

She threw a rag at his feet and spun around only to be stopped by Vince who hugged her in the tightest hug I'd ever seen. Like a mood ring, the skin on Jim's face evolved into pink followed by purple and ultimately deep, dark red. Neither Bobby nor I could breathe, let alone move; and although the drama between our older siblings shocked us beyond belief, I found comfort in solidarity with Bobby. Like old times.

"Well." Jim pursed his lips so tightly I thought they might disappear inside his big mouth. "The truth finally comes out. Sheila here thinks—"

"Bobby! Callie! Oh! Oh . . ." Greta's cry broke us from the scene in the dining room.

"Greta? What is it, honey?" Bobby said as we flanked Greta, each kneeling at her side.

"My water. I think it broke."

A gasp flew from my mouth and an instant sheen of moisture covered my cheeks and forehead, my body's attempt to cool me down. Bobby looked equally stressed. Greta's gaze whipped from him to me. "I'm the one about to push a baby out of me. C'mon. Get it together."

Bobby smacked a swift kiss on her forehead. "There's my girl. Always keeping me in line." He pulled her up while I dashed into the dining room to get the others.

Apparently Sheila had already figured what was happening. Flushed with worry, I met her at the bottom of the stairs where she landed with an oversized beach bag. At my raised brow, she said, "Things to help Greta during labor."

As much as I'd anticipated the birth of Bobby and Greta's sweet baby, I had also feared this moment. Sheila's presence, though, offered comfort in the midst of swirling confusion. Of all of us, she seemed to know exactly what to do. After helping Greta to the bathroom, Sheila put Vince in charge of the children, told Bobby to get the car ready, and asked me to wet down a washcloth, for what reason, I had no idea.

Sheila supported Greta back to the living room and flicked her chin toward the door. "Jim, open it up. Come on, Callie." She turned her gaze to me. "We need to get to the hospital ASAP."

My normally blustering eldest brother did what he was told, as did I. Cool water from the washcloth soaked into my skin as I followed Greta and Sheila out the door and to the waiting car, unsure how big a help I could actually be.

GAGE

GUS STONESBY, FROM STONESBY and Sons Construction, jingled spare change in his pocket for ten excruciating minutes, long enough for him to get the gist of the project's newest additions—and to drive Gage nuts in the process. He'd heard of guys that needed to be on their feet or squeezing a stress ball or drumming their fingers just to think, but Gage had never been one of those people. God had given him the gift of focus, meaning he could sit for hours and concentrate fully on one project. Of course, it might be said that the gift had its downsides, especially when it came to being able to free the mind enough to figure out something equally important—like women.

Specifically, like Callie.

It was Sunday and although he had planned to meet with Gus first thing Monday morning, the contractor pressed him to meet this afternoon instead. He'd been preoccupied, though, thinking about Callie, wondering how camp went, when they would speak again and how that might go. Allowing too much time to pass might backfire. Would she think that he had gotten what he'd come for? That the fire inside him had fizzled?

Dude, get it together—you don't even know if she's into you.

He shook away his thoughts, trying to concentrate as Gus started up the coin jangling again while taking another look at the schematics for the Kitteridge property. Learning that his client had crossed the line with the town council didn't make his job easier, as some might think. He had no desire to circumvent the law in any way to get his job done. Standing up to his former boss had gotten him fired, and he'd taken that as a sign that God had something new for him, something better.

But doubt had turned over inside of him. Was looking the other way as bad as participating in questionable activities?

Suz leaned into the office. "Gage, you have a call on the line."

He raised both brows and she answered by mouthing, "Redmond." With a nod, he moved to his desk and took the call. "Gage here."

Redmond's voice crackled, as usual. "You with the contractor?"

"Yes, we're meeting now."

"Make sure you tell 'im this is no free-for-all. Don't let

him make unnecessary changes that are going to cost me more money."

Surely Redmond knew Gage had little control over that.

"And you listen to the guy. He's been throwing up buildings all over the state. If he tells you something's not right, fix it."

"Of course." Why was he wasting his time? Gage would be working with the structural engineer to make sure that all aspects of the design were drawn up properly. Having Gus's input as the contractor should add another keen-eyed voice into the mix. When this project finally got off the ground, nothing within Gage's power to fix would be left to chance.

He cleared his throat, the sound of Redmond's phlegm, more than Gage wanted to hear first thing in the morning. "I'll be out at the golf course tomorrow morning with Rick and a couple of key players in this project. We have some things to iron out, and I'll be tellin 'em to expect those construction docs real soon. Nose to the grindstone, know what I mean?"

Key players? As in council members? Gage considered the consequences. "Those things you need to iron out . . . anything I can answer for you?"

"Not unless you're a legal whiz. Any experience in drafting proposed amendments?"

"Well, I—"

"That's what I thought," Redmond spat out. "You take care of your end of things—and don't delay. And I'll handle securing this property once and for all. Capiche?"

He clicked off without a goodbye and all Gage could think was that his client had spent too much time with his fast-talking realtor Rick Knutson.

Chapter Twenty-nine

 It didn't take Sheila much time to transform Greta's plain hospital room into a soothing day spa. Tranquil ocean sounds emanated from a portable CD player, flameless candles flickered on every open surface—she even rubbed lotion into Greta's feet and ankles before tucking them into a pair of fuzzy socks. As for me, I kept the washcloth saturated by running back and forth between the bathroom sink and our patient.

Sheila kept the room buzzing along. "Callie, hurry with that compress."

Doing as told, I approached the side of Greta's bed. Worry lines marked her forehead making me both want to comfort her—and run away. Shame heated my cheeks. *Pull it together! Greta needs you.*

Greta touched my clenched fist. "Where's Bobby?"

"He's filling out your paperwork, honey. They said you were too far along to sit in the hall."

"Right. I knew that. Oh!" She fixated on Sheila. "What . . . do . . . I . . . do?"

Unlike me who shrunk back into the corner, fear causing all my muscles to contract, Sheila hovered like a mother hen, cooing into Greta's face. Her voice came through like a whisper. "Breathe slowly. Keep breathing. It's all good. You and Bobby are going to have a precious baby to hold real soon. That's nice. You're doing very well."

As quickly as the etched pain on Greta's face had appeared, it drifted away. Sheila massaged Greta's temples and cheeks with her fingers, and every bit of lingering stress seemed to leave her. I marveled.

A nurse arrived with a harried Bobby following on her heels. The petite woman with brown shoulder-length hair talked to Greta from the end of the bed while stroking one of her ankles. "I see you've been having some nice contractions already. Good for you!"

Nice contractions? How can anything that painful be considered *nice*?

Sheila kept her eyes on Greta but spoke to the nurse. "I take it you have her monitor hooked up to screens at the nurse's station?"

The nurse bobbed her head. "Absolutely. Nothing gets past us. I'll just do a blood pressure check, then I'll call the doctor."

She glanced at Bobby, then at me. "Looks like you have your own pit crew here to help out. Terrific."

I lunged toward her. "Oh, but you're not leaving, are you?"

Bobby ran a hand through his disheveled head of hair, looking from me to Sheila, who scowled. Her voice belied that look, in an effort, I'd guessed, to keep Greta calm. "Thanks, Nurse. We're a great team and we're all going to help our Greta through her labor."

Greta's eyes locked with mine. "Will you really stay, Callie? I'd love it if you would." Her face took on an odd mixture of fear and hope. "Please?"

I stepped forward and held her hand. "Of course I'll stay."

"What about me?" A lopsided grin lolled on Bobby's face. "Isn't anyone going to beg me to stick around?"

"Oh, Bobby!" Greta's face crumbled into a wet mass of tears, and I lifted her hand, my eyes suggesting he get his booty over there. Fast like a spark, he moved to her side as I stepped out of the way.

After that, time zipped through space faster than a catapult shot spun through air. Greta's labor, from what I gathered by the quick succession of strong contractions and sudden entrance of a doctor and nurse, was atypical. At least, how I understood the drawn out process of labor.

Rarely had I attended a gathering of former high school friends when a glowing mom did not treat the guest list to a blow-by-painful-blow of their labor and delivery. I smiled sympathetically during those memory-charged conversations, but how easy could it be to enjoy noshing on crisp bread smeared with olive tapenade while someone described in agonizing detail their delivery of the afterbirth?

Difficult as being hemmed in between clicks of new mothers had always been, my own mom was the one to provide enough detail to solidify my desire to never ever become pregnant.

Children, I loved. Pregnancy? Not at all.

"They damage you forever!" Mom had said, in my watery memory of long ago. "Men, Oh men! They get to enjoy the process of creation while we women—yes, we *women!*—are forever altered by the audacity of childbirth. I will never forget the ripping, the tearing, the excruciation of needle and thread as it sought to repair what pregnancy had wrought."

I fought the very real urge to slip into the restroom and vomit out every inch of that speech she gave.

Greta's animal-like growl snapped me into the present. More nurses arrived with gloves and metal tools and serious expressions. Bobby had taken over labor coaching, but Sheila stayed close enough to offer support for both of them. My friend and sister-in-law looked more like a woman in the deep throes of disease rather than one about to give life. Several minutes passed along with another torturous cry from Greta before I noticed how I'd been twisting my fist into the center of my own chest.

Fat drops sprung forth over Greta's face and head, her body straining against the pressure of another contraction. Sheila's steady hand stood by, mopping. Helplessness wove its way through me, and I spun around, hiding myself from the drama.

Pray for her. The admonishment came quickly and without doubt, as sure as Greta's labored breaths. I recalled my late night chat with the young girls in my cabin and how they grappled to understand what it meant to hear God. Sometimes I did too, but I knew in this moment that *this* is what it meant.

The doctor moved into a crouched position at the end of Greta's bed, and her cries grew louder and more intense. I too moved into position, only to the far corner of the oddly shaped room, in a space just large enough to drop my head in prayer. What began as a muddle of requests slowly became more assured and specific. Bobby cheered Greta on from the sidelines. Sheila continued to give measured direction, unwavering in her encouragement. Peace began to flow through me, its warmth oozing through those places that had lain cold and barren.

The doctor's reassuring voice cut through the chaos like a beam of light in a dark room. "Almost there . . . almost . . . almost . . ."

Greta's hoarse cry turned mournful and I stepped up my prayers. Electric energy filled the room, however, peace never left.

"We're almost there, Greta." His voice so laced with both serenity and a spark of anticipation, the doctor could have been coaxing a cake to rise.

And then, as if the entire room had taken one collective breath, a pause fell over us, the kind that anticipated good news. Or in this case, great news. I held my breath, still praying, until hearing Greta's lungs gasp in one heavy sigh of relief followed by the unmistakable bleating wail of a newborn babe.

GAGE

THE MYRIAD SUGGESTIONS DROVE Gage nuts, mainly because he knew the unwillingness of his client to accept changes that might incur more costs. Surely Redmond knew the inevitability of rising prices in this business.

But the day had dawned anew. Gage hunkered down in his chair, poring over the list of updates the structural engineer had left him. Now *this* he could handle. Taking the engineer's notes and applying them to his own ideas brought his drawings closer to completion. At this point he could work out kinks and amp up the accuracy, like what an editor did for a book.

He might have stayed in that one position all day had it not been for the growl that roared through his stomach. Gage glanced at the clock and blinked unbelieving eyes: 11:30 a.m. Where was Suz?

She'd said last night that Callie had not called her back all day. Her plans were to work with him in the morning until she heard from Callie. Maybe she had.

He rubbed his eyes and the phone rang. He shook off a welling sigh. "Gage Mitchell."

"Hey, dork."

"Same to you. What are you doing, Marc?"

"Sick of working and thought I'd see what trouble my old buddy has gotten himself into lately. Seeing as you never call or write or send me a Twitter." Marc pretended to sniffle.

"Oh, man. It's crazy. This development has taken over my life. I'm sitting here right now with the schematics and engineering notes side by side."

"So that's a good thing, right? You've always wanted to head up some big project and now you are. Unfortunately we little people must suffer in your absence."

"Right. Last time I heard you and Lizzy were traveling the globe in search of Egyptian earrings or something."

"Hey, don't knock it. Egyptian collectibles are big business, my friend. Did I tell you the one about the camel and the jockey who got confused? Heh-heh. Okay, forget about all that. What's going on with the girl? Made progress there?"

"You make it sound like she's one of my drawings."

Marc laughed. "Well, I *hope* you didn't make her up." He paused. "You didn't, did you?"

Gage pressed a hand to his face and dragged it down his cheek. "No, she's as real as you and I." He sighed. "Long story."

"I got all the time in the world, man. Lizzy's out on a spa day with the girls. Hit me with it."

Gage proceeded to tell Marc about finding her dog running loose on the Kitteridge property and then Callie's ultimatum at the diner and their ultimate truce. He filled him in about the SOS team's progress, providing details about her television interview and how mesmerized he found himself while watching her on the small screen.

Marc laughed. "Welcome to small town USA. I hope she's into you because Otter Bay sounds like the shrimplike town I grew up in. Couldn't walk out the door in your undies to get the paper or the whole town'd see you."

One of Gage's eyebrows darted upward. "You step outside in your underwear?"

"Well, maybe not every day, but c'mon, sometimes it's hot."

Gage laughed, the feeling washing over him like clean water. "You never fail to crack me up."

"Hey, it's a gift. So what else? You saw her on TV and then . . . where? The Five & Dime? Laundromat? Pig Slop Café?"

Gage hauled in a deep breath. He glanced at the door, still wondering about Suz. Did he want to get into this story now?

Marc's voice dropped to a lower-pitch. "I'm waiting."

"Fine. Well, here's what happened." Gage couldn't seem to find the words, or know where to start, the whole thing sounded ludicrous even before he told the story. "I was on my way to a meeting and I discovered her hiding in the bushes outside the home where it was being held and, well, I skipped the meeting."

Marc roared. "What? Oh, man, this is priceless stuff. Price. Less." He gave way to more laughter before getting hold of himself. Gage knew it could be awhile. "Okay, so you and she were hiding in the bushes and, hey, what was she doing there anyway?"

Gage tried to corral the thoughts that collided like free floating stars in his head. What was he saying earlier about his God-given gift to focus? Callie, it seemed, had a new effect on him. "Actually, I was invited to a gathering at a town council member's home. I was exhausted that night—didn't want to go. This is between us, but Callie was, uh, spying."

"Spying? Why did she have to . . . oh. So was this a secret meeting, then?"

Gage swallowed. "Guess you could say that. Man, you're quicker than I am. I didn't suspect a thing, but like I said, I was tired and ready to leave my office for home when the invite came in."

Marc's grunt sounded grim. "This is beginning to have a familiar sound to it. Man, what are you gonna do?"

"That's just it. Nothing. I'm keeping my nose clean, staying out of whatever it is my client is doing. I'm not even sure this is anything but a bunch of rich guys all trying to one-up each other. Could be innocent as that." He paused. "No matter what, though, unlike my former employer, *my* firm will not participate in anything shady."

Marc snorted. "Yeah, that's obvious. Sounds to me like you owe Callie a favor. She kept you clean. If you had gone into that meeting, you'd have given the impression that you were cool with whatever was going on."

So much of Gage's energy had been focused on finding Callie there, teasing her, kissing her . . . well, he hadn't quite thought of it like that. Marc was right. Callie had kept him from that meeting and only now did he wonder what he would have said should he have discovered more than one council member at that meeting. Would he have walked out on the biggest paycheck he'd seen in years? Or look the other way?

Was he doing that now?

Marc broke in. "So what's going on with you and Callie now? She warm to you out there under the moon, in the bushes, with only the—"

"Quit it."

"Ooh. Testy."

"We haven't spoken since then. We . . . I sort of kissed her and she asked me to leave her alone. So I did."

Marc whistled. "Lizzy would be loving this. Our Gage Mitchell kissing a local rabble-rouser underneath pine branches in the dark of night. What else happens in the story? You gonna run into each other around town, acting like it never happened? Or are you gonna call that girl and hash things through?" He paused. "Take it from a married guy—chicks dig hashing things out."

"Thanks a lot for the advice. I don't know whether to follow it or burn it."

"Hey!"

Gage laughed. "I'll take it under advisement for next week. This week I'm too buried to be able to *hash out* anything with any kind of skill." His other line lit up. "Marc, hang on a second. My other line is ringing."

He punched the blinking button. "Gage—"

"Gage?"

"Yes?"

The voice on the line sounded distressed and warmly familiar. "It's Callie. Moondoggy's gone and . . . would you help me find him?"

He told her to hang on and clicked on over to Marc. "Gotta go, friend. Callie's on the other line and she needs me."

"Oh, man. Bringing you good luck from across the miles. You can thank me later. Bye."

He clicked back to the other line. "Callie? I'm on my way."

Chapter Thirty

 My feet had worn a path through the dust, driven by worry over Moondoggy's disappearance and the person responsible for it.

After such a beautiful night, one I will never forget for as long as I breathe, I stumbled into bed at around 5:00 a.m. When I awoke, Moondoggy was gone.

Had I not been so distraught and confused by lingering fatigue, I might have looked into a mirror before picking up the phone and calling Gage. The circles, the wild hair, the tear-stained cheeks all made for quite the picture of distress. The rest of my beleaguered family members would probably still be lost in slumber.

I heard the porch steps creak. I shook my hair as if it would matter, cinched my hoodie tighter, and opened the door. I hadn't seen Gage since the night at Jamison's and while the memory had stayed fairly tucked away within my mind, seeing him here at my home made them flood my memory again.

What had I done?

His eyes tipped at the corners, displaying his sympathy. "Would you like me to come in?"

Startled, I nodded. "Yes. Sorry. Please." I shut the door and faced him. "I'm sorry to bother you. It's just that I've been at the hospital most of the night."

"That doesn't sound good. Everything all right?"

A pin-light of peace shone in my mind. "Actually, it was amazing. My niece was born this morning. I watched her."

One of his brows rose and he tilted his head.

"Being born." My voice broke, surprising me. "Most magical thing I've ever witnessed." I cleared my throat. "When I came home I fell asleep. I finally woke up and Moondoggy was gone. I called the neighbor boy, J.D., thinking he might have come for him—"

"He didn't?"

"No. I've been everywhere: down by the water, up the hill toward camp, through town, and I can't find him."

"Was he here when you got home?"

"I figured he was asleep so I fell into bed." Tears sprang to my eyes as the reality of this situation settled deeper into my core. I dropped my gaze to my feet, shaking my head. "I'm such a terrible mother."

Gage's hand found my shoulder, giving it an awkward rub. "Not true."

"It gets worse." I held out a worn piece of paper. "When I first noticed Moondoggy was missing, I searched around the house for him. I found this in the birdbath in my front yard." The note had dried to a dirt-colored patina, crisp to the touch.

Gage reached for it, watching me. "What's this?"

I nodded for him to read it, too choked up to reply.

I warned you to leave the land alone.
Even your dog is sick of you.

Gage shot me a look. "Someone's been *threatening* you?" He pressed his fist into his bottom lip and began to pace, his gaze focused on the sparsely worded note before finding my eyes again. "How long has this been going on, Callie? Are there more notes like this?"

I retrieved the other two from my bookcase and handed them to him.

"Outrageous. Have you reported these?"

"No. I haven't. I figured it was just someone from the developer's office trying to scare me off. I never thought they would actually do anything like this—lure my dog away. They wouldn't hurt him, would they?"

Tension clouded Gage's features. Either he was annoyed with me for not reporting the two previous threats or just worried, like I was, about Moondoggy. I watched him work out his thoughts. The silence nearly shouted between us. And then he did what, instinctively, I knew he would. He wrapped both arms around me and pulled me into him, crushing me with comfort.

In this moment we weren't enemies fighting a bitter battle over property, but friends.

I had ridden endless waves of emotion lately, including the crescendo of my niece's birth last night, and the abrupt crash of this morning's events. In the silence Gage embraced me, rubbing my back and inviting some of that emotion to spill over. My tears flowed unencumbered, saturating the soft fabric of Gage's shirt and releasing those pent-up things that have a way of building forts within the soul.

One of Gage's hands dug into my hair, massaging my head. I flashed on the pain that wretched across Greta's face and coursed through her body last night and the way she later held that sweet child with the barest of available strength. She'd said, "Some things are just worth the pain, Callie." I knew she meant every word of that.

So many tears came, I could barely see. I didn't need to, though, because Gage's steady arms held me up. I hadn't experienced the support of a man for a very long time and I wondered if I ever really had. I was beginning to understand what Greta meant.

GAGE

SURREAL. THE WORD SPRANG to Gage's mind as he stood in Callie's paint-cloth draped home, cradling the distraught woman in his arms. She needed someone and she called him. *Him*. On any other day this would have rocketed his heart, but instead, agitation stirred within starting with a piercing sting of anger at the thought of the threatening notes she had received. Had Redmond done this? Or Rick? Neither seemed the type, but then again, they were hot to get this project going.

And with Moondoggy mysteriously missing, Gage didn't know what to think, but he did know this: He would canvass the entire town until he found her beloved pet.

He waited, though, and held her, sopping fresh tears with the front of his shirt. Something was different about Callie this morning. The stiff resistance that seemed to come easy for her had not made an appearance since he arrived. Morning sunlight streaming through the window fell across her hair, the moment like a snapshot. She melded into him and though a flame had fired him up to be her knight and solve the problems at her feet, Gage wanted to ride this feeling for its entirety.

Gently she pulled back and peered up at him. Despite her tear-stained skin and sad eyes, Callie was beautiful.

"I know things haven't been very good between us, Gage. Thanks for coming anyway . . ." Her words trailed off into a new spattering of sniffles and sobs until she sucked in a breath and raised her head again. "I'm not usually like this." She forced a sad laugh. "Always kind of prided myself on that."

Gage lifted her chin with his thumb. "I'm glad you called." *I dreamed you would.* He fanned his hand on her cheek, flicking tears away with his fingers. "You and I . . . there's something going on here, and I think we should shove aside our differences and face it."

She stared at him, rubbing her lips, sad eyes threatening to fill again. She nodded once and her lips parted as if to say something.

It took all his strength to hold back. He wanted to cover her mouth with his own, but a caution sign flashed in his mind. *Halt. Don't take advantage of the situation.* He leaned toward her, his voice a whisper. "But first, I want to help you, Callie. Let's go find your pup."

She pulled away abruptly, one hand covering her face. "You're right. What was I thinking letting myself get so emotional." She tucked wayward hair behind her ears. "I'll just go splash some water on my face and be right back." She turned toward the bedroom and stopped to look back. "You really don't mind, Gage?"

"Stop being a lone ranger, Callie."

Her eyes and forehead frozen in fear and sadness, she just nodded.

An hour later they left the police station with a written report and the realization that the SOS campaign was about to make the news again. Just how far would opposition to the campaign go to see this project—the one he should be in the office finalizing—built? If anyone connected with the proposed development of the Kitteridge property were the perpetrators of the threatening notes, they'd be guilty, of at the very least, harassment, and at the other end of the criminal spectrum: terrorist threats. Might also be suspected of dognapping, i.e., dog-stealing, to be precise.

Next priority—finding Moondoggy. Gage had to twist Callie's arm, so to speak, to get her into his truck. If given the choice, Gage would walk too, but they had much ground to cover and not a lot of time.

They rolled through town again, just like earlier before stopping at the police station. It didn't take long since the entire village of Otter Bay consisted of just two winding blocks with a few side streets thrown in for local color. Callie held on through the often bumpy ride, her jaw set and eyes focused on every measure of space around them. She didn't look surprised when he detoured from the village and pulled alongside the Kitteridge property.

Before he could unbuckle his seat belt, Callie had opened the door and landed on the ground holding onto the leash they'd brought with them. She jogged ahead of him, lean legs carrying her up the incline, loose hair bouncing behind her.

"Moondoggy!" She shouted through cupped hands. Without glancing at him, she spoke. "He's here. I can feel it. Let's spread out, okay?"

Doubt nudged him, but he couldn't refuse her. "Sure. I'll take the hills—" She had already begun jogging up a trail. He shrugged. "—or I could wind along the cliffs."

He set out, moving along the edge of the cliff walking close enough to view the beach below. *Wish I'd worn something with tread.* He had thrown on deck shoes this morning, for comfort, fully aware that they'd long since outlived their usefulness for grabbing unsmooth surfaces.

The land curved at this spot, providing a deep inlet to long, frothy-whipped waves. He'd passed the stairs already and knew the only way down to the beach from here came compliments of God. Rocks and wild bushes provided uneven support that only a four-legged animal could safely traverse. He glanced down. *No way.*

Callie continued to jog the upper trails, the outline of her body rigid against the threat of losing her dog. A part of Gage half-expected to leave this place dog-less and to find a ransom note back at the house. He didn't like the thought, but it had crossed his mind more than once.

A breeze from the west stirred, rustling wild poppy and sea grasses intertwined on the ledge. Sea lions and elephant seals began to bark in the distance. In his study of the area, he learned about the fragility of seal rookeries. One gross disturbance could scare the animals away forever.

He swallowed the thought. Sea lions, or otters for that matter, could live anywhere along this vast California coast. Was it up to him to worry over whether construction equipment and workers would disturb the creatures enough to make them leave?

Another bark made it to his ears and he scowled. He knew it wasn't his responsibility, but it bothered him just the same. He shielded his eyes against the flowing rays from the overhead sun, hoping to catch sight of a raft of slithery creatures lounging on the water. Instead, he saw something he had not expected.

Moondoggy.

He threw a wave into the air, catching Callie's attention until she began to run full force down the hill in his direction. On the beach Moondoggy's nose noticed the swelling excitement, and he lifted his pointed face from where it hovered over the sand, sniffing the air. Fearing the animal would run, Gage crouched down, placing one foot on a scrubby patch of sea grass that grew out from a crevice in the earth. Slowly he climbed down the face of the cliff, using his hands for balance while his feet found less-than-desirable places to land. At about halfway down, with one foot on the tip of a sharp rock and the other balanced against crumbling wall, he looked up to find Callie peering at him.

"You're crazy," she hissed. "I'm afraid to call him. He might see you hanging off that cliff and run like mad."

In one swift action he held a finger to his lips.

She frowned, still whispering. "I'll go north, in case he runs. You going to be okay?"

He nodded. If he could make it past the sheer face of the middle section of this rock, he will have made it to safety. The last quarter way down consisted of mostly plant-supported ledges and rocks. Moondoggy, for his part, had resumed his stance, sniffing the sand beneath him.

Despite the sheerness of the rock's face and the flatness of the bottom of Gage's shoes, he took a chance and ran toward the first ledge near the bottom. Actually, he slid, tried to catch his balance, and fell backward, hard, landing on his rear. If it weren't for the toughness of his jeans and the wallet in his back pocket, he'd be more sore than ever tomorrow.

Recovering, he sneaked down the rocks and sunk into the sand, thankful for minimal damage. Moondoggy lifted his head again, sniffed the air, probably catching wind of the cavalry's eminent arrival. Gage slowed and glanced into the distance, not wanting to scare the animal away. He could see Callie up on the cliff, looking for a safe way down.

He needn't have doubted, for when he caught sight of Gage watching him, Moondoggy, mouth wide open and tongue hanging free, launched into a sprint and nearly knocked him over.

Chapter Thirty-one

I DIDN'T THINK A dog could make me cry this hard or this much. By the time I reached Gage and Moondoggy, a jet skier could have skimmed my face. Heart racing, I dropped into the sand where Moondoggy had snuggled next to Gage.

I crooked my arm around Moondoggy's neck. "Come here, you." He licked my face mixing my drying tears with slobbery spit. "Where have you been? Oh I missed you—you scared me to death. Don't ever do that again? Okay? You hear me?"

Gage watched us intently.

I froze. "What? You don't think he understands?"

He shook his head, laughing. "Nah. Just thinking what a lucky dog he is."

"Oh." I measured a breath. "Some rock, uh, climbing you did over there. Impressive."

"Huh. You were going to say falling, weren't you?" He pointed at me, a teasing smile on his face. "You were going to accuse me of rock *falling*."

I shrugged, biting back a smile of my own. "But you did it so well."

He shook his head and looked out to sea, that smile still on his face. "What can I say—it seemed like the fastest way down at the time."

"I'll say." I made a swooshing sound. "Skidding's like that."

"Fine. Be that way." We both laughed as I continued to pet Moondoggy as the lapping waves inched closer to us. "I haven't done this in awhile."

My hand froze, tucked into Moondoggy's fur. "Done what? Rescued a crazy woman and her dog?"

"Never actually did that before. But I was talking about sitting on the beach. Reminds me of being a kid, building castles and moats and burying my father in the sand."

"So is that why you became an architect?" I asked, tongue in cheek. "Because you liked building things so much?"

He paused, considering. "Hmm, well, that's when I learned to site the castle so that the tide would just barely hit it when it rose to fill the moat, thus supplying the castle with enough water to use but not enough to destroy it in a high tide." He laughed. "So in answer to your question, yes, I'd have to say that my interest in architecture—green building in particular—did start then."

"And you mustn't forget about those lost-in-thought beachcombers," I said. "Or worse, big kids with heavy feet."

"Ah, yes. The ones who stomp on castles just to be mean. Then as in now, I work by simple, common sense principles."

"Which are?"

"Avoid those people at all costs."

Laughter bubbled up from some deep place within me, forcing out the stress and worry of the morning. "Gage, thank you, from the bottom of my heart. I mean it. When I woke up this morning, I knew that no one in my family could help— not after the night we all had." Fingers of relief wended their way through my body. "You may find this hard to believe, but you were the first one that came to mind. Suz always sings your praises, so somehow I knew you would come."

His eyes knit toward each other, a faint upside down V formed above the bridge of his nose. "I'm honored."

I lowered my chin. "Honored? You make me sound like the Queen of England."

His cheeks widened in a smile and those liquid-pool eyes captured me. "More like a princess."

Goose bumps danced up my arm. *Princess?* Four little words and I softened, like butter. Faint sprays from the tide landed on my skin. What could I say to that? He hadn't laughed nor scoffed after uttering those words, instead Gage Mitchell kept a never-wavering gaze on me. I'd resisted him so far (except for that one lapse in the dark in Jamison's bushes), and at this moment I didn't have an idea why.

"I feel like you and I need to start again—again. Know what I mean?"

"You mean you think we should forget about all our previous, uh, meetings."

He shook his head. "No. That's not at all what I meant. All of those times—the confrontations out at Kitteridge, the impromptu dinner—the kiss that took us both by surprise— they're all part of our history together."

My heart caught on the word *together*.

"But some of that history, especially with my work and your cause, keeps a wedge between us." He glanced out toward the horizon. "I hate it."

My lips rubbed together before I managed to eke out a response. "I hate it too."

Gage swung his gaze back to me, but I looked away. When I did, he moved closer. I knew by the way the sand shifted and Moondoggy's tail started slapping against my thigh.

Gage's fingers reached for my chin and turned me toward him, his touch sending a spark down my neck. His gaze caressed my eyes, my cheeks, my mouth, and I felt steady as a kite in a light wind. Gage kissed me then, lightly at first then more hungrily. I pulled him toward me, letting him know what I was discovering too—that I didn't want to send him away again.

A wave crashed and rolled until cold water slipped beneath us, but neither of us shied away from it. If it were not for Moondoggy's insistent pull on the leash wrapped around my forearm, we might have sat there in each other's arms past sunset.

GAGE

GAGE DROVE THE TWO miles home after dropping off Callie and Moondoggy, bouncing along as if sitting plopped in the middle of Cloud Nine. How stupid was that for a guy to say? Then again, he could hear Marc in his head now, egging him on, telling him how much chicks dig a guy's softer side.

Until recently, he wasn't aware that he had a side that was quite so . . . so . . . pliable.

This should not have surprised him, however. His and Suz's parents had the ultimate love story until their mother's sudden passing at fifty. Their father didn't live much longer after that. The doctors called it cancer, but he had always surmised that his father's heart had been too broken to beat. Gut-wrenching as losing their parents was, they'd always found a foothold of comfort knowing how intertwined their lives had been.

He pulled into the drive, aware that a grin had become embedded in his cheeks. Suz's car sat at the curb as he strolled up the path alongside his clipped lawn and bounded toward the door.

"Suz? Hello?" He stepped into the living room, only silence to greet him. He wandered into the kitchen and opened the refrigerator. In all the chaos of the morning and afternoon, he had not stopped to eat, and though he'd need to get back to work soon, the grumblings of his stomach called. Spying a plate of Suz's leftover lasagna, he retrieved it, served up a slice, and waited while his plate heated in the microwave.

A pile of envelopes and advertisements on the table caught his eye. One piece of mail, an envelope ripped at the corner, lay on top. *Heinsburgh Valley Correctional Facility*. The microwave bell rang, but he ignored it.

He climbed the stairs two at a time, calling for his sister, stopping at the closed door to the bedroom she shared with Jer. "Suz?"

A weak voice answered. "Come in."

Suz lie buried in rumpled bedding, an empty box of tissues teetering at the edge of her nightstand. If it weren't for the envelope he held between two fingers, he might have thought she was ill.

"Want to tell me about it?"

"It's from Len. He found out where I was from my old landlord."

It took considerable control to keep Gage from swearing. "Let me answer it for you—"

"No!" She sat up, her face red and puffy. "Stop trying to be my knight in shining armor—I'm not a child, Gage."

He raised both hands like paddles. "Give. Sorry." Since when did his little sister not want his help? "What did the guy want anyway?"

"Men suck, you know that?"

Gage stood. "Whoa. Don't compare me to that . . . that—"

"Say it! Len is a loser. I pick *losers* real well, don't I? If I were going to be in a beauty pageant that would be my talent: How to Choose a Loser with a capital *L*!"

"Don't say that. You're a beautiful, talented woman. And I'd say that even if you weren't my sister." He sat on the bed. "I don't know what this guy has said that has upset you this much." Well, he could *guess*. "But don't shut me out. You and Jer . . . you're my life, you know that, don't you?"

Suz released a throaty sob. "He stole drugs, leaving Jer and me to fend for ourselves. You should have *heard* how catty all the neighbors got. Did you know they called Jeremiah a criminal's spawn?"

Gage flinched.

"I never told you this but they said that Len had a girl-friend, someone he brought into our home while I worked. I denied it to everyone who spread that nasty little rumor, always tried to protect Len's reputation." She winced. "But it was all true."

Gage's heart sank lower than it had already gone since finding his sister in this state. "He never deserved you."

Suz gave a sarcastic laugh. "Yeah, well, seems you're the only one who thinks that." She shook her head and threw the covers off of her. "I don't care anymore. Forget it all—forget him."

"What did the letter say, Suz?"

"He wants a divorce." She choked back another sob. "Yeah, apparently his girlfriend wants to marry him. *In the prison.*"

He crushed the envelope in one hand and pitched it into the trash. "Let him. You don't need that guy and you know it. Now he's guaranteed to stay far away from you and from Jeremiah. Isn't that what you wanted all along?"

"What I wanted?" Suz stared like he had ordered her to jump off a bridge. "No, Gage, what I *wanted* was for the man I loved to love me back. What I wanted was for my son to have a father."

"I don't get it. The man committed a felony, he cheated on you, he's not worthy of either one of you."

Suz sank onto the edge of the bed, her head hanging low. "I guess I had this small hope that one day he'd listen to me. He'd find God and surrender his life to him, and then he'd realize what he'd lost."

He slid an arm around her. "And want you back."

She nodded, her voice dull with sorrow. "Yeah."

"You're right that anyone can be reformed." Gage shrugged and pulled her close. "Hopefully that will happen someday for Len. But your life is now. Your life, Jer's life, they're both gifts from God. Don't waste these years waiting for someone who's not ready to accept the grace of God in his life."

"I'll never stop praying for him, you know."

Something twisted inside Gage. His sister had been praying all along for her loser of a husband. There was something
so right about that simple, merciful act, and yet it had never
occurred to Gage—not even once—to do the same. He caught
eyes with his little sister, seeing the woman she had become.
"I know, Suz. I believe that you never will."

Later, after she'd gone to pick up Jeremiah from an after-
school care program, Gage sat in his kitchen, finally finding
time in this hectic and emotionally whipped day to nourish
his body. If Marc were here, he'd be on his case, urging him
to nourish his soul too. He knew he should be in the office,
head down, pencil to paper, yet he couldn't get Suz—nor
Callie—out of his head. Both women, in different ways, were
being threatened. He understood now some of what Suz had
been experiencing, that despite her husband's abandonment—
among other things—her heart had been broken by a man she
had trusted.

What about Callie? A charge ran through him that first
time they met, when she chastised the surveyor for flicking a
cigarette into the ocean. She had glared at the other men, but
when she looked at him, the sharp lines around her eyes softened. He knew he had not imagined that. Her soft gaze hard-
ened once she learned he would be designing the Kitteridge
project, though. But now that she knew him, and how similar
they really were—except for the position on the project, that
is—was that the only reason that, until today, she chafed at
his presence?

Julie Carobini

Contentment rose to the surface as he thought about how they reconnected today, and yet a sickly niggle kept him from over celebrating. Someone had been leaving threatening notes at Callie's door. They may have even lured her dog away. He set down his fork, unable to take another bite, firm in his resolve that it was time to ask his client some serious, direct questions.

Chapter Thirty-two

 Musky, hearty breathing awakened me, my eyes adjusting to the slow absence of light from the dimming sky. Moondoggy slept beside me, his slobbery snores making me question my sanity. I turned over to avoid his breath, my heart revving back up as my thoughts rolled over the past twenty-four hours. First a squabble at Sheila's, then the beautiful baby, followed by Moondoggy's disappearance and, finally, Gage. I pictured him, my knight, showing up at my first call, never giving up on finding Moondoggy . . . stumbling down that mountain.

I bit my bottom lip as it stretched into a smile. *Exactly why had I been fighting this man so long?* My smile faded as the answer quickened within me. Justin, had been attentive too— in the beginning anyway. At what point should a woman begin to believe that the prince won't abandon the castle?

I rolled onto my back, my eyes becoming lost in the textures on the ceiling altered by low light. My phone buzzed, again, and I knew that I'd have to face the messages eventually. Ruth had called three times so far, saying she had tough issues to discuss with me and *when will you be getting back to me already?*

I retrieved the phone, dialed, and pressed the phone to my ear. I waited as it rang several times.

"Hello?" Bobby's voice floated through the phone.

My own voice slipped out softly. "Hello, new papa. How's our new baby?"

"She's . . . she's the most wonderful, beautiful creature I've ever known. She already turns her head when I speak."

I laughed. "*Toward* you, I hope."

"Unlike you."

"Ha! And my sis-in-law?"

He sighed. "Greta's perfect. Okay, she's exhausted, but to me . . ." He paused. "She's perfect. I'd let you talk to her but she's asleep right now."

"I just wanted to check on you all. I would be there but . . ." I hesitated, not wanting to cloud Bobby's blissful day. "I'm still in bed, exhausted—what's my excuse?"

"Callie? Thanks so much for being here last night. Greta's so grateful. I am too."

"My pleasure. And I can't wait to hold the little sunshine again. You doing okay?"

"Better than okay. I've been holding her here for more than an hour—and yeah, my arm's asleep—but I've had an epiphany about my business."

"The storage center?"

"Yes. It's like I've been afraid of going forth at full speed, Callie. Jim's always been the smart one in the family, you know, the one with all the education. It occurred to me that I've never thought myself smart enough to be trusted with running a full-fledged business."

"You're kidding? But you've been doing that, and expanding, and—"

"And leaning on Henry as my crutch. You know what Greta said this morning? She said she can't wait to have another baby."

Part of me cringed, but another part of me grasped what she said. We all watched her go through some horrendous moments, but in the end she held a tiny, precious life, and I'd be lying if I didn't admit that envy had risen like cream to the surface. "That's beautiful, Bobby."

"Yeah, it is. I remember her saying that some things were worth the pain, but when she said that, I wasn't sure if she meant that enough to do it all over again." He chuckled.

I couldn't not smile at that.

"So my new baby girl has given me a gift. She's helping me drop the fear and offering me hope that I can make wise decisions on my own—without the obsessive need for Henry's advice. If the guy decides not to offer more financing for the expansion, so be it. I may even let him loose myself."

"Really?"

"Yeah, really. I'm sorry I gave you such a hard time, Callie.

You're driven by your passions, and I respect that. I know you're busy, but it meant a lot to us that you were here last night. We hope you know that."

Moondoggy stirred beside me, so I lowered my voice. "I wouldn't have missed out on little Heliotrope or Sumner's birth for anything."

Bobby's voice garbled into laughter, as if trying to constrain the decibel level in the hospital room.

"What have you decided to name my baby girl, anyway?"

"I forgot you hadn't heard. We've named her Callie, um, Callie." He chuckled again.

My breath held and with it a torrent of tears backed up against my eyes. I swallowed, trying to wash them back where they came from, but they only grew in number.

"You okay?"

I nodded, knowing full well Bobby could not see my response. "Yes." My voice cracked. "Are you serious about that?"

"Already told the nurse who's having it put on the birth certificate. Can't imagine what it will be like with *two* Callies in my life."

"Trouble, maybe?"

"Wouldn't have it any other way."

Buoyed by Bobby's news, I hung up the phone and pulled myself out of bed. Baby Callie? Had they really named her after me? Astonished, I shook my head, still unbelieving.

And my brother's about-face regarding his investor also stirred me, bringing out my own kind of resolve. Gage

Mitchell had been nothing but kind from the day I met him. We disagreed on the Kitteridge property, but he wasn't from here. He couldn't know what a sad loss that would be to this community. I thought about what Greta had said about pain, and how some things were worth it. Maybe it was time to let my heart take a chance again.

The phone buzzed, causing Moondoggy to snuffle and yelp. Ruth. What could she possibly say that could sully my near perfect mood?

GAGE

A VIRTUAL CHAIN-LAYERED cloak lay across Gage's shoulders. He should be at work. He had much to do and much to talk over with his client, but his heart had disconnected from the project. Instead, Marc's insistence that he get his rear end into church drove him to this stranger's home on a Monday night. It wasn't church, but it'd do.

Slowly he wove his way up to the front door of the redwood-clad house and knocked. A tan-darkened man of about fifty with a quick smile opened the door. He remembered his name was Kevin. "Good to see you, Gage. C'mon in. The guys are in the back."

He drew in a breath, hidden behind a smile that felt anything but natural, and followed Kevin to a family room in the back of the house. A flat screen TV hung from the wall playing ESPN sport's highlights as several guys looked on from a leather couch. At the other end of the room, three guys hovered over a table filled with chips and drinks, talking about whatever.

Kevin switched off the TV to a throng of groans. "All right, looks like everyone's here. Let's get started, okay?" He stopped and pointed his Bible at Gage. "By the way, that's Gage Mitchell. Gage? This is everyone."

Gage raised a hand in a wave and found a chair in the back. Even though he barely knew the men in this room, having only seen them the one time he stepped into church after moving to Otter Bay, a strange sense of belonging moved through him. He only wished Marc were here too. Marc had a way of shining a light on Scripture while entertaining him with witty and insightful questions of his own.

"Okay, so Gage, we've been working our way through Mark," Kevin said. "Just follow along and don't feel obligated to add anything unless you want to."

Gage nodded, forcing his mind to pay attention. How appropriate that they were studying the book of Mark. His friend would take that as God's way of not allowing Gage to forget his buddy. Like he ever could.

A man on the couch spoke, but Gage missed it. Another guy spoke up. "But don't forget, when Peter tried to correct Jesus—by suggesting that his prediction of his own imminent death was wrong—Jesus rebuked him."

"That's right," Kevin said. "Jesus told him flat out that he did not have in his mind the things of God, but only the things of men."

Another guy he remembered as Barry called out, "Yeah. What Jesus was telling them was so opposite of what seemed right for the Messiah. But it was all about doing the right thing, the work that Jesus had come to earth to do. And by suggesting he do otherwise, Peter was sinning against God."

Kevin took the floor again. "We do that whenever we do the opposite of what God wants, even if we're only trying to save our own butts."

"The moral of the story is God's way is hard," one guy said. "Study over."

Kevin continued. "Not so fast. It's not that his way is hard, but purposeful. Listen to this, from Mark 8:37: 'What good is it for a man to gain the whole world, yet forfeit his soul?'"

The words pounded in his brain, like a needling headache, just like the same verse had done six months earlier when he'd walked off his job—actually, he'd confronted his boss and then been *thrown out* the door. His coworkers had shaken their heads. "Let it go, man." They'd said. "Look the other way. It's not your problem."

But that's not how he was raised.

The men in the room had stopped on this one passage, the debate among them growing louder and more animated. Gage couldn't keep up and longed to dart back down the hallway and out the front door. If he were to ask the tough questions, and discover answers he could not live with, would he have the courage to walk again? Even though his sister and nephew relied on his support so much?

Or would he risk his own soul for good intentions?

A brown-haired woman with glasses and a sweet smile caught his eye as she stepped shyly into the room carrying a white-frosted cake. Quietly, she deposited the dessert on the back table, followed by a miniature replica of herself, a young girl of about ten, carrying plates and silverware. The woman left and returned again with a pot of coffee and tray of mugs.

She must have given Kevin the signal because he closed his Bible. "Let's take a break and get some dessert. We'll pick up with Mark 8:38 in a few minutes." The men clamored to the back table while Gage picked up his Bible.

Kevin approached him. "Hope we didn't scare you away."

"Not at all. I just need to head back to my office tonight."

Kevin squinted at the clock on the wall. "Tonight?" He shrugged. "Well, glad you could stop by, if only for a while."

Gage nodded. "Appreciate you having me—more than you know."

Chapter Thirty-three

I'd been living in la-la land. That was it. A fantasyland of possibilities with absolutely no grounding in reality. Funny how one call could swing the emotions from one end of the jungle to the other and cause a person to realize just how much they were beginning to resemble a monkey.

My conversation with Ruth was brief.

"Pledges have halted."

"What do you mean *halted*? Maybe they've just slowed or have come in a bit lower than others."

"No, they've stopped. Altogether. The team thinks it was your mug in the paper last week that did us in."

I breathed in and back out. "I see. How short are we?"

"Well, that's just it. Not only have the pledges stopped, but of those that had already come in, half of 'em have not been paid."

"Okay."

"That's it? *Okay?* Because if you ask me, this is not okay. Time is running out and if a miracle doesn't happen, we will have failed. Do you want that on your head?"

I should have stayed on top of things. Should have been checking my phone and answering calls and updating Stephanie with prayer requests. But I'd gotten complacent. I figured that SOS had been set in motion like a giant mill-house wheel that drew water continuously from a pond.

"Don't forget, I've got that radio interview at noon tomorrow, and hopefully I'll be able to make one last-ditch effort to save our cause."

"You mean *shores*. Save our *shores*."

"Right." We hung up, and I placed a call to June Kitteridge.

"Hello?"

"June, this is Callie Duflay. How are you and Timothy doing?"

"Oh, not good. Not good at all. Timothy's been more agitated than a washing machine on the spin cycle. Says everyone's out to get us. Are you calling to give us good news?"

I shut my eyes, trying to draw courage from some invisible place. "June, we're in trouble. The money's not coming in and without a miracle, I . . . I don't want to say what might happen."

"We'll be forced to sell our property, won't we?" Her voice sounded so small. "It is very difficult to think about, Callie.

But it is not your fault, dear. I have seen your efforts and you have tried so hard for us."

"June, please don't give up on me now. I'm not giving up. In fact, I wanted to tell you that I'm going to be on the radio tomorrow at noon. Tell everyone you know, okay?" I paused, wanting desperately to ask her one more time if I could have permission to tell the public the truth about their predicament. "Will you do that?"

"I would, dear, but so many of my friends are either dead or not speaking to me these days. They say we've sold out to developers."

Then tell them the truth—that you are being strong-armed into selling your property! I opened my mouth, willing myself to make one more plea when June's sweet voice filled the phone line again. "But I would rather hear them say that than for them to know how foolish we've been with our money. Besides, as I have said many times before, Timothy would never forgive me otherwise. Never!"

My mouth slapped shut, but not before releasing one harsh sigh.

The next day I sat across from Ham, the DJ of our local radio station, KOTR, trying to curtail a yawn. I had slept fitfully through the night, often waking from overactive dreams that pitted me against angry mobs of all types. Sometimes the opposition contained faces I recognized like Eliot, the reporter, and Jamison, the council member on the hill. Other times, they were faceless beings, some children, even, moving toward me with purpose, yet never quite able to reach me. When I awoke at seven, my mind already felt restless yet tired at the same time.

After walking Moondoggy then securing him back inside the house—too afraid to let him stay outside, I showered and stopped in to see Bobby, Greta, and baby Callie before they were released from the hospital. Finally I arrived at the station ready as could be under the circumstances. A familiar voice poured from overhead speakers, the same man I heard during the noon hour on those days I chose to drive. Only instead of hearing his voice wafting through my car speakers, he sat in this tech-infused, glassed-in room, beyond the lobby's painted walls.

He motioned for me to join him in the studio where I slipped on the earphones as I'd been instructed and waited for Ham to introduce me to his listeners. We talked briefly about the campaign and then he invited listeners to call in with questions. A string of buttons lit up.

"Caller, you're on the air."

"Hi. This is Donna Marie, and I'm wondering, will the community be building a playground for children on the property?"

Ham nodded for me to respond.

"Great question, Donna Marie. As you know, the urgency of our cause has prevented us from outlining every detail of the property's use once it's back in the hands of the community." *Good. Sound positive, like this thing was likely to happen.*

"However, once we receive enough funds to make the purchase, I'm proposing that a committee be formed to look at things like adding a playground or maybe even some soccer fields."

"Next caller."

"Hello. I heard your answer to that last caller and you don't mean to say that the property is going to be sliced and diced though, do you?"

"Not at all. Remember, there are several hundred acres of land and while most of it will stay preserved as open space, there's no reason not to consider using parts of it for more dedicated community use."

Ham announced a commercial break and I reached for a tissue, using it to wipe the sheen of moisture from my forehead. I watched as Ham pushed buttons and wiped away sweat droplets of his own with the back of one hand until strands of wet hair stuck to his forehead. Until today I hadn't realized the energy output necessary to participate in a radio program. Ham smiled at me briefly, before leaning into the microphone to give a plug for Holly's smoothie concoctions at the Red Abalone Grill. "Something smooth and cold for those up-and-coming hot summer days!"

He flashed his pudgy fingers at me . . . 3 . . . 2 . . . 1. Some callers had questions; others had opinions. I did my best to present a positive and knowledgeable response. The hour passed quickly and I felt good about the interview. We came to the last few minutes of the show. Ham led us out of the break.

"We're back with Callie Duflay of the Save Our Shores campaign. If you don't mind, Callie, we have another caller begging to speak with you."

"I don't mind at all."

"Hello. Is this Callie?" A male voice.

"Hello. Yes, it is."

"I saw you interviewed on television last week. Very impressive campaign you're running."

"Thank you very much."

"Your hard work is reminiscent of a 'hometown girl does good' story. Really, it is."

"Thank you very much."

"The Kitteridges must be thrilled with the prospect of selling their property to the community."

I hesitated. Saying they were thrilled by the forced sale of their property would be pushing it. Still, June was grateful to have found a way to stay in their home. "Hmm, well, yes."

"Now I read somewhere that prior to the SOS campaign, the Kitteridges had made a deal with another buyer. Is that true?"

"They had been talking with someone, yes."

"Okay, okay. Um, let me clarify something then: would the community be offering the Kitteridges more money for the property, then?"

I swallowed. While it was true that the developer had forced the sale, their buyer had agreed to a larger sum than the SOS team could possibly raise in such a short time. "The Kitteridges have agreed on the price offered by SOS and we are grateful."

"I see. So the Kitteridges, an elderly couple, were talked into selling prime oceanfront property at a fraction of their previous offer."

"No. Like you said, they are thrilled to know that the community will have access to the property forever."

"Even if that means that their golden years will be spent living on meager funds? Is that what you're saying?"

"No—"

"My understanding is that Tim Kitteridge is uninsured and showing signs of dementia, and that June needs money to pay for her husband's care." He paused. "I wonder how much this SOS campaign will end up costing these longtime pillars of the community."

I opened my mouth to speak—even though I wasn't sure what to say to that—but Ham took over the microphone. "That's all the time we have here, folks. I'd like to take the time to thank our guest, Ms. Callie Duflay of SOS . . ."

As he rattled on, wrapping up the show, the low throb that had started in my temple grew to encompass my head until it felt as if a vise was tightening its grip. Somehow I knew it would take more than a couple of aspirins to wipe away the effects of this interview.

GAGE

"YOU COULDN'T PAY ME to be that woman." Amelia's silver arm bracelets jangled as she tossed her shiny black hair back over one shoulder. "Cheating an old couple for her selfish cause—that's rich."

Gage turned off his office radio. The caller had baited then buried Callie with his questions about the SOS campaign. The program host announced that the barrage of calls received after the segment ran two-to-one against Callie's cause. He fought off a wince at the thought of how her voice began to shake on air.

Amelia poked his shoulder with one sharp fingernail. "Wouldn't you agree?"

He looked down one shoulder at the artist who had sidled up to him as he stood in front of his drafting table. "Excuse me?"

"The woman on the radio you were just listening to. Don't you think her cause is over with now?"

He crinkled up his forehead, trying to remember why she was here in the first place. Right. The flirty artist had some questions. "I stay out of all that." He directed her attention back to the CD on the drawing table. "I don't have much time today, so let me show you what you need to know. Here." He tapped his pencil on the document. "This is where the roof line will be drawn out. Make sense?"

When she didn't respond, he glanced at her only to discover her eyes fixed on his face, a teasing smile playing on her lips. "How about lunch?"

He set his pencil down and stepped away from the table and over to his desk. "Sorry. No can do."

She followed him, undeterred. When he sat, Amelia leaned over his desk, apparently defying gravity with her low-slung blouse. He was neither blind nor stupid, but certainly uninterested. "You have to eat, Gage. You'll waste away if you don't."

His phone rang and he grabbed the receiver, grateful for the interruption. "Gage here."

"Well, well, Mr. Mitchell. How are we doing this fine weekday morning?"

Great. More of Redmond's minions to give him grief today. "You're chipper today, Rick."

"We-hel-el, why not? Just cleared the way for my client to finally close the deal of the century."

"You did." He wanted to know but didn't want to ask.

Rick clucked his tongue. "Did you happen to catch Ham on KOTR just now? The SOS queen was on and, let's just say . . ." He paused for dramatic effect, a habit that clawed on Gage's last nerve. ". . . she didn't make her case."

Gage stopped tapping his pencil. Amelia stared at him like a hungry cat and he glanced away. "And you were somehow involved with making that happen?"

"Let's not get into semantics, now, brothah. Just wanted to give you a call, you know, to check on how the plans are shakin' down. Won't be long now."

Gage bit the inside of his cheek, willing himself to keep his mouth shut. Rick must have had someone call Callie on that radio program. Really boxed her into a corner. Made it sound like she had strong-armed the Kitteridges. He squeezed a fist. She wouldn't do that, so why didn't she defend herself?

"You there, Gage?"

Gage blinked. "Rick, I've got someone in my office right now, so if you don't mind, I'll have to get back to you. When I have something to report."

"Fine. Good. You do that. Remember—we're counting on you, man."

Gage couldn't hide the sarcastic roll to his eyes. "Yeah." *Whatever.*

Amelia leaned forward again. "Glad you got rid of him on my account. Now, about that lunch . . ."

Gage stood. "Sorry, Amelia. But I've got another meeting to run to." He picked up her sketch pad and pens and advanced around his desk, holding them out to her. "Call me if you have more questions."

Her expression dimmed in light of his dismissal, but Gage didn't care. He had a long overdue call to make—to Redmond.

Chapter Thirty-four

 For once, I wished I had driven. The way the townspeople avoided my eyes as I edged through town after my radio interview, you would have thought we were in the middle of Manhattan. No eye contact whatsoever.

A hundred retorts battled in my head as I made that walk, heart heavy over not being able to think of even one of them while being pummeled by that caller. Who was that man anyway? The developer? The person who's been threatening me? Someone who wanted to purchase an office condo with attached garage on the Kitteridge property?

Steph swung around the corner, moving toward me, her body bent but purposeful. Until she spotted me. I watched her pull up short, as if the toe of her shoe was about to connect with a mouse. Her gaze landed in several places, but never on me, and she turned to go the other way.

I raised my hand. "Steph!"

She slowed, her head bowed,

I caught up to her, dread slithering around my extremities at the flat line of her mouth. "So you heard the interview too."

She nodded. "Had it playing in the library."

I winced. "He caught me off-guard, but you know things aren't how he made it sound. The Kitteridges are good about all of this. I've spoken to June . . ."

Stephanie's leg shook and her gaze darted around. "I've been praying, Callie, but I think you should know something." Her mouth pressed into a grim line and she raised her head, looking at me with guarded eyes. "The Otter Bay Banking Association has decided to pull out."

I reached for her with both hands. "No."

She nodded over and over again. "Steve said there's nothing he can do. They were on the fence until a few minutes ago. Callie, it's become a PR nightmare for them. I'm so sorry."

"But—"

She wagged her head again. "I have to go."

She left me standing there, with nothing but embarrassment and shame to keep me company. If the association was pulling out, then the other corporate sponsors would follow. This campaign was, essentially, over.

The chill of disappointment filled my veins, making it hard to breathe, difficult to walk, but I made myself move one leg in front of the other. A knot pressed into the base of my throat, until my neck ached. Cars passed by, their occupants oblivious to the world that crumbled all around them. My world and theirs would soon be given over to those who didn't care one whit about the land or its current owners.

And I couldn't do a thing about it.

The ocean churned as if catching wind of the destruction that lay ahead. I'd made it to the Kitteridge property, drawn evermore by the smells of native brush burned into the wind by the day's sun. Few traversed the land today, and for once I was glad. I roamed along the winding path that hugged the cliff, not far from where Gage spotted Moondoggy moseying down on the beach, my mind far too overcome to caress all the good memories made that day.

Instead I sat on the ground, unconcerned that my eggshell-colored capris might never be spotless again. Another memory replaced the one from a day ago on this land. Justin and I had just agreed on a deal to release me from our business. I remember taking him in with my eyes, following the shape of his face, hoping to see some flicker of awakening. I wanted my signature on those papers to shake something up in him, to make him come to his senses. Surely he still needed me, still wanted me to work beside him, still . . . loved me. Didn't he? *Didn't* he?

I pulled in another breath, attempting to stave off the bursting of a dam that had been built, not over a couple of months, but over *years*. In an odd bit of logic, I thought signing over the business to Justin would bring him back to me. But he said goodbye as easily as if he might a business client, or one of the kids we hired during summer months. My signature on those papers failed to do anything but end the very thing I wanted to save.

And now I had failed again.

My cell phone rang in my pocket but I ignored it, switching off the ringer. It fell silent again. A formation of cormorants flew overhead toward a massive leafy tree, landing there. I'd have to find another favorite spot to sit and watch the wild birds make their nests. The cell buzzed this time, and I glanced down to find a text from Squid on the screen.

"Need to talk to you."

My eyes squeezed shut. Not now. What would I say? Six weeks ago I dabbled with the dream of dating Squid. After working with him so closely, seeing his commitment to the kids and to God, I dared to consider the possibilities. He was the first guy I'd noticed since Justin. Now those thoughts were like wisps of smoke long since dissipated.

Before I could answer, another text lit up the screen. "Can you meet at the camp first thing in the morning before the kids come?"

I shook my head and answered to the wind. "No. I can't. Leave me alone!"

My cell vibrated in my hand and would keep doing so until I acknowledged that text. Anger spiked in me. "You going to beat me up too, Squid? Going to tell me how I botched this? How I've taken down the camp along with my own reputation?"

My breathing resounded in my ears and I answered his text with a simple, "sure." Then I let the tears rip.

GAGE

"WHAT DO YOU MEAN you're not buying the property from the Kitteridges?" Gage gripped the phone receiver until his hands turned red. Slivers of white ran through his fingers.

"It's of no concern to you, Gage. You're the architect. Do your job and my staff will handle the rest."

"But if you're not purchasing the property, then who is my client?"

"Gage, Gage. Relax. I will be purchasing the property in due time. These things have a course to run, which is why I've been on you to get those plans finished. We'll break that ground the minute the property is transferred to my company. If there is nothing else then—"

"Your realtor tells me he had something to do with a phone call made today during a radio show."

"Ah, yes. The bimbo on the radio. Shut her down fast, didn't we?"

Gage gritted his teeth. "We?"

"That SOS group was getting a little too close to their goal for comfort. Had to expose them to the community, and my sources tell me it worked."

Gage's heart sank. Poor Callie. "You don't happen to know anything about some letters Callie Duflay has received?"

"Letters? From who?"

"Anonymous letters. I heard she has received several and they were threatening in nature."

Redmond chuckled. Then he swore. "Sounds like we got ourselves an ally. Just when you think the whole world is rotten, something good happens."

"I wouldn't consider threats to be a good thing."

"Well, you got me, kid. I hadn't heard about it, but can't say that I'm sorry for her."

A muscle in his jaw twitched more than once. "Getting back to the Kitteridges. If you don't know them . . . if you're not purchasing the property from them, how did you discover Tim's dementia?"

"Let me give you a bit of advice, Gage. Don't burn bridges. I get my information from people who know that I can be trusted with it. Now that information about Tim Kitteridge, that's well-known to anyone who's paying attention, but most people aren't. Most people just think he's just some doddering old crank who owns the best piece of land for miles."

"Wait a minute. If he has dementia, maybe he wasn't able to . . . Redmond, if Tim Kitteridge was forced into signing away his property while mentally unstable, that would never stand—"

"You are on the wrong track with this. Everything that Mr. Kitteridge signed occurred long before dementia settled in. His current state just makes everything simpler."

Gage shook his head, trying to get the numbers to add up. They didn't and he smelled something foul. "Redmond, I can't in good conscience go forward on this project unless you assure me that everything is being done by the book." He took a determined breath, knowing the last time he faced off with the boss, he found himself unemployed. "I need assurances that the property is being obtained legally."

Redmond's voice turned gruff. "Be careful or you might find yourself alone in a coffeehouse, wishing you had a decent job." He exhaled a garbled laugh. The sound turned Gage's stomach. "I'm pulling your leg, Gage. Relax. Everything's legal, I can assure you."

He hung up with Redmond, feeling anything but assured. His client promised him the legality of the project, but why hadn't he asked about the ethics? The more he studied what he knew, the more he turned over the facts in his head, the more perplexed he became.

Someone from his client's camp had worked awfully hard to throw Callie off her game today and they succeeded. What he could not understand was why Callie had not defended herself better. If they had never met, he might have wondered if the allegations were true—that she had twisted the old couples' arms to sell their property to her group instead. Just why hadn't she blasted that caller out of the water?

Chapter Thirty-five

 By the time I reached camp the next day, all signs of tears had stopped. The SOS team held an emergency conference call, but little transpired other than the begrudging acknowledgement that the group wanted to disband. I'd signed off with a dull heart and a pledge of my own: to believe in a miracle.

Instead of driving, I'd chosen to hike off some of the burden that weighed on my shoulders. I tugged at the cotton fabric that clung to my skin and stepped into the office.

Squid sat behind his desk, head in his hands.

"Squid?"

He lifted his head, displaying saucer-sized dark circles.

"You look exhausted." I pulled up a chair. "What's wrong?"

He sucked in a harsh breath and spit it out in one sentence: "Callie, I'm leaving camp."

I jerked up straight. He never called me by my real name. "No. Why? I don't understand."

His face took on a mixture of fear and anger. "Remember when I was telling you all that something was missing with the kids? That I didn't want the kids to have a mountaintop experience then go home and not be able to live it each day? Remember that?"

"I do."

"I figured out what was wrong. I've had problems with this series because I haven't been living it. I'm a failure, Callie."

"Squid—"

He waved me off. "Don't. I'm not finished."

I searched his face, trying to figure out what had happened with my old friend, the one who always seemed so self-assured and full of faith. He caught me watching him and his eyes turned sad. "What is it, Squid?"

He held my gaze. "My girlfriend is pregnant."

I blinked, my mind not accepting the information. A jolt ran through me. "She's pregnant? With your—"

He nodded. "Yes, the baby is mine." Squid flashed his brows at me, his mouth screwed into frown. "I'm a big disappointment to you right now, aren't I?"

New life isn't a booby prize, but I'd be lying if I did not admit the size of this blow. I stumbled to find the right words. "This isn't about me, Squid. What are you going to do?"

His hairline rose. "What do you mean? There's only one choice, of course. I'll be marrying Peyton ASAP."

I nodded. "Of course. I-I didn't mean . . . I guess I was just wondering about the logistics."

"And like I said, I'm leaving camp."

"Oh, Squid."

He held up a hand. "Might as well fire myself so the board doesn't have to, right?" His laugh sounded rueful, melancholy. "Even if they wanted me to stay, I couldn't do so in good conscience. I messed up."

"But you're doing the right thing. Facing your situation directly, not weaseling around it, or hiding it. I applaud you."

"Don't expect me to be taking any bows for this. I'm always telling the kids to build their lives on the rock, to not allow themselves to make choices that will have them sinking into sin, but I haven't been living that life. I leave here on Sunday afternoons with all the good intentions in the world and by Friday, I've pretty much turned my back on all of them."

"I see. So you're human."

"Don't you get it? I've failed those kids and this camp . . . and you."

I tilted my head to one side, watching our illustrious leader melt from the pressure. "Do you love her?"

"I think so." He scratched his beard, then shrugged. "Not sure."

I broke eye contact with him. My mind swirled. I didn't envy either one of them.

He cleared his voice. "You and I, we were a good team. I'm gonna miss that."

I nodded, my mind still a whir. We needed to find a new leader quickly, and until then I'd have to refine my understanding of the camp theme, that is if the board will still have me after the Kitteridge debacle. Squid's probably correct—the board won't be thrilled with what he has to tell them. Will they ask for my resignation too?

I exhaled one long breath. "No matter what you have done, God loves you, Squid. He wants to see you—and Peyton—restored. He's going to bless that sweet baby of yours no matter what."

"Well, that's not going to happen until I get my act together."

"What's that supposed to mean?" I stood over him, hands on my hips, reminding myself of Sheila. Yet I couldn't seem to stop myself. "Do you tell those kids that they can't go to God when they're broken? That's exactly when they need him the most."

He dropped his hands onto the desk with a slap. "I don't know. I'm just mad at myself. Feeling pretty stupid right now."

"Don't wait for your own perfection, my friend—that won't happen until heaven. You need God in all of this, so don't abandon ship now. He's not about to leave you, you know."

"This wasn't how it was supposed to be."

"When is it ever? I've got a proverb tacked up on my wall that says, 'In his heart a man plans his course, but the Lord determines his steps.' We never know our path to perfection—only that on our own, we'll screw it up. Let the Lord decide how to use this for his glory. You just have to stay on the path, my friend."

"Wow. Never knew you had the preacher in you."

I laughed. "Me neither." The proverb I'd quoted wove through my head. I'd made many plans that had not turned out like I had laid them out. Was I willing to let go of my plans too?

"Thanks for your understanding about all this." He raised his chin a little higher. "I meant it when I said I'd miss working with you."

"I know you did."

"Better get to it, right? Kids'll be here soon." He handed me a clipboard. "You might want to take a look at my notes, so you can help whoever takes over next week."

I nodded, as Squid headed out of the office, soon to be lost in new plans of his own. The office walls seem to sag from sorrow.

GAGE

THE VIEW FROM THE camp's perch at the crest of a winding hill stunned him. Miles of placid ocean shimmered as if sprinkled with sugar in the morning sun. He pulled into a parking spot at quarter till noon, hoping he'd find her here.

At the top of the steps, he leaned in through the office doorway. A woman with short brown hair and large glasses raised her head. "May I help you?"

"Looking for Callie Duflay?"

She narrowed her eyes at him. "She's had enough of reporters."

"Good thing I'm not a reporter."

The woman didn't laugh.

"Actually, we're friends." He stepped into the office. "I'm Gage."

"Gage? Haven't heard of a Gage."

"Gage Mitchell. Architect on the Kitteridge project." He cleared his throat. "Would you know where I could find her?"

Clearly this woman considered herself Callie's protector for she scrutinized him in silence for several awkward seconds. "Leave your keys on the desk and I'll tell you."

"My keys?"

"So if it turns out you're one of those paparazzis, you won't be able to get away."

He dropped his keys on her desk. "And now?"

She flicked her head toward the door. "Follow the path to the chapel. There's a sign outside."

Gage tapped his forehead with his index finger in a salute

and headed outside. The sign pointed to a flowing, planted trail. He made his way along the dirt, unable to miss the sweet smell of jasmine hanging in the air, intrigued by the artistry and uniqueness of the undulating path, and surprised by its length and "secret garden" feel. Before long, he noticed a figure, crouched behind an L-shaped bend in the path, hiding behind thick vines.

He slowed his approach, noticing the man had a camera. A reporter. Doubling his pace, Gage strode up behind him, taking a fast look through a break in the foliage at a horseshoe-shaped chapel in the woods. Callie sat alone on a stump, oblivious to her stalker. The man spun around, but not before Gage snagged him at the collar.

"What are you doing here?"

The bespeckled kid gasped. "My job."

Gage squinted at the kid, holding him at arm's length like a shirt on a hanger. "Your job is to spy on praying women?"

"I'm a reporter."

Gage shook him free. "What for? A tabloid?"

"N-no!"

"Then tell you what—stop acting like it. You want to be taken seriously, then you need to learn to be upfront with people." Gage nodded at the pile of leaves and stems that littered the ground. "You tear that hole in the vines?"

Terrified, the kid nodded more than necessary.

"You'd better pray your newspaper's willing to pay for the restoration. That's someone's work you messed with." Gage had a feeling he knew whose work that was. "Now what do you want? You're Eliot Hawl, I presume."

"Yes, sir. I wanted to find out Ms. Duflay's reaction to news that Tim Kitteridge has been hospitalized."

"Hospitalized? Why?"

"Don't know exactly—that's someone else's beat. It's news 'cuz he and his wife are at the center of the SOS campaign."

Gage's mind turned that one over. Callie had just been accused of orchestrating a campaign against the elderly couple, of taking advantage of them. This news wouldn't make her life any easier, and he wanted to be there to catch her should she fall.

Gage kept a steely gaze on the kid. "You the one who's been leaving those threatening letters at Callie's home?"

"N-no." He glanced through the man-made peephole. "Someone's been *threatening* her?"

"That's what I said. You're the only one I can think of who's been following her around. What do you know about her dog?"

Eliot's eyes popped open till they matched the size of his wire-rimmed glasses. "Nothing!"

Gage searched the kid's face for some sign of lying but found none. Yet something like recognition seemed to move across his face. Eliot looked away.

"You suddenly remember something?"

Eliot's eyes slid back toward Gage. "Maybe. I'll need to investigate—"

Gage grabbed Eliot's collar again and the kid flinched. "Hold on. Forget about any more investigation. Callie's a friend of mine, and I'm tired of seeing your byline next to her name. You just go ahead and tell me what you've thought of."

Eliot swallowed and swayed under Gage's unyielding grip. "Nothing really, just that I saw Tim Kitteridge a couple of times hanging out at Ms. Duflay's place."

Gage shifted and dropped the kid's collar. "What do you mean 'hanging out'? As in visiting her?"

Eliot straightened and threw a daggered look back at him. "She was never home when I saw him there. No, he was just walking around her garden, sniffing stuff. I think he might have brought her some mail."

"Where were you hiding during all that?"

He hesitated until Gage narrowed his eyes. "Behind her shed on the side of the house, mostly. Sometimes behind a truck on the street. Wherever I could get a good look."

Gage stepped backward, snapping a twig. A thought tore through his mind. *I think he might have brought her some mail.* Could Tim Kitteridge have been the one who had been threatening Callie? He glanced at Eliot, hoping the kid hadn't settled on the same thought.

Too late. Eliot smiled. "Poor Tim Kitteridge."

Gage quirked up his chin. "What do you mean by that?"

The kid's smile grew into a nasty grin. "Thanks a lot for the tip, Mr. Friend of Callie's. I think I just figured why old Tim Kitteridge had been hanging around her place." He looped his camera around his neck. "Guess I'll be leaving now."

"Hold on. You've got some explaining to do about the hole you've left."

Eliot had already begun to back away. "Send the paper the bill. They'll handle it."

Gage swung back toward the spray of light at the end of the path. Callie, who still sat in contemplation at the foot of that cross, had no idea how far the kid might go to win a gold star from his editor. He entered the clearing and pulled up beside her. "Callie?"

She spun around from her perch on a stump. The sober look on her face relaxed into a smile and she stood. "Gage. What are you—"

He hadn't planned to kiss her, but he did, closing her mouth with his before she could finish the question. She didn't resist and he reveled in her arms. For the moment Gage let all the questions that filled his mind fall away.

Chapter Thirty-six

 Finally I pushed him away from me, surprised by my sudden lightness of heart. "You haven't answered my question, Gage. What are you doing here?"

He smiled, but something faltered in his expression. He caressed my face with one hand. "I missed you. Been working 'round the clock but didn't want to wait another day to see you."

He wasn't exactly my boyfriend—do thirty-year-old women still use that term? What was he to me? Our hands intermingled and my fingers played with his as I stood wondering where we would go from here.

Abruptly he dropped his hand from my face and pulled me toward two tree stump seats. "Let's sit a minute, okay? I wanted to talk to you about something."

"Sure." I took my seat again. As I did, the reality of my morning whooshed through my head. The last time I stepped into this chapel, I discovered Squid and Peyton locked in an embrace of their own. Now, she's pregnant. Sobering thought.

Gage glanced at me. "You okay?"

I forced myself to brighten, which wasn't terribly difficult considering he sat next to me. "Yeah."

Gage huffed out a sigh. "I heard you on the radio the other day."

What could I say to that? If he heard the entire thing, then he heard a disaster. He probably figured I had given up, and that I would merrily take his hand and let him show me the plans for Otter Bay. Could he handle knowing I wasn't ready to compromise?

I squeezed his hand. "Sorry you had to hear that. Admittedly, not one of my best moments. Okay, actually, one of the worst."

"You were boxed into a corner. It was obvious."

I searched his eyes. "Thanks. You're right about that."

He opened his mouth, took a breath, then closed it again and pressed his lips together as if not sure of how he wanted to phrase something. His eyes were penetrating, his brows furrowed.

I cocked my chin. "What's bothering you, Gage?"

He shifted. "Just wondering why you didn't defend yourself better. I don't know, Callie. You don't seem like the type of woman who would take advantage of a little old couple."

I withdrew my hand. "Of course not!"

"Then why not say so? Why let that caller cast you in such a dark way?"

I couldn't look at him, couldn't tell him June's secret. I had promised her. I shrugged. "I don't know. Let's leave it at that, all right?"

He didn't look all right. Gage's eyes appeared cloudy and his jaw had a firm set to it. If I had more confidence about how he felt about me, I might grab that jaw of his and turn it until his mouth found mine again. As it was, I figured that he had doubts about me now and that I couldn't say anything that would make them go away.

He stood and I expected him to leave. "I need to tell you something else, Callie." He pulled me up and placed his hands on my shoulders. "I just ran that reporter out of here."

"Eliot?" I looked around. "He was here?"

Gage nodded. "Spying on you. Nearly scared the kid out of his loafers when I grabbed him by the collar."

Argh. "What did he want? Did he tell you?"

Gage paused, his face sober. "That's just it. He wanted to know your reaction to the news that Tim Kitteridge has been hospitalized."

A gasp flew out and my hands found my chest. "No. I've got to go call June. She must be beside herself."

I turned and Gage caught me by the elbow. "You and she are close, then?"

I shielded my eyes from the sunlight dripping through the canopy of pine. My voice broke. "She's become a dear friend.

★ 351 ★

I really need to go check on her . . . and the camp's going through something difficult right now. I'm sorry, but I've got to go—"

He slid his hand from my elbow to my hand. "There's more, Callie."

"Is he . . . is Tim going to make it?"

"That I don't know, but I think I may have made things harder for you."

A spike of tension shot through my shoulder. "How so?"

"I questioned the kid about why he's been following you, even suggesting that he may know something about the threatening letters you have received."

"And did he? Has he been the one leaving them?"

"No, but he said something about noticing Tim Kitteridge hanging around your place and he put two and two together."

"Tim? At my home? I don't remember . . ." My voice faded. June had spoken often about Tim's agitated state and how he didn't really seem to understand how quickly he was about to lose his property. "Oh, no. It was probably him. Poor Tim's confused, the dementia makes him think that I'm somehow after them."

"This is my fault. I'm sorry, Callie, but the community may be after you once they read about his hospitalization in the paper. That reporter's going to write about those letters, solidifying the accusation that you were pressuring the Kitteridges."

The realization crashed into my mind. Gage was right. This would not look good and any chance of SOS regaining ground might be lost. I peeked into his eyes again, heavy with concern, and reached up to touch his face. "He would have found out eventually—the letters became public record when I reported them to the police. I don't blame you."

He captured my hand and held it there against his face. "If I could fix this for you, Callie, I would. You know that, don't you?"

Words caught in my throat as I nodded. Somehow, I knew he would. If he could.

GAGE

HE HAD MADE THINGS worse for Callie. It didn't matter now that he knew Redmond had nothing to do with the threats made against her. The fact remained that Gage had helped point the way toward a story that just might drive the final nail into the SOS coffin.

He gripped the steering wheel while driving slowly down the winding hill from camp, ignoring the buzz of his phone. He knew it was Rick calling because he'd attached a special ring tone to the man's calls to warn himself. The pit of his gut felt hollow. What would it be like to draw up a "normal" project for people who found as much joy in the creative process as he did?

His boss at his last firm was crazy, had him making all kinds of changes after the permitting process had been completed. Not uncommon in the building world, but in this case Gage was asked to make dangerous, structural alterations in the plans just to save a few bucks—and that brought out the fighter in him.

His cockiness had landed that assignment in the first place, his willingness to hopscotch over anyone to succeed, but when he sat back and considered the young children who would live in the eleven thousand square foot building—he wouldn't do it. It was unconscionable. And just like that, he had been cut loose.

His phone buzzed again, this time from a text. *The guy's getting smarter, if that's possible.* Gage pulled to the road side and checked his phone:

```
Need plans to town council. Stat.
Showdown at the OK Corral blowing in.
```

Rick. The guy never met a drama he didn't like. Gage glanced at the construction documents on his passenger seat. They'd be dropped off in town this afternoon, and if all goes as expected, given rubber stamp approval.

His phone buzzed again and Gage sighed. What now? He straightened, realizing this note was from Suz:

```
At the RAG. Big powwow going on
behind me. Reporter Suz at your
service.
```

He crinkled his mouth into a tight smile and replied:

Explain yourself.

Suz: Realtor Rick seated behind me
w/Redmond & some guy named Henry.
Heated conv. They don't recognize me.
(Jer's w/me).

Must be the reason Rick got on him about the plans. How would it look if he were to show up at the RAG right now? Gage sighed and glanced to the sea before texting his sister again:

Anything I need to know about?

Suz: Redmond's worried about Tim K
being in hospital. Wants Henry to
hurry up. Henry says R keeps jumping
the gun.

Gage wracked his brain but no recollection of Henry resided there.

What's Henry's role in project?

Suz: He's buying it from Mr. & Mrs.
K, it sounds like. I think Rick's
working deal for Henry to sell
property to Redmond.

Gage's thumbs could not move quickly enough.

Anything else? I'll wait.

A breeze had kicked up, rustling through the pines. Drying needles slid across the hood of his truck.

```
Suz: There's some deadline. Next
week. If Ks don't come up with loan
payment . . .
```

He sat up. Loan payment? C'mon Suz, what else you got for me? He waited, tensing.

```
Suz: Loan payment is on their house.
If can't come up w/it, they have to
sell land to Henry. Sounds like he
will sell it to Redmond right away.
```

Gage groaned, the sound startling in the confines of his truck. "I knew it." He'd seen this type of thing before. This guy Henry must be a type of investor who got the Kitteridges into a bind with some kind of loan. They can't pay, so he takes over their house. It sounds like he also has the option of buying their additional land out from under them. Legal, but putrid to the senses.

```
Suz: They're talking about you. Do
you know Amelia?
```

An invisible pull, like a tight wire moving upwards, tugged on Gage's brow.

```
Yes.
```

Suz: She's supposed to distract you
from all this. Gross. (Hope they don't
discover me here.) Redmond's niece.
Did you know that?

Gage ground his teeth.

Didn't work. Not interested.

Suz: Redmond thinks you're squeaky
clean, but that you ask too many
questions. Says he wants to see plans
finalized soon. Wait a second.

Gage made himself breathe, otherwise the fuming anger
rising in him might have made him ill.

Suz: Henry says no worries. He's made
sure that all council members are
on his team. Once you turn in plans,
they will be okayed right away.

Gage let out a sarcastic sigh. "Of course they will." He sent
a final text to Suz.

Thanks. Off to the town council to
drop off plans. Will see you at home.

He set his phone onto the passenger seat and looked out to
the horizon. "You've really got to be a better judge of character, Mitchell." He shook his head. "Pretty desperate of you to
take on this job before investigating it thoroughly."

But what could he expect? When this job landed in his lap, he moved on it with little forethought, the same thing the mysterious Henry had accused Redmond of doing. Strangely enough, Gage had considered this job, this new company of his, as his way of setting down roots on a sure thing. He started his truck and began driving the downhill. The only thing he was sure about now was that after today, he'd have a lot of extra time on his hands.

Chapter Thirty-seven

 I made it through Day One and the campers did not appear to notice the heavy hearts in the camp staff. Squid, for his part, led by example by not letting on that this would be his last weekend of spring camp. The kids laughed and carried on during the Friday afternoon game: Are you Rock? Or are you Sand? They chose sides, sang songs, and tried not to be tricked into changing sides.

Saturday morning rolled around, and usually news of whatever happened down the hill did not make it to me until after the weekend. Usually, but not today. Luz laid the paper down in front of me, first thing this morning, *bless her heart.* My eyes swept over one of the headlines: *Tim Kitteridge Hospitalized.* The sub-head read: *Has the SOS Team Gone Too Far?*

This was not unexpected. Eliot Hawl's article went on to say that a "reputable source" confirms that Callie Duflay had been receiving unsigned, threatening notes and that Tim Kitteridge, who suffers from dementia, had been seen delivering envelopes to her home.

Good grief. Apparently the editors weren't too concerned with their paper's transformation into a tabloid. Didn't matter anyway now. The campaign was over. I confirmed this via phone this morning. Even if all the pledges made came in, we'd still be thousands of dollars short, and with only a week to go, what hope was there?

I shook off my disappointment while standing to the side of Saturday's morning game. The kids had taken turns at both the sand hill and the rock climbing wall, and Squid was working to bring down both the noise and chaos level.

"We all have to look out for weaknesses in our foundations," he told them. "Once, I was sitting on a piano bench and it crashed right out from under me. I fell on my bottom in front of my friends." The kids snickered. "That bench was made with flimsy materials, and that's how our lives will be when we don't make sure that our foundations are strong."

Squid's eyes brushed with mine and I nodded, offering him support. As he continued with his message, before leading into instructions for lunch, Natalia sidled up to me wearing camo pants, a linen blouse, and green scarf tied around her neck. I wondered when the safari would take place. "Hello, Callie."

"Natalia."

She folded her arms at her chest and watched Squid while speaking to me. "It has certainly been a rough week."

"It has."

She turned to me, her red lipstick blazing in the sun. "And for you personally, as well as Squid."

My eyes found the ground. "Yes. Tough."

She released her arms and touched my shoulder. "The SOS campaign is over, isn't it?"

It wasn't a question. Natalia was a tough businesswoman, always had been. She probably knew for weeks what I had only hours to digest. A million thoughts darted through my mind, how I might have worked harder or been smarter, maybe this wouldn't be just another failure to add to my growing list. I closed my eyes. At least Gage will be guiding the project, making it somewhat palatable.

Tidal Wave rang the lunch bell and the kids scrambled to their feet.

She touched my shoulder again. "You did what you could, Callie, but it was a tough road from the start." She dropped her hand to her side. "I'm here to discuss camp business with the board. With Squid's sudden departure imminent, we're going to have to make some tough decisions."

I let her comments sink into my mind.

"Listen, Callie, depending on what information is tossed about at the meeting, well, I'd like to meet with you, perhaps on Monday. Can you make the time?"

I pulled it together. "Sure. No problem, Natalia." *Won't have much else to do with the campaign defunct.*

She turned to go, then stopped. "By the way, Luz mentioned you know the architect on the Kitteridge property. Friend of yours?"

Hearing reference to Gage, especially when my thoughts had sunk so low, sent a ripple through me. The one bright spot in all of this mess. "Yes, I know Gage Mitchell. He's a friend."

"Gage Mitchell," she repeated. "I think I can remember that. See you Monday."

She left me to wonder if she had a remodel in the works. For the rest of the afternoon, the kids and counselors played an elaborate game of hide and seek that pitted guys against girls, cabins against cabins. Squid had disappeared for much of that time, but I hadn't looked for him knowing he had much to contemplate. When everyone had reassembled on the lawn, he reappeared and took the stage where worship leaders had begun leading campers in rounds of "Jesus Loves Me."

Squid raised the bullhorn. "Everybody hap-py?"

The kids whistled and cheered, "Yes!"

"Everybody full from lu-unch?"

More cheers. "Yes!"

"Everybody wi-ise?"

Some of the kids cracked up, a few whistled, some shouted, "Yes."

Squid lowered the bullhorn and surveyed the crowd of

children until all the noise died down. He raised the mega-phone again. "You know, the wise man, he built his house on the rock. He says: 'The rain came down, the streams rose, and the winds blew and beat against that house; yet it did not fall, because it had its foundation on the *rock*.'"

He quieted, his face serious as the evening news. "I want to be like that—how about you? You gonna build your life on what you hear on TV? Or on what your best friend tells you? Or are you gonna hear the word, learn the word, and live the word. 'Cuz that's what building on the rock means. It means that if you put into practice what God says, you will be like the wise man whose house did not fall."

I knew that Squid spoke from a fractured place within himself. He believed he had veered off the course he'd planned for himself and acted unwise.

Couldn't we all relate to that at some time in our lives? I pushed around the dirt with my foot, wishing I could stay up here on this hill and never have to face the community or my failures again. Then again, hadn't I reminded Squid that it's the Lord who determines our steps? Who am I to dish out advice to others but ignore it for myself?

GAGE

GAGE SAT ON HIS front porch, wind tickling his ears. He'd wanted to relax in the shade like this since the day he moved in, but until now, had not had the chance.

Suz leaned through the doorway, looking better with a few days rest and some needed perspective. Marc's wife Lizzie called and offered to fly her and Jer out to their lake house for some R&R in the summer, and just receiving the call had brightened his little sister. "I made some lemonade. Camille Sweet from down the road dropped off a box of lemons. Want a glass?"

"Sure. Sounds great." Homegrown foods might be an option worth looking into, now that he had zero income to expect. Of course, there was that phone call . . .

Suz brought two glasses onto the porch and plopped into the chair next to him. "How does it feel to be free as a bird?"

He took a sip, biting back the tartness, hoping his eyes didn't water enough for Suz to notice. "Stressful."

"Yeah, I figured."

"That's not entirely true. Initially, when I dropped off the approved designs at Redmond's office, I couldn't believe I was actually doing it. What am I saying—*he* couldn't believe I was doing it. But he confirmed what I suspected."

"Which was?"

"That the owners of the property had less than a week to make payment on a large loan or they would be forced to sell the property to a guy named Henry, who owns HMS Properties. He would then turn around and sell it to Redmond. Everybody wins—Henry makes a mint, Redmond stands to make his money off the sale of finished home and office condos, even the realtor will be raking it in."

"Everyone except the little old couple who didn't know better when they signed that loan."

Gage grimaced. "Had to endure a head full of swearing when I told Redmond, but you know what? I'm glad I left. Glad I had the guts to do it first this time."

"Yeah, well, I couldn't believe the way they were carrying on in the restaurant, pointing fingers. Don't they know the walls have ears?" She laughed at her own joke. "And did you really go out with Redmond's niece?"

He gave his sister a mock glare. "Please. It was a *business* meeting."

Suz laughed lightly. "Her uncle sounded mighty peeved that you wouldn't cross that line." She held up her glass. "Cheers to you, big brother."

He tipped his glass to her before taking another sip.

Suz looked over the neighborhood. "So what are you going to do now that you've pulled out of the Kitteridge project? Put an ad in the paper? Knock on some contractors doors? What?"

His brows dipped. "Can't say that I know yet. I've been paid for the completed construction docs, thankfully, so we'll have that to survive on for awhile. It's kind of hard to run a business, though, with no clients."

She peered at him. "No plans to pick up and move the company, then?"

"Nope. None." Even to him it sounded ludicrous. Half the town probably hated him for his involvement in the Kitteridge project, so what made him think he'd be able to win them over now? No one would know his reasons for pulling out of that project. If anything at all, they'd think he had been fired.

She looked at him sideways. "Really now."

"What's that look for?"

Suz shrugged. "Don't know. Just that you and Callie seem to be pretty tight lately."

"And?"

"And nothing. It's cute and, well, I told you so."

"Told me so *what*?"

She set her glass down. "That you two were perfect for each other, only that you were both too stubborn to acknowledge it; and that if only you would set aside your petty differences, you might look into each other's eyes and find true love staring back at you."

Gage's mouth gaped, his chin dropping forward. "You're saying you told me all that?"

Suz glanced off toward the horizon. "Well, maybe not in so many words. But isn't that the real reason you're so set on staying around here? I mean, I know you like the beach and all, but there are other coastal cities you could move to—if you wanted to, I mean."

Gage set down his glass on the side table and leaned forward, elbows onto his knees, staring into the clear air. "Maybe you're right."

"Yeah, maybe I am." She paused. "Anyway, I left her a message about some executive decisions I made in her house, so if she calls back, maybe you oughta be the one to answer the phone."

"Executive decisions?"

"More like design decisions." She chewed a fingernail. "I hope she likes them, but if she doesn't I can always repaint."

"Well, if the work you've done inside my place is any indication, I'd bet she'll be wild about what you've done for her."

The lines in her forehead relaxed. "Oh, and I can't believe I haven't told you this yet. I began looking for more steady work, something that will help us both until you can get more clients, so guess what I did yesterday?"

"I'm bad at guessing."

She waved her hand at him. "Fine. I applied for a job at Hearst Castle."

He forced a smile. He hated to see her give up her painting to work in the castle's touristy gift shop or sell lattes from a coffee cart. No shame in that kind of work, just not her calling. "Great. Good for you."

"I know. They've got a ton of restoration projects going on, so I'm hoping to get a spot on the crew for that. Wouldn't that be amazing?"

He twisted his chin upward. "Restoring the rooms?"

She nodded. "Yeah. So many fine details that need repainting—enough work to last for years." Suz's face glowed. Her eyes danced as she talked about the famed castle built by William Randolph Hearst. "Art treasures are in every room!"

Gage had been questioning God a lot lately, wondering why he was brought here only to see his hopes wither with the first shady detail. But then he found Callie and he watched his sister's enthusiasm grow while describing her dream job at the castle on the hill. Despite the otherwise dreary outlook for his firm, strangely enough, Gage felt nothing but hope.

Chapter Thirty-eight

Squid gave his final message to the kids, and I had to turn away to keep from crying. He'd made the right decision, stepping away from ministry for awhile as he sought to build a life with Peyton and his new child. But I'd miss him. The kids would miss him too.

As he finished with the kids, I had waited at the back of the chapel, reading over the proverb I had quoted to him the other day, the one that says the Lord determines our steps. Until then, I'd never looked at the one right before: "Better a little righteousness than much gain with injustice."

It occurred to me that although I believed the developers of the Kitteridge property had been unjust, I was not completely in the clear. I had jumped the gun when I'd first heard about the property's sale. What might have happened if I had approached both Tim and June the very moment I learned about it? If only I had gone to them first.

It was now early evening. Parked in front of Sheila's house, I debated my readiness to face everyone. The article in the paper didn't mince words yesterday and with the campaign shot, I could only imagine the comments I'd have to face. Leaning my elbows onto the steering wheel, I massaged my eyes.

My cell rang and I glanced at the number. Gage. How could the thought of one man bring on such polarized emotions?

"Hi."

"Callie, hi, it's Gage." He paused. "Are you home from camp?"

I rubbed my eyes harder. "Not yet. I stopped at my sister's for dinner."

"So I guess you've seen the paper."

I looked through my windshield at the muted sky. "First thing Saturday morning."

"Not Pulitzer prize worthy, but the kid laid it all out there. Are you okay?"

I paused to think about that, picturing Gage's penetrating eyes watching me. I wanted to tell him that I'd moved on, that I'd survive this. Of course, I would. But the whole thing still sat like an indigestible lump in my abdomen. "I'll survive."

"Callie, you gave it your all. The community couldn't have asked for more, and once things settle down, they'll find that out."

I closed my eyes. "Thanks but that doesn't matter now anyway. You won, Gage."

"No one's winning this one, Callie."

A smirk tugged at my cheek. "I wouldn't say that. You came here for a purpose, and now that purpose is in the works. So, good job."

Gage let out a sigh that revealed his exasperation. "We may have started out as opponents, but surely you know you mean more to me than that."

"Do I?" That sounded harsh, but Justin told me the same thing until one day he woke up with a changed mind. Would I ever trust in what Gage, or any other man, said? Besides, what if I had been the person to win this fight? Would Gage be professing his affection for me right now?

Silence held the line. I swallowed, waiting. Finally Gage spoke. "Don't you feel the same for me, Callie?"

My heart pricked at the heaviness in his voice and I wanted to answer him. Only I couldn't find a way. "I'm sorry. Gage, I just can't, not now. Please, give me some time."

We hung up and I continued to lean my chin against the wheel, tending to the knot in my stomach. Bobby peeked out the door and smiled at me, waving me in. The spirit was willing, but the flesh—not so much.

Still, knowing that baby Callie was beyond those doors got me out of the car.

"Hey." Bobby kissed me on the cheek. "Thought I heard something out here."

"Just planning my grand entrance."

"Nothing personal but you have a tough act to follow." He winked. "Greta and Callie made quite the entrance already."

Inside, I dropped my purse and darted across the room past Jim and Nancy and Vince, and knelt next to the same chair where Greta's water broke the previous week. It smelled freshly laundered. "How's my baby-kins?" My voice had inexplicably risen to a squeak.

Greta smiled serenely, her skin more radiant than ever. Low doses of sleep apparently agreed with her. "She's an angel."

The door flew open and in strode Mom and Dad. "Well, hello, my sweet familia!" Mom pushed her way past Bobby's waiting kiss and two-stepped across the room. "There's my babs!" She reached down and plucked Callie from her mother's arms, gently cradling the newborn in her own. We all watched as Mom cooed into the tiny pink face.

I glanced at Greta, my voice hushed, although unsure why. "I can't believe you are here. After all you went through!"

Greta shrugged. "I'd do it all over again." She leaned into me. "And you would too."

I tried to hide the doubt in my expression. Mom hadn't missed it though, and spoke up. "Yes, that is absolutely right and besides, it's really not that bad."

"Not that *bad*? Mom, you're kidding, right? You said that childbirth damages you forever!"

She shrunk back. "Me?"

"Don't you remember how you talked about all the ripping and tearing. The excruciating needles?"

Jim groaned, and Vince ducked out of the room.

Mom winced. "Darling, I don't recall any of that."

"How about this—you once said that women were forever altered by the audacity of childbirth!"

Mom gasped and looked to Dad. My normally placid father slapped his knee and laughed. I couldn't believe his callous reaction. "What could be so funny about that?"

My mother shook her head, smiling. "Callie, those were lines from a play. You must have heard me rehearsing my lines."

I froze in place and felt as if my body had shrunk to half its length. I was ten again and looking up at my mother as she paced the living room, throwing out words that had been embedded in my psyche for twenty years. Lines from a play?

Giggles filled the room as I slowly realized that some playwright wrote one of my biggest fears in life. Probably a male one. My insides overheated until I was sure the skin on my cheeks would burn right off.

Sheila placed a hand on me. "Thanks for the reminder about what I should say around the children." Even she laughed at me.

Over dinner my siblings continued to enjoy rehashing the exchange between my mother and me. Admittedly the whole thing was kind of ridiculous. It's as if my whole life I'd allowed this tiny fear to grow into a thick-rooted weed, so much that

I never even considered having children of my own. And yet I adored kids.

Funny how misperceptions could alter a person forever.

Sheila passed a platter of cookies. "I hesitated to bring this up, but now seems like the right time. Callie? How are you doing now that the SOS campaign has apparently ended?"

I shrugged, as if it didn't matter more than it did. "I'm disappointed, of course, but I'll survive."

Jim spoke up. "Like I always said, it was a lost cause."

My mother frowned at him. "What has happened to you, Jim, to make you such a prune face?"

Blakey giggled. "Prune face. That's funny, Grandma."

Mom stroked my nephew's face as Jim's chest gathered steam. His fist rested on the table with his fork piercing the air. "I'd like to point out that I am the most educated one in this room and that I—"

Dad tossed a cookie at Jim, startling my older brother as it landed on the chest of his linen dress shirt and slid into his lap, leaving a dusting of crumbs behind.

Jim's mouth flew open, wider than before. "What was that for?"

Dad sat quietly, chewing his food. He took a sip of coffee and set it back down before looking around the table. "Everything in this family seems to hinge on success, rather than on doing what is right, or more importantly, godly. I don't know where you got those ideas because it surely wasn't from me."

Mom gasped and patted Dad's shoulder. "See why I love this man?" She turned to him, her gaze unyielding. "You are so wise—and sexy!"

Bobby and Vince groaned and the table, everyone except for Jim, fell into laughter. My own shoulders lifted, not completely, but as if something weighty and cumbersome had taken flight, leaving behind a few odd pieces of my parents' mismatched luggage. Something about what my father said reminded me of the night Squid told the staff and board how he had struggled with the camp theme. Of course, none of us knew the depth of Squid's struggle and yet, wasn't I the one to point out that faith meant living for God?

To his credit, Dad didn't let up. Always the calm one in our sea of chaotic personalities, he held Jim's attention. "Son, I'm very proud of you for all that you have achieved. Very proud. But I ask that you take another look at how you measure success. Callie tried her darnedest to make a difference in the community. Maybe she made some mistakes along the way—we all do, everyday—but she makes me a proud papa." He secured me with his gaze. "I hope you know that."

Another piece of baggage disappeared from my shoulders.

Later as I stood at the door readying to leave, Sheila handed me my purse and kissed me on the cheek. "What's that for?"

My sister surprised me by cupping my cheeks with her hands. "For being you. I'm sorry that things haven't worked out the way you had hoped, Callie, but I too am proud of you for trying."

I could barely stammer a thank-you.

At home Moondoggy rocketed through his doggy door and flung himself at me. I stood in the living room, holding his head as he leaned against me, and scratching behind his ears. "So good to have you to greet me, you know that?"

He plopped his front paws back down on the floor and sat, signaling dinnertime. I filled his bowls with food and water and stopped short because there painted above his bowl were the words: "Be comforted, little dog, thou too in the Resurrection shall have a tail of gold. ~ Martin Luther."

Suz. Must be what my artist friend—Gage's sister—meant in her message when she said she hoped I didn't mind the liberties she had taken. Although she mentioned using the phrases I had pinned on the wall, this one was new to me.

I padded down the hall, chuckling to myself and thinking of Moondoggy and his tail of gold. Suz's hands had worked their magic in my little home and I adored her. I hoped my precarious relationship with Gage wouldn't stand between us.

Once again, I stopped short to take in more of Suz's handi-work flowing along the hallway wall: "I have loved you with an everlasting love."

The base of my throat grew thick as I traded laughter for what prickled in that place behind my eyes. I reached out my hand and touched the painted letters with my fingers. This familiar phrase I recognized, yet how long had it been since I had read those words—and believed them?

A vortex pulled me in. Did I believe those words? Or was I like my brother Jim, who seemed to think that accomplishments earned me access to streets of gold?

I leaned against the doorframe, lost in an endless wash of thought. I had done what I could, but maybe it was finally time to let go of this fight. Even June had accepted the finality of their plight and when Tim was well enough, her daughter planned to move them in with her.

Really, not such a bad idea at all.

Fatigue twined through me. Stepping into the bathroom, I flicked on the light, and allowed my eyes to adjust to the recently painted room. A soft hue of Bright Pearl shone on the walls, but I stepped back. Suz had once again used her artistic flair to freehand a verse onto my wall, above the mirror: "He has made everything beautiful in its time."

That last piece of baggage, the one that continued to weigh me down, disappeared, and as it did, I felt myself release the project that had ruled my waking moments for the past several months. Maybe even years.

GAGE

SUZ BENT OVER HIM, a fist in her side. "You didn't tell her that you quit the project?"

"The lady couldn't have cared less."

"She would have cared. You should have told her, Gage."

Gage shrugged. "I may not have to. One of Callie's friends gave me a call yesterday. Asked me to drive up to the camp for a meeting."

"What for?"

"Don't know really, but I can design bunkhouses as good as the next guy, so it's a start."

Suz's expression continued to twist. "I'm sure you can, and they'll be sustainable cabins with radiant heating and solar panels, I'm sure."

Gage clucked his tongue. "You mock me."

Suz dropped her arm at her side with drama. "Oh, Gage. What are you going to do? Start designing with the camp as if nothing's happened? Don't you think Callie's going to be suspicious when she sees you spending more time on that hill than on that bluff?"

"She doesn't want to talk to me."

"Gage Mitchell, you don't know what a good catch you are!"

Gage cracked a smile. "If I didn't know better, I'd think you were trying to get rid of me."

"I'd like to have some nieces and nephews, and you aren't a spring chicken, you know. Gah! Men!"

"Hey, why am I the bad guy here? Callie asked for some time, so I'm giving it to her. If anyone is tough to figure out, it's you women." He winked.

Suz flopped into a chair. Jer bounded over and she pulled him onto her lap, kissing his head. "Relationships are tough things. I just think Callie's a girl seeing her dream being dashed. I bet she knows the real reason those old people were having to sell their house."

Gage leaned forward onto his elbows. "I think so too."

Suz gaped at him. "Then she's upset. Tell her everything you know and what you've done and if she spurns you then, it's her loss." His sister reached out and touched his wrist. "Don't wait, big brother."

Chapter Thirty-nine

Although it took much longer than predicted, Ruth and I met Syd Sloan from the bank to return the pledge money that had been received for the Kitteridge property. It was the right thing to do.

At one point Syd wriggled his furry brows at me while handing me a business card with his home number scrawled on the back. The aging bank officer probably figured my prospects were as few as the dollars we had collected.

After he slouched away, Ruth cranked her head back and forth, that one eye of hers narrower than I'd ever seen it. "Be like me, honey, and forget about men. They're nothing but trouble. Now, cats—I can do cats!"

I turned to her. "Would you excuse me, Ruth? I have an important phone call to make."

Ruth stood. "Suit yourself."

When she'd gone, I pulled together what courage I had left, and dialed June Kitteridge. "Hello June? It's me, Callie."

"Hello my dear, dear friend."

I winced. "June, I have something to confess to you, something I'm, well, really quite ashamed of, and I hope you will forgive me."

"Whatever it is, consider it done."

I refused to allow myself to get off so easy. "Please, June, please hear me. When I first learned about the development of your property—" I took a breath. "Well, I'd been having a bad day. That's not a good excuse. The bottom line, June, is that from almost the minute I heard about the development, I, well I . . ."

"Yes?"

"I opened my big mouth and recruited people to fight it." There. I said it. "It didn't take long for me to realize that I should not have moved so quickly, that I should have talked with you and Tim, and helped you weigh your options. I'm ashamed of myself, June. Can you forgive me?"

Silence.

More silence.

"June?"

"Of course, Callie. You are forgiven. I'm sorry that I did not answer you right away. I was overcome by your apology. The world would be a better place if we could all start there, I believe."

Relief washed through me. "Thank you, June. You know that I would do everything possible to help you and Tim . . ."

"I know, dear. I believe you would."

After ending my talk with June, I longed to call Gage, but couldn't. Natalia expected me, so I hustled on up to camp, arriving at the same time as she.

With that deed done, I longed to call Gage but couldn't. Natalia expected me, so I hustled up to the camp, arriving at the same time as she.

Natalia beamed. "Ready for our meeting?"

"Hi, Natalia." I forced a smile to my face. "Sure."

Sitting across from me, Natalia looked noticeably perky. Her eyes shined, her makeup smoothed away lines. After several nights of little sleep, I felt like a garish stepsister next to her Cinderella. She exhaled a brisk breath. "I've been praying all night about this."

I tilted my head to one side. "Really?"

"And I believe with all my heart in what I am about to propose."

I eyed her, intrigued. "Go on."

Natalia clasped her hands on the table and smiled. "The camp would like to purchase the Kitteridge property."

I blinked, but in no other way could I respond.

"Let me explain, Callie. As you know, we have wanted to bring more kids to camp, specifically, different age groups. But space is tight, plus there are safety issues to consider when bringing in groups of vastly different ages. Are you with me?"

I nodded.

"I met with the board yesterday to discuss some grant dollars we have, and well, we'd like to make an offer to the Kitteridges to buy their property for the camp's use. At this time we intend to use that site for our high-school-aged campers. We can offer Mr. and Mrs. Kitteridge almost what the SOS group had proposed."

"Almost?"

"That's going to be key. We can't go a dime above our offer. I'm here to ask if you will talk to the Kitteridges for us and make our plea."

My head began to swirl with all the possibilities. My heart followed, with a dance of its own. Never would I have thought of this. The Kitteridges could make enough to keep their house, the camp wouldn't overfill the space with buildings, and I would be right there in the middle of it all.

As quickly as the ideas formed, dread set in. What would the community think of me now if I helped another entity develop the property? A traitor? And what about Gage and all the work he had done?

I licked my lips, biding time. "Natalia, you know I love this camp."

She nodded. "Oh, yes. We all know that."

"But time has almost run out. The camp would have to come up with the money today. Tomorrow at the latest."

She nodded, smiling "Uh-huh."

"And I'm not sure I'm the right person to handle this."

A familiar voice cut in. "You're the perfect woman to handle this."

I saw him stride into the room, his soulful eyes questioning me. "Gage?"

He pulled out the chair next to mine and sat, then stuck out his hand to Natalia. "Gage Mitchell."

"Very nice to meet you, Gage." She flicked her glance my way. "You weren't aware your friend would be here?"

Gage tipped his hand up. "That would be my fault. I hadn't had a chance to tell her yet."

My mind buzzed. More like I didn't give him the chance to tell me. Remorse, thick and muddy, seeped through me. I owed Gage an apology and yet I remained thoroughly confused. "I'm sorry. I don't understand."

Gage looked at Natalia. "May I?" He reached for my hand and it warmed me on contact. "I'm no longer associated with the Kitteridge property, Callie. I turned in the designs to the city, then pulled out of the project."

That warmth turned to tingles. "But why?"

"Let me ask you something. Did you know that the Kitteridges were being forced to sell their property by a lender? That they were put in a no-win situation?"

I glanced away, hoping he wouldn't see the answer there. When I glanced back, Natalia's eyes had narrowed right at me. "You're kidding. I had not heard that."

I exhaled and set my shoulders. "June swore me to secrecy. She was embarrassed that they'd been duped. I took the paperwork to a lawyer, to see if there was anything they could do about it, but it was all legal. Unethical, maybe, but legal."

Natalia snared me with her eyes. "But why wasn't this made public? Maybe then—"

"I tried, Natalia. But June begged me to keep quiet. Tim's dementia was becoming a problem, and she was horrified that they'd signed away their rights like that. This is the reason she agreed to take so much less from SOS. All they needed was enough to pay off the loan on their house, then they wouldn't be forced to sell the rest of the property."

"Callie, you took the brunt of criticism for this. My word."

Gage squeezed my hand. "I figured you knew but wasn't sure why you'd sat on this. I understand now. You amaze me."

I gazed at him, shrinking from his compliment. I'd taken out my frustrations on him, unwilling to let up. Ever since last night when Suz's handiwork on my bathroom wall startled me, I'd been thinking about all the places I'd looked for significance. Finding it in God and in his plans hadn't been one of them.

Until now.

I squeezed his hand back. "No, you're the amazing one, Gage. I've been stupid. I'm so sorry."

He touched my chin. "Don't."

I shut my eyes, allowing my heart to swell at this man's touch. For the first time, the thought of it didn't scare me. *He makes everything beautiful in its time.* Instead I longed to see where this connection might lead.

I opened my eyes to find Gage's fixed on mine. He grinned, sending a blush so strong through me that it threatened to electrify my nerve endings.

Natalia fanned herself with a camp brochure and I jerked upright. "Whooey, is it ever warm in here." *Had we just gotten moony-eyed in front of the boss?*

Gage laughed easily. "What can I say? Callie has a hold on me."

Natalia laughed and nodded. "No need to apologize—you sent me back to when my husband and I first fell in love. Beautiful memories."

When they *first fell in love?* My eyes flickered away from Gage's, but he squeezed my hand again.

"Getting back to the task at hand . . ." Natalia's smile grew wide and mischievous. "If you two don't mind, I'm concerned with the Kitteridge's deadline. Now more than ever, I see we must work fast. Callie, the camp can cut a check today. Here's what we propose . . ."

Epilogue

"I've heard of double weddings, but never this." Greta cradled baby Callie in her arms, a soft breeze ruffling the peach fuzz we all considered hair.

I stroked the baby's cheek as Moondoggy sat by my side. "Aw, you dressed her in the outfit I gave her."

"The only organic cotton sundress she owns!" Greta grinned. "How could I not?"

I squeezed her elbow and then, shading my eyes with my hand, searched the buzzing acreage. Familiar faces milled about the great land talking and eating and laughing. Tim, in his plaid shirt and pants hiked-up-to-there, reclined on a bench with June next to him, patting his hand. The carnival-like atmosphere quickened my heart, almost as much as the person I searched for in the throng.

Greta's mouth quirked up, teasingly. "Looking for someone?"

There. I spotted him, coming up from behind Greta. "I wouldn't say that."

My sister-in-law gasped. "Why? What's wrong?"

Laughter flowed through me. "I just meant that I'm no longer looking—already found him."

He approached, smiling, stopping only to squeeze baby Callie on her drool-smeared chin. "Hey, pretty girl."

Greta glowed. "She always starts kicking her legs when she sees you, Gage."

I laughed. "Yeah, I do that too."

Gage pulled me close, his voice a growl. "Glad to hear that." He gave me a lingering kiss.

Greta cleared her throat. "Not to be the one to douse your little reunion there, but don't look now—officials at twelve o'clock."

We turned to watch the line of men and women walking in solidarity across the Kitteridge property, parting the crowd. Council member Jamison led the way.

Bobby pulled alongside us, wrapping an arm about Greta's shoulder. "Now that's a sight I'll never forget." He shoved me with his free hand. "Good job, little sister."

I swallowed a pea-sized knot in my throat, aware of the welling going on behind my eyes. Next to me, Gage beamed. Two months had passed since the meeting with Natalia. Not only had they offered the Kitteridges enough money to make the balloon payment to HMS Properties—enabling them to keep their home—but they had decided to deed a hunk of the acquired acreage back to the town, which included a binding stipulation for community usage in perpetuity. The remainder of the land would be used to build another wing of the camp specifically for high-school-aged campers. Truly a win-win-win situation.

Bobby spoke. "So how are the new plans coming along, Gage?"

Gage continued to hold me as he addressed my brother. He'd only been gone long enough to drop Suz and Jer at the airport, but it felt like days. "Great. I already knew all aspects of this land, so this project has been a pleasure to work on. Pine Ridge is probably the best client I've ever worked with."

I hugged him, gazing up at Gage's mesmerizing face. "And you were the best man for this job. I'm so proud of you."

He smiled into my eyes. "I wouldn't be here if not for you."

Greta giggled. "My, you two are kind of sickening. But I love it." She eyed Bobby. "Don't you love these two?"

Bobby snorted as two pairs of arms wrapped around my knees. I laughed and looked down at my niece and nephew. "Hey, you two, you made it!"

Brenna wagged a finger at me. "Of course we did, Aunt Callie!"

Blakey jumped up and down while holding onto my leg as if trying to uproot me from the earth.

Sheila and Vince arrived behind them, winded, followed by our parents and, surprisingly, both Jim and Nancy. My sister hugged my neck. "Exciting day," she whispered. "Very proud of you."

I allowed her praise to filter through me, knowing that although my family seemed to have gained an appreciation for me lately, a higher authority stood at the helm of this project. I could never have come up with such a sure thing on my own.

Jamison approached me, his family in tow. After the papers reported all the backroom shenanigans involving the council and the development ring, the rest of the council resigned. Jamison, however, apologized to the community pointing out that nothing illegal actually transpired, and in typical Otter Bay fashion, the residents chose to forgive. He faced me. "Ready?"

I cast a questioning glance at Natalia. She smiled and handed me a shovel while a photographer from the local paper focused a lens in my direction.

I held it there. "I don't know what you mean."

Natalia stepped forward. "For the double ground-breaking ceremony, Callie. We would like you to break ground for the community. I will do the honors on behalf of Pine Ridge Camp."

I glanced at Jamison who surprised me with an apologetic smile and an open hand that ushered the way to a soft section of ground. "Please."

Gage released me, offering an encouraging nod, and I handed him Moondoggy's leash, my mind still trying to wrap its way around the past several months. Together, Natalia and I stuck the pointed edge of our shovels into the ground. Tears tickled my cheeks. On the count of three we pressed our blades into the soil symbolizing the start of both projects. The crowd cheered.

Ruth approached, her old floppy hat replaced by an even larger version of the last one. "Not bad, Callie. It's a compromise, but I can live with it."

Steph pulled me into her embrace, her voice laced with thickness. "Oh, Callie. What a miracle this is!"

I nodded, unable to speak without more emotion tumbling out. After she trotted away, a warm tug on my arm spun me into Gage's embrace.

My arms found their way around him as one of his hands touched my face. "You up for another celebration?"

I tipped my chin until our lips were inches apart. I breathed him in, fighting the urge to steal a kiss. "What did you have in mind?"

He paused, his eyes searching mine. The sea danced to its own serenade behind us, but a bright spark caught the corner of my vision. I turned my head slightly to investigate only to find the prettiest diamond ring in his other hand.

I whipped a look back to Gage.

He held me with his gaze. "That fiery temper of yours was the best thing to ever happen to me. Will you . . . ?"

I smiled.

". . . marry me?"

While taking in Gage's eyes, the color of sea grass in the spring, I thought back on that day we met. Who knew that a couple of snarky surveyors and their wayward tripod could lead to this?

My grip around him tightened and I threw back my head, laughing into the wind. "Yes! Of course, I will marry you." My heart fluttered and flapped around inside my body in a way I'd never known. I reveled in it, never wanting the moment to end, and yet longing for all that came along on the journey of a life well lived with the one I loved.

Moondoggy leapt to his hind legs and slapped me on the waist. I glanced down at my beloved pet and gave his silky head a swift rub.

Make that a life well lived with the *ones* I loved.